The Latin American
Cultural Studies Reader

The Latin American Cultural Studies Reader

Edited by Ana Del Sarto, Alicia Ríos, and Abril Trigo

DUKE UNIVERSITY PRESS   DURHAM AND LONDON 2004

© 2004 Duke University Press. All rights reserved.
Printed in the United States of America on acid-free paper ∞
Designed by Rebecca M. Giménez. Typeset in Quadraat by
Wilstead & Taylor. Library of Congress Cataloging-in-Publication
Data appear on the last printed page of this book.

CONTENTS

Acknowledgments, ix

ABRIL TRIGO General Introduction, 1

I. Forerunners INTRODUCTION BY ALICIA RÍOS
Traditions and Fractures in Latin American Cultural Studies, 15

ANTONIO CANDIDO Literature and Underdevelopment, 35

DARCY RIBEIRO Excerpts from *The Americas and Civilization*:
"Evolutionary Acceleration and Historical Incorporation," "The
Genuine and the Spurious," and "National Ethnic Typology," 58

ROBERTO FERNÁNDEZ RETAMAR Caliban: Notes Toward a
Discussion of Culture in Our America, 83

ANTONIO CORNEJO POLAR *Indigenismo* and Heterogeneous
Literatures: Their Double Sociocultural Statute, 100

ANTONIO CORNEJO POLAR *Mestizaje*, Transculturation,
Heterogeneity, 116

ANGEL RAMA Literature and Culture, 120

II. Foundations INTRODUCTION BY ANA DEL SARTO
The 1980s: Foundations of Latin American Cultural Studies, 153

JEAN FRANCO Plotting Women: Popular Narratives for Women
in the United States and in Latin America, 183

CARLOS MONSIVÁIS Would So Many Millions of People
Not End Up Speaking English? The North American
Culture and Mexico, 203

ROBERTO SCHWARZ Brazilian Culture: Nationalism
by Elimination, 233

BEATRIZ SARLO Intellectuals: Scission or Mimesis? 250

WALTER MIGNOLO The Movable Center: Geographical
Discourses and Territoriality During the Expansion
of the Spanish Empire, 262

JOSÉ JOAQUÍN BRUNNER Notes on Modernity and
Postmodernity in Latin American Culture, 291

JESÚS MARTÍN-BARBERO A Nocturnal Map to
Explore a New Field, 310

NÉSTOR GARCÍA CANCLINI Cultural Studies from the
1980s to the 1990s: Anthropological and Sociological
Perspectives in Latin America, 329

III. Practices INTRODUCTION BY ABRIL TRIGO
The 1990s: Practices and Polemics within Latin American
Cultural Studies, 347

IRENE SILVERBLATT Political Disfranchisement, 375

BEATRIZ GONZÁLEZ STEPHAN On Citizenship:
The Grammatology of the Body-Politic, 384

EDUARDO ARCHETTI Male Hybrids in the World of Soccer, 406

ADRIÁN GORELIK AND GRACIELA SILVESTRI The Past
as the Future: A Reactive Utopia in Buenos Aires, 427

ANA M. LÓPEZ Tears and Desire: Women and Melodrama
in the "Old" Mexican Cinema, 441

FRANCINE MASIELLO The Unbearable Lightness of
History: Bestseller Scripts for Our Times, 459

RENATO ORTIZ Legitimacy and Lifestyles, 474

DANIEL MATO The Transnational Making of Representations
of Gender, Ethnicity, and Culture: Indigenous Peoples'
Organizations at the Smithsonian Institution's Festival, 498

GUSTAVO A. REMEDI The Production of Local Public Spheres:
Community Radio Stations, 513

ROMÁN DE LA CAMPA Mimicry and the Uncanny in
Caribbean Discourse, 535

JOSÉ RABASA Of Zapatismo: Reflections on the Folkloric
and the Impossible in a Subaltern Insurrection, 561

DEBRA A. CASTILLO, MARÍA GUDELIA RANGEL GÓMEZ,
AND ARMANDO ROSAS SOLÍS Tentative Exchanges:
Tijuana Prostitutes and Their Clients, 584

JUAN FLORES The Latino Imaginary: Meanings of
Community and Identity, 606

IV. Positions and Polemics

JOHN BEVERLEY Writing in Reverse: On the Project
of the Latin American Subaltern Studies Group, 623

MABEL MORAÑA The Boom of the Subaltern, 643

GEORGE YÚDICE Latin American Intellectuals in
a Post-Hegemonic Era, 655

HUGO ACHUGAR Local/Global Latin Americanisms:
"Theoretical Babbling," apropos Roberto Fernández
Retamar, 669

NELLY RICHARD Intersecting Latin America with Latin
Americanism: Academic Knowledge, Theoretical Practice,
and Cultural Criticism, 686

ALBERTO MOREIRAS Irruption and Conservation:
Some Conditions of Latin Americanist Critique, 706

NEIL LARSEN The Cultural Studies Movement and Latin
America: An Overview, 728

JOHN KRANIAUSKAS Hybridity in a Transnational Frame:
Latin Americanist and Postcolonial Perspectives on
Cultural Studies, 736

ANTONIO CORNEJO POLAR *Mestizaje* and Hybridity:
The Risks of Metaphors—Notes, 760

Works Cited, 765
Acknowledgment of Copyrights, 805
Index, 811

ACKNOWLEDGMENTS

This book has been possible thanks to the direct participation or indirect contribution of many friends and colleagues who, over the years, have enriched the field and our own reflections. This includes, of course, our contributors to this volume, but also many other extraordinary scholars who, due to reasons of space, we have not been able to count in its pages. We would also like to thank Christine McIntyre and Christopher Dennis for their meticulous professionalism in translating some of the most difficult texts and their rigorous editing advice in the final stages of the project. We thank Ohio State University, particularly Assistant Dean Chris Zacker, and Kenyon College for their generous support in the initial steps of the project, which made possible the translation of several of the essays included. Alicia Ríos sets aside a special mention for Stanford University and Universidad Simón Bolívar. Finally, we owe special thanks to Reynolds Smith, our editor, for his confidence in this project all along, his constant encouragement, and his friendly advice, and to our anonymous reviewers for their invaluable recommendations.

For generous permission to publish these texts, totally or partially, we thank the many journals and publishers who have acceded to our requests, in many cases promptly, as indicated in the Acknowledgment of Copyrights.

ABRIL TRIGO
General Introduction

The main purpose of this reader is to provide a comprehensive view, documented through established texts and authors, of the specific problems, topics, and methodologies that characterize Latin American cultural studies vis-à-vis British and U.S. cultural studies. The reader, which includes essays by many of the most prominent intellectuals from both Latin America and abroad who specialize in this field, aims to provide scholars and students from all the disciplines in the humanities and the social sciences with a condensed but methodical and exhaustive compilation, but also to map out, from a critical perspective, the concrete sociohistorical and geopolitical circumstances as well as the specific problems and relevant polemics that make up the field in dialogue and in contest with other theoretical and critical discourses. Given its goal, the book's two axial hypotheses are first, that Latin American cultural studies are a disputed field in a global scenario, which cannot be fully understood or further advanced without considering its historical grounding in Latin American sociocultural processes, and second, that despite common interpretations, Latin American cultural studies are not just the product of an epistemological break, postmodern or otherwise, but also the result of specific historical continuities. Thus, through the introduction of selected readings, the book traces and displays the genealogical lines and epistemological crossroads that mark the sociohistorical and geocultural specificity of Latin American cultural studies by signaling its peculiar aesthetic, institutional, political, and cultural problematics, its diverse methodologies, and its historical antecedents, precursors, and founders, always in dialogue with a multiplicity of external influences. In order to offer different possible paths of reading amid the synchronic and diachronic tensions, conflicts, and transformations, as well as the overlapping critical trends and heterogeneous sociocultural realities that make up the specificity of Latin American cultural studies, the selected texts are introduced along with a map that charts the cognitive constellations, thematic networks, critical interventions, ideological fluxes, and chronological developments, as well as the position that every author in this book has in the development of the field, thus allowing the reader to choose among different routes and invent new ones.

The selection, organization, and introduction of a representative corpus of texts—an anthology, a collection, a compendium of any sort—is always a difficult task. To decide which texts and authors will be included is an agonizing process; to decide which ones will be excluded is even worse. In that sense, no definitive anthology is possible, and this reader does not intend to be the culmination of a field full of contradictions and divergent methodological, epistemological, and hermeneutic tendencies, as our own introductions clearly demonstrate. On the contrary, it has to be read as an open work, one that is in the process of becoming. However, a few words about the criteria of selection are in order. Many people would disagree with our selection, with the inclusion of certain authors or texts and the exclusion of others; many more would ask themselves why certain authors are included in one section instead of another; others might demand a better representation for women, gays, and ethnic groups, or a more nuanced balance between different disciplines or between authors from Latin America and abroad. Furthermore, some people would complain about the absence of Latino critics, but in fact, despite its many obvious connections with Latin American cultural studies, Latino cultural studies could be understood as a separate field with a different set of problems, methodologies, and intellectual traditions. As a matter of fact, the four sections in which we have organized the anthology respond to the chronological impact of certain authors or texts upon the formation and development of the field, and should not be understood as hierarchical categories. The absence of an author from any section does not imply any sort of negative judgment on her or his work. Nevertheless, after the exhausting consideration of several, sometimes opposite criteria of selection and methodological strategies, we have come up with a list of texts and authors that is not only representative of the current status of the field but, more importantly, also provides an account of its historical formation, its most outstanding ideological and methodological trends, and its main thematic axes and theoretical controversies. Therefore, we have put together a selection of texts that, for the most part, have had a significant role in the development of the field or represent a significant contribution to its current status.

An Operational Definition of
Latin American Cultural Studies

What is in a name? The name is of no importance and, nevertheless, we are not so disingenuous as to believe that names are value free, empty signifiers, because it is too well known that every name is charged, ineluctably, with sedimentations of meanings linked to concrete historical foundations and institutions of power. Partially at least, to name is to possess. So, why are we including under the rubric of Latin American cultural studies so many diverse practices, which are usually assessed by their own practitioners under differing rubrics? Given the fierce resistance to the invasion of "cultural studies" from so many camps, particularly in Latin America, we could be accused of academic opportunism, of trying to capitalize on the current popularity of "cultural studies" in the U.S. academy. Or we could be accused of miscalculation. Why publish a Latin American cultural studies reader, in English, precisely when both U.S. and Latin American cultural studies have been so harshly criticized for having become institutional gears for the global control of knowledge? Should we not adopt another rubric, or adapt one of the many Latin American historical variants? Our decision is a strategic one. We do not accept the consideration of "cultural studies" as a universal trademark; we cannot accept the historical precedence or the epistemological preeminence of any particular definition of "cultural studies," or believe it is politically prudent to cede the privilege, not of a rubric, but of the practices that that rubric names. We vindicate the specific political trajectory and the epistemological space of Latin American cultural studies, not as a branch of some universal "cultural studies" or as a supplement of British or U.S. cultural studies, but as a full-fledged field of inquiry that has its own historical problematics and trajectories. By way of summary, but with no pretense of proposing a definitive or prescriptive definition, we outline the axial features of our working interpretation of Latin American cultural studies.

Latin American cultural studies constitute a field of inquiry historically configured from the Latin American critical tradition and in constant, sometimes conflictive dialogue with Western schools of thought, such as French structuralist, poststructuralist, and postmodernist linguistics, philosophy, anthropology, and sociology of culture; German Frankfurt school and reception theory; semiotics and feminisms; and more recently, British and U.S. cultural studies. The main objects of inquiry of Latin American cultural studies are the symbolic production and living experiences of social reality in Latin America. In a word, what can be read as a cultural text, what carries a sociohistorical symbolic meaning and is intertwined with various discursive formations, could become a legitimate object of inquiry, from art and literature, to sports and media, to social lifestyles, beliefs, and feelings. Therefore, Latin American cultural studies produce their own objects of study in the process of investigation. This means that cultural studies cannot be defined exclusively by their topics of research or by any particular methodological approach, which they share with several disciplines, but instead by the epistemological construction of those topics. Precisely in this operation, which has a cognitive (heuristic, hermeneutical, explicative, analytical) and practical (prospective, critical, strategic, synthetic) value, lies their strongly political thrust. In this sense, Latin American cultural studies focus on the analysis of institutions, experiences, and symbolic production as intricately connected to social, political, and material relations, relations to which these elements in turn contribute. Consequently, *cultures* can be defined as historically and geographically overdetermined symbolic and performative institutions and lifestyles specific to concrete social formations, which develop under particular modes of production, distribution, and consumption of goods and artifacts with symbolic value. *The cultural* is perhaps a better term to capture the kaleidoscopic nature of our object of study than *culture*, which generally implies some degree of reification. Thus, *the cultural* can be conceptualized as a historically overdetermined field of struggle for the symbolic and performative production, reproduction, and contestation of social reality and political hegemony, through which collective identities evolve. As such, the cultural can be considered Latin American cultural studies' privileged field of inquiry inasmuch as it is reciprocally produced by and a producer of what is experienced at *the social* and *the political* spheres. The sociohistorical overdetermination of the cultural guarantees its inextricable connection to the political. A cultural text is always part of a wider and more complex symbolic system, a field of struggle for the symbolic reproduction of social reality that is ultimately elucidated at the political sphere. Upon this operational definition, we can summarize the central tenets of our hypotheses.

SOCIOHISTORICAL CONTEXTUALIZATION

Latin American cultural studies are a disputed field in a global scenario, which means that they must necessarily be read against the historical background of Latin American socioeconomic and geocultural enmeshment in worldwide affairs and external influences. Just as Latin American cultural phenomena cannot be fully explicated as either exclusively endogenous or exogenous processes, Latin American cultural studies cannot be fully grasped without considering their relation to British and U.S. cultural studies. This requires a dually contextual bifocal hermeneutics, capable of interpreting the text against the sociohistorical milieu in which it originated, and simultaneously against the sociohistorical milieu in which the subject's own interpretation is being produced. This critical methodology, by pitting historically set meanings and values against each other and situating the subject in the actual flux of history, prevents the entrapment of contingency politics—merely empirical and conjunctural, like identity politics—and guarantees the grasping of the contingent in comprehensive social and geopolitical formations.

RELATIONSHIP WITH BRITISH AND U.S. CULTURAL STUDIES

Latin American cultural studies did not originate in British cultural studies or in Western postmodern theories. Well before British cultural studies and postmodern writers reached Latin America, and well before British cultural studies were coined in Britain and postmodernism was born, many Latin American intellectuals were already doing some sort of cultural studies. Similarly, the genealogy of Latin American cultural studies is manifold and eclectic, and does not relate directly and solely to poststructural and postmodernist theories. They are not an offshoot of U.S. cultural studies either, which they actually antecede. Instead, they are another locally and historically grounded practice of that abstraction called "cultural studies," as, for instance, British, U.S., and Australian cultural studies are. However, the consolidation of Latin American cultural studies in the 1980s and 1990s coincided with a dramatic turn, inextricably connected to the formation of a global theoretical marketplace, from the long-lasting influence of European modern values, theories, and thinkers (particularly from France and Germany) to Anglo-American postindustrial and postmodern academic hegemony, a phenomenon further dramatized by the large number of Latin American intellectual migrants.

SOCIOHISTORICAL CONTINUITIES

Latin American cultural studies are not just the product of an epistemological break, postmodern or otherwise, but the result of specific sociohistorical continuities in the Latin American political and cultural milieus, despite the fact that some celebrities in Latin American cultural studies trace their roots directly to European schools of thought while circumventing the opulent Latin American critical tradition. Néstor

García Canclini, arguably the most internationally emblematic representative of the field, and Beatriz Sarlo, a Latin American cultural studies scholar malgré-lui, rarely credit any Latin American cultural thinker beyond their own circles. This silencing is somewhat contradicted when García Canclini claims that he "became involved in cultural studies before [he] realized this is what it was called," or when Sarlo says that she "thought [she] was doing the history of ideas" (García Canclini 1996, 84; Sarlo 1997a, 87). Obviously, if prior to becoming acquainted with cultural studies as such, they were already practicing them, it is because the field's issues and methodologies predate it as such. Both Sarlo, a literary critic, and García Canclini, a cultural anthropologist, were working in fields already permeated by theoretical, methodological, and ideological controversies that constitute pivotal issues within Latin American cultural studies.

According to Julio Ramos, a literary critic who is concerned with the discursive, disciplinary, and institutional genealogy of national literatures, and with the central role of cultural policies in the consolidation of nation-states and their national imaginaries, Latin American cultural studies deal primarily with the emergence or the survival of ethnic identities, diasporic subjects, and subaltern lores, topics that nurture an epistemology at the limits of traditional disciplinary boundaries. These topics reflect (upon) the intensification of conflicts in heterogeneous social formations, such as the border culture of U.S. Latinos and the uneven modernity of Latin America throughout its history. The difference between current Latin American cultural studies and traditional Latin American thought is that the latter bet on the integrative capability of national literatures and art, while the former questions them as apparatuses of power. The fact remains, however, that not only the topics of inquiry, but most importantly the institutions and practices of knowledge in Latin America have always been "heterogeneous, irreducible to the principles of autonomy which limited the disciplines in the United States or France, for instance." Latin American cultural thinkers since the early nineteenth century have "worked, precisely in the interstitial site of the essay, with transdisciplinary devices and ways of knowledge" (Ramos 1996, 36). They are, in the truest sense, the early precursors of Latin American cultural studies.

SOCIOPOLITICAL FRACTURES

Latin American cultural studies also originated as a hermeneutical and critical response to the economic, social, political, and cultural transformations of Latin American countries and societies under the impact of transnational finance capitalism and the globalization of culture experienced since the early 1970s. The crushing of democratic popular movements and the installation of repressive regimes paved the way for the neoliberal dismantling of local industries and social legislation, the privatization of state enterprises, the deregulation of labor and speculative capital, the twenty-fold increase of national debts, and the overall immersion in global capitalism and transnational mass culture.

Has the national question been superseded by globalization? Do new social movements and the emergence of previously suppressed identities replace national imaginaries? Is civil society outside, above, or against the nation-state? Does the deterritorialization of capital deterritorialize old territorial allegiances? Two axes intersect here. On one hand, the problematic of the nation-state and its articulation to the global markets, which leads to the core issues of citizenship and consumption, identities and the subject; on the other hand, the problematic of modernity, with the subsequent impact of the postmodern and the postnational, globalization and its articulation to the local and the national, and the passage from an international sphere to transnational networks.

The politics of the 1960s were guided (and many times dogmatically misguided) by the premise that the main contradictions of the times were *bourgeoisie versus proletariat* and *imperialism versus nation*. Such contradictions subsumed every single sociopolitical conflict and allowed for the formation of popular national blocs in order to carry out the pending national-democratic and social revolutions. Dependency theory, pedagogy of the oppressed, and theology of liberation, among the most important critical paradigms to emerge from Latin America in that period, directly nurtured and/or responded to the said premise. Later, imperialism and the nation, the main characters in this drama, faded from the scene, alongside the mere concept of social class. Imperialism, with the end of a bipolar world, the advent of flexible postindustrial capitalism, and the dispersal of its centers, lost its currency. If it is no longer possible to think in terms of modern economic and cultural imperialism, how can the peoples of the periphery name these postmodern, apparently decentered, transnational centers of power? How can they devise liberating political strategies without being able to name this imperial postmodern, this flexible, ubiquitous, omnivorous regime? Correlatively, how can these peoples name themselves, that is, create themselves as agents of their own destiny? The national question is still a capital issue in Latin America, alongside neocolonialism, the popular, modernity, and modernization. So is dependency theory, a vernacular form of post-Marxism—not to be confused with other forms of *post*-Marxism, which proclaim the demise of Marxist thought—and anticolonialism—not to be confused with postcolonial studies, which assume the demise of anticolonial struggles—whose main objectives of economic justice, popular democracy, and cultural emancipation are still unfulfilled.

This is the reason why the need to insist upon the political is medullar to any project within Latin American cultural studies. As a matter of fact, Latin American intellectuals have always been intricately linked to politics and the political, both in theory and practice. But since politics has become old-fashioned and reading culture in political terms has become a la mode, more than ever the status of the political needs to be elucidated politically (Jameson 1990a, 44). What is the articulation between culture and politics, or better yet, between the cultural and the political? The interpretation of cultures in political terms should not end up depoliticizing politics. On the contrary, a more rigorous discernment of the mutually overdetermined status of the political and the cultural should allow for a deeper and renewed politicization of both politics and cultures on the understanding that they still constitute two discernible—although never discrete or autonomous—spheres of social action. Culture is overdetermined by the political as politics is overdetermined by the cultural, but yet there is a specifically political praxis as well as a specifically cultural one. And here is where utopia comes in, because if utopia is basically a necessarily evasive horizon, it needs to be permanently reinscribed in our critical practice in the same way politics has always been inscribed in cultural studies as a tension between the intellectual and the academic, desire and knowledge (Hall 1980, 17). As Jameson has said, utopia must be named (1990a, 51), and this utopian will, renovated as practice and not just as desire, is what recreates the long tradition of Latin American thought that resonates in the intellectual adventure of Latin American cultural studies.

LATIN AMERICAN UNDISCIPLINED THOUGHT

It has become sort of commonsensical to affirm that the most characteristic feature of Latin American cultural studies is their multidisciplinary, interdisciplinary, or transdisciplinary methodology, and some of their most distinguished practitioners assume this decidedly. On one hand, John Beverley, speaking from the strong U.S. academic disciplinary tradition, stresses that "the point of cultural studies was not so much to create a dialogue between disciplines as to challenge the integrity of disciplinary boundaries per se" (1993, 20). Néstor García Canclini's position, on the other hand, is cautiously nuanced. Although he applauds cultural studies' interdisciplinary methodology, he warns that "it must not become a substitute for the different disciplines [which] should become in-volved in the study of culture, inform one another, interact, and make their respective boundaries as porous as possible. But from the peda-gogic point of view, it seems to me that at university level the differences between disciplines should be kept" (1996, 86). While Beverley cele-brates transgression, García Canclini recommends a complementary balance between the disciplined pedagogic moment and the ulterior multidisciplinary professional practice. But the core of the matter is that multi-, inter-, or transdisciplinarity are deeply engrained in Latin Ameri-can writing, in the form of an essayist thrust that evolves from the nineteenth-century polygraph intellectual (the lawyer by profession who was also a poet, a journalist, an ideologue, a politician, a statesman). It is precisely that polygraphic practice—very close indeed to the kind of contingent, impure, deprogrammed "border text" proposed by Nelly Richard, quoting exclusively European poststructuralist writers, as para-digmatic of "cultural criticism" (1998a)—which has always already tra-versed discursive formations, confused social spheres, and contami-nated the disciplines even before their academic institutional inception at the beginning of this century. For this reason, Latin American cultural studies cannot be defined either by its multi-, inter-, or transdisciplinary methodology, an issue which, as Neil Larsen correctly argues, is not "a serious issue any more" (Larsen 1998, 247). Moreover, as Walter Mignolo writes, "One could say that there is a style of intellectual production, in and from the Third World, which consists of a certain undisciplinar-ity. . . . It is not essentialism that explains this: it is rather the history of colonialism and the game of power and cultural scholarship in the his-tory of the colonial countries and in the history of the colonies" (Mignolo 1998a, 112). In this sense, the undisciplined character of Latin American critical thinking would be a byproduct of the historical unfolding of co-lonialism in its various forms, not merely as its rhetorical and stylistic inadvertent syndrome, but also as a methodological stratagem and an epistemological tactic dependent upon the uneven development of the modern relations of cultural production.

EPISTEMIC SHIFTS
Latin American cultural studies are also the aftermath of the epistemic shifts experienced by several scientific disciplines and discursive for-mations. In that manner, they are the locus where human and social sciences, such as anthropology, sociology, historiography, communica-tions, and literary criticism, converge around a new conception of the cul-tural (as a) field of struggle that began to take shape in the 1960s and

1970s. A few centers of literary research, such as the Centro Rómulo Gallegos, in Caracas, or the Institute for the Study of Ideologies and Literatures, at the University of Minnesota, and influential cultural or political journals, such as the *Revista de Casa de las Américas,* published in Havana, or *Marcha,* published in Montevideo, had a prominent role in this process. A case in point is Angel Rama's critical, methodological, ideological, and political confrontation in the 1960s with Emir Rodríguez Monegal. As Rama summarizes this intense period, Rodríguez Monegal, who practiced an extremely elegant brand of New Criticism, played an important role in disseminating Latin American literature worldwide "from the restricted appreciation of literature by a 'pure literati.'" However, says Rama, "I had to reinsert literature into a general structure of culture, which inevitably led me to its grounding in the historical, and to work with sociological methods capable of holistic constructions, reconverting criticism to the process of letters and committing it to social demands and the Latin American community." And he adds, defining in unmistakable terms the paradigm shift: "Criticism began to be historical, sociological and ideological, providing explanations that related the work to its context and scrutinized the concrete grounding of cultural phenomena. This movement emphasized the interest in a sociology of culture . . . and Marxism" (1972, 88–89, 108).

As Hernán Vidal has put it, Rama's position embodied a "social understanding of literature" according to which "the literary critic was supposed to abandon his identity as a technical analyst of privileged texts in order to take on the identity of a producer of culture from a consciously defined political position." After this turn, concludes Vidal, "literary criticism thus moved closer to symbolic anthropology, sociology, and political science" (1993, 115). The debate between these two camps, or better yet, within these two moments in the development of Latin American criticism, ranged from the status of the literary text to the composition of the canon, from the relation between literature and art to their limits with regard to the popular, and from the technologies of literary and cultural criticism to the political role of the intellectual. All of these topics would become medullar issues for Latin American cultural studies during the 1980s. The passage from the centrality of literature (and its aesthetic interpretation) to culture (and its nuanced historical, sociological, and anthropological analysis), while it signaled a new hermeneutic strategy, which required new methodologies and assigned a new epistemological status to diverse texts, discourses, and practices, should be understood, nevertheless, more as an epistemological shift than as a paradigm break.

One of the most salient features of Latin American cultural history is the continual, always renovated transformation of a few cognitive constellations (see map)— ideological, thematic, and theoretical clusters around which most of the imaginary signifiers of the first long century of Latin American postcolonial life converge. The obsessive questioning of neocolonialism, the popular, the national, modernity, and modernization, as well as national and continental identities and their internal and external others, galvanized the critical and creative efforts of generations of artists and intellectuals, thinkers and activists who were committed to the construction of modern national cultures.

In the 1960s and 1970s, Latin America went through one of its most intense historical periods, in political, economic, social, and cultural terms: from conservative and populist nationalist regimes, to revolutionary projects inspired by the Cuban Revolution and the anticolonial movement, to the military dictatorships that cleared the way for neoliberal policies and the assault of global finance capitalism; from economic neocolonialism and import substitution modernization to conservative developmentalism and its critique by dependency theory; from the urbanization and secularization of rural populations to the expansion of the middle classes and the explosion of the college population, the progressive inclusion of new social agents in political life, and the overwhelming power of the culture industry; from the expansion of national and international mass culture to the emergence of youth countercultures and ethnic subcultures, the literary boom, the new Latin American cinema, the street theater of collective creation, and the movement of the protest song. As a consequence of this sociopolitical effervescence, these were extremely fermentative intellectual times, which witnessed the emergence of diverse theoretical proposals, characterized by a strong historical and political urgency matched by anti-imperialist and anticolonialist feelings and a new Latin American utopia. Among the main theories to emerge in this period, the theories of cultural imperialism, internal colonialism, pedagogy of the oppressed, theology and philosophy of liberation, and dependency theory stand out. All these theories and sociopolitical practices were able to crystallize, up to a certain point, a utopian Latin American imaginary by rapidly spreading through the subcontinent and becoming the first Latin American theoretical product for export, particularly to other Third World regions and amid certain metropolitan academic circles. Alongside Che Guevara's mystical look and the exoticism of magical realism, they helped to fix the external image of an unruly

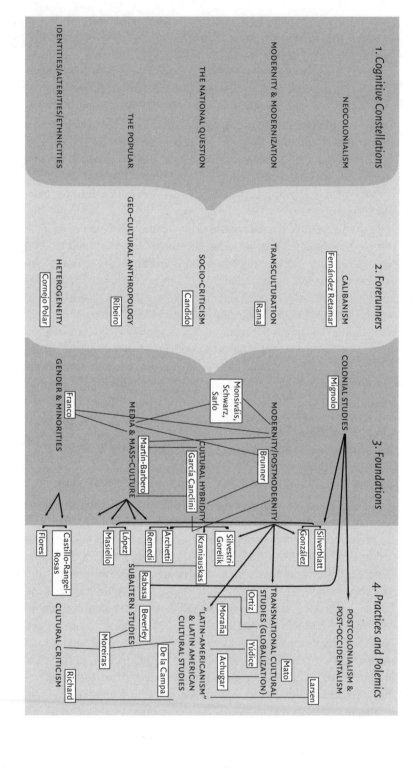

1. Cognitive Constellations

NEOCOLONIALISM

MODERNITY & MODERNIZATION

THE NATIONAL QUESTION

THE POPULAR

IDENTITIES/ALTERITIES/ETHNICITIES

2. Forerunners

CALIBANISM
Fernández Retamar

TRANSCULTURATION
Rama

SOCIO-CRITICISM
Candido

GEO-CULTURAL ANTHROPOLOGY
Ribeiro

HETEROGENEITY
Cornejo Polar

3. Foundations

COLONIAL STUDIES
Mignolo

MODERNITY/POSTMODERNITY
Monsiváis, Schwarz, Sarlo
Brunner

CULTURAL HYBRIDITY
Martín-Barbero
García Canclini

MEDIA & MASS-CULTURE

GENDER & MINORITIES
Franco

Silverblatt

Silvestri-Gorelik
González

Kraniauskas
Archetti
Remedi
López
Masiello

Castillo-Rangel-Rosas
Flores

4. Practices and Polemics

POSTCOLONIALISM & POST-OCCIDENTALISM

TRANSNATIONAL CULTURAL STUDIES (GLOBALIZATION)
Ortiz
Mato

"LATIN-AMERICANISM" & LATIN AMERICAN CULTURAL STUDIES
Moraña
Yúdice
Achugar
Larsen

Rabasa
Beverley
De la Campa

SUBALTERN STUDIES

CULTURAL CRITICISM
Moreiras
Richard

continent. In these circumstances, the old cognitive constellations drifted into new ones adapted to the times. "Forerunners," the first part in this reader, presents Antonio Candido's sociocriticism, Darcy Ribeiro's geocultural anthropology, Roberto Fernández Retamar's Calibanism, Angel Rama's transculturation, and Antonio Cornejo Polar's heterogeneity (map). These cognitive constellations amalgamate the most cogent issues and theories of the 1970s; concomitantly, these authors are direct precursors of Latin American cultural studies insofar as they function like a bridge between current practices in the field and the long tradition of Latin American critical thinking.

The 1980s repeatedly have been called the "Latin American lost decade" due to the fact that the consolidation of neoliberal socioeconomic policies, now under the blessing of neodemocratic regimes led by technocrats and electronic politicians, had terrible consequences on the national economies and the social fabrics: underemployment and flexible employment, a truly postmodern euphemism; widespread impoverishment, particularly among the lower middle sectors; the widening of the gap between rich and poor; stratification of a small, high-consuming globalized upper class and a large, low-consuming marginalized working force; and last but not least, the brutal increase of the migratory flows toward metropolitan countries. The globalization of Latin American economies, societies, and cultures reached, in the 1980s, intensity and complexity of higher proportions. In that context, Latin American cultural studies tried to elucidate and come to terms with neoliberalism as an economic model and a market ideology, with the substitution of party politics by mass-media and consumerist democracy, and with the added social and symbolic value acquired by the cultural in everyday life, as a consequence of the new economic centrality of the symbolic—and primarily of transnational mass culture—in the information age. Accordingly, this expansive foundational moment and its necessity to apprehend such deep and vertiginous transformations is framed in the ideological skirmishes of the postmodern debate, which in Latin America begins in the social sciences entrenched in research centers founded by metropolitan foundations. In other words, contemporary Latin American cultural studies are actually founded in the intersection of the Latin American tradition of cultural analysis and the postmodern self-reflexive irreverence, at the most neuralgic moment of globalization. The old cognitive constellations shifted once again, this time with completely renovated subfields of inquiry emerging, such as colonial studies, gender and minorities, modernity and/or postmodernity, media and mass culture, and cultural hybridity (map). Jean Franco, Carlos Monsiváis, Roberto

Schwarz, Beatriz Sarlo, Walter Mignolo, José Joaquín Brunner, Jesús Martín Barbero, and Néstor García Canclini, all included in the second part of this reader, are the most prominent founders of contemporary Latin American cultural studies.

Over the backdrop of these cognitive constellations, which established the main theoretical, methodological, and thematic lines of contemporary Latin American cultural studies, the 1990s staged the blooming and the subsequent implosion of the field. The third part, "Practices," includes a selection of outstanding essays that deal with some of the most recurring topics in the field, thus providing an inevitably partial though representative picture of its current status and major trends. The frantic search for new critical paradigms and the opening of epistemological frontiers nurtured an intense theoretical exchange between opposite tendencies vying for the hegemony of the field, and reached levels of theoretical oversaturation and deconstructive hypertrophy that imploded the field, leading to the present mood of uncertainty, disorientation, and fatigue. Colonial studies led to postcolonialism and postoccidentalism; studies on media and mass culture, combined in different degrees with the modernity/postmodernity debate and cultural hybridity, led to globalization and subaltern studies; gender and minorities, filtered through postmodernism, nourished cultural criticism. The debates between these different positions, recapitulated in part 4, "Positions and Polemics," exploded around the definition and the projection of Latin Americanism and Latin American cultural studies (see map). Seemingly, by the turn of the century, most of the theoretical proposals have reached their limits, which explains their gradual return to the cognitive constellations of the 1960s and 1970s, directly or indirectly connected to classic Latin American cultural paradigms, such as dependency theory, liberation theology and philosophy of liberation, the pedagogy of the oppressed, and the theories of internal colonialism, third cinema, and collective theater. The cycle, which started with the optimistic drive of the forerunners in the 1970s, is closing upon itself. After the theoretical frenzy of the 1990s, unintelligible without the explorations of the 1970s and the discoveries of the 1980s, the study of the cultures of Latin America would never be the same, and still, it will ever be what it has always already been.

I

Forerunners

Introduction by Alicia Ríos

TRADITIONS AND FRACTURES IN
LATIN AMERICAN CULTURAL STUDIES

As the preceding introduction has established, "Latin American cultural studies are a disputed field in a global scenario, which cannot be fully understood or further advanced without considering its historical grounding in Latin American sociocultural processes." Thus, "despite common interpretations, Latin American cultural studies are not just the product of an epistemological break . . . but also the result of specific historical continuities." It is a field of enquiry that has been mapped out through a series of conflicts, combining the rich Latin American critical tradition with European and North American schools of thought.

In this introduction to part 1 I would like to consider the manner in which the very long and important tradition of the Latin American critical essay has been intersected, throughout its history, by certain thematic axes and enunciative positions marking many of its pivotal concerns: questions of the national and the continental, the rural and the urban, tradition versus modernity, memory and identity, subjects and citizenships, and, especially, the role of intellectuals and institutions in the formation of discourse as well as social, cultural, and political practices. These concerns all lead into five cognitive constellations: neocolonialism, modernity and modernization, the national question, the popular, and identities/alterities/ethnicities. From the 1820s—the period immediately following independence—well into the 1960s, Latin American critical and political thought centered, directly or indirectly, on these constellations. Afterward, new critical parameters were constructed, giving rise to what we now call Latin American cultural studies.

The Latin American Critical Essay

The construct now called Latin America has always been marked by desire, perhaps even prior to the coining of this term in the nineteenth century.[1] In this context, desire must be understood doubly: as both a lack as well as a productive force arising as the result of, but also as the vehicle for, a discourse and a praxis that have felt hard-pressed to "invent" their "realities." America has been created on the empty space of a map since its origins. It has been pegged with names whose function it was to reproduce the ideal mental image of the namers—names that inevitably clashed with the other entity already there, or beginning to take shape. Even today, the contours of this map are still being drawn, from within and without, by words attempting to name something that is always managing to escape ideological boundaries.

Latin America's critical essay tradition has rested on this process of invention from Simón Rodríguez and Andrés Bello to the present. These "men of letters" had to "think" through each act, and clung to their "dreams of reason" throughout the nineteenth century. That metaphorical dream [of America] in which such men lumped together past, present, and future "authorized" them to decide what was suitable, desirable, and appropriate for the rest of the continent's inhabitants.

The wars of independence end in the mid-1820s, with the exception of those in Cuba and Puerto Rico. Once a relative peace was achieved, since throughout that first century quarrels between different ethnic and social groups abounded, the new republics committed themselves to (re-)construction, everything from roads and farm fields to, especially, the manner in which future citizens should think and express themselves. The fixation on a proper language "of their own" not only made possible the formation of a new citizenry, but also permitted control over other subjects, still in need of discipline and education. Teachers and educators, like Rodríguez and Bello, become fundamental figures. The lettered ruling class placed great faith in the role that teachers/educators would play in elaborating the premises for the successful consolidation of the new states. Rodríguez became instrumental in the development of primary education, Bello in that of the university; both left the mark of their ideas on the usage of an Americanized Spanish language (in law, grammar, and society in general). The tradition of the critical essay, a particularly Latin American form of expression, begins with these two educators and men of letters.[2]

Bello's often cited *silvas*, a poetic form from the Spanish Golden Age, *Alocución a la poesía* (1823) and *Silva a la agricultura de la zona tórrida* (1826), written in London, mark the beginning of a recurrent theme: the need to focus strictly on the American. It is, however, when writing from Chile that Bello develops a pedagogic program to be followed, especially in his articles on the manner in which to *write* and *study* history (1848), as well as in his *Discurso en el establecimiento de la Universidad de Chile* (1843). In the latter, the idea of the university as an enclave of "disinterested culture" or of "knowledge for knowledge's sake," which would later prevail, had no place. For Bello, very much in step with the beliefs of his age, "knowledge in its diverse disciplines, should be an instrument for the *supervision* of public life" (Ramos 1989, 40). Bello begins a timid reflection there on the boundaries between academic disciplines, which has nothing to do with our current conceptions. His polemic with José Victoriano Lastarria, for instance, has been catalogued by literary historiography as "literary," although at the time it was seen as cultural and, mostly, political. In his two later essays on history, Bello deepened such reflections and posited the value of the social sciences over philosophy. On the one hand, he argues, we have philosophers, politicians, and orators; on the other, historians, whose method is not speculation, but rather a "synthetic induction," or narrative, which allowed them to furnish antecedents and clarify facts. The need to construct/write national histories in order to find the "true" meaning of the national and to discover the differences between nations arises from this notion of Bello's.

Rodríguez, meanwhile, especially in his *Sociedades americanas en 1828*, coined the important phrase "Either we create or we err" (Rodríguez 1975, 343) in his pursuit of a new definition of the American. Both men promoted a "second" revolution, to which would be entrusted the happy outcome of the first one, initiated at the political level by the various liberators/heroes of independence. This new and more profound second revolution would not be led by the military, but rather by civilian men of letters, despite Bello's, Rodríguez's, and likewise Bolívar's lack of faith in their capabilities and maturity.

Domingo Faustino Sarmiento capitalized on this lack in order to focus his attack on the unlettered *caudillos* (local political war leaders) from the continent's hinterlands. Sarmiento was president of Argentina from 1868 to 1874, but not before having been twice exiled to Chile, where he wrote and published in episodic installments the political pamphlet that has undoubtedly had the widest of continental renown, his *Civilización y barbarie. Vida de Juan Facundo Quiroga* (1845). In this text, Sarmiento achieves a most accurate and vivid representation of the hatreds between his country's two opposing political parties, the federal and the unitarian, each with its own model of government. According to Sarmiento, the only way for Argentina to stay on its predestined road to success was to rid itself of its greatest enemy, the dictator Juan Manuel de Rosas, who embodied the backwardness and ignorance of the hinterlands. Similarly, he held that there would be a place only for those who were willing to overcome past limitations and to focus on the development of Buenos Aires as the nation's hub.

With the publication of *Facundo*, the constant counterpoint between the amenities/abundance of the cities and the backwardness of rural life, between modernity and tradition, between Western and local values defines itself in Latin American writing. Likewise, the conscious admixture of various literary genres and types of writing also becomes normative with its publication. *Facundo* is a fundamental text in the attempted construction of a Latin American ideal based on the hope of synthesizing all contradictions; it is at once history, sociology, moral treatise, novel, biography, political pamphlet, and, above all, essay. A strictly American representation and expression begin to take shape, thanks precisely to this mix: that is, the unavoidable coexistence of the transcultural, the heterogeneous, and the hybrid not only in the society in which it is a lived experience, but also in the expression that attempts to represent it. Given his zeal for eliminating dichotomies undoubtedly at the heart of his text's take on civilization, which is in open opposition to barbarism, it is curious that Sarmiento leaves this hybrid text of mixed genres to express "reality" as his legacy. This tendency led him, toward the end of his life, to develop an explicitly racist theory in *Conflicto y armonía de razas en América* (1883), a sort of bible for later pragmatic utilitarianism.

According to Arturo Andrés Roig's important study, *Teoría y crítica del pensamiento latinoamericano*, the word *civilization* began to be used in the sense Sarmiento gives it toward the end of the eighteenth century as a reflection of a newly evident social problematic, "a matter that comes about in direct and intimate relation to the social antagonisms such as those generated in colonized and dependent countries. . . . The nineteenth-century conflict between the pre-bourgeoisies of the Río de la Plata, avidly pursuing the processes of modernization in a bid to hasten their entrance into the sphere of industrialized nations, and the peasants and the older artisan's guilds formed at the end of the eighteenth century is well known" (Roig 1981, 67–68). The need to overcome "the barbarous" will be a theme repeated or inverted throughout Latin American history, as will the values of civilization and of "culture" along with very radical positivistic policies that find one of their highpoints in Juan Bautista Alberdi's famous dictum: "To govern means to populate." Man's duty was to conquer the immense plains, fence them in, urbanize them, and force nature to conform to human designs.

In Sarmiento, then, we find the typical Latin American man of letters: at one and the same time politician, statesman, and writer. It would have been impossible at the outset of the republics for reflection and creation not to have been tied to governmental functions, a panorama that would change with the advent of *modernismo* as a literary (and cultural) movement at the end of that first century of republican life, a life then conceived of only within the parameters of modernity and modernization, but that fell under an intense system of unequal commercial and cultural exchange with its European and North American counterparts. The accelerated process of modernization, catalyzing the transformation of the political sphere and the progressive disappearance of entire social sectors, also brought about unprecedented socioeconomic development, especially in the Río de la Plata region.

The professionalism made possible by the development of the press and its respective correspondents' posts allowed the turn-of-the-century writer, among other things, to finally become independent of his lettered function and count himself solely as an intellectual and/or a creator. In this respect, the figure of José Martí is emblematic. Martí not only continued to consolidate the long tradition of the critical essay, but also initiated with greater autonomy the so-called literary essay. Like Rubén Darío, Martí took the newspaper chronicle, that genre straddling literature and journalism, to its highest level of expression, creating a space for reflection on the hectic years at the end of the nineteenth century and the beginning of the twentieth (see Rotker 1991). One of Martí's most important contributions and a classic work of Latin American thought in its own right is his *Nuestra América* (1891), in which he posits a new "definition" of race, one of the terms most feared and most frequently appealed to in America. In this text Martí tells us that "there is no racial hatred because there are no races" (1980, 17). He did not mean to say by this that there were no whites, blacks, Indians, and *mestizos*, but rather that race did not exist in the biological sense of the word. Race existed from a rather different perspective: that of the oppressed, that of the slave. This is Martí's response to Sarmiento, whom he undoubtedly engages in dialogue here. Martí was opposed to the positivistic biological conception of race, and he would surely have also opposed José Enrique Rodós vision, clearly more "cultural" than that of Sarmiento, but based equally on Latin racial pride.

Martí proposed a different concept of "ours": pride in being who and what (Latin)Americans are. Originality and authenticity are posited as values, according to which (Latin)Americans would no longer be forced to follow foreign models of government, for example, but had, instead, to create new and more adequate models, if need be, even making wine from bananas (in many ways reiterating Simón Rodríguez's motto: "Either we create or we err"). Martí puts forth the idea of Our America as a motive for continental political unity, and as the only possible avenue of defense against the new power to the north, that "seven league monster," the United States, against which not only Cuba, but the rest of (Latin)America must also defend itself.

Yet another fundamental text in Latin American critical thought, José Enrique Rodó's Ariel (1900), makes its appearance at the turn of the century. Framed within the context of the Spanish-American War (1898), the Spanish crown's last attempt at saving its few remaining colonies— Cuba, Puerto Rico, and the Philippines—Rodó's text, again a composite of genres—essay, speech, and parable—posits the need to defend the values of "Latinness" in light of neocolonial encroachment from the new northern power. As in the case of the previously mentioned texts, this essay looks toward the future and its most valued, designated reading audience consisted of young people from all Latin American nations.

Ever an avid devotee of science and technology—as the good "modern" he was—Rodó did not align himself with positivism; his response was more in keeping with a renovated idealism attempting to salvage aesthetic and individual values in danger of extinction from imperial capitalism and utilitarian mass society. Despite being a close follower of Ernest Renan, Rodó was in favor of certain democratic ideas; when he spoke of aristocracy, it was not on the basis of economic or social privileges, but rather on that of merit earned from honest work and the cultivation of uncorrupted values. He tried "to reconcile the most stabilizing principles of European tradition with the redefinition of the social order in order to assure the mechanisms for increasing, but regulated, participation by the masses" (Moraña 1982, 658).[3] At the heart of his thought is a hidden desire for a society in which differences and heterogeneity could be overcome, thus creating a world in which Latin and criollo cultural values would prevail, including leisure in the classic sense of the term.

Throughout the nineteenth century, Latin American writers, artists, and intellectuals—of whom those just mentioned are paradigmatic and influential examples—were also practical men (and in rare cases, women) who were deeply involved in political action, always concerned with their role in society. They explicitly portray themselves not only with the intent, but also the obligation to intervene in social and cultural life. Their preoccupations, intentions, and attitudes develop as an important antecedent in what will become the thematic constellations in which later Latin American critical thought can be organized.

Latin American Critical Thought

Once Latin America, with the advent of professional journalism, had fully entered the twentieth century, the formation of more articulated, cohesive blocs of reflection on certain themes and problems began. This is not to say that the figure of individual author—or thinker—lost its relevancy, but rather that intellectual work was now conceived of within a more precise framework, since writers and thinkers now took on a new professional consciousness.

The Arielist school, including such prominent figures as Alfonso Reyes, Mariano Picón Salas, and Pedro Henríquez Ureña, emerged in the first decades of the century. Henríquez Ureña contributes fundamentally to the division of Latin American literary studies into periods, while we owe to Reyes and Picón Salas a notable theoretical development of literary criticism in general.[4] For the Arielists, American questions were associated with a tradition of their own, in keeping with a heroic past—in all cases as much indigenous as Spanish—but with a heavy dose of European values, along with a defense of certain ethical and aesthetic principles.

The problem of identities takes on new dimensions in the first half of the twentieth century: What repercussions does participation in a colonial—postcolonial or neocolonial—situation have on subjects and subjectivities, and what is to be done when such a situation is surmounted? What role do the ethnic groups who make up that desire called Latin America play? How should the local and the national, the capital cities and the heartland be connected with global metropolitan centers within a coherent development plan? The problem of how to understand the word culture—and the cultural—takes on extreme importance: How are the fuzzy boundaries between high, popular, and mass culture, and between oral and written culture to be managed? What role should the intellectual play in all of this? What should his or her commitment to the masses, to the media, and the market be? Finally, what should the relationship—and the role—of the intellectual be in diverse institutions; in the case of academic reflection, what should one's position be with respect to so-called national literatures and cultures? Distinct schools and critical practices, such as *indigenismo*, *negritud*, *criollismo*, and regionalism, each accompanied by its literary, and in most cases, political expressions arise to answer these questions.

I am most interested here in concentrating on the discourse of *indigenismo*, not only as it occurs in fiction, but also in its theoretical proposals as such. The terrible "trinity of brutalization of indigenous peoples" was to be confronted and surmounted along various fronts: anarchist in the texts of Manuel González Prada and Marxist in those of José Carlos Mariátegui. In indigenist novels and discourse, the unholy trinity of the Catholic Church, the state, and the military *(el cura, el jefe civil y el caudillo)* constitutes the principal obstacle blocking indigenous peoples from development and guaranteeing their continued subaltern condition. In general terms, intellectuals were the ones to declare themselves defenders of the dispossessed, often proposing solutions that had little to do with the lived reality of those they claimed to represent. As Antonio Cornejo Polar has pointed out so well, "given its condition as a heterogeneous story, straddling two sharply divided sociocultural worlds . . . *indigenismo* reproduces the conflict unresolved in the very history of disintegrated and torn nations. In this sense, although it may seem paradoxical, the great truth of *indigenismo*, especially the indigenist novel, is not found in what it says, but rather in the real contradiction it produces discursively" (Cornejo Polar 1994, 206). This contradiction between "reality" and its discursivity is equally evident in the case of *gauchesca* literature (Josefina Ludmer has argued as much in a now classic 1988 text on the subject, *El género gauchesco. Un tratado sobre la patria*).

González Prada, a combatant in the War of the Pacific (1879–1883), notes the painful loss of Peruvian territory to Chile at the signing of the Treaty of Ancón, ending the war, and harshly analyzes the reasons for such a disaster. In his famous *Discurso en el Politeama* (1888) he maintains: "The brutal hand of Chile tore apart our flesh and ground our bones; but the real winners, our enemy's weapons, were our own ignorance and our spirit of servitude" (González Prada 1982, 44–45). These remarks will be complemented in one of his most important, and lamentably unfinished, essays, *Nuestros Indios* (1904). Here, in line with Martí, he argues that the Indians do not represent a biological race, but a social class, dependent on their economic status. In this essay he coins one of his most celebrated and repeated phrases: "To him who would say *school*, answer him back *school and bread*. The question of the Indian is economic, it is social, rather than pedagogical" (González Prada 1982, 182). González Prada, decidedly preoccupied with the question of education, devoted some effort to the study of language and the establishment of a new system of orthography, just as had Bello and Rodríguez.

Mariátegui, founder of Peru's Socialist Party, published in 1928 what can clearly be designated as a fundamental twentieth-century Latin American text, setting the tone for what would later become a sociopolitical essayistic tradition. His *Siete ensayos de interpretación de la realidad peruana* both advances and departs from González Prada's anarchist premises. The latter had maintained that the problem of the Indian was an economic one; Mariátegui takes that premise to its ultimate consequences. His readings on Peru's defeat in the same war in which González Prada had fought shaped many of his opinions on postwar Peru. What most concerned him, however, was the elimination of the feudal state and the servility prevalent in his country: "Peru must choose between the *gamonal* [traditional landowner who acted as a feudal lord] and the Indian. This is its dilemma. There is no third way" (Mariátegui 1976, 176).

Siete ensayos begins with a reflection on the colony and the republic, what both meant from the perspective of their economic evolution and the degree to which their social stratification and their cultural values still influenced the present of Latin American countries. The essays then take up the problem of the Indian and that of land, the process of public education, the role of religion, and the positions taken on regionalism and centralism. His final essay is an analysis of Peruvian literature. Such themes have been touched on again and again by those seeking an adequate approach to the problem of Latin America; Mariátegui's decided relevance, in the context of this introduction, is the unity he achieved between reflection and political practice. His reflection always attempts to ignore conceptual limitations, allowing him to attribute due importance to both the discussion of *indigenismo* and the avant-garde, for example, thus tying together what had been until then two irreconcilable extremes. In his third and perhaps most important essay, "The Problem of Land," Mariátegui revises "written history," that is, how the problem of the Indian had been thought of and written about, in an open examination/questioning of the "lettered city." For Mariátegui, political participation was a necessary prerequisite for any theoretical position. From that point of view, his entire, admittedly Marxist, body of reflection regarding the problem of the Indian had no intent but that of the final achievement of their true social, economic, and political vindications (as he understood them at the time, and with the contradictions we might now find in them).

Other important figures and groups, all attempting to answer the questions posed earlier in this introduction, appeared throughout the first thirty years of the twentieth century. The Mexican author José Vasconcelos developed an almost delirious defense of the virtues of a future *mestizo* American *Cosmic Race* (1925), which would be increasingly superior to the rest of the world's previous cultures. It would unnecessarily lengthen this introduction to analyze the work of such important thinkers as Leopoldo Zea, Augusto Salazar Bondy, Silvio Romero, Rosario Castellanos, or Gilberto Freire, just to mention a few. I have chosen to concentrate here on those figures who, in my view, are not only the most representative, but also the most pertinent. Any genealogy must necessarily penetrate personal, affective, and disciplinary networks, to which we ascribe as much by filiation as by affiliation; it would be impossible to account for all of them, and thus, one must choose. What I do hope is clear in this brief survey of earlier Latin American critical thought, with the attendant implication of political stance in the textual selections, is its importance in the formation of current critical thought.

One of the most important and most strictly Latin American contributions to the study of culture and anthropology emerging during this period is the theory of transculturation. Fernando Ortiz first coined the term in his text, *Contrapunteo cubano del tabaco y del azúcar* (1940), another classic work of Latin American thought. This text, like Sarmiento's *Facundo*, also engages in a dialogue with various forms of expression, a sort of cross between anthropological treatise and prose poem, but an impressive musical counterpoint as well. Ortiz establishes the need to find a new word to better account for the strictly American process of the mixing and exchange of habits and cultures. He proposes a neologism, transculturation, since the word, acculturation, then used in cultural anthropology, did not meet his requirements. Acculturation implies a one-way process in which the "barbarian" is always being "civilized," while the new term, transculturation, demonstrates the manner in which coexisting cultures and cultures in conflict simultaneously both gain and lose through contact. He takes as his base a medieval Spanish text, *Libro de buen amor*, the remarkable counterpoint from Juan Ruiz, Arcipreste de Hita that features an allegorical battle between Don Carnal ("Sir Flesh," carnival) and Doña Cuaresma ("Lady Lent"), and imagines a similar battle between tobacco and sugar, that is a musical duel in which the struggle and cultural conflict between the two is made explicit. Each product represents a particular moment in the conquest and represents, respectively, African or European culture. "In the production of tobacco intelligence predominates; we have already said that tobacco is liberal, if not revolutionary. In sugar production force prevails; it is well-known that sugar is conservative, if not absolutist" (F. Ortiz 1978, 56). What is most important in Ortiz's work is the demonstration of the extent to which transculturation affects each and every instance of Cuban—and by extension Latin American—culture: its economy, institutions, jurisprudence, ethics, religion, art, language, psychology, and even its sexuality. The true history of Cuba is thus found in the intricate history of its transculturations, most especially in the violent uprooting of African peoples from their originating cultures.

The Climate of the 1960s

The second half of the twentieth century, marked by leftist struggles, especially after the triumph of the Cuban Revolution (1959), brings about the cementing of the first truly Latin American social theories. Perhaps their most interesting theoretical aspects consist of re-dimensioning the notions of superstructure and infrastructure, and interconnecting them via the most important theoretical contributions of the day. Such interconnections encompass both structural and sociological dimensions, but adapted, for the first time, in an indisputably "original" manner, molded to the particular needs of Latin American cultures and societies.

On one hand, there was a need to go beyond the limitations of Arielism and to demonstrate the falsity of its universalistic, and to an extent, essentialist, ideals. There was also a need to separate concrete political moments that moved them closer to or farther away from metropolitan centers of power. In his book *Calibán: apuntes sobre la cultura en Nuestra América*, Fernández Retamar inverts the reading of Ariel: if for Rodó the United States is Caliban and Spanish America is Ariel, we have fallen into a grave error. It is only by assuming that we are Caliban—the one who learns his oppressor's language and makes it his own, avenges his mistreatment at his master's hands, and surpasses his master's achievements—can we feel proud of who we are and leave the situation of dependence in which we have always been trapped. This colonial situation is one on which Latin American thinkers reflect time and again. Such reflections are present not only in the work of Fernández Retamar, but also in that of Puerto Rican author José Luis González's *El país de cuatro pisos* (1979), or in the important tradition of Latin American Marxist thought, especially the forgers of dependency theory, Celso Furtado, Fernando Henrique Cardoso, and Enzo Faletto, among others. Another avenue of such reflections belongs to liberation theology, especially in the works of

Gustavo Gutiérrez and Leonardo Boff. Both dependency theory and liberation theology, two strands of a particularly Latin American phenomenon, deeply influence Latin American thought.

Dependency theory, which traces its beginnings to the mid-1960s, has as perhaps its most interesting aspect the mix of both Latin American theories (those of Mariátegui, Fidel Castro, Ernesto Che Guevara) and European ones (those of Antonio Gramsci and Louis Althusser, particularly). Since that time, dependency theory has been further worked out and "appropriated," that is, both made our own and adjusted to our realities. It has undergone a re-dimensioning of its Marxist notions as well, but the vital question of identity remains as one of the theory's core elements. Its principal representatives set forth the need to defend an endogenous scientific and technological development, where national interests prevail over imperial capitalism.

Cardoso's and Faletto's principal objective is an explanation of economic processes as social and political ones, framed within the modernizing stage of Latin American countries, with their attendant particularities and peculiarities extending beyond the global study of development. Methodologically, they are interested in accentuating "the analysis of the specific conditions of the Latin American situation and the type of social integration of classes and groups as the principal conditioners of the developmental process" (Cardoso and Faletto 1978, 17). The notion of "development" is thus understood as the product of interaction between and among diverse groups and social classes all with their own manner of interrelating. Groups or classes are thus marked by distinct values and interests tied in across oppositions, conciliations, or improvements determined by the socioeconomic system in which they are inserted. The fundamental theoretical problem consists of "determining the modes the structures of domination adopt, because through them one comes to understand the dynamic of class relations" (Cardoso and Faletto 1978, 19). This notion of social processes as embedded in systemic structures is a fundamental tool in dependency analysis. The incorporation and re-definition of the concepts of centrality and periphery, as well as colonial and national formations is also of prime importance to their discussion. The idea of dependence thus "alludes directly to the conditions of existence and the functioning of the economic and political systems, demonstrating the ties between the two, on both an internal and external plane" (Cardoso and Faletto 1978, 24).

On the other end of the spectrum, liberation theology arises as a result of both the ideological and theoretical crises of diverse Christian revolutionary groups who actively participated in Latin American political struggles during the 1960s, 1970s, and 1980s. Such groups sought certain explanations, justifications, and continuity of events in which they were participants, in keeping with premises fundamental to Catholic dogma and practices, although not strictly limited to them. The contradictions between religious theory and practice led some participants to a definitive separation from the church and others to a partial one. For still others, political struggle can and should be established within the institution, as well as through political parties and lay organizations, such as Acción Católica and the Christian Democratic parties. For the most radical, it was necessary to subject biblical faith to its greatest test: to discover from within it its true relation to political practice, as well as its relation to the historic process of liberation and spiritual salvation. In this confrontation, the radical factions concluded that "there is no contradiction between historical materialism and the biblical concept of history that would impede Christians from taking up the political task of the struggle to construct socialism in its complete dimension" (Silva Gotay 1986, 121–22). As a result, such Christians began to participate actively in Latin American revolutionary processes. Leonardo and Clodovis Boff, in their widely circulated manual *Como fazer teologia da libertação* (1986), take as their point of departure the incisive question "how to be Christians in a world full of human misery?" (9). The levels of poverty and hunger to which the dispossessed of the Third World are subjected oblige the Boffs to respond with sacred ire in the face of social sin, that is, indifference to human suffering. They are further obligated to initiate a series of active measures to counteract indifference and work toward overcoming human suffering. In this manner, liberation theology establishes as its primary task the bodily and spiritual liberation of the oppressed, as well as the defense of "any and all of the oppressed: the poor, the subjugated, the discriminated [against]." Thus liberation theology struggles against racial, ethnic, and sexual oppression, as well as against economic exploitation and political repression (Boff and Boff 1986, 39).

The Forerunners

As mentioned earlier, the 1960s and 1970s in Latin America were a very intense period in terms of political, economic, social, and cultural change; these changes would seem to take on even more drastic and problematic dimensions at the beginning of this twenty-first century. Attempts at revolution inspired by the model of the Cuban Revolution, particularly during the 1960s, spread throughout the continent, at the same time as did military dictatorships and conservative regimes. This did not hinder certain democratizing attempts at national conciliation in some countries, such as Venezuela, which was then in the midst of an unprecedented economic boom. An extremely intense cultural and ideological exchange was also achieved, thanks in great part to the waves of immigration produced by unstable regional economic and political conditions, especially in the Southern Cone. In metropolitan centers, such as Mexico City and Caracas, where many of the most prominent intellectuals from regions with little prior exposure to continental exchange were forced to emigrate, an environment of important theoretical and conceptual exchange was in formation. The need for a unified Latin America, as a function of certain political and cultural interests, allowed for the consolidation of new intellectual projects that until then had been unwanted or unimagined. The five intellectuals grouped together in part 1, "Forerunners," respond to this ideal of a unified Latin America. Their discursive and methodological proposals entered into a frank dialogue that allowed the elaboration of new thematic constellations established with greater affinity for the times and its problems—without having to reject older ones outright.

On the one hand, we find Antonio Candido's sociocritical proposal, Darcy Ribeiro's geocultural anthropology, and Roberto Fernández Retamar's "calibanism"; on the other, the theories of transculturation, further developed by Angel Rama, and heterogeneity, by Antonio Cornejo Polar. The first part of this anthology's textual selections is by these five intellectuals, all direct precursors of much of what is practiced today and of what has been in the making for the past fifty years.

The works of both Brazilian authors is an obligatory reference for any Latin American or Latin Americanist cultural reflection. Antonio Candido's contributions encompass the whole of literary studies, especially his incorporation of a clearly leftist anthropological and sociological perspective into the revision of national and occidental values. Since he was a full-time academic, it became the task of his many students to put his novel manner of incorporating social, economic, and political categories into literary criticism, as well as his analysis of both "high culture" and "popular literature" into practice. Candido's readings of Brazilian literature still hold relevance, most notably because he incorporates them into the discussion of Latin American literature and culture as a whole, something rarely done before him. "Literature and Underdevelopment," the article selected for this anthology, springs from this preoccupation of his. Originally published in French in 1970, the article analyzes the problems in vogue at the moment: the role of the intellectual, the cities, the regions, and the problem of methodological models. He also revises strictly literary nomenclature (romanticism, regionalism, modernism) and distinguishes between Portuguese and Spanish usage of the same terms. One of his most important contributions is his reading of the contours and limits of what we could call "imitation," and its unquestionable sidekick, underdevelopment. Candido concludes—as do the rest of the authors in this section—by affirming the fact that we do imitate, just as everyone else does, but we also make our own additions and leave our particular marks, not only on literary texts but on the whole of cultural production.

Thus, Candido highlights the aesthetic and formal dimension of literature, without separating it from its social and ideological functions. In this way he works out the concept of (literary) "system" at the heart of his thinking: his interest is in emphasizing any works linked by common denominators that establish the pattern of a culture's dominant features (a pattern that literature unequivocally helps to construct).

Essayist, anthropologist, and sociologist, Darcy Ribeiro became one of the greatest defenders of indigenous peoples over the course of his long and checkered academic and political career. An undoubted precursor of postcolonial studies in Latin America, he set forth a theoretical proposal for the studying of what he called the civilizational processes that have mapped the history of all cultures. Ribeiro questioned the very concept of cultural autonomy, since there is an inevitable conjunction in any given ethnic expansion due to the economic, social, and ideological planes that are always involved in such processes. He identifies, as a result, four different categories among non-European peoples according to their historical and geocultural formation: Witness, New, Transplanted, and Emerging Peoples. Each of them "does not represent necessary stages in the evolutionary process, but only the conditions under which it operates" (see Ribeiro in "Forerunners"). The idea of a truly American revolution, establishing the existence of ills brought in by the civilizing process, especially as they relate to racial differences, would be—according to him—the unavoidable condition for surmounting the neocolonial situation. In order to achieve this end, Latin Americans must confront, once and for all, not only the problems generated by the European invasion, but by their own mistakes, in particular the killing rage that is still visited upon indigenous peoples and masked by unfair laws and protectionist practices.

As for Roberto Fernández Retamar, we have already mentioned his questioning of Arielism and the national liberal projects it represented. But we must also remember the particular circumstances behind the publication of his text. Due to the numerous international criticisms brought out after the Cuban government's handling of the "Padilla case," the importance of creating a manifesto outlining the revolutionary cultural project of the Cuban Revolution was clear. Fernández Retamar insists on the need to undo or overcome the perturbing inferiority complexes that have always accompanied readings on American cultural history. As a key figure in the Cuban government's cultural ensemble, he expounds on the need for literature and art, as well as the study of both, to be tied to revolutionary struggle. His indignation at the question opening his famous *Calibán* (1971), on whether or not a Latin American culture exists, can only be explained in a colonial context. That is, he states, the very formulation of such a question can only occur if we are immersed in a colonial condition; only under those conditions could any possible doubt concerning our own existence arise.

Although Fernando Ortiz coined the term *transculturation*, Angel Rama elaborates on it and takes it in a different direction. For Rama, inscribed in modern lettered discourse, the neologism serves to introduce a new reading of Latin American cultures, in which the relationship between modernity and tradition is more openly problematized, in which the mythical critical model is surmounted and in which the author sides with the counter-hegemonic potential of regional, local cultures.

In his *Transculturación narrativa en América Latina* (1982), Rama redraws the cultural map, from colonial times on, in order to outline the domination to which diverse cultural and literary systems of diverse regions have been subjected. He centers his study of Latin American literatures and cultures on three fundamental notions: originality, representativeness, and independence. According to Rama, "Literary works do not fall outside the realm of culture, but are, rather, its culmination, and to the extent that Latin American cultures are centuries-old and multitudinous inventions, they make of the writer a producer who works with the works of countless others" (see Rama in "Forerunners").

Rama's differences with Ortiz have to do with the manner in which the process of transculturation should be understood, especially when applied to literary works. He disputes Ortiz's "geometric" vision, which does not account for many factors traversing the transculturating process (e.g., those that exert a great deal of force, although not directly), and gives an impressive example. "The European transculturating impact between the two world wars did not include Marxism in its repertoire, but was, nonetheless, chosen by numerous university groups all over America" (see Rama in "Forerunners"). The selective capacity is not only applied to the foreign culture, but principally to one's own (contrary to what, in Rama's estimation, Ortiz establishes), "the site of massive destructions and losses. . . . There would be, of course, losses, selections, rediscoveries and incorporations. These four operations are concomitant and all are resolved within the overall restructuring of the cultural system, which is the highest creative function achieved in the transculturating process. Utensils, norms, objects, beliefs, customs only exist in a living and dynamic articulation, designed by the culture's functional structure" (ibid.). Rama goes on to explain how the transculturating process functions on the basis of three operations: language, literature, and worldview. These operations have always been pointed out by Latin American thinkers, both old and new, and have found their greatest representative in the figure of the Peruvian writer José María Arguedas.[5]

Antonio Cornejo Polar begins his elaborations on another of the notions most in vogue in current literary and cultural studies with Arguedas's texts as his object of study: heterogeneity, and with it, the relation between oral and written language. Cornejo proposes the resignification of the symbolic content of theoretical discourse in a departure from strictly ethnic and racial approaches in order to denounce the hidden forces behind certain approaches whose appearances belie true sociocultural exchanges. Such is the case in the notion of transculturation, which in truth, according to Cornejo, masks the category of *mestizaje* to the extent that syncretism is reinforced by the concept, omitting many cases in which conflict prevails.[6] Cornejo's reflection on heterogeneity reaches its high point in his latest book, *Escribir en el aire. Ensayo sobre la heterogeneidad socio-cultural en las culturas andinas* (1994), in which he outlines a panorama that begins strictly in colonial times with the "dialogue" between the Inca Atahualpa and Father Vicente Valverde in Cajamarca on the afternoon of Saturday, 16 November 1532, and ends with the most current discussions on subalternity and postcolonialism. Cornejo's own discussion of the issues hinges on three problems: discourse (toward which he proposes telling/writing the story of synchrony), subject (breaking down the image of the romantic/modern I, now turned into a complex, disperse, and multiple subject), and representation. His intention is to make evident the "symbolic war that corresponds to the ethno-social one between the indigenous and the *criollo* [offspring of Spanish nobility born in the colonies] worlds" (Montaldo 2000, 397). Cornejo also disjoints the colonial condition, which consists "precisely in denying the colonized his/her identity as a subject, in fragmenting/cutting into pieces all ties, and imposing others that disrupt and take/tear him/her apart" (Cornejo Polar 1994, 27).

By Way of a Pre-Epilogue . . .

The authors and texts mentioned in the previous section mark the direct beginning of theoretical reflection on the statutes of what will become Latin American cultural studies. Each of the authors approaches his object of study from a perspective that attempts not only to account for his place in the intellectual arena, but also to establish a direct dialogue with his Latin American interlocutors. The critical work of these authors takes shape from the need to question their own culture, and above all, to take academic reflection to an openly political plane (by political I don't mean solely militant participation in a given party, although this is the case for some). Each author partakes of the desire to construct a better future, to the extent that all understand that this reflection on what we have been, what we are, and what we wish to be cannot have a happy ending as long as the modalities of our own condition are not understood and confronted with honesty.

Finally, it is necessary to highlight a profound difference between what has customarily been done in the field of Latin American critical thought and what is currently being done in Latin American cultural studies. On the one hand, earlier scholars sided with and opted for the integrating capacity of national arts and literatures (as in the case of Mariátegui, whose final essay out of the seven is devoted precisely to literature). These authors also counted heavily on the strong presence of the aesthetic and strictly valuative dimensions of their cultural artifacts. One of the harshest criticisms of Latin American cultural studies has been its abandonment of that dimension, and its often arbitrary mix of methodologies and perspectives. On the other hand, current cultural scholars attempt to question literature and art precisely as part of the apparatuses of power. This is fundamental, since it is exactly here where the change in direction toward a different manner of thinking about and from Latin America occurs. If the borders between knowledges and disciplines were never altogether precise, today the argument against any such precision is open; not only are subjectivities articulated/operated simultaneously on various planes and at various depths, so are all instances of knowledge, experience, and even language. In these postmodern times, not only have master narratives lost their validity, but so have all those "natural," "historic," and/or "social" truths that allowed discourses—and their subjects—to be found in a precise context with definable, reachable limits and characteristics.

Another important difference, this time between cultural studies (from the English-speaking world) and Latin American cultural studies, is that the former usually take as their point of departure "contemporary culture," while this is not so in the case of the latter. There are, however, avenues of research that deal with the latest issues: the media, mass culture, the problems of globalization, consumption, civil society, and postmodernity. In fact, while many Latin American cultural studies scholars, such as Néstor García Canclini, Jesús Martín-Barbero, and George Yúdice, deal precisely with these topics, there is also a very fertile and active contingent of scholars devoted to earlier times, the first half of the twentieth century and all of the nineteenth, and even strictly colonial times. It is precisely the very long tradition of the critical essay in Latin America that has forced many to turn their gaze to the past, to revise the ways in which we have thought about ourselves in order to find answers—or greater problematizations—for the times we now live in.

Many of the characteristics and concerns of this field called Latin American cultural studies in effect constitute a fracture, or breach in continuity, especially when one refers to a transnational vision of the exercise of the disciplines devoted to the study of Latin America. The same is also true when one refers to a rereading of what is understood by aesthetics and a conceptualization reaching beyond rigid national parameters.

In Latin America the themes, practices, and institutions of knowledge have all been equally heterogeneous and conflictive. The Latin American cultural thinkers, represented here by Rodríguez, Bello, Sarmiento, Martí, Rodó, Henríquez Ureña, Picón Salas, Reyes, González Prada, Mariátegui, Ortiz, Cardoso, Boff, Candido, Ribeiro, Fernández Retamar, Rama, and Cornejo Polar, constitute, in a strict sense, the foremost precursors of Latin American cultural studies.

Translated by Christine McIntyre

Notes

1. Panamanian thinker Ricaute Soler holds that it would be more appropriate to use the term *Latin America* from the end of the nineteenth century on, when resistance was organized around a new world power: the United States. If we are concerned with struggles for independence, we are better off referring to *Spanish America*; in other words, the Spanish colonies in their struggle against the Spanish crown, with the notable exceptions of Cuba and Puerto Rico, which precisely define this change (Soler 1975). This is a key distinction, because the first term, *Latin America,* can include Brazil and the Caribbean, not just the Spanish-speaking areas. Conditions under North American hegemony clearly differ from those of more properly colonial times. I am not referring, then, to the etymology of these words, but rather to their conceptual and methodological possibilities.

2. Regarding *el buen decir* (a proper language) and the formation of its subjects, we cannot overlook the important contribution of Julio Ramos in his *Desencuentros de la modernidad en América Latina. Literatura y política en el siglo XIX* (1989). This text, along with Angel Rama's *La ciudad letrada* (1984a) and José Luis Romero's *Latinoamérica: las ciudades y las ideas* (1976), constitutes a crucial moment in the prelude to what we have called Latin American cultural studies.

3. For two interesting yet divergent readings questioning the traditional vision of Arielismo, see Ardao 1977 and González Echevarría 1985.

4. Rafael Gutiérrez Girardot is probably the critic who has most exhaustively and completely treated the texts of both authors, *Pedro Henríquez Ureña y Alfonso Reyes* (1994). See also Mariaca Iturri (1993, 23–26).

5. Among the many discussions of the term *transculturation*, see Antonio Benítez Rojo, *La isla que se repite: El Caribe y la perspectiva postmoderna* (1989), and Mary Louise Pratt, *Imperial Eyes: Travel Writing and Transculturation* (1992b).

6. With respect to the debate between the terms *transculturation* and *heterogeneity*, see Schmidt (1995) and Trigo (1997).

ANTONIO CANDIDO
Literature and Underdevelopment

Antonio Candido was born in Brazil in 1918. A literary and cultural critic, he is also an emeritus professor at the Universidade Estadual de Campinas in São Paulo, Brazil. His main titles include *Formação da literatura brasileira* (1969), *Literatura e sociedade* (1985), and *O discurso e a cidade* (1993).

Mário Vieira de Mello, one of the few writers to approach the problem of the relations between underdevelopment and culture, makes a distinction for the Brazilian case that is also valid for all of Latin America. He says that there has been a marked alteration of perspectives; until the 1930s the idea of "the new country," still unable to realize itself, but attributing to itself great possibilities of future progress, predominated among us. With no essential modification in the distance that separates us from the rich countries, what predominates now is the notion of an "underdeveloped country." The first perspective accentuated potential strength and, therefore, a still unrealized greatness. The second pointed out the present poverty, the atrophy; what was lacking, not what was abundant (Vieira de Mello 1963, 3–17).

The consequences Mário Vieira de Mello drew from this distinction do not seem valid to me, but taken by itself it is correct and helps us to understand certain fundamental aspects of literary creation in Latin America. In fact, the idea of a new country produces in literature some fundamental attitudes, derived from surprise, from the interest in the exotic, from a certain respect for the grandiose, and from a hopeful sense of possibilities. The idea that America constituted a privileged place was expressed in utopian projections that functioned in the physiognomy of conquest and colonization; and Pedro Henríquez Ureña reminds us that the first document about our continent, Columbus's letter, inaugurated the tone of seduction and exaltation that would be communicated to posterity. In the seventeenth century, mixing pragmatism and prophesy, Antônio Vieira recommended the transfer of the Portuguese monarchy, fated to realize the highest ends of history as the seat of the Fifth Empire, to Brazil. Later, when the contradictions of colonial status led the dominant strata to a political separation from the mother countries, there emerged the complementary idea that America had been predestined to be the country of liberty, and thus to consummate the destiny of Western man.

This state of euphoria was inherited by Latin American intellectuals, who transformed it into both instruments of national affirmation and an ideological justification. Literature became the language of celebration and tender affection, favored by Romanticism, with support from hyperbole and the transformation of exoticism into a state of the soul. Our sky was bluer, our flowers more luxuriant, our countryside more inspiring than that of other places, as in a Brazilian poem that, from this point of view, is valuable as a paradigm: the "Song of Exile," by Gonçalves Dias, who could stand for any of his Latin American contemporaries from Mexico to Tierra del Fuego.

The idea of *country* was closely linked to that *of nature* and in part drew its justification from it. Both were conducive to a literature that compensated for material backwardness and the weakness of institutions by an overvaluation of regional features, making exoticism a reason for social optimism. In the *Santos Vega*, of the Argentine Rafael Obligado, on the verge of the twentieth century, the nativist exaltation is projected onto a patriotism properly speaking, and the poet implicitly distinguishes *country* (institutional) and *land* (natural), nevertheless linking them in the same gesture of identification:

La convicción de que es mía
La patria de Echeverría,
La tierra de Santos Vega
[The conviction of what is mine
The country of Echeverría
The land of Santos Vega].

Country for the thinker, land for the singer. One of the assumptions, explicit or latent, of Latin American literature was this mutual contamination, generally euphoric, of land and country, the grandeur of the second being considered as a kind of unfolding of the strength of the first. Our literatures are nourished in the "divine promises of hope," to cite a famous verse by the Brazilian romantic poet Castro Alves.

But, the other side of the coin, the discouraged visions shared the same order of associations, as if the weakness or the disorganization of institutions constituted an inconceivable paradox in the face of the grandiose natural conditions ("In America everything is great, only man is small").

Now, given this causal link of "beautiful land—great country," it is not difficult to see the repercussions a consciousness of underdevelopment could produce in a change of perspective that made evident the reality of the poor lands, the archaic technologies, the astonishing misery of the people, the paralyzing lack of culture. The resulting vision is pessimistic with respect to the present and problematic with respect to the future, and the only remnant of the previous phase's millenarianism, perhaps, might be the confidence with which it is acknowledged that the removal of imperialism could bring, in itself, an explosion of progress. But, in general, it is no longer a matter of a passive point of view. Deprived of euphoria, the point of view is combative, and this leads to a decision to struggle, since the trauma of consciousness caused by the confirmation of how great the backwardness is catastrophic, and invites political reformulations. The preceding gigantism, based on a hyperbolic view of nature, then appears in its true essence—as an ideological construction transformed into a compensatory illusion. From this comes the disposition to combat that is diffused through the continent, the idea of underdevelopment becoming a propulsive force, which gives a new stamp to the political obligation of our intellectuals.

The consciousness of underdevelopment followed the Second World War and was manifested clearly from the 1950s on. But there had been, since the 1930s, a change in orientation, which could be taken as a thermometer, given its generality and persistence, above all in regionalist fiction. It then abandoned pleasantness and *curiosity*, anticipating or perceiving what had been disguised in the picturesque enchantment or ornamental chivalry with which rustic man had previously been approached. It is not false to say that, from this point of view, the novel acquired a demystifying force that preceded the coming-to-awareness of economists and politicians.

In this essay, I will speak, alternatively or comparatively, of the literary characteristics of the mild phase of backwardness, corresponding to the ideology of the "new country": and of the phase of catastrophic consciousness of backwardness, corresponding to the notion of "underdeveloped country." The two are intimately meshed with one another, and we see the lines of the present in both the immediate and remote past. With respect to method, it would be possible to study the conditions of the diffusion of, or of the production of, literary works. Without forgetting the first focus, I prefer to emphasize the second by means of which, though we leave aside statistical rigor, we come close, in compensation, to the specific interests of literary criticism.

IF WE THINK of the material conditions of literature's existence, the basic fact, perhaps, is illiteracy, which in the countries of advanced pre-Columbian culture is aggravated by the still present linguistic plurality, with diverse languages seeking their place in the sun. In fact, illiteracy is linked to the manifestations of cultural weakness: lack of the means of communication and diffusion (publishers, libraries, magazines, newspapers); the nonexistence, dispersion, and weakness of publics disposed to literature, due to the small number of real readers (many fewer than the already small number of literates); the impossibility, for writers, of specializing in their literary jobs, generally therefore realized as marginal, or even amateur, tasks; the lack of resistance or discrimination in the face of external influences and pressures. The picture of this weakness is completed by such economic and political factors as insufficient levels of remuneration and the financial anarchy of governments, coupled with inept or criminally disinterested educational policies. Except in the contiguous meridional countries that form "white America" (in the European phrase), there would have to be a revolution to alter the predominant condition of illiteracy, as occurred slowly and incompletely in Mexico and rapidly in Cuba.

These features are not combined mechanically, nor always in the same way, there being diverse possibilities of dissociation and grouping among them. Illiteracy is not always a sufficient explanation of the weakness in other sectors, although it is the basic feature of underdevelopment in the cultural area. Peru, to cite an example, is less badly situated than various other countries with respect to the index of schooling, but it presents the same backwardness with respect to the diffusion of culture. In another sector, the publishing boom of the 1940s in Mexico and Argentina showed that the lack of books was not uniquely a consequence of the reduced number of readers and of lower buying power, since all of Latin America, including the Portuguese-speaking part, absorbed significant numbers of its publications. Perhaps we can conclude that the bad publishing habits and the lack of communication further accentuated the inertia of the public; and that there was an unsatisfied capacity for absorption.

This last example reminds us that the problem of publics presents distinctive features in Latin America, since it is the only group of underdeveloped countries whose people speak European languages (with the exception, already noted, of the indigenous groups) and have their origins in countries that today still have underdeveloped areas themselves (Spain and Portugal). In these ancient mother countries literature was, and continues to be, a good of restricted consumption, in comparison with the fully developed countries, where publics can be classified according to the kind of reading they do, such a classification permitting comparisons with the stratification of the entire society. But, as much in Spain and Portugal as in our own countries of Latin America, there is a basic negative condition, the number of literates, that is, those who could eventually constitute the readers of works. This circumstance brings the Latin American countries nearer to the actual conditions of their mother countries than are, in relation to theirs, the underdeveloped countries of Africa and Asia, which speak different languages than those of the colonizers and confront the grave problem of choosing the language in which to display literary creation. African writers in European languages (French, like Léopold Sendar Senghor, or English, like Chinua Achebe) are doubly separated from their potential publics; and are tied either to metropolitan publics, distant in every sense, or to an incredibly reduced local public.

This is said to show that the possibilities of communication for the Latin American writer are greater, compared to the rest of the Third World, despite the present situation, which reduces greatly his eventual public. Nevertheless, we can imagine that the Latin American writer is condemned always to be what he has been: a producer of cultural goods for minorities, though in this case that does not signify groups of high aesthetic quality, but simply the few groups disposed to read. But let us not forget that modern audio-visual resources might change our processes of creation and our means of communication, so that when the great masses finally acquire education, who knows but what they will look outside the book to satisfy their needs for fiction and poetry.

Put another way: in the majority of our countries large masses, immersed in a folkloric stage of oral communication, are still beyond the reach of erudite literature. Once literate and absorbed by the process of urbanization, they come under the dominion of radio, television, and comic strips, constituting the foundation of a mass culture. Literacy would then not increase the number of readers of literature, as conceived here, proportionally, but would fling the literate, together with the illiterate, directly from the phase of folklore into this kind of urban folklore that is massified culture. During the Christianization of the continent the colonial missionaries wrote documents and poetry in the indigenous language or the vernacular in order to make the principles of religion and of the metropolitan civilization accessible to those being indoctrinated by means of consecrated literary forms, equivalent to those destined for the cultivated man of the times. In our time, a contrary process rapidly converts rural man to urban society, by means of communicative resources that even include subliminal inculcation, imposing on him dubious values quite different from those the cultivated man seeks in art and in literature.

This problem is one of the gravest in the underdeveloped countries, by virtue of the massive pressure of what could be called the cultural know-how and the very materials already elaborated for massified culture coming from the developed countries. By such means, these countries can not only diffuse their values in the normal fashion, but also act abnormally through them to orient, according to their political interests, the opinions and the sensibility—the political interests—of underdeveloped populations. It is *normal*, for example, that the image of the cowboy hero of the Western is diffused because, independent of judgments of value, it is one of the features of North American culture incorporated into the average sensibility of the contemporary world. In countries with a large Japanese immigration such as Peru and above all Brazil, there is diffused in a similarly *normal* manner the image of the samurai, especially by means of the cinema. But it is *abnormal* that such images serve as the vehicle for inculcating in the publics of the underdeveloped countries attitudes and ideas that identify them with the political and economic interests of the countries in which those images were made. When we realize that the majority of the animated cartoons and comic strips have a North American copyright, and that a large proportion of detective and adventure fiction comes from the same source, or is copied from it, it is easy to evaluate the negative effect it could eventually have, as an *abnormal* diffusion among a defenseless public.

In this respect it is convenient to point out that in erudite literature the problem of influences (as we will see later) can have either a good aesthetic effect or a deplorable one; but only in exceptional cases does it have any influence on the ethical or political behavior of the masses, since it reaches a restricted number of restricted publics. Even so, in a massified civilization, where nonliterary, preliterary, or subliterary media, such as those cited, predominate, such restricted and differentiated publics tend to unify themselves to the point of being confounded with the mass, which receives the influence on an immense scale. And, what is more, this occurs by means of vehicles whose aesthetic element is reduced to a minimum, thus rendering them capable of being confounded with ethical or political designs that, in the limiting case, penetrate the entire population.

Seeing that we are a "continent under intervention," an extreme vigilance is proper for Latin American literature, in order not to be taken in by the instruments and values of mass culture, which seduce so many contemporary artists and theorists. It is not a case of joining the "apocalyptics," but rather of alerting the "integrated"—to use Umberto Eco's expressive distinction. Certain modern experiences are fruitful from the point of view of the spirit of the vanguard and the connection of art and literature to the rhythm of the time, as in concretism and other currents. But it costs nothing to remember what can occur when they are manipulated politically by the wrong side in a mass society. In fact, even though they present at the time a hermetic and restrictive aspect, the principles in which they are based, having as resources an expressive sonority, graphical elements, and syntagmatic combinations of great suggestive power, can eventually become much more penetrating than traditional literary forms, functioning as nonliterary instruments, but more penetrating for just this reason of reaching massified publics. And there is no point, for the literary expression of Latin America, in moving from the aristocratic segregation of the era of oligarchies to the directed manipulation of the masses in an era of propaganda and total imperialism.

ILLITERACY AND CULTURAL debility influence more than the exterior aspects just mentioned. For the critic, their action in the consciousness of the writer and in the very nature of his work is more interesting.

In the time of what I called the mild consciousness of backwardness, the writer shared the *enlightened* ideology, according to which schooling automatically brought all the benefits that permitted the humanization of man and the progress of society. At first, schooling was recommended only for the *citizens*, the minority from which were recruited those who shared economic and political advantages; later, for all the people, seen dimly, vaguely, and from afar, less as a reality than as a liberal conception. Emperor Dom Pedro II said that he would have preferred to be a teacher, which denoted an attitude equivalent to the famous point of view of Sarmiento, according to which the predominance of civilization over barbarism had as a presupposition a latent urbanization based in schooling. In the continental vocation of Andrés Bello it is impossible to distinguish the political vision from the pedagogic project; and in the more recent group, Ateneo, of Caracas, the resistance to tyranny of Juan Vicente Gómez was inseparable from the desire to diffuse enlightened ideas and to create a literature full of myths of redemptive education—all projected in the figure of Rómulo Gallegos, who ended up as the first president of a renascent republic.

A curious case is that of a thinker like Manuel Bonfim, who published in 1905 a book of great interest, A *América Latina*. Unjustly forgotten (perhaps because it based itself on outmoded biological analogies, perhaps because of the troublesome radicalism of its positions), it analyzes our backwardness as a function of the prolongation of colonial status, embodied in the persistence of oligarchies and in foreign imperialism. In the end, when everything leads to a theory of the transformation of social structures as a necessary condition, a disappointing weakening of the argument occurs, and he ends by preaching schooling as a panacea. In such cases, we touch the core of the illusion of the *enlightened*, an ideology of the phase of hopeful consciousness of backwardness that, significantly, does little to bring what is hoped for to realization.

It is not surprising, then, that the idea already referred to, according to which the new continent was destined to be the country of liberty, has undergone a curious adaptation: it would be destined, equally, to be the country of the book. This is what we read in a rhetorical poem in which Castro Alves says that, while Gutenberg invented the printing press, Columbus found the ideal place for that revolutionary technique:

Quando no tosco estaleiro
Da Alemanha o velho obreiro
A ave da imprensa gerou,
O Genovês salta os mares,
Busca um ninho entre os palmares
E *a patria da imprensa* achou
[While in the rough workshop
Of Germany the old worker
Begot the bird of printing,
The Genoese leaped over the seas,
Seeking a home among the palms
and discovered the *country of printing* (the italics are the poet's)].

This poem, written in the 1860s by a young man burning with liberalism, is called, expressively, "O livro e a América," displaying the ideological position I refer to.

Thanks to this ideology, these intellectuals constructed an equally deformed vision of their own position, confronted by a dominant lack of culture. Lamenting the ignorance of the people and wishing it would disappear so that the country might automatically rise to its destined heights, they excluded themselves from the context and thought of themselves as a group apart, really "floating," in a more complete sense than that of Alfred Weber. They floated, with or without consciousness of guilt, above the lack of culture and the backwardness, certain that it could not contaminate them, or affect the quality of what they did. Since the environment could only give them limited shelter, and since their values were rooted in Europe, it was to Europe that they projected themselves, taking it unconsciously as a point of reference and a scale of values, and considering themselves the equals of the best there.

But in truth the general lack of culture produced, and produces, a much more penetrating debility, which interferes with all culture and with the quality of the works themselves. Seen from today, the situation of yesterday seems different from the illusion that reigned then, since today we can analyze it more objectively, due to the action of time and to our own efforts at unmasking.

The question will become clearer as we take up foreign influences. In order to understand them best, it is convenient to focus, in the light of these reflections on backwardness and underdevelopment, on the problem of cultural dependency. This is, so to speak, a natural fact, given our situation as peoples who are colonized, or descendants of colonizers, or who have suffered the imposition of their civilization, but a complicated fact, with positive and negative aspects.

This cultural penury caused writers to turn necessarily toward the patterns of the mother countries and of Europe in general, creating a group that was in a way aristocratic in relation to the uneducated man. In fact, to the degree that a sufficient local public did not exist, people wrote as if their ideal public was in Europe and thus often dissociated themselves from their own land. This gave birth to works that authors and readers considered highly refined, because they assimilated the forms and values of European fashion. Except that, for lack of local points of reference, they often could go no farther than exercises of mere cultural alienation, which were not justified by the excellence of their realization—and that is what occurred in what there is of the bazaar and of affectation in the so-called "modernism" of the Spanish language, and its Brazilian equivalents, Parnassianism and symbolism.[1] Clearly, there is much that is sound in Rubén Darío, as in Herrera y Reissig, Bilac, and Cruz e Sousa. But there are also many false jewels unmasked by time, much contraband that gave them an air of competitors for some international prize for beautiful writing. The refinement of the *decadents* was provincial, showing the mistaken perspective that predominates when the elite, with no base in an uncultivated people, has no way of confronting itself critically and supposes that the relative distance that separates them translates of itself into a position of absolute height. "I am the last Greek!"—so shouted theatrically in 1924 in the Brazilian Academy the enormously affected Coelho Neto, a kind of laborious local D'Annunzio, protesting against the vanguardism of the modernists, who eventually broke the aristocratic pose in art and literature.

Let us recall another aspect of alienated aristocratism, which at the time seemed an appreciable refinement: the use of foreign languages in the production of works.

Certain extreme examples were involuntarily saturated with the most paradoxical humorousness, as in the case of a belated Romantic of the lowest rank, Pires de Almeida, who published, as late as the beginning of this [the twentieth] century, in French, a nativist play, probably composed some decades earlier: La fête des crânes, drame de moeurs indiennes en trois actes et douze tableaux.[2] But this practice is really significant when it is linked to authors and works of real quality, such as those of Cláudio Manuel da Costa, who left a large and excellent body of work in Italian. Or Joaquim Nabuco, a typical example of the cosmopolitan oligarchy of liberal sentiment in the second half of the nineteenth century, who wrote autobiographical passages and a book of reflections in French—but above all a play whose conventional alexandrines debated the problems of conscience of an Alsatian after the Franco-Prussian War of 1870! A variety of minor symbolists (and also one of the most important, Alphonsus de Guimaraens) wrote all of their work, or at least a part thereof, in the same language. The Peruvian Francisco García Calderón wrote, in French, a book that had value as an attempt at an integrated vision of the Latin American countries. The Chilean Vicente Huidobro wrote part of his work and of his theory in French. The Brazilian Sérgio Milliet published his first poetic work in French. And I am certain that we could find innumerable examples of the same thing, in every country of Latin America, from the vulgar official and academic work of pedants to productions of quality.

All this did not happen without some ambivalence, since the elites, on the one hand, imitated the good and bad of European models; but, on the other hand and sometimes simultaneously, they displayed the most intransigent spiritual independence, in an oscillating movement between reality and a utopia of an ideological stamp. And thus we see that illiteracy and refinement, cosmopolitanism and regionalism, could all have roots that mingled in the soil of the lack of culture and the effort to overcome it.

More serious influences of cultural weakness on literary production are the facts of backwardness, anachronism, degradation, and the confusion of values.

All literature presents aspects of backwardness that are normal in their way, it being possible to say that the media of production of a given moment are already tributary to the past, while the vanguard prepares the future. Beyond this there is an official subliterature, marginal and provincial, generally expressed through the academies. But what demands attention in Latin America is the way aesthetically anachronistic works were considered valid; or the way secondary works were welcomed by the best critical opinion and lasted for more than a generation—while either should soon have been put in its proper place, as something valueless or the evidence of a harmless survival. We cite only the strange case of the poem *Tabaré*, by Juan Zorrilla de San Martín, an attempt at a national Uruguayan epic at the end of the nineteenth century, taken seriously by critical opinion despite having been conceived and executed according to the most obsolete patterns.

At other times the backwardness is not shocking, simply signifying a cultural tardiness. This is what occurred with naturalism in the novel, which arrived a little late and has prolonged itself until now with no essential break in continuity, though modifying its modalities. The fact of our being countries that in the greater part still have problems of adjustment and struggle with the environment, as well as problems linked to racial diversity, prolonged the naturalist preoccupation with physical and biological factors. In such cases the weight of the local reality produces a kind of legitimation of this delayed influence, which acquires a creative meaning. So, when naturalism was already only a survival of an outdated genre in Europe, among us it could still be an ingredient of legitimate literary formulas, such as the social novel of the 1930s and 1940s.

Other cases are frankly disastrous: those of cultural provincialism, which leads to a loss of a sense of measure, the result of which is to evaluate works of no value at all by the standards applied in Europe to works of quality. This leads, further, to phenomena of true cultural degradation, causing spurious work to *pass*, in the sense in which a counterfeit banknote *passes*, due to the weakness of publics and the absence of a sense of values in both publics and writers. We see here the routinization of influences already dubious in themselves, such as Oscar Wilde, D'Annunzio, and even Anatole France, in the books of our own Elísio de Carvalho and Afrânio Peixoto in the first quarter of this century. Or, bordering on the grotesque, the veritable profanation of Nietzsche by Vargas Villa, whose vogue in all of Latin America reached milieus that in principle should have been immune, on a scale that astonishes us and makes us smile. The *profundity* of the semicultured created these and other mistakes.

A PROBLEM THAT touches on the topics of this essay and is worth being discussed in light of the dependence caused by cultural backwardness is that of influences of various types, good and bad, inevitable and unnecessary.

Our Latin American literatures, like those of North America, are basically branches of the literature of a mother country. And if we give up the sensitivities of national pride, we see that, despite the autonomy gained from those mother countries, these literatures are still partly reflections. In the case of the Spanish- and Portuguese-speaking countries, the process of autonomy consisted, in good part, of transferring the dependency, in such a way that, beginning in the nineteenth century, other European literatures, not those of the metropole, and above all French, became the model; this had also occurred in the intensely Frenchified mother countries. These days it is necessary to take into account North American literature which became a new focus of attraction.

This is what could be called the inevitable influence, sociologically linked to our dependency, since the colonization itself and the at times brutally forced transfer of cultures. As the respected Juan Valera said at the end of the nineteenth century: "From both sides of the Atlantic, I see and admit it, in the people of the Spanish language, our dependence on the French, and, to a certain point, I believe it ineluctable; but I neither diminish the merit of the science and poetry of France so that we can shake off its yoke, nor want us, that we may become independent, to isolate ourselves and not accept the proper influence that civilized peoples must exert on one another. What I maintain is that our admiration must not be blind, nor our imitation uncritical, and that it is fitting that we take what we take with discernment and prudence" (1905, 9–10).

We must therefore confront our placental link to European literatures calmly, since it is not an option, but a quasi-natural fact. We never created original frameworks of expression, nor basic expressive techniques; we never created such things as romanticism, on the level of tendencies, or the psychological novel, on the level of genres, or indirect free style, on that of writing. And while we have achieved original results on the level of expressive realization, we implicitly recognize the dependency, so much so that we never see the diverse nativisms disputing the use of imported *forms*, since that would be like opposing the use of the European languages we speak. What these nativisms required was the choice of new *themes*, of different *sentiments*. Carried to an extreme, nativism (which at this level is always ridiculous, though sociologically understandable) would have implied rejecting the sonnet, the realistic story, and free associative verse.

The simple fact of the question never having been raised reveals that, at the deepest levels of creative elaboration (those that involve the choice of expressive instruments), we always recognize our inevitable dependence as natural. Besides, seen thus, it is no longer dependency, but a way of participating in a cultural universe to which we belong, which crosses the boundaries of nations and continents, allowing the exchange of experiences and the circulation of values. And when we in turn influence the Europeans through the works we do (not through the thematic suggestions our continent presents to them to elaborate in their own forms of exoticism), at such moments what we give back are not inventions but a refining of received instruments. This occurred with Rubén Darío in relation to "modernism" (in the Spanish sense); with Jorge Amado, José Lins do Rego, Graciliano Ramos in relation to Portuguese neorealism.

Spanish-American "modernism" is considered by many as a kind of rite of passage, marking a literary coming of age through the capacity for original contribution. But, if we correct our perspectives and define the fields, we see that this is more true as a psychosocial fact than as an aesthetic reality. It is evident that Darío, and eventually the entire movement, for the first time reversing the current and carrying the influence of America to Spain, represented a rupture in the literary sovereignty Spain had exercised. But the fact is that such a thing is not accomplished with original expressive resources, but rather by adapting French processes and attitudes. What the Spaniards received was the influence of France, already filtered and translated by the Latin Americans, who in this way substituted themselves as cultural mediators.

This in no way diminishes the value of the "modernists" nor the meaning of their accomplishment, based on a deep awareness of literature as art, not document, and an at times exceptional capacity for poetic realization. But it permits the interpretation of Spanish "modernism" according to the line developed here, that is, as a historically important episode in the process of creative fertilization of dependency—which is a peculiar way in which our countries are original. The corresponding Brazilian movement was not innovative at the level of general aesthetic forms either, but it was less deceptive because, by calling its two large branches "Parnassianism" and "symbolism," it made clear the French fountain from which they all drank.

A fundamental stage in overcoming dependency is the capacity to produce works of the first order, influenced by previous national examples, not by immediate foreign models. This signifies the establishment of what could be called, a little mechanically, an internal causality, which makes borrowings from other cultures more fruitful. Brazilian modernism derived in large part from European vanguard movements. But the poets of the succeeding generation, in the 1930s and 1940s, derived immediately from the modernists—as is the case with what is the fruit of these influences in Carlos Drummond de Andrade or Murilo Mendes. These, in turn, were the inspiration of João Cabral de Melo Neto, even though he also owes much to Paul Valéry, and then to the Spaniards who were his contemporaries. Nevertheless, these high-flying poets were not influential outside their own countries, and much less in the countries from which the original suggestions came.

This being the case, it is possible to say that Jorge Luis Borges represents the first case of incontestable original influence, exercised fully and recognized in the source countries, through a new mode of conceiving of writing. Machado de Assis, whose originality was no less from this point of view, and much greater as a vision of man, could have opened new directions at the end of the nineteenth century for the source countries. But he was lost in the sands of an unknown language, in a country then completely unimportant.

It is for this reason that our own affirmations of nationalism and of cultural independence are inspired by European formulations, an example being the case of Brazilian romanticism, defined in Paris by a group of youths who were there and who founded in 1836 the magazine Niterói, symbolic landmark of the movement. And we know that today contact between Latin American writers is made above all in Europe and in the United States, which, in addition, encourage, more than we do, the consciousness of our intellectual affinity.[3]

The case of the vanguards of the 1920s is interesting, because it marked an extraordinary liberation of expressive means and prepared us to alter sensitively the treatment of themes proposed to the writer's consciousness. As a matter of fact, these vanguards have been, throughout Latin America, elements of autonomy and self-affirmation; but what did they consist of, examined in the light of our theme? Huidobro established "creationism" in Paris, inspired by the French and the Italians; he wrote his poems in French and made his position public in French, in magazines like L'Esprit Nouveau. Argentine ultraism and Brazilian modernismo are directly descended from these same sources. And none of this prevented such currents from being innovative, nor those who propelled it from being, par excellence, the founders of the new literature: Huidobro, Borges, Mário de Andrade, Oswald de Andrade, and others.

We know, then, that we are part of a broader culture, in which we participate as a cultural variant. And that, contrary to what our grandparents sometimes ingenuously supposed, it is an illusion to speak of the suppression of contacts and influences, simply because, the law of the world now being interrelation and interaction, the utopias of isolationist originality no longer survive as a patriotic attitude that was understandable when the young nations were being born, a time that called for a provincial and umbilical position.

In the present phase, that of the consciousness of underdevelopment, the question presents itself, therefore, in a more nuanced way. Could there be a paradox here? Indeed, the more the free man who thinks is imbued with the tragic reality of underdevelopment, the more he is imbued with revolutionary aspirations—that is, with the desire to reject the political and economic yoke of imperialism and to promote in every country the modification of the internal structures that nourish the situation of underdevelopment. Nevertheless, he confronts the problem of influences more objectively, considering them as normal linkages on the level of culture.

The paradox is only apparent, since in fact it is a symptom of a maturity that was impossible in the closed and oligarchic world of jingoistic nationalisms. So much so that the recognition of linkage is associated with the beginning of the capacity to innovate at the level of expression, and to fight at the level of economic and political development. Conversely, the traditional affirmation of originality, with a sense of elementary particularism, led and leads, first, to the picturesque and, second, to cultural servility, two diseases of growth, perhaps inevitable, but nevertheless alienating.

Beginning with the aesthetic movements of the 1920s; the intense aesthetic-social consciousness of the 1930s and 1940s; the crisis of economic development and of technical experimentalism of recent years— we began to see that dependency was a step on the road to a cultural interdependency (if it is possible to use this expression, which has recently acquired such disagreeable meanings in the political and diplomatic vocabulary, without misunderstanding). This not only will give writers in Latin America an awareness of their unity in diversity, but will favor works of a mature and original tone, which will slowly be assimilated by other peoples, including those of the metropolitan and imperialist countries. The road of reflection on underdevelopment leads, in the field of culture, to transnational integration, since what was imitation increasingly turns into reciprocal assimilation.

One example among many: in the work of Mario Vargas Llosa there appears, extraordinarily refined, the tradition of the interior monologue, which, Proust's and Joyce's, is also that of Dorothy Richardson and Virginia Woolf, of Döblin and of Faulkner. Perhaps certain modalities preferred by Vargas Llosa are due to Faulkner, but in every case he has deepened them and made them more fruitful, to the point of making them into something of his own. An admirable example maybe found in *La ciudad y los perros*: the monologue of the non-identified character leaves the reader perplexed, since it intersects with the voice of the third person narrator and with the monologue of other named characters, thus being capable of being confused with them; and, in the end, when this character reveals himself as Jaguar, it illuminates the structure of the book retrospectively, like a fuse, requiring us to rethink everything we had established about the characters. This seems like a concretization of an image Proust uses to suggest his own technique (the Japanese figure revealing itself in the water of the bowl): but it signifies something very different, on a different plane of reality. Here, the novelist of the underdeveloped country received ingredients that came to him as a cultural loan from the countries from which we are accustomed to receive literary formulas. But he adapted them profoundly to his intention, compounding from them a peculiar formula, in order to represent problems of his own country. This is neither imitation nor mechanical reproduction. It is participation in resources that have become common through the state of dependency, contributing to turn it into an interdependency.

Awareness of these facts seems integrated into the way of seeing of Latin American writers; and one of the most original, Julio Cortázar, writes interesting things on the new appearance local fidelity and world mobility present, in an interview in *Life* (vol. 33, no. 7). And, with respect to foreign influences on recent writers, Emir Rodríguez Monegal assumes, in an article in *Tri-Quarterly* (no. 13–14), an attitude that could with justification be called a critical justification of assimilation. Nevertheless, opposing points of view, linked to a certain localism appropriate to the "gentle phase of backwardness," still survive. For those who defend them, such facts as we have mentioned here are manifestations of a lack of individuality or of cultural alienation, as can be seen in an article in the Venezuelan magazine *Zona Franca* (no. 51), where Manuel Pedro González makes clear that, in his view, the true Latin American writer would be one who not only lives in his land, but who also uses its characteristic themes and expresses, without any exterior aesthetic dependency, its peculiar features.

It seems, nevertheless, that one of the positive features of the era of the consciousness of underdevelopment is the overcoming of the attitude of apprehension, which leads to indiscriminate acceptance or the illusion of the originality of work and the charm of local themes. Whoever fights against real obstacles is more balanced and recognizes the fallacy of fictitious obstacles. In Cuba, that admirable vanguard of the Americas in the fight against underdevelopment and its causes, is there artificiality or flight in the surrealist suffusion of Alejo Carpentier, or in his complex transnational vision, including the thematic point of view, as it appears in *Siglo de las luces?* Is there alienation in the bold experiments of Guillermo Cabrera Infante or José Lezama Lima? In Brazil, the recent concrete poetry movement adopts inspirations of Ezra Pound and aesthetic principles of Max Bense and other Europeans; but it produces a redefinition of the national past, reading ignored poets, such as Joaquim de Sousa Andrade, a precursor lost among the Romantics of the nineteenth century, in a new way, or illuminating the stylistic revolution of the great modernists, Mário de Andrade and Oswald de Andrade.

TAKEN AS A derivation of backwardness and the lack of economic development, dependency has other aspects that have their repercussions in literature. Recall again the phenomenon of ambivalence, translated into impulses of copying and rejection, apparently contradictory when viewed alone, but which can be seen as complementary when confronted from this angle.

Backwardness stimulates the servile copying of everything the fashion of the advanced countries sometimes offers, as well as seducing writers with migration, an interior migration, which corrals the individual in silence and in isolation. Backwardness, nevertheless, the other side of the coin, suggests what is most specific in the local reality, insinuating a regionalism that, appearing to be an affirmation of the national identity, can in truth be an unsuspected way of offering the European sensibility the exoticism it desires, as an amusement. In this way, it becomes an acute form of dependency within independence. In the present perspective, it seems that the two tendencies are mutual, born of the same situation of retardation or underdevelopment.

In its crudest aspect, the servile imitation of styles, themes, attitudes, and literary usages, it has a comical or embarrassing air of provincialism, having been the compensatory aristocratism of a colonial country. In Brazil this reaches an extreme, with the Academia de Letras, copied from the French, installed in a building that is a reproduction of the Petit Trianon in Versailles (and the Petit Trianon is, in all seriousness, what the institution is called), with forty members who call themselves *Immortals* and, further like their French models, wear embroidered uniforms, cocked hats, and swords . . . But the functional equivalent of that academy for all of Latin America might often be, in the guise of an innovative rebellion, the imitated Bohemias of Greenwich Village or Saint-Germain-des-Prés.

Perhaps no less crude, on the other hand, are certain forms of nativism and literary regionalism, which reduce human problems to their picturesque element, making the passion and suffering of rural people, or of the populations *of color*, the equivalent of papayas or pineapples. This attitude may not only be the same as the first, but combine with it to *furnish* the urban European (or artificially Europeanized) reader the quasi-touristic reality it would please him to see in America. Without recognizing it, the most sincere nativism risks becoming an ideological manifestation of the same cultural colonialism that its practitioners would reject on the plane of clear reason, and that displays a situation of underdevelopment and consequent dependency.

Nevertheless, in light of the focus of this essay, it would be a mistake to utter, as is fashionable, an indiscriminate anathema against regionalist fiction, at least before making some distinctions that allow us to see it, on the level of judgments of reality, as a consequence of the effect of economic and social conditions on the choice of themes.[4] The areas of underdevelopment and the problems of underdevelopment (or backwardness) invade the field of consciousness and the sensibility of the writer, proposing suggestions, setting themselves up as topics impossible to avoid, becoming positive or negative stimuli to creation.

In French or English literature there have occasionally been great novels whose subject is rural, such as those of Thomas Hardy; but it is clear that this is a matter of an external framework, in which the problems are the same as those of urban novels. In the main, the different modalities of regionalism are in themselves a secondary and generally provincial form, among much richer forms that occupy a higher level. Nevertheless, in such underdeveloped countries as Greece, or those that still have major underdeveloped areas, like Italy or Spain, regionalism can be a valid manifestation, capable of producing works of quality, such as those of Giovanni Verga at the end of the nineteenth century, or of Federico García Lorca, Elio Vittorini, or Nikos Kazantzakis in our time.

For this reason, in Latin America regionalism was and still is a stimulating force in literature. In the phase of "new country" consciousness, corresponding to the situation of backwardness, it gives a place, above all, to the decoratively picturesque and functions as a discovery, a recognition of the reality of the country and its incorporation into the themes of literature. In the phase of the consciousness of underdevelopment, it functions as a premonition and then as a consciousness of crisis, motivating the documentary and, with a feeling of urgency, political engagement.

In both stages, there occurs a kind of selection of thematic areas, an attraction for certain remote regions, in which the groups marked by underdevelopment are localized. They can, without doubt, constitute a negative seduction for the urban writer, through a picturesqueness with dubious consequences; but, beyond this, they generally coincide with areas of social problems, which is significant and important in literatures as engaged as those of Latin America.

An example is the Amazonian region, which attracted such Brazilian novelists and storytellers as José Veríssimo and Inglês de Sousa, from the beginnings of naturalism, in the 1870s and 1880s, in a fully picturesque phase; it furnished the material for La vorágine, by José Eustasio Rivera, a half century later, situated between the picturesque and the denunciation (more patriotic than social); and it became an important element in La casa verde of Vargas Llosa, in the modern phase of high technical consciousness, in which exoticism and denunciation are latent in relation to the human impact that is displayed, in the construction of style, with the immanence of universal works.

It is not necessary to enumerate all the other literary areas that correspond to the panorama of backwardness and underdevelopment—such as the Andean altiplano or the Brazilian sertão. Or, also, the situations and places of the Cuban, Venezuelan, or the Brazilian Negro, in the poems of Nicolás Guillén and Jorge de Lima, in Ecué Yamba-Ô of Alejo Carpentier, Pobre negro of Rómulo Gallegos, or the Jubiabá of Jorge Amado. Or, still further, the man of the plains—llano, pampa, caatinga—the object of a tenacious compensatory idealization that comes from such Romantics as José de Alencar in the 1870s, which occurred largely among the peoples of the Río de la Plata, Uruguayans like Eduardo Acevedo Díaz, Carlos Reyles, or Javier de Viana, and Argentines, from the telluric José Hernández to the stylized Ricardo Güiraldes, which tends to the allegorical in Gallegos, in Venezuela, and reaches, in Brazil, in the full phase of preconsciousness of underdevelopment, an elevated expression in Vidas secas of Graciliano Ramos, without the vertigo of distance, without tournaments or duels, without rodeos or cattle roundups, without the centaurism that marks the others.

Regionalism was a necessary step, which made literature, above all the novel and the story, focus on local reality. At times it was an opportunity for fine literary expression, although the majority of its products have dated. But from a certain angle, perhaps, it cannot be said that it is finished; many of those who today attack it, at bottom practice it. The economic reality of underdevelopment maintains the regional dimension as a living object, despite the urban dimension's ever-increasing importance. It is enough to remember that some of the best writers find substance for books that are universally significant in it: José María Arguedas, Gabriel García Márquez, Augusto Roa Bastos, João Guimarães Rosa. Only in countries where the culture of big cities has absolute dominion, such as Argentina and Uruguay, has regional literature become a total anachronism.

For this reason, it is necessary to redefine the problem critically, seeing that it is not exhausted by the fact that, today, no one any longer considers regionalism a privileged form of national literary expression; among other reasons because, as was said, it can be especially alienating. But it is appropriate to think about its transformations, keeping in mind that the same basic reality has been prolonged under diverse names and concepts. In fact, in the euphoric phase of consciousness of the new country, characterized by the idea of backwardness, we had picturesque regionalism, which in various countries was inculcated as the literary truth. This modality was long ago left behind, or survives, if at all, at a subliterary level. Its fullest and most tenacious manifestation in the golden phase was perhaps the gauchoism of the countries of the Río de la Plata, while the most spurious form was certainly the sentimental Brazilian *sertanejismo* [from *sertão* = backlands] of the beginning of the twentieth century. And it is what has irremediably compromised certain more recent works, such as those of Rivera and Gallegos.

In the phase of preconsciousness of underdevelopment, through the 1930s and 1940s, we had problematic regionalism, which called itself the "social novel," "indigenism," "novel of the northeast [of Brazil]," depending on the countries and, though not exclusively regional, in good part it was. It interests us more for having been a precursor of the consciousness of underdevelopment—it being fair to record that, much earlier, writers like Alcides Arguedas and Mariano Azuela were already guided by a more realistic sense of the conditions of life, as well as of the problems of unprotected groups.

Among those who then proposed, with analytic vigor and at times in artistic forms of good quality, the demystification of reality are Miguel Angel Asturias, Jorge Icaza, Ciro Alegría, José Lins Rego, and others. All of them, in at least some part of their work, created a kind of social novel that was still related to the universe of regionalism, including what was negative in it, such as a sentimental picturesqueness, or kitsch; these remnants of regionalism amounted at times to a schematic and banal humanitarianism, which could compromise what they wrote.

What characterizes them, still, is the overcoming of patriotic optimism and the adoption of a kind of pessimism different from what was present in naturalist fiction. While that fiction focused on the poor man as a refractory element in the march of progress, these uncovered the situation in its complexity, turning against the dominant classes and seeing in the degradation of man a consequence of economic plunder, not of his individual *fate*. The paternalism of Doña Bárbara (which is a kind of apotheosis of the good master) suddenly seems archaic, in the face of the traces of George Grosz we observe in Icaza or the early Jorge Amado, in whose books what remains of the picturesque and exotic is dissolved by social unmasking—making it a presentiment of the passage from the "consciousness of the new country" to the "consciousness of the underdeveloped country," with the political consequences that introduces.

Even though many of these writers are characterized by spontaneous and irregular language, the weight of social consciousness acts in their styles as a positive factor, making room for the search for interesting solutions to problems of the representation of inequality and injustice. Without speaking of the consummate master Asturias is in some of his books, even a facile writer like Icaza owes his durability less to his indignant denunciations or to the exaggeration with which he characterizes the exploiters than to some stylistic resources he found to express misery. In Huasipungo it is a certain diminutive use of words, of the rhythm of weeping in speech, of the reduction to the level of the animal that, taken together, embody a kind of diminution of man, his reduction to elementary functions, which is associated with the linguistic stuttering to symbolize privation. In Vidas secas, Graciliano Ramos carries his customary verbal self-restraint to the maximum, elaborating an expression reduced to the ellipsis, to the monosyllable, to the minimum syntagmas, to express the human suffocation of the cowhand confined to minimum levels of survival.

The Brazilian case is perhaps peculiar, since here the initial regionalism, which began with Romanticism, earlier than in the other countries, never produced works considered first class, even by contemporaries, having been a secondary, when not frankly subliterary, tendency in prose and in verse. The best products of Brazilian fiction were always *urban*, most often stripped of any element of the picturesque; its major representative, Machado de Assis, showed since the 1880s the fragility of descriptivism and of local color, which he banished from his extraordinarily refined books. It was only beginning more or less around 1930, in a second phase that we are trying to characterize, that regionalist tendencies, already sublimated and transfigured by social realism, attained the level of significant works, while in other countries, above all Argentina, Uruguay, Chile, they were already being put to one side.

Overcoming these modalities, as well as the attacks they suffer from critics, is a demonstration of maturity. For this reason, many authors would reject as a blemish the name of "regionalist," which in fact no longer has meaning. But this does not prevent the regional dimension from continuing to be present in many works of major importance, though without any feeling of an imperative tendency, or of any requirement of a dubious national consciousness.

What we see now, from this point of view, is a blooming world of the novel marked by technical refinement, thanks to which regions are transfigured and their human contours subverted, causing formerly picturesque features to be shed and to acquire universality.

Discarding sentimentalism and rhetoric; nourished by nonrealist elements, such as the absurd, the magic of situations, or by antinaturalist techniques, such as the interior monologue, the simultaneous vision, the synthesis, the ellipsis—the novel nevertheless explores what used to be the very substance of nativism, of exoticism, and of social documentary. This would lead to proposing the distinguishing of a third phase, which could be (thinking of surrealism, or superrealism) called *superregionalist*. It corresponds to a consciousness distressed by underdevelopment and explodes the type of naturalism based on reference to an empirical vision of the world, a naturalism that was the aesthetic tendency peculiar to an epoch in which the bourgeois mentality triumphed and that was in harmony with the consolidation of our literatures.

To this superregionalism belongs, in Brazil, the revolutionary work of Guimarães Rosa, solidly planted in what could be called the universality of the region. And the fact that we have gone beyond the picturesque and the documentary does not make the presence of the region any less alive in works such as those of Juan Rulfo—whether in the fragmentary and obsessive reality of *Llano en llamas*, or in the fantasmal sobriety of *Pedro Páramo*. For this reason it is necessary to nuance drastic judgments that are basically fair, like those of Alejo Carpentier in the preface to *El reino de este mundo*, where he writes that our nativist novel is a kind of official high school literature that no longer finds readers in its places of origin. Carpentier's observation is true without doubt, if we think of the first phase of our attempt at classification; it is true up to a certain point, if we think of the second phase; but it is not true at all if we remind ourselves that the third phase carries a certain dose of regional ingredients, due to the very fact of underdevelopment. As was said, such ingredients constitute a stylized realization of dramatic conditions peculiar to it, intervening in the selection of themes and of topics, as well as in the very elaboration of the language.

Criticism will no longer require, as previously it would have, explicitly or implicitly, that Cortázar sing the life of Juan Moreyra, or that Clarice Lispector use the vocabulary of the Brazilian backland. But it will, equally, not fail to recognize that, writing with refinement and going beyond academic naturalism, Guimarães Rosa, Juan Rulfo, Vargas Llosa practice in their works, in the whole and in their parts, as much as Cortázar or Clarice Lispector in the universe of urban values, a new species of literature, which still is connected in a transfiguring way to the very material of what was once nativism.

Notes

1. In Latin American literature in Spanish, the reaction against romanticism at the end of the nineteenth century is called modernism. In Brazilian literature, the vanguard literary movement of the 1920s is called modernism. To distinguish the two, I use quotation marks in referring to the Spanish case.
2. I owe this citation to Decio de Almeida Prado.
3. The situation today is different and, besides, was already changing when I wrote this essay (1969). In this change the role of Cuba was decisive, promoting intensely in its territory the meeting of Latin American artists, scientists, writers, and intellectuals, who could thus meet and exchange experiences without the mediation of the imperialist countries.
4. I use the term *regionalism* here in the manner of Brazilian criticism, which extends it to all the fiction linked to the description of regions and of rural customs since Romanticism; and not in the manner of most of modern Spanish-American criticism, which generally restricts it to the era more or less between 1920 and 1950.

DARCY RIBEIRO
Excerpts from The Americas and Civilization

Darcy Ribeiro was born in Brazil in 1922 and died in 1997. An anthropologist and statesman, he was in charge of the agrarian reform in João Goulart's government (1963–1964). His main titles include O processo civilizatório. Etapas da evolução sociocultural (1968), Las Américas y la civilización. Proceso de formación y causas del desarrollo desigual de los pueblos americanos (1969), and El dilema de América Latina. Estructuras de poder y fuerzas insurgentes (1971).

Evolutionary Acceleration and Historical Incorporation

The study of the ethnic formation of the American peoples and their current problems of development demands that we first analyze the great historicocultural sequences in which they began—the technological revolutions and the civilizational processes, which correspond to the principal movements of human evolution.

We regard technological revolutions as prodigious innovations. New physical means for acting on nature and the use of new sources of energy, once attained by society, raise it to a higher stage in the evolutionary process. This occurs because the society's productive capacity expands, with consequent enlargement and changes in the distribution and composition of the population; because previous forms of social stratification are rearranged; and because the ideological contents of culture are redefined. There is also a parallel increase in the society's power to dominate and exploit the peoples within its range who have not experienced the same technological progress.

Every technological revolution spreads via successive civilizational processes that promote ethnic transfigurations of the peoples affected, remodeling them by fusion of races, confluence of culture, and economic integration to incorporate them into new ethnic conformations and into new historicocultural configurations.

The civilizational processes operate in one of two opposing ways, depending on whether the affected peoples become active instruments or passive recipients of the civilizational expansion. The first way is evolutionary acceleration, which occurs in the case of those societies that, autonomously dominating the new technology, progress socially, preserving their ethnocultural profile and, sometimes, expanding it to other peoples in the form of macroethnic groups. The second way, that of historical incorporation, occurs among peoples subjugated by societies with a more highly developed technology, thus losing their autonomy and in danger of having their culture traumatized and their ethnic profile denaturalized.

From the sixteenth century on, there have been two technological revolutions responsible for setting in motion four successive civilizational processes. The Mercantile Revolution, in an initial salvationistic-mercantile impulse, activated the Iberian peoples and the Russians and drove the former to overseas conquests and the latter to continental expansion over Eurasia. In a second impulse, more maturely capitalistic, the Mercantile Revolution, after breaking down feudal stagnation in certain areas of Europe, drove the Dutch, English, and French to overseas colonial expansion. There followed the Industrial Revolution, which, beginning in the eighteenth century, rearranged the world under the aegis of the pioneer industrial nations through two civilizational processes: imperialistic expansion and socialism.

At the same time that these successive processes commenced, the societies affected by them, either actively or passively, took shape as unequal components of different sociocultural formations, according to whether they experienced an evolutionary acceleration or a historical incorporation. So it is that, in consequence of the salvationistic-mercantile expansion, the salvationistic-mercantile empires were modeled by evolutionary acceleration and their slavistic-colonial contexts, by historical incorporation. Later, in consequence of the second civilizational process, the capitalistic mercantile formations were crystallized by acceleration and their slavistic colonial, trading colonial, and immigrant colonial dependencies, by incorporation. Finally, as the fruit of the first civilizational process initiated by the Industrial Revolution, the imperialistic industrial formations emerged through acceleration and their neocolonial counterpart, by incorporation; immediately afterward, as the result of a second civilizational process, the socialistic revolutionary, socialistic evolutionary, and nationalistic modernizing formations appeared, generated as evolutionary accelerations, although with different capacities for progress.

Historical incorporation operates by means of the domination and enslavement of alien peoples, followed by the socioeconomic structuring of the nuclei into which the dominated contingents congregate, in order to install new forms of production or exploit former productive activities. The fundamental objective of this structuring is to bind the new nuclei to the expansionist society as a part of its productive system and as an object of the intentional diffusion of its cultural tradition.

In the first stage of this process the purposeful decimation of parcels of the attacked population and the deculturation of the enslaved contingents are common. In the second stage a certain cultural creativity occurs, which permits shaping, with elements taken both from the master culture and from the subjugated, a body of common understandings, indispensable to successful coexistence and work orientation. Ethnic protocells combine fragments of the two patrimonies within the framework of domination. In a third stage these protocells enculturate persons torn from their original societies, including the native population, those transferred as slaves, and, further, the very agents of domination, and the descendants of all of them.

These new cultural cells tend to mature as protoethnic groups and to crystallize as the national identity of the area's population. In a more advanced stage of the process, the protoethnos struggles for independence in order to rise from its status as a spurious cultural variant and an exotic, subordinate component of the colonialist society to that of an autonomous society served by an authentic culture.

This restoration and emancipation are won only through a process of extreme conflict in which cultural as well as social and economic factors are conjoined. It is guided by a persistent effort at political self-affirmation on the part of the protoethnos, which hopes to win autonomy. That goal attained, a national ethnos makes itself evident—or, in other terms, the group identifies itself as a human community different from all others, with its own state and government, within which framework it lives out its destiny.

When these national ethnic groups enter in their turn into expansion into vast areas, perhaps colonizing other peoples toward whom they play a dominant role, it is possible to speak of a macroethnos. However, once a certain level of ethnoimperial expansion has been attained over a dominion, the enculturative effects and the spread of the technoscientific resources on which the domination is based tend to mature the subjugated ethnic entities, giving them the capacity for autonomous life. Thus once again the satellite turns against the ruling center, breaking the bonds of domination.

The result is autonomous national ethnic groups in interaction with one another and susceptible to the impact of new technological revolutions. These national ethnic groups display a series of discrepancies and uniformities that are highly significant in understanding their subsequent life. They vary in two basic lines: (1) according to their degree of sophistication of the productive technology and the broader or more limited prospect of development thus opened to them; (2) according to the nature of the ethnic remodeling they may have experienced and that shaped them into different historicocultural configurations, that is, into different groups that, over and above specific ethnic differences, display uniformities stemming from their parallel development. In the case of the European civilizational processes, these configurations contrast and approximate peoples according to the basic profile of European or Europeanized societies.

Classic examples of civilizational processes responsible for the rise of different historicocultural configurations are to be found in the expansion of irrigation civilizations, of such thalassocracies as the Phoenician and the Carthaginian, and of the Greek and Roman slavistic-mercantile empires, all of them responsible for the transfiguration and remodeling of innumerable peoples. More recent examples are the Islamic and Ottoman expansion and, above all, the European expansion itself, both in its Iberian salvationistic-mercantile cycle and in its capitalistic-mercantile and imperialistic-industrial cycles thereafter.

Within this perspective, studies of acculturation gain a new dimension. Instead of being limited to the results of the conjunction between autonomous cultural entities, they focus on the process whereby ethnic groups are formed in the course of imperial expansion. This process can be studied wherever the colonialist agencies of expanding societies, served by a more advanced technology and by a higher culture, act on alien sociocultural contexts. Such agencies reflect the high culture only in its instrumental, normative, and ideological aspects, which are indispensable to economic exploitation, political domination, ethnic expansion, and cultural diffusion. They generally act on more backward populations that are profoundly different culturally, socially, and, at times, racially from the dominant society. In the course of subjugation, the colonialist agencies also incorporate cultural elements from the dominated people, principally the local subsistence techniques. But essentially the new nuclei take shape as variants of the expansionist national society, whose language and culture are imposed on them. A new culture is formed, tending on the one hand to perpetuate itself as a spurious culture of a dominated society, but on the other to attend to its specific needs for survival and growth and in this way to structure itself as an autonomous ethnos.

Clearly this is not a question of autonomous cultural entities influencing each other, as in the classic studies of acculturation. What we find here is the unilateral domination of the society in expansion and the cultural asynchronism or dephasing between the colonialists and the contexts in which they implant themselves. Only in the case of interaction at the tribal level can one speak of acculturation as a process in which the respective patrimonies allow a free choice of the traits to be adopted, autonomous control of these traits, and their full integration into the old context.

The very concept of cultural autonomy requires redefinition, because one can speak of independence only in certain circumstances when it is a matter of societies affected as agents or patients in the course of civilizational processes. Neither a colonialist agency situated outside its society nor the population on which it acts constitutes an entity served by really autonomous cultures; each depends on the other and both compose, together with the metropolitan ruling center, an interdependent whole. It is hardly possible to talk of autonomy as control of one's own fate in the case of entities practicing domination, and even they, as a general thing, are part of broad sociocultural constellations whose components only partially preserve their independence. In the conjunctions resulting from ethnic expansion, there is a marked difference between the dominating entity's power to impose its tradition and the dominated subject's power to resist ethnic and cultural denaturing.

We use the term *deculturation* to designate the process operating in situations where human contingents, torn from their society (and consequently from their cultural context) through enslavement or mass removal, and hired as unskilled labor for alien enterprises, find themselves obliged to learn new ways. In these cases the emphasis is on eradicating the original culture and on the traumas that result, rather than on cultural interaction. Deculturation, in this instance, is nearly always prerequisite to the process of enculturation. Enculturation crystallizes a new body of understanding between dominators and dominated that makes social coexistence and economic exploitation viable. It expands when the socialization of the new generations of the nascent society and the assimilation of the immigrants are brought about by incorporation into the body of customs, beliefs, and values of the ethnic protocell.

Finally, we use the concept of *assimilation* to signify the processes of integration of the European into the neo-American societies whose linguistic and cultural similarities—in regard to their worldview and work experiences—do not justify employing the concepts of acculturation and deculturation. Obviously, it is assumed that this participation will be limited at first and that it may be completed in one or two generations, when the immigrant descendant is an undifferentiated member of the national ethnos. As such ethnic entities admit variable forms and degrees of participation—deriving, for example, from socialization in different cultural areas or from more or less recent immigration—these differences in degree of assimilation may assume the character of different expressions of self-identification with the national ethnos.

Another concept that we have had to reformulate is that of *genuine culture* and *spurious culture*, inspired by Edward Sapir (1924) but here used in the sense of cultures more integrated internally and more autonomous in the command of their development (authentic) in opposition to traumatized cultures corresponding to dominated societies dependent on alien decisions. The members of such societies tend toward cultural alienation or, rather, toward internalization of the dominator's view of the world and themselves (spurious).

These contrasting cultural profiles are the natural and necessary results of the civilizational process itself, which, in cases of evolutionary acceleration, preserves and strengthens cultural authenticity and, in cases of historical incorporation, frustrates the preservation of the original ethos or of its redefinition—on its own terms—of the innovations coming from the colonialist entity. The destruction of the original ethos causes, irremediably, a breakdown in cultural integration, which falls below minimum levels of internal congruence, passing into alienation through feeding on undigested ideas not pertinent to its own experience but only to the efforts at self-justification of the colonial power.

The Genuine and the Spurious

In the process of European expansion millions of men originally differentiated in language and culture, each looking at the world with his own view and governing his life by his peculiar body of customs and values, were drafted into a single economic system and uniform mode of living. The multiple faces of humanity were drastically impoverished, not integrated in a new, more advanced standard, but divested of the authority of their way of life and plunged into spurious forms of culture. Subjected to the same processes of deculturation and drafted into identical systems of production under stereotyped forms of domination, all the affected peoples became culturally impoverished, falling into incompressible conditions of wretchedness and dehumanization, which came to be the common denominator of the extra-European man.

Nevertheless, simultaneously a new basic human, common to all, gradually gained vigor, elevating and generalizing himself. The divergent aspirations of the multiplicity of differentiated peoples—each lost in an effort more aesthetic than efficacious to shape the human according to its ideals—joined together to incorporate all humanity in a single corpus of ideas shared in its essential characteristics by all peoples. One and the same view of the world, the same technology, the same methods of organizing society, and, above all, the same essential goals of abundance, leisure, freedom, education fulfilled the basic requisite for construction of a human civilization, no longer only European, nor even Western, nor yet merely Christian.

Every human contingent caught up in the overall system became simultaneously more uniform with the others and more divergent from the European model. Within the new uniformity ethnic variants much less differentiated than the earlier ones, but sufficiently marked to remain individual, were prominent. Each, as it became capable of insight and of proposing suitable plans for reorganizing society, progressively became capable also of looking at the European with a fresh view. At that moment they began to mature as national ethnic groups, breaking with the remote past and with their subjugation to the Europeans.

Since then the colonial context has turned on the former ruling center to inquire, not into the veracity of its truths nor into the justice of its ideals nor into the perfection of its models of beauty, but into the capacity of the overall social, political, and economic system to realize for all men these aspirations of prosperity, knowledge, justice, and beauty. The professed but never executed designs were laid bare. The conviction spread that the proclaimed object was associated with the profits being extracted, that the beauty and the truth being worshiped were lures to servile engagement, destined to create and maintain a world divided between wealth and misery.

This reductive process can be exemplified by analyzing what happened to the American peoples during their four centuries of association with agents of European civilization. The American peoples saw their societies made over from the foundations, their ethnic constitution altered, and their cultures debased by the loss of autonomy in the control of the transformations to which they were subjected. They were thus transmuted from a multiplicity of autonomous peoples with genuine traditions into a few spurious societies of alienated cultures, explicable in the uniformity of their new mode of being only by the dominating action exercised on them by an external force and will.

Both the survivors of the old American civilizations and the new societies generated as subproducts of the tropical trading posts resulted from European projects that sought to plunder accumulated riches or to exploit new veins of precious minerals or to produce sugar or tobacco, but, in all cases, to accumulate money. It was only incidentally, and nearly always unexpected and undesired by promoters of the colonial undertaking, that the constitution of new societies resulted from their effort. Only in the case of the colonies of settlers was there any intention of creating a new human nucleus, a decision sufficiently explicit and implemented to condition the spontaneous undertaking to the exigencies of that objective. Even in these cases, however, the new formations grew spurious like the rest, because they too resulted from alien projects and designs.

It is only through long-enduring covert effort in the least explicit spheres of life that these colonized societies have been reconstituting themselves as peoples. On these recondite levels their self-construction was practiced, as ethnic entities became differentiated from their parent populations, freed from the conditions imposed by colonial degradation, and as nationalities decided to gain control of their own destinies. This effort was being made not only far from the areas subject to control of the ruling authority but also against its operation, which was zealously dedicated to maintaining and strengthening the external bond and subjugation.

In spite of all these drawbacks the weaving of the new authentic sociocultural configuration is always continuing, as a natural and necessary reaction, within the spurious. Every step forward demands immense efforts, because everything is combining to keep it unauthentic. On the economic side, dependence on foreign trade, which coordinates the greater part of activities, is assigning nearly the entire labor force to export production. In the social orbit, the stratification is crowned by its ruling stratum, which, being at once oligarchic cupola of the new society and part of the dominant class of the colonial system, acts to maintain dependence on the metropolis, the mother country. On the ideological plane, a vast apparatus of regulating and indoctrinating institutions is being carved out, coercing all according to the religious, philosophical, and political values justifying European colonialism and ethnocultural alienation. These systems of ideological coercion become stronger through introjecting into the people, and into the elite of the subjugated society, a view of the world and of themselves serving to maintain European domination. It is this incorporation of the awareness of "the other" within oneself that determined the spurious character of the nascent cultures, impregnated in all their dimensions with exogenous values.

Besides the techniques for exploitation of gold or of sugar production, besides the installation of railroads or telegraphs, Europe exported to the peoples covered by her network of domination her whole cargo of concepts, preconceptions, and idiosyncrasies about herself and the world and even the colonial peoples themselves. The latter, not only impoverished by the plundering of their wealth and of the products of their work under the colonial regime, were also degraded when they assumed as a self-image the European view, which described them as racially inferior because they were black, indigenous, or *mestizo* and condemned to backwardness as a fatality stemming from their innate laziness, lack of ambition, tendency to lasciviousness, and so on.

Lacking control on the political and economic plane, by virtue of colonial statute, these peoples likewise lacked autonomy in the control of their cultural creativity. Any possibility of digesting and integrating into their own cultural context the innovations imposed on them was frustrated, therefore, irremediably breaking down integration between the sphere of awareness and the world of reality. In these circumstances, as they fed on undigested alien ideas not corresponding to their own experience but to the European efforts to justify rapine and to base colonial domination on moral grounds, their dependence and their alienation expanded.

Even the most enlightened strata among extra-European peoples learned to view themselves and their fellow men as a subhumanity destined to a subaltern role. Only the immigrant colonies, which carried the European racial marks through the world and settled in the climates and regions most like those of the country of origin, were not alienated by these forms of moral domination. On the contrary, they actually took pride, like the Europeans, in their whiteness, their climate, their religion, their language, also explaining by these characteristics the successes finally achieved.

For the cultures built on the old American civilizations and for those emerged from diverse environments and composed of brown or black people, these forms of alienation reinforced the backwardness from which only now is there a beginning of emancipation. In these cases the nascent culture, as far as the national ethos is concerned, was shaped by (1) the compulsory deculturation of the tribal ethnocentric concepts of the Indian and the Negro and, (2) the construction of a new conception of themselves as intrinsically inferior and therefore incapable of progress.

This spurious self-image, elaborated in the effort to find their place in the world, to explain their own experience, and to attribute to themselves a destiny, is a patchwork quilt of bits taken from their old traditions and from European beliefs, as best they could perceive them from their viewpoint as slaves or dependents.

On the plane of the national ethos this ideology explains backwardness and poverty in terms of the inclemency of the tropical climate, the inferiority of the dark races, the degradation of half-breed peoples. In the religious sphere it shapes syncretist cults in which African and native beliefs are mingled with Christianity, resulting in a variant further from the European Christian currents than any of its most combated heresies. These cults were, nevertheless, fully satisfactory for consoling man for the misery of this earthly fate and, moreover, for maintaining the system, allegorically justifying white-European domination and inducing the multitudes to a passive and resigned attitude.

On the societal plane the new ethos induces conformist attitudes toward social stratification, which explain the nobility of the whites and the subordination of the dark, or the wealth of the rich and the poverty of the poor, as natural and necessary. In the field of family organization it contraposes two family standards: (1) the dominant class, invested with all the sacraments of legitimacy and continuity, and (2) the mass strata, degraded in successive matings to anarchic matriarchal forms. In this spurious spiritual universe the very values that give meaning to life, motivating each individual to struggle for ends prescribed as socially desirable, are elaborated as justifications of rapine and idleness on the part of the oligarchic strata and as prescriptions of humility and toil for the poor.

On the racial plane the colonialist ethos is a justification of racial hierarchization, introjecting a mystified consciousness of their subjugation into the Indian, the Negro, and the *mestizo*. By it the destiny of the subordinate strata is explained through its racial characteristics and not because of the exploitation of which they are victims. In this manner the colonialist not only rules but dignifies himself at the same time he subjugates the Negro, the Indian, and their mixed breeds and debases their ethnic self-images. Besides being depersonalized—because converted into mere material requisite for the existence of the dominating stratum —the subaltern strata are alienated in the depths of their consciousness by the association of "dark" with dirtiness and "white" with cleanliness. Even the white contingents that fall into poverty, confusing themselves with other strata by their mode of living, capitalize on the "nobility" of their color. The Negro and the Indian who gained their freedom, ascending to the status of workers, continue to bear within themselves this alienated consciousness, which operates insidiously, making it impossible for them to perceive the real character of the social relations that make them inferior. While this alienating ethos prevails, the Indian, the Negro, and the various mixed breeds cannot evade these postures, which compel them to behave socially in accordance with expectations that describe them as necessarily crude and inferior and to wish to "whiten" themselves, whether through the resigned conduct of one who knows his place in society or by selective crossing with Caucasoids in order to produce offspring of "cleaner blood."

For the peoples caught in the nets of European expansion these conceptions shaped the burden of the spiritual heritage of Western and Christian civilization. Acting like distorting lenses, they made it impossible for the nascent cultures to create an authentic image of the world and of themselves, and this blinded them to the most palpable realities.

Despite their evident adaptation to the American climate, the colonial elites longed for the European climate, displaying their detestation of the "stifling" heat. Notwithstanding their evident predilection for the dark-skinned woman, they longed for the whiteness of the European female, in response to the ideal of feminine beauty that had been inculcated in them.

The intellectuals of the colonial peoples, immersed in such alienation, could operate only with these concepts and idiosyncrasies to explain the backwardness of their peoples as compared with the white-European capacity for progress. They got so entangled in weaving the web of these causes of misery and ignorance that they never perceived the greatest, most significant evidence set before their eyes, the European spoliation to which they had always been yoked, itself more explicative of their way of life and their destiny than any of the supposed defects that occupied them so much.

The break with this alienation by the dark peoples of America was initiated only after centuries of pioneer efforts to unmask the intrigue. Only in our own times is the crossbred national human accepted as such—critically appreciative of his own formative process, and having regained a cultural authenticity that is commencing to make of the national ethos, in all spheres, a reflection of the real image and concrete experiences of each people and a motivator of its effort to confront the backwardness and want to which they have been condemned for centuries.

The new ethos of the extra-European peoples, founded on their own bodies of values, is gradually restoring to them the sense of their own dignity and, at the same time, the capacity to integrate all their populations into cohesive, genuine national societies. Compared with the ethos of some archaic societies that collapsed before the attack of small bands, the new formations are different in their bold self-affirmation and their capacity for defense and aggression. To perceive that difference it is enough to compare the episodes of the Spanish sixteenth-century conquest, or those of the English, Dutch, and French appropriations in Africa and Asia three centuries later, with the struggles for American peoples' independence, the struggles for freedom of the Algerians, the Congolese, the Angolans, the Mau-Mau, and especially the Vietnamese of our days, who are facing the armies of world powers and defeating them.

The emergence of that new ethos is the most conclusive symptom of the closing of the European civilizational cycle. Precisely as has happened with Roman civilization and with so many others that operated for centuries as centers of expansion over wide contexts docile to their aggressions, Western civilization is seeing the peoples of these very contexts—by dint of their ethnic maturation and the adoption of techniques and values from the expansionist civilization—turn on them. This revolution is not destructive to the former ruling center, but libertarian rebellions of subjugated peoples resuming their ethnic image, proud of it, and defining their own roles in history.

In 1819 Bolívar inquired into the role of the Latin American peoples in the dawning new civilization, comparing the Hispano-American world with the European in these terms:

> When she freed herself from the Spanish monarchy, America was like the Roman Empire when that enormous mass fell dispersed in the ancient world. Each dismembering in that time formed an independent nation, in accordance with its situation or its interests. With the difference, however, that those members re-established once again their first associations. We do not even retain the vestige of what we formerly were; we are not Europeans, we are not indigenes; we are a species midway between the aboriginals and the Spaniards. Americans by birth, Europeans by right, we find ourselves in the conflict of disputing with the natives the titles of possession, and against the opposition of the invaders the right to support ourselves in the country where we were born; thus our case is all the more extraordinary and complicated. (Bolívar's Angostura speech, 15 February 1819)

This inquiry well depicts the perplexity of the neo-American who, becoming the active subject of historical action, asks: What are we among the world's peoples, we who are neither Europe nor the West nor the original America?

Like the peoples of extra-European context, the Europeans emerging from the Roman domination were no longer what they had been. Centuries of occupation and acculturation had transformed them culturally, ethnically, and linguistically. France is a Roman cultural enterprise, as are the Iberian peoples, all having resulted from the subjugation of tribal peoples to the consul, the merchant, and the soldier of Rome, but also from the later barbarian invasions. The Germanic and Slavic tribes most resistant to Romanization were equally impelled by the Romans' civilizational process and changed themselves during that process.

The coercive power of European civilization over its area of expansion in the Americas, however, was much superior to that of the Romans. In all Europe non-Latin languages and cultures survived, and even within Latinized areas ethnic pockets subsist to attest the viability of resistance to Romanization. In the Americas, excepting the high indigenous civilizations and the island of isolation that Paraguay became—and these Europe could not completely assimilate—all was molded into the European linguistic-cultural pattern. Thus, the Spanish, the Portuguese, and the English spoken in the Americas are more homogeneous and undifferentiated than the speech of the Iberian Peninsula and of the British Isles. This linguistic-cultural-ethnic uniformity can only be explained as the result of a much more intensive and continued civilizational process, capable of assimilating and fusing together the most disparate contingents.

The post-Roman macroethnos of the Iberian peoples, which had already endured the centuries-long domination of Moors and blacks, becoming African both racially and culturally, faced a new ordeal in America. Confronted with millions of natives and other millions of blacks, it was transfigured anew, becoming darker and more acculturated, enriching its biological and cultural patrimony, but imposing its language and its fundamental cultural image on the new ethnic entities to which it would give birth. This was the achievement of some two hundred thousand Europeans who came to the Americas during the sixteenth century and conquered millions of Indians and Negroes, fusing them into a new cultural complex that draws its uniformity principally from the Iberian cement with which it was amalgamated.

Today's Latin Americans are the offshoot of two thousand years of Latinity, melted together with Mongol and Negroid populations, tempered with the heritage of many cultural patrimonies, and crystallized under the pressure of slavery and the Iberian salvationistic expansion. That is, they are a culturally old civilization thrust on new ethnic entities. The old patrimony is expressed socially in their worst aspects: the consular and alienated posture of the dominant classes, the *caudillo* habits of command and taste for personal power, the profound social discrimination between rich and poor, which separates men more than the color of their skins, the lordly customs, such as enjoyment of leisure, the cult of courtesy between patricians, scorn of work, the conformity and resignation of the poor with their poverty. The new is expressed in the assertive energy emerging from the oppressed strata, at last awakened to the unsanctified, eradicable nature of the misery in which they have always lived; in the increasingly enlightened and proud assumption of the crossbreed ethnic image; in the equating of the causes of backwardness and want, and in rebellion against the existing order.

The impact between these two conceptions of life and society is Latin American social revolution on the march—a revolution that will one day restore to the dark-skinned peoples of America the creative impetus lost centuries ago when their Iberian intruders were slow in integrating themselves into industrial civilization, thus entering into decadence, a revolution that will signify the entrance of the Latin Americans into the world as peoples who have a specific contribution to make to civilization. This contribution will be based, essentially, on their ethnic configuration and on its potentialities, which will make them more human because they have incorporated more of man's racial and cultural facets; more generous, because they remain open to all influences and have been inspired in a panracial integrationist ideology; more progressive, because their future depends on the development of knowledge and technology; more optimistic, because, emerging from exploitation and penury, they know that tomorrow will be better than today; freer because they do not base their national projects for progress on the exploitation of other peoples.

National Ethnic Typology

The extra-European peoples of the modern world can be classified in four great historicocultural configurations. Each of them comprises highly differentiated populations sufficiently homogeneous in their basic characteristics and in the developmental problems facing them to be legitimately treated as different categories. They are the "Witness Peoples," the "New Peoples," the "Transplanted Peoples," and the "Emerging Peoples."

The Witness Peoples are the modern representatives of old original civilizations conquered in the European expansion. The New Peoples are represented by the American peoples formed in these last centuries as a subproduct of the European expansion through the fusion and acculturation of indigenous, black, and European populations. The Transplanted Peoples are the implanted European populations with their original ethnic profile, language, and culture preserved. Emerging Peoples are the new nations of Africa and Asia whose populations ascend from a tribal level or from the status of mere colonial trading posts to that of national ethnic groups.

These categories are founded on two premises: (1) the peoples composing them are what they are today in consequence of the European mercantile expansion and the reorganization of the world by industrially based civilization; (2) these peoples, formerly racially, socially, and culturally different, have a hybrid cultural inventory. They offer sufficient biological uniformity to warrant treatment as distinct configurations explicative of their mode of being.

These configurations must not be taken as independent sociocultural entities, because they lack a minimum of integration to give them internal order and permit them to act as autonomous units; nor should they be confused with econosocial formations,[1] because they do not represent necessary stages in the evolutionary process, but only conditions under which it operates. The positively acting entities are the particular societies and cultures composing them, and particularly the national states into which they are divided. These constitute the operative units, both for economic interaction and for social and political order, and also the real national ethnic frames within which the destiny of the peoples is fulfilled.

The sociocultural formations are categories of another type—such as mercantile capitalism and slavistic colonialism—equally meaningful but different from those here described.

It must be emphasized, even so, that the proposed historicocultural configurations constitute congruent categories of peoples, based on the parallelism of their historical process of national ethnic formation and on the uniformity of their social characteristics and the problems facing them. In terms of these broad configurations of peoples—rather than of the nationalities, or the respective racial compositions, or climatic, religious, and other differentiating factors—each extra-European people of the modern world can be explained. How did it develop in its current form? Why has it undergone such differentiated historical processes of socioeconomic development? What factors in each case have acted to accelerate or retard its integration into the life-style of modern industrial societies?

The typology examined below aspires to be a classification of historical categories resulting from the civilizational processes that have been loosed on all the peoples of the earth in recent centuries. As such, it seeks to be significant and instrumental in the study of the process that has led these peoples, first, from the status of autonomous societies and cultures to that of subaltern components of economic systems of world domination activated by spurious cultures and, now, to emancipation movements tending to restore their autonomy as new ethnic entities integrated into the current civilizational process.

The first of these configurations, which we have designated as "Witness Peoples," is made up of the survivors of high autonomous civilizations that suffered the impact of European expansion. They are modern survivals of the traumatizing action of that expansion and of their efforts at ethnic reconstitution as modern national societies. Reintegrated in their independence, they did not regain their former autonomy, because they had been transformed not only by the joining of their traditions to the European but by the effort to adapt to the conditions they had to face as subordinate integrants of worldwide economic systems and also by the direct and reflexive impacts of the Mercantile and Industrial revolutions.

Rather than peoples retarded in history, these are the plundered peoples of history. Originally possessing enormous accumulated wealth (which could be utilized, now, to defray the costs of their integration into the industrial systems of production), they saw their treasures sacked by the European. This sacking continued with the centuries-long spoliation of the work products of their peoples. Nearly all are enmeshed in the world imperialistic system, which fixes a place and a predetermined role for them, limiting their possibilities for autonomous development. Centuries of subjugation or of direct or indirect domination have deformed them, pauperizing their peoples and traumatizing their whole cultural life.

They face the basic problem of making the two cultural traditions to which they have become heirs—traditions not simply diverse but in many aspects mutually opposed—an integral part of themselves: (1) the European technology and ideology, whose incorporation into the old cultural patrimony was processed at the cost of redefinition of their whole way of life and of the alienation of their view of themselves and of the world; (2) their former cultural store, which, despite being drastically reduced and traumatized, preserved language, customs, forms of social organization, bodies of beliefs, and values deeply rooted in vast strata of the population, beside a heritage of common knowledge and of unique artistic styles that are now flourishing in an age of national self-assertion. Simultaneously attracted by the two traditions but incapable of fusing them meaningfully for the whole population, even today they bear within themselves the conflict between the original culture and the European civilization. Some of them have had their modernization guided by the European powers dominating them; others have seen themselves compelled to promote it designedly or to intensify it as a requisite to survival and progress in the face of the pillaging fury to which they were subjected, and also as a requisite to overcoming the obstacles represented by technological backwardness and the archaism of their social structures.

In this bloc of Witness Peoples are included India, China, Japan, Korea, Indochina, the Islamic countries, and a few others. In the Americas they are represented by Mexico, Guatemala, and the peoples of the Andean highlands, the two former being survivors of the Aztec and Maya civilizations, the latter of the Inca.

Among the Witness Peoples only Japan and, more recently and partially, China, have succeeded in incorporating modern industrial technology into their respective economies and in restructuring their societies on new foundations. All the rest are peoples divided into a more Europeanized dominant caste, sometimes biologically crossbred and culturally integrated in the modern life-styles, opposed to great masses —particularly rural—marginalized by their adherence to archaic ways of life resistant to modernization.

The two nuclei of Witness Peoples of the Americas, as peoples conquered and subjugated, suffered a process of Europeanizing compulsion much more violent than their complete ethnic transmutation turned out to be. Their present national ethnic profiles are not the original ones. They display neo-Hispanic profiles thrust on the descendants of the former society crossbred with Europeans and Negroes. Though the other extra-European peoples of high culture, despite the domination they underwent, barely colored their original ethnocultural figure with European influences, in the Americas it is the neo-European ethnos that was colored by the old cultural traditions, extracting distinctive characteristics from them.

Compared with the other American ethnic groups, the Witness Peoples are distinguished as much by the presence of the values of the old tradition that they have preserved and that bestow on them the image they present, as by their much differentiated process of ethnic reconstitution. On the Middle American and Andean societies the Spanish conquistadors established themselves from the first as an aristocracy that, succeeding the old dominant class, immediately placed the intermediary strata and the whole servile mass at its service. They could thus live in more showy palaces than the richest of the old Spanish nobility, erect sumptuous temples such as Spain had never possessed, and, particularly, set up a compulsory system of Europeanization that, starting with the elimination of the native dominant class and its learned caste, ended by installing an enormous assimilative and repressive instrumentation that ran the gamut from mass catechism to the creation of universities and the maintenance of huge military contingents ready to crush any attempt at rebellion.

Besides the tasks of socioeconomic development common to all nations retarded in history, the contemporary representatives of the Witness Peoples are faced with specific cultural problems arising from the challenge to incorporate their marginal populations into the new national and cultural being now emerging, deflecting them from the archaic traditions least compatible with the life-style of modern industrial societies. Some of their basic human contingents constitute ethnic units differing in their cultural and linguistic diversity and in being conscious of their ethnic differences from the national ethnos. Notwithstanding the centuries of oppression, both colonial and national, in the course of which every form of compulsion was used to assimilate them, these contingents remained faithful to their ethnic identity, preserving their own modes of conduct and their own conception of the world. This centuries-long resistance tells us that in all probability these contingents will remain differentiated, in the manner of the ethnic groups encysted in the majority of the present European nationalities. In the future they will probably figure as different modes of participation in the national life, like that of the Jews, or of the Gypsies, in so many nations, or as disparate ethnolinguistic pockets equivalent to those surviving in Spain, in Great Britain, in France, in Czechoslovakia, or in Yugoslavia. To reach this form of integration, however, they will need a minimum of autonomy, which has always been denied them, the suppression of the compulsory mechanism designed to force their incorporation as undifferentiated contingents of the national society, and the Witness Peoples' acceptance of their character as multiethnic entities.

The second historicocultural configuration is constituted by the New Peoples, emerging from the conjunction, deculturation, and amalgamation of African, European, and indigenous ethnic stocks. They are here designated as New Peoples because of their fundamental characteristic of being *speciei novae*, ethnic entities distinct from their formative origins, and because they represent anticipations of what, probably, the human groups of a remote future, more and more crossbred and acculturated and thus racially and culturally uniformized, will be.

The New Peoples have been constituted by the confluence of contingents profoundly disparate in their racial, cultural, and linguistic characteristics, as a subproduct of European colonial projects. Bringing together Negroes, whites, and Indians to open great plantations of tropical products or for mining operations, with the sole aim of supplying European markets and making profits, the colonizing nations ended by molding peoples profoundly different from themselves and from all the other formative peoples. Placed together in the same communities, these Negroes, whites, and Indians, though performing different roles, began mingling and culturally fusing together. Thus, beside the white, the head of the enterprise (by dint of the conditions of domination), the Negro engaged in it as slave, and the Indian, also enslaved or treated as a mere obstacle to eliminate, a crossbred population gradually arose, amalgamating these peoples in varied proportions. In that encounter people's *lingua franca* emerged as an indispensable instrument of communication, and syncretic cultures were molded, made of pieces taken from the different patrimonies that adjusted best to their conditions of life.

Not many decades after the colonial enterprises were begun, the new population, born and integrated in the plantations and mines, was no longer European or African or native, but a new ethnic body. Incorporating new contingents, these mixed populations progressively shaped the New Peoples, which shortly became aware of their specificity and finally composed new cultural configurations, ethnic entities aspiring to national autonomy.

The New Peoples, like the Witness Peoples, emerged within a hierarchy characterized by the enormous social distance separating the lordly class of plantation owners, exploiters of minerals, merchants, colonial officials, and clergy from the slave mass engaged in production. Their dominant class, however, did not become a foreign aristocracy ruling the process of Europeanization, precisely because it had not found a former noble, literate caste to replace and supplant. They were rough entrepreneurs, masters of their lands and their slaves, forced to live with their businesses and run them personally with the aid of a small intermediate class of technicians, foremen, and priests. Where the enterprise prospered greatly, as in the sugar and mining zones of Brazil and the Antilles, they could afford the luxury of lordly residences, and they had to broaden the intermediate class both at the mills and in the coastal towns, busied in trade with the outside world. These towns became cities, expressing their economic opulence principally in their churches, with less ostentation than the aristocracy of the Witness Peoples but with much more brilliance and "civilization" than the Transplanted Peoples.

As the dominant class they were also rather the managers of an economic undertaking than the acme of a genuine society. Only very slowly did they become capable of assuming the role of native leadership, and when they did so it was to impose on the entire society, transformed into nationality, an oligarchic order founded on the monopoly of land, which would assure the preservation of their sovereign role and the conscription of the people as a labor force, slave or free, in the service of their privileges.

None of the peoples of this bloc constitutes a multiethnic nationality. In all cases their formative process was violent enough to compel the fusion of the original stocks into new homogeneous units. Only Chile, because of her peculiar formation, retains in the Araucanian contingent of nearly two hundred thousand Indians a microethnos differentiated from the national, historically claiming the right to be itself, at least as a differentiated mode of participation in the national society. The Chileans and the Paraguayans also differ from the other New Peoples by the principally indigenous ancestry of their population and by the absence of both the Negro slave element and the plantation system, which played so outstanding a part in the formation of the Brazilians, the Antilleans, the Colombians, and the Venezuelans. For this reason they constitute, together with the River Plate peoples, a variant of the New Peoples. The predominantly Indio-Spanish Witness Peoples differ from them because these former original native populations had not attained a level of cultural development comparable to that of the Mexicans or the Incas.

In their finished form these peoples are the result of, first, the selection of racial and cultural qualities from the formative populations that best adapted to the conditions imposed on them; second, their effort to adapt to the environment; and, third, the compulsive force of the socioeconomic system into which they were introduced. The decisive role in their formation was played by slavery, which, operating as a detribalizing force, broke these new peoples away from ancestral traditions to turn them into the subproletariat of the nascent society. In this sense the New Peoples are the product of the reductive deculturation of their indigenous African tribal patrimonies, of the selective acculturation of these patrimonies, and of their own creativity in the face of the new environment.

Separated from their American, African, and European cultural beginnings, deviated from their cultural traditions, today they represent disengaged, available peoples, condemned to integrate into industrial civilization as people who have a future only in the future of man. That is, their progressive integration into the civilizational process gave them birth, not as slavistic colonial areas of mercantile capitalism, or as neo-colonial dependents of industrial imperialism, but as autonomous formations, whether capitalist or socialist, capacitated to incorporate the technology of modern civilization into their societies and to attain for their whole population the level of education and consumption of the more advanced peoples.

The third historicocultural configuration, the Transplanted Peoples, embraces the modern nations created by the migration of European populations to new spaces in the world where they sought to reconstitute forms of life essentially identical to those of their origins. Each structured itself according to models of economic and social life of the nation from which it came.

At first the Transplanted Peoples were recruited from among the dissident European groups, especially the religious; later they were incremented with all kinds of maladjusted persons condemned to exile by the colonizing nations; and finally, their numbers were swelled by the huge migrations of Europeans uprooted by the Industrial Revolution from their rural and urban communities who came to try their luck in the new lands. The majority of these came to America as farm workers enticed by contracts committing them to years of servitude. But a large part of them later succeeded in coming as free farmers and independent craftsmen. Their basic characteristics are cultural homogeneity, which they maintained from the start through the common origin of their population or else assimilated with new immigrants; the more egalitarian character of their societies, founded on democratic institutions of self-government and on the easier access of the farmhand to ownership of land; and their modernity as regards synchronization with the ways of life and the aspirations of the preindustrial capitalistic societies from which they had been separated.

The bloc of Transplanted Peoples is composed of Australia and New Zealand, and in a certain measure the neo-European pockets of Israel, the Union of South Africa, and Rhodesia. In the Americas they are represented by the United States, Canada, Uruguay, and Argentina. In the first cases we encounter nations resulting from colonization projects in territories where tribal populations were decimated or confined to reservations so that a new society could be installed. In the case of the River Plate countries we find an extremely peculiar Creole elite—entirely alienated and hostile to its own ethnos as a New People—which adopts as a national project the replacement of its own people by white and dark Europeans, considered to be endowed with a more decisive vocation for progress. Argentina and Uruguay are thus the result of a process of ecological succession deliberately initiated by national oligarchies, and by that process a New People configuration is transformed into a Transplanted People. By this process the *ladino* and *gaucho* population, originating in the crossbreeding of Iberian settlers with the natives, was crushed and replaced, as the basic contingent of the nation, by an avalanche of European immigrants.

Contrary to what occurred with the Witness Peoples and the New Peoples, which from their earliest years took shape as complex societies, stratified in profoundly differentiated classes ranging from a rich oligarchy of European conquistadors to the servile mass of Indians or Negroes, the majority of the Transplanted Peoples emerged as immigrant colonies, dedicated to farming, craftsmanship, and small business. They all faced long periods of privation while establishing their bases on the unpopulated land, seeking to make their existence economically viable by the production of goods for export to richer and more specialized markets. In such circumstances a local dominating minority capable of imposing an oligarchic social order does not emerge. Even though poor, even in want, they were living in a reasonably egalitarian society governed by the democratic principles of British tradition. They could not have universities or sumptuous churches or palaces; but they taught their whole population to read and write and gathered it together to read the Bible in their modest clapboard churches and to reach decisions through self-government.

In that way they were able to rise collectively, as a people, in proportion as the colony became consolidated and enriched, and finally to gain their freedom as a more homogeneous society, more capable of carrying on the Industrial Revolution. The peculiar conditions of their formation, as well as the patrimony of lands and natural resources to which they made themselves heirs, assured the Transplanted Peoples special conditions of development that, made fruitful by access to European markets and by the linguistic and cultural facilities of communication with the most progressive countries of Europe, permitted them the mastery of Industrial Revolution technology. This enabled many of them to excel their original forbears, reaching high stages of economic and social development. And it allowed all of them to progress faster than the other American nations, which were originally much more prosperous and cultured.

The fourth bloc of extra-European peoples of the modern world is the Emerging Peoples. They are the African populations nowadays rising from the tribal to the national level. In Asia there are also some cases of Emerging Peoples in transition from tribal to national status, especially in the socialist area, where a policy of greater respect for nationalities permits and stimulates their gestation.

This category has not appeared in America, in spite of the existence of thousands of tribal populations at the time of the conquest. Some of these were decimated promptly by the violence of European domination, others more slowly through subjection to slave labor, and only a few survived. These, under the most rigid forms of compulsion and national domination, have all been annulled as ethnic entities and as bases for new nationalities. Their African and Asian equivalents, on the other hand, despite the violence of the impact they experienced, are today rising to national life.

The Emerging Peoples face specific developmental problems stemming from the deformations resulting from their colonial exploitation by European powers; problems of detribalizing great segments of their population in order to incorporate them into the national life; and problems created by the imperative need to decolonize their own elites who, in the process of Westernization, became culturally alienated from their peoples or turned into local representatives of exogenous interests.

Emerging today to the status of autonomous nationalities, as the Latin Americans did a century and a half ago, these peoples are in danger of falling likewise under the yoke of new forms of economic domination. The fundamental challenge confronting them lies in compelling their elites not to make independence a selfish project by which these leaders simply replace the former foreign colonist. For this they have before them the experience of the peoples who preceded them and a more favorable world situation, which seems propitious to a more autonomous and progressive modernization process.

The four categories of peoples examined to this point, though meaningful and instrumental for the study of the modern world's populations, especially the American, do not portray pure types. Every one of the models has experienced intrusions that affected more or less extensive areas of its territory and differentiated greater or smaller parcels of its population. Thus, in the south of the United States there was a vast Negro intrusion, molded by a plantation-type productive system that gave rise to a New People configuration. A great part of the racial integration problem confronting the United States derives from the presence of this intrusion, until now irreducible and unassimilated despite being overcome and dispersed in the body of the new formation. Brazil experienced an intrusion of Transplanted People with the massive immigration of Europeans to her southern region, which gave that area a peculiar physiognomy and occasioned a differentiated mode of being. Argentina and Uruguay, as has been shown, emerged to national existence as New Peoples, characterized by a neo-Guaraní protoethnos in the case of the original Paraguay and São Paulo areas. Nevertheless, they suffered a process of pastoral specialization and ecological succession through which the national ethnic character was transmuted, originating a new entity, basically European. So it is that both took shape as Transplanted Peoples, of a special type because hindered in their socioeconomic development by the survival of an archaic oligarchy of great rural landowners. In each of the American peoples lesser intrusions color and particularize certain segments of the national population and the regions of the country where they are most concentrated.

It is to be emphasized that some populations of the modern extra-European world seem not to fit into these categories. This is the case, essentially, of such nations as South Africa, Rhodesia, Malawi (Nyasaland), and Kenya. The classificatory difficulty in this case is that rather than being nations, they are still trading colonies ruled by white groups that entered the area tardily, and even now they remain unassimilated and incapable of molding a New People configuration. Their viability as a national formation is so incontrovertible that one can predict without risk of error the inevitable uprising of the subjugated classes and the elimination of the dominant one, incapable of integrating itself racially and culturally in its own national ethnic context.

In the case of the other extra-European peoples, the national character and the basic ethnocultural profile of each unit are explicable as the result of their overall formation as Witness, New, Emerging, and Transplanted Peoples. This scale corresponds, by and large, to the current characterization of the American peoples as predominantly Indo-American, neo-American, or Euro-American. The two scales, however, are not equivalent because many other peoples, such as the Paraguayans and the Chileans, of basically indigenous form, became New Peoples and not Witness Peoples because they resulted from the fusion of the European with tribal groups that had not attained the level of the high civilizations. This is also the case of the Euro-Americans, present in all the ethnic formations of the continent; but only in the Transplanted Peoples did they stamp a clearly neo-European profile on the respective populations.

The designation of "neo-Americans" does not adequately substitute for "New Peoples," because in many senses, particularly as successors of the original populations of the continent, all these peoples today are neo-Americans.

Note

1. Concerning econosocial or sociocultural formations see Ribeiro (1968).

ROBERTO FERNÁNDEZ RETAMAR
Caliban: Notes Toward a Discussion of Culture in Our America

Roberto Fernández Retamar was born in Cuba in 1930. A poet and a literary and cultural critic, he is the director of *Casa de las Américas* in Havana, Cuba. His main titles include *Calibán. Apuntes sobre la cultura en Nuestra América* (1971), *Para una teoría de la literatura hispanoamericana y otras aproximaciones* (1975), and *Para el perfil definitivo del hombre* (1981).

A Question

An European journalist, and moreover a leftist, asked me a few days ago, "Does a Latin American culture exist?" We were discussing, naturally enough, the recent polemic regarding Cuba that ended by confronting, on the one hand, certain bourgeois European intellectuals (or aspirants to that state) with a visible colonialist nostalgia; and on the other, that body of Latin American writers and artists who reject open or veiled forms of cultural and political colonialism. The question seemed to me to reveal one of the roots of the polemic and, hence, could also be expressed another way: "Do you exist?" For to question our culture is to question our very existence, our human reality itself, and thus to be willing to take a stand in favor of our irremediable colonial condition, since it suggests that we would be but a distorted echo of what occurs elsewhere. This elsewhere is of course the metropolis, the colonizing centers, whose "right wings" have exploited us and whose supposed "left wings" have pretended and continue to pretend to guide us with pious solicitude—in both cases with the assistance of local intermediaries of varying persuasions.

While this fate is to some extent suffered by all countries emerging from colonialism—those countries of ours that enterprising metropolitan intellectuals have ineptly and successively termed *barbarians, peoples of color, underdeveloped countries, third world*—I think the phenomenon achieves a singular crudeness with respect to what Martí called our "*mestizo America.*" Although the thesis that every man and even every culture is *mestizo* could easily be defended and although this seems especially valid in the case of colonies, it is nevertheless apparent that in both their ethnic and their cultural aspects capitalist countries long ago achieved a relative homogeneity. Almost before our eyes certain readjustments have been made. The white population of the United States (diverse, but of common European origin) exterminated the aboriginal population and thrust the black population aside, thereby affording itself homogeneity in spite of diversity and offering a coherent model that its Nazi disciples attempted to apply even to other European conglomerates—an unforgivable sin that led some members of the bourgeoisie to stigmatize in Hitler what they applauded as a healthy Sunday diversion in Westerns and Tarzan films. Those movies proposed to the world—and even to those of us who are kin to the communities under attack and who rejoiced in the evocation of our own extermination—the monstrous racial criteria that have accompanied the United Sates from its beginnings to the genocide in Indochina. Less apparent (and in some cases perhaps less cruel) is the process by which other capitalist countries have also achieved relative racial and cultural homogeneity at the expense of *internal* diversity.

Nor can any necessary relationship be established between *mestizaje* and the colonial world. The latter is highly complex[1] despite basic structural affinities of its parts. It has included countries with well-defined millennial cultures, some of which have suffered (or are presently suffering) direct occupation (India, Vietnam), and others of which have suffered indirect occupation (China). It also comprehends countries with rich cultures but less political homogeneity, which have been subjected to extremely diverse forms of colonialism (the Arab world). There are other peoples, finally, whose fundamental structures were savagely dislocated by the dire activity of the European despite which they continue to preserve a certain ethnic and cultural homogeneity (black Africa). (Indeed, the latter has occurred despite the colonialists' criminal and unsuccessful attempts to prohibit it.) In these countries *mestizaje* naturally exists to a greater or lesser degree, but it is always accidental and always on the fringe of the central line of development.

But within the colonial world there exists a case unique to the entire planet: a vast zone for which *mestizaje* is not an accident but rather the essence, the central line: ourselves, "our *mestizo* America." Martí, with his excellent knowledge of the language, employed this specific adjective as the distinctive sign of our culture—a culture of descendants, both ethnically and culturally speaking, of aborigines, Africans, and Europeans. In his "Letter from Jamaica" (1815), the Liberator, Simón Bolívar, had proclaimed, "We are a small human species: we possess a world encircled by vast seas, new in almost all its arts and sciences." In his message to the Congress of Angostura (1819), he added:

> Let us bear in mind that our people is neither European nor North American, but a composite of Africa and America rather than an emanation of Europe; for even Spain fails as a European people because of her African blood, her institutions, and her character. It is impossible to assign us with any exactitude to a specific human family. The greater part of the native peoples has been annihilated; the European has mingled with the American and with the African, and the African has mingled with the Indian and with the European. Born from the womb of a common mother, our fathers, different in origin and blood, are foreigners; all differ visibly in the epidermis, and this dissimilarity leaves marks of the greatest transcendence.

Even in this century, in a book as confused as the author himself but full of intuitions (La raza cósmica, 1925), the Mexican José Vasconcelos pointed out that in Latin America a new race was being forged, "made with the treasure of all previous ones, the final race, the cosmic race." [2]

This singular fact lies at the root of countless misunderstandings. Chinese, Vietnamese, Korean, Arab, or African cultures may leave the Euro-North American enthusiastic, indifferent, or even depressed. But it would never occur to him to confuse a Chinese with a Norwegian, or a Bantu with an Italian; nor would it occur to him to ask whether they exist. Yet, on the other hand, some Latin Americans are taken at times for apprentices, for rough drafts or dull copies of Europeans, including among these latter whites who constitute what Martí called "European America." In the same way, our entire culture is taken as an apprenticeship, a rough draft or a copy of European bourgeois culture ("an emanation of Europe," as Bolívar said). This last error is more frequent than the first, since confusion of a Cuban with an Englishman, or a Guatemalan with a German, tends to be impeded by a certain ethnic tenacity. Here the *rioplatenses* appear to be less ethnically, although not culturally, differentiated. The confusion lies in the root itself, because as descendants of numerous Indian, African, and European communities, we have only a few languages with which to understand one another: those of the colonizers. While other colonials or ex-colonials in metropolitan centers speak among themselves in their own language, we Latin Americans continue to use the languages of our colonizers. These are the *linguas francas* capable of going beyond the frontiers that neither the aboriginal nor Creole languages succeed in crossing. Right now as we are discussing, as I am discussing, with those colonizers, how else can I do it except in one of their languages, which is now also *our* language, and with so many of their conceptual tools, which are now also *our* conceptual tools? This is precisely the extraordinary outcry that we read in a work by perhaps the most extraordinary writer of fiction who ever existed. In *The Tempest*, William Shakespeare's last play, the deformed Caliban—enslaved, robbed of his island, and trained to speak by Prospero—rebukes Prospero thus:

> You taught me language, and my profit on't
> Is, I know how to curse. The red plague rid you
> For learning me your language!" (1.2.363–64)

Toward the History of Caliban

Caliban is Shakespeare's anagram for "cannibal," an expression that he had already used to mean "anthropophagous," in the third part of *Henry IV* and in *Othello* and that comes in turn from the word *carib*. Before the arrival of the Europeans, whom they resisted heroically, the Carib Indians were the most valiant and warlike inhabitants of the very lands that we occupy today. Their name lives on in the name Caribbean Sea (referred to genially by some as the American Mediterranean, just as if we were to call the Mediterranean the Caribbean of Europe). But the name *carib* in itself—as well as in its deformation, *cannibal*—has been perpetuated in the eyes of Europeans above all as a defamation. It is the term in this sense that Shakespeare takes up and elaborates into a complex symbol. Because of its exceptional importance to us, it will be useful to trace its history in some detail.

In the *Diario de navegación* of Columbus there appear the first European accounts of the men who were to occasion the symbol in question. On Sunday, 4 November 1492, less than a month after Columbus arrived on the continent that was to be called America, the following entry was inscribed: "He learned also that far from the place there were men with one eye and others with dogs' muzzles, who ate human beings."[3] On 23 November, this entry: "[the island of Haiti], which they said was very large and that on it lived people who had only one eye and others called cannibals, of whom they seemed to be very afraid." On 11 December it is noted ". . . that *caniba* refers in fact to the people of El Gran Can," which explains the deformation undergone by the name *carib*—also used by Columbus. In the very letter of 15 February 1493, "dated on the caravelle off the island of Canaria" in which Columbus announces to the world his "discovery," he writes: "I have found, then, neither monsters nor news of any, save for one island [Quarives], the second upon entering the Indies, which is populated with people held by everyone on the islands to be very ferocious, and who eat human flesh" (20).

This *carib/cannibal* image contrasts with another one of the American man presented in the writings of Columbus: that of the Arauaco of the Greater Antilles—our Taino Indian primarily—whom he describes as peaceful, meek, and even timorous and cowardly. Both visions of the American aborigine will circulate vertiginously throughout Europe, each coming to know its own particular development: The Taino will be transformed into the paradisiacal inhabitant of a utopic world; by 1516 Thomas More will publish his *Utopia*, the similarities of which to the island of Cuba have been indicated, almost to the point of rapture, by Ezequiel Martínez Estrada (1965). The Carib, on the other hand, will become a *cannibal*—an anthropophagous, a bestial man situated on the margins of civilization, who must be opposed to the very death. But there is less of a contradiction than might appear at first glance between the two visions; they constitute, simply, options in the ideological arsenal of a vigorous emerging bourgeoisie. Francisco de Quevedo translated "utopia" as "there is no such place." With respect to these two visions, one might add, "There is no such man." The notion of an Edenic creature comprehends, in more contemporary terms, a working hypothesis for the bourgeois left, and, as such, offers an ideal model of the perfect society free from the constrictions of that feudal world against which the bourgeoisie is in fact struggling. Generally speaking, the utopic vision throws upon these lands projects for political reforms unrealized in the countries of origin. In this sense its line of development is far from extinguished. Indeed, it meets with certain perpetuators—apart from its radical perpetuators, who are the consequential revolutionaries—in the numerous advisers who unflaggingly propose to countries emerging from colonialism magic formulas from the metropolis to solve the grave problems colonialism has left us and which, of course, they have not yet resolved in their own countries. It goes without saying that these proponents of "There is no such place" are irritated by the insolent fact that the place *does* exist and, quite naturally, has all the virtues and defects not of a project but of genuine reality.

As for the vision of the *cannibal*, it corresponds—also in more contemporary terms—to the right wing of that same bourgeoisie. It belongs to the ideological arsenal of politicians of action, those who perform the dirty work in whose fruits the charming dreamers of utopias will equally share. That the Caribs were as Columbus (and, after him, an unending throng of followers) depicted them is about as probable as the existence of one-eyed men, men with dog muzzles or tails, or even the Amazons mentioned by the explorer in pages where Greco-Roman mythology, the medieval bestiary, and the novel of chivalry all play their part. It is a question of the typically degraded vision offered by the colonizer of the man he is colonizing. That we ourselves may have at one time believed in this version only proves to what extent we are infected with the ideology of the enemy. It is typical that we have applied the term *cannibal* not to the extinct aborigine of our isles but, above all, to the African black who appeared in those shameful Tarzan films. For it is the colonizer who brings us together, who reveals the profound similarities existing above and beyond our secondary differences. The colonizer's version explains to us that owing to the Caribs' irremediable bestiality, there was no alternative to their extermination. What it does not explain is why even before the Caribs, the peaceful and kindly Arauacos were also exterminated. Simply speaking, the two groups suffered jointly one of the greatest ethnocides recorded in history. (Needless to say, this line of action is still more alive than the earlier one.) In relation to this fact, it will always be necessary to point out the case of those men who, being on the fringe both of utopianism (which has nothing to do with the actual America) and of the shameless ideology of plunder, stood in their midst opposed to the conduct of the colonialists and passionately, lucidly, and valiantly defended the flesh-and-blood aborigine. In the forefront of such men stands the magnificent figure of Father Bartolomé de las Casas, whom Bolívar called "the apostle of America" and whom Martí extolled unreservedly. Unfortunately, such men were exceptions.

One of the most widely disseminated European utopian works is Montaigne's essay "De los caníbales," which appeared in 1580. There we find a presentation of those creatures who "retain alive and vigorous their genuine, their most useful and natural, virtues and properties" (1948, 248).

Giovanni Floro's English translation of the *Essays* was published in 1603. Not only was Floro a personal friend of Shakespeare, but the copy of the translation that Shakespeare owned and annotated is still extant. This piece of information would be of no further importance but for the fact that it proves beyond a shadow of doubt that the *Essays* was one of the direct sources of Shakespeare's last great work, *The Tempest* (1612). Even one of the characters of the play, Gonzalo, who incarnates the Renaissance humanist, at one point closely glosses entire lines from Floro's

Montaigne, originating precisely in the essay on cannibals. This fact makes the form in which Shakespeare presents his character *Caliban/cannibal* even stranger. Because if in Montaigne—in this case, as unquestionable literary source for Shakespeare—"there is nothing barbarous and savage in that nation . . . except that each man calls barbarism whatever is not in his own practice" (248), in Shakespeare, on the other hand, *Caliban/cannibal* is a savage and deformed slave who cannot be degraded enough. What has happened is simply that in depicting Caliban, Shakespeare, an implacable realist, here takes *the other option* of the emerging bourgeois world. Regarding the utopian vision, it does indeed exist in the work but is unrelated to Caliban; as was said before, it is expressed by the harmonious humanist Gonzalo. Shakespeare thus confirms that both ways of considering the American, far from being in opposition, were perfectly reconcilable. As for the concrete man, present him in the guise of an animal, rob him of his land, enslave him so as to live from his toil, and at the right moment exterminate him; this latter, of course, only if there were someone who could be depended on to perform the arduous tasks in his stead. In one revealing passage, Prospero warns his daughter that they could not do without Caliban:

> We cannot miss him: he does make our fire,
> Fetch in our wood, and serves in offices
> that profit us. (1.2.311–13)

The utopian vision can and must do without men of flesh and blood. After all, *there is no such place.*

There is no doubt at this point that *The Tempest* alludes to America, that its island is the mythification of one of our islands. Astrana Marín, who mentions the "clearly Indian (American) ambience of the island" (1930, 107–8), recalls some of the actual voyages along this continent that inspired Shakespeare and even furnished him, with slight variations, with the names of not a few of his characters: Miranda, Fernando, Sebastian, Alonso, Gonzalo, Setebos. More important than this is the knowledge that Caliban is our Carib.

We are not interested in following all the possible readings that have been made of this notable work since its appearances,[4] and shall merely point out some interpretations. The first of these comes from Ernest Renan, who published his drama *Caliban: Suite de "La Tempête"* in 1878. In this work, Caliban is the incarnation of the people presented in their worst light, except that this time his conspiracy against Prospero is successful and he achieves power—which ineptitude and corruption will surely prevent him from retaining. Prospero lurks in the darkness awaiting his revenge, and Ariel disappears. This reading owes less to Shakespeare than to the Paris Commune, which had taken place only seven years before. Naturally, Renan was among the writers of the French bourgeoisie who savagely took part against the prodigious "assault of heaven."[5] Beginning with this event, his antidemocratic feeling stiffened even further. "In his *Philosophical Dialogues*," Lidsky tells us, "he believes that the solution would lie in the creation of an *élite* of intelligent beings who alone would govern and possess the secrets of science" (1970, 82). Characteristically, Renan's aristocratic and prefascist elitism and his hatred of the common people of his country are united with an even greater hatred for the inhabitants of the colonies. It is instructive to hear him express himself along these lines: "We aspire [he says] not only to equality but to domination. The country of a foreign race must again be a country of serfs, of agricultural laborers or industrial workers. It is not a question of eliminating the inequalities among men but of broadening them and making them law" (Césaire 1955, 13).[6] And on another occasion:

> The regeneration of the inferior or bastard races by the superior races is within the providential human order. With us, the common man is nearly always a *declassé* nobleman, his heavy hand is better suited to handling the sword than the menial tool. Rather than work he chooses to fight, that is, he returns to his first state. *Regere imperio populos*—that is our vocation. Pour forth this all-consuming activity onto countries which, like China, are crying aloud for foreign conquest. . . . Nature has made a race of workers, the Chinese race, with its marvelous manual dexterity and almost no sense of honor; govern them with justice, levying from them, in return for the blessing, of such a government, an ample allowance for the conquering race, and they will be satisfied; a race of tillers of the soil, the black . . . a race of masters and soldiers, the European race. . . . *Let each do that which he is made for, and all will be well.* (Césaire 1955, 14–15)

It is unnecessary to gloss these lines, which, as Césaire rightly says, came from the pen not of Hitler but of the French humanist Ernest Renan.

The initial destiny of the Caliban myth on our own American soil is a surprising one. Twenty years after Renan had published his *Caliban*—in other words, in 1898—the United States intervened in the Cuban War of Independence against Spain and subjected Cuba to its tutelage, converting her in 1902 into her first *neocolony* (and holding her until 1959), while Puerto Rico and the Philippines became colonies of a traditional nature. The fact—which had been anticipated by Martí years before—moved the Latin American intelligentsia. Elsewhere I have recalled that "ninety-eight" is not only a Spanish date that gives its name to a complex group of writers and thinkers of that country, but it is also, and perhaps most importantly, a Latin American data that should serve to designate a no less complex group of writers and thinkers on this side of the Atlantic, generally known by the vague name of *modernistas* (Fernández Retamar 1969). It is "ninety-eight"—the visible presence of North American imperialism in Latin America—already foretold by Martí, which informs the later work of someone like Darío or Rodó.

In a speech given by Paul Groussac in Buenos Aires on 2 May 1898, we have an early example of how Latin American writers of the time would react to this situation: "Since the Civil War and the brutal invasion of the West [he says], the *Yankee* spirit had rid itself completely of its formless and 'Calibanesque' body, and the Old World has contemplated with disquiet and terror the newest civilization that intends to supplant our own, declared to be in decay" (Rodó 1957, 193).

The Franco-Argentine writer Groussac feels that "our" civilization (obviously understanding by that term the civilization of the "Old World," of which we Latin Americans would, curiously enough, be a part) is menaced by the Calibanesque Yankee. It seems highly improbable that the Algerian or Vietnamese writer of the time, trampled underfoot by French colonialism, would have been ready to subscribe to the first part of such a criterion. It is also frankly strange to see the Caliban symbol—in which Renan could with exactitude see, if only to abuse, the people—being applied to the United States. But nevertheless, despite this blurred focus—characteristic, on the other hand, of Latin America's unique situation—Groussac's reaction implies a clear rejection of the Yankee danger by Latin American writers. This is not, however, the first time that such a rejection was expressed on our continent. Apart from cases of Hispanic writers such as Bolívar and Martí, among others, Brazilian literature presents the example of Joaquín de Sousa Andrade, or Sousândrade, in whose strange poem, *O Guesa Errante*, stanza 10 is dedicated to "O inferno Wall Street," "a *Walpurgisnacht* of corrupt stockbrokers, petty politicians, and businessmen" (Franco 1967, 49). There is besides José Verissimo, who in an 1890 treatise on national education impugned the United States with his "I admire them, but I don't esteem them."

We do not know whether the Uruguayan José Enrique Rodó—whose famous phrase on the United States, "I admire them, but I don't love them," coincides literally with Verissimo's observation—knew the work of that Brazilian thinker but it is certain that he was familiar with Groussac's speech, essential portions of which were reproduced in *La Razón* of

Montevideo on 6 May 1898. Developing and embellishing the idea outlined in it, Rodó published in 1900, at the age of twenty-nine, one of the most famous works of Latin American literature: *Ariel*. North American civilization is implicitly presented there as Caliban (scarcely mentioned in the work), while Ariel would come to incarnate—or should incarnate—the best of what Rodó did not hesitate to call more than once "our civilization" (1957, 223 and 226). In his words, just as in those of Groussac, this civilization was identified not only with "our Latin America" (239) but with ancient Romania, if not with the Old World as a whole. The identification of Caliban with the United States, proposed by Groussac and popularized by Rodó, was certainly a mistake. Attacking this error from one angle, José Vasconcelos commented that "if the Yankees were only Caliban, they would not represent any great danger" (Vasconcelos n.d., xxiii). But this is doubtless of little importance next to the relevant fact that the danger in question had clearly been pointed out. As Benedetti rightly observed, "Perhaps Rodó erred in naming the danger, but he did not err in his recognition of where it lay" (1966, 95).

Sometime afterward, the French writer Jean Guéhenno—who, although surely aware of the work by the colonial Rodó, knew of course Renan's work from memory—restated the latter's Caliban thesis in his own *Caliban parle*, published in Paris in 1929. This time, however, the Renan identification of Caliban *with* the people is accompanied by a positive evaluation of Caliban. One must be grateful to Guéhenno's book—and it is about the only thing for which gratitude is due—for having offered for the first time an appealing version of the character.[7] But the theme would have required the hand or the rage of a Paul Nizan to be effectively realized.[8]

Much sharper are the observations of the Argentine Aníbal Ponce, in his 1935 work *Humanismo burgués y humanismo proletario*. The book—which a student of Che's thinking conjectures must have exercised influence on the latter (Lowly 1970, 19)—devotes the third chapter to "Ariel; or, The Agony of an Obstinate Illusion." In commenting on *The Tempest*, Ponce says that "those four beings embody an entire era: Prospero is the enlightened despot who loves the Renaissance; Miranda, his progeny; Caliban, the suffering masses [Ponce will then quote Renan, but not Guéhenno]; and Ariel, the genius of the air without any ties to life" (Ponce 1962, 83). Ponce points up the equivocal nature of Caliban's presentation, one that reveals "an enormous injustice on the part of a master." In Ariel he sees the intellectual, tied to Prospero in "less burdensome and crude a way than Caliban, but also in his service." His analysis of the conception of the intellectual ("mixture of slave and mercenary") coined by Renaissance humanism, a concept that "taught as nothing else could an indifference to action and an acceptance of the established order" and that even today is for the intellectual in the bourgeois world "the educational ideal of the governing classes," constitutes one of the most penetrating essays written on the theme in our America.

But this examination, although made by a Latin American, still took only the European world into account. For a new reading of *The Tempest*— for a new consideration of the problem—it was necessary to await the emergence of the colonial countries, which began around the time of the Second World War. That abrupt presence led the busy technicians of the United Nations to invent, between 1944 and 1945, the term *economically underdeveloped area* in order to dress in attractive (and profoundly confusing) verbal garb what had until then been called *colonial area*, or *backward area* (Zimmerman 1970, 7).

Concurrently with this emergence there appeared in Paris in 1950 Octave Mannoni's book *Psychologie de la colonisation*. Significantly, the English edition of this book (New York, 1956) was to be called *Prospero and Caliban: The Psychology of Colonization*. To approach his subject, Mannoni has created, no less, what he calls the "Prospero complex," defined as "the sum of those unconscious neurotic tendencies that delineate at the same time the 'picture' of the paternalist colonial and the portrait of 'the racist whose daughter has been the object of an [imaginary] attempted rape at the hands of an inferior being'" (quoted in Fanon 1965, 106). In this book, probably for the first time, Caliban is identified with the colonial. But the odd theory that the latter suffers from a "Prospero complex" that leads him neurotically to require, even to anticipate, and naturally to accept the presence of Prospero/colonizer is roundly rejected by Frantz Fanon in the fourth chapter ("The So-Called Dependence Complex of Colonized Peoples") of his 1952 book *Black Skin, White Masks*.

Although he is (apparently) the first writer in our world to assume our identification with Caliban, the Barbadian writer George Lamming is unable to break the circle traced by Mannoni:

Prospero [says Lamming] has given Caliban language; and with it an unstated history of consequences, an unknown history of future intentions. This gift of language meant not English, in particular, but speech and concept as a way, a method, a necessary avenue towards areas of the self which could not be reached in any other way. It is this way, entirely Prospero's enterprise, which makes Caliban aware of possibilities. Therefore, all of Caliban's future—for future is the very name of possibilities—must derive from Prospero's experiment, which is also his risk. Provided there is no extraordinary departure which explodes all of Prospero's premises, then Caliban and his future now belong to Prospero. . . . Prospero lives in the absolute certainty that Language, which is his gift to Caliban, is the very prison in which Caliban's achievements will be realized and restricted. (Lamming 1960, 109)[9]

In the decade of the 1960s, the new reading of The Tempest ultimately established its hegemony. In The Living World of Shakespeare (1964), the Englishman John Wain will tell us that Caliban

has the pathos of the exploited peoples everywhere, poignantly expressed at the beginning of a three-hundred-year wave of European colonization; even the lowest savage wishes to be left alone rather than be "educated" and made to work for someone else, and there is an undeniable justice in his complaint: "For I am all the subjects that you have, / Which once was mine own king." Prospero retorts with the inevitable answer of the colonist: Caliban has gained in knowledge and skill (though we recall that he already knew how to build dams to catch fish, and also to dig pig-nuts from the soil, as if this were the English countryside). Before being employed by Prospero, Caliban had no language: "though didst not, savage, / Know thy own meaning, but wouldst gabble like / A thing most brutish." However, this kindness has been rewarded with ingratitude. Caliban, allowed to live in Prospero's cell, has made an attempt to ravish Miranda. When sternly reminded of this, he impertinently says, with a kind of slavering guffaw, "Oh ho! Oh ho!—would it have been done! / Thou didst prevent me; I had peopled else / This isle with Calibans." Our own age [Wain concludes], which is much given to using the horrible word "miscegenation," ought to have no difficulty in understanding this passage. (226–27)

At the end of that same decade, in 1969, and in a highly significant manner, Caliban would be taken up with pride as our symbol by three Antillian writers—each of whom expresses himself in one of the three great colonial languages of the Caribbean. In that year, independently of one another, the Martinican writer Aimé Césaire published his dramatic work in French Une tempête: Adaptation de "La Tempête" de Shakespeare pour un théâtre nègre; the Barbadian Edward Brathwaite, his book of poems Islands, in English, among which there is one dedicated to "Caliban"; and the author of these lines, an essay in Spanish, "Cuba hasta Fidel," which discusses our identification with Caliban.[10] In Césaire's work the characters are the same as those of Shakespeare. Ariel, however, is a mulatto slave, and Caliban is a black slave; in addition, Eshzú, "a black god-devil" appears. Prospero's remark when Ariel returns, full of scruples, after having unleashed—following Prospero's orders but against his own conscience—the tempest with which the work begins is curious indeed: "Come now!" Prospero says to him, "Your crisis! It's always the same with intellectuals!" Brathwaite's poem called "Caliban" is dedicated, significantly, to Cuba:

> In Habana that morning
> It was December second, nineteen fifty-six.
> It was the first of August eighteen thirty-eight.
> It was the twelfth of October fourteen ninety-two.
> How many bangs how many revolutions?[11]

Our Symbol

Our symbol then is not Ariel, as Rodó thought, but rather Caliban. This is something that we, the *mestizo* inhabitants of these same isles where Caliban lived, see with particular clarity: Prospero invaded the islands, killed our ancestors, enslaved Caliban, and taught him his language to make himself understood. What else can Caliban do but use that same language—today he has no other—to curse him, to wish that the "red plague" would fall on him? I know no other metaphor more expressive of our cultural situation, of our reality. From Túpac Amaru, *Tiradentes*, Toussaint-Louverture, Simón Bolívar, Father Hidalgo, José Artigas, Bernardo O'Higgins, Benito Juárez, Antonio Maceo, and José Martí, to Emiliano Zapata, Augusto César Sandino, Julio Antonio Mella, Pedro Albizu Campos, Lázaro Cárdenas, Fidel Castro, and Ernesto Che Guevara, from the Inca Garcilaso de la Vega, the *Aleijadinho*, the popular music of the Antilles, José Hernández, Eugenio María de Hostos, Manuel González Prada, Rubén Darío (yes, when all is said and done), Baldomero Lillo, and Horacio Quiroga, to Mexican muralism, Heitor Villa-Lobos, César Vallejo, José Carlos Mariátegui, Ezequiel Martínez Estrada, Carlos Gardel, Pablo Neruda, Alejo Carpentier, Nicolás Guillén, Aimé Césaire, José María Arguedas, Violeta Parra, and Frantz Fanon—what is our history, what is our culture, if not the history and culture of Caliban?

As regards Rodó, if it is indeed true that he erred in his symbols, as has already been said, it is no less true that he was able to point with clarity to the greatest enemy of our culture in his time—and in ours—and that is enormously important. Rodó's limitations (and this is not the moment to elucidate them) are responsible for what he saw unclearly or failed to see at all.[12] But what is worthy of note in his case is what he did indeed see and what continued to retain a certain amount of validity and even virulence: "Despite his failings, omissions, and ingenuousness [Benedetti has also said], Rodó's vision of the Yankee phenomenon, rigorously situated in its historical context, was in its time the first launching pad for other less ingenuous, better informed and more foresighted formulations to come. . . . the almost prophetic substance of Rodó's Arielism still retains today a certain amount of validity" (Benedetti 1966, 109).[13]

These observations are supported by indisputable realities. We Cubans become well aware that Rodó's vision fostered later, less ingenuous, and more radical formulations when we simply consider the work of our own Julio Antonio Mella, on whose development the influence of Rodó was decisive. In "Intelectuales y tartufos" (1924), a vehement work written at the age of twenty-one, Mella violently attacks the false intellectual values of the time—opposing them with such names as Unamuno, José Vasconcelos, Ingenieros, and Varona. He writes, "The intellectual is the worker of the mind. The worker! That is, the only man who in Rodó's judgment is worthy of life, . . . he who takes up his pen against iniquity just as others take up the plow to fecundate the earth, or the sword to liberate peoples, or a dancer to execute tyrants" (1971, 12).

Mella would again quote Rodó with devotion during that year, and in the following year he was to help found the Ariel Polytechnic Institute in Havana.[14] It is opportune to recall that in this same year, 1925, Mella was also among the founders of Cuba's first Communist party. Without a doubt, Rodó's Ariel served as a "launching pad" for the meteoric revolutionary career of this first organic Marxist-Leninist in Cuba (who was also one of the first on the continent).

As further examples of the relative validity that Rodó's anti-Yankee argument retains even in our own day, we can point to enemy attempts to disarm such an argument. A strange case is that of Emir Rodríguez Monegal, for whom Ariel, in addition to "material for philosophic or sociological meditation, also contains pages of a polemic nature on political problems of the moment. And it was precisely this secondary but undeniable condition that determined its immediate popularity and dissemination." Rodó's essential position against North American penetration would thus appear to be an afterthought, a secondary fact in the work. It is known, however, that Rodó conceived it immediately after American intervention in Cuba in 1898, as a response to the deed. Rodríguez Monegal says: "The work thus projected was Ariel. In the final version only two direct allusions are found to the historical fact that was its primary motive force;

. . . both allusions enable us to appreciate how Rodó has *transcended* the initial historical circumstance to arrive fully at the essential problem: the proclaimed decadence of the Latin race" (Rodó 1957, 193; my emphasis).

The fact that a servant of imperialism such as Rodríguez Monegal, afflicted with the same "Nordo-mania" that Rodó denounced in 1900, tries so coarsely to emasculate Rodó's work, only proves that it does indeed retain a certain virulence in its formulation—something that we would approach today from other perspectives and with other means. An analysis of *Ariel*—and this is absolutely not the occasion to make one—would lead us also to stress how, despite his background and his anti-Jacobianism, Rodó combats in it the antidemocratic spirit of Renan and Nietzsche (in whom he finds "an abominable, reactionary spirit," 224) and exalts democracy, moral values, and emulation. But undoubtedly the rest of the work has lost the immediacy that its gallant confrontation of the United States and the defense of our values still retains.

Put into perspective, it is almost certain that these lines would not bear the name they have were it not for Rodó's book, and I prefer to consider them also as a homage to the great Uruguayan, whose centenary is being celebrated this year. That the homage contradicts him on not a few points is not strange. Medardo Vitier has already observed that "if there should be a return to Rodó, I do not believe that it would be to adopt the solution he offered concerning the interests of the life of the spirit, but rather to reconsider the problem" (1945, 117).

In proposing Caliban as our symbol, I am aware that it is not entirely ours, that it is also an alien elaboration, although in this case based on our concrete realities. But how can this alien quality be entirely avoided? The most venerated word in Cuba—*mambí*—was disparagingly imposed on us by our enemies at the time of the War for Independence, and we still have not totally deciphered its meaning. It seems to have an African root, and in the mouth of the Spanish colonists implied the idea that all *independentistas* were so many black slaves—emancipated by that very War for Independence—who of course constituted the bulk of the liberation army. The *independentistas*, white and black, adopted with honor something that colonialism meant as an insult. This is the dialectic of Caliban. To offend us they call us *mambí*, they call us *black*; but we reclaim as a mark of glory the honor of considering ourselves descendants of the *mambí*, descendants of the rebel, runaway, *independentista* black—*never* descendants of the slave holder. Nevertheless, Prospero, as we well know, taught his language to Caliban and, consequently, gave him a name. But is this his true name? Let us listen to this speech made in 1971: "To be completely precise, we still do not even have a name; we still have no name; we are practically unbaptized—whether as Latin Americans, Ibero-Americans, Indo-Americans. For the imperialists, we are nothing more than despised and despicable peoples. At least that was what we were. Since Girón they have begun to change their thinking. Racial contempt—to be a Creole, to be a *mestizo*, to be black, to be simply, a Latin American, is for them contemptible" (Fidel Castro, speech, 19 April 1971). This, naturally, is Fidel Castro on the tenth anniversary of the victory at Playa Girón.

To assume our condition as Caliban implies rethinking our history from the *other* side, from the viewpoint of the *other* protagonist. The *other* protagonist of *The Tempest* (or, as we might have said ourselves, *The Hurricane*) is not of course Ariel but, rather, Prospero (Kott 1967, 269). There is no real Ariel-Caliban polarity: both are slaves in the hands of Prospero, the foreign magician. But Caliban is the rude and unconquerable master of the island, while Ariel, a creature of the air, although also a child of the isle, is the intellectual—as both Ponce and Césaire have seen.

Notes

1. See Lacoste (1959, 82–84).
2. A Swedish summary of what is known on this subject can be found in Magnus Mörner's study, *La mezcla de razas en la historia de América Latina*. Here it is recognized that "no part of the world has witnessed such a gigantic mixing of races as the one that has been taking place in Latin America and the Caribbean [why this division?] since 1492" (1969, 15). Of course, what interests me in these notes is not the irrelevant biological fact of the "races" but the historical fact of the "cultures"; see Claude Lévi-Strauss (1968).
3. Cited along with subsequent references to the *Diario*, by Salas (1920). The book exposes "the irrationality of [the] charge that some American tribes devoured human flesh, maintained in the past by those interested in enslaving [the] Indians and repeated by the chroniclers and historians, many of whom were supporters of slavery" (211).
4. For example, Jan Kott notes that "there have been learned Shakespearian scholars who tried to interpret *The Tempest* as a direct autobiography, or as an allegorical political drama" (1967, 240).
5. See Adamov (1959); and especially Lidsky (1970).
6. This is a remarkable work, and I have made extensive use of its main ideas in this essay. (A part of it has been translated into Spanish in *Casa de las Américas* 36/37 [1966]: 154–67, an issue dedicated to *Africa en América*.)
7. The penetrating but negative vision of Jan Kott causes him to be irritated by this fact. "Renan saw Demos in Caliban; in his continuation of *The Tempest* he took him

to Milan and made him attempt another, victorious coup against Prospero. Gué-henno wrote an apology for Caliban-People. Both these interpretations are flat and do not do justice to Shakespeare's Caliban" (1967, 273).

8. Guéhenno's weakness in approaching this theme with any profundity is apparent from his increasingly contradictory prefaces to successive editions of the book (2d ed. 1945; 3d ed. 1962) down to his book of essays *Calibán et Próspero* (1969), where according to one critic, Guéhenno is converted into "a personage of bourgeois society and beneficiary of its culture," who judges Prospero "more equitably than in the days of *Caliban parle*" (Pierre Henri Simon in *Le Monde*, 5 July 1969).

9. In commenting on these opinions of Lamming, the German Janheinz Jahn observes their limitations and proposes an identification of Caliban/negritude (Jahn 1968, 239–42).

10. See Césaire (1969); Brathwaite (1969); Fernández Retamar (1969).

11. The new reading of *The Tempest* has become a common one throughout the colonial world of today. I want only, therefore, to mention a few examples. On concluding these notes, I find a new one in the essay by James Ngugi (of Kenya), "Africa y la descolonización cultural" in *El correo* (January 1971).

12. "It is improper," Benedetti has said, "to confront Rodó with present-day structures, statements, and ideologies. His time was different from ours . . . his true place, his true temporal homeland was the nineteenth century" (1966, 128).

13. Even greater emphasis on the current validity of Rodó will be found in Ardao 1970, which includes an excellent anthology of the author of *Ariel*. On the other hand, as early as 1928, José Carlos Mariátegui, after rightly recalling that "only a socialist Latin or Ibero-America can effectively oppose a capitalist, plutocratic, and imperialist North America," adds, "The myth of Rodó has not yet acted—nor has it ever acted—usefully and fruitfully upon our souls" (1969, 248).

14. See Dumpierre (1965, 145); Portuondo (1965).

ANTONIO CORNEJO POLAR

Indigenismo and Heterogeneous Literatures: Their Double Sociocultural Statute

The Peruvian Antonio Cornejo Polar (1936–1997) was a literary and cultural critic. Professor at several Latin American and U.S. universities, he was also the director of *Revista de Crítica Literaria Latinoamericana*. His main titles include *La novela indigenista*, *Literatura y sociedad en el Perú* (1980), *La formación de la tradición literaria en el Perú* (1989), and *Escribir en el aire. Ensayo sobre la heterogeneidad socio-cultural en las literaturas andinas* (1994).

In recent years, the urgency to adapt principles and methods of our critical work to the peculiarities of Latin American literature has been insistently required, although not always from coinciding perspectives. In general terms, it is all about the "necessity for self-interpretation" that Mario Benedetti has invoked (Fernández Moreno 1972, 367), or in a more emphatic way, the requirement for the foundation of a truly Latin American criticism.[1] In this essay, I will not attempt to determine the scientific and social validity of a project so obviously complex and risky, but nonetheless essential for the development of our own criticism. Instead, by betting on its validity, I will attempt to demonstrate one of the possible directions of a truly critical analysis of Latin American literatures subject to a double sociocultural statute.

Toward the end of the 1920s, profoundly committed to the controversy over *indigenismo* (Aquezolo 1976), José Carlos Mariátegui became aware of the urgency to devise a critical system capable of explaining heterogeneous literatures. Close to the beginning of "The Process of Peruvian Literature," the last of his *Siete ensayos de interpretación de la realidad peruana* (1928), Mariátegui affirmed the following: "The still unsolved Quechua and Spanish duality makes national literature an exceptional case that is impossible to study with the method used for organically national literatures, born and developed without the intervention of a conquest" (1963, 204).

Without a doubt, Mariátegui's judgment is pertinent to other Latin American literatures and it can elucidate not only the ruptures that originated during the Spanish conquest, in those cases in which the native population was not decimated by the impact of the metropolis, but also other forms of heterogeneity such as those that emerge from the implantation of a slave system in Latin America. The *indigenismo* of the Andean nations, the *negrismo* of Central America and the Caribbean, and even to a certain extent the *gauchesca* literature of the River Plate and literature related to the concept of the "marvelous real" can be understood as variants of the phenomenon that concerned José Carlos Mariátegui. All of these cases deal with literatures that are situated in a conflictive crossing between two societies and two cultures.

Unfortunately, Mariátegui's approach was not followed in this or other aspects by later critics. Only in very recent years, and without the possibility to determine Mariátegui's direct influence, has there been a renewed interest in the sociocultural heterogeneity of some basic areas of our literature, a heterogeneity that was barely suspected behind the already empty term of *mestizaje*. The work of Agustín Cueva on *Cien años de soledad* (1974), of Noé Jitrik on *El reino de este mundo* (1975a), and of Angel Rama on the work of José María Arguedas (1976) represent precisely the resurgence of this perspective, to which I would like to contribute with the following observations.

The Question of National Literatures

In the demarcation of its fields and tasks and in the hierarchy of its scientific objectives, literary history usually grants privilege to the concept of nation and its derivatives. Although it is sometimes an unintended assumption that likewise is subject to the confusing relations between nationality and culture, the use of the idea of national literature seems to guarantee the constitution of a relatively autonomous and homogeneous corpus and with a more or less uniform and coherent tradition. Hence, national literature would be a critically intelligible space.

However, this is not always the case. The concept of national literature is constantly submitted to a double and contradictory objection: if from certain perspectives it is judged excessively broad, since it leaves unexamined intranational variants, from opposing points of view it is rather perceived as an overly analytical category, therefore incapable of constituting a sufficient totality.

In regard to the aptitude for delimiting a truly intelligible literary field, Ernst Robert Curtius emphatically warned of the danger of an atomizing national fragmentation: "European literature can only be considered as a whole," he said in his *Literatura europea y Edad Media latina* (1955, 34, my emphasis). For Curtius, the national distinction, when specifically referring to European literature, arbitrarily breaks the compact unity of a cultural system whose borders are more open and distinct than those drawn on a political map. It is necessary to remember in this respect Curtius's objections to Dámaso Alonso's stylistic interpretations and his refusal to concede relevance to the "specificity" of certain texts that, through their *topica*, reproduce instead a generic and totalizing canon (Alonso 1958). *Topica* would be the most visible expression of a Western literary system that would constitute the only legitimate epistemological horizon for the knowledge of those units that configure and realize it.

Following in the footprints of Goethe, these problems are directly or indirectly tied to the intent of conceiving a universal literature. While it is known that the assertion of a universal literature is more desiderative than real, and even though it is also easy to recognize an abusive universalization of the Western literary order, which reveals the colonialist sign of these reflections, what is undeniable is that by resorting to such a broad category, the validity of narrower categories is put into question. From this perspective, national literature would be a false object of knowledge or, in other words, an erroneous partition of the authentic object of knowledge, which is always vaster. Similarly, it would imply the vulnerability of knowledges derived from literary history and criticism.

In the area of Latin American literature, the problem can be stated in similar terms: here too the concept of national literature is subject to pressure from wider, regional or subregional categories, which continuously gain more weight as a verifiable reality. With no need to go back to the first statements concerning the unity of Latin American literature, for the most part associated with Bolívar's political thought, it is worth remembering the most recent controversy concerning the "predominant feature" of our literature and particularly our novel (Loveluck 1969). Therefore, the following ideas should be understood within the dynamic aimed at finding the key that allows for a comprehensive understanding of Latin American literature.

Much more recently, with stronger and better historical and critical support, Roberto Fernández Retamar and Antonio Candido have insisted on this very topic. Fernández Retamar has indicated the existence of at least "three stages of regional intercommunication": romanticism, modernism, and avant-gardism, which underpinned the most solid unity forged by the new Spanish American narrative. At the same time and from a different perspective, since the 1920s, Candido has been able to detect the emergence of "an internal causality" in the process of our literatures and the development of Latin American literatures as a whole (Fernández Moreno 1972). From this point of view, Latin American literatures are included, although not necessarily undifferentiated, in the entire literary system of the region. This system would be the suitable category for the comprehension of the meaning of smaller units.

The legitimate course of expansion that is implicit in the assertion of a Latin American literature as a coherent structure is opposed to the interpretation of our literature as a simple branch of Western literature, in which case it would be a false, ultimately insufficient system. It is also opposed, understandably so, to Luis Alberto Sánchez's proposal, according to which Latin American literature mysteriously forms a unity with North American literature.[2]

Nonetheless, the concept of national literature is not only challenged due to the necessity to turn to broader categories of a more explanatory capability, but it is also challenged from the opposing view for constituting an excessively extensive order incapable of explaining what occurs within the limits of one particular country's literature. On the horizon of this demand, one can discern Marxist inferences on the coexistence of the culture of the exploited class alongside the culture of the exploiters, a coexistence that completely splits the literary field of a nation. Something similar could be said with respect to the distinction, which is always ambiguous, between "high literature" and "popular literature."

Within the framework of Latin American literature, at a still hypothetical and deductive level, Alejandro Losada has proposed to delimit three literary systems: the realist, the naturalist, and the subjectivist, which would correspond more to the social praxis of differentiated groups than to the general structure of Latin American society, and for this very reason would possess a very wide margin of autonomy. Naturally, this tripartite system, which traverses the whole structure, would also be present in the interior of each national literature (1975).

The categories highlighted up to this point—the national system, its dilution within a greater structure, and its fragmentation into smaller sectors—do not necessarily have to be contradictory. A good dialectical account could explain the coherence of their work within the real process of our literatures. It is important to caution that within all of these literatures, a sufficient degree of homogeneity is sought after, assuming that this is the indispensable condition for the formation of an object susceptible to critical elucidation. In fact, even literatures from conflicting social groups vying for power correspond to a social structure that, not because of its stratification, ceases being unique and absolute.

Homogeneity and Heterogeneity: A Few Cases

Nevertheless, not all literature presupposes the category of homogeneity. By means of a simple analysis of the literary process that allows us to discern the mode of production, the resulting text, its referent, and the system of distribution and consumption, it is feasible to determine the distance that separates homogeneous from heterogeneous literatures and to determine, consequently, the variations in critical analyses.

The mobilization of all instances of the literary process within the same sociocultural order determines the emergence of homogeneous literatures, as could be seen, paradigmatically, in important sectors of Peruvian and Chilean narratives in the 1950s. The narratives by Sebastián Salazar Bondy, Julio Ramón Ribeyro, and partly those by Carlos Eduardo Zavaleta in Peru, and the narratives by José Donoso or Jorge Edwards in Chile, bring to bear the perspectives of certain sectors of the urban middle class; employ the modern attributes that distinguish the actions of this social group, which duly translate into the renovation of the narrative technical apparatus; and referentially allude to the problems of their readership, which belongs to the same social status. The literary production thus circulates within one single social sphere, which confers to it a high degree of homogeneity: it could be said then that it is a society speaking to itself. If in some cases, like that of Donoso's El lugar sin límites and most of all in El obsceno pájaro de la noche, the meaning of the narrative seems to exceed the limits of this sphere by searching for an attractive but illegitimate universality, it is due to an ideological universalization of the particularities of a determined social sector.[3]

In contrast, the duplicity or plurality of the sociocultural signs of the productive process characterizes the heterogeneous literatures: in summary, it has to do with a process that has at least one element that does not coincide with the filiation of the others and thus necessarily creates a zone of ambiguity and conflict. Upon studying this fact in an isolated text, Cien años de soledad, Agustín Cueva has pointed out that

> the problem is expressed . . . in antonymous terms. On one hand, there is an empirical referent that cannot impose its own Weltanschauung as a hegemonic point of view capable of structuring the work into a pertinent aesthetic form . . . due to finding itself situated at a subal-

tern level within the social formation, which encompasses and rede-fines it and from which only some genre of popular literature could be engendered. . . . On the other hand, there is a *Weltanschauung* coming from the social hegemonic pole, which is not sufficient by itself and can even become an obstacle to the adequate realization of the former raw material, which naturally possesses its own thickness, or in other words its own form, and therefore requires a particular aesthetic ap-proach. (1974, 62)

Upon examining El *reino de este mundo*, Noé Jitrik has called attention to another form of heterogeneity that nonetheless is associated with the phenomenon described by Cueva. In effect, Jitrik affirms that "the writ-ing of this story has not been executed within and with relation to the co-lonial system of production, but instead, from a material point of view, it is tributary of a later historical productive circuit" (1975a, 170).

Cueva and Jitrik preferably examine the disparity between a process of production and its sociocultural conditioning, and the unequal nature of the referent that is to be revealed; or in Jitrik's words, the "fracture of the unity between the 'represented world' and 'the mode of representa-tion.'" In both cases, the object of reflection is an individual work, al-though some allusions allow its extension to the literature of "the mar-velous real." Angel Rama deals with the entire production of one writer, José María Arguedas, and he prefers to capture the heterogeneity in the productive process of the literary forms. In this respect, he affirms that

the original forms that indigenous culture provided to the writer were songs and folk short stories. Those offered by the dominant culture were the novel and the short story within the models established un-der the dual regional and social advocacy, which in turn were filiated to the European realist narrative of the second half of the nineteenth century. Given that the narrative of Arguedas yields to this line, we can infer that the battle over form, that is, in the choice of genre, in its first instance was decided in favor of Western cultural forms. But on the basis of this selection, he promotes an internal processing of those forms that modifies them notoriously while strengthening the opera-tion with contributions from the indigenous culture. (1976, 138)

These three mentioned studies are sufficient in order to understand the concept of heterogeneity, in some of its variants, and to distinguish it, along with all of the critical implications, from the concept of homo-geneity. One might be able to say that we are dealing with two distinct systems of literary production.

The Emergence of Heterogeneity: The Chronicle as a Model

Evidently, heterogeneity is manifested through many distinct forms and levels. At this time, I would like to reflect over the literatures projected toward a referent whose sociocultural identity ostensibly differs from the system that produces the literary work; in other words, I am interested in examining the facts that are generated when the production, the text, and its consumption correspond to one universe and its referent corresponds to a distinct and even opposing one. Historically and structurally this form of heterogeneity is distinctively manifest in the chronicles of the New World. These chronicles founded a type of literature that is still relevant in Latin America today.

All chronicles, even the least elaborated, implicitly articulate a subtle and complex play of distances and approximations: if, on the one hand, they produce a communicative network where before there had only been unawareness or ignorance, on the other hand, at the same time they highlight the gaps that separate and disarticulate the relation of forces they bring into play.

In the writing of chronicles there is an underlying primary motivation: that of "truthfully" revealing the nature of a bizarre, new, unknown reality; that of revealing this new reality, obviously, for a reader who either totally or partially ignores it. Although written about the Indies, the chronicles nevertheless are realized when they manage to captivate the metropolitan reader. The fact that they almost unanimously appeal to the king, or to other instances of peninsular power, is a courtesan gesture, but also more profoundly, it is a sign of a system of communication that prevails in the chroniclers' statements: the king or the metropolis is *their* reader.

At the other end of the chronicles' production process is the referent, this New World that is presented as an incomparable reality and that is offered as an opaque or dazzling enigma. Before this enigma, the chronicler feels a dual obligation: he has to be faithful to it, representing it in "truthful" terms, but at the same time, he has to submit it to an interpretation that makes it intelligible to the foreign eye, beginning with that of the chronicler himself, so frequently bewildered. The mere mentioning of this new reality implies a dual movement: Cieza de León says (and there are multiple examples) that "guanacos are sometimes larger that small donkeys with long necks, like camels," which makes clear that even the most concise description has to be processed within a comparative order that relies on the experience of a reality different from that of the referent. At more complex levels, the chronicler appeals to the whole cultural repertoire of the world that produces and receives its history; therefore, it isn't by chance that Cuzco is compared to Rome and the Inca ruler to a king or emperor, in such a way that the peculiarity of the referent remains veiled by other forms of reality, beginning, obviously, with the language itself. There is perhaps no example more instructive than Garcilaso de la Vega's Neoplatonism. With such a worldview, Inca Garcilaso wants to explain a fragmented and conflictive reality that he would like to see harmoniously synthesized in the *mestizaje* that he embodies so well. The fact that Garcilaso himself, who so fervently adhered to the Incan universe and was so proud of his maternal lineage, had to resort to a Neoplatonic philosophy in order to explain to others and to himself his personal and historical situation is a clear demonstration of how, at the base of all chronicles, there is a covering up of the referent by the cultural attributes that the chronicle materializes.

Without a doubt, it is easy in the chronicles not only to determine the cultural forces at play, but also the open and sometimes very personal economic and political interests. In each case, the mentioning of these other levels does nothing more than to underline the conflictive nature of the chronicles, since it is obvious that a coincidence does not exist between the interests expressed by the chronicler and those of the referent, on the horizon of reality. It would be erroneous, nevertheless, to extract from these facts the global condemnation of the chronicle as a genre and its authors. In essence, chronicles are limited in their capacity to reproduce, according to their specific terms, an undeniable historical event, the Spanish conquest, and to establish the beginning of what Mariátegui called not organically national literatures.

The Question of Form in Heterogeneous Literatures

In the chronicles, heterogeneity generates an unequal relationship between its system of production and consumption on one hand, and the referent on the other, granting notable supremacy to the former and obscuring the latter under the force of the interpretation that is superimposed upon it. On the formal level, this imbalance means that the referent still is not able to impose its own modes of expression and it must undergo a formalization that is alien to it, and which ends up, in a greater or lesser degree, misrepresenting it. This can be observed upon comparing the formal similarity of the Castilian chronicles and those of the New World, a similarity that implies that the American referent was submitted to the same conventions that dominated the peninsular reality.

On the contrary, if we take into account certain heterodox chronicles, especially some of those produced by Indian or *mestizo* chroniclers, formal deviations stand out that can only be explained by the effect of the referent on the chronicle's discourse. Guamán Poma de Ayala's drawings can be understood, within this framework, as fissures in the chronicle's structure in order to provide access to a second kind of language—graphic language—that responds better than verbal language to the demands of fidelity with respect to the referent. In fact, Guamán Poma's drawings tell much more about his Andean world than the rudimentary Spanish in which *Nueva Coronica y Buen Gobierno* was written,[4] and its mere existence indicates the effect of an inverse dynamic: if in some cases the productive process suffocates the referent, in this case, to the contrary, the referent can impose certain conditions and generate a modification in the formal structure of the chronicle. It can be noticed then that the form of the chronicles is not a neutral category, but to the contrary, a factor directly committed to the itinerary and the significance of heterogeneous literatures.

The chronicle genre serves as a model to heterogeneous literatures because it signals, with unparalleled intensity, the two most important alternatives: either the subjection of the referent to the rule of exogenous factors, as in regular chronicles, or, as in some exceptional cases, the capacity of that same referent to modify—and the implications are obvious—the formal order of the chronicle. Both alternatives have been extensively developed in Latin American literature.

A similar situation can be noticed in the literature related to the emancipation of Spanish American countries. In this case, the referent (the emancipative events) and the "theme" (related to the *independentista* ideology) are formalized under aesthetic norms that curiously repeat the metropolitan dictates. It is significant that the diatribes against Spain or the praise of independence and liberty are literarily processed with compliance to the values that govern Spanish literature of that period. This other manifestation of heterogeneity perhaps has its most suggestive expression in the not well-known work of Mariano Melgar (1790–1815) (Melgar 1971).[5]

One facet of Melgar's poetry is constituted by a collection of basically neoclassic texts that frequently are poetic reflections about the values presiding over the political activities of the emancipation's forerunners, like in "Oda a la Libertad." These texts, together with translations of Latin classics and his teachings as a humanist scholar, show the solid erudition of Mariano Melgar and his adherence to the "cultured" canon of the literature of his times. Significantly, next to this production, which can only be considered *independentista* because of its "topics," Melgar cultivates a "popular" poetry of an exclusively romantic theme that is known under the name of *yaraví*. Although the discussion over the origins of *yaraví* is far from over, it is undeniable that it originates from pre-Hispanic poetry, probably from the Quechua *jaray haraui*, which was extensively cultivated as an already *mestizo* form, long before Melgar used it in his erotic poetry. If it is clear that Melgar introduces in his *yaravís* resources from other styles of poetry, *yaraví* preserves its popular character, as can be noticed in its fusion of poetry and song, which implies the use and revalorization of an indigenous tradition until then despised by "cultured" Peruvian poetry.

From the perspective that concerns us here, Melgar's *yaraví* represents an act of liberation more consistent than the neoclassic poetry associated with the independence of our countries: if the latter texts thematically stand for the historical process of independence, a process that up to a point they betray because of their adherence to the metropolitan models, the *yaraví*, however, despite its apolitical themes, realizes, on the specifically literary dimension, the ideals of liberty and independence that the neoclassic poetry can only refer to in a thematic way. Contrary to what is commonly believed, neoclassic poetry represents a higher degree of heterogeneity, since the referent and the "theme" are formalized under a system defined by its strangeness and distance, while *yaraví* poetry, despite its limitations, indicates a certain advancement on the path leading to *another* homogeneity, in accordance with native tradition. Here too lies the importance of form in the delimitation, clarification, and criticism of multicultural literatures.

The Condition of *Indigenismo*

All that I have said up to now seems to focus on and to reveal itself more clearly in the case of *indigenismo*. A quote from José Carlos Mariátegui indicates the best path for understanding in-depth this vast movement:

> The greatest injustice that a critic could commit would be to hastily condemn *indigenista* literature due to its lack of integral autochthony or the presence, more or less open, of artful interpretive and expressive elements. *Indigenista* literature cannot give us a rigorously veritable version of the Indian. It has to idealize and stylize it. Nor can it give us his soul. It is still a *mestizo* literature. That is the reason why it is

called *indigenista* and not indigenous. If an indigenous literature must come, it will come in due time, when the Indians themselves are able to produce it. (1963, 292)

Although the last part of the quote is debatable, since indigenous literature has never ceased being produced on a parallel course with literature in Spanish, the demarcation between indigenous and *indigenista* literatures proposed by Mariátegui represents the abandonment of the *indigenista utopia as the alleged interior* expression of the Andean world, and it establishes the basis for founding a new and more coherent interpretation of *indigenismo*.

It is indispensable to highlight, first, the fracture between the indigenous universe and its *indigenista* representation. In the terms used here so far, this fracture signals the existence of a new case of heterogeneous literature in which the instances of production, textual realization, and consumption belong to a sociocultural universe while the referent belongs to a distinct one. This heterogeneity gains importance in *indigenismo* to the extent that both universes do not appear juxtaposed, but instead in conflict, while the indigenous universe is usually displayed precisely according to its distinctive peculiarities.

This first description presupposes a controversial sociological option, much discussed in the field of pertinent disciplines, concerning the unitary or dual structure of the Andean countries. Without directly intervening in the polemic, otherwise closely tied to concrete political positions, two key aspects should be pointed out: on one hand, the correctness of Mariátegui's position in reference to the reality of his times, when the difference between the semi-feudal sierra and the incipient capitalist coast was an obvious and irrefutable truth; on the other hand, the preservation of this duality in very recent history, when the real development of national integration cannot hide the emergence and prominence of a relationship of domination and dependence, derived from the unequal development of both social spheres. Heterogeneity persists, then, whether one accepts the coexistence of two distinct structures or one accepts the existence of a single structure where a hegemonic pole and a dependent one are distinguished.

This heterogeneity is the a priori condition of *indigenismo*. This explains why, in 1965, Sebastián Salazar Bondy could affirm the "death" of *indigenismo* as a distinguishable movement within the literatures of Andean countries: according to him, given that a general process of social indigenizing, which includes literature, has occurred, it does not make any sense to insist on a certain specificity that has been diluted and universalized.[6] Although this is obviously arguable, Salazar Bondy's position has the merit of demonstrating that *indigenismo* is only intelligible from a previous conceptualization of the Andean world as a divided and disintegrated reality. It is a heterogeneous literature inscribed in an equally heterogeneous universe.

As an insular reality or as a dependent factor within a broader social structure, the indigenous world upholds an exterior discourse that at times has been compared to the expropriation represented by the Spanish conquest. Reviving the virulence of Angel Escalante, for whom no non-indigenous writer had the "right" to write about the indigenous reality (Aquezolo 1976, 39–52), Mario Vargas Llosa maximized his condemnation to the point of affirming that "Peruvian writers discovered the Indian four centuries after the Spanish conquistadors, and their behavior toward the Indian was not less criminal than that of Pizarro." Although Vargas Llosa projects his judgment on modernist *indigenismo*, concretely referring to José Santos Chocano, Ventura García Calderón, and Enrique López Albújar, his line of thought leads him to condemn equally the subsequent *nativismo*, summarized in the poetic work of Alejandro Peralta, who would have a "vision . . . as foreign as that of any modernist" (Vargas Llosa 1964). It is clear that opinions of this nature do not contribute to the understanding of the meaning of *indigenismo*: they consider what is the most profound identity of the movement as a defect and in the long run they demand that it stops being what it is—*indigenismo*—in order to become what it cannot be: indigenous literature.

It becomes indispensable then to delve deeper into the specific nature of *indigenismo*, paying respect to its specific limits. With regard to its process of production, José Carlos Mariátegui affirmed that *indigenismo* is the work of *mestizos*. Without a doubt, the term "*mestizo*" here does not have a purely biological or racial meaning, nor is it possible to interpret it in exclusive relation to the author's ethnicity; rather, it alludes to a complex set of sociocultural questions, primarily to the fact that its process of production obeys occidentalized or "Europoid" norms, in [Alexander] Lipschütz's terms (Lipschutz 1972), as much for the sociocultural position of its producers, clearly integrated in the hegemonic pole of the societies to which they belong, as for the context in which they work and the cultural and literary conventions they employ. In order to show only the most obvious, the *indigenista* mode of production cannot be conceived at the margin of Spanish writing, while Quechua or Aymara oral traditions would be the most idiosyncratic indigenous mode of production.

Naturally, the mode of production determines the resulting characteristics of the text. In this way, *indigenista* works assume, even in their formal structure, the Westernized sign that dominates its productive process: in fact, all of the genres adopted by *indigenismo* correspond to Western literature and follow, with the non-synchronicity that character- izes Latin American literature in its entirety, the same historical rhythm. Thus, it is possible to talk about a romantic *indigenismo* and a realist *indi- genismo*, for example.

However, the Western imprint on *indigenismo* doesn't just influence the process of production and the character of its texts; it also strongly af- fects the entire communication circuit. *Indigenista* literature doesn't open a new communicative system in the Andean countries and it is limited to flow through the channels of "cultured," or "official," literature, as some would prefer, so that in no case, not even in the most radical cases, does it manage to incorporate the indigenous sectors within the commu- nication circuit. This is not an external or circumstantial factor, since the image of the ideal reader powerfully influences the work at the moment of its realization, endowing it with the requirements that that ideal reader demands in order to be incorporated into the literary chain. Like the chronicles, *indigenista* literature presupposes a distant reader, far from the universe that is presented in the text.

Nevertheless, the heterogeneity of *indigenismo* isn't exhausted in the crossing of two cultures, in the dynamics of revelation of one under the premises of another; it has the same split constitution in the decisive stratum of its social conditioning. In fact, *indigenismo* responds to the determinants of a society characterized by the underdevelopment and dependency of its capitalist structure, while the referent—the indige- nous world—appears conditioned by a rural structure still stained with feudal residues in most of the Andean countries. Otherwise, while the *indigenista* activism is a middle-class activism, especially of radicalized groups, the referent has to represent the conflicts between other classes, the belligerent opposition of the peasantry and the *gamonales*, or land- lords. Although both dimensions certainly share common characteris- tics that derive from their insertion in the class struggle, it is obvious that the social situation of the producers of *indigenismo* is different from the situation that they describe and elucidate in their texts: this explains the ideological displacements underlying *indigenismo* while it emphasizes the essential conflictive condition of their project.

Angel Rama has proposed to analyze the *indigenista* movement, in social terms, as a result of the ascendance of minority groups from the lower middle class who use indigenous claims as support and legitimiza- tion of their own grievances against the social system imposed from above by the exploiting class. In Rama's words:

What we are witnessing [in the *indigenista* movement] is a new social group, promoted by the imperatives of modernized economic development, whose education oscillates according to areas and the degree of advancement achieved by economic development, which puts forward clear demands to society. As any group that has acquired certain social mobility—as Marx already noted—it makes the demand extensive to all other oppressed social sectors and becomes the interpreter of their claims as if they were its own, in this way swelling the waters of its meager forces with multitudinous support. There is no doubt that there was a feeling of solidarity, although there is also no doubt that it served as a mask, because the injustice suffered by those masses was even more flagrant than its own, and besides, they had the undeniable prestige of having had in the past an original culture, which could not be said of the emerging groups of the lower middle class. Those multitudes were possibly more eloquent in their silence and, at any rate, comfortably representable by whoever disposed of the adequate instruments: the written word and the graphic expression. (1974a, 150)

Angel Rama's interpretation is basically correct, except for the "adverse . . . balance" that he extracts from it, since *indigenismo* effectively is a movement of certain middle sectors that assume the interests of the indigenous peasantry, and this is precisely one of the reasons for its heterogeneity. This internalization of the interests of another social class cannot be understood, however, outside the context that Mariátegui outlined in his polemic with Luis Alberto Sánchez and, later, in his "Proceso de la literatura peruana" ["Process of Peruvian Literature"]. For Mariátegui, the *indigenista* movement was related to socialism, insofar as they are both connected by a bond of "confluence or alloy," which softens the edges of their dispersed and problematical constitution. Mariátegui was even more emphatic on this point:

> Socialism organizes and defines the demands of the masses of the working class. But in Peru, the masses—the working class—are four-fifths indigenous. Then, our socialism would not be Peruvian—it would not even be socialism—if it did not solidarize, primarily, with the indigenous claims. There is no opportunism hidden within this attitude. There are no tricks either, if one reflects for two minutes on the nature of socialism. This attitude is not faked, or phony, or sly. It is nothing more than socialism. (Aquezolo 1976, 75–76)

The perspective outlined by Mariátegui does not attempt to dilute *indigenismo*'s underlying contradiction, which is a real contradiction; it tries, rather, to explain and legitimize its heteroclite condition, defining its context and granting it an ideological direction within the problems of the contemporary world. The fact that José María Arguedas explicitly recognized Mariátegui's teachings[7] helps to understand how *indigenismo*, in its greatest of realizations, confronts the difficult task of assuming productively and creatively, as Mariátegui wished, the insurmountable conflict that defines it. Instead of imagining an impossible homogeneity, *indigenismo* realizes the opposite and materializes in heterogeneity its best ideological and literary possibilities.

In this sense, it is important to emphasize that *indigenismo*, the best *indigenismo*, does not just assume the interests of the indigenous peasantry; it also assimilates, at a diverse degree, timidly or boldly, certain literary forms that organically pertain to the referent. It is understandable that this dual assimilation of social interests and aesthetic forms constitutes the dialectical correlate of the imposition that the indigenous world suffers from the productive system of *indigenismo*: in a manner of speaking, this is its response. In consequence, the critical analysis of *indigenismo* cannot continue being realized according to the exclusory criteria of "interiority." It is usual, in effect, that the critics analyze the *indigenista* texts in terms of a mimetic relationship between the referent and its literary representation, presuming that the more interior ("from within") is the author's perspective, the more valuable and clarifying the relationship between the referent and the text will be. Although *indigenismo* has an unequivocal realist vocation, and although its works effectively try to express reliable representations of the indigenous world, what is certain is that, besides its mimetic capacity, *indigenismo* attempts another form of a more complex authenticity, which is derived from the mentioned assimilation of certain forms common to the referent, an assimilation that implies a subtle artistic process that obviously is as important as, or more than, the fulfillment of the realist purpose.

In this respect, it is worth remembering that José María Arguedas's style, related to a totally invented, even artificial language, since it is made from the syntactic Quechua matrix, which then materializes lexically in Spanish, is as a result much more authentic than the massive interpolation of Quechua words, which used to be the privileged device of classical *indigenismo* in accordance with its conceptualization as a mimetic literature. With this fictitious language, Arguedas nevertheless achieves a surprising level of authenticity: if, on one hand, he can reveal the real nature of the world of reference, on the other hand, he is capable of revealing, with brilliance, the root of a major conflict, the dismembered constitution of a society and a culture that still, after centuries of coexistence in the same space, cannot tell their history without the attributes of a conflictive and often tragic dialogue. This difficult intersocial and intercultural dialogue constitutes the bedrock of *indigenismo*.

As in all heterogeneous literatures, whose specific tendencies would have to be studied separately, *indigenismo* is not exhausted in the realist representation of its referent, that is otherwise limited due to the inevitable externality of its creative point of view, but it is realized rather as a literary reproduction of the structure and history of disintegrated societies like those of the Andean countries. As a reproducer of the most genuine key to the understanding of Andean societies, *indigenismo* is deeply committed to the historic course of nations that preserve the vitality of peoples that the Spanish conquest could not eradicate. If this plurality never ceases to be conflictive, it is also, and always more so, splendidly inspiring.

Translated by Christopher Dennis

Notes

1. From a variety of not always coinciding perspectives this problem has been addressed, among others, in the following studies: Rincón (1971 and 1973); Fernández Retamar (1973 and 1975b); Jitrik (1975b); Rama (1974b); Losada (1975); and Osorio (1976).
2. It is an idea repeated many times by him, for example in Sánchez (1968, 45).
3. Cf. my articles (1975a and 1975b).
4. Cf. Wachtel (1973, especially the chapter entitled "Pensamiento salvaje y aculturación: el espacio y el tiempo en Felipe Guamán Poma de Ayala y el Inca Garcilaso de la Vega," 161–228).
5. Thanks to this critical edition Melgar's work can be known in all of its vastness and importance. Before, only the 1878 French edition—in fact an anthology that included 31 poems—was available. Now 182 texts are known. Cf. my article (1971) and Carpio Muñoz (1976).
6. Cf. Salazar's interventions in the *I Encuentro de Narradores Peruanos* (1969).
7. "Yo no soy un aculturado," speech given by Arguedas in 1968 upon receiving the Inca Garcilaso de la Vega Award, and reproduced as the epilogue of El *zorro de arriba y el zorro de abajo* (1971, 296–98).

ANTONIO CORNEJO POLAR
Mestizaje, Transculturation, Heterogeneity

I t could be said that the category of *mestizaje* is the most powerful and widespread conceptual device with which Latin America has interpreted itself, although perhaps its capacity to offer self-identifying images is at this time less penetrating than it used to be a few decades ago, and even though it cannot be forgotten that throughout history it has not ceased to elicit dissimilar but almost always radical and even apocalyptical inquiries (from Guamán Poma de Ayala to some positivists). It seems clear to me, however, that a salvational ideology of *mestizaje* and *mestizo* people has prevailed and still does prevail as a conciliating synthesis of the many mixtures that constitute the social and cultural Latin American corpus. After all, it is not by accident that here in Latin America a mythical image could be so successfully conceived, like that of the "cosmic race," which is the hymnal exacerbation of some sort of *supermestizaje* and also the legitimizing reason for the Latin American condition.

It is useless to list the innumerable uses of the *mestizo* category (and its derivatives) in order to explain Latin American literature. It is useless because they are very well known and also (and I hope not to be unfair or forgetful) because in no case has there been a consistent effort to define with a certain theoretical rigor what a "*mestizo* literature" implies. I fear that in large part there has been a certain anxiety to find some sort of *locus amoenus* in which at least two of the greatest sources of Latin America, the Hispanic and the Indian, were harmonically reconciled, although in certain regions, as in the Caribbean, aspects of African origin would obviously be included. Naturally, this yearning is neither warranted nor does it cloister itself within the literary space: its true sphere is that of the strenuous and endless processes of the formation of nations internally fractured since the Spanish conquest. To assume that there is a non-conflictive meeting point seems to be the necessary condition to think of and imagine the nation as a more or less harmonious and coherent whole, a point which continues to be a curious a priori in order to conceive (even against the painful evidence of profound disintegrations) the mere possibility of a "true" nationality. The "*mestizo* literature" would express as much as it would contribute to the shaping of this synthesis, whose expression—it is almost necessary to say it—is inextricably tied to the question of regional and/or national "identity." In this respect, the social construction of Inca Garcilaso's work and persona provides a conclusive example.

I presume that the debate over the term "*mestizo* literature" should provide, or maybe not, an effectively theoretical alternative. This explains why my first question-proposal consists of arguing whether the category of *transculturation*—either the Fernando Ortiz and Angel Rama versions or any other version—is the theoretical device that offers a reasonable epistemological base to the concept (which I consider mostly intuitive) of *mestizaje*, or involves, on the contrary, a distinct epistemological proposal. Although I have used this category many times, I believe it is the former case. *Transculturation* would imply, in the long run, the construction of a syncretic plane that finally incorporates in a more or less unproblematical totality (in spite of the conflictive character of the process) two or more languages, two or more ethnic identities, two or more aesthetic codes and historical experiences. I add that this synthesis would be configured in the space of the hegemonic culture and literature; that at times the social asymmetry of the originating contacts would be obviated; and finally, that the discourses that have not influenced the system of "enlightened" literature would be left at the margins. At the same time, it is undeniable that the concept of *transculturation* is much more sophisticated than that of *mestizaje*, and that it has an outstanding hermeneutical aptitude, as is made evident in Rama's own work.

If *transculturation* effectively implied the (dialectical?) resolution of differences in a synthesis able to overcome the originating contradictions (which is arguable), then another theoretical device would have to be formulated in order to explain sociocultural situations and discourses in which the dynamics of the multiple intercrossings *do not* operate in a syncretic way, but instead emphasize conflicts and alterities. First, it would be necessary to contemplate Néstor García Canclini's category of *hybridity*, which does not obviate syncretic instances but de-emphasizes and situates them in a precarious situational temporality that destroys them as soon as they are instated: "strategies for entering and leaving modernity." It would also be appropriate to discuss my proposal on *heterogene-*

ity, which would define vast sectors of Latin American literature. Although sometimes I went beyond the literary sphere, the truth is that my postulates were always conceived from and for literature (which is without a doubt one of their most obvious limitations). In its first version, the concept of heterogeneity attempted to clarify the nature of processes of discursive production in which at least one of the instances differed from the others, with respect to its social, cultural, and ethnical affiliation. Later, I "radicalized" my idea and proposed that each of these instances is internally heterogeneous. It is obvious that categories like those of intertext (or better, interdiscourse, to avoid problems relative to the crossing of orality and writing) or dialogism (in terms of M. M. Bakhtin not every dialogue is dialectical) would allow for the refining of this perspective. It is also obvious that it is necessary to reexamine the complex historical condition of heterogeneity: discontinuous discourses are generated within heterogeneous stratifications that, in a certain way, fragment and hierarchize history, as José María Arguedas's reformulation of the myths of Huarochirí in El zorro de arriba y el zorro de abajo, for example, demonstrates. Naturally, it will be indispensable to compare all these categories with the concept of "alternative literature" recently proposed by Martín Lienhard. Besides its many important qualities, I believe that this proposal enriches the debate over emphasizing the significance of multilingualism, diglossia, and, what is perhaps more decisive, the rejection or assimilation of orality and writing.

Beneath these intercultural dynamics remains the fact—which also should certainly be a topic of reflection and debate—of the historical and spatial coexistence of up-to-a-point autonomous "literary" systems. I think that today very few critics would exclude literatures in Quechua, Aymara, or Amazon languages from the national space of Andean literatures, but it seems to me that concerning this question, many grave problems are still unsolved. It is impossible to even state them, but I imagine that they all converge more or less directly on the conception of a "national literature," or an Andean literature, either in singular or plural. In the latter case, it would become indispensable to figure out the modes of relation (if there were any) between one system (for example, oral literature in Quechua) and another (the "cultured" literature in Spanish, if be the case). At some point regarding this question I advanced the hypothesis that the entirety of these literary systems would form a "contradictory totality," but I continue without exactly knowing how such a category would work.

Be it as it may, the essential question consists of producing theoretical and methodological devices sufficiently rigorous and sophisticated in order to better understand a literature (or more broadly, a vast gamut of discourses) whose evident multiplicity generates a copious, profound, and disturbing conflictiveness. Assuming it as such, making contradiction the object of our discipline can be the most urgent task of Latin American critical thought. Something, of course, that would have to be debated.

Translated by Christopher Dennis

ANGEL RAMA
Literature and Culture

The Uruguayan Angel Rama (1926–1983) was a literary and cultural critic. In addition to his work as a publisher and editor, he was a professor at several Latin American and U.S. universities. His main titles include *Rubén Darío y el modernismo (circunstancia socioeconómica de un arte americano)* (1970), *Transculturación narrativa en América Latina* (1982), and *La ciudad letrada* (1984).

Independence, Originality, Representativeness

The literatures of Latin America, those born under the violent imposition of a ruthless colonial regime, blind and deaf to the humanist voices who recognized the rich otherness of America; Latin American literatures, progeny of the rich, varied, elite, popular, energetic, savory Hispanic civilization, then at its zenith; Latin American literatures, offspring of the splendid languages and sumptuous literatures of Spain and Portugal; Latin American literatures have never resigned themselves to their origins, nor ever reconciled themselves with their Iberian past.

The literatures of Latin America contributed vigorously to the black legend (of Spanish atrocities in the Americas), and rightly so, but barely paused to consider that, in effect, they were only prolonging the thinking of the Spaniards who had begun the legend in the first place. Very early on, Latin American literatures attempted to re-position themselves along other cultural lineages. That is, they tried to divorce themselves totally from their birth ties to Spain. During colonial times, their "new and improved" European heritage was represented by Italy or in the guise of classicism. Since the era of independence, France and England provided a more acceptable European literary or philosophical model. Neither France nor England was perceived as yet another colonizing metropolis, although both were indeed, until the rise of North American literature's contemporary influence. Above all, beyond the legitimate search for further enrichment, Latin American letters were driven by the need to reject their primary sources, by their desire for freedom from their Spanish origins. One could even surmise that the motto of Latin American literatures, from the critical discourse of the 1750s down to the present, has been and continues to be that very independence (Velis 1980, 163–88).

The *criollos*, sons and daughters of Spaniards born in the Americas, aroused popular sentiment in favor of independence with their fervent condemnations of colonialism. They made zealous use of Latin American *indigenismo*, and marched forward under its avenging banner. These sons and daughters of Europeans and *gachupines* [derisive term for Spaniards] demagogically invoked the clichéd images of destitute Indians and black men at the whipping post in their demands for independence. Once the *criollos* held power, however, their noble proclamations became just so many empty words, exposed as mere rhetorical ploys for their own political demands.

On the continent whose most profound and enduring cultural stamp ties it inexorably to Spain and Portugal, the drive for independence has been so tenacious as to develop a literature whose autonomy, with respect to Iberian sources, is glaring. This occurs because Latin American literature forged alliances to other foreign Western literatures, rather than to its own Iberian ones. Spanish and Portuguese mother-literatures were unable to make the bonds of a common past hold sway over their colonial counterparts. These literatures were ineffective in fulfilling such a structural capacity or identifying presence in Latin American literature, because the Iberian societies out of which they arose clung fiercely to a premodern, Counter-Reformation dynamic.[1]

In other words, a shifting and capricious internationalist impulse is the driving force behind the originality of Latin American literature. But this impulse masks another more vigorous source of nurture; that is, the cultural peculiarity emerging in the continent's heartlands, not the work of literary elites alone, but rather, the tremendous striving of vast societies in the construction of their symbolic languages.

The historical moment of Latin America's uneven and haphazard political emancipation, now recognizable as such, placed the independent literatures (founded with scant backing from the Enlightenment) squarely in the mainstream of the bourgeois ideology nurturing a triumphant romantic art. Within this current, the literatures of Latin America were stamped with the tenets of romanticism's major *Dióscuros*, its twin gods of originality and representativeness, situated on a dialectical historical axis. Given that these literatures belonged to nations that had broken the ties to their motherlands in rebellion against the colonial past (where colonial offenses were still a living testimony), it was of utmost importance that literary works be *original* with respect to their sources. The clichés of "European decadence" and, a century later, "North American decadence" filtered into literature permanently, establishing the ethical principle on which both literature and the rejection of foreigners would be based. However, no consideration was given to the fact that this ethical principle was equally of foreign extraction, albeit from an ethics already considered outmoded by European standards of the day. Andrés Bello thereby justifies his "Alocución a la poesía" (1823), and begs poetry to abandon

> his region of light and misery
> in which your ambitious
> rival, Philosophy,
> who submits virtue to calculation,
> has usurped the worship of mortals from you;
> where the crowned Hydra threatens/to bring back to enslaved thought
> the ancient night of barbarism and crime.

According to Bello and his romantic successors, originality could only be achieved by means of the representative character of the region from which said originality had sprung. Such men perceived Latin American regions as notably distinct from their engendering societies in terms of physical geography, ethnic heterogeneity, and lesser degree of economic development compared to that of Europe, the sole model of progress then envisioned. Hence, Simón Rodríguez's initial motto, "either we create or we err," became a "patriotic mission" for Ignacio Altamirano, who saw in literature an appropriate tool for the forging of nationality. This ethical principle joined up with national sentiment, turning national matters into "raw material" and modeling them along emerging economic lines. Altamirano equated the writer with the farmer or the industrialist in the chain of production: "Oh! If there is anything rich in resources for the man of letters, it is this country, in the same way that it is for the farmer and the industrialist" (1949, vol. 1, 10).

In later periods, literature distanced itself very little from the formative impulses of independence, originality, and representativeness, despite major historical transformations. The internationalism of the modernizing period (1870–1910) fostered a coalescence of regionalism over and above the limited nationalities of the nineteenth century, in an attempt to re-establish the myth of a common homeland which had nurtured the independence process (the amphictyonic Congress of Panama, convened by Simón Bolívar). Internationalism served not to destroy the principle of representativeness, but rather shifted its focus from nationalism to both regionalism and a supranational vision, which would be called Latin America, placing representation of the region ahead of localisms. Internationalism could not erase the romantic criterion with regard to the appropriate scope of national subject matters (reduced simply to a question of events, characters, the country's landscapes) in literature. It did, however, manage to restrict this criterion in advocating the right to use any world stage, a thesis defended by Manuel Gutiérrez Nájera in terms deserving of Altamirano's approval (Pacheco 1978, 5). Originality, defended even more ferociously than during the romantic-realist period of the nineteenth century, was confined to individual talent, to "personal treasure" as Rubén Darío phrased it, within a cosmopolitan thematics that, nonetheless, privileged the peculiarities of "regional men" over "regional nature." Emphasis on individualism intensified and found its first success, as the continent became solidly integrated into the model of the Western world-economy, but could not wipe out the guiding principles that had given birth to national literatures during the independence movement. This was demonstrated, as never before, in a desire for originality and an attempt at autonomy, in which language was envisioned as autonomy's greatest safeguard, despite any reverence for internationalism. As the continent experienced the dynamics of modernization, its literatures were free to draw from the great wealth of accumulated Iberian tradition, without the crushing weight of colonialism. This explains the vibrant revival, underlying all detectable *mental Gallicisms*, of Spanish literatures from the Middle Ages, the Renaissance, and the Baroque. In this new international conjunction, language had once again become an instrument of independence.

The criterion of representativeness, resurgent during the social and nationalist period, from approximately 1910–1940, was stimulated by the emerging middle classes, many of whom were provincials only recently arrived in the city. The reappearance of this criterion allows one to appreciate, more so than in the romantic era, the place conceded to literature within the constituent elements of a national or a regional culture. Times now demanded literature to represent the middle classes at the very moment of their confrontation with dominant social strata, reinstating the romantic criterion of "local color." Said local color is shaped from within by a worldview and, most importantly, by the interests of a particular class which adopts the demands of the lower classes as its own, as is common in any struggle against outdated powers. Many literary movements, such as *criollismo* (regionalist reformist literary movement within realism), nativism, regionalism, *indigenismo*, negritude, as well as urban avant-garde, experimental modernization, and futurism, aid in restoring the principle of representativeness. Representativeness was again theorized as the condition of originality and independence, although now from within a schematics greatly in debt to the then haphazardly developing field of sociology. Sociology wound up both absorbing and taking the place of the national-romantic conception of representativeness, as can be seen in its founders, Domingo Faustino Sarmiento, José María Samper, and Eugenio de Hostos. The sociological conception of representativeness established regionalist limitations, which, for Alberto Zum Felde, characterize the whole continent's intellectual process: "The continent's entire essay genre seems to be linked, in greater or lesser degree, to its sociological reality. And this is nothing more than a reflection of what happens, analogously, in the novel, which is also largely sociological; both genres, the essay and the novel, differ only in form, but are identical in substance" (Zum Felde 1954, 9).

The implicit rule, however groundless it may have been, was that the middle classes were the authentic interpreters of nationality and the driving force behind national spirit, not the upper classes in power. Literature was thus defined anew by its social-patriotic mission, and legitimated in its representational capacity, but this criterion was developed with far greater sophistication. Representativeness was no longer sought in a country's geographical milieu, in national affairs, or even in national customs, but rather in the nation's animating "spirit," expressed as social behaviors that would, in turn, be recorded in literary writing. If, on the one hand, this criterion of representativeness surpassed the simplistic romantic model, on the other, it was still more rudimentary and less sophisticated than the subterranean form of representativeness that late-nineteenth-century modernizers achieved through language. Representativeness was retied, over the heads of such modernizers, to an idealizing and ethical conception of literature, held by one school of romanticism. At the same time, the new version of representativeness surpassed the romantic one in the creation of a more finely honed (and indecisive) instrument for defining nationality.

Pedro Henríquez Ureña, followed discreetly by Alfonso Reyes, read as "Mexican" the works of Juan Ruiz de Alarcón, works in which there was nary a trace of the Mexican milieu (Alatorre 1954, 161–202). Likewise, the Guillot Muñoz brothers read as "Uruguayan" Lautreamont's *Chants de Maldoror*; José Carlos Mariátegui read Ricardo Palma's works as Peruvian, as did Ventura García Calderón with Alonso Carrió de la Vandera's *El lazarillo de ciegos caminantes*. In their analyses, nationality is confined to operative modes and conceptions of life and, at times, literary devices recurrent within the course of a national literature's development. No matter how sharp such analyses may have been, they were seriously flawed. On the one hand, such analyses established the survival, sometimes over centuries, of the aforementioned works' alleged national traits, a move that forced them to discover or reveal these traits through the influence of an invariable geography rather than an unstable history. Simultaneously, on the other hand, such analyses assumed a conception of nationality that had been defined by a specific class during a specific historical period, establishing a mobile historicist criterion. This contradiction gnawed at the foundations of the new vision of representativeness, even as it maintained that same representativeness as the genealogical foundation of literary originality and also of independence. In the choice between the individual artist (on whom the nineteenth-century modernizers placed their bets) and society and nature (nineteenth-century romantic and twentieth-century regionalist favorites), the latter win. Society and nature demonstrated a greater potential, a much deeper structuring capacity, and much stronger genetic underpinnings than a purely individual creative exercise. These strengths, however, were not merely a response to the bounty of natural phenomena so many critics, including Marcelino Menéndez y Pelayo, had used to explain the distinguishing features of Hispanic American literatures in relation to other literatures of the same tongue. They were, rather, a response to the intrinsic characteristics of society—its culture—but that exact designation had yet to be coined by the incipient discipline of anthropology.

This new theoretical perspective is first proposed by Pedro Henríquez Ureña, the most perceptive literary critic of his time. Educated in the United States, he was familiar with Anglo-Saxon cultural anthropology. Henríquez Ureña aspired to integrate cultural anthropology into an exploration of Latin (Hispanic, as he preferred to say) American peculiarity, still at the service of national ideals. The title of his 1928 compilation of studies, *Seis ensayos en busca de nuestra expresión*, defines his project: The search for Latin American expression. Henríquez Ureña would pave the way for a meticulous and documented investigation of the workings of the continent's literatures. Hispanic American literatures, having arisen from the rejection of their metropolitan sources, had evolved thanks to an internationalism integrating them into a Western framework, but these same literatures continued to assert an autonomy whose cornerstone could not be found elsewhere than in the cultural singularity of the region itself. An analysis of the last two centuries would reveal a back and forth movement, alternating between two poles of attraction, one from abroad and one from the interior, less in response to freely adopted decisions than to a magnetic attraction to one or the other. The irradiating action of the two poles never paralyzed the unyielding initial project to create an independent, original, and representative literature, but situated it at a distinct level in accordance with the project's own productive capacity, predominant social tendencies, historical times, and the greater complexity of society itself. This does not mean that a faultless line of progress could be drawn; there would be drawbacks, delays, and uneven accelerations. Once diverse Latin American societies reached a high degree of evolution, a power struggle ensued between various social classes and their respective cultural formulas for control of the historical moment.

A vast intellectual inquiry into the continent, in which its writers and thinkers would actively participate, begins circa 1940. It begins earlier in some places (Argentina) and later in others (Brazil, Mexico) and seems to respond to the curb on the middle classes' ascent to power and the refluence of their gains, to the self-criticism undertaken by their leaders, and to the growing and autonomous presence of proletarian and even peasant sectors on the national scene. This long period could be analyzed historically, sociologically, and politically, as well as literarily. Attention must be paid not only to authors and their works, their worldviews, and their artistic forms, but also, preferably, to their productive peculiarities, as a means of explaining the basic norms regulating Latin American literature since its origins.

The proposal for that type of analysis at that moment in time carried with it a polemical overtone. Reacting to a heavy focus only on the content of literary works, which turned them into mere sociological documents or political manifestos, some critics have made an equally pernicious error. Under the pretext of examining literature in and of itself, such critics, in an exercise of literary autism, cut literature off from its cultural context, chose to ignore the persistent search for representativeness characterizing our historical development, and wound up ignoring the communication that any literary text necessarily entails. The reestablishment of literary works within the cultural operations carried out by American societies, the recognition of their daring signifying constructions, and the vast efforts at authenticity in the use of symbolic languages developed by Latin American writers are all ways of reinforcing the unyielding concepts of independence, originality, and representativeness. Literary works do not fall outside the realm of culture, but are, rather, its culmination. To the extent that Latin American cultures are centuries-old and multitudinous inventions, they make the writer a producer who works with the works of countless others— a compiler, as Augusto Roa Bastos would have said, a brilliant weaver in the vast historic workshop of American society.

Moreover, now that the prestige of "modernization" has waned sufficiently, along with the dazzle of technical innovation in the international avant-garde novel, one can see its accumulated effect, a hodgepodge of mere experimental imitations for a minimal audience in rarefied literary circles. Although "modernization" has produced major works of renowned splendor (Jorge Luis Borges, Julio Cortázar, Carlos Fuentes), it becomes expedient to re-examine recent literature in order to see if perhaps there weren't other sources nurturing artistic renovation, not just the "modernizing" oncs that were offloaded from the gangplanks of European ships. This point is examined in my essay "La tecnificación narrativa" (1981) as an analysis of a cosmopolitan literature disseminated in Latin America. This present study is dedicated to the exploration of another perspective, that of a literature seeking nurture in the cultural organicity attained within the continent. The only way not to invoke the name of Latin America in vain is when internal cultural accumulation is capable of providing not just "raw material," but also a worldview, a language, and a technique for producing literary works. There is nothing in this study resembling self-sufficient folklorism—ludicrous in an internationalist age. It is, rather, an attempt at spiritual decolonization: recognition of Latin America's achievements and acknowledgment of the continent's long and fecund inventive tradition, of its tenacious struggle to create one of our planet's richest sources of culture.

Response to the Conflict between the Avant-garde and Regionalism

During the 1930s, two organic narrative tendencies, one cosmopolitan and the other critical-realist, developed in Latin America's major urban centers, particularly Buenos Aires, in its day the most advanced city on the continent. Both had arisen as aesthetic proposals in the same cities where works incorporating these narrative strategies were published and disseminated, so the mere fact of their widening cultural expansion canceled out an earlier regionalist narrative movement. The regionalist movement had appeared circa 1910 and had transformed both costumbrismo [a literary movement based on the humorous or satiric depiction of local customs, dress, and typical scenes and characters] and naturalism (the case of Mariano Azuela). It had held sway over most of the continent, in areas of median or scant educational development as well as those with more advanced development, due to the success of literary works from the 1920s. La vorágine in 1924 and Doña Bárbara in 1929 are model texts whose dissemination obscured the avant-garde movement under way during this same period.

At its outset, regionalism assumed a passive-aggressive attitude in drastic confrontation with the avant-gardists, known in Brazil as modernistas. The ensuing struggle begins with Horacio Quiroga's text, "Ante el tribunal," published in 1931. Quiroga, in age and works, was the undisputed master of the regionalists: "My wounds, still fresh from the battle, are of no avail at all, when I battled against another past and other errors with a ferocity equal to that used against me today. For twenty-five years I have struggled to conquer, to the extent of my abilities, everything that is today denied me. It has been an illusion. Today I must appear before the tribunal to declare my faults, which in my estimation were virtues, and to free at least one atom of my personality from the hell into which my name has been cast" (1970, 135).

Quiroga's light tone does not hide the bitterness of the battle to which he contributed elusively in the years 1928 and 1929, culminating in a series of texts on his narrative art and influences, and unveiling his Parnassus: Joseph Conrad, William Hudson, Bret Harte, José Eustasio Rivera, Anton Chekhov, Rudyard Kipling, Benito Lynch, and others.

One could see in Quiroga's confrontation with the "tribunal" a typical generational conflict; the same could not be said, however, of the Manifiesto Regionalista, published in 1926 by Gilberto Freyre for the Regionalist Conference in Recife. Freyre's opposition to Paulista modernism [from São Paulo] not only inspired his text but also implied disagreements with writers such as Mario de Andrade, only seven years his senior, and thus part of the same generation (Freyre 1976).

Freyre's Manifiesto Regionalista attempts "a movement [in favor] of rehabilitation of regional and traditional values from this part of Brazil: a movement out of which authentic masters, such as the humanist João Ribeiro and the poet Manuel Bandeira, were becoming known." The Manifiesto restores the sense of regionalism in opposition to undue foreign influence on Brazil's capital, Rio de Janeiro, as well as on burgeoning cities like São Paulo. In his text, Freyre defined regionalism as "the meaning, eternal in its form, if such a thing can be said—the regional, not just provincial, way of being and belonging to the land—materialized or realized in a substance perhaps more historical than geographic and certainly more social than political" (1976, 52–53).

Although the manifesto, whose anthropological orientation responds visibly to the teachings of Franz Boas, attends more to the cuisine of the

Northeast and to the architecture of the *mocambos* [settlements of free blacks; later, by extension, poor urban black neighborhoods and slums] than to literature, it does not fail to highlight the influence of idiosyncratic cultural components on the spiritual formation of Brazil's Northeastern intellectuals. These components are fully manifested in the people, although Freyre skirts around any vertical, classist interpretation of cultures. Instead, Freyre advocates a regional, horizontal conception of such cultural components.

> In the Northeast, those who draw near the people descend to the roots and sources of life, of culture and of regional art. He who draws near the people is among masters and becomes an apprentice, no matter how many B.A. or M.D. degrees he may have. The power of Joaquim Nabuco, Silvio Romero, José de Alencar, Floriano Peixoto, father Ibiapina, Telles Júnior, Capistrano de Abreu, Augusto dos Anjos, or so many other great northeastern expressions of the Brazilian cultural soul, came from the contact they had as children, with the plantation or the city, or as grown men, with the people, with popular traditions, with the regional multitudes and not only with the waters, the trees, and the animals of the region. (1976, 76)

This brand of regionalism should not be confused "with separatism, or localism, with anti-internationalism, or anti-universalism or anti-nationalism," which confirm their fatal submission to the norms of national unity dictated from the capital, as well as their lack of aspiration for independence or autarchy. Such separatisms and the like are limited to attacking the capital's homogenizing social function through the application of foreign cultural models, without "attention to the conformation of Brazil, victim since its birth, of foreignisms which have been imposed upon it, with no respect for the peculiarities and disparities of its physical and social configuration" (Freyre 1976, 54–55).

The modernization of the port cities is symbolized by the incorporation of Santa Claus with his wintry dress and his sled for travel over snowy grounds. Meanwhile, Pernambucan and Northeastern culture in general is not outshone by any "in the richness of its illustrious traditions and in the sharpness of its character," and "has the right to consider itself a region that already contributed greatly in giving the culture or the civilization of Brazil authenticity and originality." A clear refutation of foreign discourses scornful of the tropics and of the anti-Lusitanian [Portuguese] stance of the modernizers, who see "in everything that Portuguese inheritance is an evil to be despised" (Freyre 1976, 58).

Not only is this conflict rigorously theorized in Brazil, from renovated and, above all, modernized perspectives, it was also simultaneously confronted in Spanish America. In the Peruvian case, José Carlos Mariátegui visualized the conflict from a social and class angle, rather than from a cultural one. In so doing, he attempted to overcome the old "centralism/regionalism" dilemma—then being resolved in administrative decentralization, which, instead of lessening, actually augmented the power of *gamonalismo* [feudal landowning system, tying indigenous peoples to plantations]—by means of a social re-evaluation that welded *indigenismo* to a new regionalism. This new regionalism could be thus defined: "This regionalism is not a mere protest against the centralist regime. It is an expression of highland consciousness and Andean sentiment. The new regionalists are, above all, *indigenistas*. One cannot confuse them with the anti-centralists of the older type. Luis Eduardo Valcárcel perceives the roots of Incan society intact beneath the weak colonial stratum. His work, more than regional, is *Cuzquian*, it is Andean, it is *Quechuan*. It is nurtured by indigenous sentiment and autochthonous tradition" (Mariátegui 1979, 140).

Mariátegui's evaluation demonstrates that regionalism not only encountered the opposition of the capital's official proposals that sought unity along international models implying the country's homogenization, but also that of the unofficial, heterodox and oppositional proposals, which were also highly internationalist. Mariátegui's disregard for regional culture in his horizontal manifestation has to do with his proximity to a third ideological force operative in the Latin American narrative of the times: the concept of social narrative. These narratives fed so-called *indigenista* social literature, as in the work of Enrique López Albújar and Jorge Icaza. Although related to critical-realist narrative, social narrative demonstrated specific characteristics that allow us to frame it separately with the publication of César Vallejo's *Tungsteno* in 1931. Dissemination of social narrative coincided with the belligerent period corresponding to the "rosy decade" of universal antifascism. Although social narrative expressed less-evolved modern traits, it still shows evidence of modernity's influence. Social narrative was affected by the urbanization of literary devices, adhered to patterns imported from Soviet socialist-realism of the Stalinist era, and expressed the worldview of the communist party's establishment. Paradoxically, some of social narrative's components belong to both critical realism and the fantastic. While popularity of the fantastic was on the rise in Buenos Aires in the 1930s (Jorge Luis Borges's Tlön, Uqbar, Tertius Orbis is a key publication), social narrative denounces its politics for their identification with conservative thought. Alejo Carpentier alludes to this third force when he states that "the era from 1930–1950 is characterized, among us, by a certain stagnation of narrative techniques. Narrative becomes nativist for the most part, but in it the new factor of denunciation appears. And whoever says denunciation, says politicization" (1981, 12). It would have been more correct to say that the social novel's narrative techniques were very simple, the opposite of those of the regional and the fantastic novel. Social narrative techniques were also less complex than those of the critical-realist novel, because the social novel expressed the perspectives of diverse sectors, classes or groups or vanguards, which had entered into a political struggle that the economic crisis could only make worse.

There was in fact a literary war, even though occasional curious contact points among the diverse currents could be seen. For example, as regionalism developed rural themes, it maintained close contact with traditional and even archaic forms of Latin American everyday life, as in folklore. Carpentier maintained a subtle appreciation for these traditional forms within the critical realism he would develop, applying them many times to the comprehension of American historical cycles. Borges, in turn, in his response to Américo Castro's book, La peculiaridad lingüística rioplatense y su sentido histórico, appropriately valued traditional forms on the linguistic front, while Mario de Andrade appealed directly to tradition in the composition of Macunaíma.

The greatest challenge in literary renovation would be presented to regionalism. By accepting this challenge, regionalism was able to safeguard important local traditions and literary values, although these values were transformed and transferred to new literary structures, similar to but not assimilable to those supplying urban narrative in its plural renovating tendencies. Regionalism realized that if it became ensconced in its dispute with the avant-garde and critical realism, it would not survive. It would lose not only scores of literary forms (bearing in mind their perennial transformation), but most importantly a broad cultural content which had achieved legitimacy through the mediation of literature, even in renovated urban centers. Regionalism would thus impede an efficient effort at national integration in a period of increasing stratification and social ruptures.

Within the general structure of Latin American societies, regionalism accentuated the cultural particularities that had been forged in the interior, contributing to the definition of its different profile and at the same time reinserting it into the heart of national cultures, which responded increasingly to urban norms. For that reason, regionalism was inclined to preserve those elements of the past that had contributed to the process of national cultural singularity and attempted to transmit the acquired configuration to the future, in order to resist foreign innovations. Tradition, one of the compulsory features for any definition of culture, was highlighted by regionalism, albeit with an evident erasure of the transformations which had been progressively imprinted on earlier traditions. Regionalism thus tended to expand a historically crystallized formula for tradition in its literary expressions.

The fragility of regionalism's values and of its expressive literary devices grew out of this tendency, as it was faced with the impact of modernization imposed from abroad via the ports and capital cities. It is well known that these literary structures, the first to cede under attack, manifested the transformations of the time, well before the worldview that inspired them, in an attempt to safeguard those same regional values without apparent change, but in reality transferring them to another cognitive viewpoint. Thus regionalism would have to incorporate new literary articulations, which were sometimes sought from the world stage, but more frequently from the much closer Latin American urban milieu. The incorporation of such new articulations avoided a drastic substitution of regionalism's bases, attempting in exchange to expand them again in order to cover the national territory if at all possible. Until this time, regionalism's message, weighted with traditionalism, had been transmitted with relative ease to the cities, largely because the cities had grown in size due to immigration from the heartlands and had incorporated strong rural cultural sectors. But now, in order to safeguard its message, regionalism had to adapt to the aesthetic conditions forged in the cities. The aesthetic articulations of the cities are so highly responsive to urban expansion that this expansion absorbs and disperses outside pressures, bending such articulations to adapt prestigious and supposedly universal models, models that originated, in fact, in the developed metropolises. One cannot say that this is only a matter of artistic operations, reserved exclusively for writers. Adoption and adaptation of foreign models are part of a much larger process of acculturation brought to bear on the entire continent, a process that, under the conjoined impact of Europe and the United States, underwent a second period of modernization between both world wars. Acculturation is more visible in the urban enclaves of Latin America undergoing modernization and in the cosmopolitan literature linked to foreign influences, but we have preferred to examine the process of acculturation in the continent's traditionalist heartlands, where this process holds greater significance.

After the First World War, a new economic and cultural expansion of the metropolises makes itself felt in Latin America. The benefits this expansion brings to one sector of Latin America's population do not hide the internal ruptures or the internal conflicts it generates, which will only become more severe after the economic crash of 1929. The process of transculturation intensifies in all orders of American life. One of its chapters takes up the conflicts between the interior regions, the continent's heartlands, and the capital cities and seaports, then undergoing modernization at the hands of urban elites who ascribed to the philosophy of progress.

The modernized culture of the cities, doubly shored up by outside, foreign sources and its own appropriation of the social surplus, dominates the hinterlands (transferring to them, in fact, its own dependence on foreign cultural systems), aided efficiently by the use of newly introduced technologies. In cultural terms, then, the commercial and industrial cities consent to the folkloric conservatism of the heartlands. Conservatism makes creativity and obligatory updating difficult, even as these updates represent a preliminary step toward national homogeneity along modernized norms. The capitals offer the heartlands, representing a plurality of cultural configurations, two fatal choices: the regions can either pull back, out of the modernizing process, which would be their death, or, alternatively, surrender their cultural values to it, that is to say, die out. [2]

Regionalist response to this conflict is, fundamentally, an attempt to avoid the rupture of national society as it undergoes a very uneven transformation, and most often the response seeks the middle ground. That is, taking modernity's achievements in hand and revising regional cultural contents in their light, regionalists create hybrid cultural forms from a variety of sources that are still capable of transmitting received inheritance. A renovated heritage, to be sure, but one that can yet be identified with its own past. The plastic regional groups intensively examine local traditions in order to revitalize their atrophied forms. Regionalists cannot renounce such traditions, but they can revise them along the lines of modernist changes, choosing only those components adaptable to the new operating system.

During the 1920s and 1930s, such adaptations are evident in all artistic fields, but most pronouncedly manifested in the period's diverse narrative trends. Alejo Carpentier, after listening to Stravinski's musical dissonances, for example, sharpens his ear and rediscovers an appreciation of the African rhythms heard for centuries in the little black town of Regla, across the harbor from Havana. Likewise Miguel Angel Asturias, stunned by the illumination of automatic writing, finds in it a useful means of saving the poetry and philosophies of Guatemala's indigenous communities. Similarly in Brazil, Gilda de Mello e Souza analyzes Mario de Andrade's modernist text *Macunaíma* and astutely hypothesizes that in order to comprehend his work, one must appreciate its dual sources, symbolically expressed in one of the poet's verses ("I am a lute-playing Tupí"): "The interest in the book results, to a great degree, from its 'simultaneous adhesion to heterogeneous terms,' or better yet, to a curious satiric play which oscillates unceasingly between the adoption of a European model and the valuation of national difference" (De Mello e Souza 75).

The modernizing impact initially generates a defensive regrouping in the fine arts and literatures, which burrow deeply into the protection of their mother culture. Once this regrouping proves incapable of resolving cultural conflict, a second transculturating moment undertakes the critical examination of regionalist values and a subsequent selection of certain components, valued for their distinctiveness or for potential viability in the new times. A comparison of the successive prologues that Gilberto Freyre writes for different editions of his *Manifiesto Regional* can be enlightening. In them, Freyre defines his work as a "regionalist, traditionalist and, *in its own way, modernist* movement" and emphasizes that "it pioneered a modernist as well as traditionalist and regionalist movement which revolutionized Brazilian art." Freyre then illustrates this with abundant names from his generous personal panoramas. Freyre's panorama cannot, however, encompass the *Semana de Arte Moderno* from São Paulo, but instead tries to find common ground with Mario de Andrade from another angle: "From the beginning, the investigation, reinterpretation and valuation of inspirations from the telluric, traditional, oral, popular, folkloric and even anthropologic intuitive roots of culture was put forward. Everyday things, spontaneous, rustic, despised by those who in art or culture are only sensitive to the refined and the erudite" (De Mello e Souza 1979, 28).

Freyre thus points out the third moment in which the modernizing impact is absorbed by regional culture. After this self-examination, reevaluation, and selection of valid components, there ensues a rediscovery of traits, which, although belonging to traditional heritage, had been unseen or unused in any systematic form but whose expressive possibilities become evident from the modernizing perspective.

An examination of Vittorio Lanternari's model, with its three different responses to the challenge of acculturation, could also be applied to regionalist literary production in terms of vulnerability, rigidity, and plasticity. "Cultural vulnerability," which accepts outside proposals and gives up its own almost without a fight, is one possibility; another, according to Lanternari, is "cultural rigidity," which is housed drastically in objects and values constitutive of its own culture, rejecting anything new. Lanternari's third possibility is "cultural plasticity," which deftly tries to incorporate the latest fads, not only as objects absorbed by the cultural complex, but above all as animating ferments in the traditional cultural structure, which is then capable of inventive responses by using its own components.[3] Of special relevance within the realm of "cultural plasticity" are those artists not limited to a syncretic composition through mere addition of contributions from one culture or the other. Rather, upon perceiving that each contribution is an autonomous structure, such artists understand that the incorporation of elements from outside sources must be coordinated with a global re-articulation of the cultural structure, making use of new focal points within it.

In order to carry out this project, a re-immersion in primary sources is necessary. From this re-immersion, the intensification of certain components of the traditional cultural structure, which seem to come from even more primitive strata than those habitually recognized, can result. These components display a signifying power that makes them invulnerable to the corrosion of modernization, as seen in the syntactic laconism of César Vallejo, and later that of Juan Rulfo, and, within other parameters, that of Graciliano Ramos. For a writer these approaches are merely artistic solutions; however, they emerge from operations carried out in the heart of a culture, and they recuperate real but previously unrecognized components, now revitalized in the face of the aggressiveness of modernizing forces.

Transculturation and Narrative Genres

The processes of acculturation are as old as the history of contacts between different human societies and as such have been studied in the crucial model of ancient cultures, like those of Crete, Greece, Alexandria, and Rome. However, the anthropological concept of acculturation is as recent as the discipline in which it has developed.[4] Given the relationship between acculturation and European colonialism, particularly English colonialism, and with twentieth-century de-colonization, the concept is dogged by ideological inferences that must not be overlooked, especially when dealing with its application to the arts and literature.

Latin American anthropology has questioned the term *acculturation* in seeking to perfect its meaning, although it has not questioned the transformations so designated. In 1947, Cuban anthropologist Fernando Ortiz proposed the term *transculturation* instead, since the new term emphasized the importance of the process designated; he proposed that transculturation was "fundamental and indispensable for an understanding of the history of Cuba, and, for analogous reasons, of that of America in general." Ortiz argued for his change in terminology within this passage: "I am of the opinion that the word *transculturation* better expresses the different phases of the process of transition from one culture to another because this does not consist of merely acquiring another culture, which is what the English term *acculturation* really implies, but the process also necessarily involves the loss or uprooting of a previous culture, which could be defined as a *deculturation*. In addition it carries the idea of the consequent creation of new cultural phenomena, which could be called *neoculturation*" (1947 102–3).

This conception of cultural transformations—enthusiastically endorsed by Bronislaw Malinowski in his prologue to Ortiz's book[5]—visibly expresses a Latin American perspective, even in what it might contain by way of incorrect interpretation.[6] It reveals resistance to the consideration of one's own traditional culture, which receives the external impact destined to modify it, as a merely passive, or even inferior entity, destined to be lost without any kind of creative response. The concept of transculturation is instead articulated along a dual verification. On the one hand, it registers that the present culture of the Latin American community (which is a product of lengthy transculturation in permanent evolution) is composed of idiosyncratic values which are acknowledged as exerting influence since the remotest of times. On the other hand, the process of *transculturation* corroborates the creative energy that powers Latin American culture, making it very distinct from a simple aggregate of norms, behaviors, beliefs, and objects. Transculturation is a force that acts with ease as much on its own particular heritage, in accordance with its developmental situation, as on external contributions. It is precisely this capacity to elaborate with originality, a feature that may be found anywhere in the territory, but most clearly in the remotest strata of the interior regions, which demonstrates, despite difficult historical circumstances, that the process of transculturation belongs to a creative and lively society.

These interior cultures can be exposed directly to the influence of external metropolises. This happens in several rural zones of the Caribbean basin during the first third of the twentieth century, in areas where companies exploiting tropical products set up shop. This history has been told from a patrician angle in *La hojarasca*, and from a social-realist angle in *Mamita Yunai*, but it can also be told through the different literary systems that were used toward these ends and their original sources, in an attempt to correlate subject matter, worldview, and literary form.

More frequently, however, the interior cultures receive their transculturating influence from their national capitals or from the area in closest contact with the outside, all of which presents an extremely varied pattern of conflicts. If it happens that the capital, which normally gives direction to the educational and cultural systems, lags behind in modernization with respect to the interior regions of the country, we will see an indictment of the capital's intellectuals by those of the interior. This is what happened in Colombia in recent decades. There, the cultural event of greatest notoriety was the insurrection of the coastal zone (Barranquilla, Cartagena) against the cultural norms of Bogotá, an insurrection that can be followed in the articles that a young Gabriel García Márquez wrote during the 1950s in El Heraldo. His articles not only pitted the coast's relaxed lifestyle against the circumspection and constriction of the capital's norms, but also took advantage of a more accelerated modernization. Speaking on "the problems of the Colombian novel," García Márquez would point out the absence of the great renovating currents of world literature, in terms of visible provocation.

> No one has yet written in Colombia a novel that is unquestionably and happily influenced by a Joyce or a Faulkner or a Virginia Woolf. And I have said happily, because I do not believe that we Colombians could be, for the moment, an exception to the play of influences. In her prologue to Orlando, Virginia confesses her influences. Faulkner himself would not deny the influence Joyce exerted over him. There is something—especially in the handling of time—between Huxley and again, Virginia Woolf. Franz Kafka and Proust are on the loose in modern world literature. If we Colombians must make a relevant decision, we would have to fall, irremediably, into this current. Lamentably, this is exactly what has not yet happened, nor are there even the faintest signs that this could ever happen. (1980, 269)

Concomitantly, in the same period this article was written, García Márquez ponders on the accusation of provincial which is attributed to him, and he turns it against the capital in a most picturesque and humorous attack on the traditionalism reigning in Bogotá, while modernization characterized the Colombian coastal zone: "An intelligent friend of mine pointed out that my position with respect to certain literary congregations in Bogotá was typically provincial. However, my well-known and very provincial modesty allows me, I believe, to affirm that in this respect, the truly worldly-wise ones are those who agree with this journalist on the parochial exclusivism of the capital's standard bearers. Literary provincialism in Colombia begins at 2,500 meters above sea level" (1980, 273).

García Márquez's position was well-founded. Not only because the La Cueva group would introduce a visible modernism into Colombian narrative (even if just barely announced in Eduardo Zalamea Borda's *Cuatro años a bordo de mi mismo*), but also because even before that, the coastal region was becoming noted for its openness to world cultures with an intensity that could not be glimpsed in the capital. The Los nuevos movement of the 1920s in Bogotá reveals that no attention was paid to new literary currents similar to that which had been seen in Ramón Vinyes's journal *Voces* toward the end of the previous decade. Artistic renovation in Colombia would result from several personal adventures (León de Griff, José Félix Fuenmayor, Arturo Vidales). The majority of contributions would arise from the interior regions of the country, where the modernizing impact defended by García Márquez would be registered, although this renovation was incorporated as a ferment stimulating the regional cultures' own expansive response to modernization.

More frequently, however, the interior regions receive impulses from the more modernized ones, in such a way that two successive transculturating processes are completed. The first process is carried out by the capital or, above all, by the port cities, which take advantage of greater resources, although it is here that the external pulsion wins its greatest battles. The second process is carried out by the interior regional culture, in response to the impact of transculturation transferred from the capital. These two processes, schematically outlined and distributed in space and time, were resolved as one in many instances, due to migration to the main cities on the part of many young provincial writers, who often associated there with other, equally provincial counterparts born in the capital. The aesthetic solutions arising from these groups of writers will mix in varying degrees both modernizing impulses and localist traditions, occasionally with very picturesque results. In the south, Pedro Leandro Ipuche coined the phrase "cosmic nativism," which metaphorizes the crossroads of cultures and had the endorsement of the early Jorge Luis Borges. The unprecedented use of world culture witnessed in the essays of José Lezama Lima is explained in Eduardo Desnoes's analysis as "the brilliant elucubrations of a genial village apothecary" (1979).

The clarification in terminology introduced by Fernando Ortiz would have pleased José María Arguedas, a fellow anthropologist from Perú and, like Ortiz, equally suspicious of foreign academic appraisal of the transformational processes of American culture. In a speech given at the reception for the Inca Garcilaso de la Vega award (1968), he belligerently objected to being considered "acculturated," as he understood the term.

That is, the loss of one's own culture, substituted by that of the colonizer, with no further possibility of expressing the unique tradition in which he had been born and raised:

> The fence should and would be destroyed: the river of wealth of both nations should and would be united. And the path need not be, nor could it have been only that which the despoiling victors imperiously demanded: that the vanquished nation renounce its soul, even if only in appearances, formally, and take on that of the victors; that is to say, that the nation become acculturated. I am not acculturated: I am a Peruvian who proudly speaks, like a happy devil, both in Christian and Indian, in Spanish and Quechua.[7]

When one applies Fernando Ortiz's description of transculturation to literary works, certain obligatory corrections must be made. His vision is geometric, in three seeming movements. His schema first implies a "partial deculturation" which can reach varying degrees and can affect different areas, from culture to literature, although always resulting in the loss of elements considered obsolete. The second facet implies incorporations from an outside culture, and the third an effort at recomposition, using surviving elements of the original culture as well as outside influences. This model does not attend sufficiently to the criteria of selectivity and invention, which should be obligatorily designated in every case as "cultural plasticity," given that this status attests to the energy and creativity of a cultural community. If the community is a living one, it will select from within itself and from the outside, and will necessarily come up with inventions with an *ars combinatoria* suitable to the autonomy of the cultural system itself. The "stripping down process," detailed by George M. Foster in his book on Spanish colonization in America, responds to a selectivity that the donor culture introduces in its contributions in order to give them greater viability. This same selectivity is found in the receiving culture in those cases in which a given norm or product is not rigidly imposed, thus permitting the recipient a choice from the rich array of donor contributions. The receiver also maintains the ability to choose from the hidden elements of the dominant culture, in their original sources. As a case in point, the European transculturating repertoire in the years between the two world wars did not include Marxism, but Marxism was chosen, nonetheless, by numerous university groups all over America, taking from it what Arnold Toynbee termed the heterodox forces of the originating European culture. Moreover, it could be said that the tendency toward independence, as the driving force behind Latin

American cultural processes, has always gravitated to the selection of elements rejected by the metropolitan European and North American systems. It pulls them out of their context and appropriates them in a daringly abstract mode. For instance, Latin American theater of recent decades has not appropriated U.S. musical comedy but has instead opted for the off-Broadway spectacle, as defined in a production like *Hair*. This kind of theater bears a critical message, which can then be adapted to the material possibilities of theatrical groups and to their vocation as social critics.

The element of selectivity is not only applied to the foreign culture but also and principally to Latin American culture, the site of massive destruction and loss. Here the task of selection is put into practice. (Further analysis along these lines may yet lead to the rediscovery of very primitive values from within cultural traditions barely remembered.) The task of selection is, in fact, a search for resistant values, those capable of confronting the spoils of transculturation. Through the prism of transculturation one can also perceive a creative task, part of the neoculturation Fernando Ortiz speaks of, a neoculturation operating simultaneously on both cultural sources in contact with each other. There would be, of course, losses, selections, rediscoveries, and incorporations. These four operations are concomitant and all are resolved within the overall restructuring of the cultural system, which is the highest creative function achieved in the transculturating process. Utensils, norms, objects, beliefs, customs, only exist in a living and dynamic articulation, designed by the culture's functional structure.

(a) *Language*. Just as had occurred during the first, late-nineteenth-century modernizing impact that produced *modernismo*, during the second modernization between the two world wars, language appeared as a defensive redoubt and as proof of independence. Linguistic performance was decisive in the case of writers, for whom the options derived from the *linguistic series* out of which they drew their raw materials determined the results of their artistic production. *Modernismo* had established two models: one, a purist reconstruction of Spanish language, especially adapted to historical subject matters (*La gloria de Don Ramiro* by Enrique Larreta, or the Mexican colonialist novel). The other established a strictly literary language by means of a cultured reconversion of the syntactic forms of American Spanish. Romantic *costumbrismo*, underlying *modernismo*, had become widespread in forms that came to be called *criollas* in which idiomatic dialectical forms of speech were first gathered. This tendency triumphed with the appearance of the regionalists, circa 1910, as *modernismo* declined. The regionalists would avail themselves of a dual system, alternating *modernismo's* cultured literary language with the dialectical register of preferably rural characters, in an attempt to create realist settings. We are not dealing with a phonetic register, but rather, with a reconstruction suggested by the use of a regional lexicon, dialectical phonetic deformations, and, to a lesser degree, local syntactic constructions. Such language, as Angel Rosenblat has already observed,[8] is situated on a secondary plane, separated from the cultured, *modernist* language still used by the narrators, and is likewise condemned within the works themselves. Santos Luzardo never tires of imparting these lessons to Marisela in *Doña Barbara*. Authorial condemnation is apparent in the use of stigmatizing quotation marks for American voices appearing in the text, a practice begun by the first romantic writers (Esteban Echeverría). It is equally apparent in the adoption of glossaries as an appendix to the novels, because the terms used were not recorded in the official Spanish Royal Academy Dictionary. These literary solutions are characterized by their linguistic ambiguity, a faithful reflection of the social structure and of the superior position within it occupied by the writer, who, if he attempts a rapprochement with inferior social strata, does not cease to affirm his own linguistically higher level, due to education and knowledge of idiomatic norms, which distance him from the popular sectors.

With respect to the performance of the regionalist writers, their heirs and transformers, under the influence of the modernizers, introduce changes. They markedly reduce the field of dialectical idioms and strictly American terms. They no longer use phonetic spelling of popular speech and compensate for it by a more confident use of the author's own spoken American language. Authors give up the use of glossaries, relying on their belief that regional words transmit their meaning within the work's linguistic context, even for those unfamiliar with them. Moreover, the distance between the author-narrator's language and that of the characters is lessened, in the belief that the use of such linguistic dualism destroys the artistic unity of the work. In the case of characters who speak a Native American language, authors seek an equivalent within Spanish, thus forging an artificial and literary language (Arguedas, Roa Bastos, Manuel Scorza) which, without breaking the unitary tonality of the work, allows the registering of a difference in language. In summary, these are some of the paths through which the linguistic unification of the text is put forward, as a response to an evidently more modern conception of artistic structuring, due in part to a very new and impetuous confidence in the American language the author uses everyday. With predictable variations, this is the guideline for all literary production after 1940. It is visible in one of the greatest exponents of literary cosmopolitanism, Julio Cortázar. His language unifies the speech of all of Rayuela's characters, whether Argentine or foreign, with the use of the spoken language of Buenos Aires (with its typical vos [used in place of the second person singular familiar tú in rioplatense Spanish] and che [hey, you, man; common interjection used alone or with vos, the use of which gave Ernesto "Che" Guevarra his nickname]). Such usage manifests minimal distancing from the language of the novel's author. This linguistic resolution can be considered drastic since it occurs after Argentine authorities imposed usage norms in elementary and high schools to eliminate these dialectical forms of speech, common in the vernacular for at least two centuries.

In the case of regionalist writers, caught in critical transculturational junctures, the lexicon, prosody, and morphosyntaxis of the regional language appeared as the favored ground for prolonging the concepts of originality and representativeness, thus simultaneously resolving the question of unity in literary composition according to the modernizing norm. What was once the language of popular characters, set up within the text against the language of the writer or the narrator, now takes on an inverted hierarchical position. Popular speech, instead of being the exception and of placing the character under the author's scrutiny, now becomes the narrating voice. This voice encompasses the totality of the text, by occupying the narrator's place and demonstrating his worldview. But this writing does not merely imitate a dialect, rather, it utilizes syntactic or lexical forms that belong within the polished colloquial language typical of the American Spanish of certain of the continent's linguistic areas. The difference between these two literary practices, even more than the linguistic ones, is given in the comparison between two excellent short stories: "Doña Santitos" by Marta Brunet, the Chilean writer and regionalism's final representative, and Juan Rulfo's "Luvina," a representation of this narrative transculturation already in progress.

Writers have returned to their linguistic community and speak from within it, freely utilizing its idiomatic resources. If it is rural or borders an indigenous community, as is frequently the case, the writer employs the linguistic system as his point of departure for his own artistic ends, not as an outsider's attempt at imitating regional speech. The moment the writer no longer sees himself as an outsider, but recognizes his own community without embarrassment or diminished regard, he abandons the copy and its emphatic registry of irregularities and variations with respect to outside academic norms. Instead, he explores the possibilities for constructing a specific literary language from within the framework of his own linguistic community. Ortiz would cite this as an example of neoculturation. On the one hand, the principle of textual unification and the construction of an aesthetically invented literary language correspond to the rationalizing spirit of modernity. On the other, the linguistic perspective the novel assumes restores a regional vision of the world, extends the validity of its interiority even more richly than before, and thus expands a more finely tuned, authentic, and artistically solvent version of the original worldview. It is, in fact, a modernized worldview, but in it regional identity is not destroyed.

(b) *Literary structure*. The linguistic solution to outside modernizing impacts would subtly reconstruct a tradition and furnish us with works now considered classics of Latin American literature, such as Juan Rulfo's *Pedro Páramo*. At the linguistic level, all in all, the problems derived from newly modernized circumstances were less difficult to resolve than those of literary structure. Here, the distance between traditional forms and modern foreign ones was much greater. The regional novel had developed along the narrative lines of nineteenth-century naturalism, adapting it to meet its own expressive needs. But it now faced an array of avant-garde literary devices initially absorbed into poetry; only later would these stimulate critical-realist narrative and practically engender cosmopolitan narrative, especially the fantastic. Avant-garde devices endowed these narratives with an imaginative dexterity, an uneasy perception of reality, and an emotional penetration, all to a much greater degree than before, while also imprinting on them a fractured worldview. One can assess regionalism's difficult adaptation to the new structures of the avant-garde novel by bearing in mind its adherence to a rigid rationalizing conception of reality, as would befit the offspring of nineteenth-century sociological and psychological currents, updated only minimally by the vitalist philosophies of the first decade of the twentieth century.

The strategic retreat into traditionalist cultural sources, also at the level of literary structure, provided its own solutions. Further retreat not only made the search for the regional novel's own literary mechanisms possible, it also made them adaptable to new circumstances, but still sufficiently resistant to modernizing erosion. The uniqueness of this solution consisted of a subtle opposition to modernizing proposals. Thus, narrative fragmentation, via the invasion of *stream of consciousness* in novelists from James Joyce to Virginia Woolf, was resisted through the reconstruction of very ancient genres. Thus, one can trace the sources of the discursive monologue (exercised in Guimarães Rosa's *Gran Sertão: Veredas*) not only back to classical literatures but to the lively oral sources of popular narration as well. Tales compartmentalized through the juxtaposition of loose pieces of narration, as in works by John Dos Pasos and Aldous Huxley, were resisted, for example, by the dispersed narrative flow of the *village women*, whose whispering voices are woven into the narrative of Juan Rulfo's *Pedro Páramo*. Both solutions are drawn from the recuperation of popular oral narrative structures. Perhaps the best example can be found in the problem encountered by García Márquez. In *Cien años de soledad*, he was forced to resolve stylistically the conjunction of historical verisimilitude with the marvelous, the plane on which the characters' point of view is situated. One must pay close attention to the author's explanation, which directs us to the oral sources of his narrative and, moreover, to the worldview governing his peculiar stylistic procedures, in his evocation of his aunt's manner of running her household:

> Once my aunt was sitting in the corridor embroidering when a girl came in with a very weird egg, a hen's egg with a lump on it. I don't know why this house was a sort of consultation room for all of the town's mysteries. Every time there was something nobody understood, they would go to my aunt's and ask her, and usually, this woman, my aunt had the answer. I was enchanted by the naturalness she had for resolving such things. Anyway, to get back to the girl with the egg, the girl says to her: "Look at this egg, why does it have a lump?" My aunt looks up at her and says: "Ah, it's because it is a basilisk's egg. Go light a good fire on the patio." So they lit the fire and burned the egg, all with great naturalness. That naturalness, I believe, gave me the key to *One Hundred Years of Solitude*, where the most horrendous, the most extraordinary things are all told deadpan, with the same straight face my aunt had when she told them to light the fire on the patio and burn the basilisk's egg. I never did find out what a basilisk was. (García Márquez and Vargas Llosa 1968, 15–16)

All things considered, there were very widespread literary losses at the level of narrative structure. A large part of the regionalist repertoire was lost and only survived in certain epigones and, curiously enough, in social narrative after 1930. These losses were occasionally replaced by the adoption of avant-garde narrative structures. García Márquez finds a well-aimed stylistic solution in *Cien años de soledad*, but also takes the inventions of Faulkner and Woolf and applies them to the series of alternate monologues in *La hojarasca*. However, such mimetic solutions did not yield an artistic dividend that would produce a return to literary structures from oral, nonwritten traditions, since the ones that were chosen had not been codified in the folkloric rule, but belonged rather, to older, albeit more hidden sources.

These two levels, language and narrative structure, acquired great importance in the Brazilian author João Guimarães Rosa, another of regionalism's followers and transformers. As Alfredo Bosi puts it: "Regionalism, which contributed some of the laxest forms of writing (the chronicle, the folkloric tale, the journalistic report), was destined to undergo a metamorphosis at the hands of this artist-demiurge that would return it to the center of Brazilian fiction" (1972, 481–82).

At these two levels, the literary operation is the same: a popular language and narrative system, deeply rooted in *Sertaneja* [inhabitant of the *sertão*, the arid Brazilian Northeast] life are Guimarães Rosa's point of departure. This is intensified by systematic investigation, which explains the retrieval of numerous archaic lexical items and the discovery of the varied points of view that the narrator employs to elaborate a text interpretive of a given reality. Both levels are projected onto a receiver-producer (Guimarães Rosa) who is the mediator between two disconnected cultural spheres: that of the regional heartlands and of the outside world. The mediating principle is inserted into the work itself: Riobaldo of *Gran Sertão: veredas* is both *jagunço* [rural Northeastern plantation owner's armed bodyguard; "hillbilly"] and lettered, a role that is likewise played by Grivo in *Carade-Bronze*, who takes the names of things to his shut-in master. The peculiar genre of Riobaldo's tale is designed here, in what Roberto Schwarz recognized as speech born of the interlocutor who promotes it (Guimarães Rosa 1965), or in what Miguel de Unamuno would have shrewdly defined as a monodialogue. This interlocutor never speaks, but without the shut in's existence the monologue could not take shape. Guimarães Rosa carries out the modernizing impulses we are familiar with through the use of "journalistic reports" in order to investigate a culture that is basically oral, not written. Throughout his works we have at our disposal his testimony on the methods of collecting information on and studying the language and the narrative forms of a cattle-raising culture. In 1947 his text "Entremeio: Com o vaqueiro Mariano" coincides with the publication of *Sagarana*. In 1962 he publishes "A Estória do Homen do Pinguelo," which also reconstructs the original scene of the rural informant who is being evaluated by the author, as he develops his story. In the 1947 text, Mariano's story about the oxen is under observation by an interlocutor who adds references to style and vocabulary ("He would think over for a moment before answering me in a colloquial mix of *guasca* and *mineiro* [dialects from Rio Grande du Sul and Minas Geráis, by implication backwoods]. Some very intense, different words open vast spaces where the real steals from the fictional"). The interlocutor finally recognizes that the narrative system itself constructs the persona, the character of the narrator. "Neither are the stories just let loose from the narrator, they create him, narration is resistance" (Guimarães Rosa 1969, 71 and 73–74). In other words, we can best witness the sustained resistance of a culture subjected to modernization at the higher level of narrative systems, in which we can detect homologous thought patterns, more than in the survival of a lexicon. As the interlocutor transcribes the message, he is simultaneously revealing the code in which it is developed. Neither part can be excised, as Bosi suggests, with supporting evidence from Lucien Sebag. The narrative system thus represents an effort at constructing a totality, within which disconnected and disperse forms of rural narration are recovered, but unified by a principle which is already prior to the impact of modernization. Thus, the impact itself has already undergone transculturation; that is, for it to be carried out at all, it had first to appeal to a traditional form of expression, spoken discourse, then extending it, in turn, homogeneously throughout the story. Walnice Nogueira Galvão has correctly observed that "speech is also a great stylistic unifier; it wipes out the multiplicity of narrative techniques: variations of the narrator's persona, letters, dialogues, other monologues—even the characters of the plot speak through Riobaldo's mouth" (1972, 70). From within the realm of speech, a higher unification operates by means of the insertion of a matrix, where the author adjusts his code to that of his narrator.

(c) *Worldview.* Yet a third and centrally important level of transculturing operations remains to be considered, that represented by a worldview, in turn engendering meanings. Works by the regionalists' "plastic" heirs provide the best examples, given that they come into being at the intimate point where values are rooted and ideologies arrayed. For this very reason, such works offer the greatest resistance to the changes brought by modernization's imposition of homogeneity to foreign models. As we have emphasized repeatedly, the period of modernization between the two world wars (referred to in Brazil as "modernism" but "avant-garde" in Spanish America) acts on the various literary tendencies, leaving a similar stamp on almost all of them, although in varying degrees of intensity. Of highest importance are their individual responses, which will determine their place in the multiplicity of Latin American cultures at the time.

The avant-garde halted the logical-rational discourse underlying literary operations, the consequence of their bourgeois origins in the nineteenth century. Three literary movements—the regional, the social and the critical-realist novels—had made use of such rationalist discourse, whether by means of a denotative referential language, or through the use of mechanical symbolic designs. The social novel remained tied to its didactic logic and preserved the bourgeois narrative model of the nineteenth century, but inverted its hierarchy of values in the development of an anti-bourgeois message. The critical-realist novel, amply represented by Juan Carlos Onetti, Graciliano Ramos, and Alejo Carpentier, took advantage of avant-garde's structural inspirations and, above all, its renovated writing. Aside from the regional novel's previously discussed response, the literary movement adapting most rapidly to the avant-garde's impact and developing under its impulse was, in fact, cosmopolitan narrative. This impact is best understood through its greatest interpreter, Jorge Luis Borges, and via the definition of his work put forward by René Etiemble. Several diverse currents, arising predominantly in Buenos Aires, are included in this tendency. One, the narrative of the fantastic, took advantage of the avant-garde's permeability to a plurality of meanings, due to its open construction as well as the underground, unconscious currents stimulating avant-garde writing. Julio Cortázar, its genuine representative, has observed that it can become rigid and logicistic, like the social novel (1970, 1 and 69–75). Another current is that which Jorge Rivera has preferred to call ambiguity, echoing José Bianco's work (1981, iv–vi), although many of Juan Carlos Onetti's texts would also fit this definition.

This is not the place to examine the causes, traits, and consequences of the European irrationalist movement that pervaded the many areas of intellectual activity. Irrationalism materialized in philosophical and political thinking, which explains its condemnation by György Lukács in his book *The Destruction of Reason*. The irrationalist movement shaped centers of artistic renovation, which included German expressionism, French surrealism, and Italian futurism, reaching its high point with the dadaists. The irrationalist movement also pervaded philosophies of life and the divergent paths of existentialism. Even those currents diametrically opposed to it, such as anthropology or psychoanalysis, made contributions useful to those who rejected reason. From these contributions, none is more intensely incorporated into contemporary culture than a new conception of myth, which, in some expressions, seemed to substitute for the deep crisis of religions in the nineteenth century. Using revisionist texts from English anthropology (Edward Taylor, James Frazer) as a point of departure, this conception of myth was taken up by the psychoanalysts of the twentieth century (Sigmund Freud, Otto Rank, Sándor Ferenczi, Carl Jung), as well as by scholars of religion (Georges Dumézil, Mircea Eliade). In fact, myth inundated the twentieth century. Circa 1962,

Mircea Eliade registered the change that has come about "in the last fifty years" in the viewpoint of scholars: "Unlike their predecessors, who treated myth in the traditional sense of the word, as 'fable,' 'invention,' 'fiction,' scholars now have accepted myth as it was understood in ancient societies. There, 'myth' means a 'true story' and, beyond that, a story that is a most precious possession because it is sacred, exemplary, significant" (1963, 1).

Among the most authoritative centers to re-establish this conception of myth and rediscover its intensive action on rationalized societies were the Germany of the philosopher Ernst Cassirer prior to Hitler's rise and the France of Lucien Lévy-Bruhl. Lévy-Bruhl's *La mentalité primitive* (1922) was the authoritative text on the subject and had provided a theoretical basis for the development of its contemporary, surrealism, until coming under the scrutiny of the structural anthropologist Claude Lévi-Strauss. Throughout the Spanish American community residing in Europe between the two world wars (our own "lost generation") and through the influence of Spanish intellectual circles (*Revista de Occidente*), this novel "object" of internationalized culture migrated to Latin America. This dissemination occurred, more than likely, with much greater rapidity than that supposed by Pierre Chaunu, who cites multiple examples of Latin American "backwardness" with respect to European inventions:

> Another sign of this long intellectual displacement: The conquest of principal Spanish American universities—Mexico and Buenos Aires —between 1940 and 1950, by German philosophical currents from the early decades of the twentieth century. At a superficial level, this is a consequence of the Spanish Republican diaspora throughout America. Its cadres from the petit and middle bourgeoisie, like José Ortega y Gasset, drank from the fountains of early twentieth century German philosophy as a reaction against the upper middle classes and French-ified aristocracy. (1964, 43)

Chaunu, in fact, refers to translations from the German published by the Fondo de Cultura Económica and to the incorporation of idealist stylistics (Karl Vossler, Leo Spitzer), which coincided with the introduction of French thought and surrealist art. Various authors, including Miguel Angel Asturias, Alejo Carpentier, and Jorge Luis Borges, adopted French mythic postulates as their own. Their exploration can be found mirrored in Cortázar's early essays, especially "Para una poética" from 1954. Myths uniquely mixed with sociological models in Asturias's work and archetypes in Carpentier's appeared as valid categories for interpreting

Latin America's distinctiveness. But even the very candid and decided appeal to the surviving popular beliefs of American indigenous and African communities on the part of these authors could not hide the appeal's origin and intellectual foundation in the European interpretive systems applied to such popular beliefs. Part of magical realism's equivocations arise from this dual source (an internal subject matter, an external signification) to such an extent that the greatest coherency achieved in Jorge Luis Borges's literature springs from its frank establishment in a cosmopolitan and worldly perspective. From the time of *Tlön, Uqbar, Tertius Orbis* (1938) on, "myth" became a bibliographic dream created from the books of the Library of Babel. In this conceptualization, Western thought is turned symmetrically on its head, as Max Horkheimer and Theodor Adorno had noted. That is, they observed the transmutation of Enlightenment into myth within the irrationalism dominating the twentieth century, thus recovering or reintegrating the original transmutation of myth into Enlightenment as the fulcrum of bourgeois civilization.

The deculturation furthered by the incorporation of this ideological corpus into regional cultures would be a violent one. Paradoxically, incorporation also served to open channels of enrichment. The regional novel's literary discourse responded basically to the cognitive structures of the European bourgeoisie. For this reason, with respect to the subject matter it developed, the discourse worked at the same distance from its subject matter as that of the narrator's educated language in relation to the characters' popular tongue. This linguistic discrepancy replicated the discrepancy between the novel's discursive structure and its content. In both cases, a distorting imposition was exercised. With the interdiction on logical-rational discourse in effect, the regionalists retreat again into local, nutritive sources and begin an exploration of the culture and its traditional practices. In their search for feedback and survival, the regionalists will draw permanent, validating resources from their cultural heritage.

This strategic retreat re-establishes a fertile contact with living sources, the inextinguishable foundations of mythic invention occurring in all human societies, but more actively so in rural communities. There is a re-discovery of energies, which until then had been held in check by regionalism's narrative systems. Recognition of the latent possibilities of popular speech and narrative structures also occurs. There is, as well, explicit recognition of a dispersed universe, of free association, of the unceasing invention of particular ambiguity and oscillation in the correlation between ideas and things. These had always existed but had been hidden by the strict literary formulas espoused in positivistic scientific and sociological thinking. To the extent that this mode of thought was unable to value a protoplasmic, discursive imaginary tied to an immediate reality sustaining oppositional models, it had been imposed rigidly on apparently erratic materials and forced them to fit into the systematic logic laid out by Spencer, Comte, or Taine. The fracturing of this logical system releases the real material belonging to the internal cultures of Latin America and permits its appreciation in other dimensions.

The sentence that Riobaldo uses to reflect on the *sertanejo* world captures the oscillation on which the novel is based: "The *sertão* is like that, you know: everything uncertain, everything certain" (Guimarães Rosa 1971, 132). The extraordinary fluidity and the constant displacement of lives and events, the transmutations of existence and the insecurity of values, will weave an underlying layer over which the interpretive discourse will be unfolded. Similarly, in Rulfo's "La cuesta de las comadres," the character's oscillating discourse is constructed upon the dispersion and contradiction of its constituent elements. In both cases, the narrator becomes the mediator who works on dispersion and constructs an equally problematic meaning. The construction of the story is reproduced by that of its discourse in such a way that plot structure equals narrative form. Benedito Nunes has seen these two superimposed movements in *Cara-de-bronze* and has perceived in the mediating function one of myth's characteristic roles: "The work's bifocal vision is attuned to the ambiguous and mediating nature of Grivo, a character who at heart is the figure of the mythic Child, one of the archetypes of the sacred, which dominates the work of Guimarães Rosa, beyond other important incarnations" (1969, 185). In this short novel the correlation between the two planes is glaring, given that the subject matter is the search for expression. But Walnice Nogueira also observes this about *Gran sertão: veredas*, bringing together the work's two leitmotifs: "Living is a very dangerous business," and "Telling something is a very, very difficult business" (Nogueira 1972, 80; Guimarães Rosa 1971, 19 and 154).

For that reason, the transculturators will discover something even more complex than myth. While the cosmopolitan narrative of the time revises literary forms in which myth has been consolidated and, in light of contemporary irrationalism, submits it to new refractions and broad universal scenarios, the transculturators facilitate the expansion of new mythic tales, removing them from their ambiguous and powerful background as precise and enigmatic creations. There is nothing more useless than trying to fit the stories of Comala into the established mold of Greco-Latin mythologies. Undoubtedly, these models are unceasingly rubbed up against or, better yet, muddied by Rulfo's inventions, but the significance of these inventions lies outside that realm; they spring from other flames and seek other dangers. These models work themselves loose from an unknown cultural background which conscious methods can only manage awkwardly.[9]

Even more important than the recuperation of these constantly emerging cognitive structures will be the inquiry into the mental mechanisms that generate myth, the rise toward the operations determining them. We find in the paradigmatic example of José María Arguedas, an anthropologist who collected and studied indigenous myths, that second level, in which not only the novel's narrator but the author himself constructs from these operations, works upon both traditional indigenous materials and Western modernized ones, indiscriminately associated, in an exercise of "mythic thinking."

Thus, the response to deculturation, which at the level of worldview and the discovery of meanings is promoted by avant-garde irrationalism, is only apparently homologous to the modernizing proposal. In truth, such a response overcomes modernization with unexpected intensity, with a breadth that few modern writers were capable of achieving. "Mythic thinking" will oppose the use of "literary myths."

At each and any of these three levels—languages, literary structure, worldview—one can see that the products resulting from the cultural contact with modernization cannot be assimilated either into the urban creations of the cosmopolitan area or into an earlier form of regionalism. One perceives that the inventions of the transculturators were widely facilitated by the existence of cultural structures the continent had attained after long processes of appropriation and adaptation. The direct contact between regional cultures and modernization would probably have been fatal for the former, given the abysmal distance between them, as in the dialectics between *indigenismo* and Europeanism, for example. Mediation was supplied by that cultural configuration which had managed to impose itself after secular efforts at accumulation and reworking. In Brazil's case, an organic national culture took shape; Spanish America, for its part, develops a fruitful intercommunication between diverse areas. Thus, the dialogue between regionalists and modernists was carried out across a broad literary system, a field of functional and self-regulated integration and mediation. This preparation, the laying of the groundwork for the construction of a common Spanish American literary system is, then, modernization's greatest contribution to the field of Latin American letters.

Translated by Christine McIntyre

Notes

Translator's additions appear in the text in brackets.

1. W. Jackson Bate has studied this issue in Anglophone literature in *The Burden of the Past and the English poet* (1970)

2. Vittorio Lanternari sees in this modernizing impact a factor of cultural disintegration: "A third factor of cultural disintegration depends on the dependent countries' process of modernization and can interfere with the process of urbanization and migration. As L. Wirht has pointed out about many societies, the sacrifice of its cultural integrity appears as a heavy tribute paid to progress. The sociological process is parallel to that of urbanization" (1966, 126). On the urban inflection of the process, see Ralph Beals: "Urbanism, urbanization and acculturation" (1951).

3. The three categories are elaborated by Lanternari, who adds: "In the innumerable cases of acculturation based on 'cultural plasticity,' the elements of crisis and disintegration are closely associated, in reality, to the elements that express or orient reintegration" (1966, 123).

4. Out of the initial problems of definition arose the "Memorandum for the Study of Acculturation," by Redfield, Linton, and Herskovits (1936, 33–36). An expansion and systematization can be found in Melville Herskovits (1938). Outside the anthropologic angle and within the philosophic tendency of German inspiration, see José Luis Romero's essay, *Bases para una morfología de los contactos culturales* (1944).

5. Malinowski says: "It is a process in which both parts of the equation are modified, a process from which a new reality emerges, transformed and complex, a reality that is not a mechanical agglomeration of traits, nor even a mosaic, but a new phenomenon, original and independent" (Ortiz 1947, xi). Ralph Beals has observed in his article "Acculturation," in A. L. Kroeber's *Anthropology Today* (1959), that Malinowski did not apply the Cuban anthropologist's concept in any of his later works.

6. A discussion of terms can be found in Gonzalo Aguirre Beltrán's *El Proceso de acul- turación* (1957). He concludes with this synthesis: "Coming back to our term: *ad- culturation* indicates union or *cultural contact*; *ab-culturation*, separation or rejection of cultures; and *trans-culturation*, the passage from one culture to another." We prefer the term *transculturation* precisely because of this definition. Beyond the arguments which Ortiz puts forward and which pertain to habitual mechanisms of linguistic determination, his felicity of expression speaks in favor of this proposition. Ortiz's sensibility to the spirit of the language makes of his books a creative linguistic experience, unlike that which occurs in many Hispano-American anthropological and sociological texts.

7. The speech, entitled "Yo no soy un aculturado," was included at the author's request as an epilogue to his posthumous and unfinished novel, *El zorro de arriba y el zorro de abajo* (1971).

8. Angel Rosenblat, "Lengua literaria y lengua popular en América" (1969), in *Sentido mágico de la palabra*. See chapter 4, "La novela social del siglo XX" (1977, 191–98).

9. Carlos Monsiváis observes this about the case of Rulfo's narrative in his essay, "Sí, tampoco los muertos retoñan. Desgraciadamente" (1980, 35–36).

Foundations

Introduction by Ana Del Sarto

THE 1980S: FOUNDATIONS OF
LATIN AMERICAN CULTURAL STUDIES

Since the middle of the twentieth century in Latin America there has been a shared belief—which reached its zenith in the 1960s and its nadir in the 1980s—that economic modernization and cultural modernism would enhance political democracy and social equality. This would allow citizens to experience modernity, that paradoxical "unity of disunity" (Berman 1982) so dearly desired by the majority of Latin Americans. According to Néstor García Canclini, the experience of modernity would boost four basic projects: emancipation, expansion, renovation, and democratization (1989a, 31). In Latin America, the intersection of these projects and their diverse formulations had generated contradictions perceived by many as doomed to failure from the very beginning: "democracy and social justice are not an easy combination." The successive implementation of different socioeconomic projects of modernization, either based on industrialization, import substitution, and developmentalist capitalism, or on a socialist system—all of which were unable to break the yoke of dependency—set the stage for present and future conflicts.

Ashes on the Hearth

From the very first decades of the twentieth century a new social formation started to take shape: mass society. This amorphous and ubiquitous phenomenon radically transformed the urban landscape as well as the real and imaginary ways in which they were lived. According to the cultural historian José L. Romero, the Great Depression "visibly unified the destiny of Latin America" (1999, 385) as far as mass society penetrated and renovated the cities and their inhabitants. In response to these transformations and as a way out of the hegemonic vacuum, different populist movements emerged during the 1930s that used the power of the state in order to incorporate this new collective subject (the masses) into national political life. It is true that populism instrumentalized "the masses" through a nationalistic, chauvinistic, and paternalistic discourse, but it is also true that for the first time large sectors of the population were given a more visible space within national life.

During the 1950s, in the context of the Cold War, the entrance of new technologies and communications systems—radio, cinema, and, especially, television—produced "revolutionary" transformations in urban society and popular cultures (see Rockefeller Report 1969). The acknowledgment of "the masses" as a social construct produced a dual interpretation, both equally disapproving: on the one hand, media and mass culture—understood as ideological apparatuses of power—generated a homogeneous and homogenizing space of recognition through which popular needs and tastes were molded; and, on the other hand, through mass media the "popular masses" expressed not only their deep desires of modernization, set according to the standards advanced by the culture industry, but also their characteristic inertia and anachronisms. Unquestionably, most Latin American nations were undergoing noteworthy, although uneven, processes of social democratization, despite obvious, sometimes blatant, exclusions and marginalizations. Citizens (according to the times, more men than women, more mestizo than criollo) were participating in and being responsible for the making of the present. In the 1960s and early 1970s, social, economic, political, and cultural contradictions reached new levels, thus thickening the social texture and producing tense political confrontations in which optimistic and utopian energies were invested. However, a retrospective critical reading of these sociopolitical and cultural radicalizations will not leave us with a sense of fulfilled justice; on the contrary, violence, terror, repression, and, many times, death drenched the whole scene.

The writings of Antonio Candido, Darcy Ribeiro, Roberto Fernández Retamar, Angel Rama, and Antonio Cornejo Polar, inspired by an overt intent of political intervention, envisioned many of these ambiguous and disguised sociopolitical and cultural transformations. Their moment was one of exploration, of opening new horizons: an effervescent euphoria which crystallized a period of intense cultural creation. These intellectuals felt as if they were experiencing the beginning of an epoch, as if they were the agents of a realized utopia. Their texts were imbued by that general feeling of modernizing and revolutionary optimism—though many times engulfed in sheer voluntarism. After the heyday of the national populisms, these were the times of fervent social and economic developmentalism, the optimistic modernization of politics, and the internationalization of national cultures. However, this keen sense of historical updating would soon be under fire and stumble upon its own limits: a worsening of economic exploitation, sociopolitical oppression, ethnic, racial, and gender discrimination, and outright commodification of cultures. It was, in a word, the beginnings of neoliberalism and globalization. Paradoxically, while it was the beginning of an epoch, it was not exactly the one radical intellectuals had envisioned.

From the North came the hegemony of mass culture, corporate consumer society, and "free market" ideology; from the South, military dictatorships based upon the not so national Doctrine of National Security, the ideological ground for the implementation of a dominant system of terror capable of adjusting national economies to the changes experienced under transnational capitalism, and whose most grotesque example could be the "Operación Cóndor," a truly transnational enterprise of disappearing coordinated by national armies. From Río Grande to Tierra del Fuego, the execution of similar strategies melted down all radical utopias. At the end of the 1980s, those utopian desires had been crushed into pieces and given way to new sensibilities at the crossroads, imbued by skepticism, pessimism, and cynicism.

At this precise moment, Latin American cultural studies were reconverted at the convergence of several strategies trying to account for the spread of global capitalism, the pervasiveness of the "American way of life," and the defeats of leftist projects, while trying to reconfigure the libidinal dialectic between the retraction of optimism and the substantiation of pessimism. The most important feedback of these intense and multiple affective interactions was the appearance of new ways of understanding, questioning, and creating objects of study, as well as experiencing modernity within peripheral, heterogeneous, and neocolonial countries instilled by postmodern discourses.

If optimism was the generalized feeling of the 1960s and early 1970s, shared by great numbers of Latin Americans, the numbing perplexity and pessimistic sensibility of the 1980s, filtered through the spectralization of neoliberalism, became a symptom of historical failure at the hands of intellectuals who had been brought up within that optimistic environment that was now vanishing. The dramatic, though blurred dividing line between these two quasi-antithetical sensibilities is definitively over-determined by a complex and multifarious crisis of capitalism, which to paraphrase Fredric Jameson, initiates its transit from the monopolistic or imperialist phase based on Fordist industrialism to its transnational or globalized phase driven by post-Fordist finance capital.

With regard to Latin America, the dominant powers erected diverse obstacles to limit the continual widening of democracy and social justice; different means were used to disarticulate hope, replacing it with the glit-ter of globalization: deregulation of markets and flexibilization of capital and labor, privatization of the public sphere, ideology of the obsoles-cence of the state, expansion of the culture industry and its most valued offshoot, mass culture. A genealogical arch could be traced by uniting six dissimilar but equally forceful historical instances that triggered and summarized in only two decades all the aforementioned side effects: from the elimination of the gold exchange standard, which freed the U.S. dollar in 1971, to the coordinated inception of authoritarian regimes throughout Latin America in the early 1970s to counteract the spread of national-socialist movements, the end of the Central American conflicts (Esquipulas II) and the Latin American debt crisis of the 1980s, the fall of the Berlin Wall in 1989, and the Gulf War in 1990. When seen in perspec-tive, these not-so-distant events, ultimately, provide a dual, not at all re-demptive, illumination: on the one hand, it sheds light back on the roots of what has been called the "lost decade" within Latin America; on the other hand, it elucidates onward the new "nature" of the global hege-monic system at the end of the millennium.

By the end of the 1980s, a consensus among intellectuals and academ-ics was reached: the world had ineluctably changed and the available epistemological macro-narratives of the 1960s, including heterodox Marxian approaches, like dependency theory or the various branches of structuralism, were inadequate to understand and impotent to transform those changing realities. How did those intellectuals work in the 1980s through the decomposition of the utopian imaginary of the 1960s? How did they imagine new horizons and new critical paradigms at those times of uncertainty? Jean Franco, Carlos Monsiváis, Beatriz Sarlo, Nelly Rich-ard, Roberto Schwarz, Silviano Santiago, Renato Ortiz, Walter Mignolo, José J. Brunner, Jesús Martín-Barbero, and Néstor García Canclini, among many others, began to revise the old theoretical models and to reformulate lines of research and methodology, in order to interpret and explain a rapidly changing reality that was constantly spinning upon itself. These intellectuals contributed to the reshaping of the main cogni-tive constellations of Latin American cultural studies (i.e., neocolonialism, modernity and modernization, the national question, the popular, identities, alterities, and ethnicities) by critically reinventing their positions, by imaginatively reconceptualizing their approaches and methodologies, and creatively mixing and re-articulating heterogeneous concepts and theories, yet always in dialogue with the long tradition of Latin American critical thought as well as with contemporary sociopolitical and cultural contexts of intervention.

That is to say that while this group of intellectuals set the actual foundations of contemporary Latin American cultural studies by venturing into new epistemological paths, they did so by renovating a long tradition of critical thinking intimately connected to sociohistorical circumstances. In other words, if Latin American cultural studies constitute a critical-epistemic field inserted in a global scenario, it cannot be fully explained let alone adequately practiced without taking into consideration their historical anchorage in Latin American sociopolitical materiality and geocultural processes. Against what has been repeatedly sustained, Latin American cultural studies are not the product of epistemological ruptures but instead of concrete historical continuities. In a word, Latin American cultural studies cannot be conceived as a mere subdivision of British or U.S. cultural studies, or an effect or a symptom of globalization, or a blatant imposition of the transnational theoretical market, or a bringing up-to-date of the "post," without running the risk of amputating its sharpness. Because, even when they operate within the framework of and in response to globalization, Latin American cultural studies are imbued with a cluster of methodologies, critical and theoretical paradigms, and cognitive constellations forged at different moments in the intricate trajectory of Latin American cultural criticism and thought. To critically recover and reconfigure said thought is today an epistemologically verifiable political need. This could be the end of the Latin American cultural studies fashion show, but the analysis, reflection, and criticism of culture in and on Latin America will continue, no matter under what name.

Coming from traditional quarters, either from the human disciplines (literary criticism, history, philosophy) or from the social sciences (sociology, anthropology, political science, communications), many intellectuals dedicated to the study of Latin American issues kept crossing disciplinary boundaries, displacing their research strategies and producing new topics and a heterogeneous amalgamation of methodologies with which they approach the changing world. Even though in the past they had denied legitimacy to the universal (anti?)discipline of cultural studies, they acknowledge today, with certain hesitancy, that what they have been doing all along is some sort of cultural studies. That is the case of García Canclini, who in a questionnaire-interview of the *Journal of Latin American Cultural Studies*, says: "I became involved in cultural studies before I realized this is what it is called" (1996, 84); or Sarlo, who, responding to the same question, affirms: "I thought I was doing the history of ideas" (1997a, 87); or Martín-Barbero, who proclaims: "I did not start talking about culture because I receive stuff from abroad. . . . We had practiced cultural studies a long time before that label appeared" (1997, 52).

Despite this resistance toward cultural studies, since the early 1970s two of our most prominent pioneers, Franco and Monsiváis, had already been involved in the study and criticism of the intricate and sometimes ambiguous relations between elite, popular, and mass culture, on one hand, and between local, regional, and international culture, on the other hand. Their works are the most fecund testimony of these initial transformations. While both Franco and Monsiváis could be listed in the previous section among the forerunners, precisely because of their pioneering work, they nevertheless articulate the transition toward the actual foundation of Latin American cultural studies.

On the wave of this transition, Martín-Barbero and García Canclini, two of the most outspoken advocates of Latin American cultural studies, acknowledged not only the imperative need to "remake the map of our 'basic concepts,'" but also the difficult challenge implied by "the task of constructing a more widely accepted theoretical model and a coherent set of research strategies" (see their essays in "Foundations"). In order to "understand the unexplored areas of reality" traditionally considered as "depoliticized, irrelevant, and insignificant," but also with the purpose of questioning the classical views on the ideological manipulation of media cultural productions, Martín-Barbero's essay analyzes the repressed aspects of media productions, such as their mediations, "the cracks in domination, the consumption dimensions of economy, and the pleasures of life." Urged by the need to "move beyond the culturalist and reproductionist interpretations," Martín-Barbero borrows from García Canclini his broadening of Pierre Bourdieu's conception of consumption and from Sarlo her elaboration of the interpretative reading of H. Robert Jauss and the reception theory of W. Iser. Rearticulating those concepts in the framework of the processes of communication and inscribing them in the Latin American context, Martín-Barbero displaces the central focus on cultural production for the analysis of creative resistance in consumption and daily practices. In *De los medios a las mediaciones. Comunicación, cultura, y hegemonía* (1987a) he celebrates the productive and liberating potential of the fissures and gaps opened by a wide range of uses and appropriations, and in a Benjaminian turn, their uneasy mediation in the configuration of a new, "plebeian" sensorium.

In his "Cultural Studies from the 1980s to the 1990s" in this volume, García Canclini critically gauges the experimental pursuits that juggled around the traditional boundaries of the disciplines to interrelate their produced knowledge. He tries to epistemologically redeploy the transdisciplinary study of cultural processes in order to "understand why in Latin America we are this mixture of heterogeneous memories and truncated innovations." Ultimately, García Canclini asserts that even though there is "a thematic inertia within each discipline" (sociology concentrated on the processes of modernization; anthropology and ethnology studying rituals, traditions, and ethnic cultural differences; the humanities devoted to the symbolic and imaginary worlds), a "precarious map of trends and main questions" will allow us to imagine the horizon of Latin American cultural studies (see García Canclini in "Foundations").

A series of crucial publications on Latin America constitute and propagate an enduring set of practices which, named Latin American cultural studies or otherwise, was already widespread: from Franco's *The Modern Culture of Latin America* (1967) to *Plotting Women* (1989) and *Marcar diferencias, cruzar fronteras* (1996c) to *The Decline and Fall of the Lettered City* (2002); from Monsiváis's *Días de guardar* (1970) to *Los rituales del caos* (1995) and *Aires de familia* (2000); from Sarlo's *Una modernidad periférica* (1989) to *Escenas de la vida posmoderna* (1994) and *Tiempo presente* (2001); from García Canclini's *Culturas híbridas* (1989a) to *La globalización imaginada* (1999b); from Richard's *La estratificación de los márgenes* (1989b) to *Residuos y metáforas* (1998a); from Mignolo's *Elementos para una teoría del texto literario* (1978) to *Teoría del texto e interpretación de textos* (1986) to *The Darker Side of the Renaissance* (1995) and *Local Histories/Global Designs* (2000); from Brunner's *El espejo trizado* (1988) to *Globalización cultural y posmodernidad* (1998); from Martín-Barbero's *De los medios a las mediaciones* (1987a) to *Al sur de la modernidad* (2001). Although most of them departed from the political urgency of their respective "national," "regional," or "local" cultures, all of these intellectuals, in one way or another, were questioning the "new" global order.

In this sense, the configuration of Latin American cultural studies as a dialogical intellectual space could be perceived as another byproduct of globalization and transnational capitalism; however, this should not lead us to conclude, in an abstract and simplified homology, that if the emergence of Latin American cultural studies goes hand-in-hand with globalization, neoliberalism, and transnational capitalism, then they only replicate, even when in resistance or in opposition to it, the nature of that very same order. We know that resistance or opposition to a certain order presupposes and shares, even for its mere existence, the conditions of possibility of that very same order. Perhaps one way to escape this double bounded binary rationality is to historically examine in the larger picture how and why in Latin America the cultural dimension has become the paramount field of struggle for the resolution of sociopolitical and ideological conflicts.

Probably, at the beginning of the twentieth-first century, the answer to this question could lack epistemological validity, since culture has always been, at least from the early nineteenth century, an openly sociopolitical realm. Nonetheless, during the 1980s, deep changes have projected "culture" to the forefront of sociopolitical events: the boundaries of the Latin American nations were internally disrupted and disputed by the sprouting of new social movements; the nation-states, now in ruins, did not have enough legitimacy to mediate between different social groups and classes; political parties were completely corrupted or disarticulated; and the overwhelming power of the media and the commodification of culture at a global scale established the market (and consumption) as the leading mechanism of social control and cultural integration. In a word, there was a double and paradoxical movement: on the one hand, the social overflowed society, opening up new ways of doing politics through culture; on the other hand, the transnational corporations in control of technology and the global markets set the rules within which culture ought to be conceived and practiced.

Amid Affiliations and Infidelities

In this section, I will consider the entangled crossing of relevant exogenous sources, currents of thought, and underlined influences eclectically translated, appropriated, and adapted to Latin America, whose complex cultural history has been intricately interconnected to the transformations triggered by Western powers since colonization. The influence of continental European thought—Spanish, French, British, or German, depending on the geopolitical and intellectual flows—went uncontested for many centuries and constituted the parameters along which American intellectual imaginaries were molded. As a consequence, Latin American cultural imaginary was multifariously embedded as a vicarious appendix mediated by "universal" culture, or better yet, as a colonized space which made possible the entire project of Western modern civilization.

It is worth mentioning that within Latin America one of the strategies unconsciously implemented to contain "total colonialism" was to disjoint the economic and the cultural predominance, acknowledging the influence of competing imperialist powers in each of them. While the United Kingdom and afterward the United States ruled the economic sphere, different aesthetic and philosophical French schools of thought —from rationalism and symbolism to existentialism and structuralism —predominated all along with an uncontested aura.

Nevertheless, significant events would completely modify the configuration of the modern–world system as well as the tides of hegemonic ideas circulating around the world. On the one hand, from its territorial expansion in the nineteenth century to its early imperial adventures at the beginning of the twentieth century, the United States accumulated so much military, economic, and political power that after World War II it simply became the uncontested leader of the capitalist world, enmeshed in a ferocious cold war against socialism. The United States, leader of the "free world," would establish its hegemony on the heels of its powerful corporate capitalism and the internationalization of its industrial pop culture. On the other hand, thwarting and resisting this incontrovertible force, the Latin American intellectual productions of the 1960s, obviously permeated by the apogee of French structuralism (Ferdinand de Saussure, Claude Lévi-Strauss, Louis Althusser, Nicolas Poulantzas, and Roland Barthes), would eclectically integrate the renewed influence of the Frankfurt school (Max Horkheimer, Theodor Adorno, and Herbert Marcuse), the emerging semiotic field (Tartu school, Italian semiotics, and French semiology), and the first poststructuralist questionings (Michel Foucault, Julia Kristeva, Jacques Derrida, and Jean Baudrillard) with the transgressive power of the rock revolution and the Beatlemania that conquered the world.

It is not by chance that cultural studies emerged in the United Kingdom right after the international system had shifted its axis of power to the United States. In other words, it is not by accident that it appeared within the context of a decadent empire resisting the invasion of an industrial pop culture born out of the emergent power. The post–World War II transformation of the international system crystallized in the early 1960s, leaving Latin America as a neocolonial region submitted to the influence of the new imperial superpower and the more complex and subtler strategies of transnational finance capitalism and media pop culture.

Undoubtedly, Anglo-Saxon cultural studies, from its origins in the 1960s to its celebrity of the 1990s, accompanies and responds to the processes of technological revolution, the expansion and flexibilization of capital, and the general reorientation of the world economy, commonly referred to in the 1990s as globalization. However, is there any cultural practice or critical discourse that could claim not to be contaminated by globalization? Even though cultural studies echo the cultural logic of transnational capitalism, or precisely because of it, their practice exceeds, problematizes, and questions that very same logic, while staging its convoluted cultural and social conflictivity. Nevertheless, I insist, Latin American cultural studies do not originate as replica, translation, or acclimatization of British or U.S. cultural studies; Latin American cultural studies acquired their consistency in the intersection of diverse traditions of Latin American critical thinking and the self-reflexive postmodern irony at a time when globalization reached Latin America in a qualitatively superior degree. They constitute, in that sense, a hermeneutic response and a critique to globalization that tries to account for neoliberalism, the substitution of the partisan mode of doing politics by the mass media and consumptive model of democracy, and the added value of the cultural in social and political daily life as a consequence of the centrality acquired by the symbolic in the wave of the communications revolution and the predominance of finance capitalism. There are two important consequences that add to these transformations: first, while the symbolic acquires a predominant role in the market, many cultural practices become mere commodities, thus losing their critical edge and transgressive value; second, the shifts and juxtapositions between the realms of politics and culture provoked ideological confrontations that range within the extremes of market neopopulists, who celebrate culture as the new space of freedom, thus minimizing politics as a purely administrative or managerial activity, and those who clearly differentiate the nature of both realms and try to rearticulate them while safeguarding their respective dynamics.

It is not my purpose here to retell the story of British cultural studies as a new critical paradigm. Many authors, from different geopolitical positions, have done so (see Dworkin 1997; Easthope 1991; Grossberg, Nelson, and Treichel 1992; During 1993; McRobbie 1994; Grossberg 1997). Moreover, it would be easy to demonstrate that a direct influence of British cultural studies on Latin American cultural studies is tenuous and, in particular, localized to the works of very few intellectuals, like Jean Franco and Beatriz Sarlo. Franco's position, for instance, is clear enough because of her British origin, formal training, and academic career.[1] Sarlo's position is interesting because of its exceptionality: the works of Raymond Williams, Richard Hoggart, and E. P. Thompson were introduced, albeit not as paladins of cultural studies per se, to an Argentine small intellectual cluster, "at that time relatively young and coming from the revolutionary left that were instinctually perceiving the horizon of cultural studies" (Sarlo 2000, 309). This group met around Jaime Rest, himself a specialist in English literature and a voracious reader of Williams, Hoggart, and Thompson. Later on, these intellectuals (among whom Sarlo and Carlos Altamirano are the most well known today) would be reunited in the oppositional cultural journal *Punto de vista* (Sarlo 2000). Therefore, instead of assessing the diffuse and eclectic influences British cultural studies may have had on the configuration of Latin American cultural studies during the second half of the 1980s, I will point out several characteristics of the British project relevant to the project delimited by this book.

According to Raymond Williams, "The relation between a project and its formation is always decisive, and . . . the emphasis of Cultural Studies is precisely that it engages with both [project and social formation]. . . . This was the crucial theoretical invention that was made: the refusal to give priority to either the project or the formation—or in older terms, the art or the society" (1989, 151–52). This affirmation probably could have been true for the Great Britain of the 1960s, where British cultural studies first emerged and promptly became institutionalized, though para-academically, in 1964 in the Center for Contemporary Cultural Studies (CCCS) at Birmingham University. Under the auspices of some intellectuals—Williams and Hoggart (literary critics) and Thompson (a historian)—this project gained consistency through two related nodal claims: first, the internal critique of traditional British high culture (and Britishness) through the vindication of the British proletarian culture (what they would call "the popular") as a source of resistance to the invasion of the "degrading" pop culture produced by the culture industry; second, their uneasiness with orthodox Marxism, deemed theoretically inadequate to further cultural critique.

What is of interest to convene my argument (and thus to compare it to the milieu in which Latin American cultural studies emerged) is that British cultural studies was a response, articulated from the locus of a decadent empire being neocolonized by its own ex-colony, to the process of its own cultural decline. In this sense, the emergence of cultural studies in the United Kingdom could be interpreted as the symptom of that particular trauma. As a response, it had a double purpose: on the one hand, it vied to renovate the fossilized power configurations of the archaic high culture, which had enmeshed them in this particular situation; on the other hand, it strived to resist the increasing commodification of culture, which was cornering, bypassing, or excluding the very live social forces (the British lower classes) that constituted the core of any possible national, popular culture.

It is quite obvious that the United Kingdom of the 1960s was very different from the Latin America of the 1980s, in regard to their respective economic development, social fabrics, ethnic compositions, cultural traditions, and geopolitical situations in the international arena. For this very same reason, the two nuclei around which British cultural studies was born as a project cannot be lightly transposed to Latin America. However, there are several sociohistorical circumstances common to both: the disarticulation of their national economies due to an international capitalist crisis, the expansive effect of U.S. pop culture, the degraded transformation of "the popular" and/or popular cultures into mass pop culture (exotic and primitive cultures ready to be folklorized), the defeat of various political and cultural projects of the left, the progressive turn to neoliberalism finally heralded by Margaret Thatcher and Ronald Reagan, and the first signs of globalization.

During the 1970s and the beginnings of the 1980s, poststructuralism and deconstruction had widely swayed the humanities and social sciences around the world, shifting their approaches and methodologies. Accompanying the globalization processes, by the end of the 1980s, British cultural studies simultaneously reached the United States and Latin America as a transdisciplinary project parallel to postmodernist discourses. Its arrival and diffusion into intellectual and academic spaces had disparate receptions, divergent agendas, and dissimilar articulations among those recipients, mainly because of the incongruent cultural configurations, the contrasting socioeconomic problematics, and the uneven influences of thinking traditions and cultural practices within each of those contexts.

Regarding the "unprecedented boom" of cultural studies within the United States, I want to emphasize that even when cultural studies were stoutly resisted by the conservative clique of the status quo within the U.S. academia, at its beginnings the progressive liberal camp welcomed and celebrated them. Despite this initial clash, after having demonstrated its enormously ambiguous and cooptative potential, cultural studies were integrated and rapidly constituted a "new," "politically correct" (inter- and trans-)discipline, which was cherishingly housed by many communications, English, comparative literature, and other departments from the humanities and the social sciences. But concomitant to the U.S. institutionalization of cultural studies , the direct influence of the British project lost its political edge. This depoliticization, on the one hand, has served the interests of those wishing to preserve the order even when its façade might have changed; on the other, it has triggered a critique from the Marxist left because of its acritical celebration of resistant consumption and the substitution of the central concept of class by other equally ideological categories, like race, gender, and ethnicity. Therefore, the conflation of cultural studies and postmodernism, primarily concentrated in the humanities where they hastily became hegemonic, produced a clear reconversion in two interrelated aspects. On the one hand, cultural studies appropriated and extended the concept of semiotic text, originally formulated regarding different kinds of languages, to any cultural phenomenon in such a way that, by being linked to the social materiality (for instance, in Roland Barthes's or the Tartu school's sense), the enlarged concept of cultural text enriched cultural analysis. Later, however, the postmodern premise that everything has a discursive nature reduced the realm of the social to a textual level, in such a way that the social ends up being textualized, losing its conflictive contingency and social materiality. On the other hand, once these methodological and hermeneutical practices were institutionalized as U.S. cultural studies, despite the inclusion of disparate projects under the same umbrella, they brought into being the ideology of multiculturalism and identity politics, which ultimately lubricate neoliberal globalization.

In contrast, within the Latin American field, both the British cultural studies project and postmodern discourses were incorporated neither as formulas ready–to–be applied, nor as methodologies, nor even as ideology, but as complex problematics that deepened even further the heterogeneity of contemporary Latin American cultures. As a result, dialogues and debates among academics and intellectuals of diverse theoretical perspectives and different disciplines were ignited. These intense polemics questioned not only very broad categories, such as modernity, modernism, and modernization; postmodernity and postmodernism; subjectivity, subject, and agency; relations between elite, popular, and mass cultures, but also their peculiar approaches, methodologies, hermeneutics, and discourses. In that sense, they definitively had an effect on the reconfiguration of the main cognitive constellations of Latin American cultural studies. This was even more the case since those problematics were crisscrossed with other discourses and practices, mainly those coming from heterodox readings of dissimilar currents within poststructuralism, French sociology of culture, and Marxism—Antonio Gramsci, Louis Althusser, and the Frankfurt school, for instance. If we consider that Latin American cultural studies have their own endogenous genealogy and eclectic and diffuse exogenous influences, with exceptional direct influence from the British project, but with correlative coincidences with respect to the peculiar situation from which similar searches and responses were arising, it is foreseeable that both projects (British and Latin American cultural studies) could be articulated, though not without detailed re-elaborations.

However, the circumstances of reception of postmodern discourses were quite different, because even in those cases when they were critically accepted as a dominant cultural condition, the most visible one being that of Nelly Richard, they were always based on localized readings mediated by a vigilant distance and they never became an ideology as it happened within U.S. cultural studies. Precisely this difference became the central issue of a fierce misperception between the two camps. During the 1990s, when U.S. cultural studies was allegedly transformed into an institutionalized paradigm with global strategies in order to become "the" model for future regional cultural studies, the influence it could have had within the Latin American field was then perceived as a threat. After a short but heated encounter with U.S.-based Latin Americanists, the transnational and global practice of cultural studies was unreservedly rejected in Latin America.

Blueprints of Displacement

Coupled with the most aggressive and homogenizing neoliberal globalization, the celebration of difference and diversity, subalternity, marginality, and heterogeneity materialized as a Latin American paradox during the "lost decade" of the 1980s. While neoliberalism, the transnationally sponsored paradigm for the region, encouraged the promotion of the market as the sole institution of sociopolitical integration and cultural homogenization, at the discursive level, the incorporation of "new" theories produced at the center—hermeneutics, semiotics, French sociology of culture, poststructuralism, and postmodernism—ignited contradictory and aporetic interpretations of this "new" Latin American heterogeneity.

It is not fortuitous that most of the articles included in the "Foundations" section were written during the second half of the 1980s, when new fields of study, such as communications, cultural anthropology, gender studies, and colonial studies evolved from different strands of Latin American critical thought. Accompanying these transformations, key concepts, such as cultural mediation, heterogeneity, and hybridity, remapped new perceptions, sensibilities, perspectives, and political positions. By the end of the decade, all these displacements had formulated the blueprints of Latin American cultural studies. Even when the most important debates would have just begun to unravel, several positions were taking shape through a few key titles: *De los medios a las mediaciones* by Martín-Barbero (1987a), *El espejo trizado* by Brunner (1988), *Cultura transnacional y culturas populares* edited by García Canclini and Rafael Roncagliolo (1988), *Una modernidad periférica* by Sarlo (1989), *Plotting Women* by Franco (1989), and *Culturas híbridas* by García Canclini (1989a).

In order to understand the constant reshaping of the most persistent obsessions concerning Latin America—neocolonialism, modernity and modernization, the national question, the popular, and identities, alterities, and ethnicities—I will try to untangle their kaleidoscopic refurbishing in the 1980s in five cognitive constellations: media and mass culture, gender and minorities, colonial studies, modernity and postmodernity, and cultural hybridity (see map). The re-elaboration of alternative concepts, theories, methods, and methodologies is directly related to the critical contribution of numerous intellectuals, who, from different countries and different disciplinary fields, have contributed to the configuration of Latin American cultural studies. For expository, hermeneutical, and methodological reasons, we have to focus our analysis on a few relevant authors, either because of their punctual influence or their particular contribution. Franco, Monsiváis, Mignolo, Schwarz, Sarlo, Brunner, Martín-Barbero, and García Canclini are key figures from this decade. Their thinking and writing, despite their dissimilar discursive strategies, critical tools, and sociopolitical agendas, give testimony to the metamorphoses of the radical optimism of the 1960s and 1970s into the critical skepticism that became visible during the 1980s.

To comment on the entire production of these prolific and creative intellectuals would be a Faustian, and doubtless fallacious, effort. During the 1980s, most of them sought different pathways to express the paradoxical sign of the modern and the dissymmetries and inequalities produced within Latin America, where ancient or premodern social relations, "backwardness," and dependency coexist with high modernisms and cutting edge modernizations. If their point of departure is the criticism of traditional metanarratives, such as nationalism, imperialism, religion, colonialism, populism, modernization, and developmentalism, most of the time they reached aporetic or paradoxical dilemmas, which make the complexities of their analyses highly intricate. Most of them continued treating and actualizing the problematics that had been identified by dissimilar Latin American schools of thought, but they also dialogued with each other so as to unravel and explain the profound Latin American heterogeneous cultural density. As I said, it is impossible to explore, summarize, and comment on all the works produced by these intellectuals. However, I will attempt to articulate a few key concepts that later on, mainly during the 1990s, would develop into new paradigms of research and analysis at the core of Latin American cultural studies.

In Latin America, the 1980s constitute a moment of profound critical reflections, theoretical reconsiderations, and paradigmatic categorical shifts: from the national to the global; from the public to the private sphere; from the state to the market; from citizenship to consumerism; from "the people" and "the popular" to civil society; from political parties to the new social movements; from cultural politics to political cultures; from modern identities to postmodern subjectivities; and from lettered, popular, and mass culture to multiple, heterogeneous, and hybrid cultures. These reconfigurations put in tension theoretical concepts, cultural practices, and political values. On the one hand, there were the intersections and overlappings between different cultural dimensions: the lettered, the popular, and the massive and the local, regional, and transnational. What are the particular domains of each of them? How do they crisscross each other? How do they work in different contexts? What are their main pitfalls and deadlocks? On the other hand, there were the blurring borders between disciplines and epistemological categories: traditions and innovations, continuities and ruptures, fragmentation of subjects and subjectivities, descentralization of power, dissemination of meanings, and diversification of cultures. Martín-Barbero, remapping the genealogy of Latin American modernity through the transformations of mass society, analyzed the uses and consumption of mass culture by the popular sectors and the opening of new spaces of subversion and liberation; Brunner studied the cultural heterogeneity of Latin America as a product of the continent's segmented and differential participation in the global modern market; and Sarlo reflected on the nature of peripheral modernity as a culture of mixtures. The extensive and intensive reflections of Franco and Monsiváis, Mignolo, Schwarz and Sarlo, Brunner and Martín-Barbero on the central issues coalescing around the cognitive constellations of modernity/postmodernity and media and mass culture, converge in García Canclini's widely adopted concept of cultural hybridity, to the point of transforming it into a sort of new cognitive constellation.

TOWARD A NEW CONCEPTION OF THE CULTURAL FIELD

Since the early 1970s, Franco and Monsiváis have criticized the homogeneous internationalization—or "Americanization," Monsiváis dixit —promoted by the media, in the belief that its expansion would erase national and popular cultures. While they were very careful in differentiating each domain—the lettered, the popular, and the massive—they also found spaces of transformation, subversion, and liberation within the gaps, fissures, and dislocations. Traditionally, mass culture productions were analyzed, following a neo-Frankfurtian position, as carriers of the ideological manipulation and social alienation embedded in the commodity form. However, both Franco and Monsiváis were prefiguring new lines of criticism, which accompanied successive developments in popular and mass cultural expressions. Their essays included in this reader explore the impact of the hegemonic U.S. pop culture on Mexican culture; however, even when they are framed as national case studies, their conclusions could be extended to the rest of Latin America. Franco's essay shows how the analysis of popular literature for women, exemplified in the United States by the Harlequin series and in Mexico by libros semanales, "makes abundantly clear not only that the plotting of women into gender roles takes on new forms when they are considered both as consumers and as reproducers of the labor force but also that the international division of labor between privileged industrialized societies and third world societies affects the way that corporate society regulates its fictions of the subject and of socialization." Most critics, mainly feminists, are interested in these cultural productions because of their alluring popularity and because of the displacements these leisure activities had performed on traditional art and literature. Franco's legitimate interest obviously took those reasons into account, but it arose mainly because "conspiracy and manipulation theories of modern mass culture have . . . failed to account for the appeal of the 'alien' products and the fact that, in certain contexts, 'alien' values could be used to resist or subvert authority" (see Franco in "Foundations"). Her conclusion leads the reader to understand not only the different effects mass culture might produce depending on the national sociohistorical context in which they are appropriated, but also that in its consumption, marginal or subaltern subjects (in this case, women) can paradoxically find spaces of subversion and empowerment.

Monsiváis's essay maps the history of U.S.-Mexican relations and its contradictory consequences on Mexican "nationalist" culture. The resistance of traditional and popular cultures was internally challenged and changed by the incorporation (expropriation and adaptation) of U.S. values into Mexican culture. He compares two specific modernization processes through which Mexican cultural nationalism was updated into the framework of mass culture: first, that of the 1920s–1940s in which radio and cinema were the main source of diffusion, and second, that of the 1950s–1970s in which rock music and television series were the propulsive forces. Americanization, says Monsiváis, "dreams of individual ascent," "ideas, images and sensations" of "the contemporary" disseminated through these media. These desires, values, and aspirations have cast an imaginary in which "modernity [perceived as] courtesy of the United States" has dissolved traditional "cultural nationalism into the show." However, it would be a mistake to consider traditional and popular cultures as relics or frozen entities; for even when they spring from the past, they are deeply rooted in residual traditions, which gain a new, "modernized" vitality articulated to a different sociohistorical context. Léopold Sédar Senghor's advice, "assimilate without being assimilated," is the motto that inspires Monsiváis's thinking. Although Americanization was emulated and introjected through these processes, Mexican nationalism and Mexican cultures did survive although under a different robe. Monsiváis's dictum is equivalent to the immigrant's prayer to the Virgin of Guadalupe: "I swear, dear Virgin, I am the same as always although now I don't even recognize myself in the mirror" (see Monsiváis in "Foundations").

Both Franco and Monsiváis are politically engaged cultural critics, with the "capacity to conceptualize and define the big picture without losing sight of the fact that this picture is known through its details: a text, a song, an advertisement, graffiti," as Pratt and Newman say in their "Introduction" to Franco's Critical Passions (1999, 1). Both have always made explicit the need for historical referentiality in order to contextualize their analyses. However, there are some differences worth highlighting. Monsiváis's mordacious irony, for instance, allowed him to build a stereoscopic gaze by which sociopolitical events and cultural flows were perceived differently. His weekly chronicles, a form in-between the journalistic article and the cultural essay that amalgamates cultural and literary criticism, history and sociology, ethnography and anthropology, and politics and economics, narrate stories that at the same time analyze central problems of our present while describing the smallest, almost insignificant details of culture as performance (as an ethnographer would do), but always inscribing them within a genealogical historical framework. Monsiváis's public reputation as a storyteller, a chronicler, and a cultural critic is undisputable. It seems that even when the role of the intellectual has been under jeopardy for a long time, this crisis does not affect Monsiváis himself, whose urban chronicles are widely read and could be considered the living emblem of the "civic intellectual." So ancient and so contemporary, the cultural criticism crafted in his chronicles-essays could easily be characterized as cultural studies.

Franco's position as an "outsider" (a Latin Americanist scholar first in the British and then in the U.S. academia) allowed her to denounce, from the inside of the metropolitan centers, the structural disadvantage of Latin American cultures. A committed intellectual, she was actively involved in the reshaping of several fields of study, such as Latin American studies, women's and gender studies, and Chicano and Latino studies. Since the early 1970s, Franco has devoted her career to studying the intricate links between Latin American cultures and their (national and regional) sociopolitical contexts of production and consumption. The social role of the cultural dimension was one of the distinctive features underlined in Franco's earlier works. For instance, in *The Modern Culture of Latin America* (1967) and in *Introduction to Spanish American Literature* (1969), to name just two of her most known works, she explores the relations between artists and intellectuals, literary and cultural movements, and society. In "Dependency Theory and Literary History: The Case of Latin America" (1975), Franco incorporates dependency theory to the study of literature and culture so as to account for the Latin American dependent condition. Her efforts to differentiate this peripheric and marginal view, with a distinct potentiality as a particular mode of cognition, defied traditional investigations, criteria, and attitudes.

Her early embracing of feminist theories and lines of investigation, such as the representation of women and other minorities, led Franco to crisscross disciplinary borders, thus challenging the hierarchization of cultural values and practices and contributing to the establishment of a whole new cognitive constellation. Franco's account of the emergence of feminism and other gendered movements, such as gays, lesbians, and transvestites (1989, 1992, 1996b, 1996c, 1997), as "new" forces within the public sphere is regarded as "a symptom of a general realignment of political and social forces" (1989, 185). Her analyses on gender performance, using the body as the space of enactment of feminine affects and emphasizing the strategies of masquerading, parody, and pastiche, challenged "the separation of sex from gender" so central to feminist theories, and undermined the "idea of socially constructed gender" (1997, 199). Besides her important role in refocusing the notion of the popular in the larger picture of literatures and cultures, Franco's most outstanding legacy to contemporary Latin American cultural studies is perhaps her insistence on vindicating the minorities' constant "struggle for interpretative power," while insisting that in Latin America, women's and minorities' rights ("individual liberation") are always linked to social and political issues ("social justice and democratization") (1989, 187).

Since the early 1980s, new ways of reading and interpreting indigenous and colonial practices, institutions, rituals, artifacts, and texts, which were a direct result of the conjunction of semiotics and cultural anthropology with poststructuralist theories, led Walter Mignolo, Rolena Adorno, José Rabasa, Maureen Ahern, and Mercedes López Baralt, among many other scholars who specialized in Latin American colonial literature, to investigate alternative literacies and to advocate for the institutionalization within the U.S. academia of a new subsection within the humanities: colonial studies. In 1989, as a kind of formalization of the field, Rolena Adorno and Walter Mignolo edited volume 36–38 of *Dispositio: Revista Americana de Estudios Semióticos y Culturales (Disposition: American Journal of Semiotic and Cultural Studies)*, in which a series of works on "colonial discourse" were published.

According to Rolena Adorno, the debate around the theorization of colonial cultural productions, with the concomitant interrelation between history and theory, materialized a transition from the field of "colonial literature" to that of "colonial discourse" (1989, iii). Different disciplines (mainly history, anthropology, and literary studies) congregated to discuss a common thread: "the study of texts [that include] a variety of media representation," such as alphabetical, visual, spatial, iconographic, cartographic, and architectural. At that moment, the "question of the other" (or alterity) decisively marked the agenda (iv). Notwithstanding the importance of these issues leading the above mentioned transition, Walter Mignolo was already prefiguring another spin: from "colonial discourse" to "colonial semiosis." He states that "the notion of 'discourse,' although embodying both oral and written interactions, may not be the best alternative to account also for semiotic interactions between different writing systems" (1989, 334). Combining hermeneutics, semiotics, and discursive analysis, Mignolo coined the concept of "colonial semiosis," which as he asserts, "indicate[s] a network of semiotic processes in which signs from different cultural systems interact in the production and interpretation of hybrid cultural artifacts. In colonial semiosis the meaning of a sign no longer depends on its original cultural context (for instance, Castilian, or Amerindian, or Chinese), but on the new set of relations generated by communicative interactions across cultural boundaries" (see Mignolo in "Foundations"). His essay included here discusses the epistemological and ideological break achieved by a new reading of Father Ricci's move during the sixteenth century, that is, the rational and strategic uncoupling of the ethnic from the geographical center in sixteenth-century modern cartography. This conception of a movable center produces a double displacement: on the one hand, it confirms that "if territoriality cannot be achieved without a center, its fixity or mobility is a sign of the position of the representing agency"; on the other hand, it allows us to detach "the arithmetic calculation . . . from the ideological and political manipulation . . . of territorial representation[s]," be it in drawings or maps. Consequently, these hybrid artifacts, he asserts, demonstrate the possibility of interpreting not only the coexistence of unsymmetrical space perceptions and geographical representations, but also the conflicts generated during the colonial expansion by the struggle between two opposite points of view, that of the colonizer and the colonized. This will be the background of Mignolo's future proposal of postoccidentalism (see Trigo's introduction to part 3, "Practices").

MODERNITY REVISITED:
THE SEARCH FOR A NEW PARADIGM

Several of the intellectuals included in this section were strongly influenced by the Frankfurt school's critical theory and diverse Marxist thinkers such as Gramsci and Althusser, and all of them were intellectually formed in the ideological atmosphere of the 1960s, which was characterized by the passionately modern politics of dependency theory, anticolonial struggles, and the critique of internal colonialism and cultural imperialism.[2] In spite of this, they were able to de-center the analysis of culture by incorporating cultural practices, uses, consumption, and reception, and deconstruct the reifying notions of culture and literature inherited from modernity and its binary rationality and foundationalist groundings. Nevertheless, this was not the result of an inter- or transdisciplinary reformulation of the concept of culture, or of the "postmodern cultural or linguistic turn," so overwhelming during the 1980s in U.S. academia. According to Beverley and Oviedo, the critique of "cultural imperialism," which was politically instrumental for several decades within Latin America, was being questioned already by the emerging "dynamics of interaction between local cultures and an instantaneous and omnipresent global culture, in which the center-periphery model of the world system dominant since the sixteenth century [had] begun to break down" (1993, 3). Therefore, is it epistemologically valid, culturally possible, politically progressive, and ideologically desirable to declare the demise *tout à court* of Latin America's most forceful theorizations for an autonomous modernity in favor of the postmodern discursive vogue coming from the metropolises?

The debate on modernity/postmodernity, which reached Latin America by the middle of the 1980s, was almost over by the early 1990s. It was largely stimulated from the social sciences, which because they were supported in great measure by international foundations (e.g., the Ford, Rockefeller, and Friedrich Ebert Foundations to name a few), and were in constant exchange with transnational organizations, were unbeatably positioned as transmitters and agents of modernization. This explains how they introduced and led the debate on the (post)modern question just as their main topic of research at that time was the politically hot questions of democratization and social integration through cultural consumption. But soon many intellectuals from other disciplines, including the humanities, were incorporated into the debate (see Calderón 1988; Casullo 1989; Follari 1990; Lechner 1991; Michellini, San Martín, and Fernando Lagrave 1991). However, while in Western metropolitan cultures the "postmodern turn" implied a profound epistemological crisis, mainly due to the fact that the recognition that that reality is necessarily heterogeneous shook the fundamental premise of a homogeneous modernity, in Latin America the debate on the postmodern helped to realize that heterogeneity was a constitutive dimension of Latin American modernity. At the centers, postmodernism turned around the validity of terms, concepts, and theories to explain a loathing and exhaustive tedium with homogeneity, hence the rejoicing with a newly discovered heterogeneity. In Latin America, even though the recognition of difference, a central postmodern tenet, was enthusiastically embraced, insofar as it threw new light on Latin American complex historical heterogeneity, the debate revolved around the pertinence of the debate. To simply celebrate cultural multiplicity, admixture, and plurality without relating them to power and social inequalities was a futile mimetic exercise.

Modernity, which in Latin America historically has adopted different shapes, tones, and degrees, has been an omnipresent utopian horizon and a central signifier, differently approached by the arts, the humanities, and the social sciences. Until the 1980s, the problem of Latin American peripheric modernities was always tackled from the axis of production, since it was believed that in the organization of an autonomous productive apparatus laid the possibilities of social transformation, cultural emancipation, and national sovereignty. The postmodern displacement from production to consumption promoted by the eclectic theoretical aggregate Benjamin-Bourdieu-de Certeau would nuance these approaches and create new perspectives.

Intellectuals within Peripheral "National" Cultures. The paradoxical dislocations produced by the configuration of cultural modernity within peripheral national cultures are the background from which Schwarz's and Sarlo's analyses would spring. Both intellectuals, following a neo-Frankfurt school (specifically Adornian) position, also inscribe their works in singular national contexts and intellectual milieus, Brazil and Argentina respectively. Even when both intellectuals' vantage points are deeply embedded in a disciplinary frame, literary criticism, their studies always transcend those limits. Following the works of Antonio Candido and Angel Rama, they further re-elaborate their sociological approach to literary and cultural analysis. Schwarz's and Sarlo's essays included here share a common subject: the criticism of intellectual traditions in their respective countries and a critique of the place and role of the intellectual within Latin American societies.

Schwarz's essay explores the constant and contradictory problematic of Brazilian intellectual life, which is historically immersed in a spurious and deceptive dialectics between the original—coming from the centers—and its copy—merely transposed to and adopted in the peripheries. This mechanism, which is based on the fallacious presupposition of a genuine and unadulterated origin, has always forced Brazilian intellectuals to "start from scratch with each generation." In spite of this, he finds several intellectuals who have broken free of this fake entanglement, as is the case of Machado de Assis, Mário de Andrade, and Antonio Candido, who have "[made] broad and critical use of their predecessor's work," highlighting "the sense of contradictions [generated] between the real Brazil and the ideological prestige of the countries used as models" and, consequently, demystifying the cultural absurdity of counterposing such unreal oppositions as the national and the foreign. For him, "copying is not a false problem, so long as we treat it pragmatically, from an aesthetic and political point of view freed from the mythical requirement of creation ex nihilo" (see Schwarz in "Foundations").

Schwarz's notion of "misplaced ideas" helps us account for the paradoxes produced by the mimetic and decontextualized absorption of foreign, modern, occidental culture (always considered as "original"), which become producers of "original" and, "by elimination," national lines of thinking once put into practice in peripheral locations (even when as mere transplantation or translation). In *Cultural Critique* 49, a special issue dedicated to "critical theory in Latin America," Silvia López has interpreted Schwarz's intellectual work as the "task of [an] editor," in which the impossibility of performing said task attests that "translation [only] finds its truth" "in its failure" (2001, 2). Building upon Candido's sociocriticism and practicing an elegant and sophisticated form of literary analysis, Schwarz laid out an inventive theoretical framework, in which the symbolic production of reality, even when it presupposes the mimicry of metropolitan originals, results in its failure in an original peripheral thinking.

Sarlo's daring essay has a dual purpose: on the one hand, to revisit and criticize the mistakes committed by Argentine leftist intellectuals during the 1950s and 1960s and, on the other hand, to produce a collective biography of Argentinean intellectuality, in which her own autobiography, and especially the account of her activities during the authoritarian period (1976–83), plays an important role. Thus, cultural, political, and ideological hypotheses are braided with the collective experiences and personal memories from those peculiarly intense years. Two dissimilar registers, the social and the personal, which in Sarlo's work are almost always present (1994, 1996, 1998, 2001), are put in tension so as to recover, or at least to reflect upon, the identity of the intellectual. What is the specificity of intellectual discourse and what should be the specific practice of the intellectual in contemporary society's public sphere? In order to answer those questions Sarlo proposes "to rethink the relationships between culture, ideology and politics, as relationships governed by a permanent tension that cannot be eliminated, since it is the key to cultural dynamics." During the 1960s, the climate of radicalization matched up intellectual practice with politics, that is, "intellectuals were transformed into political actors." Hence, to the disadvantage of the free practice of criticism, "politics became the criterion of truth." Aesthetic avant-garde and political revolution destroyed the limits of the specificity of intellectual practice and "install[ed] them within the field of social and political struggle." For Sarlo, these two practices should be differentiated not only to avoid "servility" but also to keep diversity, heterogeneity, and conflict alive. With the impasse of the 1980s, a criticism of the intellectual activity was unavoidable. If intellectuals, during the transition to democracy, were to be coopted once again by politics, their social mediation would instantly vanish. That is why, for Sarlo, the "task of the intellectual . . . is precisely that of working within and on the limits, with the idea . . . that the limits can be destroyed but also with the recognition of their existence and the weight of their inertia." Autonomous intellectuals work on and within the conditions of possibility for the transformation of societies, therefore, in "the unstable relationship between perception of the real and the lines of transformation." For the future, what the intellectuals need to accomplish is to find out "a new thesis that articulates the desire for change" (see Sarlo in "Foundations").

Notwithstanding the rethinking of the intellectuals' loci and the self-criticism brought about by Schwarz's and Sarlo's reflections, both seem to be obsessed with their ruminations on the modern role of the intellectuals as main agents and promoters of change within peripheral national cultures. Even when they acknowledge the productivity of postmodern discourses, and in times to come Sarlo more than Schwarz would incorporate a criticized version of them, both are firmly entrenched in a neo-Adornian position through which the negativity of literature, the arts, and aesthetic values are always privileged as exclusive and reclusive emancipatory social spaces. In summary, autonomous intellectuals, who articulate knowledge to social criticism, are the most valuable agents to find "the source of [revolutionary] desire" (see Sarlo in part 2, "Foundations").

Mediations: Nocturnal Maps for Multiculturality. According to Martín-Barbero, intellectuals and scholars should shift the focus of analysis so as to find the sources of those same desires for change within the gaps of the contemporary hegemonic spaces: in the mediations between the lettered, the popular, the folkloric, the indigenous, and the massive, on one hand, and the local, the regional, the national, and the transnational, on the other. Audiovisual culture has displaced the foundations on which identities were traditionally constituted, such as national languages and territories. "Therefore, [he insists] instead of starting our analysis from the logic of production and reception and studying their relationships with the logic of cultural imbrication and conflict, we propose to start with the mediations where the social materialization and the cultural expression of [media] are delimited and configured" (see Martín-Barbero in "Foundations").

His meticulous criticism of the dualist reason of *mestizajes* leads him to disentangle and remap the dense texture of Latin American modern identities in their historical dynamics as mixtures of different times and spaces, memories and imaginaries, discourses and social practices that mold new sensibilities and renewed relations between the state and its citizens, the nation and "the people," society and "the masses." Torn between two central issues for communication studies—technology, with its modern and developmentalist rationality, and culture, memories and identities—Martín-Barbero carries out a deconstruction of the main dichotomies usually attributed to the Latin American entrance to modernity: the traditional versus the modern, the rural versus the urban, the folkloric versus the popular, the popular versus the massive, the national versus the transnational. Thus, he emphasizes the need to conceive multiculturality as complex networks of relationships among conflictive and antagonistic anachronisms, mixtures, and appropriations that crisscross Latin American diversity.

With that purpose in mind, Martín-Barbero demands "a reorganization of the analytic terrain that moves the marginal issues to the centers of our concerns," therefore searching for the popular within the massive and the lettered. In that sense, he constructs a contingent liminal position between two traditional conceptions of the popular sectors, demystifying both at the same time: first, the one that considers them as the only space of liberation and political transformation, and second, the one that degrades them as completely alienated (Reguillo 1998). Equipped with a "nocturnal map," he attempts "to understand the unexplored areas of reality . . . in tentative almost groping fashion," where the most unexpected answers emerge (Herlinghauss 1998). However, Martín-Barbero notes it should not be "a map for escape, but, rather, to help us recognize our situation from the perspective of mediations and the subjects in action" (see his essay in "Foundations"). His nocturnal map is an attempt to theorize as well as criticize Latin American sociohistorical processes through culture. Martín-Barbero's "open thinking," neither apocalyptic nor integrated, would still be pondered ten years later; *Mapas nocturnos: Diálogos con la obra de Jesús Martín-Barbero* (Laverde Toscano and Reguillo 1998) is the best example.

Heterogeneity and Hybridity of Latin American cultures. José Joaquín Brunner has been studying the importance of culture to reconstruct democratic processes through sociopolitical integration since the end of the 1970s and from the point of view of the social sciences. At that time, he was directing one of the most prolific sociological institutions, FLACSO, which had undertaken the study of the cultural dimension of Southern Cone dictatorships. Perhaps he represents the clearest, though not the most progressive, position with respect to the nature of modernity and postmodernity in Latin America. According to his perspective, "The future of Latin America will not be . . . very different from its present: one of a peripheral modernity, de-centered, subject to conflicts, whose destiny will depend, to some degree, on what these societies manage to do with this modernity in the process of producing it through their own complex and changing heterogeneity." For Brunner, modernity's motor is no other than the international market; thus, it springs from the metropolitan centers and reaches Latin America always from the outside. This "fact," as he perceives it, "provokes and then reinforces an incessant movement of heterogenization of culture, employing, stimulating, and reproducing a plurality of *logics* that act simultaneously." Therefore, cultural heterogeneity refers to processes of "segmentation and segmented participation in this global market, . . . according to *local codes of reception*" (see Brunner in "Foundations"). This "differential participation" results in incessant movements of displacement and de-centering, creating constant crises. It is important to note that this notion of heterogeneity, even when it is structural and its effects propel the segmentation of markets and society, is very different from Cornejo Polar's homonymous concept. Originated within the field of literature and attempting to account for the coexistence of different ethnic cultures amid the same social formation, Cornejo's heterogeneity "attempted to clarify the nature of processes of discursive production in which at least one of the instances differed from the others, with respect to its social, cultural, and ethnical affiliation" (Cornejo Polar, "*Mestizaje*, Transculturation, Heterogeneity" in part 1, "Forerunners").

In *Cultura transnacional y culturas populares* (1988), Néstor García Canclini and Rafael Roncagliolo collected the papers presented at the Latin American Seminar on Transnational Culture, Popular Cultures, and Cultural Policies (Bogotá, August 1985). At that moment, Brunner formulated a clever methodological criticism of García Canclini's theoretical elaborations on the transformation of popular cultures under capitalism (see Trigo 2000b). According to Brunner, Canclini's eclecticism and his admixture of Bourdieu's theory of social reproduction of uneven material and symbolic relations with Gramsci's notion of hegemony occludes the possibility of thinking about the productiveness of conflicts generated by popular cultures and ends up reifying their antagonistic struggles. Hence, for Brunner, it would be "an insufficiently Gramscian interpretation of Gramsci's vision of culture" (García Canclini and Roncagliolo 1988, 159). Similarly, in "Shifting Paradigms," Abril Trigo has criticized Brunner's concept of Latin American cultural heterogeneity because it "results from the unidirectional, unidimensional action; the mechanical product of a heteronomous modernity: a partially inverted and culturalist actualization of dependency determinism from behind which a rejuvenated, developmentalist, almost neoliberal paradigm peers out" (2000b, 101). Nevertheless, beyond the exchanges, these criticisms point to deeper theoretical and methodological reconfigurations on the ways of perceiving, thinking, and analyzing Latin American cultures. The importance of Brunner's critique of García Canclini indicates a rupture that would be central for the emergence of hybridity as one of the "shifting paradigms" (Trigo 2000b).

García Canclini developed his notion of hybridity based upon his previous works on popular cultures. A philosopher reconverted into cultural anthropologist, García Canclini intermingles anthropological and sociological methodologies with art and literary criticism and discursive analysis. His *Culturas híbridas. Estrategias para entrar y salir de la modernidad* delimits the turning point of the configuration of Latin American cultural studies as a field of research, not only because he is its most straightforward promoter, but also because of the influence his works have had and continue to have on generations of practitioners (for instance, see the important work of Rowe and Schelling 1991). As the title of his book indicates, García Canclini is interested in the intercrossing of cultural manifestations that weave the density of Latin American contemporary cultures. He asserts that "the difficulty of defining what is high and what is popular derives from the contradiction that both modalities are modes of organizing the symbolic engendered by modernity, but at the same time, modernity—because of its relativism and anti-substantialism—erodes them all the time" (1989a, 339). For him, all these segmentations are "cultural constructions" that only serve to establish theoretical models that most of the time remain at the discursive level, having little to do with their present complexities in the social reality. What a Latin American cultural studies analyst needs to do is to incorporate "the procedures of hybridity through which representations of the social are elaborated" in the current cultural reconversion (339). The dangerous risk involved in the studies of these intercultural relations and juxtapositions is simply to consider that all Latin American cultures are just hybrid. To complicate the issue at hand, García Canclini deliberately avoids theorizing a definition of hybridity, affirming that it just refers to "diverse intercultural mixtures." Although it is true that in the elaboration of this category he tries to go beyond "mestizaje," which is limited to racial mixture, and "syncretism," which only denotes "religious fusions or traditional symbolic movements" (15), he neither traces a genealogy differentiating all of them, nor grounds them in their respective contexts of production and circulation.

Cornejo Polar's notion of cultural heterogeneity revises the failures of Rama's epistemological project of transculturation; Brunner's heterogeneity performs a methodological critique of García Canclini's theoretical eclecticism to study popular culture; Martín Barbero's shift from media to mediations remaps the historical anchorages and the sociopolitical underpinnings of the interrelations of lettered, popular, and mass culture as juxtaposed fields of struggle; all these re-elaborations and contributions will converge in García Canclini's notion of hybridity. Despite all its theoretical and epistemological flaws and all the criticisms to which it has been submitted, hybridity became a central paradigm during the 1990s. As a descriptive category, though not hermeneutical or analytical, its influence has been pervasive and ubiquitous within Latin American cultural studies. Almost all the practices and theorizations of the field allude directly or indirectly to this notion of hybridity, wherein the coexistence of diverse cultures and their struggle for hegemony remains always in tension.

Notes

1. Jean Franco was the first British professor of Latin American literature at Queen Mary College and King's College of the University of London and at the University of Essex. By the early 1970s, Franco had moved to the United States.
2. See Cardoso and Faletto 1978; Dorfman and Mattelart 1972; Dagnino 1973; Mattelart 1974; Franco 1975; Mattelart 1977; Franco and Burton 1978; Martín-Barbero 1987a; Sarlo 1994.

JEAN FRANCO
Plotting Women: Popular Narratives for Women in the United States and in Latin America

Jean Franco was born in Great Britain in 1924. A literary and cultural critic, she was also a professor at several Latin American and U.S. universities, including Columbia University in New York, where she is professor emeritus. Her main titles include The Modern Culture of Latin America: Society and the Artist (1967), Plotting Women: Gender and Representation in Mexico (1989), and The Decline and Fall of the Lettered City (2002).

Mass culture has frequently been explained as a conspiracy to manipulate. The reason for this is not hard to understand. In the commercial development of radio, television, and popular literature in the United States and Latin America (which was distinct from their overtly propagandist use in Nazi Germany, for example), the claim was made that they were a response to what people wanted even though it was obvious that they were also creating new needs. Particularly in the case of radio and television this innocent appeal to the market was reinforced by the apparent neutrality of the technology, which was developed in advance of any particular content. As Raymond Williams has pointed out, radio and television "were systems primarily devised for transmission and reception as abstract processes, with little or no definition of preceding content" (Williams 1974, 25). In third world countries, however, where new mass communications technologies brought in their wake a grotesquely maladjusted transnational culture, the possibility that mass culture was covert propaganda for consumer culture was more clearly appreciated. For example, Herbert Schiller's well-known study, *Mass Communications and American Empire*, detailed the way in which the U.S. technological superiority in the new media inevitably put into corporate hands the ability to disseminate values (Schiller 1971 and 1976). The term "cultural imperialism" was coined in the 1960s to describe this process, and studies began to appear that showed how even the most innocent forms of mass culture—Disney comics, women's magazines, and "Sesame Street"—covertly promoted individualism, capitalist enterprise, or simply alien traditions (Dorfman and Mattelart 1972; Dorfman 1980). That the export of these values represented a corporate conspiracy was widely canvassed[1] and, indeed, gained credibility after the war of the media and the overthrow of Allende in Chile. Even so, conspiracy and manipulation theories of modern mass culture have tended to fall out of favor, first because of their elitist assumptions about reader or viewer reception and second because they failed to account for the appeal of the "alien" products and the fact that, in certain contexts, "alien" values could be used to resist or subvert authority. It is also increasingly clear that there is no such thing as a monolithic mass culture but, rather, widely varied forms of representation, discourse, and modes of address, which constitute quite distinct organizations of fantasy and experience within the dominant culture.

At the same time, the exportability of mass culture (and particularly U.S. mass culture) is a factor of major importance in contemporary Latin American societies. In the first place, it provides a common cultural repertoire that crosses national boundaries and thus tends, superficially at least, to blur the local idiosyncracies on which the idea of national character formerly depended. Second, most mass culture forms use formulas that can readily be adjusted to local circumstances. Third, as I shall point out in this comparison between women's popular romance in the United States and Mexico, mass culture has clearly a didactic function and operates as a socializing system that is now as powerful as schooling and religion, though its methods are vastly different from the methods of these institutions.

The use of formulas—that is, ready-made plots and ready-to-hand symbols—is both a major feature of mass culture and the target of most of the critical attacks from academics and high-culture critics. Theodor Adorno's analysis of jazz (by which he meant popular American music) was prototypical in this respect (Adorno 1941). More recently, the attacks have tended to isolate the "closed narratives" that are characteristic of nineteenth century "classical realism" as well as of modern mass literature, in which plotting toward a felicitous conclusion (and therefore a closure of meaning) is the major structural device, producing functional characters, situations, and descriptions.[2] Although there are many subgenres of formula literature both in the United States and in Latin America, women's literature seems to have attracted the most attention because of its overwhelming popularity, on the one hand, and its repetitive poverty of form, on the other. These critical speculations range from the denunciation of mass literature for women as degraded to claims that the audience "reads" in a way that is different from, though not necessarily inferior to, the reading of the "high-culture" audience. In the following investigation, I shall be concerned primarily with what Peter Brooks calls "reading for the plot," and I shall deliberately play with all the ambiguities of the term plotting in English, some of which Brooks himself points out. Brooks, however, is concerned primarily with the narrative plotting of "great books," whereas my concern is also with plotting in the conspiratorial sense, for this is the crucial point where politics and fiction intersect (1984). It is no accident that Brooks devotes a whole chapter of his book to Freud and that much of the vocabulary is drawn from psychoanalysis. Especially in recent years, Freud has been of considerably more interest to literary critics, feminists, and those interested in the social constitution of gender differences than to psychologists. Feminists, in particular, have found in Freud and Lacan the outline of a course of human development that accounts for gender differences and, in particular, for the devaluation of women. Here we have another kind of plotting, one that maps out women's path in the human community and particularly in one of its major institutions—the family. The study of popular fiction in the United States and Mexico makes abundantly clear not only that the plotting of women into gender roles takes on new forms when they are considered both as consumers and as reproducers of the labor force but also that the international division of labor between privileged industrialized societies and third world societies affects the way that corporate society regulates its fictions of the subject and of socialization.

I refer to corporate society because the mass culture with which I am dealing is primarily a corporate product and thus differs radically from individual or artisan production, which, however, corporations protect selectively through patronage. The propagandist arm of corporate society is advertising, the most ubiquitous and insistent of contemporary cultural forms and one that has, in crucial ways, formed new cultural paradigms. Advertising has constituted a totally new kind of imaginary repertoire, one that recycles all the imaginary repertoires of the past (Williamson 1978). Advertising's anonymity, its use of images drawn from art, religion, patriotism, its exploitation of psychological needs, its evocation of the magic of the marketplace tend to obscure the close links (explicit in Spanish) between advertising and propaganda. As Judith Williamson has pointed out, advertising traps us in the illusion of choice.

"Freedom" is, in fact, part of the most basic ideology, the very substructure of advertising. Outside the structure of advertisements themselves, it forms the fundamental argument always used to justify advertising: that it is part of the freedom of manufacturers to compete and part of our freedom to choose between the products of that competition (42). The referent of the advertisement is the commodity sign, that is, the commodity as a sign of social distinction and discrimination and as a sign of cohesion between different groups of consumers. In similar fashion, comic strips, television shows, and radio programs carve out sectors of consumption, creating serialized communities of readers or viewers that sometimes depend on existing groupings along racial, sexual, or class lines but more often cut across them.[3]

The culture thus constituted no longer corresponds to the agrarian or industrial work cycles, to the biological span of human life, or to geographic communities. Nor does it rest on the legitimized authority of God or nation-state but rather on the apparently natural law of the marketplace. Thus, even though in the modern world people are still addressed as religious subjects (as Christians, Moslems, Jews) and as citizens (as Frenchmen or Romanians), the voice of advertising speaks to us primarily as "desiring machines," encouraging us to plug into whatever aesthetic or libidinal satisfaction is at hand. Advertising thus interpellates its subjects as no ideology has ever done before—as free subjects who appear to be unsubjected, who choose freely what they are to enjoy and to be without having to feel any special local loyalties or personal ties.[4] Perhaps the most innovative aspect of advertising, however, is its deployment of the imaginary repertoire of all previous cultures. In medieval Europe, people's cultural needs were satisfied by a single image in the local church, by sermons or histories of saints and feast days. In the nineteenth century, the intelligentsia read and reread the comparatively small number of great books (the Bible, *Paradise Lost*, *Don Quixote*, Greek and Latin classics), and they could appreciate the art of other countries only exceptionally by visiting museums or looking at engraved reproductions. In contrast, any individual today can dip into an immense archive of literature, religious beliefs, films, photographs, dance and can be transported rapidly to once exotic sites. Chinese art, Indonesian poetry, Brazilian music are readily available, giving the impression of an inexhaustible cornucopia. It is precisely this flexibility of modern culture that makes it impossible to speak of "a" dominant ideology or "a" message that it transmits. At the same time, the plurality of its deployment never adds up to "contradiction" and therefore does not produce new awareness or self-consciousness.

In fact, women's popular fiction in North and Latin America offers a guarded response to advertisement's appeal to perpetual indulgence. In contrast to advertising, its techniques and its barely disguised didacticism seem archaic. In North America, series such as Harlequin romances pave the road to wealth with all the snares and pitfalls of Christian's road to paradise in The Pilgrim's Progress. In the Mexican genres I have studied, the ethics are Victorian, and the novels plot women (and men) into lives of hard work and sacrifice. What has made mass literature of interest to critics (particularly feminists), however, is not its repetitive and anachronistic form but its popularity. Ann Barr Snitow, for instance, mentions the colossal sales figures of Harlequins and popular romances in the United States and justifies her study of books that are not art but "leisure activities that take the place of art" on the grounds that "it would be at best grossly incurious, and at worse sadly limited, for literary critics to ignore a genre that millions and millions of women read voraciously" (1983, 246). Janice Radway, in an important study of romance literature, illustrates how the corporate takeover of publishing encouraged the promotion of what she calls "category literature." Corporate publishers "believe it is easier to introduce a new author by fitting his or her work into a previously formalized chain of communication than to establish its uniqueness by locating a special audience for it. The trend has proven so powerful, in fact, that as of 1980, 40 to 50 percent of nearly every house's monthly releases were paperback originals" (1984, 36).

In their efforts to find reasons for these large sales, many feminist critics have turned to psychological explanations. Ann Barr Snitow, for instance, argues that these romances "feed certain regressive elements of female experience," but is reluctant to come down from the fence and either condemn or celebrate them: "To observe that they express primary structures of our social relations is not to claim either a cathartic usefulness for them or a dangerous power to keep women in their place" (1983, 247). Rosalind Coward, writing on romance as an expression of women's desire, believes that such fiction "restores the childhood world of sexual relations and suppresses criticism of the inadequacy of men, the suffocation of the family, or the damage inflicted by patriarchal power. Yet it simultaneously manages to avoid the guilt and fear which might come from that childhood world. Sexuality is defined firmly as the father's responsibility and fear of suffocation is overcome because women achieve a sort of power in the romantic fiction" (1984, 196). Thus, for Coward, women pay a high price for fictional power and enjoyment— a price that involves evading the pain of self-assertion by remaining perpetual children. Furthermore, any power that the heroine or reader is likely to attain, according to Coward's interpretation, has little effect on the larger structures of authority that determine the heroine's path to the paradise of consumption. In fact, most feminist critics want to have their cake and eat it, want to show that the formula is restrictive, yet want to find that it offers space for resistance. For instance, in an illuminating analysis that owes much to Freudian criticism, Tania Modleski suggests that the very tightness of the plot indicates the scope of women's resentment, which can be controlled only by making the heroine perform a "disappearing act" (1982, 37). The reader, for her part, is forced into a kind of schizoid reaction, being the surveyor of the heroine while also being invited to identify with her and hence to be the surveyed. Modleski argues that, far from achieving undiluted escape, the reader experiences a compulsion to repeat the reading because there is no real-life resolution of these contradictory feelings (57). Though Janice Radway criticizes such literary readings of romance in her book *Reading the Romance* and tries to correct them by showing how the romances are read and evaluated by real readers, her conclusions bear out some of Modleski's assertions. Radway's readers invariably stressed enjoyment of repeated readings, their need for escape from family and daily routine, and their preference for the kind of romance in which satisfactory characters and resolutions remove the anxieties and enigmas posed by the plot. In short, what we discover in recent criticism in the United States is the tendency not to blame the reader and to stress women's active participation in reading. Yet, in a way, rescuing the reader is not the point. Mass culture offers a map for integration into the system but does not imply social integration, that is, necessary compliance with corporate ideologies (Radway 1984, 176). This is a point to which I shall return later.

Any analysis of popular fiction for women must focus on the formulas and particularly on the plotting, which, as Peter Brooks notes, is inevitably bound up with questions of time-boundedness, with plot as "the internal logic of the discourse of mortality" (1984, 22). Because, however, popular literature depends on repeated schemata, it would seem to be very different from the sophisticated plotting discussed by Brooks and to have more in common with archaic oral storytelling, which depended on repetition and other mnemonic devices. The classic study of the fairy tale is Vladimir Propp's discussion of the morphology of the Russian fairy tale in which he showed how a comparatively small number of narrative functions could result in a large variety of surface realizations (1958). However, it is important to stress that the fairy tales on which Propp drew emerged within an orally transmitted culture and were related within the context of community rituals and practices. Modern romance formulas, in contrast, have been devised on the basis of market studies that are targeted to particular sectors of the population and meet well-tested needs. Moreover, they are addressed to a serialized community, which means that they are generally read in isolation by women who thus seek to make a private space in the midst of the demands of the family and everyday life. The formulas, in both cases, provide a temporal framework that encourages a reading for the plot even though the outcome can easily be anticipated. Yet as investigations of the Harlequin romances have shown (and this is probably also true of orally transmitted tales), readers or listeners identify with particular characters and are not concerned with underlying similarities to other novels.

As Borges demonstrates in his short story "Death and the Compass," formula plots are more interesting than might at first be supposed, both because they play on never satisfied desires for solution (and death) and because they link reading and writing to plotting, treachery, and conspiracy (Franco 1981a). In Borges's story, the reader's plot is worked out by Lonnrot, who reads a series of clues according to his own prejudices and comes up with a neat solution, which, unfortunately, turns out to be a trap devised by his enemy, Red Scharlach. Scharlach's plot is more ingenious because it depends on knowledge of Lonnrot's prejudices and also on the use of accidental and random elements. This story is an interesting contrast to the split mind of women's popular fiction (particularly Harlequin romances) since it suggests both the naive anxiety for a felicitous solution and the hidden resentment that powers the vengeful "author," Red Scharlach, in his bid to thwart this solution. What makes Borges's story pertinent to the study of Harlequins and other formula literature is that it suggests that the reader's plot and the author's plot do not necessarily coincide and that the latter has a distinct advantage in what is an unequal power relationship. Comparison between Borges's fiction and women's popular fiction may seem strange; yet it reveals two contrasting aspects of double plotting designed to lift the reader out of everyday life.

"Death and the Compass" is a microdemonstration of the exercise of knowledge and power: There is the reader's knowledge that structures the first plot out of the expectation of repetition, and there is the "second" plot, which can be anticipated neither by knowledge drawn from experience nor from knowledge drawn from other plots because it uses the random and the fortuitous. This is the modern plot par excellence.

On a less sophisticated level, both Harlequins and Mexican libros sema-

nales (i.e., weekly comic strip books) also present a manifest reader's plot and an authorial plot. The first can be described as a plot that incorporates elements from everyday experience, such as resentment and violence; the authorial plot resolves these tensions in a publicly acceptable form, so that plot resolution is not intended to thwart the reader's expectations but rather to suggest forms of system incorporation that not only allow women a social role but also promise social recognition. The brevity of this essay obliges me to select a single example of the Harlequins for discussion even though this appears to privilege one instance of a repetitive plot structure. Fortunately, other critics (e.g., Janice Radway) have read exhaustively in order to isolate the invariable elements. I shall therefore concentrate on one popular Harlequin, *Moonwitch* by Ann Mather. I choose this example because it explicitly plots women into corporate society.

Sara, the heroine of *Moonwitch*, has a humble background. She is an orphan, brought up by a grandfather who, on his deathbed, bequeaths her to the Kyle Textile Corporation, believing this to be controlled by his old friend J. K. In fact, the corporation has been taken over by J. K.'s son Jarrod, and the father is living in retirement in the Kyle manor house. Despite his misgivings, Jarrod accepts Sara as his ward but turns her over to J. K., who becomes her companion and guides her through the unfamiliar social world she has now entered. It is no accident that this social world is represented by the manorial space of the Kyle house, for this is the anachronistic space of patriarchy that is based on a feudal master-slave relationship. Sara's training is essentially a programming into corporate society. At the same time, she faces the typical double binds of the Harlequin heroine—that is, she is seductive and yet cannot afford to give in when Jarrod attempts to seduce her.

It should be stressed that, although the sexual encounters in such books as the Candlelight Ecstasy romances are often more titillating and "modern," the archaic formula of postponement of pleasure used by the Harlequin is still a powerful attraction to women readers all over the world. Thus, though prevented from responding sexually before marriage, Sara appears in seductive situations (half-naked on a beach in Jamaica), and it is always she, rather than the male, who must exercise self-control in order to reach the final goal of marriage. Furthermore, though she will attain upward mobility through marriage, she is not allowed to be ambitious for money. Indeed, Jarrod treats her badly as long as he believes her to be seducing him for his wealth. This double bind is transcended only when the patriarch J. K. dies, leaving Sara his valuable porcelain collection. Overcome by grief, she spurns the collection, thus

proving that she is not simply after money. Disinterestedness is the short-
est road to wealth for the Harlequin heroine.

The function of the Harlequin plot is twofold. In the first place, it reproduces anxiety situations that are insoluble, but this insoluble plot is
then overcoded by a second plot—that is, the plot we read in the light of
the successful outcome. The two plots center mainly on the hero's character, which in the first plot is enigmatic and hostile, just as adult society
is enigmatic and hostile to most women, who are forced to learn how to
behave by trial and error. This hostility is likely to cause resentment. The
second plot ensures that we read the story in order to correct any misunderstanding as to the hero's character. The corporate hero is, in reality,
benign and considerate and when successfully "read" will lift the heroine
up to her proper place as reproducer of consumer society. This clearly
suggests that anxiety is an essential element in consumer society and
shows how women are taught to use the tactics of the weak—seduction—in order to negotiate a modest place in a society whose rules they
have not made and from which they are initially estranged.

As Tania Modleski points out, the first plot is presented as an incorrect
reading, that is, the misunderstanding of the hero's true character (1982,
41–42). Thanks to the ending and the marriage contract, this misunderstanding can be corrected. Thus the marriage contract is itself of dual
significance since it recognizes that the heroine is worthy to take her
"true" place in society, while showing that this acceptance must come
from outside, from the patriarchal order itself. Misreading marks wom-
en's accession to the symbolic order; that is to say, misrecognition is a basic part of their training. Men are repressive, cruel, and powerful, and the
only way to get by is to learn what society says women "truly" want. What
is unpleasant and even unnatural can be tamed by the right tactics. Thus
the second plot maps the paths that allow the first plot to be controlled.
The powerful male figure has to be "reread" not as an oppressive tyrant
but as a master of social rules that the heroine must learn, just as the hero
has to learn to soften his will to power. At the same time, Harlequins exploit the preconstructed expectations that stem from the reader's experience of unequal gender relations in order to negotiate a more satisfactory
contract with corporate consumerism. However, it is a contract that one
can negotiate only by falling back on the tactics of the weak—that is, on
seduction rather than outright confrontation.

If women's popular fiction offers an oddly hedged response to self-
indulgence in the United States, this hedging is even more apparent in
literature produced in societies of scarcity. Mexico is particularly interesting as a vantage point from which to monitor this literature, both be-

cause it is a major producer of "photonovels" and other types of popular fiction and because the productions of corporate Mexico conflict in significant ways with an older nationalist ideology.

The *libro semanal* draws on material from the sensational press and thus implicitly acknowledges the prevalence of violence in everyday life, a violence that cannot be avoided by devising romantic plot structures. This does not mean, however, that the novels confront violence directly; rather they use it to attract the reader and then overlay an explicit moral that prompts the correct reading of such events. In this respect, the *libro semanal* is akin to the religious story in which the random persecutions and events of a holy person's life are reinterpreted by the voice of God. When this kind of utterance is deployed in a secular discourse, it produces a narrative problem, for there is no universal system of belief that will give unquestioned authority to the moral. This moral voice strives to achieve the status of an aphorism or *doxa* but lacks the power of religion. Nor does it necessarily conform to state ideology, for this overt message not only is frequently out of line with the events of the story but introduces values that have little in common with the nationalist ideology that has, for so long, dominated the discourses of postrevolutionary Mexico.

It is perhaps hardly necessary to recall the fact that in Mexico the revolution had constituted the semantic axis around which social meanings were transmitted and understood and in relation to which sexual, racial, and class categories had been defined. The power of the state to monopolize the production of meaning has now been severely challenged, however, not only by the criticism of the intelligentsia seeking to widen the democratic basis of society but also by the alternative meanings that were increasingly available in mass culture productions. As early as the 1940s, U.S. advertising firms and U.S. paperback books and magazines such as *Selecciones de Reader's Digest* had begun to attract the interest of certain sectors of the public. Though the government was able to control films (even censoring government-subsidized films like *Las abandonadas* when sectors such as the military were offended) and to place indirect pressure on publishers, there was plainly a growing gulf between the ideal image of Mexico and the culture and practices of people's everyday lives. This became painfully apparent in the 1960s, both in the use of force in the 1968 massacre of students at Tlatelolco and in the *Children of Sánchez* scandal. Though the methods and conclusion of Oscar Lewis, the compiler of *The Children of Sánchez*, are open to criticism, the government's attempted censorship of the Spanish version was an index of the wide difference that had opened up between the government's image of the Mexican and everyday reality. Lewis presents a family many members of which aspire vainly to individual realization and who are not at all spurred on by revolutionary collectivism (1963).[5] They are torn by jealousy and rivalry and dominated by a father who withholds affection but not punishment, leaving his children with an unsatisfied craving for paternal recognition. This was the Mexico into which television was introduced in 1950.

The trend away from the reformist state (*el estado de compromiso*) to a deregulated society that made scarcity the major incentive of the work force has generally been presented under the euphemistic label "modernization." Because women were now a major factor in the development of new industries, women, too, had to be modernized. Magazines and popular literature all over Latin America played a major role by showing the desirability of "modernity," as Michèle Mattelart pointed out in a study of women's magazines sold in Chile during the early 1970s. In a study of "photonovels" (i.e., novels that use photographic stills and a brief text to tell the story), Cornelia Butler Flora and Jan Flora likewise argued that this literature was an instrument for integrating the population into the labor force as well as into a consumer culture. The authors divide photonovels into three categories: (1) disintegrative/integrative, that is, as to the way they break down old patterns and integrate readers into new ways of thinking; (2) pure escape; and (3) consumer oriented. Obviously, these are not narrative categories and, as content categories, they are not clearly distinguishable. Nevertheless, the Floras' conclusion is persuasive, for it gives this literature a performative role. "Seen as an evolutionary process, these stories separate a woman from her actual environment and prepare her to accept the necessity of marginal participation as consumption is added to her function of reproduction of household labor" (1978).

In contrast to photonovels, *libros semanales*, or comic strip novels, have attracted little critical attention (except for Tatum and Hinds 1984), despite the somewhat idiosyncratic manner in which the modernization plot is written. There are two major publishers of these comic strip novels. The novels I shall discuss here are published by Novedades Editores, a subsidiary of Mex-Ameris, which is controlled by the powerful O'Farrill interests. This conglomerate also publishes such magazines as *Claudia* and *Bienestar*, two photonovels—*Rutas de pasión* and *La novela musical*—as well as fashion and sports magazines and crime literature. Romulo O'Farrill Sr. is the partner of Emilio Azcárraga in the television company Televisa (García Calderón 1984). The novels are produced under the general editorship of Ms. Ibáñez Parkman and include various genres—*vaqueros* (cowboy magazines), crime novels (directed to the male public), and sentimental novels, which are intended mainly for women.[6] Each series sold around eight hundred thousand copies per week before the recent economic crisis, which caused a dip in sales that affected novels for women more than novels for men.[7]

The comic strips are crudely drawn and often use the shorthand indices of emotion conventionalized in U.S. comics, which are left untranslated in Spanish. For instance, "Snif, Snif" indicates weeping. The color of the comics is a monotonous sepia, and the covers are often unattractive. They have neither the glossy appeal of the photonovel nor the escapist fantasy provided by the romance fiction produced under the name of Corín Tellado.[8] Precisely because the *libros semanales* are so unglamorous and are so clearly intended for women who are integrated or about to be integrated into the work place, they require a different kind of modernization plot, one that cannot simply hold out the carrot of consumption.

The distinctive feature of the *novela semanal* is its explicit moral, a moral that often strikingly conflicts with the apparent plot. In *Los nuevos ricos* (vol. 32, no. 1541, 9 March 1984), the plot appears to focus on adultery. The wife of Luis Felipe, who has married him only for his money, seduces his brother Luciano. The novel begins at the dramatic moment when Luciano, shocked at his own conduct, commits suicide. The family and Luis Felipe, who know nothing of the affair, are baffled by this tragedy, but before they discover its cause, there is an unexpected and apparently disconnected flashback to Luis Felipe's father, whose origins are now explained in some detail.

Luis Felipe's father is a *nuevo rico* who began life as a peasant. One day as he returns from work in the fields accompanied by an aunt, he finds the family home destroyed and his parents dead. A Mexican reader might immediately connect this destruction to the revolution or the Cristero War, but the novel avoids such historical specificity and turns it into an accidental tragedy. Soldiers, in search of a fugitive, had mistakenly caused the deaths. The novel thus manages at once to allude to the violence of the past without indicating that this violence brought about social change and to suggest that violence comes from the forces of the state. The "accident" drives the father and his aunt from the village and into the city, where they make a fortune selling fruit. They become the "new rich" of the title; in due time, the father marries and has two sons, Luciano and Luis Felipe, whose upbringing he neglects because of his concern with money. At the end of this flashback, we return to the adultress, who is now haunted by the dead Luciano and who dies in remorse. This second "accident" will have the same result as the first. Luis Felipe decides that he can no longer live with his parents and must make his own way in life, starting from scratch.

Now the best that can be said about this plot is that it is incoherent.

Certainly, if the reader were to draw a moral lesson, it might concern the evils of adultery. Yet the adultery turns out to be a side issue. The explicit moral printed at the end of the story is "Money and social position kill even the sincerest feeling. Luciano and Luis Felipe's parents forgot that they owed their children love and instead amassed a large fortune which, as the novel shows, was of no use to them." What seems to be the plot of the story, a plot that arouses anger at the conduct of an unscrupulous temptress, turns out to be a secondary matter that is punished by supernatural means. The "sin" of the older generation—their egoism—has to be dealt with on the level of everyday life. Egoism and moral blindness prevent them from being suitable guides for their children, who have to seek their satisfaction outside the traditional family.

This seems a strange conclusion for a country like Mexico in which the family has, at least in theory, always provided a network of support. It also contrasts in startling fashion with the Victorian treatment of sexually aberrant behavior, which was often exposed and punished, the better to cement the ties between generations. *La Traviata* is a classic example of a father-son relationship cemented by the sacrifice of the courtesan, whose death allows the family to triumph over sexuality. In the Mexican *novela semanal*, the family is an obstacle to individual progress, and adultery is one of the consequences of members of the same family inhabiting the same house. Unlike Freudianism, which makes "separation" from the mother and the oedipal conflict a crucial stage in childhood development, this novel stresses separation as an *adult* process that frees the individual from the weight of the past represented by the older generation. Though never officially stated, the official ideology of postrevolutionary Mexico, which was, at least in theory, based on the desirability of state-directed (paternalistic) reform with each generation building on the contribution of the prior generation, is here undermined by an individualistic self-help philosophy.

Though I cannot claim to have read more than a small number of these novels, I have read a sufficient number to make it clear that the attack on the older generation in *Los nuevos ricos* is not an isolated example. Again and again, such stories exploit violence, rape, and sensation only to place the blame in the end squarely on the shoulders of the older generation. In one of the novels, *Las abandonadas* (vol. 32, no. 1537, 10 February 1984), the children of a "fallen" mother and a cruel father eventually escape from the father's house and find work in the city. The moral states: "Parents must never betray their children's trust. Children are soft wax which can be molded. Unhappy children become unhappy adults but happy children will form homes that are filled with peace and love."

Clearly this moral does not follow from the logic of the conclusion, since "the abandoned girls" should be as evil as their parents. Once again the conclusion we might naturally draw from the life story is thwarted, this time because the moral of the story suggests a culture of poverty thesis according to which the older generation passes on its defects to the next. If children are "soft wax," how can they escape from evil parenting? In this case, we can only conclude that children can break the cycle by making a break with the family and going to work in the city.

In both the examples I have discussed, the focus is not so much on women as on the family as an institution. Mexican postrevolutionary policy had encouraged the secularization of public life while leaving the traditional patriarchal family untouched and absorbing machismo into its national image. The Mexican family is thus an extremely complex institution, not only a source of considerable tensions, especially among the poor, but a source of support and daily communication that the state and its institutions cannot replace. It is interesting, therefore, that many of the *novelas semanales* place less emphasis on romance than on working or on marriage as a working partnership. In *Lo que no quiso recordar* (vol. 22, no. 1557, 29 June 1984), the heroine Chelo marries a friendly architect after some misadventures with an unscrupulous brother-in-law, who had tried to blackmail her into a relationship. The moral declares that "true love means faith and trust in one's partner and the knowledge that, despite hardship, trouble, and economic difficulty, their mutual love will make them confident that all will turn out right in the end."

Though, in this case, the reader might have reached this conclusion without prompting, the suggestion that marriages face economic hardship is not reflected in the plot. Yet it is not a totally gratuitous observation, for it serves as a warning that the romantic element should not blind the reader to the fact that marriage is a working relationship. It underlines the fact that in this Mexican popular literature, unlike the Harlequin, romance is not the issue and readers are expected to use real-life experience to evaluate the story.

One explanation of the disjunction between plot and explicit moral message may be rooted in the origin of the stories—that is, everyday life as told in readers' letters or in the popular press. The latter provides a diet of violence and sensationalism that has few parallels in the rest of Latin America. Why violence should be so popular among Mexicans is not altogether clear, unless it has to do with the desire to dramatize lives that may otherwise seem pointless. At the same time, since the violence is attributed in the novels mainly to a regressive mentality, it clearly belongs to the past that the novel condemns and not to the modern life toward which the readers are supposed to aspire. In the modernization tale, it is the ingrained habits of the "typical" Mexican—violence, machismo, and drunkenness—that have to be repudiated, and since men of the older generation do not seem likely to reform themselves, women must simply break away from the traditional family and embrace the work ethic.

This is underscored by the fact that even the advertisements generally downplay the cornucopia of consumerism in order to emphasize self-help courses, utilitarian items like sheets, and door-to-door sales jobs. Women are thus addressed not primarily as consumers but as potential workers whose fulfillment will be within the work force (the plots often emphasize this) rather than in romantic marriage. In presenting this message, advertisements offer a critique of the old macho type personi-fied by Pancho Villa, whose posthumous role in the building of national-ist ideology exceeded his achievements in the revolutionary struggle. Oc-tavio Paz's El laberinto de la soledad and Carlos Fuentes's novel La muerte de Artemio Cruz, to mention two well-known examples, deal with the pro-found interpenetration of nationalism and machismo and the destructive effect on politics and everyday life.

In Mexico, the overlapping of old and new discursive formations, old and new plots, old and new proverbial wisdom gave rise to many contra-dictions that surface in popular narrative. Loyalty to the neighborhood network, to one's place of origin (Viva Jalisco), or to the extended family had been key themes in popular songs, mythology, and film. Though much nationalist and regional sentiment, especially feelings associated with place of origin and the family, is still conveyed on film and television and in popular literature, there is also a systematic parody of "tradi-tion" in the media[9] and a devaluing of the residues of more archaic ways of life—machismo, superstition, veneration of the older generation (though these may also resurface in new organizations like that of the concheros, or drug cults). In order to persuade people of the need to sepa-rate themselves from the past, the comic strip novel imitates exemplary literature in showing the evils of machismo and portraying the hard-drinking male who assesses his virility through violence, especially vio-lence against women, like a barbarian. The ideal male in the comic strip novel is the young professional or young worker who can be trusted to form a nuclear family in which the wife will also go out to work. I shall return to the apparently emancipatory aspects of this literature later. But it should again be stressed here that the organization of plot material in the novela semanal is different from that in the Harlequin novel. The novela *semanal* is not written exclusively from the female point of view and does not incorporate itself into the social norm. Rather, women are invited to see themselves as victims of a plot, the plot of the old Mexico that has passed on the tradition of machismo and thus harmed them. If, instead of reading themselves into the plot as helpless victims, they turn their resentment against the older generation of men and separate themselves from this influence, they can expect to succeed. The solution suggests the need for struggle rather than escapism. The determinism of one generation transmitting its defects to the next can be transcended, and women can start life anew as members of the work force.

It is therefore not surprising to find an explicitly feminist ideology in some of the *libros semanales*. In *Una mujer insatisfecha* (vol. 32, no. 1580, 7 December 1984) the heroine is married to a boring and impotent businessman who believes in patriarchy and the traditional values of family life. Luisa is repelled by his puritanical attitude to marital relations and quarrels with her Italian mother-in-law, whose ideas on marriage are strictly traditional. She sets up her own consultancy as a designer and meets another man but refuses to enter into a relationship that promises to be as oppressive as the one with her husband. Back in her mother's home, she hangs up the telephone when her new lover calls, feeling "free, happy and without ties." More surprising is the plot of *Desprestigiada* (vol. 32, no. 1572, 12 October 1984), in which the heroine, a flirt who likes to pick up male visitors to the pyramids, is raped by a "foreigner" (probably a Central American) who works in the post office. When she discovers that she is pregnant, she has an abortion thanks to the help of a traditional *curandera* and a woman doctor. But the foreigner rapes her a second time, because he wants a child he can adopt and take back to his own country. The rape (which is a somewhat unusual adoption procedure) is, however, less germane to the conclusion than the birth of the illegitimate child. The foreigner's plan to seize the baby is thwarted when he is picked up as illegal immigrant, and it is Luisa who brings the baby up until the child is weaned. The reader might expect this to be the ending, but this is not a story about a girl's redemption through motherhood. Rather, as soon as the child is old enough to be left with another person, she is handed over to Luisa's mother and Luisa goes back to her old life, picking up men at the pyramids. The only moral lesson is that in the future she must be more careful.

There is considerable irony in this attack on machismo in the guise of liberation. It plays on the sentiments of 1968, plays on the difference between the modernity of the young and the blind conformity of the old. It does so thanks to the anachronistic melodramatic plot, in which random acts of violence can be justified only on the grounds of the heroine's final social integration. Even so, the moral and the ending are often so arbitrary in relation to the sequence of events that they highlight the arbitrary nature of all narratives, including the master narrative of nationalism with its appeal to rootedness, to place, and to community.

In older forms of social narrative, the "story" tended to be woven out of lived experience. This term, now rightly treated with suspicion because of its empirical bias, must nevertheless be introduced because the process of human life ("the logic of mortality") cannot help but be the most powerful of paradigms. We fell in love and married and had children, and all this seemed to happen naturally. Of course, we were still woven into a social plot in which marriage and the family not only satisfied our needs for affection and recognition but also contributed to social reproduction. Nevertheless, this plot was built on events—childhood, adolescence, maturation—that appeared to be natural. The modernization plot works against this formerly "natural" state of affairs, showing that life stories are not what they seem. In Harlequins, romance is a prize available only to those who learn the conditions under which female power can be exercised. In the libros semanales, the family is not seen as the inevitable source of satisfaction for women.

It is intriguing that there are photonovels being produced in California that use real-life material to persuade Mexican men to stay in Mexico. The series, Los mojados, is based on the tragedies of Mexicans who emigrated to the United States in search of the "accursed dollar" and who found only disaster and death.[10] Thus real-life stories persuade one sector of the population—women—that the family and the province are not their only destiny, whereas Los mojados persuades men to stay at home and not swell the immigrant population of the United States. Mass culture narrative thus deals with problems that go far beyond entertainment. By addressing itself to serialized readers, it can appeal to private feelings and private lives. Yet this literature commutes private sentiments into stories that map out (plot) the way different sectors of the population can be incorporated into the international division of labor. Whereas the Harlequin romances use the powerful parallel between the stages of socialization and a ritual of passage from adolescence to womanhood, the libros semanales often depict a violent break between women as workers and women as family members. The plots of both, however, seem to depend on the fact that women experience considerable anxiety and uncertainty as to where they stand in relation to society. The libros semanales reveal that there is not a single model for the sex-gender system under capitalism, but rather multiple options. Furthermore, when these options contradict women's everyday practices or beliefs, they have to be plotted as a simulation of real life in order to persuade the readership to change its attitudes. The *libro semanal* thus bears some resemblance to the CIA guerrilla manual, which, since it could not appeal to the real-life situations of Nicaraguans, resorted to simulating events (e.g., an execution) in order to provide such experience (Omang and Neier 1985).

Far from being peculiarly postmodern, this kind of plotting belongs to the hallowed tradition of the church with its staging of miracles and marvels. The "literary resources" printed at the end of the "contra" manual could quite well have come from a Jesuit manual. But the church, whatever its capacity for manipulation, had both its transcendental signified and its moral code, which went hand in hand with belief in an afterlife. In contrast, the *libro semanal* offers travail without utopia, and self-reliance without any moral standpoint to help one deal with human relations other than that offered by the disembodied corporate voice.

Women, then, are plotted in different ways according to their position in the international division of labor. Curiously, it is women in the most affluent sectors (or those who can aspire to that affluence) who are invited most vigorously to give up their cultural capital (that which would permit them to "think like a man") and find security in their own narcissistic image. In the lower strata of the international division of labor, work or individual emancipation takes the place of romance. These novels suggest that "love" is a luxury, a fantasy not for all women but for middle- and upper-class women seeking the complementary man who will heal the split in their personality. What women want is provided by the Harlequin romance in a very efficient way, but it disguises the fact that this is the only way of being truly "incorporated." If the *libro semanal* is more problematic, it is because it does not address what women want, but rather disguises economic oppression as emancipation from the violence and oppression of working-class men. Significantly missing from mass literature is any form of female solidarity; it reinforces the serialization of women, which is the very factor that makes their exploitation both as reproducers of the labor force and as cheap labor so viable even in corporate society.

Plotting is a social as well as a literary device, and clearly, although it is important to recognize that reading the plot does not mean being committed to the social system it maps out, it is also important to understand the perplexing disjunction that is now taking place at the level of morality. "The area of belief which concerned religion, sexual and personal morality, and the sanctity and social significance of the family, has collapsed in modern bourgeois culture," according to one group of critics (Abercrombie, Hill, and Turner 1980, 138). Harlequins map out the conditions for consumerism and *libros semanales* for incorporation into the work force, but whereas the former retain traditional morality in almost nostalgic fashion within the ethical vacuum of consumerism, the latter insist on emancipation from the restraints of a family that is now a hindrance to capitalist development in Mexico.

Both kinds of mass literature I have examined seem to indicate that women find a great deal of satisfaction in stories that promise an illusory form of social recognition and provide a parenthesis to everyday life in which that recognition is withheld. Thus, even though this literature plots women's lives with regard to system integration, it also points to personal needs that arise from the ethical vacuum of late capitalism, which offers little more than raw competition, the fetishism of the commodity, or in Mexico, the exploitation of the runaway shop.

Notes

1. See, for instance, Dagnino (1973). Discussions of cultural imperialism were particularly widespread in the early 1970s. Some of these discussions are still reflected in Mattelart and Siegelaub (1979), and in publications such as *Comunicación y Cultura,* published by Galerna in Buenos Aires in the early 1970s. Seth Siegelaub also published several volumes of a bibliography of Marxism and the mass media; see *Marxism and the Mass Media: Towards a Basic Bibliography* (New York: International General). The most recent issue I have consulted is number 3 (1974).

2. There is scarcely a deconstructionist critic these days who does not have harsh words for the classical realist text. The criticism originated with Roland Barthes, see especially *S/Z* (1974). For more recent discussions, see Catherine Belsey (1980); and Kaja Silverman (1983).

3. The term *serialized* is used by Jean Paul Sartre in his *Critique of Dialectical Reason* (1976) to refer to groups of people like those in lines at bus stops who are together for a common purpose but are not otherwise bonded. He also describes radio audiences as serialized communities.

4. The notion of interpellation comes from Louis Althusser's definition in "Ideology and Ideological State Apparatuses: Notes towards an Investigation" (1971). Interpellation describes the process whereby people are constituted as subjects by such cultural agents as schooling, religion, and the media and the way they recognize themselves (are "hailed") as subjects.

5. On the transformation of everyday life under the impact of the new media, see Cremoux (1983).

6. The interview was conducted by Tununa Mercado in September 1984 in Mexico City.

7. This information was given by Ms. Ibáñez in the interview mentioned in note 6.

8. For a brief discussion of the Corín Tellado novels, see García Calderón 1984.

9. For instance, in the use of the *charro* (Mexican cowboy) who improvises poetic commentaries on the Televisa news program 24 *Horas*.

10. The publishers, who are not named, give a box number address in San Isidro, California.

CARLOS MONSIVÁIS
Would So Many Millions of People Not End Up Speaking English? The North American Culture and Mexico

Carlos Monsiváis was born in Mexico in 1938. A journalist and a cultural critic, his main titles include *Días de guardar* (1970), *Escenas de pudor y liviandad* (1981), *Entrada libre. Crónicas de la sociedad que se organiza* (1987), and *Los rituales del caos* (1995).

There is a cultural resistance unrelated to commercial inventions, superstitions, or speculations. In 1947, Daniel Cosío Villegas publishes an essay in *Cuadernos Americanos* that raises the alarm about the nation's confusions. If it relinquishes its being,

> Mexico will begin to wander adrift, wasting time that a country already lagging behind in progress cannot afford to lose, only to end up entrusting its major problems to the inspiration of, imitation of, and submission to the United States, not only because it is a rich and powerful neighbor, but also due to the success it has had, a success that we have not known how to attain. We would call upon this country in demand for money, technical training, cultural and artistic ways, political advice, and we would conclude by adopting the entirety of their values, which are so distant from our own convenience and taste. To the already domineering North American influence, the deceitful conviction of some people, the open interests of others, and the indifference and pessimism of the rest would be combined, in order to make possible the sacrifice of our nationality and, what is even worse, of the security, sovereignty, and happiness accomplished by those who forge their own destiny. In that case, many of Mexico's problems would be solved and it could even enjoy unusual material prosperity; but are we sure that our country, that we ourselves, would truly be happier?

Gradually, the most intrepid nationalism loses governmental support. The regime is uncomfortable with the anti-imperialist verbal violence (although it makes use of it in its own negotiations) and it anachronistically considers many of the demands. To the intellectual sector, old-fashioned nationalism appears to be mere *costumbrismo*. Revolutionary nationalism remains isolated, sentimental nationalism is decorative, and in the six-year term of Miguel Alemán Valdés (1946–1952), bridges are made between the modernizing aspiration and Americanization. Alemán, a believer in progress if it is concentrated on spectacular governmental works and the accumulation of individual fortunes, wants to formalize the historic reconciliation with the United States, the preamble of economic integration and social resemblance. And if the left stays in the tubes, it doesn't get any better for "the stronghold of the Hispanic and Creole morality." In command of their ideological customhouses, the traditionalists want to contain desecrating ideas (Protestantism, atheism, Marxism) and thus they do not notice the "Trojan horses" of Americanization: the yearning for an international way of life (technology and comfort) of the bourgeois and middle classes, the omnipresent cult of the contemporary, the persuasion of film and radio, and the migratory flows. The moralist resistance props up backwardness, but it doesn't go beyond that.

I Am Mexican but I Do Not Exaggerate

President Alemán is right about something: since the 1920s, North America is the secret yearning (but not quite) of many middle- and upper-class Mexicans. If that is so, in view of its political clientele, the government should foster what North America has to offer: the industrial mentality, the dogmas of individualism and privacy, the techniques of capitalist development, and the changes in social morals that do not weaken the seal of respectability. In those years, the imitation of the *American way of life* alternates with still omnipresent devotions. In his indispensable *Pueblo en vilo* (1968), Luis González describes the triumph of traditionalism over *gringophilia* among the *braceros* [seasonal farm workers] of the approximate period of 1945–1960:

Many men showed that they had been *braceros* by their loud shirts and jackets, their cowboy boots, their gringo swearwords, their rolled hat brims, their radios, their repertoire of stories brought back from the north, their admiration for the way people spent money up there, and there pretentiousness. . . . They did not come back *pochos*; hardly any of the culture or customs of their American cousin stuck to them—neither language, nor habits of sanitation, nor gestures, nor attitudes. Nor did they bring back any new ideas that might have been useful to them at home. They returned with their souls untouched—or nearly so. (1974, 243)

(This will no longer be true in the next generation. If the *braceros* educated in the strictest nationalism only become angry about the economic situation, those who succeed them will distance themselves from everything that keeps them apart from efficiency, no matter how respected it has been by their parents and grandparents.)

President Alemán hopes to eliminate "the trauma of '47," so denounced by philosophers and psychologists of *Lo Mexicano*, and the adolescents and the urban youth of the 1950s (at least their avant-garde) hope to resemble the models of the movies and magazines from the United States, adopting the youth culture, the new great industry of the United States. The teams of American football need cheerleaders who filter the satisfaction for a "modern" state of mind into the games:

La línea, el core, los halfs, y el full
la línea, el core, los halfs, y el full,
por la gloria de su equipo el Espíritu hablará
Pumas, Pumas, ra ra ra.
[The line, the core, the halves, and the full,
The line, the core, the halves, and the full,
For the glory of the team the Spirit will speak,
Pumas, Pumas, hurrah, rah, rah.]

The relocation of the Universidad Nacional Autónoma de México to the Ciudad Universitaria (inaugurated in 1952 and put into service in 1954) does the rest. In Ciudad Universitaria, President Alemán has seen the grand monument to progress that he coordinates and emblematizes, and the first generation of students in the Pedregal feel superior to their predecessors from the student neighborhood. While enjoying the "up-to-date" atmosphere, with a campus and everything, they abandon the tie, discard many of the rigid formalisms, and want to *live their youth* behaving in the manner of the gringos: there are slaloms, garden parties, bridal showers, house warmings, hulla-balloo, and miniature golf. It is "positive determinism": if the architectural space is modern, the students are also modern or will be shortly by means of atmospheric contagion. And in the urban settings, the *boleros* and tropical rhythms are mixed with the hits from Hit Parade (*"You put your right foot in / you put your right foot out . . .*"), and February 14th, the Day of Friendship and Love (St. Valentine's Day), is successfully established, while the Instituto Tecnológico de Monterrey announces educational reform, a la *gringo*, in the north of the country.

In this turn, the cinema is decisive. During the apogee of Mexican cinema, the youthful model from Hollywood, nice, funny, trapped by the mortal dilemma of whom to invite to the prom (Mickey Rooney in the Andy Hardy series) was seen as a simple *gringada*. In 1956, James Dean dazzles and shocks in *East of Eden* by Elia Kazan and *Rebel without a Cause* by Nicholas Ray. By then, the Mexican cinema has lost the battle of the middle classes, and in order to curb the avalanche of role models, the Mexican censorship prohibits, among other films, *Jailhouse Rock*, due to Elvis Presley's bad example, and *Rebel without a Cause*, because of its "harmful influence." It launches moralizing campaigns against rock and its destructive trail: long hair, "obscene" speech, and premarital sex. Everything is useless. Nothing can stop the identification of the fan with the idol, of the young person with the sincerity that she or he longs for.

Who, of those who benefit in some way from the trickle-down earnings of savage capitalism, will exclaim, as does the sorrowful character of the *costumbrista* José Rubén Romero: "Cambiaron por coca cola tus aguas de chía y limón" [They changed your waters of chía and lemon for Coca-Cola . . .]? Or who will say, like in the 1937 song by Lalo Guerrero:

Pa hacer pesos de a montones no hay como el americano
Pa conquistar corazones no hay mejor que un mexicano.
[To make big bucks, there is no one like the American
To win over hearts, there is no one better than a Mexican . . .]?

In all of Latin America, developmentalism is the god of the financial landscape, the abstract goal that is offered to the people so that in its idealization they refine their millenarian patience. Alemanism attempts to endow its pan-Americanism with a quality of structural relation to the United States and its strategy is unequivocal: technological modernization, defense of traditional values, and exaltation of the state, on which everything depends: the growth of the media and highway networks, the promotion of tourism, the expansion and strengthening of the corporate oligarchy, the permission and prohibition of behaviors that encourage or crush the popular classes, and the formal and sentimental respect of nationalism.

On 11 June 1948 President Alemán declares: "In Mexico, there is no communist problem," which is one of many ways to join the Cold War, on the eve of the Korean War and in the middle of McCarthyism. The

Cold War installs itself in Mexico, through police and administrative measures, and aims at destroying the left. The moral lynching of dissidents is institutionalized in the press, the entrance of people suspected of lefty-ism into the United States is denied (among them, Dolores del Río and Carlos Chávez for a period of time), and the Cold War spreads a deafening anticommunist tone that—as far as the socialist countries are concerned—due to an inevitable paradox is barely telling the truth while believing to reproduce calumnies. President Alemán is received in the White House, the flags captured in 1847 are returned, the Good Neighbor is complimented, and the word *gringo* is no longer a pejorative one.

For the minute history: the bourgeoisie incorporates the practice of the weekend, adopted by the North Americans in 1878 (Fussell 1983). In the childhood imagination, the traditional heroes of Jules Verne and Emilio Salgari, the Mexican comic strip characters, and the protagonists from the Walt Disney universe and the comic book (*Batman, Superman, Terry and the Pirates, The Spirit*) compete and fuse together. And *Reader's Digest* is the favorite reading material for those who don't pick up a book.

The central debate is postponed, hidden by the discussions a propos Americanization. The most urgent is found at the bottom of disputes and condemnations: the cultural internationalization of the country, stopped or mediated by educational backwardness, the country's poverty, the force of nationalism, the myth of the national exceptionality, and the grave differences between Mexico and the United States that everyone perceives and that in *El laberinto de la soledad* (1950), Octavio Paz fixes in a way that will become classic:

> But the solitude of the Mexican, under the great stone night of the high plateau, that is still inhabited by insatiable gods, is very different from that of the North American, who wanders in an abstract world of machines, fellow citizens and moral precepts. In the Valley of Mexico, man feels himself suspended between heaven and earth, and he oscillates between contrary powers and forces, and petrified eyes and devouring mouths. Reality—that is it, the world that surrounds us— exists by itself here, has a life of its own and was not invented by man like it was in the United States. (1961)

The Television: A Double-edged Impulse

On 1 September 1952, television is inaugurated in Mexico by transmitting Miguel Alemán's sixth presidential address. Upon installing channel 4 in Mexico (1954), there is no doubt: the norm will be taken from the experiences and achievements of U.S. television, almost the only conceivable television in the entire world. (The English television is the exception although its scope is more limited.) And to a high degree, U.S. television determines the family's and children's tastes, the technical vocabulary, the tyrannical notion of the show, the styles of advertisement, the ratings cult, the formats of the series, and the repertoire of genres (Westerns, sitcoms, detective series, thrillers, musical shows, children's programs).

Television channels *gringophilia* and contributes more than any other factor to the transfer of the Americanization of the well-to-do sectors to the rest of the population. The meaning of this Americanization is not to disseminate technological, scientific, cinematographic, and literary influences and adoptions, but instead to implant the dreams of individual ascent and to monopolize the keys of "the contemporary": ideas, images, and sensations. The message is categorical: modernity is courtesy of the United States.

To a great extent, television repeats the previous experience. In his book, *The American Radio and Its Latin American Activities, 1900–1939*, James Schwoch demonstrates how the expansion of radio was indispensable to the U.S. world economy. On one hand, the advertisers were the big corporations (Ford Motor Company, General Motors, Colgate-Palmolive, Westinghouse, General Electric); on the other hand, already in the 1920s—and the tendency will be maintained—only Canada is a better buyer than Mexico, which in 1925 acquires radio sets for a total value of 250,000 dollars, and in 1929 for more than a million. (At this time, 1929, more than 90 percent of the radio sets in Mexico are from the United States.) In 1925, the Radio Corporation of America (RCA) installs its affiliate, the Mexico Music Co., and in 1930, XEW is inaugurated as an associate to the National Broadcasting System, a radio division of RCA.

In the 1950s, two businessmen, Emilio Azcárraga Vidaurreta and Rómulo O'Farrill, who admire the industrial dynamic of the United States and its work ethic, see in television the summit of the spectacle that, due to its intrinsically entertaining function, provides no space for cultural programs, political debates, artistic or humanist education, or imaginative demonstrations. Television is, and can only be, the investment of free time in game shows, musical series, offerings to the Virgin, movie star interviews, *gringo* series dubbed as well as they can be, and real and mental squabbles. If the first television broadcast is a presidential address, it isn't because of an eagerness to do politics, but rather to flatter the government while granting it two securities: the omnipresent censorship and the forgetting of all controversy.

What is more important: the power of the medium or the absence of alternatives for the public? The question doesn't have any answers, television doesn't have any rivals, and family life progressively hands over its agenda to the premises and conclusions of television and its mythologies, among which is the television announcer, a mediator between the show and the family. The paradigms are the host Paco Malgesto, who carefully studies and "nationalizes" Ed Sullivan's tics and look of complacent indifference, and the series of "typical music" where cultural nationalism dissolves into the show.

Television modifies the "liberationist deed" of cinema. If cinema is the avant-garde of permissiveness, television operates according to this exterminating principle: the modern presents the traditional as "folkloric" and picturesque, which provokes paternal smiles that the present dedicates to the past. (In this respect, the Rockefeller Report for the Americas is completely frank: "A technology that tears the fabric of all existing cultures is needed.") In its virulence, censorship doesn't notice the obvious: what is permitted on television becomes familiar and "sanctifies," in a word, new forms of relationship. This function is made clear in the 1980s with melodramatic situations that badly hide the partial praise of heterodoxy, the semi-nudes, the French allusions to sex (during the times in which all children possess the keys to the obvious), and the news from diverse moral environments. But even before, television exemplifies the intransigence of censorship and the limitation of its power.

Above all, this affects provincial life, which in twenty years adapts as well as it can to Americanization, always giving ground. Since the emergence of television, behaviors are praised that imply—in various degrees—breaks with the traditional religious and social horizons. And censorship, whether official and ecclesiastic, upon assuming that the essentials of television are controlled (nothing of politics, nothing of sexual humor, nothing of "bad habits"), doesn't detect the corrosive vigor of the flow of images while accepting what will be a fixed ritual: any "liberal" or "liberating" behavior in the United States (from the relationship between kids and parents to feminine clothes, from the style of reportage to the admissible scenes on the screen) is surrounded first by an infuriating alarm, then by mockery, followed by servile imitation, and finally by the frequently creative assimilation. And the sequence of the struggle repeats itself in vain:

(a) The traditionalist groups oppose all innovation: freedom of sexual choice for women, the use of contraceptives, a more egalitarian treatment in the family and schools, frontal nudity in cinema and theater, the public use of "obscene" language, long hair, tight clothing on young people, et cetera.

(b) The avant-gardes take on fashions as moral and political battles, but the traditionalists win the initial battle by securing vetoes and prohibitions (in this field, the theater and cinema are laboratories of social change).

(c) After some time, innovation is generalized and the protesting is eliminated. Corporal pride and the anxiety to be up-to-date prevails over the fear of provocation, and the "apocalyptical," seen from up close, reveals its zones of candor and conventionalism.

The Route of the Pilgrimages: From Chalma to Disneyland

During four consecutive governments (those of Adolfo Ruiz Cortines, Adolfo López Mateos, Gustavo Díaz Ordaz, Luis Echeverría Alvarez), Americanization advances, amid nationalist and third-worldist defiance and the officialization of nostalgia. In August 1961, the Latin American governments, with the exception of Cuba, sign the Punta del Este Charter, which corresponds to the strategy of the Alliance for Progress promoted by the government of John F. Kennedy. In the opening lines, the Charter affirms: "We, the American republics, proclaim our decision to unite in a common effort that will guide our people toward accelerated economic progress and wider social justice within the framework of personal dignity and political freedom." In 1962, John and Jacqueline Kennedy arrive in Mexico City. Their Catholicism, the propagandistic rapture that surrounds them, and the historic reconciliation promoted by the government achieve the unexpected: the visit is a great popular success.

"The first generation of North Americans born in Mexico" emerges, according to the resonating phrase of an obscure elementary school teacher who drowned while crossing the Río Grande. "Denationalization" is propped up by the discrediting of the state ideology, the bureaucratization of civic education, the weakening of already "inefficient" traditions, and the commemorative use of patriotism facing U.S. protectionism and the insulting right-wing ideologies. And large social sectors sustain an idea ever more intimate of the national, sheltering the notion of patria within the affectionate mythologies of the private.

At the same time, the logic of social development requires a greater attachment to the U.S. model. And what was outward admiration in the 1950s later becomes an urgent matter. To "denationalize" is to acquire psychological solvency and social fluidity, it is to compare in an incessant way the two countries, with always favorable results for the United States.

Racism and the looting of resources are omitted, and the image of Mexicans and Latinos created in Hollywood is internalized by a certain sector as an accurate version. "Así somos . . ." [That's the way we are . . .]. It is no longer indispensable to spread the black legend of the "primitives"; the stupor of the Americanized (that is, "modernized" through reverent imitation) middle class saves measures of control. And within the dominant classes, the sensation of belonging to two countries becomes fashionable, to one country by birth, and to the other by way of life and expeditiousness in accommodating to the psychology of the "hombre de su época" [the man of the times].

The fear of contagion of "foreign cultures" does not stop, but instead exacerbates the weakness and the feeling of besiegement. The geographic vicinity to the greatest international achievement of capitalism paradoxically ends up being the greatest condemnation and the best option; the process takes place at the margin of controversies, prophetic demands, and nationalist good wishes. And if the apogee of Americanization is delayed, it is for various motives: the cultural and social heterogeneity, the weight of anti-Yankee traditions, the vigor of nationalism that during a long historic cycle is the preferential explanation of the ties between daily life and the impositions of the state, the chain of "theoretical" glimpses behind sexual gesticulation, labor anger and appeasement, the meaning of the fiesta, and the internalization of repressions.

President Díaz Ordaz wants to comply with the most dogmatic version of nationalism when he calls for an end to isolationism: "We had been provincially proud and candidly satisfied that in a world of youth disturbances, Mexico was an unaffected island" (IV Presidential Report, 1 September 1968). And he continues: "Mexico does not accept solutions that go against its own essences!" But who is authorized to speak in the name of Mexico and what are those essences? In 1968, official nationalism condemns as "unpatriotic" the student movement that demands a nationalism without manipulations that is respectful of civil human rights and free channels to internationalization, which occurs despite everything, as Octavio Paz announces in El laberinto de la soledad: "For the first time in our history, we are contemporaries of all mankind" (1961, 194).

For the majority, in a closed society, internationalization can only mean Americanization. Therefore, when President Echeverría tries, by decree, to lead a "resurrected" nationalism, he confronts the rejection and the mockery of the elites. The typical garments have become costumes and the folkloric ballets progressively depend on the creativity of designers and choreographers more informed about Hollywood and Broadway than Aztlán and Chichén-Itzá. In the other (or the same) order of things, concepts taken from sociology and sociological journalism in the United States are disseminated and continuously internalized: "Los que persuaden en la sombra" (The Hidden Persuaders) name the publicists; "El hombre-organización" (The Organizational Man) designates the employees of big corporations; "la muchedumbre solitaria" (The Lonely Crowd) alludes to the transformations that occur upon going from the "inner-directed," fundamentally autonomous individual, to the "other-directed" one, victim of the conspiracy of the examples; "la sociedad de la abundancia" (The Affluent Society) refers to the creation of artificial and gratuitous necessities. And the concept most dispersed is without a doubt that of the *status seekers*, the suddenly glorified term.

The glory of status rules the changes of address, the election of appearance, the selection of restaurants and vacation places, the pursuit of bronzed skin, and the "correct" product brands. Above all, status is defined by the automobile, which goes from being a necessity to symbolizing a declaration of wealth, a mobile advertisement of the precise position of its owner, an autobiography without rhetorical, false modesty. And in the middle-class families, status is the trip to Disneyland; the family travels so that the kids become accustomed to a "fantasy of quality."

"Their Parties Are Elegant / Dawn, What Banquets! / But I Wouldn't Want to Be with Them / Everyone Talking about Illustrious Men / And No One Ever Mentions Elvis Presley"

Young people from the middle classes find the door to contemporary sensations in rock, and one after another, from Bill Halley and Little Richard to the Beatles and the Rolling Stones, in the eternalized instant of their audition, rock idols become the augurs of a new era. Of course, the relation with other cultures is not only an attribute of rock: it emerges in various forms thanks to film, literature, theater, and dance. But in rock it goes deeper, due to the "youth ideology" and the capability of music, the sensation of belonging to a worldwide orb.

Before, the relations with the North American culture were the work of the cultural avant-garde. In the 1920s, Salvador Novo translates U.S. poets and diversifies attention, absorbed in French poetry. In the years to follow, the repercussion of some authors is very vast: Ernest Hemingway, William Faulkner, John Dos Passos, F. Scott Fitzgerald, and John Steinbeck, among the most important. In the 1960s, the rediscovery of the North American cinema, a consequence of the French theory of "auteur cinema," does away with much of the *gringada* perception and reevaluates genres and directors, such as D.W. Griffith, John Ford, Fritz Lang, George Cukor, Nicholas Ray, Raoul Walsh, Val Lewton, and Buster Keaton. Later, the thriller (represented by Dashiell Hammett, Raymond Chandler, Chester Himes) vastly influences the novel. However, regarding the history of mentalities, nothing even comes close to the seductions of rock.

In the implantation of youth culture, for the middle classes, rock is the instantaneous channel through which the youth could finally belong to the "times." In its first stage, rock is the energy that was demanded from music: Chuck Berry, Little Richard and, notoriously, Elvis Presley, indicate other forms of behavior and life rhythms. And rock's association with "contemporary vibrations" and violence are revealed, according to the authorities, upon the showing in Mexico of *King Creole* in 1958, another of Presley's vehicles. The day of its premiere there is a riot in the theater: young people dance in the aisles, the police intervene, the film is prohibited, and rock is closely watched.

The Spanish versions somewhat calm down the censoring zeal. It is a "crazy" though admissible rhythm. And upon the fading of this possibility, like everywhere, the emergence of the Beatles and the Rolling Stones progressively determines another form of youth behavior.

"Fidel, Fidel / What Is It about Fidel? / That the Americans Cannot Put Up with Him"

"In 1959, the triumph of Fidel Castro's guerrilla army proposes a new road to internationalization for Latin Americans: the revolutionary mentality in continuous advancement. (In 1965 Che Guevara will propose: "To create one, two, three, many Vietnams in Latin America.") According to the implicit theory, a revolutionary is an inevitable contemporary because there is nothing more modern than to revindicate social justice. Thanks to the impulse of the Cuban Revolution, anti-imperialism reconstitutes and foments the (ephemeral) hope of transforming violence into humanism. Upon the encounter with Latin American solidarity, in the 1960s the multitudes march in Lima, Buenos Aires, Bogotá, and Mexico with cries of victory: "Cuba, yes! Yankees, no!" The little country, ninety kilometers from the empire, which resists and searches for an identity in revindication of the exploited, is not bad news.

Also, the Cuban Revolution rehabilitates what was believed as nonexistent: the goal of an effectively Latin American culture, which diverse phenomena make credible: the literary boom, the social song, the rediscovery of radical history, and, above all, what by then was felt impossible:

the diversity of cultural options. Sectarianism grows worse, the Cuban Revolution achieves extraordinary advances in education and health care, and in the new reading of the Latin American process, the perspective from the years of the Popular Front is revived and brought up to date. Of course colonization, ethnocide, the plundering of raw materials, U.S. support of strong-hand governments, and the need to redefine the meanings of *civilization* and *barbarism* exist. Immediately afterward, the *caudillista* inertia degrades or nullifies the influence of the Cuban Revolution, which, after its open beginnings, is confined to dogmatic platforms. For example, *Calibán* (1971), the essay by Roberto Fernández Retamar, peremptorily divides the intellectual and artistic creation between supporters of Ariel (imperialism, the "northernphilia" pointed out by José E. Rodó), and those of Caliban, the false monster and true *independentista*. *How to Read Donald Duck* (1975) by Armand Mattelart and Ariel Dorfman is a more than solemn reading of cultural industry and popular culture. After reiterating what is evident (the capitalist ideologization of comics), Mattelart and Dorfman proceed to demand from the comic strip the scope of the treaty:

> It is, by now, amply proven that the Disney world is one in which all materiality has been purged. All forms of production (the material, sexual, historical) have been eliminated, and conflict has never a social base, but is conceived in terms of good versus bad, lucky versus unlucky, and intelligent versus stupid. So Disney characters can dispense with the material base underpinning every action in a concrete everyday world. Since Disney has purged himself of the secondary economic sector (industrial production, which gave rise to contemporary society and power to the bourgeoisie and imperialism), there is only one infrastructure left to give body to his fantasies and supply for his ideas. It is the one which automatically represents the economic life of his characters: *tertiary* sector. The service sector, which arose in the service of industry and remains dependent upon it. (1975, 96)

Very much influenced by the Cuban Revolution, the Marxist criticism of this period describes the subjugated masses, conquered for capitalism by the subliminal messages of the comics, especially by Superman and the symbol of plutocracy, *Tío Rico Mac Pato* [Scrooge McDuck]. These beaten armies are so unconscientious that they revere the commercial sport as if it were the very Patria, and in their gullible fervor they convert television into the pulpit of the new Great Inquisitor, whose center is U.S. imperialism and whose irradiation reaches everything. In my belief, what happens is perhaps more pressing but much less apocalyptical. Upon insisting on cultural "penetration" (an expression that presupposes the cultural virginity of Latin America), a reverse sacralization consolidates the ideological devices of the commercial offensive. The theory of the "victorious manipulation" (the deification of technology through supposedly critical means) is inexact, to say the least. Instead, the popular classes admit their lack of options, and from there they create their alternatives to the best of their abilities.

Not all of the anti-imperialist impulse is frozen in sectarian interpretations. The flow of events from 1950 to 1970 (the Korean War, the executions of Ethel and Julius Rosenberg, who were accused of atomic espionage, the daily consequences of the Cold War, the maltreatment of undocumented workers, the racist violence of the Deep South, the criminal cynicism of the CIA, the invasion of Santo Domingo, and, above all, the Bay of Pigs invasion and the intervention in Vietnam) remind Latin Americans with precision of the content of imperialism. And there is an ardent response to this in the form of demonstrations (broken up by police) and individual protests. In this way, for example, on 4 November 1965, the poets Carlos Pellicer and José Carlos Becerra are arrested in front of the U.S. embassy for passing out flyers that make public a letter addressed to the U.S. ambassador, Fulton Freeman:

> No Mr. Ambassador, things are already changing; we are now ready for anything. Do you understand? U.S. intervention, everywhere and in every sense, has brought upon you a magnificent wave of hate and disdain. Honestly, do you believe that young North Americans go to the Vietnam War with heroic spirits and patriotic enthusiasm? Isn't the tremendous problem, as inhumane as absurd, of the men of the black race born in the U.S. enough?
>
> Believe me, Mr. Ambassador, that I, as well as other Indo-Americans, will fully take advantage of the fear and stupidity of the government that you represent. (Carlos Pellicer)

Pellicer's actions are hardly considered a newsworthy fact. The control of the media is absolute. And in 1967, the death of Che Guevara in Bolivia revives the Bolivarian ideal in very diverse sectors: students, academics, writers. In "Líneas por el 'Che' Guevara" (1967), Pellicer exclaims:

> Su muerte viva nos llama a todos,
> es la llama que anuncia el fuego nuevo,
> es la participación necesaria y dichosa
> para no morir de sueños.

[His living death calls us all
It is the flame that announces the new fire
It is the necessary and joyful participation
To not die from dreaming.] (1977, 43)

In its historic sense, anti-imperialism, a central element of popular thought and feeling in Latin America, depends on the categorical experience (invasions, territorial plundering, imposition of dictators, systematization of economic looting) and on the univocal version of the North American: the other, the aggressor, the invader, the predator, and even the heretic. Already in the 1980s, the signs of the other persist: racism, police aggression, military and economic offensives, the imposition of a "unipolar world." But the notion of "empire" is assimilated in very diverse ways and, given the high number of Hispanics in the United States, for millions of Latin Americans the other stops being the other in an absolute way, and is partially converted into something that can be "expropriated" to an extent, not because his or her way of life is extremely idealized, but instead because, owing to an optical distortion, a high number of immigrants considers the horizon of great opportunities to be within its reach.

In 1965, tens of thousands of people take to the streets to protest the U.S. invasion of Santo Domingo. In 1989, although only a few (all businessmen) in Latin America approve of the invasion of Panama, the mobilization of protest is minimum in the face of an overbearing act that leaves thousands dead after the bombarding of the civil population. And the lethargy is tied to diverse facts: the feeling of worldwide impotence sharpened and certified by the War in the Persian Gulf; the scarcity or nonexistence of alternatives in countries without economic solutions for the majority or a genuinely democratic system; the highest degree of dependence on foreign investments; and the spread of Americanization.

The Counterculture in Mexico: Those Who Go Out for Fun and Those Who Are Never Included

During its expansion between 1965 and the end of the Vietnam War, the counterculture in the United States intends to be and represent the alternative to the American way of life and its landscapes of conformism, malls, conglomerates in suburbia, and strict hierarchies. The counterculture defies the "silent majority" with its own predilections:

- the search for libertarian states of spirit and thought
- the impassioned learning of expressions from Oriental cultures

- the free speech movement (to say "fuck you" in order to make language the cathartic drain of violence and the "free territory" of relationships)
- the resistance to governmental and academic authoritarianism
- the rehabilitation of utopias, in order to start a new life in the communes
- the relinquishment of "formalities"; and
- the cult of rock, an all-embracing vision and "broadening of mind" (this implies the great generational convention: the use of marijuana, amphetamines, LSD, peyote, mushrooms).

An urgent matter shapes the first stage of the counterculture: the U.S. intervention in Vietnam. "Hell, no / We won't go . . ." Instead of killing in My Lai or dying face down in the mud, it is preferable to drop out of the system, burn draft cards, protest in front of the Pentagon, and insist on the value of human life and life on the planet.

Young Mexicans who adopt the counterculture (not with this name) lack the impulse of Vietnam's tragic force. At the beginning, they are small groups who listen to rock music with mystic fervor, laugh at family conventions, observe PRI politics with sarcasm and annoyance, and become irritated in the presence of traditional versions of the country and its horizon of possibilities. They do not believe in progress, they hate destinies planned in advance by families or social conventions, and they aren't dazzled by a modernity defined only by material acquisitions. In the world of la onda [the wave], the counterculture, sensorial freedoms are exalted and the values sacred to parents and grandparents are subject to mockery. The return to nature is held as the great critique of consumer society and, without too much theoretical consistency, nationalism is declared abolished. More than theories, the counterculture in Mexico provides defiant or rebellious attitudes, among which the destruction of many moral taboos, and the repertoire of apocalyptical and anti-apocalyptical anticipations extracted from the Beatles, the Rolling Stones, the Who, Bob Dylan, Jimi Hendrix, Janis Joplin, Led Zeppelin, Jefferson Airplane, and the Grateful Dead. "The answer, my friend, is blowing in the wind." And also, "Freedom's just another word for nothing left to lose."

The year 1968 (the student movement, the massacre of Tlatelolco, the unequivocal conclusions over the nature of the governing sector) accelerates the change and multiplies the counterculture's presence. For political, sexual, and sentimental reasons, thousands of young people—commonly university students from the middle class—take the road of

Americanization proposed by the counterculture and disassociate themselves from the government and traditional morals and culture. How does one accept the conservatism that is more appropriate to the nineteenth century? How does one admit that the president of the republic is the "literal father" of Mexicans? How does one not find detestable the idea of having to reproduce without deviance the life of parents and grandparents? In its first stage, the catalogue of partial achievements and self-destructive obsessions of this counterculture is impressive. Among its central elements are

- rock, something more than just a musical genre, the source of sensations that were inconceivable some years before, the accompaniment of new ways of the body and oneiric life, and the glimpse of another kind of urban poetry as expressed by the demolition phrases: "I can't get no satisfaction, but I'll try" and "Father Mackenzie, writing the words of a sermon that no one will hear" (Rolling Stones and the Beatles)
- drugs (marijuana, acid, mushrooms), the cult of induced ecstasy, the excess of the senses, the disorder that foments the illusion of adventure, the experimentation that leads to other spiritual goals ("All your dreams are on their way / See how they shine," writes Paul Simon in "Bridge over Troubled Water")
- esotericism, the certainty of realities that can only be grasped through heterodox means; this implies a rejection of doctrines assimilated for the most part through inertia and not by conviction: Christianity, Marxism, Freudism
- the new consciousness of the body, exacerbated by music, drugs, and the idea of the destruction of moral and mental walls. This brings with it a more open and frequent sex life, less guilt ridden although still subject to machismo
- the ecotopy, the utopia of returning to nature, naturism, macrobiotic food, and so forth, which is the beginning of the ecologic movement; and
- the communes, the attempt to dissolve individuality, the self-sufficient way of life, and the ambition of a shared life.

At its peak (from 1968 to 1972 or 1973), the Mexican counterculture distinguishes itself through appearances and social hostility toward appearances. The hippi-tecs with long hair, their philosophic discourse, their backpacks, their sandals, and their disdainful "chatter" against the status quo abound in the capital or in Huautla, on their route to San Francisco or the periphery towns of Mexico City. They are struck down by governmental repression blessed by bishops and businessmen alike. The police detain and shave those who have long hair, interrupt the few parties that are permitted, and assault the young people in order to find or "plant" marijuana on them. And in 1971, in Avándaro, State of Mexico, there is a rock festival with an explosion of the forbidden language, indifference or mockery with regard to prudishness, and enthusiasm for the advantages of age (the Nation of Avándaro distrusts anyone older than thirty and praises everything that intensifies your sense of perception). During three days, among cheers of joy that make up for an inadequate sound system, crowding, beers, *toques* [marijuana smoking] and *tocadas* [parties], the *chavos* [young people] from the popular classes ratify the inevitable: their conversion to the cultural industry's model of "youth," and the expropriation of the *aliviane* [being successful in love]. They desert the government and family nationalism (which doesn't convince them), reject instituted society (which excludes them), and move to the psychological space where they can live the sensorial climax and where the "responsibilities of adulthood" are postponed or considered as ridiculous yokes. And the music organizes the stimuli. Each good *rola* [song] is an anthem to joy at maximum volume, in the middle of a gratifying trip.

In Avándaro a large part of class and nationalist control is lost to the notions of youth. And the repression, the exorcism through articles and homilies, the ban of concerts, and the call to reason make us think that the Avándaro alternative is ephemeral. In fact, in little time, the scarcity of resources, the hopelessness regarding the lack of alternatives, and the heartrending lifestyle of the *nacos* (the old bronze race) liquidate the dream of the Nation of Avándaro. But a lot of *chavos* persist in their eagerness to find their own spaces, and they transcend imitation, extracting from rock psychological advantages unheard of in their social milieu. They will not have read Carlos Castaneda and Aldous Huxley, memorized Jack Kerouac and Allen Ginsberg, meditated over shamanism, captured the European experience through the jazz records mentioned in Julio Cortázar's *Rayuela*, examined in detail *The Tibetan Book of the Dead*, investigated with scientific passion the multiple levels of meaning of *Sgt. Pepper's Lonely Hearts Club Band*, or recited the discography of Elvis Presley from Sun Records. But they are many and they know that if they are not modern, they will be nothing in their own eyes, and they assay the offers within their reach: rock, tribal life, the glances at the movies and television, the immersion in drugs, and the brutal spontaneity of sex. And they insist on their challenge: if they will let us be modern only in this way, then only in this way will we be modern.

Then, the middle-class youngsters flee from the counterculture milieus and the *nacos* relieve them. They do not share the zeal for the "doors of perception," attribute metaphysical heights to drugs (they use marijuana with the exact jubilation they grant to alcohol), scrutinize the messages of rock, or purposely create instantaneous poetry from "the dark side of the moon," but thanks to the musical euphoria and adjacent stimuli they settle where they are not rejected. They are the new "profound Mexico" that experiences urban agglomeration, school dropout, precocious and *machista* sexuality, hatred of the police, and rough slang that is the biography of the tribe. Upon finding their vital language in dreams and behaviors taken from rock, they trust to music the nature of their youth.

While the rock experience is "nationalized," the first counterculture generation fades away. The police assault continues against young people, there is proof of irrevocable damage from drug use, the hippi-tecs marry and undergo cosmetic surgery upon dispensing with their long hair, the search for security returns, the communes disintegrate, concerts are consumed only through records, and what is crucial—the mystic—evaporates. The great invention of Americanization, the youth culture, tones up consumer society, and the *onderos* [wave people] return to regimented life.

How Do You Say "Honey" in English?

In retreat, or confined to its "inexpugnable" cities, cultural nationalism, the point of convergence between the left and the right, from distinct perspectives but with very similar emphases, lavishes its anti-technological preventions, complains about the dissolution of traditions (the right: the respect for elders; the left: the class struggle), pays homage to the feudal conception of the family, and exhibits its puerile fear of the assault of *Spanglish*.

Government after government attempted to protect language through coercive measures, with laws and regulations, fining and scolding those who baptize their business *pocho* style: "Jimmy's, Charlie's." The language academicians and the wannabes call for the "purity of the language," and they attempt to isolate the word-viruses that infect speech without much success. (In this way, for example, how many really used *neblumo*, the term that was proposed in order to disallow the linguistic entrance of *smog*, or who said *balompié* and not *futbol?*) And the paternalism regarding language is a sincere act of visible desperation, which in the government of José López Portillo culminates in the bureaucratic disaster called Comité Pro-Defensa del Idioma [Defense of Language Commission], another implicit scolding to those who do not even protect the quality of what they say.

An unappealable canon that treats language like a defenseless being is sought after, and what is obvious is ignored: if English has invaded the space of other languages to such a degree, it is for hardly resistible reasons: those of the military, economic, and technological powers of the United States, which engender the lingua franca that makes inevitable the spread of new words around the world. Daily, a word—*software* or *videoclip*—is incorporated in the international dictionary, without alternative. And nevertheless, at the end of a century of Americanization, Mexican Spanish, impoverished and enriched, maintains its vital rhythm.

Will the Day Arrive When There Are More Youth Subcultures than Young People?

The counterculture *(la onda)* is only a part, albeit the most radical and independent part, of the youth cultural universe, very tied to Americanization and, at the same time, capable of producing movements of considerable originality, especially on the northern border, in regions highly marked by their migratory pulse (Jalisco, Sinaloa, Michoacán) and, in the case of the *chavos-banda* [gang-boys] and the punks, in Mexico City.

Mixture defines the *chavos-banda*, very visible in the 1980s: they are the result of the old, urban *palomillas* [gangs] and the spirit of territorial appropriation especially infused by two seminal films: *The Warriors* (1979) by Walter Hill and *The Road Warrior* (1981) by George Miller. The repercussions of *The Warriors* are collective and organizational, in contrast to the more individualistic and self-complacent resonance of *Rebel without a Cause* and Presley's first films. (*Easy Rider*, so fundamental for the counterculture, was forbidden in Mexico.)

Immediately, the movie cult accelerates and modulates the demographic explosion of the gangs, fanatics of heavy metal and of the post-apocalyptical slovenliness of *The Road Warrior* and rock groups like Kiss and the Police. The *chavos-banda*, the outgrowth of the urban culture's poor zones, combine Americanization (basically aural) and the nationalism of survival. And despite their lesser numbers, the case of the punks from Mexico City is similar, a rebellion of looks diluted in the much more tolerant megalopolis.

On the border, subcultures bloom for a time, before the call for "good youth behavior" cancels their expansion with the enticement of economic integration. In his book, *A la brava ése* (1988), José Manuel Valenzuela studies a central repertoire: *cholos*, low riders, punks, and *chavos-banda*, as well as a varied secondary cast. The first group enjoys its peak in the 1970s and goes extinct or is cornered between rituals of self-destruction and police persecutions, which make it risky to be or look like a *cholo*. In their development, the Mexican *cholos* confirm something: there is no such thing as straight Americanization. From their Californian counterparts they derive their attire, their idioms and the art of graffiti, their muralist predilection, and their attitudes and musical tastes, but nevertheless they are not a mere transplant, but the opposite: the entrenchment in border needs, the proposal of a mentality that deposits the image of the nation in the barrio, synthesizing all at once regional tendencies.

The first Mexican *cholos*, devotees of the Jefecita de Guadalupe [Patron Saint of Guadalupe], enchanted with their tattoos and their so "outdated" look, aspire to an identity that belongs to the ideal barrio, and what it is important for them is to be *carnales* [brothers, friends] or *batos locos alivianados* [crazy boys in love] without anybody fucking with them about the calendar of official nationalism and the PRI. And in Tijuana, Culiacán, Guadalajara, or Zamora, the *chavos* from the popular *colonias* [neighborhoods], anxious for migratory adventures, take flight from their attire to the promised land, and begin an odyssey wearing old shirts, the rags of the underemployed or the fruit harvesters. The outfit is a work application and the luggage to the barrios in Los Angeles.

After the *chavos-banda* and the *cholos* vanished, the pretensions of generational autonomy become lethargic, and on the surface reigns the only possible youth culture that consumer society promulgates.

Americanization: The Profound Superficial Integration

Beginning in the 1960s, what had been an elitist fervor is mass mediated, and the enthusiasm for "what is North American" is now popular. The proposal of the U.S. government, the Alliance for Progress (of evident resonance in Mexico despite its diminished role), is seen by many as a failure for not impeding the sympathy for the Cuban Revolution, but some, like the utopist Iván Illich, consider it a success:

> As an alliance for the progress of the consuming classes and the domestication of the great masses, the Alliance has been a big step in the modernization of the patterns of consumption of the Latin American

middle classes—in other words, it has been a means of integrating this colonial metastasis in the dominant culture of the U.S. metropolis. At the same time, the Alliance has modernized the levels of aspiration of the majority of the citizens and has directed their demands to products to which they neither have nor will have access. (1974, 19)

(It is very probable that the role Illich confers to the Alliance for Progress is excessive. But if we change "Alliance" to "television advertisement," the description is impeccable.)

The nationalist sectors confront Americanization with gestures and discourses that, without affecting it, facilitate its accelerated pace. The error is colossal: suddenly technological progress is identified with North American ideology, culture is confused with comfort acquisition, and, in the name of nationalism, the renunciation of innovations is almost demanded. After a slight or arduous feeling of guilt, she or he who accepts technology feels that, concomitantly, she or he has become Americanized. And "globalization" as a technique of obedience is supported in the vain fear of a feeble nationalism that overflows the nightmares of the populace. In this way, resistance to Americanization is purely declarative most of the time because the seduction is not ideological but technological: how does one say "no" to comfort? And if the meaning of the contemporary is decided in the United States (an affirmation that demands some nuances), a Latin American who asks him or herself, "How contemporary am I?," strictly speaking is asking, "How close or far away am I from the U.S. model?" The national is a variable of discomfort, as colonized as inevitable.

Daily, whether it is or isn't a conscious attitude, what is felt as anachronistic is that which is far from the U.S. paradigms. Other societies can be freer or less repressive (let's say, the Scandinavians), but according to the dominant criteria in Latin America, advancements are determined in the United States, and from there the ideological flips that go along with fashion (the bikini or the miniskirt spread when corporal pride is stronger than the fear of "what people will say"), the most uninhibited norms of family relations, the seal of "efficiency" or "inefficiency" that decides the future of traditions (from the use of indigenous languages to adultery), the increment of spaces of freedom for kids, adolescents, and women, and the minimum tolerance toward behaviors that were unmentionable before.

Exceptionally, in this case the dominant ideas of this period are those of the dominant class: Americanization [agringamiento], the people of high incomes reason, is the only known strategy that allows us to be incorporated into what really is worth the trouble. The world turns around this great life-style, and New York, Houston, Dallas, and Los Angeles are well worth the certainty that daughters abandon puberty and virginity at the same time that marital infidelity is no longer unilateral, and that planned obsolescence also affects beliefs. How much is lost by renouncing an idiosyncrasy that is not as vague as it is "devalued in the market"? And from this position pathetic consequences are generated: "Underdevelopment," affirms Iván Illich, "appears as a state of mind when human necessities are emptied in the mold of an urgent demand for new brands of canned solutions that will continually be beyond the reach of the majority" (1974, 22).

In the devastation of natural and social resources that Mexico and Latin America endure, Americanization is a decisive instrument of control. It promotes political demobilization, solidifies economic denationalization, implants consumer habits in social classes without purchasing power, and irrationally and grotesquely sharpens the distances between realities and desires. But its role changes constantly. Until recently, Americanization was the way to "become universal" by way of copying. Now, it is a place of multi-class encounters that, *grosso modo*, is defined according to the technological impact, and generally is that which is only debated from resignation or with rhetorical purposes. And upon Americanizing themselves in various ways, the young people from the popular classes believe this is the way to exorcise their resounding lack of future.

At the same time, in view of the gaudy deceit, there is a growing number of those who transform the foolishness and debasement offered in the name of Americanization into joyfully assumed popular culture and nationalist zeal. In some way, Americanization is "Mexicanized," or "Peruvianized," or however you want it, and the international is implacably fused with the very local. Something remains clear: the principles and slogans of the cultural industry are potentially "true" with respect to the masses, but inevitably false for each individual. And the nationalist revindication, either ritual or inexact from the masses' point of view, is indispensable to legions of individuals. For this reason, the unappealable conclusions about the mass media are so risky. Surely, the codes that reproduce the relations of production matter to the industry of consciousness. (That exploitation perpetuates itself through the collective interiorization of dogmas and resignations.) But also, surely, no one mechanically incorporates everything she or he hears and sees into his or her own life.

All of the Channels Will Transmit
the Genesis and the Apocalypse

Starting in the 1960s, the transnational corporations decide, without any possible rivals and in a continually expansive way, the life rituals of the bourgeoisie and the middle classes, the meaning of child amusement, the youth culture, and the prestigious use of free time. Before, the fashions used to take some time in crossing the commercial and psychological borders; afterward, time is considerably reduced—mostly due to cable television and parabolic antennas—to the point of arriving almost simultaneously in the sectors with buying power capacity or among the avant-garde youth. One after the other, the U.S. institutions of taste and consumption become the Latin American institutions of taste and consumption: the Oscar, Grammy, and Emmy awards ceremonies, the Hit Parade, the adoption of cult films, martial arts (the ambition of the Mexican Ninja), the following of movie star gossip, rock as a generational language, Nintendo as a childhood obsession.

The genuine internationalization and the pathetic or unabashed imitation coexist and fuse together. And the acquisition of a competitive mentality is added to the buying of televisions, transistor radios, blenders, tape recorders, electric washing machines, and computers. The major success of the process: the identification in some sectors of the consumption indispensable for a better life with the rejection of any idea of social justice. And such a profuse subjugation makes some critics concede to the cultural industry a greater span of influence than it actually affords. It is true that in mass society only stentorian versions fit (attires, customs, speech, sense of humor, visions of eroticism), but the hegemony of the transnational corporations will be very imperfect while the modes of experiencing it are so diverse. Television, for example, covers the entire country with its colonized formats, but its reception is very different in a popular neighborhood than in a residential one.

For the majority, the radio or the television becomes the great interlocutor, not just a zone of entertainment but a mode of life that, once taken into account (upon spurning almost any educative hierarchization: "I am so interested in you watching me that I treat everyone like children"), compensates for its social limitations. The message is clear: you do not have any alternative, audience; move closer to the paradigmatic mirror; reflect yourself over these plots, songs, phrases, attitudes; acquire, through contagion, a globalized identity and a sentimental education. And whoever speaks in this milieu of "cultural manipulation" is exact and insufficient, for speaking half-truths. The mass culture acts over the previously vanquished and, upon channeling their defeat, transforms exploitation in the backdrop that upholds the melodramatic dreams of the victims. The idea of "manipulation" is not to be used so consecratorily or deterministically, without accepting that such a tyranny forever demobilizes. And reality provides ample testimonies to the contrary.

The Dawn of Globalization:
Now Everybody Knows Who They're Working For

I'm translating an article from Esquire
on a sheet of paper from Kimberley-Clark Corporation
on an old Remington typewriter.
I'll correct the text with an Esterbrook pen.
What I am paid will add a few pesos to the profits
of Carnation, General Foods, Heinz,
Colgate-Palmolive, Gillete
and the California Packing Corporation.
—José Emilio Pacheco[1]

Cablevision. Superhero comics. Fast and badly translated humor. Countless products that satiate, invent, and modify needs. Television programs whose apotheoses depend on the victory of the U.S. justice system. Books where the selling techniques "construct" the personality of the reader. Very refined technologies. Video cassette recorders in which the community experience of cinema is buried. Satellite communication. Ideology of the MacLuhanian global village. Videodiscs. Control of telecommunications by transnational corporations. Strategies of consumption that reinvent the idea of control and the notion of the housewife. The "philosophy" of the largest salesman in the world. Movies produced in accordance with a meticulous study of the market. Audiovisual software. International news agencies that unify information and enthrone one single point of view. Disdain in the face of each nation's history. Imposition— by necessity and by prepotency—of a world language. A circuit of ideological transmission that goes from advertisement to the pedagogy of the news. Control of the "information revolution." Feminine magazines that give "femininity" the character of a shopping center. Reordering of ways of life. Malls that function like basilicas with innumerable chapels.

A Mexican whole of this landscape of subordination? The affinities between satire and reality: in the final scene of the movie Born in East L. A., a crowd that resembles the demographic explosion rushes from Tijuana toward San Diego, California. And their voracious race reveals, with allegorical emphasis, the irreversible: each year, in proportions not at all diminished, hundreds of thousands of Mexicans, Salvadorians, and Guatemalans, who must confront police brutality, the web of deceit and the fraud of the guides of the undocumented (the *polleros*), their ties to the land and feelings of insufficiency (cultural, idiomatic, technological), move forward toward their obsessive goal (the modernity whose basis is employment). And, in spite of everything, they persist.

In twenty years (1970–1990) the northern border reconstitutes itself, loses its character as a place of passing, is "morally rehabilitated," comes to know industrial development, allows drug traffickers to invade, extends its university systems and cultural groups, forgets its legends of vice in small numbers, suffers and benefits from the *maquiladoras*, aspires to full employment, and is deeply integrated into the U.S. economy while its intellectuals guarantee the vigilant preservation of national identity. The abuses of centralism persist, but the northern border gives up its mythology as the anteroom of the migratory dream.

"I Am Mexican / My Land Is Barren"

Reasons that support the arguments of determinism include the border with the United States that is three thousand kilometers long, economic dependence (72 percent of Mexican transactions are done with the U.S. market), and the migration of workers mostly, though not exclusively, to Texas and California. Before, if they wanted to orient their relation with modernity, the provinces looked toward the country's capital; now, when apparently, amid chaotic explosions, the entire country is becoming one single city, the attention—guided by mass media and the "traveler's fantasies" of the immigrants—strays from centralism.

The United States, and more precisely, the city of Los Angeles, is situated in the catalogue of idealizations, the urban monster thought to be the most plentiful in possibilities, the place already inhabited by millions of Mexicans, the paradise of freeways, assembly of ghettos, and the realization, according to the Polish writer Ryzsard Kapucinsky, of the prophecy of the Cosmic Race, the universal *mestizaje* that José Vasconcelos discerned in 1925: "The various races of the earth tend to intermix at a gradually increasing pace, and eventually will give rise to a new human type, composed of selections from each of the races already in existence" (1977, 1).

In Los Angeles, Mexicans, Nicaraguans, Salvadorians, and Hondurans are already *Hispanos*, members of the minority that in the year 2000 will be the largest in the United States. There, as hoped, they will have the employment that their countries have denied them, the house or the apartment with modern facilities, the school that will get their kids out of the low-wage jobs, and the vibration of contemporariness, impossible to obtain in their towns or popular neighborhoods. Immigrants pay their new gains (the idiomatic expansion, the initially epidermal contact with the technology that will end up being their "second skin," the reconstruction of the rural environment in milieus supposedly and wishfully postmodern) with their brutal experience of uprootedness (the abandonment of the ultimate identity: the certainty of knowing their exact place in their community).

Everything is new and seems accessible, everything is ultimately unreachable, everything is assumed with hard work and the suspension of incredulity. The undocumented, the wetback, the illegal, uses the unexpected tactic: she or he reveres the customs of which she or he lets go in order to better shake off those mental habits that make difficult his or her belonging to the hostile, racist, persecutory, and also in various ways, rewarding milieu. This could be the prayer of the immigrant:

> I thank you dear Virgin of Guadalupe, because you let me be who I've always been, although I don't know if you have noticed, Patron Saint, that I am much more tolerant toward what I don't understand or share, and capable of being faithful to you, since you are the Nation even if now I may be a Pentecostal, Jehovah's Witness, Adventist, Baptist, or Mormon, determined not to change although my appearance may be so different, and I'm always all ears to this gigantic radio, ghetto blaster, I believe that's what they call it, where I listen to these melodies that I never thought I would love so much. I swear, dear Virgin, I am the same as always although now I don't even recognize myself in the mirror.

"Americanization, Professor, Means that Mexicans, Instead of Thinking in Spanish Like Before, Think in Spanish Like Now"

I believe that the speculations over the cultural results of economic integration with the United States, the fears centered on the loss of identity, the destruction of idiosyncrasies, and so on are somewhat belated and alarmist. The process has been going on for a long time and, even though it is intensifying, what is essential is already in sight: the continent, and Mexico, will continue to Americanize, and worldviews will be refined and modified depending on how far from or close to high technology, without affecting what are still basic values, among which is the Spanish language, whose vitality and power of assimilation do not require governmental sponsors foreign to the actual educational process. (Who nowadays can define with a minimum of responsibility Mexicanness or Peruvianness?)

Upon expanding, the multiple character of the term *Americanization* becomes evident. There is an Americanization that seeks out the keys to intelligibility, the defense against what is not well understood through the imitative method that "has been nationalized," which is opposed to an Americanization that is the renouncement of all national traditions given that they obstruct the passage to personal and family modernization. And this is complemented by an oppressive fact: at the same time that its influence modifies rigidities and intolerance, U.S. society (as a whole, deeply racist and classist) provides the pattern of new racisms and classisms for Latin America.

To what extent does the force of Americanization affect current definitions of sovereignty and national culture? In answer, if one wishes to get to the bottom of the issue, the alarmism and the conditioned reflexes of chauvinists and assimilationists should be eliminated at any cost, and the evident should be considered: Americanization, in various degrees, is already a substantial part of the Latin American culture, and in the logic of survival, sovereignty cannot be renounced, in theory or in practice.

A new common place: in Mexico, the border with the United States is found everywhere, and in cultural and economic matters, we Mexicans all live on the border. Thus, for example, the migratory waves have established their "national identity" without paying tribute to the official history. Their history is distinct: loyalty to gastronomic tastes (without exaggeration), fidelity to styles of religious piety (with and without lifelong commitments), enthusiasm for songs and legends that are collective autobiographies and indulgencies of forgetfulness, and—a novelty in the incessant melting pot of regional traditions—the invention of a "northern spirit," which is self-assured, plainspoken, braggart, immoral as long as the police don't stop it, honest because of fear and conviction, and enamored with the perpetual fiesta. And, deep down, it isn't taken seriously.

How do the migratory flows from Mexico to the United States proceed? In their essay, *The Current Situation in Mexican Immigration*, Georges Verney and David Ronfeldt provide statistics: in 1920, Mexican immigration represented 11 percent of legal immigration; in 1942, the war forces a treaty between the two countries that ensures the entrance of a limited number of temporary workers *(braceros)*, and upon concluding the Bracero Program in 1964, more than 4.5 million Mexicans had taken advantage of it; in 1965, the Immigration Reform Act establishes the quotas of entrance, which in 1976 are reduced to 20,000 people per country, without including immediate family members, which sets legal entrance at 66,000 persons per year. But the numbers of illegal immigration are very high, and hundreds of thousands are deported each year. The result: in 1988 the population of Mexican origin in the United States exceeds 12 million (Verney and Ronfeldt 1991).

Mexico has changed from a sedentary country to a nomadic one. The towns are emptied every six months, and those who stay, children, women, and the elderly, retain that identity tightly made of tedium and resignation. And the emigrants, with the wealth from their cheap manual labor on their backs, live their burden in shabby buses and trailers, in the difficult and crowded crossings of the border. Due to such an intense effort and so many obstacles, life in the United States is identified with personal realization in the minds of millions, not because they ignore the mistreatment and the ghettos, but because in accordance with the immigrants' expectations, it represents the condition of third-class citizens of the future, not of the past.

Perhaps this partly explains the insistence of a sector, revealed in some surveys, that doesn't boast anymore of its patriotism, which feels disgusted with nationalism, and declares itself in favor of integration by any means. But these are the minority, and the nation does not give up on being a nation. It just happens that the new patrimony concentrates on the increase of the living standards, as an answer to the "lost decade" of the 1980s and the cruelties of neoliberalism.

Watcha Ése: From the Ghetto to the Nation

In the future, will Mexico be a country of Chicanos, of Mexican Americans? The question is of course rhetorical, but what is certain is that the considerable presence (if one wishes not to talk of influence) of the Chicano culture in Mexico is explainable due to diverse reasons: the dynamism of an educated sector in painting, theater, performance, and film; the ties activated by the incessant migratory flows; the cultural intermediation between a traditional culture, purely symbolic in many parts, and different degrees of Americanization. The Chicanos are informed on what identity (national, regional) means in a world that considers identities as variables of the picturesque; they, in the historical lapse of one or several generations, have seen traditions and language of origin persist and decline; they are unparalleled masters as much of resistance to disappearance as of the cultural and labor advantages of integration.

I am not saying that one can see Chicanos as the available "translators" of the American way of life (whatever this phrase may mean). I know of the inevitable differences between both communities, to begin with, the fact that Mexicans live in Mexico, an obvious observation that translates into a more times than not failed and epidermal Americanization, and that leads to a variety of methods to "Mexicanize" the Americanization. But in the stage of change, which in great measure will lead to definitive transformations, at a moment in which the most proven settling may be a form of nomadism, the interest in resistance and adaptation tactics increase. And in the recomposition of nationalism (which subsists despite everything) Chicano culture becomes indispensable.

Tomorrow's Nationalism Will Be Bilingual

At the beginning of the twentieth century, a phrase attributed to Porfirio Díaz ("Poor Mexico, so far from God, so close to the United States!") spreads to the point of becoming one of the slogans of the Mexican century. Afterward, there will be variants ("Poor Mexico, so far from God, so far from the United States!"), but the phrase will be fundamentally maintained as the sentence that determines the nation and nationalism. Nevertheless, in the governments of José López Portillo (1976–1982), Miguel de la Madrid (1982–1988), and Carlos Salinas de Gortari, who takes over on 1 December 1988, society (the many societies) confronts economic integration as a necessity that cannot be postponed, and which is the grand project of the state.

Everything happens at once: computerization modifies the rhythm of progress, the bourgeoisie wants to settle, at least partially, in the United States (La Jolla, Coral Gables, Miami Beach, Padre Island, MacAllen, Olympic Towers in New York), the yuppies take charge of the social scene, homogenization advances, *third worldist* becomes an insult, feminine beauty is measured through the Miss Mexico pageant, Houston is the Mecca of the sick, and if there is a McDonald's in Moscow, why can't there be one in the Oaxaca sierra? The competitive eagerness redefines the ambition of professions that from their mere name indicate new psychologies: entrepreneurs, junior executives. "First is first and second is nobody." And according to many, nationalism goes from being an essential experience to being a spectacle, which one enters and leaves at will.

An extraordinary photograph of Graciela Iturbide synthesizes the process: a Tarahumara Indian, showing her back to the camera, climbs up a mountain as she carries in her hand the equipment that will neutralize or defeat solitude: a gigantic radio. The defenders of indigenous identity will censor her for her predilection, but they are not there in the sierra to alleviate the immense monotony. For reasons similar to those of the Tarahumara woman, the youth of ethnic groups abandon their typical dress and urban adolescents adopt punk clothing. The communities remain, affected by or benefiting from (according to who is judging) the necessity to come closer to the nuclei of modernity, and everything continues the same except that it is very different.

In the era of importations, privatizations at all costs, and a unipolar world, one prediction is possible: for the most part, in the presence of the drive of Americanization, Mexicans, each in his or her own way, will pay attention to Sédar Senghor's advice: assimilate without being assimilated.

Translated by Christopher Dennis

Note

1. From the poem "Ya todos saben para quién trabajan," by José Emilio Pacheco (Pacheco, 1978, 38–39).

ROBERTO SCHWARZ

Brazilian Culture: Nationalism by Elimination

Roberto Schwarz was born in Austria in 1938. A literary and cultural critic, he is a professor at the Universidade Estadual de Campinas (São Paulo, Brazil). His main titles include *Ao Vencedor as Batatas: Forma Literaria e Processo Social nos Inícios do Romance Brasileiro* (1977), *O Pai de Família* (1978), and *Que Horas São?* (1987).

We Brazilians and other Latin Americans constantly experience artificial, inauthentic, and imitative nature of our cultural life. An essential element in our critical thought since independence, it has been variously interpreted from romantic, naturalist, modernist, right-wing, left-wing, cosmopolitan, and nationalist points of view, so we may suppose that the problem is enduring and deeply rooted. Before attempting another explanation, let us assume that this malaise is a fact. Its everyday manifestations range from the inoffensive to the horrifying. Examples of inappropriateness include Father Christmas sporting an Eskimo outfit in a tropical climate and, for traditionalists, the electric guitar in the land of samba. Representatives of the 1964 dictatorship often used to say that Brazil was not ready for democracy, that it would be out place here. In the nineteenth century people spoke of the gulf between the empire's liberal *façade*, copied from the British parliamentary system, and the actual reality of the system of labor, which was slavery. In his "Lundu do Escritor Difícil" Mário de Andrade[1] ridiculed his fellow countrymen whose knowledge spanned only foreign matters. Recently, when the São Paulo state government extended its human rights policy to the prisons, there were demonstrations of popular discontent at the idea that such guarantees should be introduced inside prisons when so many people did not enjoy them outside. In this perspective even human rights seem spurious in Brazil. These examples, taken from unrelated spheres and presupposing incompatible points of view, show how widespread the problem is. They all involve the same sense of contradiction between the real Brazil and the ideological prestige of the countries used as models.[2]

Let us examine the problem from a literary point of view. In twenty years of teaching the subject I have witnessed a transition in literary criticism from impressionism, through positivist historiography, American new criticism, stylistics, Marxism, phenomenology, structuralism, post-structuralism, and now reception theories. The list is impressive and demonstrates our university's efforts to overcome provincialism. But it is easy to see that the change from one school of thought to another rarely arises from the exhaustion of a particular project; usually it expresses the high regard that Brazilians feel for the newest doctrine from America or Europe. The disappointing impression created, therefore, is one of change and development with no inner necessity and therefore no value. The thirst for terminological and doctrinal novelty prevails over the labor of extending knowledge and is another illustration of the imitative nature of our cultural life. We shall see that the problem has not been correctly posed, although we may start by accepting its relative validity.

In Brazil intellectual life seems to start from scratch with each generation.[3] The hankering for the advanced countries' latest products nearly always has as its reverse side a lack of interest in the work of the previous generation of Brazilian writers, and results in a lack of intellectual continuity. As Machado de Assis noted in 1879: "A foreign impetus determines the direction of movement." What is the meaning of this passing over of the internal impulse, which is in any case much less inevitable than it was then? You do not have to be a traditionalist or believe in an impossible intellectual autarky to recognize the difficulties. There is a lack of conviction, both in the constantly changing theories and in their relationship to the movement of society as a whole. As a result little importance is attached to work itself or to the object of investigation. Outstanding analyses and research on the country's culture are periodically cut short and problems that have been identified and tackled with great difficulty are not developed as they deserve. This bias is negatively confirmed by the stature of such few outstanding writers as Machado de Assis,[4] Mário de Andrade, and now Antonio Candido. None of them lacked information or an openness to contemporary trends, but they all knew how to make broad and critical use of their predecessors' work, which they regarded not as dead weight but as a dynamic and unfinished element underlying present-day contradictions.

It is not a question of continuity for the sake of it. We have to identify a set of real, specific problems—with their own historical insertion and duration—which can draw together existing forces and allow fresh advances to be made. With all due respect to the theoreticians we study in our faculties, I believe we would do better to devote ourselves to a critical assessment of the ideas put forward by Silvio Romero,[5] Oswald and Mário de Andrade, Antonio Candido, the concretists and the CPCs.[6] A certain degree of cultural density arises out of alliances or disagreements between scientific disciplines, and artistic, social, and political groups, without which the idea of breaking away in pursuit of the new becomes meaningless. We should bear in mind that to many Latin Americans Brazil's intellectual life appears to have an enviably organic character, and however incredible it may seem, there may be some relative truth in this view.

Little remains of the conceptions and methods that we have passed under review, since the rhythm of change has not allowed them to attain a mature expression. There is a real problem here, part of that feeling of inappropriateness from which we started out. Nothing seems more reasonable, for those who are aware of the damage, than to steer in the opposite direction and think it is enough to avoid copying metropolitan trends in order to achieve an intellectual life with greater substance. This conclusion is illusory, as we shall see, but has strong intuitive support. For a time it was taken up by both right and left nationalists, in a convergence that boded ill for the left and, through its wide diffusion, contributed to a low intellectual level and a high estimation of ideological crudities.

The search for genuine (i.e., unadulterated) national roots leads us to ask: What would popular culture be like if it were possible to isolate it from commercial interests and particularly from the mass media? What would a national economy be like if there were no admixture? Since 1964 the internationalization of capital, the commodification of social relations, and the presence of the mass media have developed so rapidly that these very questions have come to seem implausible. Yet barely twenty years ago they still excited intellectuals and figured on their agenda. A combative frame of mind still prevailed—for which progress would result from a kind of *reconquista*, or rather from the expulsion of the invaders. Once imperialism had been pushed back, its commercial and industrial forms of culture neutralized, and its allied, anti-national section of the bourgeoisie isolated, the way would be clear for the flowering of national culture, which had *been distorted by these elements as by an alien body*. This correct emphasis on the mechanisms of U.S. domination served to mythologize the Brazilian community as an object of patriotic fervor, whereas a class analysis would have made this much more problematic. Here a qualification is necessary: such ideas reached their height in the period of the Goulart government, when extraordinary events, which brought about experimentation and democratic realignments on a large scale, were taking place. The period cannot be reduced to the inconsistencies of its self-image—indicative though they are of the illusion inherent in populist nationalism that the outside world is the source of all evil.

In 1964 the right-wing nationalists branded Marxism as an alien influence, perhaps imagining that fascism was a Brazilian invention. But over and above their differences, the two nationalist tendencies were alike in hoping to find their goal by eliminating anything that was not indigenous. The residue would be the essence of Brazil. The same illusion was popular in the last century, but at that time the new national culture owed more to diversification of the European models than to exclusion of the Portuguese. Opponents of the romantic liberal distortion of Brazilian society did not arrive at the authentic country, since once French and English imports had been rooted out, the colonial order was restored. And that was a Portuguese creation. The paradox of this kind of purism is apparent in the person of Policarpo Quaresma, whose quest for authenticity led him to write in Tupi, a language foreign to him.[7] The same goes for Antonio Callado's Quarup (1967), in which the real Brazil is found not in the colonial past—as suggested by Lima Barreto's hero—but in the heart of the interior, far from the Atlantic coast with its overseas contacts. A group of characters mark the center of the country on a map and go off in search of it. After innumerable adventures they reach their destination, where they find . . . an ants' nest.

The standard U.S. models that arrived with the new communications networks were regarded by the nationalists as an unwelcome foreign presence. The next generation, however, already breathing naturally in this air, considered nationalism to be archaic and provincial. For the first time, as far as I know, the idea spread that it was a worthless enterprise to defend national characteristics against imperialist uniformity. The culture industry would cure the sickness of Brazilian culture—at least for those who were willing to delude themselves.

In the 1960s nationalism also came under fire from those who thought of themselves as politically and artistically more advanced. Their views are now being taken up in the context of international mass media, only this time without the elements of class struggle and anti-imperialism. In this "world" environment of uniform mythology, the struggle to establish an "authentic" culture appears as a relic from the past. Its illusory nature becomes evident, and it seems a provincial phenomenon associated with archaic forms of oppression. The argument is irrefutable, but it must be said that in the new context an emphasis on the international dimension of culture becomes no more than a legitimation of the existing mass media. Just as nationalists used to condemn imperialism and hush up bourgeois oppression, so the anti-nationalists invoke the authoritarianism and backwardness of their opponents, with good reason, while suggesting that the reign of mass communication is either emancipatory or aesthetically acceptable. A modern, critical position, perhaps, but fundamentally conformist. There is another imaginary reversal of roles: although the "globalists" operate within the dominant ideology of our time, they defend their positions as if they were being hunted down, or as if they were part of the heroic vanguard, aesthetic or libertarian, of the early twentieth century; they line up with the authorities in the manner of one who is starting a revolution.

In the same order of paradox, we can see that the imposition of foreign ideology and the cultural expropriation of the people are realities which do not cease to exist just because there is mystification in the nationalists' theories about them. Whether they are right or wrong, the nationalists become involved in actual conflicts, imparting to them a certain degree of visibility. The mass media modernists, though right in their criticisms, imagine a universalist world which does not exist. It is a question of choosing between the old and the new error, both upheld in the name of progress. The sight of the Avenida Paulista is a fine illustration of what I mean: ugly mansions, once used by the rich to flaunt their wealth, now seem perversely tolerable at the foot of modern skyscrapers, both for reasons of proportion and because of that poetry which emanates from any historically superseded power.

Recent French philosophy has been another factor in the discrediting of cultural nationalism. Its anti-totalizing tendency, its preference for levels of historicity alien to the national milieu, its dismantling of conventional literary scaffolding such as authorship, "the work," influence, originality, et cetera—all these destroy, or at least discredit, that romantic correspondence between individual heroism, masterly execution, and collective redemption which imbues the nationalist schemas with their undeniable knowledge value and potential for mystification. To attack these coordinates can be exciting and partially convincing, besides appeasing national sensibility in an area where one would least expect this to be possible.

A commonplace idea suggests that the copy is secondary with regard to the original, depends upon it, is worth less, and so on. Such a view attaches a negative sign to the totality of cultural forces in Latin America and is at the root of the intellectual malaise that we are discussing. Now, contemporary French philosophers such as Foucault and Derrida have made it their speciality to show that such hierarchies have no basis. Why should the prior be worth more than the posterior, the model more than the imitation, the central more than the peripheral, the economic infrastructure more than cultural life, and so forth? According to the French philosophers, it is a question of conditioning processes (but are they all of the same order?)—prejudices which do not express the life of the spirit in its real movement but reflect the orientation inherent in the traditional human sciences. In their view it would be more accurate and unbiased to think in terms of an infinite sequence of transformations with no beginning or end, no first or last, no worse or better. One can easily appreciate how this would enhance the self-esteem and relieve the anxiety of the underdeveloped world, which is seen as tributary to the central countries. We would pass from being a backward to an advanced part of the world, from a deviation to a paradigm, from inferior to superior lands (although the analysis set out to suppress just such superiority). All this because countries which live in the humiliation of having to imitate are more willing than the metropolitan countries to give up the illusion of an original source, even though the theory originated there and not here. Above all, the problem of mirror-culture would no longer be ours alone, and instead of setting our sights on the Europeanization or Americanization of Latin America we would, in a certain sense, be participating in the Latin Americanization of the central cultures.[8]

It remains to be seen whether this conceptual break with the primacy of origins would enable us to balance out or combat relations of actual subordination. Would the innovations of the advanced world suddenly become dispensable once they had lost the distinction of originality? In order to use them in a free and non-imitative manner, it is not enough simply to divest them of their sacred aura. Contrary to what the above analysis might lead us to believe, the breaking down of cultural dazzlement in the underdeveloped countries does not go to the heart of a problem which is essentially practical in character. Solutions are reproduced from the advanced world in response to cultural, economic, and political needs, and the notion of copying, with its psychologistic connotations, throws no light whatsoever on this reality. If theory remains at this level, it will continue to suffer from the same limitations, and the radicalism of an analysis that passes over efficient causes will become in its turn largely delusive. The inevitability of cultural imitation is bound up with a specific set of historical imperatives over which abstract philosophical critiques can exercise no power. Even here nationalism is the weak part of the argument, and its supersession at the level of philosophy has no purchase on the realities to which it owes its strength. It should be noted that while nationalism has recently been almost absent from serious intellectual debate, it has a growing presence in the administration of culture, where, for better or worse, it is impossible to escape from the national dimension. Now that economic, though not political, space has become international—which is not the same as homogeneous—this return of nationalism by the back door reflects the insuperable paradox of the present day.

In the 1920s Oswald de Andrade's "anthropophagous" Pau-Brazil program also tried to give a triumphalist interpretation of our backwardness.[9] The disharmony between bourgeois models and the realities of rural patriarchy is at the very heart of his poetry—the first of these two elements appearing in the role of absurd caprice ("Rui Barbosa: A Top Hat in Senegambia").[10] Its true novelty lies in the fact that the lack of accord is a source not of distress but of optimism, evidence of the country's innocence and the possibility of an alternative, non-bourgeois historical development. This sui generis cult of progress is rounded out with a technological wager: Brazil's innocence (the result of Christianization and *embourgeoisement* barely scraping the surface) plus technology equals utopia; modern material progress will make possible a direct leap from prebourgeois society to paradise. Marx himself, in his famous letter of 1881 to Vera Zasulich, came up with a similar hypothesis that the Russian peasant commune would achieve socialism without a capitalist interregnum, thanks to the means made available by progress in the West. Similarly, albeit in a register combining jokes, provocation, philosophy of history, and prophecy (as, later, in the films of Glauber Rocha), anthropophagy set itself the aim of leaping a whole stage.

Returning once more to the idea that Western culture has been inappropriately copied in Brazil, we can see that Oswald's program introduced a change of tone. Local primitivism would give back a modern sense to tired European culture, liberating it from Christian mortification and capitalist utilitarianism. Brazil's experience would be a differentiated cornerstone, with utopian powers, on the map of contemporary history. (The poems of Mário de Andrade and Raúl Bopp[11] on Amazonian slothfulness contain a similar idea.) Modernism therefore brought about a profound change in values: for the first time the processes under way in Brazil were weighed in the context of the present-day world, as having something to offer in that larger context. Oswald de Andrade advocated cultural irreverence in place of subaltern obfuscation, using the metaphor of "swallowing up" the alien: a copy, to be sure, but with regenerative effect. Historical distance allows us to see the ingenuousness and jingoism contained in these propositions.

The new vogue for Oswald's manifestos in the 1960s and particularly the 1970s appeared in the very different context of a military dictatorship which, for all its belief in technological progress and its alliance with big capital both national and international, was less repressive than expected in regard to everyday habits and morality. In the other camp, the attempt to overthrow capitalism through revolutionary war also changed the accepted view of what could be termed "radical." This now had no connection with the provincial narrowness of the 1920s, when the Antropófago rebellion assumed a highly libertarian and enlightening role. In the new circumstances technological optimism no longer held water, while the brazen cultural irreverence of Oswald's "swallowing up" acquired a sense of exasperation close to the mentality of direct action (although often with good artistic results). Oswald's clarity of construction, penetrating vision, and sense of discovery all suffered as greater value was attached to his primal, "demoralizing" literary practices. One example of this evolution is the guiltlessness of the act of swallowing up. What was then freedom against Catholicism, the bourgeoisie, and the glare of Europe has become in the eighties an awkward excuse to handle uncritically those ambiguities of mass culture that stand in need of elucidation. How can one fail to notice that the Antropófagos—like the nationalists—take as their subject the abstract Brazilian, with no class specification; or that the analogy with the digestive process throws absolutely no light on the politics and aesthetics of contemporary cultural life?

Since the last century educated Brazilians—the concept is not meant as a compliment but refers to a social category—have had the sense of living among ideas and institutions copied from abroad that do not reflect local reality. It is not sufficient, however, to give up loans in order to think and live more authentically. Besides, one cannot so much as conceive of giving them up. Nor is the problem eliminated by a philosophical deconstruction of the concept of copy. The programmatic innocence of the Antropófagos, which allows them to ignore the malaise, does not prevent it from emerging anew. "Tupi or not Tupi, that is the question!" Oswald's famous saying, with its contradictory use of the English language, a classical line and a play on words to pursue the search for national identity, itself says a great deal about the nature of the impasse.

The problem may appear simpler in historical perspective. Silvio Romero, despite many absurdities, made a number of excellent remarks on the matter. The following extract is taken from a work on Machado de Assis, written in 1897 to prove that this greatest Brazilian writer produced nothing but a literature of Anglomania, incompetent, unattuned, slavish, et cetera.

Meanwhile a kind of absurdity developed . . . a tiny intellectual elite separated itself off from the mass of the population, and while the majority remained almost entirely uneducated, this elite, being particularly gifted in the art of learning and copying, threw itself into political and literary imitation of everything it found in the Old World. So now we have an exotic literature and politics, which live and procreate in a hothouse that has no relationship to the outside temperature and environment. This is the bad side of our feeble, illusory skill of *mestizo* southerners, passionate, given to fantasy, capable of imitation but organically unsuited to create, invent, or produce things of our own that spring from the immediate or remote depths of our life and history.

In colonial times, a skilful policy of segregation cut us off from foreigners and kept within us a certain sense of cohesion. This is what gave us Basilio,[12] Durào, Gonzaga, Alvarenga Peixoto, Claudio and Silva Alvarenga, who all worked in a milieu of exclusively Portuguese and Brazilian ideas.

With the first emperor and the Regency, the first breach [opened] in our wall of isolation by Dom João VI grew wider, and we began to copy the political and literary romanticism of the French.

We aped the Charter of 1814 and transplanted the fantasies of Benjamin Constant; we mimicked the parliamentarism and constitutional politics of the author of *Adolphe*, intermingled with the poetry and dreams of the author of *René* and *Atala*.

The people . . . remained illiterate.

The Second Reign,[13] whose policy was for fifty years vacillating, uncertain, and incompetent, gradually opened all the gates in a chaotic manner lacking any criteria or sense of discrimination. Imitation, mimicking of everything—customs, laws, codes, verse, theater, novel—was the general rule.

Regular sailings assured direct communication with the old continent and swelled the inflow of imitation and servile copying . . .

This is why, in terms of copying, mimicry, and pastiches to impress the gringos, no people has a better Constitution on paper . . . , everything is better . . . on paper. The reality is appalling. (121–23)

Silvio Romero's account and analysis are uneven, sometimes incompatible. In some instances it is the argument that is interesting, in others the ideology, so that the modern reader will want to examine them separately. The basic schema is as follows: a tiny elite devotes itself to copying Old World culture, separating itself off from the mass of the population, which remains uneducated. As a result, literature and politics come to occupy an exotic position, and we become incapable of *creating things of our own that spring from the depths of our life and history*. Implicit in this demand is the norm of an organic, reasonably homogeneous national culture with popular roots—a norm that cannot be reduced to a mere illusion of literary history or of romanticism, since in some measure it expresses the conditions of modern citizenship. It is in its opposition to this norm that the Brazilian configuration—Europeanized minority, uneducated majority—constitutes an *absurdity*. On the other hand, in order to make the picture more realistic, we should remember that the organic requirement arose at the same time as the expansion of imperialism and organized science—two tendencies which rendered obsolete the idea of a harmonious and auto-centered national culture.

The original sin, responsible for the severing of connections, was the copy. Its negative effects already made themselves felt in the social fissure between *culture* (unrelated to its surroundings) and *production* (springing from the depths of our life). However, the disproportion between cause and effects is such that it raises some doubts about the cause itself, and Silvio Romero's own remarks are an invitation to follow a different line of argument from the one he pursues. Let us also note in passing that it is in the nature of an absurdity to be avoidable, and that Romero's argument and invective actually suggest that the elite had an obligation to correct the error that had separated it from the people. His critique was seeking to make the class gulf intolerable for *educated people*, since in a country recently emancipated from slavery the weakness of the popular camp inhibited the emergence of other solutions.

It would seem, then, that the origins of our cultural absurdity are to be found in the imitative talent of *mestizo* southerners who have few creative capacities. The *petitio principii* is quite transparent: imitativeness is explained by a (racial) tendency to that very imitativeness which is supposed to be explained. (The author's argument, we should note, itself imitated the scientific naturalism then in vogue in Europe.) Today such explanations can hardly be taken seriously, although it is worth examining them as an ideological mechanism and an expression of their times. If the Brazilians' propensity for copying is racial in origin, why should the elite have been alone in indulging it? If everyone had copied, all the effects of "exoticism" (lack of relation to the environment) and "absurdity" (separation between the elite and the people) would have vanished as if by magic, and with them the whole problem. It is not copying in general but *the copying of one class* that constitutes the problem. The explanation must lie not in race but in class.

Silvio Romero goes on to sketch how the vice of imitation developed in Brazil. Absolute zero was in the colonial period, when writers "worked in a milieu of exclusively Portuguese and Brazilian ideas." Could it be that the distance between the elite and the people was smaller in that epoch? Or the fondness for copying less strong? Surely not—and anyway that is not what the text says. The "cohesion" to which it refers is of a different order, the result of a "skilful policy of segregation" (!) that separated Brazil from everything non-Portuguese. In other words, the comparison between stages lacks an object: the demand for homogeneity points, in one case, to a social structure remarkable for its inequality, and in the other case to the banning of foreign ideas. Still, if the explanation does not convince us, the observation that it seeks to clarify is accurate enough. Before the nineteenth century, the copying of the European model and the distance between educated people and the mass did not constitute an "absurdity." In highly schematic terms, we could say that educated people, in the colonial period, felt solidarity toward the metropolis, Western tradition, and their own colleagues, but not toward the local population. To base oneself on a foreign model, in cultural estrangement from the local surroundings, did not appear as a defect—quite the contrary! We should not forget that neoclassical aesthetics was itself universalist and greatly appreciated respect for canonical forms, while the theory of art current at that time set a positive value on imitation. As Antonio Candido acutely observed, the Arcadian poet who placed a nymph in the waters of the Carmo was not lacking in originality; he incorporated Minas Gerais into the traditions of the West and, quite laudably, cultivated those traditions in a remote corner of the earth (1969, 74).

The act of copying, then, did not begin with independence and the opening of the ports,[14] as Silvio Romero would have it. But it is true that only then did it become the insoluble problem which is still discussed today, and which calls forth such terms as "mimicry," "apeing" or "pastiche." How did imitation acquire these pejorative connotations?

It is well known that Brazil's gaining of independence did not involve a revolution. Apart from changes in external relations and a reorganization of the top administration, the socioeconomic structure created by colonial exploitation remained intact, though now for the benefit of local dominant classes. It was thus inevitable that modern forms of civilization entailing freedom and citizenship, which arrived together with the wave of political emancipation, should have appeared foreign and artificial, "anti-national," "borrowed," "absurd," or however else critics cared to describe them. The strength of the epithets indicates the acrobatics which the self-esteem of the Brazilian elite was forced into, since it faced the depressing alternative of deprecating the bases of its social preeminence in the name of progress, or deprecating progress in the name of its social preeminence. On the one hand, there were the slave trade, the latifundia (the landed estate), and clientelism—that is to say, a set of relations with their own rules, consolidated in colonial times and impervious to the universalism of bourgeois civilization; on the other hand, stymied by these relations, but also stymieing them, there was the law before which everyone was equal, the separation between public and private, civil liberties, parliament, romantic patriotism, and so on. The ensuring of the stable coexistence of these two conceptions, in principle so incompatible, was at the center of ideological and moral preoccupations in Brazil in the nineteenth century. For some, the colonial heritage was a relic to be superseded in the march of progress; for others, it was the real Brazil, to be preserved against absurd imitations. Some wanted to harmonize progress and slave labor, so as not to have to give up either, while still others believed that such a reconciliation already existed, with deleterious moral results. Silvio Romero, for his part, used conservative arguments with a progressive intent, focusing on the "real" Brazil as the continuation of colonial authoritarianism, but doing so in order to attack its foundations. He scorned as ineffectual the "illusory" country of laws, lawyers, and imported culture: "No people has a better Constitution on paper . . . ; the reality is appalling."

Silvio Romero's list of "imitations," not to be allowed through customs, included fashions, patterns of behavior, laws, codes, poetry, drama, and novels. Judged separately against the social reality of Brazil, these articles were indeed superfluous imports which would serve to obscure the real state of impoverishment and create an illusion of progress. In their combination, however, they entered into the formation and equipping of the new nation-state, as well as laying the ground for the participation of new elites in contemporary culture. This modernizing force—whatever its imitative appearance and its distance from the daily course of things—became more inseparably bound up with the reality of Brazil than the institution of slave labor, which was later replaced by other forms of forced labor equally incompatible with the aspiration to enlightenment. As time passed, the ubiquitous stamp of "inauthenticity" came to be seen as the most authentic part of the national drama, its very mark of identity. Grafted from nineteenth-century Europe on to a colonial social being, the various perfections of civilization began to follow different rules from those operating in the hegemonic countries. This led to a widespread sense of the indigenous pastiche. Only a great figure like Machado de Assis had the impartiality to see a peculiar mode of ideological functioning where other critics could distinguish no more than a lack of consistency. Sérgio Buarque de Holanda remarked:

> The speed at which the "new ideas" spread in the old colony, and the fervor with which they were adopted in many circles on the eve of independence, show quite unequivocally that they had the potential to satisfy an impatient desire for change and that the people were ripe for such change. But it is also clear that the social order expressed in these ideas was far from having an exact equivalent in Brazil, particularly outside the cities. The articulation of society, the basic criteria of economic exploitation, and the distribution of privileges were so different here that the "new ideas" could not have the same meaning that was attached to them in parts of Europe or ex-English America. (1977, 77–78)

When Brazil became an independent state, a permanent collaboration was established between the forms of life characteristic of colonial oppression and the innovations of bourgeois progress. The new stage of capitalism broke up the exclusive relationship with the metropolis, converting local property owners and administrators into a national ruling class (effectively part of the emergent world bourgeoisie), and yet retained the old forms of labor exploitation, which have not been fully modernized up to the present day. In other words, the discrepancy between the "two Brazils" was not due to an imitative tendency, as Silvio Romero and many others thought; nor did it correspond to a brief period of transition. It was the lasting result of the creation of a nation-state on the basis of slave labor—which, if the reader will forgive the shorthand, arose in turn out of the English Industrial Revolution and the consequent crisis of the old colonial system. That is to say, it arose out of contemporary history (Da Costa 1977; Alencastro 1979; Novais 1984). Thus Brazil's backward deformation belongs to the same order of things as the progress of the advanced countries. Silvio Romero's "absurdities"—in reality, the cyclopean discords of world capitalism—are not a historical deviation. They are linked to the finality of a single process which, in the case of Brazil, requires the continuation of forced or semi-forced labor and a corresponding cultural separation of the poor. With certain modifications, much of it has survived to this day. The panorama now seems to be changing, thanks to the desegregationist impulse of mass consumption and mass communications. These new terms of cultural oppression and expropriation have not yet been much studied.

The thesis of cultural copying thus involves an ideology in the Marxist sense of the term—that is, an illusion supported by appearances. The well-known coexistence of bourgeois principles with those of the ancien régime is here explained in accordance with a plausible and wide-ranging schema, essentially individualist in nature, in which effects and causes are systematically inverted.

For Silvio Romero imitation results in the lack of a common denominator between popular and elite culture, and in the elite's low level of permeation by the national. But why not reverse the argument? Why should the imitative character of our life not stem from forms of inequality so brutal that they lack the minimal reciprocity ("common denominator") without which modern society can only appear artificial and "imported"? At a time when the idea of the nation had become the norm, the dominant class's *unpatriotic* disregard for the lives it exploited gave it the feeling of being alien. The origins of this situation in colonialism and slavery are immediately apparent.

The defects normally associated with imitation can be explained in the same way. We can agree with its detractors that the copy is at the opposite pole from originality, from national creativity, from independent and well-adapted judgments, and so on. Absolute domination entails that culture expresses nothing of the conditions that gave it life, except for that intrinsic sense of futility on which a number of writers have been able to work artistically. Hence the "exotic" literature and politics unrelated to the "immediate or remote depths of our life and history"; hence, too, the lack of "discrimination" or "criteria" and, above all, the intense conviction that all is mere paper. In other words, the painfulness of an imitative civilization is produced not by imitation—which is present at any event—but by the social structure of the country. It is this which places culture in an untenable position, contradicting its very concept of itself, and which nevertheless was not as sterile, at that time, as Silvio Romero would have us believe. Nor did the segregated section of society remain unproductive. Its modes of expression would later acquire, for educated intellectuals, the value of a non-bourgeois component of national life, an element serving to fix Brazilian identity (with all the evident ambiguities).

The exposure of cultural transplantation has become the axis of a naive yet widespread critical perspective. Let us conclude by summarizing some of its defects.

1. It suggests that imitation is avoidable, thereby locking the reader into a false problem.
2. It presents as a national characteristic what is actually a malaise of the dominant class, bound up with the difficulty of morally reconciling the advantages of progress with those of slavery or its surrogates.
3. It implies that the elites could conduct themselves in some other way, which is tantamount to claiming that the beneficiary of a given situation will put an end to it.
4. The argument obscures the essential point, since it concentrates its fire on the relationship between elite and model whereas the real crux is the exclusion of the poor from the universe of contemporary culture.
5. Its implicit solution is that the dominant class should reform itself and give up imitation. We have argued, on the contrary, that the answer lies in the workers gaining access to the terms of contemporary life, so that they can re-define them through their own initiative. This, indeed, would be in this context a concrete definition of democracy in Brazil.
6. A copy refers to a prior original existing elsewhere, of which it is all inferior reflection. Such deprecation often corresponds to the self-consciousness of Latin American elites, who attach mythical solidity—in the form of regional intellectual specialization—to the economic, technological, and political inequalities of the international order. The authentic and the creative are to the imitative what the advanced countries are to the backward. But one cannot solve the problem by going to the opposite extreme. As we have seen, philosophical objections to the concept of originality tend to regard as nonexistent a real problem that it is absurd to dismiss. Cultural history has to be set in the world perspective of the economics and culture of the left, which attempt to explain our "backwardness" as part of the contemporary history of capital and its *advances* (Furtado 1962; Cardoso 1964). Seen in terms of the copy, the anachronistic juxtaposition of forms of modern civilization and realities originating in the colonial period is a mode of nonbeing or even a humiliating imperfect realization of a model situated elsewhere. Dialectical criticism, on the other hand, investigates the same anachronism and seeks to draw out a figure of the modern world, set on a course that is either full of promise, grotesque or catastrophic.
7. The idea of the copy that we have been discussing counterposes national and foreign, original and imitative. These are unreal oppositions which do not allow us to see the share of the foreign in the na-

tionally specific, of the imitative in the original and of the original in the imitative. (In a key study, Paulo Emilio Salles Gomes refers to our "creative lack of competence in copying" [1973].) If I am not mistaken, the theory presupposes three elements—a Brazilian subject, reality of the country, civilization of the advanced nations—such that the third helps the first to forget the second. This schema is also unreal, and it obscures the organized, cumulative nature of the process, the potent strength even of bad tradition, and the power relations, both national and international, that are in play. Whatever its unacceptable aspects—unacceptable for whom?—Brazilian cultural life has elements of dynamism which display both originality and lack of originality. Copying is not a false problem, so long as we treat it pragmatically, from an aesthetic and political point of view freed from the mythical requirement of creation ex nihilo.

Notes

1. Mário de Andrade (1893–1945), novelist, poet, and critic, was the acknowledged leader of the modernist movement in Brazil and bore the brunt of the initial scandal that it caused. The language of his *Macunaíma* (1928) synthesizes idioms and dialects from all the regions of Brazil [Translator's note].
2. For a balanced and considered opinion on the subject, see Candido in part 1, "Forerunners."
3. This observation was made by Vinícius Dantas.
4. Joaquim Maria Machado de Assis (1839–1908) is regarded as the greatest of all Portuguese-language novelists. He wrote nine novels and two hundred short stories, including *Memórias póstumas de Brás Cubas* (1880), *Dom Casmurro* (1990), and *Esaú e Jacó* (1904), which are considered to be far ahead of their time [Translator's note].
5. Silvio Romero (1851–1914) wrote the first modern history of Brazilian literature, a work which is still of interest today, despite the scientistic language of the period [Translator's note].
6. The Centro Popular de Cultura (CPC) was established in 1961 at the start of the social ferment that ended with the military coup in 1964. The movement was created under the auspices of the National Union of Students, which wanted to fuse together artistic irreverence, political teaching, and the people. It produced surprisingly inventive cinema, theater, and other stage performances. Several of its members became major artistic figures: Glauber Rocha, Joaquim Pedro de Andrade, and Ferreira Gullar among others. The convergence of the student and popular movements gave rise to completely new artistic possibilities. [Note supplied by Ana McMac.]
7. Policarpo Quaresma is the hero of the novel *Triste fim de Policarpo Quaresma* (1915), by Afonso Henriques de Lima Barreto (1881–1922). The hero is a caricature patriot,

if a sympathetic character, who gradually becomes disillusioned with the state of Brazil.

8. See Santiago (1978) and Campos (1983).

9. Oswald de Andrade introduced European avant-garde ideas into Brazil. He espoused extreme primitivism (anthropophagy) and his *Manifesto da Poesia Pau-Brasil* (1924) and *Manifesto Antropofágo* (1928) are the most daring writings of the "modern movement" which emerged in 1922, attacking academic values and respectability and seeking poetry written in the Brazilian vernacular [Translator's note].

10. Rui Barbosa (1849–1923) was a prominent liberal politician, and regarded as a model of culture, linguistic purity, and erudition in the early twentieth century: he achieved an almost mythical status, known as "the Eagle of the Hague" for his diplomacy at an international conference there in 1906. In this phrase, obviously, it is the incongruity of such false representatives of high culture in Brazil that is underlined.

11. The greatest achievement of Raúl Bopp was his "cannibalist" poem "Cobra Norato" (1921), an exploration of the Amazon jungle [Translator's note].

12. The names of a group of the so-called Minas group of Arcadian poets who flourished in the interior, gold-mining area of the country in the latter half of the eighteenth century.

13. That of the Emperor Pedro II, which lasted from 1840 to 1889.

14. In the wake of his flight to Brazil, to escape Napoleon's invasion of Portugal in 1807–1808, in which he was escorted by the British fleet, King João VI opened the ports of the colony for the first time to non-Portuguese (largely British) shipping.

BEATRIZ SARLO

Intellectuals: Scission or Mimesis?

Beatriz Sarlo was born in Argentina in 1942. A literary and cultural critic, she is a professor at the Universidad de Buenos Aires and director of the journal *Punto de vista* (Buenos Aires, Argentina). Her main titles include *El imperio de los sentimientos* (1985c), *Una modernidad periférica: Buenos Aires 1920–1930* (1989), and *Escenas de la vida posmoderna: Intelectuales, arte, y videocultura en la Argentina* (1994).

These notes are intended as one more reflection on the ideological and political transformations of the left in Argentina. They are of a polemical nature with respect to two discourses that strongly articulate the common sense of intellectual factions. On the one hand, there is the idea, proclaimed in the name of the Revolution, that it is futile, if not a covert treason, to change the political positions maintained during the last two decades; as a result, ideological and theoretical immobility is thus vindicated as merit. On the other hand, there is the assimilation of democracy and moderatism, from which I intend to distance myself.

These notes are also a form of intellectual biography, which, doubtless, is very much a sort of collective autobiography too. They are at the same time an exercise of memory and a hypothetical construction of some possible meanings concerning our most recent past. In no way do I aspire to unify experiences and discourses, but rather to point out the coexistence of contradictory aspects whose recognition prevents a rapid settlement of pending questions. As a result, all my statements are crisscrossed by fissures, and the effect is probably that of a collection of propositions reciprocally critical within the same text.

Finally, I would like to clarify that these reflections depart from the following assumption: the decisive weight that the leftist Peronist revolutionary faction had within Argentina during the cycle of ideological, political, and cultural transformations begun in 1956. It is to this faction to which I will refer principally.

WHEN AT THE END of the fifties and the beginning of the sixties, intellectuals like Oscar Masotta, Juan J. Sebreli, Abelardo Ramos, and Ismael Viñas undertook the historical and political operations that allowed for a reconsideration of Peronism, as no longer the absolute Other, the realm of evil, or the total otherness that had to be abolished, they opened another chapter in the history of Argentine intellectuals. It was not, then, a movement of exaltation, symmetrically opposed to the annihilation politics carried out by the magazine *Sur* and the oligarchic anti-Peronist movement. It was rather an attempt to make a system of productive inquiries work, governed by the idea (which seems simple but it was not) that the events which had been experienced during the first Peronist decade were resistant to summary analysis, and that finding a rationale for those events was a necessary condition to designing a political future for Argentina and the popular sectors.

"Read Peronism under a new light" became a heuristic, ideological, and practical motto. The intellectuals who engaged in this project did so with the conviction that such a collective phenomenon, which had marked their formative years, constituted the enigma that it was necessary to resolve in order to think of and act in politics.

In this case, texts such as the last issues of the magazine *Contorno* (1953–1959) or investigations on the origins of Peronism like those of Miguel Murmis and Juan Carlos Portantiero (1972) would be difficult to classify as solely historiographical or sociological endeavors. They represent instead a moment when intellectual activity and the task of producing new political perspectives had come together. This juncture was characterized by its instability, which was due to a logic, not necessarily perverse, concerning the relationship between scientific and political discourses. This relationship is, in my opinion, what makes history and the social sciences interesting discourses that go beyond the milieu in which they are produced and beyond their institutional interlocutors.

Without a doubt, during the sixties, Argentine society had to come to terms with Peronism: understanding Peronism was a precondition to modifying it or to building a left movement; understanding it also meant overcoming the period of its interdiction, in order to reincorporate it into the political spectrum. This seemed to be a central question, and intellectuals made efforts to address it not only in political terms but also within the framework of a supposedly objective discussion.

I am not going to say that this tendency culminated in a victory for either science or politics. The history of the last fifteen years does not allow me such an overstatement. But I would like to point out some features of this intellectual movement, whose current and persistent discussion adds neither depth nor intelligence to its understanding.

THE INTELLECTUALS WHO, at the beginning of the sixties, developed the theses for a "new reading of Peronism" were mobilized by the idea that if the politics of the left had to change in Argentina, that change would be brought about by the relationship between a new kind of politics and a new discourse. This meant that the truly intellectual dimension of their activity could become functional to the truly political dimension.

The expression "to become functional" is ambiguous precisely because it describes both aspects of this movement. On one hand, "to become functional" presupposes the adequacy between the discourse and the problem; but this adequacy implied the possibility that the discourse of the intellectuals might be cannibalized by political discourse. This possibility finally became a reality toward the end of the sixties. The discourse of the intellectuals, which was used to intervene in political debates despite its distinct status, ceased to be different from political discourse and became a duplication (many times degraded, because it violated its own laws) of political discourse and practice.

We had passed from the critical stage evoked at the beginning of these notes to the stage of servility, no matter who might the master be (the party, a charismatic leader, the representation of the people, or the proletariat). From the critical stage we had passed to a rationalizing stage. However, the intellectual energy and the public will shown during the critical stage make up the nucleus of a tradition that, it seems to me, we should not abandon in its totality.

What were its components? One was the idea—the epitome of modernity—that change was possible and, since it was inscribed onto the meaning of history, was going to be profound. This same idea combined features which, though they seemed mutually necessary, are not truly so. It entwined voluntaristic and deterministic elements, along with the conviction that change is inevitable. Depending on the rationale used, voluntaristic or deterministic features predominated. In brief, the deterministic elements predominated among moderates and the voluntaristic elements in the extreme wing of the intellectual and political field.

Confidence in the future (another discursive feature in those years) was the effect of either class conscience or socioeconomic structural determinism, to express it according to an opposition typical of the spirit of the times.

But this idea meant something more: change was not only possible, it was also necessary and impossible to postpone. That is to say that social, economic, and political conditions were unacceptable, because they placed the majority of the population in a position of inequality in each one of these spheres. Change was simply necessary because society was unjust. This simple phrase, however, refers to a complex reality. To state that society is unjust supposes a notion of justice that immediately evokes certain values. Silently, many times beyond political debate, the great intellectual impulses of the last decades spoke of values even when in explicit discourse they were replaced by the rhetoric of determinism, opportunism, or violence. The values that comprised the subtext of this discourse were the force that moved intellectuals toward and within politics. By transforming intellectuals into political actors, these values impelled them to find common ground between their specific practices and those of other social sectors.

The aesthetic avant-garde and political revolution, on the one hand, and psychoanalysis and Marxism, on the other, are two of the various formulas that summarize the climate of the period. Above all else, the idea was about destroying the limits of intellectual or artistic discourse and practice in order to install them within the field of social and political struggle. This movement, which affected both the left and Peronism, produced alternative networks for intellectual work and for the circulation of discourses and symbolic goods. Organizations, institutionally lax and many times ephemeral, linked the intellectuals to the popular sectors. As a result, a universe of experiences and cultural contacts was opened.

It was frequent for intellectuals to reach other sectors within society, even if they did not always manage to set up stable and organic relationships. This led to a questioning of the economy of intellectual organizations and their narrow corporativism. It was thought, perhaps to exaggerated and absurd lengths, that it was possible to change the relationship between science and politics, between art and politics. Intellectuals were placed on alert and in turn alerted society regarding the political character of scientific and aesthetic practices. Consequently, they denounced the class nature of intellectual and artistic institutions and proposed new articulations regarding their activity and social change. If this stance acquired a decidedly mechanistic character and lost all critical value due to its automatization, it was nonetheless the way in which a young contingent of intellectuals lived the limits of politics and cultural practices as an insufficiency that should be overcome.

Criticism of limits also involved criticism of specializations. Totalizing social philosophies, Hegelian versions of Marxism and of Peronism (which are still practiced today), integrating versions of politics, the party, or the state, became the unifying principles in the name of which the whole idea of diversity, coexistence, and conflict was expunged. In its most brutal form, intellectuals spoke of bourgeois science and science for the people, popular art and art of the colonial elite, as if it were simple to discriminate such divisions, either from the formal point of view or according to the content. Any idea of regimes of truth, of local truths, of partial authority was eliminated in order to organize intellectual practices and discourses under the strong rule of politics.

Nevertheless, this totalizing and frequently totalitarian unification had features that today must be rethought. There was, in the first place, the certainty that the discourse of the intellectuals should be meaningful for society and especially for the popular sectors. Thus, it should address and propose solutions to what were considered the major problems of the time, and to move from partial and specific questions to more global perspectives: consequently, intellectual discourse should install itself in the public sphere and build from there its interlocution. Resistance to considering oneself exclusively a specialist or an artist was accompanied by the impulse to convert specialized knowledge into a politically committed public patrimony. I think that criticism of specialization and closure can be read in this way, even though the totalizing elements previously mentioned ended up by imposing their unifying law.

The second feature is related to the imaginary interlocutor of the intellectuals' discourse: the people, the proletariat, the nation, or the party, according to political and programmatic divisions. This interlocutor helped to sharpen the discourse in order to occupy a public forum and play an active role in it. Discourses involving exclusively colleagues or peers produced dissatisfaction. As a consequence, the intellectuals' discourse was led toward other spaces and other dimensions of social experience, where it could contribute in the construction of new interlocutions.

On the other hand, discourses, by becoming politicized, assumed objectives of greater visibility, in collectively accessible terms, intervening in debates on questions considered significant not just for intellectuals. This process, however, was accompanied by the contradiction between intellectual logic and political logic, with the final surrender of the former. Neither Peronism nor the parties of the revolutionary left were able to act and think at the same time. As a result, action began to devour the critical reasoning on which, in some way, this vast movement to incorporate intellectuals and artists into politics had been based.

There was a certainty among us, which can be restated more or less in the following way: if that was the time of politics, if the political dimension ought by right to hegemonize over other practices and discourses, the legitimacy of the intellectuals' world depended upon an external source. Politics became the criterion of truth and assured a unique foundation for all practices.

Conversely, this one-dimensional political logic simplified to the point of parody the relationships between history and politics, between culture and politics. As the core of everything, politics embraced all public practices and tended at the same time to abolish the private, the quotidian, and the present in the name of the future. The idea of the autonomy of the spheres along with that of the specificity of practices supposes also the multiplicity of legal and logical regimes, but this was precisely what tended to be abolished. And thus, politics ensured a radial rather than multidirectional circulation of discourses; it also ensured the development of communication networks and it determined appropriate loci for culture and the arts. With respect to these loci, which were defined from without, the interlocutors, whether classified as "allies" or as "enemies," were assigned permanent positions in rigid relationships.

Nevertheless, intellectuals and artists, throughout the sixties and especially toward the end of that decade and the beginning of the seventies, accepted this pact with politics in which they entered as subordinate elements from an objective point of view and as liable parties from the moral one. (Intellectuals were blackmailed by politics, blackmail that was condensed into various metaphors, the most fortunate of which, it seems to me, was the specter of October 17.)[1] How did this happen? Although replying to this question exceeds the purposes of these notes, I would like to sketch just a few hypotheses. Argentina did not hold itself aloof, in this period, from the spirit of revolution that ran through the European capitals: the student demonstrations of the French May movement of 1968 represent a phenomenon of radicalization and leftist sympathies that unleashed the crisis of reformism. The Cuban Revolution seemed to prove at the same time that revolution was possible and that the will of a handful of men (there it was Régis Debray's theory on the transformation of the revolutionary focus into the party as a Latin American form of politics) could be a sufficient initial impulse. The Chinese Cultural Revolution, translated and sophisticated by European intellectuals, provided a model, lived as totally new, of the relationships between intellectuals and the party, intellectuals and the people, intellectual work and manual work, culture and politics. Soon, Argentina could join into this wave of transformations. Desires were neither moderate nor mediocre.

Two metaphors condense the political unconscious of the period: escalation and collapse. Politics was envisioned as an unstoppable escalade against enemy positions; the enemy seen as a fortress that was necessary to bombard until its inevitable fall. It could be said that these metaphors belong to the most elemental manifestations of politics. Quite the opposite, I would say that in the Argentinean case these metaphors gave shape to very deep political strata, configuring, precisely, a revolutionary narrative that would be told in the near future.

If, as Hayden White states, narration is the space where the opposite claims of the imaginary and the real enter into transactions, it is then possible to discover, in political narrative, traces of the mediation of conflicts between desires and the law (1978). It was, without a doubt, an optimistic narrative, though the agents of an optimistic resolution of the conflict were, in some versions, violence and death: the rebirth and purification of society would write the last chapter. It was a utopian narrative as well to the extent that, unlike the novel or the epic poem, its denouement was set in the future. It was a redemptive narration, as far as it produced an inversion of places and actors, and, in the process, the weak became strong and the strong were finally defeated by the persistence, audacity, courage, solidarity, and organization of the former. It was a magical narration, because the changes were timely and intensely categorical, in a world where the black magic of bourgeois politics (a magic of transactions and betrayals) was defeated by white magic (a magic of open confrontation and loyalty). It was also a magical narrative because some of its actors represented in condensed form the principles of historical change: a leader, a party, a class, a people, and they could imbue the remaining actors with their qualities: to pass on talents and virtues, to put oneself in someone else's shoes, to receive supernatural assistance and to invoke it. This narrative, obviously, interpellated the subjects, assuring them in a vision of history as a process whose conclusion was, significantly, inevitable.

On top, as the succession of events became ever more entangled and incomprehensible for the actors, these actors insisted on the very same narrative, which ensured them, amid present chaos, a future (revolutionary) stability.

TODAY, CERTAINTIES have deteriorated. If in the last two decades history appeared as a repository where meanings were assembled into one all-encompassing Meaning, this homogeneity can be at last called into question. The shattering of meanings is probably what induces the aesthetic admiration for the kaleidoscope of the real or the present skepticism. Nevertheless, the intellectuals who were at the forefront during crucial moments of recent history should not necessarily convert to the aesthetics of fragmentation or undertake the practice of skepticism with the same passion they had for the revolutionary perspective.

Perhaps the worst thing that can befall us, however, is to stand petrified contemplating our own past, be it in the form of the defeated revolutionary moment, or of the enormous mistake that cannot be undone. That is, we must not contemplate the past as a possibly desirable future or as the ultimate mistake. Both perspectives turn us into inexplicable subjects and, at the same time, close off the possibility of reconstructing ourselves as public intellectuals.

In this era dominated by the question of the de-centering of the subject, these notes will seem strangely archaic vis-à-vis the cultural *vogue* of postmodernism. And they will also seem guiltily post-Marxist before a recalcitrant leftist thought that, facing the present ideological and political insecurity (insecurity due to the absence of models, guiding countries, leading intellectuals, one-party systems, future begetting violence, etc.), sticks to the comforting idea that nothing has changed sufficiently, neither in the world nor in Argentina, to justify submitting the old ideas to criticism.

Indeed, certainties have been shattered. It is likely that many of the intellectuals who played a leading role during the days of the era of optimism feel relieved at this loss of political referents, insofar as the crisis of the latter constitutes an alibi for their greater indeterminacy vis-à-vis politics. To state it briefly, it is a condition for the exercise of their freedom.

Nevertheless, the determinations and the imperatives of the past were part of our relationship, as intellectuals, with other sectors and actors in the social texture. They were responsible for our sensitization to inequality and for our resolution to place ourselves in relation to these problems; they were responsible for our feeling uncomfortable with the corporate enclosure of typically intellectual or academic networks and institutions. The fact that these real questions have received imaginary resolutions in the discourse of violence and revolution does not necessarily mean that

that error should be allowed to emasculate the importance of the problems. If, by concentrating on the problems of inequality and oppression, we actually ignored the question of democracy, it does not necessarily follow that the discovery of democracy and of the construction of political institutions leave out for the next stage what was central to our past.

Above all, it would be preferable that in this our age of reason some of the affective forces that drove hundreds of artists and intellectuals into politics were not regarded with skepticism or weighed on the same scale as the one used to judge our authoritarianism, our violence, our insensitivity to the question of democracy. I mean by this that a new conformism should not substitute the revolutionary nonconformism of the sixties and seventies, and we, as intellectuals, should be always alert about the privileges that, in a society like the Argentinean one, we have as intellectuals.

A new conformism presupposes the confusion of the limits between what truly exists and what is only possible. It presupposes the rightful admission of our own limits as intellectuals, but also implies that those limits are necessarily defined from the outside by the legality of academic, cultural, and institutional practices. Academia will always speak to us of our specificity; perhaps we can find within society some other discourse that speaks to us of a more general, more public figure that is not necessarily that of the politician.

I know that I am describing a position that as soon as it gets fixed, it starts moving toward the opposite direction. This mobile and unstable perspective is precisely what I would like to emphasize.

WE HAVE FINALLY recovered our identity as intellectuals, since we now fulfill our practice and our specific discourses without the obsession that they are affected by the lack that only an Other, different from us, could fix. We have found relatively autonomous meanings with respect to other meanings produced in different places and from different practices. We accept those differences, because they are the starting point from which our locus has been rebuilt.

Ten or fifteen years ago, however, we were looking for our foundation in the people, the working class, or the party, constructs where we found the guarantee of a reason, despite their fluctuation between the real and the imaginary. This movement did not mean only the surrendering of our own reasoning to other reasons, it also meant moving beyond the perimeter of our field while renouncing, at the same time, the placid and corporative comfort. Living our identity as intellectuals with a bad conscience was not just an error.

An attempt was made to reformulate in practical terms the classic Sartrean question, "for whom do we write?" That reformulation, in its extreme form, resulted in the destruction of the specific features of the intellectual identity. But, even today, the question poses an enigma, which, in my opinion, cannot be answered by the simple expedient of denying the representativity of our discourse. If the question regarding our social interlocutors is not honestly considered, the intellectual, artistic, or academic institutions end up imposing their own rules, while we stick comfortably to our discourse, because our intellectual common sense finally absolves us: we write for our colleagues.

Doubtless this situation is a product of the experience I have tried to describe in these notes. The lack of confidence in external reasons that had erased the tensions between culture and politics is one of the forms of criticism of our past. However, conformity with the limits of our present practice does not necessarily have to be the consequence of that criticism, and likewise, criticism of our past politics does not have moderatism as its indispensable corollary. It is all about considering if we, intellectuals who emerged from the process of radicalization of previous decades, can propose something different from an obtuse reaffirmation of the past (which has ideological sclerosis as its central argument) or a criticism which, instead of deconstructing the past in order to read its various meanings, persists in burying it and, as a consequence, puts to rest those plural and contradictory meanings.

In my opinion, it would be a good idea to rethink the relationships between culture, ideology, and politics as relationships governed by a permanent tension that cannot be eliminated, since it is the key to cultural dynamics, just as culture and politics are unsymmetrical and nonhomologous processes, as a general rule. So, the idea is to consider the intellectual as a subject pierced by this tension and not subordinate to the rules of one or another of these particular spheres, ready to sacrifice in one of them what she or he would defend in another.

The romantic idea of organic continuity between culture, ideology, and politics frequently produces undesirable associations, but the claim of a radical autonomy between these spheres hinders the grasping of the formal and conceptual complexity of their links. At the same time, it does not prevent political radicalization from subordinating culture or, in periods like the one in which we are living now, culture from being endowed with regional fantasies of social independence.

Besides, fundamental questions like the relationship between the culture of intellectuals and popular culture, the system of reciprocal loans and influences, the flexion introduced in both by the mass media, the problems of distribution of cultural goods and of unequal access to formal or informal networks and institutions, the relationship (which cannot be disregarded by intellectuals) between leisure and culture resist the idea of the autonomy of the spheres as much as the summary disregard of their dissymmetries. The revolution, without a doubt, seemed to offer a paradigmatic solution to these issues. However, the long history of misunderstandings between revolutionary regimes and intellectuals, as well as the attempts to settle cultural differences, even among the popular sectors, carried out by leftist authoritarian regimes, alert us to the opportunity of imagining new roads.

There is no mimetic pact among culture, ideology, and politics. Rather, it can be said that there are different sets of relationships among always heterogeneous elements. Perhaps the recognition of this heterogeneity could constitute a motive for imagining and producing the linkages that, in previous years, could only be considered under the scheme of subordination and a unique explicative principle. This recognition would also be, in itself, a theoretical resource for building relational networks between the culture of the intellectuals and popular culture, providing that, just as in politics, heterogeneity is not necessarily radical alterity but simply difference.

The idea of heterogeneity also provides a basis for thinking that the relationships among culture, ideology, and politics are not invariable but rather the product of the forms of culture and the functions of ideology and politics at determined moments in a given society. These functions are also unstable and, accordingly, define as unstable the locus of intellectuals in the social realm.

We have learned the hard way that asking the impossible does not imply obtaining the possible, but generally, just the opposite. We are also learning that desiring the possible is not enough to get it. Perhaps a task of the intellectual (I think of the leftist intellectual, with all the ambiguity and indeterminacy that the adjective implies) is precisely that of working within and on the limits, with the idea (linked to the idea of transformation) that the limits can be destroyed but also with the recognition of their existence and the weight of their inertia. And, when I say limits, I am referring not only to the conditions for the transformation of a society into a less unequal and unjust one, but also to the limits of our practices and our knowledge regarding the practices and knowledge of other sectors. Working on the limits would be, then, working also upon our own corporative enclosure, in the recognition that the locus and the function of the intellectual can also be transformed.

It is, once again, a question of considering whether our discourse is necessary. The title of these notes posed a disjunction, scission or mimesis? Obviously, *mimesis* plays with the idea of realism, but what does *scission* really mean? A vague feeling of dissatisfaction cannot aspire to become a principle for autonomy, nor can a routine denial of the present, which only proposes the predictable affirmation of revolutionary changes whose normative contents remain deferred to a future as hazy as uncertain. Perhaps the spirit of autonomy of which Gramsci spoke can today originate from the unstable relationship between perception of the real and the lines of transformation. We need a new thesis that articulates the desire for change, endowing it with the strength that moved the revolutionary theses of the past decades. But it would also be necessary that we find the source of that desire.

Translated by Ana Del Sarto, Abril Trigo, and Alicia Ríos

Note

1. On 17 October 1945, the Argentine workers, organized in the General Workers Union (CGT, Central General de Trabajadores) and called on by Evita Perón, took over Plaza de Mayo in support of Juan Domingo Perón, who had been jailed by conservative military sectors.

WALTER MIGNOLO

The Movable Center: Geographical Discourses and Territoriality During the Expansion of the Spanish Empire

Walter Mignolo was born in Argentina. A literary and cultural critic, he is also a professor at Duke University in North Carolina. His main titles include *Teoría del texto e interpretación de textos* (1986), *The Darker Side of the Renaissance: Literacy, Territoriality, and Colonization* (1995), and *Local Histories/Global Designs: Coloniality, Subaltern Knowledges, and Border Thinking* (2000).

S everal years ago I was impressed by what I began to call "Father Ricci's move," referring to his making of what is known today as the Ricci world map as well as to his decision to transfer the center of the world from the Atlantic to the Pacific Ocean (D'Elia 1938). I began to ask myself why Ricci's world map made such an impression on me. The following account provides part of the answer. I say part of it, because this particular case became a piece of a larger puzzle I am trying to put together under the title of colonial semiosis: the production and interpretation of meaning in colonial situations. Colonial semiosis is the general term to indicate a network of semiotic processes in which signs from different cultural systems interact in the production and interpretation of hybrid cultural artifacts. In colonial semiosis the meaning of a sign no longer depends on its original cultural context (for instance, Castilian, or Amerindian, or Chinese), but on the new set of relations generated by communicative interactions across cultural boundaries.

I would like to explore a particular aspect of colonial semiosis illustrated by the mobility of the center in territorial representation. My purpose is to underline one striking although overlooked detail in a specific colonial situation: the coexistence of territorial representations that have been and are concealed by official geographical descriptions, either in verbal discourses or in map forms. During the sixteenth century, mapping as a cultural practice and the map as an object became powerful instruments of territorial representation in the West and signs correlated with the true shape of the earth (Harley 1988, 1989). My analysis rests on the belief that while territorial representation is a human need and, consequently, could be identified in every human community, geographical discourse and mapping during the modern sixteenth-century colonial expansion asserted itself as the only true representation of the earth in a way unseen before then. Thus, Father Ricci's strategy speaks for the moment European men of letters realized that the geographical center of the earth was movable, although the religious, economic, and political one was being established in Rome and in what was beginning to emerge as western Europe.

My study is divided into three parts. In the first, I will comment on what I have already called "Father Ricci's move." In the second, some observations will be made on territorial representation before 1500 and on Guamán Poma de Ayala's world map from the first years of the seventeenth century. Finally, I will explore the implications of López de Velazco's map of the Indies and of the *pinturas* collected in Jiménez de la Espada's *Relaciones Geográficas de Indias* (Geographical Accounts of the Indies), an impressive number of administrative reports planned by Juan de Ovando and López de Velazco and executed by the latter in his role as official cosmographer of the Council of the Indies. López de Velazco was mapping the Indies during the same years that Ricci was trying to convince the Chinese mandarins that the world was not exactly as they thought it was.

Father Ricci's Move

Toward 1584, according to the story told by Father Ricci himself and recently repeated by one of his biographers (D'Elia 1938), the Chinese mandarins visited the first Jesuit mission established at Shao-King. On a wall of the mission room the Chinese saw what was for them an astonishing territorial representation. Although it is not certain which map Father Ricci took with him to China, it is presumed that it was a print of Abraham Ortelius's *Theatrum Orbis Terrarum* (1570) (fig. 1). The Chinese mandarins seemed to be astonished by the fact that the earth looked like a sphere, and that it was mostly covered by water; they were still more astonished when they realized that the Chinese Empire, which up to then they had believed was not only at the center of the earth but also occupied almost its entire surface, was reduced to a small portion of land in the upper right corner of the map. D'Elia reconstructed this crucial moment in the following narrative:

> Ricci had observed that his guests, before looking at the world map in the European language, displayed on the wall of his residence in Shao-King, complained when they saw their China on the right-hand side, at the end of the known world, and near the corner, instead of at the center of the world as until then they had believed it was, in the belief that the world was square. Ricci thought it inopportune to be angry at the pride of the Chinese and afterwards, without getting any closer to the geographical truth, he saw no other alternative than merely to change the layout adopted by the European cartographers. This in fact undermined their world map from that time on by putting the two Americas on the left of the observer, Europe and Africa in the center, and Asia on the right; naturally China and Japan were represented at the extreme right of the map. Ricci, wishing to have a legitimate account of the susceptibility of his guests, placed Europe and Africa on his world map on the observer's left, with Asia in the center and the two Americas on the right. (fig. 2) (1938, 25)

According to scholars of Chinese culture and civilization (Needham and Ling 1959), Chinese conceptualization of space was based on a confederation of five directions: North, South, West, East, and Middle, with "China" meaning, in fact, "the Middle Kingdom." The Chinese universe was sometimes diagrammed as a grid of nested rectangles with the center occupied by China, as we can see in figure 3. In this "map" from about the fifth century B.C., the center stands for the imperial palace. Reading outward, the next rectangle represents the imperial domains. Then come the lands of the tributary nobles, the zone of pacification where border peoples were adjusting to Chinese customs, the land of friendly barbarians, and, finally, the outermost rectangle that separates Chinese civilization from the lands of savages who have no culture at all.

Although Father Ricci was in China almost two thousand years after the date this Chinese diagram of the world was drawn, it could be assumed that the surprise expressed by the gentry of the Ming dynasty when they saw the Ortelius-like map on the wall of the mission room was due to the fact that their conceptualization of space, as well as of the place they assigned to China in the configuration of the earth, remained attached to the rectangular matrix with China in the center. It may be difficult to believe that the kind of territorial representation prevalent in the fifth century B.C. was still relevant in China toward the end of the

1. How the world looked to European eyes toward the second half of the sixteenth century. The world map is from Ortelius's *Theatrum Orbis Terrarum*, which, supposedly, Ricci took with him to China. This and figure 2 come from the redrawing of López de Velazco's original maps in his 1574 manuscript and are reprinted in Antonio Herrera y Tordesillas, *Historia general de los hechos de los Castellanos en las Islas de Tierra Firme del mar océano*, 1601–1615. Courtesy of the Edward E. Ayer Collection, Newberry Library, Chicago.

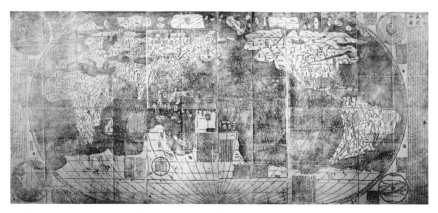

2. Ricci's redrawing of the Western *mapamundi*, placing China toward the center. Indirectly, Ricci's world map shows that notions such as East and West to identify cultures and countries are contingent on the position of the observer. In this map, the Americas are the "Orient" (unless we accept that this map is incorrect). Biblioteca Vaticana, Rome.

sixteenth century. However, the Italian traveler Gemelli Carreri claimed to have seen, circa A.D. 1700, a Chinese "map" very similar to the center-oriented representation in rectangular form shown in figure 3. This long tradition of territorial representation makes the moment Ricci showed his world map to his Chinese guests very special.

Father Ricci's move consisted in redrawing an Ortelius-like map with the projection in the Pacific Ocean and China close to the center (fig. 2). Ricci was able to detach the ethnocentric perception and conceptualization of space from geometric and arithmetic calculations, projecting the surface of the earth from different and equally valid centers of observation. However, the Chinese mandarins were not yet in a position to understand this move, and their natural reaction was to see without understanding how their ethnic center could have been de-centered. Their astonishment showed, furthermore, that the power of the center does not depend on geographical representations but, on the contrary, geographical representations are built around the power of the center. Once the ethnic perspective is detached from the geometric one, the authoritative center becomes a matter of political power rather than of ethnic subjectivity.

Although the history of Father Ricci's map in the cartographic history of the East is beyond the scope of this chapter (see Wallis 1965; Ch'en 1939), it is illustrative of the struggle between coexisting territorial representations during the economic and religious expansion of the West. While Ricci's map encountered strong opposition and resistance in China, it was more readily accepted in Japan. Current world maps printed in Japan (fig. 4) show the location of lands and water introduced by Ricci's redrawing of Western world maps. A Japanese map from the eighteenth century (fig. 5) shows the same distribution, although its drawing style is quite distinct from the European history of cartography. The Japanese cartographic tradition based on Ricci's world map began with the Shoho world map of 1645 (Wallis 1965, 42–43). In China, however, the situation was not as smooth as Ricci and the Jesuits pretended it was. Kenneth Ch'en has shown that some of the people who reported to have met Ricci did not make a distinction between the traditional "western regions" in Chinese cartography and Europe. The official history of the Ming dynasty, written while Ricci was still in China, does not follow Ricci's map. In some cases, criticism of Ricci has been quite harsh, as can be appreciated in the following evaluation:

> Lately Matteo Ricci utilized some false teachings to fool people, and scholars unanimously believed him. . . . The map of the world which

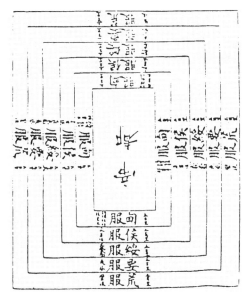

3. One kind of Chinese territorial representation before the encounter with European cartography. From Joseph Needham and Wang Ling, *Science and Civilization in China* (Cambridge: Cambridge University Press, 1959). Reproduced by permission of Cambridge University Press.

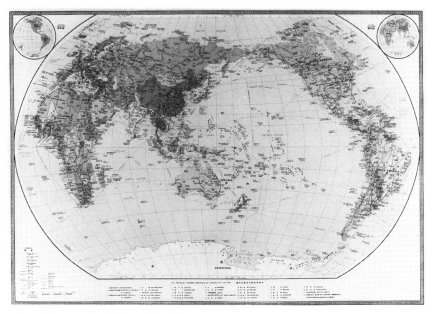

4. A world map printed in Japan in 1988.

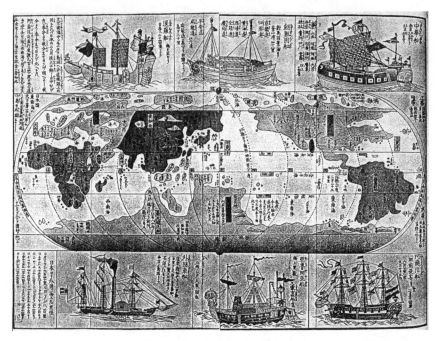

5. Ricci's legacy in Japan: an eighteenth-century world map showing Japan and China toward the center, the Americas in the East, and Europe in the Far West.

he made contains elements of the fabulous and mysterious, and is a downright attempt to deceive people on things which they personally cannot go to verify for themselves. It is really like the trick of a painter who draws ghosts in his pictures. We need not discuss other points, but just take for example the position of China on the map. He puts it not in the center but slightly to the west and inclined to the north. This is altogether far from truth, for China should be in the center of the world, which we can prove by the single fact that we can see the North Star resting at the zenith of the heaven at midnight. How can China be treated like a small unimportant country, and placed slightly to the north as in this map? This really shows how dogmatic his ideas are. Those who trust him say that the people in his country are fond of traveling afar, but such an error as this would certainly not be made by a widely-traveled man. (Chang Wei-hua, qtd. in Ch'en 1939, 348)

It is tempting (at least for me) to read the preceding paragraph as a complaint from someone who defends his rights although he is utterly in the wrong. The temptation comes from the natural tendency to judge colonial situations from the point of view of what Johannes Fabian (1983) called the "denial of coevalness." The impression the reader gets from

Ricci's account is that the Chinese cartographers and intellectuals were "behind" in time, not yet quite as developed as their European counterparts. Such an impression emerges from the dictum of serious and outstanding modern scholars who are able to say, describing Ricci's contribution to Chinese cartography, that "it gave the Chinese a true picture of the world as it was then known." Such generalizations are based on a denotative concept of sign and on a correspondence theory of truth, which disregard the locus and the subject of enunciation as well as the needs and functions of territorial representation. Instead, a universal knowing subject is presupposed and identified with the regional European cartographic perspective. If instead of saying "a true picture of the world as it was then known," we say "the true picture of the world as it was then known by Europeans and Chinese," the statement would do justice to colonial situations in which at least two perspectives on the world coexist and the attribution of true value depends on the perspective taken by the speaking subject—as can be seen in Ricci's as well as in the Chinese scholars' respective accounts. We know today that toward the end of the sixteenth century the Jesuits were not aware of or ignored the changes in the image of the cosmos introduced by Copernicus. They lived in a universe whose center was the earth and not the sun. There was a difference between the Jesuit and the Chinese scholars, nonetheless, and the difference was relevant not at the level of true correspondences between maps and the world but at the level of power. Ricci's territorial representation was more powerful than the Chinese on two accounts: first, because it went together with an economic and religious expansion that allowed Ricci to promote the European conception of the world in China while the Chinese were not in a position to promote their own territorial view to the Europeans; second, because it had the power of transcending the *ethnic* concept of the center and replacing it with a *geometric* one.

To explore this dimension of Ricci's move it is necessary to pause for a moment and review some of the constants encountered in territorial representations before the era of exploration and the mapping of the entire surface of the earth.

Human Body, Ecology, and Territorial Representations

When I began to read about the history of cartography in order to understand Ricci's move, I soon learned that the omphalos syndrome governing territorial organization, both in its spatial aspects (people believing that they are at the center of the world) and its religious one (people believing that they have been divinely appointed), was widespread, rather than a peculiarly Chinese feature. It became apparent that the ethnic center had to be grounded on some basic experience of the subject and the community such as the human body, the East-West movement of the sun and the moon (as one of the most fundamental features of spatial orientation), the place in which the human body is located as fundamental reference for territorial representation, or a combination of these factors. Arnheim's assumption that some fundamental principles of spatial organization are deeply rooted in human nature (1988, 2), and that particular concretizations take place in specific historic conditions and under the rules of enduring traditions, supports my intuitions. Lumsden and Wilson's plea for a new human science (1983, 167–84) deserves to be considered from the perspective of territoriality (see also Johnson 1987).

It is well known, for instance, that the correlation between micro- and macrocosmos was a shared belief among certain intellectuals of the Middle Ages and that the correlation was influential in depicting the earth and the universe. The micro-macrocosm theory holds that a man (or human being) is a miniature world, and that the world had the form of an immense man (or human being). The Christian version modeled this theory with the body of Christ, as illustrated in figure 6 (Wolf 1957; 1989, 66–67; Gurevich 1985, 41–92). While the human body suggests the four horizontal directions (head and feet; left and right) and the movement of the sun and the moon mark the east-west orientation (Marshcak 1972), in Christian cosmology the east (sunrise) coincides with the head of Christ and with paradise and the center with the navel, which gives rise to the metaphor "the navel of the world" and coincides with Jerusalem. The Ebstorf map (fig. 7) provides a paradigmatic illustration of territorial representation in Christian cosmology. The power of the center exemplified in such maps is very similar in conception to the rectangular Chinese world map shown in figure 3, in which the Middle Kingdom has the same function as Jerusalem in Christian representations. Thus, the geographical center appeared to be correlated both to the human body as an abstract reference point for the four directions, and to the moment in which the body becomes part of a community; consequently, the foundation of an ethnic identification.

It should come as no surprise, then, that the well-known medieval T-O maps systematically placed Jerusalem at the center. The map shown in figure 8 was used to illustrate the *Etymologiae* by Isidore of Seville, a writer who lived between A.D. 560 and 636. The map, oriented toward the east, contains the names of the three continents and identifies each with one of Noah's sons: Asia with Sem, Europe with Japhet, and Africa with Ham (spelled Cham). The Medieval T-O map was in vogue well into

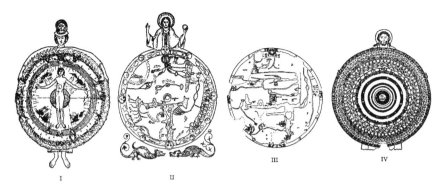

6. Various illustrations of the "map" form of the micro-macrocosm theory: (I) Hildegard of Bingen's second vision of the universe (circa 1230); (II) The London Psalter Map (circa 1250); (III) The Ebstorf Map (circa 1230); (IV) The Pisa Wall Fresco of the Creation of the Universe (from Wolf 1989, 66). Editions du Comité des Travaux Historiques et Scientifiques.

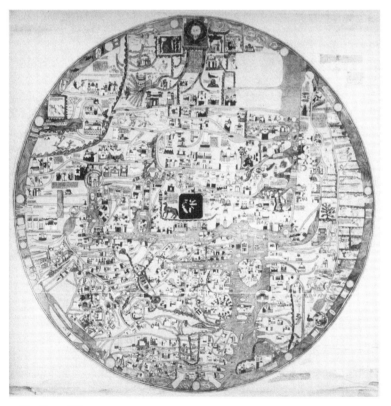

7. The Ebstorf Map.

the sixteenth century. In several fifteenth-century woodcuts from Ravenna, for instance, the world was divided into three parts; Jerusalem was in the center, and that choice was governed by either religious order or religious cosmology. Figure 9 shows St. Francis and St. Dominic in friendship sharing the possession of the world. A similar territorial representation was printed in a 1494 edition of the encyclopedia of the English Franciscan Bartolomaeus Anglicus (Bartholomew de Glanville) (fig. 10). His encyclopedia (*De proprietatibus rerum*, 1220–40) was very influential in the work of the Spanish Franciscan Bernardino de Sahagún (Robertson 1966; López Austin 1980). In the *Florentine Codex* (Sahagún 1975), a bilingual version of the material collected during a life-long project written around 1578, Sahagún drew the earth in the form you see in figure 11. Although it would be difficult to ascertain when between 1540 and 1585 Sahagún drew this T-O map, there is enough evidence to believe that as early as 1540 world maps were produced in which the surface of the earth was depicted with the Atlantic Ocean, rather than the Mediterranean and Jerusalem in the center. However, T-O maps survived at least until the sixteenth century, as illustrated by the T-O map shown in figure 12, with the New World shown in the bottom left corner.

That the Middle Kingdom and Jerusalem as the navel of the world were regional and historical representations of a more fundamental pattern rooted in human nature seems to be supported by the example of Cuzco, the capital of the Incan Empire, whose name means "navel of the world" (Sullivan 1985). It would be a mistake to think that the coincidence between Jerusalem and Cuzco exemplifies Christian influences in colonial Peru. It would be more satisfactory to think that if both Jerusalem and Cuzco are assigned a central place in territorial representations, it is because there were common features in both Christian and Incan cultures long before European explorers and men of letters changed the image of the world and the mobility of the center. Guamán Poma's world map (fig. 13) looks, at first glance, like a product of modern cartography in which parallels and meridians have been used to indicate distances and to locate places. Upon closer inspection it becomes evident that parallels and meridians are ornaments rather than basic tools of territorial representation. In the first place, the confederation of the four different directions of space (east, west, north, south) and the center can be recognized. As in the Chinese map shown in figure 3 and the T-O map shown in figure 8, Cuzco occupies the center. In contrast with the Chinese map and the social distribution correlated to it, the spectrum from the "civilized" to the "barbarian" is not represented as an increasing distance from the center to the periphery, but as opposition *between* "high" and

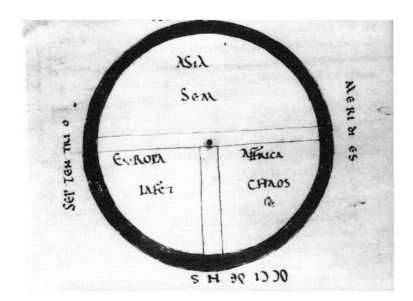

8 (above). Medieval T-O map, from Isidore of Seville's *Etymologiae*.

9 (right). St. Francis and St. Dominic on "top" of the world, represented in a T-O form from the fifteenth century. Biblioteca Classense, Ravenna.

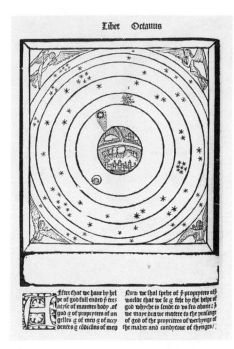

Liber Octauus

Ffter that we haue by hel pe of god full ended p treatyse of mannes body .of god p of propyrtees of angelles & of men & of acccydentes & condicions of men

Now we shal spelle of p propyrtees ofp worlde that we se & fele by the helpe of god whyche is sende to vs fro aboue : p we mape draw matere to the pralinge of god of the propyrtees of werkynge of the maker and condytour of thynges /

10 (left). T-O map from the 1492 edition of Bartolomaeus Anglicus, *De propietatibus rerum* (thirteenth century). 11 (right). Sahagún's representation of the Aztec worldview according to Christian T-O maps. Archivo Histórico Central, Mexico City.

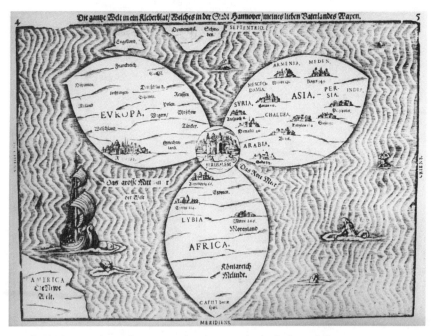

12. A late T-O map (sixteenth century), showing America in the lower left corner.

"low," on the one hand, and on the other, *within* "high" and "low." Following the works of Tom Zuidema (1964), Nathan Wachtel (1971) has summarized the double spatial structure of the "high" and the "low"— high: Chinchaysuyu (I) + Antisuyu (III); low: Collasuyu (II) + Cuntinsuyu (IV)—the four quarters of the world, and the correlation between spatial distribution and social organization. Chinchaysuyu is the privileged quarter for Guamán Poma, to which he attributes nobility, strength, and dominant position. The other pole of the "higher" division is the Antisuyu, and its people are the opposite of the Chinchaysuyu. They are barbarians, they are hostile, and they eat human flesh. The inhabitants of the Collasuyu, the quarter of the lower part, opposite the Chinchaysuyu, like their counterpart of the higher part, the Antisuyu, are amoral, lazy, and corrupt, although they are also rich. Guamán Poma located the Spaniards in this quarter of the world. Finally, the Cuntinsuyu is the exact opposite of the Collasuyu in terms of economic values: the inhabitants of the Cuntinsuyu are extremely poor. In modern terminology, civilization and barbarism distinguished the inhabitants of the two upper quarters while riches and poverty characterized the people living in the lower quarters. On the other hand, the poor but virtuous and the civilized are opposed to the rich and to the barbarians.

What seems to me still remarkable in the move made by Ricci (who was drawing his world map in China about the same time that Guamán was drawing his in Cuzco, although for different purposes), is the fact that a system of territorial representation has been achieved in which the center no longer needs to be fixed. Or, to put it another way, the power of the center has been displaced from a fixed to a movable position. If we take into account, for example, that the human body was not only the point of reference of the organization of space but also of the letters of the alphabet, science, and the cosmological order (Dubois 1970, 92–110; López Austin 1980, 1:171–95), then the passage from a system of territorial organization in which the concept of space depends on the coordination of the body with cosmogeographical markers (sunrise and sunset, for instance; human perception of the horizon; etc.) to one that depends on the eye and on arithmetic calculation acquires a specific significance during the age of the discoveries and the expansion of the Spanish Empire. For, although the coordination of the eye and arithmetic calculation goes back to Ptolemy, the confrontation during the process of the economic and religious expansion of the West between persons and institutions who were concerned with expansion and conquests on a grandiose scale and those who were not (like the Aztecs, the Chinese, the Maya, or the Incas), not only put Ptolemy into good use but also exemplified the transition from the fixed to a movable center in territorial organization.

Even if it could be said today with common sense that the center is determined by the position of the observer, it should also be possible to detach the arithmetic calculation (numeracy) from the ideological and political manipulation (literacy) of territorial representation. The world map shown in figure 4 suggests that while in Ortelius's map the observer was placed in the Atlantic, the observer in this contemporary Japanese map is placed in the Pacific. But such a reading will conceal the fact that beyond this contemporary Japanese map there is a history of colonization of space that goes back to Ricci and the effort to spread Christianity in the East. A similar argument can be made by contrasting an Arabian map from the seventeenth century, representing the Americas when the projection places the observer at the North Pole (fig. 14), with a map of the Americas (shown in fig. 15) in which it is not so much the projection that situates the observer at the South Pole, but an emphasis on the political and ideological meaning of territorial representation. If territoriality cannot be achieved without a center, its fixity or mobility is a sign of the position of the representing agency rather than of the space represented.

Mapping the Colonies: Centers, Peripheries, and Hybrid Cultural Production

I am still fascinated by the consequences of reflecting on territorial organization from the premise of an ambulatory center. Thus, if the second part of my essay took me from Ricci's adventure with his world map to the omphalos syndrome and the body as a reference point of territoriality, the replacement of the body as a reference point and of calculation as geometric projection prompted the mobility of the center and became an instrument for spatial colonization. However, while the geometric projection allowed for the mobility of the center, the economic, political, and religious center was being construed by and attached to the ethnic group in expansion (Rome or Spain, depending on the particular moment and the institutions supporting the act of enunciation). The expansion of the Spanish Empire coincided with the historical moment in the West when Christianity, after losing its religious center (Jerusalem), created another from which the campaign of Christianizing the world began. Paradoxically enough, the mobility of the religious center seems to have had some indirect consequences in the transformation of geographic discourse and of territorial representations. Although I am not in a position to prove a causal connection between the loss of the original

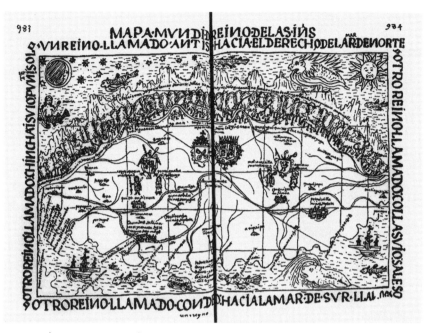

13. Guamán Poma's *mapamundi*.

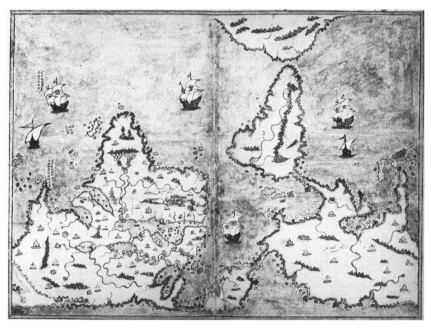

14. World map of *Tarikh-el Hind-gharbi* (Description of the Indies of the West), attributed to Mustafa ibn Abdullah, seventeenth century. Courtesy of the Edward E. Ayer Collection, Newberry Library, Chicago.

15. An ideological inversion
of the Americas.

16. López de Velazco's *Indias occidentales y del poniente*.

religious center (Jerusalem) and the creation of a new one (Rome), it would be less risky to suggest a connection between the expansion of western Christianity, its role in the colonization process after 1492, and Ricci's move.

Toward 1574, López de Velazco, who was appointed cosmographer of the Council of the Indies in 1571, was fulfilling his duties and writing the *Descripción y demarcación de las Indias Occidentales* (1574), a detailed account of the Spanish possessions from what are now called the Caribbean islands to the Philippines. He divided the Spanish territories into three parts: "Indias Septentrionales" (Northern Indies), which comprised the area from Florida to the Panama Canal; "Indias Meridionales" (Southern Indies), from the Panama Canal to Patagonia; and "Indias del Poniente" (Western Indies), which included the Philippines, Moluccas, and so on (fig. 16). López de Velazco's report came as one of the consequences of a visitation to the Council of the Indies ordered by Philip II, and the recommendation of Juan de Ovando, in charge of such an evaluation, to have a systematic way of collecting information about the colonial possessions (Carbia 1940, 109–49). If López de Velazco's verbal description and the fourteen maps attached thereto were the first step toward a systematic organization of information about the New World being construed in the colonization process, the second step was the *Instruction and Memorandum*, a list of fifty questions distributed to every corner of the Indies in which an *alcalde* (mayor) or a public notary was available to collect information and answer each of the questions. One specific question asked for a *pintura* (drawing) of the location being surveyed. As a result of this request, we have several *pinturas* attached to the *Relaciones Geográficas*, which were the written report and the reply to the *Instruction and Memorandum* (Cline 1964, 1972). Thus, we have in some of the maps drawn by the "indios viejos" (older Indians), the testimony of coexisting and conflicting territorial representations similar to the reaction of the Chinese mandarins to Ricci. Resistance to colonization of space among the Amerindians did not have the force of resistance that it had in China.

López de Velazco provided a verbal description of the information complementing the map (fig. 16): "The Indies, the islands, and *terra firma* in the Ocean which are commonly called the New World, are the lands and seas which lie within the boundaries of the kingdom of Castile, which is a hemisphere, or half of the world, beginning at 180 degrees west from a meridian circle which passes through 39 degrees longitude west of the meridian of Toledo" (1574, 5).

He believed, or at least suggested, that Nature had divided the northern and the southern parts of the West Indies at the Isthmus of Panama.

Concerning the third part of the totality of the West Indies, he coined the expression "Islas del Poniente" to designate the complex of the Spanish possessions, which he describes as follows:

> The West Indies are all the islands and terra firma which lie within the boundaries of the kingdom of Castile, to the westernmost point, whose frontiers, as I have said, extend to the other side of the world, to the city of Malaca, whence to the East and New Spain; there is a large gulf consisting of many islands, big and small, and many coastlines and much dry land, which form the Spice Islands (also called the Malucan Islands), the Philippines, the Coast of China, the Lequias and Japanese Islands, the Coast of New Guinea, the Solomon Islands, and the Thieves Islands. (1574, 5)

However, while in his own geographical discourse López de Velazco concealed native territoriality, in his massive plan to gather information implemented through the *Instruction and Memorandum*, he opened the doors—unintentionally, of course—to a kind of discourse (*The Geographical Accounts of the Indies*) that allowed for a reading of native (or subaltern) conceptualization of space. Native territoriality, which had been disregarded in López de Velazco's report as well as in the subsequent history written by Antonio Herrera y Tordesillas (1601, 15) and printed in several editions between 1601 and 1730, emerged, however, in *The Geographical Accounts* (GA). Although the GA—like many other colonial writings—did not reach the printing press until the end of the nineteenth century[1] (and during the colonial period they did not have any particular force or effect other than providing information for the official chronicler or historians), they allowed—in retrospect—for the mobility of the center fixed in the work of López de Velazco as well as in Herrera y Tordesilla's official territorial representations.

Unlike Ricci, López de Velazco was not a Jesuit with the mission of converting the Chinese to Christianity, but the geographer of the Council of the Indies with the charge to gather and organize all relevant information about the Spanish territory in the New World. Although I am comparing López de Velazco with Father Ricci because they were both active during the same years and dealt with the mobility of the center, the cases *per se* are quite dissimilar. As cosmographer of the Council of the Indies, López de Velazco was mapping the Spanish possessions in the West Indies and not making a world map, whereas Ricci was transforming Ortelius to carry on the Jesuit mission in China. Furthermore, López de Velazco was not on a mission of conversion but in charge of mapping the territories and gathering information about the native population.

Because the dialogue between the missionaries and the natives was of a nature different from that of the dialogue between geographers and public notaries (letrados, juristas), reading the *Description and Demarcation of the West Indies* as well as the *Geographical Accounts of the Indies* is quite interesting. López de Velazco's report was written with the conviction that the lands and coasts being mapped were just lumps to which no human conceptualization had been applied before the arrival of the Spaniards. He contributed to the knowledge of the periphery and to its incorporation into the ethnic center invented by those who were in a position to carry on the expansion of imperial Spain and western Christendom. This is why we can conclude that while Father Ricci—with his world map—disdained Chinese cartography and space conceptualization, López de Velazco—with his map of the West Indies—repressed Amerindian territoriality. However, the stronger tradition in Chinese cartography and narrative of the past allowed for a stronger (or at least more visible) resistance to Western territorial organization. In contrast, the liquidation of Amerindian nobility and culture left few traces of Amerindian resistance to Western territorial conceptualization. Most of them can be found in the *pinturas* of the *Geographical Accounts* or in the documents of land concession or litigations. Guamán Poma de Ayala has also left an outstanding example of resistance to territorial representation, as we will see below.

In order to understand better what the *Instruction and Memorandum* and the *Geographical Accounts* represent for interpreting the mobility of the geographical center, let me begin by counting the social and communicative situation in which the fifty questions of the *Instruction and Memorandum* were answered and by describing the context in which *pinturas* or maps were requested and subsequently drawn. At the beginning of every *Account*, the place, date, and people gathered together had to be explicitly stated. The beginning of the *Relación de Chimalhuacán Atoyac* (Account of Chimalhuacán Atoyac), from the Valley of Mexico, is as follows: "In the town of Chimalhuacán, at the holding of Jerónimo de Bustamante, on the first day of the month of December in the year 1579, this report was made by order of His Majesty the King, in accordance with the *Instrucción y Memoria* contained above, written in print. The knight commander Cristóbal de Salazar, his Majesty's chief magistrate for the town of Coatepec and its environs, was present in order to see that this was done, and with him, Francisco de Villacastín, clerk and interpreter of his court, and the chiefs were asked of their language, and of the elders who were in this said town, and of their subjects" (Acuña 1985, 155).

Although several of the fifty questions requested geographical infor-

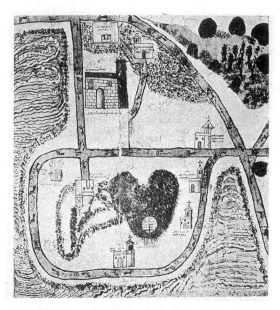

17. *Pintura* of Chimalhuacán Atoyac. Nettie Benson Latin
American Collection, University of Texas, Austin.

mation, it was only question number 10 that specifically asked for a *pintura* or map of the place. The verbal answer to this question, in the above-
mentioned *Account of Chimalhuacán*, is the following: "As has been said,
this town is located at the foot of the said Hill *of Chimalhuacán* and it is located in the direction of the West; it is not laid out in the form of a town.
In the town there is a monastery of monks of the order of Saint Dominic,
as can be seen in the painting" (Acuña 1985, 159).

The verbal description does not render what the *pintura* does.² A large
percentage of the *pinturas* in the *Accounts* were presumably done by the
hands of the "*principales indios viejos*" mentioned at the beginning of each
relation. The painting attached to the *Account of Chimalhuacán* requested in
question 10, is the one in figure 17.

Where is the center in this *pintura*? The organization of the space is
somehow alien to a Western observer. What we see are, indeed, two well-
delineated spaces facing each other. The bottom half is monopolized by
the hill (*el cerro*), more often than not a sacred place. At the top of the hill
you can see the design we have learned to identify with Aztec or Mesoamerican architecture. The caption reads: "*antigua casa de idolatría*" (the
old house of idolatrous practices). The upper half is dominated by the
monastery. The caption says: "*El monasterio.*" In between the houses of
Aztec and Christian religious practices we see roads with footsteps, a

common sign to distinguish roads from rivers as well as to indicate direction in narrative "maps" of Amerindian origins. As Western observers, we might have the impression that the monastery is more important than the hill because it is right side up and because it is located toward the upper left corner. Since in the West reading moves from left to right and from top to bottom, such a pattern could also be applied to the interpretation of the picture. However, we know that codices were usually (or also) read from bottom to top, starting at the right hand corner and moving up in a boustrophedon movement. Following this pattern will change the interpretation of the picture, since it gives the hill a more significant position than the church.

The *pintura* of Chimalhuacán provides a good illustration of colonial representation of space from the point of view of the colonized on two accounts. First, the map or painting has two centers and each center is marked by a religious place (the hill and the monastery). In that regard, the map is a paradigmatic example of a colonial hybrid cultural product in which one symbolic space is organized around two centers. Second, the map illustrates a larger domain of semiotic interactions in a colonial situation in which colonized territorial representations were possible and available, although often these were negated and silenced by the intimidating "true" territorial organization offered by those who held the power in the Council of the Indies, the religious missions, or professional cartographers and cosmographers.

Similar kinds of paintings or maps can be found from the second half of the sixteenth century to the eighteenth, attached to land disputes or land claims. The *pintura* shown in figure 18 has a disposition somehow inverted when compared to the *pintura* of Chimalhuacán. In fact, both the church or monastery as well as the native place for religious practices are right side up. Contrary to the previous *pintura*, the church is in the bottom right corner while the Aztec temple is in the upper left corner. There is, however, a feature in common with the Chimalhuacán painting that should claim our attention: the center could be conceived as an intersection of circles whose centers are the Aztec and the Christian temples. The *pintura* of the town of Huaxtepeque (State of Mexico), from the *Geographical Account* of the same town, illustrates the persistence of the pattern although in a different distribution (fig. 19). The monastery or the church shares the center of the hill, which is marked at the intersection between the signs of two cultures: the glyph of Huaxtepeque ("in the hill of guajes") and a monastery or church.

Such radically different organization of the "same" space by the cosmographer of the Council of the Indies and by representatives of the

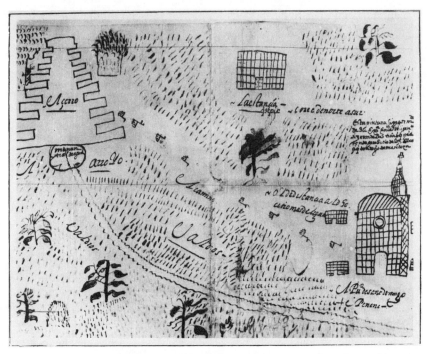

18. Santo Domingo Tepeneme. AGN, Grupo Documental: Tierras, vol. 2812, exp. 11, f. 312.

19. Pintura of Huaxtepeque. Nettie Benson Latin American Collection, University of Texas, Austin.

Amerindian cultures could be explained by looking into the Spaniards' colonization of Amerindian territories, the conflicts between ways of perceiving and representing space in Amerindian and Spanish cultures, and the power relation established between those who were in a colonizing position and those who had to accept a new spatial organization. Related to the first aspect was the substitution, in Mexico, of the local *altepeme* by the economic and religious organization of space introduced by the colonizers. The *altepeme* (from the Náhuatl Altepetl = altl [water] and tepel [hill]), is a territorial concept in the sense that while the hill and the water indicate geographical boundaries, they could also be taken for a sacred place, as we saw in the *pintura* of Chimalhuacán Atoyac. Among the many meanings attributed to the word *altepeme*, one of the most relevant for the present discussion is the one related to territoriality. *Altepeme* means, on the one hand, the land as a place as well as a living force and, on the other, the genealogy and the traditions of the people inhabiting the land (García Martínez 1987, 77ff). The *altepeme* was a concept whose corresponding precept was represented in the *pinturas* or maps. The *encomienda* was one of the pillars of economic production, distribution, and consumption of goods and of the political organization of communal life in the Spanish colonization, and it was established "on top," so to speak, of the *altepeme*, albeit keeping its structure alive. The *encomienda* and the altepeme coexisted, whereas the power was in the hands of the *encomenderos*. Parallel to the economic and political colonization centered on the *encomienda*, the church and the convents were the locus and the foundation of the colonization of the religious imagination. Churches, convents, and monasteries were sometimes placed literally on the top of a hill (the native sacred place), and sometimes in a different although prominent location. The *pintura* of Huaxtepeque (fig. 19) illustrates the first case; the *pintura* of Chimalhuacán Atoyac (fig. 17) the second.

The explanation of the second aspect (e.g., different perception of space) is related to the fact that alternative spatial representations are historical constructions rooted in basic human relationships within the environment (space, living systems, natural and human-made objects). In Amerindian cultures the representation of space was less relevant than time-reckoning and was subordinated to it (León-Portilla 1988, 65–94 and 119–162). The three main pre-Columbian cultures have left impressive documents of their concern with the organization of time, but nothing similar survived apropos the organization of space (Guzmán 1939). In contrast, in modern Europe cartography acquired a life of its own that detached more and more spatial representations (maps) from chronological ones (chronicles, history). Territorial expansion increased the need for spatial organization, a need that was not strongly felt among Amerindian communities during the same period. Finally, Western desire for economic and religious expansion not only generated more visible means of territorial representation but also produced cartographic results that expanded the perceptual image (Randles 1980) of the world and contributed to the practical control of space (Sack 1986).

Beyond the *pinturas* attached to the *Geographical Accounts* and those attached to land litigation in Mexico, Guamán Poma de Ayala in Peru documented the hybrid representation of space from the point of view of the colonized, not only in his curious and famous world map (Kusch 1970), but also in the *pintura* of the pontifical world, a representation of a coexisting Cuzco and the Kingdom of Castile (fig. 20). In this *pintura*, the familiar four-corners-of-the-world pattern common to numerous cosmological traditions (Blacker and Loewe 1975; Wheatly 1971) before the spread of Western cartography, and still existing in cultures and communities that have survived on the margins of the Western world (Gossen 1986), has been maintained. The patterns have been duplicated in order to represent Castile in the same way that Cuzco's territory is represented. Furthermore, Cuzco has been placed in the upper half, next to the sun and therefore in a privileged position, and the center has been emptied, as in the *pinturas* shown in figures 17, 18, and 20.

A preliminary conclusion can be drawn from these four alternative examples to López de Velazco's fourteen maps of the Indies: whereas the space is perceived from the point of view of the colonized as coexisting territorial organization—for reasons the examples of the *altepeme, the encomienda*, and the *monasterio* illustrate—the point of view of the colonizer conceals (or attempts to, as in Ricci's example) native non-European territorial representations. Although there is no indication in López de Velazco's map that alternative territorial representation may have existed, we cannot ignore this when looking at the *pinturas* in which space is represented by means of coexisting symbolic structures.

Chinese reactions to Western territorial representations described by Father Ricci were more visible than their Amerindian counterparts and they lasted longer. In the New World all the examples known today are from the last quarter of the sixteenth century and the first quarter of the seventeenth. It is tempting to formulate the hypothesis that the hybrid territorial representations seen in figures 17–20 are related to the *Instruction and Memorandum*, although there is no clear evidence, to my knowledge, that Guamán Poma was directly addressing question 10 of the *Instruction and Memorandum* when he drew his pontifical world map representing Cuzco and the Kingdom of Castile. Several of his drawings in

POVTIFICAL
MVVDO

las yns del piru
enlo alto de espana

castilla enlo auajo
delas yns

castilla

enesk

20. Guamán Poma's
"Pontifical mundo."

which Peruvian cities are depicted resembled so many of the *pinturas*
attached to the *Geographical Accounts* that one suspects that the official requests of the Council of the Indies transmitted via *Instruction and Memorandum* (or perhaps some examples of the *Geographical Accounts*) were
not completely unknown to Guamán Poma. Be that as it may, the fact
remains that the economic and religious expansion of the West produced—between approximately 1580 and 1620—a moment of tension in
territorial representation that turned around the mobility of the center.
Although by the last quarter of the sixteenth century Western cartographers had displaced the geographical and ethnic center from the Mediterranean (which means, incidentally, "the middle of the earth"!) to the
Atlantic, and Rome began to be more centrally located than Jerusalem,
Ricci's move consisted of disjoining the geographical from the ethnic
centers. This move certainly did not convince the Chinese, who could live
with the way their own cartographic tradition had solved the problems
and satisfied the needs of territorial representations. It convinced the Jap-

anese, however, as they saw in it the possibility of displacing the geographic and ethnic center from the Atlantic to the Pacific. The situation was different in the European expansion to the New World. López de Velazco's map of the West Indies presupposed the Atlantic as the geographical and ethnic center. Its successful reprints in Herrera y Tordesillas's *Descripción de las Indias Occidentales* (1601), also indicates that López de Velazco's map was highly satisfactory to those who charted and controlled the administration of the Indies. The Amerindian *pinturas* suggest that, contrary to the Chinese reaction, toward the end of the sixteenth century the native populations were losing their own patterns of territorial representation.

Concluding Remarks

A few concluding remarks are in order:

First, at the beginning of the sixteenth century the merging of map making and the printing industry took place. Travel and exploration awakened the curiosity of a large European audience, which the printing industry was in a position to satisfy.

Second, naturally, world maps were drawn with the Atlantic and Europe at the center, combining both the ethnic and the algebraic position of the observer. Father Ricci's move, certainly not very well known in European cartographic history, was adopted in Japan in exactly the same terms: the combination of the ethnic with the position of the observer determined by algebraic calculation. However, while this merging was ethnically "natural" for a person belonging to a community dwelling near the Pacific, it was not "natural" for Father Ricci, whose ethnic place was near the Mediterranean. In his case, the need to satisfy the audience he was attempting to convert led him to the realization that the *ethnic* and *algebraic* observer could be detached in territorial representation without losing the central religious and ideological center that was determined by political power.

Finally, when it comes to the New World, in which the encounter between missionaries and geographers with native civilizations was of a nature distinct from the experience missionaries and geographers had in China and Japan, it appears that mapping the West Indies was not contested in the same way that Ricci's world map was contested in China. It also appears that the silenced territorial representations of native populations emerged, among other cultural products, in the *pinturas* attached to GA or to land litigations.

Both the Jesuit experience in China and Japan and the geographer and

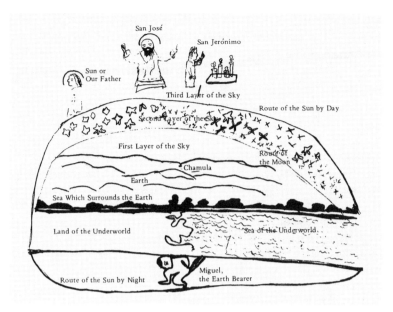

Sun or
Our Father

San José

San Jerónimo

Third Layer of the Sky

Second Layer of the Sky

First Layer of the Sky

Route of the Sun by Day

Route of
the Moon

Chamula

Earth

Sea Which Surrounds the Earth

Land of the Underworld

Sea of the Underworld

Route of the Sun by Night

Miguel,
the Earth Bearer

21. A Chamula's world map. From Gary H. Gossen, *Chamulas in the World of the Sun: Time and Space in a Maya Oral Tradition* (Cambridge: Harvard University Press, 1974).

public notary experiences in the West (Indies), illustrate one aspect of colonial semiosis: colonial cultural artifacts read in their context always reveal their hybrid dimension, even in the case in which the colonial point of view is explicitly concealed. To read the silence of European territorial representation is, perhaps, one way of reaching subaltern territoriality. I have attempted to illustrate only one case of colonial semiosis by inquiring into some of the changes in territorial representation produced during the age of exploration and expansion of the Spanish Empire.

In Latin America today there are communities still living like the Chamulas of southern Mexico (fig. 21), not yet reached by Western patterns of territoriality. In cases like this, Ricci's move comes to mind. Should they be taught to look at the world as Ortelius or López de Velazco did or should they be encouraged to develop their own alternative spatial perceptions? Can we today still hold our beliefs that a "true" territorial organization shows how the world really is or should we accept their diversity as we accept linguistic diversity (Coulmas 1984), which in an ideal or science-fiction world could lead to coexisting and equally valid organization of space, to a plural epistemology not necessarily dependent on a fixed center? The movable center would then become a metaphysical metaphor for an ideal world that resembles the state of affairs before rather than after the economic and religious expansion of the West and the consequent mapping of the earth. It could also be a methodological metaphor to understand what colonial semiosis entails. I am not proposing a romantic return to a premodern world, but rather using the image of the premodern world as an example of a de-centered epistemology that had been radically transformed during the sixteenth century.[3]

Notes

1. Jiménez de la Espada published several GAs of Peru. Since then the GAs have received more attention from scholars. Between 1984 and 1989, René Acuña published over one hundred and fifty "*relaciones*" of Mexico, all of them from the sixteenth century. Francisco de Solano edited a considerable number of GAs from the seventeenth and eighteenth centuries (1988).

2. We should keep in mind that the etymology of *map* is quite close to *pintura*. The original meaning of *map* denotes a piece of cloth or paper in which a depiction of space is drawn. In the Middle Ages, *descriptio* was a term often used to refer to what today one calls *map*.

3. I recently read Hodgson's "In the Center of the Map: Nations See Themselves as the Hub of History," an article published in 1956 (UNESCO *Courier*) that advances a thesis very similar to mine here (see Hodgson 1993, 29–35). I am grateful to Bruce Lawrence for calling Hodgson to my attention.

JOSÉ JOAQUÍN BRUNNER

Notes on Modernity and Postmodernity in Latin American Culture

José Joaquín Brunner was born in Chile in 1944. A social scientist, he is the director of the Education Program, Fundación Chile (Santiago, Chile). His main titles include *Un espejo trizado: Ensayos sobre cultura y políticas culturales* (1988), *América Latina: Cultura y modernidad* (1992), and *Globalización cultural y posmodernidad* (1998).

Starting from the vantage point of the contemporary debate about modernity, I want to discuss here some problems of Latin American culture in relation to its future.

The Ambiguous Status of Cultural Questions

I first need to explain, however, why one should be interested in such a discussion anyway. Seized as we are by the great themes of the moment—the foreign debt and the economic crisis, unemployment and the difficulties of industrialization, the Central American conflict, and the processes of redemocratization—what capacity of attraction can cultural problems have, especially if these, as is frequently the case, tend to overflow the usual categories at hand? To speak meaningfully of culture requires that we refer to collective representations, beliefs, cognitive styles, the communication of symbols, language games, the sedimentation of traditions, and so on, and not only to the quantifiable aspects of culture: namely, to the movements of the market of cultural goods.

The Latin American social sciences have only marginally preoccupied themselves with these cultural problems, perhaps because their study does not fall high enough on the ladder of academic prestige or because they do not lend themselves easily to the prevailing methodologies. Culture, as such, still appears to us as a supplement, identified, according to an old aristocratic conception, with the fine arts, with the Sunday editions of the great urban newspapers, and with the conspicuous consumption of art works and symbols invested with an aura of prestige.

This "cultured" vision of culture, otherwise absurd in an age of the primacy of the forms and contents of mass culture, of the media and the culture industry, is also sometimes a symptom of denial produced by a deeper, and typically modern, tendency: the predominance of the interests, including cognitive, of instrumental reason over the values of communicative rationality; the separation of a technical sphere of progress that includes the economy, science, and material conditions of daily life from the sphere of intersubjectively elaborated and communicated meanings, those found indissolubly anchored in a life-world where traditions, desires, beliefs, ideals, and values coexist and are expressed precisely in culture.

This reactive negation leads easily to the extreme of affirming that culture, as a symbolic domain, is incomprehensible for analytic reason and that only an empathetic approach suits it—an affirmation that leaves a considerable part of the social sciences out of the game and encloses the debate about the cultural universe in a new esotericism, this time made up of intuitions, mysteries, and, in the best of circumstances, poetry.

The attempt to conduct our own exploration within a relatively known, and shared, frame of reference, such as modernity, has as its purpose to avoid the double danger of, on the one hand, a purely functionalist vision of culture—obstacle or promoter of modernity?—and, on the other, an esoteric vision of culture, one that resists thought and cannot be thought.

The Problems of Modern Rationality

As a point of departure, I will begin with the report of the Economic Commission for Latin America (CEPAL), "Crisis and Development: The Present and Future of Latin America and the Caribbean" (1985). In this document, the cultural dimension of our problems, of crisis as well as of development, and of our time, present and future, is barely touched on. The most profound and vital issues of culture are not mentioned; nor are the more directly sociological, economic, and political issues that make up the organization of culture.

Instead, the report adopts the traditional behaviorist idea that culture needs to adapt itself to modernity and to produce the motivations and attitudes required for the optimum performance of modern systems of production, reproduction, and social rule. All this, moreover, in the context of a relatively ingenuous concept of modernity and modernization that precisely ignores the contemporary debate over these topics. Thus, the report declares: "The process of modernization is a contemporary mode of social change, of general validity, that is extended to the entire planet. It supposes a self-sustained economic growth, the total availability of social resources, the diffusion of the rational and secular norms of culture, the freedom and growth of social mobility, and the corresponding attitudinal transformations" (1985, 5).

Later, the report adds, in a similarly behaviorist vein:

> In order to have modernization it is necessary that there come into play mechanisms of empathy that incorporate values, models of behavior, and aspirations originating from the most dynamic centers of civilization and that can shape demands. Nevertheless, institutions cannot be moved, they must be transformed; life-styles cannot be changed by the free functioning of the "demonstration effect"; they must be creatively adapted so that they do not cause disturbances. The capacity of adaptation is perhaps the distinctive feature of modern societies. If modernization, because of its empathetic essence, responds to exogenous influences, our societies need to internalize it with regard to their specific histories, indigenous resources, and possibilities, through the development and free exercise of creativity. It is clear, on the other hand, that adaptive and self-sustained technological development constitutes a central component of modernization, even though the latter goes beyond it as a total social process. (1985, 6)

The CEPAL formulation is typically eclectic and limits itself to glossing over the problems of cultural adaptation that it poses. Nevertheless, it allows us to make out the questions it avoids: for example, the conflict between *formal rationality* (based on the calculability provided by the market) and *substantive rationality* (directed by values and goals). Thus, the report sustains that modernization supposes the "internalization of rational norms" but immediately adds that in order for such an internalized rationality to constitute an "integrating and stabilizing force," not destructive of those minimal prescriptive nuclei required by integration, it should "incorporate the criteria which permit it to elaborate the conflicts between growth and equity, present affluence and accumulation, social demands and the limits of expansion of supply, present and future comparative advantages." Where do these criteria come from and how are they made compatible with other criteria (of formal rationality) that are imposed by the functioning of the market? The rationality that the CEPAL document speaks about is not the same as the one, according to Max Weber, that is at the foundation of the processes of modernization, but rather is one that "makes implicit a comprehensive concept of efficiency in the administration of resources and opportunities," according to the CEPAL report.

Creativity, not as a function of the market or as the incessant revolutionizing of the means of production and all social relations that Karl Marx attributed to the bourgeoisie, but as an individually or socially acquired attribute, becomes the centerpiece of this model. The CEPAL report goes so far as to speak of creative modernization as "the stylization of a political process of the search for social efficiency," especially necessary in the conditions of crisis and profound transformations that affect the region. It is important, therefore, to ask about the sociological conditions of this creativity.

In modernity, one of the principles of creativity, the liberation of energies that transformed culture, was, as Jürgen Habermas demonstrates (1983), the separation of the spheres of science, morality, and art from the field of religious and metaphysical justifications and their conversion to esoteric domains of experts, a process that resulted in the penetration of these spheres by economic and administrative rationality, a rationality completely distinct from that which rules the transmission and reproduction of values and norms. Does the path of modernization in Latin America pass through these same forms of the rationalization of culture that have already proven to be efficient in the liberation of creativity? If it does, how can such a strategy be made compatible with the declared objective of maintaining the sought-after rationalism within a frame of values and goals that point to integration, "social efficiency," justice, and solidarity? And what does it mean, in the Latin American context, to "adapt" models of behavior and aspirations capable of shaping demands from the most advanced capitalist centers, and, at the same time, to do this "creatively," according to our "specific histories, indigenous resources, and possibilities"? If demand is not culturally autonomous—how could it be in a universe of an international market of messages and goods—can the supply of creativity and products be managed locally, and, furthermore, can it be anchored in the traditions and beliefs of the internal culture?

At heart, the CEPAL document assumes a noncontradictory conception of modernity in its supposition of an uncomplicated and "creative" access to what it calls the "rational and secular norms of culture." Of what culture? We know that neoconservatives stigmatize "irrationalist" tendencies in Western culture, inasmuch as these can no longer provide the values and motivations required by the economy; and that progressives, in the fashion of Habermas, denounce the contradictions between a technical-instrumental rationality, which permeates all of social life, and a communicative rationality, which is seen as interrupted by the first in a way that provokes a replacement of meanings by consumer goods. To whom do we appeal, then, to obtain the cultural rationalism that is made to appear as a presupposition of the advance of modernization? Or, is this proposal, in its cultural implications, nothing more than an ideological "bargain," another of the many that Latin American intellectuals and technocrats have produced in recent years in their eagerness to appropriate a modernity that does not adapt itself to their models and forecasts?

The question at hand involves, perhaps, a double misunderstanding. First, about the nature of rationality itself. What, exactly, does the CEPAL report mean when it stipulates a rational and secular culture as the foundation of the processes of modernization? The rationality of the market, for example, is very different from the rationality of politics, and both differ, in turn, from technobureaucratic rationality. In each case it is a matter of personified rationalities, institutionally mediated, tied to interests that habitually interact in a conflictive manner. In culture, these rationalities imprint cognitive styles, define values, introduce habits, and stimulate varied personality structures. Therefore, there are no "rational norms" that can be so outside of their context: the laboratory, the competitive market, the noncompetitive market, the state, the parties, et cetera. A complex culture accepts, out of necessity, these various types and forms of rationality that, according to one's adopted point of view, can also be stigmatized as irrational.

The second misunderstanding has to do with the acquisition of these rationalities. The CEPAL document emphasizes an adaptation and internalization of norms that would come initially "from outside" but, once appropriated, would form rationally oriented values, motivations, and behaviors. How will this process of transference and acquisition of rationality happen? It is easiest to imagine the process as taking place through modes of collective learning based on life experiences that condition this learning: the market, education, the multiple bureaucratic or quasi-bureaucratic structures of civil society, corporations, and unions, et cetera. But it is precisely these situations of learning, of existing, that will socialize individuals and groups in contextually conditioned and, therefore, by necessity, diversely situated "rationalisms."

In other words, there does not seem to be anything like a *homogeneously* rationalized culture.

Cultural Heterogeneity

As we understand it, Octavio Paz's critique of modernity points precisely to this *voluntarism of the ideologies* of modernism and modernization in Latin America (1974, 148–64). And Paz is not the only one who has made this point; its antecedents can be traced far back in the history of Latin American thought. What, then, is expressed by the relative malaise with modernity that recurs in the region with almost the same frequency and force with which new modernizing projects are launched? We can answer this in the following way: What produces the malaise is the periodic conflict of those forms of modernization whose supposition is invariably the adoption and extension of rational models of conduct with what, for lack of a better term, we may call the *cultural heterogeneity* of Latin America.

This is not the same thing as supposing that our societies are formed by a superimposition of historical, cultural entities in the manner of geological layers that slide on top of each other, every once in a while producing breaks and great telluric upheavals. It may be that some compelling images in Latin American literature still function within this logic, habitually departing from the even more basic opposition between nature and culture. In this sense, the whole cycle of Pablo Neruda's poetry represents better than any analysis the drama of a culture that seeks to entreat nature on its own behalf, making it participate in the loves and sorrows of individuals and peoples at the same time that it reflects as culture a superimposition of histories that have not arrived at a complete synthesis.

The notion of cultural heterogeneity refers us instead to a kind of regional postmodernism *avant la lettre* that, nevertheless, is fully constitutive of our modernity. Carlos Monsiváis, in a prose collage, has insightfully captured this:

> Cable television. Superhero comics. Quick and poorly translated humor. An infinity of products which satiate, invent, and modify necessities. Television programs whose weekly apotheosis is nourished by the victories of the North American system of justice. Books (bestsellers) where the mechanics of success program the imagination and writing. Extremely refined technologies. Videocassettes. Satellite communication. The ideology of MacLuhan's global village. Video-

discs. Strategies of consumption whose implacable logistics destroy all artisanal perspective. The "philosophy" of the biggest seller in the world. Movies which have globally imposed the rhythm, themes, and point of view of North American industry. Software and hardware. International news agencies. Contempt for the history of each nation. Homogenization of "desirable" life-styles. The imposition of a global language. A circuit of ideological transmission which goes from publicity to pedagogy. Control of the "computer revolution." Magazines which distribute "femininity." The periodic reordering of the life-styles adjustable to technological changes. (1983, 75)

The cultural heterogeneity reflected in this collage, in the "postmodernist" grafts and allegories of our modernity, is, like this modernity itself, a product of the international market. To paraphrase Raymond Williams, our identities no longer appear as such but rather as sectors of the international market, especially in the area of culture. There subsist infinite local cultural exchanges that form the framework of our daily life, that mass of more or less direct interactions in which customs, use values, images, and beliefs accumulate. But through and above this framework—can we still call it national?—flow and are articulated messages and institutions and circuits fully incorporated into a modernity whose heart is far from the heart of "our" culture.

Cultural heterogeneity, therefore, refers to a double phenomenon: (1) of segmentation and segmented participation in this global market of messages and symbols whose underlying grammar is North American hegemony over the imaginary of a great part of humanity (I will return to this point); (2) of differential participation according to *local codes of reception*, group and individual, in the incessant movement of the circuits of transmission that extend from advertising to pedagogy. What results from this double and explosive, segmented and differential participation is something similar to what is proclaimed by certain representatives of postmodernism: a de-centering, a deconstruction, of Western culture as it is represented by the manuals; of its rationalism, its secularism, its key institutions; of the cognitive habits and styles it supposedly imposes in a uniform way—something that resembles Monsiváis's collage; something that "generates meaning," but a meaning out of place, taken out of context, a graft onto another culture.

Cultural heterogeneity thus means something very different than diverse cultures (subcultures) of ethnicities, classes, groups, or regions, or than the mere superimposition of cultures, whether or not these cultures have found a way of synthesizing themselves. It means, specifically, a segmented and differential participation in an international market of messages that "penetrates" the local framework of culture on all sides and in unexpected ways, leading to an implosion of the consumed/produced/reproduced meanings and subsequent deficiencies of identity, yearnings for identification, confusion of temporal horizons, paralysis of the creative imagination, loss of utopias, atomization of local memory, and obsolescence of traditions. Thus, Monsiváis concludes, "Its values substituted . . . by others which basically modernize appearances and take advantage (for the market) of the innovations of the age, a collectivity can no longer manage to confront its experiences or verify its legitimate goals" (1983, 76).

A Multiplicity of Logics

What precise, specific meaning can the invocation of rationalism in culture and society have, then, in this "postmodernism" that characterizes Latin American modernity? Modernity cannot be read, in the fashion of Marshall Berman, as a singular collective experience of the modern, nor as variations of that same experience that in the long run tend to converge. If we were to proceed that way, we would have done no more than to transpose the conception of modernization through stages to the conception of our modernity.

What seems more reasonable is to imagine modernity as a trunk from which numerous branches and sub-branches extend in the most varied directions. In the case of Latin America, as we noted, the motor of modernity, the international market, provokes and then reinforces an incessant movement of heterogenization of culture, employing, stimulating, and reproducing a plurality of logics that act simultaneously, becoming interwoven. Logics that, from a Eurocentric and Enlightenment point of view, we could properly call modern, such as those of secularization, formal rationality, bureaucratization, individualization, futurism, alienation, et cetera. Logics of the collective imaginary, at the same time shaped by a local historical memory (which is itself sometimes varied and contradictory) and by the seductions of the mass media, as occurs with the telenovela. Logics of identification based on economic, social, and cultural positions; social logics of differentiation in a world where consumption distributes, at the same time, signs of status; sacrificial logics of giving, expenditure, and fiestas, which, by themselves, do not manage to resist the commercializing force of the market; political logics of articulation and mobilization, which are not immune to the internationalization of militancies; renewable modern logics of terror and fear in a universe of the disappeared, torture, state and private terrorism, and of the marks left on society by repression.

For this reason, proposals for modernization, whether traditional or new, that do not assume as a central fact of their "efficient" operation this cultural heterogeneity in which they are called upon to materialize themselves condemn themselves to remain on the terrain of ideological voluntarism.

Endogenous Creativity

We consider it a sign of the times that global proposals, in the manner of great laboratory tests that claim to design, on the basis of totalizing rationality, the modernization of this or that society, are not in favor, at the moment, in Latin America. On the other hand, more modest proposals for the local or partial rationalization of society are being introduced into the debate, such as CEPAL's strategy for the formation of "endogenous nuclei of technological dynamization." The CEPAL report notes apropos the future of Latin America:

> One starts from the premise that creativity is a complex process in which a wide range of agents and motivations participate: large industrial plants tied to small and medium ones, institutes of technology, institutes of basic science, the organisms which prepare qualified personnel at the different levels, the mass media, and the central state ministries and organisms which define policies and norms. . . . The interaction between these agents and their motivations is decisive for the process of creativity. (1985, 72)

This is a strategy of local rationalization that contains elements of the state and the market, of endogenous creativity, and of the appropriation of external dynamics; that supposes complex interactions between the economy, politics, the administration, and culture; that valorizes, by overlapping them, both instrumental efficiency and communicative rationality. More than the design of a modern society, or even of its economy, it is the outline of a system of relations wherein creativity encounters sociological conditions of operation.

It remains to be seen, however, whether the institutions of culture, the means of communication, institutes of training and centers of formation, research laboratories, universities, and so on, are in a condition to be incorporated into an enterprise of this sort (with an "inward" orientation, so to speak), when for a long time they have danced to the rhythm of the requirements of their differential integration into international markets. For example, universities in Latin America have been, more than anything else, enterprises of intellectual criticism, of professional certification and social mobility, leaving their participation in *enterprises of accumulation* to the mediation of complex international circuits. Their function has consisted of growing, in a sense, *against* the market, preserving at the same time, where possible, their independence from the state, under the supposition that only as such could they aspire to be the "conscience of the nation." Their politicization, not at all surprising under these circumstances, reflects a typically antimodern feature of Latin American modernity: a low level of autonomy, in general, of culture and of its institutional sphere, and, in particular, of the sciences, which runs parallel to a high degree of autonomy of politics and ideological creation.

The "new" proposals of development, which attempt to escape the globalism of certain previous designs and which insist on local rationalizations of "nuclei" that combine institutional segments of the economy, the administration, and culture, seem to better understand the fragmentary conditions of regional modernity; but at the same time, they can find themselves involved in the heterogeneity of culture and in the sometimes perverse effects that this provokes in the development of local cultural institutions.

The Social Uses of Religion

In a very different register, we know that some authors have posited a supposed tension between modernization and the "Catholic substratum" of Latin American culture. In reality, the problem proves to be more complex.

In the midst of the cultural heterogeneity that is the salient feature of our regional modernity, this religious "substratum" fulfills a variety of functions, only one of which corresponds to the supposed delegitimization of a modern work ethic. Moreover, it has already been shown that in very few parts of the developed world does the (puritan) work ethic play a key role any longer in individual motivation and performance. Everywhere, even in socialist regimes, there is an *uncoupling* of ethics and performance, and the market itself increasingly conditions directly economic behavior and performance.

On the other hand, the "Catholic substratum" continues to operate, in many parts of Latin America, as a symbolic foundation for popular religious practices and, what is more interesting, renews the exhausted deposit of symbols and desires capable of mobilizing radical (revolutionary) behaviors on the social and political plane. In many societies of the continent, a prophetic, testimonial, and revolutionary current is nourished by religion, around which are continually renewed ties of solidarity, seeds of communal life, and the principle of rebellion against the established order. The struggle in Nicaragua between the Catholic hierarchy and the "popular church" over the control of this deposit of revolutionary/counter-revolutionary legitimizations, for example, precisely emphasizes the discussion of the "uses" of this "Catholic substratum," whose importance is increasingly political, ideological, and cultural more than economic or (work) ethical.

The proposal of Puebla to evangelize Latin American culture partially recognizes this situation, but it supposes, at the same time, that the cultural heterogeneity of the region can be overcome through the elaboration of a new synthesis, wherein the dimensions of the modern could recuperate a sense of the sacred and the transcendental via a recoupling with a Christian ethic capable of interrupting the process of functionalization and "degradation" of secularized values. The proposal of Puebla imagines the "gestation of a new civilization" that, beyond modernity, "integrates the values which it has contributed but in the frame of (this) new civilization" (CELAM 1978).

Seen from the perspective of the question of modernity and modernization on the continent by the year 2000, what progress, new opening, or "solution" does this attempt to "rebaptize" Latin American culture in Catholic religious terms offer? Neoconservative proposals, following Daniel Bell's argument in *The Cultural Contradictions of Capitalism*, situate the religious question in the center of developed societies in terms of a diagnosis of the contradictions that have arisen between economy and culture in late capitalism, whereas Latin American neo-Catholic proposals, such as Morandé's (1984), still seem to reflect the classic struggle between traditionalism and modernism, secularism and religion, positivism and Catholicism. Is there not entailed here, perhaps, under the educated guise of civil tolerance, a total rejection of modernity, of its inherent dynamics and values? Is there not the risk of a new "totalizing" proposal that, precisely by ignoring the radical fact of Latin American cultural heterogeneity, seeks to base itself on religion in order to establish a cultural continuity torn to pieces long ago? And what can this proposal imply in the area of development, the economy, the new political system, the emancipation of private life, the generation of a mass culture based on the cultural industry, and the currently accepted principles of social integration and control?

Nevertheless, as we have had the opportunity to see, the question of modern secularism is not an issue that only concerns the church or a few Catholic intellectuals. It is internationally related to various currents of neoconservatism and, in Latin America, to the not at all marginal concerns of sociologists such as Gino Germani. Even among figures originating from Marxism, such as Leszek Kolakowsky, the modern "disenchantment" of the world and the subsequent "demolition" of taboos constitute the neurological point of any critical philosophy of modernity.

We find ourselves confronted here with a reactive sensibility to modernity that is widely disseminated and that, in different forms, gives rise to a critique of cultural modernism involving a range of issues, from the loss of values, the renunciation of ethics in social relations, and the erosion of national identities to the destruction of artistic canons.

As Habermas has pointed out, however, this critique is surely misguided, since it is not possible to impute to culture, and to the professionalized agents of culture, intellectuals, the effects of a secularism that has resulted from the more or less successful development of capitalism in the economy and society. The problem, in reality, is better formulated by Germani when he wonders whether, on the basis of the new conditions created in the economy and society, once their repercussions in the cultural sphere are known (i.e., secularism), it is still possible to guarantee the minimum of consensus and integration required by the functioning of democratic governments. The alternative, according to Germani, are the modern authoritarianisms, namely, regimes that impose through force a total resocialization of the population, integrating each individual into a militarized culture.

Clearly, the underlying hypothesis is that societies cannot function, indeed run the risk of disappearing altogether, without this minimum of consensus, "an agreement over foundations," as Laski put it in a phrase Germani likes to quote. Thus: "It is not surprising that the philosophy of history usually locates the beginning of the decadence of the great civilizations precisely in the phases of acute secularization, even if the latter is limited to the elite. Toynbee, Spengler, Sorokin, and others give clear examples of this theoretical orientation" (Germani et al. 1985, 31).

It is not our interest to explore the philosophical-historical implications of this thesis but rather to take up its sociological nucleus in the light of what we have said. In this sense, Germani's thesis is clear: Modernity generates serious problems of normative integration that weaken or make impossible democratic governments, leading to catastrophic solutions in the guise of authoritarian regimes of total resocialization. Modernization reduces the validity of certain traditional forms of social integration and, by pushing toward an ever-increasing secularization of culture, reduces the bases of the traditional "prescriptive nucleus," weakening the old forms of legitimization based on religious beliefs. This does not mean, however, that modernization does not generate its own forms of integration, over a full range of positions from "moral" to "organic" solidarity.

The question, especially in Latin America, is whether the cultural heterogeneity constitutive of its own specific modernity, in which a motley collection of traditional and new forms of normative prescription are mixed, still makes possible the functioning of social systems in an increasingly secularized world. This question refers us in turn, at a higher level of abstraction, to the question of the necessary degree of consensus and normative integration social systems need in order to function. If one were to go by the specialist literature on this issue, it would appear no system of society should be able to function in Latin America, so scarce are the principles of integration and agreement over foundations in the region. One could argue that precisely because of this, these societies resort with relative frequency to authoritarian regimes in order to secure their government, although not their integration.

On the other hand, it would seem possible, indeed almost obligatory, to argue that, in spite of everything, the kind of societies we have characterized by a high degree of cultural heterogeneity actually do maintain and reproduce a sufficient degree of integration, but on the basis of local and partial forms of consensus that involve only limited and differentiated areas of society. Authoritarianism would, in this perspective, be a form of "governing," of controlling this plurality of forms of consensus whenever they tend to align themselves in a catastrophic manner, polarizing society.

Such a perspective might allow us to consider our societies as societies without the need for a basic consensus, without an agreement over foundations, with scarce possibility (and necessity) of conceiving themselves as "totalities"; as societies that, more than consensus, need to organize conflict and give rise to agreements of interests; as societies that, more than recuperating a political system legitimized by a nucleus of values, need to construct and live with a necessarily unstable one, which reflects agreements over the rules of government capable of inspiring mutual respect and of avoiding the war of each against all.

Political Disenchantment

The other aspect of Germani's thesis, according to which a constant erosion of the minimum prescriptive nucleus required for social integration makes democracies vulnerable, also needs to be discussed in relation to the political future of Latin America. As Norbert Lechner has recently stated (1995), the threat of the dissolution and atomization of the social order brought on by modernization (secularism and marginalization) caused and exacerbated an "ideological inflation" in the Latin America of the sixties, favoring revolution as the means of national liberation, social integration, and economic development, as opposed to what was seen as capitalist "development of underdevelopment." The revolutionary proposal implied, as Lechner demonstrates, a messianic and fundamentalist style of doing politics, which carried within itself a germ of antisecularism in culture. By contrast, in the present climate of democratic recovery, the opposite tendency finds itself reinforced, namely, the reappraisal of secularism in culture. In opposition to what Germani sustains, Lechner suggests that secularism can be beneficial for democratic recovery in the region, relieving politics of ethical-religious compromises, disseminating values of civil tolerance, and producing a certain spirit of negotiation, a "cooling-off" of values, motivations, and affects. A new kind of realism, one that values, in Lechner's words, "the institutions and procedures, or in other words ... the forms of doing politics over its material contents," would point in this same direction.

What is suggested here is the possibility of a profane, "disenchanted" notion of politics that restricts it to specific areas, taking away its omnipotence and freeing it from its anchorage in absolute principles in order to make it more flexible and adjustable to immediate challenges. Such a concept resonates with certain tendencies, themes, and attitudes of postmodernism, as Lechner makes clear: In both, there is a criticism of the idea of complete subjects, an abandonment of the "master narratives," a conversion of time into a continuous present, a reduction of politics to an exchange of material and symbolic goods. The risk involved for Lechner, however, is that this postmodern movement of contemporary politics in Latin America may abandon the notion that society can construct itself in a deliberate manner and that the reduction of politics to a "political market" may exclude interests and goods that cannot be exchanged in the market: human rights, roots, the sense of belonging, the desire for certainty, the need for transcendental referents. Secularism then presents itself ambiguously: It reinforces tendencies that seem necessary, or at least inevitable, in the present phase of the recuperation and consolidation of democracies; but, at the same time, it generates a *deficit* of meaning, motivations, and collective construction of the social order that would impede the elaboration of a democratic culture.

These postmodern features of political culture in Latin America should be included, as I noted before, less in the context of a critique of modernity than as a consequence of the regional form of our modernity, which has tended precisely in the direction of a secularization of the area of power. The "disenchantment" *of* and *with* power in Latin America necessarily passes through a dis-dramatization of power: a reduction of its symbolic-expressive aspects and an increase in the instrumental capacities of its gestation; a loss of ideological aura in favor of the practical interests of actors, which are lost and found in the political market; in short, a greater autonomy of politics because of its differentiation and specialization. This means, of course, that politics no longer aspires to construct social identities, reserving for itself the colder terrain of changing political loyalties; that it loses its character as a "movement" in order to be reduced to "parties" that are "organization and program" but not an existential community nor an ideological-transcendental vanguard of society; that it no longer provides references of certainty nor commitments to principles, limiting itself to processing the uncertainties within a game of stipulated rules; that it retreats from the commanding heights of revolution or restoration in order to assume, in a disenchanted world and in a reality without too many illusions, the sphere of the administration of scarce means, of the negotiation between forces in conflict, of the persuasion of a public of citizens who do or do not vote.

The National as a Revolutionary Force

There is, logically and historically, an alternative to Germani's thesis about the catastrophic and authoritarian outcomes of the states of disintegration caused by the process of secularization: that of a "national-popular" revolutionary articulation tied to divergent projects of socialization and integration capable of being politically and institutionally expressed. In situations of extensive cultural heterogeneity, the very notion of *national collectivity* finds itself questioned and permanently put into tension, since there exists a latent conflict between diverse proposals of national integration. Each of these proposals resorts, for its legitimization, to a different interpretation of the national past; each mobilizes a distinct constellation of national symbols; each imagines the international insertion of the country in a different way; and each is based, in the last instance, on insufficiently secularized principles of the construction of the nation. These proposals can be mobilized indiscriminately by political parties, the armed forces, intellectual elites, leadership groups in civil society, armed revolutionary groups, charismatic leaders, and churches or sects. In each case, it is a matter of barely secularized, exclusive, and totalizing proposals. Each contains, for that very reason, a project for the socialization and resocialization of the population, under the hegemonic control of a class, group, leader, or belief.

Faced with the reality of a "disintegrated" nation, devoid of a basic or minimal consensus, permeated by the contradictions, tensions, and conflicts caused by its heterogeneity, this kind of nonsecular, quasi-religious proposal, which appeals to total commitment and mobilizes around transcendental values and goals, or around a leader who embodies these, can prove to be very powerful. These proposals habitually offer the project of a national modernization tied to a nucleus of values (the nation, the class, past splendor, liberation) that offers the minimum prescriptive nucleus around which to organize the processes of resocialization and the ceremonies and rites of integration.

As in the case we looked at earlier of the neo-Catholic proposal for Latin America's future, these are antisecular projects in the field of culture that take advantage of the diffuse, but at times extensive, criticism of modernity, of its overrationalism, its ethical pluralism, its individualism, its alienation and cultural imperialism, et cetera. Perhaps for this reason, revolutions in Latin America routinely happen in a national context: They are national-popular—national-liberation, national-security, or national-development—movements. Symbols of the national cover a wide range of political and strategic options, but in the end, they all seek the same thing: to overcome the cultural heterogeneity constitutive of society and its "internationalist" dynamic; to curb the effects of secularism; to cancel the forms, formalities, and "games" of democracy; and to reestablish a governing principle of integration through which the majority can be resocialized.

A Peripheral Modernity

One of the threads that runs through the debates about modernity and postmodernity in Latin America (but not only there, as we will see), is that of the changing poles of the modernization of the world, and of the differentiated modes of participation in modernity. Fernand Braudel studied this matter, starting from the dynamics of capitalism in the production of the modern world-system, what he called the development of a "world-economy." He found that since the fourteenth century, a continuous "partition of the world" into concentric zones, "increasingly dis-favored inasmuch as one moves away from their triumphant center," can be observed. The "long durations" are precisely processes of the center-ing, de-centering, and re-centering of the world-economy:

> The splendor, the wealth, and happiness of life are united in the cen-ter of the world-economy, in its very nucleus. That is where the sun of history gives brilliance to the most vivid colors; that is where are manifested high prices, high salaries, banking, "royal" manufac-tures, profitable industries, and capitalist agriculture; that is where the point of departure and arrival of the extensive foreign trade is situ-ated, along with a superabundance of precious metals, of solid coins, and of titles of credit. All advanced economic modernity is concen-trated in this nucleus: the traveler realizes this when he contemplates Venice in the fifteenth century, or Amsterdam in the seventeenth, or London in the eighteenth, or New York in the present. (1985, 102–3)

Farther out, in the circle of intermediate countries, which are "neigh-bors, competitors, or emulators of the center," this modernity, this level of life, decreases, and the dynamics are no longer the same as those of the center. Finally, in the marginal and dependent zones, geographically far removed from the center, "the life of men evokes purgatory, when not hell." Their subordinated integration into the division of labor and their segmented participation in the international market drags them in the wake of a modernity that only benefits them contradictorily, that pene-trates them from all sides, causing unexpected, and sometimes perverse, effects, creating and multiplying the heterogeneity that ends up being their characteristic condition of life and the barely perceptible sign of their identity. Recall Monsiváis's collage.

In the world-economy of contemporary capitalism, "North American-ization" appears as a feature inseparable from modernity. From there come the impulses of modernism; there will end up the modernists and modernisms that happen to originate in the periphery. To oppose this re-ality with a nationalism tied to traditions and values from the past, to a notion of national identity prior to any cultural contamination is, to say it in Monsiváis's own words, to declare that the resistance to cultural penetration finds itself defeated in advance" (1983, 76).

The question is, however, whether it is still meaningful to speak of cul-tural penetration in any case, since there is no doubt that in the present configuration of the capitalist world-economy, the center retains, in addition to the control over economic and military dynamics, a conclu-sive cultural hegemony. The "intermediate" countries, according to

Braudel's nomenclature, see it this way. Jean Baudrillard, referring to the relation of Europe to America, has said: "It is not only a question of a disjuncture, it is an abyss of modernity which separates us." Or again: "The United States is a realized utopia" (1985).

We have been accustomed to think the cultural problem in Latin America within the parameters of dependency theory. Cultural penetration? Dependent culture? What we observe, rather, is that modernity, as a differentiated experience in the capitalist world, has a center, which radiates a zone of marginal and dependent peripheries where this same modernity creates and re-creates a cultural heterogeneity, which, in turn, in all of its fragments, breaks, folds, collages, and displacements continues to be tied to the hegemonic center. The very identity of these peripheral zones is partially constructed with the image of this other, in the same way that its culture is elaborated with fragments of this other culture. In all fields of culture—science, technology, art, utopias—the important modern cultural syntheses are first produced in the North and descend later to us, via a process in which they are "received" and appropriated according to local codes of reception. This is how it has happened with sociology, pop art, rock music, film, data processing, models of the university, neoliberalism, the most recent medicines, armaments, and, in the long run, with our very incorporation into modernity.

Conclusions

It should be clear that these notes have no way of concluding. It is rather a question of initiating a reflection whose larger coordinates are the ongoing debate about modernity, modernism, and modernization. At a time when a confusing fog of "posts"—postmodernism, postpolitics, posthistory, postvanguard—hovers over modernity, it becomes necessary to recover the specific character of modernization in Latin America. Here, among ourselves, the malaise in culture does not, could not, spring from the exhaustion of modernity. On the contrary, it arises from an exasperation with modernity, with its infinitely ambiguous effects, with its inevitable intentionalism, with its distortions, and with the problems that it bequeaths for the future of the region, some of which I have briefly discussed.

Condemned to live in a world where all the images of modernity and modernism come to us from the outside and become obsolete before we are able to materialize them, we find ourselves trapped in a world where not all solid things but rather all symbols melt into air. Latin America: the project of echoes and fragments, of past utopias whose present we can only perceive as a continuous crisis. This sensation of the permanent crisis of everything, of the economy, institutions, political regimes, universities, art, public services, private enterprise, the armed forces, poorly and barely hides the fact that we live and think in the middle of a modernity in the process of construction, whose dynamic is increasing the heterogeneities of our very perceptions, knowledges, and information.

What happens to us is exactly the opposite of what happens in that postmodernity in which, according to Baudrillard, "things have found a way of avoiding a dialectics of meaning that was beginning to bore them: by proliferating indefinitely, increasing their potential, outbidding themselves in an ascension to the limit, an obscenity that henceforth becomes their immanent finality and senseless reason" (1982, 7). For us, it would at times seem that it is the meaning, words, and experiences that have found a way to escape a dialectic of things that bored them: infinitely proliferating, self-empowering, self-essentializing in a game of extremes and mirrors, carried along by a senseless reason . . .

But neither is it useful to exaggerate. Here, between words and things, ideology and society, symbols and instruments, there still tend to be fragile connections that permit a "coming and going" behind this dream of modernity that, only half accepted, has nevertheless already permeated the society and culture of this part of America.

The future of Latin America will not be, for this reason, very different from its present: one of a peripheral modernity, de-centered, subject to conflicts, whose destiny will depend, to some degree, on what these societies manage to do with this modernity in the process of producing it through their own complex and changing heterogeneity.

JESÚS MARTÍN-BARBERO
A Nocturnal Map to Explore a New Field

We know that struggles through cultural mediations do not
yield immediate or spectacular results. But, it is the only way to
ensure we do not go from the sham of hegemony to the sham of
democracy; to block the reappearance of a defeated domination
installed by hegemony in the complicity of our thoughts
and relationships.—*Néstor García Canclini*

Jesús Martín-Barbero was born in Spain in 1937. A philosopher and media scholar, he
is a professor emeritus of the Universidad de los Andes (Bogotá, Colombia). His
main titles include *De los medios a las mediaciones* (1987), *Pre-textos. Conversaciones sobre
la comunicación y sus contextos* (1995), and *Al sur de la modernidad. Comunicación, globalización y multiculturalidad* (2001).

Once the frontiers of our discipline were moved and we had lost
the security set up by our theoretical inertia, we have had no alternative but to follow the advice of Raymond Williams and remake the map of our "basic concepts." I do not think that this is possible, however, without changing the point from which we begin to ask
questions. This is the meaning of the recent tendency to formulate questions which transcend the "daytime" logic[1] and demand a reorganization of the analytic terrain that moves the marginal issues to the center of
our concerns. This does not imply a "carnivalization" of theory,[2] but the
acceptance that these are not times for synthesis and that reason is barely
able to understand the unexplored areas of reality that are so very near.
As Ernesto Laclau observes, "Today we realize that social history is
deeper than our instruments allow us to conceive and beyond what our
political strategies can direct" (1981, 59). Not lacking, of course, are the

tendencies toward an apocalyptic view of events and a return to the catechism. A silent but even more important tendency is moving in another direction: exploring in tentative almost groping fashion without a guiding map or with only an obscure, night-time map. This is a map which enables us to study domination, production, and labor from the other side of the picture, the side of the cracks in domination, the consumption dimensions of economy, and the pleasures of life. It is not a map for escape but, rather, to help us recognize our situation from the perspective of mediations and the subjects of action.

Daily Life, Consumption, and an Interpretative Reading

"A market perspective permeates not only society but also the explanations of society" (Durham 1980, 203). This explains why critical theories have privileged the image of the laborer-producer of merchandise not only at the moment of understanding the context of production but at the moment of trying to awaken a consciousness of the exploitation in this situation. This tendency of critical theories is not unlike the tendency of most organizations of the left truly concerned with the life of the popular classes: a preoccupation with actions of vindication of rights and movements which unite people for struggle. Everything else—the practices which make up the rhythm of daily life, the ways the popular classes exist and find meaning in life—has tended to be considered an obstacle to conscientization and mobilization for political action.

> Popular conceptions of family are considered conservative; popular traditions are looked upon as fragmentary remains of a rural and precapitalist cultural past; the tastes of the popular classes are molded by the corrupting influence of the mass media; their leisure pastimes are nothing more than escapism; their religiosity, a factor of alienation; and their life plans, no more than frustrated attempts at upward social mobility. (Cantor Magnani 1984, 19)

Forms of daily existence not directly linked with structures of economic production are looked upon as depoliticized, irrelevant, and insignificant. Nevertheless, the accounts which begin to describe what happens within the life of popular neighborhoods, accounts which do not attempt to evaluate but simply to understand the functioning of popular social relations, open up to us another reality. Here—as "scandalous" as it may seem—the attachment of the working classes to family does not appear to be necessarily or, at least, only linked to conservation of the past. Rather, as E. Durham lucidly explained, "this is an attempt to overcome a generalized state of family disorganization associated with a much more brutal and direct exploitation of the forms of labor" (1980, 202).

In the popular perception, the space of domestic activities is not limited to the tasks of the reproduction of the labor force. On the contrary, confronted with the monotonous and uncreative workplace, the family allows a minimum of freedom and initiative. In the same way, not all consumption is merely the acceptance of the values of other classes. In the popular sectors consumption expresses just aspirations to a more human and respectful life. Not all search for social betterment is a crass social climbing. It is also a form of protest and an expression of elemental rights. For this reason, it is important to develop a concept of consumption that moves beyond culturalist and reproductionist interpretations and offers a framework for research on communication and culture from the popular perspective. Such a framework would permit a comprehension of the different modes of cultural appropriation and the different social uses of communication.

In his various publications in recent years, García Canclini has brought together elements for such a new theoretical perspective (1984a, 1985b, 1988a). These approaches are close to the concepts of Bourdieu, but broaden them to allow a consideration of praxis and the forms of cultural production and transformation within the popular classes of Latin America. We must begin by identifying what we are looking for and by carefully pointing out our differences from functionalist theories of media reception. "It is not just a matter of measuring the distance between the enunciation of messages and their effects, but rather of constructing an integral analysis of consumption, understood as the overall effect of the social processes of appropriation of products" (García Canclini and Roncagliolo 1988, 493). Nor are we referring here to the much deplored "compulsive consumption" or to the repertoire of attitudes and tastes collected and classified by commercial surveys. Even less do we want to move to the airy terrain of Baudrillard's simulation. Our reflection on consumption is located in daily practices in so far as these are an area of silent interiorization of social inequality (García Canclini 1984b, 74). This is the area of each person's relationship to his or her body, use of time, habitat, and awareness of the potentialities in his or her life. It is also an area of rejection of limits to what can be legitimately hoped for, an area for the expansion of desires, a realm where one can subvert the codes and express pleasures. Consumption is not just the reproduction of forces. It is a production of meanings and the site of a struggle that does not end with the possession of the object but extends to the uses, giving objects a social form in which are registered the demands and forms of action of different cultural competencies.

The proof of the new meaning of consumption is the political relevance of the "new conflicts" centering on struggles against the forms of power which penetrate daily life and struggles over the appropriation of goods and services. The articulations between these two types of struggles become quite clear in the histories of the popular-urban culture which we have gathered.

Another theoretical stream which must be integrated into our analysis is the new conception of interpretative *reading* developed in Latin America, especially in the work of Beatriz Sarlo (1983a, 1985a, 1985b). Sarlo, carrying forward the analysis of H. Robert Jauss, proposes a study of the "different possible social readings" understood as the "activity by which meanings are organized in a unifying sense" (1983b, 11). Thus, in an interpretative reading, as in consumption, there is not just reproduction but also production, a production which questions the centrality of the dominating text and the message understood as the source of truth which circulates in a process of communication. To bring the centrality of the text and messages into critical questioning implies that we assume as constitutive the asymmetry of demands and of competencies which meet and are *negotiated* in the text. The text is no longer the machine which unifies heterogeneity, no longer a finished product, but a comprehensive space crossed by different trajectories of meaning. This concept restores to reading the legitimacy of pleasure that applies not only to cultivated, erudite interpretative reading but to any and every reading—including popular readings with their pleasure of repetition and recognition (Sarlo 1985c, 36). This concept of reading brings together both resistance and pleasure. The stubborn popular tastes that appear in a narrative are both the raw material for advertising and an activator of cultural abilities, where commercial logics and popular demand at times conflict and at times negotiate. What follows is a nocturnal map to explore this concept in the crossroads formed in Latin America by television and melodrama.

Television Understood from the Perspective of Mediations

At a time when television is at the center of technological transformations which emerge from informatics, satellites, optical fiber, et cetera, our proposal could appear to some as a bit anachronistic. We continue in this line, however, because, although the media in Latin America are experiencing many changes, the "mediations"[3] through which the media operate socially and culturally are not undergoing significant modifications. Neither the thousands of video cassette recorders invading the market each year nor the parabolic antennas that are sprouting from roofs everywhere nor the new cable networks are substantially affecting the model of production of television that we know. For most television viewers, not only in Latin America but in other parts of the world, changes in the supply, in spite of the propaganda regarding decentralization and pluralization, appear to be in the direction of making social stratification even more sharply defined, for the differentiated video products offered to the public are linked to buying capacities of individuals.[4] Producers and programmers of video technologies are mainly interested in marketing new products while the social application of technologies falls by the wayside (Moragas 1985, 68). Paradoxically, the change that appears to affect television most deeply is along the lines of our interpretation: "It is necessary to abandon *mediacentricism*, for the system of the media is losing its specificity and becoming an integral part of the economic, cultural, and political system" (60).

In Latin America, however, the abdication of mediacentricism is less the result of an industrial reconversion of the media that puts the communication functions of the media in second place behind economic and industrial considerations and is more influenced by social movements making visible the mediations. Therefore, instead of starting our analysis from the logic of production and reception and studying their relationships with the logic of cultural imbrication and conflict, we propose to start with the mediations where the social materialization and the cultural expression of television are delimited and configured. As hypotheses to bring together and structure converging areas of theoretical interpretation, we propose to analyze three places of mediation, even though some do not take television as the prime "object": the daily life of the family, social temporality, and cultural competence.

The Daily Life of the Family

If Latin American television still considers the family the "basic audience unit," it is due to the fact that for the great majority family viewing is the prime context of recognition of sociocultural identity. It is not possible to understand the specific way television appeals to the family without analyzing the daily life of the family as the social context of a fundamental appeal to the popular sectors. As we have noted earlier, this appeal is a scandal to the intellectuals who criticize the repressive aspects of family organization and for the political left which sees in the family nothing more than bourgeois ideological contamination. So far, critical analysis has been unable to understand the social mediation that the family constitutes. The family is an arena of social conflicts and tensions, but it is also "one of the few places where individuals relate as persons and where they find some possibility of revealing their anxieties and frustrations" (Durham 1980, 209).

A new conception of the family as one of the key areas of reading and of cultural codification of television is beginning to leave behind the trite moralistic conception of the relation of television and family—television as the corruptor of family traditions—and the philosophy which attributes to television nothing more than an entertainment function (see Fuenzalida 1982 and 1984). The mediation the daily life of the family exerts on television is not, however, limited to reception. It is present in the discourse of television itself. Beginning with the family as the "space of close relations," and "proximity," television carries out two key actions: the simulation of contact and the rhetoric of direct communication.[5]

We would call "simulation of contact" all those mechanisms through which television specifies its mode of communication organized around the "phatic function" (Jakobson 1956), that is, the maintenance of contact. This function of concentrating attention around interpersonal relations is important because of the dispersion of attention in the intimate daily life of the private home in contrast to the personal isolation and concentration of attention in the public atmosphere of the darkened cinema. Our emphasis here is not on the psychological dimensions of the experience but on the perspective of cultural anthropology, namely, the irruption of the world of fiction and the world of show business entertainment into the routine of daily life.[6] Given the contrast between these two worlds, intermediaries emerge in the formats of television to facilitate the transition from daily reality to the fictional world of the entertainment spectacle. Thus, television provides two basic models of intermediary: the personality who is somewhat distant from the fictional world of popular entertainment—the master of ceremonies, anchorperson, or host—and the colloquial tone of speaking which provides the right atmosphere. The anchorperson is present in newscasts; the master of ceremonies is central in game shows, musicals, educational programming, and even in the presentation of cultural events to emphasize their ritual solemnity. The function of this personality is not just to transmit information but rather to act as the intermediary who appeals to the family and becomes the spokesperson for the family. For this reason the tone is colloquial and there is a permanent simulation of dialogue which comes so close to being like the continual conversation in the family context.

For many years the "predominance of the verbal" (in contrast to the visual) in Latin American television was criticized as a proof of its underdevelopment. It was simply radio with pictures added, they said. Today, as television in many Latin American countries is reaching a very high degree of technical and expressive development, this critique is no longer acceptable. We now begin to suspect that the predominance of the verbal is part of a need to overlay a visual logic with a logic of direct contact, something that television articulates on the basis of the immediate relationship and the predominance of the spoken word in a strongly oral culture.

The "rhetoric of direct address," referred to above, includes all those mechanisms that organize the space of television around the axis of proximity and the magic of seeing, in opposition to the space of film art dominated by distance and the magic of the "image." The central communicative function of film is—quite intentionally—the poetic experience, even in low-budget films. Films are the archetypical transfiguration of reality. In spite of involvement in the plot of the film and the fascination of close-ups of personalities, the film spectator is kept at a distance. The subject matter, the actions, and the faces in film are charged with a symbolic value. Speaking of the face of Greta Garbo, Barthes summarizes the magic and specific space of action of film. "Her face was a sort of transformation of flesh into an absolute ideal which could never again be attained or lost again" (1972). In contrast to the space of film, so alluring precisely because of its distancing, the space of television is dominated by the magic of the intimacy of seeing, with a proximity constructed by means of a montage which is not so symbolic or expressive but functional and sustained on the basis of a real or simulated "direct shot." In television the experience of seeing which predominates is that produced by the sensation of immediacy which is one of the characteristics of daily life. This is especially true of advertising which is, in many ways, the synthesis of the public show and daily life experience, in spite of the fact that advertising has that uneasy, aggressive presence which gives it the air of the invading transgressor. In television, gone are the mysterious and charming faces; the faces are close, friendly, with neither alluring nor awkward features. One gains a proximity to characters and events through a discourse that makes everything "familiar" and transforms even the most strange or distant objects into something very "close." Even the most deeply rooted prejudices become impossible to confront because they are so much a part of us. It is a discourse which produces this familiarity even in the way that images are organized: for example, in the easy transparency of television imagery, the simplicity, clarity, and economy of narrative elements.

In this immediacy and directness the stamp of hegemony is at work, precisely in the construction of an appeal that speaks to people out of the familiar conditions of daily life. This is not simply the subproduct of the poverty and artifices of ideology, but a space in which operate some of the most primordial human relations and life experiences, not made less central by the fact that they are so ambiguous.

Social Temporality

In our society productive time, time valued by capital, is the time that marches on and is measured. The other time, the time of daily life, is a repetitive time that begins, ends, and begins again. It is a time of fragments rather than measurable units (Pires do Río 1984, 114ff). Is not the cultural matrix organized by television this type of time, the time of fragments and repetition? Does not television bring daily life into the marketplace by means of rituals and routines? The time by which television organizes its programming has a profit-generating commercial form and a systematic scheduling mixing many genres. Each program, each televised text, traces its meaning back to the crossing of genres and times. A program, as genre, belongs to a family of texts which are replicated and continually come back to their place within the hours of the day and the week. In so far as a program is a moment of time "occupied," each text goes back to the hourly sequence of what has preceded it and what comes after it or to what appears in the schedule on other days of the week at the same time.

From the perspective of television, leisure-time both hides and reveals the temporal rhythm work-time, the time of both fragmentation and the series. Foucault observes that power is articulated directly across time (1977). In television the movement of unification that pervades social diversity is one of the most evident features. The "time of the series" speaks the language of the system of production, a language of standardization. Underneath this language, other languages can be heard, the languages of popular story telling, songs, tales of adventure, repetitions "that belong to an aesthetic sense where recognition is an important part of pleasure and where, in consequence, repetition is the norm of the value of symbolic goods" (Sarlo 1983b, 5). Repetition, according to Benjamin, is what makes technical reproduction possible. It is the "sensorium" or cultural experience of the new public born with the masses.

It is possible to talk of an "aesthetic of repetition" that works through the variations of what is identical or what is similar in that which is different, that "conjugates the discontinuity of the time of the story and the continuity of the time that is narrated."[7] This brings us back to the important question of "sensation of duration" that, beginning with the serial in the nineteenth century, allowed the reader of the popular classes to move between the story and the novel "without getting lost." Today, the series and the genres are the mediations between the time of capital and the time of daily experience.

Cultural Competence

There are few misunderstandings as persistent and as complex as that which sustains and penetrates the relationship between television and culture. On the one hand, critics look at television in terms of the paradigm of art—the only paradigm that, in their view, deserves to be called culture—and, day after day, with the same worn out arguments, they criticize the "cultural decadence" television represents and conveys. Those critics who dare to move beyond this denunciation of television to a more positive action propose a cultural elevation of television that usually results in unbearably didactic programs. On the other hand, the folklorists, who attempt to situate "true culture" in the people—the real people who conserve the truth without contamination and mestizajes, or, in other words, without history—propose to make television the "patrimony" of native dances, music, and costumes that preserve national icons. Still another set of approaches is represented in the opposition played out between a private sector using populist arguments to defend the "demands" of the people manifest in audience ratings and a paternalistic public sector talking in the name of the true cultural "needs" of the people.

The worst aspect of the confusion is that it hides a culturalism intrinsic to all the visions and proposals, situating them outside the social meaning of cultural differences and covering up the interests that encumber their idea of culture. In no other place is the contradictory meaning of mass so explicitly challenging as it is in television. Here we find the perhaps unavoidable confluence of the deactivation of social differences—with the accompanying processes of ideological synthesis—and the presence in mass culture of the cultural matrix and a sensorium which is so nauseating to the elites. An ignorance of this tension, seeing in it only commercial interests and the efficiency of ideological mechanisms, has justified and continues to justify that, at the hour of developing cultural policies, neither governments nor the opposition take television into account. Television is not considered a question of culture but only a matter of "communication." To prove this they ask what works of lasting value television has produced. Perhaps the BBC versions of classics or the pseudohistorical melodramas of the U.S. networks? Once again, as Benjamin observes in relation to photography, the mandarins of Culture continue to debate if television can be considered culture while, like it or not, the very notion of culture and its social meaning are changing as a result of *what* is reproduced in television and *how* it is reproduced.

An interesting path out of this confusion is revealed in the unusual and pioneering work of Paolo Fabri a few years back. He brought to the debate some keys to understanding the cultural specificity of mass culture which, without ignoring the characterization of Abraham Moles,[8] go beyond systemic functionalism. The basic position of Fabri is that

> while in high culture the work of art is in dialectic contradiction with its genre, in mass culture the aesthetic norms are a question of the closest approximation to its genre. One can affirm that the genre is the basic unit of the content of mass communication (at least at the level of fiction, though not exclusively) and that the public market demands placed on producers are precisely in terms of genre. It is through the perception of the genre that researchers gain access to the latent meaning of the mass media text. (1973, 77 and 65)

A topography of culture elaborated by Yuri M. Lotman (1972) is at the root of this proposal. Here we find the differentiation between a "grammatical" culture—one that refers to the intellect and is the result of explicit rules of grammar of production—and a textual culture—where the sensation and the pleasure of the text always refer to another text and not to a specific set of rules of grammar. This is what occurs with folklore, popular culture, and mass culture. Just as most people go to the movies to see films of cops and robbers, science fiction, or a Western, so also the cultural dynamics of television operate in terms of genres. Through its genres television stimulates cultural competence and the recognition of cultural differences. The genres, articulating the narration of the serials, constitute a fundamental mediation between the logic of the system of production and that of consumption, between the logic of the format and how that format is read and used.

The Logics of Production and Use

Entering into the logic of television, that is, into the structure and dynamics of television production, does not mean falling into empty generalities as long as we stick to one basic criterion: what is important is that which structures the specific conditions of production and the ways the productive system leaves marks on the formats. Thus, the focus is on the ways in which the television industry, as a productive structure, semanticizes and recycles the demands coming from the various "publics" and the uses of television by these publics. This approach reveals a series of instances and concrete mechanisms for our study. Industrial competence, for example, is the capacity for production expressed in the degree of technological development, capacity for financial risk for innovation, and the degree of professional diversification-specialization of an enterprise. This competence should not be confused with communicative competence achieved through wider recognition and popularity of television among the publics at which it is aimed. Such competence is not based only on industrial competence nor is it measured simply in terms of audience ratings.

Another process important for our study is the levels and phases of decision in the production of genres. Who decides what is to be produced, when it is to be produced, and with what production criteria? Professional ideologies are revealed in the fields of tension between the demands of the various components of the production system, the rules of a genre, the public demands, and the initiative and creativity—itself a form of resistance—of different people in the productive process: directors, actors, scenery designers, camera operators, et cetera. There are the production routines, that is, the required repetitions of work habits in the use of time and budget, forms of acting, and the ploys by which "styles" are incorporated into practices of work. Finally, there are the "strategies of commercialization" that are not added on "later" to sell the product but are placed in the structure of the format to accommodate advertising, the position in the schedule, and the different ingredients introduced in a production that will be seen only "within" a country or used for export.

We begin our analysis of the logics (plural) of uses by differentiating our proposal from those analyses called "uses and gratifications." We are attempting to take the study of reception out of communication defined as circulation of messages, effects, and reactions, and put it into the field of culture: the conflicts which articulate culture, the *mestizajes* which weave it together, and the anachronisms which sustain it. We want to examine the workings of hegemony and resistance and, therefore, the persistent functions of appropriation and repetition by the subaltern classes. There have been attempts to rethink the space of reception from the perspective of communication, relocating it, as Miguel de Moragas has lucidly proposed, within the area of the challenges to democratization of communication that technological transformations pose. De Moragas suggests a typology based on a "field of reception" that allows us to conceive of the different types of communication competence in relation to "the activation of or blocking of social participation, a key concept for democratic media policy, implying democratization of control as well as use" (1985, 20).

The variety of logics of use are not limited only to social differences of class, but become articulated in other aspects of class. The "habitus of classes" pervades the use of television and the modes of perceiving, becoming visible—ethnographically observable—in the daily organization of time and space. Where do people watch television? Is it a public or private space? Is it the home, the neighborhood bar, or the local club? What place does the set occupy in the home? Is it a central or a marginal space? Does it rule over the living room which is the crossroads of social life in the family or does it take refuge in a bedroom or behind a cupboard from which it is removed only to watch special programs? The geography of television viewing allows us to establish a symbolic topography of class usages. With the same methods it is possible to outline a social typology of the amount of time television occupies in the home, from a context where the set is turned on all day to one in which the set is on only to watch the news or a series produced by the BBC. There are uses that are not only a question of the amount of time spent watching television but the type and social significance of the time[9] and of the demands that different social classes place on time spent watching television. Some classes only demand information because their entertainment and cultural demands are met elsewhere—sports, the theater, reading books, and in concerts—while other classes seek all this from television.

The different uses of television are not only a question of social class. Also important is the cultural competence of the groups that constitute the classes: the different levels of formal education, ethnic background, regional cultures, the local dialects with their peculiar social categorizations, and the urban *mestizajes* formed on the basis of the combination of all of these. Competence lives on in "memories"—in their narrative, gestures, and sounds—and in the pool of cultural images that nourish the growth of different social protagonist identities such as women or youth. A deeper understanding of these different modes of watching television means "watching with the people." This allows us to explain and confront the diverse forms of viewing and the competencies that those forms of viewing activate. It also allows us to examine the "stories," the life stories, that people recount and that they recognize in their viewing of television.

The genres are the mediation between the logic of the productive system and the logics of use. The rules of the genres establish the basic pattern of the formats and anchor the cultural recognition of the different groups. Admittedly, the notion of genre we are using here has little to do with the literary notion of genre as "a property of the text" or with functionalism's reduction of the genre to a taxonomy.[10] Our use of the term genre is not something that happens *to* a text but something that happens *through* and *because of* a text, for it is less a question of the structure and combinations than of competence. Let us accept, therefore, the proposal of a group of Italian researchers who consider the genre first and foremost a "strategy of communicability." The genre becomes visible as the characteristic form of this communicability and therefore can be analyzed as a text (Wolf, Casetti, and Lumbelli 1980–1, 2:147–90, 3:11–119). The consideration of genres as purely literary and not as a cultural phenomenon, reducing them to a classification scheme or a set of recipes for production, has kept us from understanding their real function in the social process and their methodological significance. This methodological role is of key importance in the analysis of texts of the mass media and especially television.

The study of genres as strategies of interaction or as ways in which senders and receivers organize and make their communicative abilities recognizable is impossible without reconceptualizing the meaning of communication. The function of the genres makes it obvious that the narrative, textual competence is not only a condition of the sender but also of the receiver. Any television viewer knows, when the text/story has been interrupted, the many ways that the story can be finished, and is capable of summarizing the work or of comparing and classifying it with other stories. As speakers of the "language" of genres, the television viewer, like the natives of a culture with no written language, are unaware of the systematic rules of grammar, but are quite capable of speaking the language. This is a new way of looking at television texts. If seen as moments of *negotiation*, genres cannot be approached in terms of semantics or syntax. They require the construction of a communicative pragmatics that can capture the operation of their recognition by a cultural community. The texts of a genre are a stock of meanings constituting an organization that is more of a complex of interrelations than a set of distinct molecules. Consequently a genre cannot be analyzed by following a list of representative categories, but by searching for the architecture which links the different semantic contents of the diverse significant topics. A genre functions by constituting a "world" in which no element has a fixed value and meaning, even more so in the case of television where each genre is defined as much by its internal architecture as by its place in the programming, that is, in the organization of the time slots and the flow of the scheduling. From this is derived a further imperative in the study of genres: the necessity of being aware of how differently the system of genres is constructed in each country. For in each country the system of genres responds to the cultural configuration, to a set of juridical demands placed on television, to the level of development of the national television industry, and to different modes of articulation to the transnational system.

Some Indicators of Latin American Identity Recognizable in the Melodrama

Seeing how we live in the midst of a melodrama—now that
the melodrama is our daily bread—I have asked myself many times
if our fear of the melodrama (as a symptom of bad taste) is not due to
a deformation resulting from our having read too many turn-of-the-
century French psychological novels. But, many of the writers we most
admire were not afraid of the melodrama. Neither Sábato nor Onetti
feared the melodrama. And when Borges himself approached the
world of the gaucho, he willingly entered the world of Juan
Moreira and the ill-bred tango.—*Alejo Carpentier*

A French melodrama is not the same as a Soviet or Spanish melodrama.
There is, however, a unity in the Latin American melodrama from the Rio
Grande to the Patagonia. The gestures, the blaming of the other, the
drunken singing of the Mexican *rancheras* or Argentine tangos, in
these the region is wholly identified.—*Hernando Salcedo*

Two expressive quotes which introduce us to the genre in which all Latin Americans of a popular background—and even the elites when they are drunk—can recognize themselves. No other genre, not horror (Latin America certainly does not lack material for the horrific!) nor adventure (there are plenty of impenetrable forests and rampaging rivers!) has managed to take shape in the region as the melodrama has. It is as if the melodrama reflected the mode of expression most open to the life-style and feelings of the people. More than the endless critique and ideological analysis, more than fashion and intellectual revivals, the melodrama continues to be a fertile ground for studying the unmatched rhythms of historical development and *mestizajes* of which we are made. Like the public marketplaces, the melodrama mixes a little bit of everything, social structures and the structures of feeling. The melodrama is much of what we are—fatalists, inclined to machismo, superstitious—and what we dream of becoming—stealing the identities of others, nostalgia, righteous anger. In the form of a tango, a soap opera, a Mexican film, or a cheap crime story, the melodrama taps into and stirs up a deep vein of collective cultural imagination. And there is no access to historical memory or projection of dreams into the future which does not pass through this cultural imagination.[11] This is where the matrix of cultural images feeding the popular recognition of itself in mass culture becomes most visible.

Of the two possible levels of meaning that are articulated in the notion of *recognition*, the dominant contemporary rationalism can make sense out of only one: the negative significance. For an epistemology operating at the level of cognition, re-cognition is nothing more than redundancy, useless effort. And if this dichotomous interpretation is projected onto the question of ideology, then the result is even more radical: the negative becomes alienation. Here, re-cognition is tantamount to being unaware and ignorant. There is another matrix, however, which gives re-cognition a very different meaning, one in which re-cognition means "to appeal to," to interpellate. Here we are dealing with subjects of action and their specific manner of constituting themselves. These subjects of action are not just individuals but collectivities, social and political actors. All these protagonists constitute themselves and reconstitute themselves within the symbolic web of interpellations and recognitions. Every subject makes a subject of another and at the same time is a subject for another. This is the living dimension of society, running through and sustaining the institutions, the dimension of the "social contract."

We can now return to the melodrama and to what is at play there, the drama of recognition:[12] son by father, mother by son. What moves the plot along is always the unawareness of identities, the struggle against bewitching spells and false appearances, trying to cut through all that hides and disguises. In short, it is a struggle to make oneself recognized. Is perhaps the secret thread between the melodrama and the history of Latin America this constant search for recognition? In any case, the melodrama's ignorance of the social contract speaks clearly of the weight that the other "primordial society" of relatives, neighborhoods, and friendships holds for those who recognize themselves in the melodrama. Would it be inappropriate to ask to what extent the success of the melodrama in Latin America is a commentary on the failure of those political institutions that have developed with an unawareness of this "other society" and are incapable of acknowledging its cultural density?

An understanding of this question brings us back to the realm of the social movements we referred to earlier as "neighborhood" movements, and the role of the daily life of the family in popular culture. These are cultures in which the rhythm of time of the family "gives rise to the idea of social, a man who is first and foremost a member of a kin group. . . . So family time joins up with community time" (Zonabend 1984, 202). "Family" time mediates and makes possible communication between "historical" time—the time of the nation and the world, the larger events that affect the community—and the time of an individual life—the time from birth to death, based on rites of passage from one age to another. Hoggart observed, referring not to backward peasants but to the poor working-class sectors of the city, that events are not perceived except when they affect the life of the family group (1972). A war is perceived as "the time when uncle died," the capital is "where my sister-in-law lives." As a result of the continuing massive waves of immigrants, the cultural uprooting, and the chronic economic instability, the popular neighborhoods of the big cities are a type of extended family. For the popular world, the family and the neighborhood are, in spite of their contradictions and conflicts, the truest forms of sociability.

When this life experience in the context of family and neighborhood is juxtaposed with a capitalism that transforms the workplace and leisure time and commercializes not only public and private time but also the most primary, intimate relationships, it might appear that that more primordial society has been abolished. In fact, capitalism has merely made it an *anachronism*. It is, however, a precious anachronism for it is this life of familial relations that, in the last analysis, gives meaning to the melodrama in Latin America—from the lasting impact of the romantic ballad to development of the *telenovela*. It is this anachronism that mediates between the time of the individual life—considered to be of no social significance, economically worthless, and a political unknown, but nevertheless culturally alive—and the time of the narrative which affirms this life and makes it possible for the popular classes to recognize themselves in this anachronism. This anachronistic perception of life, transforming into melodrama everything that it encounters, eventually gets revenge—

in its own secret way—against the abstractions imposed on them by the commercialization of their lives, their political exclusion, and their cultural dispossession.

Where does all this leave alienation, ideology, and the schemes of the businessmen? They are still there, part of the web of recognitions and nonrecognitions. They are at work not as some powerful outside force and much less as the "true" protagonists of a drama in which the poor would be nothing more than a chorus echoing the main action. The chorus rebelled long ago.[13] The signs of rebellion are found in the disquieting pleasure the poor continue to find in the melodrama. Michèle Mattelart asks herself, "What mass masochism, what suicidal class behavior can explain this fascination?" She replies with another question: "Is the power of the culture industry not also to be found outside the subjects with which it deals, the anecdotes it transmits, which are but epiphenomena of its real message?" (1982, 142). We are beginning to suspect that this is the case. What gives the culture industry force and the stories meaning is not simply ideology but culture and the profound dynamics of memory and cultural imagination.

Just as in the heyday of the serial novel, so today the telenovela—a new and more Latin American version of magical realism—is the cultural product that Latin America has managed to export to Europe and North America. The telenovela is much closer to the "narrative," in the sense given by Benjamin, than to the novel or book, and closer to the "dialogue" literature, as understood by Bakhtin, than to the monologue. Both of these themes need to be explored further.

From the tradition of oral narrative, the televised melodrama conserves a strong tie with the culture of stories and legends,[14] the literature of the cordel in Brazil and the stories sung in the corridos and vallenatos.[15] It conserves characteristics of a story told to someone, implying the presence of a narrator who, day after day, establishes a dramatic continuity. It also conserves the story's lack of boundaries and openness to time—you know when it will begin but not when it will end—and its openness to what is happening around it as well as the conditions under which it is produced. In a Peruvian telenovela, for example, a taxi strike that prevented some scenes from being filmed was incorporated into the plot. This is a paradoxical way of working for a form that is produced following the strictest rules of the industry and with the most advanced technology. It is a response, however, to a logic quite the inverse to that which controls its production: the quality of the communication it achieves has little to do with the quantity of information it provides.

A second clue to how the melodrama works can be found in the concept of literature of dialogue. According to a Brazilian analysis that goes more deeply into the proposal of Bakhtin, it is a carnivalesque genre where "the author, reader, and characters constantly change places" (Da Matta 1985, 96). It is an exchange, a confusion between story and real life, between what the actor does and what happens to the spectator. It is a literary experience open to the reactions, desires, and motivations of the public. It does not, however, bring real life events to the story. "It is not in the representation of the specific events and details that the sense of reality is created in fiction, but in a certain generality that looks in both directions and gives consistency to the specific events of reality as well as to the world of fiction" (Cantor Magnani 1984, 175).

Within its openness and confusion lies a commercial logic; likewise, the strategies of ideology it contains are irrefutable. But, to reduce this crossroads of different logics to a question of marketing and to deny the existence of other cultural experiences of matrices is methodologically incorrect and politically flawed. Without doubt, another political culture is necessary in order to accept that the melodrama is, at the same time, a form of recovery of popular memory through the cultural images produced by the culture industry and a metaphor indicating the different presence of the people in the masses.

The exploration of how a people is emerging in mass culture is the subject of the final sections of my book, *Communication, Culture, and Hegemony*, but we must again call attention to the fact that this is a "nocturnal map." This cannot be more than an indication of the new theoretical lines we are staking out and the account of some of the pioneering experiences of research along these lines in Latin America.

Notes

1. The expression is taken from Gutiérrez and Munizaga (1983, 25).

2. Used with the meaning attributed by Da Matta (1985, 92).

3. The meaning given here to the term *mediations* is that of Martín Serrano (1977).

4. Several of the chapters in Richeri (1983) touch on the deepening of social differences as a result of the new video products.

5. We take this notion from Muñiz Sodré (1981), but remove from it the apocalyptic connotations in the original text.

6. Radio had begun to bring these two worlds together but radio's nonexclusive use made it possible to carry on other activities without interruption.

7. Calabrese (1984, 70). *Análisi 9* is dedicated to "repetition" and serialization in film and television.

8. We refer to the proposal that is developed in Moles (1978).

9. Regarding the social meaning of the time occupied by television, see Thiolent et al. (1982).

10. For an example of this, see Todorov (1978).

11. There are relatively few studies, however, that approach the melodrama from the perspective of "culture": Jorge Rivera on the serialized melodrama in Argentina; Carlos Monsiváis on the melodrama in films and songs in Mexico; Beatriz Sarlo on the weekly novel in Argentina in the 1920s; M. Meyer on the serial in Brazil (1973 and 1982); Hurtado (1983).

12. This theme has already been extensively developed in part 2 of my *Communication, Culture, and Hegemony: From the Media to Mediations.*

13. The term *chorus* refers to the title of an essay by José Nun on the reductionism of the conceptions of the popular held by the left (1984).

14. We refer to the relationships of the melodrama with the legends and mystery stories that deal with mixed-up twins and changelings from unknown parents.

15. In *Comunicación y Cultura* 12 there are several articles which deal with this theme.

NÉSTOR GARCÍA CANCLINI

Cultural Studies from the 1980s to the 1990s: Anthropological and Sociological Perspectives in Latin America

Néstor García Canclini was born in Argentina. An anthropologist and cultural critic, he works at the Universidad Autónoma Metropolitana (Iztapalapa, Mexico). His main titles include *Las culturas populares en el capitalismo* (1982), *Culturas híbridas. Estrategias para entrar y salir de la modernidad* (1989a), and *Consumidores y ciudadanos. Conflictos multiculturales de la globalización* (1995a).

W hy are there so many disciplines devoted to the study of culture? My starting hypothesis is that the proliferation of trends is the outcome of unresolved problems in research, which make the task of constructing a more widely accepted theoretical model and a coherent set of research strategies difficult. But these divergences are also derived from the sociopolitical conditions and the separate institutional traditions in which the social sciences are currently practiced.

How can a comprehensive treatment of the various epistemological and social conditions under which studies on culture are developed be organized? Rather than offering an encyclopedic map of the wide array of approaches, I want to examine a few crossroads in our research. In order to do this, I suggest as a second hypothesis that the current differences between sociology and anthropology consist, fundamentally, in their incompatible conceptions of tradition and modernity. Both the incommensurability of their approaches and the attempts to overcome it must be analyzed to see if it is possible to move cultural studies out of their pre-paradigmatic condition, in the Kuhnian sense, or at least to establish why it is so difficult, when analyzing culture, to know what we are talking about. With this discussion as the starting point, we will seek to describe how the role of cultural research is being reformulated today within the academic and socioeconomic growth crisis in Latin America.

From Humanities to Social Sciences

Whereas it is not our aim here to map out the history of Latin American studies on culture, it is worthwhile remembering that the trajectories of anthropology and sociology in relation to those studies have been of different duration and have followed divergent strategies. Up until the middle of the twentieth century, when cultural questions were the almost exclusive domain of writers and philosophers, anthropologists were the only social scientists to systematically consider them as part of social processes. When studying indigenous communities and peasants, they analyzed myths and folklore with the same dedication they gave to economic and political structures. Even in the 1950s and 1960s, when sociology went beyond its essayistic stage through the empirical investigation of demographic and socioeconomic changes, cultural differences were relegated to the role of insignificant features that would be necessarily transformed by modernization. Anthropologists, in the meantime, concentrated on the proper forms of symbolization and ritualization of individual ethnic groups, in particular the most "backward" ones.

At the same time, in contrast to the specialists in high culture—art and literature historians—anthropology vindicated popular cultures. Their long familiarity with cultural problems gave anthropologists an advantage in relation to history, sociology, and other disciplines that have begun putting together a scientific body of knowledge in this area over the last twenty years. But the anthropological accumulation of knowledge, which preferably focused on the traditional popular world, hindered the contributions of this discipline to the cultural analysis of modernity.

The development of scientific sociology in the second half of our century, based on empirical studies carried out in universities and institutes independently of traditional humanities, was conceived as a venture in concurrence to the industrialization and urbanization of Latin American societies. In order to move on from the local and the traditional, that is, from "backwardness," to modern society, it was necessary to understand the macro-social laws of technological and social development. Instead of busying themselves with the old forms of social organization and symbolization (*compadrazgo*, kinship, myths, all "hindrances to development") it was necessary for the social scientists to contribute to a better understanding of migrations, relocations of people to build dams or roads, or adaptation of the peasant work force to corporate labor relations and urban structures. Within those vertiginous changes, which a biased viewpoint attributed solely to technological and economic impulses, there was no time to be distracted by cultural processes. Only in those countries with a dense indigenous population—particularly Peru and Mexico—did some sociologists see "the study and proposal of practical solutions to national problems, especially those of cultural heterogeneity, with special attention to the indigenous problem, as being their principal task" (Villa Aguilera 1975, 7). However, the sociologists who for this very reason had to work as ethnologists, thus attenuating the divide between anthropology and sociology, judged the indigenous question to be a problem, as the quotation demonstrates. Accordingly, their knowledge of indigenous cultures sought how to subordinate them to a modern national project.

One point in common between those sociological studies and those carried out by indigenist anthropologists is that, when analyzing culture, they concentrated on discerning the political meaning of modernization more than determining the theoretical and epistemological difficulties involved. The most creative work of this period, *El proceso de aculturación* by Gonzalo Aguirre Beltrán, offers a conceptually imaginative albeit theoretically precarious elaboration, because he is less concerned with elucidating epistemologically its eclecticism than with devising a narrative adequate to his political project: a "doctrine which guides and clarifies the procedures and goals of indigenist action" (1957, 9).

Is Anthropology Useful to the Study of Modernity?

With the arrival of the 1990s, the divides between anthropologists and sociologists have not disappeared, though the political and academic conditions in which knowledge is produced have changed. It seems sometimes that the degree of autonomy obtained by scientific work from external powers has only served to strengthen the historical distinctions, the departmental priorities, the strategies for growth, and the prestige of each discipline. A large part of Latin American anthropology continues to focus its research and teaching on the ethnographic description of small traditional communities. Cultural studies privilege the knowledge of those traits which give historical continuity to an ethnic group or a rural community, or which represent their resistance to modernization. The few texts dealing with technological or economic transformations or those generated by urbanization and industrialization tend to give more attention to the threats which these forces, seen as strange, represent, than to an explanation of the crossovers between heritage and innovation.

It is unusual to find research which poses the question why the indigenous groups adopt capitalist forms of production, assimilate with pleasure modern ideological structures and consumer products within their so-called "communities": we know too little about how indigenous people and peasants use bank credit and television, how they relate to tourists in the markets and the information they obtain when they go to the big cities of their own country or to the United States. There are a few articles and some unpublished theses that deal with these issues, but on checking the book-length research done about them, the classic work by Lourdes Arizpe about the Marías (1979) and the recent work by Catharine Godd Eshelman on the producers of *amate* (1988) are truly exceptions.

Even anthropological studies on working-class culture and urban marginal groups repeat, in spaces where the macro-social and modern organization of life is unavoidable, the micro-ethnographic style, characterized by intensive observation and in-depth interviews in order to learn about the "isolated" dynamics of a poor neighborhood or cultural enclave. The original dense information that this methodology provides does not manage to offer a comprehensive vision of the significance of city life. What Eunice Ribeiro Durham has to say with respect to Brazilian anthropology is applicable to the whole of Latin America: It is less "an anthropology of the city than an anthropology in the city. These are investigations which operate with anthropological topics, concepts, and methods, but which dedicate themselves to the study of urban populations. The city is, therefore, more the locus of research than its object" (1986, 19).

Given this paradigm of studies—institutionalized by organisms of research and cultural policies, by special budgets, prestigious awards, and so on—it is only reasonable that the principal role for anthropologists at the end of this Latin American century be that of the critics of modernity. Their rejection of evolutionism and ethnocentrism induces them to understand the homogenizing policies of industrialization and industrial reconversion, of national integration and subordination to transnational patterns of development, either as Western impositions on ethnic and local cultures and of the hegemonic classes on the subaltern ones, or, in the most radical cases, as simple ethnocide. Since the contradictory and dependent Latin American modernization has created vast tragedies— massive migrations, unemployment, urban sprawl, and pollution—there is no lack of data or arguments to question the candid identification of modernity with progress and of traditions with backwardness. There exists, then, an obvious place for anthropologists to function as defenders of indigenous and peasant cultures, and promoters of their knowledge and techniques, not only in academia but also in governmental and private organisms.[1] But it is also possible that anthropological thinking could be useful to render the debate on modernity, simplified by the "success" of neoliberal policies, more complex: those cultural differences difficult to reduce could be included in the discussion, along with other ways to interact with nature, promote development, and solidarily resolve collective problems.

The pending question is whether a paradigm which thinks of modernity reactively, which lacks adequate theoretical and methodological tools with which to understand industrialization (of material and symbolic goods), mass consumption, and the reorganization of national cultures in a transnational marketplace, is capable of producing a discourse with the capacity to intervene in contemporary crises.

Within Latin American anthropology, some studies able to respond affirmatively are beginning to appear. I find some examples in Brazil: Roberto de Matta's book, *Carnaváis, malandros, e hérois. Para uma sociología do dilema brasileiro*, in spite of its subtitle, it is an anthropological work because it employs theories on rituality from that discipline in order to elaborate—from the description of carnival—an interpretation of national sociability. Other innovative studies are those carried out on cultural patrimony by Antonio Augusto Arantes (1984) and Ribeiro Durham (1986), as they transcend the conservationist and fundamentalist viewpoint usual in this field, and they include the uses of patrimony in the current polemics on Brazilian development. Along these same lines, I think of the works by Renato Ortiz (1987 and 1988), which fluctuate between anthropological research on national identity and on the reformulation of traditions amid the development of cultural industries.

Within Mexican anthropology of the first half of the twentieth century there took place a reflection on national society that was very influential in the design of cultural policies, but which was interrupted when anthropology became indigenist or specialized in local communities. Some studies from the last decade resumed the global analysis of Mexico, among which there are two books with very different orientations that stand out: Guillermo Bonfil Batalla's *México profundo* and Roger Bartra's *La jaula de la melancolía*, which presents itself as an anthropological work, though in fact it is a postmodern deconstruction of discourses on national culture, thus leaving the reader desiring that that imaginative demystifying labor be accompanied, as an anthropological work should be, by an ethnography of the representations of identity and its daily performance. The most recent Mexican examples of empirical research on culture which offer in addition an innovative theoretical reflection come rather from texts whose central focus is not culture, but medical anthropology (those of Eduardo Menéndez and María Eugenia Módena), political anthropology (Esteban Krotz, Silvia Gómez Tagle, Roberto Varela), problems of social development and social reproduction (Larisa Lomnitz, Lourdes Arizpe, Guillermo de la Peña, Mario Margulis), and questions of gender (Lourdes Arizpe, Mary Goldsmith, Martha Lamas, Angeles Sánchez).

Some authors explicitly confront the emerging theoretical problems when they analyze the changes in tradition and their relocation in contemporary Mexico: this is the case with crafts and popular festivities (Victoria Novelo, García Canclini, Gobi Stromberg), religiosity and myths (Gilberto Giménez, Eckart Boege). Among current lines of research which use anthropology for the macro-social analysis of Mexico, with special attention given to its complex modern aspects, can be found studies on education and cultural policies and their reception from various social actors (Jorge González, Eduardo Nivon, Maya Lorena Pérez, Ana María Rosas, Patricia Safa, and José Manuel Valenzuela: the fact that works by these scholars are recently published articles or unpublished postgraduate theses reveals the incipient character of this tendency). It is worthwhile considering them when trying to understand which direction research is taking.

Can Sociology Think of Culture and Modernization in Concert?

Scientific sociology was born as a partner to modernization.

> When Don Lucio Mendieta y Nuñez was still a recent graduate [remembers Sara Sefchovich] and all the telephones still had the name Ericson before the number, which was made up of five figures, the first issue of the *Revista Mexicana de Sociología* appeared, published by the Instituto de Investigaciones de Ciencias Sociales de la Universidad Nacional Autónoma de México [Social Sciences Research Institute of the Autonomous National University of Mexico]. It was April 1939. (Sefchovich 1989)

Those were the years when political stability allowed Mexico to launch its industrial development, trusting that its autonomy was going to consolidate itself by import substitutions and that social and cultural fractures would heal through the integration of a national market and the export of its products abroad. Sociology, as a positive science without prejudice and dedicated to learning the facts, seemed to be a key instrument in showing how this society, which was going through an intense process of renewal and expansion, should be organized.

In the 1960s, Gino Germani, founder of scientific sociology in Argentina and one of the most respected theorists on the continent, maintained that the era of national sociologies, which were obliged to differentiate themselves one from the other by "the burden of their cultural and intellectual traditions," was coming to an end all over the world. A body of knowledge characterized by the universality of its concepts and problems, he explained, whose internal differences are due to the specialization necessary for the rigorous knowledge of the social, will find "rising practical applications" to "control change in a rational way" during "the transition from preindustrial to industrial society." The political and religious dogmas, the "descriptive values" of local and traditional groups, had to be rejected in order for sociology to fulfill its historic vocation, that which was prescribed by structural-functionalist rationality, understood at that time as the epitome of modern knowledge.[2]

What place could knowledge of the symbolic world hold in this positivist sociology, hostile to traditions, which judged cultural differences as prejudices on the verge of extinction? The study of the symbolic world seemed to be the task of humanists. By leaving the study of culture in the hands of other disciplines, scientific sociology gradually contributed to an arrangement which could be described as complicitous discrepancy: the art and literature historians sustained an idealist aesthetic according to which creative phenomena could not be explained from theories which spoke of social determinants and regularities; sociologists viewed with skepticism those pretensions of artistic production or did not realize that what occurs in art and literature goes beyond the individual relationship between a solitary author and her or his work, that is, that the production of symbolic goods is symptomatic and expressive of basic structures within society.

In any case, the study of hegemonic culture had no place among the principal objects of sociological investigation on modernization, nor was it professionally worthy within a discipline that was rapidly becoming professional based upon its "developmentalist" objectives. As for popular cultures, given that they were identified with residues destined to evaporate, it was better to leave them in the hands of the anthropologists, with whom there was also disagreement as to their value but with whom there ultimately existed that complicitous territorial distribution I mentioned above.

Toward the late 1960s, however, more or less sociological studies on culture began to transgress sociological dogmas. Meanwhile, the political and social effervescence of that decade—born partly from discontent due to the frustration of developmentalism—led artists and writers to ask themselves not so much what the relations between art and society were like, but rather what they should be like. In the midst of this overwhelmingly voluntaristic bibliography, some art and literature historians began inserting the utopias and political mottoes in sociological descriptions of the relationships among producers, intermediaries, and publics. I would like to mention, with no intention to be fair with so many writers, the texts of Antonio Candido, Noé Jitrik, Françoise Perus, Adolfo Prieto, Angel Rama, and Roberto Schwarz.

Also from the ranks of sociology there appeared studies on cultural processes. The ascendant influence of Marxism at first reduced many works to the level of ideological denunciations which "explained" symbolic goods by their connection to economic and political domination: both in the texts based on dependency theory and in those which later emerged under Marxist structuralism, the internal dynamics of cultural fields received little attention. A breath of fresh air coming from Gramscism and the French sociology of culture (especially Pierre Bourdieu) favored a more complex treatment which recognized the specificity of popular cultures and of each field of cultural production. Nonetheless, those Marxist studies most careful of the empirical diversity of symbolic processes—which managed to counteract the exaggerated emphasis on culture as the scene for domination—were, more than sociological, those carried out by anthropologists. In the last decade, the anthropological elaboration of Italian Gramscism (Alberto Cirese, Lombardi Satriani, Amalia Signorelli) found its echo in sociology and communication studies. In fact, the most important work regarding the reformulation of the problematic of domination and manipulation in terms of cultural hegemony is that of Jesús Martín-Barbero (1987a), an author whose work is decidedly transdisciplinary.

In contrast to Marxist authors, dedicated to questioning the contradictions and stumbles of modernization on dependent countries and the popular classes, some sociologists with structural-functionalist training carried out studies on culture as the expression of modernization. Their investigations are also worthy of note as they tried out the "hard" tools of sociology (surveys, polls) in their analysis of symbolic processes. Why did it occur to some sociologists to explore the laws of the artistic avant-gardes, and more precisely those works which did not give in to the marketplace, those gestures which refused to be effective actions, those experiences which were destined to subvert social regularity? I remember the pioneering studies of Regina Gibaja (1964) and Martha F. De Slemenson and Germán Kratochwill (1970)—members of the organism which led the modernization of sociology in Argentina, the Instituto Di Tella—who sought to discover the logic of relationships among artists, promoters, and publics. It is not by chance that those first empirical sociological investigations into Latin American art were made at that institute, which was at the forefront of the social sciences in the 1960s and 1970s, and promoted the artistic avant-gardes of Buenos Aires. I studied elsewhere the links between both innovative movements and their connection to industrial development in Argentina, of which the Di Tella car and electric appliances factory—the institute sponsor—was also a leader (García Canclini 1988b, chapter 4, "La producción simbólica").

These investigations were isolated. Both those inspired by Marxism as well as those with a structural-functionalist approach pointed out a *field of problems* and gathered data which helped us to catch a glimpse of it, but did not manage to configure a subdiscipline, a consistent area of studies within sociology until the 1980s. In fact, those sociological analyses of art and literature contributed to sociology of culture, but rarely does culture in its entirety appear as the object of investigation or the specific framework for those partial examinations.

Three facts, at least, allow us to say that it was not until the 1980s that cultural sociology began to exist in Latin America: (a) the accumulation of empirical research on diverse cultural processes within one country with a clear definition of the object of study and research strategies in line with international theoretical development re-elaborated according to the particular conditions in Latin American countries; (b) the dedication to the study of cultural processes by various outstanding figures in the continent's sociology (among others, José Joaquín Brunner, Sergio Miceli, Renato Ortiz, Oscar Landi, Gilberto Giménez); (c) the inclusion of the cultural problematic as a crucial and specific dimension in political and urban sociology research (Norbert Lechner, Guillermo O'Donnell, Sergio Zermeño, Roger Bartra). Some of these authors (Bartra, Giménez, Ortiz) oscillate between anthropology and sociology; others, after years of studying the state or modes of production and domination, have decided to dedicate themselves totally to culture because of the need to seek complementary clues to economic and political explanations.

The high number and the quality of works published during the last decade lead me to affirm not only that cultural sociology exists, but also that it is one of the most dynamic branches of social sciences in Latin America.[3]

Toward a Joint Revision of Research

The parallel development of sociological studies of culture and anthropological studies on cultural modernization converge in several ways, first of all, with respect to the object of study. Alongside other disciplines or trends in the social sciences, such as linguistics, semiotics, and communication studies, many anthropologists and sociologists define culture today *as the realm of production, circulation, and consumption of meanings.* This is by no means an exclusively Latin American definition, but rather it is the product of an international consensus among anthropologists such as Clifford Geertz, Edmund Leach, and Renato Rosaldo, sociologists such as Raymond Williams and Stuart Hall, semiologists such as Umberto Eco, and social scientists who are difficult to situate in only one of these disciplines, like Pierre Bourdieu and Howard S. Becker.

This socio-semiotic definition of culture allows us to approach, up to a certain point, the work of various disciplines and to establish a common platform for the study of problems which until recently have divided researchers. The discussion as to whether culture is an expression or a reflection of material structures is thus reduced as culture is conceived as a specific and necessary dimension of human practice. It does not dissolve into social totality nor does it become the idealist equivalent of the concept of social formation, as in Ruth Benedict's understanding, according to which culture is the form of a society cemented by its dominant values. Culture designates, in this perspective, the symbolic dimension of all human practices, which means that, while it is imbricated to the economic and social spheres, it is analytically distinguishable from them.[4]

Nevertheless, the divergences between sociology and anthropology are renewed when trying to define empirically the object of study and the research strategies. I want to deal with these discrepancies using as a starting point a group of studies carried out in Chile by CENECA and FLACSO. I know of no other center for sociological research on the continent that has accomplished such an extensive investigation of one country's culture—education, theater, literature, visual arts, popular culture, political culture, et cetera—with approximately fifteen researchers working continuously and in constant, creative dialogue with international trends. Let's take, for instance, the book *Chile: transformaciones culturales y modernidad* by Brunner, Barrios, and Catalán (1989), which systemizes a large part of the production from those organisms. As the most complex and elaborate sociological work on a Latin American country, it gives us the opportunity for assessing the degree of advancement and for reflecting on the difficulties of a strictly sociological perspective of culture.

The authors depart from a definition similar to that given above: they understand by culture "the processes of production and transmission of meanings that fabricate a symbolic world for individuals and society" (21). In order to structure their study they carry out two operations. The first consists in discerning two types of cultural production: one covers the symbolic goods produced in *specific fields* or institutionalized "subsectors" (education, science and technology, cultural industries, the arts and religion); at another level they place daily culture, where "the communicative effects" of the previous fields are expressed and accomplished and where the "situated interactions" between individuals and groups are carried out.

The second operation for organizing their analysis of Chilean culture is to characterize it as part of the formation of modernity. They consider that this process began in the 1920s but "it widened and deepened after 1964." The data is organized to reveal the principal traits of the modern restructuring of the symbolic markets. They also dedicate one section of the book, in which I will not linger here, to the authoritarian reorganization of Chilean society promoted by Pinochet's government, but the preference is not to insist on the conventional explanation of the changes wrought by the dictatorship. The work convincingly differentiates in what measure the transformations are the result of communicational censorship and the disciplining of daily life, but calls attention to the longer and deeper process of refunctionalization of the symbolic goods for the market, typical to modernization:

emergence of circuits for the commercialization of works; diversification of production in order to satisfy differentiated or segmented demands; overlapping of culture and industry; research carried out under contract; projects directly sold or done in exchange for subsidies; generalized use of advertising to finance cultural enterprises; obtainment of public resources in competition with other groups of producers; consumer polls and the use of instruments for the study of the cultural market. (67)

We are particularly interested in the mode in which the authors characterize the opposition between tradition and modernity. They maintain that

> traditional culture is structured around oral communications (and later printed material) which cover relatively personalized and socially familiar communicative spaces, either symmetrical (within social classes) or asymmetrical (in social relationships of domination). Cultural production is an attribute of the possession of social capital. The most important circuits of cultural communication are "networks of distinction," on the margins of which daily culture is structured, basically, as a variety of subaltern or "popular culture." Between those circuits and these subaltern cultural expressions there exists no creative interaction. Cultural production is weakly structured and professionalized. (25)

Modernity would be characterized by the substitution of those forms of traditional communication by a "predominantly institutionalized communication which makes use of ever more complex technological means" (25–26).

There are two statements here fully debatable from an anthropological perspective. One is that among the "most important" circuits of communication in traditional cultures (we suppose that it refers to literature, music, and the fine arts) and the traditional popular cultures "there exists no creative interaction." It is easy to find in any Latin American society multiple interactions and reciprocal borrowings between high culture and popular culture. In Chile, from the poetry of Pablo Neruda and Nicanor Parra to rock and the urban music of Congreso or Los Jaivas, including political graffiti and independent theater, there has been a frequent and creative interaction between the knowledge and the iconic repertoires of the different classes. To ignore these interactions seems to correspond to a style of sociological analysis that is more concerned with class and strata segmentations than with intercultural crossovers and hybridizations.

The second refutable claim from an anthropological point of view is that which affirms that traditionally "cultural production is weakly structured." Due to the context of the book, I infer that the authors understand by strong structuring that which exists within a system of clearly differentiated fields and modern institutions (education, science, television stations, etc.). But we do know from structural-functionalist anthropology, and even more so from the structural one, that all cultures organize their components into a compact system, that each component makes sense in relation to the others and according to its position in the system, and that no component can be changed without causing alterations within the totality. There is no need of "increasingly complex technological means" or a marked division of labor for a culture to be strongly structured. This structuring is produced and reproduced through institutions, like rituals and habits, which are perhaps less visible than the modern institutional or corporate apparatuses but which are no less efficient.

It is significant that this conflict between the traditional and the modern is presented only in the first of the six features that characterize current Chilean culture (24–25) and that it is done in a unidirectional, evolutionist way as if it simply consisted in the moving on from one stage to another more advanced one. In the rest of the book there is no mention about the large indigenous population in Chile, [5] or of the significance and functions of crafts, myths, and community festivities in contemporary society. Thanks to some studies published by CENECA, including those on Chilean folklore by Carlos Catalán, one of the authors of this book, we know about the vitality of popular cultures in that country. But when they are alluded to in this volume it is to state that their "consistency is increasingly weakened" by advances in education and the cultural industries. They would only offer, where they subsist, "a repertoire of resistances regarding the processes of incorporation to modernity, which momentarily can create the illusion or the myth of survival of autochthonous cultures" (33–34).

In other passages, the book recognizes that mass culture is not omnipotent: "uniformity is crossed with phenomena of differentiation; internationalization does not counteract regionalism" (36). But it does not include in its model—which covers widely and minutely modern cultural manifestations—the traditional forms of existence of popular cultures. The daily-life culture that the theoretical model, as I said, considers to be one of the two basic forms of existence of the cultural is dealt with in only a few pages (59–63 and 184–93) and only in order to cover the changes wrought by the dictatorship, in relation to politics, cultural industries, and urban milieus. Even though tensions among the local, the national, and the international are acknowledged, the local and regional dynamics of cultural development are not described.

To summarize, this sociological paradigm for the analysis of culture offers a *macro-social* characterization of the modern forms of production, communication, and consumption, which are carried out according to the laws of the market and reach mass publics. Little attention is paid to how these modalities, doubtless hegemonic, interact with daily culture and it is assumed that the traditional expressions of symbolization, ritualization, and organization are destined to disappear. Its *quantitative methodology*—which it recognizes to be "limited," as "it does not offer by itself sufficient explanation of the phenomena under study" (97)—provides a statistical chart of global development, including occasional documentary references and nonsystematic observations of the meanings which the processes hold for the subjects. Daily cultural landscapes do not generate knowledge capable of challenging the interpretations devised at the macro-analytical level. The hypotheses and basic lines of argument are developed from the quantitative acquisition of prevalent modernizing trends.

What happens now if we follow the opposite direction, that is, if we give value to the Latin American anthropological production on culture over the sociological model used to analyze the Chilean case? The first obvious thing is the almost total absence of anthropological studies on what the book by Brunner, Barrios, and Catalán denominates—in a large section's title—"the most dynamic subsector in the field": cultural industries.

Why should that which occurs in areas such as radio, television or video, or other types of industrialized production and mass consumption be the exclusive territory of sociologists and communicators? My initial hypothesis is that the indifference of anthropology toward these medullar processes, so distinctive to contemporary cultures, is due to a mistaken view of their character. Anthropological literature tends to look on cultural industries as though they serve only to homogenize societies and destroy differences. This homogenization would be carried out through the absorption of traditional and local cultures by a massive and transnational codification of symbolic processes. It should be said that this viewpoint was that of the early studies on communication, since the postwar years until the 1970s, and that it persists in sociological conceptions such as the one I have just commented on. But recent work on mass communications and reception of art and literature reveals that the expansion of the so-called mass culture, far from eliminating differences, multiplies the offer, facilitates the access of larger publics to repertoires of different cultures, and promotes diverse appropriations and interpretations of cultural goods with regard to the receivers' traditions.[6] At the same time, there exists a more fluid communication between cultural systems and nations—sometimes standardized by the transnational concentration of media power—and an intense differentiation within this transcultural system.

The second hypothesis is that anthropological reticence vis-à-vis mass culture originates in a defensive attitude with respect to what are considered to be the empirical objects belonging to this discipline more than with respect to what are its specific theoretical problems. If we think that *what distinguishes anthropological knowledge is not its interest in "primitive" peoples or in traditional ethnic groups and communities but rather its interest in studying differences, otherness, and intercultural relationships* through the generation of direct information, the transformations brought by modernity are not so threatening. It is true that in our century a reconfiguration of the empirical units of analysis, which have been the classical objects of anthropological study, is taking place. However, the relocation—more than disappearance—of peoples, ethnic groups, and traditional communities into contemporary societies implies other forms of differentiation, inequality, and cultural interaction. It is toward this reconfiguration of the *problematic* (not so much of the empirical objects of study) that, in the coming years, we should direct a renewed anthropological—and sociological—inquiry.

The Objects of Study in Postmodern Societies (in Recession) in the 1990s

Imagining the horizon for cultural studies in Latin America is even more difficult than tracing this precarious map of trends and main questions. Will the expansion of sociology and cultural anthropology, the multiplication of researchers, centers, and topics for investigation continue given the deteriorated salary and budget conditions that the economy is now imposing on scientific development? It is not just a case of predicting how the uncertainties generated by the juxtaposition of disciplines and the splitting of paradigms could be resolved. The changes in the function of the social sciences due to the neoliberal restructuring of Latin American societies (recession, mass unemployment, the replacement of the state by private corporations) have hardly begun to make themselves felt among the principal topics for research, the conditions for financing and competition, the demands for productivity and technological application of knowledge. If the dimension and character of these transformations are difficult to predict in the most consolidated fields of the social sciences, then it is much more difficult to anticipate them in culture, whose profile is less precise and whose "practical" usefulness is more doubtful.

It is possible that in the next few years the trends so profuse in topics and theoretical fashions will shrink, as will the experimental pursuits, which enjoyed their pinnacle in the 1970s and 1980s. The downsizing of national and international financial resources, the reduction of links with metropolitan production and the leading Latin American countries, will deactualize many research centers in countries of medium development and in small universities which in recent decades have shown important creativity. Without making up too depressing a list, it is enough to mention the decrease in Latin American representatives in the latest Latin Americanist congresses, such as LASA and other international events, the reduction in subscriptions to foreign magazines and even in the purchase of national books, the cuts on postgraduate grants and field work funding, and, lastly, the concentration of shrunken funds into more "productive" institutions and researchers.

It can be foreseen, however, that the greatest recognition of the social and political value of culture achieved in the last two decades will continue to favor, at least, two types of research:

(a) that which concerns the modernization of cultural development: new telecommunications and electronics technologies; production, circulation, and consumption of cultural industries; technical training of human resources for the cultural administration and retraining of workers in the context of industrial reconversion; evaluation of the role of organisms for the development of science and technology; diagnosis of intercultural conflicts in processes of rapid transformation and in border conditions

(b) that which is dedicated to traditional modalities of cultural development, as long as they cover social groups which are numerically or qualitatively significant: relationships between education and culture; political culture and new forms of hegemony; women and family; major indigenous ethnic groups; popular religiosity, especially groups in rapid expansion; arts, crafts, and other folkloric manifestations of commercial or tourist attraction.[7]

The most advanced studies on culture to which we have been referring lead us to anticipate that the topics from a) will not be absorbed only by sociologists, nor those from b) by anthropologists. There will continue to exist a thematic inertia within each discipline, but I imagine that sociology will increasingly include in its sources more prolonged observation in the field and a distinctive comprehension of the actors' lived experiences, while anthropology will use censuses and statistics in order to understand the macro-social significance of processes. Probably both groups will increase, as is already happening, their use of instruments from other disciplines—semiotics, theory of discourse, psychoanalysis—in order to understand the linguistic aspects and less apparent dimensions of social interactions. It would be only logical that the increased interest of public and private powers in culture, alongside the international requirement that all social scientists have access to modern resources, stimulates the inclusion of new technologies and the economy of culture in the university curricula and research programs. But these predictions are still so far from what is the current practice of sociology and anthropology in Latin America that we could be accused of wandering from our subject.

It should be pointed out that the purpose of interrelating the knowledge and work habits of sociologists and anthropologists does not seek to overcome an artificial division of the world of culture. In other times, it could be believed that the separation between anthropology and sociology corresponded to the existence of separate modalities of cultural development: self-sufficient indigenous communities on the one hand, and urban worlds and mass circuits of communication on the other. On a continent where 70 percent of the population lives in the cities, shaped for the most part by recent migrants who still hold to peasant habits and beliefs, and where, in contrast, capitalist economic relations, electronic culture, and sometimes tourism are daily presences in the rural areas, the traditional and the modern are no longer conceivable as independent entities. If both the hegemonic and the popular cultures are now *hybrid cultures*, if in this sense it is undeniable that we live in a postmodern age, a time of *bricolage* in which diverse epochs and cultures formerly distant now are mixed, the researcher's task cannot be to choose between tradition and modernity. It is rather to understand why in Latin America we are this mixture of heterogeneous memories and truncated innovations.

Translated by Ana Del Sarto, Alicia Ríos, and Abril Trigo

Notes

1. Among the most incisive authors it is worth mentioning Arturo Warman (1982) and Guillermo Bonfil Batalla (1990).
2. See a critical evaluation of this period in Eliseo Verón's compendium, *Imperialismo, lucha de clases y conocimiento: 25 años de sociología en la Argentina* (1974).
3. One place to corroborate this is the group of studies on *Innovación cultural y actores socioculturales* promoted by CLACSO, which appear in volumes 7 and 8 of the work *¿Hacia un nuevo orden estatal en América Latina?* (Buenos Aires: CLACSO 1989), especially those texts written by Gabriel Cohn on Brazil, Alberto Miró Quesada on Peru, Arturo Arias on Guatemala, Lourdes Yero on Venezuela, Héctor Schmucler and others on Argentina, Néstor García Canclini and Patricia Safa on Mexico, and that of José Joa-

quín Brunner, Carlos Catalán, and Alicia Barrios, whose larger version I will comment on in the following pages.

4. This is a brief summary of a point I developed in the first chapter of my book *Las culturas populares en el capitalismo* (1989b).

5. The CADAC report on indigenous groups in Latin America indicates that in Chile a decade ago there were 616,500 Indians, most of them Mapuches (cf. the annex to Guillermo Bonfil Batalla 1981).

6. I refer here to research such as that of the Birmingham Center for Contemporary Cultural Studies (cf. Stuart Hall 1980); and the English and North American "cultural studies" on active audiences (cf. James Lull 1988). In Latin America, besides the aforementioned texts by Martín-Barbero, Gibaja, and Slemenson and Kratochwill, I refer to the study on cultural consumption in various Latin American cities being carried out by the CLACSO Working Group on Cultural Policies (cf. Sunkel 1999).

7. On the prospects for research on culture see the texts by José Joaquín Brunner (1987), José Jorge de Carvalho (1989), and Jesús Martín-Barbero (1987b).

Practices
Introduction by Abril Trigo

THE 1990S: PRACTICES AND POLEMICS
WITHIN LATIN AMERICAN CULTURAL STUDIES

Over the backdrop of the cognitive constellations developed in the 1980s, the 1990s staged the blooming and the subsequent implosion of the field. However, due to a combination of factors, the front stage of Latin American cultural studies shifted from Latin America to the United States, with apparent theoretical, methodological, and geopolitical repercussions. Among these factors, we should recall the effects of globalization on the academic market, the shifts and the expansion of U.S. Latin Americanism, and the crisis of U.S. area studies. The induction of academic circuits into the logic of the market economy, with its commodification of fashion-theories and academic stars, finally reached the peripheral field of Latin Americanism, even if as an offshoot of predominant global trends. The expansion of the Spanish language market, alongside an unprecedented migration of Latin American academics to the United States during the 1970s and 1980s led to a dramatic growth of Latin American programs. Latin American studies, which had promoted, in the framework of Cold War area studies, the functionalist ideology of developmentalism, simply became obsolete with the fall of the Berlin Wall and the final shift from international geopolitics to transnational globalization. However, while promoting the instrumental knowledge of Latin America, Latin American studies had bolstered also a generation of progressive, anti-imperialist U.S. Latin Americanists, who were gradually torn between feelings of solidarity and superiority toward their object of study. Disenchanted with leftist politics and deprived of ideological ground, they had to recycle themselves in order to defend their institutional spaces, which were jeopardized by the neoliberal restructuring of universities.

Under these circumstances, the frantic search for a new critical paradigm led to the demystification of old epistemological categories, such as dependency theory, which were shaken by the shift from structuralism to poststructuralism, empirical fieldwork to discourse analysis, social sciences to humanities, interpretation to theory, and literary to cultural studies. This in turn nurtured an intense theoretical exchange between opposite tendencies vying for hegemony in the emergent field. The ensuing cross-fertilization produced high levels of theoretical oversaturation and deconstructive hypertrophy, which resulted in the partial obfuscation of the object of study, the flattening of the social materiality to its discursive texture, and the consequent emasculation of critical acuteness. It also boosted fragmentation and atomization, notwithstanding the multiple regroupings. All this made of Latin American cultural studies a versatile and dynamic field, traversed by multiple faults and constant disputes, to the point of installing an unfortunate divide between Latin American and U.S.-based scholars on Latin America. So, while Latin American cultural studies became erroneously identified with U.S. new Latin Americanism and its more trendy and presumably radical tendencies, the divide obscured the existence of a vast and vigorous production of Latin American cultural studies which, following other theoretical paths, had continued, directly or indirectly, the rocky road of Latin American critical thought.

The Revolt of the "Post"

Four main theoretical trends emerged and dominated Latin American cultural studies in the United States in the early 1990s: subaltern studies, deconstructionist discourse analysis, postcolonialism, and transnational cultural studies with an emphasis on multiculturalism and the effects of globalization. Despite notable differences between their respective theoretical foci and political agendas, modus operandi and range of diffusion, they all share a similar concern with the question of social subjects and the detection of new forms of political and cultural agency; they also depart from a critical assessment of the historical role of the nation-state as well as any form of disciplinary knowledge. These issues, ultimately stemming from their common poststructuralist and postmodernist background, materialized in the re-enhancement of the leading role of intellectuals and theoretical radicalism, and in the hailing of alternative subjects, whose epistemological and political advantage would lie on being located outside or beyond society or the nation (the subaltern, the hybrid, the marginal, the new social movements). Although both postcolonialism and deconstruction had a widespread effect on the field, theirs was a sort of diffuse, ubiquitous influence, eclectically integrated into other approaches. Deconstruction, in fact, would merge with Nelly Richard's cultural criticism, a blend of feminism and deconstruction firmly located in Latin American turf. Meanwhile, subaltern studies and transnational cultural studies, due to the militant strategy of the Latin American Subaltern Studies Group and the transnational scope of the project for the Inter-American Cultural Studies Network, behaved as catalysts of antagonism and temporary coalitions that would ultimately yield important debates.

The most ambitious enterprise of transnational cultural studies, a tendency related to the work of some Latin American cultural studies' founders, like Franco, Sarlo, and García Canclini, is the Inter-American Cultural Studies Network. The project, directed by George Yúdice, aimed to adjust the field to the logics of globalization and redefine it as cultural studies of the Americas, an "uneven transnational space of inquiry and intervention. . . . 'The Americas'—a single but incredibly complex fractal structure (re)emerging in global politics in the wake of current economic, social, and cultural reorganizations" (Inter-American Cultural Studies Network). The project's cornerstone would be CULTNET, an electronic network of scholars, artists, and activists throughout the Americas, which would serve as a forum and a clearinghouse for research and the promotion of collaborative work, anchored in four regional centers: the Universidade Federal do Rio de Janeiro (Brazil), the Center for Cultural Studies at GSUC-CUNY (New York), the Universidad Autónoma Metropolitana-Iztapalapa (Mexico), and CLACSO (Argentina). The collective produced a significant body of work, most notably the book *On Edge*, and the following conferences: "Comparative Cultural Studies" (Iztapalapa, Mexico, 1993), "Supranational Formations and the Cultural Contradictions of Globalization" (Bellagio, Italy, 1994), and "Cultural Transformations in an Age of Global Restructuring" (Rio de Janeiro, Brazil, 1994), funded by the Rockefeller Foundation. However, the project's most remarkable feature was its aim to redefine Latin American cultural studies beyond the parochial horizons of U.S. academia, and to establish some sort of institutional brokerage between U.S. cultural studies, practiced predominantly within the humanities with an emphasis on textual analysis, and cultural studies in Latin America, more definitely empirical and socially concerned due to their liaisons to the social sciences and punctual politics, in order to encourage cross-fertilization across supranational scenarios. The study of the political implications of economic and cultural relations between ethnic minorities or indigenous peoples' organizations and global institutions, and the transnational networks of brokerage and intermediation both at the global-local and the local-local levels, is the main focus of Yúdice's and Daniel Mato's research. Not only are voracious national and transnational economic and political forces avidly seeking to gain control over these peoples' territories, resources, and knowledge, but also a variety of alternative organizations, including progressive NGOs from the "developed" world are imposing their systems of representations and values upon indigenous peoples, thus distorting their lives in various ways. Mato's study on power and culture thus aims to unravel the institutional networks of cultural power while paying attention to other practices of cultural and political intervention acting locally, such as ethnic and feminist movements, human rights organizations, alternative art and music, street theater, or comics (see Mato's essay in this part).

Devised in response to the effects of globalization, transnational cultural studies focus on the passage from national modernity to global modernization, the emergence of social movements, transnational NGOs, and civil society as new axes of sociocultural action, and the transformations in popular culture and the culture industry, three areas of inquiry that draw together the circulation of commodities, media, migrants, and technologies between "the Americas," thus validating new global and/or border identities (Latinos, gays and lesbians, for instance). They intersect, in that sense, with García Canclini's nodal concepts of hybrid cultures and cultural reconversion, and relate political culture and cultural policies to the notions of civil society, citizenship, and democracy. In this scenario, civil society would disengage from geopolitical identifications and destabilize narratives of national identity, sovereignty, and citizenship, thus promoting the fragmented emergence of minor social subjectivities based upon ethnicity, gender, age, or territoriality.

The question is to what extent is it possible to formulate a global project that respects, while building upon, regional specificities; whether it is possible to accommodate global, national, and local interests and to avoid, in a hemispheric project, the dominance of the United States. These are probably insurmountable issues, due to the global and postnational scope of transnational cultural studies, in spite of their explicit denunciation of pan-Americanism (Yúdice 1992, vii). How could the extrapolation to Latin America of methodologies and cultural policies used in the metropolis, such as identity politics and multiculturalism, be not prevented, overshadowing other, more pressing issues? The three areas of interest singled out by transnational cultural studies, notwithstanding their unequivocal relevance for Latin America, reveal distinctly U.S. social problems and political solutions. Thus, the skepticism raised by this agenda among Latin American intellectuals, who, as Yúdice himself states, are suspicious of "a de-centered centrality which attempts to re-legitimize itself in a global context appealing to alterities, marginalities, subalternities, with the participation of postcolonial intellectuals from its own academic apparatuses of production of knowledge" (1994, 44–45).

Nevertheless, transnational cultural studies encompass the inquiry into globalization of several Latin American scholars, such as José Joaquín Brunner, Néstor García Canclini, Martín Hopenhayn, and Renato Ortiz. Their reflections, triggered by the neoliberal economic reforms of the 1980s and their sociopolitical sequels, and inflected by the social sciences, still carry echoes of dependency theory, although they have evolved from earlier debates on postmodernism and democratization, particularly in the Southern Cone. Brunner, for instance, who as a member of FLACSO (Latin American Foundation for the Social Sciences) elaborated a sophisticated theoretical analysis on the role of the market, the media, and the new patterns of cultural consumption in the uneven (heterogeneous) modernization of more or less traditional societies (as in *Un espejo trizado*, 1988), progressively became an advocate of globalization by default. In *Globalización cultural y posmodernidad* (1998), Brunner's liberal pragmatism grants him the necessary flexibility to rationalize the supposed inevitability and ultimate convenience of globalization while conceding that it reaches new heights in capitalist creative destructiveness, and that postmodernism, a byproduct of the pervasive transnational culture industry, amounts to the zeitgeist of global capitalism, which reproduces national social inequalities on a global scale.

García Canclini's most substantive work since *Culturas híbridas* (1989a) also has been devoted to the study of globalization in Latin America. In *Consumidores y ciudadanos* (1995a) he takes on the idea, current in U.S. cultural studies, that identity and citizenship are realized in the act of consumption. Upon this redefinition of the citizen qua consumer, García Canclini argues for a more fair distribution of material and symbolic resources, for a different kind of cultural globalization, and for a reexamination of nationhood as "an interpretive community of consumers" (50). He vindicates civil society as the site of public interest and the state as guarantor and intermediary in the formulation of cultural policies protecting national, regional, and local production, and proposes the creation of a Latin American common cultural market. In *La globalización imaginada* (1999b) García Canclini delves into the ideological forms adopted by globalization, which according to him is neither a scientific, economic, political, nor cultural paradigm, nor the only road to development, but a complex centripetal/centrifugal process in which the expansion of capital and media promotes the unification of markets, the integration of peoples, and the homogenization of minds around a global imaginary, while operating as a stratifying, marginalizing, and fragmenting machine, which perpetuates and multiplies inequality and exclusion.

This dual nature of globalization constitutes the core of Martín Hopenhayn's *Ni apocalípticos ni integrados* (1994), whose main hypothesis is that globalization reproduces, in an expanded way, the instrumental reason of modernity and the logic of capital, to the point of creating a paradoxical "disintegrating integration," characterized by an increasing asynchrony between the slow or even regressive pace of socioeconomic integration (capacity of consumption and living standard) and the accelerated integration at the ideological level (desired and symbolic consumption). This, in turn, produces two strata of people: the globally integrated, who experience postmodern life under the sign of a provisionary effect, and the marginally excluded, who experience it under the sign of a precariousness effect. Although both effects are ruled by discontinuity and contingency, unpredictability and vertigo, velocity and mutability, they bear opposite meaning: what gives joy to some gives anguish to others.

Similarly, Renato Ortiz exposes in *Mundialização e cultura* (1994) the existence of a pseudo-egalitarian ideology, which promotes outright individualism and capital flexibility as democratic values. Globalization, a totalizing system based upon the de-centering of production and the monopoly of distribution, whose strategy resides in homogenization and segmentation, standardization and fragmentation, becomes the only way to be modern, cosmopolitan, and universal. Ortiz's most arguable contribution is his distinction between globalization, which refers to economics and technology, and worldlization, which names a new civilization best represented by a high tech, sophisticated cosmopolitanism enjoyed by a transnational corporate and academic elite, and a global pop culture produced by the transnational culture industry for mass consumption. Ortiz's classification, which has obvious roots in the distinction between (material) civilization and (spiritual) culture stemming from German philosophical idealism and classical sociology, contradicts his own arguments against the autonomy between the cultural and social spheres. This means that despite its forceful critique of the perverse effects of globalization, Ortiz's strategy of disentangling cultural globalization from economic globalization could end up mystifying the latter, insofar as global pop culture—which should not be reduced to sheer Americanism—and the cosmopolitan global imaginary—an ideology of sorts for these cynical postmodern times (Sloterdijk 1987)—sustain and reproduce the logic of capital.

While studies on globalization aim toward a broader methodological range based upon their more direct inspiration in the social sciences and the founding cognitive constellations (e.g., mass media and culture, cultural hybridity, or modernity/postmodernity), cultural criticism, postcolonialism, and subaltern studies directly stem from different strands of postmodern literary criticism. This explains their emphasis on textual and discourse analysis, their staunch reaction against literature, understood as a discipline devoted to the construction of canonical national imaginaries, and their obsessive denial of modern aesthetics, which ultimately reveals a sort of residual modernism in reverse. All this materialized in the craze for *testimonio* and the prominence obtained by *I, Rigoberta Menchú* in the polemics around the literary canon that shook English and comparative literature programs at U.S. universities during the 1980s. *Testimonio* provided many U.S. Latin Americanists with the exact ammunition of an anti-literary literary genre, albeit duly canonized by Casa de las Américas's literary awards since 1970, in order to circumvent modernist aesthetics, Western teleology, and modern metanarratives, while preserving the privileged status of the text and, accordingly, their own jeopardized political and intellectual hegemonic position. As Georg Gugelberger summarizes, "*Testimonio* has been the salvational dream of a declining cultural left in hegemonic countries" (1996, 7). In fact, *testimonio* was an effective weapon against U.S. academic literary institutions, which allowed subaltern studies to argue for a radical turn "from an epistemology and politics of representation to one of solidarity" (Beverley 1996b, 220), and for studies on globalization to ascertain it as the practical manifestation of an "aesthetics of community-building, of solidarity" upon which the marginalized "wage their struggle for hegemony in the public sphere" (Yúdice 1996, 57 and 53). What provides *testimonio* with this political and epistemological counter-hegemonic potential is its dual status as a truthful account of sociohistorical events (its ethical value and epistemological veracity) and as a literary artifact (its aesthetic value and narrative verisimilitude). In spite of the problematic ambiguity of this dual status, detected early on by several critics (Sklodowska 1996,

97; Sommer 1996, 132), *testimonios*—paraliterary or nonliterary texts that long predate their critical recognition—became *testimonio*—an antiliterary literary genre—by the suspension of their literariness while being construed as a literary icon. This iconization implied the epistemological fetishization of the text as the ground of unmediated truth, and the consequent political fetishization of the poetics of solidarity that enabled the critic to identify with the testimonial subject. The literary canonization of *testimonio* ended up depoliticizing it, by converting its sociopolitical vigor in academic aura, whose final goal was to legitimize the metropolitan academic's locus of enunciation. *Testimonio* offered an extraordinary alibi for the left metropolitan Latin Americanist to bypass the mediation of local (Latin American) intellectuals in order to establish direct political alliances with the ultimate subaltern subject (natives, Indians, women, civil society), and by doing so, reinstate his metropolitan position in a devalued and de-centered field. *Testimonio* was the Real for those metropolitan academics in search of their vanishing other, in complete disregard of the real epistemological, political, or literary status of testimonial writing in Latin America. But, as much as *testimonios* existed long before the enshrining of *testimonio*, densely associated with journalism, the chronicle, and political activism, they will continue to play a part in Latin American cultural reality, despite the downfall of the "international solidarity networks." The fashion of *testimonio* provided U.S. left Latin Americanists facing the global ideological defeat of socialism, the institutional vacuum left by the obsolescence of Latin American studies, and the methodological crisis of modernist literary criticism with an object and an alibi upon which to reinvent themselves.

The Struggle Toward a Hegemonic Paradigm

On the wave of *testimonio* and deeply influenced by the political defeat of Central American revolutionary movements, the Latin American Subaltern Studies Group was founded by John Beverley, Ileana Rodríguez, and José Rabasa, among others, introducing itself in its "Founding Statement" as "one aspect, albeit a crucial one, of the larger emergent field of Latin American cultural studies" (1993, 116). Yet, the LASSG basically transposed the theoretical and methodological tenets developed by its South Asian homologue to the study of Latin America, in particular the elusive concept of subalternity, its ambiguous status as subject/object of study, and the methodology of reading "against the grain" in order to bring the subaltern to light from "the seams of the previously articulated sociocultural and administrative practices and epistemologies" (119).

The aporia of subaltern studies lies in its own definition of subalternity, a relational category flatly constructed as the opposite of sheer domination, without framing it into specific, historically constituted hegemonic formations. As a result, although John Beverley insists that it is a purely strategic device, an ontological category without ontological ground (1999, 32), the subaltern has been criticized as a dubious category, insofar as it is not the subject of (subjected to) a hegemonic formation but a leftover in the margins or the rifts of the nation-state, whose identity depends, nevertheless, on the negation of the formation from which she or he is excluded (Beverley and Sanders 1997, 243). Such ahistorical indeterminacy of subalternity and the Manichaean "center-periphery duality," which founded the subalternist's politics of solidarity, has prompted Gareth Williams to observe its "implicit essentialization," and Mabel Moraña to consider it "an all-encompassing, essentializing, and homogenizing category through which it is intended to embrace all . . . social sectors . . . subordinated to the discourses and the praxis of power" (G. Williams 1996, 237; see Moraña in "Positions and Polemics"). These critiques derive not only from the fact that the subaltern is deprived of sociopolitical agency, but that she or he only acquires it through the solitary recognition of the enlightened intellectual and only then: "The subaltern is subaltern because it can't be registered adequately in academic culture" (Beverley and Sanders 1997, 243).

And this is the contentious core of subalternism and its more important contribution: the questioning of modern conceptions of cultural agency, political representation, and the crucial role of intellectuals; more concretely, of how to represent the Latin American subaltern without fetishizing or exploiting it. In order to do so, subaltern studies proposes the self-sacrificing of its ability to represent the subaltern in an attempt to restore her or his capacity to self-representation. However, this desire carries a fundamental contradiction, inasmuch as the subaltern's voice can be restituted only through the subalternist's self-erasure, which implies that the subaltern's mere existence depends on the Latin Americanist's whim. Read against the grain, this strategy of self-erasure amounts to a neomodernist "disciplinary fantasy" of metropolitan intellectuals, whose aim to present the subaltern or postcolonial subject conceals the underlying desire to represent themselves as transparent non-agents and reassert the hegemonic position of the metropolitan intellectual: "Latinamericanist enjoyment of subaltern restitution through self-destitution paradoxically maintains the centralized site of the intellectual in the processes of restoring the subaltern to historical agency" (Beverley and Sanders 1997, 241; G. Williams 1996, 240 and 243). Or, as

Moraña rebukes, it manifests the ways in which left Latin Americanism rebuilds "its agenda, its historical mission, and its lettered centrality, looking to define a new 'otherness' in order to pass—'from outside and from above'—from representation to representativeness" (see Moraña in "Position and /Polemics"). Beverley's later move to salvage the strategy by linking it to liberation theology's preferential option for the poor while distancing it from cultural studies' "academic costumbrismo" and ideological complicity in producing a "postmodernist sublime" in line with globalization seems like a desperate maneuver (1996b, 220; see Beverley in part 4, "Positions and Polemics").

The Zapatista uprising in Chiapas provides a faultless model for subalternist analysis. Its simultaneously premodern and postmodern, nationalist and anti-statist, anti-global and internationalist features allow José Rabasa to argue that the emergence of Zapatista historical agency emanates from the indigenous people's self-awareness of their subaltern condition, thus shaping a new ethics, a new politics, and a new epistemology based upon their radical alterity: "The possibility of their call for justice, liberty, and democracy resides paradoxically in the impossibility of being understood" (see Rabasa in "Practices"). Upon this line of argument, Rabasa formulates a critique of Gramsci's notion of the subaltern as agency-less and portrays Zapatismo as an example of Antonio Negri's constituent power of the multitude as well as an experiment into new forms of commonality and toward a new internationalism.

This kind of critical analysis makes of subaltern studies one of the most forceful ideological interventions and paradigm candidates to have developed from the crisis of legitimacy within Latin Americanism (Beverley 1999, 5; Beverley and Sanders 1997, 237), and explains its function as an organizational magnet and epistemological catalyst during the 1990s. Meanwhile, the diffused character of postcolonialism and deconstructionism, in conjunction with misgivings about their relevancy regarding the Latin American scene, made them prone to the interpellation of subaltern studies. Its translation of postmodern assumptions to the periphery and its deconstructionist rereading of anticolonial political thinkers made of postcolonial studies an attractive framework for U.S. Latin Americanists trying to overcome the contestation of postmodern postulates coming from Latin America. However, both postcolonialism and deconstructionism were strongly criticized, particularly in regard to their dismissal of historically dense categories such as anticolonialism and neocolonialism, imperialism and periphery; their implicit rebuttal of Latin American historical experience of modernity; their explicit repudiation of the nation-state and the national literatures at the core of Latin

American history; and the consequent erasure of such history, partly due to postcolonial ahistoricism and partly to the extrapolation to Latin America of the decolonization patterns of the Commonwealth countries, which never experienced the protracted process of neocolonialism that has shaped the history of Latin America for the last two hundred years (De la Campa 1996 and 1999). All these criticisms necessarily led to the search for a Latin American version of postcolonial studies.

Although he eventually distanced himself from subaltern studies, whose postmodern bent relegates Latin American colonial experience to a secondary plane, Walter Mignolo was temporarily attracted by subaltern studies' intent to give voice to the voiceless. He also criticized subaltern studies' disregard for the contribution of Latin American thought to the study of colonialism, postcolonialism, and the subaltern, and for the influence of Gramscian ideas on the Latin American left, as "another example of [its] colonizing bent" (Mignolo 2000, 195). Originally interested in the production of colonial semiosis, and primarily concerned with the colonial burden of Latin American modernity, Mignolo nonetheless underlined his disagreement with postcolonialism, in particular with its Eurocentric ascertainment of modernity's foundational moment. While postcolonial studies, after Western postmodernism, establishes modernity's origins in the Enlightenment, Mignolo, following Enrique Dussel, Fernández Retamar, and other Latin American thinkers, finds it in the sixteenth century and the turning point of the conquest of America, with obvious epistemological and political implications (63). In line with Fernando Coronil, for whom occidentalism is the condition of possibility of Edward Said's notion of orientalism (Coronil 1996), Mignolo found an older version of postcolonialism in a 1976 article by Fernández Retamar, who, following the philosopher Leopoldo Zea, coined *occidentalism* as synonym of capitalist Western civilization, consequently proposing the term *postoccidentalism* to refer to the ideology "which makes possible the absolute comprehension, the absolute overcoming of the Occident," that is, Marxism-Leninism, anticolonialism, and anti-imperialism, all embodied in the Cuban Revolution (Retamar 1976, 52). Mignolo does not condone this limited interpretation, but deems that if postcolonialism embraces the decolonizing discourses in the Commonwealth, postoccidentalism would be the term that designates the intellectual decolonization moved forward by Latin American thinkers since the early nineteenth century in order to overcome occidentalism, the civilizing project of colonization of the Americas that began in the sixteenth century and continued uninterruptedly through neocolonial avatars until the present globalization (Mignolo 1998c, 144 and 152). Middle East postorientalism, Commonwealth postcolonialism, and Latin American postoccidentalism would all be part of the wider problematic of "coloniality of power," a term he borrows from Aníbal Quijano's sociology and Enrique Dussel's and Rodolfo Kusch's philosophy of liberation, in order to grasp such diverse and complex historical processes. Coloniality of power is intimately linked to historical-structural dependency, which explains the geo-economic, political, and cultural insertion of Latin America into the capitalist system of the modern world. Postoccidentalism, thus, is a critical discourse that discloses the colonial side of the modern world system and gives continuity, in a renewed form, to the critical labor of Latin American grand theories, such as dependency theory, liberation theology, and the theories of neocolonialism and internal colonialism.

It is in the conflictive intersection of local histories and cultures enacting civilizing global designs where Mignolo finds room for "border gnosis," a knowledge conceived from a subaltern perspective "somewhere else" in the exteriority of the modern/colonial world system, a barbarian theorizing for the future based upon colonial difference and community values whose paramount example would be Gloria Anzaldúa's "new *mestiza* consciousness" and Subcomandante Marcos's "double translation": a "*thinking from dichotomous concepts rather than ordering the world in dichotomies*" (Mignolo 2000, 85). The same search for a politico-epistemological vantage point beyond totalities and before essentialization drives Alberto Moreiras's brand of deconstruction analysis, "critical thought," to elaborate the notions, advanced early on by Silviano Santiago (1973) and much later by Homi Bhabha and other postcolonialists, of the "in-between." This is a "third space" between the national literatures, a *criollo* construct of internal colonialism being the first space and the metropolitan traveler theories being the second (Moreiras 1999a, 42ff). Since the globalization of flexible capitalism has weakened the nonetheless relational categories of center and periphery—argues Moreiras following Ernesto Laclau—first world countries have become dystopian, ahistorical spaces dominated by the intensity of commodity enjoyment. Lacking any center against which to articulate antagonism in order to build a counter-hegemonic popular bloc, in the centers proliferate innumerable forms of democratic struggles. In the heterogeneous peripheral countries, however, the conflictive coexistence of diverse modes of production and the awareness of an exterior center still make it possible to resist commodity fetishism and the reification of social relations, and to articulate hegemonic formations around the modern category of the "people." Paradoxically, says Moreiras, while metropolitan intellectuals long for a utopian center against which to develop antagonism—the source of historicity still effective in the periphery—intellectuals in the periphery, increasingly devoured by globalization and the concealment of its centers, desire to dispose of antagonism and their peripheral condition. In consequence, says Moreiras, neither the periphery nor the metropolis can be considered privileged loci of resistance; only from intermediate or vestibular collectivities would it be possible to grasp simultaneously transnational homogenization and practical heterogeneity, and to produce a "tenuous epistemology" capable of deconstructing the ontological hypostases of Latin American otherness, identity, and nationalities (Moreiras 1995). This intermediate location of Latin America as a third space neither metropolitan nor really peripheral is expressed in the anti-ontological literature of the continent, as represented by Jorge Luis Borges, José Lezama Lima, or Julio Cortázar, a literature which resists the cultural mimesis of metropolitan models as much as the adscription to any sort of regionalist modernization by working on the impossibility to affirm either its absolute exteriority or its absolute interiority to any structure of meaning (Moreiras 1999a, 85). Although it has been denounced as elitist, the writing of this intellectual avant-garde, located between the metropolitan and the peripheral, deconstructs populist discourses that by privileging a transcendental subject cannot truly represent subalternity without hypostasizing it.

This ideological spin drove deconstruction analysis toward subalternism, which Moreiras celebrated as "a new paradigm for Latin American cultural studies," as "the inescapable horizon of Latinamericanism," and as "the most coherent response so far to the neoliberal state" (1996a, 877–79). But this same ideological spin, by avowing that the subalternist aporia of representing the nonrepresentable is not a limitation but, on the contrary, "the basis of its mere possibility to produce knowledge" (876), took the notion of the subaltern as exterior and incommensurable to any hegemonic formation to its limits, ultimately contributing to the revision and reconversion of the subalternist agenda by Beverley and the redrawing of differences between deconstruction, postoccidentalism, and subaltern studies. At the core of these differences lies the fundamental political issue of the "arbitrary closure" and, although not always explicit, the theoretically unsolved meaning of hegemony. The entrapment of strategic sutures and the epistemological hypostasis of modernity is what Moreiras criticizes of postoccidentalism and border thinking via Kusch and Dussel, in the understanding that they only reproduce the Latin American historiographic tradition conceived in terms of identity and difference, authenticity and mimesis (1999a, 47–48). To this criticism, Mignolo responded with a further elaboration of the locus of enunciation upon the Aymaran term *utcaha* ("to be here" or "to be at home") proposed by Kusch as an alternative to Heidegger's *Dasein*, and Bernardo Canal Feijóo's reflection on Latin American schizoid identity. He transformed Canal Feijóo's nostalgia for not being where one is *(no ser donde se está)* into the celebration of "not being able to be where one is" and its consequent "I am where I think," which ambiguously oscillates from telluric nativism to the privileging of discursive practices (Mignolo 2000, 334).

And here lies the core of the criticism raised against those branches of Latin Americanism which, according to Román de la Campa, share a common postmodern legacy he brands *episthetics*, "that uncertain interplay between epistemology and aesthetics, from which criticism turns into a writing, and language metaphors translate into an immanent sense or rhetorical praxis and agency" (1999, vii). The reliance on episthetics and its privileging of discursive flows over social materiality nurtured the dismissal of more sociologically or anthropologically inspired methodologies as vulgar empiricism, and the staunch condemnation of the nation-state as well as any other form of regional or continental identity and their corresponding literatures as an errant quest for an always deferred and already differed autonomy, authenticity, and modernity in the melancholic remembrance of a foundational lack. According to this version, the truly original sin of Latin America is to have broken its colonial ties with Europe, as the philosopher Héctor A. Murena (1958) put it long ago. By some sort of reversed re-essentialization, Latin American identity becomes the impossibility of having an identity; Latin American sociohistorical complexity is thinned down to a uniform and monolithic national populist state, the supreme realization of the *criollo* elites; Latin American national literatures and cultures are condemned as hegemonic devices at the service of the populist state and a mimicking modernity. In sum, Latin America would be no more than an object of study and an ideological construal (see Moreiras in "Positions and Polemics"). This reductionist interpretation, argues de la Campa, leads also to the demonizing of Latin American critical thought, past and recent, in disregard of tendencies and nuances, contexts and circumstances, historical conditions and geocultural loci. According to this ahistorical and ultimately metaphysical ontologizing, his criticism goes, the entirety of Latin American modern history is scorned as a disposable experience and a cultural vacuum; therefore decolonization would only be possible by deconstructing the colonial logic that permeates Latin American failed history and aborted modernity, from which only certain literature and art would be worth recovering as some sort of "postmodern sublime" (see de la Campa's essay in this part). This paradoxically modernist privileging of discourse and aesthetics as the site of political and epistemological transgression, present under various guises and in different degrees in postmodern, postcolonial, and subaltern critics, has the purpose of legitimizing the privileged status of the intellectual's floating condition, as de la Campa intends to demonstrate in his comparison between Antonio Benítez Rojo's and Edouard Glissant's opposing critical strategies regarding Caribbean cultures (de la Campa 1996, 2000, and his essay in this part).

A peculiar variant of episthetic analysis is provided, from Latin America, by Nelly Richard's cultural criticism, whose main tenets are the political edge of aesthetics, the epistemological vantage of marginal art and literature, and their critical and meta-critical state of alertness. These features coalesce in the notion of the residual, which "connotes the ways in which the secondary and non-integrated is capable of displacing the act of signification toward the least favored margins of the cultural and social set of values, in order to question their discursive hierarchies from lateral positions and hybrid decenterings" (1998a, 11), and the trope of metaphor, which perforates the flatness of mass-media products with the detritus of modernization and transforms social residues into literary surplus. This neo-avant-gardist stance, posited in dialogue with the more disciplined and empirical discourse of the social sciences (and concretely that of José Joaquín Brunner) and in direct confrontation with the postdictatorial consensual politics in Chile, reveals once again not only the local overdetermination of critical discourses, but also the realization of theory into practice. The antidisciplinary, anti-academic, and antisystematic penchant of cultural criticism should materialize, in a practical and meta-critical way, in the manufacture of critical discourse itself. Thus, Richard propounds a return to the pleasure of the text and the productivity of writing, a critical writing "midway between the essay, deconstruction analysis, and theoretical criticism, mixing all these different genres to examine the intersections between social discourses, cultural symbolizations, power formations, and the construction of subjectivities" (1998a, 143). In other words, cultural criticism is proposed as a theoretical and practical political intervention in the field of culture, whose immediate objective is to activate the reader's suspicion regarding reality, to excite her or his critical imagination about the fissures in the real, and to take sides with anti-hegemonic significations.

It is important to recall, however, that despite its obvious poststructural sources, Richard's cultural criticism has been deconstructing since early on the very tenets of postmodern discourse, questioning whether it implements an actual de-centering of discursive subjects and institutions or whether it is no more than a rhetorical scheme, thus preserving the metropolitan—now postmodern—authority, a device of exclusion, a neo-imperial strategy of naming the other while denying the other the right to name itself, thus reproducing Latin America's old historical dilemma. She also denounced the postmodern strategy of appropriating the peripheral marginality and the historical eccentricity of Latin American cultures as a source of exotic and radical alterity in a renewed form of metropolitan hegemony (1987, 1989b, 1993). In consequence, Richard warned, postmodernism cannot be simply transposed to the Latin American milieu because, traversed by unevenness and underdevelopment, it differs radically from the postmodern context of post-industrial societies. The central question is: How could postmodernism's denial of originals help Latin America to overcome its condition as a pallid copy of the occidental original? Richard rejects the thesis about a Latin American postmodernism avant-la-lettre, posed by Brunner (1988, 216) and others, as an ontological relapse in reverse, according to which Latin American inauthenticity would prove to be its truest authenticity. She responds, on the contrary, with a parodic strategy, "exaggerating the copy as a self-parodying vocation, pasting over cosmetically my lack of identity-property with the devise of disguise, the allure of the borrowed or stolen, the ornamentality of the artificial" (Richard 1993, 158).

Fracturing and Implosion of the Field

The global thrust of these four tendencies—transnational cultural studies, subaltern studies, postcolonialism and postoccidentalism, and deconstructionist discourse analysis—which reached its climax in the congresses of ABRALIC (Rio de Janeiro, Brazil, 1996) and LASA (Guadalajara, Mexico, 1997), activated a chain reaction in Latin America, where many intellectuals immersed in their national and regional problematics perceived them as a new form of neocolonial intrusion and deployed, as a defensive mechanism, a fallacious dichotomy between literary criticism and cultural studies, thus inadvertently concealing and displacing the ultimate issues behind the geopolitical divide. It was a quite understandable reaction, given not only the troubled history of U.S.-Latin American relations, but also the combined effects of economic and cultural globalization, particularly with regard to the consolidation of a transnational market of academic knowledge, controlled by a network of conferences, publishers, and foundations, and ruled by the commodification of knowledge as fashion-ideas, media-style marketing, and the celebration of academic stars. Intermingled with U.S. new Latin Americanism and equated to British and U.S. cultural studies, all forms of Latin American cultural studies were flatly condemned by both sides, in the customary exercise of sweeping generalizations, in disregard of their many substantial differences. A case in point, and the most far-reaching criticism to date, is Carlos Reynoso's *Apogeo y decadencia de los estudios culturales* (2000), a meticulous condemnation of Anglo-Saxon cultural studies from an anthropological point of view that only tangentially touches on Latin American cultural studies. This criticism of Latin American cultural studies by many of its own practitioners, who are trying to distance themselves from the consumer populism and sloppy methodologies associated with the label "cultural studies," is, in fact, a constant in the field, represented in this book by Neil Larsen's contribution, as well as punctual allusions in the articles by García Canclini, Moraña, Moreiras, Cornejo Polar, and others.

From different angles and with distinct emphasis, Nelly Richard, Hugo Achugar, and Beatriz Sarlo denounced what was perceived as a new technology of knowledge on Latin America produced from the apparatuses of the U.S. academy. Feeling displaced from their respective national spaces of politico-cultural interlocution and passed over by the Latin American intellectual circuits, they adopted a defensive stance, denouncing the inequality in the transnational distribution of theoretical labor, the reification of Latin America as object of study, and the banality of a critical production less concerned with the pursuit of knowledge than with the seizing of power. From a neo-Frankfurt school position, Sarlo defended the role that national literatures, history, and language had in the configuration of republican civil education for modern and democratic societies; she also vindicated the theory and practice of the political and ideological foundations of aesthetic and literary values during the 1960s, in direct opposition to the transnational pop culture that came along with the neoliberal policies introduced by the military regimes during the 1970s. In this context, the shift from literary to cultural studies would represent, on the one hand, the recycling of critics facing the dislodgment of the reading-sphere by the video-sphere, a shifting that would arguably restore the social dimension lost in traditional literary criticism, but at the cost of the specificity of literary and linguistic practices, the historically dense social formation of aesthetic values, and the genuine cultural heritage of a people (Sarlo 1997b). It would represent also, on the other hand, the reduction of Latin American literatures and cultures to an anthropological object of study, in disregard of their history as public sites of social creativity and political struggle (Sarlo 1999). The debate of modern values would then have a dual political significance.

It is probably Achugar who has pronounced the most dramatic censure of U.S. Latin Americanism from a Latin American perspective. He scourges postmodern, postcolonial, and subaltern studies' neglect of Latin American intellectual history and tradition, and the establishment of a new geopolitical division of intellectual labor through the hegemonic use of the English language; he also criticizes transnational cultural studies' cultural brokerage and border theory's epitomizing of U.S. Latinos as the quintessence of Latin America, both ideas dangerously bordering a neo-pan-Americanism. He looks for inspiration in José Martí's "our Americanism" by asserting Latin American national and regional cultural capital and historical memories, still nurturing the emotion of the many "little motherlands" in the midst of the "great motherland" (Achugar 1997). He insists on the specificity of the peripheral locus of enunciation and the strategic value of local epistemologies, since the categories center/periphery, supposedly dismissed by postmodern decentering, are still operational: "We speak from a space configured by utopia. . . . We speak from the Latin American periphery . . . we speak from the periphery of those who bet on utopia; and we speak from Latin American discursiveness, which is another form of periphery. We speak therefore from a contaminated space" (Achugar 1998, 83). In his article included in this section, he reclaims the practice of what he calls, following Fernández Retamar's Calibanism, "theoretical babbling," in response to the division of critical labor mentioned above and the dismissal of Latin American critical thinking as un- or pre-theoretical. He thus reclaims the Latin American essay tradition as the textual ground of a locally produced theoretical thinking, although he asks himself how pertinent "theoretical babbling" is as a category of analysis, understood as a non-hegemonic "theoretical thought," or if it runs the risk of being appropriated, once again, as sheer barbarism. Achugar parodies those who abrogate for themselves an authority that is solely produced by rhetorical strategies during the act of enunciation, in a cyclical reproduction of the Prospero/Caliban divide, but then he falls into some sort of inverse reification to sustain the idea that while the periphery is a problematic locus of enunciation, the metropolis is not, thus feeding his adversaries' allegations regarding his "neo-Arielism." This difference obviously would grant to the periphery a privileged epistemological status, since everything therein produced would have a surplus of meaning, a position paradoxically similar to subalternism, postcolonialism, and deconstructionism, and with firm roots within Latin American thought.

A similar position is undertaken by Moraña, who denounces the promotion of a metropolitan agenda via the transnational academic market by a self-declared ideological vanguard (see Moraña in part 4, "Positions and Polemics"), and by Richard, who formulates a sophisticated condemnation of Latin Americanism, a device of academic knowledge of the "academic international" about Latin America, which is merely its "object of study [and] field of experience." Richard's critique rotates around the institution of an asymmetrical division of intellectual labor according to which U.S. Latin Americanism monopolizes the production of representational and theoretical knowledge over the material, experiential reality of Latin America. Hence, Latin America becomes "the primary (unmediated) source of action and imagination, of struggle and resistance . . . that supplies the metropolitan intellectuality its *plus* of popular living experiences which translates into solidary struggle, political commitment, and testimonial denouncement" (see Richard in part 4, "Positions and Polemics"). The fetishization of Latin America as a privileged epistemological locus and ethical reservoir implies its correlative containment as a pre-logical time-space, "a pre-theoretical or sub-theoretical state of consciousness" that reproduces and reaffirms, surreptitiously, the uncontested authority of a presumably de-centered center, thus keeping Latin Americans marginalized "from the battles over the metropolitan codes that decree and sanction the meaning of Latin America" (Richard 1997).

Richard admits that it is no longer possible to elaborate a theory about Latin America independently from the metropolitan conceptual fabric, insofar as the very categories of alterity, marginality, or subalternity, so central to Latin American thought, have been monopolized by U.S. Latin Americanism, even though such elaboration would carry the seal of the metropolitan academia, which explains why many Latin Americans frequently resent "cultural studies" as a globalizing metadiscourse. Instead of this explicative knowledge on Latin America, tied to the normative industrialization of papers within the academic disciplines, Richard proposes the interrogative and metacritical intervention of cultural criticism, shaped through a playful and creative, connotative and self-reflexive text, "midway between the essay, deconstructive analysis, and theoretical criticism . . . in order to examine the intersections between social discourses, cultural symbolizations, power formations, and subject constructions" (1998a, 143 and 357). She vindicates, like Achugar, the essay form, not as the bearer of Latin American critical thinking, but because of its aesthetic, anti-functionalist productivity, embodied in metaphorical thickness and intensive expressiveness. It is precisely in this emphasis on experience over representation, as expressed in the essay form, where the historical specificity of concrete localities that make "Latin American 'difference' a *differentiating* difference," is best captured (Richard 1997, 347).

These criticisms generated an immediate response from the U.S. camp. Richard, due perhaps to her postmodern affinities, her staunch criticism of social science's empiricism, and her disavowal of the Latin American critical tradition, was embraced as a strategic ally. Sarlo's nostalgia for the modern public sphere, national identity, and state politics, was deplored as a residual national populism, and her attempt to salvage literary-aesthetic values, jeopardized by market-driven global pop culture, was disparaged as the neoconservative discomfort of a liberal intellectual whose hermeneutic authority was challenged by mass media. A similar critique was held against Achugar and Moraña, whose resistance to postmodern, subaltern, and postcolonial approaches was deemed a culturalist and neo-Arielist entrenchment in the Latin American national literary traditions, in a reenactment of the conservative *criollo*-bourgeois nationalisms of the early twentieth century (Beverley 1999, 110–11; Moreiras 1999b). This resistance to radical theories, the argument goes, would be symptomatic of the Latin American intellectual's subaltern and colonial condition, which they would sublimate by reasserting the authority of the continental literary tradition, whose heritage they claim for themselves. Moreover, the vindication of national and regional identities would reproduce the historical structures of ethnic, social, and gender exclusion and subordination so characteristic of the Latin American nation-states (Beverley 1999, 18).

And here, in the completely opposite conception of the role of the nation-state, both historically and under current globalization in Latin America, lies the core of the argument. For postmodern, subaltern, and postcolonial theories, any recourse to traditional or national values is tantamount to a relapse into metaphysical, essentialist thinking, and location does not guarantee any critical position, so as Moreiras puts it, "the real difference between a radicalized, and therefore subalternist, Latin American cultural studies and what I will call a tendential neo-Arielism . . . has to do with the difference between state thinking and . . . a thinking of the 'interregnum,' " a propriety discourse and a locational thinking of expropriation (1999b, 133–34; 1997). According to this interpretation, large segments of Latin American cultural studies merely re-

produce anachronistic culturalist categories, circumscribed to the determination, evaluation, and defense of what is "properly" Latin American,
thus lacking any critical value (Moreiras, in part 4). Evidently, this strategy of epistemological maximalism of postmodern, subaltern, and postcolonial studies is only possible in connection to a wider reaction against
the nation-state and the notions of class and national identity, insofar as,
according to postmodern formulas, they embody modern forms of disciplining and discrimination inadequate to confront the challenges posed
by globalization. Because they crown both the modernist cultural edifice
and the ideological apparatus of the nation-state, national literatures are
also berated as a primordial site of hegemonic symbolic power. This explains the pretense of postmodern, subaltern, and postcolonial studies
to theoretical radicalism as the sole guarantee of epistemological autonomy (Beverley and Sanders 1997, 245), and their reliance on metaphors
ascertaining social agency beyond the margins of society and outside political hegemony, such as subalternity, nomadism, deterritorialization,
third space, space-in-between, border thinking, and so on.

The Return of the Repressed

Today, after a decade of crisscrossed hyper-theorization and intense ideological struggle, the cognitive constellations that monopolized the stage
in the 1990s show signs of uncertainty and fatigue. The period that began
with hybridization theory in 1989 and the subsequent outburst of the
"post," which officially started around 1993 with the launching of the
Inter-American Cultural Studies Network and the Latin American Subaltern Studies Group, reaching its climax in the confrontations at
ABRALIC 1996 and LASA 1997, has apparently come to an end. Under this
critical period of expansion, revision, demolition, and renewal, which
culminated the gradual loss of innocence that began with the critical pessimism of the 1980s, Latin American cultural studies reached a high level
of theoretical sophistication, critical sharpness, and methodological
flexibility, no longer enclosed in rigid disciplinary boundaries and now
more alert to epistemological traps and ideological constructs. However,
the meetings at LASA 2001 in Washington made official the breakup of
fragile alliances as well as the exhaustion of some theoretical positions;
its dramatic climax was the announcement of the disbanding of the Latin
American Subaltern Studies Group. The exhaustion of those particular
theoretical positions was posited by some, like Beverley and Moreiras, as
the exhaustion of Latin American cultural studies *tout court*, whose final
demise was triumphantly declared. This is particularly so in Moreiras's

verdict of the "exhaustion of difference," which makes of Latin American cultural studies a radical practice, suggesting that the only remaining option of any real resistance to globalization would be the critical mourning of the ruins (2001). Latin American cultural studies and any other form of political resistance are disposed of in a single blow. In our view, exactly the opposite is true. These events culminated a gradual process of readjustment of the different positions and a steady return to the vilified classics of Latin American critical thought, particularly the fecund production of the 1960s and 1970s, including dependency theory, liberation theology and philosophy of liberation, the pedagogy of the oppressed, the theories of internal colonialism, third cinema, collective theater, and transculturation. The cycle, which started with the optimistic drive of the forerunners in the 1970s, has closed upon itself.

There are many indications of this return. Taking different routes, most of the theoretical positions attempted a step backward, which reveals, even more than the exhaustion of these positions and the passing of fashions, the tenacious persistence of certain problematics embedded in the cognitive constellations of the 1960s, 1970s, and 1980s. Studies on globalization have revolved, again and again, around issues related to the stretching of the nation between global and local poles, the ongoing question of modernity and modernization, the status of the popular under the impact of transnational mass culture, and the constant reformulation of identities subjected to new forms of material and symbolic neocolonialism. With a generally pragmatic and accommodating approach, which has earned them criticism from more radical positions, they have tried to devise alternative strategies to the overwhelming spread of neoliberalism and its devastating effects, economically, socially, politically, and culturally (see García Canclini and Martín-Barbero in part 2, "Foundations"; Mato, Ortiz, and Yúdice in this part). Postoccidentalism is a clear attempt to articulate the cutting edge of postcolonial studies with the cultural memory of Latin American critical thinking, and to reinscribe, within the context of globalization but from a larger historical perspective, Latin American theories specifically designed in the 1960s as anticolonial and anti-imperialist tools for national and social emancipation (see Mignolo in part 2, "Foundations"). Meanwhile, cultural criticism cannibalizes postmodern thinking by adapting it to local conditions, the same way that Latin American critics have historically handled Western thought. Its emphasis on the local or national conditions of the possibility of thinking, on the productive tension between critical and aesthetic writing, which materializes in the essay form, and on its denunciation of metropolitan duplicitous statutes of knowledge leads to a demand for critical vigilance and a strategic suture from which to construct a "differentiating difference," in terms very similar to Stuart Hall's call for an "arbitrary closure," in the understanding that if knowledge is open, politics is impossible without some sort of strategic suture (Hall 1992, 278; see Richard 1997, 356). Finally, there is the dramatic turn of subaltern studies concerning the nation-state and the struggle for hegemony and national identity, now considered indispensable tools against globalization. Accordingly, "to construct the people/power bloc antagonism today, under the conditions of globalization . . . requires, by contrast, a *relegitimization* of the state. That is, the project of the left, to the extent that it embodies subaltern will and agency, has to be posed paradoxically as a *defense* of the nation-state, rather than as something that is 'against' or 'beyond' the nation-state" (Beverley 1999, 153). This is a complete reversal of subaltern studies' theoretical and political stance, in part forced upon subalternism by the deconstructionist wing of subaltern studies themselves. Deconstructionists stretched subaltern studies' central concept of subalternity, based upon the irrepresentability of the subaltern, inasmuch as she or he is always exterior to any hegemonic formation, to its very limits, and rejected any form of strategic suture as a mere disabling of the subaltern absolute epistemological negativity. In this manner, deconstructionists took the subalternist project to its logical consequences: the blind alley of post-hegemony and postpolitics as the ultimate radicalization (Moreiras 1996a). Cornered by its own aporias, subalternism reacted with a radical return to the very positions against which it had built its identity. This internal polemic—personal differences besides—led to the dissolution of the Latin American Subaltern Studies Group.

But if the cautious return to the precursory cognitive constellations of the 1960s and 1970s in postmodern, postcolonial, and subaltern studies indicates their relevance for the 2000s, their resilience is further demonstrated by the work of most Latin American cultural studies practitioners, who, on the sidelines of transient polemics and struggles, keep returning to and reflecting upon the core problematic embedded in them. This is the case of Kraniauskas's revisitation of major cognitive constellations through the lens of a critique of the political economy of culture. While Rama's transculturation records a process of capitalist development and cultural democratization and Cornejo Polar's heterogeneity registers a sort of "transculturation from below," given the historical absence of capital accumulation, strong civil societies, and national markets, García Canclini's hybridity points out that modernity in Latin America has been politically (rather than economically) driven, which explains why the nation-state has prevailed up to now over the market. Cultural hybridity, as best exemplified in the U.S.-Mexican border, would be the most distinctive Latin Americanist and postcolonial contribution to cultural studies, as a critique of the ideology of progress and the "time of capital." Kraniauskas foregrounds, in his essay, the theoretical and critical interlocutors kept on the side of but always underlying the most recent debates.

Continuing Practices

The theoretical debates that shaped the intellectual climate of the 1990s and are fully displayed in the "Polemics" part of this book have influenced most of the scholars directly or indirectly involved in the study of Latin American cultures and societies; these scholars continue their work in a particular disciplinary field and are inspired by a definite methodological perspective, yet their work is still infused with the inter- or transdisciplinary ingenuity that has historically nurtured Latin American cultural studies. This is precisely what the following part, "Practices," intends to illustrate.

From a different angle and in the steps of Rolena Adorno, Mary Louise Pratt, Maureen Ahern, and Regina Harrison, Irene Silverblatt studies the ambiguous socioeconomic status of Indian women belonging to the Inca aristocracy under colonial rule in Peru, and how their peculiar situation sheds light on the conflicts between Incan and Spanish cultures and on the inner contradictions of the colonial system as well. The combination of historical, anthropological, and feminist observations allows Silverblatt to produce a suggestive picture of the sociocultural dynamics of everyday life in colonial Peru, equally attentive to ethnic, class, and genre contradictions. Although the most boisterous forms of U.S. and French feminism have not prospered in Latin America, where they many times have been deemed a bourgeois and metropolitan phenomenon and where women's demands have been integrated into a wider sociopolitical agenda (Kaminsky 1997; Castillo 1997; Masiello 1996), feminism has stamped a solid though diffused imprint on Latin American cultural studies. Beatriz González's squarely Foucauldian reading of the configuration of citizenship through the disciplining of bodies and the exclusion of manners as effected in constitutional projects, grammars, and behavior manuals in nineteenth-century Venezuela injects historiography and textual analysis with a women's studies point of view. González's work, which shows clear affinities with Julio Ramos's research and Angel Rama's La ciudad letrada (1984c), investigates and questions primarily the

construction of a national identity in relation to processes of modernization and nation building. These same topics of nation and modernity
seen through a feminist glass, though with reference to twentieth-
century Mexican film and Southern Cone best-sellers, are the focus of
Ana López's and Francine Masiello's essays. López, gathering dispersed
critical notions from Monsiváis's extensive corpus, the latest on film theory and feminist criticism, and figments of Jean Franco's and Martín Barbero's cultural mappings, elaborates a sophisticated analysis of Mexican
film melodrama of the 1940s and 1950s as the cultural hinge where religion, nationalism, and modernization were processed, and social, family, and sexual identities were negotiated. Masiello, in turn, offers a poli-
faceted analysis of the construction of gender and the literary market,
female bodies and fiction, national identities and the libidinal economy
of globalization. Concretely, she studies how the best-seller, selling a
singular and unique fiction that delves into the exotic, generates feelings
of universality, supplements market needs and desires through the representation of gender, and creates the illusion of a worldwide democracy of
consumers capable of enjoying everywhere the same stories and literary
styles. By selling the identity of difference, the best-seller sells the illusion of uniqueness, singularity, and the capability of the consumer to
choose and be different; it fulfills the peremptory need to belong to the
global modern community.

  The same concern about the disputed field of the popular and the culture industry and their imbrication to the national and transnational
spheres is expressed in Gustavo Remedi's and Eduardo Archetti's contributions. Both authors use a personally involved ethnographic methodology in order to unravel the shaping of social imaginaries in local everyday
life. Remedi portrays the collective experience of illegal community radios in post-dictatorial Uruguay as an alternative way of cultural production to the globalization of culture, based upon the autonomous work of
small production units at the scale of the neighborhood and the city, and
the horizontal practice of citizenship and youth's participatory politics at
the heart of communicative networks parallel to the party political system. Archetti, meanwhile, investigates the role played by sports magazines in the construction of a popular and phallocentric soccer imaginary that contributed to the nationalization of immigrants and the
modernization of society in early-twentieth-century Argentina, and how
that imaginary is still thriving many decades later. The analysis of the urban modernization of Buenos Aires in the 1930s as the theatricalization
and ideological embodiment of a mythical past and a predestined utopia
is the topic of the essay by Graciela Silvestri and Adrián Gorelik. The pur-

pose of the authorities reacting to the uncontrollable expansion of the city, due to population growth and land speculation, was not only to contain urban sprawl and provide modern services, but also to construct a historical memory—a civic memory—for a predominantly immigrant city population. In the process, they decided to leave the development of the city to the market forces and concentrate instead on the cultural foundation and theatricalization of the city's memory, the debate about the city's obscure foundations, and the controversy between different aesthetic and architectonic schools all vying to capture the forgotten identity of the city, finally symbolized in spectacular landmarks.

The negotiation of memories and identities in the contact zones between U.S. and Latin American cultures is, precisely, what connects such dissimilar articles as Juan Flores's meditation on the Latino imaginary, and Debra A. Castillo, María Gudelia Rangel Gómez, and Armando Rosas Solís's ethnography of sex transactions at the border. Part of a larger project on prostitution in Tijuana that goes back to 1988, this essay studies the heavily racialized and exoticized transactions between Mexican prostitutes and their U.S. clients as told in the women's narratives, and in the travelogues, recommendations, and sociocultural tips posted by U.S. clients in specific Web sites, many times with the acquiescence of the prostitutes themselves, who not only take professional advantage of their unintended fame, but exert a paradoxical form of power over their virtual community of fans. Despite being more expensive than in most U.S. cities, Tijuana's sexual scene is preferred by U.S. customers, who find there certain exoticism and human connectedness that hint at the complexity of the prostitute-client relationship at the social, political, and cultural borderlands, where not only sex, race, culture, and economics are transnationally exchanged, but identities as well, through complex symbolic transactions in which subject and object positions are constantly, ambiguously shifting. From the other side of the border, Flores, meanwhile, questions the fabrication of a "Latino community" whose existence is established on the basis of demographics, either for political or for economic reasons—as a potential electorate or an emergent, homogeneous consumer market. Nevertheless, Flores sustains, there is a Latino imaginary on the make, built from the often contradictory lived experiences and historical memories of the many diverse national groups, which refer to the familiar landscapes, life-ways, and social struggles left back in Latin America, indispensable in negotiating the adaptation of immigrants to the U.S. milieu. For this reason, Latino identity cannot be thought as the negation of the non-Latino, but as the affirmation of memories and desires, deeply embedded in the Latino experience of diaspora and sociocultural awakening.

These essays, read as a corpus, demonstrate the constant and cyclical, explicit or implicit revisiting of the major cognitive constellations to have shaped the field of Latin American cultural studies, to the extent that the salient sociopolitical issues that have haunted Latin American societies throughout history remain unsolved. This is precisely the message of Cornejo Polar's almost posthumous piece, a cautionary call to prudence and vigilance with which we chose to close our selection. Is it, perhaps, pure coincidence that Angel Rama's farewell lecture at the University of Maryland was entitled "El amor por la lengua española"? After the theoretical frenzy of the 1990s, unintelligible without the explorations of the 1970s and the breakthroughs of the 1980s, the study of the literatures and cultures of Latin America would never be the same, and still, it will ever be what it has always already been.

IRENE SILVERBLATT
Political Disfranchisement

The *corregidores* [magistrates], priests, and *encomenderos*[1] . . .
take from women and their daughters, who should legitimately
govern, the rights they had since the time of the Incas, dispossessing them of their titles in order to favor rich Indian men.
—*Felipe Guamán Poma de Ayala (1956, 2:92)*

Irene Silverblatt was born in the United States. An anthropologist, she is a professor at Duke University in Durham, N.C. Her main titles include *Moon, Sun, and Witches: Gender Ideologies and Class in Inca and Colonial Peru* (1987), and *Honor, Sex, and Civilizing Missions in the Making of Seventeenth-Century Peru* (1994).

I n the years just after the Conquest, the Spanish debated incorporating
members of the Inca elite into colonial government. Final Spanish
policy was against this plan and dictated the complete dismantlement
of the power structure headed by the Cuzco nobility (Kubler 1963, 341–
47). However, once Spanish control became entrenched in the Andes, colonial authorities still faced the problem of how to govern (and profit
from) the native peasantry. The pre-Hispanic *ayllus*[2] were very dispersed,
thus impeding the collection of tribute as well as the indoctrination of
indios into the new imperial religion. The Spanish, moreover, were sensitive to the dangers that the *ayllus* might pose to their regime if allowed to
function as they had before the Conquest. The pre-Hispanic *ayllu* would
keep indigenous traditions alive, and the colonists were quite aware that
this might threaten the success of their enterprise. For these reasons, native peoples were forced in the mid-sixteenth century to regroup into nu-
cleated settlements called *reducciones*[3] (Roel 1970, 94). Colonial administrators had to elaborate a plan that would hitch indigenous peasantries

to Spain's political and economic machinery. The Spanish model of political control modified the existing politico-economic traditions of indigenous commoners to fit the needs of the colonial enterprise. A system of indirect rule was imposed: the colonial authorities recognized *curacas* (chief, headmen) as leaders of their respective communities (the colonial *ayllus*), while also installing political and religious institutions for local government which were patterned after those of Spain (Kubler 1963, 341–47).

The *Curaca*'s New Role

Curacas became the designated intermediaries between the worlds of the conquered caste and their masters. They, like the Inca elite, were granted a colonial social status equivalent to that of the European nobility. Consequently, they were relieved of tribute obligations and had the privilege of maintaining private estates. These privileges, however, were given with obligations attached. In exchange for the benefits of noble rank, *curacas* were expected to ensure that the colonial demands on the peasantry were met. The *curaca* was responsible for collecting tribute and taxes, organizing and selecting workers for colonial labor drafts, collecting the goods and salary owed the parish priest, the tithes owed the Catholic Church, and the construction and upkeep of the village church (Spalding 1974, 37).[4]

Owing to their position in the colonial politico-economic structure, and their consequent alliance with Spanish authorities, *curacas* could take personal advantage of the new channels for mobility and the new sources of wealth introduced by Spain. Often they did so to the detriment of the communities they were supposed to represent and protect. To the extent that the *curacas*' authority was derived from the external colonial power structure, they could disregard Andean norms of reciprocity and mutual obligation which had customarily mediated the relation between local headmen and *ayllu* members (Spalding 1974, 1970, 1973). The deterioration of these traditions, which also flavored pre-Hispanic gender relations, had consequences for the relations that were to emerge between *curacas* and peasant women.

We have seen how colonial village headmen participated in the economic exploitation of these women. Guamán Poma accused the *curacas* of exploiting the labor of women under their jurisdiction as well as abusing them sexually. Pérez Bocanegra forewarned priests in his confession manual for curates having native parishioners that some *curacas* illegally charged women tribute and forced them into concubinage (Pérez Bocanegra 1631, 269 and 271). Taking advantage of the new means at their disposal, *curacas* deprived women of their rights to land (ADC: AUP, Protocolos 1–2; ACC op. 8, Leg. 2).[5] Another ploy used by the *curacas*, who increasingly began to participate in the colonial mercantile economy, was to convert lands under their control to monoculture for the internal Peruvian market. *Curacas*, abusing their function as official spokesmen for their communities, in effect became *hacendados*.[6] In this process, the female members of their *ayllus* were often most vulnerable to losing water rights as well as land. In 1737, community members of San Pedro de Tacna brought suit against their *curaca* for illegally expropriating their lands. They claimed he was forcing them off communal property to facilitate the creation of a private producing estate. In testimony, witness after witness remarked that the *curaca*'s primary target was peasant women (BN C3967).

The Colonial Erosion of Women's Power

Although the Spanish formalized the *curaca*'s role as intermediary between Spanish society and the indigenous peasantry, they were not faithful to the pre-Hispanic structures, which allowed women as well as men to occupy positions of *ayllu* leadership. Theoretically, the colonial regime sanctioned pre-Conquest mechanisms through which *curacazgos*[7] were transmitted (Rostworowski 1961). In practice, though, colonial administrators did not recognize the pre-Columbian hierarchies of authority, which delegated important governing and political functions to women. Nor were they sensitive to other matrilineal patterns of succession to positions of local leadership. As a consequence, the opportunities women once had to exercise authority in the *ayllu* were undermined, as the traditional mechanisms determining their selection gave way to Spanish customs.

One of the clearest examples of this process comes from Peru's northern coast. Here pre-Columbian patterns of succession were eroded very early in the colonial period (Rostworowski 1961). The first Spaniards to arrive in Peru wrote that women, known as *capullanas*,[8] governed the North Coast ethnic groups of Peru (Anonymous 1906, 160). It seems most probable that *capullanas* succeeded to office matrilineally. For when Francisca Canapaynina, a descendant of the coastal nobility, laid claims to the *curacazgo* of Nariguala, she amassed testimony to prove that, before the Spanish conquest, women could rule. However, by 1613, testimonies are already shady regarding how women came to power. Some witnesses, backing Doña Francisca's contention, asserted in very general terms that "women could hold office like men." Others, again her supporters, also affirmed that women could rule; but they employed a different argument. By tradition, they said, a female descendant could succeed to office if a *curaca* left no male heir (Rostworowski 1961, 29). Thus, by 1613 Doña Francisca's supporters were, in effect, citing Spanish inheritance patterns to justify the legitimacy of their claim. The pre-Columbian structures were already losing their force.

Moreover, by 1625, Doña Francisca was no longer named as the *curaca* of Nariguala. Rather, her husband, Don Juan Temoche, was registered as "*curaca* and governor" of this *ayllu* (Rostworowski 1961, 29). In other words, Temoche had begun to exercise control of the *curacazgo* which originally belonged to his wife; as a married woman, Doña Francisca could no longer autonomously govern her *ayllu*. Indigenous traditions were collapsing in ways which prejudiced women's long-standing prerogative to assume positions of independent authority.

The case of Doña Francisca was not an isolated one. In the Cuzco region, as well, Spanish legal constraints and traditions impinged on the ability of native women to hold power autonomously in their *ayllus*. Although women were recorded as being the *curacas* of several *ayllus* in the Cuzco Valley, one must be aware that by the eighteenth century (the period for which I have documentary evidence) their rights to office were based on Spanish customs of succession. Women succeeded to *curacazgos* if their fathers had left no male heir. Furthermore, once married, their right to govern autonomously was compromised.

Such was the history of Doña Martina de la Paz Chiguantupa, the *cacica*[9] of the Indian commoners from Collquepata, in what is today Paucartambo Province. Her father's sole legitimate heir, she became *cacica* upon his death. Doña Martina wanted to name a woman, Doña María Juárez, as her second-in-command, or *segunda persona*, who would be responsible for the collection of tribute. But she could not give this authority to María Juárez directly, for the constraints of Spanish law dictated that, as a married woman, Doña María could exercise this post only through the tutelage of her husband (ADC: AZ, Escribano A. Chacón y Becena, Proto. 260–147).

This history repeats itself in Yucay. Doña Isidora Días was registered as the *cacica* of one of Yucay's *ayllus* (Paca) in 1770. In 1778, Melchor Haller de Gamboa sued her husband, Don Felipe Tupayache, for distributing lands to an Indian commoner which Don Melchor claimed were his. Responding to Haller de Gamboa's suit, Doña Isidora indignantly asserted that she—not her husband—had given the peasants rights to communal lands, since she was still single at the time of this land distribution (ADC: AUP Siglo XVIII, Leg. 11–2). In subsequent notarial records, the *curaca* of Paca *ayllu* is registered as Don Felipe Tupayache (ADC: AUP, Leg. II, f. 102v). The imposition of Spanish traditions on indigenous patterns of succession denied native women the chance to fill positions of autonomous authority in their communities; once married, women lost their ability to hold local office as husbands "assumed" their *curacazgos*.

In the course of colonization, the erosion of pre-Columbian patterns of governance deeply prejudiced women's political potentialities. Both Doña Isidora and Doña Martina were *curacas* by virtue of Spanish inheritance patterns. The indigenous women who once would have held posts by virtue of Andean structures of gender parallelism no longer had the chance. Guamán Poma explains: "The *corregidores*, priests, and *encomenderos* . . . take from women and their daughters, who should legitimately govern, the rights they had since the time of the Incas, dispossessing them of their titles in order to favor rich Indian men" (Guamán Poma 1956, 2:92).

Peasant Women and the Loss of Political Legitimacy

In addition to legitimizing native *curacas* by incorporating them into the colonial establishment, the Spanish also introduced political and religious institutions for local government, modeled after the municipal organizations of Spain. The civil apparatus consisted of a *cabildo* (town council) and the annual election of an *alcalde* (mayor), a *regidor* (alderman), and *alguaciles* (constables). In the religious domain, the Spanish created a hierarchy of lay assistants to the parish priests: cantor, sacristan, and treasurer (*fiscal*). As Spalding has pointed out, there were advantages for natives who decided to assume these positions and ally themselves with the provincial representatives of Spanish authority: exemption from mita[10] service and dispensations from tribute (Spalding 1974, 73). Also, since the authority on which these offices rested lay with the colonial power structure, those holding office could to some degree disregard the customary norms regulating power and wealth in traditional Andean communities.

Like *curacas*, men in village government or in the service of the parish priest could, within limits, ignore pre-Columbian structures that molded social and political life in the *ayllu*. Backed by men of power in the Spanish religious and civil establishment, these native functionaries were able to disregard traditional Andean norms which constrained the activities of those who exercised authority in the *ayllu*. Outside the restrictions of traditional society, some men who assumed these positions in the colonial *ayllu* began to exploit the opportunities their offices offered. Often this exploitation took the form of abusing indigenous women in ways inadmissible by pre-Columbian standards. Guamán Poma repeatedly accused *ayllu* civil and religious functionaries of taking unfair advantage of their posts. In league with Spanish officials, they would exploit labor and rob now vulnerable women of their *ayllus* (Guamán Poma 1956, 2:61, 111, 112, 122, 124, 152, 153, 175, 191, 3:75). And male officials did much more than participate in the economic exploitation of peasant women, as lackeys of the Spaniards and *curacas* whom they served and imitated. As the norms and structures of Western society penetrated the colonial *ayllus*, men—the "owners" of their female kin and affines—manipulated native women in order to acquire these offices of relative advantage. Guamán Poma asks the question: "Some married Indian men voluntarily take their wives, others . . . their daughters, sisters, or nieces, to the parish priest, and deposit them in their kitchen. Why? Because in this way the priests make them mayor, treasurer, or sacristan; Indian men are now accustomed to receiving favors in this way" (Guamán Poma 1956, 2:194).

Thus, as traditional structures increasingly gave way to the pressures of colonial Spain, some indigenous men turned to these positions in local government and religious institutions as a way of easing the burdens colonial society placed on them. Betraying the norms of their ancestors, men used the women who were closest in order to take advantage of the benefits which the colonial power establishment dangled in front of them: ". . . After the priest had punished the aforementioned treasurer, he asked him for one of his daughters, telling him that she would be more honored by being the wife of a priest than of an Indian, a tribute-paying man; and furthermore he would support him publicly before his *curacas* and mayors . . . and he would give him wine to drink, bread, and meat . . . and moreover he would keep the office of community treasurer for the rest of his life" (Guamán Poma 1956, 2:161).

As traditional structures yielded to such pressures, those structures which were meant to form the backbone of political and religious organization in the colonial *ayllu* became increasingly illegitimate in the eyes of many native peasants. Only peasant women, though, were forced to bear the dual burden of sexual and economic exploitation, perpetrated by indigenous men who were supposed to be their representatives. Many women must have profoundly questioned the legitimacy of the institutions which allowed their male leaders to abuse them with impunity.

Nevertheless, this is only part of the story. At the same time, *ayllu* members struggled to shape the governmental structures imposed by the Spanish to fit their traditional concepts of political and religious life. The purpose of the Toledean laws was to undercut pre-Columbian practices; yet this aim was often thwarted as the *ayllus* remodeled and adapted Spanish forms to Andean modes of organization. The resilience of the colonial *ayllu* notwithstanding, women still found themselves in a disadvantaged position. All the formal posts imposed by the Spanish were reserved for men. Consequently, the municipal and lay offices of the Iberian Peninsula could be modified or reworked in terms of the masculine components of pre-Columbian politico-religious institutions. But the women's organizations so crucial to the life of the Andean *ayllu* before the Conquest could find no equivalent Spanish forms to legitimize their existence. Even though the community apparatus of government which the Spanish imposed was being transformed by many colonial *ayllus* in accord with pre-Columbian principles of politico-religious organization, the emerging synthesis did not favor the continuance of parallel authority structures controlled by women.

Although colonial society undermined the preservation of women's ritual organizations, in some communities women (and men) discovered ways to circumvent these pressures. Some women found means—often devious—to continue participating in the official structures of community government. The Jesuit priest Pérez Bocanegra describes the development of a process in which women who held native religious posts began to link their activities with Christian practices. Inadvertently, Pérez discovered that Indians would confess to native clerics—women as well as men—before confessing to their Catholic parish priest:

Let the priest who hears confession be forewarned that in this town of Andahuaylillas, and in other towns as well, some Indian men and women, who call themselves "elder brothers" and "elder sisters" [*hermanos mayores y hermanas mayores*], do certain things, and they are considered enlightened because of certain quipus[11] . . . which they bring with them to confess, which are like lists and memorandums of what to confess. For these Indians, particularly the Indian women, teach other women to confess by means of these knots and signs, which are multicolored, in order to classify sins and the number that were committed . . . in the following way. . . . Before a penitent Indian man or woman goes to confess to the priest, he [or she] has already confessed every sin to these Indian women and men, whether they be sins he has committed, or others that he never committed, . . . and to do this, these male and female confessors tie knots in their cords which are called *caitus*, and they are the sins which they were told, and they go adding and putting in their knots others which were never committed, ordering [the penitents] and teaching them to confess a sin, when it really is not a sin, and vice versa. And commonly the [elder brothers and sisters] tell them to make an infinite number of false declarations and confess what they never did . . . and I have brought this to light by my constant questioning . . . until they finally admit: "This is what the brothers and sisters told me to say" . . . according to these knots; and they call these general confessions . . . and thus they do not confess the sins they have committed, for they do not tell the father confessor about these sins, rather only those which these Indian men and women have shown them [on the knots]; and after confessing with the priest, they go and tell these Indians what the father told them and the penance he gave them, making fun of him, saying that he does not know how to interrogate the penitent or that he does not know their language. (1631, 111–13)

Thus, under the guise of Catholic ritual, indigenous priests—men and women—were carrying out an important rite of pre-Columbian Andean religious practice, the Andean confession. Recording the "sins" of their *ayllus* on *quipus*, the native clergy would then tell the penitent which "sins," selected from those of the entire community, to reveal to the Catholic priest. Pérez Bocanegra, of course, was appalled by many aspects of this deviance from Catholic orthodoxy. It was not only the fact that women could be confessors in native rites that horrified him. More important, concealing their "heretic" activities by sending people to confess to the Catholic clergy, native priests and priestesses were able to preserve the practice of indigenous rites—rites which embodied concepts of sin, guilt, and responsibility that were radically different from Catholic dogma. Pérez found to his dismay that Catholicism was treated as a farce by his indigenous constituency, who could wear the new religion like a cloak to conceal their idolatry and heresy.

Note that the confessional process which native priestesses headed still harbored pre-Columbian patterns of religious organization. Pérez was well aware that these heterodox confessions were structured by gender divisions: "the Indian women . . . teach other women to confess by means of these knots." Pérez Bocanegra's instruction manual was written to aid clerics in their campaign against Indians who dared to continue following the religious practices of their pagan ancestors. Consequently, elder brothers and elder sisters, the *hermanos* and *hermanas mayores*, were objects of the Catholic clergy's attack; to judge from Pérez's manual, the ensuing campaign was particularly harsh in its drive against women idolators (1631, 114).

In the sixteenth and seventeenth centuries, women found themselves doubly threatened. They were hounded by the [Catholic] Church as well as by indigenous governmental and religious authorities who allied themselves with the colonial regime. These local-level officials, their power derived from alliances with Spanish authorities, no longer felt bound by the mutual obligations and normative rules that governed traditional Andean social relations; they threatened and abused women in ways that were illegitimate under pre-Columbian social and moral codes. Moreover, the local political and religious institutions imposed by the Spanish denied women direct access to the official channels of authority regulating community life. Declared Lucía Suyo Carhua, accused by the extirpators of idolatry of being a sorceress and priestess of heresy, "Now, don't you see, the universe has turned inside-out; for we are being persecuted" (AAL: Leg. 2, Exp. XIV, f. 2v). In Spanish Lucía says, "*el tiempo está al revés*"; but, in Quechua, she would likely have used the word *pacha*, denoting both space and time (space-time). She is metaphorically expressing the collapse of the Andean social and physical order as well as the social mechanisms through which that order was maintained.

Notes

1. One that receives an *encomienda* (crown grant of tribute and labor rights over specific indigenous groups).
2. Extended family or social group with territorial base; community.
3. Colonial forced settlements of indigenous groups.
4. See Stern (1982) and Spalding (1984) for excellent local histories of native responses to colonialism.
5. Abbreviations of chronicles and documents: AAL, Archivo Arzobispal de Lima; ACC, Archivo Colonial de Ciencias; ADC, Archivo Departamental de Cuzco; AUP, Archivo Urubamba, Protocolos y Expedientes; AZ, Archivo Zembrano; BN, Biblioteca Nacional de Perú.
6. Owners of wool-producing estates or agricultural properties.
7. Position or office of *curaca*.
8. Woman who governed in *varayoq* system ("one who holds a staff of office"; sponsor in a local hierarchy of civil posts).
9. Female chief, headwoman.
10. Rotation; rotated, corvée labor.
11. Knotted strings; Andean mnemonic devices used to record information.

BEATRIZ GONZÁLEZ STEPHAN

On Citizenship: The Grammatology
of the Body-Politic

Beatriz González Stephan was born in Venezuela in 1952. A literary critic, she is a professor at Rice University in Houston, Texas. Her main titles include La historiografía literaria del liberalismo latinoamericano del siglo XIX (1985), and La duda del escorpión: La tradición heterodoxa en la narrativa latinoamericana (análisis sociológico de cinco modelos narrativos) (1992).

Perhaps the borderline situation caused by the postmodern and postcolonial debates allows us to visualize—and to question—the true foundational and expansive moments of knowledge and legality, undoubtedly entwined with the culture of the book, which validated a certain type of logocentric power as well as vertical functioning patterns. From another perspective, given by new experiences that imply the disintegration of many "strong" paradigms, it means standing outside the panoptic city model,[1] a project that is very dear to the modern liberal utopias, and disassembling the formidable State machinery from its most insignificant pieces, its apparently innocuous and innocent details, and the imperceptible gears of everyday life, which are nevertheless essential not only for its functioning, but also for the consolidation and reproduction of the power that supports it.

The intense study of national issues, citizenship, the relationship between public and private, the creation of an individual and a social body, and the validity of the democratic legal order only takes into account the cultural and historic—provisional—character of these categories, which have created those identities that are still recognized as national states. Knowing that we are living within the limits of "the law," or better yet, in a limited situation; feeling the expressive possibilities of body and language, and imagining similar and different others; feeling that we belong to a land whose existence seems to be verified in cartographic representations, and trusting that we ascribe to an order whose legitimacy lies in words; these are some of the many circumstances that the post-independent State—just to mention the Latin American case—has had to face and work out.

The new political space that opened with the new republics forced a careful reappraisal of the distribution and implementation of power mechanisms which, in view of the recent civil legal order, and due to the ideas brought about by the Enlightenment, had to be less punitive and overt than during the colonial period. The violence inflicted upon Indians, blacks, *mestizos*, slaves, Masons, native dissidents and emancipators, aborigines and runaways by governors and commissioners, members of the Holy Office, foremen and landowners is well known, as is making a public spectacle of tortures and broken limbs in the name of God and the king. We must not forget the unlimited rights of teachers, parents, and husbands to inflict physical punishment upon their disciples, children, and wives; the authority and the law were violently enforced through a systematic policy of physical punishment—public and domestic—where sores, scars, and even death were part of an interplay of mixed signals: guilt and power.

However, in other areas of social life, at least well into the nineteenth century, the intensity of passions prevailed, as did violence in games, family relationships, parties, carnivals, the theater, the treatment of servants, uninhibited sexuality, in body language, sensuality, wantonness, clamor, and laughter; in sum, it was a sensitivity that was not prone to restraint, qualified by modern culture as "barbarian," and identified with an archaic and shameful past as well as with incivility, unlawfulness, and guilt. The new illustrated citizens of the republic regarded violence in prisons and in punishments as an excess of "instincts," a "savagery" that needed to be tamed or preferably prevented by activating several control and subjection mechanisms that would oversee every detail of daily life, deploying a written system of "micropenalties" that would watch each movement, gesture, and word, thus economizing strength through their docility and utility.

In this sense, we can illustrate this new sensitivity with the polemics unraveled in Caracas in 1790, due to the creation of a "House of Mercy" to provide shelter to the growing number of foundlings. Project supporters argued that since this was a women's problem, it was more urgent to "correct their habits," that is, the function of the new house would be to reeducate them: "To guide those women who vilified an occupation which should honor them, putting them to spin, weave, work with cotton, and in other activities that could help support the household" (Langue 1994, 367). Violent punishment and unrestrained passions had to be redirected to build the *homo economicus*, as well as the domestic(ated) woman, subjects of the new bourgeois society, the required prototypes for the utopia of progress and modernization. The new direction of a free and explosive vitality within the republican legal order assumed a new relationship between power and a body founded on discipline, productivity, and hygiene.[2] Not in vain do national constitutions, catechisms, and books of manners insist that idleness is the source of all vices and that public vagrancy should be persecuted.

The founding project of the nation is to civilize, first by endowing the *written word* with the power to legalize and standardize practices and individuals whose identity is limited to the written space, second by organizing a multiplicitous, automatic, and anonymous *power* that controls individuals constantly and discreetly, making them citizens of the *polis* who are contained within an invisible web of laws, rules, and policing texts—the watching and the watched in a mutual complicity that contains possible transgressions. The written word would be the decisive civilizing activity upon which the power to tame savagery and the softening of customs would rest. Words (laws, norms, books, manuals, catechisms) would constrain passions and contain violence. This was the dichotomy between reality and words that made José Martí point out, in an early critical view of Latin American modernity at the end of the nineteenth century, that "a collision with a horse cannot be avoided with a decree by Hamilton," and that "the clotted Indian blood cannot be unplugged with a phrase by Sieyés."

Evidently, the nation emerges from a purely written reality reserved for a strict minority of lettered officials—the "lettered city," as coined by Angel Rama (1984c), giving rise to important investigations (Ramos 1989). Only in this way could the effect and the game of that "imagined community" (Anderson 1983) be achieved, which was thought to be similar to the circuit established by the printed culture, which pretends, for reasons that are far from being simple, to ignore the contradictions and the multicultural character of potential readers and of a global society. However, this does not mean that communities with a strong oral tradition do not have other rules for the cohesion of an imaginary group.

The liberal model of the nation basically follows the Western formula: a strong, centralized power in a State that "uses violence without war; instead of warriors, it uses policemen and wardens; it has no arms and has no need for them; it seizes immediately and magically, 'capturing' and 'combining,' thus avoiding combat." It captures and settles the work force as it creates corporations, workshops, factories, and as it also recruits a labor force among the indigent. It regulates all movements. It limits, distributes, classifies, and arranges hierarchically territories and individuals. It creates a unified and meaningful interior that faces a savage and irrational exterior. It puts an end to wandering bands and to nomadic behavior. It identifies history and books with its victory. [3]

The creation of the National State was a slow process that originated before the nineteenth century, where some social practices anticipated modalities of the future disciplinary and liberal society. In Venezuela, during the eighteenth century, the uprisings of slaves and *mestizos* and the increasingly unbearable situation of deviants, vagrants, and beggars led the economic elite to finance a variety of establishments—a correction house for *mestizos*, blacks, and particularly unruly slaves, a jail-hospice for white and *mestizo* women "with a dissolute life," and jails for Indians—to lock up, and in some cases, isolate a population whose "idleness" led to "crime" and to "terrible vices" (Langue 1994). Another example can be found during the same time when the colonel of engineers, Don Nicolás de Castro, founded in Caracas the Academy of Geometry and Fortification, which spurred a growing interest to institutionalize mathematics, topography, and algebra in the country's universities, an interest that is closely linked to the scientific development of cartography and to an aggressive border policy (González and Donis Ríos 1992). It is obvious that the creole elite also saw itself as the subjects of a new project as well, where the strategies of scientific knowledge—calculations and measurements—and the policies to re-educate labor would serve, on the one hand, to channel its hidden fears toward a population filled with "evil otherness," and, on the other, to formalize its historic right as members of a civilized society, as the beneficiaries of modern wealth, and to redirect violence toward the surplus value of capital.

Modern societies—or those trying to be so—wield power through a series of institutions (workshops, schools, correctional facilities, hospices, sanatoriums, jails) and discursive practices (constitutions, registries, census-taking, maps, grammars, dictionaries, behavior manuals, and hygiene guides) that form a set of "specialized technologies" and public order institutions that coerce, control, subject, and softly regulate the movement of bodies to make them tamed subjectivities—subjects of the State—and neutralize the dangers of de-centralized agents. They are known as "disciplines," and their power lies precisely on a written surveillance (Foucault 1988, 139–230).

Specifically, constitutions, grammars, and manuals (to mention only the paradigms) constitute a system of surveillance and orthopedics which seizes and immobilizes the citizen through its laws and rules. Here, the "power of words" not only shapes but also creates and holds the object it prescribes. In these cases, the identification between words/discipline/power and surveillance runs parallel to the creation of citizenship. Conversely, the prerequisite for an individual to be recognized as a citizen is that he can only exist within the framework of the disciplinary writings of the constitution.

The proliferation of these disciplinary writings in their many formats—from newspaper articles, to single leaflets, to brochures, to a book—spanned the whole nineteenth century, and became stronger toward its end when modernization was tangible in the already large Latin American cities, and the population density demanded a greater propagation of these texts as well as a more thorough surveillance. This does not mean that the violence of passions—the brazenness of body and language—was ruled immediately by the constitutions, grammars, and manuals created during the first decades. Rather, there was a tension and a struggle, not always comfortably resolved, between the universes postulated by the ruling words and the dynamics of reality. Nevertheless, it is a fact that the concepts of nation and citizenship were the idea of a minority, a project postulated to be expansive which could indeed include and domesticate different communities that offered resistance to difficult negotiations. The dual task (centripetal and centrifugal) of written disciplines—including constitutions—was to incorporate and shape social groups, as well as to expel those who could not adapt to the rules. Several times, the scholastic programs of the "enlightened" governments of the last third of the century ran parallel to the policies to exterminate Indians (Argentina and Mexico) or peasant nomads (the Canudos in Brazil). Also, the concern to rid the city of dogs, hogs, and stray animals gave rise to a more generalized plan: hospices and sanitariums served to lock up vagrants and delinquents since they lacked stable jobs (and thus properties and a permanent address), with the excuse of caring for the "mentally ill" and fostering the medical sciences. And in a very particular sense, literature often served as a disciplinary practice. On the one hand, peasant "delinquents" were legally recruited as labor for landowners and as soldiers for the army; landowners and the military were obvious disciplinary institutions that instrumented difference qua illegality in order to contain the "barbaric" masses within the law. On the other hand, the "*gaucho* literature" included the voice of the illegal peasant in the written culture, returning it "civilized" and hoping to integrate it to the disciplined body of the fatherland. Books and reading were the disciplinary exercises of the new legal order (Ludmer 1988).

Of all these heterogeneous sets of normative texts, I would like to underscore a specific group of constitutions, grammars, and behavior manuals, because they represent a particular modality of discipline and written surveillance. During the nineteenth century, there were hundreds of them in every Latin American country, and their accurate reproduction was usually part of their function and nature. To read one constitution or manual is to read them all. Therefore, to speed up the purpose of this essay, I am going to refer to the Venezuelan constitutions of the nineteenth century,[4] to the *Gramática de la lengua castellana destinada al uso de los americanos* (1847) by Andrés Bello, and to the *Manual de urbanidad y buenas maneras* (1853), also by a Venezuelan, Manuel Antonio Carreño. The Constitución Federal para los Estados de Venezuela, of 1811, is the first of the Hispanic world; Bello's *Gramática* and Carreño's *Manual* became standard books for proper language and for good manners. Therefore, it is unnecessary to mention the reasons for choosing them as examples of normative and disciplinary genres.[5]

The Subjective Police Body

Constitutions, grammars, and manuals are all forms of discourse that as laws, rules, and regulations not only prevent infractions or mistakes, punishment or guilt, but also form a subjective police body that is systematically assumed through constant use, a repression that is internalized in each individual. They pursue prevention rather than punishment. They move into the area of prohibition and systematic threat to instill in every individual an adequate dose of fear of possible exclusion or discrimination from the areas deemed legal by State authorities.

It can also be said that they are basically antonomastic writings because they constitute the core that gives rise to State laws (constitutions), national language (grammars), and citizenship (manuals). From their own perspective, each determines the subject's profile and requirements according to the needs of the new legal environment. They build the legal framework of the individual to be acknowledged as a subject, to be accepted as a subject of the "City of Letters," and as an agent of the reproductive and moral forces of the national project. At this level, the modern era made a strong commitment with a *written legal order*, whose policies to bind body and language were at the service of a new economy that was more socially profitable. The police writings—writings that guide the social movement of the polis—include ethically different areas: on the one hand, city, State, industry, progress; on the other, rural areas, *caudillos*, and land-estates. But the new order, the "police" order, not only puts these areas in opposition, it also discredits the second one: "After creating a society men relinquished the *unlimited and licentious freedom* which guided their passions and belonged to *the barbaric state*. The establishment of society assumes giving up these ill-fated rights, the acquisition of others, sweeter and more peaceful, and the subjection to certain mutual duties." Later, in the same Constitution of 1811, it says: "Property is the right that every one has to enjoy and use the goods acquired through work and industry" (Mariñas Otero 1965, 149–51).

Labeling rural society as "barbaric" automatically confers on the written law, and in turn, society/citizen/property, the quality of natural values. Evidently, controlling idleness and unrestraint also implied a new ethics where virtue lies in saving passions and wealth. The desire to accumulate goods needs to go through police writing, which models bodily and linguistic passions.

The Invention of Citizenship

Among other things, the legal-political function of constitutions, and to a certain extent of grammars and manuals as well, leads to the invention of citizenship, in the sense of creating an identity that had to be built as a homogeneous space so that governing it would be more viable. It is, according to Julio Ramos, who clearly establishes the relationship between language and the policies of purity within the new legal regime of the republic, "an identity that had to be built precisely upon the transformation of the population's 'barbaric' and undisciplined materials, mostly peasants and subalterns, who resisted the political and cultural centralization required by the nation" (1993b, 21).

The constitution of a symbolic space that identifies similar subjects, whether because they use a common language, or because their symmetrical bodies adjust to the same pattern, is among the conditions that will allow the establishment of a commercial order among the nation's regions, and their link to international trade. As railroads, telegraphs, and steamships drew lands and cities closer to each other, the new forms of communication demanded the standardization of bodies and languages.

One of the attractions of the modernizing project was the efficiency of rationality, which implied a standardizing or uniformizing strategy at all levels for the benefit of the National State. Although there are many complex factors exhibited in the creation of citizenship, one of the most critical is *grammar*, because as Andrés Bello said, it is one of the ethical, legal, and political instances with the greatest power of intervention to create citizenship and the founding discourse of the modern State. Standardizing language through compulsory education would eradicate not only "nasty habits," "defects," and "rude barbarisms" from "people with little instruction," but it would also prevent the proliferation of a "host of irregular, licentious, and barbaric dialects" in the Hispanic American continent "which block the diffusion of enlightenment, the execution of the law, the administration of the State, and the national unity."[6]

Evidently, Bello thought that grammar had a civilizing mission, because when linguistic norms are distributed regularly links between the several national regions are created, not only for commercial purposes, but also for the written law (the constitution) to be divulged and fulfilled unequivocally. Establishing language rules would allow, through a transparent code, the language of trade to be conditioned by legal language (Ramos 1993b). Written law therefore required linguistic stability for the proper enforcement of law.

Grammar, in its legal-political function, creates the conditions of enunciation of the new legal subject, as it provides the structural framework of the ethics of proper language. The relationship between language and citizenship assumes the disciplinary intervention of authority—teachers and heads of family—on the "vicious practices of popular language" in order to correct the "defective" language of the "populace" and to make them citizens who "can read and write" (Bello 1981, 121–31).[7] On the contrary, the constitution demands citizens to be competent in written language, and those citizens who are closest to the law of language (to grammar) will have the authority to write the laws. Thus, the power of grammar permeates constitutions and manuals as an overdetermining instance because it governs the language of the law and the rule of the bodies.

Public and Private Space

Constitutions, grammars, and manuals share, although not exclusively, the field of regulating the civil individual. Constitutions, just as the term suggests, are in and of themselves the constitution of the Great Law. Intrinsically, they are practically a self-reflexive discourse on the law, the impersonal authority of the State, the written word that is its own boundary, the voice that designs national spaces, territories, and subjects. In this sense, a constitution is the discourse that should intervene to delimit the public space of the new legal order. Its restrictions affect the social body of the motherland, where the vast territory is apprehended as a geographic body which must be delimited, studied, and divided so that it is controlled by the war machine. Constitutions model the great physical body of nationality, the macro-subject. We are Venezuelan or Paraguayan because that identity is linked to the land whose borders, always imaginary, are designed in writing.

By expressing the great disciplinary power, constitutions have the substance of patriarchal tradition. They serve the possibilities of the masculine subject—or better yet, of a particular masculine subject—as the single privileged agent of public life (of the State's administration, elections, education, morality, jobs, goods, and freedom of expression). From this perspective, we could say that if we follow the constitutions, the founding of nations is basically phallocentric, because, for example, citizenship is built upon *male* citizens, *male* senators, *male* teachers, *male* erudites, and fathers. Constitutions open a space—the public space—as an emergency zone for a particular masculine subject, who ends up legalizing rules and norms that will govern the invisible spheres. In general, the law does not rule the feminine subject; it excludes it from public life, that is, it is a *non*-citizen.[8]

Although constitutions rule public aspects and the official dimension of civil life, manuals will act upon the physical body of the individual, and particularly on the private and familiar spaces, with their countless behavioral and hygienic rules. The civilizing project of the modern State can only organize the public sphere, because it implements many small courts in all the nooks and crannies of daily life. The great legal machine—which remains outside—is divided into a varied disciplinal anthropology. Norms—which control even the slightest insinuation of body, sight, desires, any inopportune emotion or word—penetrate homes through the school and the press, and are installed with subtlety and perseverance, not only in the core of the family or the workplace, but also in the intimacy of the individual.[9]

The creation of citizenship, necessary for the new mercantile conditions, is heavily based upon disciplining the body and its passions, and upon distributing sexual roles from within the family. It is not by chance that in disciplinary texts the greater punitive stigmas fall upon women: the severe taming of her body and will is closely related to the property of her womb—the imbrications between family, property, and State—not only to guard an education that reproduces containment and docility in her children, but also to monitor the private estate. A "good housewife," besides being discreet—which is equivalent to going unnoticed—must be thrifty in two senses: with material goods and with the desires of her body.[10] The cost of making women into objects is inversely related to the increase of private wealth—the axis of the new liberal society—and of numerous male descendants, which will enlarge, in terms of the illustrated body, the demos of the republican State.

And grammars, as we previously mentioned, will level out in one code the language of the streets and the language of the home. Grammar is the hinge that will articulate public and private issues into one project, as the two essential scenarios for the citizen's good performance. For their part, manuals will reinforce the need to know the rules of grammar, to have good pronunciation, a good tone of voice, subtle gestures, and studied movements in order to guarantee social success.

Therefore, these texts distribute, organize, and complement each other in the areas of national identity, public territories, private zones, and communication channels. They directly affect the body (physical and psychic, individual and collective) and language, with preventive, penalizing, and corrective measures. They shape the operative and enunciative conditions of the legal subject of culture. They decide the language and the body of the civilizing agent. The home prepares the citizen for the great theater of the world.

State, School, and Family: Subjects of Authority

The institutions that articulate and support a large portion of disciplinary devices are the State, with all its legal and judicial apparatus, the school, and the family. Therefore, the model individuals who are called upon to implement and fulfill the constitutional, linguistic, and behavioral order are the judge, the teacher, and the father—agents authorized to oversee the fulfillment of written norms. Therefore, obedience becomes a key exercise for body and mind to exert hegemony over the individual. Modernity will bring readjustments between sexes and power. The man still has the knowledge of language, the language of the law, and thus, the authority. From another perspective, the figure of the physician and the psychiatrist will replace the midwife and the priest as the two authorities that will rule the cleanliness of the body and the coaction of Eros.

The acquisition of citizenship is a sieve through which only those men who are competent in language, who are older than twenty-one, married, "owners of real estate whose annual rent is two hundred pesos, or who have a profession, job, or useful industry that produces three hundred pesos a year, or who have a yearly salary of four hundred pesos," can pass (Mariñas Otero 1965, 194). Therefore, the written laws and norms outline a field that gives authority to the masculine subject who is white, Catholic, married, educated, a proprietor and/or businessman; the field also inscribes in its grooves the silence of the subaltern subjects, those who are at the backside of citizenship. For example, women are referred to only as the "woman of the institutor," the governess in charge of girls "but under the rule of her husband," who is elected by the Chamber "among the most virtuous and wise of men" (ibid.). The governess (in the constitution) or the housewife (in the manuals) is subordinated, with no right to speak or to be a citizen, and together with a host of equals—children, servants, the deranged, the infirm, the poor, Indians, blacks, slaves, laborers, the illiterate, homosexuals, Jews—is regarded as a minor.

The violence of these individuals' authority will banish abuse and physical punishment for the sake of a greater and apparent softening of customs.[11] Now violence goes through the filters of several disciplines or types of knowledge that modify—repressing—bodies, languages, and emotions, as well as the appearance of the land. Pedagogy is the great preventer: the knowledge it imparts—grammar, geography, history, arithmetic, calculus, Latin—distributes in a different way the "pulsations of savagery." Education is one of the spurs of progress and the figure of the teacher holds the keys to the participation of the lettered citizen.

Geometrization of Areas: Boundaries and Frontiers

The foundation of an order ruled by writing brings about a double movement: the construction of a space closed within itself—the polis with all its educational and correctional buildings—which can be controlled and whose members can be censored; and the establishment of boundaries that outline rigid borders which create "transparent" identity zones and "dark" and incomprehensible zones, the open space of chaos and chance.

Even though the written word outlines one field over the others, for example in cultural systems that are not centered around a graphic legality, such as oral communities, its limits shape a boundary that not only separates the *inside* from the *outside*, but also provides the space that rules the area of a careful territorial geometry. In the words of Deleuze and Guattari, it is like a chess game: the power of the State encodes and decodes the space, charting and laminating it from its center of gravity.[12]

One of the tactics to tame nature is rationalization, which in this case means fractionation, division, detachment, classification, not only of the land (agronomy, geography) but also of the individual body (medicine, biology), of the social body (census, statistics, sociology), and of language (grammars, dictionaries). Geometrization transforms matter into a squared surface that can be measured in order to optimize its use, whether for natural wealth or for a human labor force. Exercise—consubstantial to discipline—works land, body, and language by sections. Arithmetic, mathematics, geometry, and algebra are now essential for the controlling power of the State and of the liberal bourgeoisie.

Contrary to a great variety of genres, from novels, photographs, and travel chronicles to painting, which delivered the illusion—always written—of a geography of "natural," "untamed," and "savage" territories, constitutions divided territories more properly, multiplying borders within its even continuum. As a "police" writing, they must be able to filter the free movement of masses and individuals, as well as to rule their contact. They "map" a territory that must be subdivided into multiple legal instances (states, governments, municipalities, mayor's offices) where custom houses oversee, inspect, and tax goods and stop the constant flow of humans and animals. Charting the territory—and not in vain did mapping and traveler's relations have a great effect on it—prepared the field for the immediate establishment of a communications network: which river was the best for the draft of large steamers; which land was the most level and furthest from savages to build railways. The nation-space is counted numerically, by regions, inhabitants, sex, occupation, abilities. To quantify is to know the potential for future wealth.

Constitutions, grammars, and manuals are, each in their own right, founding discourses for borders. Their own language is forged from prohibition, a chain of gates that allow and forbid citizenship, the right to have and to hide a body, to have a language that can be modified or silenced. The continuity of human space was separated into public and private, the individual's body parts separated to control or inhibit their function, language dissected into prolific morphological classifications. As genres of the normalizing power, these are exercises to impose boundaries.

Disciplines delimit spaces; they enclose. Laws bind and center. In contrast, manuals, in the eagerness to discipline the human body, will tame it part by part: parts that should not touch each other—fingers and hands with the mouth, ears, nose, eyes, head, legs, feet; areas, flows, gestures, and expressions that must be covered ("we should never leave our rooms if we are not fully dressed" [Carreño 1927, 53]), eliminated ("the habit of getting up at night to relieve our physical needs is highly censurable" [48]), or modified ("we should not touch our head, or put our hands under our clothes for any reason whatsoever, not even to scratch. All these acts are always filthy and highly uncivilized when performed in front of other people" [23]) in order to achieve an aseptic, hieratic, serious, distant, and contained body. Written rules flagellate passions ("we must dominate our emotions and our countenance, and must always show an affable and jovial mood"; and "we must sacrifice our taste, our dislikes, and even our comfort" [187 and 217]) until they are circumscribed to areas considered abject and guilt-ridden.

When constitutions allocate territories they create reservoirs for nomadic populations—like the North American Indians, or Venezuela's Goajiros and Yanomamis—to confine them and thus be able to locate them. In contrast, manuals stash Eros and emotions in the bottom of the dark box of the unconscious or in mental institutions, where psychiatry is challenged to channel these repressed impulses in a civilized manner.

Civilization is an internal act with contained spaces that are carefully delineated by the written word. The monumental dimensions of public works and buildings, of theaters and racetracks, squares and beach resorts, schools and academies, mansions and slaughterhouses, aqueducts and cemeteries, parcel out life in all its dimensions. Life outside the polis is "barbaric," the even surface that has not yet been stigmatized by the signs of disciplinary writing.

The Machinery of Otherness

On the flip side of writing, when the written word does not name, emerges a threatening dimension which strains this logic, which only acknowledges an imitation of the pre-written order (on this side), and negotiates "otherness" in legal, ethical, and cultural terms (on the other side), built upon a series of operations where "the other" assumes legal penalty, inquiry, judgment, and exclusion, ethical and cultural degradation ("vicious," "filthy," "repugnant," "uncivil," "unpleasant"), and social and economic failure.

Norms and laws seem to have a specular nature. Those who do not imitate them ("every individual must live under the law"; "it is an important rule of urbanity to strictly follow the uses of etiquette") will be regarded as uncivilized individuals, languages, or territories. They represent the anti-Law, the guilty body of a nonstate, prosecuted by the written word, which expels and later punishes them. The power of the State forges *otherness* because otherwise disciplinary and taming practices would not have any sense. It is the test of fire of the efficiency of the new power technologies: discipline removes inadequate excrescencies (leftovers) from individuals (because they are unmanageable), languages, and the differences in the body itself.

An indeterminate otherness accumulates on the edges of legal writing, a strange sort of "deformity" that constitutions barely name as vagrancy, insanity, banditry, or criminality, and refers only to subjects whose way of life is basically nomadic or not exactly sedentary, because they practice itinerant trade or cattle trade (in the case of llaneros, gauchos, and cangaçeiros). In other words, if being a citizen (always masculine) implied having an annual rent between one hundred and six hundred pesos, having real estate, and having a profession or a useful industry, then almost 90 percent of the population was part of that "otherness," whether because of insolvency (the poor, craftsmen, small urban and rural businessmen, debtors), inadequate professional skills (servants, slaves, peasants, the illiterate), ethnic inadequacies (Indians, blacks, mestizos), sexual differences (women, homosexuals—because formal marriage was required), or physical or mental deficiencies (the sick, the inebriated, and the insane).

Disciplines are limiting because they are limited. They are ruled by a logocentric dynamic that does not accept another logic. The edges become a contention wall against the threats from the "outside," which must be previously invalidated through a disqualifying language. The "other" becomes vulgar, rude, sick, savage, dirty: in the words of Dominique Laporte, it is "the place of shit." It is a privileged place occupied by the Indians, because since the State cannot exterminate them, the "State must provide them schools, academies, and colleges where they can learn the principles of religion, morals, politics, sciences, and useful arts . . . and try through all means to lure those natural citizens to these houses of enlightenment . . . to eliminate their dejection and rusticity" (Mariñas Otero 1965, 157),[13] because otherwise they would continue to be the social excrement of citizenship, together with domestic servants, mired with "defects" and "natural deformities."[14]

Perhaps one of the most alarming aspects of the founding of nations was the handling of *difference*. To legalize its project, the monolithic rationality imposed within the homogenizing and expansive categories could only procure several devices that quickly canceled the articulation of heterogeneity, expelling them to the area of (im)possible "savagery." I mean that the term "other"—in itself—is an unfortunate construct, which from the core of its enunciative locus rarifies *difference* as such. Power must also manufacture "otherness" because when it crushes and obliterates it, it becomes stronger and legitimized.

If we overlap some semantic areas of constitutions and manuals, and establish some basic similarities, we can see that one of the main tasks of re-educating an individual into society is the taming of his emotions, which in terms of good manners (of sanity) is equal not only to the avoidance of shouting, clapping, laughing, spitting, blowing the nose, and sucking the fingers, but also getting used to "being somewhat discreet"; in the face of offenses "we must be serenely inalterable, and must get a hold of ourselves up to the point where our anger is not even noticed in our face" (Carreño 1927, 260). That is, and getting closer to constitutions, any citizen who disputes, thinks out loud, argues, opposes, and unleashes his rage and hate is considered insane or inebriated. Citizens who have "neutralized as much as possible the exaltations of their spirit" (Carreño 1927, 256) and conquered an "elegant exterior" (254) will have political rights. Everything else—sweat, smells, closeness, hybridizations—will be called the "other."

Hygiene Policies: Cleanliness and Controlled Contact

Modernity is intimately linked to hygiene policies for individuals, languages, and territories, which complement the anatomy of surveillance and coercion, imposing pure and nonpolluted categories.[15] It is in this sense that constitutions, grammars, and manuals (including those on sexual hygiene) create pure fields of work, because they are writings that establish boundaries. It is easier to rule what has been homologated, or to control units that have been previously expunged of ethnic, linguistic, sexual, or social contamination. Dominique Laporte states that "the writer and the grammarian, no less than the prince, clean language just as they clean a city 'filled with mud, garbage, rubble, and other filth': they go down to the latrine to clean it. . . . A treasure emerges from shit: the treasure of language, of the King, and of the State" (1980, 15 and 25).

Filth—understood as humors and bodily contact, open sexuality, masturbation, carnivals, physical punishment, cock fights, bull fights, popular jargon, and the dramatization of funerals—represents one of the metaphors that complements the great axiom of "barbarism." The asepsis and the cleanliness of streets, language, body, and habits appear as the panaceas of progress and materialization in a modern nation: to clean the *res publica* of transient "unproductive" groups, of insane and sick people (i.e., Indians, *mestizos*, free blacks, and "rebels"), to clean language of "vicious" expressions ("bad words" soil the language), and the body of odors and spontaneous impulses. In this sense, "otherness" appeared as an illness, and it was feared because it could be contagious.

Hygiene was taught together with coercion policies, isolation, and disinfection of any contaminating element or subject. As part of a new sensibility, there was a phobia toward the cultural complex of "barbarism," and a compulsion for correctness and cleanliness. Carreño constantly reminds us that we should "never offer food or drink that we have touched with our lips," nor "drink from a glass that was used by someone else, nor eat what this person left on his or her plate," nor "wear used clothes," not only to avoid contact with fluids, but also a familiarity that is inappropriate for the order society wanted to impose. The body itself must be subject to a series of sterilizations—where fashion will have an important role—because all matter is associated with dirt, vulgarity, ugliness, and corruption, particularly of the female body. These modern times do not free the body, they make it the center of abjection: "It is not allowed to mention in society the different members or areas of the body, except for those that are never covered" (Carreño 1927, 124). Bodies were not the only things that should be disinfected. The modern city plan redesigned Latin American cities by redistributing buildings into discreet units, removing waste and the "vulgar" bustle of social life from the urban centers. For example, among the many redesigns made by Antonio Guzmán Blanco during his long presidential term (1870–1888), he sanitized Caracas by building the slaughterhouse and the main cemetery outside the city, by building a sewer system, aqueducts, and the municipal dump, by instituting the extermination of stray dogs, by opening a leprosarium sixty kilometers away from the city, and in another sense, by founding the Academies of Language, History, and Medicine—because the purity of the language and of patriotic heroes should be preserved as bequeathed from the times of the colony and independence. Also, the creation of schools throughout the national territory acquired an obsessive nature in his political agenda.[16] Not in vain did Guzman's government—*guzmanato*—seriously commit to the demands of civilization: cleanliness, order, and beauty. We could assume that Freud would be pleased.

As part of this general cleaning program, a series of strategies were implemented which introduced a controlled contact in all areas of public and private life. This implied a discreet distance between bodies ("We should never get so close to the person we are talking with that they can feel our breath"; or "the woman who touches a man not only commits an uncivil act, but will also appear immodest and easy; yet this fault is even worse and more vulgar if it is the man who touches a woman" [Carreño 1927, 32 and 120]). It also confined certain undesirable ethnic groups to specific territories (like the Amazon and the Goajira), and confined individuals with behaviors considered abnormal by the disciplines into correctional facilities, hospices, jails, and workshops.

Regardless of the levels of hygiene reached to improve social life, hygiene policies were often handled with irrational zeal, closer to the police methods of order and confinement than to the cleanliness itself. From another perspective, this zeal for cleanliness converged into dogmatic and conservative solutions—and perhaps pre-fascist as well—where the obtaining of purity (of body, language, and blood) gave rise to the European immigration policies to "improve the race" as well as the development of Hispanicism toward the end of the nineteenth century, as if the whitening of the population and the canonization of Castilian Spanish would guarantee the utopia of progress.[17]

An Economics of Tracing

As Carreño says, to avoid quoting Foucault, "domestic habits, due to their daily and constant repetition, acquire an irresistible power in men, dominating him forever, rising above the speculative knowledge of his chores, and finally creating a second will that subjects him to purely mechanical acts" (1927, 227–28). In order to implement the normative aspect of disciplines it is necessary to repeat movements, gestures, and attitudes mechanically, to correct the operations of body and language, thus containing force and allowing it to be docile and useful.

Laws (constitutions) and rules (grammars and manuals) pretend to achieve a maximum collective efficiency because they operate from the singularization of individuals. They thoroughly work on parts of the individual and social body. They separate, distance, classify, and regroup analogous units. They create serial *groups in series* which, in their homogeneity, are ordered progressively according to age, sex, class, knowledge, behavior, and abilities. Children are placed in different classrooms and buildings according to their age, sex, and possessions. The "insane" and the "incompetent" are placed in correctional and mental institutions. Laws and rules classify *homogenous units into hierarchically organized series*. They watch for differences in order to relocate them in the corresponding social scale. Within its species (the taxonomy rush will sweep all the crevices of knowledge and life), they neutralize disparity so that it becomes similar to the group. They regulate body movements and language use by repeating exercises endlessly. Orthography and grammar are only learned through the daily assignments that the teacher gives at school: it will be the best place to level out irregularities of expression and restlessness in the body. Therefore, keeping quiet, remaining seated, and standing in line became the mold of school orthopedia that is still in use.

Disciplines normalize the arrhythmia of social life, establishing an economics of tracing that distributes dissymmetrical relationships into a hierarchic scale. The hierarchy is maintained and every step of it is serialized through mimesis. This attempt at leveling out society in postcolonial times was just a reinstatement of monarchic power. Violence and punishment were replaced by the standardization of mechanisms that controlled analogies and watched over hierarchies. The "arboreal" system that rules the logos of the new States distributes its loads—previously washed—into differentiated compartments that are reciprocally subordinated.

The system creates overlapping singularities within the new order, isolated individualities—discrete units, though similar among themselves—easily located and interchanged within a unit—barracks, school, workshop, factory—to increase productivity or punitive efficiency. A single dimension has the advantage of creating a horizon where anomalies stand out.

Vigilant Look/Punitive Eye

The Venezuelan constitution written by Simón Bolívar in 1819 proposed a Fourth Power, the Moral Power, formed by the forty most virtuous citizens of the city. This "Areopagus," regarded as a "court of honor," would be in charge of watching over public morality and "proclaiming the names of virtuous citizens and moral educated acts, and denouncing with shame and disgrace the names of the depraved and those acts of corruption and indecency" (Mariñas Otero 1965, 189). Even though this institution was not included in later constitutions, the spirit of censorship and surveillance was adopted by other social practices, among them the manuals, which invisibly disseminated within the community an anonymous body of micropenalties that acted as a sort of infra-Law. The teacher observes, the physician examines, the father watches, each looking upon the other earnestly. Constitutions permanently invite socialized spying and denunciation ("every citizen is capable of accusing"). Manuals, in contrast, suggest a discreet observation and an elegant surveillance ("we should never look intently at the people we meet, nor those who are at their windows, nor turn our face to see those who have gone by" [Carreño 1927, 82]). Public and domestic life are destined to be a great theater where the actors and the audience are constantly under observation.

The progressive disappearance of physical punishment—or at least its softening—as well as the open and embarrassing public derision, were gradually replaced by a new punitive sensibility, more subtle and imperceptible: the development of the vigilant look.[18] Perhaps it is a sort of police *voyeurism* that represses desire, disorganized behavior, unusual uses of body and voice. Perhaps it is the flagellated eye of Thanatos. Police mechanisms, now subjectively individualized, turn each individual into a small court of inquisition facing the fear of being seen, the shame of being observed. In any event, rules and laws also weave an imaginary control where every eye becomes a judge: written norms forge watchful and watched individuals. The eye of the judge, the teacher, the father, and the physician is disseminated among many other eyes that constantly control the slightest transgression of public, private, and intimate boundaries. That is why we must watch forms, appearances, the containment of emotions, physical contact, and good rhetoric, because the eye of another person always remembers boundaries that are only imaginary.[19]

Although watching and being watched turn urban life into a great masquerade, it is also true that the city at the end of the nineteenth century became a huge observatory, not only criminal, clinical, and pedagogical, but also linguistic and literary. Modern knowledge opens its doors under an omnipresent eye that examines and classifies everything, that places individuals in a written net that seizes, explains, cures, corrects, and adapts them. The purpose of science is just as disciplinary.

THE NEW LEGAL regime of nationalities also assumed a new relationship between power and modern categories of productivity. This implied a re-definition of the implementation of power between individuals, in terms of a better use of effort, the "useful" channeling of energy, and the inspection of free mobility, in order to fulfill the desired and utopian agenda of progress.

Regardless of how the writings of the motherland interacted with the dynamics of each Latin American situation, these disciplinary texts were proposed as bastions of a civilizing project and, as such, they believed in the taming ability of words, of placing their faith in the power of the patriarchal lettered subject, and in the diffusion of pedagogy as a machine to seize/capture/castrate "inorganic" autonomies and the "confused force of barbarism." All the controlling and supervising tactics—establishing boundaries, geometrization, divisions, exclusions, serializations, and symmetrization—were never enough to build the dreamed nations and the whitened, aseptic citizens prescribed by overseas models.

Translated by Margarita Rodríguez

Notes

1. A concept taken by Michel Foucault from the *Panopticon* by Jeremiah Bentham (1748–1832), and developed in his books *Discipline and Punish: The Birth of the Prison*, and *La verdad y las formas jurídicas*, as a metaphor of disciplinary power that is best represented in the circular architectural figure of the "Panoptic," with concentric rings filled with cells and windows which face the inside as well as the outside of the building. From the central tower, the prisoner is constantly watched, never knowing who is watching him. The advantage of this construction is the power that becomes visible and unverifiable. The individual knows he is being spied upon, but not by whom or when.

2. The two volumes of José Pedro Barrán (1990–1992) are very instructive regarding a documented research that explains the change in sensitivities, from the boldest and most spontaneous forms, to more contained and constrained attitudes.

3. In Deleuze and Guattari 1988 (especially chapter 1, "Introducción: Rizoma," and chapter 12, "Tratado de Nomadología: La Máquina de Guerra").

4. The facsimile versions of the compiled and edited Venezuelan constitutions were published in *Las Constituciones de Venezuela*, vol. 17, by Luis Marinas Otero, in a collection entitled *Las Constituciones Hispanoamericanas*. For this work, we have used the constitutions of 1811, 1819 (by Simón Bolívar), 1830 (by José Antonio Páez), 1857 (by José Tadeo Monagas), and 1874 (by Antonio Guzmán Blanco). During the nineteenth century, Venezuela had about twelve constitutions.

5. The first edition of Andrés Bello's *Gramática* appeared in Chile in 1847. We use the critical edition of Ramón Trujillo, published in 1981. Manuel Antonio Carreño's *Manual* was first edited as a brochure in 1853, and was published in book form in 1854; and on 14 March 1855, the National Congress recommended its use. Throughout our work, I will use the generic names *constitutions, grammars,* and *manuals* to create specific written typologies. However, concrete examples will be taken from the above-mentioned Venezuelan models.

6. See Bello (1965, 184–206, a series of articles published by Bello between 1833 and 1834) and the "Prólogo" to the *Gramatica de la lengua castellana destinada al uso de los americanos* (Bello 1981, 184–216).

7. Being competent in reading and writing are consubstantial with citizenship. Also, constitutions regard "legal subjects" as those who are proficient in good language: "It is the exclusive domain of the Chamber to establish, organize, and direct primary schools for boys and girls, seeing that they are taught to pronounce, read,

and write correctly, together with the most common rules of arithmetic and the principles of grammar" (Mariñas Otero 1965, 193). In this sense, the "lettered intellectual" is the citizen par excellence: the "representative" of citizenship.

8. "Active" citizens—those who can vote—are those "who are more than twenty-five years old and know how to read and write"; "those who own real estate whose annual rent is two hundred pesos, or those who have a profession, job, or useful industry that produces three hundred pesos a year, or those who have a yearly salary of four hundred pesos" (Mariñas Otero 1965, 227). These requirements would remain unchanged until the constitutions of 1870.

9. The scope of this domestication/repression reaches the most unsuspected areas. Carreño's *Manual* states that "a man is not allowed to be home without his tie on, wearing a shirt, with no socks, or with bad shoes" (Carreño 1927, 55).

10. Carreño states: "The method is perhaps more important for women than for men, because . . . her destiny falls on some special functions . . . lest she bring about great harm of high transcendence. We are talking about governing a home, about directing domestic matters, the daily investment of money, and the serious and delicate assignment of the first education of children, on which their future and that of society greatly depends" (Carreño 1927, 23).

11. Already since the first constitution of 1811, physical violence is restricted in punishment: "The use of torture is permanently abolished" (Mariñas Otero 1965, 153); "Torment and any treatment that worsens the punishment established by the law, will never be used" (Mariñas Otero 1965, 252 [Constitution of 1830]). Manuals also contain a section on the "treatment of servants," suggesting that homeowners abstain from abuse, blows, and humiliations. Apparently, it was very common for servants to suffer thrashings from their masters.

12. "One of the main tasks of the State is to striate the space it rules, or to use the even spaces as a means of communication for a chartered space. For any State it is essential to overcome nomadism as well as to control migrations and more generally, to recover its rights, mostly 'exterior,' over what flows through the inhabited and cultivated areas. Indeed, the State cannot be separated, where that is possible, from the seizure of all types of flows, populations, goods or trade, money or capitals, et cetera." (Deleuze and Guattari 1988, 389). For this reason, constitutional law "promotes and decrees the creation of roads, channels, and inns; the construction of bridges, highways, and hospitals. . . . To enable an easy and speedy navigation and the promotion of agriculture and trade . . ." (Mariñas Otero 1965, 248).

13. According to this quote, the Indian population is degraded, morally deviated, promiscuous, idle, useless, depressed, and savage.

14. Cf. the section "Modo de conducirnos con nuestros domésticos" from Carreño (1927, 68–70).

15. Cf. the articles by Ramos (1993a and 1993b), to which I owe many of the ideas I pose in this essay.

16. In the Constitution, the ideas of school and hygiene, and of teacher and physician go hand in hand: "The Chamber will give special care to the shape, proportion, and location of our schools . . . taking into consideration not only [their] stability

and scope, but also the elegance, cleanliness, comfort, and recreation of the youth" (Mariñas Otero 1965, 193). Later, in the same section: "Every year, the Chamber will publish accurate charts or balances of the children born and died, their physical condition, health and diseases, their improvement, inclinations, qualities, and particular talents. To do all these observations, it will use institutors, priests, physicians, department agents, and illustrated citizens" (Mariñas Otero 1965, 194).

17. In the "Prólogo" to his *Gramática*, Bello states that the language models to follow are "the works of the Spanish Academy and the Grammar by D. Vicente Salvá," as well as his debts with Juan Antonio Puignlanch and Garcés. Although his grammar is for Hispanic Americans, "I think that preserving the language of our fathers as purely as possible is very important," to avoid, according to Bello, such hybrids as the "irregular, licentious, and barbaric dialects" that characterize American speech, which in other words would muddle communication channels, just like rubbish on the streets (Bello 1981, 128–30).

18. Foucault says about this: "Traditionally, power is what you see, what is open, what is evident. . . . Disciplinary power is invisible. . . . In discipline, those who need to be seen are subjected. Their illumination guarantees the power that is exerted over them. Being constantly watched, or the possibility of being constantly watched, maintains the disciplined individual subjected" (Foucault 1988, 192).

19. This punitive eye is interjected to the point where the most intimate privacy is controlled. We are talking now about an inward police: "It is also a bad habit to move violently while we sleep, because it sometimes makes the bed coverings fall down, and makes us assume offensive positions that go against honesty and propriety" (Carreño 1927, 48).

EDUARDO ARCHETTI

Male Hybrids in the World of Soccer

Eduardo Archetti was born in Argentina in 1943. An anthropologist, he is a professor at the Universitetet i Oslo in Norway). His main titles include *Campesinado y estructuras agrarias en América Latina* (1981), *Fútbol y Ethos* (1984), and *Masculinities: Football, Polo, and the Tango in Argentina* (1999).

Horacio, with whom I have attended so many soccer matches since 1984, and who has enlightened me about the history of Argentinean soccer, said in one of our endless conversations in October 1994:

> Argentina is a very odd country, full of contradictions. You remember, after the Falklands war, we changed all the names of the streets and places which reminded us of the British influence in our own history ... These acts are an expression of our nationalism, of our anti-British feelings. As you know, almost by definition, to be anti-British is to be a kind of anti-imperialist... However, in the park of Palermo, very close to the Planetarium, you will find a modest monument commemorating the first game of soccer played in Argentina on 20 June 1867. Those fields belonged to the Buenos Aires Cricket Club, an old British club, and all the players who played that match were British citizens. You can read all their names. They introduced the game, our national passion, and, as an act of justice, they deserve to be remembered forever ... I cannot imagine Argentinean history without this monument.

If this monument was almost unknown in 1994, it was revealed to the nation on 21 June 1997. *Clarín*, a serious and much-read newspaper of Buenos Aires, published two articles entitled, "Together with the railways arrived the English pioneers. The country of immigrants" and "Memory: The first soccer match ever played in Argentina. 130 years since the first kick." A picture of the monument illustrated both articles. The journalist concluded the second article with a clear message: soccer contributed to the integration of the immigrants and to the growth of a national soccer style and identity.

Today, we cannot imagine the Argentinean nation without this unknown monument. The spread of soccer and other sports was a product of Britain's world power status and its active presence in commerce, industrial production, territorial control, and international finance. The English Soccer Association was formed in 1863. Their founders, ex-public school and university players working in London, hoped to produce a set of clear rules from the different varieties of soccer played in Great Britain. The editor of *The Standard*, a leading British newspaper issued in Buenos Aires, received the rules of soccer in 1867 and sent them to Thomas Hogg, a well-known and enthusiastic sportsman. The Buenos Aires Soccer Club, a division of the Buenos Aires Cricket Club, was founded in 1867 by Thomas Hogg himself, together with his brother James and William Heald. They decided to play the first game on June 20th the same year. With the exception of a player named Boschetti, probably an Italian, all the other players had British names: Hogg, Forester, Ramsbottom, Smith, Bond, Heald, Best, Wilmont, Ramsay, and Simpson. It was the beginning of an unstoppable bodily habit (Escobar Bavio 1923).

Soccer expanded, and many clubs were founded. The majority of them sprang out of British schools located in Buenos Aires and surrounding neighborhoods. It is no surprise, then, that the first association was founded in Buenos Aires in 1893 with an English name: the Argentine Association Soccer League; the twenty original teams were British, and its first president was A. Watson Hutton, from 1892 the headmaster of the prestigious St. Andrews Scottish School. After 1900 it was decided that the clubs change their English names for Spanish ones. However, the association kept English as its official language until 1906 and changed its name to the Argentine Soccer Association in 1903 (Scher and Palomino 1988, 24–25).[1] From 1893 to 1900, soccer was dominated by the Lomas Athletic Club, a team composed by students from the Lomas de Zamora School, an important British boarding school.

The pioneering period of Argentinean soccer is inseparably linked to the building of the railways, beginning in the 1860s in Buenos Aires and reaching, in the course of forty years, the rest of Argentina. By 1910 there were clubs and provincial leagues as far away as Santiago del Estero in the northern part of the country. However, British and non-British clubs, located in Buenos Aires or La Plata, the city capital of the province of Buenos Aires, and the small industrial cities close to the capital dominated Argentinean soccer until the end of the 1930s; then, once professionalism was declared, clubs from Rosario, the second largest city of the country, joined the "national league." Nevertheless, the popularity of soccer was rapidly increasing, with the incorporation of the immigrants in its practice, and by 1907 twelve independent leagues of the Argentine Soccer Association, which comprised 350 teams, existed in Buenos Aires (Frydenberg 1997, 7). At the same time, contacts with the nearby Montevideo, the city capital of Uruguay, created a core of soccer in the Río de la Plata basin. Since 1902 games between Argentina and Uruguay have been played for the possession of the Lipton trophy, which had been donated by the world-famous "tea baron" and sportsman Sir Thomas Lipton, who visited Argentina in search of suitable land for tea plantations and discovered that the young British population of Buenos Aires and Montevideo loved to play soccer. In 1913 *The Standard* wrote:

> In the same manner that British capital, British brains, pluck and energy have developed the commercial stability of Argentina, so have British sport and games tended to physically develop the youth of the country and to impulse an admiration for that fair play which sport breeds. . . . An idea of the growth of sport in the Argentine is reflected in the fact that eight years ago there was not a single business in Buenos Aires to supply sporting materials and clothing and now we have three: George McHardy, Lacey and Sons and Watson Hutton & Co. (*The Standard* 1 January 1913, 22)

The British pioneer families in Argentina organized clubs and introduced and played sports but also made money. Via sports the British saw themselves as both gentlemen and players, and considered such activities as vital in achieving a very important cultural task: transferring the ethic of fair play to the native population (see Coleman 1973; Mangan 1988).

From 1901 until 1913, Association soccer was dominated by another British team, the Alumni Soccer Club, created by former students of the Buenos Aires High School. Alumni represented the best soccer played in Argentina from the time the Association began to organize the championships, and the majority of its players played for the national team. The visit of Southampton F. C. in 1904 was perceived in Buenos Aires as the test. The match of Alumni against Southampton was thus anticipated with great anxiety. The Standard defined the match as a crucial game in order to evaluate local standards, particularly as Southampton was captained by G. Molyneaux, an international player, with a "strength and comprehension of the game excelled by no other player" (8 May 1904, 5). The match, played on 26 June, saw a 3–0 victory for Southampton. According to The Standard the English team manifested "values" worthy of emulation: "exact combination," "a real display of how to head," and "fair play, the players always went for the leather" without violent charges. In turn Molyneaux was impressed by the Argentinean players, who "were a long way ahead" of many players from different European countries, like France and Denmark (29 June 1904, 1). The editorial of The Standard of 29 June recognized that soccer was the British sport that Argentineans and Anglo-Argentineans liked the most because it appealed to many of their natural talents: "courage, quickness of perception, and promptness in decision and action" and, in addition, could be played "by the youth of all classes" because the needed expenditure in equipment was insignificant compared with polo, golf, and cricket. The visit of Southampton was stressed because it permitted Argentinean players to be in contact with "the masters of the game" and to learn from them. "The young Anglo-Argentines who played against the Southampton team were defeated but they made a good fight." To learn from Southampton was possible because they displayed a "scientific style," a "systematic understanding of the game" (29 June 1904, 3). The visit also made it possible to distinguish Anglo-Argentineans born in Great Britain from Anglo-Argentineans born in Argentina. No match was played against a typical "Argentinean" team: all the Argentinean national team players had British names.

Many of my old and younger informants knew a lot about the early period of Argentinean soccer. Such accounts are periodically reproduced in the sport pages of newspapers or presented in weekly sport magazines. Recently, television programs have been showing, in a systematic way, the history of Argentinean soccer. A film documentary, Fútbol argentino, was watched by millions in the 1990s. The script, written by a well-known historian, was also published as a book with a great commercial success (Bayer 1990). Now it is possible to find in kiosks and bookshops a series of beautiful postcards introducing "the history of Argentinean soccer." Given this historical context, names of the famous early players have been conveyed, and are now part of a common memory shared by informed soccer supporters. The five Brown brothers, for instance, from the "mythical" Alumni team, are still well known because they also played for the Argentinean national team and were the architects of the early victories against Brazil and Uruguay. Bayer writes in his book that:

The first myth and the first heroes were Alumni and the Brown brothers. A team with eleven English names and ten championships won everything in twelve years. The prologue of the history of creole soccer was written by the English. But even in the first chapter names of different origin appeared. Sarmiento and Alberdi (the liberal architects of the modernizing project of Argentina) wanted Nordic and Saxon immigrants but instead arrived Italians and Spaniards, who, together with the creoles, would found the real Argentina. However, the years of Alumni were examples of morality, gentlemanship, and sport nobility. (1990, 20–21; my translation)

In writing these sentences, Bayer is reproducing a kind of synthesis of the myth of the origins of soccer in Argentina: first soccer was British, or English—because for Argentineans Englishness is the essence of Britishness, and both terms are used interchangeably—and only after a process of historical transformation become *criollo* (creole). The real Argentinean soccer, the creole way, was made by Italians, Spaniards, and the male native population. However, this pioneering time is regarded as positive because the English values of gentlemanly behavior dominated and impregnated the spirit of the game. In discussions, my informants emphasized ideas of strength, virility, and physical stamina as important aspects of the pioneers' epoch. The soccer they played, while imagined as "primitive" and lacking in sophistication, was at least honest.

Another English first-division club, Nottingham Forest, visited Argentina in 1905 and two other important teams, Tottenham and Everton, arrived in 1909 to play two exhibition games against each other and to confront the best club teams of Buenos Aires and Rosario. The next visit in 1912 confirmed the evolution registered since 1909. Swindon Town played six matches and drew in two of them. The first was against a team with players from first-division teams located in the northern area of Buenos Aires. The second was against the national team. Many English residents sent indignant letters to *The Standard* following the first draw, seeing the result not only as a defeat, but as an expression of the decadence of the quality of the soccer played in the "Old Country" (19 June 1912, 4). There were, however, other letters defending Swindon, pointing out that it is difficult to play against teams "having an entirely different style and entirely different tactics" (*The Standard* 21 June 1912, 4). After the draw against the national team, *The Standard* concluded that soccer in

Argentina had reached a "high degree of excellence" and that the national squad "played really well and there was hardly a weak spot in it" (1 July 1912, 2).

The time of learning was over and so local English dominance. In 1912, Alumni decided to leave the league; this event made it possible for other teams with players of non-British origin to dominate the local championship. The Standard commented that the road was now open to teams composed of creole and non-British immigrants. It was observed that, among first-division teams, Porteños and San Isidro had only three "anglos," Gimnasia y Esgrima one, River Plate three, Estudiantes de La Plata one, and Racing Club none (The Standard 10 June 1912, 2). In 1912 the championship was won by Quilmes, another traditional British team. The following year, however, is a historical one in the mythical construction of soccer's past because Racing Club, a team without a single player of British origin, won the championship for the first time. In the more recent history of Argentinean soccer Alumni and Racing are presented as the "founders" of a national tradition, but the virtues of Racing are of greater significance because their victories arrived when soccer was more popular, the quality of the game was higher, and more teams competed for the victory (La Nación 1994, 1:1–10).

In pioneering historical research Frydenberg (1997, 1998) has illustrated the changes in amateur soccer in Buenos Aires in the 1900s.[2] He discovered that, by 1907, three hundred soccer clubs existed outside the official championship of the Association, playing organized soccer in various competitions. The points of reference for the creation of these teams were the workplace, the street, the neighborhood, and the parish. The youth of the time were seduced by the practice of the new sport, but emphasis is placed on the importance of the search for local identity through the practice of soccer. One of the main problems for a recently created club was to find open ground upon which to play. In almost all cases a primitive ground was enough in order to establish a club. Many of the clubs formed in the city center were obliged to find open spaces in the city surroundings. Even Alumni had never had its own stadium and, from 1904, played on the pitch of the Ferro Carril Oeste club. According to Frydenberg the continuous foundations of new clubs and the permanent crisis of many older clubs reflected an unparalleled enthusiasm as well as lack of organizational realism (1997, 12–14). Many clubs disappeared, and the ones which survived were able to combine soccer with other leisure-related activities. The social space created by the clubs transformed the life of the city. The majority of the first-division clubs in today's Argentinean soccer were founded in the period 1887 to 1915, and all of them offer to their members more than soccer (Scher and Palomino 1988, 236–39).

Frydenberg describes not only the expansion of soccer but also some of the problems: the increasingly violent participation of supporters in order to influence the development of a game, the lack of discipline among the players, and the inconsistency in the definition of rules governing results (1997, 16–17). It was a common practice to protest against the result of the match, using arguments such as the partiality of the referee or the threat of the local public against the physical safety of the visiting team. Many of the conflicts were exacerbated when the clubs were located in the same neighborhood (1997, 18). However, Frydenberg concludes, "The combination of competition and desire for winning with the will to defend the identity of the club provoked a rivalry different from the one related to sport values" (1997, 18). As I have stressed above, the value of "fair play" was central to the diffusion of English sports, but Frydenberg reveals an increasing contradiction between those values and the popular practice of soccer:

> The youth admired Alumni, and the *gentlemen*. However, in reality soccer was fashioned out of the practice of daily competition, there was a constant tension between the idea of a clean game and the explosion of rivalry with certain doses of violence. . . . While the new players dyed their lives with the values of rivalry and enmity, the creators of *fair play* promoted the custom of "third time," a moment of confraternity among the players once the game was over. In the practice of competition the popular groups had a difficulty in imagining a friendly relation with the opponents when the match was over. (1997, 24; my translation)[3]

Competition with clubs composed of new immigrants and creole players, who were guided by new values, produced ambivalent feelings among the British. *The Standard* critically observed that, during the visit of Tottenham and Everton in 1909, the behavior of the Argentinean crowd was not an example of an educated public: they were booing and whistling constantly, and "a number of the crowd descended to even lower depths of insults" (27 July 1909, 3). The newspaper advised the Argentinean crowd to change their behavior if they were to remain interested in receiving visits from such famous teams in the future. This description is in sharp contrast with the one published in 1905 during the visit of Nottingham Forest. The crowd of nine thousand spectators was extremely civilized while watching the match between the professional visitors and a typical English club, the Belgrano Athletic; the grandstand was "overflowing with the elite of both English and Argentine society," and the elegance of the clothes and automobiles parked outside reminded the journalist of attending "a fashionable equestrian race meeting" (19 June 1905, 1). It seems that this highly civilized age was definitively over by 1912 when Alumni abandoned the *practice* of soccer. One by one the English upper-class clubs abandoned the practice of competitive soccer and concentrated on rugby, tennis, and cricket.

In 1914, Exeter City, a professional second-division team playing in the English Southern League, toured Argentina. It lost one match but beat the champions, Racing, 2–0, and the national team, 3–1. English soccer was still superior. During the farewell banquet the coach of Exeter said that the Argentinean amateur players should master amateur teams in England without difficulties, but they were not yet ready to defeat professional teams. He emphasized that the local players "are clever in dribbling and fast, but their weak point is that they are individualists and try to shine each above their fellows. They will never achieve real success until they recognize that it takes eleven men to score a goal" (*The Standard* 14 July 1914, 4). By 1914, if this statement holds true, two styles were constituted: the English, grounded on collective discipline and common effort, and the other, the local creole, based on individualism and lack of tactical sense. This opposition is central in the construction of the imagery of Argentinean soccer style.

Hybridity in Soccer: The Creation of a *Criollo* Style

The majority of my informants agreed upon the importance of mapping the ideological construction of soccer in the weekly magazine El Gráfico. Most of them were regular readers, and even the youngest knew the history of the magazine very well: one of the characteristics of El Gráfico is to celebrate itself with periodic publications about its own history.

Founded in May 1919 in Buenos Aires, El Gráfico was in the beginning literally a magazine "for men." It included, in different measures, political articles, news photos, sports, photos of artists, and reports on leisure and open-air activities. After 1921 El Gráfico gradually became a sports magazine, although photos of unknown and supposedly foreign female dancers would be published until the end of the 1920s. The circulation of El Gráfico increased in this decade and leveled out at one hundred thousand in the 1930s. The magazine's circulation reached its peak between the mid-1940s and the mid-1950s, with two hundred thousand copies published weekly. At that time the magazine had a continental circulation, and was read in Santiago de Chile, La Paz, Quito, Bogotá, San José, Guatemala City, and Mexico City. El Gráfico has been defined as the "Bible of sports in South America" (Sánchez León 1998, 149).

A great deal of space was devoted to soccer, but other sports such as motor racing, polo, swimming, and boxing, in which Argentineans had gained an international reputation, were also covered. At the outset, the magazine was a mouthpiece for the modernist ideology in vogue: it emphasized the importance of physical education for health, introduced notions of hygiene, incorporated recommendations on the best diet to follow and how to avoid illnesses, stressed the importance of developing hobbies such as building model aircraft, emphasized the need to encourage women to participate in sports, and, above all, persistently emphasized the moral and educational aspects of sport. According to El Gráfico, sport should be understood as the moral activity of the body, since it develops a strict code of conduct in those who play it, owing to the existence of rules, controls, and sanctions (El Gráfico 394, 1927, 18).

El Gráfico is the middle-class sports weekly which has had, and continues to have, the greatest influence in Argentina. The analysis of the content of this magazine is, therefore, an analysis of the construction of middle-class male imagery. Whether or not it was hegemonic is debatable, but there is no doubt about its decisive influence on the definition of the different areas of national and masculine moral thought. The journalists of El Gráfico, excellent writers in the main, think as members of the middle class but, at the same time, give space to the expression and dissemination of the voices, images, and performances of soccer players and other sportsmen of popular and working-class origin. The transformation of the latter into "heroes" or "villains," into "models" to be emulated or not, and the careful analysis of their performances are examples of the process of the symbolic construction of the "national" through an examination of sporting virtues.

In the context of the 1920s, when soccer was consolidated in Argentina and became part of the global world of sport, El Gráfico developed the theory of the two foundings of Argentinean soccer: the first founding was British, the second was criollo. One of the arguments used refers to the ethnic origins of the players in the most famous teams and also those playing for the national team. In the era of the British founding—from 1887 to 1911, the date when the hegemony of the Alumni, the "glorious British team" was broken—players of British origin predominated (El Gráfico 470, 1928, 5). The criollo founding began in 1913, when, as noted earlier, Racing Club, with only three marginal players of British origin—Wine, Loncan, and Prince—won the championship for the first time.

From that moment the "British" clubs declined in importance, and their players disappeared from the national teams. According to El Gráfico, this change became possible because "when soccer began to spread, the stars with British names gave way to those with purely Latin, especially Italian and Spanish, surnames like García, Martínez, Ohaco, Olazar, Chiappe, Calomino, Laforia, Isola, et cetera" (470, 1920, 5).

It is interesting to note that lo criollo is defined as having a predominance of Spanish and Italian surnames. Lo criollo is founded through the sons of Latin immigrants. The sons of "English" immigrants were never conceived of as criollos, and could not become criollo by playing soccer. They remained English, playing an English sport and, in this way, keeping their English identity. How can these differences be explained? In the interpretation of El Gráfico genealogical reasons give way to reasons based on styles of play. These styles, in turn, are based on ethnic differences conceptualized as differences in character and in the form through which feelings and bodily movements are expressed.

In the texts of El Gráfico, "British" male virtues are identified with being phlegmatic, with discipline, method, the collective ideal, force, and physical power. These virtues help to create a repetitive style like a "machine." The author recognizes that this style allows one to conceptualize British soccer as "perfect"—that is, industrially perfect. The criollo male, thanks to the Latin influence, is exactly the opposite: restless, individualistic, less disciplined, based on personal effort, agility, and skill. Owing to these characteristics, the author concludes, one can see "River Plate" soccer as being imperfect and, therefore, open to development once professionalism is established (El Gráfico 470, 1928, 15). Later, in the 1940s, the idea of the "machine" is opposed to the idea of "art" in the sense of artistic musical interpretation: Argentineans play soccer with the touch and virtuosity with which artists play the piano or the violin. For that reason, a great soccer team is like an orchestra made up of great individuals (El Gráfico 1124, 1941, 18). The most typical characteristic of Argentinean soccer would be the touch, which could be short, slow, or quick according to the tactical requirements and the intensity of the game.

The notions of opposing British and criollo male physical virtues would remain, but become modified. The English physical virtues are associated with "force and physical power," while the virtues of the criollos are those of agility and virtuoso movements. The metaphor of the "machine" as opposed to individual creativity is a constant in Argentinean soccer imagery. "Britishness" is associated with the industrial, the criollo with the preindustrial social system. Faced with the machine, or the repetitive, the typical criollo response would be the dribble. Dribbling, which would later be called the *gambeta* (a word derived from gauchesque literature which describes the running motion of an ostrich), is eminently individual and cannot be programmed; it is the opposite of the industrial, collective game of the machine.

According to El *Gráfico*, by 1928 lo *criollo* had acquired its own characteristics. The "founding" of the "*criollo* style" had to have a precise date, protagonist, and event: this was fixed in 1913 when Racing Club deposed the champions, Alumni. It is interesting to note, as in any myth, that the historical reality does not coincide with the narrative. As we saw, Alumni abandoned competition in 1912 and not in 1913. It did not participate in the championship of 1912, which was won by Quilmes, another English team. Therefore, Racing did not win over Alumni but over Quilmes. The two "foundings" are, in many ways, related to two clear historical hegemonies: Alumni dominated organized soccer from 1900 to 1911, and Racing did the same from 1913 to 1919. A concrete historical hegemony lies behind the two "mythological foundings." More interesting is the genealogy of the styles. One might conceive of a personal soccer-playing style as something totally imaginary, but, in general, style develops through comparison with other playing styles, as the texts quoted above indicate. However, in the fifteen years between 1913 and 1928 the transformation from the British to the *criollo* style was a gradual process. In this transformation the gaze of the "distant other," the Europeans, and the "near other," the Uruguayans, would be important.

El *Gráfico* argues at an early date that soccer will become the fundamental sport in Argentina, since it allows a nation to express itself through its national team (190, 1923, 4). The Uruguayan victory in the 1924 Olympic Games in Paris and the successful tour in 1925 of Boca Juniors, a first-division side, throughout many European countries would confirm the existence of a "River Plate" soccer, different from European and English soccer.[4] Until the Boca tour, the Argentineans were more English than the Uruguayans, even in the perception of the Uruguayan players themselves (El *Gráfico* 190, 1923, 4, and 205, 1923, 15). The Europeans contributed to this change through their own perception of the differences involved, through their definition of a "River Plate" soccer played by both Argentineans and Uruguayans. The visit in 1926 of Real Deportivo Español, a Barcelona club, led to the development of a theory of *criollo* soccer as something distinct. Without a trace of modesty, El *Gráfico* wrote about the visit of the Catalan team:

> We feel that the quality of the soccer played in our country is very high ... and we conclude that soccer in Spain has made surprising prog-

ress that puts it almost on a par with our own. We say almost on a par since we are convinced that our own play is technically more proficient, quicker, and more precise: it perhaps lacks effectiveness due to the individual actions of our great players, but the soccer that the Argentineans, and by extension the Uruguayans, play is more beautiful, more artistic, and more precise because approach work to the opposition penalty area is done not through long passes up-field, which are over in an instant, but through a series of short, precise, and collective actions: skillful dribbling and very delicate passes. (366, 1926, 17; my translation)

In El Gráfico's perception, the Argentinean players' skill in dribbling would be one of the fundamental aspects of criollo style. Dribbling is an individual, not a collective, activity. The collective style would therefore come to depend on the qualities of the best players, those with highly developed dribbling skills. Dribbling would be the factor that enabled the transition from the "founding" to the development of a style. Dribbling gave style a form. The gaze of the "others," the Europeans, accelerated this process. At the same time, Argentinean and Uruguayan players who began to appear in Europe in the 1920s were great dribblers. The export of Argentinean players, mostly forwards, began in 1921 when the Italian club Torino bought Julio Libonatti, a very technical and enthusiastic center forward who, during the 1920s, was a central player for the Italian national team (Brera and Sali 1975, 1: 95–97). This export of soccer players was strengthened in the 1920s and 1930s. In the process of the transformation of soccer into a "universal sport," Argentina began to export performing bodies and to be identified with soccer and performing males.

El Gráfico develops the theory of the two "foundings" in a new international context: Argentineans and Uruguayans dominated the South American championships in the 1910s and the 1920s as well as the Olympic Games of 1928. The final of the Amsterdam Olympic Games in 1928 saw the national teams of Argentina and Uruguay. The Uruguayans won their second consecutive gold medal. The soccer of "River Plate" was defined as being a world power, no longer peripheral to European soccer. This was confirmed in 1924 by the visit of Plymouth Argyll, a rather marginal professional team playing in the Southern English League, which was defeated twice by the Argentinean national team: 3–0 and 1–0. In the farewell letter written by the captain of Plymouth and published in The Standard we can read that "the class of soccer shown by your best players is very little behind that of the strongest of the English League Clubs, and we beg you to accept our congratulations" (20 July 1924, 5).

It is important to keep in mind that El Gráfico's application of the term "criollo foundation" to a game transformed by the sons of first-generation immigrants should have been considered an insult by the nationalist writers of the time. The nationalists were against massive immigration because it contaminated the "national essence" and "sullied the country" (Rock 1993, 41–42). In the world of soccer, however, the immigrants and their creativity allowed the national style to appear, strengthen, and be reproduced over time. National identity in soccer belongs to the sons of non-British immigrants: it is a cultural form created on the margins of the nationalists' criollismo. The narrative of El Gráfico is a homage to the mixing of sons of Latin Europeans with the local population and excluding, explicitly, the sons of the British, an exclusion which can be seen as a concession on the part of the writers of El Gráfico to the nationalists' "anti-British imperialism" and to the dominant anti-Anglo-Saxon ideology of Arielismo (Rodó 1957).[5] I think, however, that El Gráfico also contributed in its way, defining, in the field of sport, "Britishness" as the relevant "other" for the Argentineans. The magazine would even defend Argentinean players leaving to play abroad, even playing for national teams where they would be defined as "native." Italy made flagrant use of this, including four Argentinean players in the winning World Cup team of 1934, who would be considered as ambassadors of criollo soccer: "Stabile goes to Italy, not to defend soccer in the peninsula, but to defend criollo soccer, since he is a criollo player" (El Gráfico 589, 1930, 37).

The Criollo Male Style: Undetermined Nature or Social Amalgamation?

As I mentioned before, the documentary film Fútbol argentino, based on the theory of the two foundings of Argentinean soccer and broadcast in 1990 to much acclaim, became a kind of "master narrative" for younger generations of soccer enthusiasts. The majority of my informants accepted this historical presentation as a "true story." Matías, born in 1920 and the senior of all of them, remembered the importance of this "theory" in the 1940s, the "golden age" of Argentinean soccer, when the national team won almost every South American Cup and many clubs— after the Second World War—toured Europe with great success. He mentioned El Gráfico but also newspapers and radio programs as the main sources of this "theory." Matías insisted on the importance of creating "mythologies" and relating them to the need of having a "national style." He emphasized the competition with the Uruguayans:

The Uruguayans won the two Olympic titles, in 1924 and 1928, and the first World Cup in 1930. Argentineans got two silver medals: in 1928 and 1930. We were second twice, and we created an understanding of the defeats based on an opposition between the force and effectiveness of the Uruguayans and the elegance of ourselves. It was like a *tour de force*: the Uruguayans were suddenly more British and we were exactly the opposite. You see, Uruguayans and Argentineans learned from the British, and abruptly we had good and bad pupils. We transformed the defeats into a victory: the consolidation of a different style.

Matías knew that the concept of *rioplatense* soccer, comprising Argentina and Uruguay, had existed during the 1920s. However, he believed that this concept was not only the product of some journalists of El Gráfico but was also imposed by the gaze of the Europeans. I reminded him that in the film *Fútbol argentino* the *rioplatense* soccer was presented as something different and as a cultural export. In spite of the fact that the genealogical narrative is presented as an ideological construct, Matías and many of my informants insisted on the differences of soccer style; the question was how individual differences arose and how they developed into an imagined and "real collective style." Let me present the two interpretative models of El Gráfico.

Borocotó, a renowned journalist for decades, developed the idea of "*criollo* dribbling" in 1928 and elaborated it in 1950.[6] In his conceptualization the transformations permitting the development of the new style are open only to the descendants of Latin immigrants. His theory has two meanings: the original, in 1928, is based on the freedom of the *pibes criollos* (the "*criollo* boys") and the complementary, in 1950, on the absorption of substances. In the first theory the *pibes* learned to play spontaneously in the *potreros* (empty urban spaces of different sizes, usually small, with very uneven surfaces) without any teachers; this was unlike England where, according to Borocotó, soccer was integral to the school system (El Gráfico 480, 1928). Moreover, as we have seen above, the development of British soccer in Argentina was intimately related to the implementation and consolidation of the British educational system. The great British clubs of the pioneer time sprang out from the British schools, and many headmasters played a crucial role in improving the standards of the game. Kanitkar (1994) has argued that the imperial British created the image of the "sporting boy." The games recommended were team sports, which required qualities of leadership, cooperation, and loyalty. To be part of a team was conceived as being part of a perfect machine. The opposition between freedom—and creativity—and school—associated with discipline and pupil-teacher relations—therefore makes sense from a historical perspective. Borocotó recalls that Argentinean soccer has become known throughout the world through dribbling, and that the players leaving Argentina to play in Europe are the best dribblers. He argues emphatically that until now Argentina has been known throughout the world for exporting its valuable frozen beef and its quality cereals, "nonpopular products"—in the sense that they came from the estates of the pampa-based land-owning classes—and now it is important that it should become known for its "popular products." One of the high-quality "popular products" is dribbling, and its exponents are the refined Argentinean soccer players. The practice of soccer permits the Argentineans—and the nation—to be "seen" in the world, to be "remembered" and, above all, to be "prized." To play in the finals of 1928 and 1930 is as important as to export players (El Gráfico 467, 1928, 16). Argentineans are "global" through soccer, a bodily practice making it possible for many young athletes to take part in "transnational connections," to paraphrase the title of Hannerz's book (1996) devoted to contemporary globality.

Chantecler, another great writer of El Gráfico, also contributed to the development of a theory of lo criollo. Dribbling, an expression of the body, would become a manifestation of the essential criollo character. Dribbling expresses the wily and crafty criollo as opposed to the artless British (El Gráfico 467, 1928, 16). To the central tenets of Borocotó's thesis—the pure imagination of the pibe and the congestion of players on the field— one more component is definitely added: wiliness. Without the existence of the qualities of craftiness and wiliness, dribbling could not emerge, and there would be no space for creative improvisation. Chantecler maintains that the British are cold and mathematical and, for that reason, play "learned" soccer. In contrast, the River Plate players, who are warm and improvisers, play an "inspired" soccer. At the same time, he draws a distinction between the River Plate countries: the Argentineans play with the heart; they are faster and more aggressive; the Uruguayans play with the head; they are calmer and more romantic (El Gráfico 467, 1928, 16). Chantecler would develop the theory of the "melting pot" and amalgamation, stressing a continuous process of criollo-ization. A criollo is not born but made; he is the product of a tradition that is altered by individual contribution. In an article entitled "Viveza Criolla: The Main Characteristics of Our Game," he writes:

When our immigrant country received in its breast the great migrations of all races, it assimilated qualities from each of them and amalgamated them, giving them its own mark. This is the new race that European intellectuals talk about when they come to study the psychology of our people and cannot find a clear-cut defining characteristic because we have something from each civilization without belonging typically to any of them. (El Gráfico 654, 1932, 21; my translation)

Chantecler considers that, in the development of *criollo* "craftiness," players from the British era, like Leonard, Brown, Buchanan, and Arnold Watson Hutton, helped to change the coldness of the British. In a dictionary of *criollo* soccer Chantecler defined in a very precise way "the products of *viveza criolla*: the feint, the 'bicycle' (a special type of dribbling), a fake attack, the *túnel* (to do a 'nutmeg'), the *marianela*, and also what he calls 'disreputable cunning'" (El Gráfico 652 and 653, 1932). *Viveza criolla* becomes not just a list of inventive plays but, rather, a quality that developed historically. Behind each one of these above-mentioned acts there is a creator, a *criollo* player who developed it. Chantecler begins with amalgamation, conceptualized as the process of blending all races in soccer, and adds aggregation, imagined as the product of individual creativity.

Borocotó, on the other hand, tried to develop a theory of national soccer by cleansing it of British influence, transforming it into something purely *criollo*. His *tour de force*, his modification of the theory of nationalist writers of the time, is to have linked *criollo* soccer with immigration and the city. He maintained that the Latin immigrants nationalize soccer because they become *criollos*, inheriting the characteristics of the "authentic *criollos*." There is no melting pot; there is a transference of qualities through the absorption of fundamental substances. This perspective was fully developed in 1950.

In the World Cup of 1950 in Brazil the final was played between two South American teams: Uruguay and Brazil. Argentina did not participate, continuing a boycott initiated in 1934. The fact that these two teams reached the final and dominated the tournament created a turmoil in Argentina. The victory of Uruguay was seen as a confirmation of the superiority of "River Plate" soccer. Borocotó took part in the public debate concerning the existence of different styles and defended an essentialist point of view. He emphasized the fact that Italians and Spaniards do not play like Argentineans in spite of having many Argentinean players of Italian or Spanish descent. He refused to accept a unilineal racial interpretation of the Argentinean style: the sons of immigrants had Italian or Spanish blood, but they were transformed by their contact with unique Argentinean substances. He defined the following substances as having transformative qualities: landscape—composed of earth and air, beef, barbecued meat *(asado)*, *mate* (a local tea), and food in general. He insisted that these substances are not found in other places and that they defined Argentina as a different nation (El Gráfico 1618, 1950, 46–48). He reiterated that "there is not a single way of playing soccer," and the existence of different styles is related to "cultural traits." He continued to use the argument presented in the 1920s: contact with the pampa and its culture transformed the immigrants. In this sense, something unique and untransferable becomes naturalized: the contact with nature allows the sons of immigrants—only some sons, of course—to be transformed. The style of play is thus derived from nature—it is a natural gift; a *criollo* player is born so, and cannot be made so. The "natural," the *criollo*, appears as a barrier against cultural transference, against the importation of European styles, which was the main point of discussion in 1950. Borocotó finds symmetry between being and feeling: the natural has to do with feelings, not with reason (El Gráfico 1618, 1950, 46). From this perspective, the immigrants brought nothing of substance to help this radical transformation: their sons, born in the pampas, become *criollos*.

If Borocotó refuses to accept the idea of the melting pot, Chantecler, on the contrary, acknowledges the importance of immigration in the creation of a style in which there is even room for British craftiness. Being *criollo* is not permanent; it develops over time through a sort of successful melting pot. What is common to both theories is that the *criollo* has been divested of force and courage by making supreme virtues of the art of dribbling—that is, a play that avoids physical contact with the opposition—and cunning, the ability to hide one's true intentions by turning life (the game) into a series of continual pretences, making the opponent believe the opposite of one's true intentions, turning deceit into victory.

The Criollo Male Style as a Mechanism of Exclusion and Inclusion

I presented my historical findings to some of my informants, and we had several lively exchanges of ideas. Matías was clear in his judgment: the ideology of El Gráfico was dominant at that time, and it is still the "standard explanation of the creation of a new style." He pointed out that in other leading newspapers, especially La Nación and Crítica, the same arguments were presented. Amílcar insisted on the "middle-class and populist tone of the opposing ways of playing soccer." Roberto, a middle-aged bureaucrat, considered Borocotó's model an effective mechanism for creating some kind of solidarity and acceptance for the new immigrants. He insisted that many of his arguments were "opportunist" and a way of excluding the British in a period of increasing nationalism.

The importance of landscape, food, and blood in the creation of the style was less acceptable to my informants. However, they recognized that in order to conceive of the differences between Argentineans born of Italian parents and Italians in the motherland some central properties of the new country must be taken into account. Roberto pointed out that, at that time, the importance of the pampa and the *gaucho* was substantial: "the nationalist imagined a nation of gauchos."[7] The *criollo* was conceptualized in relation to integration but also in terms of creativity: in the world of soccer the descendants of British immigrants are less creative than the descendants of Italians and Spaniards.[8] The diversity of origins does not exclude processes of generalization in which a key factor is the continuous amalgamation of the new mixtures. The "national" is a typical hybrid product, open but exclusive because the British are eliminated from the new style. The case of Argentinean soccer illustrates the process of hybridization as the creation of a "pure form" that did not exist in the past and is historically constituted as a new form and as a tradition. Applying the term "*criollo* foundation" to a game introduced by the sons of first-generation immigrants would have been considered an insult by the nationalist writers of the time. The nationalists were against the immigrants because they contaminated the fragile "national essence." In the world of soccer, however, the immigrants and their creativity allowed the national style to appear, strengthen, and be reproduced over time. National identity in soccer belongs to the sons of immigrants; it is a cultural form created on the margins of the nationalist *criollismo*. The narrative of El Gráfico is a homage to the sons of foreigners excluding, explicitly, the sons of the British. I think that El Gráfico contributed in its way to defining "Britishness" as the relevant "other" for the Argentineans in the field of sport. Hybridization thus does not produce the chaos imagined by some of the nationalist thinkers. The virtues of the male hybrids produced in Argentinean soccer had a transgressive quality because they were able to subvert the dominant model based on English male virtues. The creolization process implied a change from the school to the street, and from the British to the new hybrids, products of the non-British immigration. In this direction, against the values of courage and willpower, the Argentinean soccer players represent almost the contrary; they were portrayed as sensitive, artistic, and great improvisers. The world of soccer gave rise to a positive image of the male immigrants, and the performances of the best players constituted important landmarks in imagining the complex relations between nationality and masculinities.

Notes

1. The Argentine Soccer Association (AFA) played a key role in the expansion of organized soccer in South America. By 1912, the most important leagues were affiliated with the AFA: the Uruguayan League, the Liga Rosarina, the leagues from the northern provinces of Argentina (Salta, Santiago del Estero, and Tucumán), the Liga del Sur (from the province of Buenos Aires), and the Brazilian Associations from São Paulo and Rio de Janeiro (The Standard 17 August 1912, 3).

2. Frydenberg's analysis is based on the reading of La Argentina, published twice a week from 1902 and transformed into a daily newspaper in 1907. The originality of La Argentina lies in the fact that the clubs not affiliated with the Association could use its pages for announcing their tournaments and results. A social world of real "aficionado soccer" was thus created. It is worth noting that Frydenberg's findings are complementary to mine, based on the reading of The Standard, which represented official organized soccer and the British values of "fair play."

3. The confraternity dinner after important soccer matches was a common practice in Argentina during the 1900s—the so-called "third half" (tercer tiempo). The Standard carefully described the dinners after international matches between Argentina and Uruguay or between the Argentinean teams and the British visitors. This practice disappeared from soccer in the 1910s. The "third half" can be regarded as a representation of a class ideology which vanished from soccer when it became popular and was appropriated by the working classes.

4. Jules Rimet, the president of the Fédération Internationale de Football Association (FIFA), visited Argentina in 1924, after the Olympic Games. He observed that victory in a universal game like soccer, like that achieved by Uruguay, was important for the new nations because they became known, gaining a prestige otherwise difficult to attain. He also lamented the absence of Argentina, because the world was deprived of a fantastic final between the two teams of the River Plate basin (La Nación 6 September 1924, 3). His premonition was right: the final of the next Olympic Games would be played by Argentina and Uruguay.

5. Arielismo was an ideology based on the famous book of José Enrique Rodó, Ariel, which was published in 1900. Rodó identified the Anglo-Saxon tradition and genius, best illustrated by the North Americans, with utilitarianism and extreme materialism, while the Latin was profoundly humanist and artistic. If we read El Gráfico with this perspective we are not surprised that the Anglo-Saxon style was presented as industrial, mechanical, and repetitive, while the Latin was sensitive, artistic, and with a creativity based on improvisation. Borocotó's analysis, perhaps a result of being the good Uruguayan he was, distilled Arielismo.

6. Borocotó—his real name was J. Lorenzo—became one of the most influential

sports journalists in Argentina. Born in 1902 in Montevideo, Uruguay, he joined El *Gráfico* in 1927 and retired, as editor, in 1955. From 1927, he was active as a radio journalist. He was the author of many best-sellers and also had success in the film world. Alabarces considers Borocotó the best sports writer of this epoch because "he understood that soccer was intimately related to the daily life of Argentineans, with their loves, their stories, their dreams" (1996, 181). He wrote the script of one of the classics of Argentinean cinema, *Pelota de trapo* (Rag Ball), made in 1948 (see Cechetto 1993), and in this way his fictional construction of Argentinean soccer mythology was transformed into "reality" through the fictional power of film. The film describes with "spontaneity and lyricism the world of children and their passion for soccer" (Maranghello 1984, 102). Alabarces maintains that *Pelota de trapo* can still be seen as the most important film on soccer made in contemporary Argentina (1996, 181).

7. The nationalists accepted immigrants if they became a part of the nation. Roberto, a descendant of Russian Jews, is right in his observation and agrees with Shumway when he writes that "Argentine nationalism is first and foremost nativistic, proud of the country's Hispanic heritage and its mixed ethnicity" (1991, 292). Given this ideological context and the influence of Arielismo, the acceptance of Latin immigrants as the creators of a national style seems plausible, although controversial.

8. The history of Argentinean soccer with the "two foundations" is comparable to the historical processes in Peru, Brazil, and Uruguay. The historical development of soccer in Peru is similar, in many ways, to the Argentinean case: British and aristocratic at the beginning, but adopted very early in the twentieth century by the working classes of Lima and Callao (Deusta Carvallo, Stein, and Stokes 1984). Mason (1995) has shown the central role of the British elite in the origins and early history in Argentina, Brazil, and Uruguay. He, however, maintains that "Britons were present at the birth of the game in Brazil . . . [but] other European migrants were important in soccer's early stages" (1995, 9). Leite Lopes (1997) has shown that in the development of Brazilian soccer the British elite was dominant. The poor whites, *mestizos*, and blacks were incorporated in organized soccer in the 1920s. This process engendered a series of conflicts when Vasco da Gama, a non-elite club founded by Portuguese immigrants, won the championship in Rio in 1923. The next year Vasco da Gama was excluded from the league. The democratization of Brazilian soccer began in the 1930s (Caldas 1989; Leite Lopes 1997). Compared with Argentina and Uruguay, Brazil had a delay of almost twenty years. This explains the dominance of both countries in the early periods of South American soccer. In spite of the similarities in the South American countries, the mechanism of exclusion of the British from the formation of a national style is particular to Argentina. The same ideological developments have not been documented in the other societies at that time. In Brazil, and I imagine in Peru and perhaps Uruguay, in contrast to the Argentinean ideology of a *criollo* foundation, the idea of "multiracialism" in sport—and in the building of a nation—became dominant in the 1930s (see Leite Lopes 1997). The important presence of the black population in the practice of soccer in Brazil and

Peru—and to a lesser degree in Uruguay—conditioned national imaginaries. Sánchez León observes that in Peru the idols in soccer are blacks or *cholos*, never white players (1993, 103). Therefore, it is possible, as a working hypothesis, to delineate "black areas" and "European areas" in the consolidation of playing styles and imageries in South America. The Argentineans never imagined that they could play like Brazilians because they never had black players on the most successful national teams.

ADRIÁN GORELIK AND GRACIELA SILVESTRI

The Past as the Future: A Reactive Utopia in Buenos Aires

Adrián Gorelik was born in Argentina in 1957. An urban historian, he is a professor at the Universidad Nacional de Quilmes in Argentina. His main titles include La sombra de la vanguardia: Hannes Meyer en México, 1938–1947 (1993, with Jorge Liernur), and La grilla y el parque: Espacio público y cultura urbana en Buenos Aires, 1887–1936 (1998). Graciela Silvestri was born in Argentina in 1954. An architect and historian, she is a professor at the Universidad Nacional de la Plata and a researcher at the Consejo de Investigaciones Científicas y Técnicas (CONICET) in Argentina. Her main titles include El umbral de la metrópolis (1993, with Jorge Liernur), and El paisaje como cifra de armonía (2001, with Fernando Aliata).

During the first half of the 1930s, the will to give a sense of identity to a process of urban development built upon the increasing social integration of new popular sectors materialized in the nostalgia for a mythical origin and a mythical destiny. With few exceptions, the urban representations inspired by Buenos Aires eschewed the central aspects that gave weight to radical modernisms, crisscrossed by Jacobin and communitarian aspirations, the pursuit of a synthesis between form and life, and the need to define a new society for the new times. Instead, a vision prevailed in which modernization and history should conflate in harmony, the former being sustained by the renewal designed by the latter. It is possible that this elitist desire to recapture the destiny inscribed in the past is what most resembles a utopia.

Toward 1936, this reactive utopia crystallized in the shape of a city: after fifty years of modernizing prefigurations it was the inexorable conclusion of an era, while investing it, ex post facto, with the attributes of the Project.[1] However, in order to do so, it was necessary to go back before the cycle began in 1880, and to turn Buenos Aires into the ideological embodiment of four hundred years of predestined utopia. It was a utopia of both origin and future. The celebrations accompanying the fourth centennial of Buenos Aires's first foundation in 1936 represent the articulated vision of a city that finally recaptured its true past because it had succeeded in glimpsing its future. It is a vision whose strength has endured until the present day despite the fact that at the very moment of its consolidation it became obsolete.

THERE IS NO ROOM for utopia in the actual construction of a city: its processes span over long periods of time and are made of small additions, of fragments of projects that have been both transformed and distorted through different urban actions, of interminable expropriations, of changes in functions and needs. Yet, the real city does not exist without utopias, without the prospect of ideal futures. Behind Central Park lie the transcendentalist dreams of an alternative, natural way of life in the city, as utopian as the capitalist speculative processes that turned New York into the fetish of metropolitan modernity. The relationship between utopia and the city could be summed up in this apparent paradox. It is an inevitable relationship given that utopia was not only always conceived of in the city, but rather it was conceived of *as* the city, generating organic associations between form and society. Moreover, every urban endeavor refers to a worldview posed as global, despite the fact that as these endeavors are incorporated into the fabric of the city they fragment, diminish, and blend into those that preceded them. The transparency of utopian anticipation becomes in the city an opaque palimpsest.

It becomes clear that every urban intervention presupposes a city project from the very moment in which the modern self-consciousness concerning *the project* is born. However, its limits are also identified: the essentially fragmentary nature of the interventions as well as the scant possibilities for an authentic transformation of the urban artifact are signs of the distinctive ambiguity of historical figures as disparate as Alberti or Piranesi. However, and perhaps because of the radical urban transformations of the nineteenth century as seen in Haussmann's modernization of Paris, an entire branch of twentieth-century city planning is exclusively sustained by the ambition of an all-encompassing Project, one that could conceivably consolidate and dominate all *real* events.

This ambiguity unfolds when we attempt to understand Argentine modernism and how it relates to the city. Firstly, if on one hand the idea of the Project seemed weakened in the European milieu after five centuries of interventions imposed on very ancient cities, in Buenos Aires, on the other hand, it was sustained not only by the speed of a modernization introduced two centuries earlier on a tabula rasa, but above all by the blistering explosion during the scarce fifty years that the formation of *modern Argentina* lasted. Secondly, the almost clinical mystique of European urbanization is directly linked to the problems posed by the old urban centers, problems that colonial planning eliminated from the outset. In contrast, the entire modernization of Buenos Aires could be limited to the question of its urban sprawl: how to control, characterize, and define it, although the urban sprawl itself was unintended and never part of the project. Within the diffuse geographical boundaries delineated by the Law of Federalization of Buenos Aires in 1880, the different municipal actions struggled until the 1930s to catch up with the problems presented by a city that steadfastly grew on a daily basis.

AS THE FIRST project to confer official existence to the suburbs, the 1925 Systematic Project for the Urbanization of the Municipality [*Proyecto Orgánico para la Urbanización del Municipio*], gave rise to a succession of debates concerning the problem of urban sprawl. Until then, the predominant attitude among the public sector toward the city's growth had been one of distrust, the origin of which could be found in the purposes of the designer of Buenos Aires-Capital City, Torcuato de Alvear. The expansion envisioned by Alvear in 1880 was not so much a product of territorial ambition as it was of the objective to surround the city with great reserves of public green spaces, which could hygienically accommodate the public services of a modern, though small and compact, city.

In 1887, the districts of Flores and Belgrano were annexed, and at the turn of the nineteenth century the first official plan to extend the city's grid appeared, going beyond those areas where construction had occurred "spontaneously," and toward the enormous open spaces and lagoons that were part of the new capital's lands. The public sector's mistrust lingered as residual evidence of the impossibility to control property speculation, and was manifested in its attempt to reform, through punctual interventions, the conditions of the city in the margins of the predominant regime of laissez-faire. Just around 1919, the undeniable existence of these neighborhoods, together with the weight of their community organizations and the democratization of the city council, bestowed political significance and public presence upon the city's expansion. However, and regardless of the socialist municipal politics—a prevailing force in the council at that time and a decisive impulse toward modernization—it is impossible not to notice the paralyzing ambivalence between the just demands made by the new residents of areas that were flooded for the greater part of the year, and the obvious unfairness of the economic interests that put these lands on the market for the exclusive benefit of the landowners. Reformists also experienced urban sprawl as a dramatic circle: the scarce improvements the state was able to bring to the suburbs to make them more habitable once the land had been parceled off only made it easier to put even more inhospitable lands on the market.

The Systematic Project of 1925 sought to provide a series of reforms already being developed for the "hygiene of the suburban neighborhoods" with an urban framework and an "architectural aesthetics"; it sought to change reality into desire: this urban expansion made it possible to identify Buenos Aires "with the ultra-modern great urban clusters, so different from traditional European cities."[2] By making it official, the Systematic Project exposed the dual nature of the process of urban sprawl: on the one hand, it implied an effective democratization of public space because it promoted the homogenization of the popular suburbs with the traditional city, which made Buenos Aires unique among Latin American cities. On the other hand, the extension of the gridiron pattern was an indication of the state's inability to deal rationally with those inhospitable lagoons and open fields. If this contradiction was brought to light, it is only because governmental administration, ideologically unable to control the always increasing property speculation, in any event considered itself more as a reformist than a modernizing agent. For the public sector, modernization just *happened*: the grid burgeoned and the urban weave of little, humble houses got stronger and thicker; reform, nevertheless, was simply necessary.

In the years following its publication, the Project's severest criticisms clearly exposed the reformist bent of the public sector. They were not critical of the dullness of the proposed improvements for the suburbs, but rather identified them as symptoms of the lack of attention paid to the city's "real" problems, those concerning downtown. The question was where to focus public action: either to invest its resources in widening the central avenues and diagonal thoroughfares, enhancing the Plaza de Mayo, or to relocate downtown to one or several "civic centers" in the outskirts, in a word, to revamp the traditional downtown or to decentralize it. The debate around these differing proposals intensified as the decade came to a close. In the midst of this polarization, there were the conflicting recommendations of two personalities who visited the country in 1930, Le Corbusier and Hegemann; the creation of institutions such as the National Commission for Civic Centers [Comisión Nacional de Centros Cívicos] of 1933; the realization of competitions such as the 1934

1. Widening of 9 de Julio Avenue. Colección Dirección de Paseos, Museo de la ciudad de Buenos Aires, 1937.

Friends of the City [Los Amigos de la Ciudad] for the Plaza de Mayo; and the realization of the First Argentine Congress of City Planning [Primer Congreso Argentino de Urbanismo] of 1935, where an entire range of projects was unveiled.

Facing this process, Mariano de Vedia y Mitre's administration (1932–38) began to formulate its own plan. On the one hand, his administration carried out many projects—of almost forgotten origin—for downtown and the suburbs: the diagonal thoroughfares were finished, as was the main stretch of the 9 de Julio Avenue and the widening of Corrientes Street; the subway network was completed; the Riachuelo riverbed was rectified and all its bridges replaced with modern structures; modern sanitation was brought to the suburbs and road surfaces were paved; the General Paz Avenue was built and the Maldonado Creek was channeled and closed off. On the other hand, because of these precise, powerful, modernizing developments, it was decided to leave the fate of the city to the control of market forces. In other words, the tension between modernization and reform was simply eliminated.

The installation of these public works validated in every case the urban structure against which, in spite of all the contradictions, every previous municipal administration had rebelled. If Buenos Aires was finally becoming "Torcuato de Alvear's city," with the Riachuelo and General Paz Avenue as boundaries of the completely urbanized outskirts, the Alvear "Project" was much more than an invention. At the very moment of fiercest debate, the possibility of solving the puzzle of the new emerging city and the new emerging society was closed. The clear-cut boundaries delineating the city were an attempt to ward off any risk of metropolitan overflow over the great conurbation that was coming into being; the attempt was, in effect, a dual denial of both the explosion of these official edges alongside the three urban axes of metropolitan sprawl, and the subsistence, inside those same boundaries, of enormous open spaces where a completely different city could have been built.

IF, FOR THE RADICAL avant-garde movements, "that which comes in the future will eclipse the past"—as Bertold Brecht suggested—then the De Vedia Project could be characterized as "that which comes in the future will establish its foundations." De Vedia y Mitre was a great founder not only because he actually completed and inaugurated long-standing public projects, thus receiving the credits, but most importantly because his main legacy was to invent a past for a city he launched into the future. The cultural gesture used to carry out this new cultural foundation of Buenos Aires was similar to his urban achievements: it brought together disparate elements and provided them with a new meaning. The celebrations held in honor of the Fourth Centennial of the First Foundation of Buenos Aires, which lasted well into 1936 with official inaugurations of public works and cultural affairs, was the crowning moment of this enterprise. These celebrations galvanized the perspectives and available topics of the new school of history, the literary avant-gardes, and the architectural modernisms, while making them functional to the construction of a Buenos Aires capable of amalgamating all of national history in the present.

The establishment by decree of the date and place of the founding of the city by Pedro de Mendoza, decided by a commission of historians appointed on an ad hoc basis by De Vedia, gave legitimacy to the event while revealing its shabbiness. It is a well-known fact that no documents attesting to the exact place (let alone the date) of that "first founding" exist. Behind the presumed scientificity of the arguments of the new school of history, required to defend its hypothesis against Paul Groussac's or Eduardo Madero's, there is an act of faith: if Buenos Aires originally had been founded in the mud on the banks of the Riachuelo as the traditional version held, the black legend that depicted the explorers as a band of adventurers would have gained more acceptance, thus depriving the city, and therefore the nation, of a glorious origin. Instead, the foundation on the plateau, as established in the decree, portrayed the founders as part of a well-ordered conquest that planned and carried out the occupation of the territory with common sense and scientific resolve. Thus, the first synthesis between the values of a zealous Spain, religious but wise and cultured, and the fertile pampas, was inscribed in the porteño locus. However, in his historiographic considerations, Ricardo Levene revealed the modernization of revisionism, arriving at a second synthesis between the cosmopolitan Buenos Aires of the 1920s ("the teeming metropolis with its diabolical hullabaloo") and the spiritual Buenos Aires of colonial times, the two souls dramatically confronting each other throughout the city's history. And thus, Levene proposed, "the synthesis that is Buenos Aires today, simultaneously action and contemplation" would have finally been attained (Levene 1936, 30).

Those were the attempts to bring to an end an intense debate that had engaged historians and intellectuals during the 1920s and 1930s: the search for the origins of Buenos Aires in order to determine its essence. In this fashion, as in countless others concerning Argentine culture, it was Jorge Luis Borges, by making the Argentine culture's mythical character explicit, who best revealed its motives. By countering "the chicanery cooked up in the Boca neighborhood" populated with immigrants with an alternative "founding," he unmasked the mythical function of this historic search: the genuine necessity to trace a direct line between origin and destiny. Why not then should a patio in the Palermo neighborhood also be proof of the national lineage, as Borges had proposed in the poem "Fundación mitológica de Buenos Aires" (1929)? Perhaps because he was who most deeply captured the construction of Buenos Aires's essence, Borges was the only one in De Vedia's series of radio lectures who allowed himself to ironize with respect to the somewhat fortuitous discoveries: "Somebody would find the substance of Buenos Aires in the deep patios of the South and the meticulous ironwork of its balustrades; others, in the brief encounters in Florida Street; some in the rough suburbs that open to the pampas or tumble down toward the Riachuelo; others in gloomy bars patronized by solitary men who experience their criollo resentment as the ensemble reels off another tango" (Borges 1936, 520).[3]

However, despite Borges's irony—or perhaps because of it—the avant-garde's quests were much more effective than Hispanism in order to define a past from the perspective of the new Buenos Aires, and not only because many avant-gardists attended De Vedia's meetings as zealously as the traditionalists did. The contribution of architectural modernism to this re-foundation is clearly seen in the role played by Alberto

Prebisch, contributor to the avant-garde journals *Martín Fierro* and *Sur*, and active participant in defining "the avant-garde urban *criollismo*" at the end of the 1920s.[4]

In the 1910s, the nationalist restoration of the centennial had looked to the neocolonial style in an attempt to develop a didactic language that would strengthen the pedagogical construction of a common origin. In the 1930s, nonetheless, modernism found in "the discreet charm" of pure and white volumes a new form of restoration (Liernur 1986). Both tendencies share a common adversary, fin de siècle eclecticism, outcome of the ostentatious whims of the parvenu immigrant, as depicted in 1930 by Prebisch in the pages of *Sur*. Both tendencies tried to recapture the constitutive harmony of "a humble city, without diagonal thoroughfares, subways, or pretensions, but endowed with the beauty of things that are precisely what they appear to be" (Prebisch 1936, 11). However, the didactic determination of the neocolonial style, which had attempted to include the diverse Latin American aesthetic patrimony in the nationalist liturgy, was, like the latter, forced into parody, in its case as a figurative recourse. Thus, neocolonialism became hyper-eclectic in its search for additional meanings. In contrast, modernism did not pursue a didactic mission but rather sought to make itself heard among the cacophony of unrefined tongues. In this sense, it was an act of restraint; accumulation was not the best response to the absence of form produced by the proliferation of forms, but instead asceticism. This is what Prebisch appears to proclaim in the quiet façade of the Grand Rex cinema, as if denouncing by contrast the *cocoliche*[5] burlesque of the other buildings at Corrientes Street.

Like the literary avant-garde in its discovery of the suburbs, modernism looked for a solution to the same problem that the neocolonial style had struggled to answer: the discovery of a distinct past, not merely Hispanic but *rioplatense*. The same austere forms admired by Prebisch in the pages of the German review *Moderne Bauformen* were similar to the noble rusticity of the local colonial buildings, whose "simple architectural shapes so faithfully matched the physical and spiritual needs of a coherent social body." In effect, "each house resembled its neighbor and the entire city moved at the same pace," described Prebisch in "La ciudad en que vivimos," an introduction to a collection of photographs by Horacio Cóppola, *Buenos Aires 1936*, with texts by Ignacio Anzoátegui and Prebisch. "The obsession with coarse competition that gripped us later, exhibited by the desire to overwhelm our neighbors with extravagant parapets and livid ornaments, had not yet taken hold" (Prebisch 1936, 11).

In contrast to classical utopias, in this local modernism, the criticism

2. Eclectic and *cocoliche* architecture, Avenida de Mayo
Photograph by Horacio Cóppola, 1936.

of the present did not emerge through the construction of an ideal model of the future, or through the description of *another* city that might bring *notices from nowhere;* instead, it focused on recapturing, morally and aesthetically, a forgotten, but nonetheless *real*, past. As the founder of *porteño* architectural modernism, Prebisch also established this conversion of the past into an operating model for the modern city, or rather the conversion of German modernism into a model for colonial Buenos Aires, thus establishing the decisive nucleus of Argentine urban ideology, one that was challenged only by isolated, marginal, *utopian* reformists.

In this regard, Prebisch's obelisk is the most outstanding emblem of the fourth centennial, the perfect synthesis between that past and the future's inclination toward "an overwhelming transformation (that rocks the city) to its very foundations," as celebrated by Leopoldo Marechal in his *Historia de la Calle Corrientes*, another of the official titles commissioned in 1936. Finished in a record time of sixty days, the obelisk is practically the only public work conceived of by this particular administration; it is

3. (left) Classical architecture, Diagonal Norte. Photograph by Horacio Cóppola, 1936.

4. (below) Plaza de Mayo, Diagonal Norte, and the obelisk in the background. Photograph by Horacio Cóppola, 1936.

the landmark with which De Vedia retrospectively elucidated in a cohesive way the first foundation, Rivadavia's "prophetic" vision of 1820, and
the "project" of the generation of 1880, even if divesting it of its notion of
progress. The obelisk symbolized the recovery of a downtown that, from
its pure forms, entered in dialogue with the pyramid of the Plaza de Mayo
and the entirety of universal culture, by connecting the expanded Corrientes Street and the brand-new 9 de Julio Avenue with the new Diagonal, which Arturo Cancela described in his conferences as grandiose
but ultimately as "white" and uniform as "the old colonial streets" (in
Levene 1936, 540).

This founding gesture brought together form and transformation; acknowledgment of these features implied reconciliation with a certain
destiny. The obelisk repeats the founding gesture, while at the same time
dodging those "passing fashions" and that futile, inapprehensible, and
fleeting time with which the modernity of the 1880s had fractured the
sluggish and amiable pace of the "big village." Linked to the past, the
obelisk symbolizes a very typical way of being modern; its form conjures
up the frenzied time of modernity itself.

"PERHAPS ONE DAY everything that we today call progress will be considered a morbid proliferation: neoplasm. There will be a return to simplicity and sluggishness itself will be revalued. There will be trains for
the rich that will be required to go very slowly. . . . Poor people will be
forced to travel at infamous speeds." This prophecy of a future appeared
in the pages of *Las dos fundaciones de Buenos Aires*, a 1933 book by Enrique
Larreta that served as the program of the competition for the remodeling
of Plaza de Mayo, organized by the Friends of the City in 1934. On its
heels, Larreta became president of the committee in charge of commis-
sioning celebrations for the fourth centennial, and his vision for the city
clearly demonstrated how the traditionalists and the avant-gardes could
come together, despite their aesthetic preferences. Two years earlier,
Borges brought to light an essential quality that stood out against the unbridled background of the avenues: "The slow horse-cart is permanently
left behind in the distance. But this same delay can be turned to victory,
as if alien speed were the horrified urgency of enslavement, and the very
delay a total possession of time, as of eternity itself. (The possession of
time is the *criollo* infinite capital, perhaps our only one. We can exalt delay
as immobility, as possession of space)" (Borges 1931, 175).

It is an anti-progressive, anti-technological, and reactive penchant
that only leaves out Roberto Arlt's or Wladimiro Acosta's utopian visions. But how does one articulate this reactive penchant with the city

that emerges from De Vedia's modernizing deeds? The obelisk can easily satisfy the request for a *return to simplicity*, while with the same gesture paying its debt to the avant-garde's principles. But what's the best way to integrate this penchant with such emblems of urban technology and speed as the subway system? What could be more artificial and soulless than this modern vehicle, which traverses the city's underground while ignoring its landscape, invalidating the peculiarities of each neighborhood, transporting the multitude at intangible speeds between points that become increasingly abstract as the perception of space, whose possession Borges reclaimed as a characteristic of the *porteño* culture is lost? It is precisely at this point that the reconciliation with the past built by De Vedia, which appeared in conspicuous places of the city naturalized by concrete references, acquired the unmistakable look of masquerading. The iconography of the murals of the D subway line—the last to be installed in De Vedia's times—didactically reconstructed the journey to be undertaken; those who arrive at the periphery travel to the present, those who start out from downtown return to the origins. Passing through the dark and uncertain tunnels, each station, with its murals facing each other and referring to each other, offers an oasis of reconciliation between tradition and progress, city and countryside. By staging an authentic and eternal sense of history, the murals seek to eradicate the senseless passage of time.[6]

This relationship between culture and technique was paramount to De Vedia's operation, and was, in turn, taken up by the majority of the participants of the 1936 radio talk shows. Nevertheless, the leading actor in these informative and celebratory lectures was the radio itself. De Vedia made use of a technology that virtually annulled time, in order to sustain, however, the meaning of time in terms of long established values. This apparent paradox perhaps concealed an even deeper ambiguity, as the advent of this technology, at once apparent and hidden, sought to eliminate time as much as the fabrication of a mythical history. The elements of this fabrication were limited to the presentation of a specific locus, in this case Buenos Aires, as the positive symbol of the ongoing transformation of the entire country, not just in terms of progress, but also of the spirit, and the avowal that this transformation in no way transgressed the destiny inscribed in its transcendental origin. In order to do so, it was most necessary to articulate without mediations the impact technology had on the national cultural essences. As Levene asserted in his lectures, Buenos Aires must first undergo the process of civilization in order to realize the equilibrium to which it was destined.

Transcending the evils of civilization constituted a goal for Buenos Aires from the very moment in which "the civilizing project" par excellence, that of the generation of 1880, started up. In the 1930s, this manifested itself as a *reactive utopia*, which materialized the process both ideologically and physically, while trying to erase the conflicts that kept up the traces of uncertainty. But, as it almost always has occurred in Argentine history, by the time the official culture identified a problem and tackled its solution, the problem had become something else. Scarcely a few years later and with the celebrations long forgotten, "Goliath's Head" would be the most accepted metaphor to refer to this modernization without reform as another lost historical opportunity, the effects of which still linger today.

Translated by Christopher Dennis and edited by Abril Trigo

Notes

1. It is important to clarify that, with the word *utopia*, we are broadly defining the ideal and accomplished anticipation of a future society. In this regard, the *Project* too, in its strongest sense, has similar connotations. In the title itself, we paraphrase Manfredo Tafuri's definition of "Project" in *Storia della architettura italiana, 1944–1985* (1986). However, we have chosen to avoid entering into the long-standing debate concerning the relationship between *Project* and *utopia*. See also Giulio Carlo Argan's suggestive *Progetto e destino* (1964).
2. Comisión de Estética Edilicia, *Proyecto orgánico para la urbanización del municipio* (1925). Although isolated, there are other voices that, from the first decade, indicated the need for expansion; for example, Benito Carrasco wrote in 1908 in *Caras y Caretas* that "on the map one can see that the real city, the grandiose city of the not too far-off future, the city that will fill America and our Race with pride, needs to develop from the streets of Callao and Entre Ríos to the West, where the design could fit the demands of modern cities, abandoning the traditional gridiron design" (Carrasco 1908).
3. Other participants in the radio series were Ignacio Anzoátegui, Luis Cané, Leónidas Barletta, Fryda Schultz, Manuel Ugarte, José Gabriel, Alfonsina Storni, Leopoldo Marechal, Roberto Giusti, and Arturo Cancela. In our opinion, the titles of Borges's conference, "Tareas y destinos de Buenos Aires," and Marechal's, "Fundación espiritual de Buenos Aires," are highly significant.
4. We have borrowed the expression "avant-garde urban *criollismo*," as well as the assumptions made about the international avant-garde movements of the 1920s, from Beatriz Sarlo's "Vanguardia y criollismo: la aventura de Martín Fierro" (Sarlo 1983c).
5. Famous comic character in Eduardo Gutiérrez and José Podestá's *gaucho* drama *Juan Moreira* (1884), whose portrayal of an Italian immigrant represented cultural difference. It came to name, sometimes with derogatory overtones, the hybrid dialect and cultural hodgepodge of urban popular sectors.

6. It is noteworthy that the murals have mostly been carried out by figures connected with the intellectual movement of *colonial renaissance,* like Martín Noel and Angel Guido, who were singled out by Ricardo Rojas in his aesthetic national program *Eurindia* and who by the 1930s were moving toward a monumentalist art deco style, as exemplified by Guido in his *Monumento a la Bandera* in Rosario. In the field of architecture, it is another example of the homogenization of *porteño* modernism.

ANA M. LÓPEZ

Tears and Desire: Women and Melodrama in the "Old" Mexican Cinema

Ana López is a Cuban American. A film critic, she is also a professor at Tulane University in New Orleans. Her main titles include *Mediating Two Worlds: Cinematic Encounters in the Americas* (1993, edited with John King and Manuel Alvarado), *The Ethnic Eye: Latino Media Arts* (1996, edited with Chon A. Noriega), and *Encyclopedia of Contemporary Latin American and Caribbean Cultures* (2000, edited with Daniel Balderston and Mike Gonzalez).

Since the 1960s the "old" Latin American cinema—produced in the 1930s, 1940s, and 1950s—has been the "other" against which the "new" cinemas struggled to define themselves. Vehemently criticized, the old cinema was rejected as imitative of Hollywood, unrealistic, alienating, and sentimental. Over the years, it became little else than a clichéd straw man in all arguments for cinematic and cultural renovation and change. Although the accomplishments of the new cinemas are enormous (and have been well chronicled elsewhere),[1] the characterization of the "old" cinema as ideologically complicit and servile to the interests of the dominant classes, albeit in many ways justified, was too broad, ignoring the subtleties and differences of cinematic practices, their audiences, and this cinema's tremendous popular appeal.

The old cinema was an easy victim: the studio systems which produced it were by the late 1950s to early 1960s ideologically and commercially bankrupt. From Vera Cruz in Brazil to Argentina Sono Films, the failed attempts to establish film production on an industrial basis demonstrated the problematic nature of the Latin American market for national films: without control of distribution and exhibition, producers could not sustain production or compete on equal terms with Hollywood imports. Latin America was a "natural" market only for Hollywood. However, awareness of the market limitations for national films (which led to a search for other, non-industrial modes of production) was not the immediate cause behind the rejection of the old cinema. The old cinema's principal sin was (as the Cuban critics Enrique Colina and Daniel Díaz Torres argued in 1971 in the pages of *Cine Cubano*) its melodramatic proclivities. Making the melodrama synonymous with the Hollywood cinema, they argued that the Latin American films of the 1930s, 1940s, and 1950s were little else than a poor imitation, "which opened the floodgates to a manifold process of cultural colonization" in Latin America (Colina and Díaz Torres 1971, 15). However, Colina and Díaz Torres did not take into account that this was the first indigenous cinema to dent the Hollywood industry's pervasive presence in Latin America; the first to consistently circulate Latin American images, voices, songs, and history; the first to capture and sustain the interest of multinational audiences throughout the continent for several decades.

The melodramatic was so easily identified with cultural colonization because of its popularity. Although Díaz and Colina argued that the melodrama was popular simply because it was the only readily available dramatic form, what most worried these and other critics was the melodrama's privileged access to popular consciousness (Díaz Torres and Colina 1972, 156–64). On the one hand, the excesses and sentimentality typical of the melodrama rankled the sensibilities of Europeanized critics, who could not understand or explain popularity as anything other than bad taste. On the other, later politicized critics simplistically reproduced an elitist mistrust of mass communication and popular culture and were unable to see in the popularity of the melodrama anything but the alienation of a mass audience controlled by the dominant classes' capitalist interests. With little differentiation or attention to the processes of reception and identification, they rejected the melodrama as "false" communication.[2] It is ironic, however, that the new cinema's efforts to establish so-called "real" communication—as important as they have been—have rarely attained the levels of popular acceptance of the old cinemas. And when that popular success has been achieved, as in *La historia oficial* (*The Official Version*, Luis Carlos Puenzo 1986, Argentina), for example, it has been precisely by recourse to the melodramatic.

Assuming that, even in underdeveloped societies, mass culture serves as an instrument of hegemony and not one of simple mass domination, my goal in this essay is to situate the melodrama of the most prolific of the "old" Latin American cinemas, the classic Mexican cinema, in some of its textual, industrial, and sociocultural contexts. The point here is not to salvage this golden age for some critical pantheon of progressive texts, but to relocate it, by highlighting its contradictory discourses, as an integral part of the Latin American and Mexican social formation of the 1930s–1950s. Emphasizing the different articulations of gender and subjectivity in a society formed by colonization and with a history marked by violence and discontinuity, this essay makes an effort to link the history of the classical Mexican cinema melodrama with Mexican society, tracing the inscription of the melodramatic alongside gendered social positioning and highlighting those moments when conflicting voices and needs visibly erupt into the cinematic and social sphere. Aware of the dangers of imposing upon the Latin American cinema critical modes that do not reflect its sociohistorical conditions, I shall not be proposing an argument based on the melodrama's ability to put into question the patriarchal codes of classic cinematic realism.[3] It is undoubtedly true, as John King argues, that Latin American cinema and literature do not participate in the strong realist tradition of their European or U.S. counterparts and that the terms of Latin American realism are still to be defined (1990, 38). On the contrary, by emphasizing the complex lines of historical and cultural affiliations that link and differentiate the social functions of the melodramatic in Mexico, my goal will be to confront conflicting, historically specific claims of national, ethnic, and gendered identity that have often gone unchallenged in Latin American film studies.[4]

The Melodrama and the Latin American Cinema

As has been extensively detailed elsewhere, the melodrama, along with music and comedy, became synonymous with the cinema in Latin America after the introduction of sound.[5] Taking advantage of Hollywood's temporary inability to satisfy the linguistic needs of the Latin American market, local producers used the new technology to exploit national characteristics. Argentina took on the tango and its melodramatic lyrics and developed the tango melodrama genre in the early 1930s. Similarly, in Mexico, the melodrama became a central genre of the sound cinema after the success of the early sound feature *Santa* (Antonio Moreno 1931), an adaptation of a well-known melodramatic novel by Federico Gamboa about an innocent girl from the provinces who is forced into prostitution in the big city and finds redemption only in death.[6]

Furthermore, the rapid establishment of a specific Latin American star system heavily dependent on radio and popular musical entertainers gave rise to melodramas, which always included at least one or two musical performances to heighten a film's "entertainment value." Starring singers-turned-actors, narratives about entertainers sprinkled with performances became de rigueur. Thus Libertad Lamarque's suffering mothers always also sang, Pedro Infante could weep over his little black child with the popular song "Angelitos negros" ("Little Black Angels") in the film of the same title, and Ninón Sevilla could vent her sexual anger and frustration dancing wild rumbas in the *cabaretera* (brothel) films of the 1950s. In these and other films the narrative stoppage usually generated by performances was reinvested with emotion, so that melodramatic pathos emerged in the moment of performance itself (through gesture, sentiment, interactions with the audience within the film, or simply music choice). In a film like *Amor en las sombras* (*Love in the Shadows*, Tito Davison 1959), which featured ten complete performances in less than two hours' screen time, music and song rather than dramatic action propel the narrative.

Despite this diversity, however, two basic melodramatic tendencies developed between 1930 and 1960: family melodramas that focused on the problems of love, sexuality, and parenting, and epic melodramas that reworked national history, especially the events of the Mexican Revolution. Although the two categories are somewhat fluid, with some family melodramas taking place in the context of the revolution and its aftermath, I shall be concerned primarily with the operations of the former. The revolutionary melodramas are perhaps as significant for the development of a gendered "Mexican" consciousness as the family ones, but I am interested in analyzing the cinematic positioning of women within the Mexican domestic sphere, and the ideological operations of the family melodramas provide us with privileged access to that realm. Set in quintessential domestic spaces (homes or similar places) that, as Laura Mulvey says, "can hold a drama in claustrophobic intensity and represent . . . the passions and antagonisms that lie behind it" (1986, 95), the family melodramas map the repressions and contradictions of interiority and interior spaces—the home and unconscious—with more urgency than is possible within the cathartic large-scale action of revolutionary dramas.

The Melodrama, Women, and Mexico

The melodramatic is deeply embedded in Mexican and Hispanic culture and intersects with the three master narratives of Mexican society: religion, nationalism, and modernization. First of all, Hispanic culture carries the burden of its Christianity which, as Susan Sontag argues, is already melodramatic (rather than tragic) in structure and intention. In Christianity, as Sontag says, "every crucifixion must be topped by a resurrection," an optimism inimical to the pessimism of tragedy (1966, 132–

39). Furthermore, the staples of the family melodrama—sin and suffering abnegation—are essential components of the Christian tradition: sin allows for passion and, although it must always be punished, passion, after all, justifies life.

Second, and perhaps most significantly, the melodrama always addresses questions of individual (gendered) identity within patriarchal culture and at the heart of the definition of Mexico as a nation. In Mexico, questions of individual identity are complicated by a colonial heritage that defines woman and her alleged instability and unreliability as the origin of *national* identity. The Mexican nation is defined, on the one hand, by Catholicism and the Virgin of Guadalupe, the Virgin Mother and patron saint, and, on the other, by the *chingada*, the national betrayal of Doña Marina (also known as La Malinche or Malintzin Tenepal), the Aztec princess who submitted to Cortés and handed her people over to the conquistadores.[7] As Cherríe Moraga succinctly puts it, "Malinche fucked the white man who conquered the Indian peoples of Mexico and destroyed their culture. Ever since, brown men have been accusing her of betraying her race, and over the centuries continue to blame her entire sex for this 'transgression'" (1986, 174–75). Raped, defiled, and abused, Malintzin/Malinche is the violated mother of modern Mexico, la *chingada* (the fucked one) or la *vendida* (the sell-out). As Octavio Paz explains, Malinche's "sons" [sic], the Mexican people, are "the sons of la *chingada*, the fruits of a rape, a farce" (1961, 85). Thus the origins of the nation are located at a site—the violated mother—which is simultaneously an altar of veneration and the place of an original shame. The victim of a rape, Malinche/la *chingada*, mother of the nation, carries the guilt of her victimization. Deeply marked by this "otherness," Mexican national identity rejects and celebrates its feminine origins while gender identity, in general, is problematized even further, as the popular saying "Viva México, hijos de la Chingada" so vividly illustrates. To be Malinche—a woman—is to be a traitor, the great whore mother of a bastard race. In fact, Mexican consciousness and gender definitions have been so intertwined and scarred by the Spanish conquest that the belief that all things of a foreign or European nature are superior to their Mexican equivalents is deprecatingly called Malinchismo. The melodramatic became the privileged place for the symbolic reenactment of this drama of identification and the only place where female desire (and the utopian dream of its realization) could be glimpsed.

Mexico's colonial heritage, first Spanish and most recently American, also affects the social functions of the melodrama. Colonialism always implies a crisis of identity for the colonial subject, caught between the impulse to imitate the colonizer and the desire for an always displaced autonomy. Like Caliban in The Tempest, the colonized must use the colonizer's "words"—the imported cinematic apparatus—and learn the colonizer's language before he or she can even think of articulating his or her own speech: "You taught me language; and my profit on't / Is, I know how to curse." Just as in Brazil the development of the parodic chanchada genre can be seen as a response to the impossibility of thinking of a national cinema without considering the Hollywood cinema as well as Brazil's own underdevelopment, in Mexico, melodrama's excess explicitly defies the Hollywood dominant: "Since there can be no nostalgic return to precolonial purity, no unproblematic recovery of national origins undefiled by alien influences, the artist in the dominated culture cannot ignore the foreign presence but must rather swallow it and recycle it to national ends."[8] As Carlos Monsiváis has said: "If competition with North America is impossible artistically or technically, the only defense is excess, the absence of limits of the melodrama" (1982, 70). Thus the melodrama's exaggerated signification and hyperbole—its emphasis on anaphoric events pointing to other implied, absent meanings or origins—become, in the Mexican case, a way of cinematically working through the problematic of an underdeveloped national cinema.

The melodrama is also formally and practically linked with the specific trajectory of Mexican national identity and the significance of the revolution for the nation-building project. If we agree with Peter Brooks that the melodrama is "a fictional system for making sense of experience as a semantic field of force" that "comes into being in a world where the traditional imperatives of truth and ethics have been violently thrown into question" (1976, xiii and 14–15), then we should not be surprised by the cultural currency of the melodrama in postrevolutionary Mexico. In the midst of the great social upheavals of the postrevolutionary period, the country seemed ungovernable and the city an unruly Mecca: the revolution changed the nature of public life, mobilized the masses, shook up the structures of the family without changing its roots, and, as Carlos Monsiváis says, "served as the inevitable mirror where the country recognized its physiognomy." The revolution may not have "invented" the Mexican nation, but "its vigor, for the first time, lent legendary characteristics to the masses that sustained it" (1982, 27). In other words, the revolution created a new class (the new urban poor soon to be a working class) whose willpower, roughness, and illiteracy became insistently visible in the formerly feudal national landscape.

The revolution also further problematized the position of women in Mexico. Women had fought alongside the men and had followed the troops cooking, healing, and providing emotional and physical solace, either as legitimate wives, lovers, or paid companions. Known generally as *soldaderas*, these women formed the backbone of an incipient feminist movement that emerged after the revolution. Yet as Jean Franco argues, "The revolution with its promise of social transformation encouraged a messianic spirit that transformed mere human beings into supermen and constituted a discourse that associated virility with social transformation in a way that marginalized women at the very moment when they were, supposedly, liberated" (1989, 102). Precisely when the nation created itself anew under the aegis of revolutionary mythology and its male superhero redeemers, women were once again relegated to the background, and in cultural production (especially in national epic allegories) represented as a terrain to be traversed in the quest for male identity. Simultaneously, while the new secular state ostensibly promoted women's emancipation to combat Catholicism and its alleged counterrevolutionary ideology (although women did not win the right to vote in national elections until 1953), Mexico also found itself caught in the wheels of capitalist modernization.

The new class thus created by the revolution—an increasingly mobile, urban, migratory class of male and female workers—was entertained by the popular theater (*teatro frívolo* or *género chico*) before it found the cinema, but after the coming of sound, Spanish-language movies became the principal discursive tool for social mapping. While the *género chico* and its carnivalesque ribaldry[9] attracted a socially but not sexually mixed audience, the cinema was family entertainment[10]—by design and by commercial imperatives, broader-based. By the late 1930s and through the 1940s and 1950s, the national cinema manifested itself as an efficient way of life, granting access not only to entertainment but to vital behaviors and attitudes: "One didn't go to the cinema to dream, but to learn" (Monsiváis 1976a, 446). There was not much room here for the carnivalesque celebration that continued to take place in the *teatro frívolo*: the cinema helped transmit new habits and reiterated codes of behavior, providing the new nation with the common bases and collective ties necessary for national unity. In fact, the cinema helped make a new postrevolutionary middle class viable.

If it is indeed true, as Monsiváis says, that film melodramas served this kind of socializing function, what exactly were the lessons they taught women? How did the melodrama mediate the postrevolutionary crisis of national and gendered identity and its subsequent institutionalization? Rather than blindly enforce or teach uncontradictory high moral values, stable codes of behavior, or obedience to the patriarchal order, the family melodramas staged specific dramas of identity which often complicated straightforward ideological identification for men and women without precluding accommodation. However, the melodrama's contradictory play of identifications constituted neither false communication nor a simple lesson imposed upon the people from above. On the contrary, these films addressed pressing contradictions and desires within Mexican society. And even when their narrative work suggests utter complicity with the work of the law, the emotional excesses set loose and the multiple desires detonated are not easily recuperated.

The narratives of the Mexican family melodrama deal with three principal conflicts: the clash between old (feudal, Porfirian) values and modern (industrialized, urban) life, the crisis of male identity that emerges as a result of this clash, and the instability of female identity that at once guarantees and threatens the passage from the old to the new. These conflicts are played out in two distinct physical and psychic spaces: the home, a private sphere valorized and sanctified by the law, and the nightclub, a barely tolerated social space as liminal as the home is central. Only marginally acceptable, the nightclub is nevertheless the part of the patriarchal public sphere where the personal (and issues of female subjectivity, emotion, identity, and desire) finds its most complex articulation in the Mexican melodrama.

The Home: Mothers, Families, and Their "Others"

Although Mexican patriarchal values insist on the sanctity of the traditional home (as an extension of the "fatherland" blessed by God), the extended families growing in them are rarely well adjusted precisely because of the rigidity of the fathers' law and in spite of the saintliness of the mothers. In Mexico, the family as an institution has a contradictory symbolic status as a site for the crystallization of tensions between traditional patriarchal values (especially the cult of machismo) and modernizing tendencies and as a source of maternal support and nurturing that the secular state could not replace (Franco 1986). This ambivalence is clearly evidenced in the deployment of the Mexican cinema's so-called mother obsession. Although it is undoubtedly true that the Mexican melodrama's fascination with saintly mother figures can be traced to the deeply conservative social impulses of the postrevolutionary middle classes, who countered their insecurity over the legitimacy of their status with aggressive nationalism and an obsessive attachment to traditional values, how this mother obsession is worked out in the melodrama complicates any straightforward assessment of the politics and social mapping of such representations.

Director Juan Oro and the actress Sara García created the archetypal mother of the Mexican melodrama in *Madre querida* (*Dear Mother*, 1935), the heart-wrenching story of a young boy who goes to a reformatory for arson and whose mother dies of grief precisely on 10 May (Mothers' Day in Mexico). Over the next decades, García played suffering, self-sacrificing mothers in countless films such as *No basta ser madre* (*It's Not Enough to Be a Mother*, 1937), *Mi madrecita* (*My Little Mother*, 1940), and *Madre adorada* (*Beloved Mother*, 1948). However, despite their self-acknowledged narrative focus on mothers and their positioning of the mother as the central ideological tool for social and moral cohesion, these and other films ostensibly glorifying mothers as repositories of conservative family values were clearly maternal melodramas rather than women's films. This distinction, invoked by E. Ann Kaplan in her discussion of Hollywood 1920s and 1930s melodramas (1987, 123–29), is significant for the Mexican case because it helps to distinguish between those films that focus on male Oedipal dramas and films that more self-consciously address female spectators and concerns.[11] Indeed, one could argue that, despite their focus on mothers, these family melodramas are patriarchal rather than maternal because they attempt to preserve patriarchal values rather than the sanctity of the mother. In attempting to reinforce the patriarchy their narrative logic breaks down: the moral crisis created in these films revolves around the fathers' identity and not the mothers', whose position is never put into question.

In *Cuando los hijos se van* (*When the Children Go Away*, Juan Bustillo Oro 1941), for example, a rigid provincial family is torn asunder by the father's (Fernando Soler) inability to see the true characters of his sons or to recognize their mother's (Sara García) more sensitive assessment of their characters. Influenced by the "bad" son, the father banishes the "good" son to the city, while the mother, with her unerring maternal instinct, never doubts his integrity and is ultimately proven right by the narrative: the banished son returns a popular radio star and saves the family from a bankruptcy engineered by his sibling. Despite the narrative's obvious privileging of the mother's sight, the film attempts to shore up a patriarchal family structure threatened not only by the patriarch's inability to see, but by the other world lying outside the patriarch's control: Mexico City, emblem of modernization and progress, and the modern and highly pleasurable world outside the family. The film attempts to idealize the family as a unit whose preservation is worth all sacrifices, even death, but its suggestion that the familial crisis is caused by the father's blindness and irrational rigidity, especially when compared with the mother's unerring instinct, puts in question the very patriarchal principle it seeks to assert.

Mothers may have a guaranteed place in the home as pillars of strength, tolerance, and self-abnegation, in other words, as Oedipal illusions, but outside the home they are prey to the male desires that the Mexican home and family disavow. As a foil to the mother's righteous suffering and masochistic respect for the law, men, especially father-figures, are self-indulgent and unable to obey the moral order. It is their desire, unleashed because of maternal asexuality, that most threatens and disturbs the stability of the family and its women. While denying desire within the family, it is a compelling and at times controlling force outside it. Thus a variant of the family melodrama focuses on the impossible attraction of "other" women: the "bad" mothers (las malas), the vamps, the mistresses.

While Sara García portrayed the archetype of the good mother, María Félix depicted her opposite, the mala mujer (bad woman), the haughty independent woman, as passionate and devilish as the mothers are asexual and saintly. The titles of Félix's films clearly reveal her star persona: Doña Bárbara (Fernando de Fuentes 1943), La mujer de todos (Everyone's Woman, Julio Bracho 1946), La devoradora (The Devourer, Fernando de Fuentes 1946), Doña Diabla (Tito Davison 1949). Doña Bárbara, her third film, most clearly defined this persona.[12] After being brutally raped as a young girl, Bárbara becomes a rich, independent landowner—la Doña—who enjoys despoiling and humiliating other human beings, especially men. She exults in her power and discards lovers and even her own daughter easily, exhibiting neither pity nor shame and relishing her hatred. Despite her power, Bárbara, like most of Félix's characters, is simply the vampiresque flip-side of the saintly mothers of the family melodramas. Easily classified as anti-family melodramas in so far as they reject the surface accoutrements of the patriarchal family, her films do so simply in order to re-inscribe the need for the standard family with great force. Despite titles which call attention to the female character, Félix's films are male-centered narratives, where the spectacular pleasure lies with the woman (and her masquerades of masculinity), but the narrative remains in the hands of the male protagonist. Even in Doña Bárbara, the principal narrative agent is Santos Luzardo, a young man (Julián Soler) who challenges la Doña's power when he refuses her seduction. The film is more concerned with how he defeats Bárbara than with Bárbara's point of view or her downfall. Bárbara remains unknowable, an enigma given a sociological raison d'être (the rape) and the face of a goddess, but whose subjectivity and desires the audience has no access to. As a star, Félix could not embody female desire, for she was an ambivalent icon, as unknowable, cold, and pitiless as the mother figure was full of abnegation and tears (Monsiváis 1988, 161–68). Her presence is simply an echo of the dangers of desire for men rather than its realization for women.

Woman's Desire on the Margins of the Home

In general, only two kinds of Mexican melodramas were structured around the issue of woman's identity and presented from a female point of view: the fallen-but-redeemed-by-motherhood women's films and the *cabaretera* subgenre. Each type of film also had its prototypical female "star": whereas the former films most often starred Dolores del Río or, somewhat later, Libertad Lamarque (two stars who specialized in characters who suffered copiously for their meager sins and relished child obsessions without equal) the latter films were epitomized by the sexy *rumberas* portrayed by the Cuban actress Ninón Sevilla. Since neither Lamarque nor Sevilla are Mexican, the relative independence achieved by Lamarque's characters and the sexual wantonness of Sevilla's could always be distanced as foreign "otherness," even when the actresses portrayed Mexican women. However, del Río, albeit Mexican-born, began her career in Hollywood, and, unlike the other two, was always considered a great actress, the *grande dame* of the Mexican cinema whose face would acquire mythical status as the archetype of the moral and physical perfection of the indigenous woman.

Lamarque, singer and Argentine stage and movie star, acquired a tango-inspired star persona after successfully competing for screen time with singing idol Jorge Negrete in Luis Buñuel's *Gran Casino* (1946): the young woman betrayed by weak men who nevertheless succeeds professionally as a high-class entertainer and manages to confront and conquer the ghost of the ideal family she could have had. Neither matriarchal mother, vampish "other," nor a symbol of indigenous purity, Lamarque was most often a prototypically innocent fallen woman. In *Soledad* (Solitude, Tito Davison 1948), for example, Lamarque plays a young orphaned servant (Argentine!) girl who is tricked into a false marriage, made pregnant, and abandoned by the willful family heir whom she loves.

Despite their innocence, however, Lamarque's characters fall uneasily into the prevailing stereotypes of the Mexican cinema. In her best films, where she portrays entertainers with tragic pasts or fates, the need to position her simultaneously in relation to family life and to public life as a performer complicates the affirmation of standard social structures and woman's position vis-à-vis the private and public spheres. Her status as a respectable performer (and the incumbent independence of a salary, relationships outside the domestic sphere, and the adoring gaze of diegetic audiences) destabilizes the apparent rigidity of her identity as a hopeless mother. Thus Soledad is unable to sustain the figurative melodramatic signification of its initial scenes (for example, prefiguring the falsity of the wedding ceremony via ominous mise-en-scène and the coup de théâtre of a candle blown out by violent wind when the couple first embrace) and depends increasingly on Soledad's performativity—on her voice rather than her silence—to unravel its melodrama. Told from her point of view and, by the film's end, literally dependent on her voice, the melodrama of Soledad ends appropriately with her long-lost daughter's anguished cry of recognition: "Mother!" But the Soledad that greets it is far more than "just a mother" and remains an outstanding model of self-sufficiency.

The Cabaret: Rumberas and Female Desire

Whereas Lamarque's characters are usually tricked or forced by circumstances into successful careers as singers while all they really want to be is wives and mothers, Ninón Sevilla and other cabareteras (María Antonieta Pons, Leticia Palma, and Meche Barba) present a different problematic. Much more sordid, their fates and entertainment activities project a virulent form of desire on to the screen. Nowhere else have screen women been so sexual, so willful, so excessive, so able to express their anger at their fate through vengeance. As François Truffaut (under the pseudonym Robert Lacheney) wrote in 1954, "From now on we must take note of Ninón Sevilla, no matter how little we may be concerned with feminine gestures on the screen or elsewhere. From her inflamed look to her fiery mouth, everything is heightened in Ninón (her forehead, her lashes, her nose, her upper lip, her throat, her voice). . . . Like so many missed arrows, [she is an] oblique challenge to bourgeois, Catholic, and all other moralities."[13] Albeit uneasily, Lamarque's sophisticated performers could be narratively recuperated within an expanded domestic sphere, but Sevilla's excessively gendered gestures engaged melodramatic tropes beyond the point of hyperbole. Thus with Sevilla, the performative excess of the "musical/performance melodrama" reaches its zenith and the boundary between performance and melodrama disappears entirely.

The most virulent of Sevilla's *cabaretera* films was Alberto Gout's 1952 *Aventurera (Adventuress)*. The plot is extraordinarily complicated and evidence of the excess associated with such films. Elena (Ninón Sevilla), a happy bourgeois girl, is left destitute when her mother runs away with a lover and her father commits suicide. Unable to find a job, she is tricked into a Juárez brothel where she is drugged and gang raped. Eventually, Elena becomes the star/prostitute of the nightclub, but she is so unruly that the madam (Andrea Palma) hires a thug to scar her in punishment. She runs away, becomes a nightclub star again, and meets and seduces Mario (Rubén Rojo), only to discover that his high-society mother is the madam of the Juárez brothel. After many other melodramatic twists and murders, the film finally ends with Mario and Elena supposedly free of their family traumas and about to enjoy a normal family life. The film's resolution imposes an end to the story, but it cannot contain the excess of signification—the malevolence of Andrea Palma's icy glance as she watches Elena's first tastes of champagne through an ominously barred lookout, Sevilla's haughty cigarette-swinging walk around the cabaret, her lascivious drunken revelry during her own wedding party, the sevenfold multiplication of her image while she sings "Arrímate cariñito" ("Come closer little love") in a Juárez nightclub—circulated by the film. This excess is narrative and visual, for the plot is only as excessive as Elena's own physical presence, the sum of Sevilla's exaggeratedly sexual glance, overabundant figure, extraordinarily tight dresses, rolling hips, excessive laughter, and menacing smoking. This excessive performance functions not so much as a parody of a mimetic performative ideal, but as an oblique affirmation of the gender identity that a mimetic repetition elides. Unlike the asexual mother-figures of García, the suffering mothers of Lamarque, or the frozen sculptural beauty of María Félix's temptresses, Sevilla is made of flesh and blood, a bundle of unrepressed instinctive desires. If, as Judith Butler argues, the performative gesture "as a certain frozen stylization of the body" is the constitutive moment of feminine gender identity (1990a, 140), Sevilla, like a drag queen, melts the style. This melt-down, her moral provocation, is much greater than the admonitions provided by the narrative.

This provocation is not, however, as straightforward as it might seem. In Mexico, the prostitute as emblem of desire, necessary evil, and mother of the nation (Malinche/Malintzin) has a prominent place in national cultural history. Prostitution might indeed be the oldest profession everywhere, but rarely have prostitutes been the preferred subject of so many popular culture texts as in Mexico. What we see in the *cabaretera* films of the late 1940s and the 1950s is the culmination of a complex process in which the figure of the prostitute (albeit cloaked with the shameful aura of Malinche) became the site of a serious challenge to the *Porfirian* moral order and an emblem of modernity.

Officially regulated and socially shunned, the postrevolutionary prostitute and her spaces—the brothel, assignation house, and cabaret—had a distinct social function: they offered men a place to escape from the burdens of home, saintly wives, and *sábanas santas*,[14] and to engage in uninhibited conversations and the ambivalent pleasures of the flesh. Mexican culture always celebrated the myth of the prostitute, but in the 1920s the prostitute also assumed a different iconic status in the wildly popular romantic visions of singer-composer Agustín Lara. Idealized and simultaneously romantic and perverse, the prostitute of Lara's songs was not pitied for falling from grace. Lara's popular songs embodied a fatalistic worship of the "fallen woman" as the only possible source of pleasure for modern man.[15] Though at first considered scandalous (and prohibited in schools by the Mexican Ministry of Public Education), Lara's audacious songs were quickly absorbed as a new popular culture idiom: the exaltation of the Lost Woman.[16]

By the late 1940s[17] the cinema had completely assumed Lara's vision of the prostitute as an object of self-serving worship, and his songs were the central dramatic impulse propelling the action of many *cabaretera* films. Thus, for example, *Aventurera* is clearly inspired by a song of the same title (sung by Pedro Vargas in the film):[18]

> Sell your love expensively, adventuress,
> Put the price of grief on your past;
> And he who wants the honey from your mouth
> Must pay with diamonds for your sin.
> Since the infamy of your destiny
> Withered your admirable spring,
> Make your road less difficult,
> Sell your love dearly, adventuress.

Lara's songs idealized woman as a purchasable receptacle for man's physical needs (the ultimate commodity for modern Mexican society) but also invested her with the power of her sexuality: to sell at will, to name her price, to choose her victim. Nevertheless, as Monsiváis says, his songs also made the object of pleasure, once used, abstract: "The deified prostitute protects the familiar one, exalts the patriarchy, and even moves the real prostitute herself to tears, granting a homey warmth to its evocation of exploited lives" (1976b, 60).

In literature, in the songs of Agustín Lara and others, and, finally, in the cinema, the prostitute and the nightlife of which she is an emblem became an anti-utopian paradigm for modern life. The exaltation of female desire and sin and of the nightlife of clubs and cabarets clearly symbolized Mexico's new (post–Second World War) cosmopolitanism and the first waves of developmentalism. The *cabaretera* films were the first decisive cinematic break with Porfirian morality. Idealized, independent, and extravagantly sexual, the exotic *rumbera* was a social fantasy, but one through which other subjectivities could be envisioned, other psychosexual and social identities forged.

But the *rumbera* is not a simple model of resistance. When analyzed as part of a specific process, a neurotic knot of determinations (Hill 1986)— and, in the context of its flip-side, the suffering mother—the image of female subjectivity that emerges is deeply contradictory and without an easy resolution. In fact, it is a fantasy. As Ninón Sevilla with much self-awareness explains to her lover in *Mulata* (Gilberto Martínez Solares 1953), another *cabaretera* film, the impossible challenge of female identity is summarized by the insecurity of "never knowing whether a man has loved me or desired me." It is not that one is necessarily preferable to the other—she can be either the wife or the sexual object—but that Mexican society nevertheless still insists that they are mutually exclusive social categories.

Notes

1. For an assessment of the last decades of Latin American film scholarship, see my "Setting Up the Stage: Latin American Film Scholarship, 1970–80s" (1992).

2. Typical of this approach is Reynaldo González's recent study of the deployment of the melodramatic in radio serials, *telenovelas*, and films, *Llorar es un placer* (1988). The papers presented at the seminar on the "old" Latin American cinema held during the 1989 Havana Film Festival also indicated that this resistance to the popularity and appeal of the melodrama is still quite alive. It was obvious, from the defensive inaugural speech by Julio García Espinosa ("this is, after all, the cinema we have been fighting against all these years") to the apologetic tone of most of the papers, that the melodramatic is still a difficult issue to sort through for Latin American critics. The papers presented at the seminar were reprinted as individual pamphlets by the Cinemateca Cubana.

3. This has been one of the principal tendencies of recent investigations of Hollywood film melodrama. See Christine Gledhill (1987, 5–39), and the other essays collected in *Home Is Where the Heart Is: Melodrama and the Woman's Film*.

4. Thus this essay needs to be situated in the context of recent work analyzing the historical and international inscription of the melodramatic in different Western and non-Western societies. See, for example, P. Petro (1989), G. Vincendeau (1989), E. Shohat (1989), and R. Vasudevan (1989).

5. This period of the Latin American cinema has generated much solid historical and archival research. For Mexico, see especially E. García Riera (1969), ten volumes to date, and M. Viñas (1987). In English, see C. J. Mora (1982). For a succinct and well-informed comparative historical analysis of this period in English, see J. King (1990).

6. Although the Mexican cinema did not take off on an industrial scale until the 1936 international success of the *comedia ranchera* (ranch comedy), *Allá en el Rancho Grande* (*Out on the "B" Ranch*, Fernando de Fuentes), melodramatic films were a basic staple from the 1930s through the 1960s. Aided by U.S. war-time policies (and U.S. resentment of Argentina's neutrality), the Mexican cinema thrived during the war and immediate post-war periods, producing as many as 124 films in 1950, the majority of which were melodramas. I am using melodrama here loosely, for the Mexican cinema (and other Latin American cinemas, especially Brazil's and its *chanchadas*) proved extraordinarily adept at generic mixing. Thus I use the melodramatic, in its broadest sense, as a structuring principle of expectations and conventions against which individual films establish their uniqueness as singular products, while recognizing that the term has a different currency in the Latin American context than in the United States or Europe.

7. An Aztec legend claimed that Quetzalcoatl, a feathered serpent god, would come from the East to redeem his people on a given day of the Aztec calendar which, coincidentally, was the same day (21 April 1519) that Cortés and his men (fitting the description of Quetzalcoatl) landed in Vera Cruz. Thus Malintzin Tenepal became Cortés's translator, strategic advisor, and eventually mistress, believing that she was saving her people. This is how recent scholarship has reinterpreted the four-hundred-year-old legacy of female betrayal that is the founding moment of the Mexican nation. See, for example, N. Alarcón (1981), A. R. del Castillo (1977), and R. Phillips (1983).

8. J. L. Vieira and R. Stam (1985), reprinted in M. Alvarado and J. O. Thompson (1990, 96).

9. The *género chico* or *teatro frívolo* was a vaudeville-like theatrical genre that developed in neighborhood playhouses and tents. While the bourgeois theater staged classical melodramas from Spain and France which outlined the parameters of decent behavior and exalted heightened sensibilities in perfect academic Spanish, the *género chico* thrived with popular characters and satire. The *género chico* was carnivalesque in the Bakhtinian sense, including in its repertory taboo words and gestures and popular speech while exalting the grotesque and demanding a constant interaction between players and audience. Benefiting from the brief lapse of traditional morals that followed the revolution, the *género chico* made the sexual body verbally visible for the first time and gave the masses who had fought in the revolution a presence and a voice. See R. S. Lamb (1975) and M. Manón (1932).

10. Each spectacle addressed and interacted with a specific sector of the population.

The *teatro frívolo* attracted a socially hybrid audience—the homeless mixed with intellectuals, artists, politicians, and military men, according to the eye-witness description of muralist José Clemente Orozco in his *An Autobiography* (1962)—but this audience was not sexually mixed. The only women mentioned in accounts of *género chico* spectatorship are prostitutes. Not only was the biting satire of the spectacle not considered morally appropriate, but women were also hardly represented on the stage. The cinema, however, was always a respectable entertainment option, appealing to men, women, and children of all classes.

11. Unlike R. Lang, who argues in *American Film Melodrama* (1989) that "in the end we learn everything about male desire from the melodrama and nothing about female desire," I maintain the distinction between those narratives explicitly motivated by female desires and organized according to a female point of view and those narratives which, despite their female "content," function according to standard male patterns of desire and identification.

12. For an extensive analysis of María Félix's career and star persona, see P. I. Taibo (1985).

13. R. Lacheney (1954) cited by García Riera (1969, 4:132–34), and J. Ayala Blanco (1968, 144–45).

14. The *sábana santa*, or holy sheet, which continued to be used well into the 1930s, was a special sheet with a round cut-out used to cover the wife's body during intercourse. Guaranteeing a minimum of pleasure, the holy sheet sustained the Catholic insistence that intercourse was sinful unless intended exclusively to procreate the race.

15. "The Perverted One"

> To you, life of my soul, perverted woman whom I love,
> To you, ungrateful woman,
> To you, who makes me suffer and makes me cry,
> I consecrate my life to you, product of evil and innocence.
> All of my life is yours, woman.
> I want you, even if they call you perverted.

> "Sinner"
> Why did fate make you a sinner
> If you do not know how to sell your heart?
> Why do those who love you pretend to hate you?
> Why does he who hated you return to love you again?
> If each of your nights is a dawn,
> If each new tear is a sun,
> Why did fate make you a sinner
> If you do not know how to sell your heart?

16. As E. Galeano summarizes it in *Century of the Wind*: "Lara exalts the Lost Woman, in whose eyes are seen sun-drunk palm trees; he beseeches Love from the Decadent One, in whose pupils boredom spreads like a peacock's tail; he dreams of the sumptuous bed of the silky-skinned Courtesan; with sublime ecstasy he deposits roses at the feet of the Sinful One and covers the Shameful Whore with incense and jewels in exchange for the honey of her mouth" (1988, 110).

17. As J. Ayala Blanco indicates, in a few months between 1947 and 1948 alone, precisely coinciding with the Mario Rodríguez Alemán *sexenio*, over twelve *cabaretera* films were produced (1968, 137).

18. The Lara song "Aventurera" had already been featured in the 1946 María Félix film *La devoradora* (Fernando de Fuentes). At the time, Lara and Félix were enjoying a much-publicized, albeit short-lived, marriage, and he ostensibly wrote the song explicitly for her.

FRANCINE MASIELLO
The Unbearable Lightness of History: Bestseller Scripts for Our Times

El mercado de fines del siglo XX es tan "democrático"
como la muerte [The market of the late twentieth century
is as "democratic" as death].—David Viñas

Francine Masiello was born in the United States in 1948. A literary critic, she is a professor at the University of California, Berkeley. Her main titles include Lenguaje e ideología. Las escuelas argentinas de vanguardia (1986), Between Civilization and Barbarism: Women, Nation, and Literary Culture in Modern Argentina (1992), and The Art of Transition: Latin American Culture and Neoliberal Crisis (2001).

In Santa Evita (1995), a best-selling novel written by Argentine Tomás Eloy Martínez, various characters ranging from necrophilic military officers to impassioned political leaders compete for the corpse of Eva Perón. The narrative movement, with its multiple obsessions over history and national destiny, is enacted upon a female cadaver; moreover, for the often sinister purposes of those characters who pretend to defend it, the body is reproduced in multiple likenesses so that few can distinguish the original corpse from its various simulacra. And while Tomás Eloy Martínez tracks a hallucinatory postmodern account of displacement and movement, he roots his narrative position as journalist and raconteur somewhere in the suburbs of New Jersey.

In truth, I am fascinated by this arrangement, not only for its engaging style, a bestseller for more than a year, but for the uses of women's bodies in this pseudo-historical narration. Santa Evita records a peculiarly paradoxical moment when documentary evidence about a national passion for a corpse appears to be stranger than fiction. Expressed alternatively through the loathing and celebration of an ambiguous social climber, a figure alternatively deified by millions or regarded as the paradigm of *mersa* (vulgar), Evita becomes a token of a larger national anxiety. Both formulaic and subversive, the corpse functions from the *"frase hecha,"* a cliché of social life which defines both a female protagonist stopped in frozen image and a political discourse congealed in the soul of the nation; but it also takes definition by a narrative of unstoppable movement. Spectacle and copy thus yield an infinite reproduction of texts defiling all sense of history. Like tourist post cards and T-shirts emblazoned with the images of popular heroes, the novel underscores the weight of a celebrity icon that paradoxically continues to circulate long after its life cycle has expired. More important still, it enters a circuit of exchange much like a commodity in the market. In this way, Tomás Eloy Martínez makes the marketplace a theme of his book; he stresses the material reproduction of signs (the reproduction of the corpse and the texts it engenders) that were destined for mass media consumption. Evita, the arch consumer of the commercial ephemera of her day, is here reduced to a talisman, a cultural symbol who passes in economic exchange. In the process, the author announces himself as the prime beneficiary of these dual systems of representation; he tags his freedom of movement inversely to Evita's paralysis as a corpse.[1] Gender and markets, female bodies and fiction, national identities and globalization: these are the topics of my project here.

In these pages, I want to address the ways in which bestseller fiction produced in Latin America travels on the North/South landscape and functions ideologically among international consumers. While it is convenient to condemn the facile readings of culture that bestseller products often supply, I wish also to consider the sense of empowerment that they offer to a wide audience of readers. In particular, I am interested in the ways in which gender enters this circuit of reading, supplying linkages in a global network of understanding, constructing an illusion of permanence, a Duchampian "ready made" of feelings in our global approximation to human experience, while also allowing readers to believe in their power of choice. Let me restate this problem. There remains, on the one hand, the circulation of bestseller discourse and its flattening effect on our critique of history, but we also have the question of draw: Why does the bestseller text pull us seductively through the North/South landscape to reconfigure local culture through international frameworks? And how does it manage to supplement market needs and desires through the representation of gender? Finally, as a transnational strategy, how does it create the illusion that we are all participants in the exchange system of the book and the market?

First, let's retreat a few steps. It is not that this bestseller phenomenon is especially new, though it seems to be registered nowadays as a primary cultural feature belonging to globalization. Think backwards, for example, to the international success of Martínez Zuviría, otherwise known as Hugo Wast, a known anti-Semite and director of the National Library in Argentina. A bestseller in the 1920s when the nationalist yearning struck populations throughout the globe, his novels reached circulations of hundreds of thousands in Latin America and Spain, and even in foreign translation. His was the *inter-American* melodrama that allowed for the reverberations of jingoist nationalism, adventure novels that promised a future of progress by suppressing dissonant forces and controlling the actions of women. This, perhaps, is the model of the early bestseller as conservative force.

More recently, international publishing markets presided over the kinds of fiction identified with the liberal-left literary boom of the 1960s. Firms such as Seix Barral and Joaquín Mortiz created an economy of literary celebrities—what Jean Franco once referred to as the phenomenon of the "*super estrella*" (1981b)—and allowed for the international circulation of images tied to a remote and lush Latin America, the repetition of a civilization and barbarism mode that was often revived through the effects of magical realism and through the intuitions of matriarchs and the libidinal fantasies of innocent girls.

What existed then, however, and in contradiction to our neoliberal times, was a (masculine?) faith in diffusing a Latin American reality and a political sense of identification. Responding to those critiques that addressed only the market aspect of the boom, Cortázar asserted with vehemence: "What is the *boom* but the most extraordinary consciousness raising experience by the Latin American people regarding their own identity? What is that consciousness raising but a very important part of an action against alienation?" (Rama 1984b, 61). Less idealistic than his compatriot, David Viñas nonetheless insisted on the urgency of a historical mission associated with the literary boom that would show the shortcomings and failure of Latin American history (1984, 21). Literature was a way to unite "*el pueblo latinoamericano*" and force a crisis of consciousness that would mark the decade of the 1960s. Beyond the promotion of a sense of the Latin American exotic or the sale of newness (we all remember "*la nueva novela narrativa*" [the new narrative] followed, of course, by the subsequent rise of "*los novísimos*" [the newest generation] or José Donoso's claims that a dozen novels were able to fill "*un espacio antes desierto*" [a space that was formerly deserted] (1972, 21), the boom also managed a critique of consumer capital and the resounding failures of colonial and neocolonial history. In its structures, we found a representational field that resisted linear narration and provided a utopian framework that celebrated the revolutions of America. At the same time, the boom permitted a certain autonomy for writers, free at last, or at least so it seemed, from local systems of meager patronage that had always held them captive (Rama 1984b, 92); the boom allowed them to become emblems of nationalist successes, individuals who could represent a modernized up-to-date Latin America and enter a system of remuneration for their creative writings.

I don't want to return to the literature of the *boom* in any celebratory mode, but to remind us that today's market scenario for literature is hardly new. Indeed, just as Andy Warhol's "factory" inaugurated a new market trend in the area of the visual arts, the Latin American boom of the same decade propelled creative writers into a multinationalist phase of translation and distribution of texts leading them to new modes of competition in markets throughout the Americas and abroad. And despite the richness of literary texts of those years, this market mode also yielded, for the purposes of consumer society, a paradoxical unification and flattening of very different literary texts so that a strange homogeneity of cultural production was used to globalize Latin American writing (Rama 1984b, 52). These points notwithstanding, the difference of outlook is important to us today in order to anticipate and track the success of bestseller logic in these current times.

Consider one example: if recognition in literature in the 1960s was assured by the prize of Casa de las Américas, today publishing firms like Planeta and Alfaguara take charge of international diffusion. The neoliberal paradigm moves away from the overtly political and instead shows the weight of the global experience on the manifestation of local culture; in the process, an anxiety for recognition in the market is everywhere to be seen. A string of essays in the cultural supplement of the Argentine daily, *Clarín*, calls attention to some of these issues. In an editorial of May 1998, Marcelo Pichón Riviere notes the recent acquisition of Sudamericana by Bertelsmann, the German firm; the new owners declare that future Argentine novels published under this multinational merger must guarantee a minimum sale of five thousand copies in order to enter their lists (17 May 1998, 2). In the same issue, other contributors reflect on the shrinkage of public spaces for art, lamenting the absence of an apparatus such as the Di Tella center that spurred so much creative energy of the 1960s. At the same time, *Clarín* carries a piece by Pierre Bourdieu on the politics of the market and its effect on the production of art and, in another essay of the same issue, a note appears on the launching of a novel

(Alberto Laiseca's *Los soria*) reliant wholly on the support of sponsors. In the following month, *Clarín* continues to express these anxieties about sales, circulation, and prestige: thus, the newspaper announces that it will inaugurate a literary prize of $50,000; it advertises the winners of the Planeta contest; it lists the new selection of this spring's Guggenheim fellows from the Latin American competition; it announces marketing strategies of the Italian publishing firm, Mondadori, showing ways to attract teen audiences to the world of books (21 June 1998); and in August, a cover story addresses the declining sales of books devoted to exposés of the dictatorship years; these books, which were popular under the first years of Menem, now barely draw an audience of readers (23 August 1998, 4–7). In that same issue, *Clarín* reveals a publishing strategy inaugurated in the United States, through which out-of-prints books can be restored upon demand to market circulation with new and rapid methods of digital printing. Meanwhile contributor Daniel Divinsky, attentive to the U.S. market and its relations to Latin American presses, reflects on the Pearson buy-out of Simon and Schuster and the Murdoch actions with Macmillan and their effect on editorial policies in Argentina. Similarly, in the Chilean journal *Cultura* (October 1996, 3), the editors remark on the circulation of national texts abroad and the ways to establish venues for new generations of writers. Along with this are the talk shows such as Skarmeta's show on Chilean television that promise to launch new books and the persistent rankings of bestsellers that allow us to participate and judge. As we know in the United States from evidence such as the much publicized list of Random House last summer, the rankings invite us as readers to be both audience and players at once; they permit us to vote for our favorite book and to receive validation for our choices. Perhaps, as one critic observed, the bestseller list allows us to find alliances with like minded consumers: Am I acceptable if my choice of readings falls among the best in the popular list? These are forms of public reading that permit us as readers to be simultaneously players and judge; they establish a community of imaginary book readers that has resonance in the form of the market. With reason then, a global canon of texts obsesses the writer insofar as it determines new modes of acceptance and carries the promise of sales.

From "Boom" to "Crash"

The exchange of texts in service of profit conditions a clear anxiety among writers and brokers. At the same time, postmodern aesthetics alters the paradigms for literary art. Thus the self-referential texts that offered allegories for writing in the 1960s are now replaced by stories about infinite simulacra which bring us to questions about the authority of the text and the power of the writer while they also test the authenticity of the objects set before us. Often this is generated over the bodies of women. Evita's frozen corpse set in multiple reproductions gives evidence of this phenomenon, but so does the dying body of Isabel Allende's daughter in her bestseller *Paula* or the history of the clitoris described in Fernando de Andahazi's novel, *El anatomista*. Images of failing women, clips of fragmented body parts, detailed studies of female sexual desire caught under the anthropologist's eye: these treatments isolate women as *parcels*, literally as objects, lifeless and beyond engagement. Though in the writings of the 1960s women were inaugurally representative of the permanence of matriarchal culture as tied to the rootedness of nation, now they are more likely frozen objects, often in need of assistance. Ursula and La Maga are replaced by cardboard figures. Helpless, infirm, dependent, these new characters rely on international brigades of readers to revive them and pump life into their ailing bodies. At the same time, writers such as David Viñas, Hugo Achugar, Charlie Feiling, and Sergio Chefjec assume female pseudonym in fiction in order to poke fun at the concept of fixed gendered identity. The crisis of feminism is articulated in fiction; the murder of women or the appropriation and exchange of their voices and bodies dominate literary form. At the same time, they enter as trump cards, empty signifiers with the ability to unite universal and particular meanings.

The cadaver, Nicolás Rosa (1997, 2) tells us, is notable for its reference to transition: movement between life and soul, between worldly life and other; it is purely inert material, but also the corporealization of movement. This double action founded on the representation of stasis can be traced in the depiction of women in Latin American literary texts. Moving between international theaters of publicity and marketing strategies, the globalized representation of femininity evokes both a call to essentialist authenticity and the universal appeal of worldwide identification. These images simultaneously compress global space by touching our sentiments as readers; at the same time, they mark the anthropological distance separating readerly subject and object. We do not face what amounts to a simple repetition of the civilization and savagery paradigm in which Europe and the United States stand as the spirit of light while Latin America is the infirm body (see Vidal 1976). Rather, the representation of Latin American women in fiction allows a transnationalization of the singular subject through which readers, drawn internationally from North and South, can participate as equals in determining questions of *value*, whether abject or unconditionally allied with the prosperity of cosmopolitan advances. Gender in literature becomes Latin America's bargaining chip to enter the poker game of global consensus.

The Neoliberal Market

Under neoliberalism, we can claim that identities are now for sale, ushered by a global force that puts all names and desires under the scrutiny of the market. The phenomenon also coincides with the attempt, advanced during the return to democratic traditions, of creating a diminished threshold of consent whereby everyone's material and ideological bases of analysis have been considerably lowered. The weight of this experience is felt in a general assessment of politics; it results in an ethical and aesthetic compromise that extends to literary culture.

I am not eager to return to a position, advanced by many, which claims this era as a period of waning historicity or indeed, in Francis Fukuyama's terms, an "end of history" itself. Rather, I am interested in the ways in which the bestseller logic distends and compresses space and time, allowing us a curious perception of "difference," alternative ways to make sense of ourselves as well as distant others, and, in the final analysis and contrary to much postmodern theory, creating the comfortable illusion of our returned insertion in history. I am concerned, in other words, about the way we are enabled to sustain strings of identification and learn to pass judgment on the political culture before us through the circulation of bestseller texts.

The 1990s bestseller constructs new versions of the intersecting relationships between local and global logic. It shrinks and distends the spatial realm, it compresses linear order (Jameson 1991, 22). This is enacted around the identification of difference and our sense that we might control it. A paradox enters, however, for just as the avant-garde lays claim to the margin, the bestseller market feeds on the same: the question of "difference" emerges from radically different fields. Consider this: recent contributors to theory, eager to flee macro-historical accounts, have turned to the power of the fragment in order to find a redemptive gesture. In this way, they privilege the *microspace* (Foucault, Deleuze, Perlongher), the *entrelugar* or *in-between* (Bhabha, Silviano Santiago), or *residuals* and *fragments* (Hugo Achugar, Nelly Richard); they celebrate *interstitiality* or *disjuncture* (Appadurai, Hopenhayn), or turn to the powers of *ungovernable subjects* (the Subaltern Studies Group in India or Latin Americanists under the same rubric working in the United States). Through these images, critics seek to excavate the potential of counter-hegemonic oppositional forces, to engage the prospect of revolt from below, to alter the monolithic discourses that dominate our *fin de siglo*. The aporia or the micro, the residuals or the margin signal a subversion of firmly encoded messages; this "dark hole" appeals to spectators and readers. It endorses our powers to reset the fragments through the practice of suture; it prompts our ability to *interpret*. In other words, as we recognize the power of the margin, we also come to terms with our powers as viewers.

As progressive intellectuals, we have claimed this as our space for battle and engagement, but bestseller logic reveals yet another terrain through which these same tools of emplotment are used. In effect, the bestseller also exploits this spatial model, but instead of positing identification as a source of resistance, located somewhere between unnameable excess and the framed limits of difference, it calls upon *singularity*; uniting the contradictions between stasis and movement, it produces a totalizing logic. In other words, the bestseller text links local and global visions; it touches our humanizing investment in the global village and strikes our needs for community linkage. Much like the merchandise of democracy, the bestseller offers this illusion of choice: as consumers we are invited to taste its range of flavors and styles, and to form an appreciation of the whole. In the end, singularity is woven from strands of "difference" and links popular subjects and metropolitan readers. This process emerges in stages.

Thus, if the boom novel emphasized the lush exotica of Latin America, and kept dramas of distant passion at bay for the curious foreign reader, the texts that circulate actively today in an international venue allow us to recognize in the difference of others an epistemological dispersion of our own. Inserted in a global arena, the foreign work still invites a fetishization of the field of difference: It can produce what Balibar once called a "transnational neo-racism" (Balibar and Wallerstein 1991, 20), which claims that difference is insurmountable, but it also supplies a fantasy of connectedness with a repressed sense of popular action.[2] It allows us to repatriate difference in the field of destination and to move toward a single field of imaging.[3]

This promotion of difference continues to be a selling point for mass-marketed texts, offering the possibility to sustain simultaneously concepts of singularity and likeness. It offers a role for our general insertion in dialogue between the Americas and potentiates us as actors through the fantasy of our identification and movement. It may be true, as many have claimed, that globalization leaves us fetishized as consumers; we are taken by an illusion of our powers to act over situations located *elsewhere*. The engagement thus allows us a fixed location in space as it also permits an entry into the quarters of shared experience, restoring us as members of a community choir that can withstand a span of difference. Commenting on the success of the market, Milagros Mata Gil observes the following:

> Assuming that Latin America is a region in such a way that, although there are subregions within, these have ties and relationships to other areas that allow us to think of the existence of a greater whole . . . confronting the possibility of giving more strength to the market or to the possible constitution of a market. So that this might come to be, so that exchange comes about, it is necessary that commodities come into play that offer a certain use value. These evoke questions of needs and the ways to satisfy them. When use value constitutes a system, as in the case of literature, with its differences and equivalences, the market comes into actions through the dialectical play of these factors . . . the market tends to alter the established order and to lead all participants toward the complementariness of common interests. (1994, 104)

Literature, in this manner, acquires a social attribute; need and unity cross the bestseller book through a range of market interests. A second caveat emerges, however: what is *merely* bestseller, nevertheless, is not to be *merely* dismissed; in fact, the symbolic imagination in these texts plays a role in regularizing a new order of common sense.

As a new global connection is established through a linkage between metropolitan and peripheral sectors, gender plays a significant role. Women often come to represent an entire field: "women's writing" becomes a marketable commodity that circulates as proof of pluralism, linking intimacy throughout the globe and supplying mirror reflections for readers of faraway lives. Thus, when Cristina Garcia's novels hit the bestseller lists in the Southern Cone, they allowed readers a glimpse of local Latin life in the Yankee metropolis. Women and sexual minorities carry the trump card of this kind of circulating fiction, a legitimation of an oppositional discourse and a point of entry to a resistant, yet global consensus.

In this context, it is no wonder that the form of memoir dominates. A touch to the realm of simple narration, which presumes no fantasy or exaggeration, the memoir presumes the equivalence of individual choice to coincide with the flow of history. As if to play with the interfacing tensions of memoir and mirror, this generic form presupposes that no additional information is needed. A psychological subject is located in the panorama of history that is available to all readers. Feelings and bodies organize history and supply a teleology that links individuals and families to a larger politics of national or international scope. They exemplify a contemporary trend of personal intervention in the failings of recent history, a way to reverse the course of time, to compress deviance through the pen, above all to alert readers to aspects of stories with which they were already exhaustively familiar. Again, the personal intervention of readers in historical events of their making allows the illusion of ongoing participation in the politics of the times; it allows them access to secret materials that expose the fallibility of the law and the violations of justice.[4] In this way, as readers we are rallied to an intervention through which secrets exchanged enable us to express choice and voice denunciation. In a time in which citizenship participation in political and civil society becomes increasingly foreclosed, the bestseller offers a possibility of intervention; our *agency* is accordingly affirmed.

Often, in the hands of women, the bestseller text offers the illusion of roots that go deeper, linking individual domesticity to a transnational agenda. Such is the case of Isabel Allende's *Aphrodite*, cook book cum family memoir, which stages not only the recipes of the author's Chilean mother, but also includes those of her literary agent, Carmen Balcells, in Spain. The book is a variant on the self-help manual, assisting the woman of the house (whether in Barcelona, Santiago de Chile, or San Francisco, California) in her plans for amorous adventure. Too, it is predicated on the recognition of a common way of life, a homogeneity of feelings and desires that promises a certain affinity among women within a global village. These linkages, of course, are joined through the feeding and nurturance of the body. Though we do not face a corpse in this instance—one might claim that awakening the erotic body is anything but!—we have nonetheless an inert form that demands, from Allende's point of view, nurturance and invigoration. The body as vessel must conform to the author's imputed meanings; it depends on sustenance provided to assume a new life in the text. Thus the self-help manual is a way of breathing life in the corpse; akin to the Snow White story, *Aphrodite* enlivens the moribund body that lies passively awaiting assistance. If as readers and authors we are awakened to agency, it is the kind that is performed on the ailing body of a randomly selected other.

Allende's book focuses on a new cultural economy that begins with a sense of intimacy. But here intimacy is clearly disciplined, identified by familiar markers and given habits, by domestic ways of structuring time and global periodicity. The author appears to tell us that even hedonism requires discipline; that consumption is a civilizing task that cannot be taken for granted. More important, the order of this new historicizing introduces the *body* as principal agent. It is this play inward to reach the global that catches my attentions here. The bestseller, in this way, links different social environments, it draws pacts of recognition; and while it often sets the ground for a common nostalgia, it provides the illusion of empowerment and action.[5] But it requires recognition of a law, if not belonging to the nation-state, then to principles of family or clan.

Appadurai writes of this double sense of history as a way that might serve us here: "*History* leads you outward, to link patterns of changes to increasingly larger universes of interaction; *genealogy* leads you inward, toward cultural dispositions and styles that might be stubbornly embedded both in local institutions and in the history of the local habitus" (1997, 32). The bestseller plays with both; its success is attributable to an inward pull that links individuals globally and the false pull of influence that individuals think they control over history. A history of the senses (in this sense, the epicurean's delight) is, in Isabel Allende's view, sufficient to correct our misrecognitions. Allende describes her project as "a mapless journey through the regions of sensual memory, in which the boundaries between love and appetite are so diffuse that at times they evaporate completely" (1998, 11). It is also her idea to supply recipes but simultaneously to override the manual, an appeal to instinct that links us all, to surpass the vagaries of distant law, a way to contemplate an alternative community based on common wisdom and the senses.

In this respect, it might be claimed that the bestseller stratifies differences, but also erases contradictions. We leap the boundaries of different communities by a bond of consumerist desire; it awakens us as readers into a global network. We are thereby linked through a spectacle of differences and held together through melodrama and nostalgia. Here, we also enter a palatable version of history. Writers such as Laura Esquivel, Angeles Mastretta, Isabel Allende, and María Esther de Miguel are exemplary in this task, ordering historical events through the bodies of women in order to link intimacy and political vision. Femininity occupies a central role in bridging global and local disjunctions, recombining messages in a new promise of unification.

Such is the case of Marcela Serrano's first novel, *Nosotras que nos queremos tanto* (1991), where women of different social positions reflect on their common memory of activism in the 1970s.[6] It is treated with a more sobering tone in Ariel Dorfman's piece of the same period, in which consensus again is the searing topic. Dorfman's wide international success through *Death and the Maiden* links ethical choices through conflict and the corporeal representation of women. In this dramatic text (I focus here on Dorfman's writing but the analysis could easily be transferred to the film), woman is situated in the realm of the irrational, identified with forces of nature; the abuses set previously upon her body arouse our compassion while, simultaneously, her revelations incite our suspicion. Though she's not a corpse as in the case of Evita, Paulina as a presence in the script nevertheless prompts similar questions: Can the female body lead to a single objective truth or does it multiply our readings of the "real"? How can we reach the end of any story so encloaked in misrepresentations of voice and law? Though her confessional draws us, she also upsets our common grounding in history; we thus tie our anxieties to a hope for common revelation. Through the female body, Dorfman leads us to consider the inadequacies of representation and the difficult reign of consensus.

"Compromise, an agreement, a negotiation. Everything in this country is done by consensus," objects Paulina (Dorfman 1991, 39). The text signals the tension between law and individual rights, between universal and local meanings, between guilt and absolution; but in the process, our judgment is halted. At the point where confrontations are suspended, we catch a fleeting moment of collective anguish; no one is allowed to indict the other, we retreat to unspoken agreements. In the best-seller, this moment is bridged by the presence of a global femininity. Women's bodies allow us to see the relationships that span ranges of difference; they allow for a drama of nonrecognition that reconciles oppositional moments in history. They show us that difference can be sustained without protracted war, but in a quandary of unresolved conflicts, they also stress inadequacies of current dialogue and debate. Reader consensus is thus achieved not just through the internal workings of the text, but by the female image that leaves us first in desperate unrest and then settles dispute through resignation.

Bestseller writing rides on a paradox: on the one hand, it proves its successful insertion in the global market; on the other hand, its strategies often challenge the very tactics that assure neoliberal success. It points to the totality of quests; it signals the necessary presence of female bodies at these locations of unrest; and, like a *trompe l'oeil*, it utilizes the tools of analysis belonging to neoliberal logic in order to strategize modes of personal resistance. In other words, clocks, weights, and yard-sticks—the measuring devices of success—are brought into much contemporary fiction to show the breadth of personal invention and even a subversion of the market. For example, Laura Esquivel's *Como agua para chocolate*, another hybrid recipe book, this time embedded in a novel, elicits a set of metaphors based on hyperbolic measure. The heroine was born to so many tears that their salt filled a ten-pound sack; she later prepares a cake with seventeen eggs and knits a bedspread that stretches a kilometer in space. These exaggerations are more than a facile attempt at magical realism; they poke fun at an economy that values numbers over qualitative form. Too, they alert us to the shortcomings of society that attempts to codify family values or love by fixed measurements or by the law.

A Measured Conclusion?

The romance of Latin American marginality offers a consumer space for particular interests to protest market-run capital. Though it calls upon premodern myths to guarantee the permanence of archaic values, it also creates the illusion of a mini–civil society within the transnational sphere.[7] It offers the possibility of a reterritorialized authority, a way to bring the experience of feeling to a new composition of readers. Of course, some may claim that mass culture places in doubt the ownership of our desires; but on the other side of this model, mass literature of the kind I've described also allows us to articulate our desires in relation to some distant other. Paradoxically, the bestseller ventilates those different positions within a single text: It consolidates memory and *contains* disruptive feelings that might stray from the law, subsuming a sense of hierarchical oppression in order to endorse individual freedom; but it also allows us to process multiple sets of verbal and corporeal linkages. It rearticulates a virtual community of readers, allowing us to shift from individual to collective subjectivity often around the signifier of gender. Thus, though the bestseller sustains an illusion of our individual power to become other than ourselves, it also allows the possibility of entertaining a postnational alliance.

The debate about bestsellers thus takes us to two forking paths: on the one hand, we can denounce its formulaic messages, seeing in its mass appeal a pluralist fantasy that echoes commodity culture and allows individuals of privilege to justify their life positions.[8] In the same critical logic, we can also share the objections sustained by an avant-garde, which claims the blank evil of the market and its deadening effect on art. In this regard, the bestseller is seen to lack the disruption of language and form belonging to experimental writing, providing instead a banal totalizing logic that ignores audacious literary practice (on this, see the recent writings of Beatriz Sarlo or Nelly Richard).

If the culture industry offers the possibility for dissonance and change, it is clear, then, that as an avant-garde our voices and desires have been already coopted. Late-twentieth-century global culture appropriates the language of these desires, leaving the countercultural movement without any claims of its own. As the corporate world absorbs counterculture and steals its language of solidarity and plans for change, we find ourselves with a loss of expression, a flattening of depth and debate. We lose the stock of images that had marked oppositional form. Unfortunately, if we accept the realities of this second path, and lament our stolen voices, we also forsake the materialized bodies intercepted in the bestseller text, and we also avoid the representational struggles used by mass culture to describe them. This countercultural position notwithstanding, we are still left to account in some plausible way for those libidinal impulses that the bestseller draws. And here I close with a final and perhaps aggressive intervention. Much of the discussion about the bestseller phenomenon confuses production and distribution of texts, but it also hints at our own ambivalence regarding our circulation as critics. In this respect, the bestseller debate becomes the scene for an enactment about our own exclusion from privilege, our academic marginality with respect to the market itself. It reminds us of our foreclosure. This situation paradoxically highlights our own susceptibility to the draw of the market and the way that we come to fetishize our intellectual difference to the detriment of others.

"We are a community, not a market," declared recent protesters at the Pride March in San Francisco in June, as they objected to the commercialization of images of gayness to the detriment of political alliance. Is the alternative to stay at home, to remove ourselves from the street, to withdraw from the appeal of art that satisfies general yearnings? To dismiss the bodies of figures who draw the interests of masses? The answer, it seems, is to be found in a practice that reads through and beyond the market, to supply an analysis that does not stop merely at the doorsteps of commercial success and corporate fanfare, one that surpasses our sanctimonious fantasies of an aesthetic existence outside of consumption. The cultural miracle of this fin de siglo may well be that as the bestseller engages with questions of permanence and ethics, we as supporters of an avant-garde remain increasingly remote and distant to the temperaments of our times. Our solution may be found not in a retreat to the entrelugar or the fragment, but in a return to direct participation in major spaces of action. From here we might work not simply from the gaps and fissures of discourse, but seek the relationships between whole yet complementary figures that may bring these opposing worlds into alignment.

Notes

1. Graciela Michelotti-Cristóbal makes a similar point when she writes of *Santa Evita*: "El único personaje que se mantiene activo y lúcido es el narrador" [The only person who remains active and lucid is the narrator] (1998, 141).

2. Carlos Rincón takes another perspective on this matter and studies the transference of stories from periphery to periphery to explain cultural competency. It also spreads the range of illusions that link members of peripheral communities in action.

3. Appadurai refers to a "repatriation of difference" (1990) to signal the ways in which the global/local divisions are shown in a single territorial nucleus; I am using this term in another manner to claim that mass culture texts, while signaling foreign difference *elsewhere*, also invite the readers to reflect on internal differences at home.

4. On public appetite for the scandals of current politics, see Marcos Meyer (1998), where various commentators call attention to the bestseller appeal of political revelation; Meyer reminds us, for example, of *Nunca Más*, the bestseller of the Alfonsín years, which sold in its Argentine edition 206,038 copies; or Ricardo Kirschenbaum's *Malvinas, la trama secreta*, which was a foundational text of this genre.

5. Susan Frenk insists on this empowerment, though for reasons that differ from mine (1996).

6. Serrano's most recent novel, *El albergue de las mujeres tristes* (1997), takes the bestseller formula in a different direction, to help the reader identify a common thread and easy sense of permanence in "*los saberes femeninos.*"

7. The liberating effects of mass culture as a way to create a miniature version of civil society has been articulated, with different emphasis than mine, by George Yúdice (1995). On the danger of this illusion, see Jameson's critique of Yúdice (1998b).

8. See for example Fredric Jameson, who writes about reader privilege under late capitalism: "Your privileges seal you off from other people, but by the same token they constitute a protective wall through which you cannot see, and behind which therefore all kinds of envious forces may be imagined in the process of assembling, plotting, preparing to give assault" (1991, 289). On the bestseller, see also Jean Franco (1996a).

RENATO ORTIZ
Legitimacy and Lifestyles

Renato Ortiz was born in Brazil in 1947. A sociologist and anthropologist, he works at the Universidade Estadual de Campinas (São Paulo, Brazil). His main titles include *Cultura brasileira e identidade nacional* (1987), *A moderna tradição brasileira. Cultura brasileira e industria cultural* (1988), and *Mundialização e cultura* (1994).

When sociologists discuss culture they take for granted at least two important points of reference in their debates: tradition and the arts. Both are seen as sources of legitimation, establishing, as Weber would say, differential modes of domination. In this way tradition and the arts emerge as specific spheres of culture, assembling a set of values which guide behavior, channeling the aspirations or the mind and will of the people. Tradition seeks to paralyze history, evoking the collective memory as a privileged institution of authority—"customs have always existed." The arts view society in a different way. They underline the existence of a "superior" cultured universe, inhabited by education, feeling, and artistic enjoyment. For anyone interested in contemporary culture there is still a question to be raised: To what extent do these two dimensions constitute enduring levels of legitimacy? Can they be "valid" conceptions of the world (that is to say, socially dominant) in the context of a worldwide culture?

In the case of popular traditions, we can say that the impact of modernity displaces them as sources of legitimacy. In European countries, with the Industrial Revolution, traditional cultures crumbled. Industrialism and nation formation definitively jeopardized the old ways of regional and local life, whose literary, poetic, and spiritual manifestations had very special characteristics.[1] It is for this reason that folklorists are an invention of the nineteenth century. They discovered that "superstitions" are remnants of a distant past, but which found themselves to be threatened. Faced with a changing society, folklorists desperately searched for a means to save them. Curious about popular customs they collected the pieces of this fragmented memory, seeking to reify it in museums, books, and exhibitions (Cocchiara 1952; Dorson 1968). At heart all their efforts consisted in the construction of an encyclopedic knowledge whose social roots were eradicated.

In Latin America the scenario is evidently different. There the constitution of modernity is a complex and difficult process. Yet, even so, the crisis of legitimacy for popular cultures is visible. Unlike the example of Europe, this did not happen in the nineteenth century, but crystallized later with the formation of national societies. In Argentina, Brazil, and Mexico social changes and the constitution of the nation-state rearticulated the strength of traditions. The modernization of society has as its counterpart a reorganization of the cultural sphere, particularly with the consolidation of the culture industries in the 1960s and 1970s (Televisa and Rede Globo). I do not wish to give the reader the impression that the process is analogous to that of Europe. That would be absurd. However, I emphasize the aspect that concerns us for this discussion. Even though the presence of popular traditions is a fact, their presence can only be felt at a local level. We know that there is not just one tradition but rather a fragmented, complex set of popular cultures whose sphere of action is short-circuited by the nation-state and the culture industries. Festivals, crafts, and pastimes are shot through by the totality of capitalist relations (García Canclini 1983). Tradition is penetrated and modified in its fundamental elements, as in the cult of the dead in Mexico. In the past, the cult of the dead established a link between man and his ancestors, a means of vitalizing social relations. Nowadays, the changes are drastic. The cult has become a celebration in which tradition and a monetary economy (including the exploitation of tourism) have merged. Something similar happens with indigenous or Afro-American beliefs. Throughout the history of Latin America these beliefs have survived, but they are generally syncretized with the most diverse influences. Nevertheless, it would be difficult for them to be claimed as the only traditions of the popular classes. Penetrated by the de-centering of modernity, these beliefs suffer from direct competition with other creeds (Pentecostalism, popular Catholicism, Allen Kardec's spiritualism, etc.). It is a plurality that, far from confirming the continuity of tradition, exposes a contemporary picture of diversity in which religious authority fragments.

If popular traditions are in conflict with industrial societies, it is with the advent of the latter that the autonomy of the arts arises. I do not propose to expand on this point, which has been worked through extensively by sociologists and historians, but I emphasize: it is only in the transition from the eighteenth to the nineteenth century that the artistic universe became independent from political and religious influences (Sartre 1972; R. Williams 1958). Until then, the work of art fulfilled a religious function (in churches and convents), a political one (the struggle between the Enlightenment bourgeoisie and aristocratic power), or an ornamental one (court portraits or those of the families of the great merchants). This constraint was further reinforced by patronage. The artist depended materially on his patron. Modernity reformulated this framework. What emerges is the artist as a free individual (that is, capable of choosing his own themes and language) and an autonomous (almost sacred) sphere of art. Political, religious, or commercial judgments (an antagonism between the romantics and "mass" literature; the serial novel) are replaced by purely aesthetic criteria. Flaubert's statement, "art for art's sake," reveals a new spirit, the presence of a domain closed in on itself, whose operational rules escape outside intervention.

The autonomy of the arts (literature, music, the plastic arts) makes possible the creation of a new level of cultural legitimacy, a legitimacy which does not derive just from intrinsically artistic values, but which is associated with a certain social class. As Lukács and Lucien Goldman show us, in some way "great art" represents a structure in which the bourgeoisie retains a predominant role. The authority of the artistic sphere is simultaneously aesthetic and social. Much of the debate about "bourgeois culture versus proletarian culture," "erudite culture versus popular culture," "good taste versus massification," despite the limitations that these polarities induce, is a consequence of culture's link to a specific kind of domination: aesthetic values and predispositions, which are reproduced by the institutions which link together society and the general public. I am thinking of museums and schools, spaces for transmission of a legitimately consecrated knowledge. In this way individuals can be hierarchized as being "more" or "less" cultured, as the erudite sphere acts as a scale in relation to which tastes and people are gauged. These are the assumptions in Bourdieu's analyses. In *La distinction*, aesthetic judgments are ordered according to "classical" values (that is to say, whose validity is historically defined by nineteenth-century bourgeois society) transmitted through education (schooling, museums, books, cultural programs on the radio and the television, etc.) (Bourdieu 1979). It is a conception of the world which allows individuals to distinguish themselves socially, but which conceals a profound mechanism of discrimination. All of Bourdieu's work serves to show how this social segregation is inscribed into the materiality inherent in the selection of artistic objects. When someone from the middle class, deciding between Ravel's "Concerto for the Left Hand" and Charles Aznavour (a popular singer), chooses the latter, his judgment does not just reveal an individual preference. Unconsciously, such a person unmasks his lack of culture, his class condition. He "could not have acted any differently." His cultural capital is sufficient for this low "taste," but incapable of applying it to Ravel (at least to a concerto so little known, different to the "Bolero" that nowadays is so well publicized by the cinematographic industry and by popular radio broadcasts of classical music). The mechanism is analogous in the popular classes. A worker manages to discern between some names of famous painters, for example Picasso, but without really understanding the nature of their works. He recognizes a sign (transmitted by school and the media), without exactly knowing it. On the other hand, the members of the upper classes do possess this cultural capital. In addition they can argue about the stages of a painter's life, or cubism in Picasso, displaying the familiarity and the cultural competence which characterizes them.

When we read about the sociology of culture, everything happens as if the autonomization of the art world were an all-embracing and universal phenomenon. But is this true? Suffice it to look at Latin America to understand that it is not. In Brazil, when the modernist poets in the 1920s celebrated the wings of an airplane, electric trams, cinema, the jazz band and industry, they were searching for signs of modernity. Modernism wanted to be a radically new movement, and it was out of this that the European avant-gardes' fascination with it arose. However, modernism's view of technique, of speed, was rather unfocused. It concealed the existence of a provincial country that adapted poorly to the sculpted ideal. Brazil had no shortage of "tradition." The process of industrialization was incipient and the modernization project, carried out by the state, was found to be a still distant prospect (it was only consolidated in the 1950s). Modernism happened without modernization, exposing a hiatus between its expression and the society which gave it sustenance (R. Ortiz 1988). In western Europe, modernism revealed the dynamism of industrial society, of material progress and the mobility of urban life. The world which arose from the Industrial Revolution imposed a rethinking of ideas on intellectuals and artists. Impressionism and art nouveau corresponded to the social reality which surrounded them, translating the materiality of modern life. Brazilian intellectuals had only the intention of being modern. Their proposal, far from being something palpable, was above all a projection. It is not by chance that from 1924 onward modernism identified itself with the national question as it tried to con-

struct a country that could reflect the utopian project that had been imagined as a reality. The same could be said of the Mexican muralists. As
García Canclini points out, "Rivera, Siqueiros, and Orozco proposed an
iconographic synthesis of national identity, inspired by the works of the
Mayans and Aztecs, the designs and the colors of pottery from Puebla,
the colors of the lakes of Michoacán, and the experimental advances
of the European avant-gardes" (1989a, 78–79). The mixture of elements
is not an anachronism, but the possible response of Mexican modernity,
which only existed as potential, channeled by state action and shaped in
the search for a national identity. The appeal to tradition was a social
necessity. The reclaiming of popular culture was the means which was
found to express avant-garde ideals and the project of national construction. Latin American artists found themselves to be far from Flaubert's
ideal. The political component constantly cuts across nationalist ideas,
jeopardizing the process of autonomization. Art and politics are complementary terms. The artist is a "committed" intellectual, whose commitment to the national destiny is found ineffaceably expressed in his text,
painting, music, and poetry (see Franco 1967). However, the Latin American example can seem questionable. After all, we could take it as a symptom of underdevelopment, as a sign of an incomplete modernity.

A counter-example helps us to dispel any doubts. The panorama is
also similar in the United States. North American cultural evolution is
determined by two principles: a puritan concept of life and the workings
of capitalist society. This adverse environment induced numerous American intellectuals to exile themselves in Europe, where they found a favorable climate for their ideas (Henry James, Ezra Pound, T. S. Eliot, Ger-
trude Stein, Ernest Hemingway). Strictly speaking, the great modernist
innovations in the United States were jazz and cinema, both centralized
by the culture industry and ignored by the "cultured" universe. Until the
1940s American museums mainly exhibited European paintings, conse-
crating Europe's hegemony among artists. Only with abstract expressionism was European dominance broken. For the first time a group of
American painters became constituted as an avant-garde, defining an independent aesthetic universe in which the impositions of society and foreign determinism were contested (Guilbaut 1989). As Daniel Bell oppor-
tunely observes:

> While there were modernist currents in the United States, until World
> War II there was no modernist culture in any coherent form that domi-
> nated any genre or field. The rise—and swift dominance—of mod-
> ernism in American culture occurred well after World War II. It came

about with the collapse of the small towns, the Protestant hold on American life, the rise of a new urban development and the explosive expansion of the universities, the emergence of New York intellectuals as cultural arbiters, and the growth of a new middle-class public. . . . For the first time in American life the artist, not the public, dictated the definition of culture and the appreciation of cultural objects. (1990, 67–68)

However it must be added that this dominance is temporary. In the 1950s pop art undertook to reorient the course of things, returning to society as the main source of inspiration and reference.

To say that the sphere of arts is partially autonomized means that it would be inappropriate to consider a clear separation between a pole of restricted production and a pole of expanded production. This contradiction, which in France is constituted in the nucleus of the opposition between the artist and the market, becomes diluted. In the case of Brazil, owing to the fragility of existing capitalism, a certain dimension of the symbolic goods does not manage to fully express itself. The example of literature is enlightening (Candido 1985; Machado Neto 1973). It would be difficult for us to have, as in Europe, the formation of a reading public that could, on the one hand, free the writer from patronage, and on the other, promote him according to strictly aesthetic criteria. The low level of schooling and the high level of illiteracy of the population (1890: 84 percent; 1920: 75 percent; 1940: 57 percent) immediately contributed to this. In this context the book trade could only be incipient. The print-run of a novel was on average one thousand copies, and in the 1920s the print-run of a bestseller did not exceed eight thousand copies.[2] A writer could not "make a living from literature," leading him to take up teaching posts and public positions. The relationship of intellectuals with the sphere of mass-produced goods, like the newspaper, had to be specific. As was said during the period, newspapers were the only means by which a writer could ensure that he was read. In Brazil, an intellectual's relationship with his public started through the mass media. For the writer, the newspaper performed important economic and social functions; it was the source of income and prestige. Due to the insufficient institutionalization of the literary sphere, a "mass" institution plays a role whereby it instantly legitimizes the literary work. In the case of the United States, it is not fragility which jeopardizes the process of autonomization. The vigor of its capitalism builds up the market as a source of artistic and cultural authority. The example of Hollywood, where mediocre and talented writers work, is striking. As we have seen, in the

United States the notion of modernity is linked to advertising, to the market, to "mass culture." The arts thus have difficulty in establishing themselves as a hegemonic model for cultural activity.

In fact, the reading which the sociological tradition makes of the autonomy of the artistic sphere represents a Eurocentric view. The Latin American and North American cases show that, from the point of view of a global history, the artistic universe faces contradictions as it emerges and consolidates itself as a legitimate source of cultural life. In this sense, I would say that there is not a "modern" phase, in which the arts dictate the norms of cultural production, substituted by another "postmodern" phase in which this authority is weakened. Strictly speaking, within this perspective, the majority of the planet has always been "postmodern," as such an ideal has never been achieved. It is for this reason that the hierarchies between being "cultured" or "uncultured" cannot be those suggested by the European reality. The mechanisms of distinction as noted by Bourdieu evidently exist (I will attempt to deal with them shortly) but they affect a different kind of cultural material. Opera, classical music, literature, and painting are not dominant and universal forms of social distinction.

Now I can resume my reflection on globalization. If my reasoning is correct, it necessarily leads us to a question. Tradition and the arts are not shaped according to worldwide norms of legitimacy. But what substitutes for them? I want to argue that world-modernity brings these values with it. Because they are global, independent of the specific histories of each place, because of their breadth, these values embrace the planet as a whole, and because they express a socioeconomic movement which crosses nations and peoples, the new standards of legitimacy supersede the previous ones. Once again the examples of language and food are suggestive.

English, as it becomes characterized as a worldwide language, ceases to be British or American. The language loses its original status to become a "bastard" language, adapted to the "distortions" which cultures inflict upon it. English, either spoken or written, in Japan or in the Philippines, is basically a linguistic variant; in the variant the British or American standard is distant. Nowadays, there is even an African literature in which nativized English is used as a register of literary creation. Another interesting case is that of popular music. Dave Laing, in reference to heavy metal, reflects that, "Although it has grown out of American rock music, the evolution of its vocal style has produced an accent detached from any geographical roots in the United States or Britain. This is part of the reason why, of all pop genres, heavy metal is probably the most international in appeal" (Laing 1992, 137). The musical sonority of a language becomes the link of solidarity (in the Durkheimian sense) between young people of different cultures. We should not, however, imagine that the striking presence of English in the international scenario emerges only through a desire for communication by the inhabitants of a global village. On the contrary, we are confronting a global level of authority in which other sources of authority are crystallized. Suffice it to note the prestige of English words—teenager, sex, jazz, thriller, in, out, made in, rock-and-roll, cult; in sport (rugby, windsurf, jet-ski), and in computer science (save, cut, paste). The absorption of these terms does not correspond to any Anglicism; this would presuppose the taking of loanwords from a language considered to be foreign, by one which receives them. It is a question of conforming to a hegemonic model of prestige. Some studies show that in advertising and in newspapers terms are used in English even when there are corresponding ones in the national language (Groupe de l'Etudes sur le Plurilinguisme Européen 1986 14; Gorbach and Schroder 1985, 231), so its use is not due to questions of communication. We should relate it, as some studies say, "to snob appeal, and it has in fact been shown that readers or listeners who use English often understand it poorly or not at all" (Gorbach and Schroder 1985, 231). The lack of understanding does not seem to constitute an obstacle to communication in this way. This is clear in the case of rock music, broadcast on a planetary scale, regardless of the difficulty of decodification faced by the listener. But what would a language that is not understood mean? Bourdieu, in his critique of linguistic structuralism, has reminded us that "to listen is to believe." The symbolic forces which determine the linguistic market define those who speak and those who listen. The source of authority is reinforced in the moment in which communication takes place. Paradoxically, we find ourselves in a situation in which people appreciate what they do not understand. They listen because they believe. That is, the legitimacy of English is such that in these cases the need for understanding is dispensed with for those who use it.

Anthropologists also show us how worldwide values affect traditional societies, reorganizing old hierarchical systems. Jack Goody shows how in Ghana the penetration of industrial cuisine becomes a reference point for lifestyles. The introduction of industrial foodstuffs—tomato sauce, tinned sardines, drinks (Coca-Cola, whisky, beer)—and new technologies for the preparation of food (cookers) change food habits (boxes of matches led to the loss of fire-making techniques in just a few years). The result was not the standardization of customs, but a social diglossia, similar to the linguistic one (the use both of English and the local

	Lower class	Middle class	Upper class
Food preparation (heat source)	Stone hearth	Wood burning stove	Electric cooker
Receptacles	Pots	Metal utensils	—
Who prepares food	Wife and relations	Wife and servants	Domestic servants and cooks
Tools for food consumption	Fingers	Fingers and spoons	Cutlery
Place	Floor	Table	Table
People	Men are served by their wives; there is separation of the sexes	—	There is no separation of the sexes

language). Within the ruling classes, the sphere of public life was "modernized" quickly, and in it another kind of social difference was formed. This new stratification is reflected in the consumption of foodstuffs and drinks. Among rural populations, cider and palm-oil wine prevail. In the cities there is a real hierarchical ranking that goes from the lower to the upper classes: (-) cheap spirits, beer, whisky, and cognac (+). "The emergence of this linguistic and culinary diglossia produced a situation that seems to be relatively stable, rather than simply being a stage of continual evolution of one monolinguistic state to another. So the diglossia participates in a system of sociocultural stratification which emerges and constitutes an authentic hierarchy" (Goody 1984, 302). Goody summarizes this social form in the table above. The products and means of cooking are thus associated with social classes. The electric cooker, cutlery, whisky, the table, the nonseparation of sexes at meal times become signs of social difference, and they distance themselves from eating with their hands, from pots, from the floor where the food is placed, from palm wine, in short, from tradition. The legitimacy of objects establishes a way of living, which sometimes we have a tendency to consider as "European," but which basically translates the far-reaching nature and authority of a world modernity.[3]

Coca-Cola wanted to change the shape of its bottles—there were protests. But their marketing research indicated the need for this action. What was to be done? The solution was ingenious and wise. Beside the new packaging introduced on the market, the old format was christened "Classic Coke." The episode is uncommon, but it makes us reflect on the meaning of tradition. Usually we see it as being something of the past, a set of practices preserved in society's collective memory. Tradition is associated with folklore, patrimony, the bygone. Rarely does it occur to us to think of the traditional as a set of institutions and values, arising from a recent history, and which are imposed on us as a modern tradition, a way of being—tradition as a norm, although mediated by the speed of exchanges and by the mobility of the people. However, when we say that a bottle has become classic, we are affirming that the bottle should not be forgotten, as it is part of a heritage. The qualifier delineates within different temporalities out of the very terrain of modernity; it refers us to a re-actualized past.

There exists, therefore, a history of objects, of things which surround us. The example of drama, worked on by Raymond Williams, is interesting. He tells us:

> In most parts of the world, since the spread of television, there has been a scale and intensity of dramatic performance which is without any precedent in the history of human culture. Many though not all societies have a long history of dramatic performance of some kind; but characteristically in most societies, it has been occasional or seasonal. In the last few centuries regular performances have been available in large cities and resorts. But there has never been a time, until the last fifty years, when a majority of any population had regular and constant access to drama, and used this access. (R. Williams 1975, 59)

Books, theatrical performances, but above all cinema and television generalize the use of dramas in modern societies. However, Raymond Williams was referring to dramatic performances in the generic sense (from Shakespeare to *Dallas*); it is those centered on the market, those which predominate at the global level, which interest us. It is these which best reveal the mechanisms of a global consumer society. In a certain way we relate to these dramatic performances as if they had always existed, as if they did not have a past. But for this a work of creation, of arrangements and rearrangements, was necessary, which would transform them into performances that nowadays are easily assimilated by the cinema-television-radio-video viewers. The emergence of each one of these techniques demanded a differentiated treatment. The transition from theater to radio drama presupposes an adaptation of the text to voices, the sound quality suppressing the absence of the physical presence of the actors. The adaptation of literature and theater for the cinema and television involves problems of time, cutting, lighting, recording, and production or editing. To make a soap opera or a radio serial, a complete training was demanded, adjusting the story to the kind of medium employed. Writers and cinema and television directors and businessmen all had to invent and crystallize given formats so as to be widely distributed. A history of fictional genres exists, made with successes and mistakes, in the context of culture industries. The stereotyped formats that we know nowadays (like the hard-boiled detective) were refined day by day, answering the demands of textual and market forces. The Western, mystery, melodrama, and adventure are specific articulations, a narrative mode which balances characters, action, plot, atmospheres, and, of course, commercial interests. The formats of the drama scripts could thus emerge, articulating popular taste with the narrative.[4] As John Cawelti observes: "Audiences find satisfaction and a basic emotional security in a familiar form; in addition, the audience's past experience with a formula gives it a sense of what to expect in new individual examples, thereby increasing its capacity for understanding and enjoying the details of a work" (1976, 9). The familiarity derives from repetition. This, in turn, reinforces and predicts what is expected. Expressed in another way, industrialized dramas, if they are to be understood as an everyday experience, must adapt to the formats and be delivered pedagogically to individuals, molding the audience's taste and palate. The construction of the tradition of a world-modernity lies, therefore, in a broad process of socialization of forms and cultural objects. In the constitution of this history, the United States must be seen as playing a role of the utmost importance. Not so much because of imperialism, but rather because it has been one of the first countries to invest in the globalized segments of culture. The experiences put into practice with soap operas, films, and television serials, globally distributed, demarcate a model for orienting the public and the producers.

In this sense, worldwide traditions are counterposed to national traditions (whether they are popular or not). The example of Indian cinema is revealing. From a quantitative point of view, India has the largest cinematographic industry in the world. However, as global traders say, Indian movies are not "exportable."[5] Why not? A possible answer is found at the level of distribution. The market is shared between a few transnationals, whose interest in Indian films is nonexistent. But I believe that there are other reasons. Indian film, like American, is an industrialized, highly stereotyped product. It has its own characteristics. The most popular films, musicals, are made starting from a formula dictated by the star system: a star, six songs, three dances. These are long films, on average three hours long, whose subjects vary from corruption to the subaltern role of women in society. Music has a central presence. "Often a film is judged just for its seductive music, even when it is about something dramatic. Because of the songs, the spectator sometimes sees the film again and again. He could, for his convenience, listen to them on records or cassettes, but he prefers to see them being sung" (quoted in Manuel 1991, 160). In the 1940s songs were sung by actor-singers, but with technological advances they could be recorded in play-back and dubbed: "With this the actor could begin a song at any time and anywhere. A couple, digressing in a park, sing accompanied by an orchestra of invisible strings; or during a song, the actor is shown in his flat in Bombay and, immediately after, at a waterfall in Kashmir. This use of music seems implausible for educated Indians, not to mention Westerners, who are used to the grammar of verisimilitude. But for the majority of spectators such effects seem natural" (Okada 1991, 290). The singers, absent from the images, therefore enjoy a prestige, similar or greater, to the actors. With their voices they participate in this star system, whose basis is a reinterpretation of Indian tradition. The songs are modals (they are not based on the harmonic scale) and they are presented in Urdu or Hindi, the languages of greatest diffusion in the country. The musicians thus perform a function of solidarity, uniting the different ethnic groups which make up the nation-state.

Another example is Japanese "enka" music. Like Indian film, it does not belong to the ancestral Japanese tradition, but it is the fruit of an adjustment to modernity initiated by the Meiji Revolution. Its main determining features are a pentatonic scale (without the fourth and seventh degrees) and a melismatic vocal style. The scale is different from that of the Indian modal, and from the harmonic scale (major and minor), which for non-Japanese makes it difficult to understand. The melismatic style—the vowels extend along the set of notes, beyond the aesthetic dimension—has a specific function: to transmit the text to the listener. "As a consequence, the rhythm of enka remains in an intimate relationship with the Japanese language. In Japanese, the majority of consonants are followed by vowels. The word is a result of the sequences linking consonant-vowel units. To each of these syllables the same metric cadenza is attributed. This uniformity is reflected in its turn in the music. The rhythm of enka finds its basis in the Japanese language" (Kawataba 1991; Oshima 1988). Text, music, and rhythm are united in a single harmony. Undoubtedly a musicality of this nature has barriers to understanding. For this reason Japan, despite its privileged position in the world ranking—it is the second largest producer of records—does not manage to "export" its music (see Martín Barbero 1987a).

The examples of Indian cinema and "enka" suggest two things. First, the mode of industrial production of culture is not sufficient for it to become globalized. Cinema can be exploited commercially in this way, linking Indian traditions to the demands of a modern technical medium. This also happens in Latin America, where radio and television recycle popular traditions, introducing them, resemantized, into the text of stories to be told. This is a pattern of underdevelopment that is repeated in several countries. In each one of them, the culture industries combine technologies, monetary interests, and cultural specificities. However, they are limited to national contexts. Second, the markedly nationalized productions contrast with the process of globalization. This means that the international market contains aesthetic assets in which tastes are predetermined. The richness of cultural expressions, which are specific to certain peoples, faces an unbridgeable barrier. Its authenticity is limiting. Hence the interest of large corporations in making cultural products more far-reaching, or what businessmen would call "universal." This is the case with the Brazilian soap opera. Once exported, it underwent a huge change. The number of episodes was cut (from 180–200 episodes to an average of 60), the story was compressed, merchandizing was withdrawn, likewise everything that reminded one too much of local color was cut. What was excessively Brazilian became superfluous, and was therefore eliminated. The soundtrack was modified, and an easy soundtrack for an international public was introduced. Soap opera producers reinterpret the scenes in an aesthetic code, derived from the language of video, which is shared by consumers in the external market. Toei Animation does the same with Japanese cartoons (Comier-Rodier and Fleury-Vilatte 1992). Toei draws on a worldwide tradition, the cartoon, adapting it to the consecrated stories of science fiction, adventures, and melodramas. The introduction of techniques such as "limited animation" still allows the adaptation of the story to economic imperatives; they save time and money, restricting the flow of images. But for the product to be able to adapt completely to the expectations of the global audience, their producers could not forget a small detail—graphic modifications eliminated the excessively oriental features from the characters' eyes.

International exchanges are not, however, simple economic exchanges, they determine a scale of appraisal, in which specific national or regional elements are relegated to the category of local color. The case of "enka" music is suggestive here. In Japan "enka" music is undervalued by the young as a worn out, dated manifestation. The young prefer a kind of sound-oriented listening, in which sonority dominates over the richness of the text. In this way the listener ceases to be interested in the content, in the melismatically constructed message, concentrating on the rhythmic sequence (Kitagawa 1991). Pop music, especially when broadcast in English, is ideal for this purpose. It relegates the text to the background, promoting the sonority of the songs. We could imagine the opposition between "enka" and "pop music" as a clash between "East" and "West." The young, in rejecting their past, have thus become "Westernized." But I believe that this is a narrow interpretation of what is happening. The same antagonism appears elsewhere. Pop music is superseding the "old" songs in France as well. It is therefore not a matter of a mere preference on the part of the young, but is associated with a whole way of life—frequent visits to nightclubs, concerts, and shopping centers, et cetera (Donnat and Cogneau 1990). FM radio stations that broadcast pop music on a mass scale are not just a medium of communication, but sites of consecration of a certain taste that is incompatible with the *chansonnier* style. In Brazil, the conflict between rock and samba reveals the same contradiction. As a symbol of national identity, that is to say, an internally accepted value, samba finds itself threatened by a musicality that is alien to its historical roots. In reality, we are facing a worldwide phenomenon, in which the new generations, in order to differentiate themselves from their predecessors, are using globalized symbols. In this way the notion of tuning in becomes an element of social distinction. To listen to rock-and-roll means to be tuned into a set of values, lived and thought of as being superior. To prefer other kinds of songs is synonymous with being out of step, with a form of behavior that is inappropriate to "modern times." In this way samba, "enka," and French song are relegated to the past, a sign of the limiting localism of "universal" communication.

Global versus national, worldwide versus local. These dichotomies do not just circumscribe spatial boundaries, but are invested with a symbolic value. The movement of globalization associates them with pairings such as worldwide/specific, cosmopolitan/provincial. Within this perspective, Indian cinema is "parochial," "provincial," as its reach respects the country's frontiers. Its sin is not to be "exportable." Meanwhile, this economic reductionism conceals an ideological operation, that of equating the worldwide with the global market. This is why businessmen, when they refer to their products and their strategies, do so using these terms. The strange thing is that, just as branches of the humanities are questioning the validity of universal knowledge, the administrators of the large corporations, practical men, are insisting on the theme. For them the world is a differentiated system, in which rational, systematic, and instrumental action is possible, despite the disbelief of some academics. But what do we understand as universality within this context? Businessmen are obviously not talking about religions, art, or philosophy; they are not so much concerned with democracy or equality. In fact, globalization conceals a movement in which words and concepts are being re-signified. Its universality belongs to the realm of quantity, and it can be scientifically measured by businesses and by public opinion surveys. Universality is synonymous with the global. A product is "universal" when it embraces the planet. In this sense, an "exportable" film is considered to be "more universal," "more cosmopolitan" than cinema by a specific director (Federico Fellini, Wim Wenders, Alain Resnais). Its worldwide distribution (which cannot be questioned, for it is measurable) guarantees it an ontological value. A usurpation takes place, an inversion of meanings. When philosophers of the Enlightenment said that "man is universal," they had in mind that, despite the deep differences which exist between peoples (civilized or barbarian), they shared something in common. The affirmation of universality could be made in spite of the cleavages. The worldization of consumption modifies this statement. The frontiers of universality should now coincide with those of globality. The frontiers are concrete, no longer abstract. In this way the universal ceases to be an opening, an intangible point of reference, for thought and for action. It becomes material, in effect being shared (businessmen would say consumed) by "everyone." In this way the world market becomes the only "true" universal, in the face of which any other manifestation would be the mere symptom of an incongruous localism.

In recent years, advertising agencies have tried to re-define their criteria for market evaluation. Since the 1970s, in the United States, advertising agencies have started to give up demographic descriptions which grouped people together according to income levels. With the process of segmentation of the market, sociographic categories seemed insufficient to the advertising agencies for an understanding of market dynamics. Some research on the consumption of automobiles already indicated that different kinds of attitudes existed within groups who were in the same income brackets. According to certain values and opinions—exciting lifestyle, equality, self-respect, intellectual, opposed to national security, politeness, social recognition—consumers could be divided into two groups. One, more liberal, preferring compact cars, in principle tending more to "intellectual" attributes and an "exciting lifestyle"; another, traditional, made up of more conservative individuals, concerned with the "national security" of the country, who tended to choose large standard-sized cars as a more appropriate means of expressing a need for social recognition. The result of these investigations was clear:

Knowledge of consumer values provides an efficient set of variables which, closely related to needs, expands the marketeer's knowledge beyond demographic and psychographic differences. If large market segments can be identified on the basis of value profiles, the marketing strategist could develop programs which would maximally enhance the most important values of each segment of the market. Thus, in addition to the more traditional variables, values could be employed as a standard consideration in market analysis and as a tool to achieve greater precision and effectiveness in diagnosing market segmentation. (Vinson 1977, 48)

Demography and sociology would give way to social psychology, a more efficient discipline for linking consumer habits to lifestyles.

It was this calculation which led marketing departments in various organizations to adopt values and lifestyles (VALS), designed by Stanford Research Institute, as a means of classifying people. AT&T, the *New York Times*, *Penthouse*, National Bank, and Boeing Commercial Airplane sought to diagnose market tendencies in the best possible way. What does VALS teach us? In a simplistic way, it divides society into groups of lifestyles: integrated individuals, emulators, fulfilled emulators, socially aware, led by necessity. Those led by necessity are almost on the threshold of poverty, and the advertisers have little regard for them. The integrated individual is a typical traditionalist, cautious and conformist. "In the United States he generally drives a Dodge or a Plymouth; he drinks Coca-Cola, Pepsi, or Budweiser; he eats in McDonald's with his family, he likes Jell-O, and his wife cleans the bathroom with Lestoil or Spic and Span" (Meyers 1991, 26). The emulators are a small group of young people, desperately searching for an identity. On the other hand, the socially aware are the legitimate representatives of the "modern" consumer spirit. Open, personally developed [sic], they dress in clothes from the best boutiques, drive foreign cars, drink wine, and love to travel.

I do not intend to discuss the scientific status of these categories, since this is a primitive classificatory system (despite being devised in the universities). But what is striking is its wholly deterritorialized character. To say that someone is "integrated" or "developed socio-consciously" means considering him purely from a psychosocial point of view. We are faced with an entity devoid of any roots. Demography would link individuals to geographic regions and social classes. The consumer was American, English, Japanese, and belonged to classes A, B, C, or D. To take lifestyles as a unit of grouping is to compare related segments, despite their geographical locations. This kind of categorization can therefore be expanded. When European advertising executives, by analogy to the Americans, examine the market of the European Union, they establish a ranking which oscillates between two extremes: the traditional and the modern. The *défricheurs* are "young people, with a relatively high level of education, found mainly among executives [sic]. Their dominant characteristics are spontaneity, flexibility, and a talent for making decisions. They take risks, they are committed, they are hedonists, and their culture is universal" (Hasson 1989, 66). At the other extreme there are the "traditionalists, who are evidently different as regards their group identities, and as regards to consumption, this being most definitely local; they are hostile toward Europe, and introspective" (Hasson 1989, 66).

The emergence of transnational categories translates, even if in an unsatisfactory way, a broader vision. It is not by chance that Alain Touraine, when he examines the beginning of post-industrial societies, points toward recent changes in the cultural sphere (1969). Even in the nineteenth century, particularly in Europe, the existence of different cultural media, and the distance between them, allowed ways of life to subsist within their specific contexts, like the antagonism between the bourgeois and proletarian classes. The bourgeois universe, with its mannerisms and idiosyncrasies, its openness to "high" culture, opera, picture galleries, classical music, and theater, was closed in on itself. At the other extreme, the popular medium, particularly the proletarian, secreted a kind of culture which revolved around trade union organizations, the factory, popular amusements (football, dances, fairs), and the pub. As Hobsbawm suggests, in the case of England there was a working-class culture with characteristic patterns which differed from the predilections of the bourgeoisie (1987). But with what Touraine judges to be "the disappearance of the cultural basis of the old social classes" there is a radical change. "Ways of life" are substituted by the "levels of life" of a consumer society, levels which, in freeing individuals from their social origins, regroup them as "lifestyles." However, in using their globalized categories, the marketing men are not just classifying people; they are placing them within a hierarchy. We see how an advertisement paints the picture of hamburger consumers in the United States:

> During the 1970s and 1980s, McDonald's and other hamburger and fast food chains employed psychological advertisements to convince the integrated North Americans that their restaurants were a paradise of family harmony, much more so than the dirty and greasy road-side cafés. The traditionalists reacted positively to this strong advertising,

full of promises and zeal; during all this time there was a possibility that fast-food businesses would branch out along the national highways. (Meyers 1991, 124)

However, with market changes, new forms of consumerism appeared:

The socially aware, driven by healthier and natural foods, considered beefburgers, or whatever, milk shakes, chips, as a nutritional absurdity. When they decided to eat out, they would do so in a bar or in a European style restaurant, and not in McDonald's or Burger King, with their plastic chairs, their yellow, orange, or red decoration. The clinical and automatic methods of hamburger chains reinforced the sense of repulsion felt by the Woodstock generation in relation to fast-food. Socially aware consumers want to be treated as individuals, not as part of a mass. (Meyers 1991, 125–26)

We are not faced here with a simple understanding of the market, but a universe of values, a symbolic order which distinguishes between "superior" and "inferior" individuals. Standardized food, a family atmosphere, tacky decoration, and mass production are counterposed to eating in restaurants, individual service, healthy foods, good taste. This all happens as if a Fordist period had been ousted by another, which was flexible and adapted to good taste and the individuality of the customers. In this way fast-food arises as a value superseded by the modernity of customized products.

Research on the female market also expresses this hierarchy of values. The research divides women into two opposed groups: traditional and modern. Attitudes toward the home are, in this case, fundamental to making distinctions.

Housekeeping activities often are viewed as the socially "undervalued" aspects of homemaking. Egalitarian females are less inclined to enjoy such tasks and are more inclined to avoid them than are traditional women. Modern women are apt to agree that meal preparation should take as little time as possible. They are more likely to transfer such tasks to others by eating away from home. (Reynolds 1977, 40)

However, the differences are not restricted to domestic life. They reveal a complete lifestyle. "Modern women, when compared with traditional women, are more likely to identify with a youthful as well as fashionable lifestyle: they are more likely to think of themselves as swingers, unwinding with a drink, or having wine with their dinner" (Reynolds 1977, 40).

However, there are also, on the one hand, "liberated" women, "their own bosses," "egalitarians," inclined to travel; and on the other, the "homebodies," "dominated by men," "reconciled to living a day-to-day existence." Obviously, these ways of being are expressed in consumer objects: travel, sports cars, luxury clothes, in opposition to the banal opportunities offered by supermarkets and department stores.

These classifications, although generated in the United States, have become widespread with the advent of global marketing. The category of woman, liberated from the weight of nationalities and from social classes, is displaced. What one might imagine is that "all women," reduced to the same denominator, could be ordered according to a continuum which would oscillate between modern and traditional. Some investigations, comparing female consumerism in the United States, the United Kingdom, and France, demonstrate these assumptions (scientifically?):

> In all three countries, the basic pattern of life-style centers around women's acceptance or rejection of their traditional home-making role. The fundamental dimension differentiating women in all three countries concerns attitudes toward, and involvement in, home-oriented activities, and this dimension also appears to be closely linked to conservative and traditional moral values. (Douglas 1977, 47)

The world market for female consumer objects can be equated in this way in terms of the opposition between modern and traditional, guiding marketeers in their entrepreneurial activities (Bartos 1989).

The categories of VALS can be applied to different contexts. Let us take by way of example a survey carried out in Brazil on reading habits.[6] Summarizing the results from the collection of data, the survey shows two scenes. In the first, a young couple watching television; in the second, another young couple reading. The commentaries follow through a comparative picture. The couple watching television is "lower middle class," "he is a civil servant," "she is a housewife," "they are repressed, the television transports them into a world outside the home," "they talk with the television on but the conversation is never profound, they chat about trivial things, his day at work," they are "a square and conservative couple." Evidently people like this could only have a mediocre life, which our investigators would not hesitate in describing: "beach holidays," "they are badly dressed, they are ugly, she seems older than him," "they are tense"; like the majority of people they like to eat well but, the text warns us, only "occasionally." "They are watching the national news and they are going to watch soap operas." The judgments about the other couple are of a different nature: "upper middle class," "he is an entrepreneur," "she has a liberal profession," "they are married or they just live together," "they have a broad understanding of the world, and open opinions," "they immerse themselves in the things which they read together and then they discuss them," they are "an in-couple." In the face of qualities such as these, only a marvelous world can unfold: "holidays abroad," they are "relaxed, comfortable, calm, they have a more stable economic and emotional situation," "they are doing their own thing, they have a deep respect for each other," "an elegant and pretty couple, his shirt and trousers are made of fine material." Evidently such people often go to the theater and the cinema, they eat out, practice sport, and they do not forget to read "*Iacocca*, some book or other by Kundera, *The Name of the Rose.*"

This discriminatory vision in relation to people and social classes is common among advertisers but beyond a distorted ideology it displays a range of signs which value a certain lifestyle. The picture sculpted by our agency, its description of reading habits, mainly in the case of bestsellers, acts as an element of participation within a special cosmos. The picture is of "foreign holidays," "of fashionable trousers," "of the shirt made of fine material," of a "pretty," "healthy" universe, where people can have "a profound conversation," a "stable emotional situation," and "get to know themselves." This idyllic vision of a harmonious world is very well expressed in the study's conclusion: "The comparative picture shows the perception of those interviewed in relation to the image of the reader. The reader's characteristics are similar to the stereotype of a modern person; success on a personal and professional level, control of information (even superficial information), introspection, but not shyness, and an organized and rich inner world."[7]

The world-modernity brings with it a hierarchy of likes and aesthetic tendencies, but neither tradition nor the arts are the structural forces in this globalized "cultural field." Although for many years in western Europe the universe of the arts had always exerted its authority, strictly speaking it is now in a fragile situation. Recent studies on French cultural practices demonstrate this facet (Donnat and Cogneau 1990). It is no longer "classical" values which organize cultural life, but what some authors call "the culture of going out." The art of living no longer takes "high" culture as a reference point, but the kinds of "going out" done by individuals—going to a rock concert, to the opera, to restaurants, the cinema, theater, holiday travel. The opposition "erudite culture" versus "popular culture" is substituted by another: "those who go out a lot" versus "those who stay at home." On the one hand there are the sedentary people who watch television almost all the time, and leave the house just to go to work. On the other there are those who "enjoy life." Mobility, characteristic of modern life, becomes a sign of difference. This explains why eating in a fast-food restaurant is "worth" less than eating in restaurants. A fast-food restaurant is a place where the domestic routine is extended; restaurants, on the other hand, are places of modernity, as the department stores in nineteenth-century Paris were for Walter Benjamin. However, the idea of "going out" does not differentiate between the various kinds of movement. Going to the theater, the cinema, the opera, or a rock concert are equivalent to one another (at least in principle). Regular attendance at, and an intimacy with, the world of the arts ceases to be seen as a sign of distinction. The authority of the arts is diluted in the midst of other activities. But the rearticulation of legitimacies is penetrating. Within this "culture of going out" a certain amount of gradation is insinuated:

> The analyses of listeners, readers, and of going out reveal a modern versus old dimension, that is to say, in schematic terms, an opposition between genres and practices, which has recently emerged in the sphere of old and classical practices. In the case of listening (classical music, tangos, waltzes, songs, in opposition to rock or contemporary French hits) we are talking about the use of the walkman, the CD, and the radio (FM versus educational radio stations), among those who assiduously listen to or record music. Among readers, the reading of comic strips, science fiction, scientific and technical books is in opposition to the reading of classical romances, the classics of literature. In the field of going out, going to rock concerts, jazz concerts, constant visits to the cinema, nightclubs, and sporting events are opposed to going to classical concerts, the opera, and visits to historical monuments. (Donnat and Cogneau 1990, 154)

The same contradictions which we found in "enka" music are present, but these contradictions are not only applied to "old" French songs. It is a whole cultural field which is defined from the dichotomy of old versus new. In this field, "cultured" practices are re-signified as old, passé, outdated forms of behavior. From the prospect of modern dynamism, these practices are devalued in comparison with going to the cinema, to nightclubs, to jazz concerts.

The worldization of culture redefines the meaning of tradition. We now have two possible interpretations for the same concept. Tradition is seen as the permanence of a distant past, as a form of social organization in opposition to the modernization of societies. Popular cultures in Latin America (with their respective black and indigenous influences), and in Japan the practices inherited from oriental history, make up part of this range of expressions which we usually label as being traditional. The expressions point to a kind of social structure which, even though fragmented by technological change, represents a world predating the Industrial Revolution. In these expressions, social, demographic, and ethnic segmentation is predominant, and the presence of the countryside, of rural activities, is striking. For the sake of convenience sociologists call these formations "traditional societies"; but besides this understanding there emerges another—a tradition of modernity, as a form of structuring social life, a tradition displayed in electronic goods, in a quickened concept of time, and of a "dislocated" space, a modern tradition which carries within it a popular-international memory, whose structural components are ready to be recycled at any moment. Like Coca-Cola bottles, the orchestras from the 1940s (Glenn Miller), or posters of Bogart or Garbo are equally "classic" examples. The past mixes with the present, determining ways of being, conceptions of the world. Culture-identity, a behavioral reference, roots human beings in their mobility.

Meanwhile, this tradition of modernity has a history, an evolution. Many of its components were forged "a long time ago." They emerge in this way as a memory of a past moment, yet without being part of folklore, or of popular cultures, they will be understood as "traditional." The "new" technologies (fax, satellites, airplanes, computers) contrast in this way with the "old" (the telephone, cars, the typewriter). They make up part of the technical "traditionalism" of the second Industrial Revolution, which came about in the nineteenth century. In its formation the tradition of modernity thus settles down in geological layers. The deepest layers do not disappear in the face of the dynamic of the present, but are articulated with it, although they are "already" perceived as customs, as something "out of time." A century ago the telephone became part of man's routine, its presence became familiar. Beside the fax, which presupposes its use, the telephone is seen as "out of date." I am not suggesting that modernity has fashion as its paradigm, changing with each season. No society lives this state of permanent revolution. Modernity, in this sense, is not ephemeral. Its changes take place on firm soil, which gives them sustenance. This solidity grants it the status of civilization, whose cultural standard is differentiated from past "traditions." But the globalization of societies also modifies the concept of modernity. To be modern is to belong to a contemporary culture, not in the sense of an "affirmative culture" as Marcuse would have it, rather its opposite (1970).

For Marcuse, eighteenth-century bourgeois society did not identify only with class domination; it carried within it a contradiction that was expressed through universal values of beauty, happiness, and liberty. The bourgeois imaginary bore a hope in relation to the very capitalist order that had engendered it. The "affirmative culture," as negativity, unveiled the possibility of a future in which values such as "liberty, equality, fraternity," could be achieved. To say that modernity has become an affirmation involves understanding that a certain kind of culture (which claims to be modern) has ceased to be an element of negativity, of change. Culture is no longer characterized as a "tradition of rupture" as Octavio Paz (1984) thought, but as a kind of capsule by means of which a social order is affirmed: modernity as lifestyle, whose concept is not far from that used by the culture industries when they classify their products as being "out of" or "in" fashion. A dress, a car, a technique, a habit are modern in the sense that they adapt to a contemporary situation; they become obsolete with the "passing of time." For this reason the idea of the modern, as a form, arises as an element of distinction between objects, aspirations, and ways of living. The term acquires an imperative dimension, ordering individuals and social practices. A modern attitude "bears more weight" than traditional behavior. The opposition past versus present thus corresponds to the dichotomy out versus in, determining the adjustment or neglect of activities and of tastes. In this sense modernity is no more than a way of being, a cultural expression which translates and takes root in a specific social organization. Modernity is also ideology, a set of values that orders individuals within a hierarchy, concealing the differences and unevennesses of a modernity that seeks to be global.

Translated by Anna Reid

Notes

1. On traditional European culture, see Muchembled (1978).
2. These figures are comparable to those of the French publishing movement during the transition from the eighteenth century to the nineteenth.
3. An interesting study of the transformation of legitimacies in the context of global society is that of Yves Dezalay (1992). The author shows how the globalization of the economy transforms the production of Law. Faced with the demands of transnational firms, the field of juridical authority begins to create a tension between a source of worldwide authority and another traditional authority, confined to nationally based rules.
4. For a history of soap opera as a fictional genre, see Allen (1985).

5. In 1989 India produced 781 feature films as against just 345 in the United States. However, as American films completely penetrate the worldwide market, Indian films are almost exclusively restricted to national territory. See *Statistical Yearbook* 1990 and 1991 (Paris: UNESCO).

6. *Estudo motivacional sobre os hábitos de leitura* (São Paulo: Sadiva Associação de Propaganda Ltda., 1988).

7. Ibid., 16.

DANIEL MATO

The Transnational Making of Representations of Gender, Ethnicity, and Culture: Indigenous Peoples' Organizations at the Smithsonian Institution's Festival

Most people don't know, but it takes a lot of work to be an indigenous leader in these days. One has to send and receive a lot of faxes, attend numerous international meetings; and now, one also has to learn to handle e-mail.—*A sarcastic comment made by an indigenous leader in the course of a personal conversation; my translation.*

Daniel Mato was born in Argentina. He is a professor at the Universidad Central de Venezuela in Caracas. His main titles include *Crítica de la modernidad, globalización y construcción de identidades en América Latina y el Caribe* (1995).

Ongoing globalization processes challenge indigenous peoples' lives in diverse ways. These processes seem to be to a significant extent fuelled by "global" agents whose practices are in one way or another informed by the systems of representations, values, and beliefs of so-called "developed" Western societies, those of the United States, Canada, and western Europe. Not only are voracious national and transnational economic and political forces avidly seeking to gain control over these peoples' territories, resources, and knowledge, but also a variety of self-considered alternative organizations from the "developed" world (some of which actually advance agendas that in certain ways may be regarded as more or less alternative to those of mainstream agencies) are actively exposing these peoples to their systems of values, beliefs, and representations. Not surprisingly, at least some of these values, beliefs, and representations become part of these peoples' experiences, and therefore are more or less critically appropriated, or at the very least become unavoidable references from which to differentiate themselves, in the social processes of producing their representations of both their collective selves and of diverse aspects of experience. Among these more or less alternative organizations are, for example, conservationist organizations, indigenous peoples' advocacy organizations, museums, anthropologists, journalists, musicians, filmmakers, et cetera.

This essay discusses the participation of various indigenous peoples' political and economic organizations from "Latin" America in the Culture and Development (C&D) Program of the 1994 edition of the Smithsonian's Festival of American Folklife.[1] This festival was an occasion to observe how certain "world class" events are both the result of and the occasion for the development of transnational relations and how these peoples' representations of themselves and of aspects of their lives are affected—it does not matter whether "for good" or "for bad"; the issue cannot and must not be reduced to such a simplistic opposition—by their participation in these systems of global-local and transnational local-local relations. Although it may not be logically assumed, I have also observed during my field research that other participating agents' representations also change through these relations and events, but these other changes are not the subject of this essay.

A Transnational Festival and the Significance of Transnational Relations

Since its founding in 1967 the Festival of American Folklife has been organized annually by the Center for Folklife Programs and Cultural Studies of the Smithsonian Institution; it takes place every summer on the Mall in Washington, D.C. The C&D Program was one of the four programs of the 1994 festival's edition.[2] The interesting point here is that this festival program, as some others before it, was a manifestation of larger fields of transnational relations and a locus for transnational cultural-political representations, confrontations, and negotiations connected with indigenous peoples' struggles for their rights in "Latin" American countries.

The production of the C&D Program directly involved two U.S. agencies whose practices usually extend beyond the U.S. borders: the Smithsonian Institution's Center for Folklife Programs and Cultural Studies (CFPCS), which yearly organizes the festival; and the Inter-American Foundation (IAF), a U.S. agency specializing in grassroots development that reports directly to the U.S. Congress, which was the program's co-organizer and sponsor. In addition, the program involved the practices of six indigenous peoples' political organizations, eight indigenous communities' grassroots development organizations, and four "local" development support—or service provider—nongovernmental organizations (NGOs) working with indigenous peoples' communities from seven "Latin" American countries.[3]

The program was an occasion for the interaction not only of the members and employees of all these organizations among themselves, but also with other individuals and institutions in the United States; among them were representatives of the World Bank and of the Inter-American Development Bank as well as of environmentalist, human rights, and alternative development advocacy NGOs, which took part in diverse activities of dialogue and networking initiated either by some of them or by some of the participating indigenous peoples' organizations, and/or the "local" NGOs.

The encounter of all these agents at the festival program was not coincidental. In recent years this festival has increasingly become a manifestation and locus of transnational relations. For the Smithsonian's Center of Folklife Programs and Cultural Studies, developing collaborative relationships with foreign institutions, communities, and individuals is an institutional practice and a prerequisite for producing the festivals, as is acknowledged by their staff members and directors (Cadaval 1993; Kurin 1991). Developing transnational relations is not only a practice of this Smithsonian Center, but also and very especially of the Inter-American Foundation (IAF), whose particular goal is the fulfillment of a transnational mission: to sponsor grassroots development organizations in Latin America. In this regard, it is significant that those relations linking the IAF and the festival participants are not at all conjunctural, but have been cultivated for years.

The inclusion of foreign participants in the festival has resulted from the Smithsonian institutional mission in its dynamic relation with the evolving circumstances of U.S. society, and particularly with conflicts and negotiations regarding the participation in the U.S. public spheres of social groups that, in this country, have been depicted as "minorities." According to the respective festivals' preparatory documentation and yearbooks, the inclusion of participants from abroad has been—at least at the beginning—linked to decisions to represent the home town/countries' cultures of those "minorities," as conceived in the 1973–76 program suggestively named "Old Ways in the New World."

In order to understand the transnational character and global signifi-cance of the C&D Program it must be stressed that the politics of culture and representations shaping this program—and many other programs and activities of U.S. organizations, both private and public—has been influenced by issues related to the debates on multiculturalism and af-firmative action. The recognition of these shaping influences is signi-ficant, because it suggests ways in which this and other programs pro-moted by governmental and nongovernmental U.S. organizations are part of the various means by which U.S. society—or different segments of it—tends to "export" its own system of representations, problems, and solutions to the rest of the world, or at least to influentially expose other peoples of the world to them. It does not matter whether or not such exportations or exposures are planned endeavors of the involved social agents. Of course, this is not just the case of the festival; it is a phe-nomenon that forms part of larger social dynamics, and not only involves matters of race and ethnic identities but also representations of civil-society democracy, the market, progress, et cetera, as myself and other authors have already pointed out in other instances (Mato 1996a, b; Yú-dice 1995).

At this point, it is necessary to differentiate between at least two main kinds of agents linked through transnational relations. We must distin-guish those that may be called "global" agents from those that may be called "local" agents. I call "global" those agents that in spite of having their headquarters in a particular locality—usually, but not necessarily, in the United States or western Europe—have an almost worldwide scope of action. I call "local" those agents whose actions are locally planned and largely carried out in the same locality that constitutes its basis of op-erations. Within this schematic opposition, we might also distinguish between national and more narrowly local agents, and to make all the in-termediate level distinctions that may be useful for a particular analysis. Nevertheless, the name "local agents" should not lead anyone to think of them as locally limited, because such a situation is rapidly declining in the context of ongoing globalization processes.

I have proposed the idea of transnational complexes of intermediation elsewhere (Mato 1996c).[4] I think this idea may help us in directing our attention to the study of the connections, conflicts, and negotiations among all these kinds of agents in specific local-global and local-local transnational connections, and thus to the ways in which tendencies to-ward globalization—that is to say, tendencies to the increasing develop-ment of closer interconnections among peoples, their cultures, and institutions at worldwide levels—take place and are worked through. As illustrated in this article, as well as in some former literature, these complexes involve agents from both sides of the imaginary North-South dividing line. The name of complexes of transnational intermediation must not create the false idea that they are established and closed arrangements of agents. Although there may be some more or less stable arrangements operating on particular subjects and in particular areas of the world, the cases already examined rather show the existence of mutating arrangements (Mato 1996c, 1997b). It seems necessary to emphasize that transnational intermediation processes are shaped by both "local" and "global" agents, although the relations among transnational intermediaries involve differences in power. That is, there are relations of power between these different agents, as emerges not only from my own research but also from the analysis of cases presented in other current literature (e.g., Clark 1991; Fisher 1993; Schuurman and Heer 1992).

One might say that certain "world class" events are both a result of the work of and a locus for the development of some complexes of transnational intermediation. The C&D Program is one of them. Transnational intermediation and globalization processes take place not only through events, but experience shows that some of these events have been particularly significant in contributing to shape aspects of these processes. An important peculiarity of the Smithsonian Festival's program is that it has involved the practices of agents linked to two salient kinds of complexes of transnational intermediation: those organized around "development" issues and those organized around "cultural" issues.

As I have said, the production of this particular program has involved two agencies from the United States and eighteen organizations from "Latin" America. It must be emphasized that documents studied and interviews conducted lead me to affirm that all twenty involved organizations have had significant experience in developing transnational relations before the festival. Nevertheless, there are qualitative differences in both the extent of transnational experience and the knowledge about regional and global tendencies managed by diverse agents, and particularly when comparing "global" vis-à-vis "local" agents. Global agents usually have a notable advantage in both regarding the amount of experience and the management of information about the other side of the relationship and its circumstances; that is, those of "local agents." Strikingly, this advantage is not only assured through the very involved global agent's direct experience and research but also through privileged access to libraries and documentation sources which store the products of other global agents and scholarly research. This latter point deserves our close attention and reflection about the roles of scholars and scholarly institutions in this regard (see Mato 1996b, 1996c).

The fact that small and local grassroots organizations and service-provider NGOs have important experience in maintaining transnational relations and developing global strategies should not surprise anyone. These have been part of their institutional practices, in some cases since their inception and in others for many years. The creation of many of the participating organizations, like that of many others in the region, has been significantly linked to the practice of a variety of "global" agents. These have been, to mention a few examples, the cases of the Asociación Nativos de Taquile, Cooperativa de Productores Molas, and the work of the U.S. Peace Corps, and of the Federación Shuar-Achuar, and Radio Latacunga, and the work of Catholic Church missionaries, all of them justified through institutional rationales of "assisting the poor" or "assisting the indigenous communities." Besides, ISMAM (Social Solidarity Society of the Indigenous Persons of the Sierra Madre of Motozintla) and El Ceibo, on their part, are producers of organic beans (coffee and cocoa respectively), which they almost fully export to the United States and western European countries respectively, and their relations with trade agents in these countries are stable and a key factor of their survival. It should also be noted that their marketing strategies have successfully appealed not only to their customers' interests in consuming "organic products," but also in "helping the poor" or "the indigenous communities," which also reveals the relevance of other systems of production of meaning connected to those that constitute the focus of this essay. In addition, in the cases of these and other participating organizations, they have in recent years received direct economic assistance not only from the Inter-American Foundation but also from other sources from abroad, both governmental and nongovernmental, which in every case has been framed within institutional rationales similar to those mentioned above.

It is important to note that these organizations do not constitute exceptions to the rule. Developing transnational relations has been a regular practice of numerous "Latin" American grassroots organizations as well as of several kinds of NGOs—service-provider, research, and advocacy and issue-driven—since the 1970s, due to political repression and difficult economic conditions that have been diversely but closely associated not only with domestic but also with global factors, like U.S. government-supported *coups d'état* and military regimes, external debt crises, so-called structural adjustment programs, and associated compensatory social programs involving local organizations and NGOs, et cetera (Bello, Cunningham, and Rau 1994; Development GAP 1993; Schuurman and Heer 1992).

If we ignore these political and economic factors we run the risk of seeing the participation of these organizations in the C&D Program as merely defined by issues of cultural representation. Nevertheless, we must not commit the complementary—and surely more general—mistake of understanding their participation in this or similar programs as if it were driven only by economic or political issues. In any case, and given this essay's privileged focus on cultural issues, I have to underline that my interviews with festival participants demonstrated that their decisions to participate in the program were due not only to cultural factors, but also to other issues usually regarded as economic and political, which in some cases—and due to specific factors—were even more a determinant of their decisions.

Developing global strategies and transnational relations has been even more imperative and significant for the cases of most indigenous peoples' organizations in the region than for other grassroots and diverse kinds of NGOs. They have gained notable experience in acting globally and networking transnationally in recent years. Not incidentally, this is true of several of those participating in the festival, for example, the Shuar-Achuar Federation and the Kuna General Congress, of Ecuador and Panama respectively. Furthermore, the Shuar-Achuar Federation had already participated in the festival in 1991, and the Kuna Congress maintains a permanent relation not only with the Inter-American Foundation (as do the other participating organizations), but also with the Smithsonian Institution. Moreover, it is known that the U.S. government has been a key factor in the Kuna people succeeding in gaining the relative autonomic status they presently hold in Panama.

Transnational networking both for developing their own projects and/or raising support for ongoing conflicts with the governments of the countries in which indigenous peoples live is an important motive for their leadership's participation in events organized by global agents, as I learned through interviews with representatives of indigenous peoples' organizations participating in the festival.[5] Their comments during these interviews were not only relevant to the festival but also to other events in which they had participated before. In addition, interviews I conducted with numerous indigenous leaders participating in other "world class" events, like the Amazon Week in New York in May 1994, and the Workshop on Identity, Community Museums, and Development organized by the Smithsonian's National Museum of the American Indian in Washington in September 1995, also highlighted the importance that accomplishing these kinds of goals has in shaping their interest in participating in these events. In fact, not only did they explain to me the importance of achieving transnational cooperation and support for their ongoing projects and struggles in our privately conducted interviews, but they also openly requested such support in their public speeches at all the mentioned events.

As I said above, the most visible and important goals for indigenous peoples' leaders participating in the festival and in other "world class" events are experiencing recognition and building international legitimacy for their representations of culture as well as obtaining political support and mediating financial and technical resources for their organizations' projects. I have discussed specific examples of how achieving these goals directly contributes to shaping their agendas elsewhere (Mato 1996a, b, 1997a), an important matter which I cannot expand here. However, at the same time these events also entail for them personal and institutional experiences that become part of the sources of their making of representations, both of diverse aspects of life and of personal and collective selves.

At an organizational level, my research of this and comparable experiences has shown that involved organizations are stimulated and demanded by their participation in these experiences to present their representations in sharper ways. This research has also shown that they subsequently experience diverse kinds of responses to different elements of these representations, ranging from reinforcing to rejecting reactions. For example, during the festival preparation and celebration, participant organizations and individuals received innumerable explicit reinforcing responses—both from the public and the festival organizers—for what in these contexts is usually regarded and called "cultural uniqueness," and/or for their "cultural conservation" efforts. In addition, and at a more personal level, each individual draws his or her own conclusions and sometimes modifies his or her own representations according to these experiences. These individuals take home these new or transformed representations and, given their influential positions in their local societies, it may well happen that they successfully promote these representations and associated cultural changes in their home communities. Through these two levels—individual and organizational—participation in these "world class" events and preparatory and follow-up transnational relations become sources of possible sociocultural change. I will devote the rest of this essay to illustrating these kinds of phenomena through two brief examples.

Transnational Experience and the Making of
Representations of Culture and Ethnicity

The first example is provided by the case of Facundo Sanapí, an Emberá land surveyor, from the region of the Darien Gulf in Panama. His participation was part of a program section dedicated to presenting the experiences of two indigenous peoples' organizations in mapping their own territories as a procedure of validating their peoples' land rights claims. It is significant that both experiences were initiated with the support of global agents. One of the involved indigenous peoples was the Shuar from Ecuador and the other the Emberá from Panama. What the public would find in this particular site of the festival was a large tent open on two sides, within which various maps and photographs were displayed on the tent's wall and in a showcase. In attendance at this site as well as being responsible for the scheduled presentations were two Emberá and one Shuar specialist in the subject, explaining their peoples' experiences, and whose words were translated by a U.S. translator, this latter role being alternately played by one of two members of the U.S.-based NGO Tierras Nativas/Native Lands. Although the subject being presented in this C&D Program section was strikingly important, it did not typically attract as many visitors as did most of the others. Facundo Sanapí—reasonably—attributed this difference to the fact that the most visited sections of the festival were those in which the indigenous peoples' representatives were wearing colorful "traditional" costumes, performing their dances, singing their songs, or displaying beautiful handicrafts. Facundo Sanapí was worried about this state of affairs. He concluded, and reiterated during his presentations:

> I am here in foreign clothes, because this costume (at which point he indicated the regular trousers, shirt, and shoes that he was wearing) is not mine. It is not my *culture*, I am in foreign *culture*. I left my *culture* at home, because, to tell you the truth, in my home I use my *culture*. Here I get surprised that everyone, every *ethnie* (he used the word "etnia" in Spanish) has their *culture* while I am in foreign clothes, and this is very painful to me (emphases added; my translation).

Facundo Sanapí expressed distress about this situation when I later interviewed him privately. He told me:

> Wearing their *own indigenous clothes* (the *guayuco* that would only cover men's genitals) and body-painting would have been very important for them in order to *demonstrate that there also are indigenous peoples who*

truly still conserve their tradition in the Darien [the region of Panama that constitutes their territory]. [Because] the work we are presenting here is very important, it is a process and a document that is very important for us. But we should present them *as indigenous peoples* in order to make the public see that he who presents this document is *a true indigenous person* (emphases added; my translation).

While I do not know what really happened about this reflection of Mr. Sanapí when he returned home, I do know he told me that if the Smithsonian were to invite them again they would wear their *own costumes*. Significantly, this was a matter about which Sanapí and his colleague, Manuel Ortega, devoted some time to elaborate, and both agreed that this was what they would have to do in the future. Indeed, they came the last day of the festival with their bodies painted with some improvised materials, but they were not satisfied with the result and did not cover their skin apart from their chests and backs, and this only for a few hours. What is significant about this example is that this experience seemed to have told them that in order to be effective they not only had to be indigenous but to *appear* as such before the eyes of their potential allies, and that they had to represent their Indianness in terms that had already been coded by their potential allies. They seemed to have learned that wearing exotic costumes and body-painting plays a significant role in this regard. It seemed to me that this apparently freshly acquired knowledge combined very well with aspects of their discourse that seemed to have been elaborated from older exchanges with "western culture" representatives and institutions (see Mato 1996b, 1997a)—as for example their recurrent use of the words—and ideas—of "culture" and "ethnicity" as kinds of standardized categories (representations) through which they would not only experience life, but also represent experience.

Transnational Experience and the Making of Representations of Gender Issues

The second example is the case of Indígenas de la Sierra Madre de Motozintla Sociedad de Solidaridad Social (ISMAM). The organization is a cooperative of indigenous organic coffee producers from the state of Chiapas, Mexico, close to the area of the Zapatista uprising that began in January 1994. While most of ISMAM's members may be considered to be Mam individuals there are also members of other indigenous peoples in the cooperative. Five members of this cooperative attended the festival, three of whom were male farmers who were also members of the men-only cooperative governing body. The other two were women, whose main responsibilities in their homeland were the family, the household, and several coffee-producing activities. The members were accompanied by the organization's administrative and economic adviser, a young and very active Catholic priest. They were the main protagonists of their presentations, although they were also assisted by the distributor of their coffee in the United States, the official presenter and translator, who was also a Mexican sociologist, and the Inter-American Foundation country representative. All five Mam participated in the presentations but the men held more protagonistic roles than the women, and a sort of gender division of labor was evident among them. While the men talked about organic agriculture and problems of contamination before they adopted their kind of "organic" practice, which was repeatedly presented as the legacy of their ancestors, as well as about aspects of their organizational and international trade experience, the women talked about the household, the family, and their specific roles in the productive process. The demonstration area included coffee terrace models, a compost heap, a coffee-drying patio, and a small wooden house where they displayed samples of coffee beans, posters, certificates, and other items. On one side of the house there was an area reserved to represent household practices. This was where the two women involved themselves in diverse cooking activities, and where they spent most of their time while not involved in the presentations.

Two months after the festival the curator of the festival's program received a letter from ISMAM expressing their satisfaction and appreciation for their participation in the festival. Attached to the letter was a summary of a recent meeting of the cooperative, which included a brief report of the presentation made by the festival participants to their cooperative fellows at a recent assembly. The report detailed their experience of the festival and what conclusions they had drawn from this experience. For example, it suggested that people should think more carefully before migrating to the United States because of the penury that "the wetbacks" (they used the Spanish expression *los mojados*) experience in the United States, and also made an important statement regarding the importance of women's work. It is worthwhile discussing what this report said about the latter. Although it is difficult for me to translate the wording because of the Mams' particular use of the Spanish language, one might say that the report talks about the need, or the pertinence, of recognizing the worth of women's work as being as valuable as men's work (in Spanish: *"También se habló para las mujeres como organización para poder valorizar todo sus trabajos como todos los seres masculinos"*).

The recognition of the importance of women's contributions is an important advancement in this "local" context (and surely in many others too), as may easily be deduced from the above-mentioned gender division of labor displayed at the festival. Let us discuss some factors that may contribute to understanding how this has happened. First, one must take into account the sensitivity of the ISMAM's representatives toward this issue. This sensitivity must be interpreted in connection with the demonstrated capacity of the contemporary Mam people—and the cooperative members—for reformulating diverse elements of their collective representations in a dynamic interaction with a variety of external factors. But, very particularly, this sensitivity must be regarded in relation to the important organizational experiences of women's groups in the region, which in the specific case of the Mam communities has taken place since the 1970s in connection with the practices of some progressive sectors of the Catholic Church (see e.g., Cadaval 1995; Hernández Castillo 1995; Hernández Castillo and Nigh 1995). Although I cannot provide specific evidence, it also seems relevant to point out that both the development of this sensitivity and the increasing importance of women's activities in the region may also have been influenced by the Zapatistas' and associated indigenous peoples' organizations' discourses and practices regarding gender issues, which more recently have had crucial relevance (Mato 1996c).

The role played by the female—although, as she has pointed out, not a feminist activist—program "curator" (according to the Smithsonian's vocabulary) may constitute another factor in understanding why and how these festival participants reached such a significant conclusion regarding the importance of women's place in their society and organization. As I understood from both my interviews with the program curator and my observance of her performance during the festival, she placed special emphasis on ensuring women's presence in all the participant organizations. This was particularly important and usually hard work; during her field trips to prep she did everything possible to ensure women's participation. It seems to me that it may be assumed without much argument that during these field trips her practice was not only inspired by her personal feelings and convictions, but also framed by both unavoidable public debates in U.S. society and the institutional discourse of the Smithsonian Institution as an affirmative action/equal opportunities organization—and at the very least the goals of many officers within the Smithsonian. Although in some cases ensuring women's participation was an easy task, in other cases it was not, as she explained to me during the course of our interviews. That ISMAM was one of these latter cases seems obvious after considering the above-mentioned gender division of labor both at home and at the festival.

Finally, another factor in understanding this conclusion made explicit by ISMAM in its communication to the C&D Program curator may be the festival's ambiance regarding gender relations. I would swiftly point out that this ambiance was shaped by various relevant forces: (1) again, the curator's socially equitable attitude and her consequent way of discussing gender issues with everyone, including the indigenous participants; (2) a similar attitude on the part of most festival presenters and other staff members of the Smithsonian Institution and the Inter-American Foundation; and (3) a gender equality discourse and very clearly associated role model provided by at least some of the female participants from "Latin" America, from both indigenous organizations and diverse kinds of NGOs.

It seems feasible to assert that for these ISMAM members, participating in the festival at the very least involved being exposed to other gender relations' representations, gender divisions of labor, and valorization of women's work. It also seems possible to argue that this exposure may at least have served to reinforce certain tendencies to change that were already being advanced by certain women's groups in their communities.

On the Transnational Making of Representations in the Age of Globalization

The examples of the ISMAM representatives and that of the Emberá delegates illustrate the fact that these festival participants, as participants in other comparable transnational experiences, are exposed to and potentially affected by other individuals' and organizations' representations that turn out to be either relatively new or at least unexpected, according to their own reports and behavior during the festival. Although these two examples basically illustrate representations of *gender, culture,* and *ethnicity* issues, other cases in this same festival program illustrate representations of *development.*

One may reflect that there is nothing very peculiar in these two stories, because the confrontation with, the demarcation from, and the borrowing and adaptation of other peoples' representations and institutions is a very ancient phenomenon. Nevertheless, I would say that what is notable is that the frequency and intensity of the intercultural transnational encounters that make these confrontations, demarcations, borrowings, and adaptation possible are rapidly growing and that they increasingly involve geographically more distant peoples. Moreover, I would also argue that what is notable is that "local" peoples are increasingly adapting systems of representations that are exhibited and/or promoted by "global" agents based in a few world-dominant societies. What is also notable is that these two cases, as well as others I have studied, do not represent examples of imperial impositions. Rather, these two specific cases represent examples of the outcomes resulting from the global-local as well as from transnational local-local exchanges that usually take place within the context of more or less informal and mutating complexes of intermediation of resources and representations constituted by "global" and "local" agents. These examples, as do others I have studied, show that these "global" and "local" agents actively shape current globalization processes in terms not only of representations of gender culture and ethnicity, but also of race, and diverse forms of economic and political organizing.

Finally, I would say that what is also notable is that the examples discussed above, as with those other studies I have referred to, show the significance of a relatively curious kind of "global" agent involved in these processes, and about which we do not hear or read very much in the specialized literature more focused in the mass media, the corporations, or the mainstream government agents. I say "curious" precisely because these agents must be considered as non-mainstream, at least in relation to certain matters, like those of "gender" or "culture." As a consequence, it is also possible to observe the existence of differences and even conflicts among the representations that this diversity of "global" agents promotes. And to make things even more complex and incompatible with any fantasy of adopting dualistic theoretical models, it even happens that some governmental agencies in the United States and western Europe (for example, the Smithsonian Institution and the Inter-American Foundation in the cases discussed above) may be counted among those promoting non-mainstream representations—along with many "progressive" nongovernmental organizations—at least regarding matters of ethnicity and gender, although usually not involving political issues related to international and transnational relations of power.

Notes

1. While I use the term "Latin America," I find it very problematic. The word "Latin" in this context recalls a long-term process of social construction of identities and differences and still serves as a subtle legitimating device in the present system of exclusion of large population groups in the Americas. So-called *Latinoamericanismo*

may be seen as a nationalism building a quasi-continental "nation." Its roots—not the expression itself—come from the period of the anticolonial movements. At that time, the local elites constituted by the descendants of the European colonizers—including both "pure" European and diverse *mestizo* elements—began building the new nation-states upon the system of exclusions of the colonial period. These elites assumed that they, not the so-called *indios*, nor the imported African slaves and/or their descendants, were "the people." The alliances developed among these elites during the quasi-continental anticolonial war were the origin of the interdependent formation of official national identities and the interstate-crafted representations of what began to be called "Latin America" and a "Latin American culture." Although today the expression "Latin America" has several and even contested meanings, this interdependent system of representations still legitimizes social inequality, cultural discrimination, and economic disadvantage to particular population groups and in particular to indigenous peoples and some populations of African descent—throughout the region—and that is why this note of caution is needed.

2. Some significant book-length studies about the festival are by Bauman, Sawin, and Carpenter (1992), Cantwell (1993), and Price and Price (1994).

3. The program also involved the participation of two organizations that were not self-defined as indigenous peoples' ones, the first providing international trade services to Haitian artisans, the second a cooperative of rural producers in Brazil. Here, however, I will focus only on the indigenous peoples' and indigenous communities' organizations, which constituted the vast majority of the program's participants.

4. In the referred text I used the expression "brokering" instead of "intermediation," but several colleagues convincingly insisted on the fact that the expression "brokering" carries too many financial connotations, which is not the intended meaning. As this article illustrates, agents taking part in these complexes intermediate both resources (not only financial) and representations. Remarkably, these representations are significant in the setting up of these agent's agendas (for example, representation of "development," "democracy," "human rights," etc.).

5. Including the Shuar-Achuar Federation from Ecuador, the Organization of Indigenous Peoples of Beni from Bolivia, the Emberá from Panama, and Mapuche from Chile, among others; interviews with M. Tankamash (2 July 1994), F. Tsenkush (1 July 1994), M. Fabricano (1 July 1994), and M. Ortega (5 July 1994).

GUSTAVO A. REMEDI
The Production of Local Public Spheres:
Community Radio Stations

Gustavo A. Remedi was born in Uruguay in 1962. A literary and cultural critic, he is a professor at Trinity College in Hartford, Conn. His main titles include *Murgas: el teatro de los tablados. Interpretación de la cultura nacional* (1996).

Adrift/A la deriva

In the face of cultural globalization, there seems to be a growing concern regarding the importance of democratizing the access to *the means of cultural production* for the construction and maintenance of truly democratic societies and polities. It is only such access that makes possible the meaningful exercise of the right to be informed and the ability to express oneself—a basic condition for the participation of citizens in decision-making processes—as well as the development of the *human personality* that results from these and other related cultural experiences. Yet we live in a time when the cultural industries are owned and commanded by a handful of giant corporations (such as Disney, AOL Time Warner, News Corp., Bertelsmann, Sony, Vivendi, Viacom, and so on), and when most of us have been turned into consumers and spectators.

I certainly recognize that as consumers and spectators we still engage in various kinds of cultural action and production. Given choices, people make choices. Also, as interpreters that read selectively, that produce and inject contexts and meanings, and that re-elaborate and transform what we are being exposed to—at times radically and completely altering that which is given to us in the first place—we can also be thought of as "cultural producers" of a kind. (We complete "the hermeneutic circle" and momentarily close "the open work.") Yet all these kinds of cultural production are excessively dependent upon a given symbolic supply—lim-

1. Graffiti across from the bus stop with the inscription of Emisora de la Villa's frequency, Villa del Cerro, Montevideo. Photograph by author.

ited, framed, and orchestrated by others. Indeed, much of this kind of "consumers' production" is little more than a response, even if critical, to power; it is, in other words, an acceptance of powerlessness and of a subordinate position. Now, for people to be empowered—to access the level of power—and to challenge *and* replace the current cultural hegemony, we need to be able to engage in other kinds of cultural production, that is, other than merely choosing from, or responding to mainstream cultural flows.

It is in this context that it should not surprise us to discover various ways of *public sphere-building*. The Movement of Community Based Radio Stations in Montevideo could be thought of as one of them. Indeed, technological advances in electronics, combined with mass production, global circulation of technology, and lower costs, have made it much easier for almost anybody to operate a low potency, small-scale radio station of sorts. And this has been, in part, what has turned low budget and experimental radio broadcasting into an attractive form of expression for the youth and neighborhood organizations.

When I began to look into this emerging cultural formation in June of 1996 there were more than a dozen of these radio stations in Montevideo alone, all transmitting in FM. These were El Puente (103.5), Radio FEUU

(102.5, of the Uruguayan Federation of University Students), Emisora de la Villa (104.9), FM Alternativa (97.9, Radio Oeste (105.1), Lejano Oeste (97.5), Radio Demente (103.5), La Esquina (104.1), Emisora de Emergencia (101), Radio Uyuyuy (107.5), La Teja Libre (105.3), Al Sur, Parque Batlle, FM Jardines del Hipódromo, Sembrando FM (all 103.5), and Voces de Belvedere (the latter born in the summer of 1995). Radio Subrreta (104.1) from Las Piedras and Radio Oxígeno in the small town of La Paloma, Durazno, give testimony to the fact that the movement is also present beyond Montevideo. By October of 1996, and as a result of the high school student protest of August of 1996, three high schools, the Instituto Alfredo Vázquez Acevedo (IAVA), Liceo No. 4, and Liceo No. 34, formed their own radio stations. By late October, there was a second community radio station broadcasting in Las Piedras and a new radio station was organized in Barros Blancos (L.L. 1996a; personal interviews 1996).

Many, if not most, radio stations are practically and symbolically anchored in a particular neighborhood: FM Alternativa is associated with Belvedere; Emisora de Emergencia with Prado, Parque Posadas, and Paso Molino; La Esquina with El Cerrito de la Victoria; Uyuyuy with La Unión, Villa Española, and the surroundings of El Cilindro; El Puente and La Teja Libre with La Teja and Pueblo Victoria; Lejano Oeste with Paso de la Arena; IAVA with Centro and Cordón. Radio Demente, however, can be heard from Parque Batlle to Malvín and in its case its members do not see themselves as associated with any particular neighborhood. They simply want to "be on the air." They also prefer to call themselves a radio trucha (fake) and do not want to become legal for fear of becoming "too institutionalized" and "ceasing to be spontaneous" (L. L. 1996a).

In August of 1996, I traveled to Montevideo and visited Radio FEUU, El Puente, and Emisora de la Villa. I got acquainted with their members, their history, their goals, as well as with a body of concepts and arguments already in circulation. This also gave me the chance of producing some primary documentation (interviews, photographs) and collecting other existing materials (newspaper clips, communiqués, fliers, handouts, stickers, recordings of radio stations' "IDs," and the like).

Community-based radio stations are not simply the result of changes in communication technology nor are they limited to a passing "urban tribe" of sorts (Costa, Pérez, and Tropea 1996). They are at the intersection of a whole series of questions very much central to Latin American societies and cultures today, such as the increasing sense of alienation and marginalization experienced by youth; the articulation of age, class, and ethnic claims in contemporary cultural and spatial politics; the structure of ownership of the media apparatus at the national and local levels; postdictatorial cultural policies in general, and in particular, with regard to mass media; and lastly, the status of the practice of citizenship as it is being challenged by the combined action of the neoliberal state and "the corporate takeover of public expression" (Schiller 1989).

Writings on the Air

22 July 1996. I asked Roberto Elissalde, of *Brecha*, to put me in touch with Raúl Zibechi, Nelson Cesin, Samuel Blixen, and other journalists who had covered various episodes involving "pirate" and "clandestine" radio stations. They, I thought, could in turn put me in touch with the radio stations themselves. Just hours later I received an e-mail from "Walter," a member of *la coordinadora*. When I told him of my interest in the movement and of my upcoming trip to Montevideo, he offered me a complete tour through all the member radio stations.

Wednesday, 7 P.M. We are all sitting and chatting around a table, outside the broadcasting room. They are all incredibly young, articulate, and sharp. We drank *mate* and shared the last pack of cigarettes. They loved to talk and explain their history, their motives, and their view on the entire matter. They also asked me about the United States, the youth, the music, the media, the FCC regulations. It was definitively the kind of fieldwork that fills you with energy, enthusiasm, and hope. As I returned home I took a picture of graffiti placed right across from the bus stop announcing the frequency, the days, and the times of Emisora de la Villa broadcasts.

Saturday morning. "Why do you do this?" I asked Rosana up front. "Well, first and foremost, we enjoy doing it! We come to realize that radio is a great invention, and a quite socially useful tool. It's cheap at both ends. It has the potential of becoming a democratic means of communication. But above all, it is fun. We get together, we make a lot of friends, we learn a lot, and we get a lot of things done. We also have had some positive impact in the life of the neighborhood: people know they can come to us. We want to give people the chance to come here and talk. We also have things to say. We also want to give ourselves the chance to hear about the things we care for, that is, about local news, bands, or sports. Some people and organizations also need this kind of space to communicate with one another. Montevideo has grown and we have grown apart. So we need to hear from each other, learn from each other, and care for each other. We all live in the same city and share the same past and the same future. We all talk a lot about democracy but democracy can only flourish by bringing people together, so we can all participate, discuss and decide things collectively. In the end, we do it because 'the public opinion' and 'a democratic way of life' are not something given: both are what people make of them. We make them possible by doing radio, inviting people to participate, building our audiences and networks, mobilizing the neighborhood to do something about the things that matter to us as a collective. Otherwise public discussion and participation would not exist. People would drop out of society; they would stop caring about things that matter to them." Rosana is seventeen years old and is responsible for an evening program about carnival. As I finish interviewing her, she claims that it is her turn to interview me. "It is only fair," she smiles. I was, after all, in Montevideo presenting a book about carnivalesque theater—and Carnival is *big time* in La Teja.

Friday, 7 P.M. That evening was Seba's and Nico's turn to sit out at the front door. "It was pretty boring," Nico later confessed, as he smoked a Fiesta Light, "up until things started to go wrong." They saw the police car driving around the block for a second time and then the same Volkswagen Gol that was seen last week parked across the street when they stormed into the popular kitchen just one block away. Everybody started moving fast. Fer grabbed the tape recorder and the tapes. Meche put the mixing console into her backpack and biked her way out. In just minutes the amplifier and transmitter were also put away at a safe distance. Manu took the CDs and the newspapers. Gabi was the last to leave through the back door, with the thermos, the pastries, and the cigarettes. By the time Corradi of the DNC and Sergeant Muñoz stepped in there was very little left: a little stove, a full ashtray, a cow's skull, a poster of Metallica, a homemade antenna lying on the floor against the wall, a notebook containing that week's results of the local soccer tournament. "Well, they know we are around. They'll think it twice next time," a neighbor reported them saying as they stepped into their Volkswagen.

Saturday, 10 P.M. By the time Seba opened the door it was already "too late." There were four policemen, Corradi, Muñoz, and the guy with the blue jacket—the bald one. "All they said was: 'We warned you!' They took everything, including the radio flag Ana had made up on the occasion of the student protest. It was a disaster . . . Man, it was scary! The only thing we could save was the CDs and the mics. We felt terrible. Why do they do this? They know what we are about: They know that all we want is to have a space of our own; that's all."

The morning after. That Sunday I woke up early. Walter was waiting for me at Plaza Lafone, the heart of La Teja. As we stepped in I saw Leti on the mics. She was happy to announce that 104.9 FM El Puente was back on the air "as usual." Emisora lent them their spare amplifier and mics, La Esquina gave them their extra earphones. The rest they borrowed from *la coordinadora*, which had acquired some back-up equipment for situations like this. As we ride his motorcycle Walter explains to me: "The idea is that no radio station must ever be shut down and silenced. As a collective we need to be sure that all of us can be on the air no matter what."

27 *August*. "Why do you think the government does not authorize alternative, low potency radio stations?" I asked Gabi. "To be honest, we cannot exactly tell. We don't understand. To start with, we cannot understand why Uruguay is the only country in Latin America where alternative radio stations are not allowed to function. We have very small equipment, use very little power, provide a social service—basically within our own community. On the other hand, we think that the current regulations—made during the dictatorship—need to be changed. . . . Last April, in a surprising move, President Sanguinetti acknowledged that we do serve a cultural purpose and he authorized us to broadcast live from the Encounter. Then, again, he changed his mind and went back to persecuting us. It is all very erratic and unpredictable." "It's political," adds Rosana. "They tell us that there is not enough room for so many radio stations but on the other hand they keep on giving away lots of permits to their friends. The commercial radio stations and their organizations also dislike us. While we do not represent any real competition vis-à-vis their advertisers they feel threatened by us. They also try to be sure that the common folks, and the youth in particular, are excluded from having access to the airwaves. But I don't know. In the end, I don't quite understand. Yet, there must be reasons why they come after us so viciously and why they do not want changes, don't you think? So, going back to your question, in truth we are not exactly sure why it is that they won't let us be. You may want to look into this and ask them."

The Field of Broadcasting

Community-based radio stations are the latest newcomers to the field of radio broadcasting, which in Uruguay was born and organized in the late 1920s. Some of its pioneers were Radio General Electric in 1922 (later CX 14 El Espectador), Radio Paradizábal, CX 20 Radio Monte Carlo, and CX 16 Radio Carve. Many of these pioneer cultural enterprises—a few of which were later to become local media empires—were the outgrowth of small import, retail, and repair shops dealing in electronic equipment such as radio receivers and transmitters. Also born in the 20s were CX 12 Radio Westinghouse, CX 10 International Broadcasting, CX 26 Radio Uruguay, CX 30 Radio Nacional, CX 34 Radio Artigas, and CX 40 Radio Fénix. Since the state needed to regulate and control this emerging field, most of the legislation was produced in the late 1920s and mid-1930s. In 1933 the eleven existing radio stations founded the Asociación Nacional de Broadcasters (ANDEBU) (Pallares and Stolovich 1991; Alvarez 1992; Imperio 1992). FM transmissions started in 1938, and FM stereo in the 60s. Television broadcastings, which in Uruguay started around 1960, were the offspring of these early radio broadcasting ventures. Thus, Radio Monte Carlo led to Canal 4, Radio Carve to Canal 10, General Electric to Canal 5 (Beceiro 1994; Alvarez 1992).

From the start radio played a central role in the cultural and political life of the country. To begin with, radio broadcasts play a central part in Uruguayans' everyday lives—whether at home, at work, at the bar, driving, or on the bus. While most people do watch television in the evenings—after work, until midnight—radio is "the companion of choice" and the source of ideas and information throughout the day. More importantly, radio has always been a key segment of the public sphere, that is, the realm of everyday life in which social matters and matters of state are discussed, where people learn about the world and express their ideas, and in sum, where national sentiments and public opinion are formed. In 1967, ANDEBU's president Jiménez de Aréchaga was very optimistic: "(Latin) America put radio in the hands of the people so people could use it, just as they used the printed press, as an instrument in the struggle for democracy. . . . Freedom to use the means of communication is the essence of a democratic society; restriction and control of the media pertains only to totalitarian regimes" (Imperio 1992). Yet Benito Nardone, a populist and conservative *caudillo* was elected president in 1960 due largely to CX 4 Radio Rural broadcasts. Indeed, the mass media apparatus proved to be equally pivotal to both the military regime propagandists as well as to the anti-dictatorship opposition (as in the case, for example, of CX 30 La Radio of the late 70s and early 1980s).

By 1978 there were 86 radio stations nationwide (22 in Montevideo) and 17 television channels (4 in the capital). By 1986, the number had risen to 30 radio stations in Montevideo alone, distributed as follows: 18 AM stations (3 large, 7 medium-sized, and 8 small) and 12 FM stations (4 large and 8 small). And by 1990, there were 90 (nationwide): 51 AM stations, 25 FM stations, and 14 television stations. With the exception of one television channel and a few radio stations managed by the Servicio Oficial de Difusión Radio Eléctrica (SODRE), most means of communication are privately owned and operated. In addition to ANDEBU, these entrepreneurs formed various corporate organizations and operational networks such as RAMI (Asociación de Radioemisoras del Interior) and CORI (Cadena de Oro de Radioemisoras del Interior).

While for Luciano Alvarez the field of the mass media in Uruguay is "ruled by the market" (Alvarez 1992) for other authors it is pretty much in the hands of a private media oligopoly (Pallares and Stolovich 1991, 92). In fact, a tiny circle of families forming oligopolistic economic groups (Scheck, Romay-Salvo, and Fontaina-De Feo) has always controlled the lion's share of the field of mass media in Uruguay (Pallares and Stolovich 1991, 139). Until very recently, these three groups not only owned the main television channels (Canal 12 Teledoce, Canal 10 Saeta, and Canal 4 Monte Carlo, respectively), they also owned other means of communication (radio stations, newspapers, film distribution companies, advertising companies) as well as ranches, industries, retail companies, and so on. The Romay-Salvo group, for example, owns CX 20 Radio Monte Carlo and CX 12 Radio Oriental, two of the radio stations with the greatest power and reach. Fontaina-De Feo owns CX 16 Radio Carve and CX 24 Radio El Tiempo. Scheck and Associates controls the major national newspaper El País, and integrates RBS, the main film distribution company. During the 80s these same three local corporations formed the Red Uruguaya de Televisión (Uruguayan Television Network), and in the 90s, they formed Equital, the three-headed sole cable TV provider in Montevideo (itself an outlet for a handful of global and regional "infotainment" corporations), thus securing the monopolistic intermediation of cable television. The situation seems to have changed slightly with the arrival of DirecTV of Hughes Electronic Corp.—President Jorge Batlle's response to a media oligopoly that historically had favored his rivals within his own Colorado Party.

Outside these main groups at the core of the national mass media apparatus, radio stations have also been treated as a sort of prize to be given by the powers-that-be to loyal entrepreneurs and friends. In 1984, only months before the end of the military dictatorship, twenty-nine FM licenses were allocated to individuals associated with the military regime (Pallares and Stolovich 1991, 122). Prior to the 1998 elections, and following what seems to be a pattern preceding every national election, the second Sanguinetti administration (1994–1999) also authorized up to sixty new commercial radio stations, mostly FM ("Y las ondas son ajenas . . ." 1999).

Children of the Underground?

Community radio stations emerged in the late 1980s, right after the end of the military dictatorship, as a means of denouncing police raids (raz-zias) against youth in the working-class neighborhoods and shanty towns (barrios marginales) of the periphery of Montevideo, those zones most affected by the increase of unemployment, poverty, and marginalization brought about by the neoliberal economic policies of the 1980s and 1990s. Indeed, today 45 percent of children and youth (up to the age of fourteen) live below the line of poverty, and the percentages of high school dropouts and of youth interested neither in studying nor in looking for a job have skyrocketed, reaching worrisome figures. Thus, police raids routinely target the young population because of how they dress, wear their hair, practice their sexuality, talk or behave in public, or simply because of the music they listen to. While at times that subculture may be associated with drug and alcohol abuse, and violent and criminal acts, such behavior is obviously not the monopoly of youth in these peripheral neighborhoods. It is just that this sector of the population is an easy target, and that these neighborhoods are less visible, and police abuses go unnoticed and unchecked.

As with the so-called underground magazines of the mid-1980s, the very first "pirate radio stations" of the late 1980s were a vehicle to expose and protest police repression as much as a symbolic and discursive referent for the subculture of the youth (see Pallares and Stolovich 1991, 47n.9). In 1996, there was a sharp increase in the number of community-based and low potency radio stations in Montevideo, many of which are, precisely, developments of earlier cultural projects and experiences, such as underground magazines, neighborhood newspapers, theater groups, cultural centers, and the like. El Puente FM, for example, born in 1994, was the offspring of the local newspaper El Tejano (created in 1989), itself the result of the cultural activities deployed by the Coordinadora Anti-Razzias and other neighborhood organizations that constitute their advisory board (El Hurgador no. 2, August 1996, 2). In this sense, the community radio stations of today are an expression of affirmative cultural positions and have cultural and political projects of their own rather than being simply a reaction against state repression.

In the mid-1990s low potency radio stations gained further visibility and presence within social, cultural, and even political life due to the coverage they got in the mainstream press. With exceptions, most press reports tried to create a negative aura around their activities and to capitalize on the shock value of headlines and labels such as "pirate," "underground," "illegal," or "clandestine" radios, which evoke the turbulent 1960s and the exotic image of "the rebel radios"—like the legendary Radio Venceremos of El Salvador and other "guerrilla radios" in Central America, the anarchist Radio Libertaire in France, or the hundreds of "free radios" or "micro-radio" stations that exist in the United States, such as Free Radio Berkeley, Radio New York International, or the Tampa-based Party Pirate and Radio Mutiny. To such catchy and romantic labels, most radio activists reply: "Neither pirate, illegal, or underground, but alternative, low potency, local and community-based radio stations."

Of particular public interest and outrage was the infamous case of April 1996, when the interim city mayor, Alberto Roselli, collaborated with the Dirección de Comunicaciones (National Communications Board) and the police in the closure of a community radio station in the La Teja neighborhood. This political action was all the more contradictory considering that while this was happening the same city government was sponsoring the First Encounter of Community Radio Stations at the city hall of Montevideo ("Con los pies en la tierra y la voz en el aire," 25–28 April 1996). Needless to say, the board of the Frente Amplio, the center-left coalition, pointed out this contradiction and loudly criticized this embarrassing episode.

Another, yet related, piece of news that attracted equal attention was an incident in 1995 involving Radio FEUU. Created in 1988 and revamped in December of 1995, Radio FEUU broadcasted student positions and student-led debates. This time the debate was about the allocation of public funds to the university, which the government wanted to cut down as part of an overall IMF-sponsored "free-market" program to reduce the size and functions of the welfare state. As FEUU considered the debate on the university budget to be a matter of public interest and concern, it decided to put Radio FEUU back to work. First, it started broadcasting from the roof of the school of architecture using equipment of just one watt of power. It later moved to the school of chemistry, then to the school of social sciences, and finally to the nineteenth floor of the hospital of the school of medicine, with a transmitter with 25 watts, by means of which it was able to reach listeners located up to 30 kilometers away.

While university authorities gave permission to Radio FEUU to use the facilities of the hospital, the minister of defense, Raúl Iturria, asked students to stop its broadcasts. When Jorge Brovetto, rector of the university, under pressure from the ministry of defense, asked Radio FEUU to stop transmitting from university buildings, FEUU reminded Brovetto that the university was under occupation. As Radio FEUU was forced out

of the hospital, it first moved to the school of sciences, and then it continued to transmit underground from an unspecified place ("desde un lugar
de Montevideo") (Blixen 1995).

Temporarily interrupted after the budget debate, Radio FEUU resumed on 27 June 1996, as a result of a decision made by the university
"to generate a much needed debate about constructing a truly democratic
society and what that means in terms of the right to the freedom of expression" for, according to FEUU delegates Damián Osta and Andrés
Dean, "it seems that we have inherited a semi-democracy" (una democracia
a medias). The Radio FEUU affair shed light upon the persecution of community stations, which increased in 1996 (Zibechi 1996).

The climate worsened even further in August 1996 when community
radio stations decided to give support to the Federation of High School
Students (FES), as the latter occupied their high school buildings. The
measure came in response to an educational reform imposed without
much discussion and consent by the Public Education Central Authority
(Concejo Directivo Central) under the auspices of the Inter-American Development Bank in Washington (Urruzola 1996). As the protest escalated
it helped to forge an alliance between student organizations, neighborhood organizations, and community-based radio stations. This was
done in a very orderly fashion, as la coordinadora de radios comunitarias allocated each member station (its equipment and personnel) to a different
high school facility. Radio El Puente served IPA (Instituto de Profesores
Artigas), Radio La Esquina served Liceo Dámaso A. Larrañaga, Emisora
de la Villa helped Liceo No. 11, la coordinadora assisted IAVA (Instituto Alfredo Vázquez Acevedo), and so on (El Hurgador no. 2, August 1996, 3).

As community radios became "high school radio stations," they not
only proved to be of tactical political value (forcing the authorities to enter into a dialogue) but also they prevented the government from using
force and going unnoticed. They also kept students, family members,
and neighbors interconnected and informed of what was going on within
the buildings and in other high school facilities. They provided a social
and cultural activity during the occupation. Most importantly, they
helped to sustain an uninterrupted public debate, which helped educate
people on this issue within and beyond the high school student movement.

Later, community-based radio stations also participated in both the
International Workers Day mass gathering of 1 May 1997, as the National
Workers Union (Plenario Intersindical de Trabajadores-Central Nacional
de Trabajadores) authorized community radio stations to be at the side of
the main stage and to broadcast live, and in the Day of Solidarity Work

organized by the movement of housing cooperatives (Federación Unifi-
cadora de Cooperativas de Viviendas por Ayuda Mutua) in celebration of
their twenty-seventh anniversary. The presence of community radio stations in both events was important in bringing people face to face, introducing people to each other, and generating opportunities for dialogue,
cooperation, and coordination between different groups and social
movements. Moreover, social interactions and occasions such as these
have also helped to dissipate fears about "pirate radios" injected into the
popular imagination by the government, and have contributed to extending the social roots as well as the legitimacy of the community radio stations movement (Curuchet 1997).

In November, following the successful First Encounter of April 1996,
la coordinadora organized an even more successful Foro sobre medios de comunicación social en democracia (Forum on Democracy and Mass Media).
This second forum took place at the university, and it was declared "of
national interest" by the government of Montevideo. The forum was of
the highest possible level in terms of the personalities, sponsoring institutions, and the number of people that participated. The agenda included
presentations and discussions of (1) technical matters regarding the use
of the radio-electric field, (2) the forms of property of the means of communication, (3) the right to communication, (4) the need for new and
different kinds of means of communication, (5) the relationship between
communication and democracy, (6) broadcasting rights in Uruguay and
other countries of the region, (7) the existing legal framework, (8) the relationship between local development, political decentralization, and
communication (Agenda del Foro, e-mail 20 November 1996).

Doing Radio as Community-Building

In terms of technology, these radio stations are fairly simple and elementary. They consist of a room, a table, a few chairs, and a power source.
Because of recent advances in the field of electronics, all the necessary
equipment is now inexpensive, light, and small. It consists basically of a
double tape deck recorder and player, a CD player, an amplifier, a radio
transmitter, a mixing console, a couple of microphones and earphones,
and an antenna. While there are usually three or four persons at work,
outside other small groups prepare their up-coming program and "get
ready." The latter are, in turn, surrounded by a circle of friends, guests,
and fans "just hanging around," chatting, making suggestions and music requests, and simply having a good time. Due to its simplicity radio
stations are relatively easy to install and move around. This explains why

when radio stations need to change their location, neighbors, local organizations, and institutions find it easy to lend them space.

Most broadcast on the FM band, utilizing empty frequencies. At times, they even share the same empty frequencies. According to a student interviewed, "there are up to four or five channels per 800 Khz, so there is plenty of Hertzian space available for all." While they have relatively powerful equipment (from 25 watts up to 300 watts) radio stations only use a very minimal amount of power (between 0.75 and 5 watts), voluntarily limiting their range of transmission to "their targeted zones" in order not to interfere with the commercial radio stations (which, in any case, use much more powerful equipment).

Some community radio stations broadcast daily, usually in the evening or late at night. Oeste, for example, transmits everyday, starting at 7 P.M. Others are on the air only two or three days a week, mostly on Friday evenings and weekends. Radio FEUU can be heard Fridays from 5 to 10 P.M. and Saturdays from 10 A.M. to midnight. El Puente airs Fridays from 7 P.M. to midnight, Saturdays from 9 A.M. to midnight, and Sundays from 5 P.M. to midnight. Emisora de la Villa broadcasts on Saturdays and Sundays. Uyuyuy broadcasts Sundays from 8 to 11 P.M. and Emisora de Emergencia, Sundays from 6 to 9 P.M. These choices result from the fact that both producers and listeners have jobs or need to attend school, and operation and programming must fit around their schedules.

The people that produce, work, and listen to community radio are mostly youth: high school students, university students, working-class youth, and even younger teenagers, as in the case of Las Fatales de La Teja (El Puente). While some parents and older neighbors are occasionally involved, the average age seems to be in the late teens and early twenties. All of them are volunteers and "amateur," even if they are acquiring professional skills through practice.

Programs include music, news, sports, interviews, social commentary, debates, and variety. Some are intended for the general public, others are just for their fans and friends. Some radio stations have formed a programming board, which reviews and allocates space and time to projects presented to them by people from the neighborhood. El Puente, for example, includes people from different local organizations on its board. Once a month, the programming board calls a meeting of all participants; programming is discussed and new proposals may be added or replace other programs. El Puente organized its First General Assembly on Programming on 7 August 1996, an occasion for the various participants to finally meet each other face to face, exchange experiences and ideas, and discuss "the fundamental questions," such as "What is a communitarian practice? Must everybody take to the streets with a tape recorder? Who is the targeted audience? What is communitarian, the radio or the programs? Only the local matters?" (see Karina in El Hurgador no. 2, August 1996, 3).

All in all, programming necessarily reflects the world of the community of users: their culture and worldview, their everyday life and style, their success stories and problems, their concerns and critiques of society, their anxieties and fears. News broadcasts are both local news and a selection and commentary of news published in the printed press. Some radio stations also make use of the information distributed at no cost by Pulsar and other alternative news agencies (mostly via internet and e-mail). Cultural programs stress events in the neighborhood or things considered of interest to the community. Sports programs deal—although not exclusively—with the performance of local teams in various tournaments. Music is one of the distinct features that characterize these radio stations as they broadcast, in the words of Jorge Lobo (22), of Radio Emergencia, "music that nobody else broadcasts here" (L. L. 1996a). Discussion of social and political themes goes from local issues and issues specific to the groups that participate in, or listen to, these stations, to national and international politics.

Though forced to move around, most radio stations are deeply rooted in a particular neighborhood, functioning amid a fairly developed social and cultural network of people, groups, and organizations (El Tejano: Periódico barrial de La Teja y Pueblo Victoria no. 37, April 1996). These include the local theater, policlinic and public kitchen, the local soccer club or housing co-op, the local parishes and carnival troupes, as well as other occasional partners such as the local newsstand, Jumbo (the local supermarket), the Federation of Workers of ANCAP (the oil refinery), or the Taxi Driver's Union.

Geographical attachments and development of local networks are not, however, features or goals necessarily shared by all. Jorge Lobo of Emisora de Emergencia explains that "they have not yet developed any links to their community, and that they do not want to rush it or force it either." Radio Demente enjoys its condition of anonymity and the "mystique" of being underground, emphasizing the mere pleasure of doing radio regardless of who is listening or from where they are transmitting. Radio Oeste also sees itself playing a broader role. For sixteen-year-old Jorge Doprich, "We do not want to talk only about local issues, we also want to talk about Montevideo. If you only tackle your own neighborhood there are still many other neighborhoods that also have things to say and may not have the means to have a radio of their own." Mauricio de los Santos, of La Esquina del Cerrito, also prefers to use radio "as a means of connecting the various parts of the city and of effecting neighborhood integration" (L. L. 1996a).

Changing addresses pose various logistical problems for community-based radio stations. First of all, it forces the entire team to keep in touch and to tell each other the new location. Second, it somewhat weakens the relationship with the community because neighbors wishing to say something on the air, help out, or simply hang around may not know where to go. Third, it creates problems with the transmission as the topography and form of the city impose certain physical limitations on radio transmissions, thus forcing the radio to change band or frequency. In any case, stations always need to let their audience know their frequencies, their program schedules, and if possible, the place from where they are going to be broadcasting. One way of conveying this information is mouth-to-mouth, which certainly works to a degree, since participants and their audiences are, for the most part, friends, classmates, and neighbors. Other than that, they have also developed a whole repertoire of ways of reaching their public. These include billboards strategically located on nearby bus routes; graffiti on the walls next to, or in front of, bus stops; fliers and handouts advertising the content and time of particular programs; stickers often placed on windows, cars, bikes, and thermoses as well as notebooks and folders. Some, like El Puente, have their own outlet press (El Hurgador), a space in local newsletters (El Tejano), and even their own electronic mailing list and internet Web site.

All in all, four main characteristics seem to be shared by most. First, their sense of being part of a larger entity, bigger than the neighborhood and smaller than the country: the city of Montevideo. Second, the social and cultural "void" they fill. Third, the generational and countercultural twist most of these radio stations express. These translate into a particular style of doing radio: the privileging of certain themes, music, or sociocultural phenomena (those things that youth repeatedly encounter in their everyday lives); a distinct approach to those issues and themes; and linguistic markers and attitudes typical of the youth and of the times. Finally, observance of the "ten principles" according to which community radio stations need to be: (1) controlled by the community that participates in it, and listens to it, (2) instruments of direct popular expression, (3) nonprofit, (4) a form of social property, (5) collectively managed, (6) independent from political parties, religious organizations, and the institutions of the state, (7) pluralistic so as to make room for all the cur-

2. Billboard on Carlos María Ramírez Avenue, entering la Villa del Cerro, August 1996. Photograph by author.

rents of opinion existing within their community, (8) producing programs that mirror the diversity of cultural interests in the community, (9) giving space to the various social organizations of the neighborhood, (10) not isolated entities but parts of a collective movement ("Principios de la Coordinadora de Radios Comunitarias," 8 October 1996, e-mail 16 October 1996).

The Politics of Speaking in Public

Hertzian waves are a patrimony of humankind. The International Telecommunication Union, a specialized agency of the United Nations based in Geneva, coordinates the usage of radio frequencies worldwide by giving each member state a limited amount of band space and of satellite orbits to be allocated to their nationals. Uruguay, however, is one of the few countries in Latin America that does not authorize community-based radio stations (Fonseca 1996).

In Uruguay, the allocation (*concesión de uso*) of Hertzian waves in the form of a given frequency and the authorization of radio stations is the function of the National Bureau of Communications (Dirección Nacional de Comunicaciones), which is supervised by the Ministry of National Defense.[1] Frequencies are allocated to a private user or concession-holder (*concesionario*) with no time limit, who, in turn, can sublet parts of that space (short periods of time) to a third party (or leaser). Indeed, subletting (public) frequencies from a private concession-holder is another way of gaining access to radio broadcasting, although this option, in addition to being expensive, subordinates leasers to private parties and interests.

According to the 1978 regulations, in order to be authorized to operate a radio station, a set of conditions must be met. These include passing a close "examination," presenting "moral credentials," "proof of economic strength," a detailed description of how this resource is going to be "exploited," "making a cash deposit to be decided by the executive," and more (Pallares and Stolovich 1991, 187). Once given, permits can also be revoked if radio stations use the "wrong kind" of language, "disrupt public tranquility, undermine the morality, decorum, and good manners," "pose a risk to public security, or affect the image and prestige of the republic" (Decree-Law 14.670 of June 1977 and Regulatory Decree 734 of 1978). Needless to say, these are all vague rules and criteria by means of which state officials intend to influence the behavior of radio stations.

This current institutional and legal framework often stands as an insurmountable obstacle for those requesting access to the waves (unless they are "well connected") and a form of coercion and censorship used upon those who have gained access to the waves. All in all, these rules favor certain individuals and groups while making sure that other social groups, forces, and cultural projects are kept away from having their own means of communication. Community broadcasters claim that the government "does not have any social or legal criteria regulating the allocation of radio frequencies except arbitrariness and favors to political allies and friends" (L. L. 1996b). For Federico Fasano, director of the daily *La República*, "The problem (here) is not a technical problem but a political one" (Fasano Mertens 1992).

Although not authorized by state officials, community radio stations claim to be "legitimate" and perfectly constitutional under the rights of freedom of association, expression, and the press guaranteed by the Constitution, as well as by the various international agreements on human rights signed and ratified by Uruguay (*El Tejano: Periódico barrial de La Teja y Pueblo Victoria* no. 38, May 1996). To begin with, Article 29 of the Constitution of 1967 clearly states that "all the matters related to the communication of thoughts and ideas by means of words, private writings, published in the press or via *any other means of diffusion* are entirely free, and there is no need for any prior censorship; the authors, however, are to be held responsible for abuses, previously and properly defined and typified as such by the law, in which they may incur" (emphasis added). The Constitution echoes none other than the Universal Charter of Human Rights itself: Article 27 establishes that "every person has the right to participate freely in the cultural life of the community." More to the point, Article 19 clearly states that "everyone has the right to freedom of opinion and expression; this right includes freedom to hold opinions without interference and to seek, receive, and impart information and ideas *through any media*." Finally, according to Article 13 of the American Convention on Human Rights, also known as the Pact of San José de Costa Rica of 1969 (signed *and* ratified by the Uruguayan government, and incorporated in Law 15.737 of March 1985), that means: "either orally, in writing, in print, in the form of art, or through *any other medium of one's choice.* " Thus, citing Article 13, law school professor Alberto Pérez Pérez concludes that

> the right of expression cannot be restricted by any indirect methods or means such as the abuse of government or private control over . . . radio broadcasting frequencies, or over equipment used in the dissemination of information, or by any other means tending to impede the communication and circulation of ideas and opinions. . . . There is absolutely no possibility that the state may set conditions prior to the exercise of the right of freedom of expression and communication; . . . limitations and restrictions in the allocation of radio waves should only be admitted when and if the new radio stations cause some kind of technical interference with other existing radio stations, which is not certainly the case (El *Tejano* no. 38, May 1996; L. L. 1996b).

Contrary to this, the current practice of organizing the field of mass media in Uruguay still has its roots in the 1928 Radio Broadcasting Law (Ley de radiodifusión de 1928), the 1929 Decree (Decreto reglamentario de 1929), and the 1935 Law of the Press (Ley de prensa de 1935) passed during the dictatorship of Gabriel Terra. Worse still, the pillars of the present system are none other than the Radio Broadcasting Decree-Law 14.670 of June 1977 (also known as Ley de radiodifusión de 1977); Decree 734 of December 1978; Decree 327 of 1980; and Decree-Law 15.671 of November 1984 (Decreto de ley de prensa de 1984), all four decrees introduced during an unconstitutional and totalitarian regime guided by the infamous Doctrine of National Security (1973–1985). The first Sanguinetti administration, itself the outcome of the restricted elections of 1984, ratified by decree most of these regulations (Decree 350 of July

1986) (Pais Bermúdez 1992, 10; Fasano Mertens 1992, 170). Few people are aware that this legal framework is largely unchanged in spite of minor modifications introduced in 1990. Thus, when asked about their legal status, pointing to the fact that the current legislation is the product of a de facto power, and standing on the shoulders of a body of international agreements and constitutional laws, radio station activists reply: "They are illegal" *(los ilegales son ellos)*.

The Criminalization of Community

Community radios are often the target of police raids and searches *(alla-namientos)*. Searches are supposed to be "inspections" to check whether radio stations have permits and are observing state regulations, but because these radio stations are not authorized and are of an amateur nature these "inspections" automatically lead to closure and confiscation of their equipment. Between June and November 1996 a series of raids led to the confiscation of the equipment of several radio stations: Emisora de la Villa, El Puente, La Teja Libre, FM Alternativa, and Radio FEUU, most of which hardly hide at all. Police raids are ordered by the Ministry of National Defense, signed by the director of Dirección Nacional de Comunicaciones and authorized by a judge (Barreche 1996).

In addition to the raids, the government seeks to turn public opinion against community radios by means of distorting their image, motives, and nature: "They want to make the general public believe that we are 'subversive' and that not a few of us are moved by depressive and imbalanced psyches, 'souls out of control' *(descontrol anímico)*. . . . We know that some people do not want to listen, or give reasons, and are obsessed with putting labels on us. In the *barrio* we call this 'foul play' *(jugar sucio)*" ("Mensaje de la Coordinadora de Radios," 8 October 1996, e-mail 16 October 1996).

On 23 September 1996, the daily El País wrote that Raúl Iturria, then minister of defense, had stated that the armed forces had confiscated the equipment of Radio La Intrusa of La Teja, which was apparently "transmitting messages originating in the Lacandona Jungle, home of the Mexican EZLN, and in Nicaragua . . . presumably coming from Uruguayan journalists stationed there . . . containing subversive plans and tactics . . . which military intelligence is trying to decipher [since they] may be related to possible armed riots and eventual terrorist attacks" ("Confiscaron en Uruguay equipo de radio que difundía mensaje del EZLN" [AP, DPA], La Jornada [Mexico] and El País [Montevideo], 23 September 1996, e-mail 2 October 1996). According to the report the armed forces had found "a song with a Central American rhythm giving instructions on how to make a home-made bomb" as well as "components that could be used in the fabrication of Molotov cocktails (which) were used at an earlier time against police patrolling the zone." According to other radio activists, however, this incident had to do with "a group of anarco-punk youngsters, also residents of the neighborhood," which "had indeed played some revolutionary tunes of the 1970s and read some EZLN declarations but nothing more. There were no bombs or anything like that, except for some kerosene and nails; the father of one of these kids is a carpenter," they explained. Yet, "unfortunately, this incident played right into the government propaganda, made us lose some ground in the community, and did substantial damage to the image of the entire movement" ("Saludos tejanos," e-mail 16 October 1996).

While broadcasters are persecuted by the police, informal radio transmissions are not, nor ever were against the law. Participants were briefly detained and given a warning, and saw their equipment repeatedly confiscated, but they never were in danger of being incarcerated. In 1997, however, the government coalition—pressed by private interest groups such as ANDEBU, RAMI, and other broadcasters' organizations—wanted to pass a law criminalizing all unauthorized radio broadcasts (they would not, of course, authorize them either). According to this law anyone working at these radio stations, lending either their homes or their means of transportation, giving technical assistance, or making economic contributions to them could face up to ten years in prison.

Community broadcasters condemned this law and reminded government officials of their constitutional rights. Some, like Adriana Alegría, of Uyuyuy, think that the government should not be regulating these activities and that there should not be a need to request authorization. Others, like Mauricio de los Santos, of La Esquina, see legalization as a way of ceasing to be clandestine and stopping police raids, which in addition to being antidemocratic "scare our people away." In fact, he does not plan to remain underground forever. For de los Santos "at our radio station nobody hides, we always say where we are." Radio Oeste broadcasters also read their address and telephone numbers during transmissions. According to Jorge Doprich, "We have requested authorization from the DNC because we never meant to be clandestine nor do we want to hide from anyone" (L. L. 1996a).

In October of 1996, a press release issued by la coordinadora included the name of all the directors and the locations of all the member radio stations while insisting that the government recognize and accept the existence of a "third kind" of radio station that is neither profit seeking and privately owned nor state-owned and managed, but experimental, socially oriented, community operated, and nonprofit. The message demanded that a special legal accommodation be found that considered the existence of low power, community-based radio stations, and that, in fact, the state assist in their development ("Mensaje de la Coordinadora de Radios," 8 October 1996, e-mail 16 October 1996).

Globalization and Citizenship

Community-based radio stations matter because people have the right to become cultural producers beyond the point of creative consumption and active reception. In today's largely post-urban, electronically mediated public life, our own development as persons and citizens depends on access to these and other ways of producing and partaking in the public sphere. Such cultural activities are also fundamental when it comes to bringing together the various zones, subcultures, and movements that conform the city, and to community-building and organizing. Ultimately, the very notions of local and national cultures are going to depend more and more on the way local actors, organizations, and institutions are able to intervene and mediate (both ways) in the national and global traffic of culture—that is, in their capacity to contextualize, nationalize, and localize the global, as well as to nationalize and globalize the local.

All this seems to be particularly important in the context of the monopolistic character of the national and global cultural industry. And it is even more important in light of the fact that, today, the printed press, books, computers, and higher education have been turned into expensive and exclusive commodities, inaccessible to an increasing segment of the younger population. Indeed, this is one of the causes that seem to be at the root of the current tendency toward social disintegration, alienation, marginalization, and class polarization.

Needless to say, the legal and political questions regarding the cultural industries and the field of electronic means of cultural production also seem to be central at this stage. However, the ultimate question goes well beyond this or that particular aspect of the law or, for that matter, this or that particular cultural movement. The ultimate question lies with "the possibility of citizenship"—and of a truly democratic cultural model—at a time when global corporate capital seems to have succeeded in taking over public expression, hence making the practice of citizenship devoid of content, marginal, and obsolete in the face of "market determinations" or technocratically dictated goals, programs, and procedures.

For cultural critics, educators, and activists the challenge is to begin to pay attention to these emerging local cultural practices, neither envisioned or problematized in isolation of global flows, nor confined to be mere instances of "creative reception." Perhaps we might need to move up to a second wave of reception studies, devoted to the study of the reception of these emerging local cultural practices aimed at producing (resuscitating?) a democratic public sphere, in response to the somber spectacle of cultural globalization.

Note

1. Until 1968, communications and broadcasting were supervised by the Control de Servicios Radioeléctricos, a dependency of the Ministry of National Defense. From 1968 to 1974, the Control was placed in the sphere of the Ministry of Transportation, Communications, and Tourism. Between 1974 and 1984, the Control was placed within the National Administration of Electric Telecommunications (ANTEL), a decentralized public enterprise then supervised by the Ministry of Defense. Finally, before leaving office, the dictatorship created the Dirección Nacional de Comunicaciones, an organism supervised by the Ministry of Defense yet financed by ANTEL. Many of its authorities were military officers. In September 1985, only months after assuming office, President Sanguinetti made an attempt to place the DNC under the Ministry of Interior—a bill, however, never approved by Parliament, thus keeping the DNC within the sphere of the Ministry of Defense (Pallares and Stolovich 1991, 122; Pais Bermúdez 1992; Fonseca 1996). Today the Dirección has been substituted by the URSEC (Unidad Reguladora de Servicios de Comunicaciones).

ROMÁN DE LA CAMPA

Mimicry and the Uncanny
in Caribbean Discourse

The only theory worth having is that which
you have to fight off. —*Stuart Hall*

Román de la Campa was born in Cuba in 1946. A literary and cultural critic, he is a professor at the State University of New York, Stony Brook. His main titles include *LatinAmericanism* (1999), and *Cuba on My Mind: Journeys to a Severed Nation* (2000).

Mapping Caribbean culture has always conjured images of hybridity, mimicry, syncretism, and transculturation. Long before the advent of postmodern troping, the names Frantz Fanon, Aimé Césaire, Nicolas Guillén, C. L. R. James, and Fernando Ortiz gave meaning to such categories. But these very terms are now used to designate an imploded sense of otherness in a late-capitalist culture seeking to understand itself amid the cultural shifts of globalization, mass migrations, and a generalized condition of diaspora. That could possibly explain why contemporary Euro-American discourses of self-critique, deconstruction, and epistemological unfixity display a tantalizing ambiguity. Unsure whether to celebrate the end of the Cold War or mourn the twilight of its modern legacy, these discourses now inform a grammar of globalized difference whose main tropes encode such concepts as liminality, in-betweenness, and otherness as rhetorical space. Yet, it is not altogether clear how such a grammar speaks to the Caribbean and other sites of colonial legacies. Whose image is reflected, or doubled, in the mirror of this transposed lexicon? Will it still recognize the voices and images of a Caribbean that is clinging to the need for "opacity" in order for "anxiety to have a full existence"? Will the new grammar of difference speak to a culture that must now "confront the ideal of transparent universality, imposed by the West, with secretive and multiple manifestations of Diversity" (Glissant 1989, 2)? Are there various Caribbeans, one Spanish, closer to postmodern Latin Americanism, the others English and French, closer to diasporic, postcolonial theorizing?

Fissures, aporias, chaos, and epistemic contradictions—these are now the primary foci of a critical paradigm that has gained considerable prominence in humanistic research during the past several decades. Paramount in such work is the argument that history, as either experience or discursive flow, undermines the pretense of teleological certainty. For third world or postcolonial societies whose histories defy homogeneous definitions of modernity, rethinking the world through the lens of indeterminacy and disruptions seems apt, at least at the level of theory. But such insights become more pertinent still when distinguishing between third world cultural production and the globalizing machinery of conceptual dissemination, a "techno-mediatic power that threatens any democracy," according to Jacques Derrida (1994, 54). Postmodernism in the late 1990s, particularly in the hegemonic neoliberal formation that concerns Derrida, seemed to move farther away from the still somewhat open cultural logic that Fredric Jameson observed a decade earlier, to a more distinctly set of self-enclosed marketing features (1986). Can postmodern writing distinguish itself from the avant-garde cultural effects of late capitalism and focus on lingering structural hierarchies? Is this the terrain, or the promise, of postcolonialism? Are the two "posts" mutually intelligible?

Shifts in critical thinking are generally thought to assume a central position in Western capitals first, only later being consigned to peripheral areas such as Latin America and the Caribbean. The avant-garde does not seize epistemological status so readily at the margins. Indeed, the rate of production and dissemination of critical work stemming from Euro-American academic institutions, and the disciplinary boundaries that speak through them, impose a commanding presence. In peripheral sites, often devoid of well-financed research universities, it is frequently said that newness accrues more readily to the artistic than conceptual domains. Such stratified relations between codification and performativity have often placed Caribbean culture on a secondary or derivative plane of signification—bespeaking perhaps a fissure inherent in the constitution of peripherally modern societies, a characteristic indelibly marked by legacies of struggle, including revolutions, in the arts and in politics. The effects of this peripheral status have also been implicit in various forms of homogenizing programs throughout the area's history, such as the constant pursuit of cultural identity, nationhood, and other familiar modes of imagining modern societies. They all continue both to elude and to inform the Caribbean, in ambiguous yet enriching ways, constituting perhaps one of those "stubborn shadows where repetition leads to perpetual concealment" (Glissant 1989, 4).

How, then, does one read third world stories with lingering claims on the universalizing discourses of modernity? Are they mostly national allegories, a form of mimesis somehow bound to older and aesthetically simpler Western models? Are they exotic and nostalgic narratives prone to a magic realism that mystifies identitarian longings for multicultural mass marketing? Or should we look on such stories as cultural objects whose only value lies in their need for deconstructive demystification of foundational pretenses? Is there a postmodern way of reading that avoids modern and postmodern forms of reductionism and trivialization, an approach that does not resist the complex double coding of continuity and rupture implicit in postcolonial textuality?

One can no longer ignore the fact that shifting from a structural understanding of history, culture, and literature to an emphasis on postmodern discursivity avoids many pitfalls, particularly the tendency to impose an enclosing system on the texts and phenomena under study. But this theoretical turn deserves some scrutiny as well, especially insofar as it claims to speak in the name of both diversity and heterogeneity. Arif Dirlik, for instance, argues for the need to understand how neoliberal capitalism still structures postmodern logic. Although nations have been largely displaced by markets in the new global configuration, its boundaries are still structurally defined (Dirlik 1994). Yet, whether one insists on the structural category of Third World or opts for the discursive notion implicit in postcolonial, large regions of the world, including some within the industrialized West, still cling to the fallen utopian discourses of democratization, modernization, and national renovation. Postmodernity has not yet managed to bridge the gap between an absolute first world critique of such utopias and the ongoing hierarchy of material differences within the global village construct.

Signification, like investing, can be absorbed too loosely by the portfolio of floating metaphors and postmodern dissemination, thereby resulting in a critical space where undifferentiated abstractions take up the space of diversity. Debate over the meaning of Frantz Fanon's work today provides a telling example. For Homi Bhabha, Fanon's exceptional moments of rhetorical excess embody an exhilarating ambiguity, splitting, and rhetorical transgression that betray his otherwise banal propensity to existential humanism (Bhabha 1994c). For Henry Louis Gates Jr.,

Fanon has become an object of appropriation for postmodern and post-colonial theorists bent on escalating a process of "epistemological hygiene" that dismisses the historical value of his colonial discourse (Gates 1991). Stuart Hall strikes a somewhat intermediate position in what is perhaps one of the most important essays on the topic of identity, and argues that Fanon calls for a double coding, a reading through both continuity and rupture, a dialogism that still informs the Caribbean and other postcolonial societies (Hall 1994a).

An emerging concept of world literature (or culture) is often implicit in the globalization of the literary marketplace. It offers evidence of an interesting but contradictory market of literariness, mostly codified through the English language, which encompasses discursive communities that no longer depend on their most immediate point of referential enunciation. To speak of "Caribbean literature," for example, is to conjure an object of study that is more than ever before free from local entanglements. This splitting from immediate referentiality allows such texts to circulate as signifiers suddenly capable of floating in multiple contexts. But an absence of boundaries also begins to codify the Other's world of lived experiences according to the expectations of a new and somewhat distanced readership. Texts, images, and discursive communities inevitably respond to the greater logic of marketable forms, a referential field of force that inscribes itself into the work of writers and critics. Imagined communities written largely from abroad can indeed amount to sameness. Yet, Caribbeanness still designates a difference, that certain cultural quality Glissant calls "our hesitant clairvoyance," derived from a long history of creolization that has yet to be globally embraced (1989, 3).

These and other problems implicit in cultural globalization still lie beyond the grasp of standard deconstructive insights. A non-identitarian cultural politics is not as easily attained as one would like to think from first world academic positions of relative wealth, stability, and inchoate pluralism. Specificity in time and space must be constitutive in any valuation of writing from the Third World, lest we impose on it a cultural logic of exchange lacking any trace of resistance or claims on the world of life experiences. Obviously, the first world/third world binarism often fails to account for many positions in between, but global structures retain certain hierarchies that are often left unattended by cultural theorization from afar. One could argue that Euro-America's postmodern investment in declaring an end to modernity holds crucial insights for societies still striving for new ways of modernizing, but the two predicaments could not be more distinct: Euro-American postmodernism reflects on a legacy of abundance no longer taken for granted and searches for a new horizon within a position of prominence, not to mention privilege, while third world or postcolonial societies struggle in a new void still fraught with a history of material necessities and modernizing entanglements. Even if one accounts for various intermediary positions between these two poles, it seems clear that postmodernism, globalization, and neoliberalism must necessarily entail substantially different strategies, particularly as these apply to literature, history, and the politics of identity.

The central aim of this essay is to unearth these differences within contemporary Caribbean theoretical discourse. The work of Sylvia Wynter, Stuart Hall, Wilson Harris, C. L. R. James, Benita Parry, Neil Lazarus, Franklin Knight, Roberto Márquez, J. Michael Dash, and A. James Arnold, among others, has been of particular interest and value in this pursuit. Collectively, they offer a Caribbean purchase on the line between structural and poststructural epistemologies that cannot be denied, as evidenced by the increasing attention their work commands from the postcolonial and postmodern readership. Each of these writers or critics merits individual attention, but my main focus in this essay will be Antonio Benítez-Rojo's The Repeating Island and Édouard Glissant's Carribbean Discourse, two ambitious attempts to encompass the cultural history of the Caribbean primarily as discourse. My specific interest is not to locate these two established writers in conformity with new conceptual paradigms, nor with each other, but rather to probe how the difficulty within their work itself reveals surprising degrees of problematization, counterarguments, and specifically Caribbean modes of responding to current theoretical junctures. Benítez-Rojo's and Glissant's differing discourses reveal different Caribbean claims on signification as well as performance, and thus offer a concrete interpellation of the globalizing tendencies implicit in poststructural understanding.[1]

Antonio Benítez-Rojo

The Repeating Island, published in 1992, is the English version of La isla que se repite (1989), which Antonio Benítez-Rojo wrote after migrating to the United States from Cuba in 1980. The book's explicit attempt to rewrite Caribbean culture as a postmodern performance had an immediate impact in the fields of Latin American and Caribbean literary and cultural studies. Though not quite a cultural history of the Caribbean, The Repeating Island composes a rich and at times daring combination of literary criticism, theory, and creative writing. Among its most innovative critical essays are those addressing the work of Nicolas Guillén, Fernando Ortiz, and Bartolomé de las Casas. The latter deserves special commentary because it is arguably Benítez-Rojo's most original and far-reaching attempt to mix creative writing and textual analysis.

Interspersed among these critical pieces, however, one also finds large sections of traditional historicism that, although quite informative in their own right, evidently betray the author's commitment to novel modes of narration. Such a historicist voice reappears with much greater force and frequency than Benítez-Rojo's narrative voice is willing to acknowledge. The introductory essay, in turn, showcases the author's talents as a creative writer, despite its tendency toward speculative, and at times impressionistic, theoreticism. It nevertheless conjoins the book's plurality of forms, tones, and historical ranges in a somewhat daring, suggestive, and equivocal attempt to engage the Caribbean as an island always bound to repeat itself.

Benítez-Rojo's discourse on the Caribbean emerges from a postmodern perspective that he loosely constructs through a string of metasignifiers such as chaos, free play, supersyncretism, and polyrhythms, leading to his ultimate category of "performance"—which he portrays as a Caribbean cultural disposition, an ontology of sorts that is always already postmodern, particularly when viewed from the vantage point of a reader already fully versed in deconstructive insights. Although Benítez-Rojo calls on the force of well-known theorists such as Jean-François Lyotard, Gilles Deleuze, Félix Guattari, and various specialists in chaos theory, his understanding of the Caribbean comes largely—if not solely—from a critique of literary history, a theoretical framework much more closely bound to the work of Paul de Man. Furthermore, it is evident that Benítez-Rojo's most important rhetorical devices are his vast knowledge of Caribbean syncretism (particularly religious myths and iconography), his use of philological skills to retrace the colonial history of such syncretism, and, most important, his freewheeling narrative techniques.

Cuba, a nation caught in many contemporary debates, does not appear to hold a central place in The Repeating Island. But it does loom large as the author's main point of reference in his attempt to deconstruct the modern legacy implicit in the Cuban literary canon, and as a site from which he extrapolates a broader engagement with the entire Caribbean. Nor is there an absence of political import in the book's main articulations, although it never drifts far from an epistemological/aesthetic understanding of politics. Benítez-Rojo's ultimate aim is to retrace the history of modern teleologies and developmental strategies in the Caribbean, both capitalist and socialist, revealing them as ineffective but violent projects prone to fail a culture whose virtuosity and resilience might best be described as *postmodern sublime.*

Unlike the work of other exiled Cuban writers, *The Repeating Island* is neither immediately political nor a clear testimony of dissidence. What drives the book is not an account of life in a country ruled by one party and the same leader since 1959 but rather the newly gathered critical insights of an author whose reputation as a novelist and short-story writer had been well established in Cuba by the time he moved to the United States. Indeed Benítez-Rojo's enthusiasm for critical frontiers constitutes an unbridled celebration of new intellectual horizons that should provide the basis for our own critique, for it is that pursuit of theoretical insights that circumscribes the book and the author in various significant ways.

The Repeating Island contains the story of a novelist turned theorist; it evidences the dramatic adjustment of a writing career that suddenly attempts to absorb the postmodernist theoretical canon of U.S. research universities after twenty years of writing literature from within Cuba's paradigm of nationalist and historical realisms; and it reveals a continued, albeit radically transformed, reflection on Caribbean culture for a writer whose narrative work since the late 1960s already manifested a deep interest in the area's colonial discourse. It is therefore important to probe whether *The Repeating Island* manages to forego Cuban-centeredness and how the critical tools it deploys allow it to encompass the Caribbean at large. In its immediate scope, in terms of which texts it submits to exegetical rigor, the book appears limited to the established corpus of a mostly Hispanic and largely Cuban configuration of the Caribbean (half of one essay out of nine is devoted to Wilson Harris, none to the French or Dutch-language Caribbean). The work does contain, however, various philological incursions into a pan-Caribbean syncretism that entails a broader, albeit undifferentiated, reading of the Caribbean constrained by an emphasis on premodern and colonial textuality. Equally important is the need to test the relationship between the practice of textual deconstruction deployed by Benítez-Rojo, and the claims it makes on a historical understanding of the Caribbean as a living cultural entity.

Modernity and the Cuban Canon

While providing close readings of Guillén, Carpentier, and Ortiz, *The Repeating Island* thus appears to evade a thorough consideration of how these writers continue to inform various contemporary national and regional debates on Caribbean cultural understanding. In stark contrast to other contemporary Cuban writers and artists, even those such as Tomás Gutiérrez Alea (see, for example, his film Strawberry and Chocolate [1994]) who have remained working within Cuba's more limited space for artistic exploration, Benítez-Rojo seems unwilling to look at Caribbean culture as an ongoing set of social, political, and economic problems in any way affected by his postmodern literary appreciation. His Caribbean remains always distant, always sedimented in canonical texts that become the object of a form of literary history seeking to free the reader from afar.

Benítez-Rojo's depiction of the Cuban Revolution in broad, sketchy, strictly epistemological strokes is a telling example of a postmodern view that tends to evade contemporary history. He defines the socialist regime as a modernizing force equally as incapable of forming an organic bond with Caribbean culture as the capitalist regimes that preceded it. Both socialist and capitalist socioeconomic programs are seen as part of a failed modernity, a series of plantation systems or machines, one substituting for the other, tending toward the imposition of violence without hope for change under any conceivable political definition. Such a broad form of historical periodization may provide some insights, allowing one to seize upon the epistemic features of the entire modern period, but its pitfalls soon become apparent when so many centuries are indiscriminately conflated. One is led to ask whether the entire world is trapped in the dead-end flows of violent machines, or has this malaise affected only the peripheral areas that failed to modernize according to Western precepts?

The author's investment in postmodern theory seems to fail him precisely at this crucial juncture, because his postmodern understanding seems bound only to a literary appreciation of the negative socioeconomic outcomes of third world or postcolonial societies such as the Caribbean. Nowhere does Benítez-Rojo draw any links between postmodernism and global capitalism as an ongoing process; nor does he show how the reading of modernity differs when it focuses on the history of more highly modernized societies. This becomes an important omission, for Jean-François Lyotard, the theorist whose work informs Benítez-Rojo's work most prominently, has engaged closely with postcapitalist culture as a living entity through concepts such as "differends" and "phrase-regimes" (Lyotard 1984, 1988).

Choteo and the Uncanny

It has been often noted that The Repeating Island fashions a Caribbean culture through notions such as polyrhythms, chaos, and performativity,

which together aim to display a primary form of resistance to modernization processes. The entire book evolves according to this performative
principle. But it should be mentioned that rhetorical figures such as polyrhythms also seem to correspond, in this book, to modes of coping with
reality that are portrayed as instinctive, in the sense that they invoke cultural experiences dating back to premodern times. An enactment of this
ambiguity comes about at a crucial passage of ludic transparency in
which the author, while reminiscing about the imminent danger of the
Cuban missile crisis in 1962, explains how he came to dispel his own
fears that a nuclear catastrophe would engulf the Caribbean:

> While the state bureaucracy searched for news off the shortwave or
> hid behind official speeches and communiqués, two old black women
> passed "in a certain way" beneath my balcony. I cannot describe this
> "certain kind of way"; I will say only that there was a kind of ancient
> and golden powder between their gnarled legs, a scent of basil and
> mint in their dress, a symbolic, ritual wisdom in their gesture and
> their gay chatter. I knew then at once that there would be no apoca-
> lypse. The words and the archangels and the beasts and the trumpets
> and the breaking of the last seal were not going to come, for the sim-
> ple reason that the Caribbean is not an apocalyptic world; it is not a
> phallic world in pursuit of the vertical desires of ejaculation and cas-
> tration. (Benítez-Rojo 1992, 10)

It is not clear exactly how or why the author felt liberated from apocalyptic doom upon witnessing the swagger of the two black women, unless racial and sexual stereotypes can be turned into postmodern literary
exorcism. Benítez-Rojo's use of the postmodern seems here less inflected
by the thought of Lyotard, Guattari, or other theorists of the postmodern
than by de Man's conflation of history and textuality. The passage does
not seek an example of culture as a dynamic entity, but rather an understanding of history as a series of tropes against which close readings of a
few chosen texts stand for all of history as a distant text.[2] But there is yet
another aspect of this vignette that presents a notion of Cuban *choteo* as a
playful narrative technique, an interesting and potentially innovative
form of mimicry whose relation to Homi K. Bhabha's postcolonial troping and Glissant's notion of "diversion" are discussed in detail in the last
section of this essay. *Choteo*, a tendency to joke around, a dismissal of all
that pretends to be profound, or simply a failure to take seriously serious
matters, has been historically seen as an inherent defect of Cuba's national culture first articulated by Jorge Mañach in his well-known *Indagación del choteo* (*On Cuban Wit*). But in this street scene Benítez-Rojo at-

tempts to deploy *choteo* as a posture of indifference struck by the two black women, that is, as contestation rather than resignation. They—or rather, their attitude—become a figure of *choteo* as wisdom or resistance before the menacing gaze of a history governed by East-West conflicts. A form of mimicry or "diversion," as Glissant would call it, is turned over, as it were, into a literary device. Apocalypse is thus rendered harmless and disarmed, albeit somewhat simplistically, by the mere swagger of two otherwise unimpressed Cubans. Mimicry is thus also shown as a form of disdain, not just imitation or intimidation. Yet, one must still wonder if and how this particular use of *choteo* as deep instinctive wisdom accrues value as a figure of postmodern writing. It would seem that fantasizing about black women, vaginal fluids, and gastronomic delights draws directly from a phallic racialist tradition well entrenched in the Caribbean, most particularly during the modern history that Benítez-Rojo aims to leave behind.

But the most challenging and emblematic articulation of *The Repeating Island*'s governing hypothesis must be found in the essay on Bartolomé de las Casas; indeed, it is an elaborate and systematic instance of Benítez-Rojo's deconstructive enterprise. Slowly and very methodically, the author suggests how a contemporary reader should understand the (proto-) postmodern qualities of a sixteenth-century text such as *Historia de las Indias (History of the Indies)*. Las Casas's lengthy and unruly text is submitted to a series of interesting sleuthing maneuvers, which are then juxtaposed to the way this historic chronicle was read during Cuba's abolitionist epoch in the nineteenth century. From there, Benítez-Rojo reconstructs a passage filled with complex and suggestive ambiguity. It begins by underscoring why the *Historia de las Indias* was outwardly repressed or dismissed as digressive by Spanish colonialist historiography up to and during the nineteenth century. From there, the author walks the contemporary reader through a carefully woven process of textual reconstruction and decipherment that is both a discovery and a performance.

Crucial elements of this unearthing surround the advent of a series of plagues on the island of Hispaniola as chronicled by Las Casas. Reference to smallpox is first made and understood as divine intervention: a plan to put an end to the torment suffered by the Indians forced to do slave labor. Later, after Las Casas has also acknowledged the error of African slavery, he writes of another "plague," a symbol of punishment also available from within his own discourse: rebellious slaves begin to descend on the colonizers with untold fury. But Benítez-Rojo's interest lies in a brief reference to another inscription of a plague narrated by Las Casas in such a way as to require a literary, rather than a historical or theological, unpacking. An "uncanny" story thus unfolds from *Historia de las Indias*—a sort of fable that encodes repressed contents of personal, political, and historical import for Las Casas's chronicle and our understanding of colonialism. It is the plague of the ants and the *solimán* stone, a rock made of mercuric chloride intended to attract and exterminate the ants even as it magically decreases in size with each ant bite. This image, in Benítez-Rojo's carefully crafted essay, becomes an in-between moment of extreme complexity in Las Casas's writing, in which the priest ciphers his misgivings about African slavery and his own guilt about having supported it for the sake of liberating the Indians. More important, in the process Benítez-Rojo also unearths the relationship between slavery and the sugar plantation system symbolized by the *solimán* stone, an allegory of exploitation bound to repeat itself over and over throughout the subsequent centuries. Ants/slaves are drawn to the stone/plantation that attracts/exterminates: in this allegory, a foundational tale of the plantation machine, a mythological combat of modernity, finds origination.

For Benítez-Rojo, Caribbeanness is best understood through such uncanny articulations as conjuring violence with artistry, unearthing the ambiguity of repressed forms and contents, and demarcating the extraordinary value of writing as the originary site of Caribbean performative culture, from the time of the colonial chronicles to our own day. Las Casas's writing is thus given a new voice by exhuming, as in an archaeological expedition, its self-referential inscriptions: his confessional guilt, his ambiguity toward African slavery, his fear of monarchical rule, his symbolic fable. All of these elements become emblematic of much more, according to Benítez-Rojo. They constitute a mode of writing that has epistemic value as chaos; that is, as a mode that encompasses both literary transgressions of history's repressive iterations, etched in the colonial chronicle, and our equivocal attempts to reread and rewrite ourselves against the grain of such forces. Chaos unfolds into an agonistic celebration in Benítez-Rojo's pursuit of textual processes that always already affirm literariness as a special place of discovery. Las Casas thus becomes proto-postmodernist and proto-Caribbean at once, in the panhistoric logic of *The Repeating Island*.

The Postmodern as Caribbean Destiny

There should be no question that Benítez-Rojo's reading of Las Casas holds considerable heuristic value for a closer examination of the relationship between literary deconstruction and postmodernity, a nexus that is not always as clear or direct as one might assume.[3] But behind the textual sleuthing and the interest in chaos or historical uncertainty as new modes of looking at writing in The Repeating Island, there lies a narrative and a conceptual strategy bound to certain repetitions of somewhat lesser reach. As narrative, Benítez-Rojo's deconstructive work seeks to become a literary performance that turns critical discoveries into an unfolding tale of ambiguity and textual decipherment. As conceptual or theoretical strategy, on the other hand, Benítez-Rojo's deconstruction is perhaps more prone to a general pattern whose steps, if not its outcome, become rather predictable: (1) identifying key moments of excess, aporia, and contradiction within the texts that have been privileged or repressed by modernity becomes the index that problematizes it; (2) exegetical work or close readings on such texts or fragments provides a basis for a different pattern of anticanonical generalization that privileges indeterminacy; (3) substantive epistemic refutations can be made on the basis of designification once these counter-readings are carefully crafted to show history as an ongoing discursive battle prone to scrutiny as literary prowess. Only a closer look at the historical and cultural boundaries drawn by The Repeating Island will illuminate the specific claims it makes on Caribbean postmodernity.

Benítez-Rojo's understanding of the "uncanny" as specially constitutive of literary dissemination finds a special moment in Bartolomé de Las Casas's text. Yet, such fragments of symbolic repression are hardly absent from other texts, societies, and historical times. Defining its presence in Historia de las Indias as a specifically postmodern quality, and then linking it to contemporary Caribbean culture, would seem to require a more precise and extended explanation than Benítez-Rojo is prepared to offer. Yet, such a claim is precisely the central idea of his book: postmodernism becomes the panhistoric shadow of modernity, a witness to the latter's repressive legacy, which is given a voice through the work of deconstruction in such a way as to allow any text since colonial times to understand itself as postmodern and, by extension, Caribbean.

If we understand Benítez-Rojo along these lines, it remains somewhat obscure how the Caribbean becomes the only heir to this method of reading against the grain of modernity. Moreover, one immediately wonders if medieval, pre-Columbian, and classical texts will conform to the ever-expansive category of Caribbean postmodernity conjured by Benítez-Rojo. His version of Caribbean postmodernity appears as an all-encompassing aquatic essence capable of drifting toward all ages and places, through open-ended metaphors such as chaos, meta-archipelagos, "the semi-pagan hagiography of the Middle Ages and African beliefs," and the "turbulent and erratic rhythms" of the entire Third World ("copper, black, and yellow rhythms") that belong to the "Peoples of the Sea" (1992, 23 and 29). This newly configured Caribbean ultimately flirts with an essentialized view of itself, even if it is designed as a process of literary dissemination that reaches its maximum intensity in what Benítez-Rojo calls "a certain kind of way" in which "both the text and the reader will transcend their statistical limits and will drift toward the decentered center of the paradoxical":

> Caribbean discourse is in many respects prestructuralist and preindustrial, and to make matters worse, a contrapuntal discourse that when seen à la Caribbean would look like a rumba, and when seen à la Europe like a perpetually moving baroque fugue, in which the voices meet once never to meet again. I mean by this that the space of "a certain kind of way" is explained by poststructuralist thought as episteme—for example, Derrida's notion of différance—while Caribbean discourse, as well as being capable of occupying it in theoretical terms, floods it with a poetic and vital stream navigated by Eros and Dionysus, by Oshun and Elegua, by the Great Mother of the Arawaks and the Virgen de la Caridad del Cobre, all of them defusing violence, the blind violence with which the Caribbean social dynamics collide, the violence organized by slavery, despotic colonialism, and the Plantation. (1992, 23)

This celebration of Caribbean as an all encompassing site relies on a strategy of leaping back and forth from oral, preindustrial temporalities to postmodern discursivity, specifically aimed at erasing the cultural legacy of modernity as historically specific or variegated. Modernity is thus deconstructed in three related ways: as the repository of pain and violence implicit in exploitative regimes (plantation machines) that failed to produce modern industrialized states; as the root of disillusionment and historical failure to which premodern rituals, rhythms, and performativity become the antidote; and as the archive of texts whose major, if not only, remaining value lies in the possibility of unearthing their rhetorical and literary excess.

Accordingly, the flow of Caribbeanness in The Repeating Island swings back and forth from colonial to postmodern times—from Las Casas to Benítez-Rojo. In the process, this flow engulfs the modern explicitness of Guillén and Ortiz, slipping above and beyond the narratives of state formation, anticolonialism, anti-imperialism, socialist and capitalist dependency, literacy campaigns, and other traces of social textuality that still pertain to modernizing needs in the Caribbean, even if they are now devoid of modernity's utopian legacy. The specificity of all such historical traces comes under erasure in The Repeating Island. One could counter that these narratives are quite worthy of deconstructive work in their own right, and that Benítez-Rojo aims to do just that in a very general sense. But a postmodern reading of the Caribbean would need to resist the tendency to lump the rich and multifarious history of modernity into an undifferentiated chronology encompassing four hundred years. For the Caribbean, as well as other postcolonial societies, the narratives implicit in modernization remain rich in the dialogic entanglements of postmodern sociopolitical as well as literary textualization.

Needless to say, cultural mapping can no longer simply rely on designators such as nation, patriarchy, party, class, race, and ethnicity, particularly in their now standard definitions as modern foundational narratives, with their concomitant notions of fixed identities and subject positions. The need to disturb these resting places of traditionalism remains paramount, even if calling for such work sometimes takes the form of an obligatory ritual aiming no further than to exorcise the easily found demons of essentialism. Yet, a certain utopian impulse also lurks behind a postmodernism that is strictly bound to a new celebration of literariness. Does not such a celebration also implicate certain identitarian tendencies in its complacent aestheticism, unperturbed as it is by the grave distance between its radical epistemological claims and its general indifference toward the contemporary social world?

Benítez-Rojo never raises this doubt in The Repeating Island, where the contemporary social fabric of Caribbeanness remains largely absent from theoretical insights, and where cultural mapping relies considerably on a rather antiquarian gaze that essentializes the premodern and erases the modern in its literary pursuit of the postmodern. This utopian impulse is perhaps the only way to explain Benítez-Rojo's predominant emphasis on a religious syncretism whose transcendent value he never questions, most particularly the cult of the Virgin as a predominant signifier in Caribbean history. Its function in The Repeating Island is to create a privileged moment of cultural origination, whose symbolic value will be transferred from the field of religion to that of postmodern writing.

We should note, moreover, that within the protocol of religiosity, the author's position is quite different from that of the people whose culture he describes in The Repeating Island. For these people, religion seems to constitute an unconscious animistic behavior meant to exorcise the demons of modernity, much like the swagger of the two black women recalled at the time of the missile crisis. For the author, however, access to such a protocol of popular religious images is always presented as a finished intellectual product of historicism, a newly gathered critical consciousness. Benítez-Rojo deploys ethnological, philological, and literary research to reconstruct a colonial, and even precolonial, origination point for Caribbean culture and its religious rituals. He often presents this information as incontestable facts of historiography, not as religious rituals that he himself practices, although one could surmise that for Benítez-Rojo there is a certain exorcism at work in a literary articulation that aims to link premodern animism with literary free play. Thus, postmodernity and premodernity come together through the power of traditional historicism and creative performance to constitute a new horizon of intertextuality.

Against this fusion of vastly dissimilar temporalities, cosmologies, and disciplines, the Caribbean's equivocal but rich experience with modernity is reduced to a literary archive, or to a selection of texts awaiting deconstructive appreciation. The narratives of emancipation, nationalism, cultural identity, developmentalism, political reform, educational campaigns, and revolutions, among others, all turn into profound errors. Benítez-Rojo prefers a historical void to the failed discourses of the past, and calls on postmodernity only to unearth the literary or rhetorical value left behind by such failures. In the meantime, conjuring the idea of a living community from this theoretical cul-de-sac becomes unlikely, if not irrelevant. The people of the Caribbean engaged in ongoing life experiences are left with an invitation to levitate from the coffin of their modern struggles, to leave their bodies behind as relics of a sad case of mistaken identity, and to join the celebration of a newly found and largely premodern indeterminacy.

Édouard Glissant

During the past decade or so, the importance of Édouard Glissant's theoretical work seems to have reached an audience beyond France and the Francophone world of the Caribbean and Canada. The appearance of the English translation of Le discours antillais (Caribbean Discourse 1989), his most ambitious theoretical treatise, was perhaps the turning point. Glissant's preeminence as a writer is now widely acknowledged in the Caribbean, and is rapidly gaining in the United States and Latin America. In any case, Glissant's artistry and his prolific output in nearly all narrative genres are extraordinary achievements. A simple look at his oeuvre reveals a commitment to all forms of writing over a career spanning more than thirty years.

It has been said that Caribbean Discourse constitutes an attempt to "read the Caribbean and the New World Experience, not as a response to a fixed, univocal meaning imposed by the past, but as an infinitely varied, dauntingly inexhaustible text" (Dash 1989, xi). *Caribbean Discourse* has also been considered a "fascinating but frustrating read" that, like Benítez-Rojo's *The Repeating Island*, requires the reader to engage the Caribbean in the context of current theoretical discourses, and vice versa (L. Taylor 1994, 99). My aim here is to probe further into *Caribbean Discourse*, this ambitious, difficult, and comprehensive text that continues to command so much attention in Caribbean studies. More specifically, I will focus on the ways in which Glissant's writing on the Caribbean intersects with the work of Benítez-Rojo and cultural globalization, as well as with the postcolonial work of Homi Bhabha and certain Derridean aspects of postmodern writing.

Glissant's novelistic, poetic, and theoretical work during the late 1980s and early 1990s continues to augment, in a process he calls spiral repetition, the massive body of writing that was ultimately abridged for publication in English as *Caribbean Discourse*. His latest collection of essays, *Poétique de la relation* (1990), places greater emphasis on chaos as a category of particular theoretical value for the Caribbean. This book also expresses a much greater concern with the role and history of women in the formation of mimicry, camouflage, and other forms of what Glissant calls *cultural diversion*. Yet, *Poétique de la relation* continues to draw mainly on the notions developed in *Caribbean Discourse*, particularly those of crosscultural poetics, opacity, baroque, and creoleness, figures that Glissant extends beyond the context of the Caribbean itself to seek an understanding of globalization as chaos.

Diasporic Cartography and Street Theater

Caribbean Discourse presents a hybrid compilation of writerly forms imbued by a deep but fluid understanding of contemporary French theory and by repeated excursions into Caribbean literature and history. Although many contemporary philosophers and theorists have brought to the world of discourse an aesthetic awareness, Glissant has managed to distinguish himself as a creative writer who laces his art with epistemological acumen. This provides an intriguing tension, for Glissant's language and performativity constitute attempts to occupy the space of contemporary theory derived from life experiences and popular Caribbean art forms.

Glissant's discourse is thus, to a large extent, the reverse of what one finds in much contemporary theoretical work on postcolonial culture, which is more directly, if not solely, informed by the language and constructs of European and North American theorists. Glissant's construction of the Caribbean also attempts to link theory with historical experience through terms such as *opacity, otherness,* and *diversion,* categories that invoke neither identitarian complacency nor an easily deconstructed play on differences. These terms are read against the background of historical entanglements whose potential complicity with language and representation Glissant does not take for granted. *Caribbean Discourse* also calls on the writing and rewriting of history through complex imbrications absent from much postmodern theorizing, such as the continuous play of memory on orality, the need for a "prophetic vision of the past," and the refusal to relinquish the desire for imagining a community (64).

What Glissant offers is a coiled text made of nothing but fragments, a spiraling spring of scatterings in which *Caribbean Discourse* looks on itself as fragmentation incarnate. Content becomes secondary to a formal obsession with naming, splitting, and tidbits of "stubborn shadows where repetition leads to perpetual concealment" (4). A poetics of fragmentation comes into being, a process of nominalization that labels, or titles, each item as a species of discourse in need of preservation: litanies, interludes, fragments, aphorisms, graffiti, graphs, mappings, riddles, feigned dialogues, juxtaposed voices, historical overtures, tables, news reports, anonymous voices, events, dates, land, landscapes, outlines, a theatrical proposition, and so forth. This naming is neither a collage nor a pastiche, but rather an enactment of supplementarity and marginality, fused with an obsession for historical consciousness. *Caribbean Discourse* is a riddle that aims to frustrate and fascinate, or perhaps a form of historicized mimicry that seeks to complicate our understanding of colonial history during postmodern times.

A decisive moment is found in a section titled "The Table of the Diaspora." At first glance it looks like a simple map of the Caribbean's cultural geography since colonial times, structured along a horizontal axis that includes continental America, the Caribbean, and Africa. Yet, the map has no visible vertical axis as such, though there are many cultural (music, poetry, and religion) signifiers spread about on different levels and planes. Political and economic categories (Plantation America, names of countries) occupy the lower strata of this cultural spacing, but its predominant element is a series of arrows and lines suggesting multiple ways of connecting to myriad cultural, economic, and even geographic signifiers. For example, Plantation America, Marcus Garvey, and salsa music occupy, in ascending order, the borderline between continental America and the Caribbean.

The map's most important features are uncertain zones filled with a dizzying array of crisscrossing lines and other indicators of potential interconnections. The table thus becomes an aesthetic representation of Glissant's theoretical poetics. It comes close to Benítez-Rojo's literary postmodernism in that it resists linearity, base-superstructure ordering, and other forms of historical and geographic representation as such, yet it contrasts with his postmodernism in that Glissant's formulation also resists relinquishing historical circumscription altogether. Glissant presents critical elements of the Caribbean's historical experience in nonsynchronous (or polyrhythmic, in Benítez-Rojo's terms) fashion, but unlike the Cuban writer, he gives the modern period of history a crucial role in determining the future. Contemporary cultural mapping for Glissant assumes its role as an act of discourse along the lines generally associated with the poststructuralist thinking that also informs Benítez-Rojo, but this does not lead Glissant to posit an exclusive emphasis on the premodern or colonial archive of Caribbean texts. Glissant's cartography revolts against both identitarian myths of origin and deconstructive dismissals of the Caribbean's stories of dispossession, decolonization, and other brushes with modernity.

Glissant's aesthetics of fragmentation always begins by calling on the cultural history of Martinique, his motherland, followed by the French Caribbean, the greater Caribbean, Latin America, and ultimately the world at large. Such a framework reveals a global awareness that is richly informed by specific international contrasts, not merely by synchronizing abstractions. The role of the West appears prominently in the brutal colonial legacy implicit in this story, but Glissant is equally incisive, if not harsh, in his views on the participation of Martinican society in this process. He warns that "the West is not in the West. It is a project, not a place" (1989, 2). He also devotes numerous passages to Martinique's own ruling cast of bekés and their role in shaping various forms of mimetic culture; and he is nothing less than scathing about any attempt to romanticize or mystify certain forms of popular culture, particularly folklore.

Theatricalization, delirium, community, consciousness, and resistance—these are some of the salient terms through which Glissant pursues the interplay between theoretical opacity and clairvoyance, a specular movement of ambivalence that runs from the street to his discourse, interspersed with critical pronouncements. For this, Glissant offers, as historical background, a carefully crafted outline of the formative relationship between theater and nationhood in Western culture. He then emphasizes that this history has been always already absent, thwarted, or diverted from taking place in Martinique and in the Caribbean as a whole.

The focus on Western theater as a cultural model of universal value, however, must be seen as part of Glissant's own ambivalent performance. The passage bemoans Martinique's failure to have traveled the Western road to national or collective consciousness through theatrical forms, but it is also a pretext for Glissant's own theoretical dramaturgy. The enactment of a developmental cultural reference that has become an impossibility in the Caribbean turns into a script with deconstructive potential. From the precepts of Greek tragedy, through Hegelian aesthetics, to Brechtian principles of modern alienation, Glissant's review turns into an invocation of the performative, by taking the tone of stage directions for a future Caribbean dramaturgy.

In an apparent attempt to fill that gap, Glissant turns to a neighboring cultural formation: the Latin American theater of collective creation, a different dramaturgy that flourished during the late 1970s and early 1980s. This is a theatrical form that forgoes the need for tragedy and alienated heroes, but reconfirms Glissant's investment in the value of collective performativity as resistance and awareness: "A theater springing from a 'collective politics' would banish such debasement. It is emerging everywhere in South America with the same provisional characteristics: a schematic conception of 'character' (there is no 'profound' psychological examination), exemplary situations, historical implications, audience participation, elementary decor and costume, importance of physical gesture" (1989, 220). Latin American theater of collective creation, like *testimonio* literature, constitutes an innovative form of cultural engagement that incorporates but also goes beyond deconstructive precepts to posit new ways of understanding subjectivity within subalternity. Yet, because of the confinement of postmodern articulations of the Caribbean and Latin America almost exclusively to the literary domain, collective creation theater has never received much critical attention in U.S. research universities where Latin Americanism is largely codified today. Collective creation theater clings to notions of social agency that postmodernity proper tends to find naive or too closely bound to modern metanarratives; this trait may well have contributed to academic disinterest. Although collective creation theater, like *testimonio*, has waned considerably, it was contemporaneous with the emergence of postmodernity as an epochal construct in the 1970s.

Glissant's interest in popular theater points to a series of crucial questions regarding the articulation of "collective consciousness" through artistic means. It foregrounds the question of whether deconstructive modes of configuring postcolonial subjectivity recognize the value of collective empowerment in any concrete way. Can Foucault's notions of self-care as self-knowledge, for example, or various forms of deconstruction inspired by Derrida's work, call upon individuals to act on the social text from a set of shared and generalizable principles? If so, do such theoretical constructs constitute forms of awareness that approach the notion of resistance beyond individual acts or the pursuit of collective goals? These and similar questions are defining the difference between postmodernism proper and postcolonialism.[4]

Glissant's reaffirmation of the quest for national and regional Caribbean models invokes the need to account for the ways in which Caribbean societies continue to conceive and imagine themselves at a time when all metanarratives have become suspect. One could ask, nonetheless, whether his continuous use of the idea of consciousness itself corresponds to a lingering vestige of Western metaphysics, which Glissant has failed to sufficiently examine. More specifically, does *Caribbean Discourse* fail to acknowledge individual ways of cohabiting with neocolonization in its call for a collective consciousness as a prelude to a liberating collective will? Are delirium, folklore, the street scene, impulsive theatricalization, as well as other forms of diversion or mimicry described by Glissant, something more than the unconscious and submissive mimetic devaluations of a utopian Martinican culture conceived out of modern fantasies? Finally, does Glissant's notion of "diversion," like Benítez-Rojo's *choteo*, come close to more ambiguous strategies of survival and resistance, or does it only suggest the absence of more totalizing programs for a distant or absolute liberation?

Diversion, Mimicry, and Mimesis

The practice of diversion, writes Glissant,

> is not a systematic refusal to see. No, it is not a kind of self-inflicted blindness nor a conscious strategy of flight in the face of reality. Rather, we would say that it is formed, like a habit, from an interweaving of negative forces that go unchallenged. . . . Diversion is the ultimate resort of a population whose domination by an Other is concealed: it then must search *elsewhere* for the principle of domination, which is not evident in the country itself. Diversion is the parallactic displacement of this strategy. Its deception is not therefore systematic, just as the *other world* that is frequented can indeed be on the "inside." It is an "attitude of collective release." (Glissant 1989, 19–20)

For Glissant, the possibility of resistance is always already present in the complex notion of "diversion" (*détour*), which composes the central construct in his understanding of Caribbean cultural formations. In time, he expands the notion of diversion to include creole, syncretism, orality, crosscultural poetics, the Caribbean folktale—indeed, all the major aspects of his discourse—as creative forms of diversion. Most important, Glissant distinguishes diversion from mimeticism in a considerably different way than Bhabha, Achille Mbembe, and other established postcolonial critics draw distinctions between mimicry and mimesis. This is unquestionably the crucial point in which *Caribbean Discourse* intervenes and contends with the constellation of postmodern and postcolonial discourses on the Caribbean. The distinction between diversion and mimeticism forces the reader into a theoretical territory that is often equivocal, and itself not devoid of its own opacity.

Diversion, like the lines in Glissant's "Table of the Diaspora," points in various directions at once. Its possibilities include resistance, but only in terms of a broader historical inscription of Caribbean history (*retour*). Lucien Taylor's ambivalence toward Glissant's notion of creolization reveals the difficulty of locating Glissant's thought within the boundaries of contemporary deconstructive theory, but still finds no other frame of comparison than the highly deconstructive writing of Homi Bhabha. J. Michael Dash is much more categorical in his assessment of the theoretical value of *Caribbean Discourse:* "With these ideas on creolization and *Antilla-nité* Glissant fully enters the arena of postcolonial theory" (Dash 1995, 148). Yet, Dash does not revisit his understanding of diversion itself in this new appraisal. His understanding of the term remains somewhat cryptic and closely bound to Glissant's notion of "reversion" (*retour*), in a movement Dash understands as "the dialectic of withdrawal and return" (Dash 1989, ix). This connection is no doubt important, but one needs to look more closely at the inner side of diversion, its puzzling interplay with mimesis, its ambiguously productive nature, and its possible inscription of mimicry, which is precisely the arena of contemporary debates within postcolonial theory.

A brief reference to my earlier discussion of Benítez-Rojo's own use of mimicry seems fitting at this point—that crucial moment when the reader is asked to observe a magnificent gesture of indifference on the part of two anonymous black women walking past the author during the darkest moments of the Cuban missile crisis. Benítez-Rojo clearly presents this gesture as a form of popular disdain toward the very source of apocalyptic power from which such dangers derive, a sort of native wisdom understood as a mocking or an exorcism. Yet, it is not clear whether the author's appropriation of this form of mimicry as writing also constitutes a strategy of resistance on the part of the two women he portrays. They do not speak, but their bodies are written into the author's construction of performativity as mockery. One wonders, however, if they are as conscious of the implicit power of indifference as the writer is of its discursive subversion. Is the body language of these two women not different from a critical discourse that reads them into a complex theoretical construct? Must they be black, women, and anonymous? Does this scene constitute a form of passive mimesis (or *choteo*, in the discourse of Jorge Mañach), or is it a form of mimicry that entails a more active participation in a regime of power?

The most elaborate and influential theorization of mimicry as an active strategy of postcolonial engagement is found in the work of Homi Bhabha. In his deconstructive formulation, he calls it "a writing, a mode of representation that marginalizes the monumentality of history" (1984, 128). Bhabha warns that it is not the "familiar exercise of *dependent* colonial relations" but rather

the figures of a doubling, the part-objects of a metonymy of colonial desire which alienates the modality and normality of those dominant discourses in which they emerge as "inappropriate" colonial subjects. A desire that, through the repetition of *partial presence*, which is the basis of mimicry, articulates those disturbances of cultural, racial, and historical difference that menace the narcissistic demand of colonial authority. It is a desire that reverses "in part" the colonial appropriation by now producing a partial vision of the colonizer's presence. (Bhabha 1984, 129)

In addition to his own commitment to creative theoretical discourse, Bhabha brings an array of contemporary theoretical insights to bear on this construct, especially Foucauldian notions of power as an ascending order that always implies individual subjects, Derridean observance of slippage and supplementarity in the critique of totalizing ontologies, and Lacanian troping of desire, splitting, and imaging. Bhabha finds in mimicry a deconstructive potential that goes far beyond the idea of resistance: "A strategy of subversion emerges. It is a mode of negation that seeks not to unveil the fullness of Man but to manipulate his representation. It is a form of power that is exercised at the very limits of identity and authority, in the mocking spirit of mask and image" (Bhabha 1994b, 298).

Glissant's notion of diversion, on the other hand, straddles the line between mimesis and mimicry. Individual acts of diversion may indeed be seen as being nothing more than floating signifiers awaiting some form of inscription into narrative engagements. In this sense, diversion comes close to Bhabha's concept of mimicry in his construction of post-coloniality as a form of writing. But, as collective expression, these signifiers entangle more complex and fundamental cultural formations such as the folktale, creolization, syncretism—indeed, the entire spectrum of Caribbean culture. From this particular point, Glissant moves strategically to recast the stories of national and cultural formation that have produced a sense of nonhistory in Martinique and the Carribean into a rewriting of the area's errant "irruption into modernity."

These moments constitute the points of historical "entanglements" inscribed in the archive of diversion, to which one must return without essentializing its contents. Glissant carefully acknowledges that this awareness does not represent a return to identitarian forms of thinking, negritude, or even a nondiscursive understanding of creolization. What these entanglements ultimately invoke for him is "a prophetic view of the past," that is, the need to historicize errancy through artistic imagination and charge it with a constructionist role after the task of deconstruction is done. Two key examples would be a recognition of creolization as a global signifier that emphasizes cultural heterogeneity rather than race, and a radical valorization of orality in an age of performativity in which writing is no longer a narrowly defined practice.

Glissant's diversion thus provides an elaborate critique of both modern and postmodern notions of mimesis: neither the powerless subordination to colonial power often associated with the culture of underdevelopment nor an empowering deconstructive figure limited to theoretical work. Indeed, Caribbean Discourse could be read as a treatise on what Glissant calls parallactics (the displacement strategies of diversion). More specifically, Glissant explores through his study of Martinique the question of whether mimesis/mimicry—that intricate doubling that informs postcolonial culture—can find a historical grounding. In doing so, he presents a set of crucial theoretical problems whose value continued to increase for postcolonial criticism in the 1990s. As postmodern theorization moves beyond its initial stages of literary and epistemological avant-gardism, re-elaborations of community, nationalism, and the social text, as well as other political applications of deconstructive insights, are coming to the fore.[5]

In Caribbean Discourse, Glissant manages to engage the world of theory through the specificity of the local without recurring to historicist forms of narration. The complexity of his work lies precisely in the commitment to a theory that cultivates both edges of that performative impulse.

In this context, the substantial differences between Bhabha's and Glissant's modes of mapping what could be called postcolonial societies could not be of greater significance to contemporary critical thinking. Bhabha's entire critical project embodies a new type of writing as theory that aims to gather new force from the deconstruction of third world narratives. It is both creative and incisive, though it understands these aims only from within the aesthetics of de-signification that has evolved in continental philosophy since Martin Heidegger. His postcoloniality emphasizes a writerly frontier in which otherness finds its place mainly as signifier, concrete historical entanglements implode into an invigorated but still universalizing theoretical troping, and political subversion becomes suggestive only as a rhetorical figure. Although he is aware of the value of writing as a form of de-signification within the tradition of Western metanarratives, Glissant views writing from contradictory perspectives, most particularly by questioning its capacity to trope third world historical entanglements.

It is in Glissant's grave doubts about the conception of writing as a new liberating frontier that we find his most striking critique of mainstream poststructural thinking. Indeed, he is eager to submit the privileged practice of writing, which he sees as an intricate part of the colonizing legacy, to a different deconstructive rigor, in which orality and performativity figure prominently. Glissant's critique of writing dramatizes the need to account for a new postmodern orality, as well as video culture and other performative arts that resist strict scriptural containment. His critique also extends to include the body in relation to orality in a manner that moves beyond Foucauldian notions of self-knowledge as sedimented technologies. Glissant intuits that postcolonial thinking must provide a different critical account of this global moment, its opportunities as well as its pitfalls. His search for a new understanding of collective agencies, and for the promise buried with ghosts of the past, retains a hope of renewal that has been mostly absent from postmodern insights. His work does include a stable first world state endowed by centuries of institutionalized nationhood, property systems, and democratic traditions and his call for theoretical difference thus has a different concern for historical evolvement:

> The methodological and fundamental distinction between diachrony and synchrony could also be seen as a trick; that, no longer capable of dominating the History of the world, the West chose this method of refining the idea that histories would no longer weigh so heavily on consciousness and self-expression. It is, however, simpler to consider

this transformation, not as a trick, but as a kind of logical eventuality. In the face of a now shattered notion of History, the whole of which no one can claim to master nor even conceive, it was normal that the Western mind should advance a diversified Literature, which is scattered in all directions but whose meaning no one could claim to have mastered. Now, to follow the logic of these ideas to its conclusion, we should let the weight of lived experience "slip in." Literature is not only fragmented, it is henceforth shared. In it lie histories and the voice of peoples. We must reflect on a new relationship between history and literature. We need to live it differently. (Glissant 1989, 76–77)

Glissant's call to allow the weight of experience to "slip in" to literature is a very poignant moment in his essay on history and literature. It signals a state of literary affairs that goes beyond de-signification toward a state in which narratives, performances, and oralities in the Third World construct a daily life aiming to a better future. *Caribbean Discourse* can therefore be seen as a liberationist text, and indeed, some may find this aspect somewhat naive. It does not call, however, for a nostalgic return to aesthetic values stemming from humanistic precepts. Furthermore, its optimistic moments are not reserved for the academic theorist, or even for the Caribbean. It speaks to the global village itself:

One could imagine—this is, moreover, a movement that is emerging almost everywhere—a kind of revenge by oral languages over written ones, in the context of a global civilization of the nonwritten. Writing seems linked to the transcendental notion of the individual, which today is threatened by and giving way to a crosscultural process. In such a context will perhaps appear global systems using imaginative strategies, not conceptual structures, languages that dazzle or shimmer instead of simply "reflecting." Whatever we think of such an eventuality, we must examine from this point on what conditions creole must satisfy in order to have a place in this new order. (Glissant 1989, 126–27)

"Slipping in," then, is perhaps Glissant's most artful appropriation of postmodern perspectives on language and the body. It could be read as a devious exercise of his brand of mimicry, or a Caribbean gaze at poststructuralist discursivity from within. It is thus a figure that comes full circle, back to the world, from postcolonial experiences to the First World as a shared legacy of experiences as well as rhetorical devices. Freeing the body through new oral discourses, mobilizing diversity, and imagining a future where our understanding of culture is not exclusively ruled by the boundaries of writing—these are some of its constitutive moves. "Whatever we think of such an eventuality," as Glissant himself seems to wonder, it is a construct that delves into the contradictory links between globalization and postmodernity. It is also Glissant's daring conjuration of a postdeconstructivist horizon, a different technology of the self, where art, theory, and history seek to defamiliarize postmodern cartographies that continue to pursue tantalizing but mainstreamed modes of implosion. For Glissant, Caribbean opaqueness provides a way out of this fashionable cul-de-sac.

Notes

1. An elaborate discussion of these pressures on Caribbean discursivity and feminism is found in Sylvia Wynter, "Beyond the World of Man: Glissant and the New Discourse of the Antilles" (1989).
2. See, in particular, de Man's chapter "Literary History and Literary Modernity," in Blindness and Insight (1971).
3. Judith Butler writes about this doubt in "Contingent Foundations: Feminism and the Question of 'Postmodernism'" (1990b).
4. See the questions raised in this regard by Amaryll Chanady in the introduction to Latin American Identity and Constructions of Difference (1994).
5. Two different but insightful new formulations are Neil Lazarus, "National Consciousness and the Specificity of (Post-)Colonial Intellectualism" (1994), and Ernesto Laclau, New Reflections on the Revolution of Our Time (1990). See also Ernesto Laclau, ed., The Making of Political Identities (1994).

JOSÉ RABASA

Of Zapatismo: Reflections on the Folkloric and the Impossible in a Subaltern Insurrection

Usted se está equivocando demasiado con la decisión que ha tomado
en contra de nosotros, usted cree que matando los Zapatistas de Chiapas
o matando al subcomandante Marcos puede acabar con esta lucha. No
señor Zedillo, la lucha Zapatista está en todo México, Zapata no ha
muerto, vive y vivirá siempre.—*Comité Clandestino Revolucionario Indígena*[1]

In seeking to learn to speak to (rather than listen to or speak for) the historically muted subject of the subaltern woman, the postcolonial intellectual
systematically "unlearns" privilege.—*Gayatri Chakravorty Spivak*

"Todos somos indios." La consigna es inobjetable en la medida en
que asume el orgullo (novedad histórica) por un componente básico de la
nacionalidad. Pero qué decir de "¿Todos somos Marcos?" La frase parece
en exceso retórica, fruto de la pasión militarista, del frenesí romántico,
o de la escenografía mesiánica.[2]—*Carlos Monsiváis*

José Rabasa was born in Mexico in 1948. A literary and cultural critic, he is a professor
at the University of California, Berkeley. His main titles include *Inventing America:
Spanish Historiography and the Formation of Eurocentrism* (1993), and *Writing Violence on
the Northern Frontier: The Historiography of Sixteenth-Century New Mexico and Florida and
the Legacy of Conquest* (2000).

One of the urgent tasks in the study of subaltern insurrections is
to find ways of understanding the compatibility of modern
and nonmodern cultural and political practices.[3] Although the
"Carta a Zedillo" by the Comité Clandestino Revolucionario Indígena,
Comandancia General [Clandestine Indigenous Revolutionary Commit-

tee, General Command, CCRI-CG], reached me in Ann Arbor, through the internet, that most modern—perhaps postmodern—form of communication, it manifests a folkloric understanding of revolutionary agency ("Zapata no ha muerto, vive y vivirá para siempre" [Zapata is not dead; he is alive and will live forever]) and a willingness to taunt the *impossible* by asserting a communicable Indian discourse beyond its immediate, local situation (an effort to internationalize the Zapatista call for democracy, liberty, and justice). Another communiqué from the CCRI-CG, printed in *La Jornada*, 16 April 1995, further illustrates a folkloric Zapatismo with a millenarian evocation of Votán Zapata: "Votán Zapata is the one that walks in the heart of all and each of the true men and women. We are all one in Votán Zapata and he is one in all of us." Votán, "guardian and heart of the people," a pre-Columbian Tzeltal and Tzotzil god, also names the third day of the twenty-day period and is the night lord of the third *trecena* (thirteen twenty-day periods) of the Tonalamatl ("count of the days," the Mesoamerican divinatory calendar), and merges with Emiliano Zapata within a poignant view of the power inherent in the multitude as one and the one as the multitude. This communiqué commemorates the betrayal and death of Zapata on 10 April 1919. A communiqué from 1994, also communicating Zapata's death, places Votán Zapata within a 501-year-period of resistance ("Votán Zapata, tímido fuego que en nuestra muerte vivió 501 años" [Votán Zapata, timid fire that in our death has lived 501 years]) and elaborates in more detail on the one/multitude nature of Votán Zapata: "Is and is not everything in us . . . He is walking . . . Votán Zapata, guardian and heart of the people. Master of the night . . . Lord of the mountains . . . Us . . . Votán Zapata, guardian and heart of the people. None and all . . . As being is coming . . . Votán Zapata, guardian and heart of the people"] (ellipses in original; EZLN 1994, 212). According to Eduard Seler, Votán may very well correspond not only to Tepeyollotl of the Nahuas and Pitao-Xoo of the Zapotecs, but also to the bat god of the Calchiqueles (1990–1993, 295).

Of all the communiqués, this is the one that appears to have struck a vital chord among the radicalized youth, whose preference for rock and roll has very little in common with the oral traditions and music choices of the young Indians comprising the Ejército Zapatista de la Liberación Nacional [Zapatista Army of National Liberation, EZLN]. The impact of this communiqué can perhaps be attested by the prominence given to Votán and the archetypical resonance of the ubiquitous ski masks in articles published in *La Guillotina* (March–April 1995) a student publication from UNAM [Universidad Nacional Autónoma de México]. By the way, the motto of *La Guillotina* is "¡Exigid lo imposible!" [Demand the impossible!]. In reflecting on Zapatismo, we ought to avoid reductive readings of folklore and retain the impossible as a utopian horizon of alternative rationalities to those dominant in the West. This reflection informs our critique of the ideological constraints that have kept intellectual discourse from giving serious consideration to hybrid cultural and political practices that combine modern and nonmodern forms.

The Zapatista rebellion in Chiapas makes full use of the new technologies that circulate local news in global contexts—their political and physical survival depends on this flow of information. The Zapatistas, furthermore, deploy the new modes of communication along with consensus politics based on ancestral communalism, just as the indigenous peoples of Chiapas use Western medicine along with *naguales* [animal soul companions] and shamans (Gossen 1994, 566). Gary Gossen argues that shamans and *naguales* have as much to do with the spiritual health of the self as of the community. The factors that determine individual destinies are "predetermined but also, secondarily, subject to the agency of and will of others, both human and supernatural." Indians' beliefs in co-essences, according to Gossen, should be understood as "a fluid language of social analysis and social integration" (1994, 567). They complement Western medicine: Whereas antibiotics cure the individual, shamans also have the task of situating the individual in the cosmos and guiding him or her through the surrounding social reality. These possibilities of using modern science and technology without being forced to disavow one's knowledge is a new historical configuration. It can be argued that the three Ladinos who immersed themselves in the Selva Lacandona ten years ago were able to tap into Indians' long history of rebellion only as a result of *learning to talk to* the community and subjecting themselves to its authority.[4] With a few modifications (not only *women* subalterns or *female* privilege), the epigraph from Gayatri Spivak applies to the three anonymous Ladinos (for all the speaking Marcos does) who unlearned privilege in the formation of the EZLN.

Carlos Monsiváis's comments on the slogans shouted in *yesterday's* march in Mexico City would seem to reiterate the uniqueness of this new historical configuration. Monsiváis goes on to make the distinction between those who might very well have conflicting vocation and those who identify themselves with Marcos in the sense of "if you condemn Marcos for wanting a better world, a more just Mexico, you might as well condemn me and all of us who want the same." Given the circumstances of the offensive by the army (the witch hunts, the tortures), it is understandable (strategically correct) to call for peace, but to place all the emphasis on sharing the condemnation (and ultimately the martyrdom) is to ignore the military nature of the EZLN. In the "Todos somos Marcos," we ought to also hear a will to resist and fight back. For there is, if not a messianic, an eschatological note in the Zapatista call for justice that goes well beyond a "more just Mexico." Monsiváis's remarks, though clearly sympathetic with the cause, manifest the impossibility of the EZLN's subaltern narrative: impossibility in the sense of its incompatibility with "modern" narratives. If this issue of the impossibility of subaltern narratives clearly removes us from the urgency of the immediate events in Chiapas, it also helps us focus on the philosophical significance of the indigenous discursive modalities of the EZLN.

To clear the ground for a serious consideration of the subaltern discourse of the Zapatistas, this essay draws a critique of Gramsci's blindness to the folkloric (I owe this posing of the question to David Lloyd) and addresses recent scholarship that has begun to supersede this interpretative limitation. This theoretical reexamination seeks to understand how the EZLN can constitute itself as a vanguard that is precisely grounded in its self-conscious subalternity, that is, as an instance of the counter-hegemony of the diverse. On the basis of a new ethics, politics, and epistemology of subaltern studies, the second part of this essay moves on to examine the discourse on subalternity that Marcos and the CCRI-CG have elaborated since their revolt on 1 January 1995. It examines how their communiqués have been interpreted from several perspectives that range from condemnations of the violence and illegality of the Zapatistas to understandings of the EZLN in terms of a history of guerrilla warfare in Mexico since the 1960s (Guillermoprieto 1995; Romero 1994; Trejo Delarbre 1994). These articles and books have tended to be written either as a privileging of Marcos over the indigenous communities (it was Marcos's ethnographic acumen that enabled the mobilization of the Indians) or as an unmasking of the Zapatistas that reveals their links to Bishop Samuel Ruiz, Marcos's appropriation of the Indian "voices" in the communiqués from the CCRI-CG, and the absence of a "real" army. The critique of these readings enables us, however, to elucidate the subaltern nature of the EZLN and a narrative of the impossible in the communiqués. The apparent impossibility of the project has as much to do with the denial of a credible Indian-led insurgency as with a hegemonic consensus among Mexican intellectuals that revolution was not an option anymore in Latin America, leaving reform as the only viable political process. As for the government's delegation in the negotiations, Mayor Rolando has put it succinctly: "Es imposible que el gobierno comprenda lo que estamos pidiendo" [It is impossible for the government to understand what we are asking] (La Jornada, 16 May 1995). As we will see in this essay, the Zapatistas attribute the incapacity of the government—as well as of intellectuals—to address their demands to a mixture of moral ineptness (cannot understand what dignity means), racism (cannot dialogue with Indians on an equal basis), and intellectual torpidity (cannot understand the terms of a new communist revolution). The peace talks are proving to be hard lessons for the government on how to speak to subalterns.

As we reflect on Zapatismo we must go beyond representation or even performance, which is ultimately a modality of the former. There is much to gain if we view the insurrection in terms of Antonio Negri's concept of constituent subjectivities: "Constituent power against constituted power, constituent power as singular subjectivity, as productivity and cooperation, that asks how to be situated in society—how to develop its own creativity" (Negri and Hardt 1994, 310). In one of his most recent communiqués Subcomandante Marcos establishes a connection with labor movements in Italy that suggests a connection with Negri. Under the figure of his literary interlocutor Durito (the Little Hard One), a scarab, Marcos conveys his solidarity with the Fiat workers in Turin by giving to their cause the pay he received for a contribution to a collection of essays. I will return to this communiqué later on, but for now I would like to give as an example of Negri's concept of emergent subjectivities, in addition to the "Todos somos Marcos" slogan in Monsiváis's letter, the massive demonstration on 1 May where the unemployed, street children, housewives, alternative unions, small businessmen, and radicalized high school students marched together. Chiapas turns out to be a metonym for the nation: beyond the Zapatistas' local struggle, the EZLN demands a national debate over the meaning and future of democracy in Mexico. A recent communiqué from the CCRI-CG, moreover, suggests the basis for a new internationalism: "We call on all, legal and clandestine, armed and pacifist, civilian and military, on all who struggle, by all means, on every level and everywhere for democracy, liberty, and justice in the world" (La Jornada, 11 June 1995). As we will see later on, the political program of the Zapatistas calls for the multiple engagements of democratic groups, for the creation of a political space where different positions may confront each other rather than a pluralistic centrist position.

Less concerned with identifying and studying "subalterns" as positive entities, the project as I envision it would call for an analysis of the mechanisms that produce subalternity as well as the formulation of political and cultural practices that would end it. But before dwelling on issues pertaining to the ethics, politics, and epistemologies of subaltern studies, I will draw a critique of Gramsci's blindness to the folkloric.

Antonio Gramsci first used the term *subaltern* in his *Notes on Italian History*. His writings also inaugurated the concept of hegemony as a new mode of understanding ideology. Although readings of Gramsci have a long history in Latin America (including Laclau's early work, *Politics* and *Ideology*), they have tended not to be critical of his finally elitist conception of Culture or his conception of the corresponding counter-hegemonic blocs.[5] Gramsci's notion of the folkloric, which he opposes to the modern conception of the historical emergence of national Culture, needs to be critiqued to make space to comprehend the dynamics of subaltern movements. What is at stake in this critique is the compatibility of modern and nonmodern forms of culture and politics and not the celebration of some sort of pristine indigenous community. We must keep in mind, nonetheless, that the possibility of critiquing the ideology of progress is a recent phenomenon not readily available to Gramsci.

For Gramsci, notions of popular culture and indigenous knowledge were incompatible with his understanding of a Culture that could be established as a counter-hegemony. As Gramsci put it in "The Modern Prince," one must study elements of popular psychology "in order to transform them, by educating them, into a modern mentality" (1971, 197). His understanding of cultural politics unavoidably privileged Western conceptions of knowledge, art, and ethics—and, evidently, of History. The elaboration of a counter-hegemonic culture signified an alternative modernity that would transform premodern subjects. In "On Education," Gramsci wrote:

> The first, primary grade should not last longer than three or four years, and in addition to imparting the first "instrumental" notions of schooling—reading, writing, sums, geography, history—ought in particular to deal with an aspect of education which is now neglected—i.e., with "rights" and "duties," with the first notions of the State and society as primordial elements of a new conception of the world which challenges the conceptions that are imparted by the various traditional social environments, i.e., the conceptions which can be termed folkloristic. (1971, 30)

The "folkloristic" would reduce all forms of knowledge not bound by Western criteria of truth to superstition at worst and to unexamined "common sense" at best. "Common sense," in this regard, would parallel what semioticians call natural signs, that is, an uncritical understanding of the world where the signifier bypasses the signified and is thus identified with its referents. The history of philosophy, in itself, would be a chronicle of the institutionalization of "common sense": "Every philosophical current leaves behind a sedimentation of 'common sense': this is the document of its historical effectiveness."[6] For Gramsci, "common sense" continually transforms itself as it incorporates scientific ideas and philosophical opinions into everyday life: "'Common sense' is the folklore of philosophy, and is always half way between folklore properly speaking and the philosophy, science, and economics of the specialists" (1971, 326). This understanding of "common sense" as the folklore of philosophy enables us to turn this concept against Gramsci by pointing out that the reduction of what he terms "traditional social environments" to folklore is in itself a manifestation of philosophical folklore. I term this critical gesture a form of *enlightened de-enlightenment.*

Although "common sense" and folklore were clearly inferior forms of knowledge in Gramsci's assessment, their role in rebellions and insurrections—especially of the peasant—cannot be ignored. If he was critical of voluntarism, of instinct (and called for a transformation of peasants' mentality by modernity), subaltern insurgencies would call for a theoretical reflection rather than a dismissal on grounds of insufficient consciousness—lacking plans in advance or not following a theoretical line. Theory, then, should hold a dialectical relation with movements of revolt that fall out of the schema of historic-philosophical outlooks. The task of subaltern studies, as defined in this essay, would be to conceptualize multiple possibilities of creative political action rather than requiring a more "mature" political type of formation. Subaltern studies, therefore, would not pretend to have a privileged access to subalterns; rather, it would define intellectual work as one more intervention in insurgent movements. In developing practices the intellectual would grow parallel to the emergent social actors and their interventions in everyday life.

We may now consider Gramsci's position and the prominence subaltern studies gives to negation in the context of Gautam Bhadra's analysis of the 1857 rebellion in India.[7] Bhadra concludes his study with a brief allusion to fragmentary leadership in peasant insurrections: "Yet this episodic and fragmentary narrative points to the existence in 1857 of what Gramsci has called 'multiple elements of conscious leadership' at the popular level" (Guha and Spivak 1988, 173–74). Bhadra's account works against dismissals of the indigenous leaders' role in the insurrection as "minor incidents" by academic historians like S. N. Sen in *Eighteen Fifty Seven,* or their mockery of "mushroom dignities" by soldier historians like R. H. W. Dunlop in *Service and Adventure with the Khakee Ressalah or, Meerut Volunteer Horse, during the Mutinies of 1857–58.* In Bhadra's account, the indigenous leaders played an integral role in the popular insurrection. The four leaders shared ordinariness and had learned to use the logic of insurrection in the practice of everyday life: "The consciousness with which they all fought had been 'formed through everyday experience'; it was an 'elementary historical acquisition.'" Bhadra's analysis of this rebellion differs in the tone and details of the insurrection from Gramsci's historical examples: "It was the perception and day-to-day experience of the authority of the alien state in his immediate surroundings that determined the rebel's action" (Guha and Spivak 1988, 175). Though one could argue that the situation of Sardinia and the Italian south in general was one of internal colonialism, Gramsci's counter-hegemonic state and project of modernity would re-inscribe the south within a narrative that posits historical development. In the case of the British Empire the colonial situation foreclosed a connection, and the consciousness of the rebels was one of insurgency against a colonial power—not against a landed aristocracy, as in the case of what Gramsci conceptualizes as a progressive peasantry, that is, one that does not align itself with the local landlords against the urban leadership of both South and North. In this regard, the work of the Indian subalternists falls within a postcolonial subject position that is fully aware of the colonial impulses that accompany the project of modernity.

This transformation of historiography, however, still believes that the task of tertiary discourse is to recover the place in history *for* subalterns. Its task is to prove that the insurgent can rely on the historian's performance and not that the performance of the insurgent itself can recover his or her place in history. This faith in the historian has less felicitous consequences.

Colonial documents on indigenous rebellions without fail give prominence to the leadership of women and make mention of blacks, mulattoes, and *mestizos* joining ranks with Indians; in the case of the Zapatistas, they find support among urban lumpenproletarians who wear the ubiquitous ski mask at rock concerts or in the recent demonstrations as a symbol of solidarity. Marcos's characterization of the *México de abajo*, from below (vis-à-vis the Mexico of the penthouse, the middle floor, and the basement), vividly portrays subaltern rage: "El México de abajo tiene vocación de lucha, es solidario, es banda, es barrio, es palomilla, es raza, es cuate, es huelga, es marcha y mitín, es toma tierras, es cierre de carreteras, es 'ino les creo!' es 'no me dejo,' es 'iórale!'" (*La Jornada*, 22 September 1994). This popular language cannot be translated without distortion (Rabasa 1994, v–xi; 245–70). For instance, *banda* or *palomilla* would call for "gang," but Marcos emphasizes a vocation for solidarity. The "no les creo" [I don't believe you], "no me dejo" [I will not take it] sums up the

"¡órale!," which something like "enough" would hardly do justice to. Elsewhere I have traced this same *México de abajo* in the context of a 1692 rebellion in Mexico City (Rabasa, Sanjinés, and Carr 1994, 245–70). There, as in the case of the demonstrators, there is a solidarity with the Indians: "Todos somos indios," "Todos somos Marcos." One can hear the "¡órale!"

The state-sponsored ideology of *mestizaje* after the 1910 Revolution theoretically should have extended bonds of solidarity with Indians, but its historical effect was to promote a systematic denial of Indian roots—though the pre-Columbian past was idealized—and a program of acculturation that aimed to destroy indigenous languages and cultures. Only *mestizos* were deemed by the state to be authentic Mexicans. In this regard the "Todos somos indios" would seem to augur (at least on a symbolic plane) the possibility of a radical change in the structures of feeling where the plurality of the Indian peoples of Mexico would be recognized and respected. This emergent sensibility would ultimately depend on the indigenous leadership and its capacity to negotiate on its own with the government. In this regard the porosity among Indian groups in rural Mexico and the corresponding responses from urban subalterns would differ from subalterns in India, who seem to be less mobile, communicative, and communicable. This difference, however, has as much to do with a long history of insurrections in Mexico where Indians occupied the same urban and rural spaces with the *castas* (racial mixtures that colonial documents laboriously break up ad infinitum—namely, beyond *mestizos* and mulattoes, documents identify *zambaigos* [Indian and Chinese], *lobos* [Indian and African], *pardos* [mestizo and African], *castizos* [mestizo and Spaniard], and so on). These classifications clearly have a very different meaning than the caste system in India, and a very different history. Not only is there a memory continuum (obviously with different interpretations in time, as in any other culture) in the remembrance of past Indian insurrections, but also of the *México de abajo*.

We should heed, nevertheless, the CCRI-CG's constant insistence on the Indian leadership of the EZLN in the face of the government's and the press's accusations of manipulation by "profesionales de la violencia" [professionals of violence]: "We reiterate it, the EZLN is an organization of Mexicans, with an Indian majority, directed by a committee that gathers all the different ethnic groups of Chiapas and does not have, in its composition, one single member that is not an Indian" (*La Jornada*, 9 February 1995). This statement suggests that nationalism as a mode of relating communities without erasing their linguistic and cultural specificities should be taken seriously as a subaltern political program that should not be "folklorized." If the specificity of the Zapatistas and the history of Mexico should not be erased through a reading that draws parallelisms with rebellions in India and elsewhere in Southeast Asia, the rhetorics of counterinsurgency that Ranajit Guha has identified are nonetheless germane to the Mexican government's policies that have attempted to contain Marcos and infantilize the Zapatistas. For instance, some sectors of the press in the days that followed the rebellion dismissed the first communiqués that listed NAFTA as one of the motivations for the rebellion. How could Indians understand NAFTA without foreign advisors? This same press has consistently condemned the insurgency as illegal violence.[8] A recent collection of articles condemning the violence, proscribing the utopian impulse, suggesting that international drug dealers financed the EZLN, blaming liberation theology and the bishop of San Cristóbal de Las Casas, Samuel Ruiz, for the violence, and unmasking the manipulation of the Indians by Marcos has been published with the title La guerra de las ideas [The war of ideas]. The title gives the impression that its contributors are the only ones who carry out a legitimate "war of ideas." The question is against whom, for at least some of the articles—even though they do not fully sympathize with the taking up of arms by the EZLN—suggest that they are also waging a "war of ideas" against the government. But the editor of the book never seems to consider the violent nature and implications of the moral superiority he ascribes to the contributors to the volume. What do you do to outlaws? What about the communiqués of Marcos and the CCRI-CG that call for dialogue and carry out war by other means, as Clausewitz would put in? In spite of the communiqués' mastery of media, some quarters of the press still disparage their literary quality. Most of the contributors chose to ignore that NAFTA was the culmination—the icing on the cake— of neoliberal policies that Salinas had been implementing during his sexenio.

Of particular relevance to Chiapas was Salinas's reform of Article 27 of the Constitution that had "guaranteed that villages had the right to hold property as corporations, that the pueblo was a legitimate institution in the new order [of the 1910 Mexican Revolution]" (Womack 1972, 375). Marcos underscored this point several times in the February 1995 interviews held with Blanche Petrich and Elio Henríquez for La Jornada:

Those reforms canceled all legal possibilities of their holding land. And that possibility is what had kept them functioning as paramilitary self-defense groups. Then came the electoral fraud of 1988. The compañeros saw that voting didn't matter either because there was no respect for basic things. These were the two detonators, but in my view it was the reform of Article 27 that most radicalized the *compañeros*. That reform closed the door on the indigenous people's strategies for surviving legally and peacefully. That's why they rose up in arms, so that they would be heard. (*La Jornada*, 4–7 February 1994)

The Zapatista uprising in January presented itself as a response to the sellout of the country to transnational corporations. El Sup (the nickname often given to Marcos, mocking Superman as in *superclinton*) names the Indians in Chiapas as among the last few patriots who are willing to fight for the country. In the interview Marcos cites the CCRI-CG's motivation for taking arms: "We disagree with selling our country to foreigners. Although we can live with starvation, we cannot accept that this country be ruled by someone that is not a Mexican" (ibid.). This nationalist statement has very little to do with the state-sponsored nationalism of the PRI—a nationalism that, by the way, also informs the tourist industry that has confined indigenous cultures to curio shops, museums, and archaeological sites.

As in the case of Bhadra's rebels, the Zapatista leadership has a clear understanding of the national situation based on a historical experience. Unlike Bhadra's individualized rebels, the Zapatista contingent includes, besides Marcos, a number of leaders *sin cara* (faceless) and *sin nombre* (nameless)—with the *noms de guerre* of Comandantes Tacho, David, and Trinidad, and Mayor Rolando—who have, nevertheless, gained visibility and a voice in interviews they have held with the press. It is important to note that the CCRI-CG has kept Marcos from participating in the recent peace negotiations with the government. This subordination of Marcos has as much to do with safeguarding him as with keeping in check his protagonist tendencies. The representatives in the round of talks of April and May 1995 were once more infantilized, and in the discussions in July there seems to have been a breakdown with regard to the Zapatista demands for respect for their dignity. Tacho deplores but also mocks the ineptness of the representatives from the government: "They also told us that they were studying very much what is dignity, that they are doing research and studies on dignity. What they could understand more was that dignity was service to others. And they asked us to tell them what dignity means to us. We answered them that they should go on with their research. It makes us laugh, and we laughed in their faces" (*La Jornada*, 10 June 1995). The collective memory of five hundred years of oppression enables the Zapatista leadership to link local demands to a national agenda. When blamed for wasting time in the negotiations with such issues as respect for dignity, the Zapatista delegation, according to Tacho, responded that "nosotros no somos los culpables, todos los indígenas de México llevamos cinco siglos con la pobreza, el desprecio, y con la marginación" [we told them that we were not to be blamed because all the Indians of Mexico have lived for the last five hundred years in poverty, disdain, and marginalization] (ibid.).

The emergence of the Zapatista movement with an Indian feminine leadership also signals a re-centering of rationality and the nation in and on Indian terms. Marcos is subordinated to the CCRI-CG, which in turn arrived at the decision of going to war after the committee of each community consulted its members: "Los Comités pasaron a preguntar a cada hombre, a cada mujer, a cada niño si ya era tiempo de hacer la guerra o no" [the committees went on to ask each man, each woman, each child if it was time to go to war or not] (Blanche Petrich and Elio Hernández, interview of Marcos for La Jornada, 4–7 February 1994). When queried why women and children participated in the revolutionary organization, Ramona, who is described as a small monolingual Tzotzil comandante, responded: "Because women are also living in a difficult situation, because women are the most exploited ones, still strongly oppressed. Why? Because women for many years, indeed for the last five hundred years, have not had the freedom to speak, to participate in an assembly" (Blanche Petrich and Elio Hernández, interview of the CCRI-CG for La Jornada, 3–4 February 1994). Because of a severe illness, Ramona has been replaced at the table of negotiations by Comandante Trinidad, who is in her sixties and has been described thus: "con el rostro parcialmente cubierto por un paliacate rojo y una larga cabellera entrecana y lacia" [with her face partially covered with a red bandana and long and straight hair] (La Jornada, 13 May 1995). Trinidad has demanded a special table to discuss women's issues and denounced the response of the government that mocked her by asking why they should not also have a "mesa de jóvenes, de niños, o de ancianos" [table of youth, of children, or of the elderly] (ibid.). If the indigenous leadership has gained prominence in the past few months, the indigenous leaders since the earliest interviews have underscored the subordinate role of Marcos. For instance, in the very early interview of 3–4 February 1994, a member of the CCRI-CG states that Marcos is a spokesperson and a military strategist, but not the political theorist: "Pues Marcos es como subcomandante. Marcos tiene la facilidad del castilla. Nosotros todavía fallan un chingo . . . (El manda en lo militar.) Nosotros, pues, más la cuestión política, organizativa" [Well, Marcos is like a subcomandante. Marcos has the facility of the castilla. We still make a chingo of mistakes . . . (He leads the military aspect.) We are in charge of the political and organizational questions]. Because of their flawed Spanish, Marcos functions as a spokesperson, and at least in this interview the *chingo* of mistakes of the Indians' *castilla* are not corrected. Marcos at first, undoubtedly, was indispensable for placing the Zapatistas on a national and international front.

While in one set of texts or statements, Marcos and the CCRI-CG develop a lively rhetoric, often irreverent and mocking of the government, and a critique of the political economy as well as the ideological warfare conducted by the government, in another set, they underscore how the political positions and decisions to go to war were made after consensus was reached in every indigenous community. Marcos's pen might very well be involved in some of the CCRI-CG texts, but it is only in bad faith that some members of the national and international press have ascribed authorship to him. So much ink has flowed trying to unmask Marcos, that is, to peg an identity and a proper name on El Sup. At a time when most Mexican intellectuals were willing to believe that revolution, Marxism, and guerrillas were dead, and that the left in Latin America could only be reformist, the emergence of the Zapatistas had to be explained away. The theories that informed these views were either wrong or the EZLN was an anomaly if not a historical aberration that tried to exhume Marx and the rest. Thus, Jorge Castañeda reduces the Zapatistas to an "armed reformism" (Castañeda 1994, 44–45). It does not occur to Castañeda that the EZLN might at once be reformist (seek specific democratic transformations) and revolutionary (express a sense of injustice that calls for a radical new time). In a letter responding to Zedillo's inaugural speech, Marcos underscored the revolutionary character of the Zapatistas:

> You are not yourself anymore. You are now the personification of an unjust system, antidemocratic and criminal. We, the "illegal," the "transgressors of the law," the "professionals of violence," the "nameless," are now and have always been the hope of all. It is nothing personal, Mr. Zedillo. It is simply that we have proposed ourselves to change the world, and the political system that you represent is the main obstacle to achieving it." (*La Jornada*, 7 December 1994)

The end of changing the world presupposes the destruction of the PRI and the state apparatuses that support it. It does not mean, however, that the EZLN aspires to take over the state. It remains a revolutionary movement, but the strategy that informs it is not any longer inspired by the Cuban Revolution.

When the press reduces the EZLN to the personal history of Marcos-the-militant-in-previous-armed-movements-in-Mexico, it ends up re-inscribing the Zapatistas as a variation and advancement of the guerrillas in Guatemala, the FSLN in Nicaragua, and the last instance in a series of armed movements in Mexico. Marcos inevitably assumes the image of a *caudillo*, a role he has contested, but the press insists on it: "Marcos es el caudillo—aunque él lo niega—de un levantamiento armado en el país del surrealismo" [Marcos is the *caudillo*—even if he denies it—of an uprising in the country of surrealism] (Romero 1994, 23). This is seemingly an empathetic version of the unmasking—with an exoticizing turn: "el país del surrealismo." But the rhetoric of counterinsurgency can be traced in the reference to Marcos as *caudillo*. In the ranks of those who seek to unmask Marcos to discredit him figures prominently Alma Guillermoprieto's article in the *New York Review of Books*. Her article (though signed on 2 February 1995) appeared in a suspicious moment that inevitably (regardless of her intentions) would come into play with a "Political Update" from the Chase Bank that called for the extermination of the Zapatistas ("The national government will need to eliminate the Zapatista to demonstrate their effective control of the national territory and of security policy" [quoted in Silverstein and Cockburn 1995]) and the apparent compliance to this demand by the Mexican government that revealed the "true" identity of Marcos, printed "his" photograph, and placed an order for his arrest and that of the other leaders of the EZLN. Marcos emerges as a professional of violence who manipulates the Indians, and, perhaps, more in tune with the Chase Bank memorandum, the EZLN as hardly a military force. The government justified its decision to send the army into Zapatista territories because arms caches had been found in the states of Veracruz and Mexico.

Critics of Marcos who attempt to identify him manifest a will to control the meaning of texts by means of the construction of their authors. Poststructuralist concepts of the author-function as developed by Foucault offer another way of reading the "authority" in the communiqués by Marcos and the CCRI-CG. Instead of insisting on who the real Marcos is, one should understand the particular author-function he as well as the CCRI-CG occupy and produce. The communiqués by the CCRI-CG are ascribed to a collective body and as such manifest the values and position of the indigenous community. They derive their authority and legitimacy inasmuch as they are the expression of a collective body that by definition is subaltern: For dominant discourse, Indians, as long as they speak and think as Indians, cannot write or formulate a coherent political program. Beyond the obvious racism, this dismissal of indigenous intellectuality entails structural determinants that date back to the early colonization of the Americas—the subjection of native knowledges as superstitious or idolatrous. Indians had to abandon indigenous forms of life in order to make sense. In this regard, the CCRI-CG manifests an instance of writing the impossible in its affirmation that the EZLN is an Indian-led insurgency.

The Zapatistas' call for justice has ancestral roots that cannot be reduced to an immediate program of reforms. Their call for justice is in the realm of the incalculable, as defined by Derrida: "The law is the element of calculation and it is just that there be law. But justice is incalculable. It requires us to calculate with the incalculable" (quoted in Spivak 1995, 111). Tacho's demand for respect for dignity conveys this call for justice as incalculable. What could make amends for the oppression of indigenous peoples over the past five hundred years? But equally radical are CCRI-CG calls for a broad national and international front to struggle for the transition to a radical democracy, which, perhaps, is nowhere better defined than in Durito's text—the one I mentioned earlier in this essay, the one stating that Marcos's pay went to the Fiat workers in Turin.

Marcos refutes the characterization of the EZLN as an armed reformist movement: "Any attempt at 'reform' or 'equilibrium' of this deformation is impossible FROM THE STATE PARTY SYSTEM . . . A REVOLUTION IS NECESSARY, a new revolution" (La Jornada, 11 June 1995; Marcos's emphasis). Durito reminds us that this call for revolution actually went back to a communiqué from 20 January 1994, where Marcos had first spoken of "un espacio democrático de resolución de la confrontación entre diversas propuestas políticas" [a democratic space for the confrontation of diverse political proposals]. Durito criticizes Marcos's obscure and indigestible style and goes on to clarify what should be understood by revolution. It is "una concepción incluyente, antivanguardista, y colectiva" [an inclusive, anti-vanguardist, and collective conception] that is no longer a problem "de LA organizacion, EL método, y de EL caudillo (ojo con las mayúsculas)" [of THE organization, THE method, and THE caudillo (beware the capitals)] but a task that pertains to all those who see the revolution as necessary and possible and for its realization everyone is important (ibid., Marcos's emphasis). The end of the revolution would not be anymore "the conquest of Power or the implantation (by means of peaceful or violent means) of a new social system, but of something anterior to one and the other thing. It is a question of building the antechamber of a new world, a space where, with equal rights and obligations, the different political forces would 'dispute' the support of society's majority" (ibid.).

This proposition contains striking parallelisms with Negri's understanding of communism and the constituent power of the multitude: "We may conceive the multitude: as minoritarian or sutbaltern, or more accurately as exploited, but the multitude is always already central to the dynamics of social production; it is always already in a position of power. The power it is endowed with, however, is a power qualitatively different from the power of the State" (Negri and Hardt 1994, 307). These calls for revolution do not have in common an alternative socialist state, but a political space that is not bound by the logic of capitalism and socialism as alternative administrations of capital (Spivak 1988b, 115). Both Negri and the Zapatistas call for the formation of strong subjectivities that would resist any transfer of power to a transcendental institution, that is, to any form of political mediation that resides outside the processes of the masses. It could be argued that this commonality could be traced back to a shared affinity with the Zapatismo of the Plan de Ayala. Nevertheless, the connections between the EZLN and the Italian labor movement bear the auspices of a new internationalism that would no longer be grounded in a party or follow the program of a socialist model.

Within the long memory of indigenous oppression, grief, mourning, and rebellion, socialism is but one particular political form, one of the many regimes of laws that have been available from the West. Marcos is but one of the many Western interlocutors that have advocated justice for the Indians. We must here recall Bartolomé de Las Casas, the bishop after whom the town of San Cristóbal is named, who, at the end of his long life of struggle against the injustices committed against the Indians, called for a restoration of all sovereignty to the indigenous leaders and condemned the colonial enterprise in its entirety. Las Casas's radicalism extended to threatening Philip II with excommunication (Parish and Weidman 1992) and calling for a restitution of all stolen goods and sovereignty to the Indians. Because the colonial enterprise was wrong, the Indians had the right to make war against the Spaniards and uproot them from their territories: "The eighth [conclusion is] that the native people of these parts and of every one where we have entered in the Indies have the right to make a most just war against us and to erase us from the face of the earth, and they hold this right until doomsday" (Las Casas 1992, 218).

One might very well wonder if this position is even within the realm of the impossible today. Indian histories have kept a record of both those institutions of the West that have sought to restore justice as well as those that have oppressed them. This is not the first indigenous rebellion in Mexican history, and one of the tasks of subaltern studies would be to call for a recuperation of the communities' memories of earlier Indian insurgencies and an understanding of how they were subjected to dominant forms of the nation-state. This *knowledge* (not of positivistic data but of the discursive devices that subject Indian cultures and a parallel indigenous awareness that their histories are figures of the impossible) would spare us the banal characterization of the Zapatistas as the first postmodern or, for that matter, postcommunist revolutionary movement. It is precisely in terms of this long history that one can define the subaltern subject position of the CCRI-CG, of the Zapatista insurgency in general, and of Marcos himself as exterior to the logic of capitalism or socialism.

One of the tasks of subaltern studies would consist of writing histories of Indian insurgencies in Mexico that would not be interpreted according to supposedly more advanced or developed political movements. These histories would practice what Guha calls writing in reverse, that is, against the grain of the documents that first recorded rebellions, but also against the counterinsurgent histories that sought to explain and contain insurrection. This would include tertiary histories that would privilege the wars of independence, the revolution, or Marxist theory as providing categories to evaluate earlier movements as ineffectual. The Zapatistas respond to the specific conditions of postmodernity (globalization, transnationalism, the "demise" of socialism, neoliberalism, and so on). And if their response is determined by these political and economic conditions, the EZLN should not be reduced to a postmodern phenomenon: Zapatismo is and is not (post)modern; as I pointed out at the beginning of this essay, subaltern movements should be seen as cultural forms where the modern and nonmodern are compatible. Indeed, the EZLN manifests, in its interpretation of the sources of their oppression and counterinsurgent modes of containment, a lucidity that has been from the start a part of Indian resistance to colonialism. It also entails, at least implicitly in the Zapatista denunciation of paternalism, a critique of Gramsci's "folklorization" of popular culture. Subaltern studies would, therefore, also make it its business to draw an inventory of modes of colonial discourse, of forms of writing violence, that have sedimented in "commonsense" developmentalist tropes.[9]

In addressing the subject positions of Marcos (and by extension the CCRI-CG) we must keep in mind that "he" is a series of communiqués, interviews, and speeches that have been recorded on video, and not some sort of coherent and consistent self behind the statements he utters. And let's also not forget that these multiple subject positions have little to do with a celebration of a postmodern fragmented self. Furthermore, Marcos's and the CCRI-CG's understanding of history, and their role within it, is profoundly tragic and eschatological (though not teleological). It is worth recalling here Walter Benjamin's distinction between progress and *jetztzeit*, "the 'time of the now' which is shot through with the chips of Messianic time" (1969, 263). The Zapatistas, like Benjamin, would confront "mythical violence," the violence of the storm (progress) that keeps the angel from redeeming the past; "awaken[ing] the dead, and mak[ing] whole what has been smashed" (1969, 257), with "divine violence," a revolutionary violence conceived as "the highest manifestation of unalloyed violence" (1986, 300). Marcos's and the CCRI-CG's communiqués evoke a history in which the enemy has been victorious, but they also formulate a discourse on violence that grounds its purity in the impossibility (paradoxically, also the condition of possibility) of its demands. Though the Zapatistas are a military force, the power of their violence resides in the new world they call forth—a sense of justice, democracy, and liberty that the government *cannot* understand because it calls for its demise. Marcos's multiple subject positions fulfill tactical and strategic functions within his discourse. Within one communiqué he might very well open his text with a poem by Paul Éluard (a gesture that situates his voice within a long-standing Marxist aesthetic), move on to evoke millenarian indigenous narratives (thus asserting that the EZLN struggle for justice has ancestral roots), elaborate a critique of the political economy of Mexico in terms of the four main social classes (the social scientist here complements the intellectual and the "anthropologist"), "include multiple voices in the critique where the social scientist" gains force from popular speech (IMF data are made palatable by satire, humor, evocations of the populace—the "¡órale!" cited above). I could go on and on and draw an exhaustive map of the author-functions in Marcos's communiqués, but there is a danger that in doing so we might reiterate the same closures that author-criticism imposes on texts. An inventory of Marcos's subject position, hence author-functions, runs the risk of neutralizing his discourse.

As an intellectual, Marcos no longer defines his task as one of representation. He does not speak for the Zapatistas (he is one more Zapatista and, as an intellectual, a subordinate), nor does he portray them (Spivak 1988a, 276 and passim). This does not mean that Marcos has not functioned as a spokesperson nor that he has not literarily recreated guerrilla life in the Selva Lacandona or provided explanations of how Power operates today. But these "mirrors," as he calls them (we must keep in mind that the numerous communiqués from the CCRI-CG as well as the interviews of the indigenous leadership have also produced mirrors), of who the Zapatistas are, what they want, and who oppresses them must give way to a "crystal ball," which he understands as the production of revolutionary spaces that systematically would undermine the constitution of a vanguard.

Marcos's understanding of the role of the intellectual from within an illegal army can be extended to others working through legal channels. Intellectual work would run parallel to emergent social movements rather than articulate for them a political program. Thereby, intellectual work would operate on one of the multiple spaces of intervention. If as an intellectual Marcos might define the ends of the Zapatista insurrection, its realization would ultimately depend on the constituent power of the multitude: "To sum up, we are not proposing an orthodox revolution, but something much more difficult: a revolution that will make the revolution possible . . ." (*La Jornada*, 11 June 1995). The ellipses are his, and suggest that this open-ended closing of the communiqué must be completed with the political creativity of the different groups struggling for democracy, liberty, and justice—to repeat once more the Zapatistas' three main demands, demands that define the need to retain the impossible alive in the face of forms of "writing violence" that have systematically infantilized subalterns.

The notion of *writing violence* paradoxically points to the constitution of forms of life that follow a different logic as violent, that is, as devoid of Reason. It also refers to objects of representation, that is, massacres, tortures, rapes, and other forms of material terror. There is an aesthetic, an epistemology, and an ethics of colonial violence. The aesthetic of colonial violence has at hand a whole series of epic topoi that have circulated in Western literature at least since Homer and still are used in denigratory representations of third world peoples (Rabasa 1993). A colonialist ethics informs the laws and regulations that different colonial and neocolonial enterprises have formulated to control voyages of exploration, justify wars of aggression, and rationalize permanent occupations of territories. Clear instances of epistemic violence have been the colonialists' subjections of indigenous knowledges as irrational, superstitious, and idolatrous. In the Zapatista communiqués we have seen how Marcos and indigenous leaders like Tacho, Trinidad, and David have responded to colonialist forms of writing violence by seeing through them, by laughing at counterinsurgent rhetorical moves, and by denouncing the cynical duplicity of the state.

Such is the predicament of postcolonial intellectuals practicing subaltern studies. The specific categories of aesthetic, ethical, and epistemological forms of colonial violence comprise a culture of conquest that still informs the history of the present, of what Foucault has defined as the ontohistory of what makes us subjects (Foucault 1984). In our case it is the history of what makes of intellectuals oppressive subjects. This ontohistory, as I have suggested above, would consist of an *enlightened de-enlightenment*. Subaltern studies would thus first have the task of elaborating an inventory of the colonial legacy of modernity, before even beginning to conceptualize "elsewheres" to dominant Western rationalities (to borrow Donna Haraway's utopian phrase [Grossberg, Nelson, and Treichel 1992, 295–337]). Historical narratives are hardly "insignificant" events in the cultural identities of people. As the Zapatistas put it, "Un pueblo con memoria es un pueblo rebelde" [A people with a memory is a rebel people]. Also consider Rigoberta Menchú's Quiche community's refusal to accept a Ladino version of the conquest and colonization (Menchú and Burgos-Debray 1983). Clearly it is not *inconsequential* for her community to "turn the clocks back" and claim a clear understanding of colonialism—a subalternist reading of the rises of developmentalist ideologies. Both Menchú's *testimonio* and the communiqués of the EZLN are forms of subaltern discourse that should not be confused with what subaltern studies produces in elite intellectual centers.

Subaltern politics and revolutionary interventions are obviously not dependent on or inspired by academic theory. In the case of Marcos, however, there is a likelihood that he has read Gramsci and, perhaps, elaborated a critique of Gramsci's blindness toward the folkloric. In his interview with Blanche Petrich and Elio Henríquez, Marcos, furthermore, evokes Zapatismo as he critiques the vanguardism of the Cuban-inspired *foquismo* prevalent in the 1970s guerrilla: "Our military instruction comes from Villa, principally from Zapata. It also comes by way of negative example from what was done by the guerrillas of the 1970s. They started with a local military movement and expected that the base would slowly join in or that they would be enlightened by this guerrilla *foco*" (*La Jornada*, 5–7 February 1994).

In the manner of a coda, I would like to underscore that my approach to issues pertaining to the *folkloric* and the *impossible* clearly does not presume the transparency for which Spivak criticizes Foucault and Deleuze in their claim that they "know far better than [the intellectual] and certainly say it very well" (quoted in Spivak, 1988a, 274). The impossibility of speaking and the eminent folklorization that has haunted the discourse of Zapatistas at every stage of their dialogue with the government—exchanges that could very well be understood as colonial encounters caught in a struggle to the death—do not manifest subalterns who "know far better" and "say it well," but a clear understanding that the possibility of their call for justice, liberty, and democracy resides paradoxically in the impossibility of being understood. The point of departure is not that "subalterns speak very well, but that they 'cannot speak' and choose not to learn how"—indeed, they demand that the discourse of power "learn how to speak to them." This position is, perhaps, nowhere better exemplified than in Comandante Trinidad, who, at a session with the government, chose to address the official representatives in Tojolobal and then asked them in Spanish if all was clear (Vera Herrera 1995). Rather than seeing Trinidad's intervention as a symbolic statement about the difficulties of negotiating in another language, we ought to see it as an allegory of the inevitable subalternization of Indian discourse. Obviously, her denunciation of the oppressive situation of women and children living under the military occupation of the Selva cannot be a mere question of translation, but at a more elemental level must be seen as criticism of deep-seated colonialist attitudes that cannot accept that an old Indian woman could have anything to say and would be able to say it. This allegory of the impossibility of communication implies that the Subject of the West is not only dying but that its demise will come only as a result of specific struggles that make manifest its colonialist (read sexist, classist, racist) worldview that remains concealed in its claims to universality. In discussing Zapatismo, I have brought into play and critiqued theoretical points derived from Gramsci, Foucault, and Spivak. My point has not been to understand Zapatismo in light of these thinkers, but to sustain a dialogue in which Zapatismo ultimately provides a critique of the discourses we produce as privileged intellectuals.

Notes

1. "You are equivocating too much with the decision you have taken against us. You believe that killing the Zapatistas of Chiapas or killing Subcomandante Marcos can end this struggle. No, Mr. Zedillo, the Zapatista struggle is in all of Mexico. Zapata is not dead; he is alive and will live forever." Comité Clandestino Revolucionario Indígena, Comandancia General del EZLN, "Carta a Zedillo," Chiapas, Mexico, 10 February 1995. Marcos, one of the three non-Indians within the Zapatista ranks, bears the title of subcomandante in contradistinction to the higher-ranking Indian comandantes. From the beginning of the rebellion on 4 January 1994—the same day the North American Free Trade Agreement (NAFTA) was implemented—Marcos has expressed his subordination to CCRI-CG, composed of Tzotzil, Tzeltal, Chol, Tojolobal, Mam, and Zoque Indians, who are in turn obliged to consult their own communities. All translations from Spanish are mine.
2. "'We are all Indians.' The slogan of the demonstrations is unobjectionable insofar as it expresses pride (a historical novelty) for a basic component of nationality. But what can we say about 'We are all Marcos'? This phrase seems to be too rhetori-

cal, the fruit of militaristic passion, of a romantic frenzy or of a messianic sce-nography."

3. For a sustained formulation of strategies and methods to understand, interpret, and grasp the politics of popular movements from the perspective of the masses themselves see Ileto (1979). Although the subject of this essay is a contemporary in-surrection and not a historical event, Ileto's assessment of the failure to understand popular movements applies to the letter (Ileto 1979, 13).

4. Carlos Urzua and Tótoro Taulis have written a detailed history of the movement since the early 1980s (1994). Their history establishes a connection to earlier guer-rilla movements as well as differentiates the nature of the Zapatistas precisely in terms of the subordination of the Ladinos to the recommendations of the Indian committees. John Ross has written a most detailed and empathetic chronicle of the early days of the insurrection (1995). For an analysis of the socioeconomic causes of the insurrection see Collier and Lowery Quarantiello (1994). This present essay seeks to examine the political discourse of Zapatismo. The sources for this reflec-tion are the communiqués by Marcos and the CCRI-CG, as well as the invaluable re-ports from the Selva Lacandona of journalists for La Jornada: Hermann Belling-hausen, Elio Henríquez, Epigmenio Ibarra, and Blanche Petrich, to mention the most prominent and indefatigable.

5. My critique of Gramsci has many affinities with David Lloyd's critique of Gram-sci's view that the history of subaltern groups is episodic and fragmentary (Lloyd 1993, 127 and passim).

6. This passage from Gli intellectuali e l'organizzazione della cultura is quoted in Gramsci (1971, 326n.5).

7. On the centrality of negation in subaltern studies, see Guha (1983, 19–76). Guha finds in the following passages by Gramsci a starting point for an understanding of negation in subaltern insurgencies:

Not only does the people have no precise consciousness of its own historical iden-tity, it is not even conscious of the historical identity or the exact limits of its adver-sary. The lower classes, historically on the defensive, can only achieve self-awareness via a series of negations, via their consciousness of the identity and class limits of their enemy; but it is precisely this process which has not yet come to the surface, at least not nationally. (Guha and Spivak 1983, 273)

Guha's chapter "Negation" goes on to document modalities and instances of actual negations in the history of Indian peasant insurgencies. But Guha, from the con-cluding remarks, seems to suggest an incompatibility of nonmodern social forma-tions with modern political concepts, that is, with "advanced ideas of democracy" (Guha and Spivak 1983, 76). As we will see, in the Zapatistas we find a negation of this teleology that privileges supposedly more developed political forms in the inter-pretation of subaltern identities. Reynaldo Ileto, as I have pointed out above, pre-sents a lucid argument for approaching popular movements in their own terms.

8. The press repeats what I suggest is a constant form of counterinsurgency that Lloyd has defined as follows:

Of course from the perspective of dominant history, the subaltern must be represented as violence. "Must" in two senses: that which cannot be assimilated to the state can be understood only as outside the law, disruptive and discontinuous, unavailable for narration; secondly, the history of the state requires a substrate which is counter to its laws of civility and which it represents as outrageous and violent, in order that the history of domination and criminalization appear as a legitimate process of civilization and the triumph of law. (Lloyd 1993, 127)

9. For a critique of developmentalist discourse as the imaginary of our time, see Escobar (1992).

DEBRA A. CASTILLO, MARÍA GUDELIA

RANGEL GÓMEZ, AND ARMANDO ROSAS SOLÍS

Tentative Exchanges: Tijuana Prostitutes and Their Clients

Debra A. Castillo was born in the United States in 1953. A literary and cultural critic, she is a professor at Cornell University in Ithaca, N.Y. Her main titles include *Talking Back: Toward a Latin American Feminist Literary Criticism* (1992) and *Easy Women: Sex and Gender in Modern Mexican Fiction* (1998). María Gudelia Rangel Gómez was born in Mexico in 1965. She is a health scientist at the Instituto Nacional de Salud Pública in Cuernavaca, Morelos, México. Her main titles include "Antecedentes de los servicios de salud e imágenes de las comunidades de los centros de la secretaría de Salud en Tijuana" (1999) and "Border Lives: Prostitute Women in Tijuana" (1999, with Debra Castillo and Bonnie Delgado). Armando Rosas Solís was born in México in 1950. He is an economist in Cuernavaca, Morelos, México.

Prostitution has been a defining characteristic of Tijuana's vast tourist industry since the growth boom at the beginning of the century, and serves as the basis for its infamous reputation—on the U.S. side of the border—as a sin city and giant brothel existing to serve the San Diego naval base, and on the Mexican side as a rest stop, point of departure, and haven for the Mexican field workers coming up from the south of the country. Nowadays, the presence of drug dealers and the fifteen thousand prostitutes[1] continue to feed this ugly stereotype, despite efforts by long-time residents to change the way people both in Mexico and in the United States think of the city and to encourage the image of the city as a modern metropolis that welcomes family-type tourism. These revisionary intentions, however, seem to be caught up in a tacit conflict with traditional expectations and with economic realities. Thus, for example, there is the curious phenomenon of Revolution Avenue and its attached "Zona Norte," the old center of the brothel-cum-nightclub industry, which currently by day functions as a family-oriented tourist area with restaurants and handicraft shops, and by night transforms back into its old identity as an area of discotheques/bars/brothels.

One reason the Zona Norte is so important for all sorts of commercial transactions is that it is not only the site of the city's official "red zone," it is also here that a large number of contacts are made between prospective border crossers and the *polleros* (the person who makes a living guiding illegal immigrants into the United States). These contacts usually occur in the area's restaurants, in the billiard rooms, and in the run-down hotels. The Zona Norte is a major way-station for those people who hope to immigrate illegally into the United States. These are poor people, transient people, who come to the area, stay in the hotels and boarding houses, and make use of all the wide panoply of services offered in the area: not only sexual services, but also second-hand clothing and hardware, food and pharmaceuticals. There is in the Zona Norte a wide range of shops not found in the nearby downtown area, making this an obligatory stop for both transients and the permanent population living in the area. This is a doubly captive audience for products; both the temporary and the permanent residents are equally users of the many and varied services, so that internal immigrants and local people, tourists and clients for sexual services all fall into the same vast network.

Zalduondo, Hernández Avila, and Uribe Zúñiga remind us that an understanding of the social context of paid sex requires the perspectives of clients, pimps and bar owners, rooming house owners, and police and other authorities as well as sex workers (1991, 173). To take into account this full perspective is beyond the scope of this essay, and is in fact the task of our book-length study currently in the final stages of revision for publication. Our more modest task in the pages that follow is to draw a narrower sketch, one that puts together complementary aspects of sex workers' narratives about their profession with what we have been able to glean about the narratives that their clients construct of their encounters.

In addition to published research and consultation with health and municipal officials, direct information from the women themselves came from a two-phase qualitative project. The first phase involved ethnographic work in 1988, including visits to different zones of Tijuana to compile a list, as complete as possible, of places where prostitution occurs and to learn the social characteristics and study the dynamics of each of these places. This phase of the project included interviews with 184 women working in prostitution in Tijuana. The principal goals of the interviews were to evaluate their knowledge of HIV/AIDS and to take blood samples to test for seropositivity. During this process (1) a complete census was made of all the places in which prostitution is practiced in Tijuana; (2) researchers surveyed the areas to observe the working dynamics in each site; (3) through participant observation, researchers studied the characteristics of women working both in establishments and on the street; (4) researchers classified the zones based on the social characteristics of the sites in which prostitution is practiced and of the women who work in them. The second phase took place in 1994–95 and consisted of in-depth interviews conducted in their workplaces with thirty Tijuanan prostitutes; these women were chosen by taking into account this complete census of places in which prostitution is practiced and the types of services offered. This information has been continuously updated by the researchers.

In general, scholarship on clients is even sparser than available information on women in prostitution, for if the women are frequently reluctant to speak to outsiders, the men who hire women for prostitution are even more elusive. Efforts to speak to clients in the Tijuana bars have been unproductive, even without taking into account the language barrier between potential interviewers and many of the clients, some of whom are Mexican, but many of whom are international sex tourists from the United States as well as other countries. The men tend to be incommunicative or incoherent in the bar setting, and it is difficult to imagine other settings in which interviews with this diverse and largely nomadic population might take place.

We have been able to obtain a partial understanding of a particular set of Tijuana sex workers' U.S. clients through reviewing postings on the internet, and especially though the relatively large body of reports available on two main text-based sites: the usenet site <alt.sex.prostitution .tijuana> and the Tijuana listings on the World Wide Web's extremely complete "World Sex Guide."[2] In addition to these two main sites, there are a growing number of other websites focusing on prostitution in Tijuana, ranging from an entire site dedicated to narrative fictions set in Tijuana, to an evolving set of websites that include scanned photographs of bars, hotels, and women, to several webpages written in hypertext markup language to allow readers to click on highlighted words (streets, bars, women's names) and link to images. Through these sites we have been able to glean reactions from several hundred clients, as well as to gain stronger and more individualized accounts from a couple of dozen more frequent commentators.

In cyberspace, clients of Tijuana prostitutes not only exchange information about women and places to find them, but also find themselves in occasionally rancorous, but usually cordial, dialogue. At the same time, internal evidence suggests that this dialogue occurs mostly in the net, where strangers can establish a pseudo-community of prostitutes' clients, while generally—though not always—ignoring each other in the Tijuana nightclubs themselves. Although some of the novice writers ask for assistance or a guide to the nightclubs, and <tecman@pacbell.net> offers his credentials as the guide for the very finest sex tours ("I sell these out very fast . . . Space is very limited"), O'Toole's conclusion represents the general consensus: "You're right to recommend seeking out a colleague. But I have found that many guys lack the collegial approach to a Zona Norte visit. In fact, they seem almost ashamed to be in the Zona and they're loathed to interact with others. That's why I started the FAQ."

For the prospective client, the undoubted premier guide to Tijuana's prostitutes is "Brockton O'Toole," who has not only authored the definitive FAQ on Tijuana, but who also frequently serves as the intermediary for other men who have comments, but do not want to risk posting in their own name or who do not want to deal with the hassle of anonymous posting. Brockton O'Toole is also one of the most frequent contributors to <alt.sex.prostitution.tijuana>, and his cool, detached style sets the tone for other clients as well, who are made the objects of his chastising, elder statesman response if they step out of line. This mock-ponderous tone is clearly a highly mannered, self-consciously literary style. In response to one usenet note, for example, he writes: "Take care my friend, Sir Brockton may get excited and spill his Earl Grey all over the keyboard!" Not all of the readers appreciate O'Toole's literary style. As one fellow reporter complains: "I don't know if it's just me or what, but I think you're getting to be a bit full of yourself. 'World Famous FAQ'? Jesus Christ man, you're a guy that's written a few pages on how to get to TJ and get laid. Are you expecting the Pulitzer prize soon? I remember when you first began to frequent ASP . . . Little did I know what a pretentious little dweeb you would become."

Studied mannerisms aside, O'Toole's Tijuana FAQ takes itself very seriously indeed. He recommends only two clubs, Adelita and Chicago, though he mentions in a late January 1997 usenet note "during my last several visits to the Miami Club, I was 'quite' impressed with the selection of girls. Accordingly, I am considering recommending it." Thus, O'Toole does not exactly recommend the club yet, nor does he modify his October 1996 FAQ to add the Miami; the usenet note hints that it is being posted as a trial balloon for comments before he takes the grave step of making a major change in his formal document, which is located not on the usenet, but on the World Wide Web's research tool, the "World Sex Guide." O'Toole divides his FAQ into seven sections: location and lodging, changing money, getting to Tijuana, the *zona roja*, Adelita, Chicago, and returning home. The document as a whole is a model of the concise, restrained travelogue; each subsection offers specific directions and useful hints. His hotel recommendations come with prices and phone numbers; his advice on changing money (he is against it) remind the client to carry small bills; his discussion of getting to Tijuana reviews Mexican automobile insurance code. He tells his readers where to park their cars on the U.S. side, reminds them to have exactly $5 cash to pay for the taxi, and how to tell the driver "you want to go to Adelitas (ah-day-LEE-tas)."

For each of the two clubs he recommends, he describes the place, the women, the kinds of services offered, and the price a client can expect to pay. O'Toole calls Adelita "pure South of the Border," and another anonymous researcher elaborates: "When the taxi dropped us off. . . we knew we weren't in Kansas anymore. This was the Mexico of the movies . . . steamy streets, food vendors everywhere, ladies more then [sic] everywhere." Still another writer describes it as "like walking into a brothel in some old Western." If the Adelita Club stands in for the internet-aware clients as the representation of authentic Mexicanness, that is, of a living culture read as if it were a movie set created to respond to U.S. consumer dreams of the picturesque, then the Chicago Club is the Adelita's absolute contrast. O'Toole calls Chicago "easily the finest hooker bar in Tijuana," but he warns that the women are in high demand and "the competition can be tough." Papa Dave tells readers that for his taste the Chicago Club is "cold and unfriendly" and other readers comment that the women are so uniformly beautiful that they can be intimidating. Jayhawk, for example, mentions that one woman, a stunning brunette beauty, "had a really nice dress on and reeked of class. I was actually a little scared off by this." Another writes of an attractive woman named Jessica, "I couldn't even get near her the last time I tried." Clearly, for the clubs that O'Toole recommends as the most desirable, the message he gets across in the FAQ is that clients will need the benefit of his advice in order to connect with the woman of their choice. Indeed, much of his discussion of the two nightclubs involves elaborate descriptions (other clients even include rudimentary maps in their reports) of where to stand, what to say, and who to tip in order to make contact.

Though we have not been able to identify any postings on the more commonly used sites as originating in Tijuana, several of them originate in Mexico, and one of the (now disappeared) websites was clearly sponsored by a Tijuana establishment known for catering to U.S. sex tourists. Likewise there are several self-identified Mexicans who participate frequently in the exchanges. Interestingly enough, while the women involved in sex work tend to be almost illiterate and certainly not computer users themselves, a number of clients comment that there is, at least at some levels in the sex worker community, an awareness of the possibilities of the internet and of the way the "World Sex Guide" and other internet exchanges have mediated the women's contacts with some of their clients. Several years ago (dinosaur times in computer years) there was already a growing awareness of the possibilities of the internet. "MR ESO" reports on a conversation he held with a woman he met in early February 1997: "I met a very cute girl at Adelitas at the end of the night that particularly intrigued me . . . Turns out she used to work at the Chicago Club. She also spoke perfect English and spent a lot of time living in the states. She was also familiar with the internet and recited the FAQ almost word for word." Another client recommends a woman named Veronica in the bar Nuevo Río Rosas and says, "I told her I'd be telling my friends about her so if you want to take her back to a room tell her you're a amigo de jeff and I'm sure she'll understand." Enigma tells of asking another woman if he could take her picture and post it on the internet; "she said she'd be OK with it," and shortly afterward, pictures of "Heidi" appeared on a popular website, along with images of a dozen other women. Heidi, apparently, kept track of the status of her postings through conversations with her clients. Another man, "The Seeker," describes a conversation with a fellow netizen at a border checkpoint: "He claims to have hooked up with Heidi, who he told me was great . . . He told me he talked to her for an hour B4 the main event, and she sat with him for a long while after they were done. He told me she was flattered that Americans would come to look for her by name from posting in this newsgroup." "Sr. T. Jota" adds a first-person account of a similar dialogue: "She shyly asked me if I had a computer. 'Yes.' 'Did you read my name on it?' 'Yes.' She seemed somewhat embarrassed and unbelieving that she was 'muy famosa.' Gentlemen have often come in asking for her."

A final example of such canny and mediated exchanges involves a popular young woman named "Rosie" from the Chicago Club. Clients frequently comment on her excellent English—"I've discussed everything from Gangsta' Rap to Beavis and Butthead with Rosie" says "señor Pendejo." "Oliver" writes about his encounter with the legendary "zona norte superstar," "the idea that this was 'the' Rosie made me even more excited. On the way to the hotel, I told her I'd heard about her. 'From the waiter?' she asked. 'No . . . uhh . . . have you heard of the internet?' She had, of course." After a description of his sexual relations with her, Oliver continues: "Rosie asked me if I'd write about her on the internet; I said of course, so here you have it. She wondered if any of her internet fans were asking questions about her hair." This brief and suggestive note opens up an entirely unexpected realm, in which the concrete exchanges between certain Tijuana prostitutes and their clients have been for several years already inflected by a metadiscourse occurring on the World Wide Web.

The contents of the usenet group listings change continually and the site is flooded by and plagued with enormous amounts of spam—out of 150 messages there may be only 2 or 3 relevant ones at any given time— hence users more and more frequently access the favored sites through search engines like Altavista, Metacrawler, and (for the usenet) Dejanews, thus screening out unwanted materials.[3] Furthermore, while the usenet contents are constantly changing, only a few of the relevant messages are long enough to contain sufficient material to allow for a sustained discussion. For example, one complete exchange consists of "Harold" querying: "Would love to do oral sex on a young girl from TJ. Please e-mail me with way to contact you." <hotjr@mail.earthlink.net> and David Start's response: "The best way to do that is to go there" <travagt@primenet.com>.

And go there they do: sometimes several times a week, often posting cryptic rankings of the "hottest" women each visit. The general perception of Tijuana from the clients' point of view is that Tijuana is both accessible and safe (both physically and sexually), and that standardization of fees for services prevents price gouging while still allowing the client an opportunity for a certain amount of negotiation. It is also clear that the "World Sex Guide" FAQs as well as the more experienced clients on the usenet are responding to an understood generalized perception about Mexico in general, and Tijuana in particular, that is quite different from the safe space they describe. Novice clients continually write in to the usenet asking not only about places and women, but more generally to inquire if Tijuana is really as dangerous as everyone says. Brockton O'Toole's "World Sex Guide" Tijuana FAQ sets the tone with its reassurances. "Don't be concerned about your safety," he writes, clearly imagining an audience whose first reaction would be precisely such a concern. "You won't have trouble if you behave yourself. The TJ cops do NOT care about prostitution, but they DO notice if you act like an asshole." Atta's shorter report confirms this perception: "Tijuana is generally a pretty safe place. Just make sure you don't look too rich. If you start a fight or drink alcohol on the street, la policia will be there and you can decide between la casa and a hefty tip." Still another client agrees: "If Tijuana was known as an unsafe place or a ripoff joint, no one would go there. They go an extra mile (at least by Mexican standards) to make it clean and safe." To a usenet message's worried posting, "I was wanting to go down to TJ but everyone I have talked to say it's not that safe at night," Cachondo responds: "I live in San Diego and have been to the TJ clubs literally hundreds of times over the last few years . . . Show respect and you'll be respected."

Still, muggings do occur, though the clients' reports suggest that they happen more frequently at the international border than in the Zona Norte, and for this reason clients writing to the internet sites advise their readers to take a cab to that area even though it is within walking distance. Cachondo's comments stand for the general perception among experienced clients:

> Behind most every story of someone being hassled by cops there is another story untold. For example—I know a guy that said he was through [sic] in jail and his car impounded by the police. Upon further questioning, I found out that he was completely drunk, tried to drive out of a parking lot without paying the $5 parking fee, tried to outrun the cops, tried to run out of the jail area where he was being questioned, etc. He spent one night in jail, paid a fine (I think less than $200) and got his car out of impound the next day.
>
> Take a cab to and from the clubs and you'll avoid walking through some bad areas where someone could mug you. I've made the walk myself many times, but usually not alone. The area around Adelitas and the Chicago Club looks scary, but it's not that bad, it's just poor. Use common sense, don't look down on the people, don't get completely shit-faced, and you'll be fine.

Like other experienced clients, Cachondo reminds his novice interlocutor that poverty in Mexico has different connotations than in the United States, where areas in which prostitution is openly practiced are often extremely dangerous as well as poor. In Tijuana, by contrast, the police, as well as the sex workers and all the others who profit from Tijuana's major tourist draw, are complicitous in their concern for maintaining good relations and encouraging repeat customers. In turn, the U.S. tourist has to act with a minimal amount of common sense and respect for another culture. In another long letter, he adds: "Just pretend you're in the States and that there are laws (as there are) and that you're not any better than the Mexican people (which you aren't) and you'll be just fine."

Interestingly, given a general perception of Mexico as the place to go for cheap everything, the general consensus of the clients is that Tijuana's commercial sex scene is attractive as a different kind of experience but not as an inexpensive one. While a few of the men talk about going with women who work on the streets, and who charge them as little as ten dollars for service, the overwhelming majority of them have stated preferences for women who work in a very narrow range of bars (Adelitas and Chicago are by far the two favorites). Papa Dave, who identifies himself as a thirty-year veteran of the Tijuana sex scene, bemoans the fact that "Tijuana is NOT cheap. A short-time, as I indicated, with a girl from the Chicago Club will cost you AT MINIMUM $80. You could get the same thing on the streets of most U.S. cities for $50," and he also comments that drinks in the bars are charged at U.S. prices. Other clients agree: in the United States, commercial sex is cheaper than in Tijuana or at least similarly priced. The question the clients frequently ask themselves and each other is, "Was it worth it?" Their answers range from a disappointed "not really" to an enthusiastic "yes," with the majority of the clients agreeing that all-in-all the experience is worth the extra outlay of cash if only because it offers something different—usually defined as a taste of real Mexico—in a setting that is clean and safe.

In this sense, the clients' perceptions of Tijuana's relative safety dovetails precisely with the image that the prostitutes hope to convey in their interviews; they provide safe sex in clean surroundings, where the men do not have to worry about assault. In one of the few messages from a client who was mugged, the man emphasizes exactly how unusual it was, not only because of the infrequency of such a happening, but also because of the bystanders' response. He describes an attack in the Zona Norte in which someone came up behind him, choked him, grabbed his wallet, and disappeared. What is particularly surprising about this report, and which offers an absolute contrast with similar stories from the United States, is that the man comments, "after the attack several people including a couple of prostitutes ran up to me to make sure I was OK. One of the prostitutes even offered to give me some spare change— which was very nice of her to try to help me!" Another client tells of spending a few minutes talking to one of the prostitutes after they finished. He says, "She was fairly open and she asked me how I was getting back to the border. When I said I was walking, she asked why not take a taxi. I replied that I had spent my last dollar on her. She then handed me a $5 for taxi fare." The client concludes, "My heart melted immediately." Stories like these are sufficiently common to establish the women's commitment to their clients' safety, a factor the women also emphasize in their commentaries on their relations with their clients as only making good business sense besides promoting a better working environment for them. Even more, such comments hint at a complexity to the prostitute-client relationship that is generally unaccounted for in the literature.

Occasionally, these stories develop into full-fledged narratives. "MR ESO," a frequent contributor to the usenet and one whose net persona was that of a detached "researcher" cum stud, suddenly reveals another side of his personality in a long and involved story about an ongoing relationship with a particular woman from Adelitas and his concern that he was both hurting her and complicating his own life impossibly by raising expectations he could not fulfill: "I wouldn't mind being a preferred customer but there seems to be no way back to that . . . It is not that I am afraid of a relationship, I just don't have the money, I have cancer, I am old, and I cannot promise anybody much . . . It was my last wish to fuck up the place I like to play. I have never really hurt anybody in there, I don't get drunk or rude . . . yet I have fucked it up just as much as any asshole." El Chamuco writes back that MR ESO should remember that the usenet is "to talk business, not relationship problems," but gives his interlocutor a several page primer:

> OK, first of all I am Mexican, so I do know what I'm doing. Second: WHAT THE FUCK IS YOUR PROBLEM MAN!!?? DON'T YOU KNOW ANYTHING?? YOU "DO NOT GET INVOLVED EMOTIONALLY WITH PROSTITUTES!!" . . . First item: Just because they are prostitutes does NOT mean they don't have feelings . . . Second item: Some girls are TOO nice, and if they like you PHYSICALLY they will think that body and mind are the same . . . Third item: Once a Mexican girl gets emotionally attached to you BEWARE. Things are very different in Mexico.

The various comments on and responses to MR ESO's dilemma run the range from suggestions that he get his therapy elsewhere, to reminders such as El Chamuco's about differing cultural expectations for relationships between U.S. men and Mexican women, to comments about the desperation of many of these women who are living in miserable economic circumstances and quite naturally hope to find a way out of prostitution. In their work on Thai sex tourism, O'Connell Davidson and Sánchez Taylor conclude that the power that sex tourists exercise is not "simply or even primarily patriarchal. Their power is also 'racialised' and its currency is economic. . . . Women's sexual labor often wholly or partly supports the households that furnish both national and international capital with a cheap, disposable workforce" (1996, 18–19). While British sex tourists in O'Connell Davidson and Sánchez Taylor's account willfully ignore these complicating factors, in stories such as MR ESO's, where both Tijuana prostitute and client are given a human face, the longer, thoughtful exchanges accompanying the narrative show client awareness of how these factors of race, culture, and local and international economics affect individual dilemmas. MR ESO, thus, has been playing out a fantasy, both as a narrator on the internet and as a client in Tijuana, but it is a fantasy that falls apart in the face of his own imbrication in an increasingly complex relationship with a Mexican woman, a relationship in which he became involved in a failed attempt to hold his ill health and encroaching death at bay.

Inevitably, however, most of the comments on both the World Wide Web and the usenet sites are concerned with the more superficial qualities of the women themselves: who are the "hottest," who are the most beautiful, where they can be found. As a number of the men note, the Tijuana sex scene is extremely fluid, echoing women's comments about stepping into, and dropping out of, the sex work environment based on personal or family economic need. "Do the girls when you can," advises one writer, "because you never know if you will ever see them again." From the clients' point of view the internet provides an ideal medium for the continuous updating that cannot occur in other formats, such as the book and the video that Atta recommends in his introduction to Mexico in the "World Sex Guide," or the other books on Tijuana hawked on the Web by "sexlatino" and "proball." A number of the men speak nostalgically about the "TJ Superstar, Rosie," who until a few months ago worked out of the Chicago Club and who reportedly combined a perfect body, a great face, superior taste in clothes, excellent English, and a terrific style in bed (as some of the clients suspect, Rosie's extreme popularity earned her a good deal of money by Mexican standards; what they don't take into account, however, and her friends in Tijuana know, is that it seriously compromised her health as well).

Mostly the clients trade anecdotes about "looks" versus "attitude"— U.S.-style beautiful women versus abilities in bed—and argue in favor of one or the other, with the more experienced clients firmly stating their preferences for the more experienced, if less immediately drop-dead gorgeous, women. They air differences of opinion about "newbies" or "diamonds in the rough" and discuss body type preferences, at times in terms that betray racism and stereotyping thinly masked by a presumed knowledge of Mexico and Mexican customs. For example, one client asks why there are so many "overweight unattractive women who are practically

GIVING it away" and another responds, "Mexican tastes are different. They're not giving it away, they just go with fat, ugly Mexican men." Here again, the usenet offers its own internal policing; to questions about availability of American women in Mexico one writer responds: "The fact that you are asking for American girls in MEXICO not only sounds stupid, but plain racist," and another contributor even reproduces material drawn from an author profile (easily obtainable through Dejanews) with the comment: "Have we noticed CuteGuy's other posts? . . . Another racist moron . . . Yet another correlation between racism and low I. Q."

Some writers have specific preferences about sex with women whom they know have children: "I do not like having sex with hookers that are mothers," says one, apparently not aware that almost all women working in prostitution in Tijuana have children to support; while another disagrees: "You'll meet the friendliest women during the day. These are the women that want to go home early to be with their children," and several others comment on particularly good experiences with women who are still lactating. One man, who is clearly aware that maternity is a precondition for most women working in prostitution, even shares his technique for getting particularly good service for those fellow clients whose Spanish extends to conversation beyond basic phrases: "After buying her one drink and complimenting her generously on her looks, her demeanor, and inner strength in raising her son as a single mother, we ended up in 'el cuarto.' It was nice, very nice."

These brief recommendations also have their accompanying typical narratives, usually of the sort that involves steamy sex with women who (a) come to orgasm, and/or (b) allow the client to remove his condom. Since "researchers" are urged to post "reports," there is a clear built-in interest in the homoerotic and voyeuristic possibilities of these tales quite beyond the satisfaction of the request for basic information about the best and hottest women of the moment. At the same time, tolerance for fantasy is finite. El Chamuco responds to one man's tale of hot sex with two women with the comment:

> You are the guy who posted the bullshit story about fucking a 14-year-old on your way to TJ, right? Well, this one isn't working either . . . I suggest you stop pretending to be so 'lucky.' You aren't impressing anyone. If you have a thing for writing fiction then just say it's fiction and END IT. Or go to alt.sex.stories and post all the fiction you want . . . Nobody is buying it . . . It's getting annoying.

Interestingly enough, it is not the explicit content that provokes irritation, but the underlying fantasy representation of the hot Mexican woman slavering over the white gringo. Alt.sex.prostitution.tijuana has developed a low tolerance for certain kinds of fantasy, and while clients frequently comment on the appeal of the exotic aspects of Mexico in racist terms, the corresponding fantasy about the attractiveness and superiority of white men as lovers is sure to be shot down, as is any suggestion that the women suddenly and inexplicably offer free service to desirable studs met in bars. While the men are quite willing to describe their techniques for manipulating the women and receiving either superior service or favored client status, and they do accept stories of ongoing relationships, they do not subscribe to fantasies in which the women forget the compulsion of those economic factors that have driven them into prostitution in the first place.

One of the most important findings of this admittedly unscientific sample of client responses is the degree to which their statements about sexual practices correlate with those of the women interviewed. While some of the men report occasional encounters with women willing to work in pairs ("lesbian" encounters are much discussed on the usenet) or to perform anal sex or other specialties for an extra fee, by and large the reports are remarkably consistent. Sex with women in Tijuana is a standard twenty-minute half-and-half session, involving oral followed by vaginal sex, often using two or more condoms. While Marta Lamas's study of street prostitution in Mexico City arrives at the conclusion that "ninguna chica se niega a hacerlo sin condón, pues eso representa perder al cliente" [no girl would refuse to do it without a condom, since that would mean losing the client] (1993, 123),[4] the Tijuanan women interviewed are far more united and adamant about condom use, to the degree that one of the more common topics of conversation among the women in interviews and focus groups involved an exchange of stories and suggestions of methods to convince reluctant clients or, as a last resort, techniques for applying the condom without the client's knowledge. We do not attempt to resolve the question of whether the women are lying or not (though the client reports also firmly indicate that condom use is universal with the women they frequent), but would like to point out in evaluating these responses merely that these women's awareness of the importance of condom use indicates a consciousness of the issues involved in safe sex practices and serves implicitly to define two important ideological spaces: (1) of the woman interviewed as wholesome and intelligent, (2) of the space of prostitution as an infection-free site where knowledge is put into practice, in contrast to the less professional, less careful practices of the general population.

As one of the women notes, it is important to have an unbreakable agreement among the women that they will only accept clients with con-doms since, as she says, 99 percent of the men try to get out of using one: "Vamos a suponer que yo aceptara irme con un cliente sin condón, al ra-tito ya le gustó otra y también sin condón. Y es donde va el contagie" [Let's suppose that I agreed to go with a client without a condom, and then after a while he likes another woman and also without a condom. And that is where contagions start]. One of the more common argu-ments is to state that the sex worker knows she is disease-free because of her regular check-ups, but that the client can give no such assurances. As one woman comments, she tells her clients, "¿A ver tú traes una tarjeta o un permiso de que acabas de hacer un análisis como yo traigo la mía? No, pues que no" [So, do you have a card or a permission that you've just done an analysis like the one I have here? If not, then no]. This argument has the benefit of reinforcing the message that the professional sex worker offers advantages to a man careful of his health and that the red zone is a safer environment for non-monogamous men than the larger commu-nity. The alternative argument is also common: that the client may be-lieve he is disease-free, but since he cannot have the same confidence about his partner, condom use is in his best interests.

O'Toole's FAQ is adamant: "Condoms are an absolute must for both oral sex and anything else," and his admonition is repeated in report after report. Even Cachondo, who describes Tijuana as "a sexual play-ground where almost everything goes" admits that the line is drawn pre-cisely at condom use. In his infamous usenet description of his hot ses-sion with two women, he notes: "The one thing I hadn't considered was the condom situation. They changed my condom every time I switched from fucking one to the other, so I ended up with 6 condoms on the floor at the end. They were very good at changing them quickly, so it wasn't even a bother." When one man complains about a woman as having "way too many rules" by insisting that the man wash his hands and put on a condom before sex, the response on the net was completely unsympa-thetic, ranging from O'Toole's mannered there's "no excuse for not washing your hands before you get down to business. As for the rest of your body, I know this is a class group and I'm going to assume you bathed completely before heading out on the town . . . I expect no less from the cultured gentlemen who assemble here" to another client's straightforward: "So get up and wash your fucking hands, you lazy sack of shit."

Both women and men recognize that the problem with condoms is not their use—the educated client will use them, the uneducated client can generally have a condom put on him without him even realizing it—

but their tendency to break. One of the women interviewed says that about one in four condoms breaks during use, causing her to worry continually about possible infection, and a frequent client seems to agree with this high failure rate, as well as offer a reason. He advises newbies to the Tijuana prostitution scene that "you should buy your condoms yourself—and preferably in the U.S. . . . Simple reason: condoms have due dates, and some of the stuff they sell in Mexico is way past overdue . . . Remember if the condom is overdue the risk of breaking it is VERY HIGH, so make sure you check the due date."

One of the curious results of this generalized condom use is that the removal of the condom at some point in the session has acquired a highly erotic significance. A particularly "hot" session that provides the occasion for much male bragging is one in which the woman allows a particularly favored man or regular client to remove his condom before ejaculation on some location on her body. The women are understandably more reluctant to talk about such activities, but when pressed, will agree that sometimes, with a very clean, well-known, favored client or with their non-client boyfriend, they will sometimes remove the condom for non-vaginal sex. Thus, removal of the condom becomes a particularly coded action, one that takes places only at the woman's discretion and that culminates an unusually successful sex act, or that offers the titillating spectacle of a powerfully transgressive one. "How times change," laments veteran Tijuana client Papa Dave, "in the 60s in TJ it was not uncommon for a girl to REFUSE to have sex if you insisted upon wearing a condom . . . I find myself thinking back to the great places like the Brooklyn Bar, where things were jumping 24 hours a day and the place was always full of gringos. I remember how hard it was (we used to make drunken bets on it) to come up with something the girl would say 'no' to . . . ." Papa Dave's nostalgia tells us exactly how far distant those halcyon days are, but also suggests how the universality of condom use has created opportunities for a whole new set of erotic fantasies.

Another correlation between the clients' reports and the prostitutes' perceptions is that a number of the men are looking for conversation as much as they are anticipating the sex act itself. Both the women and their clients frequently comment on the awkwardness of the highly international nature of Tijuana prostitution, in which most of the women speak only Spanish, and a large number of the clients speak, for example, only English or Japanese, two of the more common languages among non-Mexican or Mexican-American clients. Many of the women in this very international sex market indicate that they prefer Mexican clients, since the common cultural grounding gives them a certain comfort zone both in knowing what to expect of the sex act and in establishing a relation beyond sex that involves some conversation. As one woman says, "americanos poco, porque estoy estudiando inglés entre otras cosas, no lo domino bien. Además me dan un poquito de desconfianza porque hay señores muy tranquilos y como no son mexicanos no conoce uno muy bien la reacción. Es otra cultura pues. Otra todo" [Few Americans, because while I am studying English among other things, I don't speak it well. Besides, they make me a little uncomfortable because there are very calm men, but because they are not Mexicans, you don't know how they will react. It's another culture. Another everything]. For many of the women, talking to clients not only alleviates their natural anxieties about exposing themselves to unknown men, but also helps reduce the tedium and disgust of their jobs: "Yo platico, cuento, o sea me doy amistad primero y luego. Para que no me tomen como lo que, ta, rápido y lo que viene . . . Y ya pues se va formando la cosa más bonita para que no sea tan, vaya, tan fastidioso" [I talk, tell stories, that is, I give friendship first and then. So that they don't just grab me like, quick and then do it . . . And that way, well, something nicer develops so that it is not, so, so boring]. Another comments that even if she does not know the language, conversation helps ease the awkwardness of the sexual encounter as well as earning her better fees. Describing herself as "international," she says, "Siempre los recibo con una sonrisa en los labios, les doy su lugar para que ellos también me den mi lugar así y yo puedo sacarle más. Yo no sé hablar inglés pero con todo . . . ni sé lo que platico. Ni sé si me entiende o no me entiende" [I always receive them with a smile on my lips and I treat them respectfully so that they will also treat me respectfully and I can get more money out of them. I don't know how to speak English but whatever . . . I don't even know what I talk about. Nor do I know if they understand me or don't understand me]. One woman says, shortly, succinctly, "necesito el trato" [I need the exchange].

Several of the women indicate that this dialogue is equally important to the men, in some cases overriding their ostensible purpose for seeking out a sex worker. Whether foreign or national, the men often come to a prostitute because they need moral support, one woman says, or are looking for a spiritual companionship. Ninety percent of the clients, says one woman, are men with very little education; thus, she helps them to think and to analyze by asking them questions and demonstrating an interest in their lives. Another woman adds that typically the client is lonely, and needs to connect with another person and unburden himself: "Muchas veces ya a la hora de hacer la relación ya no es tan importante para mí el sexo o sea porque yo les introduzco una cierta terapia mental del cual muchas mujeres ni en su casa . . . El cliente mentalmente cambia lo que es el sexo por una convivencia" [Often when the time comes to have the relation sex is not so important for me because I offer them a certain mental therapy that many women don't even in their homes . . . The client mentally changes from what is sex to conviviality]. Yet another woman prides herself on her excellent memory, so that she can refer back to previous conversations and ask her clients if they have been able to solve a particular problem. This technique, she proudly comments, has earned her a solid living and frequent offers of matrimony. For a fourth woman, conversation with clients has become her specialty, to the degree that many of them seek her out primarily for her sympathetic ear. In these cases, she suggests that she and her client go to a more congenial setting—a restaurant or cafe—and talk for a while, with sex as an open option, paying her a modest rate for her time.

Thus, if for women specializing in Spanish-speaking clients or, alternatively, speaking at least some English (or, in one case, reported by a client, good Vietnamese) is a tremendous anxiety reliever as well as a guarantee of higher fees; from the men's point of view, ability to converse with the women makes the sessions both more interesting and more intensely erotic. Frequently, internet reporters lament their lack of fluent Spanish as an icebreaker. Several of the men comment on a particularly successful session as one in which they involve the women in conversation both before and after the "main event," and in which the woman shows "tenderness" rather than "matter-of-factness." A first-time Tijuana visitor complains, "I have been with a few professional women in my time and I always have big hopes that they are going to do something incredible but they seem to fall short. Maybe I expect too much from them." This comment precipitates a number of responses from other readers on the usenet. One suggests that he gets better results by allowing anticipation to play a role; another comments, "I try to blend romance, conversation, shows, and fucking" because in that way—especially on less busy weekdays—he is more likely to get an extended session "rather than the usual business fucks." A third client reminds the whining newbie that most of the women working in prostitution are really very nice ladies, but they have no particular brief for clients who don't cultivate them:

> What would you do for a measly fifty bucks? If you can answer that, then you kinda know how they feel screwing one hopeful guy after another . . . A lot of it is up to you . . . if they like you . . . and stay away from the hardcore business. You actually have to spend some time to

cultivate these good times you desire . . . Bottom line . . . you are the "trick," the sooner they pop you, the sooner they can get on to the next "trick."

Julia O'Connell and Jacqueline Sánchez Taylor's work on sex tourism in Thailand and elsewhere suggest that "one of the more curious findings of research on prostitution (at least for those who are surprised by the extent of human hypocrisy and capacity for self-deceit) is that many sex clients in European countries bemoan the impersonal approach of prostitutes" (1996, 7). While this kind of self-deceit also shows up on the Tijuana nets, it is immediately associated with immaturity and inexperience; more frequently the client shows that he is very well aware of the interlapping boundaries within the prostitutes' own world, in which the personal only rarely comes into contact with the commercial aspects, and where only certain favored clients are allowed the privilege of tenderness and of the kind of confidence in her partner that allows the woman to enjoy the encounter.

One of the things that becomes very clear in both the prostitutes' narratives about themselves as well as in the clients' representations of them is that while most exchanges involve straightforward sexual service in a heavily racialized and exoticized environment, the stereotypes seldom hold entirely. These women, who are so often portrayed in mainstream studies as nothing more than sexual objects, in the context of their professional activities frequently have the opportunity and flexibility to resist such conversion into objects, at least at some level, turning the tables on their clients and assuming a position of relative power. Their provocative looks and arousing dancing (not to mention the fact that the most highly solicited of these women may earn considerably more money than even the more affluent of their customers) may strategically turn the tables on the men, turning the potential clients into their supplicants.

Still further; at least one insightful study points out the degree to which both the prostitute and her client engage in a kind of transa, or con game, in which roles are consciously manipulated. Holzman and Pines note that "the position accorded customers in the occupational ideology of prostitutes is not one of respect. Johns are considered 'marks' in what is perceived by prostitutes to be a sexually based con game. . . . Prostitutes are taught different pitches or stories to tell the mark so as to extract more money from him" (1982, 92). In this respect, the women see the client as an exploitable object. In Holzman and Pines's study of U.S. clients, however, they learn that while the client is often amused by such tactics, he is seldom taken in by them. These researchers find that whether the client is an infrequent user of prostitutes or a very experienced one, he understands the delicate rules of the game in which they are engaged; he will listen to the stories and "routinely modifies his behavior to help create or maintain a good rapport" (95). In the back and forth negotiation of this *transa*, both the woman and the man shift continually between subject and object positions, sometimes occupying both at the same time, but from different perspectives. In the simulacrum of a social relationship, both remain on guard, and both imagine that they are fooling the other. If the woman tells a particular story to try to elicit more money, the client seems perfectly aware of the fictionality of the narrative, though he may give her the money anyway, just to ensure a more agreeable encounter.

And yet, at some point, the studied fictionality can turn into a real conversation with a woman who "seems like a nice person," and where there is a sexual relationship involving mutual enjoyment and even a simulated or real tenderness between client and sex worker. In the midst of the usenet reports ranking women by numbers, there are also comments like this one: "I've always wanted to really get into the head of some of these women and figure out what they're really feeling, but my Spanish isn't perfect and my communication with them is strained. The life of a prostitute has got to be a strange life to say the least. Couple that with cultural differences and who knows what they're really feeling." El Chamuco talks about how some of the most daring strippers and the hottest prostitutes have deep concerns about how their work might affect their private and family lives. Someone else writes about a Catholic woman and mother of seven working in prostitution who was always very upset about the mortal sin she was committing, and the terrible conundrum of having no education and not being able to feed her large family in any other way. Cachondo—a frequent contributor who writes numerous explicit reports to the usenet and the "World Sex Guide," including his comments on fulfilling his fantasy of being with two women—also writes meditative reports, such as this one in which he discusses his ongoing relationship with a former regular of his who quit prostitution for a time, and who was now back in Tijuana working on an occasional basis: "She told me she had breast cancer. She's getting chemotherapy now in Mexico DF. Really quite sad. She has to come to TJ once every month or two to make some money to support herself, two kids, and her mother. She's worried that her hair will fall out and she won't be able to work any more." In comments such as these, we can see how easily an artificially defined encounter, in an ugly setting, can somehow slip into some other kind of human relationship—transient, but nonetheless real.

Thus, the interviews and the client reports both describe a world that combines horror and personal agency, in which from the women's point of view the fundamental paradox is defined by a position in which they are experiencing at the same time blatant exploitation as sexual objects and a kind of personal freedom to choose the best remuneration for their labor. From the clients' point of view, the women are both living dolls that they use for sex, and queens for whose attention they compete. And, too, both the men and women are frail and complex human beings: the women are mothers and caretakers who sometimes find sexual satisfaction with the clients; the clients at times establish more complex, human contact with the prostitutes. There is also a paradox imposed by the very nature of the commercial exchange. Holzman and Pines describe the median income of the U.S. client as $30,000 a year, with a range from $8,000–$75,000 (1982, 101). In this context, Cachondo's realization of the kind of money that can be potentially earned in prostitution by women in Tijuana comes as a real shock: "I spoke with a woman working in Adelitas that I've been with several times now so we're a bit more open with each other. I asked her how much she makes working there. She said a good week's $2,500. Sometimes only $1,500 though. She works six-day weeks. Figure an average of $2,000 per week. That's $100,000 per year if she takes no more than two weeks vacation." Furthermore, Cachondo reminds us, this putative income is tax free.

Just as there is no single image of the woman who works in prostitution, so too there is no single characterization of the client. A number of the more self-reflective threads on the usenet describe the men's feelings about their own roles in these transactions, quite apart from bragging about particularly "hot" sessions or recommendations for specific women. One series of comments is sparked by the question, "How many of you guys would marry a prostitute?"; another by the comment of a client that he frequently feels depressed when he reflects on his "expensive hobby" and wonders, "Does anyone else experience feelings like this? And how do you deal with them?"; still another by a writer who broadcasts to the net his challenge: "I am astounded by these guys who go to TJ to get lucky—and pay for it. What a bunch of losers . . . Get a life— and a good therapist." The responses to these questions and comments remind us that many of these men have given considerable thought to their activities. The answers to these questions are: (1) yes, a fair number of the clients marry or are tempted to marry prostitutes: "Turns out that these women have MUCHO opportunities to settle down with their customers. In fact, they get tired of men falling in love with them . . . though I don't know what kind of husband material most johns would be. Not at all what I expected the situation would be" (a response confirmed by the women who talk about their many offers of marriage, and about the women they know who have—successfully or not—taken up clients on these offers); (2) yes, the feeling of depression is common since the men are often aware that they are trading a sex life for a love life and that this activity is not in the long run healthy either physically or emotionally, even though it fulfills a specific immediate yearning to touch and be touched—responses that echo the women's sense that men want to talk as much as they want to have sex; and (3) the writer who calls them "losers" is uninformed: "You know nothing of what you're talking about and are basing your opinion on 'feelings' rather than facts. In short, you're stupid and you're stereotyping." In each of these answers, the writer's comments complicate the stereotypical picture of the prostitute-client transaction. The client's feelings of inadequacy and depression, the questioning of his own fitness as husband material, his defensiveness about oversimplifying his motivations all point to specific locations at which subcultural values resist and recognize dominant culture morality. These paradoxes remind us that as investigators coming to the world of sex work from the outside, we are too often apt to reduce its complexities to a single, and much flattened, vision. One of the women brought us up short with the poignant reminder: "Mi vida es mía. Yo vivo una vida normal, como Ud., como cualquier otro ser humano" [My life is my own. I live a normal life, like you, like any other human being].

James Clifford describes the predicament of postcolonial ethnography as an unnerving process of negotiating across resistances while at the same time dealing with the moral tensions, inherent violence, and tactical dissimulations of modern fieldwork. His comments seem apposite to the way we undertake a study of Tijuana prostitutes and their clients as well:

> Some "authentic encounter," in Geertz's phrase, seems a prerequisite for intensive research; but initiatory claims to speak as a knowledgeable insider revealing essential cultural truths are no longer credible. Fieldwork . . . must be seen as a historically contingent, unruly dialogic encounter involving to some degree both conflict and collaboration in the production of texts. Ethnographers seem to be condemned to strive for true encounter while simultaneously recognizing the political, ethical, and personal cross-purposes that undermine any transmission of intercultural knowledge. (Clifford 1988, 90)

Here too, in commenting upon the prostitutes' stories—created in dialogue with an interviewer who is not a sex worker, and upon the clients' stories—created in dialogue with each other, we find ourselves striving for some version of "true encounter" in the realization that the stories we hear, or eavesdrop upon, are narratives shaped for a particular audience and with a particular political, ethical, and personal stake. Wendy Chapkis suggests, "We need new tools that allow us to listen to the different stories told without simply asking 'is this True.' We need tools that help us listen for meaning rather than fact—to ask what it means that a story is told in this way . . ." (1997, 2). The question is still open.

Notes

1. There is no particular consistency to our use of terms for the women engaged in paid sex work in Tijuana. Some of the women accept the term "sex worker," others find it a silly academic affectation. Some prefer the straightforward term "prostitute," many find it harsh and suggest the circumlocution "work in the (night) scene."

2. We have consulted numerous other sites as well, but find in general that they are far less complete. Most of the material tends to be cross-posted in one of the main sites, though it is most efficiently gleaned through use of World Wide Web search engines like Dejanews.

3. The pervasiveness of search engine use can be attested by this sample note from O'Toole, making reference to an earlier query: "On Fri, 15 Nov 1996 . . . *proball@electriciti.com* made what appeared to be a typical newbie clueless 'wanna' post . . . Obviously someone who can't use Dejanews or Altavista. So I ignored him."

4. Lamas's conclusion is also consistent with other local studies, though not with the statements made by the women interviewed in depth for the Tijuana study. For example, the CONASIDA report on sex workers in the area of Tuxtla Gutiérrez in the south of Mexico indicates that women in that area "do not include negotiations about condom use as part of their daily practice, and their experience is slight. They reiterate a rejection of condom use in almost all types of clients, except 'rich boys'" (1995b, 13). Similarly, clients interviewed in Ciudad Hidalgo, also in the south of Mexico, tell interviewers that in that city the reported condom use by sex workers is much higher than actual condom use by clients (1995a, 19).

JUAN FLORES

The Latino Imaginary:
Meanings of Community and Identity

Juan Flores was born in Puerto Rico in 1943. A literary and cultural critic, he is a professor at Hunter College, CUNY in New York City. His main titles include *Divided Borders: Essays on Puerto Rican Identity* (1993), and *From Bomba to Hip-Hop: Puerto Rican Culture and Latino Identity* (2000).

Is that Hispanic or Latino? What's in a name? A bewildered public puzzles over alternative signifiers, and even over who is being so designated, and how. "What do we call them? What do they want to be called? What do they call themselves?" Or, as the title of a thoughtful article on just this problem of megalabels has it, "What's the Problem with 'Hispanic'? Just Ask a 'Latino'" (D. González 1992, 6).

The broadest identifying term, of course, long used as shorthand even by many Latinos themselves, has been "Spanish," as in Spanish restaurant or Spanish television, where the idea of a unifying language culture conspires with the suggestion of Iberian origins and characteristics. The ideological undertones of that label, which are of course retained in slight variation in both "Hispanic" and "Latino," go unquestioned, as does the reality that many of those so designated do not even speak Spanish as a first language, or at all. The need for elastic and flexible usages stretches the field of reference so far that Spaniards, and even Italians and French, sometimes find their place under that hopelessly porous umbrella. The signifying net is cast so wide that what would seem the defining experiences, migration and resettlement, become of secondary importance, and all of Latin America is swept conveniently into the "Hispanic" bin. Or, to complicate the picture beyond recognition, there is even the suggestion that "Latinos" be used "to refer to those citizens from the Spanish-speaking world living in the United States" and "Hispanics" to "those living elsewhere" (Stavans 1995, 27).[1]

With all the slippages and evident arbitrariness, though, what would seem a terminological free-for-all actually does mark off limits and contexts, and pressing issues of power. "Where I come from, in New Mexico, nobody uses Latino, most people never even heard the term. We're Mexicanos, Chicanos, Mexican-Americans, Raza, Hispanic, but never Latino. Anyone who comes around talking about Latino this or Latino that is obviously an outsider." Or, from a contrary perspective, it is "Hispanic" that raises the red flag: "Hispanic? For me, a Hispanic is basically a sell-out, un *vendido*. Anyone who calls himself Hispanic, or refers to our community as Hispanic, just wants to be an American and forget about our roots."

Bits of conversation like these point up the range of contention over the choice of words to name a people, a culture, a community.[2] Behind the war of words, of course, there lurks the real battle, which has to do with attitudes, interpretations, and positions. In the dismissive indifference of many Americans there is often that undertone of annoyance which, when probed a little further, only turns out to be a cover for other, submerged emotions like ignorance, fear, and of course disdain. The gaps among Latinos or Hispanics themselves can be as polarized as they appear here, with one usage thoroughly discrediting the other. But usually the options are more flexible, operational, and mediated by a whole span of qualifying terms, tones, and situations. And over against those who use the words at all, there are many Mexican Americans, Puerto Ricans, Colombians, Cubans, or Dominicans who have no use for any such catchall phrases and would rather stick to distinct national designations.[3]

Yet this disparity over nomenclature, sharp as it is in the case of Latinos, should not be mistaken for a total lack of consensus or collective identity, nor as proof that any identification of the group or "community" is no more than a label imposed from outside, and above. Regardless of what anyone chooses to name it, the Latino or Hispanic community exists because for much of the history of the hemisphere, and multiplying exponentially the closer we approach the present, people have moved from Latin America to the United States, while portions of Latin America have been incorporated into what has become the United States. Along with their increase in numbers there has also been a deepening of their impact, real and potential, on the doings, and the destiny, of this country.

It is becoming clear that any discussion of an "American community" must be inclusive of Latinos and cognizant of the existence of a "Latino community" intrinsic to historical discourses about U.S. culture. The real challenge, though, is that the Latino presence makes it necessary to recognize that the very meaning of the word, the concept of community itself, is relative according to the perspective or position of the group in question: there is both a "Latino community" and a "community" in the Latino sense of the word.

Comunidad: the Spanish word, even more clearly than the English, calls to mind two of the key terms—común and unidad—in the conceptualization of this notoriously elusive idea. What do we have in "common," and what "unites" us, what are our commonalities and what makes for our unity? It is important to note that though the two terms point in the same semantic direction they are not synonymous, and their apparent coupling in the same word, comunidad, is not a redundancy. For while común refers to sharing—that is, those aspects in the cultures of the various constitutive groups that overlap—the sense of unidad is that which bonds the groups above and beyond the diverse particular commonalities. The point of this admittedly rather willful deconstruction is, once again, that the Latino "experience," the group's demonstrable reality and existence, includes but is not coterminous with its self-consciousness: común stands for the community in itself, while unidad refers to the community for itself, the way that it thinks, conceives of, imagines itself.

The "Latino community" is an "imagined community"—to summon Benedict Anderson's well-worn though useful phrase—a compelling present-day example of a social group being etched and composed out of a larger, impinging geopolitical landscaper (Anderson 1983).[4] The role of the social imagination and the imaginary in the self-conception of nationally, ethnically, and "racially" kindred groups is of course central, but must always be assessed with a view toward how they are being imagined (i.e., from "within" or "without") and to what ends and outcomes. Distinguishing between interior and exterior perspectives is thus a necessary step, and given that in the case of Latinos the outside representation is the dominant one, any instance of cultural expression by Latinos themselves may serve as a healthy corrective to the ceaseless barrage of stereotypes that go to define what is "Latino" in the public mind.

But the marking off of "us" and "them," though the foundational exercise in "imagining" communities, has its own limits, as it becomes evident that there is from both angles as much blurring involved as clear and meaningful bounding. Vexing questions like who's Latino and who isn't, and what kind of Latina(o)(s) we are talking about, quickly press in on any too facile dichotomy. Beyond the issue of names and labels, and even who is using them, there are differing levels or modes of meaning simultaneously at work in the very act of apprehending and conceptualizing the "community" and "identity" in question. "Latino" or "Hispanic" not only mean different things to different people; they also "mean" in different ways and refer to different dimensions of collective social experience.

I would suggest that by distinguishing between a *demographic*, an analytic, and an *imaginary* approach to Latino unity and diversity it is possible effectively to complicate and deepen our understanding of cultural expression, identity, and politics without becoming paralyzed by the sheer complexity and contradictoriness of it all. Whether Latinos or Hispanics are thought of as an enumerated aggregate of people, an analytically differentiated set of constituent groups, or a historically imagined cultural "community" or "ethnoscape" is at the core of ongoing debates and confusions.[5] Not that these diverse conceptualizations are mutually exclusive, nor are they to be considered in any mechanically sequential or hierarchical way. On the contrary, as I seek to describe them it will be obvious that all three are necessary, and that they are complementary. That is, they are really different methodological and epistemological emphases rather than discrete forms of explanation. But scrutinizing them in hypothetical discreteness not only helps understand their interrelation but may also enhance our analysis and appreciation of the voices and images of Latino art.[6]

The demographic conception of Latinos, or of a "Latino community," refers to an aggregate of people whose existence is established on the basis of numerical presence: count them, therefore they are. Here Latinos—or more commonly at this level, Hispanics—comprise not so much a community as a "population," a quantified slice of the social whole. As limited as such a means of identification may seem, it is nevertheless the dominant one, serving as it does both government bureaucracies and corporate researchers in setting public taste and policy. This definition of the Hispanic community by official measurement is thus inherently instrumental, since the immediate goal is really to identify, not so much social groups or lines of cultural unity and diversity, but voting blocs and consumer markets. From this angle, Latinos appear as a homogeneous, passive mass, a "target" public, without any concern for internal differentiation or possible social agency itself geared toward those same pragmatic goals of electoral or commercial utility.[7]

But it is not only campaign managers and admen for whom Latinos are, first of all, numbers. The labels and tallies they arrive at for their convenience—be it Hispanic or Latino, at whatever percentile—are made visible, credible, "real" by means of a whole sensorium of images, sounds, and flavors. The demographic label thus aims not only to buy the Hispanic package but to sell it; it targets not only potential customers but merchandise, or even movers of merchandise. Whatever the particular purpose, though, the means and result are usually the same—stereotyped images offering up distorted, usually offensive, and in any case, superficial portrayals of Latino people.[8] And these are the only images of Latinos that many people in the United States, and around the world, are ever exposed to, which makes it difficult for the public to gauge their accuracy. It is important to recognize these images as products not just of opportunist politicians or greedy marketeers but also of the demographic mentality itself. Numbers call forth labels, which in turn engender generic, homogenized representations—stereotypes. According to the same logic, holding economic and political power relies on the work of both the census-taker and the cameraman.

The most loudly proclaimed finding of this aggregative endeavor, by now a demographic truism of our times, is that Hispanics are the nation's "fastest-growing minority," on course to become the "largest" minority at some (variously defined) point early in the twenty-first century. Whether greeted by alarmist jitters or triumphalist joy, this momentous news item rests on an abiding confidence in the validity of the count, and an unquestioned consensus that like social units are being summed and demarcated from unlike, incompatible ones. The often unspoken allusion, of course, is to African Americans, who are thus cast as the main rival in the numbers race and the main instance, among "minorities," of the non-Hispanic other. Asian Americans, too, are in the running, with all lines of historical interaction and congruency again erased from the calculation. In both cases, it is clear how tools of advertent inclusion and conjunction may at the same time serve as wedges between and among groups whose social placement and experience in the United States could just as well, given a different political agenda, point to commonalities as to differences. The tactics of divide and conquer are still prominent in the arsenal of power, and nowhere more so in the contemporary equation than in the talk of Hispanics as undifferentiated numeraries.

The process of adding up is accompanied by the need to break down, to identify not the sum total but the constituent parts. The analytical approach—the business, above all, of positivist social science—is bent on deaggregation; it presumes to move closer to Latino "reality" by recognizing and tabulating the evident diversity of Latino groups and experiences. Such varying factors as country of origin, time in the United States (generation), region or place of settlement, occupation and socioeconomic status, educational background, and the like move into focus as the only meaningful units or vantages of analysis, with any cohesion among Latinos referred to only in the plural: typically, there are only Latino "populations," groups, or at best "communities."

This analytical account of Latino multiplicity is indeed often helpful in counteracting stereotypes and monolithic categories, and the elaborate discussion of "modes of incorporation" certainly allows for a sense of the dynamic relation among a too hastily posited aggregate of structurally differentiated social experiences (Portes and Bach 1985; Portes and Rumbaut 1996). But resting, as it overwhelmingly does on socially constructed statistical evidence and an objectification of collective historical actors, it is still close kin to the demographic approach. Even the census evidences an increasing official need to break the composite down, with "Hispanics" now grouped into Mexican, Puerto Rican, Cuban-origin, Central and South American origin, and "other Hispanic," subcategories which then serve as the basis for much quantitative research. Commercially geared demographics are also far along in their analytical enterprise, having persuasively charted both a "pan-Hispanic" as well as regionally differentiated Los Angeles, Miami, and New York centered markets, along with countless other target-specific variables.

To this extent, and in many social scientific studies, the pluralizing "analysis" of Latino reality is still dealing with a community "in itself," constructed in terms of relatively inert categories with their appropriate labels and generic representations. The focus on "labor market experience" as the "key factor in the structuring of [Hispanic] ethnicity," for example, while an invaluable starting point for differentiating social positions among the groups and subgroups in question, leaves unaddressed what would seem the crucial issue of "the complexities of the interaction between social and ethnic identities," that is, the "interdependency between socioeconomic placement and cultural (self-)identification" (Nelson and Tienda 1997, 26).

Ultimately, the limitation of analytical methodologies of this kind is not the act of differentiation itself, but a failure to differentiate among differences, and among kinds and levels of difference. For example, the vast research on Latinos as part of immigration studies, perhaps the most prevalent paradigm for treating Latino social experience, tends to stumble in the face of the glaring fact that the majority of Latinos, comprising the largest national groups within the composite, are not even "immigrants" in any quantifiable or recognized sense: because of their citizenship status, Puerto Ricans are not counted among the nation's immigrant populations, and a large share of the Mexican Americans are here not because they crossed the border, but because "the border crossed them." Characteristically, this most severe and telling divide among the Latino pan-ethnicity, the difference between immigrant and "resident minority" Latinos having much to do with issues of colonial status and class, tends to elude even the most thorough and cautious scrutiny of Latino realities, which as a result arrive at misleading conclusions. Even historically informed and critically "balanced" accounts of Latino immigration and communities, such as those of Roberto Suro and Rubén G. Rumbaut among others, lose interpretive cogency because of this overly "objectivist" method and inattention to such structurally larger but less readily quantifiable dimensions of contrastive analysis, and lead to continual equivocation and inconsistency—like that of Rumbaut—as to the validity of any unifying concept at all, or, in the case of Suro's *Strangers Among Us*, to an inadequately critical relation to "culture of poverty" and "underclass" theory in speaking of "Puerto Rican-like poverty," a central message of his book being that "the entire nation will suffer if the Puerto Rican fate is repeated" by "today's Latino newcomers" (1998, 146–47).[9]

Yet Latinos are also social agents and not just passive objects in this analyzing process, nor do they tend to sidestep the task of "telling Hispanics apart." Consciously and intuitively, personally and collectively, Puerto Ricans, Mexicans, Cubans, Dominicans, and each of the other groups most often project their own respective national backgrounds as a first and primary axis of identity and on that basis, fully mindful of differences and distances, negotiate their relation to some more embracing "Latino" or "Hispanic" composite. Here the force of analysis, rather than an extension of demographic aggregation and labeling, stands in direct opposition to it, an instinctive reaction against instrumental measuring and its pernicious consequences. Of course, there are interests involved here too, but in this case they are the interests of the "object" of analysis itself, the Latino peoples and communities.

From a Latino perspective understood in this way, analysis is guided above all by lived experience and historical memory, factors that tend to be relegated by prevailing sociological approaches as either inaccessible or inconsequential. Rather than as slices or cross-sections, the various groups and their association may be seen in dynamic, relational terms, with traditions and continuities weighing off subtly against changes and reconfigurations. At this level of conceptualization, differences are drawn among and within the groups not so as to divide or categorize for the sake of more efficient manipulation, but to assure that social identi-

ties, actions, and alliances are adequately grounded in the specific historical experiences and cultural practices that people recognize as their
own, with appropriate attention to the sometimes sharp class and racial
cleavages that always crosscut any too hasty presumption of equivalence.
The logic is that solidarity can only be posited when the lines of social
differentiation are fully in view but the goal, nevertheless, is solidarity.

It is this critical, historically based approach to diverse and changing
Latino realities that underlies and sustains what I refer to as the "Latino
imaginary," another sense or conceptual space of pan-group aggregation
that is too often and too easily confused with the official, demographic
version. Not that calculation is itself foreign to an "imagined" Latino
community; in fact it is at this epistemological level that the very act and
authority of counting and measuring become issues of vital social contestation. The "imaginary" in this sense does not signify the "not real,"
some make-believe realm oblivious to the facts, but a projection beyond
the "real" as the immediately present and rationally discernible. It is the
"community" represented "for itself," a unity fashioned creatively on the
basis of shared memory and desire, congruent histories of misery and
struggle, and intertwining utopias.

The Latino historical imaginary refers, first of all, to home countries
in Latin America, the landscapes, life-ways, and social struggles familiar,
if not personally, at least to one's family and people, and in any case indispensable to Latinos in situating themselves in U.S. society. Mexico,
Puerto Rico, and Cuba are very different points of imaginative reference,
to be sure, and again, it is always through their particular national optics
that Latinos tend to envision some generic Latin American or Latino
"We." But the features of José Martí's "nuestra América" do stand out in
the Latino historical unconscious in that long narrative of Spanish and
North American colonial conquest, the enslavement and subjugation of
indigenous and African peoples, the troubled consolidation of nations
under the thumb of international power, and the constant migratory
movement of peoples, cultures, and things which has been attendant to
all aspects of the Latino saga. For Latinos in the United States, the passage to, and from, "el Norte" assumes such prominence in the social
imaginary that migration is often confounded with life itself, and any
fixity of the referential homeland gives way to an image of departure and
arrival, the abandoned and the re-encountered.

This nomadic, migratory dimension of the Latino imaginary is anchored in the historical reasons for coming here, and in the placement
assigned most Latinos in U.S. society. Unlike earlier waves of European
immigrants, Latinos typically move to this country as a direct result of

the economic and political relationship of their homelands, and home region, to the United States. However much Cuba, Mexico, and Puerto Rico may vary in status and social arrangement—and if we add the Dominican Republic and Colombia the range could hardly be wider in present-day geopolitics—huge portions of their respective populations have come to live in the United States because of the gravitational pull of metropolitan power and dependency at work in each and all of their histories. Since World War II, its economy on a course of shrinkage and transition rather than unbridled expansion, the United States has been tapping its colonial reserves to fill in its lower ranks, and its Latin American and Caribbean neighbors have proven to be the closest and most abundant sources at hand.

Colonial relations of hemispheric inequality underlie not only the historical logic of Latino migration but also the position and conditions of Latinos here in this society. Differential treatment is of course rampant, as has been dramatically evident in recent years in the contrasting fates of Cubans and Haitians arriving on the same rafts from their beleaguered home islands. Yet today even many Cuban Americans, recent arrivals and long-standing citizens alike, are finding the red carpets and gold-paved streets illusory at best, and are coming to resent being cited as the exception to the rule of Latino disadvantage. For the Latino imaginary, even when the relatively "privileged" Cuban Americans are reckoned in, rests on the recognition of ongoing oppression and discrimination, racism and exploitation, closed doors and patrolled borders. Whether sanguine or enraged, this recognition structures the negotiated relations among Latinos, between Latinos and the dominant culture, and with other groups such as African Americans and Native Americans.

Memory fuels desire: the past as imagined from a Latino perspective awakens an anticipatory sense of what is, or might be, in store. The alarmist hysteria over the prospect of "America's fastest-growing minority" overrunning the society is directed not only at Latino people themselves but at the ground shift in power relations implied in that new calculus. For the desire that these demographic trends awaken in Latinos is directed first of all toward recognition and justice in this society, but wider, hemispheric changes always figure somewhere on the agenda. The Latino imaginary infuses the clamor for civil rights with a claim to sovereignty on an international scale; retribution involves reversing the history of conquest and subordination, including its inherent migratory imperative. A full century after its initial pronouncement, Martí's profile of "nuestra América" still looms like a grid over the map of the entire continent, with the northern co-optation of the name America demanding special scrutiny and revision.

But Latino memory and desire, though standing as a challenge to prevailing structures of power, are not just reactive. The imaginary articulates more than a reflexive response to negative conditions and unfavorably weighted relations, which, though oppositional, is as a response still ultimately mimetic and confined to extrinsically set terms. It is important to recognize that the Latino imaginary, like that of other oppressed groups, harbors the elements of an alternative ethos, an ensemble of cultural values and practices created in its own right and to its own ends. Latinos listen to their own kinds of music, eat their own kinds of food, dream their dreams, and snap their photos not just to express their difference from, or opposition to, the way the "gringos" do it. These choices and preferences, though arrived at under circumstances of dependency and imposition, also attest to a deep sense of autonomy and self-referentiality. Latino identity is imagined not as the negation of the non-Latino, but as the affirmation of cultural and social realities, myths, and possibilities, as they are inscribed in their own human trajectory.

The conditions for the emergence of a Latino cultural ethos were set around mid-century, as it began to become clear that these "new immigrants" filing in from the southern backyard make for a different kind of social presence than that constituted by European arrivals of earlier years. Of course, the histories of each of the major U.S. Latino groups extend much further back than that: Cubans and Puerto Ricans to the mid- to later nineteenth century, when colonies of artisans and political exiles formed in New York and Florida, while today's "Chicanos" were "here" all along, for centuries before the fateful year 1848 when the northern third of their nation was rudely moved in on and annexed by the bearers of manifest destiny. In fact, in the long historical view, the literary and cultural presence of Spanish-speaking people in the territory now called the United States actually precedes that of the English. And if we add to that the Indian American and Afro-American dimensions of "nuestra América," a full-scale revision, or inversion, of the national history results, with the supposed "core," Anglo-Saxon culture appearing as the real intruder, the original illegal alien.

It is a serious fallacy, therefore, to think of Latinos in the United States as "recent arrivals," as is often the tendency in their treatment in scholarly research on immigration.[10] But despite their long-standing, constitutive role in North American history, sheer demographic growth and diversification point to a markedly new structural positioning and cultural dynamic for Latinos in the second half of the twentieth century. Now more than ever, in the present, "postcolonial" era, many Latinos are here as colonial migrants, whose very locations and movements are defined by the status of their "home" countries within the system of transnational economic power. Rather than an ethnic, minority, or immigrant group, those trusty old concepts of cultural pluralism, Latinos may now be more accurately described as a diasporic community or, more suggestively in view of the intensified transnational linkages, as an "ethnoscape" or "world tribe." But a still more satisfactory neologism to characterize the social and cultural space occupied by Latinos is that of the "delocalized transnation," of whom it is also said that they "become doubly loyal to their nations of origin and thus ambivalent about their loyalties to America" (Appadurai 1996, 158–77). Precisely because of the persisting hierarchies of transnational power, if convergences among today's Latinos involve the formation of a "Hispanic nation," it promises to be decidedly less an "American" nation, less a "step toward joining America," than commentators like Geoffrey Fox might propose (1996, 237ff).

The social consciousness and cultural expression of this new geopolitical reality burst forth in the late 1960s and early 1970s, surely the watershed years in the construction of a new language of Latino identity. Inspired by the Civil Rights movement, the opposition to the war against Vietnam, and the Cuban Revolution, countless movements, causes, and organizations rallied thousands of Chicanos and Puerto Ricans to the cries of "Viva la Raza!" and "Despierta Boricua!" The political horizon of the Latino imaginary was set in those spirited movements and found vibrant artistic expression in such diverse forms as wall murals, bilingual poetry and street theater, and hybrid music and dance styles like boogaloo, Chicano rock, Latin soul, and salsa. *Talleres* (workshops) and *conjuntos* (musical groups), readings and *actos* (dramatic sketches) proliferated, lending voice and vision to the fervent political struggles of Latino and Latin American peoples and often attesting to close cultural affinities and political solidarities with other, non-Latino groups, notably African Americans and American Indians.

By our time, in the 1990s, that heyday is long past, hardly even a living memory for many young Latinos; all too frequently in the burgeoning scholarly and journalistic literature on Latinos of recent years, the importance of that foundational period in the story of Latino identity formation is minimized or erased. But the Brown Berets and the Young Lords Party, the Chicano Moratorium and the Lincoln Hospital takeover, the causes of the farm workers and Puerto Rican independence, along with many other manifestations of cultural and political activism, are still an inspiration

and a model of militancy and righteous defiance for the present generation of Latinos of all nationalities as they sharpen their social awareness.
For although the immediacy, intensity, and cultural effervescence have
no doubt waned in the intervening decades, Latinos in the United States
have just as assuredly continued to grow as a social movement to be reckoned with, nationally and internationally, in the years ahead. This is true
demographically in the striking (for some startling) multiplication in
their numbers, and analytically in the equally sharp diversification of
their places of origin and settlement. As contrasted with earlier stages,
the Latino concept is today a far more differentiated site of intersecting
social identities, especially along sexual, racial, and class lines.

But the persistence and expansion of the Latino social movements are
most prominent as a cultural imaginary, a still emergent space or "community" of memory and desire. In the present generation, Latino youth
from many backgrounds have played a formative role in the creation of
hip-hop and its inflection toward Latino expression and experience;
though not always explicitly political in intention, the Latino contribution to contemporary popular music, dance, performance, and visual imaging has accompanied important signs of social organization and self-
identification among young Latinos in many parts of the country. The
emergence of "Latino literature," though in important ways a marketing
and canonizing category having the effect of concealing distinctions necessary for purposes of literary history and criticism, has also involved expanded horizons and greater intercultural exchange than had been true
in the previous Nuyorican and Chicano generation. In the case of the
"casitas" in the New York barrios—another richly suggestive and often-
cited example from recent Latino experience—entire neighborhoods
across generational and many other lines are drawn together by way of
sharing in the enactment of collective cultural memory.[11] Present-day
considerations and representations of Latino life which would do justice
to that complex reality find it necessary to incorporate such instances of
cultural innovation and "invented traditions" by way of complementing
their reliance on social scientific insights.[12]

Hispanic? Latino? Settling on a name never comes easy, and when it
comes to an all-embracing term for Mexicans, Puerto Ricans, Cubans,
Dominicans, Colombians, Salvadorans, Panamanians, and an array of
other Latin American and Caribbean peoples in the United States, consensus does not seem to be near at hand. But the search for a name, more
than an act of classification, is actually a process of historical imagination and a struggle over social meaning at diverse levels of interpretation.
Rigorous demographic and social science analysis is no doubt essential

to the task of circumscribing that process, and especially for identifying structural variations in the placement of the different national groups relative to hierarchies of power and attendant histories of racialization. But only a fully interdisciplinary approach, guided by an attention to cultural expression and identity claims and transcending the bounds set by positivist analysis, allows for an integral understanding of Latino experience. In that sense the search for Latino identity and community, the ongoing articulation of a pan-ethnic and transnational imaginary, is also a search for a new map, a new ethos, a new *América*.

Notes

1. Another such unusual, and in my view confusing, usage of the terms may be found in William Luis (1997, x–xi); here "Latino" refers to those of Latin American background born and raised in the United States, while "Hispanic" is taken to refer to those "born and raised in their parents' home country." Though the terminological distinction is questionable and remote from common parlance, Luis is accurate in calling for distinctions in group denomination when he states that "it would be incongruous to group Hispanics from privileged families who have superior educational backgrounds, traveling to the United States to pursue a post-secondary education, with Latinos living in the ghettos of East Harlem or East Los Angeles, attending inferior schools and lacking the economic support necessary to overcome the limitations of their existence" (xi). For an example of the overemphasis on language and an excessively expansive sense of "Latino" and "Hispanic," see Fox (1996).
2. The opening citations are renderings of statements I have encountered during the course of conversations and interviews, or in newspaper accounts. Examples of the abundant published discussion of the terms *Hispanic* and *Latino* may be found in Oboler (1995) and Shorris (1992). See also my essay, "Pan-Latino/Trans-Latino: Puerto Ricans in the 'New Nueva York,'" ch. 7 of *From Bomba to Hip-Hop* (2000).
3. Documentation of this widespread preference for national designations may be found in de la Garza (1992). For a response, see Fraga, Gallegos and López (1994).
4. As useful as Anderson's coinage may be for characterizing the cultural convergences among Latinos, to posit the idea of a "Hispanic nation," as in Geoffrey Fox's book of that title, would seem premature at best, and misleading in taking Anderson's analysis too literally (see Fox 1996, 1–18).
5. The range of theoretical approaches from strictly quantitative to comparative to ideological is evident in the growing published literature on "Hispanics" or "Latinos." See for example, Tienda and Ortiz (1986, 3–20); Padilla (1985); Morales and Bonilla (1993). The concept of "ethnoscape" is set forth by Arjun Appadurai (1996, 27–65).
6. The present essay was originally intended as a general theoretical introduction to the projected catalogue of "Latino Voices," the first international festival of Latino

photography, which opened in Houston in November 1994. The idea of conceptualizing and circumscribing a "Latino imaginary" arose while previewing slides of images by Chicano, Puerto Rican, and Cuban photographers included in that historic exhibition, and deciding how best to present their theoretical and cultural significance to a broad United States audience of the 1990s. Although the catalogue did not materialize, I have presented the paper in a variety of settings across the country, incorporating insights as I went along. I especially thank Wendy Watriss, Frances Aparicio, and Marvette Pérez for their critical responses, though they are in no way to be held responsible for the arguments of the essay as it stands.

7. The most extended discussion of these instrumental uses of the "Hispanic" label may be found in Oboler (1995), though I also find of some interest the exchange between Fernando Treviño and David Hayes-Bautista (1987).

8. For examples of "Hispanics" in advertisements and other commercial uses, see Flores and Yúdice (1990). That essay also appeared in my book *Divided Borders* (1993). See also Arlene Dávila (1999).

9. For Rumbaut, see the valuable essay, "The Americans: Latin American and Caribbean Peoples in the United States" (1992); it is worth noting that while the author seems to have little difficulty speaking of "Latinos" as a group when contrasting them with African Americans, he otherwise voices skepticism as to the value of panethnic, or what he terms "supranational," identities.

10. See, for example, Pedraza (1998). Even broad historical overviews of Latino immigration may tend to abbreviate the duration of Latino presence in the United States; see, for example, Rumbaut (1992), where preponderant attention goes to the post-1960s period.

11. On Latino rap, see "Puerto Rocks: Rap, Roots, and Amnesia," chapter 6 of Flores (2000). For an interpretation of the *casita* phenomenon, see "Salvación Casita: Space, Performance, and Community," chapter 4 of Flores (2000).

12. See, for example, Winn (1992, 550–600). This chapter, like the book as a whole, is intended as the accompaniment to the ten-part public television series on contemporary Latin America. "North of the Border," the final chapter and segment, is about U.S. Latinos and is based on the research of Alejandro Portes and Rubén G. Rumbaut. Their social science findings are significantly amplified by extensive references to rap music, *casitas*, and other cultural phenomena. See also Fox (1996, 223ff).

IV
Positions and Polemics

JOHN BEVERLEY

Writing in Reverse: On the Project of the Latin American Subaltern Studies Group

John Beverley was born in the United States in 1943. A literary and cultural critic, he is a professor at the University of Pittsburgh in Pennsylvania. His main titles include *Against Literature* (1993), and *Subalternity and Representation: Arguments in Cultural Theory* (1999).

The work of subaltern studies begins, Ranajit Guha insists, with necessary transgression of the intentions and rules of decorum that regulate scholarly activity (Guha 1989, 135). Accordingly, this is not an essay in the formal or "finished" sense, but rather a set of scattered—"migrating"—observations that are meant above all to provoke discussion and reflection. I will cite a passage from Guha's *Elementary Aspects of Peasant Insurgency in Colonial India* that gives the phrase of my title—for those of you who are unfamiliar with him, Guha is the founder of the South Asian Subaltern Studies Group. In this connection, I will say a few words about the project of the Latin American Subaltern Studies Group, which I have been closely involved with,[1] and then discuss a case that illustrates what I think are the main issues involved in this project—it has to do with three literary texts associated with the Tupac Amaru rebellion of 1780 in the Peruvian highlands. I will conclude with some remarks on the problematic relation between subaltern studies and cultural studies and on the implications of subaltern studies for our roles and work in the university.

The passage from Guha goes as follows:

> The historical phenomenon of [peasant] insurgency meets the eye for the first time as an image framed in the prose, hence the outlook, of counterinsurgency—an image caught in a distorting mirror. However, the distortion has a logic to it. That is the logic of the opposition between the rebels and their enemies not only as parties engaged in active hostility on a particular occasion but as the mutually antagonistic elements of a semi-feudal society under colonial rule. The antagonism is rooted deeply enough in the material and spiritual conditions of their existence to reduce the difference between elite and subaltern perceptions of a radical peasant movement to a difference between the terms of a binary pair. A rural uprising thus turns into a site for two rival cognitions to meet and to define each other negatively. . . . Inscribed in elite discourse, it [the uprising] had to be read as a writing in reverse. (Guha 1983, 333)

I want to draw out the implications of this statement in relation to four interrelated areas that the project of subaltern studies touches: intellectuals, literature, the nation, and the university.

First, intellectuals. We have been having an internal debate in our group about the question of intellectuals. I say this to underscore that the group is not one thing but a forum for discussions around a shared concern, so that while I think I am representing the nature of this concern adequately, there are also elements of my own particular take on it in what I am going to say. When the group announced its interest in pursuing the model of subaltern studies in Latin American and Caribbean contexts—for example, in our founding statement, which we submitted as part of an ultimately unsuccessful grant proposal to the Rockefeller Foundation, or at our public forum at the 1993 meeting of the Latin American Studies Association in Atlanta—we encountered variations on the following set of hostile questions: What is the point of importing into Latin American studies a problematic elaborated under other cultural and historical circumstances? Given the work of figures like Fernando Ortiz, José Carlos Mariátegui, Ezequiel Martínez Estrada, Rodolfo Kush, Édouard Glissant, José María Arguedas, Miguel Barnet, Ernesto Galarza, or Xavier Albó (the list could, of course, be varied or multiplied almost at will), has there not already been an engagement by Latin American, Caribbean, and U.S. Latino intellectuals—on native grounds, so to speak—of the problems of historical and cultural study identified by Guha and the South Asian group? Is it not a kind of theoretical "colonialism" to ignore this? Aren't we simply being trendy? What about the problem of "traveling theory"?

Our founding statement explains in detail some of the general historical and personal contingencies that led us to re-evaluate our own work in the direction of subaltern studies; we point there above all to the crisis of the great left projects of the last two decades, like the Cuban and Nicaraguan revolutions, and the revisionary or deconstructive effect on Marxism of new theoretical perspectives coming from feminism and poststructuralism, particularly the work on the nexus of power and knowledge associated with Foucault. What was at stake in our move to subaltern studies was, in other words, a growing sense of the inadequacy of the models of intellectual and political protagonism in which many of us were in fact formed. In the field of literary and cultural criticism, which many of the initial members of the group come from, one of the most influential of these models was undoubtedly the concept of transculturation, introduced by Fernando Ortiz in his ethnographic studies in Cuba in the twenties and thirties, and then adapted in the sixties by Angel Rama to the field of literature in the form of what he called "narrative transculturation" (Rama 1982). If for Ortiz transculturation designated a social process in which European and African elements—food, customs, religious practices, manners, dress, et cetera—became fused in Cuban everyday life, in Rama's version, which was based on the conjunctural coincidence between the literary practice of the boom writers and the new political energies released by the impact of the Cuban Revolution, transculturation became something like an ideology for intellectual work in general—positing a quasi-Leninist relation between a "lettered" vanguard of social scientists, humanists, artists, writers, critics, and a new type of politician—and subaltern social classes and groups, in which the first would serve as an agent of the second by constructing new cultural and political forms in which the formative presence of the subaltern in Latin American history and society could be made manifest. Pablo Neruda's claim to "speak for" a transhistorical popular subject in *Canto General* (and the Popular Front politics that it was the vehicle of), or the work of the Peruvian novelist José María Arguedas at the boundary between indigenous and European cultural forms, and Quechua and Spanish, are exemplary of transculturation in this sense, as is the earlier notion of cultural *mestizaje* or creolization first advanced by Pedro Henríquez Ureña, the founder of modern Latin American criticism, which underlies the writing practices of both magic realism and the neobaroque.[2]

What I think is wrong with the transculturation model is that it is based on and continues to privilege a fundamentally literary notion of the actual or potential representational adequacy of intellectuals and elite culture in relation to the subaltern—I mean representational in both a mimetic and a political sense, in the way Gayatri Spivak explains in "Can the Subaltern Speak?" (1988a). As Spivak points out there, subalternity is a relational rather than an ontological identity, which implies that it is a socially constructed identity (or, since it is not *one* thing, a set of constantly shifting identities). What we liked about the South Asian group was its acute sense of the limitations of elite discourse, whether historiographic, anthropological, or literary, colonial, liberal, or even Marxist, limits imposed, as the passage from Guha suggests, by the inescapable fact that elite discourse and the institutions that contain it, like the university or literature, are themselves complicit in the construction and maintenance of subalternity.

The slogan "writing in reverse" indicates in particular a point of difference between the subaltern studies proposal, as we understand it, and the projects of Edward Said or Roberto Fernández Retamar, with which it obviously shares many concerns. In his foreword to the anthology of the Indian group, *Selected Subaltern Studies*, Said puts Guha and his colleagues in the company of writers like Frantz Fanon, Salman Rushdie, Gabriel García Márquez, C. L. R. James, Aimé Cesaire, Ngugi Wa Thiongo, Toni Morrison, and Mahmud Darwish, in the sense that the group's work is like theirs, in Said's words, a "hybrid," partaking jointly of Western and non-Western concerns and theory and adumbrating the shape of a new, postcolonial humanism (Guha and Spivak 1988, ix–x). But where Said and Retamar (in his essay "Calibán") envision a new type of intellectual as the protagonist of decolonization, the admittedly paradoxical intention of subaltern studies as an intellectual project is to displace the centrality of intellectuals, and what intellectuals recognize as culture and the written record, in social history and policy generation.

I realize that this will sound a little too Manichean. Said notes in particular the danger that the project risks becoming a separatist one, in the manner (he claims) of radical feminism. But if only because subaltern culture and politics tend themselves to be Manichean, it might be worth assuming this risk. Intellectuals like ourselves are given to preserving and nurturing the written record, whereas peasant rebels, such as those Guha studies in *Elementary Aspects of Peasant Insurgency* or the Zapatistas in Chiapas today, often want to destroy it (by burning the municipal archives, for example) for good reason: they understand that the written record is the record of their conditions of subordination and exploitation.

I will come back to this point at the end, because it also concerns the way we think of our roles in the university and research and policy institutes. Let me move now, however, to the—not unrelated—question of the nation and nationalism. Guha has defined the central problematic of his own work as

> the study of [the] *historical failure of the nation to come to its own*, a failure due to the inadequacy of the bourgeoisie as well as of the working class to lead it into a decisive victory over colonialism and a bourgeois-democratic revolution of either the classic nineteenth-century type under the hegemony of the bourgeoisie or a more modern type under the hegemony of workers and peasants, that is, a "new democracy." (Guha and Spivak 1988, 43)

Those of us who come from Marxist backgrounds, like myself, may admire the conceptual precision of this formulation, but otherwise it will come as no particular surprise in the various disciplinary strands that make up Latin American studies, which have long worked with the assumption that *nation and national* are not popular, all-inclusive terms. Indeed, we noted in our founding statement that "the force behind the problem of the subaltern in Latin America could be said to arise directly out of the need to reconceptualize the relation of nation, state, and 'people' in the three social movements that have centrally shaped the concerns of Latin American studies (as of modern Latin America itself): the Mexican, Cuban, and Nicaraguan revolutions" (Beverley and Oviedo 1993, 112).[3]

What we have added to the South Asian group's concern with the "monism" (the phrase is Guha's) of colonial and postcolonial historiography is a postmodernist concern with the effects of the current processes of economic, demographic, and cultural transnationalization on Latin America. We stipulated, however, that

> the "deterritorialization" of the nation-state under the impact of the new permeability of frontiers to capital-labor flows merely replicates, in effect, the *genetic process of implantation of a colonial economy* in Latin America. . . . It is not only that we can *no longer* operate solely within the prototype of nationhood; the concept of the nation, itself tied to the protagonism of creole elites concerned to dominate and/or manage other social groups or classes in their own societies, has obscured, *from the start*, the presence of subaltern social subjects in Latin American history. (Beverley and Oviedo 1993, 118)

This emphasis on the logic of the present is a key point in our approach to subaltern studies, one that differentiates us in particular from

Florencia Mallon's vision of subaltern studies as fundamentally a new historiography (1999). We conceive our project as an intervention along the dividing line that produces subaltern and elite identities: that is, as a *politics* as well as a new kind of knowledge production. In that sense, we judge its components strategically. While we start, like Guha and his South Asian colleagues, from the fact of the non-coincidence of "nation" and "people" in the historical past of Latin America, we are acutely aware that the possibility of articulating the Gramscian copula *national-popular* is still the central question of how to construct political hegemony.[4] We are also aware that we work from a cosmopolitan position of extreme privilege, and that there is a danger that what we do will contribute, "behind our backs," so to speak, to those forces that are acting to disorganize Latin American (national) spaces and populations to the advantage of new and perhaps more virulent forms of domination and exploitation.

Nevertheless, even at the risk of one-sidedness, we need to distinguish our project from those that continue to depend on a nationalist claim. While the theoretical force of dependency theory is certainly long spent, some of its underlying assumptions are still very much with us. One is that it is somehow the responsibility of the left—and here I mean both the organized political left and the left intelligentsia—to carry forward the project of elaboration of a national culture left incomplete by the Latin American bourgeoisies, because of their dependent or—to recall André Gunder Frank's apt characterization—"lumpen" character.[5] Let me give a concrete example. My friend Nelson Osorio, who was active in the Chilean Communist Party during the Allende years and was arrested, tortured, and exiled after the coup, has been working in Venezuela for something close to a decade to compose an encyclopedia of Latin American literature, the *Diccionario Enciclopédico de Literatura Latinoamericana*, or DELAL for short. The project involves coordinating the participation of hundreds of scholars all over the world, under his direction. Its aim is to produce a totalization of Latin American literature within an overall center-left ideological perspective.

Several members of our group, including myself, have been involved with the DELAL. While in agreeing to be part of it we recognize its "progressive" character, however, we also share to one degree or another the assumption, current since Rama's *La ciudad letrada* (1984a), that literature has been in Latin America a practice that is constitutive of elite identity, and, as such, precisely part of the problem we want to address, rather than part of the solution. In particular, the equation of elites-literature-city-nation Rama makes in *La ciudad letrada* is modified but doesn't necessarily go away with attempts to democratize literary culture such as the literacy campaigns instituted by the Cuban and Nicaraguan revolutions, or Ernesto Cardenal's workshop poetry project in Nicaragua; in fact, the crisis of these revolutions, with which many of us were identified and involved in one way or another, was precisely one of our starting points.[6]

What has undermined effectively the hegemony of the "lettered city," by contrast, is the mutation of the public sphere caused by the audiovisual mass media, which, as Antonio Candido observed somewhat despairingly in a seminal essay on literature and underdevelopment in the early seventies (1973), implied a renewed deferral of the idea of literary culture as a model or formative practice of informed citizenship.

Candido spoke as a *modern*, one of those moderns who, like Lukács and Adorno, believed that it was the task of a Marxist-oriented intelligentsia to preserve and defend the institutions of the national culture, including literature, formed by the bourgeoisie in their rise to power, from their degeneration in the hands of that same bourgeoisie, and in particular from the destructive inroads of the mass media and cultural commodification. The DELAL project comes out of a similar logic, and it stands to reason that Osorio, who has created something like an academic version of Allende's Unidad Popular to sustain it, should want to resist our efforts to de-center the status of literature as a cultural signifier. He would observe against us that in order to deconstruct the canon of Latin American literature, it must first be constructed as such. I take the point. But the strategic thrust of the subaltern studies project is that it is necessary to move beyond the parameters of *both* the nation and written literature, at least as these are conventionally understood. Where Candido saw a crisis of civic identity in the inability of the newly urbanized "masses" to accede to literature, which they pass by, so to speak, on the way to what he called the "urban folklore" of the media, we are more inclined to see a possibility of cultural democratization.

I believe that the antagonism our project encounters may also arise from the fact that it threatens—or in fact competes with—other initiatives to introduce "multicultural" perspectives in education: for example, those, like Henry Louis Gates's effort to construct, or reconstruct, the canon of Afro-American literature, that assume that literature can be made into an adequate cultural representation of subaltern groups.[7] The fact that we can compete at all reflects the problems caused for public policy by the incomprehension or misunderstanding of subaltern social subjects by previously dominant academic methodologies and disciplines, as well as the new role of the university and the research centers in the administration of transnational capitalism, especially in the face

of the demographic, political, and cultural transformations it has involved. What exactly is it, however, that a project like ours does for
pedagogy?

Here, my own answer has to be somewhat ambiguous. On the one
hand, I am tempted to say—because it is the sort of claim administrators
and foundations would notice—that we offer a newer and finer conceptual instrument for retrieving and registering the presence of the subaltern. Two classic examples are Guha's own ingenious (although not unproblematic) reconstruction of an "alternative solidarity" of women in
nineteenth-century rural Bengal in "Chandra's Death" (Guha 1989) or
Michael Taussig's spectacular account of the "devil contract" among
field workers in the Cauca Valley of Colombia (Taussig 1980). In a related
way, there is also the question of the contribution of a subalternist perspective to the formation of a new pedagogy in the humanities and social
sciences based on the incorporation of the "other," with its manifold implications of interdisciplinary research, teaching, textbook publishing,
and the like.[8]

But there is a more negative or purely critical side to the subaltern
studies project—related to the central place Guha gives the category of
negation in subaltern identity in *Elementary Aspects*—that I would prefer
to emphasize here. That is its concern to register where the power of the
university to understand and represent the subaltern breaks down or
reaches a limit. This involves recognizing the contradiction—or to use a
more properly deconstructive term, the catachresis—built into the very
idea of "studying" the subaltern. We put it this way in our founding
statement:

> Our project, in which a team of researchers and their collaborators in
> elite metropolitan universities want to extricate from documents and
> practices the oral world of the subaltern, the structural presence of the
> unavoidable, indestructible, and effective subject who has proven us
> wrong—she/he who has demonstrated that we did not know them—
> must itself confront the dilemma of subaltern resistance to and insur-
> gency against elite conceptions. (Beverley and Oviedo 1993, 121)

The concluding words of I, *Rigoberta Menchú* express the nature of this
resistance very well. "I'm still keeping secret what I think no-one should
know," the narrator says. "Not even anthropologists or intellectuals, no
matter how many books they have, can find out all our secrets" (Menchú
1984, 247). Doris Sommer has argued that it is not so much a question
here of *real* secrets that Rigoberta Menchú needs to keep from us in the

interest of protecting herself and her community, as of *strategic* insistence that, despite her claim, proper to *testimonio* as a genre, she is telling us "toda la verdad de mi pueblo," there is something she will in fact *not* tell, that we cannot know (Sommer 1993b). Recognizing the nature and force of subaltern resistance to being "known," which is what is implied by Guha's idea of writing in reverse, involves in turn learning how to work against the grain of our own interests and prejudices—undoing the authority of the academy and knowledge centers at the same time that we continue to participate fully in them and to deploy their authority as teachers, researchers, and theorists. Spivak calls this process "unlearning privilege," and offers an example of it in her own recent essay, "Responsibility" (Spivak 1994).

I can illustrate more concretely what is at stake here by turning to the three texts associated with the Tupac Amaru rebellion I mentioned at the start. These are the *Genealogía*, written in Spanish by the leader of the rebellion, José Gabriel Condorcanqui Tupac Amaru, which is the text of a legal petition defending his claim to be descended from the last Inca that he presented to the Real Audiencia de Lima in 1777, three years before the rebellion; the *Memorias* (also known as *Cuarenta años de cautiverio* or *El cautiverio dilatado*) of his brother, Juan Bautista Tupac Amaru, which appeared in Buenos Aires in 1825, also in Spanish; and the play *Ollantay*, written and performed in Quechua before indigenous audiences—one was said to have included José Gabriel himself—around 1780, but formally modeled on the conventions of the Spanish Golden Age drama, including the three act form of the *comedia* and the figure of the *gracioso*.

The *Genealogía* is a text immersed in the baroque rhetoric of colonial legalism. It was inspired to a certain extent, although with a more immediately utilitarian purpose, by the sort of genealogy that Garcilaso constructed a century and a half earlier in the *Comentarios reales* to justify the right of the Inca aristocracy to share in the administration of the viceroyalty with the representatives of the Spanish crown. In the light of José Gabriel's subsequent role in the rebellion of 1780, one can see latent in his intention of securing his claim to be the direct descendant of the last Inca the possibility of displacing the colonial regime itself and occupying himself the position of Inca in a restoration of the Inca state.

Though, like Sor Juana's *Respuesta a Sor Filotea*, the *Genealogía* has elements of autobiography and family history, it is more like an expanded version of a *prueba de limpieza de sangre* than an autobiography as such. The rhetorical elaboration of the document, which seems excessive for what is after all a formal legal petition, is intended to establish José Gabriel's mastery of the aristocratizing codes of the viceregal *ciudad letrada*. It defines a parity between himself and his Spanish and creole interlocutors. By contrast, his brother's *Memorias*, which appeared some fifty years later, is an autobiography in the modern sense and reveals an entirely new rhetoric and persona. The *Memorias* posits Juan Bautista's experience in Spanish prisons after the defeat of the rebellion as a metonymy of the degradation to which Spanish colonial rule has subjected America. If the *Genealogía* anticipates the rebellion of 1780 by establishing the legitimacy of José Gabriel's claim to be the descendant of Tupac Amaru I, the *Memorias* articulates a sense of the continuity between that rebellion and the liberal revolutions of the creoles nearly half a century later. It is the sort of text that Bolívar or San Martín would have read with pleasure.[9]

If, however, we try to study these texts as examples of the appropriation of European literary models by representatives of an Indian rebellion against colonial authority—that is, under the aegis of the transculturation model—we will rapidly encounter an impasse. Neither the *Genealogía* nor the *Memorias* figure in the canon of Latin American or, for that matter, Peruvian literature, but it is not simply a question of including these texts and others like them in the canon (although it goes without saying that they should be included in the canon). Rather, the impasse results from a problem Paul de Man identified in a text that bears a family resemblance to the *Memorias* in particular, Rousseau's *Confessions*. Although in their construction of an allegory of the subject the *Genealogía* and the *Memorias* evidently "generate history" (the phrase is de Man's)[10]—in the language of speech act theory, they are *performative*, they are part of the ideological *mise en scène* of the rebellion and its aftermath—they do not *represent* history (in the double sense Spivak's article articulates: that is, either politically or mimetically). The autobiographical subjects they configure are simply incommensurate with the actual character of the rebellion, which involves the collective action of large and heterogeneous sectors of both indigenous and creole populations. The metonymic chain that we have learned to identify in a *testimonio* like I, *Rigoberta Menchú*, which connects the textual representation of an individual life experience of the narrator to the collective destiny of the class or social group, cannot be completed here.

There is a related problem that the historian Leon Campbell has noted. Campbell agrees with scholars of Andean literature like Martin Lienhardt or Rolena Adorno that there existed since the Conquest a written Andean Quechua-Spanish "resistance literature," based on adaptations of European models, which nourished the worldview of the leaders of the indigenous communities like the Tupac Amaru family (we know, for example, that Tupac Amaru himself carried on his person an edition of the *Comentarios reales* of Garcilaso). But the documentary evidence that has been amassed around the rebellion also reveals the existence of a radically different culture of rebellion, a predominantly Andean-based and oral (or, more accurately, despite the apparent anachronism, *audiovisual*) culture, developed for and by the rebels—mainly peasants and artisans and members of their families—who made up the great *tupamarista* and *katarista* armies, and who (on the whole) neither read nor spoke Spanish, nor were particularly concerned to learn how to. Campbell concludes that there existed what he calls a "dual idiom" of rebellion: on the one hand, texts written in Spanish like the *Genealogía* or the proclamations and letters issued by the rebel leadership to the creoles or colonial authorities; on the other, the non-, or even anti-literary cultural practices deployed by the rebels themselves.[11] For the leaders of the rebellion, like the Tupac Amaru family itself, such an ambivalence evidently responded to contradictions in their own ideological formation and position within the colonial system and in their efforts to semiotize themselves as leaders (Tupac Amaru sometimes wore Inca clothing, at other times European-style military uniforms, for example).

But Campbell's idea of a dual idiom is not merely conjunctural or tactical, nor does it only refer to divisions in the practices of the leadership. It also coincides with the terms of a well-known historical debate about the nature—reformist or revolutionary?—of the uprising itself. As Campbell puts it,

> When one takes only the Spanish-language literary record into account, the focus of the rebellion appears to be directed exclusively toward the cities and their creole inhabitants and the rebel program focused on material issues, concerned primarily with dismantling the harsh economic reforms of the Bourbons, which impoverished many Peruvians through increased taxes and commercial restrictions. . . . If, on the other hand, the roles of myth, symbolism, and ceremony, of ritual and response, are also examined and their interior meanings better defined, it is clear that not only did these comprise an important part of the literature of the rebellion but that these ideas were often at variance with what the rebels seemed to be asking for in the written proposals. Because the rebel's Spanish language directives were focused on the major commercial centers that had remained loyal to the crown or creole areas under rebel control . . . they give the rebellion a

"tactical rationalism" very characteristic of the times. . . . They also fit nicely with Western definitions of eighteenth-century rebellion as it developed in Europe and America. (Campbell 1987)

In other words, the historian who chooses literary texts like the *Genealogía* or the *Memorias* as representative of the culture and goals of the rebellion will see an essentially reformist movement, conceived within the language and the legal and cultural codes imposed by the process of European colonization of the Andes, now creolized or (to use the postmodernist term) "refunctioned," while the historian who looks beyond these texts to other cultural practices will see something that looks more like a revolution from below of the poorest and most exploited sectors of the indigenous population, with conjunctural allies among the creoles and the *caciques*, aimed at restoring the Inca state.

I have kept in reserve the question of *Ollantay*, because it is directly connected to this last issue in a way that is strikingly different from José Gabriel's claim to be the Inca in the *Genealogía*. In some ways, *Ollantay* is in fact the most derivative and "European" of the three texts, combining as it does the baroque allegorical model of state theater—as in Calderón's *La vida es sueño* with what came to be known as the *comedia tierna* in the Spanish Enlightenment—Jovellanos's *El delincuente honrado* is the best-known example of the genre, which anticipates bourgeois melodrama. The play is based on an Inca legend set in the period before the Spanish Conquest about a commoner, Ollantay, who is one of the leading generals of the Inca army and who falls in love illicitly with the daughter of the Inca and has a child with her. When the Inca learns of this, he reacts by imprisoning his daughter and forcing Ollantay to flee to his native province. There Ollantay raises an army to challenge the Inca's authority and recuperate his wife. In the course of the war, the old Inca dies and is replaced by his son, Tupac Yupanqui, the brother of Ollantay's wife. Ollantay's army is eventually defeated, however, and Ollantay himself is brought in chains to Cuzco to stand trial for treason. In the legend, Ollantay is put to death for his transgression; in the play, however, he is (partly through the mediation of his daughter, Yma Sumac) forgiven by Tupac Yupanqui and appointed as, in effect, a sort of vice-Inca (he will rule in Tupac Yupanqui's place when the latter is away), and reunited with his wife and child.

If we were to read *Ollantay* in the same spirit as the *Memorias* of Juan Bautista, that is, as a "national allegory"—in the sense Fredric Jameson uses this term—anticipating the Wars of Independence of the early nineteenth century, the hero's frustrated love affair and eventual rebellion against the old Inca would symbolize the dissatisfaction of an emergent creole class with the still dominant structures of power of the colonial *ancien régime*, represented by the Bourbon dynasty and its viceroyalties. What is interesting about *Ollantay* for our purposes here, however, is (1) that it was written in Quechua—and therefore for all practical purposes was inaccessible to a creole audience—and (2) that, despite its reliance on the formula of the Spanish *comedia*, its models of cultural and political authority are ultimately Andean, rather than European. While the representation of the old Inca against whom Ollantay rebels can certainly be read as a symbol for the Spanish Bourbons, it might also have suggested to the local audiences who saw the play in 1780, as the Tupac Amaru rebellion was spreading, the more immediate and not at all "symbolic" possibility of restoring the Inca state as such. With an important twist, however: the new Inca state suggested at the end of *Ollantay* is no longer based on a principle of strict *caste* authority such as that dominating the traditional Inca system; it is, rather, a state that allows precisely for the accession to power of non-aristocratic subjects like Ollantay.

Is it a question here of an infiltration into or contamination of a "purely" Andean conception of the state by proto-Jacobin ideology or the idea of enlightened despotism (which itself was based historically in part on Enlightenment concepts of the Inca state)? *Ollantay* is in this ideological sense too a case of transculturation; it involves at both formal and ideological levels an explosive combination of Andean and European elements that could only have been stabilized into the form of a new national-popular had the 1780 rebellion succeeded. But it is important to see this as a transculturation from *below* that involves not so much the ways in which an emerging creole "lettered city" becomes progressively more adequate to the task of representing the interests of the indigenous peasantry, but rather how that population appropriates aspects of European and creole literary and philosophical culture to serve *its* interests.

What is involved here is not the distinction between a project that has a concept of "nation," articulated in literature and print culture, as in Benedict Anderson's well-known hypothesis, and one that does not, that is simply tribal or community based, or regional, precisely because it lacks the representational capacity to project an "imagined community" beyond those limits. It is a question, rather, of *different* conceptions of the subject-form of the nation (and of different types of intellectuals and intellectual culture). Steve Stern explains that in Peru-Bolivia, in the late colonial period, peasants did not live, struggle, or think in terms that isolated them from the emerging "national question." On the contrary, protonational symbols had great importance in the life of peasants and small-holders. Yet *these protonational symbols were tied not to an emerging creole nationalism, but to no*tions of an Andean—or Inca-led social order. Andean peasants saw themselves as part of a wider protonational culture, and sought their liberation on terms that, far from isolating them from an overarching state, would link them to a new and just state. (1982, 76; italics mine)

To see texts like the *Genealogía* or the *Memorias* as adequately representative of the interests at stake in the Tupac Amaru rebellion, then, not only obscures the fact of an indigenous production of a sense of the national-popular that, while it undoubtedly involved elements of European culture, did so in a way subordinate to its own struggle for hegemony and its own conceptions of community, rationality, and government.[12] It also amounts to an act of appropriation that excludes the indigenous peasantry as a subject conscious of its own history, incorporating that population only as a contingent element of *another* history (of the modern nation-state, of the Enlightenment, of Peruvian literature), whose subject is also an Other (creole, Spanish-speaking, *letrado*, male).

I would like to move at this point, however, to consider briefly a contemporary text about indigenous resistance and rebellion in the Americas that I have already had occasion to mention more than once here, *I, Rigoberta Menchú*. As you know, Menchú's narrative begins with a strategic disavowal of both literature and the liberal concept of the authority of private experience that literature can engender: "My name is Rigoberta Menchú. I am twenty-three years old. This is my testimony. I didn't learn it from a book, and I didn't learn it alone." Any number of subsequent passages imply a critique of what literacy and books represent in the power systems that affect the narrator's possibilities of liberation or even survival. At the same time, however, it is clear that Menchú constructs her account not only from an oral, non-Western, precapitalist model of story telling, of the sort Walter Benjamin portrayed in his essay "The Storyteller." In narrating her own *testimonio*, she is clearly drawing on her experience as a lay catechist, whose function (which involves the Book of Books of Western culture, so to speak) is to dramatize and allegorize the biblical stories she tells in order to provoke discussion about their present-day relevance to the lives of her congregation.

I have argued elsewhere that it would be yet another version of the native informant of classical anthropology to grant testimonial narrators like Rigoberta Menchú only the possibility of being witnesses, not the power to create their own narrative authority and negotiate its conditions of truth and representativity. "This would be a way of saying that the subaltern can of course speak, but only through the institutionally sanctioned authority—itself dependent on and implicated in colonialism and imperialism—of the journalist or ethnographer, who alone has the power to decide what counts in the narrator's 'raw material' and to turn it into literature (or 'evidence')" (Beverley 1993, 97).

What a text like *I, Rigoberta Menchú* forces us to confront is the subaltern not only as a "represented" subject but also as agent of a transformative project that aspires itself to become hegemonic. In terms of this project, which is not our own in any immediate sense and which in fact involves structurally a contradiction with our position of relative privilege and authority, the testimonial text is a *means* rather than an end in itself. In particular, becoming a writer, producing a literary text, reading and discussing that text in a classroom cannot be *in themselves* the solution demanded by what René Jara calls the "situation of urgency" that generates the *testimonio*, whether or not these things actually happen. That solution has to be something other than the *testimonio*'s own existence as a written text. In other words, it is not only our purposes that count in relation to a *testimonio* like *I, Rigoberta Menchú*.

The key thing to understand and accept in this respect is that *the subaltern does not want to be subaltern*: inscribed on its banner are the words of the Sermon on the Mount: the first shall be last, and the last shall be first. This recognition is what distinguished our project from one which would seek simply to "represent" the subaltern or register its presence in social history.[13] It is also at the heart of the unanticipated polarization we have experienced with the larger project of Latin American cultural studies, within which we initially inscribed the work of our group.[14] It is not only that cultural studies perpetuates, as I suggested earlier, an essentially modernist ideology of cultural agency. Although animated by theoretical and political concerns coming from feminism, Marxism, deconstruction, postcolonial thought, the practice of the new social movements, and the like, cultural studies can have, and, in fact, tends to have an essentially *descriptive* relation to the emerging "scapes"—to borrow Arjun Appadurai's term (as in technoscapes, demoscapes, culturescapes, etc.)—of global culture it seeks to map. As such, I would argue that it risks becoming a form of academic *costumbrismo*. Even more: I think we are all beginning to understand that what we do in critical theory, cultural studies, new historicism, postcolonial critique, and the like, can be—according to the logic of what Bourdieu calls "effects not desired"—complicit in producing discursively a kind of postmodernist sublime (Beverley 1993, 44). The phrase is only partly ironic: the function of such a sublime—as a new sensorium or aesthetic-cognitive remapping—would be to adjust the humanities and the field of culture generally to the new patterns of domination, exploitation, and immiseration produced by globalization, just as the romantic sublime of Kant and company did for an earlier stage of capitalism in the nineteenth century. The trajectory of Appadurai's own work and of the transnational cultural studies journal he coedits, *Public Culture*, is itself symptomatic of this danger, as is in a different way something like the Benetton ad campaign that used in sophisticated ways testimonial and documentary material drawn from subaltern situations to persuade affluent transnational consumers to buy that company's clothes.

Cultural studies may or may not have political consequences, depending on how it is articulated (its capacity to draw the left away from what García Canclini calls a "Gutembergian" concept of cultural agency is salutory, in my opinion). By contrast, the subalternist project is *necessarily* a partisan one, something like a secular version of what liberation theology calls the "preferential option for the poor," and it shares with liberation theology the essential methodology of "listening to the poor," to use Gustavo Gutiérrez's phrase.[15] Here I am speaking only for myself; other members of the group aren't comfortable with this comparison, mistrusting a rhetoric that relies on the claim of organized religion to speak for the poor. What we do agree about, however, is that subaltern studies is—to quote our founding statement again—"a question not only of new ways of *looking* at the subaltern, new and more powerful forms of information retrieval, but also of building new relations between ourselves and those human contemporaries[16] whom we posit as objects of study" (Beverley and Oviedo 1993, 121).

We do not, in this sense, claim to represent the subaltern; we register instead the way in which the knowledge we construct and impart as academics is structured by the absence or difficulty or impossibility of representation of the subaltern. This is to recognize, however, the fundamental inadequacy of this knowledge and of the institutions that contain it, including the university, and therefore the need for social change in the direction of a more radically democratic and nonhierarchical social order.

Notes

1. Several of us had been discussing informally the implications of subaltern studies for our own work and decided to form an affinity group similar to the South Asian

one in the Latin American area. Our first meeting was at George Mason University in the spring of 1992, followed by a larger conference at Ohio State University in 1994 organized by Ileana Rodríguez. The group's founding statement, which was written and edited collectively for the George Mason meeting, is reproduced in Beverley and Oviedo (1993). We are aware that other groups of this kind have come into being around the country and in Latin America, and by no means want to claim that we have the franchise on the name or the idea.

2. Let me note in this respect that I regard more recent theories of postmodernist or postcolonial cultural agency, such as Antonio Cornejo Polar's idea of the Andean cultural system as a "contradictory totality," Michael Taussig's "epistemic murk," Homi Bhabha's "colonial mimicry," Barbara Harlow's "resistance literature," Gloria Anzaldúa's "borderlands," Mary Louise Pratt's "contact zone," or Néstor García Canclini's "cultural hybridity," as variations—sometimes consciously so—of the transculturation model, even where they seem to transfer its evidently modernist sense of aesthetic and ideological agency to the popular sectors and pop culture.

3. We also observed that the constitution of Latin American studies itself as a multi-disciplinary formation in the sixties (and of LASA as its organizational expression) anticipated the way in which Guha and his colleagues found it necessary to conceptualize the subaltern as a subject that emerges across, or at the intersections of, a wide range of academic disciplines as well as social positions.

4. The success or failure of the new ANC government in South Africa or of Aristide in Haiti, for example, will depend on their ability to embody hegemonically a sense of the national-popular. Forgacs (1984) offers a useful introduction to Gramsci's elaboration of this concept, which is deeply connected with his thoughts in The Prison Notebooks on the problem of the subaltern classes in Italian history.

5. Rama's Transculturación narrativa (1982) was itself not unrelated to dependency theory, in the sense that it pointed to the need to produce a radically "new" culture and literature that would break with previous patterns, just as dependentista economists were arguing that Latin America needed to "delink" from the world market.

6. I am inclined to read La ciudad letrada in fact as Rama's self-criticism of the efficacy of the ideology of the literary inherent in his own idea of narrative transculturation, a criticism framed by the incipient crisis of the project of the Latin American left in the early eighties (Rama himself was expelled from the United States by the Reagan administration). My book with Marc Zimmerman, Literature and Politics in the Central American Revolutions (1990) began with the hypothesis that certain forms of Central American literature had been a material factor—as an "ideological practice," in the Althusserian sense—in the construction of revolutionary movements in that region. However, it was our growing sense as we worked on the book of the limitations of literature (and after 1985 of the revolutionary movements themselves) as a model of popular empowerment—limitations revealed dramatically in the debates around the poetry workshop experiment in Nicaragua, for example—that led me in part to the work of the Asian Subaltern Studies Group and to the position I am elaborating here.

7. See on this point the critique of Gates's project, particularly around the question of canonizing slave narratives, in Judy (1993).

8. One place to study these implications is in the debate around the course Mary Louise Pratt and Renato Rosaldo developed for the Stanford Western Culture undergraduate requirement (D'Souza 1991; Pratt 1992a). Subalternist perspectives also impact in significant ways on education ideology and methodology generally, particularly in the area of literacy training and English: see, for example, Stuckey (1991) and Knoblauch and Brannon (1993).

9. There exists a perhaps apocryphal letter of Juan Bautista Tupac Amaru to Bolívar, in which he writes among other things that the blood of "mi tierno y venerado hermano . . . fue el ruego que había preparado aquella tierra para fructificar los mejores frutos que el gran Bolívar habrá de recoger con su mano valerosa y llena de la mayor generosidad" [my loving and venerable brother . . . had tilled the land whose best fruits will be harvested by Bolívar's courageous and generous hand]. Several historians have suggested a link between the *Memorias* and the program advanced by the party of Belgrano in the Wars of Independence, which included the idea of restoring the Inca empire.

10. "Just like any other reader, he (Rousseau) is bound to misread his text as the promise of political change. The error is not within the reader; language itself dissociates the cognition from the act. *Die Sprache verspricht (sich)*; to the extent that it is necessarily misleading, language just as necessarily conveys the promise of its own truth. This is also why textual allegories on this level of rhetorical complexity generate history" (de Man 1979, 277).

11. *Anti-literary* because writing was one of the symbols of colonial power itself. Guha notes, for example, that in the Indian peasant rebellions of the nineteenth century, "the want of literacy also made the peasants relate occasionally to a written utterance in such a way as to destroy its original motivation by deverbalizing it and exploit the resulting opacity in order to provide that graphic representation with new 'signifieds.'" He cites in particular the case of a leader of the Santal rebellion of 1855 who, as a sign of his authority, waved before his followers a sheaf of papers, "which proved on scrutiny to contain among other things 'an old Book on locomotives, a few visiting cards of Mr. Burn Engineer' and . . . a translation in some Indian language of the Gospel according to St. John. What is even more remarkable is that the rest of the papers said to have dropped from heaven and regarded by the Santal leaders as evidence of divine support for the insurrection had nothing inscribed on them at all either in writing or in print" (Guha 1983, 248–49).

12. Anibal Quijano has argued that there is an "Andean rationality" that parallels the project of the Enlightenment, but on a different historical "track," so to speak (in Beverley and Oviedo 1993, 154). In the case of South Africa, it is worth recalling that the Afrikaans white minority was also "creole" and anticolonial (in its relations to the British). In contrast to what is going on in South Africa today, one could say that, *mutatis mutandis*, apartheid "won" historically in Latin America. Indeed, apartheid may be a more accurate model of what happens in many parts of Latin American culture than the idea, which has been a mainstay of Latin American nationalism (and which is connected to the notion of transculturation, as I noted earlier), of a relatively benevolent racial-cultural *mestizaje*.

13. See, again, the carefully argued observations on the implications of a subalternist perspective for historical method and technique in Mallon 1994, which also contains a critique of our founding statement.

14. In our founding statement, we wrote that "the project of developing a Latin American Subaltern Studies Group such as the one we are proposing represents one aspect, albeit a crucial one, of the larger emergent field of Latin American Cultural Studies" (Beverley and Oviedo 1993, 116).

15. In a series of lectures on the new evangelism delivered at the Pittsburgh Theological Seminary in 1993, Gutiérrez noted that liberation theology means by "the poor" essentially the same thing as the subaltern, that is, those who do not have access to full "significance" as subjects in the dominant cultural codes. In the definition preferred by Guha, the subaltern is "the general attribute of subordination . . . whether this is expressed in terms of class, caste, age, gender, and office, or in any other way" (Guha and Spivak 1988, 35).

16. Today I would say "human and nonhuman contemporaries."

MABEL MORAÑA

The Boom of the Subaltern

Mabel Moraña was born in Uruguay in 1948. A literary and cultural critic, she is a professor at the University of Pittsburgh in Pennsylvania. Her main titles include *Literatura y cultura nacional en Hispanoamérica (1910–1940)* (1984), *Políticas de la escritura en
América Latina* (1997), and *De la colonia a la modernidad. Viaje al silencio: Exploraciones del
discurso barroco* (1998).

In recent years, cultural criticism has focused obsessively, from different
perspectives, on the concept of hybridity, extending its boundaries,
challenging its limits, and examining its theoretical value. Until this
revision started to take place, the concept appeared as an unquestionably
operative category in capturing the distinct and defining qualities of
Latin American history, a history marked since its Western origins by the
violence of colonial appropriation, and the coexistence of multiple cultures and conflicting political agendas. Within this context, cultural diversity has been approached from new perspectives that shed new light
on the ideological implication of categories that are proposed to capture
the Latin American condition.

Postcolonial debates have made us well aware of the enduring dichotomies established by imperial authority between colonizer and colonized, civilized and barbaric, developed and underdeveloped. At the
same time, those debates have shown that the multiplicity of exchanges
that take place both in colonial and in modern societies impose innumerable displacements, negotiations, and crossings between hegemonic and
dominated models, both culturally and politically. The importance of
these exchanges should not be understated. Nevertheless, the concepts
that are currently used to make reference to the processes and results of
multicultural interweaving, such as hybridity, miscegenation, heterogeneity, transculturation, should not be adopted without revision. Indeed,

they are constructs that are subject to multiple uses and articulations, and which have been the focus of comparative analysis as well as of theoretical, ideological, and political deconstruction in the last decade.

These notes are meant to be understood as a contribution to cultural debates focused on the production, reproduction, and appropriation of both central and peripheral knowledge in the transnational field of Latin Americanism. At the same time, throughout these pages I would like to make reference to the relationship between the notions of hybridity and subalternity, and particularly to the implications that occur with the appropriation of both concepts in this field of study. That is, I would like to consider the elaborations of these concepts from and on Latin America in connection to the creation of the "Third Space" that Homi Bhabha brings about when referring to the contradictory and ambivalent places from which one enunciates, discriminates, and interprets cultural practices.[1]

Since the decade of the 1960s, Latin Americans have assumed that the concept of *hybridity* captures the most salient trait of quotidian experience and cultural production in social formations that, from colonial times to the present, have had to negotiate their existence by defining projects and agendas in terms of their *locality* and their *foreignness*. Nevertheless, it is obvious that the interchanges between one and the other implied the understanding of complex processes of symbolic representation as well as the implementation of interpretative strategies that, as Althusser so long ago pointed out, allowed one to complement one's ignorance with the benefits of interdisciplinary shuffling.

The notion of hybridity was utilized in an "outright" way, as a synonym for syncretism, as a way to indicate a point of intersection or cultural exchange, and as a form of countervailing the colonialist ideology in America. As is well known, this ideology applied, from the time of the Discovery—with few variations—the principle of "one God, one king, one language" as a form of political subjugation and cultural equalization. I would like to concentrate here on contemporary appropriations of this notion, particularly in the field of Latin American studies in the second half of the twentieth century, keeping in mind the historical significance of the concept, inscribed from the beginning in the cultural history of Latin America.

In the decade of the 1970s, Antonio Cornejo Polar formalized a semantic field around the concept of heterogeneity that included and surpassed the descriptive level that was implicit in the notion of hybridity. His studies on the Andean region emphasized the coexistence of distinct and conflicting sociocultural systems that reveal the nation as a contradictory and fragmented totality (totalidad contradictoria), crossed over by multiple communicational forms, economic and cultural modes of production, and political agendas that contradict the liberal utopia of nationalist unification.[2]

In the same decade, the anthropological concept of transculturation extrapolated by Angel Rama from that field to the area of literary studies, constituted a new attempt to explore the topic of cultural transitivity in order to understand, in the context of political developmental policies, the place and function of Latin American intellectuals, as well as the possibilities and risks of their collaboration with state projects and national institutions in the context of modernity.[3]

With the micro-sociology practiced by Néstor García Canclini, hybridity becomes a central feature in processes of cultural transnationalization and systemic exchanges that take place in contemporary Latin American societies (1995a). The notion of hybridity contributes to the replacement of essentialist identitarian discourses with the new mystification of material and symbolic markets that propose a new space for the construction of collective subjectivity and the redefinition of citizenship. The market is proposed as the site where diverse subjects, projects, and agendas interweave, but also as a conciliatory civil space, where the exchange value of cultural goods incorporates new social and ideological dynamics on the basis of cultural reconversion and "democratization by consumption" (1995b). In the context of globalization, hybridity is again the discursive device that incorporates particularities into the new universality of transnational capitalism. More than a vindicating concept of social difference, hybridity appears in García Canclini as a formula for (re)conciliation and ideological negotiation between the main centers of world capitalism, the political entity of the nation-state, and the distinct social sectors that make up civil society in Latin America, each one from its own economic, political, and cultural affiliations.[4]

Up until this point, Latin American criticism utilized the notion of hybridity to elaborate a critique of modernity and liberal nationalism "from within," in an attempt to overcome the limitations of dependency theory, as well as the dichotomies that oppose popular and "high" cultures, vernacular and foreign cultural trends, central and peripheral spaces. Without having brought about a radical epistemological shift, the notion of hybridity incorporated a certain form of cultural fluidity into the vertical analysis of class. It permitted, for example, the topographical inscription of ethnic, linguistic, and gender diversity into the Latin American political map, only relatively challenging the limits of a cartography imposed from outside, with the instruments that imperialism has always used to mark territory, establish borders, and define the routes of access to the heart of the colonies.

In this sense, more than an ideological notion that situates itself in the interstitial point between hegemonic projects and discourses, the notion of hybridity seemed to open up an alternative space for Latin America, thus de-centering the parameters of aesthetic value and bourgeois political pragmatism, homogeneity, and centralization. The notion also opened up a theoretical route in the cultural narrative of the continent for the leadership of a collective *personage* that had been elaborated for a long time, from very different cultural and political fronts: *the masses, the people, the citizen,* the subaltern (according to different denominations). This political and cultural collective subject had been—partially and vicariously—represented before in the epic of anti-imperialist discourses and national social movements, but it was now being incorporated in its own right, into the ambiguous and often paradoxical performance of postmodern cultural politics.

With the end of the Cold War, the crisis of state socialism, and the consequent weakening of Marxist thought as a theoretical and political platform for the offsetting of neoliberalism and capitalist globalization, two phenomena gain particular relevance in the field of international Latin Americanism: first, the need to reestablish the centrality of spaces and discourses that define the position and the function of Latin America at a transnational level; second, the urgency to re-define forms of political agency in Latin America, along with the correlative problem of the representation of an *otherness* capable of subverting the new order (the new hegemony) in postmodern times.

It should not seem strange that, given this situation, the notion of hybridity has been the object of "central" readings that award it an increasing interpelative quality, a sort of "added value" that permits the reconstruction of Latin America's sociocultural image in the terms of occidentalist theorization. It is also not fortuitous that this appropriation of the concept coincides with the theme of political agency, debates on the role of the intellectual in the context of globalization, the re-definition of disciplinary boundaries, and the reflections on the ethics of cultural representation (see Castro Gómez and Mendieta 1998).

Particularly in the United States, the notion of hybridity is articulated to postcolonial thought as much as to the ideology of "minorities discourse," and to what Homi Bhabha rightfully calls the "anodyne liberal notion of multiculturalism."[5] Therefore, the notion of hybridity finds its place within a transdisciplinary debate that constructs Latin America, once again, as an object to be (re)presented from outside, that is, as an image that verifies the existence and function of the eye that watches it. In this context, hybridity has then become one of the ideological axes of postcolonial thought, marking the space of the periphery with the perspective of a critical neo-exoticism that maintains Latin America in the place of the other, a pre-theoretical place, calibanesque and marginal, with respect to metropolitan discourses.

Finally, hybridity facilitates a pseudo-integration of "Latin Americanness" into a theoretical apparatus created for other historical-cultural realities, thus providing the illusion of a rescue of third world specificities that does not surpass, in many cases, the rhetorical and discursive repertoires that were characteristic of cultural criticism of the 1960s. To provide an example, in The Post-Colonial Studies Reader edited by Bill Ashcroft, Gareth Griffiths, and Helen Tiffin (1995)—one of the most widely used texts for the academic diffusion of postcolonial theory—Latin America is only represented through the category provided by the notion of hybridity, a notion that provides a title for one of the sections of this critical anthology. But even in this minimal inclusion, only the notion of "magical realism" is mentioned in an attempt to demonstrate how postcolonial thought integrates the forms of the past into new cultural processes (e.g., the process of creolization), without relinquishing the epistemological bases from which otherness was constructed in the developmental horizon of modernity.[6] Gayatri Spivak and Fredric Jameson have also made reference to Latin American hybridity, connecting it to the works of Alejo Carpentier, Gabriel García Márquez, and other representatives of the boom, thus manipulating the inscription of the Latin American question into the theoretical context of postcolonialism.[7] This is a new demonstration that Latin America has never completely recovered from the "magical realism syndrome" that in the middle of the liberation struggles and anti-imperialist resistance of the 1960s endowed it with an exportable image of a celebrated and only moderately defiant neocolonial hybridity capable of brilliantly captivating the Western imagination and pricing itself on international markets, including the Swedish academy.

In this context of ideological negotiations and theoretical appropriations, and taking into account the unprecedented rupture of modernity's cultural and social paradigms, who are the actors that define cultural agency in Latin America, and which are the practices that allow us to identify their political agendas? How is it possible, in a panorama marked by the collapse of the grand narratives, to recuperate the value of small regional accounts—the vindications, uprisings, and agendas elaborated by groups that resist the control of a transnationalized power from positions that go beyond the rigidity of class structures without completely overcoming it? How should heterogeneity be understood in light of the fragmentation of the centers that are faced with the challenge of propounding new ideological bases for a postcolonial, postoccidental, posthistorical hegemony? From what positions is it possible to reinstate political agendas in analyses marked by radical culturalism? How can North-South relations be redefined in the context of globalization? Should this connection be perceived as the *in-between* ideological location from which one thinks and one constructs Latin America as the inevitable space of an *otherness* without which the "I" that speaks (that *can* speak, as Spivak has indicated) is de-centered as well as epistemologically and politically destabilized? How can the entry of premodern (hybrid) social formations into postmodernity be arbitrated, when neo-feudal enclaves still exist, when economic dependency, patriarchalism, and political authoritarianism still leave space for torture, internal colonialism, political impunity, exploitation, and marginality? How should the role of the intellectual be (re)established along with his or her unyielding messianic aspirations while a radical critique of the nation-state, of metropolitan centralism, of lettered practices is being undertaken and denounced as a symptom of the violence of the elites? Finally, from what position of *authority* (from which *authorial* definition, throughout which channels of *authorization*) should one vindicate the agenda of the new *lettered* left, which is well enthroned in academia, and which is part of the technocracy of postmodern humanism, without turning one's back to human rights, to submerged classes and marginalized subjectivities, and without abandoning the hopes of a truly equal integration of diverse Latin American regions in the global context?

I believe it remains clear that these questions intend to suggest at least two interconnected problems. The first is related to the necessity of rethinking the role that will be played in the current era by the centers that, due to their own internal development and international influence, identify themselves with the program of postmodernity. The second is related to the responsibility and (self-)legitimation that central and peripheral *intelligentsias* will assume, in this process of political-ideological re-articulation, with respect to the interpretation of new social movements in Latin America.[8] In spite of the fact that the theorization of globalization incorporates, without a doubt, new parameters into the problem of Latin American representation, many aspects related to this problem still create a situation of déjà vu that is worth analyzing.

In the era that was opened in Latin America at the beginning of the twentieth century, Angel Rama has observed the development of what he called a trend of "critical opposition thought" with concepts that could be used, almost unchanged, to explain the current situation. In that context, Rama described the power and the limits of the *opposing intellectual's* critical agenda as follows:

> During the ensuing decades, this current of opposition thought flowed into an idealistic, emotional, and spiritualized doctrine of social regeneration, contributed to an acerbic critique of late-nineteenth-century modernization (ignoring the opposition's own roots in that process), and launched a concerted assault on the lettered city. This assault was aimed at ousting its current occupants and at altering its ideological orientation, but not at abolishing its hierarchical function. (1996, 92–93)

The construction of a new postmodern version of Latin America elaborated from the "center" responds in large part to these same intentions: to make a *construct* out of Latin America that confirms the globalizing centrality and the theoretical (and even political) "avant-gardism" of those who interpret it and who aspire to (re)present it discursively.

The notion of *subalternity* has taken hold in the last decade mainly as a consequence of the epistemological re-centralization originating in the social changes that include the weakening of the Marxist model at the historical and theoretical levels. When marginalized and exploited sectors lose their voice and political representation, the multifaceted image of Indian, women, peasants, "lumpen," and vagabonds all flow together in a totalizing and "redemptorist" discourse destined to fill out the void left by setbacks suffered by socialist utopia. Through music, videos, *testimonios*, novels, an image is provided that rapidly penetrates the international market, giving rise not only to the commercialization of this cultural product from international centers, but also to a theoretical reshuffling that intends to totalize the Latin American hybrid empirical reality with homogenizing and universalizing concepts and principles.

When I make reference to the "boom of the subaltern" I am referring to the phenomenon of ideological dissemination of an all-encompassing, essentializing, and homogenizing category through which it is intended to embrace all of the above-mentioned social sectors, which exist subordinated to the discourses and the praxis of power. I understand that the concept of subalternity has been used as a relational and "migratory" category, that it is defined in situational terms, in an attempt to liberate it from both ahistorical essentialism and theoretical rigidity. Nonetheless, what new knowledge does this concept offer us? Where is the "other" located, and from what systems of ideological control is this placement legitimized?

The concept of subalternity is not new in the Latin American theoretical imagination. In the discourse of the independence—a discourse "authorized" by the legitimacy that derives from political praxis—the term is used to make reference to the dispossessed sectors that were marginalized by the colonial regime. Nevertheless, the derogatory connotation of the term impeded its utilization as an interpellation of the vast sectors to which the utopianism of the emancipation was supposed to address. In current theorizations the concept of subalternity becomes empowered by Gramscian elaboration, in which the Italian Marxist made reference to the popular strata that, in view of the historical unity of hegemonic classes, made themselves "present" through episodic movements and social disruptions. Gramsci makes specific reference to these disseminated and discontinuous popular movements, which showed variable and negotiable degrees of adhesion to the hegemonic discourses, and which could not yet be perceived as an articulated and organized form of political resistance.

The current elaboration of the concept violates, somehow, this discontinuous and episodic quality, converting subalternity into a globalizing narrative applied to a great variety of social subjects. In this manner, the political activism that laid the foundations for the texts included in the *Prison Notebooks* is being replaced by an intellectual exercise from which one can read, more than the story of the strategies of resistance of the dominated in the South, the history of representational hegemony of the North, in its new era of postcolonial re-articulation.

With the expression "the boom of the subaltern" I intend to put three levels in articulation: first, "boom" makes allusion to the ideological-conceptual montage that promotes subalternity as part of an exterior agenda, tied to a market where the notion is affirmed in terms of its use-value, in an ideological exchange that recognizes it as the name brand of a product that incorporates itself, through diverse strategies of promotion and ideological reproduction, into globalized cultural consumption. On the second level, the expression refers to the mode in which relations of sociopolitical subalternity (exploitation, subjection, exclusion, dependency) are transformed into *fields of knowledge*, where they are reproduced as objects of interpretation and spaces of representational power. On the third level, the expression refers to the way in which this object of knowledge is elaborated (transformed into a *theme*) from a determined discursive locality or place of enunciation: academia, cultural institutions at the international level, the ideological "vanguard," where the hierarchical location of the speaker seems to exempt him or her from the necessity of legitimizing the space from which she or he speaks.[9]

I would dare to say that for the Latin American subject—who all throughout history has been successively conquered, colonized, emancipated, civilized, modernized, Europeanized, developed, given consciousness, un-democratized (and with all impunity, re-democratized), and now globalized and subalternized by discourses that promised, each one in its context, the liberation of its soul—the current era could be interpreted as the way in which the left that lost the revolution intends to rebuild its agenda, its historical mission, and its lettered centrality, looking to define a new "otherness" in order to pass—"from outside and from above"—from representation to representativeness. This same individual that was, in time, subject, citizen, *hombre nuevo* enters now into the neocolonial epic by the false door of a denigrating condition elevated to the status of a theoretical category that, just now, in the middle of the vacancy left by the left that is starting to rebuild its political project, promises his or her discursive vindication. But one could always say that the tricks of alienation are, once again, preventing this subject from recognizing his image in the elaborations that objectify him.

Since hybridity has been converted into profitable material in discourses that intend to surpass and replace the ideology of the melting pot and *mestizaje* with the new ideology of multiculturalism and difference, the Latin American question has become part of the pastiche of postmodernity. In the new elaborations on hybridity and subalternity, in some ways, history has been dissolved (insofar as the distrust in bourgeois historiography continues to increase). In other cases, history appears subsumed in hermeneutic and culturalist montages, and heterogeneity is converted, paradoxically, into a leveling category that sacrifices empirical particularity to the necessity of theoretical coherence and equalization.

In this panorama of transdisciplinary and transnationalized impulses, there survives what Jean Franco—among others—pointed out some time ago with respect to the place occupied by Latin America in the intellectual mapping redefined by cultural criticism. Franco indicated the effects and the dangers of theoretical domination exercised from the main centers of neoliberal capitalism. From those, cultural institutions and intellectuals still assume—more often than not—the necessity of theorizing not only on but *for* Latin America, which is still considered incapable of producing its own parameters of knowledge. The supposed virginity of America, a continent that has been presented since the Conquest as a blank sheet where Western history should be inscribed, provided the matrix for the conception of the continent as an "*other*" world, *a place of desire* situated in the alterity that was assigned to it by successive empires that appropriated it economically, politically, and culturally, with different strategies and in various degrees, all throughout a development that alienated American peoples from their own memory and notion of historical origin, except for the ones that the imperial agendas successively assigned them.

Theoretically localized as the "subcontinent," a portion of a "Third World," "the backyard" of the United States, a union of "young" nations that arrived late to the banquet of modernity, Latin American countries were always suspended in the uncertain process of satisfying exterior models, and considered an unfulfilled society, always in the process of development. For many, Latin America still continues to be a pretheoretical and virginal space, without history (in the Hegelian sense), a place of subalternity that opens itself to theoretical voracity as well as to economic appropriation. It continues to be seen, in this sense, as the exporter of primary cultural materials and the importer of theoretical paradigms, manufactured in the centers that become wealthy with the products that they place in the same markets that supply them in the first place.

In summary, hybridity and subalternity are, at this moment, more than productive concepts for a more profound and decolonized comprehension of Latin America, important notions for the understanding of North-South relations, and for the re-foundation of the "epistemological privilege" that certain places of enunciation continue to maintain in the context of globalization. Those notions propose, among other things, the question about the position that postmodernity has assigned to Latin America as a space of observation and cultural representation, and as a laboratory for new neoliberal hermeneutics. Finally, Latin America is included as part of the agenda of a new left that, while in search of its voice and its new historical mission, proposes itself as the vanguard of globalization, thus reinforcing its own centrality and the predominance of a technocratic intellectuality. The binomial hybridity-subalternity compels one to think of two other related notions: *sub-identity and sub-alterity*, and of the new fundamentalisms to which these ideas can lead us.

Both notions offer themselves to theoretical reflection and, once again, they reopen the challenge of thinking the nation as a "global village" (that is, as a conflictive grouping of regions, cultural spaces, languages, and political projects) from which resistance to new forms of cultural colonization and hegemony can be exercised, resistance, mainly, to the politics of exclusion, authoritarianism, and colonialist exploitation that will be added in this new era to the exclusionary strategies of modernity.

Translated by Susan Hallstead

Notes

1. Homi Bhabha refers to the "Third Space" as the nonrepresentable area between the I and the You in which discursive conditions are established. It is the space in which meaning is created as a communicational and ideological process of exchange and negotiation, where signs are appropriated, translated, and received, without fixation or necessary unity (1994a, 37).

2. Cornejo Polar developed the concept of heterogeneity beginning in the late 1970s, in combination with the ideas of "contradictory and nondialectic social totalities." Later on, he complemented this with the study on migration and construction of collective subjectivities. For an evolution of the concept see Moraña (1995).

3. As is well known, Rama elaborates Fernando Ortiz's idea of transculturation, which had already been appropriated by Mariano Picón Salas, to study the connection between modernity and vernacular cultures in Latin America, particularly in the literary production of the 1940s. For a discussion of the concept see Moraña (1997).

4. It is very interesting to see the "dialogue" between García Canclini (1999a) and Cornejo Polar's posthumous article "Mestizaje e hibridez: los riesgos de las metáforas" (1997), in which both critics discuss the limits and theoretical implications of the concept of hybridity. For a comparative approach to the concepts of hybridity, heterogeneity, *mestizaje*, and transculturation, see the articles by Friedhelm Schmidt, Martín Lienhard, and Raúl Bueno (Mazzotti and Zevallos Aguilar 1996).

5. "Cultural diversity is the recognition of pre-given cultural 'contents' and customs, held in a time-frame of relativism; it gives rise to anodyne liberal notions of multiculturalism, cultural exchange, or the culture of humanity" (Bhabha 1995a, 206).

6. For a connection of the ideology of magical realism with Latin American studies see Von der Walde (1998) and Zamora and Faris (1995).

7. Spivak has interpreted Latin American magical realism in terms of the allegorization of a continent that cannot achieve decolonization. In her own words:

Why is "magical realism" paradigmatic of Third World literary production? In a bit, and in the hands of the less gifted teacher, only that literary style will begin to count as ethnically authentic. There is, after all, a reason why Latin America qualifies as the norm of "the Third World" from the United States, even as India used to be the authentic margin for the British. It is interesting that "magical realism," a style of Latin American provenance, has been used to great effect by some expatriate or diasporic subcontinentals writing in English. Yet, as the Ariel-Caliban debates dramatize, Latin America has not participated in decolonization. Certainly this formal conduct of magical realism can be said to allegorize, in the strictest possible sense, a socius and a political configuration where "decolonization" cannot be narrativized. . . . In the greater part of the Third World, the problem is that the declared rupture of "decolonization" boringly repeats the rhythms of colonization with the consolidation of recognizable styles. (1990, 297)

For a discussion of Spivak's and Jameson's positions on this issue see De la Campa (1999, 7–14).

8. It would be interesting to relate these problems to Nelly Richard's analysis of disciplinary changes in the field of Latin Americanism (1998c).

9. For a critical approach of the concept of subalternity and of subaltern studies see G. Williams (1996) and Mallon (1994). For an overview of articles from the perspective of subaltern studies see the articles offered in Spanish translation by Rivera Cusicanqui and Barragan (1997).

GEORGE YÚDICE

Latin American Intellectuals in a Post-Hegemonic Era

George Yúdice was born in the United States in 1947. A literary and cultural critic, he is a professor at New York University. His main publications include *On Edge: The Crisis of Contemporary Latin American Culture*, coedited with Jean Franco and Juan Flores (1992), "Transnational Brokering of Art" (1995), "Globalización de la cultura y nueva sociedad civil" (1997), and *Cultural Policy*, coedited with Toby Miller (2002).

Much has been written about Latin American intellectuals who established epochal ideologies from the early nineteenth century until the late 1960s. For example, the anticolonialist Americanism of the independence period; the elite liberal or positivist republicanism of the period of national consolidation, largely exclusive of Indians and blacks, in the second half of the nineteenth century; the critique of U.S. forms of progress in the late nineteenth century and early twentieth; the construction of a national-popular and revolutionary ideology in the first two or three decades of the twentieth century; the rise of *mestizo* national identities in the late 1930s and 1940s, which sought to integrate popular classes, Indians, and blacks; and the development of a revolutionary utopianism at the end of the 1950s and throughout the 1960s. Curiously, little has been written about intellectuals as such for the period ranging from the military dictatorships of the late 1960s to the so-called transition to democracy in the 1980s and 1990s. In this latter period, we witness much talk about the agency of social movements and civil society organizations. I think it would be safe to say that for the period before the 1970s, intellectuals were thought of predominantly as the *letrados*, the poets and artists whose opinion-shaping writing and work circulated in journals, universities, political parties, civic forums, conferences, and so on. The social movement or civil society activist is generally not thought of as an intellectual in the same terms, unless, of course, one applies Gramsci's understanding of that figure.

According to Gramsci, every social group that plays a role in economic production "creates together with itself, organically, one or more strata of intellectuals which give it homogeneity and an awareness of its own function not only in the economic but also in the social and political fields." Such unified awareness requires "cultural battle," not only to create a class consciousness but also to generalize that consciousness to other classes to achieve hegemony, which is a historical act. "A historical act can only be performed by 'collective man,' and this presupposes the attainment of a 'cultural-social' unity through which a multiplicity of dispersed wills, with heterogeneous aims, are welded together with a single aim, on the basis of an equal and common conception of the world. . . . Great importance is assumed by the general question of language, that is, the question of collectively attaining a single cultural 'climate.'" This broadening of the sphere of intellectual action leads Gramsci to declare that "all men are intellectuals" insofar as they "participate . . . in a particular conception of the world . . . and therefore contribute . . . to sustain a conception of the world or to modify it, that is, to bring into being new modes of thought" (1971, 3, 348–49, and 9).

This brief account of the pre-1970s is of course inadequate. It excludes, among other things, other-than-progressive intellectuals, who seemed to come to prominence with the Vargas Llosas and Octavio Pazes of the 1970s and later. The focus on intellectuals who may have spoken in behalf of the popular classes also excludes popular figures themselves who led working-class movements among peasants and miners. But it does capture the prevailing image of the pre-1970s intellectual, who presumably engaged in mental and cultural work to attain what Gramsci referred to as a "single cultural 'climate,'" something that is difficult to say about the movements of the 1980s and 1990s, with the exception, perhaps, of Sandinismo and the FMLN, which in any case, made some nods in the direction of women's movements and were forced to recognize other than national groups living in what they thought to be their territory (think of the Miskitos).

While there has been a revival of populism or neopopulism in the 1990s (Menem, Fujimori, Chávez), this is clearly not the same as the national popular struggles of the 1930s and 1940s. Yet the notion of the popular continues to set the tenor of our (i.e., of progressives') ideas of whom intellectuals should work in behalf of. I would argue that the popular has transformed into the mass (with the emergence of the mass culture industries of the 1960s) and civil society actors in the transition to democracy. The notion of the popular was used by Gramsci in his diagnosis of the rise of fascism in 1920s Italy and as part of his program for moving Italian politics in a more revolutionary direction. In his estimation, progressive Italian intellectuals were out of touch with the social forces, particularly the "popular masses," necessary for the construction of a "national-popular" consciousness and "collective will" that in turn were necessary for revolution. Unlike the French Jacobins, the intellectuals of the Risorgimento were absorbed into the Action Party that served the interests of the northern (Piedmontese) capitalists (1971, 204). Gramsci calls this northern dominance a "dictatorship without hegemony," in which Piedmont stood in for but did not properly function as a "leading" social group (1971, 106).

The construction of a national-popular will in Latin American societies faced similar challenges to those outlined by Gramsci. Juan Carlos Portantiero, for example, considered Gramsci's analysis of "Caesarism" and "Bonapartism" applicable to Latin America nationalist populisms, particularly Varguismo in Brazil, Cardenismo in Mexico, Peronismo in Argentina, and Aprismo in Peru (1981). This situation results when a potentially catastrophic contention between social forces is intervened in by a third actor, for example the military, which brings into play an array of "auxiliary (often popular) forces directed by, or subjected to, their hegemonic influence," and "succeeds in permeating the state with its interests, up to a certain point, and in replacing a part of the leading personnel" (Gramsci 1971, 219–20). In this case, the popular forces do not, obviously, take power, but some of their agendas, particularly those which have been articulated into the third actor's ideological offensive against dominant forces, are incorporated into state policies. The abovementioned populisms have left deep marks, which were suppressed by the dictatorships and are only now, under neoliberalism, being fully scuffed into oblivion as the clientelist and corporatist welfare states are dismantled.

The historical circumstances that enabled the rise of this classic Latin American populism changed in the 1960s. Import substitution industrialization was no longer viable in the world economy and power blocs were reunited under the control of transnational capitalism. Leftist articulations of populism, transmuted into guerrilla movements in many contexts, were energetically countered by new military dictatorships (Southern Cone) or authoritarian governments (Mexico). The anti-insurgency policies of the United States were an important intervention in these circumstances, offering the carrot of aid for development (e.g., the Alliance for Progress) and the stick of military intervention (e.g., the Chilean coup) and training (e.g., the School of the Americas). Analytically, as the dominant classes could no longer transform and neutralize these radicalized populisms, outright coercion (torture, massacres, disappearances) became the prescribed instruments to rein in the threats. At the same time, new media industries, especially television, whose reorganization under conglomerates like Mexico's Televisa and Brazil's TV Globo were facilitated by these repressive governments, began to transform the *popular* into the *mass*. The mass media, of course, have a longer history in Latin America than this turning point in the 1960s; they became significant players in modernization and education as early as the beginning of the century in some countries.

According to Renato Ortiz, the 1960s represent the crystallization of a common cultural consciousness among so-called popular sectors and leftist intellectuals with the potential to create an alternative hegemony which might change the "equilibrium" between political and civil society within the state. In countries like those of the Southern Cone, Brazil, and Mexico, it is not possible to speak of hegemony as an equilibrium between political and civil society. Ortiz, for example, writes of the "precariousness of the very idea of hegemony among us" (R. Ortiz 1988, 65). Instead, what characterized countries such as Argentina, Brazil, and Mexico was a pact between state-aligned elites who promoted import substitution industrialization and an equally state-aligned popular nationalism that sought state welfare, delivered in corporatist forms since the 1920s and 1930s. The origins of "popular culture" in Latin America can be traced to this paradoxical state, which recreated those institutions most responsible for supporting that culture: education, radio, film, museums, and anthropological institutions. It is through these institutions that a good deal of "people's culture" was disseminated, not outside of the market but squarely within the culture industries. The most salient examples are samba and carnival in Brazil and *rancheras* on radio and in film in Mexico. The nationalization of samba, for example, involved the intervention of the Vargas regime in the 1930s, the radio broadcasting and recording industries, as well as various social institutions, such as carnival, and "popular" networks (Raphael 1980; Vianna 1995). The shift that took place in the 1960s was the incipient accommodation of Brazilian and Mexican media to international standards. This mass mediated internationalization, often considered "Americanization," has had significant consequences for the rearticulation of the "national popular."

By the time the dictatorships gave way to a new phase of democratization under a neoliberal consensus, the media and a host of new civil society forms of organization articulated the new logic under which popular antagonisms would be negotiated. This does not mean that the racialized popular mass of the population ceased to be a force to contend with; it did mean that the possibility of radicalizing their demands in socialist terms became increasingly unlikely. Neoliberal populisms in the 1980s and 1990s in Argentina (Menem), Brazil (Collor), and Peru (Fujimori) revealed the degree to which the form of incorporating popular classes had changed. Furthermore, the defeat of the Central American revolutions, the utter marginalization of Cuba, particularly after the demise of the Soviet Union, and the "fundamentalization" or criminalization of several guerrilla struggles, especially in Peru and Colombia, signaled the unworkability of change by means of armed insurrection. Indeed, many "national liberation fronts" (e.g., the Sandinistas and the Salvadoran FMLN transformed themselves into civil society organizations after more than a decade of struggle, as did the neo-Zapatistas almost immediately. I have argued elsewhere that the recourse to civil society (succored by U.S. foundations and European and global nongovernmental organizations) is fully compatible with neoliberalism (1998, 372). As state budgets for social programs are cut, it makes sense to free market advocates to have civil society "organize itself," a turn of events examined by the Mexican intellectual Carlos Monsiváis in *Entrada libre: crónicas de la sociedad que se organiza* (1987).

The rethinking of the popular comes with an exuberant rejection of its incorporation into a national discourse. This is no doubt due to the fear that a radicalization of populism will engender those forces to which the dictatorships reacted. It is also due to the recognition that globalization has altered the circumstances under which it was politically viable to appeal to the popular for progressive ends. Without progressive potential, the popular—and the claims that it serves as the ground for opposition to imperialism—becomes a fetishized symbol of Latin America's hybrid temporality, caught between the magic of the traditional and the indigenous or African and the realist "rationality" of modernity. For example, José Joaquín Brunner, one of the most influential intellectuals of the transition to democracy in Chile, reviles the national-popular as an outdated myth. Echoing García Canclini's recognition of the hybridization of popular traditions with the market and mass culture, Brunner breathes a sigh of relief as the national-popular subject recedes into insignificance (1990, 21).

Let me briefly focus on one intellectual's change of view with respect to the popular. Throughout the 1980s, García Canclini's interests developed gradually from policies that presume that popular groups can take control of the production and consumption process to a more mediated understanding of how appropriation works in fragmented urban settings in the context of an increasing tendency to consume "international popular" culture.[1]

> Consider that today no "national" cinema can recoup investment in a film from ticket sales within its own borders. It has to target multiple sales venues: satellite and cable television, networks of video and laser disk rental outlets. All of these systems, structured transnationally, facilitate the "defolklorization" of messages they put into circulation. (García Canclini 1995a, 111; my translation)

These conditions foster a collective memory made from the fragments of different nations, making it difficult for that memory to be distilled from any one particular group, although "American" references may predominate (R. Ortiz 1994, 139). We are reminded here of Appadurai's suggestion that supranational cultural formations (e.g., the Indian diaspora or Latinos in the United States) emerge from processes of deterritorialization of peoples, commodities, money, images, and ideologies (Appadurai 1996, 38). Under these conditions, of what some have considered a "global ecumene" and others Armageddon, the familiar "national-popular" constructions of medium-scale nations (Spain, Yugoslavia, Britain, Italy) obviously founder and give way to a range of smaller nationalisms (Catalonian, Basque, Serbian, Albanian, Scottish, Padanian) and supranational federations (the European Union) and trade agreements in search of a supranational cultural cement (Mercosur).

The "popular" has also given way to a social movement framework, at first associated with opposition to dictatorships and subsequently to democratization in the context of the postdictatorial and postauthoritarian transition. In this latter context and under the sway of neoliberalizing economies and polities, social movements have tended to accommodate to a civil society paradigm, according to which citizens engage in voluntary associations, often organized as nongovernmental organizations (predominant in Latin America) or nonprofit organizations (typical of the United States), to perform a myriad of social services, including cultural activities. Fiscal and juridical forms of organization have begun to take precedence over the local political bosses who integrated "popular sectors" into clientelist networks. Civil society networks and NGOs are flexible and nomadic, capable of producing a sense of participation, if not always meeting the needs of the population. There are, of course, many situations in which this model does not seem to correspond to the antagonisms brought forth by subordinated groups. The Colombian guerrillas and the Sendero Luminoso in Peru certainly are not good examples of democratic organizations. There is, however, no theory of civil society that can easily exclude those associations that manifest undemocratic behavior. García Canclini recognizes the paradox that the effort to institute democracy may already be tainted by the inclusion of nondemocratic groups. "How can a program that is democratic and respectful of groups structures be established if the structures in question are paternalistic, authoritarian, and based on bonds of blood rather than affinity? Moreover, what if the state that promotes democratization is also racked by these same nondemocratic characteristics?" (1995a, 178). One might, following David Ronfeldt, characterize these as manifestations of "uncivil society," which are just as likely as democratizing social movements to emerge in a polity in which state authority is undervalued and a premium is put on difference, decentralization, and voluntary association (1995). The focus of attention, however, has been on those mobilizations that further the democratization of national societies, such as the neo-Zapatistas or the Brazilian movement of the landless (Movimento dos Sem Terra). While the latter two seem to have maintained a certain autonomy from the state and capital, most civil society organizations are permeable by institutions of the corporate sector, the government, and the "globalized civil society" of international NGOs. The supposed autonomy of social movements—their particularly social, as opposed to political agendas—does not obtain independently of channeling by capital and the state.

As we shall see, what we have commonly thought of as the often contentious new social movements have made common cause with international foundations and many government agencies in creating a "collaborative" civil society (Yúdice 1998). This tendency is global and local at the same time and indeed marks a new development in conceptualizing the scope of culture, politics, and agency. Indeed, civil society, often theorized as independent of the state, is in contrast defined by Foucault as the "concrete ensemble within which these abstract points, economic men, need to be positioned in order to be made adequately manageable" (Foucault 1979). In the Brazilian case, and indeed for many Latin American countries, it has been pointed out that governments have sought to shift the question of welfare from the traditional clientelist model to civil society. International foundations and NGOs are complicit with this shift, for they have fostered what Sonia Alvarez calls the "NGOization." We might say that in Brazil it is only with NGOization that there is an institutional place for social movements. Nongovernmental organizations articulated the political-communicative networks that sustained the larger oppositional field and new social movements. Various forms of "participatory" citizen councils proliferated in the 1980s—innovative spaces for civil society intervention in public policymaking, many actively promoted by Workers Party (PT) administrations. Popular movements and feminist versions thereof became key sites for enacting cultural politics, that is, for publicizing disputes over received and alternative meanings of notions such as participation and representation.

By the 1990s, these movements were reshaped by what Fernando Henrique Cardoso had once called a new "pact of domination," grounded in qualified democracy and neoliberal social and economic policies. Civil society wasn't suppressed; it was subjected to a new regime of discipline as NGOs were largely absorbed into partnerships with the state. Their result is that the express official preference for civil(ized) civil society—quite pronounced under the Cardoso administration—has narrowed the political space for contentious politics. In the meantime, cultural politics has burgeoned.

Let me turn to one example, which expresses well how neopopular intellectuals negotiate with NGOs and the state, making culture an activist resource as well as a "good business." The "cultural turn" in social movement activism is conditioned both by mobilization of "non-normative" groups as it is by governmentalization, as I will explain later in this essay. The recent transformation of cultural policy along neoliberal lines in Brazil—that is, seeing it as fully compatible with an entrepreneurial, business ethos—has contributed to both the cultural activism and its governmentalization. Consider that renovation of the Pelourinho, Bahia's highly symbolic colonial site for trading and punishing slaves, and for the past two decades the major tourist center, was conceived in partnership with the Inter-American Development Bank, UNESCO, and local community activist and corporate groups. As a recent brochure introducing the new tax incentives for cultural support known as the Rouanet Law expresses it, "Cultura É Um Bom Negócio" [Culture Is Good for Business]. Both of the cultural groups or networks examined here have "capitalized on" these incentives.

Most Americans have probably heard of the music group from Bahia called Olodum. They played on Paul Simon's "The Obvious Child" in his 1991 *Rhythm of the Saints* album. More recently, they appeared in Michael Jackson's music video "They Don't Really Care about Us," directed by

Spike Lee. What Americans are less likely to know is that Olodum is also at the center of a civil society movement whose objective is to better life conditions for the poorer, mostly black residents of Salvador. Olodum, in fact, gained official NGO status in order to carry out its activism on behalf of Afro-Brazilians. As an NGO, Olodum conducts campaigns to find solutions for racism, AIDS, cholera, urban blight, and youth homelessness. Moreover, Olodum spearheaded the renovation of the Pelourinho, taking leadership in a partnership that included corporations, foundations, international NGOs, government institutions, banks, the church, and tourist enterprises that collaborated on this expensive project. Parlayed into the most vibrant site of heritage tourism in Brazil, the Pelourinho has afforded Olodum a veritable mall for its outlet of heritage accessories.

Most Americans have not heard of the Grupo Cultural AfroReggae, formed by young residents of the *favela* Vigário Geral in Rio de Janeiro. Like Olodum, it is also part of a network of heterogeneous institutions. It was founded to combat the escalating violence which, as in many other large urban centers, most affects racialized poor youth. AfroReggae's self-description begins with the following statement: "The work carried out by the Núcleo de Vigário Geral acquired salience due to international awareness that this community is racked by violence, by the action of the police and narcotraffickers" (AfroReggae, *Campanha do Metro*). Subsequently, the group enlarged its scope beyond its consciousness-raising activities, its bang-on-drum band, and fundraising activities on behalf of the poor to take on a wide range of actions, in partnership with other organizations and institutions from the corporate sector to the government and other social actors. Like Olodum, it has made its performances of cultural identity—Afro-diasporic identity linked to music—compatible with business, even earning awards from Reebok and other transnational corporations.

The historical conjuncture in which these networks arise is comprised of the following features: (1) the eradication of revolutionary populism by the Brazilian and Southern Cone dictatorships of the 1960s, 1970s, and 1980s, or the authoritarian-paternalistic rule characteristic of countries like Mexico; (2) the emergence of social movements that could not appeal directly to politics, yet stretched the significance of the cultural and the personal to the point of having political effects; (3) (re-)democratization and incorporation of social movements under the international hegemony of neoliberalism in the 1980s and 1990s; (4) the demise of socialism, which left little opposition to the legitimacy claimed by neoliberals in their program to transform (through structural adjustment, privatization, and downsizing of the public sector) the legacy of the national-popular or national-populist state (a process which is still taking place); (5) increasing dispersion of so-called popular sectors due to urbanization and urban sprawl, to the point, as García Canclini has argued, that there is little communication across difficult-to-reach sections of the megalopolis; (6) the abandonment of public spaces for traditional forms of congregation due, again, to urban sprawl but more significantly to a preference for home delivery of entertainment via television, video, and cable; and (7) the concomitant transnationalization of publicness due to various forms of supranational linkages, from migrant circuits to multinational networks and supranational regional integration agreements like NAFTA and MERCOSUR that are rearticulating one of the most powerful forms of cultural affiliation: national identity.

Under these circumstances, the "popular" has lost its significance. Using Ernesto Laclau's terminology we might say that it is no longer politically significant for the struggle for hegemony; it no longer serves as a means to articulate "the people" into class discourse. The groups that he writes about do not characterize themselves by making recourse to "the people." You will remember that Laclau's account of ideology turns on the creation or negotiation of a sociosemantic space by nonclass elements (such as the nation or the people) whose meaningfulness would be delivered by class discourse. Any class can make claims on these symbols and values or ideologemes. And hegemony would be achieved when the horizon of meaning in a social formation is established because it is compelling to subjects who respond to those symbols and values. What makes an ideology compelling is, precisely, the *articulation* of diverse agendas such that, for example, at a particular historical moment domination or opposition can be articulated with specific projects. Laclau gives the following example:

> Let us imagine a semi-colonial social formation in which a dominant fraction of landowners exploits indigenous peasant communities. The ideology of the dominant bloc is liberal and Europeanist, while that of the exploited peasantry is anti-European, indigenist, and communitarian. This second ideology—the sole opponent of the power bloc—has therefore, a clear peasant origin. In that society develops a growing urban opposition of middle and working classes who challenge the hegemonic landowning fraction's monopoly of power. In these circumstances, the organic intellectuals of these new groups, trying to make their political opposition consistent and systematic,

increasingly appeal to the symbols and values of peasant groups because they constitute the only ideological raw materials which, in this social formation, express a radical confrontation with the power bloc. (Laclau 1977,
171–72)

My argument is that in societies in which social movements are
thought of in terms of civil society rather than "popular movements," the
ideological struggle no longer takes the form that Laclau elucidated. Political struggle under neoliberalism increasingly works from the basis of
a civil society paradigm, which prioritizes difference over the kind of
imaginary totalizing that national identity presumed in the era of the
popular. This means that the expression of antagonism will change. It
also means that the cultural sphere, as a generator of difference in post-
transition Latin America, will have priority as well. The expansion or reconversion of human rights to civil rights in the aftermath of dictatorship and authoritarianism has produced a situation in which rights are
increasingly claimed on the basis of cultural difference, something that
would have been meaningless and indeed counterproductive in the age of
the popular. While the expansion of human rights has given some
strength to civil society-type activism, the claims made on the basis of
difference have, paradoxically, weakened the potential for mass mobilization and instead foster a diversity of movements, often with competing
agendas. Furthermore, the logic of the popular is no longer compelling,
no longer enables opposition that can be channeled by a clear ideology.
The fit between this curious development of "civil society" (associations
that act in their own interest) and neoliberalism (which remodels the
state to serve as the broker for international capital, with minimal attention to social welfare demands) functions as the seemingly noncoercive
successor of the repressive means by which authoritarian dictatorships
dealt with the problem of what Laclau calls transformism (1977, 172–73).

These new civil society groups, and especially the ones that I call networks, are, unlike their predecessors, not absorbed in the machinations
of populist leaders or tied to the state through corporatist structures.
While personalist politicians like Brizola have had the loyalty of a large
percentage of favela or barrio residents and the rural poor, the new networks have charted a different path. They are not incorporated corpora-
tistically into the state, for there is no reason for this. Most members of
these networks do not have formal employment. In fact, one of their activities is to train favela youth to get jobs, many in the informal economy,
such as working in entertainment, particularly music and dance.

Popular groups absorbed into corporatist and populist circuits were,

unlike Olodum or AfroReggae, not structured as a network of articulations that extends from the barrio to the largest NGOs and foundations
from the United States (I interviewed the coordinator, José Júnior, at the
Ford Foundation's regional office in Rio) and from Europe (Médecins
sans frontières), linked as well to municipal, state, national, and transnational agencies (from the local tourist board to UNESCO). They also
are linked to other networks, like the ones that connect them to various
musical and cultural groups of the African diaspora in the Caribbean and
the United States. In Rio itself, AfroReggae is linked to IBASE (Instituto
Brasileiro para a Análise da Sociedade e da Economia, a social science research think tank that, like the Washington-based Institute for Policy
Studies, monitors political activity), the Caixa Econômica Federal, the
citizen action initiative Viva Rio, the CEAP (Centro de Articulação das
Populações Marginalizadas), and many other NGOs, corporations, and
parties.

When one reads the documents these groups disseminate, or talks to
them about their projects, one can't help but notice their use of terminology as advocates of civil society. Olodum's Social Program has as a fundamental task the enabling of the exercise of citizenship, especially
through cultural incentives as well as education. It develops educational
activities that emphasize the practice of human rights, democracy, and
an entrepreneurial self-reliance. Olodum touts the "Carnival Associations (that) are emerging as building blocks for black economic and political power," and has even founded a factory and a chain of boutiques.
Business and civil society go together; de Tocqueville lurks in the cultural
unconscious of such groups. Moreover, Olodum has developed the exper-
tise to capitalize on the new incentives for culture recently passed by the
Brazilian legislature. It is consistent with major international initiatives,
such as UNESCO's Culture and Development Task Force, to transform
culture into a major resource. AfroReggae has as its guiding premises
"communication, combating violence, the recuperation of self-esteem
and citizenship for the youths" of the *favelas*, and networking with other
NGOs. This "deepening" of civil society (social formation, professional-
ization, cultural development) will keep these youths from the very kind
of clientelist circuits that revolve around *caudillos*, only in this case, the
chefões or chiefs of narcotraffic, prostitution, and informal employment
(AfroReggae, *Campanha do Metro*). Like Olodum, AfroReggae publishes a
newspaper and has a listserve with a global list of subscribers and a home
page, announcing activities and conducting further outreach.

These groups are capable of very sophisticated self-analysis. In an article on its own activities, AfroReggae assesses the dangers of putting all

the eggs of their activism in the basket of civil society. The article warns of the "dilemma in which all nongovernmental organizations find themselves. On the one hand, they help construct the process of civil society democratization, which is laudable. . . . On the other hand, however, they run the risk of facilitating the state's retreat from social programs. Consequently, NGOs should not aim to take over state functions. The ideal is to establish an interface between civil society and the government" ("AfroReggae vira tese de mestrado").

This is not a language that is learned spontaneously in popular mobilization, but is part and parcel of the activities of the networks brought together by such *citizen action initiatives* like Ação da Cidadania, founded and coordinated until his death in 1997 by Herbert de Souza, and Viva Rio, coordinated by Rubem César Fernandes. Both of these men have also either worked in academia or collaborated on important work on social mobilization with academics. They form an important linkage between practice, analysis, and theory. And they both have been directors of major research institutions. Betinho led IBASE, and Rubem is director of the ISER (Institute for the Study of Religion).

It does not make much sense then to assimilate social movements to the traditional category of the popular, and its role in processes of hegemony, when the state is undergoing a sea change, in relation to the economic projects of neoliberal elites and the processes of economic and technological globalization. Certainly, the response of the state to the international economy is not new, as Polanyi demonstrated long ago. But there is a difference in the degree to which the state can stay in control of the economy and other transnational processes such as migration. But the most important change in Latin American states is certainly not the dependent economic status, but rather the move away from centralization to de-centering or dispersion of decision making (Chalmers et al. 558). If the state was the major broker of the public sector, from the times of Vasconcelos's reorganization of education in Mexico to those of Cárdenas's wholesale revamping of the public sector—we could also refer to Vargas in Brazil (e.g., his Estado Novo's intervention in popular music), and Perón in Argentina—today decision making about all aspects of economic, social, and cultural life is beginning to take place in many sites, inducing social and political actors, "including those from the popular sectors, to target those varied, and often changing, centers of decision making" (558). In some cases, these sites extend beyond the boundaries of the nation-state, such as when private actors from one country find it more effective to lobby in the deliberative bodies of another country.

I would like to end this essay with a comment on governmentality and agency. Foucault used the notion of governmentality to characterize the ways in which people's action is channeled by the institutions of the state as well as those of what we have been calling civil society (Foucault 1991, 53). An example is the very use of NGO and foundation categories in the discourse of AfroReggae and Olodum. Scholars interested in effective opposition to domination are correctly concerned that characterizations of action as being dictated from the top down are a mischaracterization and perpetuate the harm of domination. Agency—the ability to take up action—is usually wielded against this kind of top-down view. However, it should be clear that there is no unilateral action. Agency in this sense is a faulty concept. We might say the same about agency that Bakhtin said about language—it is never wholly one's own. One has to appropriate it by re-articulating others' voices. Agency succeeds to the degree that an individual or a group can make one's own the multiplicity of institutional venues through which initiative, action, policy, and so forth are negotiated. This notion of an orchestrated and negotiated agency is recognized by the groups I have been studying, from Olodum and AfroReggae to Ação da Cidadania and Viva Rio. But orchestration and negotiation require work and effort. They do not happen simply through the action of a given group. They require a range of individuals, groups, organizations, and intermediaries to help provide interfaces among diverse agendas, say those of a neighborhood group vis-à-vis a church, a local government, a national or regional NGO, and international foundations. It is for this reason that the groups I have presented here prefer to present themselves as networks. Like the figure of the author many years ago, the figure of the intellectual has been deconstructed, not to eliminate the products formerly attributed to it, but rather to show that they are produced in contradictory and collaborative action.

Note

1. García Canclini (1995a) borrows the phrase from Renato Ortiz, who in A moderna tradição brasileira (1988) uses it to refer to the integration of Brazil into an international order of mass media that requires certain standards of production. The fact that Brazil is one of the largest producers of television programs for export has been internalized into the styles of popular consumption and in ways that do not correspond to the cultural imperialism hypothesis (R. Ortiz, "Do popular-nacional ao internacional-popular?," 1988, 182–206). Of course, this sleight of phrase does not carry with it the Gramscian assumptions about the ability of popular groups to influence the "leading" groups, which in any case have been internationalized.

HUGO ACHUGAR
Local/Global Latin Americanisms: "Theoretical Babbling," apropos Roberto Fernández Retamar

Quel sera l'avenir?
La révolte des peuples sans histoire.
—E. M. *Cioran*

Hugo Achugar was born in Uruguay in 1944. A literary and cultural critic, he is a professor at the Universidad de la República in Montevideo, Uruguay. His main titles include *Poesía y sociedad (Uruguay 1888–1911)* (1986), *La balsa de la medusa. Ensayos sobre
identidad, cultura y fin de siglo en Uruguay* (1992), and *La biblioteca en ruinas. Reflexiones
culturales desde la periferia* (1994).

In Uruguay, in January and February 1999, the discussion about disappearances during the dictatorship and also about the confrontation
between civilian power and the military took an unprecedented turn.
The so-called Sanitation Plan III aims to ensure that 95 percent of the
population of the Montevideo region has access to the benefits of a sewerage system, and not only those in the city. The construction connected
with the plan caused discussions between the national army, the regional
administration—currently lead by the Frente Amplio, a left-wing coalition—and various other sectors of the national political spectrum. The
discussion questioned whether the sewerage pipes should follow their
projected route, which involved crossing a barracks, or whether it should
be modified. The barracks in question has been named as one of the
places where numerous disappeared people were buried during the military dictatorship (1973–85). The matters at stake, which were debated by

both sides, touched on the revision of the past, the theme of human rights, the authority of the army and of the regional government, the preservation of any possible human remains, quite aside from technical matters, security issues, and questions of authority.[1]

So, why begin an essay on the critical work of Fernández Retamar—and its theoretical implications, dating from the early 1970s—with a reference to the vicissitudes of Montevideo's Sanitation Plan III from the late 1990s? The answer has to do with so-called "local histories" and their importance in the production of theoretical discourses linked with "Latin Americanism(s)." The answer is also related to what Nadia Lie notes in her development of the idea of "the rhetoric of colony":

> It follows that the much advocated attention to "the rhetoric of empire" (Spurr 1995) might have to be complemented by what could be termed "the rhetoric of the colony." It goes without saying that this does not imply that colonialism continues to be visible. What it does, however, hint at is that those people that live in the "margins," are not "better readers"—if they are at all—simply on the basis of their oppression by the West, *but also because of concrete, local interests*. (Lie and D'haen 1997, 265, emphasis mine)

It is not that I agree word for word with Lie's argument, however I do agree that those "concrete, local interests" form the basis of readings from the margins or the periphery. It is also true that concrete, local interests are not exclusively relevant to "those people that live in the 'margins.'" In this sense, I find relevant Walter Mignolo's comments about the four critical projects that aim to overcome modernity—the postmodern, the postcolonial, the postoriental, and the postoccidental—because they contribute to the restitution of local histories as producers of knowledge that challenges, substitutes, and displaces global histories and epistemologies, in a moment when the subject, stripped of the knowledge postulated by Descartes and articulated by modernity, is increasingly difficult to sustain (1998c, 43).

The idea that the "restitution of local histories as producers of knowledge" and the condition of reading from the periphery according to "concrete, local interests" could both eventually function in the same way does not necessarily imply that local histories would be the same for all, even in the "margins" or the "peripheries." The "local history" of one social subject is not the "local history" of another even when both belong to the same community. Its production is not only dependent on a "local history" but also on the concrete "positioning" of local interests within those local histories. The families of those who disappeared are not positioned in the same way as the military even though both groups, to some extent, share the same "local history" of the dictatorship.

The "post" of the postdictatorships of the Southern Cone enters into dialogue with the four "posts" indicated by Mignolo. It is a "post" that plays a central role in the production of knowledge, in particular because of its relation to political history and to the national and cultural imaginaries of the "pre"-dictatorship era, as well as of all the narratives that organized it. That is to say that the centrality of this "post" is due to the ruptures it introduces with a past, the reconfiguration of cultural agendas, and the repositioning of social subjects.

The "concrete, local interests" that form the place of reflection for Fernández Retamar, myself, and many others are not necessarily equivalent. It is not only the "concrete, local interests" that differ, but following Walter Mignolo's argument, the languages used are not equivalent either. Despite his validation of "local histories" as producers of knowledge that displaces global epistemologies, Mignolo maintains (when he refers to an attempt to contextualize Fernández Retamar's discourse by the Argentinean del Barco) that "the moment of energy and intellectual production in Latin America" (supposedly the 1970s) "tends to get blurred in the international theoretical scene because of the hegemony of the English language and the discussion about postmodernism and postcolonialism, which is fundamentally conducted in English" (1998c, 39). Mignolo's proposal seems to suggest that the vindication and restitution of "'local histories' as producers of meaning that challenge . . . global histories and epistemologies" is only possible in English. This begs the question as to whether the statement is related to the "local histories" of Mignolo's place of writing and reflection—the North American academy—and the emergence of a Latino-North American theoretical "market," as well as the growing "Anglo-Saxonization" of reflection about Latin America.[2] Whether "pre" or "post," "local histories," like any story, presuppose heroes and villains, strategies and narrative models.

On Histories and Filiations

Cannibals, barbarians, natives, savages, subalterns, slaves, "people without history," marginalized, colonized, dominated; the list of descriptions or assessments of some of the characters of Latin American history—heroes or villains, depending on the storyteller—is even longer. They are nouns and adjectives that, without necessarily being synonymous, evoke different archives, traditions, and narratives.

Some of those archives propose that in the beginning was William Shakespeare and his well-known work *The Tempest*, the creator of the vision of the "original inhabitants" of the American continent. A more long-winded tradition includes Columbus, Montaigne, and other Europeans who elaborated visions of the "original inhabitants" of the American continent, which would soon be inherited in order to characterize future generations of "hybrid" or "transculturated" Latin Americans. It would be possible to go back even further and to maintain that the original archive is to be sought in Herodotus or in Xenophon's and Arrian's *Anabasis*. We could even dream of traveling back in time in order to witness the moment when a person not belonging to a tribe was first labeled "foreign." We could seek out the first document or human being to identify another person as an object to conquer, as a threat, or as a convenient enemy on the basis of language, skin color, or religion. Or, as occurred during the Uruguayan dictatorship, that document or norm that established categories of citizens—A, B, C—and permitted some of them to speak but not others; or, as occurred with the Indians and then with black people during the Conquest; as seems to occur today with the division of intellectual labor and the "hegemony" of certain languages.

There is no single history of the genealogies of the "Other." Some include Herodotus, Columbus, Shakespeare, Montaigne, and Renan as links in a complex weave that in Latin America continues into the late twentieth century. Among others, this weave incorporates Domingo Faustino Sarmiento, José Enrique Rodó, and Fernández Retamar. Other variants would include Vicente de Valverde, Inca Garcilaso de la Vega, Bartolomé de las Casas, Guamán Poma de Ayala, José Martí, José Carlos Mariátegui, Frantz Fanon, or "Che" Guevara. While some writers like Harold Bloom include Aimé Cesaire, John Dryden, and Jan Kott, they do not even mention Rodó, Fernández Retamar, or George Lamming— and Lamming does not even write in Spanish, but in Prospero's own language. There are yet others who include Fidel Castro without taking account of the fact that other "others" rule this out. The archives, filiations, and genealogies are numerous, as has been indicated, and they are not only nourished by "writers" but they can also include mapmakers, painters, and sculptors.

Hegel thought that theoretical discourse was impossible in the Americas (1946, 171–80). So, can "Latin Americans" in Latin America have "theory," whether minor or major? Who are those Latin Americans? Can they formulate a theoretical discourse, or are they only capable of "emotion," of producing "magical realism," "carnival," "hyperinflation," "tango," "enchiladas," "murals," "drugs traffic," and "coups d'état"? Can marginalized and subaltern Latin Americans produce theoretical discourses, or should they limit themselves to translating them from English, like they used to do from French or German?

Can it be that anything that is not part of the written and prescribed tradition that follows Shakespeare, Columbus, and many others cannot be heard? Can it be that on a theoretical or scientific level the Northern Hemisphere ears will always perceive discourse from Latin America— whether major or minor, learned or popular, left-wing or right-wing, from men or women, miners or academics—to be like incoherent or inconsistent theorizing?

"Theoretical Babbling" and Caliban's "Incoherence"

PROSPERO: Abhorred slave,
Which any print of goodness wilt not take,
Being capable of all ill! I pitied thee,
Took pains to make thee speak, taught thee each hour
One thing or other: when thou didst not, savage,
Know thine own meaning, but wouldst gabble like
A thing most brutish, I endow'd thy purposes
With words that made them known. But thy vile race,
Though thou didst learn, had that in't which good natures
Could not abide to be with; therefore wast thou
Deservedly confined into this rock,
Who hadst deserved more than a prison.

CALIBAN: You taught me language; and my profit on't
Is, I know how to curse. The red plague rid you
For learning me your language!
(The Tempest 1.2. 352–365)

Prospero interprets and qualifies Caliban's speech as "gabble"—that is, as "incoherent speech." In fact, Prospero's judgment of Caliban's "incoherence" refers not only to the incoherence he perceives in human "babbling." It is the incoherence of a turkey, "a thing most brutish" that does not know how to talk. Prospero has tried to teach Caliban to talk but all he has learned to do is to "talk incoherently," to "talk rubbish/gabble," to "gabble/*babble*" like "a thing most brutish." According to Prospero, Caliban has only learned to make "inarticulate sounds . . . as of fowls." The movement from "gabbling" to "babbling" takes us from the animal to the child, but both terms imply, for Prospero, degraded speech, as is clear from the affirmation that Caliban cannot "talk coherently" and therefore does not qualify as a competent speaker. Caliban cannot speak the conquerors' language correctly, although he can curse. He cannot carry on a major discourse but can only "maldecir" / "decir mal," that is, curse/speak awry or, rather, carry on a discourse of resistance, a minor discourse.

Caliban's speech, qualified as "gabble," would strike the hegemonic ears as a poor imitation of the dominant discourse. Is this true, or is it the case that Caliban does have a discourse of his own that Prospero cannot understand?[3] There is no reference to Caliban's own, original language. There is no record of it because the "aboriginal" language has been wiped out, silenced. The only one that remains and is recorded is the language he has learned. By the same token, what has been learned badly can only produce—to Prospero's kind of ears—a bad imitation, a "babbling," a mere "gabbling."

The linguistic scene of The Tempest does not raise ambiguities: "gabbling" and "babbling" are negative. But the negative only exists as such for Prospero, and Caliban does not apprehend it this way. "Babbling" for Caliban is affirmative: it states his resistance to Prospero's power. In Shakespeare's adumbration of the linguistic scene in the seventeenth century, "babbling" is negative; Caliban's interpretation is not valid. But such a scene did not end with The Tempest in the seventeenth century but has continued into our days.

In Calibán: Apuntes sobre la cultura en nuestra América, when Fernández Retamar refers to the "linguas francas" that (we) Latin Americans speak, he argues:

> Right now, that we are discussing, that I am discussing with those colonizers, how else can I do it except in one of their languages, which is now also our language, and with so many of their conceptual tools, which are also now our conceptual tools? This is the extraordinary cry that we read in . . . The Tempest. . . . The deformed Caliban, whose island Prospero had stolen, and whom Prospero would enslave and teach his language, this Caliban reprimands him. . . . Knowing how to curse. (1971, 12)

A learned language, which is now our language, one in which it is only possible to "curse," "speak awry," babble and which therefore is a "minor language," "minor discourse." The language scenario designed in The Tempest has continued into the present. The "babbling" that the minor language can produce is not capable of what is perceived as "systematic" and "methodic" thought. At the beginning of Para una teoría de la literatura hispanoamericana y otras aproximaciones, Fernández Retamar subscribes to José Gaos's contention that in Spanish and Spanish American thought the "most original and valuable aspect is the essay, the article, and the speech" (1975a, 43). He highlights constraints in systematic and methodic thinking: ". . . In what pertains to studies of literary theory in our America, we should not limit ourselves to works that take the form of 'the systematic and methodical tract or course,' and rather we should consider others, apparently less rigorously structured around this discipline" (ibid.).

Such a scenario seems to repeat itself. Latin American theoretical discourse tends to appear in other forms and those who elaborate it include not only "pure theorists" or "critics"—such as Alfonso Reyes, Henríquez Ureña, et cetera—but also, in Fernández Retamar's words, "protagonists of our literature"—like Martí and Rubén Darío. Apparently—for Gaos and Fernández Retamar—the "systematic and methodical tract or course" is not suitable or not characteristic of Latin Americans (although it is more than possible that they were only thinking of Spanish America); instead, what is recommended is "theoretical babbling" as Latin American thought appears in essays, articles, and speeches. Those who think that there is only one way to do theoretical work—their way or what their institutions define as the way, cannot recognize the discourse of the Other as "structured" and will qualify whatever they interpret as unsystematic and unmethodical as mere "babbling." Once again it seems that there is a hegemonic or Prosperean way to theorize and a cannibal, subordinate, or minor way. But Caliban's reply to Prospero implies the vindication of his speech, implies his right to babble not as an invalid or incoherent speech, but as his own valid and structured discourse. What is it that is being established: a difference or the Prosperean use of difference as a mark of disqualification? Both: difference and disqualification. For Fernández Retamar, theoretical activity in Latin America is different. For Gaos, theoretical activity in Latin America is different and worthy of disqualification. However, as Fernández Retamar subscribes to Gaos's contention of difference, the latter's further emphasis on difference qua disqualification punctually contaminates the former's discourse with traces of ambiguities, which might have momentarily undermined the force of his argument. Fernández Retamar's second observation runs in a different direction: "The works that I mentioned at the beginning (El deslinde by Alfonso Reyes and La estructura de la obra literaria by Félix Martínez Bonatti) are attempts at literary theory written in Spanish America, but not theories of Spanish American literature. The reason for this is simple: they aspire to be general theories" (1975a, 43, Fernández Retamar's emphasis).

This second observation, which to my mind is the weightier and the more intrinsically interesting of the two, allows Fernández Retamar to stress "local history" (the place from where one speaks) as determining the production of knowledge and of theories and also to revise the idea of a "universal literature" in terms of the postcolonial world:

> The theories of Spanish American literature could not be made by taking over and imposing en masse criteria that were forged in relation to other literatures, metropolitan literatures. Such criteria, as we know, have been proposed—and introjected by us—as having universal validity. But we also know that this is altogether false, and represents no more than another manifestation of the cultural colonialism that we have suffered, and that we have not completely stopped suffering, as a natural sequel of political and economic colonialism. In the face of this pseudo-universality, we must proclaim the simple and necessary truth that *a theory of literature is the theory of one literature.* (1975a, 48, Fernández Retamar's emphasis)

He goes further and argues—as is logical given the historical moment that the Cuban Revolution was going through—that, by virtue of its colonial past, the Third World has everything in common.[4] This homogenization of the colonial past—perhaps tributary to the political needs of the revolution in the 1970s—does not seem to maintain the line of argument that "local history" determines the production of knowledge. In this sense, in the essay "Brazilian Culture: Nationalism by Elimination," originally published in 1986 in *Folha de São Paulo*, the critic Roberto Schwarz seemed to offer another line of argument, holding that the class variable in local histories becomes preponderant in the moment when "originality" or colonial impositions (copies) are to be established (Schwarz 1992). A paraphrase of both Schwarz and Fernández Retamar would allow us to affirm that theoretical discourse is the theoretical discourse of one class—an idea that also draws on a long tradition of Marxist thought.[5]

But there is another dimension to Fernández Retamar's thesis regarding the necessity to react "in the face of that pseudo-universality" by proclaiming "the simple and necessary truth that *a theory of literature is a theory of one literature.*" Situating theoretical literary discourse as "the theory of one literature" does not only presuppose a "local history," or following Schwarz, the reality of class projects (or those of a particular class), but also proclaims the pseudo-universality of certain theoretical propositions. This is something that feminism, among other projects, has signaled time and again. In fact, it questions the very idea of "globalization."

This line of argument would seem to run the risk of rendering theoretical discourse unviable for more than one local history, or even for more than one class or gender. This is not however the thrust of Fernández Retamar's argument. He problematizes the very notion of "Spanish America" and foregrounds its historical condition. Moreover, taking up propositions made by José Carlos Mariátegui, he argues that the unity of Spanish or Latin America will not be achieved within the bourgeois order. That is to say, the possibility of scientific or universal knowledge is not rejected, but projected into a future in which the bourgeois order will have been defeated (and, although he does not extend his discussion to include it, when a "subject" capable of producing a truly universal scientific discourse will have arisen: the proletariat).

He problematizes the idea of a universal literature when he meditates, "does that literature already exist, that world literature, not as a mechanical addition but as a systematic reality?" (1975a, 44). Interrogating Goethe's idea of a "*Weltliteratur*" he maintains that "European capitalist expansion had established the premises for a world literature, because it had established the premises for the genuine *globalization of the world*" (ibid., Fernández Retamar's emphasis). He adds, "But these premises could not be crowned within the capitalist framework: such a task would correspond precisely to the system that would dismantle that framework—at the moment, still incomplete" (ibid.).

He based the impossibility of a universal theory on the fact that the world still was not united—neither in Goethe's time nor in 1972 when he was writing his essay. Read today, in 1999, after the fall of the Soviet Union and in the midst of the age of "economic and financial globalization" or of the "'globalization' of culture," Fernández Retamar's affirmation sounds like wishful thinking. Without discussing the more general theme of possible "globalization," which, as Appadurai argues, is often little more than a synonym for "North Americanization," "Japanization," et cetera, it would seem apposite to recall the near commonplace that, alongside these "global" processes, there are also "local" or "localization" processes (Appadurai 1990). In this respect the term "glocal" is extremely eloquent.

The preceding point does not, however, resolve the question about the possibility of a theoretical or scientific discourse with universal validity. From another perspective, the question of global or local discourse also presupposes that of the subject—unless, given the present balance of power and the location of economic and military hegemony, it is to be maintained that knowledge production can only take place in the Northern Hemisphere, particularly in the United States, and that only subjects living in the North are capable of producing knowledge, even if they were originally from Latin America, India, Pakistan, Australia, or, even "minor" European countries. On this matter, it is interesting to consider what Fernández Retamar indicated in 1971, commenting on the "legacy" of Martí and Rodó, a legacy that carries Martí's idea of "Our America," as opposed to Anglo or North America, and Rodó's idea of a "spiritual" (Ariel-like) Latin America in opposition to a "material, nonspiritual" (Caliban-like) Anglo or North America:

> So, if, because of the strange circumstances mentioned, that knowledge (of Martí's work) was forbidden or was only permitted in a limited way . . . what then can we say about more recent authors who have editions of Martí to hand but, nevertheless, insist on denying him? I am not thinking, of course, *of scholars who are more or less foreign to our problems, but, on the contrary of those who maintain a consistent anticolonial attitude* [my emphasis]. The only explanation for this fact is painful: colonialism has penetrated us so deeply that we only read anticolonial authors *disseminated from the metropolises* [his emphasis] with real respect. (1971, 39–40)

However, even if the site of knowledge were to be identified with, or rather, decided by the new Prosperos of the North American or Commonwealth academies, the universality of theoretical discourse would continue to be a problem, at least in the human sciences. For Fernández Retamar, the problem of universality weaves into the discussion of the theme of the West; thus, the West and "occidentalism" are categories that belong with the dichotomy bourgeois order/socialism. In fact, he claims the right to theoretical discourse of those who belong to the margins of the capitalist world.

Once again, the problem seems to be between Caliban and Prospero, between speaking or not, thinking or not. Spivak has claimed that the subaltern cannot speak and that at the point of speaking he abandons or is no longer in the situation of the subaltern (1988a). From different positions and with different implications Bhabha (1994a) and Irigaray (1977) have posited that the option available to certain "marginal" and "hybrid" subjects is "imitation" (mimicry).[6] Can barbaric Latin Americans theorize? Should they "Prospereanly" speak or can they "barbarically" babble? Speaking differently used to mark one off as a barbarian; it was, literally, "to babble." Is there only one way of theorizing? Can I as a barbarian have the right to my own discourse? Or should I theorize as Prospero does?

Latin American Critical Discourse as Intervention?

How pertinent as a category of analysis is "theoretical babbling," understood as a non-hegemonic "theoretical thought," for referencing Latin American discourse in its non-European, North American, or Commonwealth specificity? Is it possible to think of a "minor use" of theory, making a free paraphrase of Deleuze's proposition, and "theoretical babbling" as a positive and valid category? Or does it run the risk of being appropriated as barbarism, as just another way of disqualifying any discourse produced outside the rules of theoretical discourse of the "center," or of the "Northern Hemisphere universities"? Will Latin American cultural criticism, "essay writing" (ensayismo), or thought thus be seen as worthless theorization because they do not fall within the academic parameters of "scholarly" thought—in the double sense of the word "school"—from the Commonwealth and the gardens of academia? That is to say, to what extent are those who do not theorize like "I" do barbarians who cannot speak Greek, or, who are just perceived to "babble" because they do not theorize within my system? Who determines and disqualifies a discourse as barbaric "babbling": the speaking subject or the one who listens? [7]

Isn't something similar happening in the dialogue between Latin Americanists from the North and the South to what was happening in the dialogue between Prospero and Caliban? Does it not keep happening today when Latin American discourse is heard from the perspective of the "Prosperean" Commonwealth theoretical discourse, of Anglo-Saxon postcolonialism, or of certain positions of "Latin-North Americanism"? Isn't it the case that, as Fernández Retamar said, the only ones to merit real respect (are) "anticolonial authors *disseminated from the metropolises*" and that those who are disseminated from Latin America are just "gabble" to metropolitan ears, or for those of us whose ears have been so deeply silenced by colonialism? To put it another way, how is this matter related to other problems: the problem of the savage, of the cannibal or of Caliban; the problem of the Latin American subject or speaker, and with the problem of "theory" in relation to Latin America? To what extent do Fernández Retamar's claims constitute a specific way of thinking and to what extent do they reveal a more general situation?

In 1975, when Fernández Retamar published *Para una teoría*, the Latin American critical project—labeled by Antonio Cornejo Polar as "the great epistemological project of the 70s" (1994, 14)—included many other voices and seemed to have reached a climax. In fact, Fernández Retamar's formulation arose in the context of critical restlessness and theoretical proposals from many countries in Latin America. There is the evidence of the so-called "Conversatorio de Lima de 1974" in which, among others, Nelson Osorio and Antonio Cornejo Polar participated, and also the earlier polemic between Oscar Collazos, Mario Vargas Llosa, and Julio Cortázar, as well as many editorial projects and various of Angel Rama's essays of the early 1970s. In Argentina, different critical projects consolidated, some of which were later carried on in Mexico, the United States, and other countries, although under more difficult circumstances, in Argentina itself.[8] In Peru, and then in Germany, Alejandro Losada aspired to give an account of social and literary systems. In Brazil, apart from the work of Antonio Candido (and his polemics with Haroldo de Campos), a whole critical endeavor was developing that included Roberto Schwarz. To the former there should be added the work developed in the Rómulo Gallegos Center of Latin American Studies by Domingo Miliani and the research group comprising members from various Latin American countries. Toward the end of the 1970s, works like Carlos Rincón's *El cambio de la noción de literatura* or Roberto Schwarz's *Ao vencedor as batatas: forma literária e proceso social*, among many others, signaled that "the Latin American critical project" had a multiple presence. Finally, the colloquia and essays convened and published by Casa de las Américas in Havana and by Biblioteca Ayacucho in Caracas indicated if not a conscious "project"— the idea of a project could imply a sense of "conspiracy" or "strategy" that never existed—a kind of convergence of efforts that were not necessarily identical or homogenous. In fact, Fernández Retamar's proposals met with resistance from many active critics of the time, some of whom, like Rama and Miliani, believed that *Para una teoría* risked proposing a "critical Ameghinism."[9]

The importance of the text published in 1975 and its articulation with the situation in Latin America—particularly the Southern Cone, including Brazil and Cuba—are confirmed by both the enthusiastic responses and the criticism provoked by its claims from the different participants in the Latin American critical debate—both inside and outside Latin America. So, to what extent did the proposal of *Para una teoría* represent an intervention in Cuba's internal debate and also in the Latin American debate? Moreover, to what extent did these essays constitute the theoretical foundations of Caliban's "theoretical babbling"? In other words, to what extent did Latin America's theoretical babbling constitute a minor discourse? Before attempting to answer this question it is necessary to turn back and consider the relationship between Ariel, Caliban, and Prospero.

On Ariel, Caliban, and Prospero and the Function of the Latin American Intellectual

For a sector of first world and Latin American academy, the Uruguayan José Rodó and his *Ariel* (1900)—a book that was to dominate the intellectual scene during the first decades of the twentieth century because of its aesthetic, anti-utilitarian, and anti-North American spirit—symbolize the position of the elitist intellectual linked to the power system and who carries out its orders, characteristic of the "lettered city" as described by Angel Rama: "In the center of every city, passing through various stages that reached their plenitude in the vice-regal capitals, there was a lettered city forming a circle that was protective of the power system and that carried out its orders" (1979, 33).

The questioning of Rodó is old and has a long history (a large part of which can be found in Fernández Retamar's *Caliban*), the same way that the accusation of Arielism is not new. In 1967, some years before Fernández Retamar published his rereading of Rodó's *Ariel*, Carlos Real de Azúa, referring to a colloquium and subsequent book edited by Lipset, maintained: "The first and most used (of an abundant set of stereotypes) consists in attributing resistance to Yankeeization to the fact that intellectuals are 'Arielists' " (1987, 306). Rather than Rodó's *Ariel* itself, the problem resides in what was done with the book—or rather, if Arielism should be viewed as a synonym of antidemocratic and elitist discourse. It is true that such a reading of *Ariel* and Arielism is valid; but it is just one way of reading Rodó. *Ariel* and, therefore, Rodó himself can and have been read differently. Among other things, *Caliban* is such a rereading of Rodó's *Ariel*. Most importantly, however, are a rereading and a substantial modification of the view of the function of the Latin American intellectual. Moreover, *Caliban* questions a metropolitan discourse that puts in doubt the existence of Latin American discourse, or that considers it of little importance as mere reproduction. It is not in vain that the essay begins and presents itself as a response to the question, formulated by "a European journalist, seemingly of the left," "Does a Latin American culture exist?":

> The question seemed to me to reveal one of the roots of the polemic, and it could be expressed in another way: "Do you exist?" Because to

question our culture is to question our existence, our very human reality, and as such, it indicates a readiness to take the part of our irremediable colonial condition, suspecting that we are only a disfigured echo of what is going on elsewhere. That elsewhere, of course, is found in the metropolises, the colonizing centers. (Fernández Retamar 1971, 7)

The clear provocation establishes its situation of enunciation: "the recent polemic about Cuba"; the identity of a *them*—"some bourgeois European intellectuals (or aspiring to be so), with visible colonialist nostalgia"—and of an *us*—"the major writers and artists of Latin America who reject open and veiled forms of political and economic slavery."

At the beginning of the 1970s, Cuba was at a particular political moment. Following the Cultural Congress and after the Padilla "case," the polemic referred to by Fernández Retamar at the beginning of *Caliban* was unleashed, and intellectuals were divided between those who supported the Cuban Revolution and those who criticized it. In the following quotation Ambrosio Fornet described that stage of the Cuban Revolution, which produced intense debate inside and outside of Cuba: "Everyone took the existence of the other for self-justification. The offensive of dogmatism only made the liberals more cohesive; the cohesion of the liberals worsened dogmatism. Every time the dinosaurs moved—as Jorge Ibarra would say—the butterflies jumped; every time the butterflies jumped, the dinosaurs moved. In this vicious circle the only things that got damaged were the insects on the ground, the plants that had already been planted, and the ground itself" (Dalton 1969, 51).

It would be productive to read *Caliban* in this context, which also allows us to understand Fernández Retamar's proposed rereading of the Ariel-Caliban-Prospero triad and his proposal as to the function of the Latin American intellectual. It is in this context that he affirms, at the beginning of the second part of *Caliban* and after his archaeology of the character, "Our symbol is not, then, Ariel as Rodó thought, but Caliban. . . . I do not know a metaphor better fitted to our cultural situation, to our reality" (1971, 30). He immediately goes on to elaborate a long list that functions as a filiation of "our cultural situation." The list includes independence leaders, martyrs like Tupac Amaru, social activists, poets, sculptors, popular musicians from the Antilles, as well as Carlos Gardel and Heitor Villalobos, Mexican muralism, Violeta Parra, Fidel Castro, Che Guevara, et cetera. It is Fernández Retamar's filiation and that of anyone who identifies with it.

What is interesting is not so much the postmodern mixture of this un-chaotic "enumeration," but rather the implicit elaboration of a "them" and an "us," of Ariels and Calibans. According to Fernández Retamar, they are the Ariels, "bourgeois European intellectuals (or aspiring to be so), with visible colonialist nostalgia." We, Calibans, are, for Fernández Retamar, "the major writers and artists of Latin America who reject open and veiled forms of political and economic slavery." However, the "them" and "us" that his text sets out from the beginning and maintains for a long time are then reformulated into another opposition where Ariel is less of an enemy than Prospero.

An important part of the essay's argument does aim to dismantle Rodó's Ariel, and the very symbol of the intellectual who is occupied in Prospero's service. The fundamental force of rejection or questioning, however, is directed toward Prospero rather than Ariel. As has been seen, the fact that Rodó's proposal is forcefully and unmistakably called into question does not imply that the essay's historical function and usefulness are ignored. Following Mario Benedetti, in the following quote, Fernández Retamar affirms: "Despite its lacks, omissions, and naiveties . . . Rodó's vision about the Yankee phenomenon, rigorously located in its historical context, was in its time the first spring-board for other later claims which were less naive, better informed, more far-sighted . . . today, the almost prophetic substance of Rodo's Arielism conserves some of its relevance" (1971, 31). And then he adds, "These observations are supported by incontrovertible realities" (31). Further on, and after strongly questioning Rodríguez Monegal's interpretation, he affirms, that "all things considered, it is almost certain that these lines would not carry the name they do if it were not for Rodó's book, and I prefer to see them as a homage to the great Uruguayan whose centenary is being celebrated this year. It is not strange that the homage should contradict him on more than a few points" (34).

Ariel and Caliban are two forms of our culture for Fernández Retamar. The fact that one represents the traditional, belletristic intellectual and the other the organic intellectual or revolutionary (82) does not imply that both could not be, in his words, merely "servants in the hands of Prospero, the foreign sorcerer" (35). This is what allowed him to affirm earlier in relation to Rodó that "even if he got the symbols wrong, as has been said, it is no less true that he was able clearly to point out the great enemy that our culture had in his time—and in ours—and that is massively more important" (31). Prospero, the greatest enemy, is for Fernández Retamar "the foreign sorcerer." However, Prospero also represents or constitutes the site of knowledge, as has already been said. This is the knowledge that can disqualify Caliban and "dazzle" Ariel, the knowledge that allows him to dominate the island that they "all" inhabit. Moreover, Prospero also represents or constitutes the knowledge of power, knowledge fitting for a "foreign sorcerer."

Fernández Retamar's proposals are taken up by some, adulterated by others, appropriated by yet others, and even translated into English. The sanitation plan that is crossing the barracks in Montevideo is celebrated by some, lamented by others, and demonized by still others. How are we to read the present that is a form of reading the past and of constructing the future? From where is the future to be read? Whose future?

"What will the future be? The revolt of the people without history," Cioran asked and answered himself (1997). What cultural tradition does Cioran belong to? Is it valid for a Latin American to quote him? One possible answer—to which the present meditation does not aspire—would be negative. The optimism that could be read as inspiring the passage by Cioran is surprising in a writer who does not often turn to thoughts that are, if not utopian, at least "happy." Although the answer seems simple and direct it raises various problems. Who are those peoples without history? What does it mean to have no history? Are they those who live on the margins of history in a Western sense—that is, outside "Western (European) historical time"? Or those who live within the history of the West (including the Latin American periphery) but in a marginal or subordinate position and therefore have "an invisible history"? Is it possible to conceive of the history of peoples without history? Would it be possible to express it in one language or should it be done in many languages at the same time?

Could it be that those who have no history or whose history is invisible (in Arendt's sense) are those who cannot talk and can only "babble" in Prospero's sense? Could it be that the new Prosperos who hold power and who will rewrite history are prepared to proceed as Arnoldo de Regensburg proposed around 1030? Are the current Prosperos ready to uphold a version of Regensburg's affirmations that would read: "It is not only appropriate for new things to change old ones, but also that if the old things are disordered, they should be thrown out and forgotten; or if, on the other hand, the old things fit in with the proper order of things but are seldom used, then they ought to be buried with a salute to the flag. After all, I, Prospero know what is best for both Caliban and Ariel, and, as if that was not enough, the present and the future belong to me"?

Let me finish by proposing two further questions: Could it be true that there is not only one postcolonial discourse and that it does not remain self-identical through history and across languages and cultures? Could it be that "theoretical babbling" is the place that present Anglo-Saxon postcolonial discourse reserves for postcolonial discourse in other languages? Clearly the answer is not simple. It is particularly complex if the peculiar situations in which North-Latin Americans live are taken into consideration, as José D. Saldívar does, which leads him to inscribe his theoretical discourse in a "space of hybridity and *betweenness* in our global Borderlands composed of historically connected postcolonial spaces" (1991, 153). This is a space that is not only composed of historically connected postcolonial ones but also of colonizing spaces, since for Latin America the United States continues to be a colonizing force.

What remains unsettled and without resolution is the past of our own present. What remains unsettled and without resolution is a multiple dialogue between the numerous interlocutors. What remains unsettled and without resolution is the need to transform Prospero's monologue into a truly democratic assembly in which all voices can be spoken.

Notes

1. On various positions and arguments see the Montevidean press, especially the newspapers El *Observador* and La *República*, from January and February 1999.
2. It is worth remembering what Antonio Cornejo Polar pointed out in his (posthumous) essay "Mestizaje and Hybridity: The Risks of Metaphors. Notes," and his questioning of, and unease with, the growing production of work about Latin America in English.
3. It would be appropriate to discuss Roberto Schwarz's propositions about copying and imitation in "Brazilian culture" here, but it exceeds the limits of the present essay.
4. This opens up a line of discussion that we will not follow on this occasion as it supposes the problematic of the homogenization of the "Third World."
5. It is not possible to enter into the discussion of class versus ethnic group, gender, et cetera.
6. At present we cannot discuss Bhabha's and Irigaray's ideas in depth, but it would be productive to confront them with Roberto Schwarz's arguments on the topic.
7. "Gregor, in Kafka's *Metamorphosis*, warbles more than he speaks, but *this again is according to the testimony of others*" (Deleuze and Guattari 1986, 23; my emphasis).
8. I am referring to the work of David Viñas, Noé Jitrik, Adolfo Prieto, Beatriz Sarlo, Josefina Ludmer, Ricardo Piglia.
9. This refers to the ideas of the Argentine paleontologist and anthropologist Florentino Ameghino (1853–1911), who asserted that all mammals, including humans, had originated in the Argentine pampas.

NELLY RICHARD

Intersecting Latin America with Latin Americanism: Academic Knowledge, Theoretical Practice, and Cultural Criticism

Nelly Richard was born in France in 1948. A literary and art critic, she is the director of *Revista de Crítica Cultural* in Santiago, Chile. Her main titles include *La estratificación de los márgenes* (1989b), *La insubordinación de los signos. Cambio político, transformaciones culturales y poéticas de la crisis* (1994), and *Residuos y metáforas. (Ensayos de crítica cultural sobre el Chile de la Transición)* (1998a).

S ince a LASA conference is somehow a "contact zone" between Latin Americanism—a device of academic knowledge—and Latin America—an object of study, a field of experience, a position of enunciation—I would like to organize these reflections around the traffic between divergent positions which nonetheless intersect, dialogue, or even interpellate with one another. These intersected positions between metropolitan academia and their more or less peripheral "others" put into play the question of the relationship between academic knowledge, theoretical practice, and critical discourse, convened by different geographical-cultural contexts and institutional locations where we situate ourselves in order to speak "about" or "from" Latin America through complex systems of representation and politics of signs.

Asymmetries of Discursive Power: Speaking about and Speaking from Latin America

The constitution of Latin American studies—and of the Latin American [lo latinoamericano] as object of study—is connected to the problem of subalternity that, according to John Beverley, "emerges across, or at the intersections of, a wide range of academic disciplines as well as social positions" (1994, 285), thus making Latin Americanism and cultural studies converge around topics such as the relationship between metropolitan Western power and peripheral formations; the dynamics of cultural resistance that oppose non-hegemonic identities to dominant social codes; the reconversion of the popular and the national under the globalizing effect of mass communication; the thought of the hybrid (borders, impurity, alterity) that crosses non-homogenous constituents of fragmented community registers; et cetera.

Consequently, we could say that cultural studies and Latin American studies share the project of mixing—collaboratively—multidisciplinarity and transculturality in order to respond to the new categorical shifts between the dominant and the subaltern, the educated and the popular, the central and the peripheral, the global and the local: shifts that travel through geopolitical territorialities, identity symbolizations, sexual representations, and social classifications. These overlapping categorical shifts have altered the dichotomic relationship between the same and the other, the identical and the different, that which is one's own and that which belongs to another, the colonizer and the colonized, which founded the oppositional and contesting conscience of Latin America. Today this conscience undoes and redoes itself by means of mixed appropriations, translations, and reconversions of statements that also force theory to reformulate itself in a hybrid way.

A Latin American theory able to think itself independently from the conceptual fabric of the metropolitan academic discourse is no longer possible, because, among other things, the very category of peripheral subalternity that modulates current Latin American thought is being monopolized, in its postcolonial key, by the agenda of cultural studies and Latin Americanism, whose globalized theoretical model not only overdetermines the local use of categories such as the subaltern and the peripheral, but also threatens to erase, with its generalizations, the specific feature of memories and localities distinctive of each cultural singularity.

Therefore, we do not have any way to think of the complexity of forces that produce tension in the academic-cultural scenario of "the Latin American" without passing through the theoretical diagram (alterity, marginality, subalternity) that cultural studies elaborates in its dispute against hierarchic knowledges, even though this elaboration carries contradictorily, for us, the seal of the metropolitan academia. This is to say that today Latin Americanism takes the Latin American all the way through an ambiguous map of shifted localities between center and periphery: between metropolitan academia and the borders of conflictive dissemination of the global knowledge produced about Latin America, which function simultaneously as borders of tensional re-inscription of said knowledge in multiple sites of tactical confrontation. The ambiguities and contradictions of this new map require us to rethink, more thoroughly than ever, the value of each theoretical location: that is to say, the condition of experience that emerges, for each one of us, from the act of thinking about theory while immersed in a particular geocultural locality through the (constructed) relationship between the positioning of the subject and the mediation of codes, between contextual location and discursive positionality.

Cultural studies debate the problems which provide more critical vitality to its redefinitions of academic knowledge, informed by the postmodernist agenda and its notions on the heterogeneous, the multiple, and the local. Nevertheless, those of us who incarnate these notions of otherness in our material condition of subjects both different and distant from the centers of authority and discursive control frequently resent cultural studies as a globalizing metadiscourse sanctioned by a circuit of metropolitan guaranties that reinstitutionalize new forms of international dominance through academia. It is true that postmodernity (if that is the name we give to the crisis of authority of the monocultural pattern of dominant modern reason) has contributed in liberating the discordant folds of many margins and peripheries, and it is also true that the postmodern revindication of the multiplicity of ethnic, social, and gender-sexual otherness has put pressure on the borders of the cultural institution, forcing it to include voices that up until now have been underrepresented or devalued by the Western-metropolitan dominant. This proliferation of margins has created multiple interruptions and discontinuities on the surface of representation of cultural power that have shattered (fragmented, disintegrated) the image of the Center, making this image no longer conceivable as an absolute point of homogeneous dominance and control. This new fragmentation and disintegration of the metropolitan authority system has modified the binary scheme of hierarchy and subordination that, according to the contesting ideology of underdevelopment theories, opposed "center" to "periphery" as fixed and contrary polarities, in rigid confrontation with each other as a result of lineal antagonisms. The geographical opposition between "center" and "periphery," as points radically separated by an irreversible distance between two extremes, has been rearticulated in a more fluid and transverse way due to the new segmented and disseminated condition of the (translocal) power of the media and mediations. The swift displacement of borders traversed by multiple currents of communicative globalization that ubiquitously deliver global ideologies, brands, theories, and styles; the alterations experienced by the cartographies of cultural power due to the internal reconfiguration and recombination of divisions between dominant and subordinate according to mobile coordinates no longer limited to geographic locations produce certain effects that try to make us believe that the limits no longer limit, the divisions of power have become immaterial, and the subject positions are infinitely reversible and interchangeable. Nevertheless, our actions as well as our "linguistic games" are still conditioned by divisions and asymmetries of power that, in the case of the cultural peripheries, obstruct the multilateral flow of signs, blocking the routes of reciprocity that would activate the exchange of messages between recognized and equally valid interlocutors. These divisions and asymmetries are now reinforced by academia as the machine of international production and validation of the postcolonial theory that, among other functions, "mediates the exchange of cultural commodities of global capitalism in peripheral zones" (Kwane Anthony Appiah, as quoted by de la Campa 1996, 715).

We can agree with Walter Mignolo that "a fundamental transformation of the intellectual space is under way as a result of the configuration of a postcolonial reason, both in the locus of oppositional practice within the public sphere and in the theoretical battle within academia," as well as "a displacement of the *locus* of enunciation from the First World to the Third World" (Mignolo 1996a, 112). But along with favoring to some extent this displacement, the metropolitan academia also simulates a deterritorialization of its power of representation through refined stratagems according to which "a de-centered centrality tries to relegitimize itself within a globalizing context by appealing to alterities, marginalities, and subalternities from its own academic apparatuses of production of knowledge, with the involvement of postcolonial intellectuals located in them" (Yúdice 1994, 44).

Deconstructing such stratagems and exposing the internal contradiction of the globalizing metadiscourse that construes them involves the highlighting of the living and changing materiality of contextual specificities that that discourse names (feigns to recognize) and at the same time de-identifies. It involves the insistence on the signs of particular historicities and localities, of practical territorialities, of specific contingencies, in order to make the Latin American "difference" a *differentiating* difference: that is to say a multiple and relational process of negotiated and conflictive reinscriptions of the identity-alterity tension, which are capable of intervening in every new context of discourse that speaks about difference.

We know that it is not enough that postcolonial theory incorporates the *notion of otherness* in its new anti-hegemonic discourse so that the *real other* (the concrete subject formed by historical and social plots of censorship and exclusion) is able to participate in the metropolitan debate with its own voice. It is also not enough that the postmodernist theory of marginality and difference, elaborated by metropolitan academia, speaks *in representation of* the periphery, even though it does it with the good intention of occupying the role of political-institutional mediator in the struggle for the right to self-expression, so that the rules of cultural power become more equal or so that the Center's "fantasizing with otherness" translates into "a stable commitment with the political or aesthetic projects that Latin America could offer" (Masiello 1996, 747).

The hierarchy of the Center is not just based upon a maximum concentration of means reinforced by the monopoly of economic distribution. The authority that the Center exercises as symbolic power comes from the investitures of authority that allow it to work as "center-function": that is to say, as the core or the network which operates an infinite number of substitutions, conversions, and translations of signs regulated by a unique code of value homologation. The theoretical authority of the center-function resides in this monopoly of power-of-representation according to which "representing" means controlling the discursive means that subordinate the object of knowledge to a conceptual economy self-pronounced as superior. And even though Latin America is regularly invited to debate on the crisis of centrality of the cultural institution as the apparent protagonist of the subversion of the metropolitan canon, the network which articulates the postcolonial debate is the one certified by the factual power of the academic international, whose coordinated series of study programs, publishing lines, and systems of scholarships establish and sanction the theoretical validity and the remunerability of the investigations under way in agreement with export values.[1]

Then, what is the scenario in which *the* Latin American is debated nowadays? It is a scenario marked by the insidious complexity of this new postcolonial articulation made out of intermediary powers which move *between* the de-centered centrality of the metropolis, on one hand, and, on the other, the cultural re-signification of the periphery, conflictively carried out by the metropolitan theory of the subaltern.

The critical reinterpretation of *the* Latin American as an active differential bearing in this scenario of complex intersections of forces and categories demands the articulation of a situated knowledge, which, as Walter Mignolo points out, is able to "establish epistemological connections between the geocultural location and theoretical production" (1996a, 119) without falling into the ontological determinism that postulates a natural equivalence (fixed because of not being constructed) between place, experience, discourse, and truth. The critical valence of the Latin American in relation—and tension—with Latin Americanism (understood as a "social relationship" of knowledge administration [Moreiras 1995, 48]) then would depend on our ability to re-signify the experience in the formulation of a theoretical-discursive query about contextual conditionings: about the difference between *speaking from* and *speaking about* Latin America as two enunciative situations, institutionally crossed by an unequal relation of power-knowledge. It is a politically modifiable relationship, from both sides, in so far as a vigilant self-critical awareness about the "where" and the "how" allows us, in every utterance, to review our own game of enunciation.

The Subtheoretical Notion of Latin American Otherness

The conceptual authority involved in the act of speaking about Latin America from the international academia is exercised through a division of labor that, in the unconscious of many of the discourses of Latin Americanism, usually opposes theory and practice: reason and matter, knowledge and reality, discourse and experience, mediation and immediacy. The first series of this sequence of oppositions (reason, knowledge, theory, discourse, mediation) designates the intellectual power of abstraction and symbolization that defines the supremacy of the Center, while the second series (matter, reality, practice, experience, immediacy) confines Latin America to the spontaneity of lived experience. In Jean Franco's words, this division of labor "puts Latin America in the place of the body while the North is the place that thinks of it" (Richard and Eltit 1995, 20). The ideologem of the body (physical matter, concrete reality, practical experience) supports the fantasy of a Latin America whose "authenticity" would reside in the primordial force of lived experience. Following along this line of oppositions, Latin American otherness would constitute itself as the reverse of the concept and the reason fetishized by academic knowledge: a natural reversal that would compensate for the abstractive and reifying coldness of the Center's theory (prisoner of university cloistering itself) thus infusing it, imaginarily, with a borrowed energy. Latin America would be that primary (unmediated) source of action and imagination, of struggle and resistance: the radical and primary "outside" (radical *because* of being primary) of the Latin Americanism that supplies the metropolitan intellectuality with its *plus* of popular living experiences, which translates into solidary struggle, political commitment, and testimonial denouncement. This *plus* would operate, according to the economy of symbolic compensation that regulates the typical discourse about Latin America, as a supplement of the Real ambiguously charged with a value of surplus and of residue as far as it would designate—emblematically—the untranslatable to the conceptual language of the Center's theory: a prediscursive or extradiscursive force that resists the Center and that Latin Americanism tries to capture or declare uncapturable.

This force would be the raw negative that best contrasts with the polished metropolitan image of theoretical metropolitan work: a negative which generates distancing and whose remote codelessness would transgress the domesticating effect of the Center's theory. Perhaps it is in the recent and successful rescue of Latin American *testimonio* brought about by the metropolitan academia where the complexity of tensions that run through the marrow of Latin Americanism is best illustrated.[2] This complexity of tensions is split between: (1) the political will for a solidary intermediation with the voice of the subaltern, (2) the epistemological challenge of reformulating reading positions that neither subject nor reduce the social heterogeneity of the subaltern text to an authoritative code, and (3) the academic conditioning of a metropolitan discipline compelled to theorize otherness through categories forged by the dominant language of institutional knowledge. It is enough to take the example of the extensive academic discussion with regard to the text *I, Rigoberta Menchú* in order to observe the overlapping of power and resistance that play—and negotiate—on the limits of the institutionalization of the subaltern text, especially when the resistance of that text to institutional capture (a value coded in its ability to symbolize the vital commitment to the unsubmissive outside of academia) is awarded precisely by the same institution that *internally* grants this value.

Doris Sommer's analysis of *I, Rigoberta Menchú* defends the secret of "inviolable areas" in the narration, which are capable of frustrating or disappointing "any intellectual eager for an assimilable authenticity" (Sommer 1994, 234) with a strategy of obstructing the knowledge of another's life story, whose otherness would thus remain unappropriable. John Beverley tracks down the voice of the Real within Rigoberta's *testimonio*, in the Lacanian sense of a traumatic Otherness that challenges all cultural symbolization and codification (Beverley 1996a). Both authors appeal to a provocative dimension of unrepresentability that would make of *testimonio* the limit-experience of a metropolitan reading attracted to—and challenged by—this border, silent and rebellious to any literary domestication. The Real of *testimonio* would be the social heterogeneity and conflictiveness that subaltern practice puts in opposition to academic decodification, according to an opposition based on how that heterogeneity of life experiences would produce a popular value that always exceeds the academic competence of a cultured knowledge declared incapable, by its own advocates, of achieving the political intensity of third world struggle.

We know that the Real is not the raw reality, but rather a retroactive reconstruction of the process of symbolization that goes back to that which it could not incorporate, that designates as Real that which had escaped from the categories that language uses to name—and to dominate—its object: "The Real is at the same time presupposed and proposed by the symbolic" that reconstructs it after failing to integrate it in order to explain the deficiencies of its structure (Žižek 1992, 221). Therefore, *testimonio*'s Real would also be a "fantasy-construct" presupposed and proposed by Latin Americanism in order to designate as otherness what is unassimilable to the disciplinary categories of methodical knowledge, while it consecrates that unassimilability, paradoxically, through the institutional supremacy of the academic machine, which certifies the theoretical definition of the other and the other [lo otro].

The disturbing or traumatic effect of the *testimonio*'s rebellious opaqueness, of the secret or unknown force of something (an enigma, a problem, a resistance) that distorts the rituals of academic training, would be connected—for many of its defenders—to the declared condition of unpenetrability of this combative distance that opposes real *testimonio* (or the Real of *testimonio*) to its metropolitan reading. The popular struggle symbolized by *testimonio* would be the most radical—and emblematic—"outside" of academia: an "outside" in whose imaginary support the Center's Latin Americanism projects its political will of aperture and change blocked by university cloistering. Perhaps the political consciousness of Latin Americanism requires, in order to continue being mobilized by utopias of change, this mechanism of production of an Other that takes the form of a radical exteriority (distance and foreignness) with respect to the all too familiar metropolitan bibliography. Perhaps it needs to declare this Real untranslatable to the academic language of the Center, in order to convert the theoretical fiction of a supposedly unassimilable otherness into the counter-text that promises to defamiliarize the metropolitan routine from the competency of knowledge. However, when this operation is brought to an emblematic rank, it produces the problem of confining the value of the Latin American in a (silent or savage) exteriority to the discursive norm and its cultural mediations: an exteriority that retains and detains the Latin American in the limits of a (prediscursive or extradiscursive) "before" the codes of symbolic operation, condemning it to remain distanced from the battles of categories, readings, and representations protagonized by the metropolitan critical knowledge developed *about* Latin America.

With the success of *testimonio*, the Latin American would seem to effectively enjoy, in the new postcolonial context, the epistemological advantage of symbolizing a decolonizing alternative at the same time it enjoys the ethical privilege of expressing social commitment with the dispossessed. But it would seem that such exemplariness only radicalizes itself on the condition that the Latin American remains in a situation of pre-theoretical or sub-theoretical conscience; that is to say, marginalized from the battles between models and readings that decree and sanction the cultural significance of Latin American practices. To participate in these battles between knowledge and representation supposes abandoning the assigned place of the unrepresentable as the (only) resistant place of the Latin American, and trying out other approaches of counter-representation or derepresentation, as shown by actively discordant textualities: "*ladino*" textualities whose tactical movements, in the figurative sense of the term *ladino* used by Pablo Oyarzún, reveal them as astute, clever, sly practices. These practices are recalcitrant to the central order of academic classification of knowledge and are experts in mocking its systems of valuation with unpredictable ingenuity that confuses or disorganizes the general control over the limits between what is translatable and what is not.[3]

Contingent Knowledges, Microexperiences of Knowledge

The opposition between representation (abstraction, theory, discursivity) and experience (concretion, practice, vivenciality) affirms the inequality of powers traced between, on one hand, those who establish the codes of theoretical construction that will endow their objects of study with academic legitimacy and, on the other hand, the subjects represented by these codes, *spoken by* the theorization of otherness, and without much access to the institutional benefits of the metropolitan theory nor the right to be consulted about the validity of the categories that describe and interpret them. Subverting this dichotomy of power requires the production of local theory, situated knowledge, situational discourse, and conscience, which generate an instability of functions in the interior of the system supposedly regulated by the division between the Latin American proliferation of differences (as an excess of irrationality) and the installation of an "order restituting narrative" that Latin American-ism uses in order to control those differences, placing each one in a classifiable and interpretable place (Masiello 1996, 751).

The defense of the value of "experience" in opposition to the category of "representation" generally supposes, in humanist terms, a reality lived from the body or the biography that as such escapes the discursive mediation of signs. However, not every recovery of experience should be confused with the naturalism of the primary fact. Taken in its non-ontological but rather epistemological dimension, the notion of experience has the critical value of postulating the historical-social concretion of subjectivities-in-context, the specific materiality of institutional positions through which these subjectivities communicate and recreate their meanings *in action*. Transferred to the realm of knowledge, resorting to experience tells us of a theoretical knowledge that produces itself as multiarticulated through local effects of signification.

Theorizing experience (to confer to it the analytical status of a construction of meanings) affirms the strategic value of a localized knowledge as much as becoming aware of the particular theoretical experiences that cultural criticism carries out in specific contexts.

Stuart Hall refers to the strategic value of this situated knowledge when he insists time and time again on the definition of cultural studies as a "contingent practice." This definition speaks to us of a theory of culture according to which culture creates itself by means of pacts of signification and struggles of interpretation always materialized in specific positions and situations, in "local histories" whose experiential density we should protect against the "global design" of theories which threaten to erase the real-concreteness of each practice of difference (Mignolo 1996b, 691). This model of cultural studies as a "contingent practice" would demand detailed attention to the localized microexperiences in certain folds of the cultural systems, which are not necessarily perceptible or decipherable from the academic-institutional reticulate.

In the case of Latin Americanism, this definition of "contingent practice" implies going through differentiated fields of critical experience, which do not allow themselves to be easily synthesized by the unified terms of the metropolitan reading device: broken planes that disarrange the topography of the academic discourse *about* Latin America, whose theoretical generalizations tend to skip the concrete function of the signs-in-use that, within each cultural geography, particularize the value of a knowledge that intervenes in its context.

I would like to illustrate the defense of these microexperiences localized in the irregular folds of the institutional weave with a reference to the Chilean case, mediated by a discussion about the divergent potential of local (peripheric) uses of certain authors internationalized today by the academic criticism of the Center. I want to use this Chilean example, mediated by a reference to the Argentinean discussion, in order to illustrate how the margins of theoretical competence are stratified according to different economies of intellectual labor that crisscross the Latin American context.

In a text entitled "Forgetting Benjamin," Beatriz Sarlo complains about the "indifferent banalizing" to which Walter Benjamin is submitted and whose name suffers, today, the simplifying usury sentenced by cultural studies. It is true that cultural studies' apparatus of technical reproduction not only requires a uniform reading regulated by mandatory lists of authors, but also requires an operation standardized by the theoretical styles of the academic international against which Beatriz Sarlo alleges. And one of the operations regulated by this new theoretical formulism urges us to dissolve all of the limits of disciplinary competence so that a new promiscuity of fields and methods would guarantee the *official* novelty of transdisciplinarity, making "texts that belong to the tradition of literary criticism put themselves under the advocacy of the new academic religion. Texts that have been classically inscribed in the theoretical discussion of literature move, via Bakhtin or Benjamin, to the overpopulated republic of cultural analysis" (Sarlo 1995, 19).

Beatriz Sarlo's argument is structured from the strong tradition of a university intellectuality that admits that certain texts like those of Benjamin have been circulating for a long time in the departments of humanities in Argentina, becoming academic references. Beatriz Sarlo's complaint against the deficient or trivial interpretations of Benjamin in the international academia makes use of the academic certification of her own disciplinary tradition and the rigorous antecedents of a knowledge authorized by that same tradition. If we had to confront Sarlo's criticism of the international academicism, in Chile, we could not do anything but contrast the strong and authorized tradition of university knowledge, whose legitimacy she resorts to, with our own constellation of unassembled motives that the critical discourse of the eighties in Chile put together, combining Benjamin with heteroclitic residues of cultural languages strongly unaffiliated with the whole university-theoretical legacy.[4] The experimental discourse of the eighties in Chile not only was gestated outside of the academic space (in illegal proximity to unsheltered works) but rather it also questioned the formalization of the exclusive—and excluding—disciplinary chart that Beatriz Sarlo evokes as the effective safeguard of the pertinence of her criticism. That is to say that, in Chile, they were discourses and theories intensely disarmed, which incorporated Benjamin as an eccentric piece in a collage that, without a doubt, represents a critical antecedent opposed to the present academic-international establishment that Sarlo criticizes, but that also distances itself from the disciplinary systematicity and propriety of the customary knowledge of the Argentinean intellectual tradition. Benjamin's unorthodox theorization, adapted in Chile within the confines of legitimate knowledge, would establish its controversial difference not only with the metropolitan centrality but also with the disciplined universe of academic competence of the Argentinean intellectual tradition. In opposition to that tradition they would place a renegade knowledge whose theoretical nonconformity questioned the local literary academicism as well as the cultural sociologism of the alternative centers of study in dictatorial Chile.

To mention the radical extra-systematicity of this "discourse of crisis," which theorized about the most convulsive borders of art and literature during the eighties in Chile, helps us to remember knowledges interwoven outside of the canon of the humanities but in dispute with the explicative paradigm of the social sciences, and it also helps us to highlight how the map of established disciplines and catalogued knowledges is disordered in contexts disturbed by multiple ruptures as in the case of dictatorial Chile. These were contexts in which cultural criticism had to try unexpected localizations, surfaces of emergency that don't figure into the institutional map of established studies, transversal gestures which locate themselves in the breeches and fissures of traditional disciplines long before they had any knowledge that that is the way it was prescribed by the new designs of the international academia.

These startling theoretical directionalities opened by knowledges that have escaped into the margins of the university systematizations, that rebel against the protected equilibrium of disciplines under contract, should also convoke the attention of Latin Americanism, to the extent that it wishes to respond to the task of realizing particularized readings specific to localities and localizations of language, whose force and significance depend on their concrete inscription in a determined field of intellectual positions.

In order to discover these widespread localities generally hidden behind the landscape of compiled resonant (strong and clear) voices collected in the prestigious anthologies published in the Center, Latin Americanism should learn to shade the centered protagonism of the social sciences, which, by virtue of the traditional post of observation and supervision they have occupied during the transition from dictatorship to postdictatorship, appear as official guarantors of the general debate about modernity-postmodernity in Latin America. Only a stroll through the lateral forking paths of the most eccentric fields of debate in its configuration of voices would give an account of other forms of distribution of the critical energies that don't necessarily coincide with the disciplinary distribution of knowledges obliged to a bibliographical systematization.[5] This would show how, in the Chilean case, those de-centered practices that used to fight against the executive and bureaucratic macrorationality of cultural sociology were the ones that knew how to inaugurate provocative forms of cultural criticism.

Marginalities, Classifications, and Revolts of Meaning

Upon speaking about the new circumstances under which the critical and theoretical practices at the times of Chilean dictatorship exercised their thinking in active demand against the technical formalism of university knowledge, I am referring to an argument which leads us to the question of how to define "cultural criticism": Is it a new game of academic pioneering carried out within a territory mapped by institutional pluralism or is it a rigorous border practice capable of thinking, critically, about the political and intellectual tensions between knowledge, discourse, language, and society?

The leitmotif of the "trans" fabricated by the new script of the academic culture speaks about borders, crossings, and mixtures, but many times it erases the "unrest of classification" (Barthes 1987, 73) that apparently would have wanted to exalt the critical will for nomadism and errancy indicated by a prefix that appeals to traffics and moves as opposed to sedentary formations of institutional knowledge. Today, transdisciplinarity is one of the theoretical fashions inciting the systems of knowledge to extend and to diversify the field of their objects of study in order to better understand an increasingly mobile and complex reality. But this larger plurality of methods of reading and analysis that cultural studies, for instance, revindicate, doesn't necessarily lead them to worry about the changes in discourse that these disciplinary intersections, summoned to participate in a new zone of free trade of knowledge, should produce. Roland Barthes already warned that "interdisciplinarity" "can't be carried out through the simple confrontation of specific knowledges; interdisciplinarity is not stress-free: it effectively begins . . . when the solidarity amid the old disciplines is broken, perhaps even violently . . . for the benefit of a new object, of a new language" (Barthes 1987, 73). The "unrest of classification" could, as a result, mark the difference between interdisciplinarity, conceived simply as the peaceful sum of complementary knowledges integrated into a new body of knowledge that is more inclusive and functional vis-à-vis the dynamics of change, and transdisciplinarity, which would entail the risk of becoming an *antidiscipline* upon trying to inaugurate new ways of knowledge that perturb the contented adaptation between knowledge, method, and objectivity.

Perhaps one of the most problematic subjects for thinking about the relationship between marginal and peripheral knowledges that cultural studies try to incorporate into the academic machine, and about the risks of re-institutionalization of knowledge involved in the search for academic legitimacy, has to do with the "politics of identity" and its reclassifications of the minor. According to George Yúdice, cultural studies were consolidated in the United States based on the "politics of representation" of "identity groups" (Yúdice 1993b, 17) struggling to democratize the institutions of civil society, and on the academic will to reinterpret the rights and necessities of subjects discriminated against by multiple grammars of exclusion, at the level of knowledge. And there is no doubt that the anti-discriminatory struggles that promote the insertion of minority groups in different public structures have required a more ample and flexible redefinition of the traditionally established criteria for selection, valuation, and recognition of cultural identities that have effectively pluralized the traditional academic model. But the "politics of representation" of "identity groups" have also simplified the questions of identity and representation, upon reducing them to the monodic formulation of a predetermined and easily synthesized condition by a unique coordinate of sexual or social identification (being a woman, gay, Latino, etc.) that apparently needs to be illustrated in always lineal and revindicating terms.

The tyranny of exemplarity, which cultural studies exercise when speaking the typifying language of classified marginalities, dominates when the characteristic traits of class, race, or gender are summoned to establish the univocity and transparency of an identity or a difference (being a woman, gay, Latino, etc.) that is expected to serve in the unique register of orthodox ownership. It is as if collective identity were repressing the free and changing deployment of the "I's" *to be created* in the fractured interior of each subject in order to comply with the normative awareness of well-learned and recited "We's." It is as if that public "we" only understood the monovalent language of functional correspondences between *being* and *talking as*: a language forced to follow a pedagogical maxim of an identity (being a woman, gay, Latino, etc.) that doesn't want to see its demonstrative goal interrupted with possible fantasy zigzags that let the subject gravitate toward mistakes in meaning.[6]

Quite possibly, feminism has most provocatively lived the discussion that deals with how to reconcile a policy of social action of the feminine "we" with a theoretical-cultural reflection about the symbolics and poetics of the "I" capable of converting the *difference* into a scenario of *multiple variations* that—intensively—goes through not just the bodies but also the vocabularies and the grammars. The challenge of having to know how to combine the concrete reference to women as the *real* subject of a work of social emancipation, on one hand, with, on the other hand, the postmetaphysical criticism of any categorical unity (for example, *the* woman) that reproduces the illusion of a semantic cohesion that we already know is disintegrated by the crisis of meaning led feminism to refine its strategy of thought and intervention in the intersected direction of a *double game:* a game that should combine the need for the subject to affirm itself (politically) as "identity" with the need for language to question itself (metadiscursively) as a "representation-of-identity." It is this double game alone that allows feminism to respond to the challenge of not having to renounce the collective struggles activated by a politics of identity that needs a community of reference, while, at the same time, exercising a constant theoretical and critical vigilance over the homogenizing weight of a re-foundational feminine "we" that could once again close the difference upon itself through a new identitary totalization.

If identity and difference are categories in process formed and articulated in the—mobile and provisional—intersections opened by each subject between the given and the created; if identity and difference are not fixed inventories of natural attributes but rather interpretative games that resort to multiple stagings and theatricalities, we shouldn't allow the necessity for a "politics of representation" to close down all the breeches of indefinition that fortunately maintain the categories in suspense and knowledge incomplete. The call of "identity politics"—divulged by cultural studies—for the subjects to reduce themselves to or coincide with the predominant trait of their class, identity, or gender representation (no matter how minor their contents are) usually blocks the lines of flight and rupture that the symbolic imaginary of cultural poetics is capable of unleashing in the conventional registers of social identification boosting the internal difference of each subject as a possibility to enter and leave the homogenous discourse of identity repeatedly.

As Yúdice states, cultural studies mobilize their university knowledge in alliance with the politics of identity and representation. But if we believe that cultural criticism should constitute an exercise that transversely questions the institutionalization of knowledge, it would have to be in charge of carrying out the deconstructive gesture capable of converting the relationship between politics, identity, and discourse into a relationship not only open to experimentations of content, as recommended by the politically democratizing tendency of cultural studies, but also interested in expressive explorations, in mutations of speech, and innovations of style. For this, the relationship between politics, identity, and discourse should not resign itself to lineally confirm and validate meanings of identity already classified as minor by the politics of institutional representation. It should rather enter into certain—opaque, diffused, and reticent—margins of nonrepresentation that question the dominant regime of visibility of the socially admissible roles in agreement with correspondences of other legitimate knowledges. These partially shifted margins of identity or difference in revolt with typologies and languages thwart the simplifying will of the academic institution to translate it all into a distribution of roles according to the raw classification of cultural sociology. These creatively dissident margins scoff—through its ambiguities and paradoxes of representation—at the call of institutional politics to follow a straight and continuous line of contents of identity to be conveyed through a language without twists and revolts of meaning. Exploring these margins is only possible when we put the institutional language of normalizing knowledge that doesn't dare to show "the tearings and perplexity of writing" into crisis (Tununa Mercado as quoted by Masiello 1996, 756).

Describing Changes, Changing Knowledge

Multidisciplinary knowledge, normalized nowadays by the academic standard of cultural studies, tends to generate investigative materials that have reduced the Text—a symbol of a dense essay tradition—to the utilitarian variant of the *paper*. This bureaucratic reduction has surrendered the rhetoric and figurative thickness of the language of "theory as writing" that thinks about *how* it is said, in favor of the techno-informative smoothness of facts. Against the *paper*, this methodological dominant in cultural studies, which pursues the mere calculability of signification and the manipulability of information, it would also be necessary to practice cultural criticism as an escaping zone capable of questioning the relationship between *subject of knowledge, language* and *knowledge*, without renouncing the undisciplined aesthetic torsion that averts a convenient and verifiable knowledge toward borders recharged with intense opaqueness that preserve truth as an enigma in suspense.

Literary studies have seen themselves violently shaken by the de-centering of the modern ideology of literature that, in Latin America, founded the critical conscience of the continental and the national, now threatened by the dispersive effect of the mass-media global networks, which fragment the integrative weave of the nation and its citizenry (Ramos 1996, 34).[7] Literary studies have also resented the confusion generated by the project of cultural studies that wishes to expand the notion of text to the semiotic articulation of any social practice, without dealing with the difference between *narration* (volume) and *information* (surface), which separates the indirect from the direct, the aesthetic symbolization from the communicative process. The crisis of the literary paradigm has raised the question—posed by Beverley—of "what would happen if literature were simply one of many discourses" (1995, 39), that is to say, when the border between everyday language (instrumentality of the message) and poetic language (self-reflexivity and polyvalence of the sign) dissolves. In other words, when all that is spoken and written come together under the same banal register of a mortal de-intensification of meaning, because the word will have stopped being theater or an event, becoming instead a simple currency of practical exchange without any luster, glow, or dramatic effect. I believe that the question about the future of the literary-aesthetic as the figurative will of a shattered and plural sign that criticizes mass communication also falls back on the imaginative dimension of the critical text, seriously threatened by a dispassionate bureaucratic language that erases from its notifying transactions any "pleasure of the text": any emotion or sparkle still linked to the trembling profile of suggestive, beautiful, or inefficient words. Words capable of acting out their *incongruity of styles* with regard to the "calculation of the categorical knowledge that tries to entrap the in-apprehensibility of the *who* of each subject in the *what* of its functions" dismissing—in passing—"the heterogeneity of the *other*, the prodigious episode of the *other*, all of which that *other* is when it is not just a useful life, summoning it to appear in the category" (Galende 1996, 53).

I agree with Federico Galende's criticism about the ingenuity of a certain knowledge of cultural studies that believes to be performing an act of knowledge through simply describing the real transformed with a language so in line with itself—and with its indexes of legibility largely approved—that it never asks about what the new agitates: for all that compels the new to break conventions and the verisimilitude of accepted vocabularies with the critical force of that which separates, disturbs, divides, shocks the interior of the established systems of designation. Cultural criticism should be attentive to this difference between "dogmatic knowledge," which formulates and displays the reasons why the present is like it is, and (interrogative) "critical knowledge," which doesn't conform to the conceptual generality of an explicative truth and perforates that order of rationalization with the—speculative—slash of doubt, conjecture, or utopia, thus claiming for writing against the didacticism of knowledge contented with applying a teaching technique.

But the idea of a knowledge that writhes in the arabesques of doubt, of (its) eternal questioning, is insufficient, without running the risk of an affirmation or a negation that, no matter how provisional it may be, subscribes or contradicts a determined act of meaning. To lose yourself in the infinite displacement of significations frustrating any encounter of the signifier with the signified and avoiding the whereabouts of names or categories conspires against the possibility that knowledge can exercise a transformative action over the institutional material structures since such an action requires for dubious thoughts to come out of their self-absorption in order to declare themselves in favor of or against certain meanings. Such a pronouncement requires the interruption of the unlimited chain of indefinitions in order to anchor itself in a locatable (referable) site from which it can toss out lines, mark positions, signify changes, since the organizing moment of an institutional struggle depends upon the capacity knowledge has (as an institutionalizable practice) to operate on concrete textures of meaning and references in order to intervene with its practical materiality.

While the agenda of "criticizing the disciplines, democratizing structures, modifying requirements, dismantling the canon, creating new spaces to work with more freedom" that John Beverley defends (1996b, 48) remains unfulfilled—within academia—cultural studies will be justified in fighting for criteria of practical effectiveness in order to transform the dynamic of university programs, departments, and curricula. However, the criticism of cultural studies should envision a combined double gesture that, on one hand, makes them name the change with recognizable words (even though the names may be already suspected of raising too much unanimity) because change should be nameable and communicable as a shared reference so that it may be inscribed politically and prevent, on the other hand, the danger of language and knowledge coming to illustrate the new institutional realism of the politics of academic change, under suspicion of an inadvertent stylistic conformism.

The "criticism of criticism" to which cultural studies should submit its agenda of reorganization of academic knowledge requires that many words currently intended to conceptualize the other and the other—

marginality, de-centering, heterogeneity, difference, subalternity, hybridity—keep available not only their potential for flexible articulation but also the most unruly force of a polyvalent language supplemented by local variations capable of misadjusting the planning of the metropolitan academia. Applied to the field of Latin Americanism, the means to keep the creativity of the concept alive, the only force capable of respecting the precariousness and the discontinuity of cultural formations in constant splitting of planes and disarray of series, could have to do with what Alberto Moreiras has called "a criticism of a tenuous object" (1995, 50): a criticism made possible after the weakening of those principles of identity that used to regulate the Latin American discourse of the sixties based on strong national allegories and third world emblems. This "criticism of a tenuous object" suggested by Moreiras would be opposed to the categorical endings of a dogmatic knowledge of the "efficient object," sustained by its opposites: in the lack of completion of a Latin American theory of borders and the in-betweenness particularly sensitive to the undoing and redoing of border significations; in the small heterologies of differential knowledges that escape through the cracks of the master disciplines; in the plural action of certain nonsensical peripheral writings that contort themselves in order to make fun of the recapitulating synthesis of the academic script.

Translated by Micah J. Mercurio

Notes

1. For instance, the asymmetries and inequalities that circulate and traverse the international theoretical network are related to the fact that "the study of Latin America is being globalized, its main texts are incorporated to the Western canon, but research opportunities are diminishing or vanishing for many Latin American intellectuals. . . . The Latin American intellectuality, sooner or later, finds out that the necessary conditions to practice literary and cultural criticism are largely met through fellowships and jobs abroad"; or that, "80 per cent of world journals devoted to Latin American literary criticism are published in the United States" (de la Campa 1996, 701).
2. For a powerful discussion on *testimonio* and its academic recovery, see Moreiras (1996b) and Williams (1996).
3. As an example of these recalcitrant, astute, and sly practices, I would like to quote Diamela Eltit's book, El padre mío (1989), whose literary rhetoricity denaturalizes the authentifying premise of *testimonio*, transgressing the "Latin Americanist" gender stereotyped by the North American academia.
4. For a critical reading of heterodox theorizations developed during the eighties by the Chilean artistic-cultural "new scene," see Richard (1994).

5. With respect to this point, I share Mignolo's opinion according to which "the reorganization of the production of knowledge, from a postoccidentalist perspective, would have to be formulated as a *border epistemology* in which the (philosophic, literary, essayist) reflection, incorporated to local histories, finds its place in the unincorporated knowledge of the social sciences global design" (Mignolo 1996b, 692).

6. With respect to this point, Françoise Collin, in her article "Praxis de la diferencia," points out: "How to be a political movement which does not reduce those female and male individuals who are consecrated to it to their definition as political subjects? What encloses them in the collective identity they have to constitute to affirm themselves? To escape within the political from political reductionism could only be done by constantly reinscribing the political rupture within the political, sheltering . . . that which escapes from it and transgresses it, making the infinite heterogeneity of language resonate within the homogeneous empire of discourse, preserving the memory of the undoing in the doing" (Collin 1995, 11).

7. Julio Ramos poses the issue in this way: "Probably, at the end of this century marked by the distinctive globalization of mass-media societies, social formations do not require the legitimizing intervention of those discourses which mold national integration, to the extent that the state pulls back from the republican contract of the representation of 'common welfare' and in that the media and consumption intertwine other parameters for citizen identification and its multiple exclusions. What then could be 'the future of literary studies' in the middle of such transformations?" (1996, 34–35).

ALBERTO MOREIRAS

Irruption and Conservation: Some Conditions of Latin Americanist Critique

Alberto Moreiras was born in Spain in 1956. A literary and cultural critic, he is a professor at Duke University in Durham, N.C. His main titles include *Tercer espacio: literatura y duelo en América Latina* (1999a), and *The Exhaustion of Difference: The Politics of
Latin American Cultural Studies* (2001).

Latin Americanist reflection today, understood as the sum total of academic discourse on Latin America, whether carried out in Latin America, in the United States, in Europe, or elsewhere, is one of the sites where the separation of intellectual labor from its very means of production is forcefully revealed. This separation shows up as a kind of expropriation, as an expropriating symptom, in the constitutive gap between theoretical discourse and the field of reflection. Granted that Latin Americanism seeks, in every case, something like an appropriation of a (Latin American) found object, the distance between the object and the appropriative intention remains irreducible. This irreducibility has today become thematized as the very name of the Latin Americanist game in an ongoing debate or series of debates involving the relative replacement of the traditional apparatus of literary studies by cultural studies in transnational reflection on Latin American culture; and also involving the weight within Latin Americanist reflection of intellectual currents that seem to flow all too unilaterally from U.S. university discourse toward the different Latin American academies.[1]

The conditions of possibility for Latin Americanist discourse have shifted over the last decade. What could still be understood in, say, 1985 as a crossing between our Americanist drives (in the footsteps of the well-known 1891 essay by José Martí) and the centripetal forces of scientific universalism—in other words, the whole apparatus of identity discourse to be paradigmatically applied whenever it was a question of attuning specific histories to general epistemologies and vice versa—is in 2000 an even more perplexing endeavor. The change is not merely due to the fact that the very concept of a "general epistemology" has consistently come under critical fire. It is also that, inverting Freud's definition of melancholy, whenever it is now a matter of reflecting upon historical specificity, the shadow of the reflecting subject is found to have always already fallen upon the object. Just as the disappearance of any "true" world ends up destroying the very possibility of thinking appearance, the failure of epistemic certainty drives the concreteness of the concrete into its grave. That is to say, Latin Americanism lives, if it is living, in a certain precariousness of experience—that unleashed by the fact that the waning of the critical subject involves the dissolution of the critical object itself.

Old philology arose in eighteenth-century Europe as the means the modern university gave itself to think about the social from the cultural legacies of the national community. It was soon hegemonized by the powerful literary apparatus, which came to exclude or subordinate attention to symbolic elements that could have shed some light on processes of cultural constitution. But contemporary Latin American cultural studies—lightly and hurriedly accused of being a mere transplant of British and North American provenance—are not understood by their critics to be, at least partially, a sort of return to the philological sources at the twilight of the modern Latin American state form.[2] They are rather said to start off from a blind or one-eyed will to negate literature—the latter taken as a promise of aesthetic autonomy and spiritual transformation of existence. Cultural studies, it is said, politicize everything, and thus nothing, and pay no heed to the preservation of the properly aesthetic values that have grounded the self-reproducing possibility of the humanist intellectual since romanticism. We will have to ask about the status of the aesthetic in contemporary reflection, and whether or not it can still provide, as it did in previous historical times, a paradoxical opening to some outside of history in relation to which reason could pursue its will to truth against the fetishizing of the real. What is at issue in the debate on literature and cultural studies is nothing but the specific valences of the critical function in the humanities. No doubt such a function cannot be exclusively claimed by any of the sides in the debate: but the function of critical reason is the dead center of the discussion.

Those who refuse to indulge in the mere denunciation of emerging reflection should also refuse to validate the nevertheless understandable desire of those who seek to preserve through their critique, but at all costs, their unchanged capacity for self-reproduction. Self-reproduction without mutation is no longer politically viable. Of course, in the last instance, the gesture whose possibility opens in cultural studies cannot be reduced to a simple return to the classical—that is, romantic—roots of philology. If politico-intellectual activity must be understood as the development of a critical relationship with the present, then academic politics in the humanities are fundamentally conditioned by the latter. A critical relationship with the present cannot be sustained on the insistence upon modalities of cultural discourse that have passed on to the historical archive after having exhausted their analytical productivity. I do not mean literature here, but rather literary studies, in the same way that we do not refer directly to culture when we say cultural studies (but to the apparatus for the study of culture). Literary criticism is today unsatisfactory in its traditional forms and objects, and it can no longer claim the position it once held as the arbiter of national culture. This is not an unannounced phenomenon. The irruption of so-called "theory" in literature departments—the unprecedented relevance of theoretical reflection for literary studies—after the 1960s was its first clear sign. Thirty years later we witness a new turn in the crisis: theory itself seems threatened, and withdraws. Cultural studies are apparently the new tool for hegemonic articulation. Literary criticism is powerless and cannot develop viable counter-hegemonic strategies, and something similar happens to theory. The problem of succession to the old is open, and it involves and interpellates all of us.

But we need to move beyond stating the obvious. I find Charles Taylor's differentiation between "cultural" and "acultural" theories of modernity useful because it enables us to establish a distinction between modernity as "modernization," that is, as a teleological tool or set of tools for the instrumental rationalization of the world, and the more properly historical usage of modernity as what results from the diversified impact of capitalism upon social formations across the world (1999, 152–53). For Taylor the ideological notion of modernity as modernization is today obsolete and lacking in philosophical value. He is therefore more concerned with "cultural" notions of modernity. From the acknowledgment that the world-system, in its imperial expansion, determines modernity, he goes on to suggest that there is not one modernity but many alternative ones, and that it is the task of reflection in the humanities to understand them all in their historical specificities. But the notion of alternative modernities is not an exhaustively culturalist notion: it merely registers the fact that the history of capital and the history of social power—understood as the constitutive state of the symbolic sphere in any given social formation—are not the same thing. To investigate their non-identity is then to investigate alternative modernities, or what is alternative or multiple within modernity.

Taylor's notion could curiously constitute a basis for the rigorous meta-critical defense both of the literary-critical apparatus and of cultural studies, especially in reference to the theoretical analysis of the symbolic production of peripheral and semi-peripheral societies in the world-system (see Wallerstein 1974 and 1991). The Latin American literary tradition is in point of fact almost exhaustively definable as the quasi-systematic exploration of the specificity of the Latin American alternative modernity from today's outdated concepts of identity and difference. Latin Americanist tradition never really subscribed other than marginally to "acultural" theories of modernity. All the great figures of this tradition, from Clavijero, Bello, Sarmiento, and Martí to Rama or Cornejo Polar through Reyes, Henríquez Ureña, Candido, Rodríguez Monegal, and Fernández Retamar, were culturalists in Taylor's sense. But the master concepts of identity and difference keep finding a new if precarious life in the new space of cultural studies. It could in fact be said that a large part of Latin American cultural studies work is nothing but an engaged reproduction and transplantation of the old historiographic categories to new texts: the literary referent is often rather mechanically substituted with alternative referents, but the questions remain—a bit farcically— the same.

It is true—it has the truth of tautology—that something is gained when criteria for inclusion are expanded and it becomes possible, for a literary scholar, to read the cinematographic text, or the text of the new social movements, in a situation where it had not previously been allowed to move beyond the essay, the novel, or the poem. In this cultural studies do return to the philological spring, since philology wanted to explore cultural specificity through an ample repertoire of discursive traces. And it is also tautologically true that something is lost when those who read such texts—the preservers—do it on the limiting basis of a certain weakening of their technical capacity. Their reading capacity is in principle weakened because readers educated in an exhaustive attention to the literary cannot simply transfer their attention to the nonliterary and expect to produce results of a similar strength. But there is no reason to think that the history of reading is ecstatic and that adequate tools for the kind of reading which is pertinent to the widening of textual space will not be developed soon. It is, however, truer, and more interesting, and not tautological, to conclude that, if the simple considerations above are more or less accurate, then cultural studies today, from a literary perspective, is still far from having created a new paradigm for Latin Americanist reflection. Cultural studies, from the point of view of its reading practices, its master concepts, and its geopolitical inscription, is, to a certain extent, more of the same. The old and the new thus share a similar anachronism—or a similar novelty. [3]

We then have to wonder about the real motives underlying the dispute between cultural studies and literary studies. If both practices are to a large extent the same, and only the textual object changes, why the mutual antagonism? A perhaps more provoking way of asking the same question is to say: If the old literary-critical and the new culturalist apparatuses use the same concept of critical reason, and if such a concept is circumscribed to the determination, evaluation, and defense of what is properly Latin American or intra–Latin American in the specific Latin American alternative modernity, if the concept of critical reason used by all sides of the disputation cannot go beyond the affirmation of an identitarian space-in-resistance, whether from a continental, national, or intranational perspective, then how is any real concept of critique at stake in the debates? And how are the debates handling the potentiality of a renewal of reason attuned to the needs of thinking for the present? Can critical reason dissolve in identitarian or differential description? Has Latin Americanist reflection ever done anything but engage in the attempt at precisely such descriptions? Can it ever do anything else? Are the debates in question looking for something else?

A certain aporetics has become everyday currency. Take your average non–Latin American Latin Americanists: they must hear, as a constant background murmuring, that their efforts to think Latin America from their location in the cosmopolitan university have, as a damning condition of possibility, their all-too-comfortable installation in the methodological trends and fashions of world-hegemonic university discourse. The problem is not that those trends and fashions are "foreign," but rather that they are excessively familiar as "foreign." Latin American Latin Americanists can invariably confront their boreal counterparts with the disquieting thought that, whatever the intended novelty in their discourse, it is never novel enough: "I already know where you are coming from; before you speak, I already know what you will say—because I know what produces you. What you want to give me is not even yours; it belongs to someone else. I cannot then make it mine."

But look now at your stereotypical Latin American Latin Americanist and you will realize that she is by no means off the hook: if the problem of her alien friend was an excessively comfortable installation in the privileges of Northern knowledge, and if such sinister installation in knowledge (sinister because "excessively comfortable," and thus not comfortable at all) was inverted as a mark of unredeemable ignorance, Latin American Latin Americanists may find a dubious legitimation in the positing of location as final redemption. But then location was precisely what always already delegitimized their outsiding others. How can location function simultaneously as a source of legitimation and as its opposite? The apparent answer is that "proper" location works, improper location does not. The Latin American Latin Americanist must find her or his truth in a discourse of propriety which is however never secure as such: it is simply based on the expropriation of the impropriety of the other. "Take this, since it does not come from elsewhere," she says, without realizing that, if it is not to come from elsewhere, then nobody (else) can take it. She is therefore herself expropriated.

One of the first large institutional fora devoted to the mutual display of less than friendly emotion between Latin Americanist literary and cultural studies scholars was the meeting of the Brazilian Comparative Literature Association (ABRALIC) in Rio de Janeiro in August 1996. The conference theme called for the defense of a space for thinking culture beyond the re-inscription of the literary understood as a reactive formation. Or, from the alternative perspective, it was a matter of protecting a space of thinking called literary studies from the intrusion of an emergent field called cultural studies. For the audience and panelists alike, a decision had to be made if it had not been previously made. That is, one had to make a decision insofar as what was at stake was not simply to fulfill a program for the acquisition and maintenance of academic or symbolic power for some people or their antagonists. At the Rio meeting literature—but it never was literature; it was rather the literary discipline in all of its archival wealth but also in all of its misery—held the place of truth from the institutional perspective. Therefore it had to guard itself against a graphematic structure that was threatening to divest it of subjective power or even to eliminate its subject position—in other words, that was threatening to turn it into a lie. But, whatever the power negotiations within the Brazilian academy, for an outside observer it soon became obvious that the disputation could not be considered a confrontation between autonomous knowledges or autonomous subjects of knowledge. It was not a confrontation between alternative but already constituted codifications of institutional value. The discursive battle brought face-to-face two armies that had been born into themselves out of their mutual opposition: two instances or vectors of force whose dissimilarity or heterogeneity was a direct result of the need to cut or divide a territory that had previously been indifferently occupied. In any case a

certain violence became visible and it embodied two empirical characterizations: on the one hand, the dividing and founding violence of cultural
studies, which I will call force; on the other hand, the divided and con-
serving violence of literary studies, which I will call power. It was not,
and it is not, a pure division: the division was marked from its inception
by mutual contamination. "Power" makes reference to the hegemonic
site of the literary in the Brazilian discussion; "force" to the irruptive position of cultural studies. But we will indeed see the precariousness of
such distinctions. The irruption of the new soon became conservative,
and the preservation of the old revealed itself, through its very spirit of
resistance, as the site for potentially new forms of irruption.

The structure that thus came to light was from the beginning complicated by the fact that both power and force were not merely originary instances, endowed with a full capacity for autonomous self-inscription.
They were conditioned, and overdetermined, by their previous form of
presence in a space that was not the same institutional space that was
now hosting the battle, even if it was not totally heterogeneous to it. The
mode of pre-inscription of both power and force at the Rio meeting was
chiasmatic, and it depended upon a transnational frame that in itself
seemed to have undergone a hegemonic mutation in which a historically
previous relationship had been inverted. What in the transnational context was emergent power had become irruptive force in Brazil; and what
was residual force in the transnational sphere was occupying the space of
threatened power in Brazil. Thus part of the mutual contamination between dividing and divided violence came from the fact that force and
power in Brazil respectively translated power and force in the transnational space. Or thus ran the story of the Rio discussion.

At the sessions, at the halls, at the bars, during the walks along the
beach it was possible to think that the defense of the literary apparatus
was at the same time a defense of the national or the regional order
against an interference that could only be understood as neocolonial,
since it emanated from a transnational space that was hegemonized by
the U.S. metropolis; and it was possible to think that the transnationaliz-
ing cosmopolitanism of the irruptors could be defined, in at least one
and not the least significant of its facets, as imperial serfdom. On the opposite side, that is, on the side of the irruptors, it could be thought that
the defense of the literary space, granted that it was the defense of a previously constituted national space, was compromised by the concomitant
ideological defense of established social domination within the nation
against new interpellations that would want to dismantle it. And then of
course both positions are simultaneously true and false: they are true be-

cause they describe factual phenomena; and they are false because they do not describe them well enough.

I do not know in any detail how the situation that became schematic at the Rio meeting has evolved in Brazil since 1996 (see Miranda 1998 and Souza 1998). Within Spanish-language Latin Americanism the controversy, which also began around the same year, turned quickly and effectively hot, and it soon drew a peculiar pattern: the open and explicit accusation made against U.S.-based Latin Americanist cultural studies scholars of engaging in cultural colonialism on the basis of an undue appropriation and reproduction of the Latin American cultural object. An element that was absent in Rio should now be added to this story, and it may prove to be a decisive element even if at first it may appear as merely confusing: the attack against U.S.-based cultural studies did not primarily come from literary scholars, that is, it did not primarily come from members of the various Latin American national intelligentsias that could be identified with a defense of more or less residual power positions.[4] It came from prominent academic intellectuals whose credentials as thinkers in the tradition of cultural studies are rather impeccable. They seemed to have substituted conservation, a certain conservation, for irruption—which is, certainly, not necessarily a bad thing. Everything depends upon what it is that is trying to emerge, and on what it is that one wishes to preserve.

Thus the 1996 ABRALIC discussion between power and force, between literary and cultural studies, took a different turn upon reproducing itself as a transnational complaint from some significant Latin American practitioners of cultural studies force against the constituted power of the largely North American academy. But I think this was still a turn within the same controversy, and not an alternative or supplementary one. In both cases, we have the two forms of violence, one dividing and founding, the other divided and conservative, and in both cases we have a reaction against a tendential displacement caused by the irruption within the institutional field of a graphematic structure that is both threatening and invasive. The tactical variation that led Spanish-language Latin American critics to launch their attack against their Latin Americanist friends from the North springs from the mutual contamination of the two instituting violences, and it marks simply a second phase of the same dispute.

The growing accumulation of a series of polemical writings within the last few years—and, still more significantly, the impact of the controversy on field formation and development: conference discussions, seminar conversations, dissertation topics, and so forth—constitutes something like a minor scandal, the effective comprehension of which is still not quite accessible but will have to be pursued. To the extent that we cannot trivialize these accusations by considering them totally justified on the basis of the fact that they attack poorly conceived work, it is necessary to foreground their importance, which encompasses not just cultural and intellectual but also historical, political, and geopolitical fields of reflection and action. A thoroughly fundamental question is at stake, and it is a question as to the minimal conditions for an effective critique of knowledge in the contemporary world. Latin American critics of the U.S. academic establishment are quite right that the post-1989 crisis of the area studies apparatus released a spectrum or two into the world. If area studies were centrally committed to the productive containment of thought within the geopolitical parameters of the Cold War, the current situation of area-based (but not area-bound) university discourse in the U.S. academy—what we could call the disorientation and disoccidentalization of post-area studies—has broken containment and expanded into a diffuse borderlands where all cows seem equally colored and no single cat stands out. Under those conditions, there is indeed a risk that the de-Americanization of knowledge, which is ostensibly pursued, can at times appear undecidably as its opposite; there is also the risk that the calls for diversity and cultural creativity, the abandonment of the national referent, and a newly found theoretical interest in the subaltern may constitute a new avatar of more traditional tools for U.S. cultural domination. It may be that U.S. post-area studies, in other words, far from being a new space of experimentation in the freedom of knowledge, is little more than yet another "cunning of imperialist reason," in Pierre Bourdieu's sense (Bourdieu and Wacquant 1999, 41)—indeed, imperial reason itself.

And yet that suspicion may itself be implicated in the very same logic it ostensibly fights when it moves by means of blanket indictments that make no differentiations and establish no boundaries. There must be a difference after all between, say, postcolonial studies and neoliberal thought, and the distinction between critical race theory and rational choice conceits is not a mere trifle when it comes to investigating or contesting the American domination of epistemic fields concerning any and all areas of the world. We all know enough about the interrelationship between blindness and insight in critical work to understand that no one is free from errors and prejudices that necessarily contaminate that work. But the ongoing controversy, which is now mostly reduced to repeating what everybody already knows for the most part, may be stagnating or may have reached an impasse: a certain disorientation has come to affect all sides and it is apparently impossible to move beyond an endless drawing and redrawing of already staked-out positions and a vague commitment to the necessary reestablishment of redemptive macro-narratives. But the fundamental question remains: Is it possible to reaffirm the non-imperial destiny of critical reason, or is such a pretension nothing but the final movement of an exhausted Enlightenment that can barely survive by holding onto the illusion that thought and power are not the same, against all kinds of historical evidence? No call for a more adequate historicization, no pretense about the epistemic privileges of location, and no suspicions about political bad faith can adequately deal with that question: those things are not enough.

We must understand the current discussions as symptomatic of a geo-cultural change, which is as such necessarily destabilizing for all, but for an understanding of which the old parameters of cultural imperialism are seriously inadequate. Ways of thinking developed in the North in order to deal critically with ongoing changes are not to be mechanically defined as imperialist for the simple fact that they hope to attain some influence in the South. I understand "geoculture" in Immanuel Wallerstein's sense, that is to say, as the "cultural frame" for the current world-system, today undergoing transition according to Wallerstein, and in respect of which 1989, the year that ciphers the end of the Cold War, remains "a door closed upon the past" (Wallerstein 1991, 11 and 15). I want to propose three hypotheses about such geocultural change, which I will offer briefly and without drawing from them all pertinent considerations.

First Hypothesis

The first hypothesis is the most obvious: the presentation of this polemic as a polemic between literary and cultural studies is a decoy whose constitution is ideological and which therefore ought not to deceive anyone—perhaps paradoxically. What is at stake is not literature, nor its study, nor even aesthetics. What is at stake is not the text nor any of the ways of reading developed through the many years of hegemony of the literary field. It is rather a matter of dealing with a geocultural displacement that is in the last instance motivated and sustained by a substantive change in the structure of capitalism at the planetary level. I do not want to suggest that there is a relationship of simple causality between mode of production and cultural superstructure. I am, rather, interested in the mediations that have been taking place over the last decades concerning the expansion and globalization of capital accumulation; in the changes in the financial structures of capital, changes in the state form, in the sociopolitical regimes of rule, in the end of the division of the world into power blocs; in the development of new antisystemic movements in what some would still call civil society, and in their combined effects upon the production, distribution, circulation, and consumption of knowledge. All of that amounts to a massive geocultural shift in the specific codifications and recodifications of sociohistorical value. We must cipher the origins of the polemic that so markedly affects the until recently leading function of literary studies in a change in the structures of knowledge, a paradigmatic slide whose consequences, although everywhere noticeable, cannot yet be understood with sufficient clarity.

If capitalism in its previous stage produced affective territorializations on the basis of an encoding of social value where literary studies had a key function as preservers of the unified space of the nation, the contemporary mode of production codetermines an alternative kind of affective identifications for the rationalization and processing of which literary studies are grossly insufficient.[5] That does not mean one can no longer study literature, even understand literature within the horizon of a thinking of irruption and force—it only means that literary studies have lost their hegemonic function for the ideological production of social value. The game of irruption and conservation must be understood, in all its complexity, within that schematics.

The academic apparatus called cultural studies will thus tendentially substitute literary studies in the ideological articulation of the present. The latter will now assume a subaltern function. This process will not occur without problems, since it involves a restructuring of academic power and the subsequent redistribution of cultural capital within university discourse. Interpretative wars are therefore inevitable. But they are also to a certain extent useless if they are only meant to vent resentment against ongoing social processes. We can understand and resist the latter—we can proceed, for instance, toward the critique of the emerging apparatus—but we cannot deny that those processes are taking place lest we condemn ourselves to maintaining nonviable critical positions (which lose henceforth all critical power). That is my first hypothesis. As a corollary, I want to say that the new subaltern function of literary studies endows it with a forceful irruptive potential. We are far from having "dealt with" the literary—but the tools proper to literary reflection must be redesigned in view of the emerging configurations of knowledge. Literary reflection can find a new role in a potential counter-hegemonic articulation, an articulation that we could also call "ultrapostmodern," using Perry Anderson's admittedly clumsy term, and which still needs to be conceptually developed (1998, 102 passim). I should refer from this perspective to some questions that I left pending above.

There is an implied possibility in Taylor's distinction that I have not yet commented upon: the possibility according to which what is fundamentally important for the study of alternative modernities has to do with the lag or lack of overlap between the history of capital and the history of social power. If the notion of critical reason still holds irruptive power and is not simply a citation from some obsolete ideologeme, then critical reason must exert itself, through historical imagination, in the attempt to understand the totality of the social relations that condition us as well as our past. Our immediate past's critical project, at least for those of us who were formed in the Latin Americanist humanities, was very precisely to understand the Latin American alternative modernities in their various specificities. We were trained to do so through the understanding and exploration of an aesthetic mode of production that was determined by a historicist modernism whose first emblematic productions could well be José Martí's "Nuestra América," Rubén Darío's "A Roosevelt," or José Enrique Rodó's *Ariel*. Within that configuration the aesthetic was never an end in itself or was already fundamentally loaded by historicist weight. Only historicism could allow for an understanding and a strengthening of Latin American social power against the incursions of monopoly capital—the latter blamed as a source of sociohistorical alienation.

The aesthetic was therefore a means toward historicism although no doubt one could also say that historicism, insofar as it was a culturalist historicism, could simultaneously be understood as a tool for aesthetic satisfaction.[6] The Latin American national-popular state, which defined or sutured symbolic production in the region from the beginning of the twentieth century until the late 1970s, was a form of aesthetization of the political—certainly so for José Vasconcelos, but also, say, for Fernando Ortiz and for Angel Rama, not to mention Jorge Luis Borges, Octavio Paz, or the boom literature. Critical reason for that period was an aesthetic-historicist project that looked to preserve and reinforce the specificity of Latin American (and Argentinean, Mexican, et cetera) social power against an invasive and threatening outside.

What has changed? How is it now sayable that the project of critical reason has undergone a fundamental modification, one of whose symptoms is the contemporary dispute between literary and cultural studies? And in what sense can it be said that cultural studies will only come into its own, that is, will only be able to understand itself as a critical relationship with the present, if it manage to determine a specificity of its own? Can cultural studies develop a style of thinking that will no longer be associated with a mere expansion of the textual corpus within aesthetic-historicist postulates for the sake of the construction and strengthening of the national-popular state and against monopoly capital?

One wishes that the problem would end there: that one could simply proceed toward an answer that would solve the issue. "All right," the Latin American Latin Americanist says, "if those self-appointed cosmopolitans and neocosmopolitans are right, if we can no longer think clearly against capital and for the nation, if the old location of thinking has become a problem and not the solution, let's solve the problem by imagining alternative locations." But there is a further element of destabilization in the fact that the very discourse of location, that is, the substitution of the national or the regional by the local, which only a few years ago seemed to give us a new beginning to think about/from/of Latin America under the geopolitical conditions of university discourse in the time of post-area studies, has finally revealed itself as a ruinous thinking, or a thinking in the ruins of thinking.

Taylor's culturalist theory of modernity, like all historicisms, depends upon a determinate tropology that Martin Heidegger may have defined for our time on the basis of Wilhelm Dilthey's work: the tropology of the hermeneutic circle (Heidegger 1962, 188–95 passim). The hermeneutic circle marks, for culturalism, the epistemological limit of human existence as such. To understand one's own culture, or even somebody else's culture, means to enter and dwell within that culture's hermeneutic circle. But Taylor's presentation of his culturalist theory of modernity on the basis of a theorization of the lag between the history of capital and the history of social power seems tendentially to dismantle his own constitutive tropology. In other words, if the sphere of social power within any given culture is subjected to historical change, and if historical change is not simply a function of that culture's internal dynamics, but also or above all a function of heterogeneous factors (such as spatial contaminations from the outside in the form of military conquest or political or economic domination), then the hermeneutic circle never closes. That is, the hermeneutic circle, insofar as a cultural world goes, is never a circle, but simply a circle's catachresis. But then the culturalist theory of modernity loses its necessity and becomes a mere tropological approximation to an ideology of the truth of the world. What goes for the national goes for any conceivable locality as well, since locational thinking simply alters the expanse of the hermeneutic circle but does not destroy it.

The first tendential contribution of cultural studies to the destruction of the aesthetic-historicist paradigm is no doubt the vague intuition that the understanding of a given social formation's culture as a hermeneutic circle is a mere ideological prejudice. That seems to me the great and quasi-inaugural contribution of Néstor García Canclini's *Culturas híbridas* (1989a). To use Deleuzian/Guattarian vocabulary, the hermeneutic circle would stand revealed, in every case, as a striated or segmented space under the pretense of smoothness. The hermeneutic circle is a circle of hegemony. It is in fact a function of the constitution of the public sphere or of the space of social power as a hegemonic relation. Hegemony, as one of the master concepts to represent political modernity, was always itself understood as an imaginary circle, or rather, as a sphere. Power and subordination within the hegemonic sphere were very precisely intraspheric. The constitution of the political sphere around the notion of the nation-state within the political tropology of modernity is no doubt not a circumstantial fact, but rather an essential and all-determining one.

But the threat to or the destabilization of the hermeneutic notion of culture on the basis of its insufficiency is a contribution of cultural studies that cultural studies itself does not seem to understand all too well. In the specific case of Latin American historicity cultural studies must engage in the radicalization of its own postulates and look for the remainder beyond transculturation, the outside of hermeneutic circularity, and what has been subalternized as the constitutive outside of the hegemonic relation. This amounts to a proposal for a fundamental revision of the goal of critical reason. Critical reason in cultural studies is no longer (or should not be) aesthetic-historicist, but it is rather fundamentally committed to the deconstruction of the inside/outside relationship on which any and all historicisms, including the historicisms of intranational or diasporic locality, and therefore all cultural theories of modernity, have always been structurally established. In my opinion such a proposal has not yet come to fruition, whether on the Latin Americanist side or on the side of British or American (or Australian) cultural studies.

What kind of tropology could today replace the master tropology of the hermeneutic circle, with its corollary, which is the supplemental tropology of the outside as a savage space? What kind of thinking could think the abandonment of the hegemony as the master concept to think about culture in our own time, to think modernity alternatively, and to think postmodernity? A fundamental revision of critical reason must abandon its aestheticist or historicist horizon, a legacy of the modernist past, and seek the undoing of the inside/outside polarity on which all aesthetic historicisms and all culturalist theories of modernity rest. We could think then of the irruptive possibilities of the postaesthetic and posthistoricist language that the literary promise still withholds and could provide—but not without a certain effort.

There is nothing, in my opinion, wrong in principle with any kind of ruinous thinking, and thinking in the ruins of thinking may in fact define the conditions of intellectual labor for our age. The problem, here, is also elsewhere. Locational thinking, to the extent that it thought of itself as something other than a thinking of or in the ruins of the local, thought of itself as what we could call translational or translative thinking. For a thinking of location it was always a matter of vindicating the sheer (utopian) possibility of a retrieval of what Walter Benjamin would have called "pure language" by means of the literary labor of translation—understanding translation radically, as the infinite opening to history. If history is, among other things, the story of power and resistance, then locational thinking undertook to retrieve the historicity of resistance as itself a form of power. We could alternately describe this by suggesting that locational thinking was already a thinking of expropriation, of history's expropriation, and of the expropriation of the thinker as well. The labor of translation undertook to liberate what the later Julio Cortázar would have referred to as a sort of intersemiotic ghost: if the ghost is precisely that which can never leave the place of erstwhile dwelling, the rooted trace of history, then the locational thinker is the thinker for whom what remains at stake is precisely what remains. And what remains can only be found, through translative digging, at the very crossing of the intersemiotic systems—for instance, at the crossing of colonial discourse and subaltern negation in Latin America.

If the crossing of colonial discourse and subaltern negation is the very object of this thinking of expropriation, then it is clear that no thinking of propriety is an adequate rendition of it. The fight between the stereotypical Latin Americanists from the South and from the North is a staged fight, a wrestling match between jokers, since what is at stake there, in that match, is anything but, precisely, what remains. The Latin American Latin Americanist, or one who assumes that position, has no real right to assume the representation of subaltern negation, because he or she also thinks from colonial discourse, just as, for example, the U.S. Latin Americanist (and all other cosmopolitans and neocosmopolitans, to the extent that they are Latin Americanists) is no impeccable representative of the system of epistemic domination. Location, here, is always already crossed, and crisscrossed. A critical position is no automatic gift of commodified location.

Second Hypothesis

The second hypothesis is the following: cultural studies, in an accelerated process of expansion and transnationalization, is already losing its unity as an irruptive and dividing force. As it happened to literary studies, cultural studies has been captured by its very iterability and is today in a large measure in a process of consolidation as epistemic power, within each of its alternative possibilities, at the service of the ideological reproduction of late capitalism. This no doubt fuels what was earlier called the "second phase" of ongoing debates. If cultural studies' irruptive strategies could at first present or conceive of themselves as endowed with some founding violence—it happened to literature in Latin America some one hundred and fifty years ago—such irruptive possibilities are today largely tamed, at the service of new encodings of social value. The differential and mutual contamination of the two forms of violence, the fact that they grow by division of a given territory, means that the present violence of consolidation will be followed by new forms of founding. It is then a matter of understanding the game so that we can avoid being caught unawares by the reification of social values that accompanies the ideological reproduction of the movement of capital. It is still critical reason that can mobilize thought and make it a producer rather than a reproducer.

The defense of cultural studies, still necessary in the face of archaic or reactionary forms of intellectual labor, is not in any case an unconditional defense. In that sense discussions between intellectuals from the South and the North are as essential as those between North and North or South and South. But they should not be undertaken in the name of the preservation of reactive cultural capital. In other words, effective attacks come from the dividing force that determines critical reason—critiques must come from the grapheme against entrenched truth, and not the opposite. Some of the protests come from Latin American cultural studies scholars against a certain excess—against the tendential or potential radicalization of cultural studies into, for instance, subalternism. Historical imagination, which was the condition of possibility of philology, still appears today as the specific strength of reflection in the humanities. Only historical imagination can meditate on the difference between what is coming and what could come, and between the present and the past. Holding on to historical imagination is a point of departure for any emergent rearticulation of critical reason. It is essential to fight the tendential reduction of thinking to the condition of a means for the technical reproduction of what there is. In that sense, the division of the intellectual field, or of the humanities, between literature and culture, between literary reflection and cultural critique, between what is radical, or too radical, and what attempts to preserve—the reification of that division into two fields with opposing interests collaborates with the shrinking of thought, and can only lead to further disasters of various kinds.

This is perhaps the place to mention two recent books, which in a sense belong to my own critical location, Fredric Jameson's *The Cultural Turn* (1998a) and Perry Anderson's *The Origins of Postmodernity* (1998), as both of them have something to say that affects my argument directly. Anderson's book is substantially a re-evaluation of Jameson's theory of postmodernism as the theoretical horizon of our time. Anderson generally limits himself to an exposition and endorsement of Jameson's thought, which he considers the culmination of Western Marxism. I will focus upon the last section of his book, entitled "Politics," and concretely on two remarks that will allow me to develop my position.

Elaborating upon the notion that Jameson's theory of postmodernity finds its ground in the systematic counterpoint between "a plane of substance (political economy) and a plane of form (the aesthetic)" (P. Anderson 1998, 125), Anderson detects what he considers a certain reduction of the political into a minor or subsidiary role within the system. He notes the absence of any sustained study of Antonio Gramsci in Jameson's work. About Gramsci's work Anderson says: "It was eminently political, as a theory of the state and civil society, and a strategy for their qualitative transformation. This body of thought is bypassed in Jameson's . . . resumption of Western Marxism" (131). In the Marxist tradition Gramsci was the great thinker of the hegemonic circle and of its counterpart, subaltern power. The omission of this thematic in postmodernism theory is not just casual neglect: it has to do very precisely with the determination of postmodernity as the moment in capitalist development when "culture becomes in effect coextensive with the economic" (131). In Jameson's own words, postmodernist language suggests "a new cultural realm or dimension which is independent of the former real world, not because, as in the modern (or even the romantic) period, culture withdrew from that real world into an autonomous space of art, but rather because the real world has already been suffused with it and colonized by it, so that it has no outside in terms of which it could be found lacking" (Jameson 1998a, 161).

Jameson's postmodernism theory implies the necessary deconstruction of the notion of hegemonic circle, or even of the hermeneutic circle understood as a definition of culture, because it involves a radical reduction of the notion of an outside, without which a hermeneutic circle cannot constitute itself as such. A maximum reduction of the possibility of an outside pushed toward their limit the political possibilities of a theoretical reflection on culture in modernist terms. If in full-blown postmodernism the history of capital and the history of social power become one and the same, then the very project of critical reason, which was in modernity based upon the non-identity of social form and social content, as Taylor might put it, is undermined in its very formulation. And the same happens to aesthetic thinking, which is always necessarily based upon the possibility of an existing if unreachable outside, upon the Borgesian "imminence of a revelation that never arrives," which is aesthetically posited as the transaesthetic foundation of the real and therefore as foundation of the aesthetic itself. In one of his more striking formulations Jameson says: "The image is the commodity today, and that is why it is vain to expect a negation of the logic of commodity production from it, that is why, finally, all beauty today is meretricious and the appeal to it by contemporary pseudo-aestheticism is an ideological manoeuvre and not a creative resource" (Jameson 1998a, 135).

What is then the type of historical imagination that could warrant a reformulation of the project of critical reason as a properly politico-epistemological project? In other words, where can we find a force for intrasystemic irruption if the system has expanded in such a way that no productive notion of an outside is permitted? A second remark by Anderson attempts to save the possibility of political articulation in postmodernity as an intrasystemic movement, in reference to Carl Schmitt's theorization of the political field as the field of division between friends and enemies. Anderson says:

> The aesthetic and the political are certainly not to be equated or confused. But if they can be mediated, it is because they share one thing in common. Both are inherently committed to critical judgment: discrimination between works of art, forms of state. Abstention from criticism, in either, is subscription. Postmodernism . . . is a field of tensions. Division is an inescapable condition of engagement with it. (P. Anderson 1998, 134–35)

I will finish this commentary to my second hypothesis by foregrounding that strange possibility of a critical reason that becomes irruptive or disruptive on the basis of the apparent impossibility of any irruption, of any disruption. Friendship and enmity become for Anderson the figures for a perpetual redivisioning of the social field. The critical possibility is thus given in the possibility of friendship, of which Jacques

Derrida says that it can constitute, in its radicalization, "when . . . we come to call the friend by a name that is no longer that of the near one or the neighbor, and undoubtedly no longer the name of man," "an unprecedented thought of rupture and interruption" (1997, 293).

Jameson does not negate, but rather postpones, such interruptive possibility, which for him must arrive in some yet unimaginable future after a dialectical modification of the system. Derrida's words, which take here their departure from the Nietzschean thought of the "perhaps," are merely tentative and preparatory: what he imagines as a radical opening to the friend is also based upon the absolute subsumption of otherness into sameness, which is an intrinsic part of Jameson's postmodernism. When there is no longer an imaginable outside, by the same token we lose the possibility of an inside that would permit the simple division of the territory of the political between friends and enemies. The collapse of the classical distinction, the end of the friend and the end of the enemy, inaugurates the new aporetic possibility of the friend—as well as the new aporetic possibility of the enemy. A chance must be taken, on the basis of the Nietzschean perhaps, which does not entirely reduce the sinister possibility of the utterly dystopian or monstrous future—a future ruled over by the figure of the new enemy, rather than the figure of the new friend. Something like a Nietzschean "grand politics" comes then to establish a watch and keep vigilant over the possibility of a political reason and a critique of knowledge that Derrida entrusts to the "literary community" (1997, 293), but in a sense which is now to be considered postaesthetic and no longer simply modern.

The commodification of location in locational thinking—the conversion of expropriation into propriety and, finally, into property—is an undesirable but structural by-product of the literary labor of translation. That it haunts Latin Americanist reflection today is a given. The irreducibility of a critical distance between conditions of reflection and field of reflection—or, if you want, the critical irreducibility of such a distance—finds itself put to work at the service of a betrayal of translation. How, then, to undo such structural betrayal? How can we preserve the promise of locational thinking—for instance, Latin Americanism—and at the same time avoid the pitfalls of its recommodification? Is it possible to do both if we insist upon translation as the ultimate horizon of Latin Americanist thinking?

But the minute translation comes to its own end, the minute the labor of translation transmutes into a result, fulfilling its structural goal, is also the minute when locational thinking abandons its vocation as a ruinous thinking, a thinking of the ruins of thinking, and becomes ruined thinking: no place left for the intersemiotic ghost, who chokes and must return to the underground. A fulfilled translation cancels the crossing at the cost of the structural conversion of subaltern negation into colonial discourse. A fulfilled translation, a work of appropriation, is always necessarily colonial discourse. There is only one thing that becomes historically more damaging than the separation of intellectual labor from its means of production, and that is their final identification—because it marks the absolute subsumption of intellectual labor into capital.

Third Hypothesis

Meanwhile, and just as my first hypothesis involved the first moment of the epochal dispute in the disciplinary fields of the humanities between literary and cultural studies, and as my second hypothesis referred to a second moment when what was attacked was the tendential radicalization of cultural studies toward alternative encodings, the third hypothesis refers to a third moment that we are perhaps entering. The very same catastrophe of the conservative paralysis and reification of what was emerging force only a few years ago, sad as it may be, is also the dawning promise of a real task for thinking. That is my third hypothesis. The task in our present is clearer and more urgent precisely in view of its opacity and obscurity—in view of its aporetic obscurity. The critique of cultural studies must give way to projects for theoretical reformulations that might allow us to advance toward that "literary" dream of unprecedented interruption and rupture. I understand a theoretical practice as the resistance to all processes of commodification or reification of forms, whether aesthetic forms, forms of valuation, or conceptual forms. In that sense only a theoretical practice can preserve the possibility of an irruption of thinking—against conservation there where conservation is a reactionary practice.

I also believe that Latin Americanist reflection is now in a privileged position to attempt such projects of reformulation. The Latin American civilizational crossings, together with the Latin American threshold or intermediate position vis-à-vis globalization processes, give it a potential role at the crossroads of planetary history. Wanting to think such crossroads as they require to be thought means assuming a certain risk and a certain danger: the risk and the danger of failure. But not wanting it, that is, preferring to continue within intellectual and academic practices that no longer satisfy even ourselves, is gambling even more strongly for a greater danger: the danger of absolute redundancy, of the infinite iterability of the same. Whether all of this, and to what an extent, is a matter of personal decision or a matter of carrying out the programmatic calculability of what is already before us, even if in darkness, remains itself undecidable. But there is no critical possibility that does not embrace undecidability—the opposite case is to proceed to the mechanical deployment of a program for the encoding and recoding of value: a service indeed.

The maximum accomplishment of translational thinking is also its total defeat: an adequate integration into the circuits of conformity, when all further translation becomes unnecessary, when language no longer exists as such, when there can be no literary community any more. If it is necessary to translate so that what is alien does not expropriate us, and if it is necessary to translate so that what is ours does not kill us (and, finally, both of those are the very conditions of possibility of the cultural practice of Latin Americanism), it is also necessary to understand that translation is not the final horizon of thinking. An untranslative excess, then, must mark Latin Americanist reflection as its last and first condition of critical existence: as the possibility of its existence as a theoretical practice and a community of friends. For the same reason, locational thinking must give way to a sort of dirty atopianism, a supplement to location, without which location comes to the end of itself and becomes a ruin of thought. Dirty atopianism is here the name for a nonprogrammable program of thinking that refuses to find satisfaction in expropriation at the same time that it refuses to fall into appropriative drives. It is dirty because no thinking proceeds from disembodiment. And it is atopian because no thinking exhausts itself in its conditions of enunciation. This does not free us from criticism: rather, it makes critique possible.

Notes

1. It would be difficult to mention all of the participants in these debates, many of whom have not yet published their work. But see recent issues of *Revista de Crítica Cultural*, *Revista Iberoamericana*, *Journal of Latin American Cultural Studies*, *Cuadernos Americanos*. The debates, in plural, may however be one and the same debate, since they share so many intersecting characteristics. The most recent contribution at the time of handing my typescript to the press is Abril Trigo's, "Why Do I Do Cultural Studies?" (2000a), a level-headed and useful attempt to navigate conflictive options that will nevertheless not go beyond staking out one possible position among others. Latin Americanists know that the discussions I refer to go well beyond published work and manifest themselves almost obsessively at professional conferences and in e-mail discussions. Four recently published books will have influence in fueling them, but I have myself not been able to include them in my musings here: Román de la Campa (1999), Doris Sommer (1999), John Beverley (1999), and Walter Mignolo (2000).

2. Of course "cultural studies" developed in Britain during the 1960s and 1970s and was reinstitutionalized in the United States in the late 1980s. See Dworkin (1997) for a history of its early development. See Grossberg, Nelson, and Treichel (1992) for its first major U.S. manifestation. The history of Latin American cultural studies is yet unwritten. My point is that what is now emerging as a full-blown field of inquiry in Latin American studies has its own regional history, which is only partially indebted to the British and North American and Australian precursors. That history also has a totally different genealogy as well as different conditions of social and intellectual inscription.

3. I am bracketing the otherwise obvious fact that cultural studies not only interacts with and develops from the literary field but also from history, sociology, anthropology, and communication studies in particular. But I must leave it to scholars from those disciplines to elucidate the impact of cultural studies upon them (and vice versa).

4. This is not to say that some Spanish-language literary Latin Americanists, whether U.S.-based or not, are not putting up a fierce opposition. They are, but their contributions tend to be more subdued and behind the scenes. I would venture to say that it was easier for the Brazilians to thematize the literary/cultural studies debate because of the existence of the vast network of scholars associated to ABRALIC. In the United States, unfortunately, and in spite of the existence here of similar networks, the division of the previously unified field continues with little mediation but with at times considerable effects at various levels of professional life.

5. On contemporary financial capitalism see Arrighi (1994) and Jameson (1998a).

6. I do not mean to condemn all historicisms, as there is one I like: absolute historicism, in Jameson's sense. By the same token I am not opposed to aesthetics. It is rather the combination of aesthetics and historicism as theoretico-political horizon which I find lacking today. See Jameson, "Marxism and Historicism" (1988) for an interesting structural-historical differentiation of historicisms in European thinking.

NEIL LARSEN

The Cultural Studies Movement
and Latin America: An Overview

Neil Larsen was born in the United States in 1952. A literary and cultural critic, he is a
professor at the University of California, Davis. His main titles include *Modernism and
Hegemony: A Materialist Critique of Aesthetic Agencies* (1990), *Reading North by South: On
Latin American Literature, Culture, and Politics* (1995), and *Determinations: Essays on Theory, Narrative, and Nation in the Americas* (2001).

Since roughly the mid-1980s, students, critics, and theorists of
Latin American culture and literature have found themselves
dogged by the question of Latin America and postmodernism. Is
there a Latin American postmodernism or a Latin postmodernity? If so,
is it merely an extension of the metropolitan version, or is it an alternative
to it? Do the various critical theories often termed "postmodern" enable
us to make better sense of contemporary Latin American reality, or do
they merely continue a covertly imperializing practice of assimilating
Latin American or postcolonial culture itself to critical canons that the
latter have had no hand in establishing? Many positions, including my
own, have by now been staked out on these questions.[1] I will not take the
time to sum them up here, except to say that haunting the debate as a
whole seems to be a persistent nervousness about its legitimacy. I, at
least, have often found myself wondering in private whether we ought
even to bother with the question at all, whether just consenting to raise
the "issue" of "Latin America and postmodernism" is already to fall into
a clever sort of neocolonizing trap.

In any case, the issue soon becomes practically unavoidable, whether
ultimately legitimate or not. Still, I have to admit at the outset to the same
sort of uneasiness about the question of Latin America and "cultural
studies." As with postmodernism, the question can take various forms:

Is there a Latin American "cultural studies"? If not, should there be one? And if there is, what is its relationship to cultural studies as practiced in metropolitan settings such as Britain or the United States? Yet no matter what form it takes, it always seems to be preempted by another set of questions, namely, what is "cultural studies" anyway, and why should Latin Americans, or Latin Americanists, bother with it in the first place?

The questions of postmodernism and cultural studies with respect to contemporary Latin America are not, of course, precisely analogous. Postmodernism evokes both a certain, if perhaps hypothetical, cultural reality and a set of intellectual and critical approaches to it. "Cultural studies" connotes only the second of these. So the question would seem to be a simpler one: Is the method or theory of "cultural studies" adequate or appropriate to the particular cultural object here?

But is it quite so simple as this? For to answer either yes or no presupposes that cultural studies is finally adequate to some other cultural object, whether metropolitan mass culture or just culture in a general, global sense. And that is something that I, for reasons I will indicate, am unwilling simply to concede. So the place to begin, I suggest, is with "cultural studies" itself and the claims that are often made on its behalf.

What is "cultural studies," then? The term itself, like "postmodernism," seems to cause no end of wrangling and confusion (Nelson 1991). For some, especially those trained in literature departments, it appears to mean simply utilizing techniques of formal analysis developed by linguistics and poetics—semiotics and deconstruction, to name just two— to interpret texts or "discourses" of a cultural but not necessarily literary or linguistic character. For others, it refers much more strictly to a specific mode of radical cultural analysis and critique developed by the Centre for Contemporary Cultural Studies (CCCS) at the University of Birmingham in Britain. Associated with the CCCS or "Birmingham school" are Raymond Williams and Stuart Hall, among many others.

Insofar as the term itself is a matter of importance here—and I suggest that we avoid getting too preoccupied with its legitimate and illegitimate uses—I would propose the following empirical generalization: "cultural studies," when not simply an explicit reference to the tradition of the Birmingham school, is the Anglo-North American name we now generally give to the dominant current of left-tending poststructuralist criticism—especially, for practical purposes, that stemming from the work of Michel Foucault—as it crosses from the humanities into the social sciences. Of course, to say "crosses" implies the existence of a disciplinary boundary that many practitioners of "cultural studies" treat as nonexistent. Perhaps it would be more precise to say that the rise of "cultural studies" marks the disappearance of at least one component of the humanities/social sciences division of labor and "knowledge." But the trajectory of the change remains important here. If, as one might put it, both a certain class of humanists and a certain class of social scientists now look to thinkers such as Foucault for a common conception of what it is they study, it is the latter group for whom this stance has required the more serious "breach" of discipline.

But the basic impulse behind cultural studies predates the current vogue attaching to the rubric. My view here—which I will have to present only on the most general plane—is that cultural studies grows out of the long-germinating dissatisfaction on the left wing both of the humanities and of the social sciences with a current of cultural criticism most often associated with the tradition of the Frankfurt school. The latter tradition, as is well known, tended to view contemporary, late-capitalist mass and popular culture as irredeemably lost, even hostile, to any project of human emancipation. With the advent of modern monopoly capitalism, even culture had become, in Adorno and Horkheimer's expression, an "industry," feeding what were merely the fetishized images of traditional culture to a society locked into an attitude of passive consumption. As the one remaining locus of negativity, and hence of possible resistance to the culture industry, Frankfurt school "critical theory" pointed to the modernist or avant-garde "work of art": by rendering itself opaque to the debased consciousness of the commodity world, and thus in a sense unconsumable, the work of a Schoenberg or a Beckett could at least hope, if not to represent the "administered universe," then to make negatively palpable its true horrors. Or so the reasoning went.

Cultural studies dissents from this adverse stigmatization and urges the recognition of an oppositional, emancipatory dimension in mass capitalist culture. Although neither its more degraded aspects nor its commodity character are denied per se, the primary conceptual status of mass culture within Frankfurt school theory is challenged. Thus, where theorists like Adorno viewed culture as a monolithically controlled compartment of the social whole, cultural studies theorists such as Williams or Hall emphasize its ubiquitous presence in the multiple areas of social life, including work and politics. Culture comes to be thought of more as practice than as product. At the same time, the simultaneous elevation of the aesthetic and denigration of the cultural—the Frankfurt school's seemingly radical redeployment of "high" and "low" art hierarchies—is suspended by Birmingham-style cultural studies. Mass culture is proposed as embodying its own scale of values to which notions of aesthetic autonomy are fundamentally irrelevant.

In form, then, cultural studies suggests a politically and practically oriented dissension from Frankfurt school criticism, a refusal of what is fairly obviously the dead end of radical aestheticism from the standpoint of progressive social change. The at times almost apocalyptic mood of pessimism that pervades much of the Frankfurt school gives way to the casual, upbeat, and even celebratory tone of cultural studies. A "sixties" accent is unmistakable.

But the change here, I would maintain, is less radical than it appears. And in a certain sense, I think, it presents the danger of a move further to the right. Why so? Above all because, despite the fact that it drops the elitist and aestheticist ban on mass culture, cultural studies nevertheless duplicates the conceptual *premise* of such a ban for thinkers like Adorno: that of the historical impossibility of advancing, through the revolutionary negation of the existing order, to a higher stage of social existence as such—the disavowal, in short, of social classlessness as historical telos. If Adorno, hostile to the "existing socialism" of his day and dismayed by what appeared to him to be the fascist seduction of the Western proletariat, abandoned the revolutionary, class critique of culture, cultural studies, despite advocating a "cultural politic," does nothing to restore this class critique and threatens, in some ways, to bury it even deeper. While, from his residence in what Lukács sarcastically described as the Hotel Abyss, Adorno paints a picture of frank hopelessness, cultural studies broadcasts the false hopes of emancipation through the spontaneous cultural subversions of dominant order, leaving class relations intact. If there is an Adornian politics, its militants must be relatively few. The politics of cultural studies, however, given its seemingly affirmative radicalism, exerts a potentially much greater mass appeal.

No doubt it can be objected here that the mere insistence on capitalist mass culture as a field of contention rather than an iron cage does not per se rule out a class critique of culture and may even be seen as inviting it. But it is, in my observation, the parallel practice of cultural studies to posit, along with the politicization of culture, the *culturalization of class*. So as to avoid what is purportedly an outmoded tendency to class reductionism, cultural studies effectively *reduces* the question of class itself to that of the culturally constructed nature of class identities. For social and political theorists such as Ernesto Laclau and Chantal Mouffe—not central figures in the cultural studies movement as such, but certainly an important influence on an articulation of the present-day movement's central concerns—this then becomes grounds for revoking the "ontological privilege" of class altogether and proclaiming a politics with no other objective but the "articulation" and rearticulation of new, presumably less oppressive forms of "hegemonic" identity (Laclau and Mouffe 1985). "Culture," that is, in appearing to take on an emancipatory, political dimension purged by the dismal aestheticism of the Frankfurt school, in reality becomes a surrogate for a politics of social emancipation. The Adornian withdrawal from history and its often painful realities of class conflict and revolutionary disappointment into what seemed the still marginally hopeful resistance of autonomous art to a debased culture continues, in my view, to foreground the "cultural politics" of the Birmingham school and its emulators. (And with the fall of Eastern bloc "socialism"—that is, of its pseudo-Marxist state-capitalist elites—to the "free market forces" decreed by the IMF and the Deutsche Bank, the tendency to political withdrawal becomes, if anything, even stronger.) The fact that it is popular culture rather than the aesthetic that now constitutes the field and defines the meaning of the emancipatory simply makes the implicit surrender to existing class relations more subtle and difficult to confront. Adorno, at least, knew what he was missing.

The close affinities of cultural studies for poststructuralism must be seen in this light. Adorno's position was, in essence, that a realist or representationally based mode of cognition, including a realist aesthetics, had become tainted by the dominant instrumental reason of monopoly capitalism and was thus useless for purposes of emancipation. But note that even so, the obsolescence of representation has nothing to do with any intrinsic property of meaning or signification but rather with the putative *nonrepresentability* of society itself in its objective totality. If it was only the radically nonrepresentational structure of modern, abstract art that could escape assimilation into the socially dominant categories, this was still, in the final analysis, a result of what were theorized to be objective social and historical transformations. Cultural studies, with the experience of the 1960s in its rearview mirror, becomes understandably uneasy with this dystopian posture and implicitly requires an epistemology that, while still excluding society itself as an object of rational, conceptual representation, is nevertheless more attuned to a mood of social activism. This it finds in poststructuralism, given its general depiction of knowledge as a process of signification rather than representation, together with its theory of meaning itself as a pure, constitutive, and even playful activity, free of all fixity or objective constraints. The subsequent, superficially plausible inference—now a matter of dogma on the culturalist left—that forms of subjectivity and identity, and even "facts" themselves, are therefore "culturally constructed" becomes, in this epistemological context, a basis for radical affirmation rather than, under the Adornian sociology, a cause for despair.[2] But the price of this Foucauldian optimism is the tacit reduction of society itself to a semiotic or "discursive" existence. In this context, the possibility of transforming society in its totality as an *objective* structure, in which Adorno declared himself a nonbeliever, is not even posed.

Proponents of cultural studies may perhaps counter here that even despite this loss of a historical and a social-revolutionary perspective, the emphasis on culture as a signifying practice or—to use John Brenkman's phrase—a "value-interpretation" that can be "articulated" to a range of political projects is still preferable to the "old left" tendency to treat culture as merely the passive reflection of intrinsic class interests (Brenkman 1987). To the extent that Marxists have in fact been guilty of this latter practice, I would at least agree that between Dick Hebdige and, say, G.V. Plekhanov there is really no meaningful basis for choice. At the same time, however, part of the cultural studies shtick is to convey the impression that up until now the left has ignored the radical possibilities inherent in mass or popular culture. (The one seeming exception to the rule here is said to be Gramsci.) If we take "left" to mean Adorno and company, then of course the notion is understandable. But this is, in essence, a falsification, resting on the same Cold War modernism that undergirds Adorno's elitist aestheticism. From Brecht and Eisenstein to socialist and Popular Front realisms, from the Mexican muralists to the Beijing Opera, the old, communist, left consistently struggled to establish a mass cultural presence. If the effort sometimes failed, or resulted in boring erudities, it just as often succeeded. The old left was not adverse to a certain, class-aligned "cultural politics." Among the reasons for its historical demise, the old left's neglect of mass culture as a political arena does not, I think, weigh very heavily.

But to turn now from Frankfurt-Birmingham to a more North-South axis: Is Latin America, barely recovered from postmodern bombardment, about to be invaded by cultural studies? If this were the actual scenario, then I would certainly advocate a posture of militant resistance. But the implicit suggestion here—perhaps reinforced at the time of the first "postmodernism" debates by the then upcoming Columbian quincentennial—that Latin Americans are once again in danger of selling themselves for a handful of glass beads is both patronizing and naive. In the first place, the modern Latin American tradition of cultural criticism was never a stranger to Frankfurt school-style critique, even if, in the heat of the anti-imperialist movements of the 1960s, it was less apt to see it as something viable. (I think here, for example, of the Brazilian critic Roberto Schwarz or of the Argentine Josefina Ludmer.) Nor has this tradition been less involved in the structuralist and poststructuralist moments, as witness the huge impact of Althusser and the somewhat lesser but still significant impact of Foucault on theorists from Ernesto Laclau to Angel Rama. And it certainly seems to me that one can speak of a Latin American "cultural politics," especially in the wake of the smashing of *foquismo* and the left-populism of the late 1960s and early 1970s. (See, inter alia, Néstor García Canclini, Nelly Richard, John Beverley, George Yúdice, and Jean Franco.) With U.S. and other imperial corporate interests poised to remove what few barriers to mass cultural imports still exist in Latin America, who knows but that we will find the culturalist left groping for a way to interpret the ousting of Che or Sandino by Madonna as somehow still enabling a subtle form of "resistance"? The point is that once we accept the political and historical premises of the cultural studies style of critique—and, North or South, the conditions for acceptance are fundamentally similar—we are all pretty much in the same boat.

But perhaps we *are* seeing such an invasion in a less suspected quarter: I am thinking here of the noticeably higher profile accorded by the North American metropolis in recent years to images of Latin American popular culture—especially peasant and religious culture. This has become a phenomenon not only in advertisements for such things as airlines and coffee, where one would expect it, but also in trendier, cultural consumption patterns in cities like New York and Los Angeles, where a limited market has developed for Latin American images of saints, religious paraphernalia, and other quasi-kitsch items. In 1991, for example, I attended a celebration-cum-art exhibit on the occasion of the Day of the Dead hosted by the Cambridge, Massachusetts, Multicultural Arts Center, complete with a variety of retablo-style personal memorials, papier-mâché skulls, and a mariachi band. The crowd, mostly but not exclusively non-Latin, visibly enjoyed itself but also seemed uncertain whether to play the role of sympathetic observer or celebrant. Meanwhile, a show at Boston's Institute of Contemporary Art, bilingually titled "El *Corazón Sangrante*/The Bleeding Heart," was featuring a collection of mostly modern and contemporary works by Mexican and Chicano artists, including Frida Kahlo, David Avalos, and Nahum Zenil, but also a sampling of Aztec figurines and colonial-period religious paintings. With the possible exception of the Kahlos, most of the modern work was engaged in an ironic, highly self-conscious but nevertheless cynical pandering to this same metropolitan taste for the artifacts and icons of Latin popular culture and religious mysticism.[3]

One can hardly blame this sort of trend on the Birmingham school, but the curiously indulgent and uncritical reception accorded to spectacles such as these by what is, in my experience, a largely educated, progressive, and pro-multiculturalist audience ultimately springs, I think, from an ideological basis shared by cultural studies. True, the marketing of Latin American popular culture can have a certain positive impact; I am thinking, here, of the superb collections of Latin dance music put together in the 1980s by the rock performer and musicologist David Byrne. But at what point does the sympathetic and progressive cultural consumer-celebrant perhaps unwittingly revert to the reactionary who regrets the passing of the semi-feudal, paternalist, and mystifying order that frames the exotic images?

In any case, it is striking to me how the dominant narrative of Latin America among progressive intellectuals in the United States seems to have shifted from that of a no doubt excessively romanticized political militance to what might be termed a neo-exoticist story of popular culture, politically sanctioned by a liberal multiculturalism. Whereas the old new left played at being Che or Sandino, now it dresses itself up in peasant garb—á la Frida Kahlo but minus the hammer and sickle on her lapel.

Notes

1. See chapter 13, "Latin America and Postmodernism: A Brief Theoretical Inquiry," and chapter 14, "Postmodernism and Imperialism: Theory and Politics in Latin America" (Larsen 1995).
2. See, to take only one random example, Donna Haraway's remark that "biology is the fiction appropriate to objects called organisms; biology fashions the facts 'discovered' from organic beings" (1989, 5).
3. See Patricia Hills's useful review of the show "Bleeding Hearts, Borders and Postmodernism" (1991–92).

JOHN KRANIAUSKAS
Hybridity in a Transnational Frame: Latin Americanist and Postcolonial Perspectives on Cultural Studies

John Kraniauskas was born in Great Britain in 1956. A literary and cultural critic, he is a professor at Birkbeck College of Humanities in London. His main titles include *The Essay in Latin America* (1992), and *Literature and the Nation in Latin America* (1993).

In "Marxism after Marx: History, Subalternity, and Difference" (1996), the Indian historian Dipesh Chakrabarty provides a subalternist reading of the historicity of capital. Just as his *Subaltern Studies* colleague Ranajit Guha recovers the trace of subaltern agency in the historical narratives of the colonial and postcolonial Indian states, Chakrabarty here reflects also on the coexistence of different temporalities within the time of capital: the temporality of commodified abstract labor that, in his view, underpins imperial history writing, and the heterogeneous temporalities of subaltern "real" labor that capital subsumes and overcodes, but which it cannot quite contain. "If 'real' labor . . . belongs to a world of heterogeneity whose various temporalities cannot be enclosed in the sign History," he suggests, "then it can find a place in a historical narrative of capitalist transition (or commodity production) only as a Derridean trace of something that cannot be enclosed, an element that constantly challenges from within capital's and commodity's—and by implication History's—claim to unity and universality" (Chakrabarty 1996, 60). Such heterogeneous social forms ("worlds") are thus only ever, for example, pre-capitalist from the point of view of capital's self-narration in a Euro-centered historicism—in Chakrabarty's words: "secular History"—and its nation-based teleologies of progress (be they evolutionary or developmental) as they are imposed upon them. From a subalternist point of view, however, they mark the place of what Guha calls a "semiotic break" (Guha 1983, 36) with such disciplinary history, of alternative memories and nonsecular temporalizations of experience, as well as alternative futures too:

> Subaltern histories are therefore constructed within a particular kind of historicized memory, one that remembers History itself as a violation, an imperious code that accompanied the civilizing process (here: the de-differentiation of labor[1]) that the European Enlightenment inaugurated in the eighteenth century as a world historical task. It is not enough, however, to historicize History, the discipline, for that only uncritically perpetuates the temporal code which enables us to historicize. The point is to ask how this imperious, seemingly all-embracing code might be deployed or thought so that we have at least a glimpse of its own finitude, a vision of which might constitute an "outside" to it. To hold history, the discipline, and other forms of memory together so that they can help in the interrogation of each other. (Chakrabarty 1996, 61)

But this "outside" of the time of capital encoded as History, Chakrabarty insists in a Bhabhian rhetorical formulation, is grafted into the category "capital," "fractur[ing] from within the signs that tell of the insertion of the historian (as a speaking subject) into the global narratives of capital":

> I think of it as . . . something that straddles a borderland of temporality, something that conforms to the temporal code within which 'capital' comes into being while violating it at the same time, something we are able to see only because we can think/theorize capital, but something that also reminds us that other temporalities, other forms of worlding, coexist and are possible. (Chakrabarty 1996, 62)

From the subalternist perspective of Guha and his colleagues, History as an institutionalized practice of writing emerged as a regulative apparatus of the colonial state in India. The presence of the subaltern within its historiography is thus defined by its negativity.[2] Here Chakrabarty gives this political story an economic twist, rereading commodification and value (abstract labor time)—the time of capital—as the site for possible re-memoration rather than reification (forgetting), and finding alternative histories in the heartland of ideology. In other words, cultural practices rather than mere false consciousnesses. Such, it seems to me, was the kind of critical space once opened up by the practices of history "from below" and cultural studies in the United Kingdom, and now offered up anew by a post-Gramscian concept of "the subaltern" as refashioned by Indian critical historians in their critique of the imperial political (state) economy (capital) of history.[3]

This is one reason why I have begun with Chakrabarty's reading of Marx against his evolutionary grain. Another is because it displays a set of ideas and images that underlies a tendential conceptual convergence in the increasingly institutionalized and interdisciplinary field of contemporary cultural studies in British and U.S. universities (and beyond), particularly around the contributions of postcolonial criticism, on the one hand, and Latin Americanist and Latino/a critical traditions, on the other. The work of Paul Gilroy and Angel Rama are important cases in point in such an intertext, for both, in their different ways, are concerned with reflecting on the processes by which historical memory is sedimented into contemporary cultural forms—novels and music—in ways that undermine "civilizing" ideologemes of development: in Gilroy's work, the conventional sociological opposition between the temporalities of "tradition" and "modernity" and, in Rama's, the processes described in anthropology by "acculturation." Referring to black popular music and story telling, Gilroy observes:

> Narratives of loss, exile, and journeying . . . like particular elements of musical performance, serve a mnemonic function: directing the group back to significant, nodal points in its common history and its social memory. The telling and retelling of these stories plays a special role, organizing the consciousness of the "racial" group socially and striking the important balance between inside and outside activity— the different practices, cognitive, habitual, and performative, that are required to invent, maintain, and renew identity. These have constituted the black Atlantic as a nontraditional tradition, an irreducibly modern, ex-centric, unstable, and asymmetrical cultural ensemble that cannot be apprehended through the Manichean logic of binary coding. (1993, 198)

These "tactics of sound," he goes on to say, become sedimented performatively in "an alternative public sphere" that is also "an integral component of insubordinate racial countercultures" (Gilroy 1993, 201 and 200). What is alluded to in Chakrabarty as "other temporalities, other forms of worlding" is thus concretely embodied and made present in dynamic cultural practices and alternative musical institutions in Gilroy.[4] Rama, meanwhile, writing in the early 1970s, finds the sounds of popular peasant and Indian cultures structuring the novels of writers like

José María Arguedas, Juan Rulfo, and Gabriel García Márquez—not now "magical realists," but rather constitutive of what he calls a "transcultural avant-garde" that rewrites the novel form with the resources of nonsecular histories and alternative means of communication. From this point of view, Arguedas's novel *Ríos profundos* is not just a bildungsroman in(to) the European tradition, but also an "opera of the poor" founded on Andean song. The key concept that enables Rama's rereading of Latin American literary history is that of "transculturation," coined originally by the Cuban anthropologist Fernando Ortiz to describe—in Gilroy's terms—the insertion of the black Atlantic into Cuba, the cultural counterpoint of the labor processes associated with the production of (American) tobacco and (imperial) sugar. For Rama the concept of "transculturation" "describes a Latin American perspective" on the experience conventionally referred to as "acculturation," that is:

> resistance to being considered the passive or inferior element in the contact between cultures, the one destined to suffer most losses. The concept was born from a double recognition: on the one hand it confirmed the existence, in an already transculturated contemporary culture, of a set of idiosyncratic values which could also be found in the remotest of its past history; and on the other, it simultaneously affirmed the existence of a creative energy acting not only on its own inherited traditions, but on ones coming from outside too. (Rama 1997, 158–59)

Fundamental to Rama, therefore, was the critical registering in the concept of "transculturation" of processes disavowed by the neocolonialist concept of "acculturation": of, in other words, the violent processes of *deculturation* associated with cultural colonialism and capitalist development in the countryside and, especially, the inventive ones of *neoculturation* associated with the transcultural renewal of cultural practices—and of which the novels of the "transcultural avant-garde" are an example. In the interpretations of Rama and Gilroy, so-called "tradition" produces the "new" and thus confounds the narrative order and hierarchies of the ideologies of modernization and modernism.

Different, although overlapping, historical forms of racism and subordination of "heterogeneous worlds" to the time of capital are evoked in the work of these critics: slavery and debt-peonage in plantations, mines, and haciendas at the colonial beginnings of modernity, as well as continuing processes of uprooting and dispossession, nation-building, proletarianization, and racist marginalization. The memories of such processes, meanwhile, are recorded in and through cultural form. The difference, however, is that in the case of Rama, while the popular memories of and resistance to the "civilizing" processes of ongoing primitive accumulation ("modernization")—which, arguably, accompany capitalism rather than merely precede it—coexist with and interrupt the time of capital in a transculturated novel form, the latter does not return them to insubordinate alternative public spheres, as it does in the musical tradition described by Gilroy. Narrative transculturation thus possibly figures a process of contradictory cultural democratization and integration, the widening of hegemony's cultural parameters under the impact of the expanded reproduction of capital and the ideology of development. Which, of course, also says something about the particular socialities of the literature and music analyzed by both critics—Rama is not analyzing a process of transculturation "from below."[5]

The work of both Rama and Gilroy concretizes Chakrabarty's deconstruction of History through reference to specific cultural practices, while Chakrabarty provides their work with a clear anti-capitalist and even utopian frame. All also partake, as I have suggested, of the kinds of interests, images, and tropes marshalled in the critique of the rhetoric of "progress" and "development" that hold together important components of the field of contemporary cultural studies traversed by post colonial and Latin Americanist concerns and are centered on the idea of the production of a "break" or "disjuncture" in the dominant order, a "trace of something that cannot be enclosed, an element that constantly challenges from within." An "outside" that is "inside," and an "inside" that is "outside"[6]: in Chakrabarty this oxymoronic outside-inside is real labor; in Gilroy and Rama it is the "tactics of sound" carrying alternative memories. At another level, contemporary reflection on cultural forms and practices in an increasingly globalized world—the hybrid as specific global-local configurations—also stresses cultural mixture, and underlines the ways in which subjects are always already marked by "others," identity by alterity. Indeed, this is a long tradition in Latin American critical thought. Similarly, while in her critique of sexual identity Judith Butler foregrounds the ways in which the hegemonic imaginary is structured by what it excludes, Ernesto Laclau also theorizes the mythic unification of the social around its "constitutive outside."[7] The keyword stitching together this field, however, is arguably the term "hybridity," operating polysemantically at a number of levels, both inside and outside academic institutions. In this sense, as Alberto Moreiras has pointed out, one could say that it is a working, hegemonic idea (Moreiras 1998): becoming part of critical common sense, unifying and gathering together disparate themes—from the experiences of imperialism to subjectification—and different strands of thought—psychoanalytic and literary, sociological and historical, passing through the philosophic—and fastening them into the interdisciplinary core of an increasingly internationalized and codified cultural studies. Which means that the idea is also the site of a politics of theory in which alternative uses of the term—and alternatives to the term—fight it out, are articulated, and unraveled.

Hybrid Time

I would like to turn here to the work of a further two key writers in this field, Homi K. Bhabha and Néstor García Canclini who, to simplify, we may take as representing the two halves of this—hybrid—interdisciplinary whole: the psychoanalytic and literary, on the one hand (Bhabha), and the anthropological and sociological, on the other (García Canclini). Their work also traverses the field of cultural studies from both postcolonial criticism (Bhabha) and Latin Americanism (García Canclini)—which each has transformed considerably. The notion of "hybridity" is central to both thinkers, and fundamental to their respective critical analyses of the cultural politics of the coexistence of different temporalities within modernity—that is, the kinds of issues and ideas set out by Chakrabarty on the disjunctive time of capital (although, as we shall see, neither Bhabha nor García Canclini think capital as such). Chakrabarty's image of a "border-land of temporality" is especially apposite, for both García Canclini and Bhabha not only visit borders in their texts—indeed, their work meets and overlaps at one such border, the very particular border between the United States of America and Mexico—but develop "border epistemologies" too.

"What is in modernity *more* than modernity is the disjunctive 'postcolonial' time and space that makes its presence felt *at the level of enunciation*" (Bhabha 1994a, 251). Apart from its rhetorical and formal similarities to Chakrabarty and others' formulations of disjuncture, this brief quotation contains in condensed form some of the central ideas developed in the work of Homi Bhabha over the course of approximately fifteen years, and collected in his book *The Location of Culture*. I am thinking of the later, more recent essays in particular—including those that have been published since the book—in which the idea of "hybridity" has become increasingly rethought from the point of view of time or, rather, "the geopolitics of the historical present" (Bhabha 1994b, 210).[8] What emerges is an attempt to think an alternative temporality to established grand narratives, not from the point of view of their crisis as established by conventional postmodernist critique, but their putting into question, their interruption from the point of view of a counter-modernity or, more specifically, a *postcolonial agency*. This agency is thought spatiotemporally in the concept of *time-lag*, and involves the hybridization of time—which means, paraphrasing Chakrabarty, that it "fractures the time of modernity" from within (Bhabha 1994a, 174, 252). In the paragraphs that follow I would like to trace a diagram of the mechanics of Bhabha's interpretative machine for reading/making this hybrid time.

Enunciation and Disjuncture

As Benita Parry points out at the beginning of her recent critical review of *The Location of Culture*, the collection constitutes "a strong articulation of the linguistic turn in cultural studies, distinguished by (his) recourse to Lacanian theories and hence foregrounding the instabilities of enunciation" (Parry 1994, 5). The specifically epistemological force of her subsequent critique then hinges on Bhabha's semiotic idealism, what she calls "the autarchy of the signifier," whereby "the generation of meaning [is] located in the enunciative act, and not in the substance of the narrated event" (9). Parry is right to foreground the act of enunciation. What is missing from her account of Bhabha's work, however, is precisely the intimate connection between it and a psychoanalytic account of the workings of the ego and unconscious—which she notes, but then immediately forgets. The point is that Bhabha's notion of postcoloniality actually *works* like the Freudian unconscious—its most basic dynamic being that of the return of the repressed in response to disavowal—and the site of this work is "enunciation": enunciation without the unconscious is like postcolonialism without colonialism. Further: enunciation is to the unconscious as postcolonialism is to colonialism. Thus, what returns to modernity to make "its presence felt" is precisely its colonial unconscious. Which means that postcoloniality is, in his account, "structured like a language" (Lacan), and the "colonial," a mythical origin that is—like the unconscious—without history, but always already present, here and now. In this sense, Bhabha's interpretations approximate classic "symptomatic readings," scanning the postcolonial present for the trace of its absent(ed) colonial cause (which it "repeats"). [9]

When Bhabha writes of enunciation he is articulating a specific conception of culture and thus intervening in the field of cultural studies itself. He is clearly uninterested in culture conceived as a given, pre-constituted "epistemological object," that is, "as an object of empirical knowledge" (Bhabha 1994a, 34). Taking the contemporary experience of racism and the historical experience of colonialism as his points of departure, culture becomes a specific kind of power-knowledge: "Culture only emerges as a problem, or a problematic, at the point at which there is a loss of meaning in the contestation and articulation of everyday life, between classes, genders, races, nations" (34). It is a practice; more specifically, an enunciative practice that emerges in a context marked by conflictual difference—which it attempts to negotiate and overcome (for example, in appeals to organic or homogenizing notions of culture and community). The substance of the "narrated event" referred to by Parry cannot, therefore, be unproblematically separated out from its performance or enunciation. "The concept of cultural difference focuses," he goes on to say, "on the problem of the ambivalence of cultural authority: the attempt to dominate in the *name* of a cultural supremacy which is itself produced only in the moment of differentiation. And it is this very authority of culture as knowledge of referential truth which is at issue in the concept and moment of *enunciation*" (Bhabha 1994a, 34–35). In uttering *that* culture, authority is *intimately* (and this is the force of Bhabha's use of enunciation to think the subject) implicated *in* and *by* it: outside-inside.

Why does Bhabha talk of the "*ambivalence* in colonial authority," of the "*attempt* to dominate"? It is almost as if in Bhabha's avenging gesture colonial authority *qua* culture was defeated from its very inception. This is because the very practice of enunciation, the discourse of culture itself, undermines any attempt at narrative closure or cultural self-constitution on the part of the subject of power—here, the ideological constitution of colonial authority—even though this may have been what motivated its articulation in the first instance: "The enunciative process," he says, "introduces a split in the performative present of cultural identification" (Bhabha 1994a, 35).[10] Indeed, we are dealing here with something like transculturation in psychoanalytic mode. For example, the very articulation or performance of colonial stereotypification is marked by the cultural difference (the "other") it negotiates. And it is this constitutive non-identity of the subject of/within enunciation—this splitting and this "gap"—that provides Bhabha with his most important interpretative and critical resource: it makes the postcolonial perspective, its time and space, possible. In his chapter "The Commitment to Theory," from which I have quoted above, he calls this space "third space."[11]

Disjuncture and Disavowal

We can now return to the relation Bhabha establishes between modernity and postcolonial time and space. He is concerned firstly, it has become clear, with modernity *as and when* it is enunciated, that is, with a particular narrative ordering of cultural difference (in the form, for example, of "progress" or "development"); and secondly, with a supplementary force located within such discourse in the form of a disjuncture, which splits the subject of enunciation (for example, in Chakrabarty's terms, the authority of imperial history). Disjunctive enunciation, therefore, does have a content—the differential object of narrative ordering and self-constitution—and it works as the discourse of culture's—in this case, modernity's—unconscious. In other words, the process of disavowal is welded into disjuncture.

The importance of the Freudian concept of "disavowal" for Bhabha's work cannot be stressed enough. It provides a critic committed to a politics of cultural difference with an extremely simple but highly productive mechanism for generating critical interpretations from the "postcolonial perspective." Indeed, the idea surfaces in almost all of his essays, from his early "The Other Question: Stereotype, Discrimination, and the Discourse of Colonialism" (1994a)—which I have referred to above—through "'Race,' Time, and the Revision of Modernity" (1994a)—from which I took the brief passage we are looking at—to his more recent "In a Spirit of Calm Violence" (1995b) where he "discover(s) the postcolonial symptom of Foucault's discourse"—and in which his focus shifts from the ambivalence of colonial authority ("hybridity" and "mimicry") as such to the question of postcoloniality ("time-lag"). Foucault, Bhabha insists, disavows, "'the colonial moment' as an enunciative present in the historical and epistemological condition of Western modernity" through a "massive forgetting" (Bhabha 1995b, 327–28), which, nevertheless, leaves its traces within his text. Freud's concept of disavowal emerges most clearly in his discussion of fetishism, and involves the simultaneous recognition and negation of difference in a displaced making of identity. In Freud's case, sexual identity. But in Bhabha's, racial and cultural identities: colonial stereotypification is the uneasy, anxious result of the recognition of difference, the generation of fear and attraction, and its negotiation through denial. But from the point of view of disavowal, and this is the crucial point, the recognition of difference does not disappear, it rather—as in Foucault's "colonial moment"—haunts identity, making "its presence felt," precisely, "at the level of enunciation." Cultural difference thus accompanies the discourse of its negation and can be read symptomatically within the texts of both colonialism and modernity. This is a key idea, essential to Bhabhian critique.

The gap or disjunction within enunciation, the intersubjective, now has a dynamic of disavowal that provides space—a "third space"—for "another place of enunciation": the "other," so-to-speak, enunciates with(in) the "self." This is the effect of "foregrounding the instabilities of enunciation" (Parry 1994). Such a haunting, in Bhabha's view, opens up "a narrative strategy for the emergence and negotiation of those agencies of the marginal, minority, subaltern, or diasporic that incite us to think through—and beyond—theory" (Bhabha 1994a, 181). Returning to our passage, then, it is possible to appreciate how colonialism and the cultures of "resistance" and "survival" accompany modernity in the form of a supplementary force (which will become "agency") that has been disavowed, but which makes its presence felt—indeed, showing this, in a number of interesting and increasingly complex ways, is what Bhabha's critical practice is all about. But what is it that makes the colonial unconscious that interrupts narratives of modernity "postcolonial"? In other words, what is it that makes it a question of time? This question may be answered in two parts. The first refers to Bhabha's attempt to "rename the postmodern from the position of the postcolonial" (175). The second refers to a politics of time, that is, what Bhabha calls the "time-lag." Both are, of course, connected.

Time Lag

In his chapter "The Postcolonial and the Postmodern: The Question of Agency," Bhabha informs the reader that it is his "growing conviction . . . that the encounters and negotiations of differential meanings and values within 'colonial' textuality, its governmental discourses and cultural practices, have anticipated, *avant la lettre*, many of the problematics of signification and judgment that have become current in contemporary theory—aporia, ambivalence, indeterminacy" (Bhabha 1994a, 173). The colonial past as interpreted by Bhabha thus illuminates the postmodern present, the crisis and critique of enlightenment paradigms and narratives—especially ideologies of progress—all of which were implicated in colonialism. But such a colonial "unconscious" is not to be revealed in Bhabha's work through an inquiry into a set of historical determinations sedimented into the present as in the transcultural "tactics of sound" that emerge in the criticism of Gilroy and Rama (although histories of the political economy of migration might provide such a possibility in his work[12]), but rather through symptomatic and deconstructive readings that reveal the traces of disavowal in the discourses of culture articulated in the present, our present, marked by cultural difference. Contemporary neo-racism thus "repeats" past colonialism, and it is the job of the postcolonial critic to articulate this "unconscious" relation and to track the work of such repetition. The colonial past is thus *repeated*, echoed, though—more often than not—displaced into the metropolis.[13] This is the postcolonial time-space that interrupts the present: it is temporal insofar as it recombines the past and present as a deferred re-inscription, and it is spatial insofar as postcolonial repetition travels—or migrates—and is experienced mainly in the metropolis. But how does this repetition work? Well, as expected, through the enunciative act, the re-articulating of discourses in the present such that it is interrupted, stalled or, as Bhabha says, "lagged": "disjunctive temporality is," he writes, "of the utmost importance for the politics of difference. It creates a signifying time (via disjunctive enunciation) for the description of cultural incommensurability where differences cannot be sublated or totalized" (Bhabha 1994a, 177). This is why Bhabha underlines the fact that disjuncture—the return of the colonial repressed—happens in and through the *present* of enunciation. The time-lag is a "temporal break in representation," the sign of temporal hybridity that, in Walter Benjamin's words, "blast[s] open the continuum of history" (in the forms of historicism and progress), bringing it to a standstill (Benjamin 1979, 257). And this, of course, is where Bhabha also joins Chakrabarty in his critique of Euro-centered History. Postcoloniality is a form of counter-modernity, a disavowed colonialism made present, in the present, through the "gap" (or "fracture") in the enunciation of modern culture. Such also is Bhabha's heterogeneous temporality: it makes modernity *stutter*. In sum: "the time-lag of postcolonial modernity moves *forward*, erasing that compliant past tethered to the myth of progress, ordered in the binarisms of its cultural logic: past/present, inside/outside" (Bhabha 1994a, 253).

What kind of agency is it that emerges from Bhabha's "postcolonial archeology of modernity," his critical rereading of the conflictual present for the presence of the colonial? As his references to Walter Benjamin's "Theses on the Philosophy of History" in his later essays on postcoloniality suggest, Bhabha is concerned with thinking about the materiality of the past in a nonpositivist fashion. "*Time-lag keeps alive the meaning of the past*": it "*impels the 'past,' projects it*" (Bhabha 1994a, 254; his emphasis) into the present that sparks it off. And insofar as it "impels" and "projects" the past through the speaking subject, the hybridizing time of postcolonial agency would seem to take on the form of memory. It is not, however, a question of conscious memorization, but rather—as we have seen—an unmediated force that brings the past to bear on the present *unconsciously*: the colonial past "flashes up at a moment of [racist] danger" (Benjamin 1979, 257). In this respect, although responding to social conflict, it is an asocial agency. From Chakrabarty's point of view—which is influenced by Bhabha's—it is a temporality which may remind us of other "forms of worlding," but which does not itself "world." There is, in other words, no equivalents to "real" labor in Bhabha's symptomatic and revelatory readings, such as can be found in Gilroy's and Rama's analyses of the historicity of cultural forms where heterogeneous histories flow into and nourish vibrant alternative and/or insubordinate worlds. On the contrary, in Bhabha's work the colonial—which, of course, has a variety of concrete instantiations—stands in *mythically* for such histories, as always already given and always already present, engulfing its future, our present, now. The only labor to be found is the critical labor of the analyst, which may explain the apparent voluntarism with which, despite the historical experiences of the colonized in the past, Bhabha refers to the "ambivalence" of colonial domination (because, of course, on the one hand, a very anxious and ambivalent colonial *discourse* may play itself out in extremely unambiguous *violence* and, on the other, be experienced fairly unambivalently by the colonized themselves).[14] In his "Theses on the Philosophy of History," however, Benjamin writes of the "oppressed class itself"—which Chakrabarty might call "the subaltern"—"as the depository of historical knowledge." Its task is social emancipation "in the name of generations of the downtrodden" and for which, rather than images of redeemed "future generations," the "image[s] of enslaved ancestors" are crucial (Benjamin 1979, 262). Although Bhabha explicitly refuses alternative grand narratives to those of modernity, it is clear that Benjamin's allusions to historical forms of thinking *continuity* beyond "now-time"—the idea of a class as a "depository of historical knowledge" as well as the reference to "generations"[15]—suggest that the "flashes" of memory to be found in the reflections on history in both writers work best when fed into or read alongside (that is, mediating) alternative social forms of *conscious* memorization. These are forms which carry ongoing and renewed responses— narratives, images, and histories—figuring (temporalizing) experiences of subalternization to the abstract "time of capital."

Differential Historical Time

Psychoanalysis has—in a variety of guises—played a key role in metropolitan cultural studies, and coupled with semiotics has proven fundamental in reflections on questions of subjectivity, desire, and identity.[16] In Bhabha's work it provides the space opened up by *différence* with a very particular contents and time—the past—which haunts and hybridizes the present and the subject of enunciation. Indeed, I have suggested that in fact the workings of the unconscious in his writings ontologize hauntology outside history—dominant and alternative—and do so through the mythification of the experience of the colonial. Within the context of Latin American cultural criticism, however, psychoanalysis is barely visible at all. This is so despite its very evident presence in a number of capital cities in the region as a clinical practice very much in demand among the middle classes, and notwithstanding the central importance of cultural identity to its traditions of thought and politics. Structuralist linguistics and semiotics have, on the contrary, been very important and, for example, transformed—dictatorships permitting—the disciplines of literary and media studies in institutions of higher education throughout the region between the mid-1960s and the early 1980s. The work of Néstor García Canclini comes out of this context—including the experiences of dictatorship in Argentina and exile in Mexico—and interconnects, moreover, with both sociology and anthropology, the other key disciplines associated with cultural studies. From the point of view of any discussion of "hybridity" his recently translated work, *Culturas híbridas: Estrategias para entrar y salir de la modernidad* (1989a) is not only central but also helpful insofar as it uses the term at a number of levels, thus illustrating the conceptual field of its operation beyond psychoanalysis and deconstruction. The book presents itself as a socioanthropological study of Latin American modernity, and insofar as it also attempts to provide for a historical account of cultural hybridizations, it may also be read as a critical counterpoint to Bhabha's psychoanalytic one.

Culturas híbridas is grounded in a set of hypotheses which attempt to formulate a theoretical approach to Latin American cultural history that is adequate to its object (that is, to a particular set of historical experiences). The object, as the title makes clear, is modernity; while García Canclini's proposal for theoretical adequacy is suggested in another word included in the title: hybridity. The point is, of course, that not only is hybridity a feature of García Canclini's design for a "transdisciplinary gaze" (that is, interpretation), but of modernity in Latin America itself (the object of such interpretation): a transdisciplinary gaze for transculturated worlds. "Nomadic" or "hybridized" forms of critique would, he suggests in his first hypothesis, facilitate "an alternative way of thinking about Latin American modernization: not as an alien and dominant force operating through the substitution of tradition and traditional identities ('lo propio'), but rather," and this is García Canclini's second—and in my view, most important—hypothesis, "as the projects of renovation with which diverse sectors take charge of the multi-temporal heterogeneity of each nation"—in other words, the specific character of Latin American modernity and its relation to tradition. Thirdly, and finally, recognition of the cultural hybridity of modern Latin American nations illuminates "the oblique powers that are involved in the mixing of liberal institutions and authoritarian habits, social democratic governments with paternalist regimes." The political importance of the idea of hybridity as formulated in García Canclini's *Culturas híbridas* thus emerges as a response to the demands on the present made by "this mixture of heterogeneous memory and truncated innovation" that is modernity in Latin America (García Canclini 1989a, 14–15). The concept of "hybridity" thus pertains to an epistemology of modernity, its specific local characteristics, and, finally, to its political significance.

It is clear that the demands made by García Canclini on the idea of "hybridity" are substantial, for it is set to work at different levels. Hybridity as a form of transdisciplinarity, for example, does not simply mean the use of concepts derived from a variety of disciplines but, in some instances, their mutual transformation. For this reason, when investigating the "theatricalization of the popular" (García Canclini 1989a, 191–235), he accompanies his deconstruction of the art-handicraft ("*artesanía*") opposition with a sociological critique of anthropological conceptions of the popular (associated with tribal and rural tradition) and an anthropological critique of sociological conceptions of the popular (associated with urban modernity). The effect of this conceptual confrontation and transformation is to illuminate what is conventionally thought to be a series of contradictions in terms: the aestheticizing effects of commodification on a handicraft industry (now in the process of massification) usually thought of as traditional, folkloric, and inimical to modernization. In other words, cultural continuity and change through renewal, as in Gilroy's analysis of black popular music (although, in this case, without insubordination). Elsewhere, he similarly confronts and transforms Gramsci's political concept of "hegemony" with Bourdieu's sociological concept of "reproduction." At a more empirical level, the idea of "hybridity" also has a more familiar function in García Canclini's descriptions of new urban landscapes, communities, and identities— particularly at the U.S./Mexican border—that have been disconnected from specific locations and spatially reinvented through newly accessible communication technologies—processes associated, but at the level of practices and objects, with forms of cultural re-articulation he calls "reconversion" and "de-collection." It is at these levels that the idea of hybridity as a critical strategy (interpretation and description) is, in my view, most productive.

More fundamental for his theory of Latin American modernity as such, however, and this is where García Canclini's reflections bring his work into the same conceptual space as Chakrabarty, Rama, Gilroy, and Bhabha, are his references to "intercultural hybridization," "hybrid sociability," and "hybrid history" (García Canclini 1989a, 264, 332, and 69). Taken together, these references to culture, society, and history testify to the apparent need to lift the idea of "hybridity" from the realm of empirical description, via conceptual "transdisciplinarity," into a totalizing domain of theory that is adequate to the task of studying "the hybrid cultures that constitute modernity and give it its specific Latin American profile" (15).[17] It is this theory of the particularity of Latin American modernity—its "hybridity"—that is my principle concern in what follows.

Like the Brazilian critic Roberto Schwarz (1992), García Canclini correctly dismisses the idea held by many that modernism (and modernization) is in some sense foreign to Latin America, or is a superficial transplant. He too points to the process through which "misplaced ideas" (like, for Schwarz, liberalism's concept of "citizenship" in a Brazil still dominated by slavery) become "improperly" adopted but structuring components of national and regional cultural formations, and outlines "how to interpret a hybrid history." It is here that the question of multitemporal heterogeneity is discussed. Following in the footsteps of Perry Anderson's (1992) critique of Marshall Berman's homogeneous, unilinear, and developmentalist theory of European modernism, García Canclini locates Latin American modernism at the intersection of "different historical temporalities" so as to maintain, in an echo of his second hypothesis concerning Latin American modernity, that it "is not the expression of socioeconomic modernization (as in Berman) but rather the way in which the elites take charge of the intersection of different historical temporalities and attempt to elaborate a global project with them" (García Canclini 1989a, 71).

In his reading of Marshall Berman's All That Is Solid Melts into Air, Perry Anderson suggests that an explanation of modernism can only be found in the uneven development of capitalism. Evoking Louis Althusser's conceptualization of both conjunctural "overdetermination" and the "differential" historical time characteristic of all social structures, as well as Raymond Williams's temporalization of cultural formations in terms of the "residual," "dominant," and "emergent," he notes that "such an explanation would involve the intersection of different historical temporalities, to compose a typically overdetermined configuration" (Anderson 1992, 34): a still usable—aristocratic—past (in the form of artistic academicism), an unstable—bourgeois—present (characterized by technological revolution), and an uncertain—revolutionary?—*future* (revealed in the Russian Revolution).[18] What, then, constitutes the cultural content of such temporalities in Latin America? According to García Canclini, "Latin American countries now are the product of the sedimentation, juxtaposition, and intercrossing of Indian traditions (especially in the Mesoamerican and Andean areas), of colonial Catholic hispanism and of modern political, educational, and communicative practices" (García Canclini 1989a, 71). This, it must be said, is quite a conventional picture of Latin American syncretism, separating out and identifying what is thought to be either "traditional" or "modern," so as to then—and only then—mix them. He goes on to maintain, however, that the dynamic of cultural hybridity results from the fact that the "modern" has failed to "substitute" the "traditional." Indeed, processes of modernization have rather tended to reproduce and re-articulate "tradition"—as in the case of the production of handicrafts—so that what has been usually defined socially, culturally, or politically as "traditional" and "past" are still active in the present (such that they too are endowed with futuricity). Yet the key to Latin American modernity contained in García Canclini's outline of its modernisms is not to be found only in such transculturation, but rather in the ways it feeds into "the way in which elites *take charge of* the intersection of different historical temporalities" (my emphasis)—the key hypothesis, as we have seen, concerning the particularity of Latin American modernity that motivates the book as a whole. The main point here is that, given the historical absence of local centers of capital accumulation, strong civil societies, and national markets—local manifestations of capitalism in a context of dependency—both modernism and modernization have been thought of as *projects* whose concern is *to take charge* of temporal heterogeneity. In sum, what emerges without being explicitly addressed in *Culturas híbridas*—that is, despite García Canclini's culturalism—is the *political*, state- (rather than commodity-) centered dialectic of cultural modernity in Latin America. There are thus two interconnected levels of overdetermination at work here: firstly, the conjunctural intersection of different historical times (hybridity), which produces—and is at the same time reproduced by—a modernity in which, secondly, from the point of view of culture and the making or "formation" of subjects, social relations with the nation-state (the political) predominate over social relations with the market (the economic).

This does not mean that a political history of modernity replaces García Canclini's hybrid history, but rather that each feeds on and informs the other. For as he points out, "Despite the attempts to give elite culture a modern profile, confining the Indian and the colonial to popular sectors, an interclass *mestizaje* has generated hybrid formations in all social strata" (García Canclini 1989a, 71). It is this continual reproduction of cultural and social hybridity that provides the dynamic for the political character of Latin American modernity: "truncated innovation" periodically demands processes of modernity that are conceived in political terms by Latin American elites, that is, as *projects* (modeled, in the main, on imperial conceptions of "development"—the time of capital). And this is because each attempt at renovation fails to "substitute tradition." From this point of view, *Culturas híbridas* may be read as a response to Habermas's question: "modernity—an incomplete project?" In Latin America, however, modernity is not "incomplete," it is "truncated," and truncation—perceived as an effect of sociocultural hybridity—is constitutive of its political logic.

What is missing from García Canclini's account of hybrid history— although given the theoretical and empirical density of the text, it is perhaps asking too much—is some reflection on the history of the ways in which this truncated modernity has been thought, both culturally and politically, in postcolonial Latin America from, for example, D. F. Sarmiento in the 1840s to Angel Rama in the 1970s. For this may have critically illuminated the way in which the temporal and political logics of modernity as "development" informed his own perspective on processes of hybridization. Sarmiento is particularly relevant since he specifically addresses the question of the coexistence of at least two historical times in post-independence Argentina—he called them "civilization" and "barbarism"—and set out "to take charge" of them militarily and pedagogically: "Both the nineteenth and twelfth century live alongside each other: one in the cities and the other in the countryside" (Sarmiento 1970, 63). Sarmiento's project was to reverse the situation in which, in his view, the Middle Ages had the upper hand and taken control of the state in the form of dictatorship. In other words, he proposes imposing the "time of capital," the Europeanized city onto the countryside, so as to bring the nation up to date by abolishing that "other" heterogeneous time. The ideologeme under which such a project to "take control of" heterogeneous time was to occur, of course, was "progress." Rama, meanwhile—as we have seen—populistically inverts Sarmiento's problematic and attempts to read the dominant against the grain, looking for the transformative effects of the heterogeneous.

From the point of view of this tradition of political and cultural interpretation in Latin America, it is thus not surprising that *Culturas híbridas* should suggest a modernizing politics of its own that—with the help of recent postmodern critiques of modernist grand narratives of progress—attempts to overcome this opposition between modernization and "traditions that persist" (García Canclini 1989a, 331). "Perhaps the central theme of cultural politics today," says García Canclini, "is how to build societies on the basis of democratic projects that are shared by all without equalizing them, where disaggregation becomes diversity, and where inequalities (between classes, ethnic or social groups) are transformed into difference" (148). García Canclini recognizes that one cannot just enter and leave modernity, that "it is a condition that contains us, in cities and in the countryside, in the metropolis and the underdeveloped countries." Here, however, he does not follow Anderson and advocate political rupture with modernity. He rather suggests that the only answer may be "to radicalize the project of modernity . . . to renovate . . . to create new possibilities so that modernity can be something else and something more" (333). In García Canclini's view, such a politics would be new and arise from the contemporary "cultural reorganization of power . . . of the political consequences of passing from a vertical and bipolar conception of sociopolitical relations to a de-centered, multidetermined one" (323). In other words, I assume, the replacement of class politics by the disenchanted politics of social movements. What emerges, however, is a cultural politics in which a self-styled modernity identifies its own opposites, that is, those traditions it must overcome. Culturas híbridas may thus itself also be read politically—and "obliquely"—as providing intellectual resources for such a democratic social and cultural project, for—in other words—"taking charge of" the more recent configurations of modernity in Latin America.

Border Times

In this context some of the transformations or hybridizations described by García Canclini in Culturas híbridas and elsewhere would seem to be over-optimistic and, curiously, subjectless, despite the importance of the concept of identity in his work (see García Canclini 1992a and 1995a). This may be because of an overemphasis on national and postnational identitites at the expense of others, and the fact that the culture of the Mexican/U.S. border—more specifically, the city of Tijuana—acts as a paradigm for his analysis of contemporary processes of hybridization: "The hybridizations described throughout this book lead us to conclude that today all cultures are frontier cultures," he says (García Canclini 1989a, 325). This is a view shared by Bhabha. Indeed, he goes even further, inscribing his own thoughts on postcoloniality and counter-modernity in *The Location of Culture* into a politics of the "borderline condition":

> Postcolonial critique bears witness to those countries and communities—in the North and in the South, urban and rural—constituted, if I may coin a phrase, 'otherwise than modernity.' Such cultures of a postcolonial contra-modernity may be contingent to modernity, discontinuous or in contention with it, resistant to its oppressive, assimilationist technologies; but they also deploy the cultural hybridity of their borderline condition to 'translate,' and therefore re-inscribe, the social imaginary of both metropolis and modernity. (Bhabha 1994a, 6)

Thus, from the point of view of the working concept of "hybridity" in the texts of both Bhabha and García Canclini, the border—especially the U.S./Mexican border where their texts meet—becomes both culturally exemplary, a "third space," and an explicit epistemological position from which to read the texts and times of contemporary cultural formations. Indeed, the realities of the U.S./Mexican border would seem to actualize in almost paradigmatic form what Chakrabarty calls a "borderland of temporality" (see above) as well as the spatiotemporal tropes of "transculturation," "heterogeneity," "inside-outsides"—that is, of "hybridity"—that distinguish Latin Americanist and postcolonial contributions to cultural studies in the form of critiques of the ideologies of progress and development, the "time of capital." The problem, however, and this is another characteristic the critical discourses of both Bhabha and García Canclini share, is that this "time" is thought in such a way that cultural concerns—however dislocated and/or unconscious they may be—obliterate political economy, that is, capital as a determining—temporalizing—instance (both of and by cultural form).[19] And this emerges particularly clearly in the way García Canclini's recourse to the idea of hybridity to analyze the temporal heterogeneity of Latin American modernity seems paradoxically to reconfigure and maintain, rather than subvert, the temporalization of modernity and tradition as signs of the present and past it criticizes. In his account of handicrafts, for example, a renovated traditional cultural form acquires the attributes of the modern and becomes new (via state subsidy and the comparative advantage of the marketplace). In such a context, what fails to renovate—including those branches of the handicraft industry that do not modernize—fails—and becomes "past" due to the truncating effects of a tradition "that persists." What this would seem to provide is not a critique of the logics of development but rather an example of *cultural* development in which, from the subalternist perspective of Chakrabarty, the chronological "time of capital" not only remains intact but may even be strengthened.

The interrelated ideas of "deterritorialization" and "reterritorialization" used by García Canclini to describe the transformations of contemporary culture may provide a further illustration of the "times" of García Canclini's critique as well as a point of entry for critical reflection on both his and Bhabha's optimism with regard to the border chronotope—that is, a point at which, in García Canclini's own terms, sociopolitical bipolarity returns to organize multidetermination (García Canclini 1989a, 288–305). According to Deleuze and Guattari, "The social axiomatic of modern societies is caught between two poles, and is constantly oscillating from one pole to another" (Deleuze and Guattari 1977, 260). Capitalism, in their view, "is continually reterritorializing with one hand what it is deterritorializing with the other" producing "neoterritorialities" (259 and 257). So enmeshed are these processes that, they insist, "it may be all but impossible to distinguish deterritorialization from reterritorialization . . . they are . . . like opposite faces of one and the same process": what Marx described as the tendency, and counter-tendencies, of the rate of profit to fall, a law immanent in the expanded reproduction of capital (258 and 259–60). The cultural content of Deleuze and Guattari's observations on processes of social abstraction—and what I have referred to above as "ongoing primitive accumulation"—are glossed in the form of a culturalism by García Canclini as follows: "I am referring to two processes: the loss of "natural" relations between culture and geographical and social territories, and, at the same time, certain relative and partial territorial relocalizations of old and new symbolic productions" (García Canclini 1989a, 288). Migration is important to both Bhabha and García Canclini, in whose view the "multidirectional migration" characteristic of contemporary transnational capitalism undermines bipolar—and "relocalizing"—conceptions of intercultural relations thought of in terms of dependency, centers and peripheries, and imperialism. It is in this context that the frontier, as a space of hybrid cultural intercrossings, a "neoterritoriality," becomes paradigmatic.

But, as I have suggested, it is also the point at which the cultural contents of capitalist forms of social abstraction are lost. García Canclini does, momentarily, recognize that there may be suffering at the border: "Intercultural movements show their faces of pain on both sides of the frontier: underemployment and the uprootedness of peasants and Indians who had to leave their lands so as to survive. But," he rapidly goes on to point out, "a dynamic cultural production is emerging there too"

(García Canclini 1989a, 290–91). And he is right: hybridity, especially its border culture variant, is of increasing international exchange and exhibition value (see Coombes 1992). However, it seems to me that the suffering involved—what Benjamin may have called the "barbarism," and by which I am referring to the violence contained in relations of exploitation and domination, the subordination to the "time of capital"—is passed over too quickly and, curiously, this is because the processes of deterritorialization and reterritorialization described by García Canclini become binarized and, most importantly here, temporalized. He reports that in reactions to a series of photographs of Tijuana "we saw a complex movement that we would call reterritorialization. The same people that praise the city for its open and cosmopolitan character want to fix signs of identification, rituals that would differentiate them from those who are just passing through, be they tourists or . . . anthropologists interested in understanding intercultural mixing" (García Canclini 1989a, 304). From the point of view of a contemporary modern (that is, what the author calls a "de-centered multidetermined") cultural politics, such fixing becomes a thing of the past—tradition, ritual—a politics signifying a time to be "take[n] charge of" if it does not successfully "develop" and become up-to-date.

The problem, however, may be that capitalist reterritorialization does not only present itself today as *tradition*, or as what Deleuze and Guattari call "neoarchaisms," but as the production of the new subjects of a sociocultural order which is both specifically transnational (postnational) and one in which, from the point of view of time, the disavowal of coevalness that structures narratives of progress and development is being tendentially undermined by the new technologies allied to capital itself (see Mignolo 1998a).[20] In other words, reterritorialization may also be located—indeed, especially so—in a certain mobility—migration—and neocosmopolitanism—the ability, indeed the necessity at the Mexican/ U.S. border, to adopt a multiplicity of identitites. That is, in Deleuze and Guattari's terms, reterritorialization accompanies the ever-increasing need for social abstraction—what Chakrabarty refers to as "abstract" rather than "real" labor—of the capitalist machine (Deleuze and Guattari 1977, 258–59). As Stuart Hall has also reminded us, "the so-called 'logic of capital' has operated as much through difference —preserving and transforming difference . . . not by undermining it" (Hall 1994b, 353) but by subordinating it to the logics of "development," the time of capital that seeks to overcome traditions "that persist." If this were the case, the suffering García Canclini mentions so briefly may be more than just symptomatic of the "loss" of traditional identities—that is, nostalgia. It may have critical content too, registering, at the border, resistance and even possible alternatives to the new reterritorialized "border" subjectivities being produced and replicated throughout the cities of the United States, and elsewhere, as "disciplinary societies" are transformed into "societies of control" (see Davis 1990 and Deleuze 1992).

Notes

1. "This abstraction of labor as such is not merely the mental product of a concrete totality of labors. Indifference toward specific labors corresponds to a form of society in which individuals can with ease transfer from one labor to another, and where the specific kind is a matter of chance for them, hence of indifference. Not only the category, labor, but labor in reality has here become the means of creating wealth in general, and has ceased to be organically linked with particular individuals in any specific form. Such a state of affairs is at its most developed in the most modern form of existence of bourgeois society—in the United States" (Marx 1977, 104).

2. "The peasant obviously knew what he was doing when he rose in revolt. The fact that this was designed primarily to destroy the authority of the superordinate elite and carried no elaborate blueprint for its replacement doesn't put it outside the realm of politics. On the contrary, insurgency affirmed its political character precisely by its negative and inversive procedure" (Guha 1983, 9). On the other hand, Guha underlines the fact that the colonial historiography documenting insurgency was a "vital discourse for the state." In it "causality was harnessed to counterinsurgency and the sense of history converted into an element of administrative concern" (2–3).

3. See my "Globalisation Is Ordinary: The Transnationalisation of Cultural Studies" (1998).

4. Other examples might, for instance, include working-class institutions that keep the realities of "real" labor alive. The question I am alluding to with this example is whether "real" labor coexists with abstract labor for the working class in contexts of real—or complete (if such a thing exists)—subsumption of labor to capital; that is, when labor is fully incorporated into the production process as variable capital.

5. See Antonio Cornejo Polar (1998). In Cornejo Polar's work the difference of "heterogeneity"—both at the level of culture and modes of production—constitutes the thorn in the side of transculturation itself.

6. See, for example, Jacques Derrida (whom Chakrabarty mentions): "But this inside must also enclose the spectral duplicity, an immanent outside or an intestine exteriority, a sort of evil genius which slips into spirit's monologue to haunt it, ventriloquizing it and thus dooming it to a sort of self-persecuting disidentification" (Derrida 1989, 62). This philosophical formulation of "hauntology" by Derrida—later developed in *Spectres of Marx* (1994)—is remarkably similar to Homi Bhabha's discussion of "disjunctive enunciation" (see below).

7. In the words of Butler: "In this sense, then, the subject is constituted through the force of exclusion and abjection, one which produces a constitutive outside to the subject, an abjected outside, which is, after all, 'inside' the subject as its own founding repudiation" (Butler 1993, 3); and Laclau: "We are faced with a 'constitutive outside.' It is an 'outside' which blocks the identity of the 'inside' (and is, nonetheless, the prerequisite for its constitution at the same time). . . . The effectiveness of myth is essentially hegemonic: it involves forming a new objectivity by means of the re-articulation of the dislocated elements" (Laclau 1990, 17 and 61).

8. In this sense, my account and critique of Bhabha's work is slightly different from Robert Young's in both *White Mythologies: Writing History and the West* (1990) and *Colonial Desire: Hybridity in Theory, Culture, and Race* (1995), which are concerned with the ideas of hybridity in what we may call the "early" Bhabha.

9. This is why, for example, one way of symptomatically describing the shift in the critical analysis of colonial discourse between Edward Said's *Orientalism* (1978) and Bhabha's own work is to note how Gramsci's notion of "hegemony"—so important for Said's approach to colonialism—is dropped in favor of a psychoanalysis of politics.

10. Such an undermining of authority is central to Bhabha's concerns. As he puts it: "I attempt to represent a certain defeat, or even impossibility, of the 'West' in its authorization of the 'idea' of colonization" (Bhabha 1994a, 175).

11. In this chapter the full importance of Derrida's concept of "*différance*" for Bhabha's own analyses becomes very clear (see Bhabha 1994a, 19–39).

12. Many critics of postcolonial theory have related its emergence to migrant intellectuals that have risen in the academies of England and the United States. See, for example, Ahmad (1992).

13. See P. Osborne (1995, 199). This book has proved invaluable in helping me to think through some of the issues of this essay.

14. See note 10 above and Bart Moore-Gilbert (1997).

15. The problem of thinking the continuity of subaltern cultural practices over time, and their significance, is tackled head on by Gilroy. For example:

I believe it is possible to approach the music as a *changing* rather than an unchanging same. Today, this involves the difficult task of striving to comprehend the reproduction of cultural traditions not in the unproblematic transmission of a fixed essence through time but in the breaks and interruptions which suggest that the invocation of a tradition may itself be a distinct, though covert, response to the destabilizing flux of the post-contemporary world. (Gilroy 1993, 101)

16. This section is an amended version of Kraniauskas (1992). For a response, see García Canclini (1992a).

17. It is with the empirical and interdisciplinary meanings of "hybridity" that U.S. and U. K. cultural studies have been mainly concerned. As we have seen, its temporal meaning, on the other hand, has been the concern of critics of the practices and

rhetorics of modernity, progress, and development experienced as colonialism and imperialism.

18. See Louis Althusser (1969 and 1979, 91–118) and Raymond Williams (1977, 121–27). Postcolonial agency is, in Bhabha's account, a form of cultural "emergent."

19. For example, in their analysis of the Los Angeles uprising following the Rodney King verdict, Melvin L. Oliver, James H. Johnson Jr., and Walter C. Farrell Jr. (1992, 122) refer to the contemporary political economy of the U.S.-Mexican border:

> At the same time . . . well-paying and stable jobs were disappearing from South Central Los Angeles, local employers were seeking alternative sites for their manufacturing activities. As a consequence of these seemingly routine decisions, new employment growth nodes or "technopoles" emerged in the San Fernando Valley. . . . In addition, a number of Los Angeles-based employers established production facilities in the Mexican border towns of Tijuana, Ensenada, and Tecate. Between 1978 and 1982, over two hundred Los Angeles-based firms . . . participated in this deconcentration process. Such capital flight, in conjunction with the plant closings, has essentially closed off to the residents of South Central Los Angeles access to what were formerly well-paying unionized jobs. It is important to note that, while new industrial spaces were being established elsewhere in Los Angeles County (. . . as well as along the U.S.-Mexican border), new employment opportunities were emerging within or near the traditional industrial core in South Central Los Angeles. But, unlike the manufacturing jobs that disappeared from this area, the new jobs are in competitive sector industries, which rely primarily on undocumented labor and pay, at best, minimum wage. Meanwhile, the territorial frontier provides very real opportunities for super-profits: on the Mexican side, in the *maquilas* (export-orientated assembly plants), forging, according to Leslie Sklair (1992), the formation of new transnational bourgeois strata mediating and linking national and international capital; and on the U.S. side, in the use of cheap—and illegal—immigrant labor power subject to increasingly racist legislation and discrimination. A slogan daubed on the border fence "Ni ilegales, ni criminales/Trabajadores internacionales" captures the contradiction produced there between a law that separates and an economic dynamic which joins, and that makes of the border zone it creates a place of extreme violence and exploitation.

On the ideology of cultural studies, see Kraniauskas (1998).

20. I say "disavowal" rather than the more usual "denial" to underline the fact that coevalness is momentarily recognized before its denial (see Fabian 1983).

ANTONIO CORNEJO POLAR

Mestizaje and Hybridity: The Risks of Metaphors—Notes

Not too long ago, Roberto Fernández Retamar warned against the implicit dangers of using categories from other domains in cultural and literary studies. Metaphoric and/or metonymic borrowing can lead to innumerable confusions. As for myself, I remember that a significant segment of Marxist aesthetic stiffness derived from the literal reading of what were actually metaphors taken from nineteenth-century science, like the concept of "reflection," for example.

It is evident that categories like *mestizaje* and hybridity basically stem from biology and other disciplines unrelated to cultural and literary analysis, with the aggravating factor—in the case of *mestizaje*—that it is an extremely ideological concept. As far as hybridity is concerned, it is almost spontaneously associated with the sterility of hybrid products, an objection so often repeated that today Néstor García Canclini has gathered an impressive list of hybrid and fecund products . . . At any rate, this association cannot be easily overcome. In fact, in the Velázquez English-Spanish dictionary, the word hybrid immediately provokes a somewhat brutal meaning: "mule." Of course I recognize that the use of these semantic borrowings has inevitable risks; at the same time, I consider that behind them there is a dense layer of meanings moving around, which include and justify every single worldview. I would even be tempted to affirm that in order to clarify a concrete point, a good reading of that substratum of meaning is more productive than the simple declaration of the inaptness and irrelevancy of categories in use.

Many times I have said that the concept of *mestizaje*, despite its prestigious tradition, is a concept that falsifies the condition of our culture and our literature in the most drastic way. In effect, what *mestizaje* does is to offer a harmonious image of what is obviously disjointed and confrontational, proposing representations that deep down are only relevant to those for whom it is convenient to imagine our societies as smooth and non-conflictive spaces of coexistence. In another occasion, I have also considered the inappropriate use of the life and work of Inca Garcilaso as an exemplary *mestizo*, emblematic of a nation so mixed that it would already be a non-fissured totality.

I add—despite my unrestricted respect for Angel Rama—that the idea of transculturation has become more and more the most sophisticated disguise of the category of *mestizaje*. After all, Fernando Ortiz's symbol of the "*ajiaco*" that Rama assumes could very well be the greatest emblem of the deceptive harmony in which a multiple process of mixing would have concluded. I want to make clear that I am not denying in any way the obvious or subterranean relations that exist between the diverse sociocultural strata of Latin America; what I object to is the interpretation according to which everything would have been brought into harmony within the supposedly placid and pleasant (and certainly enchanting) spaces of our America.

I notice, on the one hand, that García Canclini's theory of hybridity, although sometimes spoiled by the celebratory tone in which it is presented and the excessive use of examples that seem to refer preferably to certain strata of Latin American societies, has a less acknowledged but unquestionable virtue: its immersion in history, which makes it possible to enter and leave hybridity, in one way or another, the same way one "leaves and exits modernity," even though these movements do not always obey the needs, interests, or freedom of those who experience them.

On the other hand, I would like to highlight that these categories, whose semantic anchorage corresponds to other disciplines, are as conflictive as those categories that seem to support themselves on critical practice itself, such as "heterogeneous literature," "alternative literature," or "diglossic literature." I will not bring to mind the known phrase of [Johann Wolfgang von] Goethe about the tree of life, but I will emphasize what is obvious to me: no critical category unveils the totality of the material under study and—above all—the category in question corresponds to a different order vis-à-vis its object of study. To insist on what is evident, not a single one of the above-mentioned categories resolves the problems that they raise and all of them work from an epistemological locus inevitably distant and distinct.

There probably exists diverse degrees of proximity among these mentioned concepts and the sphere of aesthetic production, but it is a proximity somewhat deceitful, because in one way or another both the critical concepts and the sphere of aesthetic production will remain fixed on their own epistemological order. In these regards, I am enormously interested in the attempt to investigate certain ethnic literatures using the forms of knowledge inherent to those same ethnicities; nevertheless, the problem—if it were a problem—is still unsolved. I am not referring to the philological attempt to define the genres that would have been used before the Conquest, which is part of the meritorious work of [Angel María] Garibay, [Miguel León] Portilla, [Jesús] Lara, or Vidal Martínez, but instead I am referring to the clarification of certain dimensions of the American peoples' knowledge, which would explain the nature of some of their more complex discursive manifestations. *Tinku, pachakuti, wakcha,* for instance, would be the basis that would make possible a more intimate understanding of the discursive universes of the Andean world.

As I have said, this idea attracts me and I believe that it can be effectively productive. However, I wonder if by leaving behind one eccentricity we are not entering another; or what would be even worse, if we are not just repeating the metaphysical stance of theorists like [Arnald] Steiger, for whom each literary genre corresponded to a particular form of life experience. I do not easily see how experiences such as helplessness, poverty, and foreignness (*wakcha*) could be transferred to the configuration of ethnic discourses that allude to or depart from these experiences. In other words, I enthusiastically admit their hermeneutical competence, but I do not perceive their theoretical productivity. Finally, I want to point out that perhaps deep down the relation between critical epistemology and aesthetic production is inevitably metaphorical.

At this point, I would like to make a tangential, though—I hope—clarifying proposal. The entry to or exit from modernity and hybridity also has a particularly frequented route in cultural and literary studies. I am not now alluding to the old claim of theoretical-methodological autonomy; I am referring—more succinctly—to the difficult coexistence of texts and discourses in Spanish and Portuguese (and eventually in Amerindian languages) with the uncontainable dissemination of critical texts in English (or in other European languages). Of course I am not even remotely trying to postulate a linguistic fundamentalism that would only allow one to speak of literature in its own language, but I am cautioning against the excessive disparity of criticism in English that—under old industrial models—seems to take Hispano-American literature as a raw material to be turned into sophisticated critical artifacts. At this moment, I cannot go through all of the repercussions involved, but allow me to randomly point out some of them:

(a) Criticism in English usually use a bibliography in the same language and disregard, or do not mention, what has been done in Latin America with so much effort during so many years. Besides, its extreme preference for the narrow, theoretical postmodern canon is a compulsion that verges on the preposterous.

(b) Since the "natural" space of Latin American studies is Latin America, some sort of subdivision of the discipline is under way, taking into consideration that it is absolutely erroneous that the majority of professors of Hispano-American literature are proficient in English. Thus, certain Saxon contributions are not incorporated, or are incorporated too late, to the Latin American critical tradition. Naturally, meanwhile the other side of the discipline acquires its own rhythm and defines its own canons.

(c) The massive use of a foreign language for the study of Hispano-American literature is generating—even though perhaps nobody wants it—a strange hierarchy in which texts written in a foreign language end up leading the common field of Hispano-American studies. I am afraid we are generating a strange diglossic criticism.

(d) Though perhaps it is an independent phenomenon, there is no way of not mentioning that there has been a dramatic decline in the use of Spanish by both professors and students. It is probable that this is one of the reasons explaining the proliferous production in English—which without a doubt goes hand in hand with the prestige of writing in that language. I feel somewhat archaic saying this, but the truth is that I am nostalgic for those old times in which the first requirement, but also the ultimate pride of both professors and/or students of Spanish was to be perfectly proficient in Spanish. Of course I am not at all referring to the nationality of the professor and/or the student. It doesn't escape me that professors of Hispanic origin have—and even sometimes more acutely—this same problem.

(e) All the aforementioned also relates to the remarkable increment, in Spanish departments, of academic activities and courses that are currently conducted in English. I cannot address now such a touchy issue, but I am very afraid that cultural, postcolonial, and/or subaltern studies have not calibrated the implications of practicing these disciplines predominantly in English regardless of the language of the discourses under study. In a certain sense, the most general problems begin to be perceived from the partial viewpoint of the culture whose language is used, with the aggravating factor that for obvious reasons the original texts remain displaced by not always reliable translations.

(f) I confess that I don't have any solution on how to resolve the problem that I have just mentioned, but I am fully aware that behind the
best intentions a false universalization of literature is being fashioned from the mere preference of a linguistic tool. Involuntarily,
we are again approaching the idea of a "universal literature," with
the only difference that this time it is a strange artifact totally
manufactured in English, precisely the language of hegemony that
speaks for itself about the marginal, the subaltern, and the postcolonial.

(g) I do not want to finish without mentioning that my words do not
imply that criticism written in Spanish is always good. First, the
military dictatorships, through censorship or even more brutal
methods, and afterward neoliberalism with its politics of depletion
of public cultural institutions (universities, libraries, archives) have
practically destroyed the material basis for the development of the
discipline, although it is also necessary to recognize the dissimilar
situation between countries and the obvious differences between
collective and individual projects.

I confess that in my words there may be an excess of pessimism. When
I began my academic experience in the United States, I did it with a paper
that, paraphrasing César Vallejo, I entitled, "Against the Professional
Secret." There I explained my disappointment with a profession that
seemed to have lost all capacity for self-critique, and in which, without a
doubt, a worrisome permissiveness was in progress. I think that at that
time my observations were exaggerated, because although my examples
were forcefully conclusive, they came from a reduced number of sources.
I would not want my words to be considered now as a premonition, but
instead as a distressed and cordial indication of what could be the frayed
and not very honorable ending of Hispano-Americanism.

Translated by Christopher Dennis

WORKS CITED

Abercrombie, Nicolas, Stephen Hill, and Bryan S. Turner. 1980. *The Dominant Ideology Thesis*. London: Allen and Unwin.

Achugar, Hugo. 1986. *Poesía y sociedad (Uruguay 1888–1911)*. Montevideo: Arca.

———. 1997. "Leones, cazadores, e historiadores: A propósito de las políticas de la memoria y del conocimiento." *Revista Iberoamericana* 180: 379–87.

———. 1998. "Fin de Siglo: Reflections from the Periphery." In *New World [Dis]Orders and Peripheral Strains Specifying Cultural Dimensions in Latin American and Latino Studies*, edited by M. Piazza and M. Zimmerman. Chicago: March/Abrazo Press.

Acuña, René. 1985. *Arte de la lengua mexicana y vocabulario (Andrés de Olmos)*. México: Instituto de Investigaciones Filológicas, Universidad Nacional Autónoma de México.

Adamov, V. Arthur. 1959. *La Commune de Paris (8 mars–28 mars 1871): Anthologie*. Paris: Editions Sociales.

Adorno, Rolena. 1989. "Foreword." *Dispositio/n* 36/38: iii–iv.

Adorno, Rolena, and Walter Mignolo, eds. 1989. *Dispositio/n* 36/38.

Adorno, Theodor. 1941. "On Popular Music." *Studies in Philosophy and Social Science* 9: 17–28.

Aguirre Beltrán, Gonzalo. 1957. *El proceso de aculturación*. México: UNAM.

———. 1982. *El proceso de aculturación*. México: Ediciones de la Casa Chata.

Ahmad, Aijaz. 1992. *In Theory: Classes, Nations, Literatures*. London: Verso.

Alabarces, Pablo. 1996. "Fútbol y cine." In *Cuestión de pelotas*, edited by P. Alabarces and M. G. Rodríguez. Buenos Aires: Atuel.

Alarcón, Norma. 1981. "Chicana's Feminist Literature: A Re-Vision through Malintzin, or, Malintzin: Putting Flesh Back on the Object." In *This Bridge Called My Back: Writings by Radical Women of Color*, edited by C. Moraga and G. Anzaldúa. Watertown, Mass.: Persephone Press.

Alatorre, Antonio. 1964. "Para la historia de un problema: la mexicanidad de Ruiz de Alarcón." *Anuario de Letras Mexicanas* 4: 161–202.

Alencastro, Luiz Felipe de. 1979. "La traite négrière et l'unité nationale brésilienne." *Revue Française de l'Historie de l'Outre-Mer* 46.

Allen, Robert. 1985. *Speaking of Soap Operas*. Chapel Hill: University of North Carolina Press.

Allende, Isabel. 1998. *Aphrodite*. New York: Harper Collins.

Alonso, Dámaso. 1958. "Berceo y los topoi." In *De los siglos oscuros al de oro*. Madrid: Gredos.

Altamirano, Ignacio. 1949. *La literatura nacional*. Edited by J. Martínez. Vol. 1. México: Porrúa.

Althusser, Louis. 1969. "Contradiction and Overdetermination." In *For Marx*. London: New Left Books.

———. *Lenin and Philosophy, and Other Essays*. London: New Left Books.

———. 1979. *Reading Capital*. London: Verso.

Alvarado, Manuel, and John O. Thompson, eds. 1990. *The Media Reader*. London: British Film Institute.

Alvarez, Luciano. 1992. "Breve panorama de la comunicación en el Uruguay." In *Industrias culturales en el Uruguay*, edited by C. Rama. Montevideo: Arca.

Anderson, Benedict. 1983. *Imagined Communities: Reflections on the Spread of Nationalism*. London: Verso.

Anderson, Perry. 1992. "Marshall Berman: Modernity and Revolution." In *A Zone of Engagement*. London: Verso.

———. 1998. *The Origins of Postmodernity*. New York: Verso.

Anonymous. 1906. "Discursos de la sucesión y gobiernos de las yngas" (1570). In *Juicio de límites entre Perú y Bolivia*, edited by Víctor Maurtua. Vol. 8. Barcelona: Henrich y Compañía.

Anonymous (attributed to Antonio Valdez, ca. 1780). 1971. *Ollantay: Drama quechua del tiempo de los Inkas*. La Paz: Editorial Juventud.

Appadurai, Arjun. 1990. "Disjuncture and Difference in the Global Cultural Economy." *Public Culture* 2.2: 1–11 and 15–24.

———. 1996. *Modernity at Large: Cultural Dimensions of Globalization*. Minneapolis: University of Minnesota Press.

———. 1997. "Consumption, Duration, History." In *Streams of Cultural Capital: Transnational Cultural Studies*, edited by D. Palumbo-Liu and H. Gumbrecht. Stanford, Calif.: Stanford University Press.

Aquezolo, Manuel, ed. 1976. *La polémica del indigenismo*. Lima: Mosca Azul.

Aranguren, José Luis. 1966. *Moral y sociedad. La moral española en el siglo XIX*. Madrid: Taurus.

Arantes, Antonio Augusto, ed. 1984. *Produzindo o passado. Estratégias de construção do patrimonio cultural*. São Paulo: Editora Brasiliense.

Araújo, José Germán. 1992. "La radio como producto coherente." In *Industrias culturales en el Uruguay*, edited by C. Rama. Montevideo: Arca.

Ardao, Arturo. 1970. *Rodó. Su americanismo*. Montevideo: Biblioteca de Marcha.

———. 1977. "Del mito ariel al mito anti-ariel." *Actualidades* 7: 7–27.

Argan, Giulio. 1964. *Progretto e destino*. Milan: Il Saggiatore.

Arguedas, José María. 1971. *El zorro de arriba y el zorro de abajo*. Buenos Aires: Losada.

Aricó, José, ed. 1978. *Mariátegui y los orígenes del marxismo latinoamericano*. México: Siglo XXI.

Arizpe, Lourdes. 1979. *Indígenas en la ciudad de México. El caso de las "Marías."* México: SepSetentas.

Arnheim, Rudolf. 1988. *The Power of the Center: A Study of Composition in the Visual Arts.* Berkeley: University of California Press.

Arrian. 1893. *Anabasis of Alexander.* London: George Bell and Sons.

Arrighi, Giovanni. 1994. *The Long Twentieth Century: Money, Power, and the Origins of Our Times.* New York: Verso.

Ashcroft, Bill, Gareth Griffiths, and Helen Tiffin, eds. 1995. *The Post-Colonial Studies Reader.* London: Routledge.

Astrana Marín, Luis. 1930. *William Shakespeare.* Madrid: Aguilar.

Ayala Blanco, Jorge. 1968. *La aventura del cine mexicano.* México: Ediciones Era.

Balibar, Renée, and Dominique Laporte. 1974. *Le Français National: Politique et pratiques de la langue nationale sous la Révolution Française.* Paris: Hachette.

Balibar, Renée, and Immanuel Wallerstein. 1991. *Race, Nation, Class: Ambiguous Identities.* London: Verso.

Barker, Francis. 1993. *The Culture of Violence: Essays on Tragedy and History.* Chicago: University of Chicago Press.

Barrán, José Pedro. 1990–1992. *Historia de la sensibilidad en el Uruguay.* Vols. 1–2. Montevideo: Ediciones de la Banda Oriental.

Barreche, Eduardo. 1996. "Allanan radios comunitarias." *La República,* 17 June.

Barthes, Roland. 1972. *Mythologies.* London: Cape.

———. 1974. *S/Z.* New York: Hill and Wang.

———. 1987. *El susurro del lenguaje.* Barcelona: Paidós.

Bartos, Rena. 1989. *Marketing to Women around the World.* Boston: Harvard Business School Press.

Bartra, Roger. 1987. *La jaula de la melancolía. Identidad y metamorfosis del mexicano.* México: Grijalbo.

Bate, W. Jackson. 1970. *The Burden of the Past and the English Poet.* New York: W.W. Norton.

Baudrillard, Jean. 1982. *Fatal Strategies.* New York: Semiotext(e).

———. 1985. "La utopía realizada." Paper delivered at the Congress on the European Cultural Space, Madrid, 17–19 October.

Bauman, Richard, Patricia Sawin, and Inta Gale Carpenter. 1992. *Reflections on the Folklife Festival.* Bloomington: Folklore Institute, Indiana University.

Bayer, Osvaldo. 1990. *Fútbol argentino.* Buenos Aires: Editorial Sudamericana.

Beals, Ralph. 1951. "Urbanism, Urbanization, and Acculturation." *American Anthropologist* 53: 1–10.

Beceiro, Ildefonso. 1994. *La radio y la televisión de los pioneros. Cronología y anécdotas de un fenómeno uruguayo.* Montevideo: Ediciones de la Banda Oriental.

Bell, Daniel. 1990. "Resolving the Contradictions of Modernity and Modernism." *Society* 27: 43–50.

Bello, Andrés. 1965. "Advertencias sobre el uso de la lengua castellana." In *Antología de Andrés Bello,* edited by R. Silva Castro. Santiago: Zig-Zag.

———. 1981. "Prólogo." In *Gramática de la lengua castellana destinada al uso de los ameri-*

canos, edited by R. Trujillo. Tenerife: Instituto Universitario de Lingüística Andrés Bello.

Bello, Walden, Shea Cunningham, and Bill Rau. 1994. *Dark Victory: The United States, Structural Adjustment, and Global Poverty*. London: Pluto Press.

Belsey, Catherine. 1980. *Critical Practice*. New York: Methuen.

Benedetti, Mario. 1966. *Genio y figura de José Enrique Rodó*. Buenos Aires: Universitaria.

Benítez Rojo, Antonio. 1989. *La isla que se repite: el Caribe y la perspectiva posmoderna*. Hanover, N.H.: Ediciones del Norte.

———. 1992. *The Repeating Island*. Durham, N.C.: Duke University Press.

Benjamin, Walter. 1969. "Theses of the Philosophy of History." In *Illuminations*. New York: Schocken Books.

———. 1979. "Theses on the Philosophy of History." In *Illuminations*. London: Fontana/Collins.

———. 1986. "Critique of Violence." In *Reflections*. New York: Schocken Books.

Bensmaïa, Réda. 1994. "On the Concept of Minor Literature: From Kafka to Kateb Yacine." In *Gilles Deleuze and the Theater of Philosophy*, edited by C. Boundas and D. Olkowski. New York: Routledge.

Berman, Marshall. 1982. *All That Is Solid Melts into Air*. New York: Penguin Books.

Beverley, John. 1993. *Against Literature*. Minneapolis: University of Minnesota Press.

———. 1994. "Writing in Reverse: On the Project of the Latin American Subaltern Studies Group." *Dispositio/n* 46: 271–88.

———. 1995. "¿Hay vida más allá de la literatura?" *Estudios* 6: 23–40.

———. 1996a. "Estudios culturales y vocación política." *Revista de Crítica Cultural* 12: 46–53.

———. 1996b. "On What We Do: Postmodernism and Cultural Studies." In *The Postmodern in Latin and Latino American Cultural Narratives*, edited by Claudia Ferman. New York: Garland.

———. 1996c. "The Real Thing (Our Rigoberta)." *MLQ* 57: 129–39.

———. 1999. *Subalternity and Representation: Arguments in Cultural Theory*. Durham, N.C.: Duke University Press.

Beverley, John, and José Oviedo, eds. 1993. *The Postmodernism Debate in Latin America*. *boundary 2* 20.3: 1–231.

Beverley, John, and James Sanders. 1997. "Negotiating with the Disciplines: A Conversation on Latin American Subaltern Studies." *Journal of Latin American Cultural Studies* 6.2: 233–57.

Beverley, John, and Marc Zimmerman. 1990. *Literature and Politics in the Central American Revolutions*. Austin: University of Texas Press.

Bhabha, Homi. 1984. "Of Mimicry and Man: The Ambivalence of Colonial Discourse." *October* 28: 125–33.

———. 1994a. *The Location of Culture*. London: Routledge.

———. 1994b. "Anxious Nations, Nervous States." In *Supposing the Subject*, edited by Joan Copjec. London: Verso.

———. 1994c. "Remembering Fanon: Self, Psyche, and the Colonial Condition."

In *Colonial Discourse and Post- Colonial Theory*, edited by P. Williams and L. Chrisman. New York: Columbia University Press.

———. 1995a. "Cultural Diversity and Cultural Difference." In *The Post-Colonial Studies Reader*, edited by B. Ashcroft, G. Griffiths, and H. Tiffin. London: Routledge.

———. 1995b. "In a Spirit of Calm Violence." In *After Colonialism: Imperial Histories and Postcolonial Displacements*, edited by G. Prakash. Princeton, N.J.: Princeton University Press.

Blacker, Carmen, and Michael Loewe, eds. 1975. *Ancient Cosmologies*. London: Allen and Unwin.

Blixen, Samuel. 1995. "Radio FEUU: Qué culpa tiene el tomate . . . ." *Brecha*, 22 December.

———. 1997. "Suspendido por molestar al gobierno." *Brecha*, 5 December.

Bloom, Harold, ed. 1992. *Caliban*. New York: Chelsea House Publishers.

Boff, Leonardo, and Clodovis Boff. 1986. *Como fazer teologia da libertação*. Brazil: Vozes.

Bonfil Batalla, Guillermo. 1981. *Utopía y revolución*. México: Nueva Imagen.

———. 1990. *México profundo*. México: Grijalbo.

Borges, Jorge Luis. 1931. "Séneca en las orillas." *Sur* 1: 174–79.

———. 1936. "Tareas y destino de Buenos Aires." In *Homenaje a Buenos Aires en el IV Centenario de su fundación*. Radio Conference Series. Buenos Aires: Intendencia Municipal.

Bosi, Alfredo. 1972. *Historia concisa da literatura brasileira*. São Paulo: Editora Cultrix.

Bouissa, Alfredo, Eduardo Curuchet, and Oscar Orcajo. 1998. *Las otras radios: entre la legitimidad y la legalidad*. Montevideo: Nordan.

Bourdieu, Pierre. 1979. *La distinction*. Paris: Minuit.

Bourdieu, Pierre, and Loïs Wacquant. 1999. "On the Cunning of Imperialist Reason." *Theory, Culture, and Society* 16.1: 41–58.

Brathwaite, Edward. 1969. *Islands*. London: Oxford University Press.

Braudel, Fernand. 1985. *La dinámica del capitalismo*. Madrid: Alianza.

Brenkman, John. 1987. *Culture and Domination*. Ithaca, N.Y.: Cornell University Press.

Brera, Gianni, and Giorgio Sali. 1975. *Storia critica del calcio italiano*. Milano: Tascabili Bompiani.

Brooks, Peter. 1976. *The Melodramatic Imagination*. New Haven, Conn.: Yale University Press.

———. 1984. *Reading for the Plot*. New York: Knopf.

Brunk, Samuel. 1993. "Zapata and the City Boys: In Search of a Piece of the Revolution." *Hispanic American Historical Review* 73.1: 33–65.

Brunner, José Joaquín. 1987. *Ciencias sociales y el tema de la cultura. Notas para una agenda de investigación*. Santiago: FLACSO.

———. 1988. *Un espejo trizado: ensayos sobre cultura y políticas culturales*. Santiago: FLACSO.

———. 1990. "Seis preguntas a José Joaquín Brunner." *Revista de Crítica Cultural* 1: 20–25.

———. 1992. *América Latina: cultura y modernidad*. México: Grijalbo.

———. 1998. *Globalización cultural y posmodernidad*. Santiago: Fondo de Cultura Económica.

Brunner, José Joaquín, Alicia Barrios, and Carlos Catalán. 1989. *Chile: Transformaciones culturales y modernidad*. Santiago: FLACSO.

Buarque de Holanda, Sérgio. 1977. *Do imperio à republica II*. São Paulo: Companhia Editora Nacional.

Butler, Judith. 1990a. *Gender Trouble*. New York: Routledge.

———. 1990b. "Contigent Foundations: Feminism and the Question of 'Postmodernism.'" In *Feminists Theorize the Political*, edited by J. Butler and J. Scott. New York: Routledge.

———. 1993. *Bodies that Matter*. London: Routledge.

Cadaval, Olivia. 1993. "Patterns of Collaboration: The Festival of American Folklife U.S.-Mexico Borderlands Program." Paper presented at the AAA Annual Meeting, Washington, 17–21 November.

———. 1995. "Negotiating Cultural Representations through the Smithsonian Festival of American Folklife." Paper prepared for delivery at the 1995 International Meeting of the Latin American Studies Association, Washington, 30 September.

Calabrese, O. 1984. "Los replicantes." *Análisi* 9.

Caldas, Waldenyr. 1989. *O pontapé inicial: Memoria do futebol brasileiro (1894–1933)*. São Paulo: IBRASA.

Calderón, Fernando, comp. 1988. *Imágenes desconocidas. La modernidad en la encrucijada postmoderna*. Buenos Aires: CLACSO.

Campbell, Leon. 1987. "The Influence of Books and Literature on the Tupac Amaru Rebellion." Copy of author's manuscript of a talk presented at a Brown University conference titled "The Book in the Americas."

Campos, Haroldo de. 1983. "Da razão antropofágica: Diálogo e diferença na cultura brasileira." *Boletim Bibliográfico Biblioteca Mário de Andrade* 44.

Candido, Antonio. 1969. *Formação da literatura brasileira*. São Paulo: Martins.

———. 1973. "Literatura e subdesenvolvimento." *Argumento* 1: 6–24.

———. 1985. *Literatura e sociedade*. São Paulo: Cia. Ed. Nacional.

Cantor Magnani, José Guilherme. 1984. *Festa no pedaço. Cultura popular e lazer na cidade*. São Paulo: Editora Brasiliense.

Cantwell, Robert. 1993. *Ethnomimesis: Folklife and the Representation of Culture*. Chapel Hill: University of North Carolina Press.

Carbia, Rómulo. 1940. *La crónica oficial de Indias Occidentales. Estudio histórico y crítico acerca de la historiografía mayor de Hispano América en los siglos XVI a XVIII, con una introducción sobre la crónica oficial de Castilla*. Buenos Aires: Ediciones Buenos Aires.

Cardoso, Fernando. 1964. *Empresario industrial e desenvolvimento econômico no Brasil*. São Paulo: Difusão Européia do Livro.

Cardoso, Fernando, and Enzo Faletto. 1978. *Dependencia y desarrollo en América Latina*. México: Siglo XIX.

Carpentier, Alejo. 1981. *La novela latinoamericana en vísperas de un nuevo siglo*. México: Siglo XXI.

Carpio Muñoz, Juan Guillermo. 1976. *El yaraví arequipeño*. Arequipa: La Colmena.

Carrasco, Benito. 1908. "La ciudad del porvenir." *Caras y Caretas*, 22 February.

Carreño, Manuel Antonio. 1927. *Manual de urbanidad y buenas maneras*. París: Garnier Hermanos.

Carvalho, José Jorge de. 1989. *O lugar da cultura tradicional na sociedade moderna*. Antropología 77. Brasilia: Fundación Universidad de Brasilia.

Castañeda, Jorge. 1994. *Sorpresas te da la vida: México 1994*. México: Aguilar.

Castillo, Debra A. 1997. "Figuring Feminisms in Latin American Contexts." *Dispositio/n* 49: 155–73.

Castro Gómez, Santiago, and Eduardo Mendieta, eds. 1998. *Teorías sin disciplina: Latinoamericanismo, poscolonialidad, y globalización en debate*. México: Porrúa/USF.

Casullo, Nicolás, ed. 1989. *El debate modernidad-posmodernidad*. Buenos Aires: Puntosur.

Cawelti, John G. 1976. *Adventure, Mystery, and Romance: Formula Stories as Art and Popular Culture*. Chicago: Chicago University Press.

Cechetto, C. 1993. *Borocotó*. Buenos Aires: Taller Escuela Agencia.

CELAM. 1978. *Document of Consultation to the Episcopal Conferences*. III Conferencia General del Episcopado Latinoamericano.

CEPAL. 1985. *Crisis y desarrollo: presente y futuro de América Latina y el Caribe*. Vols. 1–3. Santiago: CEPAL.

Césaire, Aimé. 1955. *Discours sur le colonialisme*. Paris: Réclame.

———. 1969. *Une tempête. Adptation de "La tempête" de Shakespeare pour un théâtre nègre*. Paris Editions du Seuil.

Cesin, Nelson. 1996. "Encuentro de radios comunitarias: periodistas sin patente." *Brecha*, 3 May.

Chakrabarty, Dipesh. 1996. "Marxism after Marx: History, Subalternity, and Difference." In *Marxism beyond Marxism*, edited by S. Makdisi, C. Casarino, and R. E. Karl. New York: Routledge.

Chanady, Amaryll, ed. 1994. *Latin American Identity and Constructions of Difference*. Hispanic Issues, vol. 10. Minneapolis: Minnesota University Press.

Chapkis, Wendy. 1997. *Live Sex Acts: Women Performing Erotic Labor*. New York: Routledge.

Chaunu, Pierre. 1964. *Amérique et les Amériques*. Paris: Armand Colin.

Ch'en, Kenneth. 1939. "Matteo Ricci's Contribution to, and Influence on, Geographical Knowledge in China." *Journal of the American Oriental Society* 59: 325–509.

Cioran, Emile. 1997. *Cahiers (1957–1972)*. Paris: Gallimard.

CLACSO. 1989. *¿Hacia un nuevo orden estatal en América Latina?* Santiago: CLACSO.

Clark, John. 1991. *Democratizing Development: The Role of Voluntary Organizations*. West Hartford, Conn.: Kumarian Press.

Clifford, James. 1988. *The Predicament of Culture: Twentieth-Century Ethnography, Literature, and Art*. Cambridge: Harvard University Press.

Cline, Howard. 1964. "The *Relaciones Geográficas* of Spanish Indies, 1577–1586." *Hispanic American Historical Review* 3: 341–74.

———. 1972. "The *Relaciones Geográficas* of Spain, New Spain, and the Spanish Index: An Annotated Bibliography." In *Guide to Ethnohistorical Sources*, edited by Howad Cline. Vol. 12, part 1, of *Handbook of Middle American Indians*, edited by Robert Wauchope. Austin: University of Texas Press.

Cocchiara, Giuseppe. 1952. *Storia del folklore in Europa*. Torino: Einauldi.

COLEF-CONAPO-STPS. "Síntesis Ejecutiva." In *Encuesta sobre Migración en la Frontera Norte*. Tijuana: COLEF.

Coleman, David C. 1973. "Gentleman and Players." *The Economic History Review* 26.1: 92–116.

Colina, Enrique, and Daniel Díaz Torres. 1971. "Ideología del melodrama en el viejo cine latinoamericano." *Cine cubano* 73/74/75: 15.

Collier, George A., and Elizabeth Lowery Quarantiello. 1994. *Basta! Land and the Zapatista Rebellion in Chiapas*. Oakland: Institute for Food and Development Policy.

Collin, Françoise. 1995. "Praxis de la diferencia: Notas sobre lo trágico del sujeto." *Revista Mora* 1: 2–17.

Colón, Cristóbal. 1956. *La carta de Colón anunciando el descubrimiento del nuevo mundo, 15 de febrero de 1493*. Madrid: Edición Facsimilar.

———. 1982. *Textos y documentos completos. Prólogo y notas de Consulo Varela*. Madrid: Alianza Universidad.

Comier-Rodier, B., and B. Fleury-Vilatte. 1992. "The Cartoon Boom." *The Unesco Courier* (October): n.p.

Comisión de Estética Edilicia. 1925. *Proyecto orgánico para la urbanización del municipio*. Buenos Aires: MCBA.

CONASIDA (Consejo Nacional para la Prevención y Control del SIDA). 1989. "Encuesta sobre sexualidad y SIDA en mujeres dedicadas a la prostitución." Final Report. México, D. F.

———. 1995a. "Análisis de la situación de Ciudad Hidalgo, Chiapas." Internal Technical Report.

———. 1995b. "Resultados del análisis de la situación y propuesta para desarrollar una intervención para aumentar la seguridad del sexo comercial en Chiapas, área de Tuxtla Gutiérrez." Internal Technical Report.

———. 1995c. *SIDA/ETS* 1.1: 1–20.

Coombes, Annie. 1992. "Inventing the 'Post-Colonial': Hybridity and Constituency in Contemporary Curating." *New Formations* 18: n.p.

Cornejo Polar, Antonio. 1971. "Mariano Melgar y la poesía de la Emancipación." *El Peruano*, 28 July.

———. 1975a. "José Donoso y los problemas de la nueva narrativa hispanoamericana." *Acta Litteraria Academiae Scientiarum Hungaricae* 17: 215–26.

———. 1975b. "Los geniecillos dominicales: sus fortunas y adversidades." *San Marcos* 13.

———. 1977. "Para una interpretación de la novela indigenista." *Casa de las Américas* 100: 40–48.

———. 1978. "El indigenismo y las literaturas heterogéneas: su doble estatuto socio-cultural." *Revista de Crítica Literaria Latinoamericana* 7/8: 7–21.

————. 1994. *Escribir en el aire: ensayo sobre la heterogeneidad socio-cultural en las literaturas andinas*. Lima: Ed. Horizonte.

————. 1996. "Una heterogeneidad no dialéctica: sujeto y discurso migrantes en el Perú moderno." *Revista Iberoamericana* 176/177: 837–44.

————. 1997. "Mestizaje e hibridez: los riesgos de las metáforas. Apuntes." *Revista Iberoamericana* 180: 341–44.

————. 1998. "Indigenismo and Heterogeneous Literatures: Their Dual Socio-Cultural Logic." *Journal of Latin American Cultural Studies* 7.1: 15–27.

Corominas, Joan. 1967. *Breve diccionario etimológico de la lengua castellana*. Madrid: Gredos.

Coronil, Fernando. 1995. "Transculturation and Politics of Theory: Countering the Center, Cuban Counterpoint." In *Cuban Counterpoint: Tobacco and Sugar*, by Fernando Ortiz. Durham, N.C.: Duke University Press.

————. 1996. "Beyond Occidentalism: Toward Nonimperial Geohistorical Categories." *Cultural Anthropology* 111: 52–87.

Cortázar, Julio. 1970. "Del sentimiento de lo fantástico." In *La vuelta al día en ochenta mundos*. Madrid: Siglo XXI.

Costa, Pere-Oriol, José Pérez, and Fabio Tropea. 1996. *Tribus urbanas*. Barcelona: Paidós.

Coulmas, Florian, ed. 1984. *Linguistic Minorities and Literacy: Language Policy Issues in Developing Countries*. Amsterdam: Mounton.

Coward, Rosalind. 1984. *Female Desire: Women's Sexuality Today*. New York: Paladin.

Cremoux, Raúl. 1983. "El poder de la cultura en la televisión." In *Política cultural del estado Mexicano*, edited by Moisés Ladrón de Guevara. México: GEFE/SEP.

"Cuando el 85 por ciento era nacional." 1997. *Brecha*, 6 June.

Cueva, Agustín. 1974. "Para una interpretación sociológica de *Cien años de soledad*." *Revista Mexicana de Sociología* 1: 59–76.

————. 1989. "El marxismo latinoamericano: historia y problemas actuales." *Homines* 6: 428–41.

Curtius, Ernest. 1955. *Literatura europea y Edad Media latina*. México: Fondo de Cultura Económica.

Curuchet, Eduardo. 1997. "Gente en obra: El ladrillo y el micrófono." *Brecha*, 6 June.

Da Costa, Emilia Viotti. 1977. *Da monarquia à república: Momentos decisivos*. São Paulo: Grijalbo.

Dagnino, Evelina. 1973. "Cultural and Ideological Dependence: Building a Theoretical Framework." In *Structures of Dependency*, edited by F. Bonilla and R. Girling. Stanford, Calif.: Stanford University Press.

D'Allemand, Patricia. 1997. "Art and Culture in the Discourse of José Carlos Mariátegui." *Travesia. Journal of Latin American Cultural Studies* 1.2: 299–311.

Dalton, Roque. 1969. *El intelectual y la sociedad*. México: Siglo XXI.

Da Matta, Roberto. 1981. *Carnaváis, malandros, e heróis: Para uma sociología do dilema brasileiro*. Rio de Janeiro: Zahar.

————. 1985. *A casa e a rua: Espaço, ciudadania, mulher, e morte no Brasil*. São Paulo: Editora Brasiliense.

Dash, J. Michael. 1989. "Introduction" to *Caribbean Discourse*, by Édouard Glissant. Charlottesville: University of Virginia Press.

———. 1995. *Édouard Glissant*. New York: Cambridge University Press.

Dávila, Arlene. 1999. "The *Othered* Nation: The Marketing and Making of U.S. Latinidad." Unpublished manuscript.

Davis, Mike. 1990. *City of Quartz: Excavating the Future in Los Angeles*. London: Verso.

de la Campa, Román. 1996. "Latinoamérica y sus nuevos cartógrafos: discurso poscolonial, diásporas intelectuales y enunciación fronteriza." *Revista Iberoamericana* 176/177: 697–718.

———. 1999. *LatinAmericanism*. Minneapolis: University of Minnesota Press.

———. 2000. "América Latina: Confección y marketing de un campo de estudios." *Revista de Crítica Literaria Latinoamericana* 51: 177–88.

de la Garza, Rodolfo O. 1992. "The Latino National Political Survey." In *Latino Voices: Mexican, Puerto Rican, and Cuban Perspectives on American Politics*, edited by R. de la Garza. Boulder, Colo.: Westview Press.

de la Peña, Guillermo. 1981. *A Legacy of Promises: Agriculture, Politics, and Ritual in the Morelos Highlands of Mexico*. Austin: University of Texas Press.

de las Casas, Bartolomé. 1992. *El Tratado de las "Doce Dudas."* In *Obras Completas*, edited by J. B. Lassegue. Vol. 2. Madrid: Alianza.

del Castillo, Adelaida R. 1977. "Malintzin Tenepal: A Preliminary Look into a New Perspective." In *Essays on La Mujer*, edited by R. Sánchez and R. Martínez Cruz. Los Angeles: University of California Chicano Studies Center.

D'Elia, Pascuale, ed. 1938. *Il mappamondo cinese del p. Matteo Rici*. Citta del Vaticano: Biblioteca Apostolica Vaticana.

Deleuze, Gilles. 1992. "Postscript on the Societies of Control." *October* 59: 3–8.

Deleuze, Gilles, and Félix Guattari. 1977. *Anti-Oedipus: Capitalism and Schizophrenia*. New York: Viking Press.

———. 1986. *Kafka: Toward a Minor Literature*. Minneapolis: University of Minnesota Press.

———. 1988. *Mil mesetas: capitalismo y esquizofrenia*. Barcelona: Pre-Textos.

de Man, Paul. 1971. *Blindness and Insight: Essays in the Rhetoric of Contemporary Criticism*. Oxford: Oxford University Press.

———. 1979. *Allegories of Reading: Figural Language in Rousseau, Nietzsche, Rilke, and Proust*. New Haven, Conn.: Yale University Press.

De Mello e Souza, Gilda. 1979. *O Tupi e o Alaude: Uma interpretação de Macunaima*. São Paulo: Duas Cidades.

Derrida, Jacques. 1989. *Of Spirit: Heidegger and the Question*. Chicago: University of Chicago Press.

———. 1994. *Spectres of Marx: The State of the Debt, the Work of Mourning, and the New International*. New York: Routledge.

———. 1997. *Politics of Friendship*. New York: Verso.

De Slemenson, Martha, and Germán Kratochwill. 1970. "Un arte de difusores: apuntes para la comprensión de un movimiento plástico de vanguardia en Buenos Aires, de sus creadores, sus difusores, y su público." In El intelectual latino-

americano. Un simposio sobre sociología de los intelectuales, edited by J. Marsal. Buenos Aires: Editorial del Instituto Di Tella.

Desnoes, Edmundo. 1979. "A falta de otras palabras." Paper presented at the symposium "The Rise of the New Latin American Narrative, 1950–1976." Washington, Wilson Center, 18–20 October.

Deusta Carvallo, J., S. Stein, and S. C. Stokes. 1984. "Soccer and Social Change in Early Twentieth-Century Peru." *Studies in Latin American Popular Culture* 3: 17–21.

Development GAP. 1993. *The Other Side of the Story: The Real Impact of World Bank and IMF Structural Adjustment Programs*. Washington: The Development GAP.

Dezalay, Yves. 1992. *Marchants de droit: la restructuration de l'ordre juridique international par les multinationales du droit*. Paris: Fayard.

Díaz Torres, Daniel, and Enrique Colina. 1972. "El melodrama en la obra de Luis Buñuel." *Cine cubano* 78/80: 156–64.

Dirlik, Arif. 1994. *After the Revolution: Waking to Global Capitalism*. Hanover, N.H: New England University Press.

Donnat, Olivier, and Dennis Cogneau. 1990. *Les pratiques culturelles de Français: 1973– 1989*. Paris: La Découverte.

Donoso, José. 1972. *Historia personal del boom*. Barcelona: Anagrama.

Dorfman, Ariel. 1980. *Reader's Nuestro que estás en la tierra: ensayos sobre el imperialismo cultural*. México: Nueva Imagen.

———. 1991. *Death and the Maiden*. New York: Penguin.

Dorfman, Ariel, and Armand Mattelart. 1972. *Para leer el pato Donald*. México: Siglo XXI.

Dorson, Richard. 1968. *The British Folklorist: A History*. Chicago: University of Chicago Press.

Douglas, Susan. 1977. "Life-style Analysis to Profile Women in International Markets." *Journal of Marketing* 41.3: 46–54.

D'Souza, Dinesh. 1991. *Illiberal Education: The Politics of Race and Sex on Campus*. New York: Free Press.

Dubois, Claude-Gilbert. 1970. *Mythe et langage au seiziéme siècle*. Paris: Editions Ducrot.

Dumpierre, Eramos. 1965. *Mella*. La Habana: Instituto de Historia, Academia de Ciencias de Cuba.

Dunlop, Robert. 1858. *Service and Adventure with the Khakee Ressalah or, Meerut Volunteer Horse, during the Mutinies of 1857–58*. London: R. Bentley.

Durham, E. R. 1980. "A familia operaria: Consciencia e ideologia." *Dados* 23.2: 201–14.

During, Simon. 1993. *Cultural Studies Reader*. Melbourne: Routledge.

Dworkin, Dennis. 1997. *Cultural Marxism in Post-War Britain: History, the New Left, and the Origins of Cultural Studies*. Durham, N.C.: Duke University Press.

Easthope, Anthony. 1991. *Literary into Cultural Studies*. London: Routledge.

Eliade, Mircea. 1963. *Myth and Reality*. New York: Harper and Row.

Eltit, Diamela. 1989. *El padre mío*. Santiago: Francisco Zegers Editor.

Escobar, Arturo. 1992. "Imagining a Post-Development Era? Critical Thought, Development, and Social Movements." *Social Text* 31/32: 20–56.

Escobar Bavio, E. 1923. *Historia del fútbol en el Río de la Plata*. Buenos Aires: Sports.

Esquivel, Laura. 1989. *Como agua para chocolate. Novela de entregas mensuales con recetas, amores, y remedios caseros*. México: Editorial Planeta.

Estediario. 1996. "Con los pies en la tierra y la voz en el aire. Encuentro por el desarrollo de radios comunitarias." 16 April.

EZLN: *Documentos y comunicados, 1 de enero/8 de agosto de 1994*. 1994. México: Era.

Fabian, Johannes. 1983. *Time and the Other: How Anthropology Makes Its Object*. New York: Columbia University Press.

Fabri, Paolo. 1973. "Le communicazioni di massa in Italia: Sguardo semiotico e malocchio de la sociologia." *Versus* 5: 57–109.

Fanon, Frantz. 1952. *Black Skin, White Masks*. New York: Grove Press.

Fasano Mertens, Federico. 1992. "Ante la crisis sin retorno de la prensa uruguaya. El problema de la redistribución de la palabra no es un problema técnico sino político." In *Industrias culturales en el Uruguay*, edited by C. Rama. Montevideo: Arca.

Fernández Moreno, César. 1972. *América Latina en su literatura*. México: UNESCO-Siglo XXI.

Fernández Retamar, Roberto. 1969. "Cuba hasta Fidel." *Bohemia*, 19 September.

———. 1969. "Modernismo, noventiocho, subdesarrollo." In *Ensayo de otro mundo*. Santiago: Universitaria.

———. 1971. *Calibán. Apuntes sobre la cultura en Nuestra América*. México: Diógenes.

———. 1973. "Para una teoría de la literatura hispanoamericana." *Casa de las Américas* 80: 128–34.

———. 1975a. *Para una teoría de la literatura hispanoamericana y otras aproximaciones*. La Habana: Casa de las Américas.

———. 1975b. "Algunos problemas teóricos de la literatura hispanoamericana." *Revista de Crítica Literaria Latinoamericana* 1: 7–38.

———. 1976. "Nuestra América y Occidente." *Casa de las Américas* 98: 36–57.

Fisher, Julie. 1993. *The Road from Rio: Sustainable Development and the Nongovernmental Movement in the Third World*. Westport, Conn.: Praeger.

Flora, Cornelia Butler, and Jan Flora. 1978. "The Fotonovela as a Tool for Class and Cultural Domination." *Latin American Perspectives* 16: 134–50.

Flores, Juan. 1993. *Divided Borders: Essays on Puerto Rican Identity*. Houston: Arte Público.

———. 2000. *From Bomba to Hip-Hop: Puerto Rican Culture and Latino Identity*. New York: Columbia University Press.

Flores, Juan, and George Yúdice. 1990. "Living Borders/Buscando América: Languages of Latino Self-Formation." *Social Text* 24: 57–84.

Follari, Roberto. 1990. *Modernidad y posmodernidad. Una óptica desde América Latina*. Buenos Aires: REI Argentina.

Fonseca, Elena. 1996. "Encuentro para el desarrollo de las radios comunitarias en el Uruguay: 'Con los pies en la tierra y la voz en el aire.'" *Estediario* (Rocha), 16 April.

Forgacs, David. 1984. "National-Popular: Genealogy of a Concept." In *Formations of Nation and People*, edited by T. Bennett. London: Routledge.

Foster, George M. 1960. *Culture and Conquest: America's Spanish Heritage.* New York: Wenner Gren Foundation for Anthropological Research.

Foucault, Michel. 1977. *Discipline and Punish: The Birth of the Prison.* London: Allen Lane.

———. 1979. *Discipline and Punish: The Birth of the Prison.* New York: Vintage Books.

———. 1980a. *Power/Knowledge: Selected Interviews and Other Writings, 1972–1977.* New York: Pantheon.

———. 1980b. *La verdad y las formas jurídicas.* Barcelona: Gedisa.

———. 1983. "The Subject and Power." In *Michel Foucault: Beyond Structuralism and Hermeneutics*, edited by Hubert L. Dreyfus and Paul Rabinow. Chicago: University of Chicago Press.

———. 1984. *The Foucault Reader.* Edited by Paul Rabinow. New York: Pantheon.

———. 1988. *Vigilar y castigar. Nacimiento de la prisión.* México: Siglo XXI.

———. 1991. "Theatrum Politicum: The Genealogy of Capital: Police and the State of Prosperity." In *The Foucault Effect: Studies in Governmentality*, edited by G. Burchell, C. Gordon, and P. Miller. Chicago: University of Chicago Press.

Fox, Geoffrey. 1996. *Hispanic Nation: Culture, Politics, and the Construction of Identity.* Secaucus, N.J.: Carol.

Fraga, Luis, Herman Gallegos, and Gerald López. 1994. *Still Looking for America: Beyond the Latino National Political Survey.* Stanford, Calif.: Stanford Center for Chicano Research.

Franco, Jean. 1967. *The Modern Culture of Latin America: Society and the Artist.* New York: F. A. Praeger.

———. 1969. *An Introduction to Spanish American Literature.* London: Cambridge University Press.

———. 1975. "Dependency Theory and Literary History: The Case of Latin America." *Minnesota Review* 5: 65–80.

———. 1981a. "The Utopia of a Tired Man: Jorge Luis Borges." *Social Text* 4: 52–78.

———. 1981b. "Narrador, autor, super-estrella. La narrativa latinoamericana en la época de cultura de masas." *Revista Iberoamerica* 114/115: 129–48.

———. 1986. "The Incorporation of Women: A Comparison of North American and Mexican Popular Narrative." In *Studies in Entertainment: Critical Approaches to Mass Culture*, edited by T. Modleski. Bloomington: Indiana University Press.

———. 1989. *Plotting Women: Gender and Representation in Mexico.* New York: Columbia University Press.

———. 1992. "Going Public: Reinhabiting the Private." In *On Edge: The Crisis of Contemporary Latin American Culture*, edited by G. Yúdice, J. Franco, and J. Flores. Minneapolis: University of Minnesota Press.

———. 1994. "Beyond Ethnocentrism: Gender, Power, and the Third-World Intelligentsia." In *Colonial Discourse and Postcolonial Theory: A Reader*, edited by P. Williams and L. Chrisman. New York: Columbia University Press.

———. 1996a. "From Romance to Refractory Aesthetic." In *Latin American Women's*

Writing: Feminist Readings in Theory and Crisis, edited by A. Brooksbank Jones and C. Davis. Oxford: Clarendon Press.

———. 1996b. "The Gender Wars." NACLA *Report on the Americas* 29.4: 6–9.

———. 1996c. *Marcar diferencias, cruzar fronteras: Ensayos.* Santiago: Cuarto Propio.

———. 1997. "From the Margins to the Center: Recent Trends in Feminist Theory in the United States and Latin America." In *Gender Politics in Latin America: Debates in Theory and Practice*, edited by E. Dore. New York: Monthly Review Press.

———. 1999. *Critical Passions: Selected Essays.* Edited by M. L. Pratt and K. Newman. Durham, N.C.: Duke University Press.

———. 2002. *The Decline and Fall of the Lettered City: Latin America in the Cold War.* Cambridge, Mass.: Harvard University Press.

Franco, Jean, and Julianne Burton. 1978. "Culture and Imperialism." *Latin American Perspectives* 16: 77–97.

Frenk, Susan. 1996. "The Wandering Text: Situating the Novels of Isabel Allende." In *Latin American Women's Writing: Feminist Readings in Theory and Crisis*, edited by A. Brooksbank Jones and C. Davis. Oxford: Clarendon Press.

Freyre, Gilberto. 1976. *Manifiesto regionalista.* Recife: Instituto Joaquim Nabuco de Pesquisas Sociais.

Frydenberg, J. 1997. "Prácticas y valores en el proceso de popularización del fútbol: Buenos Aires 1900–1910." *Entrepasados. Revista de Historia* 6.12: 7–31.

———. 1998. "Redefinición del fútbol aficionado y del fútbol oficial: Buenos Aires, 1912." In *Deporte y sociedad*, edited by P. Alabarces, R. Di Giano, and J. Frydenberg. Buenos Aires: Eudeba.

Fuenzalida, Valerio. 1982. *La télé: Un affair de famille.* Paris: n.p.

———. 1984. *Televisión: Padres-hijos.* Santiago: CENECA.

Furtado, Celso. 1962. *A pre-revolução brasileira.* Rio de Janeiro: Editora Fondo de Cultura.

Fussell, Paul. 1983. *Class: A Guide through the American Status System.* New York: Summit Books.

Galeano, Eduardo. 1988. *Century of the Wind.* New York: Pantheon.

Galende, Federico. 1996. "Un desmemoriado espíritu de época." *Revista de Crítica Cultural* 13: 52–55.

García Calderón, Carola. 1984. *Revistas femeninas. La mujer como objeto de consumo.* México: El Caballito.

García Canclini, Néstor. 1982. *Las culturas populares en el capitalismo.* México: Nueva Imagen.

———. 1983. *As culturas populares no capitalismo.* São Paulo: Editora Brasiliense.

———. 1984a. *Desigualdad cultural y poder simbólico.* México. Mimeographed.

———. 1984b. "Gramsci con Bourdieu." *Nueva Sociedad* 71: 69–78.

———. 1985a. "Cultura y poder: ¿dónde está la investigación?" Paper read at the symposium "Cultura popular y resistencia política," New York.

———. 1985b. "Cultura transnacional y culturas populares en México." Paper read at Congreso de Americanistas, Bogotá.

———. 1988a. "Culture and Power: The State of Research." *Media, Culture, and Society* 10: 467–97.

———. 1988b. *Teoría y método en sociología del arte.* México: Siglo XXI.

———. 1989a. *Culturas híbridas. Estrategias para entrar y salir de la modernidad.* México: Grijalbo.

———. 1989b. *Las culturas populares en el capitalismo.* México: Nueva Imagen.

———. 1992a. "Too Much Determination or Too Much Hybridization?" *Travesía. Journal of Latin American Cultural Studies* 1.2: 161–70.

———. 1992b. "Museos, aeropuertos, y ventas de garage: la cultura ante el Tratado de Libre Comercio." *La Jornada Semanal,* 14 June.

———. 1995a. *Consumidores y ciudadanos. Conflictos multiculturales de la globalización.* México: Grijalbo.

———. 1995b. *Hybrid Cultures: Strategies for Entering and Leaving Modernity.* Minneapolis: Minnesota University Press.

———. 1996. "Cultural Studies Questionnaire." *Journal of Latin American Cultural Studies* 5.1: 83–87.

———. 1999a. "Entrar y salir de la hibridación." *Revista de Crítica Literaria Latinoamericana* 50: 53–58.

———. 1999b. *La globalización imaginada.* Buenos Aires: Paidós.

García Canclini, Néstor, and Rafael Roncagliolo, eds. 1988. *Cultura transnacional y culturas populares.* Lima: IPAL.

García Márquez, Gabriel. 1980. *Obra periodística. Vol. 1: Textos costeños.* Edited by J. Gilard. Barcelona: Bruguera.

García Márquez, Gabriel, and Mario Vargas Llosa. 1968. *La novela en América Latina. Diálogo.* Lima: Carlos Milla Batres, Ediciones UNI.

García Riera, Emilio. 1969. *Historia documental del cine mexicano.* México: Ediciones Era.

Gates, Henry Louis, Jr. 1991. "Critical Fanonism." *Critical Inquiry* 17: 457–70.

Gatti, Daniel. 1996. "Francia: la legalización y después." *Brecha,* 3 May.

Geary, Patrick J. 1994. *Phantoms of Remembrance: Memory and Oblivion at the End of the First Millennium.* Princeton, N.J.: Princeton University Press.

Germani, Gino, et al. 1985. "Democracia y autoritarismo en la sociedad moderna." In *Los límites de la democracia.* Buenos Aires: CLACSO.

Gibaja, Regina. 1964. *El público de arte.* Buenos Aires: Eudeba.

Gilroy, Paul. 1993. *The Black Atlantic: Modernity and Double Consciousness.* London: Verso.

Gledhill, Christine. 1987. "The Melodramatic Field: An Investigation." In *Home Is Where the Heart Is: Melodrama and the Woman's Film,* edited by C. Gledhill. London: British Film Institute.

Glissant, Édouard. 1989. *Caribbean Discourse.* Charlottesville: University of Virginia Press.

———. 1990. *Poétique de la relation.* Paris: Gallimard.

Godd Eshelman, Catherine. 1988. *Haciendo la lucha. Arte y comercio nahuas de Guerrero.* México: Fondo de Cultura Económica.

González, David. 1992. "What's the Problem with 'Hispanic'? Just Ask a 'Latino.'" *New York Times*, 15 November, sec. 4, 6.

González, Hermann, and Manuel Alberto Donis Ríos. 1992. "Cartografía y cartógrafos en la Venezuela colonial: Siglo XVIII." In *Memoria del V Congreso Venezolano de Historia*. Vol. 3. Caracas: Academia Nacional de la Historia.

González, Luis. 1974. *San José de Gracia: Mexican Village in Transition*. Austin: University of Texas Press.

González, Reynaldo. 1988. *Llorar es un placer*. La Habana: Editorial Letras Cubanas.

González Echevarría, Roberto. 1985. "The Case of the Speaking Statue: *Ariel* and the Magisterial Rhetoric of the Latin American Essay." In *The Voice of the Masters: Writing and Authority in Modern Latin American Literature*. Austin: University of Texas Press.

González Prada, Manuel. 1982. *Textos: una antología general*. México: UNAM.

Goody, Jack. 1985. *Cuisines, cuisine et classes*. Paris: Centre George Pompidou.

Gorbach, M., and K. Schroder. 1984. "Good Usage in EFK Context." In *The English Language Today*, edited by S. Greenbaum. Oxford: Pergamon Press.

Gossen, Gary, ed. 1986. *Symbol and Meaning beyond the Closed Community: Essays in Mesoamerican Ideas*. Albany: SUNY-Albany Institute of Mesoamerican Studies.

———. 1994. "From Olmecas to Zapatistas: A Once and Future History of Souls." *American Anthropologist* 96: 553–70.

Gracia Martínez, Bernardo. 1987. *Los pueblos de la sierra. El poder y el espacio entre los indios del norte de Puebla hasta 1700*. México: El Colegio de México.

Gramsci, Antonio. 1971. *Selections from the Prison Notebooks*. New York: International Publishers.

———. 1992. *Prison Notebooks*. New York: Columbia University Press.

Grossberg, Lawrence. 1997. *Bringing It All Back Home*. Durham, N.C.: Duke University Press.

Grossberg, Lawrence, Cary Nelson, and Paula Treichel, eds. 1992. *Cultural Studies*. New York: Routledge.

Groupe de l'Etudes sur le Plurilinguisme Européen. 1986. *Actes du Deuxième Colloqué, Langue français-langue anglaise: Contacts et conflits*. Strasbourg: Université des Sciences Humaines de Strasbourg.

Guamán Poma de Ayala, Felipe. 1956. *La corónica y buen gobierno*. Lima: Editorial Cultura.

Guéhenno, Jean. 1969. *Calibán y Próspero*. Paris: B. Grasset.

Gugelberger, John, ed. 1996. *The Real Thing: Testimonial Discourse and Latin America*. Durham, N.C.: Duke University Press.

———. 1996. "Introduction: Institutionalization of Transgression: Testimonial Discourse and Beyond." In *The Real Thing: Testimonial Discourse and Latin America*. Durham, N.C.: Duke University Press.

Guha, Ranajit. 1983. *Elementary Aspects of Peasant Insurgency in Colonial India*. Delhi: Oxford University Press.

———. 1989. "Chandra's Death." In *Subaltern Studies V: Writings on South Asian History and Society*, edited by Ranajit Guha. Delhi: Oxford University Press.

Guha, Ranajit, and Gayatri Chakravorty Spivak, eds. 1988. *Selected Subaltern Studies*. New York: Oxford University Press.

Guilbaut, Serge. 1989. *Comment New York vola l'idée d'art moderne*. Marseille: Ed Jacqueline Chambon.

Guillermoprieto, Alma. 1995. "The Shadow War." *New York Review of Books* 42.4: 34–43.

Guimarães Rosa, João. 1965. *A sereia e o desconfiado*. Río de Janeiro: Editora Civilização Brasileira.

——. 1967. *Gran sertón: Veredas*. Barcelona: Seix Barral.

——. 1969. *Estas estórias*. Río de Janeiro: Livraria José Olympio.

——. 1971. *The Devil to Pay in the Backlands*. New York: Knopf.

Gurevich, Aaron. 1985. *Categories of Medieval Culture*. London: Routledge and Kegan Paul.

Gutiérrez, Gustavo. 1992. "The New Evangelization." Lecture series at the Pittsburgh Theological Seminary, May.

Gutiérrez, Paulina, and Giselle Munizaga. 1983. *Radio y cultura popular de masas*. Santiago: CENECA.

Gutiérrez Girardot, Rafael. 1994. *Cuestiones*. México: Fondo de Cultura Económica.

Gutierrez-Jones, Carl. 1991. "Rethinking the Borderlands: Between Literary and Legal Discourse." *Dispositio/n* 41: 45–60.

Guzmán, Eulalia. 1939. "The Art of Map-Making among the Ancient Mexicans." *Imago Mundi* 3: 1–6.

Habermas, Jürgen. 1983. "Modernity, an Incomplete Project." In *The Anti-Aesthetic: Essays on Postmodern Culture*, edited by H. Foster. Port Townsend, Wash.: Bay Press.

Hall, Stuart. 1980. "Cultural Studies and the Centre: Some Problematics and Problems." *Culture, Media, Language: Working Papers in Cultural Studies, 1972–79*, edited by S. Hall, D. Hobson, A. Lowe, and P. Willis. London: Hutchinson.

——. 1984. "Estudios culturales: dos paradigmas." *Hueso Húmero* 19: 69–97.

——. 1992. "Cultural Studies and Its Theoretical Legacies." In *Cultural Studies*, edited by L. Grossberg, C. Nelson, and P. Treichler. New York: Routledge.

——. 1994a. "Cultural Identity and Diaspora." In *Colonial Discourse and Post-Colonial Theory*, edited by P. Williams and L. Chrisman. New York: Columbia University Press.

——. 1994b. "Culture, Community, Nation." *Cultural Studies* 7.3: 349–63.

Hannerz, Ulf. 1996. *Transnational Connections: Culture, People, Places*. London: Routledge.

Haraway, Donna. 1989. *Primate Visions: Gender, Race, and Nature in the World of Modern Science*. London: Routledge.

Harley, John Bryan. 1988. "Maps, Knowledge, and Power." In *The Iconography of Landscapes: Essays on the Symbolic Representation, Design, and Use of Past Environments*, edited by D. Cosgrove and S. Daniel. London: Cambridge.

——. 1989. "Desconstructing the Map." *Cartographica* 26.2: 1–20.

Hasson, H. 1989. "Les tendances émergentes dans les comportements des consommateurs en Europe." *Revue Française de Marketing* 4.

Hayes-Bautista, David, and Jorge Chapa. 1987. "Latino Terminology : Conceptual Bases for Standardized Terminology." *American Journal of Public Health* 77.1 : 61–68.

Hegel, Georg Wilhelm Friedrich. 1946. *Filosofía de la historia universal.* Madrid: Revista de Occidente.

Heidegger, Martin. 1962. *Being and Time.* New York: Harper and Row.

Herlinghauss, Hermann. 1998. "La modernidad ha comenzado a hablarnos desde donde jamás lo esperábamos. Una nueva epistemología política de la cultura en *De los medios a las mediaciones* de Jesús Martín Barbero." In *Mapas nocturnos,* edited by M. Laverde Toscano and R. Reguillo. Colombia: Siglo del Hombre Editores.

Hernández Castillo, Rosalva Aida. 1995. "De la comunidad a la convención nacional de mujeres. Las campesinas chiapanecas y sus demandas de género." In *La explosión de las comunidades en Chiapas,* edited by J. Nash and A. Parellada. Documento IWGIA No. 16. Copenhagen: IWGIA.

Hernández Castillo, Rosalva Aida, and Ronald Nigh. 1995. "Global Processes and Local Identity: Indians of the Sierra Madre of Chiapas and the International Organic Market." Paper presented at the AAA Annual Meeting, Washington, D.C., 18 November.

Herrera y Tordesillas, Antonio. 1601–1615. *Historia general de los hechos de los castellanos en las Islas y Tierra Firme del Mar Océano, por Antonio de Herrera coronista mayor de Su majestad, de las Indias y su coronista oficial de Castilla, en quatro décadas desde el año 1492 hasta el de 1531.* 8 vols. Madrid: Imprenta Real.

Herskovits, Melville. 1938. *Acculturation: The Study of Cultural Contacts.* New York: J. J. Augustins.

Hill, John. 1986. *Sex, Class, and Realism: British Cinema, 1956–1963.* London: British Film Institute.

Hills, Patricia. 1991–1992. "Bleeding Hearts, Borders, and Postmodernism." *Art New England* 21 (December/January): 35–39.

Hobsbawm, Eric. 1987. *Mundos de Trabalho.* Rio de Janeiro: Paz e Terra.

Hodgson, Marshall. 1993. *Rethinking World History: Essays on Europe, Islam, and World History.* New York: Cambridge University Press.

Hoggart, Richard. 1958. *The Uses of Literacy.* London: Penguin.

———. 1972. *On Culture and Communication.* New York: Oxford University Press.

Holzman, Harold R., and Sharon Pines. 1982. "Buying Sex: The Phenomenology of Being a John." *Deviant Behavior* 4.1: 89–116.

Hopenhayn, Martín. 1994. *Ni apocalípticos ni integrados. Aventuras de la modernidad en América Latina.* Santiago: Fondo de Cultura Económica.

Horkheimer, Max, and Theodor Adorno. 1972. *Dialectic of Enlightenment.* New York: Seabury Press.

Hurtado, María de la Luz. 1983. *Teatro y sociedad chilena en la mitad del siglo XX.* Santiago: Universidad Católica.

Huyssen, Andreas. 1986. *After the Great Divide: Modernism, Mass Culture, Postmodernism.* Bloomington: Indiana University Press.

Ileto, Reynaldo. 1979. *Passion and Revolution: Popular Movements in the Philippines, 1840–1910.* Quezon: Ateneo de Manila.

Illich, Iván. 1974. *Alternativas.* Tabasco: Joaquín Mortiz.

Imperio, Oscar. 1992. "ANDEBU: 60 años de historia." In *Industrias culturales en el Uruguay,* edited by C. Rama. Montevideo: Arca.

Inter-American Cultural Studies Network. ca. 1992. "Proposal for the Establishment of an Electronic Network Relating to Cultural Studies (CULTNET)."

Irigaray, Luce. 1977. *Ce sexe qui n'en est pas un.* Paris: Editions de Minuit.

Jahn, Janheinz. 1968. *Neo-African Literature: A History of Black Writing.* New York: Grove Press.

Jakobson, Roman, and Morris Halle. 1956. *Fundamentals of Language.* 's Gravenhage: Mouton.

Jameson, Fredric. 1986. "Third World Literature in an Era of Multinational Capitalism." *Social Text* 15: 65–88.

———. 1988. "Marxism and Historicism." In *The Ideologies of Theory: Essays, 1971–1986.* Vol. 2. Minneapolis: University of Minnesota Press.

———. 1990a. "Modernism and Imperialism." In *Nationalism, Colonialism, and Literature* by Terry Eagleton, Fredric Jameson, and Edward Said. Minneapolis: University of Minnesota Press.

———. 1990b. *Signatures of the Visible.* New York: Routledge.

———. 1991. *Postmodernism or the Cultural Logic of Late Capitalism.* Durham, N.C.: Duke University Press.

———. 1998a. *The Cultural Turn: Selected Writings on the Postmodern, 1983–98.* New York: Verso.

———. 1998b. "Notes on Globalization as a Philosophical Issue." In *The Cultures of Globalization,* edited by Fredric Jameson and Masao Miyoshi. Durham, N.C.: Duke University Press.

JanMohamed, Abdul R., and David Lloyd. 1990. "Introduction: Toward a Theory of Minority Discourse: What Is to Be Done?" In *The Nature and Context of Minority Discourse,* edited by A. R. JanMohamed and D. Lloyd. Oxford: Oxford University Press.

Jiménez de la Espada, Marcos. 1881–1897. *Relaciones geográficas de Indias.* Madrid: Tip. de M. G. Hernández.

Jitrik, Noé. 1975a. "Blanco, negro, ¿mulato? Lectura de El reino de este mundo de Alejo Carpentier." In *Araisa.* Caracas: Centro de Estudios Latinoamericanos.

———. 1975b. *Producción literaria y producción social.* Buenos Aires: Sudamericana.

Johnson, Mark. 1987. *The Body in the Mind: The Bodily Basis of Meaning, Imagination, and Reason.* Chicago: Chicago University Press.

Judy, Ronald. 1993. *(Dis)forming the American Canon: African-Arabic Slave Narratives and the Vernacular.* Minneapolis: University of Minnesota Press.

Kaminsky, Amy. 1997. "Feminist Criticism and Latin American Literary Scholarship." *Dispositio/n* 49: 135–53.

Kanitkar, Helen. 1993. "'Real True Boys': Moulding the Cadets of Imperialism."
In *Dislocating Masculinity: Comparative Ethnographies*, edited by A. Cornwall and
N. Lindisfarne. London: Routledge.

Kaplan, E. Ann. 1987. "Mothering, Feminism, and Representation: The Maternal in
Melodrama and the Woman's Film, 1910–40." In *Home Is Where the Heart Is: Melodrama and the Woman's Film*, edited by C. Gledhill. London: British Film Institute.

Kawataba, Shigeru. 1991. "The Japanese Record Industry." *Popular Music* 10.3:
327–45.

King, John. 1990. *Magical Reels: A History of Cinema in Latin America*. London: Verso.

Kitagawa, Junko. 1991. "Some Aspects of Japanese Popular Music." *Popular Music*
10.3: 305–15.

Knoblauch, C. H., and Lil Brannon. 1993. *Critical Teaching and the Idea of Literacy*.
Portsmouth, N.H.: Boynton/Cook-Heinemann.

Kott, Jan. 1967. *Shakespeare, Our Contemporary*. Garden City, N.Y.: Anchor Books.

Kraniauskas, John. 1992. "Hybridity and Reterritorialization." *Travesia. Journal of
Latin American Cultural Studies* 1.2: 143–51.

———. 1998. "Globalisation Is Ordinary: The Transnationalisation of Cultural
Studies." Mimeographed.

Kroeber, Alfred, ed. 1959. *Anthropology Today*. Chicago: University of Chicago
Press.

Kubler, George. 1963. "The Quechua in the Colonial World." In *The Handbook of
South American Indians*, edited by J. H. Steward. Vol. 2. New York: Cooper Square
Publications.

Kurin, Richard. 1991. "The Festival of American Folklife: Building on Tradition."
In *1991 Festival of American Folklife*. Washington: Smithsonian Institution.

Kusch, Rodolfo. 1970. *El pensamiento indígena y popular en América*. Buenos Aires:
Hachette.

Lacheney, Robert. 1954. "L'amour aux champs." *Cahiers du Cinéma* 30: 45–48.

Laclau, Ernesto. 1977. *Politics and Ideology in Marxist Theory: Capitalism, Fascism, Populism*. London: New Left Books.

———. 1981. "Teoría marxista del Estado: debates y perspectivas." In *Estado y política en América Latina*. México: Siglo XXI.

———. 1990. *New Reflections on the Revolution of Our Time*. London: Verso.

———, ed. 1994. *The Making of Political Identities*. London: Verso.

Laclau, Ernesto, and Chantal Mouffe. 1985. *Hegemony and Socialist Strategy: Towards a
Radical Democratic Politics*. London: Verso.

Lacoste, Yves. 1959. *Le pays sous-developpés*. Paris: Presses Universitaires de France.

Laing, Dave. 1992. "Sadness, Scorpions, and Single Market: National and Transnational Trends in European Popular Music." *Popular Music* 11.1: 127–40.

La Jornada. 1994–1995. México, February to December.

Lamas, Martha. 1993. "El fulgor de noche. Algunos aspectos de la prostitución
callejera en la ciudad de México." *Debate Feminista* 8: 103–33.

Lamb, Ruth S. 1975. *Mexican Theater of the Twentieth Century*. Claremont, Calif.: Ocelot
Press.

Lamming, George. 1960. *The Pleasures of Exile*. London: Blackwell.

Lang, Robert. 1989. *American Film Melodrama*. Princeton, N.J.: Princeton University Press.

Langue, Frédérique. 1994. "Desterrar el vicio y serenar las conciencias. Mendicidad y pobreza en la Caracas del siglo XVIII." *Revista de Indias* 54.201: 355–81.

Lanternari, Vittorio. 1966. "Désintégration culturelle et processus d'acculturation." *Cahiers Internationaux de Sociologie* 41: 117–32.

Laporte, Dominique. 1980. *Historia de la mierda*. Barcelona: Pre-Textos.

Larsen, Neil. 1995. *Reading North by South: On Latin American Literature, Culture, and Politics*. Minneapolis: University of Minnesota Press.

———. 1998. "Cultural Studies Questionnaire." *Journal of Latin American Cultural Studies* 7.2: 245–48.

Latin American Subaltern Studies Group. 1993. "Founding Statement." In *The Postmodernism Debate in Latin America*, edited by J. Beverley and J. Oviedo. *boundary 2* 20.3: 110–21.

Laverde Toscano, María C., and Rossana Reguillo, eds. 1998. *Mapas nocturnos. Diálogos con la obra de Jesús Martín Barbero*. Santafé de Bogotá: Universidad Central and Siglo del Hombre Editores.

Lazarus, Neil. 1994. "National Consciousness and the Specificity of (Post)-Colonial Intellectualism." In *Colonial Discourse, Postcolonial Theory*, edited by F. Barker, P. Hulme, and M. Iversen. New York: Manchester University Press.

Lechner, Norbert, ed. 1991. *Debates sobre modernidad y posmodernidad*. Quito: Nariz del Diablo.

———. 1995. "A Disenchantment Called Postmodernity." In *The Postmodernism Debate in Latin America*, edited by J. Beverley, M. Aronna, and J. Oviedo. Durham, N.C.: Duke University Press.

Leite Lopes, Jorge. 1997. "Successes and Contradictions in 'Multiracial' Brazilian Football." In *Entering the Field: New Perspectives on World Football*, edited by G. Armstrong and R. Giulianotti. Oxford: Berg.

León Portilla, Miguel. 1988. *Tiempo y realidad en el pensamiento maya*. México: UNAM.

Levene, Ricardo. 1936. "La Conquista de América y la expedición de Don Pedro de Mendoza." In *Homenaje a Buenos Aires en el IV Centenario de su fundación*. Radio Conference Series. Buenos Aires: Intendencia Municipal.

Lévi-Strauss, Claude. 1968. *Race et histoire*. Paris: UNESCO.

Lewis, Oscar. 1963. *The Children of Sánchez*. New York: Random House.

Lidsky, Paul. 1970. *Les écrivains contre la Commune*. Paris: F. Maspero.

Lie, Nadia, and Theo D'haen, ed. 1997. *Constellation Caliban: Figuration of a Character*. Amsterdam: Rodopi.

Liernur, Jorge Francisco. 1986. "El discreto encanto de nuestra arquitectura." *Summa*, April.

Lipschutz, Alexander. 1972. *Perfil de Indoamérica en nuestro tiempo*. La Habana: Instituto Cubano del Libro.

L. L. 1996a. "Más radios ilegales." *Revista 3*, 16 August.

———. 1996b. "Legitimidad versus legalidad." *Brecha*, 5 March.

Lloyd, David. 1993. *Anomalous States: Irish Writing and the Post-Colonial Moment.* Durham, N.C.: Duke University Press.

López, Ana. 1992. "Setting Up the Stage: Latin American Film Scholarship, 1970–80s." *Quarterly Review of Film and Video* 13.1/3: 239–60.

López, Silvia. 2001. "Introduction: The Task of the Editor." *Cultural Critique* 49: 1–17.

López Austin, Alfredo. 1980. *Cuerpo humano e ideología. Conceptos de los antiguos Nahuas.* 2 vols. México: UNAM.

López de Velazco, Juan. 1574. *Descripción y demarcación de las Indias Occidentales.* Manuscript. John Carter Brown Library, Brown University, Providence, Rhode Island.

Losada, Alejandro. 1975. "Los sistemas literarios como instituciones sociales en América Latina." *Revista de Crítica Literaria Latinoamericana* 1: 39–60.

Lotman, Jury. 1972. *Los sistemas de signos.* Madrid: Alberto Corazón.

Loveluck, Juan, ed. 1969. *La novela hispanoamericana.* Santiago: Universitaria.

Lowy, Michael. 1970. *La pensée de la colonization.* Paris: Editions Universitaires.

Ludmer, Josefina. 1988. *El género gauchesco: un tratado sobre la patria.* Buenos Aires: Sudamericana.

Luis, William. 1997. *Dance between Two Cultures: Latino Caribbean Literature Written in the United States.* Nashville, Tenn.: Vanderbilt University Press.

Lull, James, ed. 1988. *World Families Watch Television.* Newbury Park, Calif.: Sage.

Lumsden, Charles, and Edward Wilson. 1983. *Promethean Fire: Reflections on the Origin of the Mind.* Cambridge: Harvard University Press.

Lyotard, Jean-François. 1984. *The Postmodern Condition: A Report on Knowledge.* Minneapolis: University of Minnesota Press.

———. 1988. *The Differend: Phrases in Dispute.* Minneapolis: University of Minnesota Press.

Machado Neto, Antonio Luiz. 1973. *Estrutura social da república das letras. Sociologia da vida intelectual brasileira, 1870–1930.* São Paulo: Editora da Universidade de São Paulo.

Mallon, Florencia. 1994. "The Promise and Dilemma of Latin American Subaltern Studies: Perspectives from Latin American History." *American Historical Review* 99.5: 1491–1515.

Mangan, J. A., ed. 1988. *Pleasure, Profit, Proselytism: British Culture and Sport at Home and Abroad, 1700–1914.* London: Frank Cass.

Mannoni, Octave. 1950. *Psychologie de la colonization.* Paris: Editions Universitaires.

Manón, Manuel. 1932. *Historia del teatro popular de México.* México: Editorial Cultura.

Manuel, Peter. 1991. "The Cassette Industry and Popular Music in Northern India." *Popular Music* 10.2: 189–204.

Mañach, Jorge. 1969. *Indagación del choteo.* Miami: Mnemosyne.

Maranghello, César. 1984. "La pantalla y el estado." In *Historia del cine argentino.* Buenos Aires: CEAL.

Marcuse, Herbert. 1970. "Le caractère affirmatif de la culture." In *Culture et société.* Paris: Minuit.

Mariaca Iturri, Guillermo. 1993. *El poder de la palabra. Ensayos sobre la modernidad de la crítica literaria hispanoamericana.* La Habana: Casa de las Américas.

Mariátegui, José Carlos. 1963. *Siete ensayos de interpretación de la realidad peruana*. Lima: Amauta.

———. 1969. "Aniversario y balance." In *Ideología y política*. Lima: Biblioteca "Amauta."

———. 1976. *Siete ensayos de interpretación de la realidad peruana*. Barcelona: Crítica.

———. 1979. *Siete ensayos de interpretación de la realidad peruana*. Caracas: Biblioteca Ayacucho.

Mariñas Otero, Luis, ed. 1965. *Las Constituciones de Venezuela*. Madrid: Centro de Estudios Jurídicos Hispanoamericanos del Instituto de Cultura Hispánica.

Marshack, Alexander. 1972. *The Roots of Civilization: The Cognitive Beginnings of Man's First Art, Symbol, and Notation*. New York: McGraw-Hill.

Martí, José. 1980. "Nuestra América." In *Nuestra América*. Buenos Aires: Losada.

———. 1999. "Our America." In *José Martí Reader: Writings on the Americas*, edited by D. Shnookal and M. Muñiz. New York: Ocean Press.

Martín, JoAnn. 1993. "Contesting Authenticity: Battles over the Representation of History in Morelos, Mexico." *Ethnohistory* 40.3: 438–65.

Martín-Barbero, Jesús. 1987a. *De los medios a las mediaciones. Comunicación, cultura, y hegemonía*. México: Gustavo Gili.

———. 1987b. "Retos a la investigación de comunicación en América Latina." In *Procesos de comunicación y matrices de cultura. Itinerarios para salir de la razón dualista*. México: G. Gili-Felafacs.

———. 1993. *Communication, Culture and Hegemony: From the Media to Mediations*. London: Sage Publications.

———. 1997. "Nosotros habíamos hecho estudios culturales mucho antes que esta etiqueta apareciera. Entrevista a Jesús Martín Barbero." *Dissens* 3: 47–53.

———. 2001. *Al sur de la modernidad. Comunicación, globalización, y multiculturalidad*. Pittsburgh: IILI.

Martín Serrano, Manuel. 1977. *La mediación social*. Madrid: Ramón Akal.

Martínez, Tomás Eloy. 1995. *Santa Evita*. Buenos Aires: Planeta.

Martínez Carril, Manuel. 1992. "Reflexiones sobre las industrias audiovisuales." In *Industrias culturales en el Uruguay*, edited by C. Rama. Montevideo: Arca.

Martínez Estrada, Ezequiel. 1965. "El Nuevo Mundo, la isla de Utopía y la isla de Cuba." *Casa de las Américas* 33.

Marx, Karl. 1977. "Introduction." In *Grundrisse*. Harmondsworth: Penguin.

Masiello, Francine. 1996. "Tráfico de identidades: mujeres, cultura y política de representación en la era neoliberal." *Revista Iberoamericana* 176/177: 745–66.

Mason, Tony. 1995. *Passion of the People? Football in South America*. London: Verso.

Mata Gil, Milagros. 1994. *El pregón mercadero*. Caracas: Monte Avila.

Mato, Daniel. 1995. "Complexes of Brokering and the Global-Local Connections: Considerations Based on Cases in 'Latin' America." Paper prepared for presentation at the Nineteenth Congress of Latin American Studies Association, Washington, 28–30 September.

———. 1996a. "Globalización, procesos culturales y cambios sociopolíticos en América Latina." In *América Latina en tiempos de globalización. Procesos culturales y cambios sociopolíticos*, edited by D. Mato, M. Montero, and E. Amodio. Caracas: UNESCO-Asociación Latinoamericana de Sociología.

———. 1996b. "On the Theory, Epistemology, and Politics of the Social Construction of 'Cultural Identities' in the Age of Globalization." In *Indigenous Peoples: Global Terrains*, edited by J. Beckett and D. Mato. Special issue of *Identities: Global Studies in Culture and Power* 3.1/2: 61–72.

———. 1996c. "The Indigenous Uprising in Chiapas: The Politics of Institutionalized Knowledge and Mexican Perspectives." In *Indigenous Peoples: Global Terrains*, edited by J. Beckett and D. Mato. Special issue of *Identities: Global Studies in Culture and Power* 3.1/2: 205–18.

———. 1997a. "On Global-Local Connections and the Transnational Making of Identities and Associated Agendas in 'Latin' America." *Identities: Global Studies in Culture and Power* 4: 4.

———. 1997b. "A Research Based Framework for Analyzing Processes of (Re)Construction of 'Civil Societies' in the Age of Globalization." In *Media and Politics in Transition: Cultural Identity in the Age of Globalization*, edited by J. Servaes and Rico Lie. Louvain. Belgium: ACCO Publishers and Katholteke Universiteit Brussel.

Mattelart, Armand. 1974. *La cultura como empresa multinacional*. México: Ediciones Era.

———. 1977. *Multinacionales y sistemas de comunicación. Los aparatos ideológicos del imperialismo*. México: Siglo XXI.

Mattelart, Armand, and Ariel Dorfman. 1975. *How to Read Donald Duck: Imperialist Ideology in the Disney Comic*. New York: International General.

Mattelart, Armand, and Seth Siegelaub, eds. 1979. *Communication and Class Struggle: An Anthology*. New York: International Mass Media.

Mattelart, Michèle. 1982. "Women and the Cultural Industries." *Media, Culture, and Society* 4.2: 133–51.

Mazzotti, José Antonio, and Juan Zevallos Aguilar, eds. 1996. *Asedios a la heterogeneidad cultural. Libro de homenaje a Antonio Cornejo Polar*. Philadelphia: Asociación Internacional de Peruanistas.

Mbembe, Achille. 1992. "The Banality of Power and the Aesthetic of Vulgarity in the Postcolony." *Public Culture* 4.2: 1–30.

McRobbie, Angela. 1994. *Postmodernism and Popular Culture*. London: Routledge.

Melgar, Mariano. 1971. *Poesías completas*. Lima: Academia Peruana de la Lengua.

Mella, Julio Antonio. 1971. *Hombres de la revolución*. La Habana: Editorial de Ciencias Sociales, Instituto Cubano del Libro.

Menchú, Rigoberta, and Elizabeth Burgos-Debray. 1983. *Me llamo Rigoberta Menchú y así me nació la conciencia*. México: Siglo XXI.

———. 1984. *I, Rigoberta Menchú: An Indian Woman in Guatemala*. London: Verso.

Meyer, M. 1973. "O que é, ou quem foi Sinclair das ilhas." *Revista del Instituto de Studos Brasileiros* 14.

———. 1982. "Vaudeviles, melodramas, e quejandos." Mimeograph.

Meyer, Marcos. 1998. "La crisis del libro periodístico." *Clarín*, 23 August.

Meyers, W. 1991. *Los creadores de imágenes*. Barcelona: Ariel.

Michellini, Dorando, José San Martín, and Fernando Lagrave, eds. 1991. *Modernidad y Posmodernidad en América Latina*. Río Cuarto, Argentina: Ediciones del ICALA.

Michelotti-Cristóbal, Graciela. 1998. "Eva Perón: Mujer, personaje, mito." *Confluencia* 13.2: 135–44.

Mignolo, Walter. 1978. *Elementos para una teoría del texto literario*. Barcelona: Crítica-Grijalbo.

——. 1986. *Teoría del texto e interpretación de textos*. México: UNAM.

——. 1989. "Afterword: From Colonial Discourse to Colonial Semiosis." *Dispositio/n* 36/38: 333–37.

——. 1995. *The Darker Side of the Renaissance: Literacy, Territoriality, and Colonization*. Ann Arbor: University of Michigan Press.

——. 1996a. "Postoccidentalismo: las epistemologías fronterizas y el dilema de los estudios (latinoamericanos) de áreas." *Revista Iberoamericana* 176/177: 679–96.

——. 1996b. "Herencias coloniales y teorías poscoloniales." In *Cultura y Tercer Mundo I*, edited by B. González. Caracas: Nueva Sociedad.

——. 1998a. "Cultural Studies Questionnaire." *Journal of Latin American Cultural Studies* 7.1: 111–19.

——. 1998b. "Postoccidentalismo: el argumento desde América Latina." In *Teoría sin disciplinas*, edited by S. Castro Gómez and E. Mendieta. México: Porrúa/USF.

——. 1998c. "Postoccidentalismo: el argumento desde América Latina." *Cuadernos Americanos* 67: 143–65.

——. 2000. *Local Histories/Global Designs: Coloniality, Subaltern Knowledges, and Border Thinking*. Princeton, N.J.: Princeton University Press.

Miranda, Wander Melo. 1998. "Projeções de um debate." *Revista Brasileira de Literatura Comparada* 4: 11–17.

Modleski, Tania. 1982. *Loving with a Vengeance: Mass Produced Fantasies for Women*. Hamden, Conn.: Archon Books.

Moles, Abraham. 1978. *Sociodinámica de la cultura*. Buenos Aires: Paidós.

Monsiváis, Carlos. 1970. *Días de guardar*. México: Ediciones Era.

——. 1976a. "El cine nacional." In *Historia general de México*, coordinated by Daniel Cosío Villegas. Vol. 4. México: El Colegio de México.

——. 1976b. *Amor perdido*. México: Ediciones Era.

——. 1980. "Sí, tampoco los muertos retoñan. Desgraciadamente." In *Juan Rulfo. Homenaje nacional*. México: Instituto Nacional de Bellas Artes.

——. 1982. "Reír llorando (Notas sobre la cultura popular urbana)." In *Política cultural del estado mexicano*, edited by Moisés Ladrón de Guevara. México: Ed. GEFE/SEP.

——. 1983. "Penetración cultural y nacionalismo." In *No intervención, autodeterminación y democracia en América Latina*, edited by P. González Casanova. México: Siglo XXI.

——. 1987. *Entrada libre. Crónicas de la sociedad que se organiza*. México: Ediciones Era.

———. 1988. "Crónica de sociales: María Félix en dos tiempos." In *Escenas de Pudor y Liviandad*. México: Grijalbo.

———. 1995. *Los rituales del caos*. México: Ediciones Era.

———. 2000. *Aires de familia. Cultura y sociedad en América Latina*. Barcelona: Anagrama.

Montaigne, Michel de. 1948. *Ensayos*. Vol. 1. Buenos Aires: Aguilar.

Montaldo, Graciela. 2000. "Nuevas reflexiones sobre la cultura de nuestro tiempo." *Estudios* 14/15: 395–405.

Moore-Gilbert, Bart. 1997. *Postcolonial Theory: Contexts, Practices, Politics*. London: Verso.

Mora, Carl J. 1982. *Mexican Cinema: Reflections of a Society, 1896–1980*. Berkeley: University of California Press.

Moraga, Cherrie. 1986. "From a Long Line of Vendidas: Chicanas and Feminism." In *Feminist Studies/Critical Studies*, edited by T. de Lauretis. Bloomington: Indiana University Press.

Moragas, Miguel de. 1981. *Teorías de la comunicación*. Barcelona: Gustavo Gili.

———, ed. 1985. *Sociología de la comunicación de masas*. Barcelona: Gustavo Gili.

Morales, Rebecca, and Frank Bonilla, eds. 1993. *Latinos in a Changing U.S. Economy*. Newbury Park, Calif.: Sage.

Morandé, Pedro. 1984. *Cultura y modernización en América Latina*. Santiago: Universidad Católica de Chile.

Moraña, Mabel. 1982. "José Enrique Rodó." In *Historia de la literatura hispanoamericana*, edited by L. Iñigo Madrigal. Madrid: Cátedra.

———. 1995. "Escribir en el aire: heterogeneidad y estudios culturales." *Revista Iberoamericana* 170/171: 279–86.

———. 1997. "Ideología de la transculturación." In *Angel Rama y los estudios latinoamericanos*, edited by M. Moraña. Pittsburgh: IILI.

———, ed. 2000. *Nuevas perspectivas desde/sobre América Latina: el desafío de los estudios culturales*. Santiago: Cuarto Propio/IILI.

Moreiras, Alberto. 1995. "Epistemología tenue (sobre el latinoamericanismo)." *Revista de Crítica Cultural* 10: 48–54.

———. 1996a. "Elementos de articulación teórica para el subalternismo latinoamericano Candido y Borges." *Revista Iberoamericana* 176/177: 875–92.

———. 1996b. "The Aura of Testimonio." In *The Real Thing: Testimonial Discourse and Latin America*, edited by G. Gugelberger. Durham, N.C.: Duke University Press.

———. 1997. "From Locational Thinking to Dirty Atopianism." Introduction to "The Cultural Practice of Latin Americanism I," edited by A. Moreiras and M. Embry. *Dispositio/n* 49: v–ix.

———. 1998. "Hegemonía y subalternidad." *Nuevas perspectivas desde/sobre América Latina: el desafío de los estudios culturales*, edited by M. Moraña. Santiago: Cuarto Propio-IILI.

———. 1999a. *Tercer espacio: literatura y duelo en América Latina*. Santiago: Universidad ARCIS/LOM Ediciones.

———. 1999b. "The Order of Order: On the Reluctant Culturalism of Anti-Subalternist Critiques." *Journal of Latin American Cultural Studies* 8: 125–45.

———. 2001. *The Exhaustion of Difference: The Politics of Latin American Cultural Studies.* Durham, N.C.: Duke University Press.

Mörner, Magnus. 1969. *La mezcla de razas en la historia de América Latina.* Buenos Aires: Paidós.

Muchembled, Robert. 1978. *Culture populaire et culture des élites dans la France moderne (XVe–XVIIIe siècles).* Paris: Flammarion.

Mulvey, Laura. 1986. "Melodrama in and out of the Home." In *High Theory/Low Culture,* edited by C. McCabe. New York: St. Martin's Press.

Murena, Héctor A. 1958. *El pecado original de América.* Buenos Aires: Sur.

Murmis, Miguel, and Juan Carlos Portantiero. 1972. *Estudio sobre los orígenes del peronismo.* Buenos Aires: Siglo XXI.

Nedelsky, Jennifer. 1990. "Law, Boundaries, and the Bounded Self." *Representations* 3: 162–89.

Needham, Joseph, and Wang Ling. 1959. *Science and Civilization in China.* Cambridge: Cambridge University Press.

Negri, Antonio, and Michael Hardt. 1994. *Labor of Dionysus: Communism as Critique of the Capitalist and Socialist State-Form.* Minneapolis: University of Minnesota Press.

Nelson, Candace, and Marta Tienda. 1997. "The Structuring of Hispanic Ethnicity: Historical and Contemporary Perspectives." In *Challenging Fronteras,* edited by M. Romero, P. Hondagneu-Sotelo, and V. Ortiz. New York: Routledge.

Nelson, Cary. 1991. "Always Already Cultural Studies: Two Conferences and a Manifesto." *Journal of the Midwest Modern Languages Association* 24.1: 24–38.

Nogueira Galvão, Walnice. 1972. *As formas do falso.* São Paulo: Editora Perspectiva.

Novais, Fernando. 1984. "Passagens para o Novo Mundo." *Novos Estudos Cebrap* 9: 2–8.

Nun, José. 1984. "La rebelión del coro." *Punto de Vista* 20: 6–11.

Nunes, Benedito. 1969. *O dorso do tigre.* São Paulo: Editora Perspectiva.

Oboler, Suzanne. 1995. *Ethnic Labels, Latino Lives: Identity and the Politics of (Re)Presentation in the United States.* Minneapolis: University of Minnesota Press.

O'Connell Davidson, Julia, and Jacqueline Sánchez Taylor. 1996. "British Sex Tourists in Thailand." Bangkok: ECPAT International.

Okada, Maki. 1991. "Musical Characteristics of Enka." *Popular Music* 10.3: 283–303.

Oliver, Melvin L., James H. Johnson Jr., and Walter C. Farrell Jr. "Anatomy of a Rebellion: A Political-Economic Analysis." In *Reading Rodney King/Reading Urban Uprising,* edited by R. Gooding-Williams. New York: Routledge.

Omang, Joanne, and Aryeh Neier. 1985. *Psychological Operations in Guerrilla Warfare.* New York: Vintage Books.

Orozco, José Clemente. 1962. *An Autobiography.* Austin: University of Texas Press.

Ortiz, Fernando. 1947. *Cuban Counterpoint: Tobacco and Sugar.* Translated by Harriet de Onís. New York: Knopf.

———. 1978. *Contrapunteo cubano del tabaco y el azúcar.* Caracas: Biblioteca Ayacucho.

Ortiz, Renato. 1987. *Cultura brasileira e identidade nacional.* São Paulo: Editora Brasiliense.

———. 1988. *A moderna tradição brasileira: Cultura brasileira e industria cultural.* São Paulo: Editora Brasiliense.

———. 1994. *Mundialização e cultura.* São Paulo: Editora Brasiliense.

Osborne, Lawrence. 1997. "Does Man Eat Man?" *Lingua Franca* 7.4: 28–38.

Osborne, Peter. 1995. *The Politics of Time: Modernity and Avant-Garde.* London: Verso.

Oshima, Y. 1988. "Stratégies des industries audiovisuelles japonaises." Ph.D. diss., Université de Paris X.

Osorio, Nelson. 1976. "Las ideologías y los estudios de la literatura hispanoamericana." *Casa de las Américas* 94: 63–75.

Oyarzún, Pablo. 1994. "Identidad, diferencia, mezcla: ¿pensar Latinoamérica?" Suplementos Temas, *La Época* (Santiago) 16 January.

Pacheco, José Emilio. 1978. *Antología del modernismo (1884–1921).* México: UNAM.

Padilla, Félix. 1985. *Latino Ethnic Consciousness: The Case of Mexican-Americans and Puerto Ricans in Chicago.* Notre Dame: Notre Dame University Press.

Pais Bermúdez, Ronald. 1992. "Aspectos jurídicos de la televisión (y la radio) en el Uruguay." In *Industrias culturales en el Uruguay,* edited by C. Rama Montevideo: Arca.

Palumbo-Liu, David, and Hans Ulrich Gumbrecht, eds. 1997. *Streams of Cultural Capital: Transnational Cultural Studies.* Stanford, Calif.: Stanford University Press.

Pallares, Laura, and Luis Stolovich. 1991. *Medios masivos de comunicación en el Uruguay: tecnología, poder y crisis.* Montevideo: Centro Uruguay Independiente.

Parish, Helen-Rand, and Harold E. Weidman. 1992. *Las Casas en México: historia y obra desconocidas.* México: Fondo de Cultura Económica.

Parry, Benita. 1994. "Signs of Our Times." *Third Text* 28/29: 5–24.

Paz, Octavio. 1950. *El laberinto de la soledad.* México: Cuadernos Americanos.

———. 1961. *The Labyrinth of Solitude: Life and Thought in Mexico.* New York: Grove Press.

———. 1974. *Children of the Mire.* Cambridge, Mass.: Harvard University Press.

———. 1984. *Os filhos do barro.* Rio de Janeiro: Nova Fronteira.

Pedraza, Silvia. 1998. "The Contribution of Latino Studies to Social Science Research on Immigration." JSRI Occasional Paper 36. East Lansing: Julian Samora Research Institute, Michigan State University.

Pellicer, Carlos. 1977. "Líneas por el 'Che' Guevara." In *Cuerdas, Percusión y Aliento.* Tabasco, México: Universidad Autónoma Juárez.

Pérez Bocanegra. 1631. *Ritual formulario, e institucion de curas, para administrar a los naturales de este Reyno, los sanctos sacramentos del baptismo, confirmacion, eucaristia, y viatico, penitencia, extremauncion, y matrimonio, con advertencias muy necessarias.* Lima: G. de Contreras.

Petro, Patrice. 1989. *Joyless Streets: Women and Melodramatic Representation in Weimar Germany.* Princeton, N.J.: Princeton University Press.

Phillips, Rachel. 1983. "Marina/Malinche: Masks and Shadows." In *Women in Hispanic Literature: Icons and Fallen Idols,* edited by B. Miller. Berkeley: University of California Press.

Pires do Rio, Teresa. 1984. *A política dos outros.* São Paulo: Editora Brasiliense.

Ponce, Aníbal. 1962. *Humanismo burgués y humanismo proletario*. La Habana: Imprenta Nacional de Cuba.

Portantiero, Juan Carlos. 1981. *Los usos de Gramsci*. México: Folios Ediciones.

Portes, Alejandro, and Robert L. Bach. 1985. *Latin Journey: Cuban and Mexican Immigrants in the United States*. Berkeley: University of California Press.

Portes, Alejandro, and Rubén G. Rumbaut. 1996. *Immigrant America: A Portrait*. Berkeley: University of California Press.

Portuondo, José Antonio. 1965. "Mella y los intelectuales." In *Crítica de la época*. La Habana: Editora del Consejo Nacional de Universidades, Universidad Central de Las Villas.

Posadas, Juan Martín. 1992. "El papel del estado respecto a la televisión uruguaya." In *Industrias culturales en el Uruguay*, edited by C. Rama. Montevideo: Arca.

Pratt, Mary Louise. 1992a. "Humanities for the Future: Reflections on the Western Culture Debate at Stanford." In *The Politics of Liberal Education*, edited by D. Gates and B. Herrnstein Smith. Durham, N.C.: Duke University Press.

———. 1992b. *Imperial Eyes: Travel Writing and Transculturation*. London: Routledge.

Pratt, Mary Louise, and Kathleen Newman. 1999. "Introduction: The Committed Critic." In *Critical Passions: Selected Essays*, by J. Franco. Durham, N.C.: Duke University Press.

Prebisch, Alberto. 1936. "La ciudad en que vivimos." In *Buenos Aires 1936*. Buenos Aires: MCBA.

Price, Richard, and Sally Price. 1994. *On the Mall: Presenting Maroon Tradition-Bearers at the 1992 Festival of American Folklife*. Bloomington: Folklore Institute, Indiana University Press.

Propp, Vladimir. 1958. *Morphology of the Folktale*. Bloomington: Research Center in Anthropology, Indiana University Press.

Quijano, Aníbal. 1993. "Modernity, Identity, and Utopia in Latin America." In *The Postmodernism Debate in Latin America*, edited by J. Beverley and J. Oviedo. *boundary 2* 20.3: 140–55.

Quiroga, Horacio. 1970. *Sobre literatura*. Vol. 7 of *Obras inéditas y desconocidas*. Montevideo: Arca.

Rabasa, José. 1993. "Aesthetics of Colonial Violence: The Massacre of Acoma in Gaspar de Villagrá's *Historia de la Nueva México*." *College Literature* 20.3: 96–114.

———. 1995. " 'Porque soy indio': Subjectivity in *La Florida del Inca*." *Poetics Today* 16.1: 79–108.

Rabasa, José, Robert Carr, and Javier Sanjinés, eds. 1994. *Subaltern Studies in the Americas*. *Dispositio/n* 46: 1–288.

Rabinow, Paul, ed. 1984. *The Foucault Reader*. New York: Pantheon.

Radway, Janice A. 1984. *Reading the Romance: Women, Patriarchy, and Popular Literature*. Chapel Hill: University of North Carolina Press.

Rama, Angel. 1972. *La generación crítica: 1939–1969*. Montevideo: Arca.

———. 1974a. "El área cultural andina (hispanismo, mesticismo, indigenismo)." *Cuadernos Americanos* 6: 136–73.

———. 1974b. "Sistema literario y sistema social en Hispanoamérica." *Literatura y praxis social en América Latina.* Caracas: Monte Avila.

———. 1976. "Recuperación del pensamiento mítico en José María Arguedas." *Latino América Anuario* 9.

———. 1979. *Aportación original de una comarca del tercer mundo: Latinoamérica.* Cuadernos de cultura latinoamericana 73. México: UNAM, Coordinación de Humanidades, Centro de Estudios Latinoamericanos, Facultad de Filosofía y Letras: Unión de Universidades de América Latina.

———. 1981. "La tecnificación narrativa." *Hispamérica* 30: 29–82.

———. 1982. *Transculturación narrativa en América Latina.* México: Siglo XXI.

———. 1984a. *La ciudad letrada.* Montevideo: F. I. A.R.

———. 1984b. "El 'boom' en perspectiva." In *Más allá del boom: Literatura y mercado,* edited by Angel Rama et al. Buenos Aires: Folios.

———. 1984c. *La ciudad letrada.* Hanover, N.H.: Ediciones del Norte.

———. 1996. *The Lettered City.* Durham, N.C.: Duke University Press.

———. 1997. "Processes of Transculturation in Latin American Narrative." *Journal of Latin American Cultural Studies* 6.2: 155–71.

Rama, Claudio, ed. 1992. *Industrias culturales en el Uruguay.* Montevideo: Arca.

Ramos, Julio. 1989. *Desencuentros de la modernidad en América Latina. Literatura y política en el siglo XIX.* México: Fondo de Cultura Económica.

———. 1993a. "Cuerpo, lengua, subjetividad." *Revista de Crítica Literaria Latinoamericana* 38: 225–37.

———. 1993b. "El don de la lengua." *Casa de las Américas* 34.193: 13–25.

———. 1996. "El proceso de Alberto Mendoza: poesía y subjetivación." *Revista de Crítica Cultural* 13: 34–41.

Randles, W. G. L. 1980. *De la terre plate au globe terrestre: Une mutation épistemologique rapide (1480–1520).* Paris: Armand Colin.

Rangel, Gudelia. 1993. "Diagnóstico Preliminar del Problema del SIDA en la ciudad de Tijuana, Baja California." COLEF I, *Urbanización y Servicios* 7: 143–54.

Raphael, Alison. 1980. "Samba and Social Control: Popular Culture and Racial Democracy in Rio de Janeiro." Ph.D. diss., Columbia University.

Real de Azúa, Carlos. 1987. "Elites y desarrollos en América Latina." In *Escritos.* Montevideo: Arca.

Redfield, Robert, Ralph Linton, and Melville J. Herskovits. 1936. "Memorandum for the Study of Acculturation." *American Anthropologist* 38: 33–36.

Reguillo, Rossana. 1998. "Rompecabezas de una escritura: Jesús Martín-Barbero y la cultura en América Latina." In *Mapas nocturnos,* edited by M. Laverde Toscano and R. Reguillo. Bogotá: Siglo del Hombre Editores.

Renan, Ernest. 1878. *Caliban: Suite de "La Tempête." Drame Philosophique.* Paris: Calmann Lévy.

Reynolds, Fred. 1977. "The Modern Feminine Life Style." *Journal of Marketing* 41.3: 38–45.

Reynoso, Carlos. 2000. *Apogeo y decadencia de los estudios culturales.* Barcelona: Editorial Gedisa.

Ribeiro, Darcy. 1968. *The Civilizational Process*. Washington: Smithsonian Institution Press.

Ribeiro Durham, Eunice. 1986. "A pesquisa antropológica con populações urbanas: Problemas y perspectivas." In *A aventura antropológica*, edited by R. Cardoso. São Paulo: Paz e Terra.

Richard, Nelly. 1987. "Modernidad/Postmodernismo: un debate en curso." *Estudios públicos* 27: 307–13.

———. 1989a. *Masculino/Femenino. Prácticas de la diferencia y cultura democrática*. Santiago: Francisco Zegers.

———. 1989b. *La estratificación de los márgenes*. Santiago: Francisco Zegers.

———. 1993. "Cultural Peripheries: Latin America and Postmodernist De-centering." In *The Postmodernism Debate in Latin America*, edited by J. Beverley and J. Oviedo. boundary 2 20.3: 156–61.

———. 1994. *La insubordinación de los signos. Cambio político, transformaciones culturales, y poéticas de la crisis*. Santiago: Cuarto Propio.

———. 1997. "Intersectando Latinoamérica con el latinoamericanismo: discurso académico y crítica cultural." Paper delivered at the Latin American Studies Association conference, Guadalajara, 6 March.

———. 1998a. *Residuos y metáforas (Ensayos de crítica cultural sobre el Chile de la Transición)*. Santiago: Cuarto Propio.

———. 1998b. "Introducción a la crítica cultural: notas en borrador." Mimeograph.

———. 1998c. "Intersectando Latinoamérica con el latinoamericanismo: discurso académico y crítica cultural." In *Teorías sin disciplina. Latinoamericanismo, poscolonialidad y globalización en debate*, edited by S. Castro Gómez and E. Mendieta. México: Porrúa/USF.

Richard, Nelly, and Diamela Eltit. 1995. "Jean Franco: Un retrato." *Revista de Crítica Cultural* 11: 18–21.

Richeri, Giuseppe, ed. 1983. *La televisión: entre servicio público y negocio*. Barcelona: Gustavo Gil.

Rincón, Carlos. 1971. "Para un plano de batalla por una nueva crítica en Latinoamérica." *Casa de las Américas* 6: n.p.

———. 1973. "Sobre crítica e historia de la literatura hoy en Latinoamérica." *Casa de las Américas* 80: 135–47.

———. 1978. *El cambio de la noción de literatura y otros estudios de teoría y crítica latinoamericana*. Bogotá: Instituto Colombiano de Cultura.

———. 1997. "Streams out of Control: The Latin American Plot." In *Streams of Cultural Capital: Transnational Cultural Studies*, edited by D. Palumbo-Liu and H. Gumbrecht. Stanford, Calif.: Stanford University Press.

Rivera, Jorge. 1981. "La nueva novela argentina de los años 40." Prologue to José Bianco's *Las ratas*. Buenos Aires: Editor de Centro América Latina.

Rivera Cusicanqui, Silvia, and Rossana Barragan, comps. 1997. *Debates Post-Coloniales: una introducción a los estudios de la subalternidad*. La Paz: Editorial Historias/SEPHIS/Aruwiyiri.

Robertson, Donald. 1966. "The Sixteenth-Century Mexican Encyclopedia of Fray Bernardino de Sahagún." *Cahier d'Historie Mondiale* 9.3: 617–26.

Rock, David. 1993. *La Argentina autoritaria. Los nacionalistas, su historia y su influencia en la vida pública.* Buenos Aires: Ariel.

Rockefeller Report. 1969. *Rockefeller Report on Latin America.* New York: Quadrangle Books.

Rodó, José Enrique. 1957. *Obras completas.* Edited by E. Rodríguez Monegal. Madrid: Aguilar.

Rodríguez, Simón. 1975. *Obras completas.* Vol. 1. Caracas: Universidad Simón Rodríguez.

Roel, Virgilio. 1970. *Historia social y económica de la colonia.* Lima: Editorial Gráfica Labor.

Roig, Arturo Andrés. 1981. *Teoría y crítica del pensamiento latinoamericano.* México: Fondo de Cultura Económica.

Roldós, Enrique. 1996. "Telepresentes y teleausentes." *Brecha,* 22 March.

Romero, César. 1994. *Marcos: ¿un profesional de la esperanza?* México: Planeta.

Romero, José Luis. 1944. *Bases para una morfología de los contactos culturales.* Buenos Aires: Institución Cultural Española.

———. 1976. *Latinoamérica: las ciudades y las ideas.* Bogotá: Universidad Nacional de Antioquia.

Romero, Silvio. 1897. *Machado de Assis.* Rio de Janeiro: Livraria José Olympio.

Ronfeldt, David. 1995. "The Battle for the Mind of Mexico." Rand Corporation, June. *chiapas@mundo.eco.utexas.edu.*

Rosa, Nicolás. 1997. "La lección de anatomía." *Gandhi* 2: 1–5.

Rosenblat, Angel. 1969. "Lengua literaria y lengua popular en América." In *Sentido mágico de la palabra.* Caracas: Universidad Central de Venezuela.

———. 1977. *Sentido mágico de la palabra.* Caracas: Universidad Central de Venezuela.

Ross, John. 1995. *Rebellion from the Roots: Indian Uprising in Chiapas.* Monroe, Me.: Common Courage Press.

Rostworowski de Diez Canseco, María. 1961. *Curacas y sucesiones, Costa Norte.* Lima: Minerva.

Rotker, Susana. 1991. *Fundación de una escritura: las crónicas de José Martí.* La Habana: Casas de las Américas.

Rowe, William, and Vivian Schelling. 1991. *Memory and Modernity: Popular Culture in Latin America.* London: Verso.

Rumbaut, Rubén. 1992. "The Americans: Latin American and Caribbean Peoples in the United States." In *Americas: New Interpretive Essays,* edited by A. Stepan. New York: Oxford University Press.

Sack, Robert David. 1986. *Human Territoriality: Its Theory and History.* New York: Cambridge University Press.

Sahagún, Bernardino de. 1975. *General History of the Things of New Spain: Florentine Codex. Book 12, The Conquest of Mexico.* Sante Fe: University of New Mexico Press.

Said, Edward. 1978. *Orientalism.* New York: Pantheon Books.

———. 1988. "Foreword." In *Selected Subaltern Studies*, edited by R. Guha and G. Spivak. Delhi: Oxford University Press, iii–x.

———. 1993. *Culture and Imperialism*. New York: Knopf.

———. 1996. *Representations of the Intellectual*. New York: Vintage Books.

Salas, Julio C. 1920. *Etnografía americana. Los indios caribes—Estudio sobre el origen del mito de la antropofagia*. Madrid: América.

Saldívar, José David. 1991. *The Dialectics of Our America: Genealogy, Cultural Critique, and Literary History*. Durham, N.C.: Duke University Press.

Salles Gomes, Paulo Emilio. 1973. "Cinema: Trajectória no subdesenvolvimento." *Argumento* 1: 55–67.

Sánchez, Luis Alberto. 1968. *Proceso y contenido de la novela hispanoamericana*. Madrid: Gredos.

Sánchez León, Abelardo. 1993. *La balada del gol perdido*. Lima: Ediciones Noviembre Trece.

———. 1998. "El gol de América Latina." *Nueva Sociedad* 154: 147–56.

Santiago, Silviano. 1973. *Latin American Literature: The Space in Between*. Buffalo, N.Y.: Council on International Studies.

———. 1978. "O Entre-lugar do discurso latino-americano." In *Uma literatura nos trópicos*. São Paulo: Editora Perspectiva.

Sarlo, Beatriz. 1983a. "Del lector." In *Literatura/Sociedad*, edited by C. Altamirano and B. Sarlo. Buenos Aires: Hachette.

———. 1983b. "Lo popular como dimensión: tópica, retórica y política de la recepción." Mimeograph.

———. 1983c. "Vanguardia y criollismo: la aventura de *Martín Fierro*." In *Ensayos Argentinos. De Sarmiento a la vanguardia*, edited by C. Altamirano and B. Sarlo. Buenos Aires: CEAL.

———. 1985a. "Crítica de la lectura: ¿un nuevo canon?" *Punto de Vista* 24: 7–11.

———. 1985b. "Los lectores: una vez más ese enigma." In *El imperio de los sentimientos*. Buenos Aires: Catálogos.

———. 1985c. *El imperio de los sentimientos*. Buenos Aires: Catálogos.

———. 1989. *Una modernidad periférica: Buenos Aires 1920–1930*. Buenos Aires: Nueva Visión.

———. 1994. *Escenas de la vida posmoderna: intelectuales, arte y videocultura en la Argentina*. Buenos Aires: Ariel.

———. 1995. "Olvidar a Benjamín." *Punto de vista* 53: 16–19.

———. 1996. *Instantáneas*. Buenos Aires: Ariel.

———. 1997a. "Cultural Studies Questionnaire." *Journal of Latin American Cultural Studies* 6.1: 85–91.

———. 1997b. "Los estudios culturales y la crítica literaria en la encrucijada valorativa." *Revista de Crítica Cultural* 15: 32–8.

———. 1998. *La máquina cultural: maestras, traductores, y vanguardistas*. Buenos Aires: Ariel.

———. 1999. "Cultural Studies and Literary Criticism at the Crossroads of Values." *Journal of Latin American Cultural Studies* 8: 115–24.

———. 2000. "Raymond Williams: una relectura." In *Nuevas perspectivas desde/sobre América Latina: El desafío de los estudios culturales*, edited by M. Moraña. Santiago: Cuarto Propio-IILI.

———. 2001. *Tiempo presente: notas sobre el cambio de una cultura*. Buenos Aires: Siglo XXI.

Sarmiento, Domingo. 1970. *Facundo: Civilización y barbarie*. Madrid: Alianza Editorial.

Sartre, Jean Paul. 1972. *L'idiot de la famille*. Paris: Gallimard.

———. 1976. *Critique of Dialectical Reason*. London: New Left Books.

Scher, Ariel, and Héctor Palomino. 1988. *Fútbol: pasión de multitudes y de elites. Un estudio institucional de la Asociación de Fútbol Argentino (1934–1986)*. Buenos Aires: Centro de Investigaciones Sociales sobre el Estado y la Administración.

Schiller, Herbert. 1971. *Mass Communications and American Empire*. Boston. Beacon Press.

———. 1976. *Communications and Cultural Domination*. New York: International Arts and Science Press.

———. 1989. *Culture Inc.: The Corporate Takeover of American Expression*. New York: Oxford University Press.

Schmidt, Friedhelm. 1995. "¿Literaturas heterogéneas o literaturas de la transculturación?" *Nuevo Texto Crítico* 14/15: 193–99.

Schuurman, Frans J., and Ellen Heer. 1992. *Social Movements and NGOs in Latin America*. Saarbrukcn: Verlag Breitenbach Publishers.

Schwarz, Roberto. 1992. *Misplaced Ideas: Essays on Brazilian Culture*. London: Verso.

Schwoch, James. 1990. *The American Radio and Its Latin American Activities, 1900–1939*. Urbana: University of Illinois Press.

Sefchovich, Sara. 1989. "Los caminos de la sociología en el laberinto de la *Revista Mexicana de Sociología*." *Revista Mexicana de Sociología* 51.1: 5–101.

Seler, Eduard. 1990–1993. "Wall Paintings of Mitla: A Mexican Picture Writing in Fresca." In *Eduard Seler: Collected Works in Mesoamerican Linguistics and Archeology*. Vol. 1. Culver City, Calif.: Labyrinthos.

Sen, Surendra Nath. 1957. *Eighteen-Fifty-Seven*. Delhi: Publications Division, Ministry of Information and Broadcasting, Government of India.

Serrano, Marcela. 1997. *El albergue de las mujeres tristes*. Buenos Aires: Alfaguara.

Shakespeare, William. 1955. *The Tempest*. New Haven, Conn.: Yale University Press.

———. 1961. *Obras completas*. Madrid: Aguilar.

Shohat, Ella. 1989. *Israeli Cinema: East/West and the Politics of Representation*. Austin: University of Texas Press.

Shorris, Earl. 1992. *Latinos: A Biography of the People*. New York: Norton.

Shumway, Nicolas. 1991. *The Invention of Argentina*. Berkeley: University of California Press.

Silva Castro, Raúl. 1915. *Antología de Andrés Bello*. Santiago: Zig-Zag.

Silva Gotay, Samuel. 1986. "El pensamiento religioso." In *América Latina en sus ideas*, edited by L. Zea. México: Siglo XXI.

Silverman, Kaja. 1983. *The Subject of Semiotics*. New York: Oxford University Press.

Silverstein, Ken, and Alexander Cockburn. 1995. "The Killers and the Killing." *The Nation* 260.9: 306.

Simon, Pierre Henri. 1969. *Le Monde*, 5 July.

Sklair, Leslie. 1992. "The Maquilas in Mexico: A Global Perspective." *Bulletin of Latin American Research* 11.1: 91–107.

Sklodowska, Elzbieta. 1996. "Spanish American Testimonial Novel: Some After-thoughts." In *The Real Thing: Testimonial Discourse in Latin America*, edited by G. Gugelberger. Durham, N.C.: Duke University Press.

Sloterdijk, Peter. 1987. *Critique of Cynical Reason*. Minneapolis: University of Minnesota Press.

Snitow, Ann Barr. 1983. "Mass Market Romance: Pornography for Women Is Different." In *Powers of Desire: The Politics of Sexuality*, edited by A. Snitow, C. Stansell, and S. Thompson. New York: Monthly Review Press.

Sodré, Muniz. 1981. *O monopoliza da Fala: Função e Linguagem da Televisão no Brasil*. Petrópolis: Vozes.

Solano, Francisco de. 1988. *Relaciones geográficas del arzobispado de México*. Madrid: Consejo Superior de Investigaciones Científicas.

Soler, Ricaute. 1975. *Clase y nación en Hispanoamérica*. Panamá: Educa.

Sommer, Doris. 1993a. *Cultures of U.S. Imperialism*, edited by Amy Kaplan and Donald E. Pease. Durham, N.C.: Duke University Press.

———. 1993b. "Sin secretos." In *La voz del otro: Testimonio, subalternidad y verdad narrativa*, edited by J. Beverley and H. Achugar. Lima: Latinoamericana Editores.

———. 1994. "Conocimiento interruptus: una ética de lectura." In *Las culturas del fin de siglo en América Latina*, edited by J. Ludmer. Rosario: Beatriz Viterbo Editora.

———. 1996. "No Secrets." In *The Real Thing: Testimonial Discourse in Latin America*, edited by G. Gugelberger. Durham, N.C.: Duke University Press.

———. 1999. *Proceed with Caution When Engaged with Minority Writing in the Americas*. Cambridge, Mass.: Harvard University Press.

Sontag, Susan. 1966. "Death of Tragedy." In *Against Interpretation: And Other Essays*. New York: Dell.

Souza, Eneida Maria de. 1998. "A teoria em crise." *Revista Brasileira de Literatura Comparada* 4: 19–29.

Spalding, Karen. 1970. "Social Climbers: Changing Patterns of Mobility among the Indians of Colonial Peru." *Hispanic American Historical Review* 50: 645–54.

———. 1973. "Kurakas and Commerce: A Chapter in the Evolution of Andean Society." *Hispanic American Historical Review* 54: 581–99.

———. 1974. *De indio a campesino*. Lima: Instituto de Estudios Peruanos.

———. 1984. *Huarochirí: An Andean Society under Inca and Spanish Rule*. Stanford, Calif.: Stanford University Press.

Spivak, Gayatri Chakravorty. 1988a. "Can the Subaltern Speak?" In *Marxism and the Interpretation of Culture*, edited by C. Nelson and L. Grossberg. Urbana: University of Illinois Press.

———. 1988b. "Subaltern Studies: Deconstructing Historiography." In *In Other Worlds: Essays in Cultural Politics*. New York: Routledge.

———. 1990. "Poststructuralism, Marginality, Postcoloniality, and Value." In *Literary Theory Today*, edited by P. Collier and H. Geyer-Ryan. New York: Cornell University Press.

———. 1994. "Responsibility." *boundary 2* 21.3: 19–64.

———. 1995. "Supplementing Marx." *Whither Marxism?: Global Crises in International Perspective*, edited by B. Magnus and S. Cullenberg. New York: Routledge.

Spurr, David. 1995. *The Rhetoric of Empire*. Durham, N.C.: Duke University Press.

Stavans, Ilan. 1995. *The Hispanic Condition: Reflections on Culture and Identity in America*. New York: HarperCollins.

Stern, Steven. 1982. *Peru's Indian Peoples and the Challenge of Spanish Conquest: Huamanga to 1640*. Madison: University of Wisconsin Press.

Stuckey, J. Elspeth. 1991. *The Violence of Literacy*. Portsmouth, N.H.: Boynton/Cook-Heinemann.

Sullivan, Lawrence E. 1985. "Above, Below, or Far Away: Andean Cosmogony and Ethical Order." In *Cosmogony and Ethical Order: New Studies in Comparative Ethics*, edited by R. W. Lovin and F. E. Reynolds. Chicago: Chicago University Press.

Sunkel, Guillermo, ed. 1999. *El consumo cultural en América Latina*. Santafé de Bogotá: Convenio Andrés Bello.

Suro, Roberto. 1998. *Strangers among Us: How Latino Immigration Is Transforming America*. New York: Knopf.

Tafuri, Manfredo. 1986. *Storia della architettura italiana, 1944–1985*. Turin: Einaudi.

Taibo, Paco Ignacio. 1985. *María Félix: 47 pasos por el cine*. México: Joaquín Mortiz/Planeta.

Tatum, Charles, and Harold E. Hinds. 1984. "Mexican and American Comic Books in a Comparative Perspective." In *Mexico and the United States: Intercultural Relations in the Humanities*, edited by J. Luna-Lawhn, J. Bruce-Novoa, G. Campos, and R. Saldívar. San Antonio, Tex.: San Antonio College Press.

Taussig, Michael. 1980. *The Devil and Commodity Fetishism in South America*. Chapel Hill: University of North Carolina Press.

Taylor, Charles. 1999. "Two Theories of Modernity." *Public Culture* 11.1: 153–74.

Taylor, Lucien. 1994. "The Same Difference." *Transition* 63: 98–111.

Terray, Emmanuel. 1992. *Le mmunisme*. Arles: Actes Sud.

Thiolent, Michel, et al. 1982. *Televisão, poder, e clases trabalhadoras*. São Paulo: Intercom.

Tienda, Marta, and Vilma Ortiz. 1986. " 'Hispanicity' and the 1980 Census." *Social Science Quarterly* 67: 3–20.

Todorov, Tzvetan. 1978. "Tipologie du roman policier." In *Poétique de la prose*. Paris: Editions du Seuil.

Touraine, Alain. 1969. *La société post-industrielle*. Paris: Denoël.

Trejo Delarbre, Raúl, ed. 1994. *Chiapas: la guerra de las ideas*. México: Diana.

Treviño, Fernando. 1987. "Standardized Terminology for Hispanic Populations." *American Journal of Public Health* 77.1: 66–72.

Trigo, Abril. 1997. "De la transculturación (a/en) lo transnacional." In *Angel Rama y los estudios latinoamericanos*, edited by M. Moraña. Pittsburgh: IILI.

———. 2000a. "Why Do I Do Cultural Studies?" *Journal of Latin American Cultural Studies* 9.1: 73–93.

———. 2000b. "Shifting Paradigms: From Transculturation to Hybridity: A Theoretical Critique." In *Unforeseeable Americas: Questioning Cultural Hybridity in the Americas*, edited by R. De Grandis and Z. Bernd. *Critical Studies* 13: 85–111.

Tupac Amaru, José Gabriel Condorcanqui. 1946. *Genealogía de Túpac Amaru*. Lima: Los Pequeños Grandes Libros.

Tupac Amaru, Juan Bautista. 1976. *Memorias*. Buenos Aires: Editorial Boedo.

Urruzola, María. 1996. "Entrevista a Nancy Birsdall, Vice-President of the Inter-American Development Bank." *Brecha*, 12 April.

Urzua, Carlos, and Tótoro Taulis. 1994. EZLN, *el ejército que salió de la selva*. México: Planeta.

Valenzuela, José Manuel. 1988. *A la brava ése*. Tijuana: El Colegio de la Frontera Norte.

Valera, Juan. 1905. "Juicio crítico." Prologue to Juan Zorrilla de San Martín's *Tabaré*. México: Casas Editoriales.

Vargas Llosa, Mario. 1964. "José María Arguedas descubre al indio auténtico." *Visión del Perú* 1: n.p.

Vasconcelos, José. n.d. *Indología. Una interpretación de la cultura ibero-americana*. Barcelona: Academia Mundial de Librería.

———. 1977. *La raza cósmica. Misión de la raza iberoamericana, Argentina y Brasil*. México: Espasa-Calpe.

———. 1997. *The Cosmic Race/La raza cósmica*. Baltimore: Johns Hopkins University Press.

Vasudevan, Ravi. 1989. "The Melodramatic Mode and the Commercial Hindi Cinema." *Screen* 30.3: 29–50.

Velis, Claudio. 1980. "Outward-looking Nationalism and the Liberal Cause." In *The Centralist Tradition of Latin America*. Princeton, N.J.: Princeton University Press.

Vera Herrera, Ramón. 1995. "Relojes japoneses." *Ojarasca* 44: 20–25.

Verney, Georges, and David Ronfeldt. 1991. *The Current Situation in Mexican Immigration*. Santa Mónica, Calif.: Rand.

Verón, Eliseo. 1974. *Imperialismo, lucha de clases y conocimiento. 25 años de sociología en la Argentina*. Buenos Aires: Editorial Tiempo Contemporáneo.

Vianna, Hermano. 1995. *O mistério do samba*. Rio de Janeiro: Zahar.

Vidal, Hernán. 1976. *Literatura hispanoamericana e ideología liberal: surgimiento y crisis*. Buenos Aires: Hispamérica.

———. 1993. "The Concept of Colonial and Postcolonial Discourse: A Perspective from Literary Criticism." *Latin American Research Review* 28.3: 113–19.

Vieira, João Luiz, and Robert Stam. 1985. "Parody and Marginality: The Case of Brazilian Cinema." *Framework* 28: n.p.

———. 1990. "Parody and Marginality: The Case of Brazilian Cinema." In *The Media Reader*, edited by M. Alvarado and J. O. Thompson. London: British Film Institute.

Vieira de Mello, Mário. 1963. *Desenvolvimento e cultura: O problema do estetismo no Brasil.* São Paulo: Nacional.

Vigarello, Georges. 1988. *Concepts of Cleanliness: Changing Attitudes in France since the Middle Ages.* New York: Cambridge Press-Editions de la Maison des Sciences de L'Homme.

Villa Aguilera, Manuel. 1975. *Ideología oficial y sociología crítica en México, 1950–1970.* México: UNAM, Facultad de Ciencias Políticas.

Villegas, Abelardo. 1986. "Panorama de los procesos de cambio: revolución, reformismo y lucha de clases." In *América Latina en sus ideas*, edited by L. Zea. México: Siglo XXI.

Vincendeau, Ginette. 1989. "Melodramatic Realism: On Some French Women's Films of the 1930s." *Screen* 30.3: 51–65.

Vinson, Donald. 1977. "The Role of Personal Values in Marketing and Consumer Behaviour." *Journal of Marketing* 41.2: 44–50.

Viñas, David. 1984. "Pareceres y digresiones en torno a la nueva narrativa latinoamericana." In *Más allá del boom: literatura y mercado*, edited by Angel Rama. Buenos Aires: Folios.

Viñas, Moisés, ed. 1987. *Historia del cine mexicano.* México: UNAM/UNESCO.

Vitier, Medardo. 1945. *Del ensayo americano.* México: Fondo de Cultura Económica.

Von der Walde, Erna. 1998. "Realismo mágico y poscolonialismo: construcciones del otro desde la otredad." In *Teorías sin disciplina: Latinoamericanismo, poscolonialidad, y globalización en debate*, edited by S. Castro Gómez and E. Mendieta. México: Porrúa/USF.

Wachtel, Nathan. 1973. *Sociedad e ideología.* Lima: Instituto de Estudios Peruanos.

Wain, John. 1967. *El mundo vivo de Shakespeare.* Madrid: Espasa-Calpe.

Walker, Cheryl. 1990. "Feminist Criticism and the Author." *Critical Inquiry* 16: 551–71.

Wallerstein, Immanuel. 1974. *The Modern World-System.* San Diego: Academic Press.

———. 1991. *Geopolitics and Geoculture: Essays on the Changing World-System.* Cambridge: Cambridge University Press.

Wallis, Helen. 1965. "The Influence of Father Ricci on Far Eastern Cartography." *Imago Mundi* 19: 38–45.

Warman, Arturo. 1980. *"We Came to Object": The Peasants of Morelos and the National State.* Baltimore: Johns Hopkins University Press.

———. 1982. "Modernizarse ¿para qué?" *Nexos* 50.5: 11–14.

Wheatly, Paul. 1971. *The Pivot of the Four Quarters: A Preliminary Enquiry into the Origins and Character of the Ancient Chinese City.* Chicago: Aldin.

White, Hayden. 1978. *Tropics of Discourse: Essays in Cultural Criticism.* Baltimore: Johns Hopkins University Press.

Williams, Gareth. 1996. "Fantasies of Cultural Exchange in Latin American Subaltern Studies." *The Real Thing: Testimonial Discourse in Latin America*, edited by G. Gugelberger. Durham, N.C.: Duke University Press.

Williams, Raymond. 1958. *Culture and Society.* New York: Columbia University Press.

————. 1974. *Television: Technology and Cultural Form*. London: Penguin.

————. 1975. *Television: Technology and Cultural Form*. New York: Schocken Books.

————. 1977. *Marxism and Literature*. Oxford: Oxford University Press.

————. 1989. *The Politics of Modernism*. London: Verso.

Williamson, Judith. 1978. *Decoding Advertisements: Ideology and Meaning in Advertising*. London: Mario Boyas.

Winn, Peter. 1992. "North of the Border." In *Americas: The Changing Face of Latin America and the Caribbean*. New York: Pantheon.

Wolf, Armin. 1957. "Die Ebstorfer Weltkarte als Denkmal einer Mitterlalterlichen Welt und Geschichtsbildes." *Geschichte in Wissenschaft und Unterricht* 8: 316–34.

————. 1989. "News on the Ebstorf World Map: Date, Origin, Authorship." In *Géographie du Monde au Moyen Age et à la Renaissance*, edited by M. Pelletier. Paris: Editions du CTHS.

Wolf, M., F. Casetti, and L. Lumbelli. 1980–1981. "Indagine su alcune Regole di Genere Televisivo." *Ricerche sulla Comunicazione* 1–2, vol. 2.

Womack, John. 1972. *Zapata and the Mexican Revolution*. Harmondsworth: Penguin.

Wynter, Sylvia. 1989. "Beyond the World of Man: Glissant and the New Discourse of the Antilles." *World Literature Today* 63.4: 637–47.

"Y las ondas son ajenas. Sesenta nuevas emisoras radiales en un año." 1999. *Brecha*, 9 July.

Young, Robert. 1990. *White Mythologies: Writing History and the West*. London: Routledge.

————. 1995. *Colonial Desire: Hybridity in Theory, Culture, and Race*. London: Routledge.

Yúdice, George. 1992. "Postmodernity and Transnational Capitalism in Latin America." In *On Edge: The Crisis of Contemporary Latin American Culture*, edited by G. Yúdice, J. Franco, and J. Flores. Minneapolis: University of Minnesota Press.

————. 1993a. "Civil Society, Consumption, and Governability in an Age of Global Restructuring." *Social Text* 45: 1–25.

————. 1993b. "Tradiciones comparativas de estudios culturales: América Latina y los Estados Unidos." *Alteridades* 5: 9–20.

————. 1994. "Estudios culturales y sociedad civil." *Revista de Crítica Cultural* 8: 44–45.

————. 1995. "Transnational Brokering of Art." Paper prepared for presentation at the 19th Congress of Latin American Studies Association, Washington, 28–30 September.

————. 1996. "Testimonio and Postmodernism." In *The Real Thing: Testimonial Discourse in Latin America*, edited by G. Gugelberger. Durham, N.C.: Duke University Press.

————. 1998. "The Globalization of Culture and the New Civil Society." *Cultures of Politics/Politics of Cultures: Re-Visioning Latin American Social Movements*, edited by S. Alvarez, E. Dagnino, and A. Escobar. Boulder, Colo.: Westview Press.

Zalduondo, Bárbara O. de, Mauricio Hernández Avila, Patricia Uribe Zúñiga. 1991. "Intervention Research Needs for AIDS Prevention among Commercial Sex

Workers and Their Clients." In AIDS and Women's Reproductive Health, edited by
L. Chen, J. Sepúlveda Amor, and S. Segal. New York: Plenum.

Zamora, Lois Parkinson, and Wendy B. Faris, eds. 1995. Magical Realism: Theory,
History, Community. Durham, N.C.: Duke University Press.

Zea, Leopoldo. 1988. Discurso desde la marginación y la barbarie. Barcelona: Anthropos.

Zibechi, Raúl. 1996a. "Radios comunitarias: voces en el aire." Brecha, 21 June.

———. 1996b. "Siempre en domingo: ofensiva contra radios comunitarias."
Brecha, 1 November.

Zimmerman, José Luis. 1970. Países pobres, países ricos. La brecha que se ensancha.
La Habana: Editorial de Ciencias Sociales, Instituto del Libro Cubano.

Žižek, Slavoj. 1992. El sublime objeto de la ideología. México: Siglo XXI.

Zonabend, Françoise. 1984. The Enduring Memory: Time and History in a French Village.
Manchester: Manchester University Press.

Zuidema, Tom. 1964. The Ceque System of Cuzco: The Social Organization of the Capital of
the Inca. International Archives of Ethnography. Leiden: E. J. Brill.

Zum Felde, Alberto. 1954. Índice crítico de la literatura hispanoamericana: los ensayistas.
México: Guaranía.

ACKNOWLEDGMENT OF COPYRIGHTS

Part 1. Forerunners

Candido, "Literature and Underdevelopment" – From *Antonio Candido: On Literature and Society*, translated, edited, and introduced by Howard S. Becker (Princeton, N.J.: Princeton University Press, 1995), 119–41. Originally published as "Sous-développement et littérature en Amérique Latine," in *Cahiers d'Histoire Mondiale* 4 (Paris: UNESCO, 1970), 618–40; and as "Literatura y subdesarrollo," in *América Latina en su literatura*, coordinated by César Fernández Moreno (México: UNESCO/Siglo XXI, 1972), 335–53; and reprinted in Antonio Candido, *A educação pela noite e outros ensaios* (São Paulo: Ática, 1987), 140–62.

Ribeiro, "Evolutionary Acceleration and Historical Incorporation," "The Genuine and the Spurious," and "National Ethnic Typology" – Three excerpts from *The Americas and Civilization*, translated by Linton Lomas Barret and Marie McDavid Barret (New York: E. P. Dutton and Co., 1971), 34–39 and 71–89. Originally published as *Las Américas y la civilización: Proceso de formación y causas del desarrollo desigual de los pueblos americanos* (Buenos Aires: Centro Editor de América Latina, 1969) and as *Américas e a Civilização* (Rio de Janeiro: Civilização Brasileira, 1970).

Fernández Retamar, "Caliban: Notes Toward a Discussion of Culture in Our America" – Excerpts from *Caliban and Other Essays* (Minneapolis: University of Minnesota Press, 1989), 3–16. These excerpts were translated by Lynn Garafola, David Arthur McMurray, and Roberto Márquez. This essay appeared for the first time in *Casa de las Américas* 68 (1971): 124–51.

Cornejo Polar, "*Indigenismo* and Heterogeneous Literatures: Their Double Sociocultural Statute" – This text was read at the seminar "Algunos enfoques de la crítica literaria en Latinoamérica," which was organized by the Centro de Estudios Latinoamericanos Rómulo Gallegos of Caracas, in March 1977. It is in part a re-elaboration of "Para una interpretación de la novela indigenista," *Casa de las Américas* 100 (1977): 40–48. The essay was originally published as "El indigenismo y las literaturas heterogéneas: su doble estatuto socio-cultural," *Revista de Crítica Literaria Latinoamericana* 7/8 (1978): 7–21.

Cornejo Polar, "*Mestizaje*, Transculturation, Heterogeneity" – Originally published as "*Mestizaje, transculturación, heterogeneidad,*" *Revista de Crítica Literaria Latino-americana* 21.42 (1995): 368–371.

Rama, "Literature and Culture" – Originally published as "Literatura y cultura," chap. 1 of *Transculturación narrativa en América Latina* (México: Siglo XXI, 1982), 11–56.

Part 2. Foundations

Franco, "Plotting Women: Popular Narratives for Women in the United States and in Latin America" – From *Reinventing the Americas: Comparative Studies of Literature of the United States and Spanish America*, ed. Bell Gale Chevigny and Gari Laguardia (New York: Cambridge University Press, 1986), 249–68.

Monsiváis, "Would So Many Millions of People Not End Up Speaking English? (The North American Culture and Mexico)" – Extracted from "¿Tantos millones de hombres no hablaremos inglés? (La cultura norteamericana y México)," in *Simbiosis de culturas: los inmigrantes y su cultura en México*, comp. Guillermo Bonfil Batalla (México: Consejo Nacional para la Cultura y las Artes-Fondo de Cultura Económica, 1993), 455–516.

Schwarz, "Brazilian Culture: Nationalism by Elimination" – From *Misplaced Ideas: Essays on Brazilian Culture* (London: Verso, 1992), 1–18. It began as a lecture in a series entitled "Tradição/Contradição," organized by Adauto Neves for Funarte, and was first published as "Nacional por subtração," *Folha de São Paulo* (7 June 1986). The English translation by Linda Briggs first appeared in *New Left Review* 167 (1988): 77–90.

Sarlo, "Intellectuals: Scission or Mimesis?" – Originally published as "Intelectuales: ¿Escisión o mimesis?" *Punto de vista* 25 (1985): 1–6.

Mignolo, "The Movable Center: Geographical Discourses and Territoriality During the Expansion of the Spanish Empire" – From *Coded Encounters: Writing, Gender, and Ethnicity in Colonial Latin America*, ed. Francisco Javier Cevallos-Candau, Jeffrey A. Cole, Nina M. Scott, and Nicomedes Suárez-Araúz (Amherst: University of Massachusetts Press, 1994), 15–45.

Brunner, "Notes on Modernity and Postmodernity in Latin American Culture" – From *The Postmodernism Debate in Latin America*, ed. John Beverley and José Oviedo, *boundary 2* 20.3 (1993): 34–54. Originally published as "Notas sobre la modernidad y lo posmoderno en la cultura latinoamericana," *David y Goliath* 17.52 (1987): 30–39. It was also published as "Modernidad y posmodernidad en la cultura latinoamericana," in *El espejo trizado: ensayos sobre la cultura y políticas culturales* (Santiago: FLACSO, 1988), 207–39; a longer version appeared as "Experiencias de la modernidad," in *América Latina: cultura y modernidad* (México: Grijalbo, 1992), 73–121.

Martín-Barbero, "A Nocturnal Map to Explore a New Field" – From *Communication, Culture and Hegemony: From the Media to Mediations*, trans. Elizabeth Fox and Robert A. White (London: Sage, 1993), 211–28. It was also published as "Mapa nocturno para explorar el nuevo campo," in *De los medios a las mediaciones. Comunicación, cultura, y hegemonía* (México: G. Gili, 1987), 229–47.

García Canclini, "Cultural Studies from the 1980s to the 1990s: Anthropological and Sociological Perspectives in Latin America" – This essay first appeared as a paper for the Latin American Studies Association Congress in April 1991, in panels on cultural studies organized by Jean Franco. It was originally published as "Los estudios culturales de los 80 a los 90: perspectivas antropológicas y sociológicas en América Latina," *Punto de Vista* 40 (1991): 41–48.

Part 3. Practices

Silverblatt, "Political Disfranchisement" – Chapter 8 of *Moon, Sun, and Witches: Gender Ideologies and Class in Inca and Colonial Peru* (Princeton, N.J.: Princeton University Press, 1987), 148–58.

González Stephan, "On Citizenship: The Grammatology of the Body-Politic" – Originally published as "Las disciplinas escriturarias de la patria: constituciones, gramáticas y manuales," *Estudios* 5 (1995): 19–46.

Archetti, "Male Hybrids in the World of Soccer" – Originally published as a chapter in *Masculinities: Football, Polo, and the Tango in Argentina* (Oxford: Berg, 1999), 46–76.

Gorelík and Silvestri, "The Past as the Future: A Reactive Utopia in Buenos Aires" – Originally published as "El pasado como futuro. Una utopía reactiva en Buenos Aires," *Punto de vista* 42 (1992): 22–26.

López, "Women and Melodrama in the 'Old' Mexican Cinema" – Originally published in *Mediating Two Worlds: Cinematic Encounters in the Americas*, ed. John King, Ana M. López, and Manuel Alvarado (London: British Film Institute, 1993), 147–63.

Masiello, "The Unbearable Lightness of History: Bestseller Scripts for Our Times" – Another version of this essay was published under the title "La insoportable levedad de la historia," *Revista Iberoamericana* 66, no. 193 (Oct.–Dec. 2000): 799–814.

Ortiz, "Legitimacy and Lifestyles" – Originally published as chapter 6 of *Mundialização e cultura* (São Paulo: Brasiliense, 1994), 183–215. The version in this volume is reprinted from the *Journal of Latin American Cultural Studies* 5.2 (1996): 155–73.

Mato, "The Transnational Making of Representations of Gender, Ethnicity, and Culture: Indigenous Peoples' Organizations at the Smithsonian Institution's Festival" – Originally published under the same title in *Cultural Studies* 12.2 (1998): 193–209.

De la Campa, "Mimicry and the Uncanny in Caribbean Discourse" – Originally published in *LatinAmericanism* (Minneapolis: University of Minnesota Press, 1999),
85–120.

Rabasa, "Of Zapatismo: Reflections on the Folkloric and the Impossible in a Subaltern Insurrection" – A longer version of this essay was published in *The Politics of
Culture in the Shadow of Capital*, ed. Lisa Lowe and David Lloyd (Durham, N.C.:
Duke University Press, 1997), 399–431. A shorter version, entitled "Del Zapatismo (Reflexiones sobre lo folklórico y lo imposible en la insurrección subal-
terna del EZLN)," was published in *Estudios* 11 (1998): 203–18.

Flores, "The Latino Imaginary: Meanings of Community and Identity" – Originally
published in *From Bomba to Hip-Hop: Puerto Rican Culture and Latino Identity* (New
York: Columbia University Press, 2000), 193–203.

Part 4. Positions and Polemics

Beverley, "Writing in Reverse: On the Project of the Latin American Subaltern Studies Group" – Originally published with the same title in *Subaltern Studies in the
Americas*, ed. José Rabasa, Javier Sanjinés C., and Robert Carr, *Dispositio/n* 46
(1994): 271–88.

Moraña, "The Boom of the Subaltern" – This essay is a revision of previous versions
of a paper originally presented at the 1996 LASA Conference in Guadalajara.
Some of the publications now cited in the essay were published after the original text was written, but have been included in this version without substantially
altering the arguments developed in the original.

Yúdice, "Latin American Intellectuals in a Post-Hegemonic Era" – Prepared for the
symposium "Recentering the Periphery: Latin American Intellectuals in the
New Millenium," The New School for Social Research, 7 April 2000.

Achugar, "Local/Global Latin Americanisms: 'Theoretical Babbling,' apropos
Roberto Fernández Retamar" – This essay originally appeared with this title in
Interventions 5, no. 1 (2003): 125–41. It is included in this volume by permission
of Taylor & Francis Ltd., http://www.tandf.co.uk/journals/routledge/
1369801X.html.

Richard, "Intersecting Latin America with Latin Americanism: Academic Knowledge, Theoretical Practice, and Cultural Criticism" – Originally published as
"Intersectando Latinoamérica con el Latinoamericanismo: saberes académicos,
práctica teórica, y crítica cultural," *Revista Iberoamericana* 180 (1997): 345–61.

Moreiras, "Irruption and Conservation: Some Conditions of Latin Americanist Critique" – A shorter version of this text was published as "Irrupción y conser-
vación en las guerras culturales," *Revista de Crítica Cultural* 17 (1998): 68–71.

A similar version appears in the first chapter of Moreiras's book *The Exhaustion of Difference: Politics of Latin American Cultural Studies* (Durham, N.C.: Duke University Press, 2001), 1–25.

Larsen, "The Cultural Studies Movement and Latin America: An Overview" – Originally published in *Reading North by South* (Minneapolis: University of Minnesota Press, 1995), 189–96.

Kraniauskas, "Hybridity in a Transnational Frame: Latin Americanist and Postcolonial Perspectives on Cultural Studies" – Originally published as "Hybridity in a Transnational Frame: Latin Americanist and Postcolonial Perspectives on Cultural Studies," *Nepantla: Views from South* 1.1 (2000): 111–37.

Cornejo Polar, "*Mestizaje* and Hybridity: The Risks of Metaphors. Notes" – Originally published as "Mestizaje e Hibridez: los riesgos de las metáforas. Apuntes," *Revista de Crítica Literaria Latinoamericana* 63.180 (1997): 341–44.

INDEX

Acculturation, 24, 61–63, 70–72, 77, 132–36, 152, 569, 738–39
Achugar, Hugo, 363–64, 366, 464–65
Adorno, Rolena, 172, 370, 632
Adorno, Theodor, 161, 184, 627, 730–31
Aesthetics, 161, 243, 335, 353, 360–63, 366, 465, 472, 476–79, 485–86, 537, 540, 548–53, 558–59, 578–79, 638–39, 646, 681; architectural, 430, 434–35, 437, 440; avant-garde, 237; politics and, 175–77, 240, 248, 360–63, 690, 701–2; postmodern, 463, 707–27
Alterity, 172, 260, 356, 362, 365, 652, 687–89
Althusser, Louis, 26, 161, 165, 173, 734, 750
Americanization, 168–70, 238, 307, 677
Anderson, Perry, 717, 722
Andrade, Mario de, 49, 51, 128, 131, 133–34, 175, 233–35, 239
Andrade, Oswald de, 49, 51, 235, 239
Anthropology, 3, 9–12, 125, 135, 147, 152, 157–59, 170, 315, 363, 392, 464, 658, 738–39; cultural, 166, 172; geo-cultural anthropology, as a cognitive constellation, 12; and sociology, 329–346, 739, 746–47, 754
Anticolonialism, 7, 173, 356–57, 368, 512, 547, 640, 655, 678–79
Anti-imperialism, 235–37, 357, 407, 547, 646–47, 733

Archetti, Eduardo, 371
Area studies, 347, 712, 716
Arguedas, José María, 31, 54, 95, 101, 105, 114, 118, 138, 141, 151, 625, 739
Arielism, 25, 29, 96, 214, 364–66, 418, 424–25, 653, 678–84, 717
Avant-garde, 176, 205, 209–12, 225, 249, 253, 337, 432–39, 465, 471–72, 477–78, 536, 557, 649, 730, 739, 745; postmodern, 359–62

Bakhtin, Mikhail, 326, 696
Barthes, Roland, 161, 316, 698
Baudrillard, Jean, 161, 308, 312
Bello, Andrés, 16–17, 23, 122, 389, 391, 709
Benítez-Rojo, Antonio, 361, 539–41
Benjamin, Walter, 175, 317, 319, 326, 578, 636, 696–97, 720
Berman, Marshall, 153, 298
Bestseller, 371, 459–73
Beverley, John, 8, 9, 354–55, 359, 367, 684, 702–3, 734
Bhabha, Homi, 358, 537, 543, 550, 555, 644, 646, 678, 741–47; and García Canclini, 753–56
Bhadra, Gautam, 567–68
Bolívar, Simón, 17, 69, 85, 88, 91, 95, 123, 401, 632
Border studies, 221, 227–30, 364, 370, 584–92, 612–14, 619, 639, 737, 741,

749, 753–59; and border culture, 6; and border gnosis, 358; borderlands of, 372, 714; and border text, 9; thinking in, 359, 367, 685, 687–88, 697–705

Borges, Jorge Luis, 48, 49, 127, 130–31, 138, 147–49, 433, 437–38, 717

Borocotó, J. Lorenzo, 419–23

Bourdieu, Pierre, 158, 312, 336, 338, 462, 476, 480–81, 638, 714

Braudel, Fernand, 306–7, 308

Brooks, Peter, 185–88, 446

Brunner, José J., 13, 156, 159, 167–68, 178–79, 337–39, 351, 362–63, 659

Caliban and Calibanism, 25, 28, 83–99, 214, 364, 647, 672–75, 678–84

Candido, Antonio, 12, 28–29, 102–3, 175, 234–35, 243, 336, 629, 680, 709

Carnivalization, 385, 398

Carpentier, Alejo, 51, 53, 56–7, 131, 133, 147–49, 541, 647

Carreño, Manuel Antonio, 389, 395, 398–400, 402

Castillo, Debra, 372

Césaire, Aimé, 90, 94–95, 98, 535, 672

Chakrabarty, Dipesh, 736–38, 741, 746, 755

Chantecler, 420–22

Chicano/a, 171, 230–31, 607, 615–19

Cinema, 11, 13, 154, 169, 206–12, 226, 368, 441–58

Citizenship, 7, 168, 223, 230, 350–51, 370–71, 611, 614, 645–46, 651, 672, 702, 705, 750; in relation to the state, 384–405

Civilization and barbarism, 18–19, 41, 385, 389–91, 396–99, 402, 405, 461, 464, 645

Civil society, 7, 168, 216, 295, 301, 304, 306, 350–54, 369, 385–402, 468, 471,

516, 533, 699, 716, 722; networks and organizations in, 660–67

Colonialism, 9, 59–68, 72, 75–78, 83–88, 91–94, 97–99, 105, 121–23, 135, 140, 236, 243–47, 445, 545, 576–81, 627, 631–37, 643–52, 670, 676–79, 682–83, 739–58; and colonial subject, 445; condition of, 30–31, 568, 612–14; cultural, 52, 676, 713, 739; discourse of, 172, 538, 541, 555, 577, 720, 725; internal, 11, 13, 173, 568

Colonial semiosis, 262, 289–90, 538, 541

Colonial society, 120, 380–81

Colonial studies, as a cognitive constellation, 12–13, 166–67, 172–73

Communications, 9, 157, 162, 164, 172, 226, 236–37, 241, 246, 296, 299, 312–16, 319–22, 325, 28, 336–45, 371, 442, 513–34, 749; systems of, 154

Communications studies, 166, 177

Consumer culture, 168–69, 183, 191–93, 224, 351, 363, 371–72, 460–63, 466, 469, 471, 513–14, 588

Consumer society, 155, 185–86, 191–93, 217, 222, 462, 636

Consumption, 7, 186–88, 193–94, 222, 225–26, 292, 297–98, 311–13, 319, 333, 338, 341–44, 460, 468, 472, 533, 609, 649, 660, 668, 705, 734–35; and consumerism, 191, 197, 201; cultural, 351–52; modes of, 4

Cornejo Polar, Antonio, 12, 22, 28, 31, 363, 369, 373, 644, 680, 709

Cosmopolitanism, 123, 127, 132, 142–43, 147, 149–51, 352–53, 455, 465, 626, 708, 710, 716–18

Creolization, 410–13, 538, 550, 555–59, 625–27, 632–36, 647

Criollo, 22, 123, 358, 360, 366, 410–25, 433–39

Critical thought, 9, 12, 157, 162, 166, 255, 348, 358–60, 364, 366, 368,

706–27, 740, 763; Latin American,
21–25
Cuban revolution, 11, 25–30, 213–14,
222, 357, 542, 625, 627, 629, 676,
682
Cultural, the, 4, 8–9, 12, 353, 359–61,
368, 371–72; brokerage, 349–50, 364,
501–02, 511–12; criticism, 9–10, 13,
349, 353, 361, 365, 368, 625, 643,
647, 651, 679, 686–705, 730, 733,
748; dependency, 43–52; formation,
59, 72, 82, 475–80, 490–94, 514,
553–57, 660, 750, 754, 756; globalization, 513, 534, 538, 550; system,
133, 137, 139–40, 262, 394, 647–651,
688
Cultural capital, 364, 477, 714, 719
Cultural imperialism, 7, 11, 173, 184,
201, 306, 668, 715
Cultural politics, 6, 168, 176, 179, 319,
332–34, 346, 350–51, 516, 538, 566,
646, 655–62, 741, 753, 756
Cultural production, 513–34, 565–66,
613, 644–49, 739–40, 745, 755, 758
Cultural studies, 1–13, 153–81, 329–46,
348–50, 623, 637–38, 686–705, 706–
27, 728–35, 736–59, 758–60; British,
1–13, 157, 160–66, 363, 738; Latin
American, 1–13, 15–34, 153–81, 343,
347–73, 637, 641, 707, 709, 721, 726–
27, 728–35; U.S., 1–13, 157, 160–66,
346, 363
Culture: Caribbean, 535–60; counterculture, 216–21, 472, 527, 738; mass,
7, 11–12, 183–85, 188, 192, 199, 226,
292, 301, 318–19, 324, 327, 341–43,
368, 442, 480, 656–58, 729–33;
national, 11, 131, 151, 155, 175–77,
229, 235–36, 242, 333, 433, 438–39,
543, 566, 628, 636; pop, 161–64, 169,
352–53, 363, 366; popular, 214, 224,
319, 325, 330, 335–41, 345, 350, 442,
454, 475–78, 493–95, 552, 566, 577,
658, 730–35; subculture, 221, 297,

604; transnational, 179, 183, 225,
348–52, 362–64, 366, 368, 371, 637,
639, 660
Culture industries, 161–63, 214, 219,
224–25, 235–36, 292, 301, 320, 323,
326–27, 333, 339–44, 350–52, 362,
371, 441–42, 471, 475–78, 481, 484–
86, 490, 496, 533, 658–66, 730

Deconstruction, 164, 177, 201, 348–49,
356–62, 365, 369, 552–60, 719, 722,
740, 745, 748
Deculturation, 60–63, 66, 75, 77, 136,
139, 149, 151
De la Campa, Román, 360
De las Casas, Bartolomé, 88, 540, 544–
47, 672
Deleuze, Gilles, 394, 540, 580, 679
Democracy, 153, 156, 162, 176, 233, 247,
250, 258, 306, 321, 350, 356, 429–30,
460, 466, 517–24; and civil society,
655–66; and consumption, 352, 371;
radical, 562, 565, 575, 578–82
Dependency theory, 7, 11, 13, 25–26,
156, 171–73, 308, 336, 348, 351, 358,
365, 368, 626, 637, 643
Derrida, Jacques, 161, 238, 536, 547,
554, 723–24
De Vedia y Mitre, Mariano, 431–33,
437–38
Dussel, Enrique, 357–59

Ethnicity, 111, 117–18, 165, 179, 266–70,
287–88, 330–32, 343–44, 350, 366,
414–15, 425, 506–11, 611–19, 762;
as a cognitive constellation, 157, 167

Fanon, Frantz, 93, 95, 535, 537–38, 672
Feminism, 169–71, 185–88, 198, 349–
50, 370–71, 392, 447, 464, 469–70,
625–26, 700
Fernández Retamar, Roberto, 12, 25,
28–30, 102, 357, 364, 626, 670–72,
674–75, 678–80, 760

Flores, Juan, 372
Foucault, Michel, 161, 400, 554, 574, 579, 580–81, 624, 668, 729, 734
Franco, Jean, 13, 156, 158–59, 167–68, 169–71, 349, 447–48, 461, 478, 651, 734
Freyre, Gilberto, 24, 128–29, 134

García Canclini, Néstor, 5–6, 8, 9, 13, 117, 153, 156, 158–59, 167–68, 179–81, 310, 312, 349–52, 363, 368, 478, 638, 645, 661, 664, 719, 734, 760–61, 741, 748; and Bhabha, 752–56
Gender, 165–71, 183–85, 191, 200, 350, 366, 371, 443–47, 452–53, 460, 464–67, 471, 507–11, 688, 699, 704; gender and minorities, as a cognitive constellation, 12–13, 167
Gender studies, 166
Germani, Gino, 302, 304, 335
Gilroy, Paul, 738, 740, 745, 747, 749
Glissant, Edouard, 361, 539, 544, 549–60
Globalization, 179, 223–26, 237, 296–300, 333, 342, 460–73, 480–96, 498–504, 510–11, 533–34, 535–60, 577, 638, 645–52, 659–61, 666–67, 669–85, 687–89, 695, 702–5, 716, 725, 737, 740, 750, 757; and cultural studies, 1–13, 155–62, 164–68, 173, 347–59; of culture, 6; 347–59, 362, 365–71; studies, 13, 349–56
González-Stephan, Beatriz, 370
Gorelik, Adrián, 372
Governmentality, 375–83, 655–66
Gramsci, Antonio, 26, 165, 173, 261, 564–68, 577, 580–81, 650, 656, 722, 733, 749
Groussac, Paul, 91–92, 432
Guamán Poma de Ayala, Felipe, 108, 116, 263, 272, 275, 281, 286–87, 375, 672

Guattari, Félix, 755–56
Guevara, Ernesto ("Che"), 26, 95, 670, 734–35
Guha, Ranajit, 567–68, 570, 577, 623, 626, 631, 736–37
Guimarães Rosa, João, 54, 56–57, 145–46, 150

Habermas, Jürgen, 294–95, 302, 752
Hall, Stuart, 338, 369, 535, 538–39, 695, 729–30
Hegemonic formations, 355, 358–59, 361, 365, 369
Henríquez-Ureña, Pedro, 20, 35, 124–25, 625, 675, 709
Heterogeneity, 12, 100–115, 116–18, 122, 165–68, 211, 331, 345, 358–59, 397, 537, 557, 643–44, 648, 653, 692–93, 702–5, 736, 739, 746–57, 761; according to Brunner, 167–68, 291–309, 351; as a cognitive constellation, 166, 174, 176, 178–80; according to Cornejo Polar, 28, 31, 34, 369, 644; social, 20; 165–66
Hoggart, Richard, 162–63, 325
Hopenhayn, Martín, 351–52
Horkheimer, Max, 730
Hybridity, 117, 166–68, 178–81, 262, 276, 283, 289, 340, 345, 349–50, 367, 398, 405, 413, 423, 457, 535, 550, 639, 643–53, 659, 672, 678, 685, 687, 704, 740–58, 760–62; cultural hybridity, as a cognitive constellation, 13, 353, 369–70

Identity, 15, 31, 106, 111, 213, 222, 228–30, 258–59, 297–98, 305, 307–8, 314, 321, 323–24, 334, 355, 368–72, 385–86, 390–94, 465, 495, 511–12, 537–39, 548–52, 556–60, 573, 580–82, 607, 626–30, 663, 687–89, 699–705, 709, 731–32, 738–40, 743–44, 747–49, 753, 756–58; border, 350; as a cognitive constellation, 11, 21, 157,

167–68; ethnic, 6, 75, 151, 501, 611; formation of, 4, 7, 10–11, 176–177; gender, 407, 411–12, 415, 427, 443–55, 464; Latin American, 359–62; Latino, 372, 615–18; national, 51, 60, 117, 227, 229, 240, 244, 246, 302, 307, 333, 350, 366–71, 418, 423, 445–46, 460–61, 478, 487, 653, 664–65; question of, 21, 26

Identity politics, 5, 165, 351, 700

Illich, Iván, 222–23, 224

Imaginary, 150, 170, 256–58, 298, 371, 413–15, 524, 583, 608, 671, 700; global, 352–53; Latin American, 156, 160; Latino, 372, 606–19; national, 6–7, 353; signifier, 11

Indigenism, 54, 100–115, 121, 124, 130, 151

Intellectuals, 15, 36–37, 42, 57, 68, 83–84, 92–98, 204, 214, 227, 234–47, 250–61, 315, 348, 433, 466, 472, 477–79, 488, 541, 561–83, 655–68, 706–7, 713–14, 720–25, 735, 758; Latin American, 5, 8–11, 19–23, 28–29, 645–52, 671–72, 681–83, 686–705; questions about, 155–177, 351, 353–66, 623–35, 645–52, 671–72, 681–83, 686–705

Jameson, Fredric, 8, 156, 632, 645, 720

Kraniauskas, John, 370

Kristeva, Julia, 161

Laclau, Ernesto, 310, 358, 566, 664, 734, 740

Larsen, Neil, 9, 363

Latin Americanism, 13, 347–48, 356, 360, 363–65, 536, 553, 644–46, 654, 706–8, 713, 724, 726

Latin American studies, 171, 624, 627, 669–85, 686–705, 738–41, 754, 763

Lettered city, 23, 386, 394, 402–3, 629, 635, 649, 681

Levene, Ricardo, 433, 437–38

Lewis, Oscar, 192–93

Liberation theology, 13, 25–27, 356–58, 368, 638, 641

Literary criticism, 353–54, 362–63, 645, 653, 696, 705, 760–62

Local, the, 7, 21, 158–59, 173, 177, 184–86, 330, 341, 350, 368, 517–33, 557, 669–85, 687–88, 695–97

López, Ana, 371

López de Velasco, Juan, 263, 279–81, 287–89

Marginalization, 307–8, 447–48, 451, 471–72, 515, 521, 533, 572, 670–73, 678, 684, 739

Margins, 103, 111, 117, 465–66, 536, 686–705, 745; and marginality, 166, 169, 171, 178, 349–55, 361–62, 365–67, 551, 556, 648–50

Mariátegui, José Carlos, 22–23, 26, 32, 95, 100–01, 107, 109–10, 111, 113–14, 124, 130, 672, 677

Martí, José, 19–20, 22, 84, 85, 88, 90–91, 95, 364, 386, 672, 675, 678, 706, 709, 717

Martín-Barbero, Jesús, 13, 156, 158–59, 167–68, 177–78, 180, 336, 368, 485

Martínez, Tomás Eloy, 459–60

Marx, Karl, 239, 294, 753

Masiello, Francine, 371, 690, 695, 700

Mato, Daniel, 350

Mbembe, Achilles, 555

Media, 21, 40, 154, 197, 201–2, 206, 215, 222–27, 235–37, 241, 259, 292, 298–99, 361–63, 460, 477–79, 490, 516–33, 629, 659–60, 668, 688, 702–5, 748; mass, 3, 33, 366; media and mass culture, as a cognitive constellation, 12–13, 158–62, 167–68, 176–80, 350–54

Mediations, 45–47, 131, 145, 150–51, 158–62, 166–70, 176–80, 315–25, 350–51, 354, 520, 688–96

Melodrama, 313, 319, 323–28, 371, 441–58, 469, 484–86, 615–19

Memory, 15, 469–71, 737–40, 746–49; collective, 474–75, 483, 571, 576, 580, 660; cultural, 326–27, 368, 617; historical, 298, 324, 372, 612, 738; international-popular, 495; local, 298

Menchú, Rigoberta, 580, 630, 636, 692

Mestizaje, 31, 84, 101, 107, 115–18, 177–80, 227, 318–21, 324, 569, 625, 640, 651–53, 655, 752, 760–63

Mignolo, Walter, 9, 13, 156, 159, 167–68, 172–73, 357, 360, 368, 671, 689

Migrants, 216, 227–30, 325, 345, 350, 371–72, 407–12, 415, 418–25, 663, 758–59

Mimicry, 535–60, 639, 744

Modernism, 29, 128, 133–34, 153, 165, 167, 296, 301–2, 307–8, 353–55, 361, 367, 414, 427–40, 477–78, 717–19, 739, 750–51; Brazilian modernismo, 19, 43, 47–48, 57, 120, 140–41

Modernity, 7, 11–13, 15, 78, 117, 133, 143, 193, 199, 208, 217, 227, 232, 252, 290, 291–309, 329–33, 339–45, 350–53, 368–71, 393, 398, 437, 454, 474–97, 535–60, 566–68, 580, 645–47, 670, 708–10, 768–69, 722–23, 761–62; as a cognitive constellation, 11, 15, 157, 173–80; in Latin America, 6, 168, 356–60, 369, 734–57; and postcolonialism, 734–57; and tradition, 18–19, 30

Modernization, 7, 11, 74, 78, 123–27, 129, 132–35, 137–38, 140, 146, 151–52, 153–59, 165–69, 174, 193–99, 206, 222, 229, 293–308, 350–51, 359–61, 368, 371, 388, 444, 447, 449, 475–77, 708, 739–40, 748–53; in Buenos Aires, 427–39

Modleski, Tania, 188, 191

Monsiváis, Carlos, 13, 156, 158–59, 167–68, 169–70, 296–98, 307, 446–47, 451, 454, 561, 563, 659

Moraña, Mabel, 356, 363, 365–66

Moreiras, Alberto, 358–9, 363, 366, 368, 691, 704, 740

Mouffe, Chantal, 731

Multiculturalism, 165, 348, 351, 501, 537, 629, 643, 646, 651–53

Nationalism, 48–49, 123, 167–70, 192–93, 197–99, 204–11, 217–24, 230–31, 236–39, 366, 371, 406, 418–25, 444, 448, 461–62, 549, 557, 569–71, 627–28, 636, 645

National question, 7, 36–56, 124, 175–78, 210, 223, 246–48, 305–7, 333–35, 341, 366–71, 387–91, 477, 606–19, 627–40, 687, 702; as a cognitive constellation, 11, 15, 157, 167–69; and national ethos, 59–81, 116–17; and national literature, 6, 100–103, 107, 118, 123–25, 356–58, 360, 366–367; and "national popular," 360, 366, 635–39, 645–68, 717–18

Neocolonialism, 7, 59, 78, 155–56, 161, 356–58, 362, 368, 462, 554, 579, 647, 651, 712, 739; as a cognitive constellation, 11, 15, 167

Neoliberalism, 12, 155, 159, 162–66, 179, 230, 308, 333, 343, 348, 351, 359, 363, 368, 461–65, 470, 516, 521, 536–39, 570, 577, 646, 651–52, 657–67, 714, 764

NGOs (nongovernmental organizations), 350, 500–511, 659–68

Olodúm, 662–66

Ortelius, Abraham, 263, 280, 289

Ortiz, Fernando, 24–25, 30–31, 117, 135–36, 138–39, 140, 142, 535, 539, 541, 625, 717, 761, 739

Ortiz, Renato, 156, 333, 337, 351–53, 368, 658

Otherness, 356, 359, 387, 396–99,
445, 451, 535, 551, 558, 688–94,
724

Patriarchy, 187, 190–91, 196, 198, 392,
402, 443–54, 548, 593
Pérez Bocanegra, 376, 381–82
Popular, the, 7, 10, 163–64, 168–71,
177–78, 474–80, 484–86, 490, 493–
95, 645, 656–67, 687, 691–93, 749;
as a cognitive constellation, 11, 15,
157, 167
Populism, 154–55, 167, 363, 366, 422,
656–59, 734
Postcolonialism, 8, 13, 31, 348–51, 353,
355–58, 362, 365, 368, 384, 401,
535–61, 568, 579, 604, 629–30, 637–
39, 643–51, 671, 676, 679, 684–85,
687–94, 714, 728, 736–59, 763–64
Postmodernism, 200, 228, 257, 296–98,
304, 308, 333, 343–45, 459, 463, 465,
480, 536–42, 545–58, 552–54, 627,
634, 637–39, 648–52, 671, 688–90,
722–24, 728–29, 733–35; in Benítez-
Rojo's work, 545–49; and cultural
studies, 5, 13, 164–66, 174, 348, 356,
366–69; debate on, 351; in Glissant's
work, 549–55
Postmodernity, 33, 537, 545, 549, 553,
560, 577, 688, 698; as a cognitive
constellation, 12–13, 353
Post-occidentalism, 173, 357–58
Poststructuralism, 161, 164–66, 172, 348

Rabasa, José, 172, 354, 356
Radway, Janice, 187–88, 190
Rama, Angel, 10, 101, 105, 112–13, 117,
336, 371, 373, 386, 461, 625, 628,
645, 649, 709, 717, 734, 761, 738–40,
745–47, 751, 752; on transculturation, 12, 28, 30–33, 368–69, 625,
639, 739–40, 743–45, 748, 751
Ramos, Julio, 6, 386, 390–91, 702
Rangel Gómez, María Gudelia, 372

Remedi, Gustavo, 371
Renan, Ernest, 20, 89–92, 97, 672
Reyes, Alfonso, 20, 124, 675, 709
Ribeiro, Darcy, 12, 28–29
Ricci, Matteo (father), 262–69, 275–76,
279–81, 287–88
Richard, Nelly, 9, 156, 159, 166, 349,
361–62, 363, 365–6, 471, 734
Rock, 161, 170, 206, 212–13, 217–21,
225, 480–81, 487, 493–94
Rodó, José Enrique, 20, 25, 91–92,
95–97, 672, 678, 681, 717
Rodríguez, Simón, 16–7, 20, 23, 122
Rosas Solís, Armando, 372

Sarlo, Beatriz, 5–6, 13, 156, 158, 159,
163, 167–68, 175–77, 313, 349, 363,
471, 696–97
Sarmiento, Domingo, 17–20, 24, 124,
672, 752
Schwarz, Roberto, 13, 156, 167–68,
175–77, 336, 676, 680, 750
Senghor, Léopold Sédar, 170, 232
Sevilla, Ninón, 444, 451–53, 455
Shakespeare, William, 86–90, 94–95,
483, 672
Silverblatt, Irene, 370
Silvestri, Graciela, 372
Soap opera, 324, 483–86, 493, 496
Soccer, 371, 406–26, 517, 526
Social formations, 4–7, 72, 105, 153,
163, 179, 338
Social movements, 7, 565–67, 572–82,
650, 655–67
Social sciences, 10, 12, 17, 157, 164, 174,
178
Solís, Armando Rosas, 372
Subalternity, 166, 321, 332, 340, 354–
355, 359–369, 390, 394, 465, 553,
561–83, 623–41, 673, 678, 686–87,
689–93, 704, 714–25, 736–38, 745–
47, 755, 758, 763–64; concept of,
649–51, 652–54; Latin American
Subaltern Studies Group, 623–30

Subaltern studies, 13, 348–49, 351–69

Subcomandante Marcos, 358, 561

Taylor, Charles, 708, 717–18

Telenovela, 325–26, 455

Television, 183, 186, 193, 197, 209, 214, 219, 223–26, 313–28, 342, 476, 483–86, 492–94, 519–20, 658–60, 664, 668

Testimonio, 353–54, 580, 631–32, 636–37

Third space, 358–59, 367, 743–44, 754

Thompson, E. P., 162–63

Transculturation, 116–17, 133–42, 146, 152, 535, 623, 630, 633, 639, 640, 641–43, 651, 670, 717, 752, 755; according to Ortiz, 24–25, 625; according to Rama, 12, 28, 30–33, 368–69, 625, 639, 739–40, 743–45, 748, 751

Transdisciplinarity, 6–9, 159, 164, 173, 336, 361, 365, 367, 370, 627–29, 639, 644–47, 651, 687–88, 692–93, 696–704, 729–30, 738, 741, 748–50, 758

Transnational, the, 166–68, 174, 177–79, 184, 225–26, 323, 332–33, 342, 359, 442, 460–71, 481, 484–86, 490, 496, 498–511, 535, 571, 577, 627–29, 638, 644–48, 657–68, 706, 712–13, 721, 755–56; academic market, 362, 365; capitalism, 155–62; cultural studies, 347–52, 362, 364; pop culture, 352, 363

Underdevelopment, 35–57, 112, 224, 238, 304, 316, 362, 442, 446, 478, 486, 557, 629

Utopias, 8, 89, 110, 174, 217–18, 239, 256, 298, 308, 336, 359, 613, 645, 649–50, 684, 693, 703, 720; Latin American, 11, 155–56, 364, 371; modern, 384–86, 400, 402, 427–40, 445, 455, 478, 537; postmodern, 548, 554; revolutionary, 563, 570, 580, 655

Vasconcelos, José, 24, 85, 92, 96, 717

Vidal, Hernán, 10

Virgin of Guadalupe, 222, 228, 445

Wallerstein, Immanuel, 713

Williams, Raymond, 162–63, 183, 185, 297, 310, 338, 476, 483, 729–30, 750

Yúdice, George, 349–50, 368, 689, 699–700, 734

Zapata, Emiliano, 95, 562

Zapatistas, 356, 561–83, 626; EZLN, 562, 564

Ana Del Sarto is an assistant professor of romance languages at Bowling Green State University. She has published several articles on Latin American literary and cultural theory, emphasizing the relations between the humanities and the social sciences.

Alicia Ríos is an associate professor in the Department of Language and Literature at Universidad Simón Bolívar, Venezuela. She is the coeditor, with Tomás Eloy Martínez, of *Historia de la conquista y población de la Provincia de Venezuela* (1993).

Abril Trigo is an associate professor in the Department of Spanish and Portuguese at Ohio State University. He is the author of *Memorias migrantes. Testimonios y ensayos sobre la diáspora uruguaya* (2003), *¿Cultura uruguaya o culturas linyeras? Para una cartografía de la neomodernidad posturuguaya* (1997), and *Caudillo, estado, nación: literatura, historia e ideología en el Uruguay* (1990).

Library of Congress Cataloging-in-Publication Data

The Latin American cultural studies reader /

Ana del Sarto, Alicia Ríos and Abril Trigo, eds.

p. cm. Includes bibliographical references and index.

ISBN 0-8223-3328-7 (cloth : alk. paper)

ISBN 0-8223-3340-6 (pbk. : alk. paper)

1. Latin America—Civilization. 2. Culture—Study and teaching. I. Sarto, Ana del. Ríos, Alicia. Trigo, Abril.

F1408.3.L38 2004   980—dc22—2004006056